ART AT AUCTION
IN
AMERICA

1993 EDITION

The comprehensive, up-to-date annual art
price guide to over 10,000 artists and 20,000 works
of art sold at America's major auction houses
from August 1991 through August 1992.

KREXPRESS
10169 New Hampshire Ave./Suite 195
Silver Spring, MD 20903

Library of Congress   ISSN 1046-4999
ISBN 0-9624926-3-9

If additional copies of this valuable art collecting tool are needed they can be ordered directly from the publisher at $35.00 per copy plus $2.50 handling and shipping. For quantity orders of 5 or more copies please contact the publisher by mail or phone.

KREXPRESS
10169 New Hampshire Ave./# 195
Silver Spring, MD 20903
(301) 445-6009

Cover reproduction: William Merritt Post (American 1856 - 1935)
Quiet Inlet
Oil on Canvas
12″ x 16″

PRINTED IN THE UNITED STATES OF AMERICA

TABLE OF CONTENTS

INTRODUCTION

Welcome to the 1993 Edition of ART AT AUCTION IN AMERICA — now America's most popular art auction price annual.

The 1991-1992 auction year was one of continued caution and conservatism on the part of dealers and collectors alike. Prices remained relatively stable, although exceptional works in all fields still found a ready market and often record prices. Two areas in particular, old Masters and Latin American art, continued a broad-based upward movement. Buy ins were down from the 1990-1991 years, but much of this is probably attributable to lower estimates and reserves accepted by consignors. It remains to be seen how a new administration in Washington next year will affect the economy and, ultimately, the art market.

In a continuing effort to broaden our coverage, we have added three more auction houses to our listings - **Alderfer Auction Co.** of Hatfield, Pennslyvania (strong in New Hope School artists); **Illustration House, Inc.** of New York (specializes in original work by illustrators) and **Mystic Fine Arts** of Mystic, Connecticut (strong in Connecticut and New England artists)

If you are unfamiliar with this important publication, ART AT AUCTION IN AMERICA is designed to give both the novice and the expert the power of portable knowledge so that they can be more informed and confident art collectors. The listings contain the key data pertinent to each work's value with the exception of subjective aspects such as condition and attractiveness or quality of the piece.

The art sales information has been collected from major auction houses in the United States and Canada, and includes both foreign and American artists. Much art, of course, is also sold through dealers, galleries and brokers. These sales represent the art retail market and actual selling prices are rarely available to the public. The auction market, on the other hand, represents the art wholesale market to a large degree. This being said, it is important that beginning collectors and investors understand that prices paid at auction for a particular artists work are only a guide and can be somewhat different than those quoted by a dealer. These reasons include: 1) The auction market is generally less susceptible to (but not immune from) artificial manipulation of prices— particularly for the works of contemporary artists. 2) Dealers and brokers obviously must make a profit on a sale, whereas an auction house automatically receives a commission on each painting sold ranging from 20% to 30% of the selling price. Also, many dealers guarantee the authenticity of their inventory, in effect providing you insurance. Most auction houses do too, but have many disclaimers in their terms of sale. 3) The auction market will often reflect up and down price swings in an artist's value before the retail market shows a similar trend. Many a dealer has run back to his gallery to reprice stock immediately after auction results have set new records.

It is not practical or possible to provide the novice a complete background with regard to art values in the limited space available here. However, it is important to briefly review some general observations about how certain factors affect the value of a work of art. Although it may not be new information for experienced dealers and collectors, it will be of value to most others.

Disclaimer

Every effort has been made to assure the accuracy of the information included here. However, in a mass of data this large, all of it initially compiled by auction houses outside our control, a few errors are inevitable. If you question any information, please contact us or the auction house involved for corroboration before relying on it. We do, in fact, encourage you to notify us of any errors you may find since this information will all be retained in an historical data bank.

Additionally, as is explained in more detail in the text of this guide, many factors may contribute to the value of a particular artwork. Therefore, you should not rely upon these ranges to purchase a particular piece of artwork, but should instead obtain an appraisal from a reputable dealer or art professional. The Publisher and Writer accept no responsibility and/or liability for any purchase of a work of art which is later appraised at a value less than the values set forth in this guide. This guide is provided for informational purposes only.

IMPORTANT FEATURES OF
ART AT AUCTION IN AMERICA

ART AT AUCTION IN AMERICA is the most comprehensive portable guide available.

Any work by any artist which sells for twenty-five dollars or more is included.

ART AT AUCTION IN AMERICA is easy to use.

Prioritizes works of art within each artist's listing by descending price which allows you to see what effect variables such as medium, size, subject, auction house and date of sale may have on a painting's value.

ART AT AUCTION IN AMERICA includes only practical information.

Artists are listed alphabetically without regard to nationality or painting style. However, nationalities and birth and death dates are indicated whenever available. Paintings identified by subjective attributions such as "attributed to," "circle of," "style of," "manner of," or "school of" are not included.

ART AT AUCTION IN AMERICA is user friendly.

A key to the abbreviations in the listings is included in two places, near the end of the introductory material, and also on the inside of the back cover.

ART AT AUCTION IN AMERICA retains all original titles of art work.

Titles provided by the auction house in the language of the artist, usually French, Spanish, German or Italian, are retained as referenced in the original auction catalogue.

Each succeeding edition of Art At Auction in America will include an expanded list of artists.

If there are no current sales of works by an important artist who was listed in a previous edition, the artist's name will still be included in the 1993 Edition, with a notation of which edition to check for information. There are over 3000 such artists listed this year.

Art At Auction in America lists all sales prices in U.S. Dollars.

Canadian auction prices have already been converted for you at 1.0 Canadian Dollars = 0.85 U.S. Dollars.

Art At Auction in America includes private sales of auction houses.

Occasionally, auction house price lists indicate that some paintings, which did not sell at auction, were sold privately after the sale. These sales, while not strictly an auction price, are of useful reference value and have been included in this book.

IMPORTANT FACTORS AFFECTING ART VALUES

Most popular collectibles such as prints, stamps, coins, furniture, toys, etc., are produced in multiples with no discernable difference between like items. This produces a market and values which usually reflect simple supply and demand for each given item, and the resultant confidence that an item can be bought or sold for a certain price.

Fine arts, on the other hand, are more complicated to value because each item is unique. There can be no absolute value because no two items are exactly alike. The best that can be done is to look at similar items to get a feel for the approximate value of a particular piece. It is this subjectivity and inherent uncertainty which intimidates many would-be art collectors. ART AT AUCTION IN AMERICA provides specific information about each individual work which then can be compared to similar items in question. This can significantly increase the confidence of the buyer and seller of art.

The following key factors generally determine art values (in no particular order):

1. The Artist (name, nationality and dates of activity)
2. The Mediums Used (e.g., oil on canvas, watercolor on paper)
3. The Size of the Work
4. The Subject Matter
5. The Date Painted (if known)
6. The Auction House (or dealer) selling the work and its location
7. The Date of Sale
8. The Condition of the Piece
9. The Authenticity
10. The "Attractiveness" or General Quality of Work
11. Provenance
12. Historical Considerations

1. The Artist

This can often be the most important factor in art values. A painting by Renoir, for example, will be worth considerably more than an otherwise similar painting by a relatively minor impressionist artist simply because of the name. Like all artists, however, Renoir produced some works I'm sure he would like to have forgotten.

In this guide artist's names are listed alphabetically. Occasionally, paintings resulted from the collaborative efforts of two artists. In these cases, the paintings are included under both artists' listings. Among some Old Masters particularly, and occasionally others, artists went by a pseudonym, as did Tiziano Vecellio, better known as Titian. In these cases, the paintings are listed under both names. Paintings described as "attributed to," "circle of," "style of," or "manner of" a particular artist and "School" paintings such as "American School," are not included in this catalogue. There is little value in listing this information because of its subjectivity.

For example, a Hudson River Scene, unsigned and described as "American School" could be worth anything from $25 to $10,000 or more depending on the overall size, artistic quality and attractiveness of the painting. In any guide such as this, without a photo of each painting, the information would be useless to a buyer or seller.

We have also provided nationality information and dates of activity where possible. Nationalities can be hard to pin down since many artists emigrated during their lifetimes and others lived and painted in distant lands. We have tried to follow the precedent of others in assigning nationality but some variations are inevitable. Among the lesser-known European artists, so little may be known they are simply described as European or Continental.

The birth and death dates of artists are included where available. Obviously, among living artists only the birth date is listed, but sometimes even among older artists only one date is known. In some cases, if neither their birth nor death dates are known, but all their known paintings fall into a particular range of dates, they are described by their active dates (in which case the dates in the catalogue are preceded by the letter "a."). The artists of whom even less is known, are assigned a century which corresponds to what little may be known about them or their painting style.

2. The Mediums Used

This factor includes both the material applied to convey an artistic idea and the material or substrate onto which it is applied. Prior to the 20th Century, there were only a limited number of mediums used with oil paints, watercolor, tempera, charcoal, chalk, and ink, typical

10

examples applied to such materials as canvas, linen, panel, board, or paper. The advent of so-called modern art has expanded the available mediums dramatically (and I might add complicated the cataloguing of these works). The mediums are thus divided into two categories, a) the classical painting mediums, and b) the modern/contemporary mediums. This will simplify using the key to abbreviations.

Abbreviations for the material(s) applied are always listed first on the left, followed by a slash (/), which can be translated as meaning "on." The material or substrate onto which they are applied is listed to the right of the slash (again in abbreviated form). If that substrate is laid onto another substrate, another slash follows with that second substrate listed. For those readers familiar with normal convention of listing mediums, those conventions are followed as much as possible. The limited space available, however, requires some changes to be made. The abbreviations are still done as logically and mnemonically as possible.

Some typical examples of classical mediums:

O/C	oil on canvas
W/Pa	watercolor on paper
O/C/B	oil on canvas laid down on board
Pe&W/Pa	Pencil and Watercolor on paper

Some typical examples of modern mediums:

Mk/Pa	Marker on paper
L/C	Collage on canvas
Sp Ss/C	Synthetic Polymer Silkscreened on canvas

The mediums used often have a major effect on value. In general, oil paintings by a given artist command higher prices than watercolors, which in turn command higher prices than the ink drawings. There are plenty of exceptions, however, so it's important that an entire artist's listing be reviewed before developing any conclusions. If the medium is omitted from a specific listing, it means this information was not included in the auction catalogue.

3. The Size of the Work

The size of a piece often has a significant effect on its value. Everything else being equal, larger typically means more expensive. If paintings get too large, however, the size of the market that can accommodate such a painting shrinks dramatically, another factor that affects value. Paintings produced in horizontal format, where the width (horizontal dimension) exceeds the height (vertical dimension), are more common and apparently more desirable for many collectors than paintings produced in a vertical format, where height exceeds the width.

This guide states dimensions in inches rounded to the nearest whole inch, with the vertical dimension the first number and the horizontal dimension the second number. Round paintings are described with a single number followed by the abbreviation "dia" for diameter. The only exception to the use of inches is in the listing of some Old Master drawings which are more commonly described in millimeters (mm). (Dividing the mm number by 25 will give you a close approximation in inches.)

If the size dimension is missing from a listing, that means it was omitted from the auction catalogue.

4. The Subject Matter

The subject may range from a brief description of the painting by the auction house to an actual title assigned by the artist. We have been as descriptive as possible given the limited space available.

We opted not to simply list the paintings by category such as still life, landscape, portrait, etc. The title usually indicates its general category and provides additional useful information. For example, if a portrait of George Washington by Rembrandt Peale were to be listed simply as Portrait, it wouldn't explain to the reader why it went for what may appear to be a very high price.

Among modern art works, some are simply "Untitled" and an apt verbal description impossible. Those works are usually of the abstract genre. Some foreign works, particularly French, German and Latin American, are often titled in the artist's language. Many of these are not translated into English in this guide.

It is also important to be aware that while many artists painted a variety of subjects, often one or more of those subject areas is considered more desirable by collectors and/or experts and hence may command a higher price. A variety of reasons for these differences apply. It may be that the artist simply painted a particular type of subject better. It also may be that a particular subject area may be more desirable in today's market. An example of this is the current popularity of beach scenes. Any beach scene by an artist like Edward Potthast (Am 1857-1927) will usually sell for more than his other landscapes. In his case, Potthast has become well known for his impressionistic beach scenes, which in turn creates additional demand for the type of scene he is famous for.

John F. Francis (Am 1808-1886) is known as a major 19th Century American still-life painter but he also did many studio portraits of average people. Since this subject area is not popular today, his still lifes bring significantly higher prices than his portraits.

The point is to be aware that the subject area, or even a subgrouping within the subject area, can have a great impact on the price of an individual work of art. The way prices are prioritized in any artist's listing in this guide allows one to see how and to what extent the subject can affect prices. Another item of note is that American painters often generate higher prices for paintings of American scenes than foreign scenes, although the gap seems to be closing.

A review of general subject areas includes:

Landscape - Outdoor vistas which may or may not contain figures, buildings, etc.

Marine - Subjects relating to ships and / or the sea.

Genre - Scenes of everyday life from some time period.

Still Lifes - Picked fruit or flowers, dead game, pottery, etc.

Trompe l'oeil - "Fool the eye" images created on a flat surface appearing to be three-dimensional.

Figure - Single person or groups of people.

Hunting/Sporting - Typically fox-hunting scenes, horses.

Wildlife - Wild animals in native habitat.

Illustrations - Pieces produced for ads, magazine covers, etc.

Primitives (folk art) - Art done by amateurs without any training.

Modern - Avant-garde, abstract, non-traditional.

There are, of course, gray areas, and paintings that don't easily fit into one subject or are combinations of two or more areas.

5. The Date Painted

Some works are dated by the artist and, if so, that date is provided in the catalogue following the title or description. This factor, while usually of less importance than other variables, can identify during which period of the artist's life the work was done. For artists who went through distinct periods of changing style—for example, George Inness and Pablo Picasso—the time periods can have an impact on value.

The majority of works, however, are not dated by the artist.

Dating can also provide valuable information for those researching a particular artist. For example, dated landscapes can sometimes help determine when the artist may have traveled to certain locations or worked with other artists.

6. The Auction House Selling the Painting

The auction house often impacts prices. For important paintings, this difference is usually not significant. For middle-range and less expensive paintings, however, prices are often higher in large metropolitan areas, New York City being the most notable. There is more money there, a higher concentration of collectors, and more contact with the general art-buying public particularly because of their name recognition and the sheer mass of art which is traded. The larger auction houses included in this price guide also have a reputation to protect, can afford larger staffs, and are able to do more research in cataloguing paintings and determining authenticity. "Local" artists, who are not well known nationally, usually sell more easily and at higher prices in auction houses nearer their home base where they are better known. For example, many early- to mid-20th Century "California Artists" sell best in California.

This price guide includes most major auction houses from coast to coast. There are scores of additional smaller auction houses and while each could add a couple of "local" artists to the overall listings, this advantage is outweighed by our efforts to keep the book relatively small and portable.

7. The Date of Sale

Like much of business and commerce, art sales and auctions slow during the summer months. Competing diversions, like vacations, contribute to this trend. For the buyer, this can mean some bargains at auction since there are fewer people to compete with. The seller, however, should stick to the prime auction season of October to May if intending to consign paintings for sale. It is rare for any major works to be auctioned in the summer months.

This price guide lists the month and year of sales following the abbreviated name of the auction house. If there has been an increase in value for a particular artist's work during the year, the trend may be seen by comparing prices to dates sold.

The date also allows the reader the opportunity to find the catalogue of the actual sale cited and perhaps see a photo of a painting of interest if reproduced in that catalogue.

The next five key factors, Numbers 8 through 12, all relatively subjective, are often not available and thus are not included among the data in this price guide. However, they still should be considered important factors.

---

8. The Condition of the Piece

Obviously, condition can have a major effect on anything you buy. The more pristine and nearly flawless, the better—and often more expensive. It's not any different with works of art. Examples of less-than- perfect condition can range from paint loss for oil paintings to "foxing" of watercolors to outright damage such as holes in canvas or paper tears. The extent of damage and the difficulty of repair are most important. A small bit of paint loss and expert restoration in the sky, say, of a large landscape will have little effect on value. The same loss and restoration in a key part of the painting, such as figures or buildings, can have a more significant impact. A qualified restorer can repair almost any damage, but, the costs can be quite high. For your sake, never let an unqualified person touch any work of art!

Condition is a variable not included in most auction catalogues and hence is not included in this guide. It can usually be provided by the auction house for a specific piece if you request it and any buyer should always do so before bidding. If restoration has been done well, it will be invisible to the naked eye. An ultraviolet (black) light will often show up restored areas and other problems with a painting. It can be a useful tool for collectors and dealers alike.

9. The Authenticity

The question of authenticity of a piece is always a problem. I've found it to be one of the biggest deterrents to collectors entering the fine arts field.

There is no way for a guide such as this to guarantee authenticity. Signed works generally are safer choices for any buyers but even signatures are obviously not foolproof. This guide does not indicate whether works are signed or unsigned due to space limitations and also because most works (with the exception of Old Masters) are signed.

Large and reputable dealers are probably the safest choice here for the newer collector, and although you may pay more for this "insurance" it's a good way to get started. This price guide can still help the collector and dealer determine if the prices asked or offered are at least reasonable. Once one becomes more knowledgeable and confident, auctions can become an enjoyable and useful alternative. My feeling is that the major auction houses, at least, do the best job they can in assuring the authenticity of pieces they sell.

Among lower-priced works, the question of authenticity becomes far less important. There just isn't much incentive to counterfeit works that sell for under $1000 to $2000. Anyone talented enough to forge such works probably could sell his or her own works for at least that much or would likely forge more valuable pieces. Analogously, counterfeiters do not produce bogus paper money in denominations smaller than $20 or $50 dollar bills.

10. The "Attractiveness" or General Quality of the Work

As discussed in the section about artists, even the best has days when everything works out and days when nothing seems to work out. This, "quality" of a work is very subjective and obviously cannot be catalogued or reported in a guide such as this. Only if you look at enough art, especially enough works by a particular artist, will you be able to differentiate between the exceptional, the average, and the terrible. Experienced dealers and collectors can tell the difference, which may help explain drastic contrast in the listings in this guide for certain artists with similar paintings in the same auction.

The "attractiveness" can also relate to the subject matter. There are numerous examples of "pretty" pictures by obscure artists reaching prices ten times or more their projected value. This is often not because they were particularly well painted but because they were pleasant, "pretty" pictures of romantic scenes at the park or beach, both popular subjects today.

11. Provenance

Provenance is defined as the origin or source. In art, it is essentially the history of ownership or lineage from as near to the artist's hand as possible. This really could be included within the review of authenticity since it serves to authenticate by tracing backward.

Major works of art sometimes have a clear provenance but most works do not. It is not available for most paintings and hence is not included in this price guide.

12. Historical Significance

Most works of art have no historical significance but a painting such as Monet's "Impression Sunrise" obviously does, at least within the field of art history. Other paintings with true historical significance are some of the paintings of the American West produced in the 19th Century, and of famous statesmen like George Washington.

Sometimes, the historical significance can affect value and other times it may just be interesting—how interesting determines the effect on value.

The painting by James Hamilton, reproduced on the cover of the 1990 Premiere Edition, for example, has an interesting history which could affect it's value. It was one of several small paintings purchased by the U.S. Government and presented by Abraham Lincoln to Charlotte Saunders Cushman, the leading American actress of her day, in appreciation for her work with the fledgling American Red Cross during the Civil War.

In other cases, paintings were reproduced as popular engraved prints and thus became far more famous than would ever occur otherwise. Here, the actual original painting may have a higher value than normally expected.

Other Suggested Resources Relating to the Auction Market

A well developed and more detailed background and review of art value considerations for the novice can be found in *Curriers Art Price Guides*. These guides also contain a general price range for each artist but no specific information on individual paintings sold. [Currier Publications, P. O. Box 2098, Brockton, MA 02403]

For keeping abreast of the market between editions of ART AT AUCTION IN AMERICA...

Our own *ART PRICE QUARTERLY* provides reports covering every work sold at three month intervals throughout the year. The format is the same as used in this book. [KREXPRESS, 10169 New Hampshire Avenue, #195, Silver Spring, MD 20903]

Art and Auction Magazine provides monthly updates of both the American and foreign auction markets. Its coverage tends to be focused on the higher priced more newsworthy happenings, but it includes interesting inside information on the art market in general. [Art & Auction, 250 W. 57th St., New York, NY 10107]

Maine Antique Digest, published monthly, and *Antiques and the Arts Weekly* are large tabloid publications which are read by many collectors and professionals in the collectibles business. Both publications contain information about upcoming auctions as well as highlights of those just past. They are not limited in scope to New England, but are nationwide in coverage. [Maine Antique Digest, P. O. Box 645, Waldoboro, ME 04572] [Antiques & the Arts Weekly, The Bee Publishing Co., 5 Church Hill Rd., Newtown, CT 06470]

There are many more regional antique and arts publications in each area of the country and these can also often be of great value to collectors.

EXPLANATION OF PRICING

The prices listed in this guide are all in U.S. dollars, rounded to the nearest dollar. The lower cutoff point is $25; i.e., paintings selling for less than $25 are not included. There is no maximum. Works selling for one million dollars or more are priced using the capital letter M to signify millions; e.g., 3.0M would be $3,000,000 and 3.025M would be $3,025,000. Canadian dollars have been converted to U.S. dollars at a rate of 1.0 CD = 0.85 USD.

Nearly all auction houses add their own ten percent commission to the hammer price. Some of the auction houses include this ten percent in their published prices, some do not. It is usually easy to determine if any price listed includes the ten percent. If the prices are simple round numbers like $4,000 or $20,000, the commissions are probably not included. On the other hand, if the prices listed are $4,400 or $22,000, then the commissions probably are included. The following reviews which auction houses include commissions in their price lists and which do not:

Auction Houses Listed with 10% Commissions Included	*Auction Houses Listed with Commissions Not Included*
Barridoff	Alderfer
Butterfield & Butterfield	Bourne
Christie's/Christie's East	Doyle
Eldred's	DuMouchelles
Mystic	Freeman/Fine Arts
Skinner's	Hanzel Galleries
Sotheby's/Sotheby's Arcade	Illustration House
Sotheby's Toronto	Leslie Hindman
Weschler's	Louisiana Auction Exchange
	John Moran
	Selkirk's
	C. G. Sloan
	Wolf's
	Young Fine Arts

Arguments can be made as to whether it is more accurate to include the commissions paid or not. However, it is felt that the ten percent difference is not important enough to be too concerned about given the subjectivity of art valuations anyway. Therefore, to reiterate, the prices listed in this guide include the ten percent commission where the auction house includes it in their published prices and it is not included where they do not.

The prices are listed in descending price order independent of the other variables. There are several other ways to organize the data, but this is a *price* guide, and the simplest way for the user to determine which variables have the most significant affect on the price of a particular artist's work is through prioritization by descending price. Any other method of organization would be useful in looking at that one variable; e.g., date sold, but it would be very difficult to draw any other conclusions.

Again, it is important to note that the prices come from the auction houses and are entered into our database. Thus errors, although rare, are undoubtedly inevitable. In fact, we have questioned a few suspicious numbers on the price lists and have, indeed, gotten corrections. If any information looks questionable, please contact us or the auction house before relying on it.

KEYS TO USING THIS GUIDE

The key to the abbreviations used in ART AT AUCTION IN AMERICA, and included below, is also reproduced on inside of the back cover so the user does not have to flip back and forth in this book.

Artist's Name

Artist's names are listed alphabetically irrespective of nationality or dates of activity. Some names are difficult to alphabetize such as Willem De Kooning and Vincent Van Gogh. Van Gogh is listed under Van, and De Kooning is listed under De. French surnames which contain de are usually listed following convention, e.g., Diaz de la Pena is listed under Diaz....

Artists who used or were known by a pseudonym are usually listed under both their family name and pseudonym.

Artist's Nationality

Am	American	Hun	Hungarian
Arg	Argentinean	In	Indian
Aut	Australian	Irs	Irish
Aus	Austrian	Isr	Israeli
Bel	Belgian	It	Italian
Bol	Bolivian	LA	Latin American
Brz	Brazilian	Jap	Japanese
Br	British	Mex	Mexican
Bul	Bulgarian	Nz	New Zealander
Can	Canadian	Nic	Nicaraguan
Chl	Chilean	Nor	Norwegian
Chi	Chinese	Per	Peruvian
Col	Columbian	Phi	Philippino
Con	Continental	Pol	Polish
Cos	Costa Rican	Por	Portuguese
Cub	Cuban	PR	Puerto Rican
Czk	Czechoslovakian	Rom	Romanian
Dan	Danish	Rus	Russian
Dut	Dutch	Scn	Scandinavian
Ecu	Ecuadorian	Sco	Scottish
Eng	English	Spa	Spanish
Eur	European	Swd	Swedish
Fin	Finnish	Sws	Swiss
Flm	Flemish	Tha	Thai
Fr	French	Tur	Turkish
Ger	German	Uru	Uruguayan
Grk	Greek	Ven	Venezuelan
Hai	Haitian	Yug	Yugoslavian

Artist's Dates

1) If:
    a) Birth and Death Dates are known   1810-1888
    b) Only Birth Date known or still living   1810-
    c) Only Death Date known   -1888
2) If only Active Dates known   a 1830-1848
3) If only Century known   19C

Reference to other editions

Such a reference under an artist's name indicates there were no sales of that artist's work during the 1991-1992 auction year, but sales information can be found in the noted edition of ART AT AUCTION IN AMERICA.

Size of Work

In inches rounded to the nearest whole inch.
    First Dimension = height of work (vertical dimension)
                     x = by
    Second Dimension = width of work (horizontal dimension)
    Round Paintings = a number followed by "dia" indicating diameter

Mediums Used in the Work

In the interest of accuracy and completeness, we have included more mediums than most similar publications. Please do not be intimidated by the size of the listings as most actually occur infrequently, and the common ones are easily committed to memory.

Traditional Mediums

Q	Aquatint	Et	Egg Tempera	Pnc	Peinture a la Colle
Bc	Body Color	E	Enamel	Pal	Peinture a l'essence
Br	Brush	Gd	Gold Leaf/Gold Paint	Pl	Pen and Ink
K	Chalk	G	Gouache	Pe	Pencil
C	Charcoal	H	Graphite	B	Sepia
Cw	Chinese White	R	Grisaille	T	Tempera
Kc	Colored Chalk	I	Ink	V	Varnish
Y	Crayon	O	Oil	S	Wash
D	Drypoint	P	Pastel	W	Watercolor

Modern Mediums

A	Acrylic	Os	Oil Stick
Ar	Air Brush	Pt	Paint
Bp	Ball Point Pen	Pts	Paint Stick
Cs	Casein	Pp	Petroplastic
Cg	Chromogesso	Ph	Photograph
L	Collage	Pg	Pigment
Cp	Colored Pencil	Pol	Politec
Ct	Copper Paint	Pr	Polyester Resin
Det	Detrempe	Py	Polymer
Dis	Dispersion	Px	Proxylin
Du	Duco	Rn	Resin
Em	Emulsion	Rs	Rubber Stamp
N	Encaustic	Sd	Sand
Fx	Fax	Sg	Sanguine
Fp	Felt Pen	Ss	Silkscreen
Gp	Gun Powder	Sv	Silverpoint
Lx	Latex	Slt	Solvent Transfer
Lq	Liquitex	Sp	Synthetic Polymer
Mg	Magna	Vy	Vinylite
Mk	Marker	Wx	Wax
MM	Mixed Media		

Mediums Applied To

Ab	Academy Board/Artist's Board	L	Linen
A	Acetate	Mb	Marble
Al	Aluminum	M	Masonite
B	Board	Me	Metal
Bu	Burlap	My	Mylar
C	Canvas	Pn	Panel
Cb	Canvas Board	Pa	Paper
Cd	Cardboard	Pb	Paperboard
Cel	Celluloid	Ph	Parchment
Clx	Celotex	Pl	Plaster
Ce	Cement	Pls	Plastic
Cer	Ceramic	Pw	Plywood
Cl	Cloth	Por	Porcelain
Cp	Copper	Rb	Ragboard
Cot	Cotton	S	Silk
F	Fabric	Sl	Slate
Fg	Fibreglass	St	Steel
Frs	Fresco	Tn	Tin
Gl	Glass	Wd	Wood
Iv	Ivory	Wb	Woodboard
Ju	Jute	V	Vellum
Lh	Leather	Vl	Vinyl

Auction House

Ald	**Sanford A. Alderfer Auction Co.**	
	501 Fairgrounds Road, Hatfield, PA 19440	(215) 368-5477
Brd	**Barridoff Galleries**	
	P.O. Box 9715, Portland, ME 04104	(207) 772-5011
Bor	**Richard A. Bourne Co.**	
	P. O. Box 141, Hyannisport, MA 02647	(508) 775-0797
But	**Butterfield and Butterfield**	
	220 San Bruno Avenue, San Francisco, CA 94103	(415) 861-7500
Chr	**Christie's**	
	502 Park Avenue, New York, NY 10022	(212) 546-1000
	Christie's East	
	219 East 67th Street, New York, NY 10021	(212) 606-0400
Doy	**William Doyle Galleries**	
	175 East 87th Street, New York, NY 10128	(212) 427-2730
Dum	**DuMouchelles Art Galleries Co.**	
	409 E. Jefferson Avenue, Detroit, MI 48226	(313) 963-6255
Eld	**Robert C. Eldred Co.**	
	Route 6A, East Dennis, MA 02641	(508) 385-3116
Fre	**Freeman/Fine Arts of Philadelphia, Inc.**	
	1808-10 Chestnut Street, Philadelphia, PA 19103	(215) 563-9275
Hnd	**Leslie Hindman Auctioneers**	
	215 W. Ohio St., Chicago, IL 60610	(312) 670-0010
Hnz	**Hanzel Galleries**	
	1220 South Michigan Avenue, Chicago, IL 60605	(312) 922-6234
Ilh	**Illustration House, Inc.**	
	96 Spring Street, New York, NY 10012	(212) 966-9444
Lou	**Louisiana Auction Exchange, Inc.**	
	2031 Government Street, Baton Rouge, LA 70806	(504) 924-1803
Mor	**John Moran Auctioneers**	
	3202 E. Foothill Blvd., Pasadena, CA 91107	(818) 793-1833
Mys	**Mystic Fine Arts**	
	47 Holmes Street, Mystic CT 06355	(203) 572-8873
Sel	**Selkirk's**	
	4166 Olive Street, St. Louis, MO 63108	(314) 533-1700
Skn	**Skinner, Inc.**	
	357 Main Street, Bolton, MA 01740	(508) 779-6241
Slo	**C. G. Sloan & Co., Inc.**	
	4920 Wyaconda Road, North Bethesda, MD 20852	(301) 468-4911
Sby	**Sotheby's**	
	1334 York Avenue, New York, NY 10021	(212) 606-7000
	Sotheby's Arcade	
	1334 York Avenue, New York, NY 10021	(212) 606-7516
Sbt	**Sotheby's Toronto**	
	9 Hazelton Ave., Toronto, Ontario M5R2E1, Canada	(416) 926-1774
Wes	**Weschler's**	
	909 E Street, N.W., Washington, DC 20004	(202) 628-1281
Wlf	**Wolf's**	
	1239 West 6th Street, Cleveland, OH 44113	(216) 575-9653
Yng	**Young Fine Arts Gallery, Inc.**	
	P. O. Box 313, North Berwick, ME 03906	(207) 676-3104

Title or Description of work

Self-explanatory, though some titles are in the language of the artist. Some modern works are untitled.

Date Painted

The year date as actually inscribed on the work. May be complete such as 1864 or partial such as 64. Occasionally, only part of a date may be legible and may be listed as 186?.

Date of Auction

Month and year of auction.

Prices

All in U.S. dollars in descending price order. Some include ten percent buyer's commission, some do not, depending on auction house. M means million; e.g., 4.05M =$4,050,000. Canadian dollars are converted at 1.0 CD = 0.85 USD.

SEE HOW EASY IT IS TO FIND JUST THE INFORMATION YOU NEED

Artist's nationality

Artist's full name (listed alphabetically)

Medium

Size in inches

Description or title of the work

John, Augustus Eng 1878-1961
Pe/Pa 13x8 Seated Female Nude Skn 11/88........................ 250
Johns, Jasper Am 1930-
O/C 68x53 False Start Spb 11/88............................. 17.05M
N/C 60x60 Gray Rectangles Spb 11/88........................... 4.29M
O/C 72x50 Screen Piece II 1968 Spb 11/88...................... 1.37M
Johnson, David Am 1827-1908
O/C 10x18 Ocean Beach, New Jersey 1877 Chr 9/88........ 13200
O/B 6x9 On Esopus Creek 1876 Chr 9/88...................... 3850
Johnson, Jonathan Eastman Am 1824-1906
O/C 40x33 Honorable Morgan O'Brian Wes 10/88.............. 2000
Johnson, Marshall Am 1850-1921
O/C 18x24 Beating to Windward Bor 8/88....................... 2900
Johnson, Roy Am 1890-1963
W/Pa 14x11 Dutch Girl By Window Wes 10/88................... 225
O/M 20x16 Lady In Garden Wes 10/88........................... 125
O/CB 16x12 Woman Holding Fan Wes 10/88....................... 75
Jones, Hugh Bolton Am 1848-1907
O/C 14x20 A Lush Spring Chr 9/88............................. 4400

Artist's birth and death date or century

Date of work (if artist dated it)

Auction house

Date of auction

Prices realized in dollars and in descending price order

Abades, E. Martinez   Con 20C
* See 1992 Edition ....
Abades, Juan Martinez   Spa 1862-
O/C 40x24 Moored on the Beach Sby 2/92 11,000
O/C 40x24 The Mooring Sby 2/92 8,800
Abakanowicz, Magdalena   1930-
C/Pa 32x47 Untitled 84 Chr 5/92 5,500
Abbatt, Agnes Dean   Am 1847-1917
W/Pa 8x29 Yellow Dandelions Chr 11/91 2,200
Abbema, Louise   Fr 1858-1927
* See 1992 Edition ....
Abbey, Edwin Austin   Am 1852-1911
P/B 21x18 The Jester 1887 Chr 3/92 4,950
Pl/Pa 7x11 Woman Sitting in Church 1886 llh 5/92 1,700
W,I&Pe/Pa 9x14 Resting on a Park Bench 1874 Sby 12/91 .. 880
G&R/Pa 10x18 Jeere 1881 Dum 5/92 650
Pl/Pa 7x9 Three Figures in an Interior 1888 Wes 3/92 ... 220
Abbott   Am 20C
G/Pa 14x10 Lovers Hnd 6/92 50
Abbott, Samuel Nelson   Am 1874-1953
O/C 27x42 Football Player Tackling Bag llh 5/92 6,500
Abbott, Yarnall   Am 1870-1938
O/C 30x37 Sea and Derricks Chr 11/91 1,320
Abdy, Rowena Meeks   Am 1887-1945
C/Pa 12x18 Mission San Juan Bautista But 10/91 1,650
Abel-Boulineau, N.   Fr 20C
* See 1990 Edition ....
Abelard, Gesner   Hai 20C
O/M 24x40 Park Wes 3/92 578
Ableta, James   Am 20C
* See 1991 Edition ....
Abramovsky, Israel   1888-
O/B 9x12 A Shore Road Yng 4/92 350
Abrams, Lucien   Am 1870-1941
* See 1992 Edition ....
Abreu, Mario   Ven 1918-
* See 1990 Edition ....
Abry, Leon Eugene Auguste   Bel 1857-1905
* See 1990 Edition ....
Absolon, John   Eng 1815-1895
* See 1992 Edition ....
Abularach, Rodolfo
* See 1992 Edition ....
Accard, Eugene   Fr 1824-1888
O/C 27x23 Admiring the Pearls Chr 5/92 7,700
Accardi, Carla   1924-
O/C 24x64 Untitled Chr 11/91 24,200
Acconci, Vito   1940-
K,Pt&L/Pa 36x144 Stills for Home Movies 1973 Chr 2/92 . 16,500
Aceves, Gustavo   20C
* See 1992 Edition ....
Acheff, William   Am 1947-
O/C 12x18 Santo Domingo Dipper 1982 Sby 12/91 10,450
Achenbach, Andreas   Ger 1815-1910
* See 1992 Edition ....
Achenbach, Oswald   Ger 1827-1905
O/C 52x44 Sicilian Village Mount Aetna Chr 5/92 .. 60,500
Achille-Fould, Mlle. Georges   Fr 1865-
O/C 46x35 The Answer Hnd 5/92 4,000
Achtschellinck, Lucas   Flm 1626-1699
* See 1990 Edition ....
Acquivito   It 20C
O/C 24x36 Harbor Scene Yng 2/92 200
Adam, Benno   Ger 1812-1892
* See 1991 Edition ....
Adam, Franz   Ger 1815-1886
* See 1991 Edition ....
Adam, Joseph Denovan   Br 1842-1896
O/C 30x50 Children Playing on a Hillside Chr 2/92 4,620
Adam, Julius   Ger 1852-1913
O/C 11x17 Woher Kommst Denn Du? 08 Sby 10/91 40,700
O/Pn 6x8 Tug of War Sby 2/92 29,700
O/Pn 6x8 The Playful Kittens 1887 Sby 2/92 26,400

Adam, Richard Benno   Ger 1873-1936
O/C 45x33 Frohes Jagen 1923 Sby 6/92 5,500
Adams, Charles Partridge   Am 1858-1942
O/C 19x26 River Valley Sby 12/91 2,750
O/C 14x18 Mountainous Landscape Wlf 9/91 1,600
O/C 24x24 Landscape Mor 6/92 750
Adams, John Clayton   Br 1840-1906
* See 1992 Edition ....
Adams, John Ottis   Am 1851-1927
O/C 29x22 Spring Landscape 1895 Chr 12/91 33,000
Adams, John Quincy   Aus 1874-1933
* See 1991 Edition ....
Adams, Lillian   Am 1899-
O/C 18x24 October Landscape Fre 12/91 400
Adams, Wayman   Am 1883-1959
O/Pn 10x7 Playing on the Steps Chr 6/92 9,350
O/Pn 15x12 A Carriage Ride Chr 6/92 3,300
Adams, Willis Seaver   Am 1842-1921
* See 1992 Edition ....
Adamson, Dorothy   Br -1934
* See 1992 Edition ....
Adamson, Harry Curleux   Am 20C
* See 1992 Edition ....
Adamson, John
* See 1991 Edition ....
Adamson, Sydney   Br 20C
O/C 27x40 The Rebel Charge 1899 Sby 4/92 2,640
Adan, Louis Emile   Fr 1839-1937
* See 1992 Edition ....
Addams, Charles   Am 1912-1988
I&S/Pa 13x15 Fishermen Capture Submarine 47 llh 5/92 ... 1,700
Adler, Edmund   Ger 1871-1957
O/C 22x27 Preparing the Flag Sby 2/92 14,850
O/C 18x23 The Young Seamstress Sby 2/92 13,750
Adler, Jankel   Pol 1895-1949
* See 1991 Edition ....
Adler, Jules   Fr 1865-1952
* See 1991 Edition ....
Adler, Oscar   20C
O/C 20x28 Farm Scene in Winter Yng 2/92 600
Adler, Samuel   Am 1898-1979
O/C 50x38 Figure in Blue Mys 6/92 550
Adolphe, Albert Jean   Am 1865-1940
* See 1991 Edition ....
Adriani, Camille   Am 20C
O/B 20x16 Ladies In A Garden Hnd 6/92 400
Adrion, Lucien   Fr 1889-1953
O/C 32x25 Jardin du Luxembourg Chr 11/91 6,050
O/C 24x36 Notre Dame de Paris Chr 11/91 3,960
O/C 26x32 La Seine 37 Doy 11/91 3,500
O/C 20x24 Village Street Sby 2/92 2,200
O/C 16x20 Route de Chevreuse a Bievres Sby 2/92 ... 2,090
Aertsen, Pieter   1507-1575
* See 1992 Edition ....
Affleck, William   Br 1869-
W/Pa/B 13x17 English Cottage in the Cotswolds Sby 1/92 . 4,125
Africano, Nicholas   1948-
O&E/C 65x82 Raise Your Arm 1978 Chr 2/92 6,050
A,O&Mg/M 14x26 This is a God-Forsaken Place Sby 10/91 . 4,400
Afro (Basaldella)   1912-1976
O/C 43x27 La Citta Morta 1953 Chr 5/92 60,500
O/C 21x29 Untitled 52 Sby 2/92 60,500
Agam, Yaacov
* See 1992 Edition ....
Agard, Charles Jean   Fr 1866-
* See 1991 Edition ....
Agnesti   It 20C
O/C 12x16 Cardinal Flirting with a Maid Hnd 12/91 800
Agnew, Clark   Am 19C
* See 1990 Edition ....
Agostinelli, A.   Am 20C
O/B 12x9 Three Little Girls Fre 12/91 140
Agostini, Guido   It 19C
O/C 17x13 Sesto Calenda sul Ticino But 5/92 2,200

Agostini, S. It 20C
O/C 10x18 On the African Plains 1969 Hnz 5/92 130
Agostini, Tony It 1916-
O/C 18x22 Three Paintings Chr 2/92 3,300
O/C 14x11 Still Life Chair and Flowers Sby 2/92 1,210
O/C 24x29 Fruit in a Compote Sel 4/92 150
Agrasot Y Juan, Joaquin Spa 1836-1907
O/C 29x18 The Serenade Sby 10/91 27,500
O/C 13x21 The Sultan and His Harem Sby 2/92 6,600
Agresti, R. It 19C
O/C 26x22 Nursing the Baby Chr 5/92 2,750
Agthe, Curt Ger 1862-
* See 1992 Edition . . . .
Aguilar, Homero
* See 1990 Edition . . . .
Aguste, Phillipe Hai 20C
* See 1992 Edition . . . .
Ahl, Henry Curtis Am 1905-
* See 1991 Edition . . . .
Ahl, Henry Hammond Am 1869-1953
* See 1992 Edition . . . .
Ahlborn, August Wilhelm Ger 1796-1857
* See 1991 Edition . . . .
Ainsley, Dennis Am 20C
O/C 24x36 Book Stands, Paris Dum 10/91 400
Airth, T.
W/Pa 20x16 Hunting Dogs Dum 4/92 200
Aitken Am 20C
O/B 19x12 Two Still Lifes Slo 12/91 550
Aitken, J. Eng 19C
O/C 18x24 Return of the Prodigal 1858 Wes 11/91 1,045
Aivasovsky, Ivan Constantin. Rus 1817-1900
* See 1992 Edition . . . .
Aizenberg, Roberto Arg 1928-
O/C/B 36x22 Torre 1982 Chr 5/92 11,000
Aizpiri, Paul Fr 1919-
O/C 21x26 Saint Maxime Sby 6/92 16,500
Ajdukiewicz, Zygmund Pol 1861-1917
* See 1992 Edition . . . .
Akers, Vivian M. Am 1886-1966
O/B 6x5 Passing Showers 1953 Brd 8/92 798
O/B 12x16 Streaked Mountain 1929 Brd 5/92 522
Akkeringa, Johannes Evert Dut 1894-
W/Pa 15x21 Women Drying Nets Hnd 10/91 3,600
Akkersdijk, Jacob Dut 1815-1862
* See 1992 Edition . . . .
Alajalov, Constantin Am 1900-1987
O/C 16x13 Man Tending Barbeque 51 Ilh 5/92 7,500
Alberici, Augusto It 1846-
* See 1992 Edition . . . .
Alberola, Jean-Michel 1953-
O/C 59x64 Suzanne et les Vieillards 1984 Chr 5/92 6,050
K&H/Pa 58x66 Melampus III 83 Chr 2/92 5,280
K/Pa 66x58 Ichnobates Chr 2/92 4,950
K/Pa 40x51 Hilaeus II 83 Chr 5/92 2,860
K&C/Pa 53x41 Laelaps Chr 5/92 2,640
Albers, Josef Am 1888-1976
O/M 48x48 Homage to the Square: Guarded 59 Chr 5/92 . . 143,000
O/M 24x24 Homage to the Square 69 Chr 5/92 66,000
O/M 32x32 Homage to Square: Saturated 1961 Sby 5/92 . . 55,000
O/M 24x24 Homage to Square: Gate C 1957 Sby 10/91 . . 44,000
O/M 16x16 RI-A2 1968 Sby 11/91 38,500
O/M 18x18 Homage to the Square 63 Chr 11/91 28,600
O/M 18x18 Homage Square: Extend Center 1956 Chr 5/92 . . 24,200
O/Al 24x24 Homage to the Square 65 Chr 11/91 24,200
H/Pa 5x8 Untitled 50 Sby 2/92 3,575
Albert De Gesne, Jean Victor Fr 1834-1903
* See 1991 Edition . . . .
Albert, Adolphe Fr 20C
* See 1992 Edition . . . .
Albert, E. Maxwell Am 19C
O/C 15x18 Mother and Child in Garden Mys 11/91 2,530

Albert, Ernest Am 1857-1946
O/C 24x24 Rock Bound Brook Hnd 3/92 17,000
O/C 30x40 Old Lyme Landscape Skn 11/91 4,125
Albert, Karl Am 1911-
O/M 20x24 Mexico Village Mor 6/92 1,500
O/C 20x30 Three-Arch Bay Mor 6/92 750
O/B 12x16 Boli Miki Bakery Lou 12/91 625
Alberti, Giuseppe Vizzotto It 19C
* See 1992 Edition . . . .
Albina, Luca It 20C
O/Pn 14x20 The Day's Catch Sby 7/92 3,025
Albinson, Dewey Ernest Am 1898-
O/C 30x40 Farm in the Hills Hnd 3/92 1,600
Albotto, Francesco 1721-1753
* See 1992 Edition . . . .
Albrecht, Carl Ger 1862-1926
O/B 9x11 Still Life of Pansies Slo 4/92 150
Albridge, F. J.
W/Pa 12x10 Sailboat Dum 2/92 150
Albright, Adam Emory Am 1862-1957
O/C 18x28 Children on a Hill 1933 But 4/92 22,000
O/C 28x23 Two Boys Fishing But 4/92 8,800
O/Cb 20x13 Young Boy Fishing Wlf 9/91 1,000
O/B 12x14 The Old Homestead Hnz 10/91 700
Albright, Gertrude Partington Am 1883-1959
O/C 20x26 Bird Rock, Monterey But 2/92 1,650
Albright, Ivan Le Lorraine Am 1897-1985
W/Pa 14x20 Town Scene 1941 Hnz 5/92 1,100
Alcazar Y Ruiz, Manuel Spa 19C
* See 1991 Edition . . . .
Aldershot, * *
O/C 114x195 Santa Maria Wes 5/92 1,980
Alderton, Henry A. Am 1896-1961
O/C 12x16 Oahu Beach 1928 Mor 3/92 900
Aldin, Cecil Eng 1870-1935
* See 1992 Edition . . . .
Aldine, Marc It 1917-
O/C 32x21 Venetian Canal Sby 7/92 3,850
Aldrich, George Ames Am 1872-1941
O/B 24x29 Creek in Winter Hnd 10/91 5,000
O/C 30x24 Woman with Water Pail But 4/92 4,400
O/B 20x24 Nocturne, Montreuil sur Mer Hnd 10/91 . . . 1,700
O/B 20x24 Old Mill Sel 4/92 1,300
O/C 16x20 Le Soir Rivier Elaune Sel 12/91 750
O/C/B 24x24 Wooded Landscape Sel 4/92 650
Alechinsky, Pierre Bel 1927-
A/Pa/C 46x37 Carre de Ciel 1978 Chr 5/92 55,000
O/C 16x13 Le Langage Des Liens 1962 Sby 11/91 . . . 16,500
I&G/Pa 49x35 Untitled 1980 Sby 11/91 16,500
Br&I/Pa 13x8 Untitled 61 Chr 2/92 2,640
Alegiani, Francesco It 19C
* See 1992 Edition . . . .
Alexander, Clifford Grear Am 1870-1954
* See 1990 Edition . . . .
Alexander, Francesca Am 1837-1917
* See 1991 Edition . . . .
Alexander, Francis Am 1800-1880
O/C 26x22 Pair: Portrait 1821 Sel 9/91 700
Alexander, Henry Am 1860-1895
* See 1991 Edition . . . .
Alexander, John 1945-
O/C 90x100 The Annunciation Chr 11/91 11,000
Alexander, John White Am 1856-1915
* See 1991 Edition . . . .
Alexieff, Alexander I. Rus 1842-
O/Pn 16x10 Portrait of a Woman Sby 7/92 3,410
Alfani, Domenico It 16C
* See 1990 Edition . . . .
Alfonzo, Carlos Cub 1950-1991
W&G/Pa 48x32 Untitled 87 Sby 11/91 3,575
Alfredson, A.
O/C 19x23 Autumn Landscape Wlf 6/92 400
Alfredson, P. Am 19C
O/C 16x20 Farmhouse Hnz 5/92 200

Alger, John   Am 1879-
O/C 22x27 Cows in a Pasture Wlf 10/91 250
O/C 20x25 Cows in a Pasture Wlf 10/91 200
Alix, Gabriel   Hai
O/M 24x20 Arbre en Fleur Chr 5/92 715
Alken, Henry Thomas   Br 1785-1851
O/C 17x24 Meet, Halloo, Full Cry, Death: 4 1847 But 5/92 209,000
O/C 17x21 The Belvoir Hunt Slo 10/91 5,250
W/Pa 11x15 Horses and Riders: Four Sby 6/92 4,950
W/Pa 6x9 Five Watercolors 1840 Wlf 3/92 3,250
W/Pa 9x13 On the Scent Slo 4/92 1,000
Alken, Samuel (Jr.)   Br 1784-1825
K&W/Pa 11x18 Black and Bay: Pair 1812 Sby 6/92 4,950
Alken, Samuel Henry   Br 1810-1894
* See 1992 Edition . . . .
Allak, Gustave
O/C/B 26x37 Romantic Landscape Dum 9/91 200
Allan
O/C 36x42 Abstract Dum 1/92 90
Allan, Donald F.   Am 20C
O/B 12x12 Still Life: Two Slo 10/91 140
Allan, R.   Eng 20C
O/C 20x30 River Scene Sel 5/92 220
Alleaume, Ludovic   Fr 1859-
* See 1991 Edition . . . .
Allen   Br 19C
O/C 8x12 Fishing Boats Yng 2/92 125
Allen, Charles Curtis   Am 1886-1950
O/C 20x24 Vermont Autumn Skn 5/92 2,090
Allen, Courtney   Am 1896-1969
O/C 29x34 Woman Bailing Out of Plane Ilh 11/91 1,600
O/C 27x21 Still Life Flowers, Tree, Dead Bird Eld 7/92 330
Allen, E. A.
O/Cb 19x29 Venice Canal Scene Dum 8/92 150
Allen, Greta   Am 1881-
* See 1992 Edition . . . .
Allen, J.   Am 20C
O/C 30x40 Interior Scene Hnd 6/92 160
Allen, Junius   Am 1896-1962
O/Cb 12x16 On Monhegan Island 1955 Sby 12/91 2,640
O/C 24x34 Down East 1953 Sby 12/91 1,980
Allen, Pearl Wright   Am 1880-
O/C 9x12 American Coastal Scene 1921 Sel 12/91 80
Allen, Robert Weir   Eng 1852-1942
* See 1992 Edition . . . .
Allen, Thomas   Am 20C
O/Pn 10x13 Rocky Landscape at Sunset Dum 7/92 650
Allievi, Fernando   Arg 1954-
* See 1992 Edition . . . .
Allis, C. Harry   Am 1876-1938
* See 1992 Edition . . . .
Allori, Alessandro   It 1535-1607
* See 1991 Edition . . . .
Allori, Cristofano   It 1577-1621
* See 1992 Edition . . . .
Alma-Tadema, Lady Laura (Epps)   Br 1852-1909
* See 1992 Edition . . . .
Alma-Tadema, Sir Lawrence   Br 1836-1912
* See 1992 Edition . . . .
Almanza, Cleofas   Mex 1850-1915
O/C 14x20 Colina del Tepeyac 1885 Chr 5/92 38,500
Almaraz, Carlos   1941-
O/C 60x50 Kauai 84 Chr 11/91 4,950
Alonso, Carlos   Arg 1929-
O/Pn 21x33 Desnudo de Mujer 86 Chr 5/92 8,800
Alott, Rudolf   Fr 19C
* See 1990 Edition . . . .
Alpuy, Julio   Uru 1919-
O/B 16x20 Naturaleza Muerta Chr 11/91 7,700
Alsina, J.   Fr 20C
* See 1992 Edition . . . .
Alston, Abbey   Br 19C
* See 1991 Edition . . . .

Alt, Franz   Aus 1821-1914
* See 1992 Edition . . . .
Alt, Otmar
A/C 59x47 Der Verlaufen Eisel Prinz 1971 Sby 2/92 4,675
Altamirano, Arturo Pacheco   Chl 20C
O/C 24x29 Costa de Antofagasta 1971 Chr 5/92 3,080
Altenkirsh, Otto   Ger 20C
O/C 24x27 Winter Landscape Slo 12/91 400
Altieri, E.   It 20C
O/C 12x18 Piazzale Michelangelo But 11/91 1,980
Altmann, Alexander   Rus 1885-1932
* See 1992 Edition . . . .
Altoon, John   Am 1925-1969
O/C 36x48 Abstract Composition But 5/92 5,500
O/C 34x48 Three Flies 54 Chr 2/92 935
Altson, Abbey   Br a 1890-1899
O/C 24x20 Portrait Woman with a Feather Boa But 5/92 . . . 7,700
O/C 24x20 Portrait Woman with Red Hair But 5/92 6,600
O/C 20x24 Spring Flood But 11/91 4,675
O/C 24x20 Maude Wlf 6/92 2,300
Alvardi, Carlo
O/C 30x40 Madonna and Child Chr 5/92 7,150
Alvarez, Luis Catala   Spa 1841-1901
* See 1992 Edition . . . .
Alvarez, Mabel   Am 1891-1985
O/B 20x16 Belle of Portugese Roses But 6/92 7,150
O/C 17x15 Musical Reverie But 10/91 3,025
O/B 14x16 Rocking Chair But 6/92 3,025
O/Cb 14x18 Rainy Day - Hawaii Mor 3/92 1,100
O/B 10x14 Hawaiian Fields Mor 3/92 950
O/B 18x14 Floral Still Life Mor 3/92 475
W/Pa 12x9 Flowers in Vase Mor 3/92 350
MM/Pa 15x12 San Juan DeDois-El Templo Mor 3/92 300
Aman-Jean, Edmond   Fr 1860-1935
* See 1992 Edition . . . .
Amar, Joseph   1954-
W&H/Wd 24x19 Untitled 1986 Chr 5/92 550
Amaral, Antonio Henrique   Brz 1935-
O/C 51x67 Banana No Prato 1970 Sby 11/91 17,600
O/C 39x32 Naturaleza Muerta 73 Chr 5/92 16,500
Amberg, Wilhelm   Ger 1822-1899
O/C 25x19 Stealing a Smoke Chr 5/92 2,750
Ambramovic, Ulay & Marina   20C
Ph 30x22 Marina & Charcoal Chr 11/91 165
Ameglio, Mario   Fr 1897-1970
O/C 26x32 Les Halles 1956 Sby 2/92 4,400
Amen, Irving   Am 1918-
O/C 42x24 Ballerinas Fre 12/91 250
A/C 30x40 Chess Game Hnd 5/92 250
A/C 40x30 Serenade Hnd 5/92 250
A/C 40x30 Young Mother Hnd 5/92 250
A/C 24x30 Tea and Music Hnd 5/92 150
A/C 20x24 Young Girl Drawing Hnd 5/92 100
Amenoff, Gregory   1948-
O/C 90x90 Groundswell 85 Sby 10/91 7,700
O/C 60x70 Facing North 80 Chr 5/92 4,400
O/C 78x84 Evenfall 1983 Chr 11/91 2,860
O/C 17x21 Painting for Summer II 81 Chr 2/92 1,210
Ames, Ezra   Am 1768-1836
* See 1990 Edition . . . .
Ames, Wally   Am 20C
O/B 12x16 Garden Scene Mys 11/91 302
O/C 16x20 Woodland Scene Mys 11/91 220
Amherst, Jeffrey
O/C 26x36 Judgement of Paris Wlf 3/92 50
Amigoni, Jacopo   It 1675-1752
* See 1992 Edition . . . .
Amorosi, Antonio   It 1660-1738
O/C 17x13 Young Baker Sby 7/92 4,675
Amorsolo, Fernando   Phi 1892-1972
O/B 20x16 Young Woman with Mangoes 1951 But 5/92 . . . 7,150
O/C 24x34 Winnowing 1961 Wes 11/91 6,710
O/B 16x20 Young Woman 1950 But 5/92 6,600
O/Pn 10x13 The Burning of Manila 1946 Wes 3/92 660

29

Amos, G. T.   Eng 19C
O/C 34x44 Watering Cows Slo 10/91 900
Anaf, C.   Con 19C
O/Pn 10x8 The Proposal 1872 Slo 7/92 375
Anbreine, J. C.
O/C 15x17 Le Comes 1864 Durn 6/92 1,200
Ancelet, Gabriel-Auguste   Fr 19C
* See 1992 Edition ....
Ancelot, Eugene J.   Fr 19C
O/Pn 15x23 Couple Watching Sailboats Wlf 6/92 500
Ancinelli, Dagli   1621-1661
* See 1992 Edition ....
Anders, Ernst   Ger 1845-1911
* See 1991 Edition ....
Andersen, Carl Christian   Dan 1849-1906
* See 1991 Edition ....
Anderson, Doug   20C
* See 1991 Edition ....
Anderson, Grace   Am a 1914-1948
O/B 16x12 Brook in Autumn Brd 8/92 440
Anderson, Harry   Am 1906-
W&G/Pa 16x21 Illustration Farthest Hill 1953 Fre 10/91 650
G/Pa 18x21 My Last Night Dad Fre 10/91 325
Anderson, J.   20C
W/Pa 11x14 Moonlit Harbor Scene Slo 12/91 275
Anderson, Karl J.   Am 1874-1956
C&P/Pa 21x13 Man Feeding Birds Ilh 11/91 950
Anderson, Lennart   Am 1928-
* See 1991 Edition ....
Anderson, Lyman M.   Am 1907-
O/C 18x14 Woman in White at Ship's Wheel Ilh 5/92 950
Anderson, M.   Swd 20C
O/C 26x20 Nude in a Landscape Fre 4/92 475
Anderson, Millie   Am 20C
O&W/B 14x17 Carter's Peanut Farm 1977 Slo 7/92 90
Anderson, Oscar   Am 1873-1941
O/C 20x24 Spring Yng 4/92 125
W/Pa 12x15 Bass Rocks 1942 Yng 2/92 124
Anderson, Ruth A.   Am 1884-1939
O/C 20x16 Young Girl in Pink Slo 4/92 650
Anderson, Victor C.   Am 1882-1937
* See 1992 Edition ....
Anderson, Walter   Br a 1856-1886
O/C 21x17 A Stitch in Time Sby 2/92 27,500
O/C 23x17 The Straw Hat Sby 5/92 9,900
Anderson, William   Br 1757-1837
* See 1992 Edition ....
Andoe, Joe   1955-
O&V/L 40x48 Tulip--left #1 Chr 11/91 6,600
O/L 40x48 Untitled (Beehive) Sby 5/92 3,850
O/L 40x48 Untitled (Laurel) Chr 5/92 3,300
O/L 20x24 Untitled (Landscape) Chr 5/92 2,860
Andrade, Magdan   Am 20C
O/C 20x24 Landscape with Figures Sel 9/91 300
Andre, Albert   Fr 1869-1954
O/C 29x25 Tulips Roses et Jaunes Doy 11/91 7,500
Andre, Carl
* See 1992 Edition ....
Andre, Charles Hippolyte   Fr a 1877-1913
* See 1992 Edition ....
Andre, Gaston   Fr 20C
W/Pa 15x10 Surreal Beach Scene Mys 6/92 220
Andrejevic, Milet   Yug 1925-
* See 1991 Edition ....
Andreotti, Federigo   It 1847-1930
O/C 26x19 Cappello Di Paglia Sby 10/91 19,800
O/C 26x19 Cappello di Paglia Papaveri Sby 5/92 16,500
Andrews, Ambrose   Am 1824-1859
O/C 26x36 Ox Drawn Cart 59 Chr 11/91 1,100
Andrews, Eliphalat F.   Am 19C
* See 1991 Edition ....
Andrews, George Henry   Br 1816-1898
* See 1992 Edition ....
Andrews, Henry   Br 1816-1869
O/C 38x54 A Formal Party Hnz 5/92 2,500

Andrews, Marietta Minnigerode   Am 1869-1931
O/C 27x22 Japanese Tea Room Wes 3/92 880
Andriessen, Hendrick   Bel 1607-1655
* See 1991 Edition ....
Anesi, Carlos   Arg 1965-
A/C 36x51 Caballo Chr 5/92 18,700
Anesi, Paolo   It 1700-1761
* See 1991 Edition ....
Anfosso, Pierre   Fr 20C
O/C 18x22 At the Beach But 5/92 880
Angelis, Pieter   1685-1735
O/Cp 9x11 Figures Merry-Making Tavern Chr 10/91 18,150
Anglada-Camarasa, Hermen   Spa 1873-1959
C/Pa 22x18 Five Male Portrait Studies 1904 Sby 10/91 9,900
Anglade, Gaston   Fr 1854-
O/C 17x22 Hilly River Landscape Chr 2/92 3,850
O/C 20x26 Shepherdess and her Flock Chr 5/92 2,420
Ango, Jean-Robert   Fr a 1760-1769
K/Pa 14x18 Le Jeu de la Palette Chr 1/92 7,700
Anguiano, Raul   Mex 1915-
O/C 36x34 El Mendigo 1945 Chr 5/92 8,250
T/Pa 18x24 Mujer en Paisaje Arido 1943 Sby 5/92 3,850
O/C 30x11 Portrait of a Woman 1940 But 5/92 3,025
Anisfeld, Boris   1878-1973
O/C 25x30 Coastal Scene Chr 11/91 770
Anivitti, Filippo   It 1876-
W/Pb 16x11 Flower Market by the Spanish Steps Chr 5/92 . 1,310
Annenkoff, Georges   Rus 1890-1971
* See 1992 Edition ....
Annot, Madame (Mrs. R. Jocobi)   Am 1894-
O/C 22x18 Floral Still Life Lou 12/91 325
Anquetin, Louis
* See 1992 Edition ....
Ansdell, Richard   Br 1815-1885
O/C 44x34 Feeding the Dogs 1866 Sby 10/91 13,200
O/C 36x28 Gentleman in Riding Attire Fre 10/91 350
Ansell, M. D.   Eng 20C
O/C 20x30 Lochness Scotland Sel 5/92 800
Anshutz, Thomas Pollock   Am 1851-1912
O/C 16x24 Lumber Boat Chr 12/91 12,100
C/Pa 25x19 Group of Figure Studies Chr 11/91 7,700
C/Pa 25x19 Group of Figure Studies Chr 11/91 6,600
P/C 48x30 Meditation Chr 3/92 6,600
C/Pa 25x19 Group of Figure Studies Chr 11/91 6,050
P/Pa 20x16 Woman in Yellow, Seated Chr 3/92 5,500
W/Pa 8x14 Beached Sailboats Chr 11/91 2,090
W/Pa 14x11 Extensive Landscape Chr 11/91 1,760
O/B 10x8 Artist, Farmyard, Flower Garden (3) Chr 11/91 .. 1,430
W/Pa 14x11 Study of 'The Winged Victory' Chr 11/91 ... 1,430
W/Pa 9x12 Coast Scene Rowboat Chr 11/91 1,100
W/Pa 7x10 Green Meadow Chr 11/91 1,100
Antes, Horst   Ger 1936-
O/C 51x39 Rot in Blauen Mann 1965 Sby 5/92 51,700
G/Pa 38x27 Untitled Sby 11/91 14,300
O/M 32x36 Stillebin Mit Bim 1965 Sby 10/91 11,000
W/Pa 18x14 Untitled 63 Sby 2/92 1,760
Antigna, Alexandre   Fr 1817-1878
O/C 21x30 Rest for the Weary Sby 5/92 5,280
Antoine, Montas   Hai 20C
O/M 24x32 Village Chr 5/92 1,700
Antonissen, Henri-Joseph   Dut 1734-1794
O/Pn 12x17 Peasants on a Country Road 1794 Sby 5/92 .. 8,250
Antrobus, Edmond G.   19C
O/C 33x55 Fiesta En El Lago De Texcoco 1865 Sby 11/91 88,000
Antunez, Nemesio   Chl 1918-
O/C 26x39 Eclipse 60 Chr 5/92 4,400
Antwerp, Henry Loos   Am
* See 1992 Edition ....
Anuszkiewicz, Richard   Am 1930-
A/C 49x60 Untitled 1976 Chr 5/92 6,050
A/C 36x36 Color Temper (307) 1970 Sby 10/91 4,400
A/Pn 11x11 Four Generations 1968 Chr 2/92 2,420

Anvitti, Filippo   It 1876-
O/C 16x18 Flower Market Doy 11/91   3,600
Aoyama, Yoshio   Jap 1894-
* See 1992 Edition . . . .
Apol, Louis   Dut 1850-1936
W&G/Pa 6x8 Winter Scene (2) Lou 12/91   650
Appel, Charles P.   Am 1857-
O/C 12x18 End of the Day Doy 12/91   1,100
O/C 14x20 Stormy Landscape Wlf 6/92   800
O/C 12x16 Autumn Landscape, Evening Hnz 5/92   275
Appel, Karel   Dut 1921-
O/C 22x18 Animal 1955 Sby 2/92   46,750
O/B 32x26 Tete Bleu Sby 5/92   38,500
A&Os/Pa/Cd 83x54 Le Fou de Trifle 83 Chr 2/92   22,000
G&I/Pa 19x26 Creeping Cat 53 Sby 2/92   17,600
G,W&Y/Pa 22x30 Couple with Bird 61 Chr 2/92   14,300
G&Y/Pa 21x30 Untitled 59 Sby 2/92   13,200
A/Pa/C 30x22 Untitled 69 Sby 2/92   13,200
A/C 18x21 Untitled Dum 5/92   12,000
G/Pa 23x30 Untitled 61 Sby 2/92   11,000
A/Pa/B 25x19 Head of a Man Sby 10/91   10,450
MM/Pa/C 19x24 Untitled 75 Sby 10/91   7,700
O/Pa/C 23x31 Three Faces Like Clouds 78 Hnd 3/92   5,750
Y&H/Pa 9x11 Two drawings Chr 5/92   5,720
Apperley, George Owen   Br 1884-1960
W/B 8x6 Fortress in the Mountains 1925 Chr 10/91   330
Appleby, John F.   Br 19C
O/B 12x19 Moonlit Mountains '88 Sby 7/92   660
Arakawa, Shusaku   Jap 1936-
* See 1992 Edition . . . .
Arana, Alfonso
* See 1992 Edition . . . .
Aranda, Jose Jimenez   Spa 1837-1903
O/Pn 19x24 The Pedicure But 11/91   3,850
Arapoff, Alexis P.   Rus 1904-1948
O/C 24x20 Portrait William H. Littlefield 1933 Skn 9/91   825
G,W&H/Pa 16x22 Flowers with Teapot 1931 Skn 11/91   330
Araujo, Carlos   Brz 1950-
O/Pn 55x39 Esperando Roberta Chr 5/92   14,300
O/Pn 63x47 Apocalypse Chr 11/91   12,100
Arbant, Louis   Fr 19C
O/C 16x13 Still Life of Fruit Wes 5/92   742
Arbuckle, George Franklin   Can 1909-
O/C 30x40 Assisi, Italy, with Cathedral 1974 Sbt 5/92   2,338
Arcambot, Pierre   Fr 1914-
O/C 22x32 Metro Skn 11/91   1,320
Archipenko, Alexander   Rus 1887-1964
MM/Wd 12x9 Vase with Flower 19 Sby 5/92   275,000
O/C 18x14 Portrait de Femme Sby 5/92   39,600
Arcieri, Charles F.   Am
* See 1991 Edition . . . .
Ardon, Mordecai
* See 1992 Edition . . . .
Arends, Jan   1728-1805
* See 1992 Edition . . . .
Arentino, Spinello   It
* See 1991 Edition . . . .
Arias, Miguel   Cub 19C
O/C 22x40 Paisaje Cubano 1883 Sby 5/92   4,400
Arikha, Avigdor   20C
O/C 58x35 Standing Nude with Mirror Sby 10/91   49,500
Ariza, Gonzalo   Col 1912-
* See 1991 Edition . . . .
Arman (Pierre Fernandez)   Fr 1928-
* See 1992 Edition . . . .
Armet Y Portanel, Jose   Spa 1843-1911
O/C 18x32 Houses by a Stream Chr 10/91   4,180
Armfield, Edward   Br 19C
O/C 24x36 Spaniels Retrieving a Pheasant Sby 7/92   2,310
Armfield, George   Br 1808-1893
O/C 17x21 The Fox at Bay 1865 Sby 6/92   5,500
Armfield, Maxwell   Am 20C
* See 1991 Edition . . . .
Armfield, Stuart
O/Pn 22x30 Prayer 56 Sby 2/92   2,200

Armin, Emil   Am 1883-
O/C 24x30 Sunlit River Hnd 5/92   400
Armington, Caroline   Fr 1875-1939
O/Pn 9x7 Summer Landscape 1920 Wlf 3/92   225
Armington, Franklin Milton   Can 1846-1941
* See 1991 Edition . . . .
Armitage, Thomas Liddall   Br 19C
* See 1990 Edition . . . .
Armodio
O/Pn 28x20 Two Paintings Sel 5/92   150
A/Pn 20x28 Metamorfismo Sel 5/92   125
Armor, Charles   Am a 1865-1911
O/C 37x27 Wide Water Slo 9/91   100
Armour, Mary Nicol Neill   1902-
* See 1992 Edition . . . .
Armstrong, David   Am 1836-1918
O/C 15x22 Bakers Shop at Pont Aven 1878 Fre 4/92   3,700
Armstrong, William   Can 1822-1914
* See 1992 Edition . . . .
Arnald, George   Br 1763-1841
* See 1992 Edition . . . .
Arnautoff, Victor M.   Am 1896-1979
* See 1992 Edition . . . .
Arndt, Paul Wesley   Am 1881-
O/C 28x38 Early Thaw, Vermont Slo 2/92   550
Arnegger, Alois   Aus 1879-1967
O/C 39x29 A Woodland Stream Sby 2/92   15,400
O/Pn 29x39 Cherry Trees Sby 10/91   14,300
O/C 36x49 Villa Overlooking Mediterranean 1907 Sby 1/92 .   4,675
O/C 24x36 Evening in a Mountainous Village Sby 7/92 . . .   1,320
O/C 27x41 Water's Edge, Capri Hnz 5/92   1,250
O/C 27x39 Alpine Landscape 1943 Sby 1/92   990
O/C 27x39 San Remo Dum 5/92   700
Arnegger, Gottfried   Aus 1905-
O/C 28x39 View of the Gulf of Naples Chr 5/92   1,980
Arner, Robert   Am 20C
O/C 10x13 Still Life Slo 7/92   150
O/C 27x22 Lilacs Slo 7/92   125
Arnet
O/C 60x48 Bavarian Landscape Dum 4/92   350
Arnholt, Waldon Sylvester   Am 1909-
O/Pn 24x26 Panoramic Landscapes: Two 1964 Wlf 10/91 . .   375
Arnold, Carl Johann   Ger 1829-1916
* See 1992 Edition . . . .
Arnold, Reginald Ernest   Eng 1853-1938
* See 1992 Edition . . . .
Arnold-Kaiser, Bernita
* See 1990 Edition . . . .
Arnoldi, Charles   1946-
K/Pa 29x23 Untitled 1978 Chr 5/92   6,050
Arnolt, Gustav Muss   Am 1858-1927
O/C 22x30 Chestnut Horse in Landscape Slo 4/92   1,200
Arnosa, Jose Gallegos   Spa 1859-1917
O/Pn 14x21 La Botica Sby 2/92   198,000
Arnull, George   Br 19C
* See 1990 Edition . . . .
Aron (Michael Gottlieb)   Rus 1908-
O/B 6x5 Middle Eastern Scene Skn 9/91   55
Arp, Jean   Fr 1887-1966
Br&I/Pa 8x11 Composition Chr 2/92   6,050
L/Pa 14x11 Tiermarchen Chr 2/92   5,500
W&Pe/Pa 14x10 Die Menschen Gleichen Chr 2/92   4,620
Arpa Y Perea, Jose   Spa 1862-1903
* See 1990 Edition . . . .
Arrieta, Jose Agustin   Mex 1802-1879
O/C 46x36 Soldado Y Dama Sby 11/91   176,000
O/C 46x36 Intervencion Sby 11/91   137,500
Arrighi, S.   It 19C
O/C 22x30 Preparing the Meal Chr 2/92   4,620
Arriolla, Fortunato   Am 1827-1872
* See 1992 Edition . . . .
Arsenius, Johann Georg   Swd 1818-1903
O/C 16x20 Horse and Groom Sby 6/92   5,775

Arthur, Reginald   Br 19C
* See 1991 Edition . . . .
Arthurs, Stanley Massey   Am 1877-1950
G/B 14x11 Four Watercolors Wes 11/91   1,430
G/Pa 14x11 Two Mural Studies 1946 Ilh 5/92   800
Artigue, Albert-Emile   Fr a 1875-1901
* See 1992 Edition . . . .
Artschwager, Richard   Am 1924-
A/Clx 42x43 Untitled (Office Scene) Sby 5/92   71,500
A/Clx 24x19 Eight Rat Holes Sby 11/91   55,000
Lq/Clx 36x30 Small Picture on South Wall 1974 Chr 2/92 .   36,300
A/Clx 54x37 Soviet Accelerator 80 Sby 10/91   30,250
A/Clx 27x33 Expression Impression 66 Sby 2/92   20,900
A/Clx 27x33 Upper Right Corner Hit 1969 Sby 10/91 . . . .   19,800 ·
C/Pa 19x25 Untitled 87 Sby 10/91   4,400
Pe/Pa 30x24 Untitled 74 Sby 5/92   4,400
Artz, Constant   Dut 1870-1951
O/C 20x16 Ducks Wading Chr 10/91   4,400
Artz, David Adolf Constant   Dut 1837-1890
W/Pa 29x17 The Fisherman's Family But 5/92   4,125
Artz, William   Con
O/B 12x9 Coastal Village Lou 6/92   60
Artzybasheff, Boris   Am 1899-1965
H/Pls 7x5 Anthropomorphic Taping Machine Ilh 5/92   750
Asada, Takashi
O/C 64x51 Fille au Miroir 32 Sby 2/92   4,400
Ascenzi   Con 20C
* See 1992 Edition . . . .
Ascenzi, Giuseppe   It 20C
W/Pa 15x21 A Game of Cards 1901 But 5/92   1,870
Aschenbach, Ernst   Nor 1872-1954
O/C 20x28 Mountain Lake Scene Lou 9/91   350
Ashley, Frank N.   Am 1920-
O/C 20x24 Jazz Singer Mor 3/92   3,250
W/Pa 18x24 Morning Run #3 1959 But 2/92   990
Ashton, Ethel V.   Am 20C
O/C 30x37 4th of July, Philadelphia Chr 6/92   2,750
Askenazy, Mischa (Maurice)   Am 1888-1961
O/C 25x30 Sailboats But 2/92   11,000
O/C 40x54 The Children's Party But 2/92   7,700
O/C 32x40 Boats, Chioggia, Italy But 6/92   5,500
O/C 16x20 Nude Reading But 2/92   4,125
O/B 22x24 Landscape Mor 3/92   3,750
O/B 17x14 Figural Mor 11/91   2,000
O/B 48x30 Nude at Window Mor 3/92   2,000
O/C 40x28 Nude in Interior Mor 6/92   1,800
O/M 14x10 Seated Nude Mor 3/92   1,700
O/M 14x10 Nude at Window Mor 6/92   1,500
O/C 17x13 Boy in Brown Shirt Mor 6/92   1,100
O/C 24x18 Man Under a Tree But 6/92   1,100
W/Pa 28x22 Figures-Canal Scene Mor 6/92   1,000
O/Cb 16x21 Landscape Mor 3/92   1,000
O/Pw 18x24 Landscape - Chavez Ravine Mor 3/92   1,000
O/C 22x16 Portrait Mor 3/92   1,000
O/C 17x13 California Coastal Mor 11/91   900
O/B 18x14 Portrait Woman Mor 11/91   800
P/Pa 19x17 Rooftops of the City Mor 11/91   700
Askevold, Anders Monsen   Swd 1834-1900
* See 1991 Edition . . . .
Aslanian, Pierre Bedros   Can 1937-
O/C 8x10 Baie St-Paul; St-Saveur: Pair '91 Sbt 5/92   842
Asoma, Tadashi   Jap 20C
O/C 50x50 Early Evening 73 Sby 6/92   3,575
Asplund, Tore   Am 20C
W/Pa 13x29 Hilly Landscape Mys 11/91   688
Asselijn, Jan   Dut 1610-1652
* See 1990 Edition . . . .
Assereti, Gvo   18C**
* See 1992 Edition . . . .
Assereto, Giuacchino   It 1600-1649
* See 1990 Edition . . . .
Asther, Nils
* See 1992 Edition . . . .

Asti, Angelo   Fr 1847-1903
O/C 13x10 Bust of a Young Woman Hnd 3/92   1,400
O/Pn 12x8 Portrait of a Young Lady Hnd 10/91   650
Astrup, Nikolai   Nor 1880-1928
* See 1992 Edition . . . .
Atalaya, Enrique   Spa -1914
O/Pn 18x24 Preparing the Trousseau 1877 Hnd 10/91 . . .   6,000
Atamian, Charles Garabed   Tur 1872-
* See 1992 Edition . . . .
Atherton, C.
O/C 21x32 Gravel Pit Hnz 10/91   750
Atherton, John   Am 1900-1952
O/C 25x30 Shasta Dam Lou 3/92   1,200
Atkins, Arthur   Am 1873-1899
O/C/B 14x18 Eze from Villa St. Hospice But 6/92   3,300
O/C/B 14x18 Pont Neuf...L'Horloge But 6/92   3,300
Atkins, Lee   Am 1913-1987
O/Cb 20x24 Blue Barn--Bedford, Pa. 1946 Slo 9/91   300
O/Cb 18x24 Hunters--Pennsylvania 1955 Slo 9/91   275
W/Pa 16x23 Coal Trestle 1945 Slo 9/91   250
W/Pa 14x21 Country Road; Rainy Day 1945 Slo 9/91   225
G/Pa 23x18 Still Life--Field Flowers 1954 Slo 9/91   225
W/Pa 19x24 Mountain Lake--Spring 54 Slo 9/91   175
I&W/Pa 25x18 Architectural Rendering 32 Slo 9/91   125
Atkinson, Jacob   Am 1864-1938
* See 1992 Edition . . . .
Atkinson, Nancy James   Am 20C
O/Pn 8x10 Trompe L'Oeil Hnz 5/92   100
Atkinson, W. A.   Eng 19C
O/C 10x20 Courting Couple 1901 Dum 1/92   250
Atkinson, William Edwin   Can 1862-1926
W/Pa 15x21 Haywagon '97 Sbt 11/91   468
Atl, Dr.   Mex 1875-1964
O/Pn 21x29 Valle De Mexico 1937 Sby 11/91   57,750
O/M 20x24 Paisaje con Volcan 1946 Chr 5/92   52,800
O/Bu 16x24 Amanecer Chr 11/91   41,800
C&S/Pa 27x38 Paisaje Con Maguey 1932 Sby 11/91   22,000
C/Pa 23x22 Paisaje con Volcan 1950 Chr 5/92   16,500
C/Pa 19x24 Paricutin Sby 5/92   15,400
C/Pa 11x18 Paisaje Montanoso con Nubes 1940 Chr 11/91   9,900
Atlan, Jean   Fr 1913-1960
* See 1991 Edition . . . .
Attendu, Antoine Ferdinand   Fr 19C
O/C 24x36 Nature Morte a la Lampe Sby 10/91   11,000
Atwood, C.   Am 20C
* See 1992 Edition . . . .
Atwood, Jesse   Am 19C
O/C 30x25 Portrait of Franklin Pierce Fre 10/91   525
Aubert, Jean Ernest   Fr 1824-1906
* See 1990 Edition . . . .
Aublet, Albert   Fr 1851-1938
* See 1992 Edition . . . .
Aubudon, John Woodhouse   Am 1812-1868
* See 1991 Edition . . . .
Audubon, John James   Am 1785-1851
P&Pe/Pa 14x18 Ruffed Grouse Chr 5/92   143,000
Audy, Jonny   Fr a 1872-1976
* See 1991 Edition . . . .
Auerbach, Frank   1931-
O/C 41x48 To the Studio Sby 11/91   308,000
O/C 24x28 Figure Seated on a Bed Sby 11/91   77,000
O/B 22x20 Head of Jym Sby 2/92   49,500
Auerbach-Levy, William   Am 1889-1964
O/C 25x30 Self-Portrait with Cokie 1935 Hnd 6/92   1,200
Aufray, Joseph   Fr 1836-
O/C 21x16 Snowball Fight Fre 12/91   1,500
Auge, Philippe   Fr 1935-
* See 1992 Edition . . . .
Augusta, George   Am 20C
P/Pa 12x16 Quiet Street Scene in Summer Bor 8/92   250
Auguste, Clervaux   Hai
O/C 36x59 Paradis Terrestre 1953 Chr 5/92   4,950
O/C 30x51 Marche 1948 Chr 5/92   3,080

ult, George Copeland   Am 1891-1948
Pe/Pa 15x10 Kitchen Stove Chr 9/91 4,400
C/Pa 12x9 Tree on the Square '33 Chr 3/92 3,080
umonier, James   Br 1832-1911
* See 1992 Edition . . . .
ureli, Giuseppe   It 1858-1929
W/Pa 10x16 Ladies of the Seraglio Wlf 9/91 5,000
W/Pa 22x15 Awaiting His Arrival But 5/92 1,870
W&Pe/Pa/B 17x24 Tying Her Skate Sby 7/92 1,540
ussandon, Joseph Nicolas H.   Fr 1836-
O/C 46x29 La Nymphe en Hiver 1866 Slo 7/92 4,500
usten, Alexander   Br 20C
O/C 18x14 Darby and Joan Slo 2/92 600
O/C 20x30 The Fish Tale Wes 3/92 385
usten, Carl Frederick   Am 1917-
W&G/Pa 17x11 Pair Watercolors 43 Slo 9/91 400
usten, Edward J.   Am 1850-1930
O/C 20x14 Floral Still Life '95 Wes 11/91 825
ustin, Charles Percy   Am 1883-1948
O/Ab 12x14 New Mexico Sunset '40 Wlf 10/91 375
ustin, Roy   Am 20C
O/C 29x23 Female Nude Sel 2/92 50
ustrian, Ben   Am 1870-1921
O/C 74x38 After a South Wind 1901 Chr 5/92 30,800
O/C 15x20 Chicks in a Blue Basket 1900 Wlf 9/91 15,000
O/C 14x18 Pup and Chick 1912 Wlf 9/91 5,000
O/Pn 10x8 Curiosity 1914 Sby 6/92 3,300
H/Pn 9x7 Sunset Hour 1916 Chr 6/92 880
Aved, Jacques Andre   Fr 1702-1766
* See 1990 Edition . . . .
Avercamp, Barent   Dut 1612-1679
* See 1992 Edition . . . .
Avercamp, Hendrick   Dut 1585-1663
* See 1992 Edition . . . .
Avery, Kenneth Newell   Am 1882-
* See 1990 Edition . . . .
Avery, Milton   Am 1893-1965
O&Pe/C 30x40 Adolescence 1947 Chr 12/91 352,000
G&Pe/Pa 31x23 Girl in a Brown Hat Chr 5/92 41,800
O/C 20x24 Goat by the Sea '59 Sby 5/92 37,400
O/Cb 28x22 Spring Time 1957 Chr 9/91 19,800
G,W&Pe/Pa 16x23 By the Waterfall Chr 12/91 17,600
O/Cb 14x18 Barnyard 1958 Sby 9/91 15,400
G&Pa 22x17 Still Life with Flowers 1950 Chr 12/91 15,400
G&Pe/Pa 9x23 Dark Bird, Dark Sea 1960 Chr 3/92 13,200
Y/Pa 22x17 Road Through the Trees 1955 Sby 9/91 8,800
O/C 14x11 The Dandy 1944 Sby 12/91 5,225
Pl/Pa 11x9 Young Mother Sby 4/92 2,860
Mk/Pa 17x14 Life Drawing Class 1956 Sby 4/92 2,640
H/Pa 11x9 Mother and Child #3 Sby 4/92 2,420
Avitabile, Gennaro   It 1864-
O/Pn 16x13 Una Partita a Scacchi Sby 2/92 6,050
Axentowicz, Theodor   Pol 1859-1938
* See 1990 Edition . . . .
Ayotte, Leo   Can 1909-1977
* See 1992 Edition . . . .
Baadsgaard, Alfrida   Dan 1839-
* See 1991 Edition . . . .
Babb, John Staines   Br 1870-1900
* See 1991 Edition . . . .
Babcock, Paul   Am 20C
O/C 20x26 Pasadena Bridge 1936 Mor 11/91 425
Baboulene, Eugene   Fr 1905-
O/C 13x18 Pasteque Chr 11/91 4,400
O/C 13x18 Le Mourillon Chr 11/91 4,180
O/C 13x18 Maison de Pecheur a Giens Chr 11/91 4,180
Bacardy, Don   20C
* See 1991 Edition . . . .
Bacci, Edmondo   It 1913-
O&Sd/C 55x55 Avvenimento No. 286 Chr 11/91 10,450
O&Sd/C 55x55 Avvenimento No. 360 Chr 11/91 9,900
MM/C 72x58 Avvenimento #228 But 5/92 6,050
O/C 34x40 Ayvenimento No. 268 Chr 2/92 3,080
O/C 25x39 Avvenimento No. 115 Sby 10/91 2,860

Bach, Elvira   20C
* See 1991 Edition . . . .
Bache, Martha Moffett   Am 1893-
O/C 20x16 Georgetown, Winter Slo 2/92 950
Bache, Otto   Dan 1839-1914
* See 1990 Edition . . . .
Bachelier, Jean-Jacques   Fr 1724-1806
* See 1991 Edition . . . .
Bacher, Otto H.   Am 1839-1927
C/Pa 11x18 Landscape 19 Wlf 3/92 100
Bachmann, Otto
A/M 16x47 Surrealistic Beach Scene 1964 Sby 2/92 2,200
Bachrach-Baree, Emmanuel   Aus 1863-
O/Pn 13x10 Uniformed Drummer Boy 1891 Sel 4/92 750
Backhuysen, Ludolf   Dut 1631-1708
O/C 27x29 Dutch Frigate Flying Banner 1696 Sby 1/92 . . . 55,000
Backus, Claire   Am 20C
O/B 12x18 California Landscape Lou 6/92 125
Backus, Standish   Am 1910-
O/B 24x32 Hawaiian Canoes 1950 But 6/92 1,320
Backvis, Francois   Bel 19C
* See 1990 Edition . . . .
Bacon, Charles Roswell   Am 1868-1913
* See 1990 Edition . . . .
Bacon, Francis   Am 1909-
* See 1992 Edition . . . .
Bacon, Henry   Am 1839-1912
O/Pn 18x14 Christmas Prayers 1872 Chr 9/91 7,700
O/Pn 11x14 Reading on Deck; Young Boy: (2) 91 Sby 12/91 7,700
O/C/B 15x22 Departure of the Fishing Fleet 1884 Sby 12/91 6,875
O/Pn 11x14 Beach Scene; Washerwoman: Pair Sby 12/91 . 6,600
O/C 19x28 Bird Song and Reverie Skn 5/92 6,050
O/Pn 10x7 A Breton 1877 Sby 12/91 3,300
W/Pb 16x25 An Arab Encampment 1909 Chr 11/91 990
Bacon, Peggy   Am 1895-1987
O/B 24x30 Camp Alas 1958 Wlf 9/91 3,000
P/Pa 26x17 Alley Cats Sby 12/91 1,980
P/Pa 22x18 All Hallow's Eve 1945 Brd 8/92 1,100
Pe/Pa 6x8 Self-Portrait 1931 Wes 11/91 330
Badger, Samuel Finley Morse   Am 19C
O/C 22x36 The Edith G. Folwell Brd 5/92 11,000
Badura, Faye Swengel
O/B 10x12 Canal and River Ald 3/92 425
Baechler, Donald   Am 1956-
O,H&L/C 110x159 Conversazione 89 Chr 5/92 52,800
A/C 111x66 Untitled (Zagreb) 82 Chr 2/92 20,900
O,A&L/C 24x24 Untitled 88 Chr 2/92 7,260
E/C 24x24 Sphinx #1 81 Chr 5/92 7,150
A/C 18x24 Abstract with Four Trees 85 Sby 2/92 6,600
I,H&L/Pa 27x21 Untitled 90 Chr 5/92 3,520
A&Ph/Pa 11x9 Untitled 86 Chr 11/91 935
Baeder, John   Am 1938-
* See 1991 Edition . . . .
Baer, Fritz   Ger 1850-1919
O/C 26x34 A Poppy Field Chr 5/92 4,950
Baer, Jo   Am 1929-
O/C 60x86 Untitled Diptych 66 Sby 10/91 5,775
Baes, Emile   Bel 1879-1953
* See 1992 Edition . . . .
Bahieu, Jules G.   Bel 19C
O/C 35x48 Attack of the Bird of Prey 1908 Dum 1/92 4,500
Bail, Franck Antoine   Fr 1858-1924
* See 1992 Edition . . . .
Bail, Joseph   Fr 1862-1921
O/C 47x26 The Young Chef Chr 5/92 16,500
Bailey, Frederick Victor   Br 20C
* See 1992 Edition . . . .
Bailey, Harry L.   Am 1879-1933
O/C 20x28 Farm Horses in Landscape Mor 3/92 425
O/B 7x10 High Sierras Mor 11/91 125
Bailey, T.   Am 20C
O/C 31x24 The Bark, "Isabella" Eld 7/92 275
O/C 12x16 Sailing Schooner Dum 9/91 200
O/C 28x36 American Full-Rigged Ship Eld 7/92 193

Bailey, Thomas Br 20C
O/C 24x36 Pointers Fre 10/91 275
Bailey, Walter Am 1894-
O/B 22x30 Untitled Wlf 6/92 375
Bailey, William Am 1930-
O/C 32x39 Still Life 1973 Chr 11/91 68,200
O/C 26x32 Natura Morta, Orvieto 1977 Chr 5/92 66,000
H/Pa 15x11 Two Untitled Drawings Chr 11/91 8,800
H/Pa 15x11 Untitled 1974 Chr 2/92 3,300
W&H/Pa 15x11 Untitled Chr 11/91 2,750
Baillio, R. Fr a 1790-1810
Pe/Pa 17x12 Male Nude Holding Bow Sby 7/92 2,475
Baird, William Baptiste Am 1847-
O/Pn 6x9 Horses Grazing Chr 6/92 1,320
O/B 6x8 Androscoggin River 1874 Yng 4/92 1,200
O/B 6x8 Mt Washington/White Horse Ledge 1874 Yng 4/92 . 300
Baj, Enrico It 1924-
O&L/F/C 39x35 General Tres Decore Sby 10/91 34,100
O&MM/F/C 17x27 I'm Waiting for You Chr 2/92 12,100
L/C 28x31 Montagne Portrait 58 Sby 6/92 4,950
Bakalowicz, Ladislaus Pol 1833-
O/Pn 44x31 The Serenade 1875 Sby 10/91 20,900
Baker, Elizabeth Gowdy Am -1927
W/Pa 45x28 Mr. Henry Rogers Malorey 1908 Chr 6/92 2,090
W/Pa 45x28 Mrs. Henry Rogers Malorey 1908 Chr 6/92 . . . 2,090
Baker, Ernest Am 19C
* See 1992 Edition
Baker, Laura B. Am 20C
O/C 18x14 Portrait of Ellen Paige Butcher Fre 4/92 275
Baker, Ralph Am 1908-1976
W/Pa 21x29 House in Landscape Mor 6/92 600
Baker, T. E. S. Am 20C
O/C 30x25 Native American Camp @ Sunset Sby 4/92 . . . 1,430
Bakhuyzen, Alexandre H. Dut 1830-
* See 1990 Edition
Bakhuyzen, G. J. Van De Sande Dut 1826-1895
* See 1992 Edition
Bakhuyzen, Hendrik Van De Sand Dut 1795-1860
O/C 55x75 Cattle Resting 1859 Sby 5/92 25,300
Bakhuyzen, Julius Van De Sande Dut 1835-1925
* See 1991 Edition
Bakhuyzen, Ludolf Dut 1631-1708
* See 1991 Edition
Bakker, Jan Dut 1879-1944
O/C 16x24 Dutch Canal With Bridge But 11/91 770
Bakos, Jozef G. Am 1891-
* See 1992 Edition
Bakst, Leon Rus 1866-1924
G,W&Gd/Pa 25x18 Helene de Sparte: Costume Sby 2/92 . 16,500
G&Pe/Pa 12x9 Costume Design for a Slave Sby 2/92 12,100
W&l/Pa/B 18x12 Costume Design for May '23 Sby 10/91 . 10,120
W&G/Pa/B 18x12 Costume Design for Ersilia '23 Sby 10/91 . 5,500
W,Pe&G/Pa 11x17 Phaedre: Design for Decor 1915 Sby 2/92 3,850
G/Pa 13x10 Six Costume Designs Sby 6/92 1,980
G&Gd/Pa 18x25 Moskwa: A Textile Design Sby 2/92 1,650
G&Pe/Pa 19x24 Textile Design Sby 6/92 1,045
G/Pa 18x24 Isba: A Textile Design Sby 6/92 990
Balande, Gaston Fr 1880-1971
* See 1992 Edition
Balassi, Mario It 1604-1667
* See 1991 Edition
Baldessari, John 1931-
Ph/B 87x60 Horizontal Women Chr 11/91 38,500
A&Ph 62x95 A Healthy Life (With Jogger) Chr 5/92 30,800
Ph&A/Al 96x72 Three Figures (with manhole) Chr 11/91 . . . 30,800
Ph,Pt&O/Bd 61x200 Stares Sby 11/91 29,700
Pt,O&Ph/Pb 90x57 Stain Sby 2/92 18,700
Balducci, Giovanni It 1560-1631
O/Cp 4x10 The First Passover Seder Sby 1/92 33,000
Bale, Charles Thomas Eng a 1868-1875
O/C 30x50 Autumn's Bounty 1884 Doy 11/91 5,750
O/C 18x14 Still Life with Tankard and Grapes Chr 10/91 . . . 4,950

O/C 37x28 Still Life Fruit and Game 1890 Hnd 3/92 4,20
O/C 20x30 Still Life Fruit and Jug Sby 7/92 3,85
O/C 37x28 Still Life Fruit and Game 1890 Hnd 12/91 3,00
O/C 18x14 Pair of Still Lifes Hnd 12/91 1,40
Balestra, Antonio It 1660-1740
* See 1992 Edition
Ball, Adrien Joseph Verhoeven Bel 1824-1882
* See 1990 Edition
Ball, Alice Worthington Am -1929
O/C 30x32 Still Life Skn 5/92 60
Ball, Arthur Br 19C
O/C 14x20 An Afternoon Rest 93 Chr 2/92 2,20
Ball, Thomas Raymond Am 1896-1943
O/B 8x8 Portrait Elvira Foot Fre 10/91 80
Balla, Giacomo It 1871-1958
C/Pa 13x18 Velocity of an Auto + Space Sby 5/92 57,75
T/B 10 dia Motivo Decorativo Chr 2/92 26,40
Ballard, Harry Am 20C
W/Pa 11x18 Two Watercolors Sel 4/92 7
Ballard, Jim Am 20C
L 21x16 A Peaceful Nest 1991 Skn 3/92 16
Ballavoine, Jules Frederic Fr 19C
O/C 32x22 Love's Whisperings Sby 5/92 16,50
Balleroy, Jerome Fr 1915-
O/B 16x22 White House Fre 4/92 20
Ballesio, Federico It 19C
W/B 22x30 Concert for the Cardinal But 11/91 8,80
W/Pa 22x15 Playing with the Baby Chr 10/91 3,74
W/Pa 22x16 Amusing the Baby Chr 2/92 2,75
W/Pa 15x22 The New Poem Chr 10/91 1,54
Ballesio, G. It 19C
* See 1992 Edition
Ballon, J. Spa 20C
O/C 16x13 Village Lane Slo 7/92 13
Balthus (Balthasar Klossowski) Fr 1908-
Pe&Fp/Pa 15x20 Etude de Figures 64 Chr 11/91 4,95
Bama, James E. Am 1926-
O/B 25x33 The Science Fair Sby 4/92 4,180
W/Pa 7x6 Mountain Man 1985 Doy 12/91 2,400
O/B 22x33 Acme Grocery Sel 9/91 1,200
Bamberger, Fritz Ger 1814-1873
* See 1991 Edition
Bamfylde, Copleston Warre -1791
* See 1992 Edition
Banchev, Jakim
O/C 21x28 Dunes in Indiana Dum 9/91 250
Banchi, Giorgio It 1789-1853
* See 1992 Edition
Bancroft, Milton Herbert Am 1867-1947
* See 1991 Edition
Bandinelli, Baccio It 1493-1560
* See 1991 Edition
Banfield, Elizabeth Am 20C
O/B Size? House by a River Mys 11/91 110
Banier, E. S. Eur 19C
O/C 18x14 Sheep in Meadow Slo 9/91 475
Banks, Thomas J. Br 19C
O/C 36x52 South Pass of Killiecrankie 80 Sby 7/92 7,700
Bannister, Thaddeus Am 1915-
O/C 22x28 Schooner Grayling Fre 4/92 4,500
O/C 19x25 The Schooner Alert Fre 4/92 3,700
O/C 22x36 Schooner Ada Bailey Hnd 6/92 3,200
O/C 25x30 The Schooner Elsie Hnd 6/92 3,200
O/C 23x32 Bark Charles P. Howe Wes 11/91 2,310
O/C 28x40 Schooner Marion F. Sprague Wes 11/91 1,100
Banting, Sir Frederick Grant Can 1891-1941
* See 1992 Edition
Bantzer, Carl Ludwig Noah Ger 1857-
O/C 49x31 Portrait Woman in a White Gown 1883 But 5/92 . 3,575
Baptista Da Costa, Joao Brz 1865-1926
O/C 38x50 Paisagem Perto do Petropolis Chr 5/92 33,000
Baquero, Marlano Spa 19C
* See 1991 Edition

34

Barauss, Emile Fr 1851-1930
* See 1992 Edition . . . .

Barbarini, Emil Aus 1855-1930
O/Pn 8x12 A Flower Market Wlf 9/91 6,500
O/Pn 8x12 The Marketplace Wlf 9/91 6,500
O/C 17x21 Feeding the Chickens Chr 5/92 3,740

Barbarini, Ernst Ger 20C
* See 1992 Edition . . . .

Barbasan, Mariano Spa 1864-1924
O/Pn 10x7 Venetian Canal Scene Chr 10/91 28,600

Barbeau, Marcel Can 1925-
G/Pa 20x25 Three Verticals and Blue '72 Sbt 5/92 1,215

Barber, Alfred R. Br a 1879-1893
* See 1992 Edition . . . .

Barber, Bill Am 20C
O/M 24x36 Riders on Horseback Mor 6/92 650

Barber, Charles Burton Br 1845-1894
* See 1992 Edition . . . .

Barber, Della J.
MM 26x18 Winter Town 1927 Ald 5/92 35

Barbieri, Giovanni Francesco It 1591-1666
* See 1991 Edition . . . .

Barbieri, Vittorio It 19C
O/C 16x23 A Gift of Flowers Chr 2/92 2,200

Barbosa, Mario Brz 19C
O/C 16x13 Brittany Market Scene But 11/91 2,750

Barbudo, Salvador Sanchez Spa 1858-1919
O/Pn 24x15 Visit to the Artist's Studio 1881 Sby 2/92 . . . 44,000
O/C 15x22 Presentation to the Cardinal 1877 Chr 10/91 . . 4,180

Barcelo, Miguel 1957-
A&MM/C 79x120 Le Feu Sur la Plage 84 Chr 5/92 121,000
MM&O/C 51x77 Chao Chr 5/92 55,000

Barcelo, Miguel Spa 17C
* See 1991 Edition . . . .

Barchus, Eliza Am 1857-1959
O/C Var Mount Hood (2) Mys 6/92 550

Barclay, McClelland Am 1891-1943
O/C 28x50 Dinner Under the Stars Chr 9/91 3,300
O&R/C 30x26 Woman and Man from Rowboat Dum 7/92 . . 2,000
C/Pa 33x27 Woman in Gown with Tuxedoed Men 34 Ilh 5/92 1,500

Bard, James Am 1815-1897
* See 1992 Edition . . . .

Bardone, Guy Fr 1927-
O/C 40x29 Marguerites Sby 6/92 3,300
O/C 32x26 Apres-rnidi a la plage, Arcachon Chr 5/92 2,860
O/C 21x32 Orage sur la Giudecca, Venise Chr 5/92 2,860
O/C 32x25 Le Bocal De Soucis Sby 10/91 2,090

Bardwell, Thomas Eng a 1735-1780
* See 1990 Edition . . . .

Barella, Jose Puigdengolas
* See 1992 Edition . . . .

Barend, Johannes Hermanus Dut 1840-1912
O/Pn 8x12 The Little Fisherman Skn 9/91 2,750

Barenger, James Br 1745-1813
* See 1991 Edition . . . .

Bargue, Charles Fr 1825-1883
* See 1992 Edition . . . .

Barilari, Enrique Arg 1931-
* See 1990 Edition . . . .

Barile, Xavier Am 1891-1981
O/B 20x16 Snowballs Yng 4/92 100

Barillot, Leon Fr 1844-1929
* See 1992 Edition . . . .

Barkentin, G. S. Con 20C
O/C 24x36 River Landscape 1935 Fre 10/91 175

Barker of Bath, Benjamin Br 1776-1836
* See 1992 Edition . . . .

Barker, John Br 19C
O/C 30x40 Cottages and Market: Pair Sby 10/91 8,800
O/C 24x36 After the Hunt But 5/92 4,950

Barker, Thomas Jones Br 1769-1847
* See 1991 Edition . . . .

Barlach, Ernst Ger 1870-1938
* See 1991 Edition . . . .

Barlow, J. Noble
O/C 16x21 Figures in a Riverboat Wlf 3/92 1,400

Barlow, Myron A. Am 1873-1937
O/C 30x29 Two Women at Table Dum 9/91 7,000
O/C 37x37 Young Woman Reading Chr 11/91 3,740
O/C 36x28 Two Female Figures 1900 Dum 9/91 2,500
O/C 29x29 Two Women Around Outdoor Fire Dum 9/91 . . 2,250
O/C 48x36 Woman by a Small Waterfall Dum 9/91 2,000
O/C 17x22 Moonlight Scene Dum 11/91 1,100

Barnabe, Duilio It 1914-1961
O/C 20x21 Nature Morte au Bol Blanc Sby 10/91 6,600

Barnard, Edward Herbert Am 1855-1909
* See 1991 Edition . . . .

Barnes, Archibald Georges Br 1887-
* See 1992 Edition . . . .

Barnes, D. De Mars Am 20C
G/Pa 14x22 The Yankee Clipper Slo 9/91 250

Barnes, Ernest Am 1873-
O/B 12x18 Landscape Mys 6/92 412

Barnes, Ernest Harrison Am
O/C 25x30 Landscape Fre 4/92 750
O/C 25x30 The Mountain Yng 2/92 425

Barnes, Frank Nz 19C
* See 1991 Edition . . . .

Barnet, Wil Am 1911-
G/Pa 12x9 Children Painting 42- Chr 11/91 1,870
O/C 12x16 Two Nudes Fre 10/91 175

Barnett, Thomas P. Am 1870-1929
O/C 40x44 Stone Industries '24 Sel 9/91 2,600
O/C Size? Snowy Winter Landscape 1913 Sel 4/92 1,250
O/C 18x24 Floral Still Life Fre 12/91 300

Barnoin, Henri Alphonse Fr 1882-1935
W&C/Pa/B 11x12 Marche a Quimper Chr 10/91 605

Barnsley, James MacDonald Can 1861-1929
O/C 26x17 Mountain Stream 1889 Sbt 11/91 2,338
O/C 17x31 Old Bridge at Grez Sbt 11/91 2,104

Baron, Henri Charles Antoine Fr 1816-1885
* See 1990 Edition . . . .

Barone, Antonio Am 1889-
O/C 45x36 The Little Mother 1914 Chr 6/92 8,800
O/B 20x16 Portrait of a Girl 1959 Wlf 10/91 250

Barr, E. Con 19C
O/Pn 9x6 The Boulevard Sby 1/92 2,200

Barr, William Am 1867-1933
* See 1992 Edition . . . .

Barraband, Jacques Fr 1767-1809
G/Pa 22x16 Male Lesser Bird of Paradise But 5/92 33,000
G/Pa 20x16 Red Bird of Paradise But 5/92 33,000

Barralet, John James Am 1747-1815
Pl&S/Pa 11x9 George Washington's Resignation Chr 11/91 . 1,320

Barraud, Francois Sws 1899-1934
* See 1991 Edition . . . .

Barraud, Henry Br 1811-1874
* See 1992 Edition . . . .

Barraud, Maurice 20C
Pl&S/Pa 9x7 At the Bullfight Sby 11/91 990

Barraud, William Br 1810-1850
O/C 36x48 Chestnut Pony and Dog 1840 Sby 6/92 20,900
O/C 19x24 Cob with Terriers in a Landscape 1832 Chr 2/92 5,280
O/C 21x17 Bay Stallion 1841 Wlf 9/91 2,100

Barreda, Ernesto Fr 1927-
* See 1991 Edition . . . .

Barrera, Antonio Col 1948-
* See 1992 Edition . . . .

Barrera, Antonio It 20C
O/C 47x37 Passa Il Duce Slo 12/91 2,500

Barret, George (Sr.) Br 1728-1784
O/C 71x75 Waterfall and Figures Chr 10/91 92,400
Bc/Pa 23x18 Hauling Timber Through a Wood Chr 1/92 . . 6,600

Barret, Marius Antoine Fr 1865-
* See 1992 Edition . . . .

Barrett, J.   Br 19C
 * See 1992 Edition ....
Barrett, Oliver Glenn   Am 1903-1970
 O/Cb 20x24 Monterey Surf Mor 11/91 150
Barrier, Gustave   Fr 20C
 O/Pa/C 36x29 Still Life with Violets, an Urn Chr 2/92 .. 1,980
Barrios, Armando   Ven 1920-
 * See 1991 Edition ....
Barron, Hugh   Br 1745-1791
 * See 1992 Edition ....
Barsotti, Hercules   Brz 1914-
 * See 1992 Edition ....
Barth, Eugene Field   Am 1904-
 O/C 22x18 Chinese Dream/Still Life Skn 5/92 358
Barth, Karl   Ger 1787-1853
 H&K/Pa 8x7 Portrait Sculptor Ludwig Schaller Sby 1/92 ... 2,200
Barthalot, Marius   Fr 1861-
 O/C 13x18 View of a City Lou 9/91 750
Bartholdi, Frederic-Auguste   Fr 19C
 * See 1991 Edition ....
**Bartholomew, William Newton   Am
1822-1898**
 W/Pa 9x15 Chicken Coop Yng 4/92 750
Bartlett, Dana   Am 1878-1957
 O/C 24x32 Verdugo Canyon Mor 3/92 7,000
 O/C 20x24 Saddleback Mountain Mor 11/91 5,500
 O/C 25x30 Mountain Landscape Chr 11/91 3,080
 O/C 20x24 Springtime But 10/91 2,750
 O/C 44x32 Yosemite Falls 1912 But 6/92 2,750
 O/C 16x20 Along the Riverbed But 2/92 2,090
 O/B 32x32 Desert Scene But 10/91 2,090
 O/C 16x20 California Hills Mor 6/92 1,500
 O/C 20x24 Jacinto Range Near Palm Springs Mor 3/92 ... 1,500
 W/Pa 16x20 Mission San Antonio De Padua Mor 11/91 ... 1,000
 O/C 12x15 River Landscape Mor 8/92 750
 MM/Pa 11x8 L.A. Street Scene 47 Mor 6/92 250
 W&Pe/Pa 9x12 Trees by a Country Brook Wes 3/92 138
Bartlett, Frederic Clay   Am 1873-
 * See 1992 Edition ....
Bartlett, Gray   Am 1885-1951
 * See 1992 Edition ....
Bartlett, Jennifer   Am 1941-
 O/C 108x157 The Island Sby 10/91 132,000
 E&Ss/St 38x129 22 East 10 Street Sby 11/91 82,500
 E&Ss/St 72x259 392 Broadway Chr 11/91 82,500
 MM 36x115 In the Garden #1 Chr 5/92 44,000
 O/C 57x50 Fire Table Cone D Sby 5/92 33,000
Bartlett, William Henry   Am 1809-1854
 * See 1992 Edition ....
Bartolini, Frederico   It 20C
 * See 1992 Edition ....
Bartolozzi, Francesco   1725-1815
 K&Sg/Pa 21x17 Study of a Male Nude 1778 Sby 7/92 935
Bartoluzzi, Millo   It 20C
 W/Pa 10x19 The Fisherman Hnz 5/92 625
Barton, Ralph   Am 1891-1931
 Pl&S/Pa 12x17 Many Characters with Wings Ih 5/92 400
 Pl/Pa 7x12 Three Men Talking in General Store 21 Ih 11/91 . 200
Barttenbach, Hans   Ger 1908-
 O/Pn 9x7 Pair: Bavarian Couple Native Attire Sel 12/91 .. 1,100
Barucci, Pietro   It 1845-1917
 O/C 24x36 Neapolitan Seaweed Gatherers Chr 2/92 22,000
 O/C 21x42 A Roadside Stop Chr 2/92 11,000
 O/C 24x47 Travelling to Market Roman Campagna Sby 2/92 9,900
 O/C 20x43 Spring Landscape with Cattle Hnz 5/92 6,750
 O/C 21x15 Landscape with Fishers in a Boat Sby 1/92 ... 3,520
Baruchello, Gianfranco   It 1924-
 MM/Pa 13x19 Abstract 63 Wes 3/92 880
Barwolf, Georges   Bel 1872-1935
 * See 1992 Edition ....
Barye, Antoine Louis   Fr 1795-1875
 * See 1990 Edition ....
Basbian, Alfred   Dut 20C
 O/B 20x16 Floral Hnz 5/92 110

Basch, Gyula   Hun 1851-
 O/B 4x4 Boy and the Frog Yng 4/92 30
Baselitz, Georg   Ger 1938-
 O/C 64x51 Ludwig Richter Auf Dem Weg '66 Sby 11/91 ... 1.1
 O/C 99x79 Schlafzimmer '75 Sby 11/91 462,00
 O/C 86x86 Franz im Bett 82 Chr 5/92 440,00
 O/C 64x51 Graue Hunde, Drei Streifen 68 Sby 5/92 407,00
 O/C 64x58 Hommage A Wrubel 1963 Sby 11/91 297,00
 O/C 79x64 Orangenesser 81 Sby 5/92 242,00
 O/C 58x45 Orangenesser V 81 Chr 5/92 220,00
 O/C 98x78 Strandbild 4 Frau am Strand 80 Sby 5/92 ... 159,50
 O/C 79x55 Fliederstrasse '70 Sby 11/91 154,00
 O/C 68x55 Motivschimmel Zerbrochene Brucke 86 Chr 5/92 143,00
 O/C/C 86x45 Untitled Sby 11/91 99,00
 O/C 64x51 Blumen 82 Sby 5/92 88,00
 W,G&Y/Pa 25x19 Untitled 64 Sby 5/92 82,50
 C,Y&W/Pa 17x14 Untitled (Zwei Streifen Kopf) 66 Sby 5/92 63,25
 H/Pa 19x14 Untitled (Neuer Type) Sby 5/92 44,00
 Y&Pe/Pa 19x10 Untitled (Kullervo) Sby 5/92 29,70
 I,W&Y/Pa 19x13 Untitled (Fahne/Im Fenster) 65 Sby 5/92 . 28,60
 I/Pa 11x10 Untitled (Grobes Herz) 64 Sby 5/92 28,60
 Y&G/Pa 17x14 Untitled (Kahlschlag) 67 Sby 5/92 28,60
 Pe&W/Pa 20x13 Hunde 68 Sby 5/92 27,50
 Y&Pe/Pa 19x10 Untitled (Walderbeiter) 67 Sby 5/92 ... 27,50
 Pe,Y&W/Pa 24x17 Untitled (Zeichung) Sby 5/92 27,50
 I/Pa 28x20 Untitled (Kind Mit Enten) Sby 5/92 25,30
 I/Pa 12x8 Blutleuchte 61 Sby 5/92 24,20
 Y/Pa 16x10 Untitled (Kullervo) Sby 5/92 24,20
 Y&Pe/Pa 15x10 Untitled (Held) 66 Sby 5/92 23,10
 I&W/Pa 12x8 Untitled 59 Sby 5/92 22,00
 I/Pa 26x20 Tierstuck 65 Sby 5/92 20,90
 I/Pa 19x13 Untitled (Fahn) Sby 5/92 19,80
 I,W&C/Pa 17x12 Untitled (Im Fenster) Sby 5/92 19,80
 I/Pa 17x17 Untitled (Kopf) 64 Sby 5/92 19,80
 H/Pa 14x9 Untitled (Held) Sby 5/92 17,60
 C/Pa 11x13 Untitled (Figuren Im Raum) Sby 5/92 15,40
 I/Pa 14x13 Kreuz 64 Sby 5/92 14,30
 I/Pa 12x9 Ofen 62 Sby 5/92 14,30
 O/Pa 24x17 Untitled 76 Sby 11/91 13,20
 Y,W&Pe/Pa 17x12 Untitled (Frau) Sby 5/92 12,10
 I/Pa 19x13 Untitled (Schweinekopf) Sby 5/92 11,00
 W/Pa 24x17 Stations of the Cross Series 83 Chr 11/91 .. 10,450
 H,C&Y/Pa 24x17 Strassenbild 80 Chr 2/92 9,90
 I&C/Pa 30x23 Untitled 89 Chr 5/92 9,350
 Y/Pa 12x10 Kreuz 63 Sby 5/92 8,800
 I&Pe/Pa 19x13 Untitled (Gesicht) Sby 5/92 8,800
 C/Pa 15x14 Mann Mit Hund 1967 Sby 2/92 5,500
 C&P/Pa 21x30 Untitled 85 Sby 10/91 5,225
 W/Pa 26x20 Untitled 86 Sby 10/91 4,950
Basing, Charles   Am 1865-1933
 O/B 9x11 Staten Island Village and Dock Chr 6/92 1,540
 O/C/B 19x15 Venetian Street 1905 Wes 11/91 220
Baskin, Leonard   Am 1922-
 I/Pa 40x27 Birdman in Profile 1962 Skn 9/91 1,100
 S/Pa 40x27 Tiresias Dancing 1965 But 11/91 990
 I/Pa 40x27 The Coward 1961 Sby 12/91 770
Basoll, Antonio   It 1774-1848
 * See 1991 Edition ....
Basquiat, Jean-Michel   Fr 1961-1988
 A&L/C 86x68 ISBN 85 Chr 5/92 187,000
 A,Os&L/C 74x96 Part Wolf Chr 5/92 154,000
 A&O/C 83x118 TBT Chr 5/92 154,000
 O,Os&L/Wd 96x55 Anthony Clarke 1985 Chr 11/91 112,200
 A&Os/C 84x84 Thesis 1983 Chr 11/91 85,800
 O,A&Os/C 69x64 Red Rabbit 1982 Sby 11/91 71,500
 A&Os/C 72x47 Loin 82 Chr 2/92 68,200
 A&L/C 68x86 Dog Man 86 Chr 2/92 66,000
 A,Os&Pt/C 60x48 Orange Sports Figure Sby 5/92 66,000
 MM/Pa 30x42 Untitled 81 Chr 5/92 30,800
 O/C 36x48 59 Cents (2 for a Dollar) Sby 5/92 22,000
 Y/Pa 25x36 Alfred E. Neuman 1983 Chr 2/92 19,800
 Os&Fp/Pa 22x30 Father-Mother Chr 5/92 17,600
 Y/Pa 30x23 Two Drawings 87 Sby 11/91 16,500
 O&Pts/Pa 19x17 Untitled Sby 10/91 13,200
 Y&L/Pa 42x30 Untitled Sby 10/91 10,450

Os/Pa 30x24 Did the First Man Eat Pig? 1982 Chr 2/92 ... 7,700
Os/Pa 30x22 Untitled Sby 5/92 7,700
Pe&Cp/Pa 30x22 Untitled 85 Sby 11/91 7,150
I&Y/Pa 30x22 Untitled Chr 11/91 7,150
W,Os&Fp/Pa 22x15 Untitled Chr 5/92 7,150
Y/Pa 30x22 Formaggi Chr 5/92 5,500
Y/Pa 11x9 Untitled Chr 11/91 4,400
Y/Pa 12x9 Untitled Sby 10/91 1,760

Bassano It 1549-1592
O/C 32x45 Return of the Prodigal Son Sby 10/91 33,000

Bassano, Francesc (the Younger) It 1549-1592
O/Cp 37x35 Hercules and Cerberus Chr 5/92 20,900

Bassano, Jacopo It 1510-1592
* See 1992 Edition ....

Bassano, Leandro It 1557-1622
* See 1992 Edition ....

Basseporte, Madeleine-Francois Fr 1701-1780
* See 1990 Edition ....

Bassi, E. It 20C
W/Pa 13x8 Man Playing the Guitar 1899 Wlf 6/92 325

Bastard, Marc-Auguste Fr 1863-1926
O/B 14x18 Bridge Over the Seine River Lou 9/91 275

Bastiani, Lazzaro Di Jacopo It a 1425-1512
* See 1990 Edition ....

Bastien, Alfred Bel 1873-1955
* See 1992 Edition ....

Bastien-Lepage, Jules Fr 1848-1884
* See 1990 Edition ....

Bastogy, Charles-Albert-Hector Fr 20C
P/Pa 17x22 Fishermen near Concarneau Yng 4/92 325

Batcheller, Frederick S. Am 1837-1889
O/C 12x18 Still Life with Currants Skn 9/91 2,530

Bate, Stanley 20C
O/C 36x48 Runway and Orly: Two Sby 10/91 2,090

Bateman, James Br 1814-1849
O/C 36x28 The Kill 42 Sby 6/92 8,250
O/C 9x12 A False Scent 1845 Sby 6/92 3,080

Bateman, Robert Br 19C
* See 1991 Edition ....

Bates, David 1952-
O/C 78x90 Jetty Fishing Chr 11/91 17,600

Bates, David Br 1841-1921
O/C 27x38 Swamp and Animals 1890 Wlf 6/92 4,000
O/C 20x30 A Reed Bed, Spetchley Park 1885 Sby 2/92 ... 3,850
O/C 20x30 In Glen Malin 1901 Sby 7/92 3,850
O/C 18x14 At Dolwyddelen 1895 Chr 10/91 2,420
O/C 8x10 Brook in a Welsh Valley 1889 Slo 10/91 800

Bates, Dewey Am 1851-1891
* See 1991 Edition ....

Bates, Kenneth Am 1895-1973
O/C 25x30 Mystic Factory Scene Mys 6/92 495

Bates, Maxwell Bennett Can 1906-1980
O/B 20x16 Young Girl Sbt 11/91 1,122

Baton, Claude Am 20C
* See 1992 Edition ....

Battaglie, Oracolo Delle It 1600-1658
O/C 59x59 Battle Scene Sby 10/91 77,000

Battaglioli, Francesco It 18C
O/C 21x17 Company in a Classical Villa But 11/91 2,475

Battista, Giovanni It 1858-1925
G&W/Pb 9x15 Bay of Naples Chr 10/91 1,210
G&C/Pa 26x14 View of Naples and Monk Reading Chr 5/92 . 770

Battistello It 17C
* See 1990 Edition ....

Bauchant, Andre Fr 1873-1958
O/C 35x46 Les Enfants dans la Campagne 1929 Chr 2/92 . 42,900
O/C 18x25 La Pirogue 1925 Sby 6/92 12,100

Baudet, ***
* See 1992 Edition ....

Baudit, Amedee Sws 1825-1890
O/C 36x60 Evening Harbor Scene 1889 Slo 2/92 3,250

Baudouin, Pierre-Antoine Fr 1723-1769
K/Pa 5x4 Lovers in a Park Chr 1/92 1,760

Baudry, Paul Fr 1828-1886
* See 1991 Edition ....

Bauer
O/C 11x18 Still Life with Peaches & Bananas Dum 4/92 350

Bauer, Carl Ferdinand Aus 1879-1954
* See 1990 Edition ....

Bauer, Johann Balthasar Ger 1811-1883
* See 1992 Edition ....

Bauer, Rudolf Ger 1889-1953
O/C 51x61 Third Symphony in 3 Movements Chr 5/92 ... 66,000
O/Pn 29x41 Presto 7 Sby 2/92 39,600
O/C 46x32 Spirituality Sby 2/92 16,500

Bauer, Will Ger 20C
O/C 24x36 Mountain Landscape Slo 4/92 500

Bauer, William Am 1888-
W/Pa 10x29 Shoreline, Ship Hnz 5/92 200

Bauerle, Carl Wilhelm F. Ger 1831-1912
* See 1992 Edition ....

Bauermeister, Mary Am 1934-
MM 12x16 Fetiches 1961 But 5/92 1,760

Bauernfeind, Gustave Aus 1848-1904
O/C 19x16 A Side Court in Jerusalem 1884 Sby 5/92 46,750

Baugin, Lubin Eur 1612-1633
* See 1990 Edition ....

Baugniet, Charles Bel 1814-1886
* See 1992 Edition ....

Baum, Charles Am 1812-1878
* See 1992 Edition ....

Baum, Paul Ger 1859-1932
* See 1992 Edition ....

Baum, Walter Emerson Am 1884-1956
O/C 32x40 The Creek in Winter 1923 Chr 5/92 22,000
O/B 25x30 The Creek in Winter 1921 Chr 12/91 19,800
O/C 30x36 Bethlehem 1929 Ald 5/92 12,500
O/C 30x36 Green Street Ald 5/92 3,800
O/B 27x36 The Creeks Meet 1923 Slo 10/91 3,750
O/Cb 16x20 Ice Dam, Haycock Mountain 1935 Chr 9/91 ... 3,520
O/C 16x20 Blooming Glen Road Ald 5/92 3,100
O/Cb 25x30 Snowy Landscape with River Sby 4/92 3,080
O/C 16x20 Berks County Farms Ald 5/92 2,600
O/B 16x27 A Snowy Village Chr 11/91 2,420
O/M 12x16 Snowbound; Winter Landscape: (2) Sby 4/92 .. 2,420
O/B 14x18 Trees on Riverside Ald 5/92 2,400
O/M 16x20 Sunday; Street Scene: (2) Sby 4/92 2,200
O/B 4x5 Winter Landscape Ald 5/92 2,000
O/B 12x16 Winter Near Hellertown Ald 5/92 2,000
O/M 16x20 Allentown; Farmhouse: (2) Sby 4/92 1,980
O/B 12x16 Wile Street Manayunk 46 Sby 4/92 1,980
O/C 16x20 Lehigh County Scene 1941 Ald 3/92 1,500
O/B 5x7 Bridge; Creek Winter: 2 Miniatures Ald 3/92 ... 1,100
O/B 10x12 Philadelphia Street Ald 5/92 1,100
O/B 9x11 Easton Bridge Ald 5/92 1,050
W/Pa 25x33 Fishing Boats 1935 Ald 5/92 1,000
O/C 24x20 My Studio 1948 Ald 3/92 650
P/Pa 6x8 Bridge at Bethlehem Ald 3/92 550
P/Pa 8x10 Brook in Winter 1939 Ald 3/92 550
O/B 12x19 Lessig's School Sby 12/91 550
O/C/B 20x16 Portrait Ald 5/92 550
O/C 29x23 Amish Man at the Capital 1940 Ald 5/92 400
O/C 14x18 The Post Farm 1946 Ald 5/92 400
W&G/Pa 18x12 Lois Berrodini Wes 11/91 275

Baumann, Karl Herman Am 1911-1984
* See 1990 Edition ....

Baumeister, K. Ger 19C
O/C 39x58 Mary Magdalene and Angel 1865 Slo 2/92 650

Baumeister, Willi Ger 1889-1955
* See 1991 Edition ....

Baumes, Amedee Fr 1820-
* See 1991 Edition ....

Baumgartner, H. Ger 19C
* See 1992 Edition ....

Baumgartner, Johann Wolfgang
1712-1761
O/C 11x8 Martyrdom of Saint Venantius Chr 10/91 12,100
O/C 13x9 Saint Augustine Chr 10/91 11,000
Baumgartner, Peter Ger 1834-1898
O/C 36x29 The Marriage Instructions 1866 Chr 2/92 44,000
O/Pn 9x11 Ready to Serve Sby 2/92 13,200
Baumgartner, Warren Am 1894-1963
G/Pa 17x25 Virgin Sacrifice Ilh 5/92 1,200
W/Pa 20x24 Taxidermist Tying Feathers on Bird Ilh 5/92 550
Baumhofer, Walter M. Am 1904-
* See 1991 Edition
Baur, Joh. Ger 19C
O/Pn 9x6 Feeding the Bird Chr 10/91 1,540
Bayeu, Ramon
* See 1990 Edition
Baylinson, A. S. Am 1882-1950
C&K/Pa 20x15 Standing Nude and a Seated Nude (2) 1935 Chr
6/92 1,320
Bayliss, Sydney H.
O/C 16x24 Tropical Paradise Eld 7/92 825
Bayrer, Wilhelm & Muller, A. Ger 1836-
W&G/Pa/B 12x16 Two Sporting Scenes 1900 Skn 5/92 . . . 1,320
Bazaine, Jean Fr 1904-
* See 1990 Edition
Bazanni, Luigi It 1836-1927
W/Pa 30x24 La Fontana di Pompeii 1882 Sby 10/91 4,950
Bazile, Alberoi Hai 20C
O/M 10x12 The Day's Work Skn 3/92 330
Bazile, Castera Hai 20C
O/M 24x15 Self Portrait as a Drummer 50 Chr 5/92 44,000
O/M 19x26 Annunciation Chr 5/92 16,500
O/M 24x16 Caritas 52 Sby 2/92 15,950
O/M 24x20 Village Scene 58 Chr 5/92 12,100
Baziotes, William A. Am 1912-1963
O/C 30x38 Phantom 1953 Sby 11/91 110,000
O/C 40x50 October 1960 Sby 11/91 99,000
W&G/Pa 11x14 Puppet Forms Chr 9/91 10,450
O/B 18x14 Fleur du Mal 1944 Sby 10/91 8,250
Bazzani, Giuseppe It 1690-1769
* See 1991 Edition
Bazzani, Luigi
O/Pn 29x20 An Offering of Flowers 1883 Hnz 10/91 5,250
Bazzaro, Leonardo It 1853-1937
O/Pn 36x24 Lady in a Garden Chr 10/91 8,800
Bazzicaluva, Ercole It 1600-1638
K&PV/Pa 16x22 Figures on a Bridge Chr 1/92 1,980
Beach, Thomas Br 1738-1806
O/C 50x40 Portrait of John Edwin Brd 5/92 7,700
O/C 30x25 Portrait of a Lady 1790 Chr 10/91 2,200
Beal, Gifford Am 1879-1956
O/Pn 24x36 The Elegant Lawn Party Sby 5/92 46,750
W&PV/Pa 14x20 Topsfield Fair Chr 9/91 4,950
O/C 13x17 After the Market 1922 Sby 12/91 1,760
Beal, Jack Am 1931-
* See 1991 Edition
Beal, Reynolds Am 1867-1951
O/C Size? Wellfleet Mys 6/92 3,960
MM 21x28 The Ferris Wheel 1915 Brd 5/92 2,750
Cp/Pa 13x18 Circus 1929 Yng 2/92 2,500
W/Pa 13x18 Elephants, Cole Brothers Circus Brd 8/92 2,200
Y/Pa 13x20 Circus Scene, 1929 Brd 8/92 2,090
P&Pe/Pa 10x12 Picnic of 'Sells Floto' Circus 1929 Skn 11/91 2,090
Pe/Pa 14x18 Sells Floto Circus, 1929 Yng 4/92 2,000
W/Pa 7x9 Monhegan Island 1939 Lou 3/92 1,900
Y/Pa 12x20 Sparks Circus, 1930 Brd 8/92 1,870
Y/Pa 10x14 Pagliacci 1918 Brd 8/92 1,760
W/Pa 13x17 Sparks Circus 1927 Chr 11/91 1,760
Cp/Pa 9x12 Circus Yng 2/92 1,600
Y/Pa 12x14 Circus Scene Mys 11/91 1,540
G,P&Pe/Pa 11x13 Gloucester--Carnival 1944 Skn 11/91 . . . 1,430
Y/Pa 11x11 Circus Scene Mys 11/91 1,045
Pe/Pa 8x10 Spark Circus, Salem Ma 1929 Chr 11/91 1,045
W&Pe/Pa 10x12 Circus Scene Mys 6/92 605

Beal, William T.
* See 1991 Edition
Beale, Mary 1633-1697
* See 1992 Edition
Beaman, Waldo Gamaliel Am 1852-1937
O/B 9x13 Still Life with Peaches '93 Skn 11/91 880
Bean, Ainslie Br a 1880-1890
W/Pa 18x13 Mediterranean Waterfront Yng 2/92 200
Beard, James Henry Am 1812-1893
O/Ab 5x10 Ohio Landscape with River View 1864 Slo 7/92 . 1,700
O/C 27x22 Bearded Gentleman 1867 Wes 3/92 660
Beard, William Holbrook Am 1824-1900
O/C 20x16 Home from the Hunt Mys 6/92 1,650
Bearden, Romare Am 1914-1988
W&L/B 23x26 The Family Sby 5/92 28,600
W&L/B 8x12 Caribbean Mermaid Sby 2/92 13,200
W/Pa 9x11 The Eel Fishers Sby 2/92 7,700
Beare, George Eng a 1744-1749
* See 1990 Edition
Beaton, Cecil
W&G/Pa 24x19 Elegant Lady with a Whippet Sby 2/92 1,760
W&Gd/Pa 19x14 Caribbean Fruit Seller Sby 6/92 880
Beatty, John William Can 1869-1941
O/C 20x24 Landscape, Evening '13 Sbt 11/91 7,714
O/B 10x13 Thatched Cottage '07 Sbt 11/91 1,028
O/C 13x22 Harbour View '94 Sbt 11/91 654
Beaudin, Andre Fr 1895-1979
W/Pa 15x18 Path Through the Forest 1972 Hnd 12/91 1,600
Beauduin, Jean Bel 1851-1916
O/C 29x24 The Flower Garden 1903 Chr 2/92 7,150
O/C 24x29 The End of the Day Chr 10/91 5,500
Beaugureau, Francis Henry Am 1920-
O/C 22x34 The Buffalo Soldiers Chr 3/92 4,180
Beaulieu, Paul Vanier Can 1910-
O/C 25x32 Still Life Pears and Grapes '50 Sbt 11/91 11,220
O/C 18x24 Boats in the Harbour 1958 Sbt 11/91 7,012
W/Pa 22x18 Study of a Rooster '68 Sbt 11/91 1,870
O/C 20x24 Rural Village in Winter Sbt 5/92 1,496
Beaumont, Arthur Am 1879-1978
* See 1992 Edition
Beaumont, Arthur Edwaine Am 1890-
O/C 18x24 Coastal Scene with Figures Slo 12/91 550
Beaumont, Thomas D. Br 20C
O/C 20x30 Return of the Flock Hnd 6/92 375
Beauquesne, Wilfrid Constant Fr
1847-1913
O/C 44x74 At the Height of Battle Sby 5/92 11,000
O/C 42x75 The Defeat Sby 5/92 11,000
O/C 75x43 Ambush on the Vosges, 1870 Sby 5/92 6,600
O/C 51x38 Abduction During the War 1891 Sby 7/92 5,500
O/C 22x26 French Army Gathered in Town Slo 10/91 5,000
Beauregard, C. G. 19C
O/C 12x9 Portraits: Pair Dum 9/91 450
Beauvais, Armand Fr 1840-1911
* See 1992 Edition
Beaux, Cecilia Am 1861-1942
* See 1992 Edition
Beavis, Richard Br 1824-1896
* See 1992 Edition
Beccafumi, Domenico It 1486-1551
O/Pn 35 dia Holy Family with Infant St. John Chr 5/92 . . . 308,000
Beccaria, Angelo It 1820-1897
* See 1992 Edition
Becher, Arthur E. Am 1877-1960
O/C 34x24 Baby's First Christmas Chr 11/91 8,250
C/Pa 18x20 Three Story Illustrations Ilh 11/91 300
O/Pn 22x18 Blue and Gold/Oriental Still Life '56 Skn 3/92 . . . 275
Becher, Bernd and Hilla 20C
Ph 17x21 Steelplant, France Chr 11/91 22,000
Ph 66x55 9 Postwar Houses, Germany Chr 11/91 16,500
Ph 25x22 Silos fur Gerrent 1963 Chr 11/91 15,400
Ph 16x12 Water Towers Sby 10/91 12,100
Ph/B 16x12 Textile Factory, Mettmann, Germany Chr 5/92 . . 7,150
Ph/B 12x16 East Chicago--Three Views Chr 5/92 6,600
Ph/B 16x12 Water Tower Sby 10/91 2,200

Becher, Carl Ludwig G. Ger 19C
O/C 30x22 Girl Holding Dog Mys 6/92 110
Bechi, Luigi It 1830-1919
O/C 47x33 Boy Playing a Clarinet Chr 5/92 15,400
O/Pn 10x7 Courtyard Flirtation Sby 7/92 5,500
O/C 9x12 A Children's Game Sby 1/92 2,420
Bechtle, Robert Am 1932-
O/C 72x69 Vacuum Cleaner Salesman 67 Chr 5/92 16,500
Beck, A. R. Am 20C
* See 1992 Edition
Beck, Dunbar D. Am 1902-1986
* See 1992 Edition
Beck, I. F. Scn 19C
* See 1990 Edition
Beck, Jacob Samuel 1715-1778
* See 1992 Edition
Becker, Carl Ludwig Friedrich Ger 1829-1900
O/C 29x39 Appealing to the Monarch But 11/91 2,475
Becker, Charlotte Am 1907-
O/B 18x17 Girl with Doll on Shoulder Ih 11/91 1,600
O/B 21x17 Baby in Crib, Blue Shoe in Mouth Ih 5/92 850
Becker, Joseph Am 1841-1910
W/Pa 10x14 Coastal Scene 97 Brd 8/92 632
Becker, Maurice Am 1889-
O/C 24x20 At the Racetrack '36 But 4/92 1,650
Becker, W. Br 20C
O/C 30x30 Moonlight in Arabia Wlf 11/91 300
Beckett, Charles E. Am 1814-1856
O/C 13x18 Wild River Bridge, Bethel, Maine 1852 Brd 8/92 . 4,290
O/C 10x13 Waterfall, Autumn Brd 8/92 1,210
Beckhoff, Harry Am 1901-1979
I&W/Pa 9x20 Boy Following Dandy 1930 Ih 5/92 325
Beckman, William 20C
* See 1991 Edition
Beckmann, Max Am 1884-1950
O/C 24x16 Gelbes Cafe 41 Chr 5/92 264,000
Beckwith, Arthur Am 1860-1930
O/C 12x17 Basket of Peaches But 6/92 825
Beckwith, James Carroll Am 1852-1917
O/C 31x27 Portrait of Evelyn Nesbitt 1900 Sby 3/92 22,000
O/Pn 8x6 The Straw Hat Chr 3/92 13,200
O/Pn 14x11 Spanish Dancer '90 Sby 5/92 11,000
O/Pn 16x10 Old Boathouse in Central Park Chr 12/91 7,700
O/C 26x20 Woman with Tiara Lou 3/92 3,000
O/C 26x20 Mrs. Leland Cofer But 11/91 1,650
Beechey, Richard Brydges Br 1808-1895
* See 1990 Edition
Beechey, Sir William Br 1753-1839
O/C 88x54 Portrait of Lady Reade Chr 10/91 5,500
O/C 24x20 Portrait of Master Collier Sby 5/92 4,950
O/C 30x25 Portrait of Lord Stannard Wes 11/91 990
Beelt, Cornelis Dut 1660-1702
* See 1991 Edition
Beer, Wilhelm-Amandus Ger 1837-1890
O/C 38x45 Napoleon's Retreat fr Moscow 1888 Hnd 12/91 . 4,000
Beerstraten, Jan Dut 1622-1666
* See 1992 Edition
Beert I, Osias Flm 1570-1624
* See 1990 Edition
Beert, Osias Flm 1622-1678
* See 1990 Edition
Bega, Cornelis Dut 1631-1664
* See 1990 Edition
Behrens, Howard Am 20C
O/C 32x48 Tidal Pool 80 Hnd 10/91 1,900
Beich, Joachim Franz 1665-1748
O/C 22x35 Moses and the Israelites Red Sea Chr 10/91 . . 22,000
Beigel, Peter Br 1913-
* See 1990 Edition
Beinke, Fritz Ger 1842-1907
O/Pn 13x9 Watching a Hot Air Balloon Skn 9/91 2,475
Beisen, Kubota Jap 1852-1906
W/Pa 37x26 Ducks Fre 4/92 350

Bekker, D. Ger 20C
O/C 56x40 Beggars Hnz 5/92 300
Bel-Geddes, Norman 20C
* See 1991 Edition
Bela, Kontuly 20C
O/C 31x23 Still Life Flowers, Tomatoes & Corn 1962 Slo 4/92 200
Belanger, Louis Fr 1736-1816
K&Bc/Pa 13x19 A Mansion in a Park 1792 Chr 1/92 9,900
Belarski, Rudolph Am 1900-1983
O/C 28x24 Man Aiming Rifle at Two Others 39 Ih 5/92 . . . 1,800
Belimbau, Adolfo It 1845-
O/C 18x14 Portrait of a Lady Hnd 12/91 325
Belknap, Zedekiah Am 1781-1858
* See 1992 Edition
Bell, Cecil C. Am 1906-1970
O/C 24x30 Italian Fiesta '39 But 4/92 6,050
O/C 20x16 Going Home But 4/92 5,500
O/Cb 10x14 Two City Genre Scenes Skn 3/92 1,040
Bell, Charles Am 1874-1935
* See 1991 Edition
Bell, Edward August Am 1862-1953
* See 1992 Edition
Bell, George Am 20C
O/C 11x14 Landscape Mys 11/91 220
Bell, John W. Am 19C
O/Pn 5x7 Harbor Scene with Sailboat 1874 Slo 10/91 900
Bell, Larry 1939-
MM/Pa 39x32 Three Drawings '79 Chr 11/91 1,650
Bell, Phillip Am 1907-
O/C 55x40 Frontier Rhythm 1935 Slo 12/91 2,500
Bell-Smith, Frederic Marlett Can 1846-1923
W/Pa 20x13 Lake in the Rockies 1889 Sbt 5/92 3,740
W/Pa 11x8 Camp on Bow River 1889 Sbt 11/91 3,039
W/Pa 10x7 Street Scene, England 1891 Sbt 5/92 2,571
W/Pa 8x13 River Near the Rocky Mountains Sbt 11/91 . . . 1,770
W/Pa 13x9 Rocky Mountain Gorge Sbt 5/92 1,309
W/Pa 5x5 Westminster, London Sbt 5/92 654
W/Pa 11x17 European Harbour Scene Mys 6/92 385
Bellange, Joseph Louis Hippoly Fr 1800-1866
* See 1991 Edition
Bellanger, Camille Felix Fr 1853-1923
O/C 32x26 The Basket of Cherries 1920 Slo 9/91 8,000
Bellanger, Georges Fr 1847-1918
* See 1991 Edition
Bellefleur, Leon Can 1910-
O/C 24x20 Abstract Composition '61 Sbt 5/92 6,078
G/Pa 14x18 Midi Octobre, 1960 '60 Sbt 11/91 2,338
O/C 12x9 Carousel '82 Sbt 5/92 1,776
Bellei, Gaetano It 1857-1922
O/C 28x20 A Sweet Singer Sby 7/92 13,200
O/C 25x22 A Look Through the Door Chr 2/92 4,620
Bellel, Jean Joseph Francois Fr 1816-1898
* See 1992 Edition
Bellenge, Michel-Bruno Fr 1726-1793
* See 1990 Edition
Bellerman, Ferdinand Ger 1814-1889
* See 1990 Edition
Bellevois, Jacob Adriaensz. Dut 1621-1675
O/Pn 24x33 Dutch Ship Floundering Sby 1/92 22,000
Belli, A***
* See 1992 Edition
Belli, Giovacchino It 1756-1882
* See 1990 Edition
Bellini, Giovanni It 1430-1516
* See 1991 Edition
Bellis, Hubert Bel 1831-1902
O/C 18x15 Chrysanthemums Chr 2/92 6,600
O/C 26x19 Still Life with Oranges Hnd 3/92 2,000
Bellmer, Hans Fr 1902-1975
Pe/Pa 16x9 Multi-Eyed Figure Wlf 3/92 800

39

Belloli, Andrei Franzowitsch   Rus -1881
* See 1992 Edition ....
Bellon, Jean   Fr 1941-
* See 1992 Edition ....
Bellotti, Pietro   It 1627-1700
* See 1991 Edition ....
Bellows, Albert Fitch   Am 1829-1883
O/C 10x8 The Fisherman Bor 8/92 2,600
Bellows, George Wesley   Am 1882-1925
O/Pn 18x22 The Fisherman Sby 12/91 82,500
O/Pn 15x20 Flaming Breaker Chr 12/91 55,000
Bellucci, Antonio   It 1654-1726
* See 1992 Edition ....
Bellynck, Hubert Emile   Fr 1859-
O/C 18x13 Reading by Oil Lamp Hnz 5/92 1,250
Beloff, Angelina   Rus 1884-1967
W/Pa 16x13 Salto De San Anton, Cuernavaca 57 Sby 11/91   7,975
Belois, J.   Fr 20C
O/C 25x20 Lady at the Opera Mys 6/92 220
Beltran-Masses, Frederico   Spa 1885-1949
* See 1992 Edition ....
Beman, Walter   20C
W/Pa 7x10 Sunset through Woods Yng 4/92 60
Bemelmans, Ludwig   Am 1898-1963
O/C 26x36 Bateaux Restaurants Chr 11/91 4,950
W/Pa 6x8 New York City Lou 9/91 475
W/Pa 14x11 Cafe along the River Wlf 3/92 325
W/Pa 14x21 Scene with Chickens 1938 Ald 5/92 150
Bemis, E.   Am 20C
O/B 16x20 Fishing Dock Yng 2/92 50
Benard, Jean-Baptiste   18C
* See 1992 Edition ....
Benassit, Louis Emile   Fr 1833-1902
* See 1992 Edition ....
Bendiner, Alfred
W/Pa 16x23 Venice Sby 2/92 550
Benedetti, Andrea   It 1615-1649
* See 1991 Edition ....
Beneduce, Antimo   Am 1900-
W/Pa 14x20 Figures Resting by Columns Slo 7/92 90
Beneker, Gerrit A.   Am 1882-1934
O/C 31x22 Pirate with Guns Drawn 1913 Ilh 11/91 2,000
O/B 10x8 Afternoon in Provincetown 1925 But 4/92 1,320
Benessit, Emanuel   Fr 19C
O/Pn 10x14 French Cavalry Officer Slo 9/91 1,100
Benfatti, Alvise   It 1550-1609
O/C 56x74 The Nativity Chr 1/92 16,500
Bengston, Billy Al   Am 1934-
* See 1992 Edition ....
Benito   Eur 20C
O/Pn 12x7 The Guitar Player Wlf 11/91 200
Benlliure Y Gil, Jose   Spa 1855-1914
* See 1992 Edition ....
Benlliure Y Gil, Mariano   Spa 1862-
W/Pa 40x27 At the Wine Cellar 85 Sby 10/91 15,400
Benlliure Y Ortiz, Jose   Spa 1884-1916
O/Pn 12x9 Break From Work Sby 10/91 27,500
Benn, Ben   Am 1884-1983
W&Pe/Pa 17x12 Woman in a Brimmed Hat 1915 Chr 6/92 . 1,320
O/C 18x24 The Sea 55 Chr 11/91 770
O/C 10x8 Gladiola 56 Skn 5/92 220
Benninghaus, Julius Charles   Am 1905-
O/Cb 7x9 Indian on Horseback 1923 Hnd 10/91 950
Benois, Alexander Nikolaevich   Rus 1870-1960
G&Pe/Pa 12x9 Two Costume Designs 1931 Sby 2/92 1,540
G&Pe/Pa 12x9 Petrouchka: Costume Design Sby 6/92 880
G&Pe/Pa 12x9 Sadko: Costume Design Sby 6/92 550
Benois, Nicolai   Rus 1902-
* See 1992 Edition ....
Benoit, Rigaud   Hai 20C
O/B 30x24 Waterfall Chr 11/91 11,000
Benoit-Levy, Jules   Fr 1866-
O/C 74x99 La Bonne Peche 1903 Wes 5/92 3,080

Benoldi, Walter   It 20C
O/Pn 12x6 Two Compositions Hnd 12/91 500
O/C 36x28 Shelf Still Life Wes 3/92 440
Bensa, Ernesto   It 19C
W/Pa 24x16 Church Courtyard Wes 3/92 550
W/Pa 26x17 Church Interior Wes 3/92 550
Bensell, George F.   Am 1837-1879
O/C 30x50 Forceful River Fre 4/92 3,700
Bensing, Frank   Am 1893-1983
O/C 14x32 Nurse & Two Women in Hospital Room Ilh 5/92 . 550
Benson, Frank Weston   Am 1862-1951
W/Pa 21x15 The Maine Coast Hnd 10/91 7,000
Benson, John P.   Am 1865-1947
O/B 8x10 Ships at Sea Mys 6/92 385
Bentley, Claude
* See 1992 Edition ....
Bentley, John William   Am 1880-1951
O/C 25x30 On the Rondout Chr 9/91 10,450
O/C 16x20 Spring 1917 But 6/92 3,300
Benton, Dwight   Am 1834-
O/C 14x26 Boys by the Shore '78 Yng 4/92 2,000
O/Pn 4x8 Stormy Day at Viareggio '87 Wes 3/92 550
Benton, Fletcher   Am 1931-
O/C 40x32 Rural Crossroads But 5/92 2,090
Benton, Thomas Hart   Am 1889-1975
Et/C/Pn 48x31 T.P. and Jake Sby 12/91 275,000
Lq/M 9x15 Rice Threshing Sby 5/92 77,000
W/Pa/B 16x14 Cove; Martha's Vineyard Chr 5/92 17,600
O/M 7x4 Still Life Sby 9/91 15,400
O/M 5x6 Southwest Landscape Sby 9/91 8,800
G/Pa 7x11 Train and Landscape: Double '52 Sby 5/92 .. 8,800
Pl&S/Pa 12x9 Waiting It Out Wlf 10/91 7,000
Pe/Pa 6x5 Four Drawings Chr 11/91 1,100
Pe/Pa 9x11 An Indian in Movement Chr 6/92 198
Benwell, Austin Joseph   Br 19C
* See 1991 Edition ....
Berard, Christian   Fr 1902-1949
W&Pl/Pa 13x10 Six Drawings Chr 11/91 2,000
I,S&G/Pa 14x13 La Beaute de Noel Sby 10/91 1,650
Berard, Desire Honore   Fr 1845-
* See 1992 Edition ....
Beraud, Jean   Fr 1849-1936
O/C 16x22 Une Avenue Parisienne Chr 5/92 308,000
O/Pn 10x14 Scene de Grand Boulevard Sby 10/91 110,000
O/C 15x11 Une Parisienne Chr 5/92 71,500
Berchem, Nicolaes Pietersz.   Ger 1620-1683
O/Pn 15x21 Landscape w/Shepherdess (2) Chr 1/92 ... 165,000
O/Pn 17x22 Landscape with a Shepherd Sby 5/92 55,000
Berchere, Narcisse   Fr 1819-1891
* See 1992 Edition ....
Berczy, William Von Moll   Can 1744-1813
* See 1991 Edition ....
Berea, Dimitri   Am 1908-1975
O/C 27x36 Woman in an Interior Sby 10/91 7,150
O/C 22x18 Still Life with Roses Sby 10/91 3,300
Berentz, Christian   Ger 1658-1722
O/C 14x18 Still Lifes Peaches on Plate: Pair Sby 1/92 ... 55,000
Beresford, Frank Ernest   Eng 1881-1962
O/C 19x26 Express Train at Sunset 1905 Wes 11/91 302
Berg, David   Am 1920-
Pl&S/Pa 20x17 Barbershop Fantasy Ilh 5/92 750
Berg, George Louis   Am 1870-1941
* See 1992 Edition ....
Berg, Joan   Dut 20C
O/C/B 40x10 Two Noblemen Hnd 6/92 120
Bergamann, Julius Hugo   Ger 1861-1940
* See 1990 Edition ....
Bergamini, Francesco   It 1815-1883
O/C 15x21 Mischief Sby 10/91 2,750
Berge, Stephen   Am 1908-
O/C 30x25 Waiting for Her Suitor Mys 11/91 138
Bergen, Claus   Ger 20C
* See 1992 Edition ....

Berger, Ernst Aus 1857-1919
 * See 1991 Edition . . . .
Berger, G. Ger 1917-
 O/C 12x20 Pair Landscapes Sel 9/91 450
Berger, H. Ger 19C
 O/C 26x22 Historische Muhle in Konigswinter Hnd 3/92 400
Berger, Hans Sws 1882-
 O/C 34x70 Peacocks in a Wooded Landscape 1917 Sel 4/92 3,250
Bergeret, Denis Pierre Fr 1846-1910
 O/C 94x55 Still Life with Game Sby 6/92 6,600
Bergey, Earle K. Am 1901-1952
 O/C 28x25 Skater in Yellow Lying on Her Back Ih 5/92 . . . 2,600
Bergier, Joseph Dut 1753-1829
 * See 1991 Edition . . . .
Bergmann, Julius H. Ger 1861-1940
 O/C 38x45 Leading the Flock Sel 4/92 6,500
Berhas, Frans Bel 1827-1897
 * See 1990 Edition . . . .
Beringuier, Eugene Fr 1874-1949
 O/C 46x59 The Rehearsal Sel 4/92 6,500
Berjon, Antoine Fr 1754-1843
 * See 1992 Edition . . . .
Berk, Henrietta
 * See 1992 Edition . . . .
Berke, Ernest Am 1921-
 O/C 22x30 Evening Serenade 1963 But 4/92 1,430
Berke, Troy Am 20C
 * See 1992 Edition . . . .
Berkeley, Stanley Br 1855-1909
 * See 1992 Edition . . . .
Berkes, Antal Hun 1874-1938
 O/C 21x27 Street Scene in Winter Slo 4/92 1,300
Berlant, Tony 20C
 L/Pn 10x10 Hi Fly 1964 Sby 6/92 1,760
Berman, E.
 W/Pa 12x9 Irish Setter Ald 5/92 70
Berman, Eugene Am 1889-1972
 O/C 24x20 Vue D'Un Port de Mer en Ruines 1933 Sby 10/91 7,425
 O/Pn 9x7 Porte Rustique; Porte Ecroulee:Pair 38 Sby 2/92 . 7,150
 O/C 16x12 Trio 1954 Sby 6/92 4,950
 O/C 40x28 Lady From Parma 1942 Sby 6/92 3,575
 O/C 18x12 Antique Fragments Roman Garden 1954 Sby 6/92 3,300
 Pl/Pa 10x14 Don Quixote; Scene VI: Two Sby 2/92 3,300
 W&I/Pa 10x16 Design for the Front Curtain Sby 2/92 2,750
 W/Pa 15x12 Four Costume Designs 1945 But 11/91 2,475
 W,G&PI/Pa 13x10 Costume Design for Giselle 1946 Chr 2/92 1,980
 G,W&I/Pa 12x9 Costume Design for Giselle 1946 Chr 2/92 . 1,430
 W&G/Pa/B 28x20 Fountain 1932 Sby 2/92 1,430
 W&I/Pa 9x7 Four Drawings 1943 Sby 10/91 1,320
 W,I&G/Pa 9x13 Don Quixote, Wedding Chr 11/91 935
 I/Pa 13x10 Villa Adriana: Two 1951 Sby 10/91 880
 I&W/Pa 9x7 Roma: Three Costume Designs 1955 Sby 6/92 . 770
 G&S/Pa 6x19 Stage Design 1955 Sby 6/92 660
Berman, Leonid Am 1896-1976
 O/C 16x31 Rice Field Near Tokyo 58 Sby 10/91 3,300
 O/Cb 7x9 Bear Island 62 Sby 6/92 550
Berman, Wallace Am 1926-1976
 * See 1991 Edition . . . .
Bermudez, Cundo Cub 1914-
 O/C 35x43 Harlequins Sby 5/92 20,900
 O/C 35x24 Interior Sby 5/92 11,000
 G/Pa 31x27 La Adivinadora 56 Chr 11/91 9,900
 G/Pa 37x29 Mujer 44 Chr 5/92 7,700
 G/B 26x20 Mujer Sentada Chr 5/92 5,500
 T/Pa 29x35 Figures in a Barber Shop 44 Doy 11/91 3,000
Bernadotte, Prins Eugen Swd 20C
 * See 1991 Edition . . . .
Bernard, Emile Fr 1868-1941
 * See 1991 Edition . . . .
Bernard, Jean Joseph Fr 1864-1933
 * See 1991 Edition . . . .
Bernardo Con 19C
 O/C 18x15 Woman Wearing a Plumed Hat Chr 2/92 550
Bernardo, Monsu Dan 1624-1687
 * See 1992 Edition . . . .

Bernath, Sandor Am 1892-
 W/Pa 18x18 Racing Off the Point Wes 5/92 770
 W/Pa 17x19 Port Tack Wes 5/92 715
 W/Pa 16x19 Seven Sails Wes 5/92 605
 W&G/Pa 13x17 Smooth Sailing Skn 5/92 440
Berndtson, Gunnar Swd 1854-1895
 * See 1992 Edition . . . .
Berne-Bellecour, Etienne P. Fr 1838-1910
 O/C 32x46 A Cavalry Halt 1878 Sby 10/91 17,600
 O/Pn 15x10 Officer in Landscape Sby 1/92 4,400
 O/Pn 10x12 A Welcome Respite Sby 1/92 4,125
Berneker, Louis Frederick Am 1876-1937
 * See 1992 Edition . . . .
Berni, Antonio Arg 1905-
 O/C 18x14 Mujer con Panuelo 51 Chr 5/92 6,600
Berninger, Edmund Ger 1843-
 O/C 19x24 The Amalfi Coast But 5/92 5,500
Berninghaus, Charles Am 1905-1971
 O/Cb 14x18 Taos Landscape But 11/91 1,650
Berninghaus, Oscar E. Am 1874-1952
 O/M 16x20 Valley of the Sun Sby 5/92 36,300
 O/C 30x40 The Watering Hole 15 But 4/92 33,000
 O/C 20x24 Five Miles to Taos Chr 9/91 22,000
 O/C 30x20 Mountainous Winter Landscape Sel 12/91 18,000
 O/Cb 9x13 Two Horses Sby 12/91 10,450
 O/B 12x8 Indian with Striated Blanket Sel 9/91 5,500
 W/Pa/B 6x9 Indian on a Mustang '99 Sel 9/91 3,500
Bernstein, Theresa Am 1890-
 O/C 30x40 Armistice Day Celebration 19 Chr 12/91 26,400
 O/C 28x36 Balcony at Carnegie Hall Sby 12/91 13,200
 O/B 9x12 Beach Scene Sby 12/91 13,200
 O/C 24x17 Lenore Lloyd Lou 12/91 2,900
 O/C 17x20 Still Life Chianti and Grapes Lou 12/91 1,900
 O/B 9x12 New York Roof Tops 1912 Lou 9/91 1,400
 O/C 20x25 Sheep Meadow, Central Park Skn 11/91 1,320
 O/B 6x8 In the Berkshires '15 Wlf 9/91 650
Beroud, Louis Fr 1852-1910
 O/C 45x58 Symphonie en Rouge et Or 1895 Sby 2/92 . . . 28,600
 O/C 26x21 Interieur du Louvre 1898 Sby 2/92 7,700
Berrelmans, Ludwig Am 1898-1963
 G/Cd 20x27 High Wind Wlf 10/91 800
Berry, Nathaniel L. Am 1859-
 O/B 10x12 Landscape Mys 11/91 60
Berry, Patrick Vincent Am 1852-1922
 O/C 10x14 Grazing Cows Slo 7/92 425
Bert, Emile Bel 1814-1847
 * See 1992 Edition . . . .
Bertauld, P. Fr 19C
 * See 1992 Edition . . . .
Bertaux, Jacques Fr 1745-1818
 * See 1991 Edition . . . .
Berthelemy, Jean-Simon Fr 1743-1811
 * See 1990 Edition . . . .
Berthelsen, Johann Am 1883-1969
 O/C 17x13 New York Snow Scenes: Pair Sby 4/92 4,125
 O/C 22x16 Old Trinity Doy 12/91 3,250
 O/C 24x30 Winter, Washington Square Sel 9/91 3,000
 O/C 16x20 Snow at the United Nations Lou 9/91 2,750
 O/Cb 16x12 Fifth Avenue Sby 12/91 2,530
 O/C 16x20 Washington Square in Snow Wlf 4/92 2,500
 O/C 20x16 New York City Street Scene, Winter Slo 7/92 . . 2,200
 O/B 8x6 Trinity Church Fre 4/92 2,200
 O/Cb 22x18 New York in Winter But 11/91 1,650
 O/Cb 14x10 Up Fifth Avenue But 4/92 1,650
 O/B 14x18 United Nations But 4/92 1,540
 O/Cb 10x8 St. Paul at Park Ave. Wlf 9/91 1,500
 O/Cb 12x9 Washington Square in the Snow Skn 11/91 1,430
 O/Cb 12x9 Winter, New York City Skn 11/91 1,430
 O/M 18x22 Winter in New York Hnz 10/91 1,400
 O/C 24x20 Cathedral in Winter 1941 Hnz 10/91 1,300
Berthot, Jake Am 1939-
 A&H/Pa 30x22 Man Goat with a Pipe 81 Chr 5/92 1,980
Bertin, Jean Victor Fr 1775-1842
 O/C 19x14 A L'Ombre Sby 5/92 3,850

Bertin, Roger Fr 1915-
  * See 1990 Edition . . . .
Berton, Louis Fr 19C
  * See 1991 Edition . . . .
Bertoni, Mae Am 1929-
  O/Cb 10x12 Sur la plage Skn 5/92   880
Bertrand, James Fr 1823-1887
  O/C 54x28 Folie D'Ophelie 1872 Sby 10/91 18,150
Bertrand, Paulin Andre Fr 1852-1940
  O/C 20x36 Promenade under Apple Blossoms Chr 5/92 . . 14,300
Bertrand, Pierre-Philippe Fr 1884-
  * See 1992 Edition . . . .
Bertzy Con 19C
  * See 1992 Edition . . . .
Beschey, Balthasar Flm 1708-1776
  * See 1991 Edition . . . .
Besnard, Paul Albert Fr 1849-1934
  O/C 24x20 Modele au Collier 1915 Wlf 9/91   2,500
  W&C/B 22x19 Nymph 1889 Chr 5/92   1,540
Bess, Forrest Am 1911-1977
  O/M 20x9 Untitled 53 Zne 2/92   3,300
Besser, Arne 20C
  A/C 40x30 Untitled Chr 11/91   2,200
Bessier
  O/C 24x20 French Street Scene Dum 6/92   300
Bessinger, Frederick Am 1886-1975
  * See 1992 Edition . . . .
Bessire, Dale Philip Am 1892-
  * See 1992 Edition . . . .
Bessonot, Boris Rus 19C
  * See 1990 Edition . . . .
Best, Arthur William Am 1859-1935
  O/C 15x24 Marin County Landscape But 6/92   1,760
  O/C/B 12x16 Flowers on the Dune But 6/92   1,210
Best, Harry Cassie Am 1863-1936
  * See 1992 Edition . . . .
Bethell, James Br 19C
  O/C 31x48 The Death of Lucretia But 11/91   5,225
Bethell, Worden Am 1899-1951
  P/Pa 6x7 Landscapes (2) Mor 6/92   375
Betsberg, Ernestine Am 20C
  W/Pa 22x30 Flowers Sel 5/92   550
Betts, Ethel-Franklin Am 20C
  O/Cb 17x16 An Afternoon Snack Wlf 9/91   1,700
Betts, H. A. Am 20C
  O/C 14x22 River Landscape Slo 2/92   150
Betts, Harold Harrington Am 1881-
  O/C 50x43 Portrait Mrs. George F. Harding 1917 Hnd 12/91 .   100
Betts, Louis Am 1873-1961
  O/C 30x21 Nude in Landscape Lou 12/91   3,300
  O/C 30x25 Boy in Blue Hnd 5/92   1,300
Beuys, Joseph Ger 1921-1986
  K/B 39x79 Untitled Sby 5/92 35,200
  Ph/Gl 42x32 Show Your Wound Sby 11/91 27,500
  Ph/B 28x39 Due Conigli Chr 11/91 13,200
Bevacqua, Francesco It 20C
  O/C 20x16 Soleil Dum 6/92   1,000
  O/C 20x16 Le Soleil Yng 4/92   350
Bevin, Alice Am 20C
  O/C 24x18 Central Park Mys 11/91   82
Bewley, Murray Percival Am 1884-
  O/C 20x16 Memories Lou 12/91   700
Beyle, Pierre Marie Fr 1838-1902
  * See 1992 Edition . . . .
Beyschlag, Robert Ger 1838-1903
  O/C 28x22 Lovers in a Sylvan Wood Chr 5/92   7,700
  O/Pn 7x5 Picking Grapes Chr 2/92   2,860
Bezombes, Roger 20C
  * See 1992 Edition . . . .
Bezzi, Bartolomeo It 1851-1925
  O/C 20x27 Italian Fishing Village Doy 11/91   4,500
Bezzuoli, Giuseppe It 1784-1855
  O/C/B 31x37 The Weary Travelers Sby 7/92   4,400
Bhengu, Gerard Am 20C
  W/Pa 14x10 Zulu Woman Mys 6/92   110

Biagabegs, Roland
  O/B 20x24 Abstract Landscape Dum 11/91   175
Bianchi, C. It 20C
  * See 1992 Edition . . . .
Bianchi, Isidoro It 1602-1690
  * See 1991 Edition . . . .
Bianchi, Mose It 1840-1904
  * See 1991 Edition . . . .
Bianchi, Pietro It a 1640-1650
  Pl/Pa 7x11 San Carlo Borromeo But 5/92   2,200
Bianchine, Virginie
  O/C 24x32 Monk and Lady Dum 1/92   450
Bianchini, Antonio It 20C
  * See 1992 Edition . . . .
Bianchini, E. 20C
  O/C 16x12 Still Life of Flowers Slo 4/92   160
Bianco, Pierreto Bortuluzzi It 1875-1937
  W/Pa 12x18 Midday, Grand Canal Slo 2/92   1,500
Biard, Francois Auguste Fr 1799-1882
  * See 1992 Edition . . . .
Biblena, Giuseppe Galli It 1696-1756
  Pl&W/Pa 17x26 Circular Courtyard and Colonnade Chr 1/92 28,600
  Pl&S/Pa 17x26 A Palatial Loggia Chr 1/92 14,300
  Pl&S/Pa 17x26 Courtyard with Elaborate Arcades Chr 1/92 13,200
  Pl&W/Pa 17x26 Arcaded Hall Chr 1/92   7,150
Bickerstaff, George S. Am 1893-1954
  O/Cb 10x14 Landscape Mor 11/91   350
Bicknell, Albion Harris Am 1837-1915
  O/C 22x18 Pink Roses in a Glass Vase Chr 3/92   3,850
  W/Pa 12x9 Lakeside Brd 8/92   660
Bicknell, Frank Alfred Am 1866-1943
  O/C 32x40 Connecticut Valley Autumn Skn 11/91   4,180
  O/C 20x24 Autumn Landscape Wlf 9/91   1,800
Bidauld, Jean-Joseph-Xavier Fr 1758-1846
  * See 1991 Edition . . . .
Bidlo, Mike Am 1954-
  A/C 12x64 Study for #7, ca. 1948 83 Chr 11/91   3,300
Biedermann, Eduard Am
  * See 1992 Edition . . . .
Biegel, Peter Br 1913-
  * See 1992 Edition . . . .
Biehle, August F. Am 1885-1979
  * See 1992 Edition . . . .
Biehn, Joshua (Joseph) Can a 1891-1899
  * See 1992 Edition . . . .
Bieler, Andre Charles Can 1896-1989
  T/Pa 13x16 The Fish Stall 1952 Sbt 11/91   654
Biennourry, Victor Francois E. Fr 1823-1893
  * See 1992 Edition . . . .
Bienvetu, Gustav Fr 20C
  * See 1992 Edition . . . .
Bierhals, Otto Am 1879-1935
  O/B 18x22 A Winter Sleigh Ride Chr 11/91   2,860
  O/B 4x5 Still Life Vases and Jugs Skn 9/91   330
  O/C 8x10 Flowes by a Stone Wall Yng 4/92   250
  O/B 10x8 Forest Pathway Hnz 10/91   180
Bierstadt, Albert Am 1830-1902
  O/B 15x22 Approaching Storm/Hay Wagon 61 Skn 5/92 . 154,000
  O/C 29x20 Storm Among the Alps Chr 5/92 66,000
  O/Pa/C 14x20 Deer at Sunset Chr 5/92 52,800
  O/Pa/Pn 14x19 Sunset on the Lake Sby 3/92 34,100
  O/Pa/B 14x19 The Grand Tetons Chr 12/91 24,200
  O/Pa/C 14x20 Chilcotin Indian Camp But 4/92 10,450
  O/Pa/C 19x14 Snow-Capped Mountains Sby 9/91   6,600
  O/Pa/B 11x16 Sunset Sby 9/91   6,600
  O/B 7x6 Portrait of a Man Sby 4/92   5,500
  O/Pa/B 14x19 Snowcapped Mountain Landscape Sby 9/91 .   4,675
  C&Cw/Pa 9x11 Two Scottish Bulls '75 Wes 11/91   1,100
Biesel, Charles Am 1865-1945
  W/Pa 16x12 Fish House-New Bedford 1916 Mor 6/92   200
Biessy, Marie-Gabriel Fr 1854-1935
  * See 1992 Edition . . . .

Bigaud, Wilson   Hai 20C
O/M 13x19 La Ronde 1953 Chr 5/92   10,120
O/M 12x16 Apparition de la Sirene Chr 5/92   6,600
O/M 12x10 Chef Section 1951 Chr 5/92   4,950
O/C 29x40 Haitian Scene Wlf 9/91   2,700
Bigazzi, L.   19C
O/C 14x14 Madonna of the Chair 1877 Yng 2/92   60
Bigelow, Daniel Folger   Am 1823-1910
O/C 16x30 Adirondack Lake Sby 4/92   1,100
Biggs, Robert Oldham   Am 1920-
Pe/Pa 30x17 Mid City 1972 Sel 9/91   300
O/M 41x58 View of St. Louis Sel 9/91   300
Biggs, Walter   Am 1886-1968
O/C 28x48 Group of Elderly People Ih 5/92   5,500
O/C 18x22 Morning in Charleston Sby 12/91   3,300
W&C/Pa 24x28 Woman at Sidewalk Cafe 1938 Ih 11/91 .   3,250
Bigot, Trophime   Fr 1579-1650
O/C 40x54 Liberation of Saint Peter Chr 5/92   49,500
Bihan, D. L.   Br a 1850-
* See 1991 Edition
Bihet, G.   Fr 19C
* See 1992 Edition . . . .
Bill, Max   Am 20C
* See 1992 Edition . . . .
Bille, Carl   Dan 1815-1898
O/C 36x55 Ships at Sunset 1869 Chr 10/91   12,100
Billet, Etienne   Fr 1821-1881
O/C 32x51 The Desert Hunt Chr 2/92   8,800
Billet, Pierre   Fr 1837-1922
O/C 44x32 Young Shepherdess 1890 Chr 10/91   8,800
Biltius, Jacobus   Dut 1633-1681
* See 1991 Edition . . . .
Bimmermann, Caesar   Ger 19C
* See 1991 Edition . . . .
Binder, Jacob   Ger 20C
* See 1992 Edition . . . .
Binet, Adolphe Gustave   Fr 1854-1897
* See 1992 Edition . . . .
Binet, Georges   Fr 1865-1949
* See 1992 Edition . . . .
Binet, Victor Baptiste B.   Fr 1849-1924
O/C 15x25 On the Riverbank Chr 2/92   6,600
Binford, Julien   Am 1909-
O/C 43x29 Repairing the Green Dress Sby 12/91   3,300
Bingham, George Caleb   Am 1811-1879
Pl/Pa 7x6 Sleeping Child and a Dog 1846 Chr 11/91   3,300
Binks, Reuben Ward   Br 1860-1940
O/C 24x36 Five Bulldogs on a Beach 1914 Sby 6/92   17,600
G/Pa 9x12 Sealyham Terrior Sby 6/92   1,100
G/Pa 11x14 Pointer in a Landscape 1929 Sby 6/92   990
Binolt, Peter   Ger 1590-1632
* See 1991 Edition . . . .
Birch, Samuel John Lamorna   Br 1869-1955
* See 1990 Edition . . . .
Birch, Thomas   Am 1799-1851
O/C 18x23 Commodore Perry Leaving Lawrence Chr 5/92   264,000
O/C 36x54 Monongahela Passing Great Western Fre 4/92 .   52,000
O/C 23x30 Strolling Along Country Road Sby 5/92   11,000
O/C 19x29 Robinson Crusoe 1839 Sby 9/91   3,850
Birch, William   Br -1795
K,Pl&W/Pa 8x3 Design for Garden for G. Reed Chr 1/92 . . .   1,430
Birchall, William Minshall   Eng 1884-1940
W&G/Pb 10x15 Whaling Barks 1924 Chr 5/92   880
W/Pa 13x19 Sovereign of the Seas 1927 Yng 2/92   650
W/Pa 10x14 Off Lizard Head 1921 Slo 9/91   500
W&G/Pa 7x11 Outward Bound Slo 2/92   500
W&G/Pa 7x11 Pilot Wanted Slo 2/92   500
W/Pa 9x11 American Whaleship Eld 7/92   385
Bird, F.   Am 19C
W/Pa 7x14 Mountain '98 Fre 4/92   30
Birdsall, Amos (Jr.)   Am 1865-1938
O/C 25x30 Seascape Yng 2/92   250
Birkhammer, Axel   Dan 1871-
O/C 28x40 Himmelbjerget, Denmark Doy 11/91   2,800

Birkmeyer, Fritz   Ger 1848-1897
O/C 17x24 The Officer's Greeting Sby 1/92   3,960
Birley, Sir Oswald   Nz 1880-1979
* See 1990 Edition
Birney, William Verplanck   Am 1858-1909
O/C 19x26 The Knitting Lesson Sby 12/91   880
Biro, Geza   Hun 1919-
* See 1990 Edition
Birolli, Renato   It 1906-1959
O/C 28x24 Street Scene with Church Sby 2/92   6,050
O/C/B 11x14 Study of Two Men 1952 Sby 2/92   3,080
Birren, Joseph P.   Am 1865-1933
* See 1992 Edition . . . .
Bisbing, Henry Singlewood   Am 1849-1919
O/C 15x30 Cows by Windmills Ald 5/92   475
Biscaino, Bartolommeo   It 1632-1657
* See 1992 Edition . . . .
Bischoff, Elmer   Am 1916-1991
O/C 24x20 Woman in Bathrobe 58 But 5/92   79,750
Bischoff, Franz A.   Am 1864-1929
O/C 30x24 Bouquet of Roses But 10/91   66,000
O/C 27x42 Grapes But 2/92   10,450
O/B 13x19 Monterey Farm But 2/92   8,800
W/Pa 12x18 Roses But 2/92   6,600
O/B 13x19 Houses by the Sea But 2/92   5,500
O/C 13x18 Bulls But 2/92   5,225
O/B 13x19 Autumn, Monterey Valley But 2/92   4,950
O/C 24x30 Landscape But 10/91   4,950
O/B 13x19 Cottage Through the Trees But 2/92   4,400
O/C 15x20 Arroyo Seco But 2/92   4,125
O/C 24x34 Coastal Scene But 10/91   3,300
O/C 18x24 Valley Trees But 6/92   2,750
O/B 13x19 Trees in a Landscape But 10/91   2,475
O/C 14x18 Farm House But 10/91   1,980
W&G/Pa 19x25 Mediterranean Village But 6/92   1,870
W&G/Pa 8x10 Study Porcelain Plate, Violets But 2/92   1,540
G&G/Pa 6x8 Valley of Romance Mor 9/92   1,500
G&G/Pa 6x8 Valley of Romance Mor 11/91   1,300
O/B 13x10 Houses with Eucalyptus But 6/92   1,100
Bischoff, Friedrich   Ger 1819-1873
* See 1992 Edition . . . .
Bishop, Isabel   Am 1902-1988
O&T/Pn 20x14 Two Men Standing Sby 12/91   11,550
Bishop, Richard Evett   Am 1887-1975
O/C 24x32 Mallards Allighting Chr 6/92   5,280
Bison, Giuseppe Bernardino   It 1762-1844
Pl&S/Pa 7x9 Study Three Standing Figures Sby 1/92   1,760
Bisschop, Abraham   1670-1731
* See 1991 Edition . . . .
Bissi, Sergio Cirno   It 1902-
O/C 24x36 Un Ballo in Maschera But 11/91   6,600
Bissier, Jules   Sws 1893-1965
W/Pa 7x10 27.6.61 61 Chr 2/92   17,600
Br,I&G/Pa 15x21 29.XII 58 I 58 Chr 2/92   11,000
O&T/L/B 8x9 Untitled 60 Sby 10/91   11,000
Bissiere, Roger   Fr 1886-1964
* See 1992 Edition . . . .
Bissolo, Francesco Di Vittore   a 1492-1554
* See 1992 Edition . . . .
Bisson, Edouard   Fr 1856-
* See 1992 Edition . . . .
Bisttram, Emil   Am 1895-1976
* See 1992 Edition . . . .
Bittar, Antoine   Can 1957-
O/Pn 8x6 Evening Vendor, Ottawa 1991 Sbt 5/92   468
O/Pn 9x10 Freedom 1991 Sbt 11/91   468
Bittar, Pierre   Fr 20C
* See 1991 Edition . . . .
Biva, Henri   Fr 1848-1928
O/C 35x45 Roses Sby 10/91   22,000
O/C 26x22 Day by the River Chr 10/91   7,700
O/B 15x18 View of Garches Sby 2/92   3,410

Bixbee, William Johnson Am 1850-1921
O/B 9x13 Sailboats in the Fog Slo 4/92 650
Bjulf, Soren Christian Dan 1890-1958
O/C 31x38 A Fishmarket Chr 10/91 1,100
Black, LaVerne Nelson Am 1887-1938
* See 1991 Edition
Black, Olive Parker Am 1868-1948
O/C 24x30 Summer Landscapes: Pair Chr 3/92 6,050
O/C 24x36 Summer Landscape Sby 4/92 3,850
O/C 16x24 The Farm by a Stream Sby 12/91 2,090
O/C 24x30 The Pasture Stream Skn 5/92 2,090
O/C 24x20 A Wooded Stream Chr 6/92 1,650
O/C 24x20 Old Home Brook Skn 9/91 1,540
Black, Paul Am 20C
O/C 36x40 Clark Pond Slo 4/92 2,500
Blackburn, Clarence E. Eng 1914-1984
O/C 30x40 The Harbour at Brixham Slo 9/91 1,100
Blackburn, Morris Am 1902-1979
O/C 28x36 Still Life with Plate Chr 6/92 3,520
Blackman, Robert Am 20C
O/C 16x20 Woman Adorning a Hat But 11/91 2,090
Blackman, Walter Am 1847-1928
O/C 22x18 A Gypsy Woman Chr 6/92 2,090
Bladen, Ronald 20C
Pe/Pa 19x23 Two Views Vertical Walls Sby 11/91 880
Blaine, Mahlon Am 20C
MM 15x19 California Mission Mys 11/91 220
Blair, Lee Everett Am 1911-
O/Pa 14x20 Horseback Riders Mor 6/92 2,000
Blais, Jean-Charles 1956-
A/Pa 54x76 L'isle 81 Chr 2/92 7,700
Blaize, Candide Fr 1795-1885
* See 1992 Edition
Blake, Peter
* See 1992 Edition
Blakelock, Ralph Albert Am 1847-1919
O/B 9x13 Indian Encampment Chr 9/91 3,520
O/C 15x22 River Landscape Sel 4/92 2,000
O/Pn 4x5 The Last Glow But 4/92 1,430
Blampied, Edmund Br 1886-1966
* See 1992 Edition
Blanch, Arnold Am 1896-1968
A/C 28x20 Women Feeding Birds 1952 Skn 11/91 880
Blanchard, Antoine Fr 1910-
O/C 13x18 Paris, Le Quais de Louvre Doy 11/91 6,000
O/C 20x24 Paris Street Scene Lou 6/92 3,700
O/C 24x36 Les Champs Elysees Hnd 5/92 3,400
O/C 24x30 Parisian Street Scene Wlf 3/92 3,000
O/C 12x16 La Madeleine At Dusk Wes 11/91 2,750
O/C 20x24 Parisian Street Scene Dum 10/91 2,500
O/C 8x10 Parisian Street Scene Wlf 6/92 1,200
O/C 8x10 Parisian Street Scene Wlf 6/92 1,050
W/Pa 10x18 Paris StreetScene Yng 2/92 250
Blanchard, Antoine (Jr.)
O/C 20x24 Parisian Street Scene Hnz 10/91 425
Blanchard, Carol Am 20C
O/Pn 18x10 A Fish Story Wlf 9/91 450
Blanchard, Maria Fr 1881-1932
* See 1991 Edition
Blanchard, Remy 1958-
A/C 81x52 Monstre, Brisseur de Chaines Chr 5/92 1,100
O/C 51x45 Chats 82 Chr 5/92 550
Blanche, Jacques Emile Fr 1861-1942
O/B 24x20 Bouquet de Fleurs Chr 2/92 19,800
O/C 18x22 Boulogne-Sur-Mer Sby 2/92 6,050
Blanco, Dionisio 20C
* See 1991 Edition
Blas 20C
W/Pa 13x18 Ships in the Bay of Naples '49 Hnd 3/92 190
Blashfield, Edwin Howland Am 1848-1936
O/C 18x14 Sweet Vanity Hnd 3/92 4,500
O/C 14x10 Nobleman Mys 6/92 880
Blatas, Arbit 1908-
O/C 26x32 Venetian Canal Sby 10/91 1,540

Blauvelt, Charles F. Am 1824-1900
* See 1992 Edition
Blechen, Carl Ger 1798-1840
O/C 9x12 Piediluco Mountain Landscape Sby 10/91 22,000
Bleckner, Ross Am 1949-
O&Wx/C 120x96 The Forest Sby 5/92 60,500
O/L 48x40 Untitled 1987 Sby 11/91 30,800
O/C 87x88 Deceased 81 Sby 10/91 27,500
O&Wx/C 108x78 Untitled 1981 Sby 2/92 16,500
A/C 26x26 Untitled Chr 5/92 12,100
W/Pa 30x22 Untitled 89 Chr 11/91 8,580
O/C 10x8 Untitled 1986 Chr 5/92 7,700
Br,I&W/Pa 30x22 Untitled 1990 Chr 2/92 7,150
O/Pa 16x12 Untitled Chr 11/91 3,520
Bleger, Paul-Leon Fr 20C
* See 1992 Edition
Bleker, Dirck Dut 1622-1672
* See 1990 Edition
Blenner, Carle John Am 1864-1952
O/C 22x28 Asters Mor 6/92 6,500
O/Pn 12x10 Woman with a Red Rose But 4/92 3,300
O/Cb 7x9 The Harvest Chr 11/91 1,650
O/Pn 10x8 Model in Guise of a Bacchante Skn 11/91 . . . 1,210
O/C 30x25 Still Life White Peonies, Lilies Sby 4/92 825
O/B 12x16 Landscape with Ocean in Distance Wlf 11/91 . . 500
Bleser, August (Jr.) Am
O/C 33x30 Man Over Reclining Woman 1938 Ih 11/91 . . . 3,250
W/Pa 21x17 People by Ice Boat and Car Ih 5/92 2,000
Bleuler, Johann Ludwig Sws 1792-1850
G/Pa 13x19 Schaffhouse: Pair Sby 10/91 14,300
Blinks, Thomas Br 1860-1912
O/C 32x51 The Chase Sby 6/92 33,000
O/C 14x18 Portrait of a Huntsman's Dog Skn 9/91 6,600
O/Ab 14x10 Hunting Dogs Running Down Hill Dum 12/91 . 3,250
Bliss, Robert Am 20C
O/B 30x35 Tawny Beach 55 Bor 8/92 700
Bloch, Julius Thiengen Am 1888-1966
O/C 40x30 The Hitch Hiker Wlf 3/92 2,900
Pl/Pa 8x10 People in the Park Ald 3/92 200
Bloemaert, Abraham Dut 1564-1651
* See 1992 Edition
Bloemaert, Hendrick Dut 1601-1672
O/C 39x32 The Poulterer Sby 5/92 23,100
Bloemaert, The Pseudo-Hendrick Dut 17C
* See 1991 Edition
Bloemers, Arnoldus Dut 1786-1844
* See 1992 Edition
Blommers, Bernardus Johannes Dut 1845-1914
O/Pn 10x14 Laundry Day Chr 2/92 5,280
W/Pa 16x20 Mother and Child in a Kitchen Hnd 10/91 . . . 3,400
Blondel, Emile
O/C 18x15 Rue du Chevalier de la Barre '51 Sby 2/92 . . . 1,100
Blondel, Merry-Joseph Fr 19C
* See 1990 Edition
Bloom, Hyman Am 1913-
P/Pa 24x18 Purgatory Slo 2/92 400
Bloomer, Hiram Reynolds Am 1845-1911
O/C 11x17 High Sierra But 2/92 1,100
Bloomfield, Harry Am 20C
* See 1992 Edition
Bloomfield, Harry Eng 1870-
O/B 35x28 Nu Couche 1928 Wes 5/92 220
Blow, Thomas R. Am 1897-
O/B 12x9 Roses and House (2) Mor 6/92 175
Blower, David H. Am 1901-1976
W/Pa 15x22 Beneath the Bridge, San Pedro But 6/92 . . . 825
W/Pa 22x29 Wilmington Houseboat Mor 3/92 650
O/C 16x20 Santa Fe Hotel - Pasadena Mor 3/92 475
Bluemner, Oscar Florianus Am 1867-1938
G/Pa 5x7 Buildings Sby 9/91 8,250
W&Pe/Pa 3x4 Red Houses Along River Landscape Sby 9/91 8,250
Pe/Pa 5x6 Bloomfield Canal & Plain: Pair '17 Sby 9/91 . . 2,750

44

C&K/Pa 4x6 Jersey Canal, Lindhurst: Two Chr 11/91 2,420
Y/Pa 5x7 Bloomfield, New Jersey 18 Chr 11/91 1,045
Y/Pa 4x6 Along the North Newark Canal 1920 Wes 3/92 275

Bluhm, Norman Am 1920-
O/C 72x80 Sun Storms 1957 Chr 11/91 24,200
O/C 45x57 Deep Waters 1956 Sby 6/92 11,550
O/C 79x113 Noir 54 Chr 11/91 8,800
O/Pa/B 24x72 Study #1 '60 Sby 2/92 6,600
O/Pa/M 36x47 Abstraction '61 Sby 2/92 4,125
O/C 24x36 Untitled '74 Chr 5/92 2,200

Blum Am 19C
W/Pa 40x28 Cairo Street Scene 1891 Hnd 10/91 850

Blum, Jerome S. Am 1884-1956
O/C 21x26 Bay at Audierne Brd 5/92 4,400

Blum, Robert Frederick Am 1857-1903
P/Pa 19x13 A Japanese Woman Chr 12/91 66,000
O/Pn 7x9 Stringing Beads, Venice Chr 5/92 9,900

Blume, Peter 20C
* See 1991 Edition

Blumenschein, Ernest L. Am 1874-1960
O/C 16x20 Church at Chimayo Chr 5/92 88,000
O/C 20x16 Indian in a White Robe But 11/91 66,000

Blumenschein, Helen Green Am 1909-
G/Pa 7x9 Taos, New Mexico But 4/92 2,200

Blythe, David Gilmour Am 1815-1865
* See 1992 Edition

Boardman, William Am 1815-1895
* See 1991 Edition

Bobak, Molly Joan Lamb Can 1922-
O/C 12x16 St. John's, Newfoundland Sbt 11/91 1,963

Boccherini Am 20C
* See 1992 Edition

Bocchetta It 20C
O/M 10x7 Study Roman Doorway Hnd 6/92 100

Boccioni, Umberto It 1882-1916
* See 1992 Edition

Bochner, Mel Am 1940-
Bp/Pa 5x6 Meditation Theorem of Pythagorus 1972 Sby 2/92 990

Bock, Charles Peter Am 1872-
O/C 28x23 Sand and Water Meet 1904 Wlf 10/91 500
O/C 18x24 Lake Michigan Beach 1910 Wlf 10/91 300

Boddington, E. H. Br 19C
O/C 20x12 Fisherman 1859 Fre 4/92 1,400

Boddington, Henry John Br 1811-1865
* See 1992 Edition

Bodeman, Willem Dut 1806-1880
* See 1992 Edition

Bodenmuller, Frederich Ger 1845-
O/Pn 23x18 Lady in Sixteenth C. Dress 1879 But 5/92 6,050
O/Pn 17x13 Elegant Woman 1879 Slo 7/92 2,500

Bodley, Josselin Br 20C
O/C 20x16 St. Tropez '59 Hnd 3/92 500

Bodmer, Karl Am 1809-1893
O/Pn 13x10 Fox in a Forest Interior But 11/91 5,500

Bodrero, James S. Am 1900-1980
W/Pa 11x17 Steeplechase '31 Mor 6/92 200

Bodrigi, A. Eur 20C
O/C/B 20x24 Jewish Scholar Reading Slo 2/92 60

Boers, Sebastian Theodoros V. Dut 1828-1893
* See 1992 Edition . . . .

Boesen, Johannes Dan 1847-1916
O/C 26x38 A Wooded Path 1885 Chr 10/91 2,750

Boetti, Alighiero E. 20C
* See 1992 Edition

Bogaert, Hendrik Dut 1627-1672
O/Pn 20x17 Interior of Barn w/Earthenware 1649 Chr 1/92 13,200

Bogart, Waldo L. Am 20C
O/C 24x19 Distributing the Food Rations Slo 2/92 550

Bogdani, Jacob Hun 1660-1724
* See 1992 Edition

Bogdanov-Bjelsky, Nikolai P. Rus 1868-1945
* See 1990 Edition . . . .

Bogdanove, Abraham J. Am 1888-1946
* See 1992 Edition . . . .

Bogdanovich, Borislav 20C
O/B/B 45x28 Goldenrods Sby 6/92 1,650

Bogert, George Hirst Am 1864-1944
O/C 22x28 Sailboats Anchored at Dusk Chr 11/91 2,200
O/C 13x16 Landscape-White Birches Ald 3/92 525
O/C 28x36 River Landscape at Sunset Slo 4/92 500

Boggio, Emilio Fr 1857-1920
* See 1992 Edition

Boggs, Frank Myers Am 1855-1926
O/C 22x29 Le Pont Des Arts Sby 3/92 11,000
O/C 15x23 Boats Anchored in a Harbor Sby 12/91 5,500
O/C 15x22 Low Tide at St. Vaast-la-Rougue 82 Sby 12/91 . 4,400
O/C 22x18 Le Pavillon Royal Chr 11/91 2,200
O/C 18x12 New York, Staten Island Wlf 6/92 1,000
W&C/Pa 11x17 Mantes Sby 12/91 990

Bogh, Carl Henrik Dan 1827-1893
* See 1992 Edition

Bohatsch, Erwin 1951-
O/C 57x67 Obne Titel 84 Chr 5/92 3,520

Bohm, Francois Bel 19C
O/C 24x18 Dutch Village Slo 10/91 900

Bohm, Max Am 1868-1923
O/C 44x70 The Idlers 1889 Wlf 3/92 5,200
O/C 39x53 Preparing Supper Chr 6/92 2,420

Bohm, Pal Hun 1839-1905
* See 1992 Edition

Bohmen, Karl Ger 20C
O/C 50x35 Lady in a Rowboat Hnd 5/92 2,000

Bohnenberger, L.
O/C 14x20 Barn Interior w/Sheep & Chickens Hnz 10/91 . . . 575

Bohrod, Aaron Am 1907-
O/M 31x23 Still Life with Ferdinarnd 1938 Hnd 6/92 6,000
O/M 22x40 Algonquin, Illinois Doy 12/91 5,000
O/M 18x14 The Kitchen: A Trompe l'Oeil Sby 12/91 3,410
O/B 16x20 Maid in Japan But 11/91 3,025
O/M 30x16 The Green House Sby 12/91 2,970
O/B 24x32 The Lake But 11/91 2,750
O/B 16x20 Sea Chest Hnd 10/91 2,000
G/Pa 16x14 Street in Madison 1948 Hnd 5/92 2,000
O/Pn 14x20 The Grotto 1964 Hnd 6/92 2,000
var. 11x9 Five Figure Drawings Hnd 10/91 1,200
PI/Pa 12x8 Five Figure Drawings Hnd 6/92 1,200
PI&S/Pa 12x8 Five Figure Drawings Hnd 6/92 1,000
S/Pa 11x9 In Belgium 1940 Hnd 5/92 700
I,Y&S/Pa 11x8 Pittsburgh Highway Hnd 5/92 550
S&PI/Pa 12x8 Bronx Sailor '43 Hnd 10/91 350
W/Pa 18x14 Two Houses and a Mailbox Lou 3/92 225

Boille, Luigi 1926-
O/C 87x71 Untitled 1960 Chr 11/91 2,200
O/Bu 77x63 Untitled 61 Chr 11/91 1,870

Boilly, Jules Fr 1796-1874
O/C 24x29 Le Parlant Tableau Sby 7/92 3,300
K/Pa 19x12 A Nude Woman Chr 1/92 1,320

Boilly, Louis-Leopold Fr 1761-1845
O/Pn 13x11 Still Life Flowers in Glass Vase Sby 1/92 . . 253,000

Boisrond, Francois 1959-
A&T/Pa 62x34 Three paintings 82 Chr 5/92 3,080
A&Fp/Pa 62x45 Trompette 81 Chr 5/92 1,210

Boisselier, Felix Fr 1776-1811
* See 1992 Edition . . . .

Boissier, Gaston Maurice E. Fr 19C
* See 1990 Edition . . . .

Boit, Edward Darley Am 1840-1916
W/Pa 9x13 The Shore, Biarritz 93 Skn 5/92 605

Boizard, C. U.
O/B 48x39 Christ on the Cross (2) Ald 5/92 210

Boizot, Antoine Honore Louis 1744-1800
O/C 12x16 Riders on Horseback in a Park Sby 1/92 4,500

Bol, Ferdinand Dut 1616-1680
* See 1991 Edition . . . .

Bol, Hans Dut 1534-1593
* See 1991 Edition . . . .

Boland, Charles   Con 20C
   * See 1992 Edition . . . .
Boldini, Giovanni   It 1842-1931
   W/Pa 7x6 Portrait Mrs. A. T. Stewart 73 Sby 10/91   41,250
Bolduc, David   Can 1945-
   * See 1992 Edition . . . .
Bole, Comtesse Jeanne   Fr a 1870-1883
   * See 1992 Edition . . . .
Bolegard, Joseph
   O/C 20x23 Three Boys at Swimming Hole Ilh 11/91   950
Bollendonk, Walter   Am 20C
   O/C 20x24 Swirling Tide 1961 Fre 10/91   125
Bolles, Enoch
   O/C 30x22 Blonde in Bikini Putting on Robe Ilh 5/92   5,000
Bolotowsky, Ilya   Am 1907-1981
   O/C 33x23 Variations in Blue 1958 Sby 2/92   8,800
   O/C 10x5 Untitled 44 Sby 2/92   7,425
   O/Wd 8 dia Four Top Tondo 1976 Sby 10/91   5,500
   O/C 32x22 Linear 1959 Sby 2/92   5,500
   l/Pa 12x16 Untitled Study for Mural Sby 2/92   4,675
   A/C 36 dia Golden Tondo II '75 Chr 5/92   3,300
Bolt, M. C.
   * See 1991 Edition . . . .
Bolt, Ron   Can 1938-
   O/C 48x54 Vial of Wrath '79 Sbt 11/91   3,272
Boltanski, Christian   1944-
   Ph/Pa 12x37 The First Communion Chr 5/92   13,200
Bolton, Hale William   Am 1885-1920
   * See 1992 Edition . . . .
Boltraffio, Giovanni Antonio   It 1467-1516
   * See 1990 Edition . . . .
Bombled, Louis Charles   Fr 1862-1927
   O/C 21x32 La Chasse au Cerf Sby 7/92   3,300
   O/C 20x26 La Poursuite Sby 1/92   2,970
Bombois, Camille   Fr 1883-1970
   O/C 36x51 Laveuses au Bord d'Une Riviere Sby 5/92   60,500
   O/C 22x18 Au bistro Chr 5/92   49,500
   O/C 21x26 Le lac aux cypres Chr 5/92   46,200
   O/C 22x18 Jeune Fille Sautant a la Corde Sby 10/91   38,500
   O/C 16x13 La Facade Jaune Chr 11/91   38,500
   O/C 18x26 Chateau en Bourgogne Sby 10/91   30,800
   O/C 9x13 L'entree du marais, Poitevin Chr 5/92   30,800
   O/C/M 13x17 Arcy-Sur-Oise Sby 10/91   11,000
   O/C 26x21 Clown Sby 5/92   11,000
   O/C 7x10 La Seine a Bougival Chr 5/92   11,000
   O/Pn 6x10 Vue de la Marne Chr 5/92   9,350
   O/C 6x9 Fisherman by the Seine Hnd 5/92   7,400
   O/Pn 4x5 L'isle Chr 5/92   3,850
Bompard, Maurice   Fr 1857-1936
   * See 1991 Edition . . . .
Bompiani, Augusto   It 1852-1930
   W/Pa 25x19 Portrait Young Italian Woman Fre 4/92   1,600
Bompiani, Roberto   It 1821-1908
   * See 1992 Edition . . . .
Bompiani-Battaglia, Cecelia   It 1847-1927
   W/Pa 20x14 Young Peasant Boy Wes 11/91   715
Bonamici, Louis   Fr 20C
   O/C 26x20 Mending the Nets Hnd 3/92   600
Bonane, E.
   O/C 20x24 The Chess Game Dum 4/92   1,100
Bonar, Lester M.   Am 1896-1973
   W/Pa 23x17 Purse Seiner Fishing Mor 6/92   200
Bonavia, Carlo   It a 1740-1786
   * See 1991 Edition . . . .
Bonbright, Sybil   Am 1906-1968
   O/C 20x16 Interior, Cascais Slo 7/92   275
Bond, H.   Eng 19C
   O/C 12x20 Malsmead near Brendon Fre 4/92   300
Bond, W H**   Eng a 1896-1907**
   O/C 16x22 Marsh Landscape '93 Wes 3/92   1,100
Bond, William J. J. C.   Br 19C
   O/B 12x18 Rocky Coast 1909 Sby 7/92   770
Bondoux, Jules Georges   Eur -1920
   * See 1991 Edition . . . .

Bonevardi, Marcelo   Arg 1929-
   O/Wd 48x30 Table with Objects 68 Chr 11/91   5,500
   MM/Pn 18x25 Object 1973 Sby 10/91   3,850
Bonfield, William Van De Velde   Am 19C
   * See 1990 Edition . . . .
Bonfils, Gaston   Fr 19C
   O/C 18x13 The Jolly Fiddle Player Wlf 11/91   675
Bongart, Sergei   Am 1918-1985
   * See 1992 Edition . . . .
Bonham, Horace   Am 1835-1892
   * See 1991 Edition . . . .
Bonheur, Auguste   Fr 1824-1884
   O/C 24x32 Cattle Watering Chr 5/92   9,350
Bonheur, Rosa   Fr 1822-1899
   O/C 26x32 Highland Cattle 1876 But 5/92   16,500
   Y&P/Pa 20x26 Deer in the Forest at Dusk 67 Sby 10/91 . . .   4,400
Bonifazio Veronese   It 1487-1553
   O/Pn 18 dia The Crowning of the Poet Chr 5/92   28,600
Bonington, Richard Parkes   Eng 1801-1828
   O/Ab 11x9 Scene from Gil-Blas Slo 10/91   3,250
Bonirote, Pierre   Fr 1811-1891
   * See 1990 Edition . . . .
Bonito, Giuseppe   It 1707-1789
   * See 1992 Edition . . . .
Bonnal, Felicie Palade   Fr 19C
   O/C 37x29 Jeune Bretonne au Rouet Chr 10/91   7,150
Bonnar, James King   Am 1885-1961
   * See 1992 Edition . . . .
Bonnard, Pierre   Fr 1867-1947
   O/C 15x18 Antibes Sby 5/92   121,000
   W/Pa/C 13x10 Paysage a Vernon Chr 11/91   22,000
   Pe/Pa 13x10 Nu Dans la Salle de Bain Chr 11/91   9,350
   l/Pa 8x5 Girl and Goat Sby 6/92   2,200
   H/Pa 6x4 Marthe Bonnard Sby 6/92   1,980
Bonnefond, Claude   Fr 1796-1860
   O/C 21x17 Une Pelerine Soutenue Sby 7/92   3,850
Bonnier, Alice
   P/Pa 14x11 Pair of Female Portraits 1922 Sby 2/92   440
Bontecou, Lee   1931-
   O/C 10x8 Untitled Chr 11/91   6,050
Bonvin, Francois   Fr 1817-1887
   O/C 17x11 Woman Knitting 1850 Chr 5/92   12,100
Bonvin, Leon   Fr 1834-1866
   * See 1991 Edition . . . .
Boog, Carle Michel   Am 1877-1967
   W/Pa 16x23 The Equestrians Wes 11/91   1,980
Boogaard, Willem-Jacobus Dut 1842-1887
   * See 1992 Edition . . . .
Book, Harry M.   Am 20C
   O/C 22x27 Autumn Landscape Fre 4/92   180
Booth, Franklin   Am 1874-1948
   Pl/Pa 11x7 Woman Seated on Bench in Garden Ilh 5/92 . . .   4,500
Borchand, Edmund   Fr 1848-1922
   O/C 13x19 Target Practice But 11/91   3,300
Bordencherxxx, J.   Con 19C
   O/Pn 25x16 In Piping Times of Peace Chr 10/91   1,650
Bordes, Leonard   1898-1969
   O/B/Pn 21x26 Le Village Chr 2/92   1,000
Bordignon, Noe   It 1834-1920
   * See 1991 Edition . . . .
Bordone, Paris   It 1500-1571
   O/C 42x32 A Courtesan Chr 5/92   132,000
Borduas, Paul-Emile   Can 1905-1960
   O/C 15x18 Treillis Blanc Chr 11/91   52,800
   O/C 22x18 La Naissance de l'Etang '53 Sbt 11/91   32,725
Borein, Edward   Am 1873-1945
   W/Pa 8x10 Crossing the Plain Sby 12/91   12,100
   Pe&G/Pa 7x10 Cowboy on Horseback Sby 12/91   5,225
   Pl&Cw/Pa 13x16 The Painted Moonbeam 1923 But 4/92 . . .   4,950
   S&Pe/Pa 11x11 Stage Coach But 4/92   1,650
   l/Pa 11x9 Three Indians on Horseback Hnd 12/91   1,000
   Pl/Pa 6x9 An Indian Village But 4/92   990
   W/Pa 9x12 Palomino and Cowboy Slo 7/92   950

46

Borelli, Arthur   Am a 1930-1939
O/B 24x36 Chicago Scene Dum 11/91 500
Boren, James   Am 1921-
* See 1991 Edition . . . .
Bores, Francisco   Spa 1898-1972
O/C 21x26 Interieur 48 Sby 10/91 17,600
G/Pa 10x13 Abstract '47 '47 Sby 2/92 3,300
Borg, Axel   Am 20C
O/C 26x40 Landscape with Mouse Wlf 10/91 175
Borg, Carl Oscar   Am 1879-1947
O/C 28x37 Boats on the Nile But 4/92 7,150
O&G/B 16x20 Navajo Home But 10/91 7,150
O/C 24x30 Foothills of Santa Barbara But 6/92 6,050
G/Pa 5x7 Indian on Horseback Sby 12/91 935
Borges, Jacobo   Ven 1931-
P&C/Pa 23x30 Untitled 89 Chr 11/91 4,620
Pl,S&Sg/Pa 20x28 Estudio de Miguel Angel 79 Chr 11/91 . . 3,850
Pl/Pa 8x6 Pequena pero Elegante Chr 5/92 1,650
Borie, Adolphe   Am 1877-1934
O/Pn 13x10 Portrait of a Lady Skn 11/91 5,500
Borione, Bernard Louis   Fr 1865-
O/Pn 16x13 A Pinch of Snuff 1912 But 5/92 4,400
O/C/Pn 18x13 Humming a Tune Chr 2/92 2,310
W/Pa 11x8 Seated Man with Lute But 5/92 1,320
Borker, K. V.   Con 20C
O/C 28x39 Venetian Canal Scene Hnd 3/92 475
Borman, Johannes   Dut a 1653-1659
* See 1991 Edition . . . .
Borofsky, Jonathan   Am 1942-
A/C 109x83 2,841,780 Painting w/Hand Shadow Sby 11/91 55,000
A/C 110x84 Male Aggression Now Playing Chr 5/92 . . . 24,200
I/Pb 60x40 Self-Portrait at 2,600,631 Sby 11/91 23,100
MM/Pa 52x32 Man Eating Breadfruit 1977 Sby 5/92 . . . 15,400
A&Pe/C 36x21 Pencil Head Chr 2/92 12,100
Borrani, Odoardo   It 1834-1905
* See 1991 Edition . . . .
Borstein, Elena   20C
* See 1991 Edition . . . .
Bortnyik, Sandor
* See 1990 Edition . . . .
Bortoluzzi, Millo   It 1868-1933
W&G/Pb 18x10 Flowering Wisteria on a Canal 92 Chr 5/92 . . 990
Bos, F.   Con 19C
O/C 21x17 An Afternoon Reverie 1876 Chr 2/92 1,320
Bos, Hendrik   Dut 1901-
* See 1992 Edition . . . .
Bos, M.
O/C 18x26 Cattle Resting Hnz 10/91 1,000
Bosa, Louis   Am 1905-
O/B 7x12 Skaters Chr 11/91 1,100
Boscoli, Andrea   It 1560-1607
O/C 54x78 Triumph of Mordecai Sby 5/92 41,250
Boshier, Derek
* See 1992 Edition . . . .
Bosley, Frederick A.   Am 1881-1942
O/C 28x30 Looking at Prints 1918 Chr 5/92 24,200
O/C 36x35 Spirit of the Antique 1913 Skn 9/91 4,675
Bosman, Richard   Am 1944-
O/C 54x42 Poison Sby 5/92 6,600
O/C 60x60 Rip Tide Sby 10/91 6,600
O/C 48x72 Combatants 84 Chr 11/91 5,500
Boss
O/C 24x36 Forest Clearing with Herd of Cattle '91 Hnz 10/91   475
Bosschaert, Jean-Baptiste   Flm 1667-1746
O/C 32x26 Sculpted Urn Draped with Garland Chr 1/92 . . 11,000
Bossoli, Carlo   It 1815-1874
G/Pa 10x16 Sebastopol From the Northern Fort Sby 2/92 . 12,100
G/Pa 11x18 A Passing Storm 1873 Chr 10/91 7,150
Bossuet, Francois Antoine   Bel 1800-1889
* See 1992 Edition . . . .
Boston, Frederick James   Am 1855-1932
O/C 24x20 Lady with Rose Yng 2/92 300
Boston, Joseph H.   Am 1860-1954
O/C 25x30 Moonlight on the Hudson Eld 7/92 1,100

O/C 12x16 Country Road Wes 11/91 770
O/C 14x10 Young Woman Dum 4/92 700
O/C/B 10x8 Portrait of a Lady 1920 Hnd 6/92 250
Botello, Angel   Spa 1913-1986
O/Pn 42x48 Ninas Peinandose Chr 11/91 19,800
O/Pn 56x30 Madre e Hija Chr 11/91 18,700
O/Pn 30x48 Mujeres en la Playa Chr 11/91 16,500
O/Pn 47x35 Silla II Sby 6/92 11,550
O/Pn 48x54 Two Children with Mother Sby 6/92 11,550
O/M 33x48 Still Life with Jugs Sby 2/92 11,500
O/M 23x19 Cabeza de Mujer Chr 5/92 9,350
O/Pn 24x18 Still Life of Daisies in a Red Jug Sby 2/92 . . . 9,350
O/C 20x40 Des Nudo de Olga Hnd 10/91 8,000
O/Pn 48x36 Trees Sby 6/92 6,600
O/B 44x22 Female Nude Sel 4/92 6,000
O/M 19x15 Haitiana Chr 5/92 5,500
O/M 19x15 Cabeza de Muchacha Sby 10/91 4,950
O/Pn 24x20 Nina con Espejo Sby 6/92 4,950
O/C 20x40 Des Nudo de Olga Hnd 5/92 4,800
O/Cb 20x16 Portrait of Francoise Sby 6/92 3,300
O/M 24x19 Girl with Blonde Hair Sel 9/91 2,600
O/M 20x16 Head of a Girl Sel 9/91 2,400
MM 14x13 Dancers Mys 6/92 1,650
Botero, Fernando   Col 1932-
O/C 71x75 Dejeuner Sur L'Herbe 69 Sby 11/91 . . . . . 1.045M
O/C 66x76 Los Amantes 77 Chr 11/91 440,000
O/C 65x50 El Guitarrista 89 Chr 5/92 352,000
O/C 64x76 Naturaleza Muerta 1974 Chr 5/92 330,000
O/C 74x76 El Paseo Del Presidente 67 Chr 11/91 . . . 308,000
O&C/C 60x60 Cabeza de Nina 66 Chr 11/91 220,000
O/C 30x32 Bodegon en Azules Chr 11/91 143,000
W/Pa 59x43 Naturaleza Muerta con Guitarra 80 Chr 5/92 143,000
O/C 52x21 Nina Montada a Caballo 61 Sby 5/92 . . . 121,000
O/C 47x51 L' Atelier de Zurbaran 63 Chr 5/92 99,000
O/C/Pn 21x22 Cabeza de Cristo 64 Chr 11/91 88,000
O&P/Pa 24x32 Pareja en el Valle 77 Chr 5/92 60,500
Pe/Pa 17x14 Fiesta 71 Chr 11/91 35,200
O/C 13x12 Nina Chr 11/91 35,200
Pl/Pa 17x14 La Amazona 80 Chr 5/92 18,700
H/Pa 17x14 Santa Gertrudis 71 Sby 11/91 17,600
Pe/Pa 16x14 Nina con Fruta 73 Chr 11/91 13,200
Both, Andries Dirksz.   Dut 1611-1641
* See 1992 Edition . . . .
Both, Jan   Dut 1615-1652
* See 1990 Edition . . . .
Botilotto, S.   It 20C
O/C 20x24 Fishing Boats on Beach Hnz 5/92 200
Botke, Cornelius   Am 1887-1954
O/B 25x30 Alsation Platter But 6/92 2,475
Botke, Jessie Arms   Am 1883-1971
O/M 33x40 Geese in a Garden 1932 Skn 11/91 20,900
O/B 24x20 White Peacock and Day Lilies But 6/92 8,250
O/C/B 8x10 White Birds But 10/91 5,500
O&Gd/B 20x16 Pink Flamingos But 6/92 4,675
O/C/B 6x9 Geese But 2/92 2,200
O&G/Cb 8x10 Swans But 2/92 1,540
O&G/B 8x10 Springtime But 2/92 1,320
O/C/B 11x8 Trees But 2/92 1,320
O/Cb 10x8 Wisteria But 2/92 1,210
MM/B 8x10 Coastal-Springtime Mor 6/92 800
Botkin, Henry Albert   Am 1896-1983
O/C 40x32 Hollow Green 1966 Mys 6/92 605
Bott, Emil   Am 19C
O/C 16x31 The Idlewild 1881 Sby 12/91 17,600
Bottex, Jean-Baptiste   Hai 20C
O/M 36x48 Les Bourgeois de Cap Haitien Chr 5/92 . . . 2,420
Bottex, Seymour   Hai 20C
O/M 24x20 Adam and Eve Chr 5/92 660
Botticelli, Sandro   It 1445-1510
O/Pn 19x15 Madonna & Child w/Yng St. John Chr 5/92 . 440,000
Botticini, Francesco   It 1446-1497
* See 1991 Edition . . . .
Bottini, Georges   Fr 1874-1907
G,W&H/Pa 10x11 Au Cafe 99 Sby 7/92 3,575

Botto, Otto Am 1903-
O/Pn 33x23 Clown with Mandolin Wlf 10/91 200
Boucart, Gaston H. Fr 1878-1962
O/C 26x32 The Gondola Race Chr 2/92 2,750
Bouchard, Lorne Holland Can 1913-1978
O/B 12x16 Laurentides en Octobre 1975 Sbt 5/92 842
Bouchard, Paul Louis Fr 1853-1937
G/B 13x18 Landscape with Birches Hnd 10/91 600
Bouche, Louis Am 1896-1969
O/C 18x28 Progression, 1944 1944 Chr 6/92 1,760
Bouche, Louis Alexandre Fr 1838-1911
* See 1992 Edition . . . .
Bouchene, Dimitri
* See 1992 Edition . . . .
Boucher, Alfred Fr 1850-1934
* See 1990 Edition . . . .
Boucher, Francois Fr 1703-1770
K/Pa 13x8 Young Gentleman Peering Around Chr 1/92 . . . 36,300
Bouchet, Jules Frederic Fr 1799-1860
* See 1992 Edition . . . .
Bouchot, Francois Fr 1800-1842
* See 1992 Edition . . . .
Boucie, Pierre Flm 1610-1673
* See 1991 Edition . . . .
Boudet, Pierre Fr 1925-
* See 1992 Edition . . . .
Boudewijns, Adriaen Frans Flm 1644-1711
O/C 12x17 A Southern Port Sby 10/91 11,000
Boudin, Eugene Fr 1824-1898
O/C 20x29 Petit Port de Saint-Jean 1892 Sby 5/92 143,000
O/Pn 8x11 Port de Trouville 86 Chr i1/91 132,000
O/C 14x23 Scheveningen 75 Sby 5/92 104,500
O/C 20x29 Antibes, La Pointe de L'llette 93 Chr 11/91 . . . 79,200
O/Pn 10x16 Le Phare de Honfleur Chr 2/92 71,500
O/Pn 15x18 Etretat/La falaise d'Amont 90 Skn 11/91 69,300
O/C 9x13 Le Port du Havre Sby 5/92 57,750
W&Pe/Pa 6x9 La Cabine de Bain 1865 Sby 5/92 24,200
O/Pa/Pn 9x13 Vaches au Paturage Sby 11/91 22,000
P/Pa 6x8 Soleil Couchant Chr 11/91 13,200
Br&S/Pa 4x5 Quai en Bretagne Chr 11/91 3,300
Boudry, Alois Bel 1851-1938
O/C 25x22 The Fishmonger Slo 10/91 2,000
Bouel, Louis Francois Numance Fr 19C
* See 1992 Edition . . . .
Bouet, Pierre Henri Fr 1828-1889
O/Pn 12x9 Village at the Base of a Mountain Fre 4/92 350
Bough, Samuel Sco 1822-1878
O/C 24x36 View Near Killarney 1875 But 5/92 5,225
O/C 12x17 Loading the Cargo 1865 But 11/91 3,850
O/C 10x14 River Landscape Fre 4/92 800
Boughton, George Henry Am 1833-1905
O/C 20x30 A Spring Idyll 1901 Chr 5/92 18,700
O/Pn 13x9 Winter, A Cautious Step Chr 5/92 11,000
W&G/Pa 6x10 One More Goodbye Slo 7/92 750
O/Pn 10x12 Cathedral in Moonlight: Winter Slo 4/92 650
Bouguereau, William Adolphe Fr 1825-1905
O/C 62x35 L'Orage 1874 Sby 10/91 220,000
O/C 51x28 Retour des Champs 1898 Chr 2/92 198,000
O/C 53x30 Jeune Fille Mettant Ses Bas 1900 Sby 10/91 . . 165,000
O/C 62x34 Jeune Fille Portant Une Cruche 1885 Sby 5/92 . . 132,000
O/C 35x21 Paquerette 1894 Sby 10/91 126,500
O/C 26x40 Enfants Endormis 1868 Sby 2/92 99,000
O/C 18x15 Fortunata 1879 Sby 2/92 46,750
Pe&K/Pa 13x8 Diana Sby 7/92 4,675
Pe/Pa 13x9 Study of a Peasant Girl Sby 1/92 2,090
Pe&K/Pa 13x10 Study Standing Man Sby 7/92 935
Bouilion, Michel Fr 17C
* See 1991 Edition . . . .
Bouillier, Amable Fr 1867-
* See 1992 Edition . . . .
Boulanger, Graciela Rodo Bol 1935-
O/C 29x24 Le Vol Sby 10/91 7,150
O/C 24x18 El Paso Volante 1967 Sby 10/91 4,675

Boulanger, Gustave Clarence R. Fr 1824-1888
K/Pa 21x11 Standing Female Nude Sby 7/92 990
Boulanger, Louis & Coignard, L Fr 1806-1867
O/Pn 17x24 Le Berger et Ses Vaches Hnd 5/92 1,600
Boulet, Cyprien-Eugene Fr 1877-1927
O/C 70x86 Triage Scene at Verdun 1915 Sby 1/92 2,750
O/C 26x22 La Femme au Chapeau Vert Chr 10/91 2,420
Boulier, Lucien Fr 1882-1963
O/C/B 8x10 Bouquet de fleurs Chr 5/92 1,430
O/C 14x11 Girl with Flowers Wlf 3/92 100
O/Cd 12x11 Portrait of a Young Girl Wlf 3/92 100
Boult, F. Cecil Br 19C
O/C 12x18 The Chase 1882 Chr 5/92 3,080
Boundey, Burton S. Am 1887-1954
* See 1991 Edition . . . .
Bourdelle, Emile-Antoine Fr 1861-1921
Pl/Pa 12x8 Cinq etudes de la main de l'artiste 1902 Hnd 12/91 300
Bourdon, Charles Fr 19C
O/C 32x20 In the Rose Garden Sby 7/92 1,100
Bourdon, Sebastian Fr 1616-1671
* See 1992 Edition . . . .
Bourgain, Gustave Fr -1921
* See 1990 Edition . . . .
Bourgeois, Denis Can 1938-
O/C 16x20 Le Jardin de Ma Maison Sbt 11/91 468
O/C 16x20 Ste. Anne Sbt 11/91 468
Bourgeois, Louise Am 1911-
Br&l/Pa 11x9 Untitled 48 Chr 5/92 11,000
Bourgogne, Pierre Fr 1838-1904
* See 1992 Edition . . . .
Bourke, J. H. Am 19C
P/Pa 19 dia Girl with a Parrot '91 Hnz 5/92 300
Bourlard, Antoine Joseph Bel 1826-1899
* See 1992 Edition . . . .
Bourne, Jean Baptiste C. Fr a 1815-1900
* See 1992 Edition . . . .
Bout, Pieter Flm 1658-1719
O/C 23x32 Hawking Party 1719 Sby 10/91 19,800
O/C 12x17 A Southern Port Sby 10/91 11,000
Boutelle, Dewitt Clinton Am 1820-1884
O/C 9x12 Woodland Stream 1862 Wes 11/91 660
Bouter, Cornelis Dut 1888-1966
O/C 24x30 Mother with Children in Garden Sby 7/92 4,400
O/C 21x44 Interior Scene Dum 6/92 3,000
O/C 14x20 Children in a Garden Hnz 5/92 2,200
Bouterwek, Friedrich Ger 1806-1876
* See 1990 Edition . . . .
Boutibonne, Charles Edouard Hun 1816-1897
* See 1992 Edition . . . .
Boutigny, Paul Emile Fr 1854-1929
O/C 24x20 The Martyr Sby 1/92 3,860
O/C 24x20 Mort du Colonel Desgrees du Lou Sby 1/92 . . 3,575
O/C 29x36 Arrival for the Wedding 1928 Sby 7/92 3,190
O/C 24x20 Les Delivrees Hors Concourse Sby 1/92 2,860
O/C 24x20 Dans Les Tranchees Sous Verdun Sby 1/92 . . 1,650
Bouttats, Frederik (the Elder) Flm a 1612-1661
* See 1990 Edition . . . .
Bouvard, Antoine Fr -1956
O/C 14x19 Views of Venice: Pair Sby 7/92 12,650
O/C 20x26 View of the Doges Palaces Skn 9/91 11,000
O/C 20x26 Venetian Sunset Skn 5/92 8,800
O/C 24x32 Venetian Canal Scene Brd 8/92 7,975
O/C 20x26 View of Venice from Rialto Bridge Chr 2/92 7,150
O/C 14x11 Venetian Canal Sby 7/92 3,850
Bouyssou, Jacques Fr 1926-
O/C 29x36 La Plage a Grandchamp Chr 2/92 5,280
O/C 26x32 Grandcamp Maree Base Sby 2/92 4,400
O/C 21x26 Le Bassin a Honfleur 1964 Sby 10/91 4,400
O/C 24x32 GrandCamp Chr 5/92 3,520
O/C 18x24 Outing by the Shore Sby 6/92 2,200
O/C 28x35 Ships at Harbour Sby 6/92 2,200

Bovam, Sam   Am 19C
O/B 9x12 Rocky Coast 1848 Sby 4/92   1,210
Boverie, L.   Bel a 1888-
W/Pa 21x29 Sunlit Beach Scene Sel 9/91   1,350
Boville, E.
O/Pn 13x18 Harbor Scene Hnz 10/91   160
Bovkun, Vladimir
O/C 51x51 Smile of a Ancestor Hnz 10/91   1,000
Bower, Alexander   Am 1875-1952
O/C 40x48 Maine Coast, Sun and Snow Brd 8/92   13,200
O/C 18x18 Maine Lighthouse Brd 8/92   550
O/B 10x8 Forest Scene Brd 8/92   187
Bowers, George Newall   Am 1849-1909
* See 1992 Edition . . . .
Bowes, David   20C
T/C 39x39 Portrait of Sabina Mirri 1983 Chr 2/92   1,870
Bowie, Frank Louville   Am 1857-1936
O/C 14x18 Winter Snow Scene 1914 Mys 11/91   605
O/C 14x18 Crab Traps at Casco Bay Lou 3/92   275
O/C 14x18 Lobster Traps, Casco Bay 1928 Brd 8/92   143
Bowles, R. H.   Am 20C
O/B 12x16 Narragansett View Mys 11/91   138
Bowser, David Bustill   Am 1820-1900
* See 1991 Edition . . . .
Boxer, Stanley Robert   Am 1926-
A/C 91x8 Summer Whisper 74 Sby 2/92   3,300
G&Y/Pa/B 14x11 Untitled 50 Chr 2/92   418
Boyce, George Price
* See 1991 Edition . . . .
Boyd, Fiske   Am 1895-1975
O/C 21x29 Low Tide, Martha's Vineyard 1925 Sby 12/91 . . .   330
Boyd, Rutherford   Am 1884-1951
Pe/Pa 8x10 Manhattan Bridge Under Construction Wes 3/92 .   192
C/Pa 19x13 Sunset, Lower Manhattan Wes 3/92   138
Boyer-Breton, Marthe Marie L.   Fr 19C
* See 1992 Edition . . . .
Boyle, Charles Wellington   Am 1861-1925
* See 1992 Edition . . . .
Boyle, George A.   Eng 19C
O/C 16x20 Figures by a Brook; Spring Slo 7/92   700
Boynton, Ray
O/C 25x30 Plaza Havana 1950 Ald 5/92   250
Boze, Honore   Br 1830-1908
* See 1990 Edition . . . .
Bozzalla, Giuseppe   It 1874-1958
* See 1992 Edition . . . .
Brabazon, Hercules Brabazon   Br 1821-1906
W&Pe/Pa 5x8 Boats and Fishing Village: Pair Sby 1/92   1,045
Bracho Y Murillo, Jose Maria   Spa 19C
* See 1992 Edition . . . .
Brack, Emil   Ger 1860-1905
* See 1992 Edition . . . .
Brackenburg, Richard   Dut 1650-1702
* See 1991 Edition . . . .
Brackett, Sidney Lawrence   Am 19C
O/C 12x15 Kittens and Rabbit Skn 3/92   880
Brackett, Walter M.   Am 1823-1919
O/C 26x42 The Big Catch 1878 Sby 6/92   9,900
O/C 20x32 Catch of the Day 1906 Skn 9/91   5,500
O/C 20x32 Catch of Lake Trout 1860 Skn 11/91   4,950
O/C 12x20 A Pair of Trout 1887 Skn 3/92   2,200
Brackman
P/Pa 18x24 Women on Beach Dum 5/92   625
Brackman, David   Br 19C
* See 1991 Edition . . . .
Brackman, Robert   Am 1898-1980
O/C 40x50 After the Mask Wlf 3/92   26,000
O/C 28x36 Arrangement No. 9 with Figure Chr 9/91   7,700
O/C 25x30 Still Life with Plant Chr 11/91   5,280
O/C 30x24 Young Girl Holding Fruit Mys 6/92   4,400
O/C 28x32 Still Life with Primrose Sby 12/91   3,300
O/C 10x8 Self Portrait Chr 9/91   2,640
P/Pa 15x12 Female Nude Sel 9/91   1,900
O/C 20x12 Early Fall #3 Wlf 9/91   1,800

P/Pa 20x25 Figure Studies Sby 12/91   1,650
Bracy, Arthur E.
O/C 30x24 Elderly Man Reading Dum 5/92   250
Bradbury, Bennett   Am 20C
O/C 24x36 Coastal Mor 11/91   1,700
O/C 24x40 The Minarets - High Sierra Mor 3/92   1,000
O/C 30x48 Seascape-October Morning Mor 6/92   700
O/C 24x36 Coast Royal-Laguna Mor 6/92   450
O/C 18x24 Evening Breakers Mor 6/92   325
Bradbury, Gideon Elden   Am 1837-1904
O/C 24x19 Logging on the Saco Brd 8/92   3,410
O/C 12x20 Mount Tom on the Saco 1878 Brd 8/92   2,310
Braddon, Paul   Eng 1864-1938
W&G/Pa 20x21 St. Peter's, Rome Slo 9/91   300
Bradfield, *   Am 20C**
O/Cb 17x12 Still Life 1923 Slo 7/92   160
Bradford, William   Am 1823-1892
O/C 24x36 Edge of the Storm 1863 Skn 5/92   49,500
O/C 20x30 Fishing Boat in the Bay of Fundy Chr 5/92   26,400
O/C 20x30 Entrance to Battle Harbor Fre 4/92   17,500
O/C 9x14 Land of the Midnight Sun Hnd 5/92   10,000
Bradley, Susan H.   1851-1929
W/Pa 12x10 City Square Yng 4/92   200
Bradley, William   Br 1801-1857
* See 1992 Edition . . . .
Bradstreet, Julia E.   Am 19C
O/C 18x33 Floral Still Life Mys 11/91   165
Brady, Mary   Am a 1880-1913
O/C 22x17 Child and Her Doll But 2/92   880
Bragazzi, Olive   Am 20C
W/Pa 11x14 Study Lou 3/92   250
Braginton-Smith, Heather   Am 20C
O/B 6x12 Beach Scene with Artist '91 Eld 7/92   193
Brail, Achille Jean Theodore   Fr 19C
* See 1991 Edition . . . .
Braith, Anton   Ger 1836-1905
O/Pn Size? Sheep and Rooster Sel 9/91   700
Braley, Clarence E.   Am 1858-1925
* See 1992 Edition . . . .
Bramer, Leonard   Dut 1594-1674
* See 1990 Edition . . . .
Bramtot, Alfred Henri   Fr 1852-1894
* See 1992 Edition . . . .
Brancaccio, Carlo   It 1861-1920
O/C 32x39 Stamboul Sby 10/91   29,700
O/C 22x36 Vicino Di Napoli Sby 2/92   15,400
O/C 22x18 A Gondolier Chr 2/92   8,800
Branchard, Emile Pierre   Am 1881-1938
* See 1992 Edition . . . .
Brancusi, Constantin   Rom 1876-1957
* See 1991 Edition . . . .
Brandani, Enrico   It 1914-
O/B 28x20 Camerata Academica Wes 3/92   1,430
O/B 27x20 Symphonie Pour Orgues Wes 3/92   1,210
O/B 30x20 Les Poissons Volants Wes 3/92   908
O/Pn 29x24 L'Institutrice Wes 3/92   742
O/Pn 14x10 Les Regrets 67 Wes 3/92   742
O/M 27x18 Les Fous 1961 Wes 3/92   688
O/B 13x19 La Promenade Wes 3/92   330
Brandao-Giono, Wilson   20C
* See 1992 Edition . . . .
Brandeis, Antonietta   Aus 1849-1920
O/Pn 9x22 View of the Ponte Vecchio Chr 2/92   33,000
O/Pn 6x10 Canal Grande, S. Maria Della Salute Sby 10/91 .   7,700
O/Pn 5x9 View of the Piazza San Marco Chr 10/91   7,150
O/B 7x9 Grand Canal, Venice Hnd 10/91   3,800
Brandi, Giacinto   It 1623-1691
* See 1992 Edition . . . .
Brandner, Karl C.   Am 1898-1961
O/B 16x20 Fall, Oregon, Illinois Hnd 12/91   225
O/B 18x20 Landscape with Church Hnd 12/91   150
O/B 12x15 Landscape Hnd 12/91   140
Brandriff, George Kennedy   Am 1890-1936
O/C 25x30 A Busy Quay Chr 6/92   13,200

O/C 48x30 The Fish that Got Away Chr 6/92 8,800

Brandt, Rexford Elson   Am 1914-
* See 1991 Edition . . . .

Brandtner, Fritz   Can 1896-1969
O/B 40x30 Spirit Ka Ku, Quatsino Sound, B.C. '50 Sbt 5/92   7,480
W/Pa 14x10 Spirit of Ka Ku 1930 Sbt 5/92   3,740
W&Y/Pa 14x11 After Visiting Night Club Sbt 11/91   2,805

Brangwyn, Sir Frank   Br 1867-1956
G&W/Pa 18x14 A Cathedral Interior Chr 10/91   825
W/Pa 8x15 At Half Sail '25 Hnd 6/92   550
W/Pa 19x24 Italian Bridge 1911 Hnd 10/91   475

Branner, Martin   Am 1888-1970
Pl/Pa 24x17 Perry Winkle and His Friends 1924 Ih 11/91 . .   1,000

Braque, Georges   Fr 1882-1963
O/C 52x78 Atelier VIII Chr 5/92 . . . .   7.7M
O/C 20x37 La Rose Noire 27 Chr 11/91 . . . .   1.1M
O/C 12x10 Verre, Bouteille et Carte Bar Sby 5/92   632,500
C,Pt&L/Pa 11x13 Nature Morte a la Pipe et Verre Sby 5/92 550,000
O/C 10x14 Bouteille et verre Chr 5/92   352,000
O/C 14x26 Nature Morte a la Serviette Sby 11/91   341,000
O/C 13x22 Pichet Noir et Poissons Sby 11/91   286,000
Pl/Pa/Pa 8x11 Nature morte a la guitare Chr 5/92   49,500
C/Pa 19x24 Nature Morte avec Chaise Chr 5/92   35,200
Pl/Pa 12x8 Nu debout Chr 5/92   28,600
Pl/Pa/Pa 8x11 Nature morte aux fruits Chr 5/92   26,400
G&L/Pa/B 10x8 Couverture d'Un Catalogue Chr 5/92   9,900

Brascassat, Jacques Raymond   Fr 1804-1867
O/C 18x24 Cattle in a Country Meadow Wes 11/91   2,310

Brasilier, Andre   Fr 1929-
O/C 58x45 Chevaux au Pied d'un Arbre 1966 Sby 10/91 .   49,500
O/C 38x51 Voiliers au Grand Ciel Bleu 1970 Sby 10/91 . .   46,200
O/C 29x21 Repos des Cavaliers 1969 Sby 2/92   38,500
O/C 58x38 Delphiniums 1963 Sby 10/91   33,000
O/C 37x29 L'Arbre Jaune, Maisons Laffitte 1961 Sby 5/92   22,000
O/C 22x15 Les Chevaux Oranges 1963 Chr 11/91   19,800
O/C 38x51 Le Pont des Arts 1966 Sby 5/92   17,600

Braun, Ludwig   Ger 1836-1916
P/Pa 17x24 La Femme en Repose But 5/92   1,100

Braun, Maurice   Am 1877-1941
O/C 25x30 Lifting Fog But 10/91   14,300
O/C 42x36 Windswept Pine But 10/91   14,300
O/C 14x18 The Oak Mor 11/91   9,000
O/C 20x24 Along the Shore Chr 3/92   8,250
O/B 14x16 Distant Mountain Mor 3/92   8,000
O/C 16x20 San Diego Hills Chr 9/91   7,150
O/C 12x16 From Point Loma Mor 3/92   7,000
O/C 16x20 San Diego Harbor But 6/92   6,600
O/Cb 10x14 Fall Landscape Mor 3/92   6,000
O/C 16x20 Cuyamaca Mts. San Diego Mor 11/91   5,500
O/C 25x30 Fishing Shacks But 10/91   2,750

Brauner, Victor   Rom 1903-1966
O/C 41x61 Personnages sur la plage 1955 Chr 5/92 . . .   198,000
O/C 32x26 La substance du sommeil 1959 Chr 5/92   99,000
N/B 30x22 Fixation des vents 1958 Chr 5/92   77,000
O/Pn 26x32 Ruptures et conciliations 1959 Chr 5/92   41,800

Brauntuch, Troy   1954-
Pe/Cot 98x111 Untitled 83 Sby 2/92   6,930
I&P/L 120x96 Balcony '84 Sby 5/92   3,300

Bravo, Claudio   Chl 1936-
O/C 58x45 Self Portrait 1971 Sby 11/91   495,000
O/C 40x30 Beyond 1970 Sby 11/91   74,250
P/Pa 20x26 Bread Sby 5/92   36,300
H/Pa/Pn 15x19 Infantas Chr 5/92   26,400
C&P/Pa 26x20 Untitled 1970 Sby 11/91   26,400
C,P&Pe/Pa 18x24 Vivian Sentada Chr 11/91   25,300
W/Pa 18x12 Nina Sentada 1959 Chr 11/91   5,500

Bray, Arnold   Am 1892-1972
O/C 24x30 Rocky Coast But 10/91   1,540

Brayer, Yves   Fr 1907-1990
O/C 21x26 Maisons Blanches En Espagne Sby 10/91   9,625

Breakell, Mary Louise   Br a 1879-1912
O/Pn 7x10 Lake Maelog, Wales 1906 But 11/91   660

Breakspeare, William A.   Eng 1855-1914
O/C 14x11 Long Haired Beauty Chr 2/92   1,210

Brear, John William   Am 1906-1981
S&Pe/Pa 26x18 Door, Doric Temple at Cora 1926 Hnd 12/91   110

Brebiette, Pierre   Fr 1598-1650
K/Pa 11x15 Elijah in his Fiery Chariot Chr 1/92   19,800

Brecher, Samuel   Am 1897-
O&W/Pa 15x12 Portrait of a Man Sby 12/91   825

Breck, John Leslie   Am 1861-1899
* See 1992 Edition . . . .

Breckenridge, Hugh Henry   Am 1870-1937
O/C 24x25 Italian Fruit Dish Sby 5/92   29,700
O/C 21x18 Portrait of Edward Chambers Fre 4/92   375

Bredin, Christine   Am 20C
O/B 11x8 Girl with Bonnet Dum 11/91   650

Bredin, Rae Sloan   Am 1881-1933
O/C 20x16 Little Miss Short Chr 3/92   8,800

Breen, Marguerite   Am 1885-1964
O/C 14x18 The Practice Hour Chr 6/92   3,080

Breenbergh, Bartholomeus   Dut 1598-1657
O/Pn 19x32 Finding of Moses 1633 Sby 1/92   440,000

Breham, Paul Henri   Fr 1850-1933
* See 1992 Edition . . . .

Breitbach, Carl   Ger 1833-1904
* See 1992 Edition . . . .

Breitner, George Hendrik   Dut 1857-1923
* See 1991 Edition . . . .

Brendekilde, Andersen   Dan 1857-1920
O/C 30x40 Sunlit Farm Scene Sel 2/92   9,500
O/C 30x40 White Thatched Cottage Chr 10/91   5,500

Brenner, Carl C.   Am 1838-1888
* See 1992 Edition . . . .

Bretland, Thomas   Br 1802-1874
* See 1992 Edition . . . .

Breton, Andre   Fr 20C
* See 1990 Edition . . . .

Breton, Jules   Fr 1827-1905
O/C 34x54 The Haymakers at Rest 1873 Chr 10/91   88,000
O/C 24x30 Lavandiere au Foret '73 Sby 1/92   6,050

Brett, Dorothy Eugenie   Am 1882-1977
* See 1991 Edition . . . .

Brett, Harold Mathews   Am 1880-1955
O/B 25x30 Old Cape Cod Skn 3/92   660

Breu, Max   Ger 20C
O/C 30x36 Sheep and Chickens 1908 Wes 11/91   1,980

Breuer, Henry Joseph   Am 1860-1932
O/C 26x20 Majestic Mountains 1912 But 6/92   1,540
O/C 36x42 Forest Clearing But 2/92   1,045
O/C 11x12 Sand Dunes Monterey 1916 Mor 11/91   600
O/B 7x10 Landscape 1915 Mor 6/92   350

Breul, Hugo   Am 1854-1910
O/C 14x12 Gentleman Mys 11/91   82

Brevoort, James Renwick   Am 1832-1918
* See 1992 Edition . . . .

Brewer, Nicholas Richard   Am 1857-1949
O/C 25x30 Harvesting Scene Wes 11/91   468

Brewster, Amanda   Am 1859-
O/C 40x32 Incident au Village 1887 Fre 10/91   2,800

Brewster, Anna Richards   Am 1870-1952
O/C 25x17 Youth and the Moon Chr 11/91   2,860

Brewtrall, Edward Frederick   Eng 1846-1902
W/B 30x19 Frog Princess 1880 Wlf 6/92   2,500

Breydel, Karel   Flm 1678-1733
* See 1992 Edition . . . .

Brianchon, Maurice   Fr 1899-1979
O/C 26x36 Le Verger au Printemps Sby 5/92   39,600
O/C 24x36 Nature Morte a l'Ananas Chr 2/92   35,200
W&H/Pa 12x19 Courtyard View Skn 5/92   1,650

Briante, Ezelino   It 1901-1970
O/C 20x28 Seascape Fre 4/92   1,000

Briante, L.
O/Ab 18x12 Genre Scene: Pair Dum 6/92   350

Brice, William   Am 1921-
* See 1992 Edition . . . .

Bricher, Alfred Thompson Am 1837-1908
O/C 9x18 Autumn Boating 1870 Chr 9/91 24,200
O/C 22x32 White Island, Isle of Shoals Slo 10/91 23,000
O/C 13x29 Headlands Chr 5/92 18,700
O/C 24x20 Dusk on the Hill Side 1872 Chr 9/91 17,600
O/C 12x20 Mule Island, Isle of Shoals Chr 5/92 16,500
O/B 9x7 A Wintry Day 62 Chr 12/91 13,200
O/C 13x29 Seascape at Sunset Sby 9/91 11,000
W&Pe/Pa 10x22 Along Southampton Beach Chr 12/91 6,600
G/Pa 14x20 Portrait of Alice Bricher But 4/92 5,500
O/Ab 6x10 Mt. Kearsarge from Intervale 63 Brd 8/92 4,180
W&G/Pb 21x17 Cattails in a Meadow Sby 3/92 3,850
W/Pa 10x21 Walk on the Beach Skn 5/92 2,200
W/Pa 5x10 The Sunlit Cove Skn 5/92 1,870
W/Pb 13x20 Sailboats in the Distance Chr 6/92 1,210
Pe&G/Pa 8x12 Seascape Brd 5/92 935
Pl/Pa 4x9 Coastal Village, New Jersey Slo 7/92 850
Br&I/Pa 3x7 Breaking Waves Wes 5/92 825
W/Pa 7x9 Figure on a Cliff Wlf 3/92 750
W/Pa 8x12 Seascape Lou 3/92 750
W/Pa 7x15 Rocky Coastline Scene Dum 10/91 700
W/Pa 13x7 St. Duncan Ald 5/92 370

Bridges, Fidelia Am 1835-1923
S&G/Pa 9x13 Pink Wild Flowers 1874 Chr 6/92 2,860

Bridgman, Frederick Arthur Am 1847-1928
O/C 27x44 A Bistro in Algiers 1884 Dum 4/92 40,000
O/C 20x29 Afternoon on the Balcony 1901 Sby 10/91 . . . 22,000
O/C 13x16 Young Boy with Black Ram 1874 Skn 11/91 . . . 8,250
O/C 24x38 La Cote De Tanger L'Atantique 1925 Wlf 9/91 . . 8,000
O/C 11x16 Odalisque 1878 But 11/91 5,500
O/C/B 10x8 Head of a Young Boy with Turban Sby 4/92 . . . 4,400

Briede, Alex
O/Pn 7x10 Sailboat in Storm Dum 9/91 175

Briganti, Nicolas P. Am 1895-1989
O/C 27x36 Merchant Ships, Venice Doy 12/91 2,400
O/C 23x36 Autumn Wlf 3/92 475
O/B 4x6 Pair Still Lifes Mys 11/91 385
O/C 18x40 Landscape with a Cow Fre 4/92 375

Briggs, Warren C. Am 1867-1903
O/C 10x10 River Landscape with Fisherman Fre 4/92 700
O/C 14x20 Landscape with Sheep Lou 3/92 350

Brigham, William Cole Am 1870-1941
O/B 6x8 Three Seascapes 36 Skn 9/91 248

Brignoni, Sergio 20C
* See 1991 Edition

Bril, Paul Flm 1554-1626
* See 1991 Edition

Briscoe, Franklin Dulin Am 1844-1903
O/C 15x27 Off the Bank Sby 9/91 5,500
O/C 15x27 Homeward Bound 1870 Sby 12/91 4,840
O/C 28x50 Ship Wreck off the Coast Chr 11/91 4,180
O/C 26x40 Seascape 1895 Wes 11/91 3,850
O/C 15x27 Sunset in the Tropics 1870 Sby 12/91 2,530
O/C 15x27 Tropical Idyll 1870 Sby 12/91 2,530
O/C 8x13 Canoeing and Cows: Pair 76 Sby 12/91 1,760
O/C 10x16 Fishing Boats Sby 12/91 1,650
O/C 36x22 Figures Along Coast 1883 Fre 10/91 1,150
O/C 14x24 Ocean Ald 5/92 375

Brissot De Warville, Felix S. Fr 1818-1892
O/C 21x25 Bringing Home the Flock Sby 2/92 8,800
W/Pa 10x14 Sheep Herder Mys 6/92 880

Bristol, John Bunyan Am 1826-1909
O/C 17x29 Housatonic Meadows, NY Chr 6/92 4,620
O/C 10x15 Figure by Mountain Lake Yng 4/92 2,000
O/C 10x15 A Connecticut View Skn 5/92 1,100
O/C 14x24 Lake George Sby 12/91 550

Bristow, Edmund Eng 1787-1876
O/C 20x24 Mousey 1824 Slo 7/92 2,000

Brito, Ramon Vasquez 20C
* See 1991 Edition

Brittain, Miller Gore Can 1912-1968
Y/Pa 17x9 Three Figural Studies '65 Sbt 11/91 1,964

Britton, Harry Can 1878-1958
O/C 20x16 Harbour Scene Sbt 11/91 935

Broadhead, George H.
W/Pa 13x18 River Landscape Eld 7/92 55

Broadhead, W. Smithson Br 19C
* See 1992 Edition

Brochart, Constant-Joseph Fr 1816-1899
O/C 17x12 Children with Infant and Dog Yng 2/92 1,400

Brock, Richard H. Br 20C
* See 1992 Edition

Brockhurst, Gerald Leslie Br 1890-
* See 1992 Edition

Broderson, Morris Am 1928-
W/Pa 10x8 Summer, 1978 '78 Lou 9/91 250

Broe, Vern Am 20C
O/B 18x24 Catboats Eld 7/92 825
A/C 18x22 Catboats Eld 4/92 578
O/C 12x16 Girls by the Seashore Eld 4/92 550
O/C 11x14 Two Girls in a Garden Eld 7/92 440

Broedelet, Andre Dut 1872-1936
O/Pn 18x11 Blowing Bubbles But 11/91 2,750

Broge, Alfred Dan 1870-1955
O/C 25x22 Interior with a Harpsicord Fre 12/91 3,200

Bromley, Frank C. Am 1860-1890
O/C 13x21 Herding Cows Lou 12/91 750

Bromley, William Br 19C
* See 1992 Edition

Brook, Alexander Am 1898-1980
O/C 16x12 Half Nude Seated Female Chr 6/92 2,420
G&P/Pa 21x16 Two Women Embracing Chr 6/92 1,100
O/C 19x36 Verdant Landscape Skn 5/92 990
O/C 12x9 Chrysanthemums Chr 9/91 770

Brooke, E. Adveno Br 19C
* See 1992 Edition

Brooker, Harry Br 1876-1902
* See 1991 Edition

Brookes, Samuel Marsden Am 1816-1892
O/C 29x36 Still Life Hare, Fowl, Antelope 18** But 2/92 . . 3,850

Brooks, Henry Howard Am
* See 1991 Edition

Brooks, James Am 1906-1992
O/C 36x24 Untitled Slo 7/92 1,200

Brooks, Leonard Frank Can 1911-
O/C 24x30 Minden Hills Sbt 11/91 841

Brooks, Maria Br a 1869-1890
* See 1990 Edition

Brooks, Nicholas Alden Am 1849-1904
O/Pn 14x11 Ten Dollars on First Race, Saratoga Chr 5/92 . 38,500
O/C 16x20 Tabletop Still Life With Books 1891 Wes 11/91 . 3,850
O/C 9x11 Still Life with Fife 1880 Chr 9/91 2,860

Brooks, Thomas Br 1818-1892
* See 1991 Edition

Brooks, W. W. Eng a 1838-1870
O/C 21x17 Prie Dieu 1865 Wes 11/91 1,320

Broulliet, Pierre Andre Fr 1857-1914
* See 1990 Edition

Browaski, E. Am 20C
O/B 10x12 Still Life with Pipe Mys 6/92 165

Browere, Alburtus Del Orient Am 1814-1887
O/C 14x25 Majestic Vista But 10/91 8,250

Brown, Amy Difley Am 20C
O/C 20x30 Atmospheric Landscape Mor 6/92 600

Brown, Anna Wood Am 20C
O/C 18x21 Mother with Baby Hnd 3/92 800

Brown, Arthur Kellock Eng 1849-1922
W/Pa 10x14 Cummertrees Kirk, Dumfrieshire Slo 2/92 170

Brown, Arthur W. Am 1881-1966
Pe&S/Pa 13x21 Lawyer/Between Two Women 1935 Ih 11/91 . 550

Brown, Benjamin Chambers Am 1865-1942
O/C/C 22x30 The Rose of Dawn Mor 3/92 11,000
O/Cb 20x16 Old Pines - Sierra Trail But 2/92 6,050
O/C 18x24 Desert Sunset Near Phoenix Mor 3/92 6,000
O/Cb 11x15 Spring-Time, Arroyo Seco Path Mor 3/92 . . . 4,500
O/C 28x36 Spring Landscape Wlf 6/92 2,400
W/Pa 10x14 Flower Market Mor 11/91 1,400

O/B 16x20 California Salt Hnz 5/92 1,000

Brown, Byron   Am 1907-1961
* See 1992 Edition . . . .

Brown, Carlyle   Am 1919-1964
* See 1992 Edition . . . .

Brown, F. C.   Am 19C
* See 1992 Edition . . . .

Brown, Frank E.   Am 20C
O/C 16x20 Still Life Rifle and Powder Horn 1955 Eld 4/92 . . 110

Brown, George Elmer   Am 1871-1946
W/Pa 32x25 Column of Saint Mark's Lion But 11/91 1,870
O/C 26x21 Church in Montreal But 4/92 1,760

Brown, George Loring   Am 1814-1889
O/C 32x57 Catching Sardines 1869 Chr 6/92 7,700
O/C 18x24 Sunrise, White Mountains 1862 Chr 12/91 . . 6,050
O/C 22x36 Morning near Rome (Italy) 1884 Chr 6/92 . . . 1,100
W/Pa 9x12 Lake Nemi, 1858 Yng 4/92 900
O/C 11x15 Sunset on the Mystic River 1862 Eld 7/92 605
W/Pa 10x13 Italian Landscape Yng 4/92 375

Brown, Harrison Bird   Am 1831-1915
O/C 13x24 White Mountain, Naples 1862 Brd 8/92 20,350
O/C 26x43 White Mountains fr Jones Farm 1861 Brd 8/92 . 15,400
O/C 30x58 Climbing the Cliffs, Grand Manan 73 Brd 8/92 . 10,120
O/C 12x22 Picnic, Casco Bay 70 Brd 8/92 6,380
O/C 12x20 Indians Drying and Smoking Fish Brd 8/92 . . . 5,940
O/C 28x42 River Valley, White Mountain Brd 8/92 5,940
O/C 27x50 Alpine Village Brd 8/92 5,500
O/C 13x24 Farm in the Foothills Brd 8/92 5,500
O/C 26x42 To the Rescue, Grand Manan 1859 Brd 8/92 . . 5,500
O/C 13x24 Hotel Tiberio '72 Yng 4/92 4,250
O/C 21x36 Maine Coast 1866 Brd 8/92 4,180
O/C 13x23 White Mountains from a River Yng 2/92 3,750
O/C 13x25 Natural Pool Brd 8/92 3,410
O/C 14x24 Overlooking Casco Bay Brd 8/92 2,970
O/C 13x20 Picnic at Snow Falls, South Paris Brd 8/92 . . . 2,750
O/C 13x23 Artist at Work, Whitehead, Cushing Brd 8/92 . . 2,200
O/C 25x48 Entrance to Bar Harbor 71 Skn 11/91 2,200
O/C 11x17 Pastoral Landscape With Cows 1859 Brd 8/92 . 1,760
O/C 11x19 White Mountain Landscape Brd 8/92 1,650
O/C 13x24 Castle Ruins by the Sea 70 Brd 8/92 1,430
O/C 21x36 Rugged Coast, Maine Brd 8/92 1,430
O/C 12x22 Castle on the Cliffs 72 Brd 8/92 1,320
O/N 2x4 Seascape Brd 8/92 578
W/Pa 9x12 Seascape Brd 8/92 132

Brown, Horace   Am 1876-
O/C/M 14x27 Winter in the Valley Skn 9/91 1,320
O/C 24x20 Nocturnal Silo Fre 4/92 350

Brown, Howard V.   Am 1878-
O/C 24x16 Battle Scene Wlf 11/91 550

Brown, James   Am 1951-
A/Me/B 51x36 Stabat Mater (Brown) XIII 1988 Chr 11/91 . 24,200
O&E/Cd 65x61 Untitled 1983 Sby 11/91 23,100
E&H/Pa 40x26 Untitled 1984 Chr 5/92 14,300
A&H/Pa 60x50 Angels and Spirits 2 1982 Chr 11/91 9,900
O&L/L 36x28 Stabat Mater 96 1988 Chr 5/92 5,280
H/Pa 26x20 Untitled 1983 Chr 5/92 3,850
Pe/Pa 50x38 Self-Portrait Sby 6/92 3,025
H/Pa 26x20 Untitled 1983 Chr 11/91 2,200
H/L/Pa 9x6 Untitled: Three Drawings Sby 10/91 2,200

Brown, Joan   Am 1938-
* See 1992 Edition . . . .

Brown, John Appleton   Am 1844-1902
O/C 16x30 Picking Wildflowers 1865 Skn 5/92 5,610
O/C 31x42 Landscape with River '76 Sby 12/91 4,125
O/C 17x21 Summer Meadow Wildflowers Skn 3/92 1,870
P/Pb 17x21 Springtime Skn 3/92 1,320

Brown, John George   Am 1831-1913
O/C 18x44 Watching the Circus 1881 But 11/91 253,000
O/C 16x26 Look Out While Bell Rings 1863 Chr 12/91 . . . 71,500
O/C 21x17 Delivery Boy 1863 Chr 5/92 55,000
O/C 17x14 The Young Artist 1867 Chr 5/92 55,000
O/C 40x32 The Rush for Evening Papers 1912 Sby 5/92 . . 17,600
O/C 24x16 Frank and His Dog Sby 9/91 15,400
O/C 22x16 A Leisure Hour 1881 Chr 12/91 12,100
O/C 24x16 Bright as a Dollar Chr 3/92 11,000

O/C 25x20 I'll Share With You Chr 3/92 11,000
O/C 25x16 Shoeshine Boy Writing on the Wall Sby 3/92 . . . 9,350
O/C 24x16 Portrait Douglas B. Wesson 1895 But 11/91 . . 8,800
O/C 25x30 Thanksgiving Time Eld 7/92 7,700
O/C 27x20 Wedding Dress 1869 Hnd 10/91 5,000
O/C 30x20 Woman by a Stream 1885 Sby 12/91 4,675
O/C 25x20 Self-Portrait 1902 Sby 12/91 2,640
O/C 22x14 The Maine Woods Chr 6/92 2,200
Pe&K/Pa 7x10 Three Drawings of Children 1875 But 4/92 . . 1,870
O/C 15x10 Oscar and Mabel But 4/92 1,760
Pe/Pa 13x9 Little Greedy Wes 11/91 825

Brown, John Lewis   Fr 1829-1890
O/C 20x26 Le Rendez-Vous de Chasse Sby 6/92 2,200

Brown, Joseph Randolph   1861-
W/Pa 9x7 Path Through the Trees 1900 Yng 2/92 275

Brown, Lucille Rosemary Greene   Am 1905-
W/Pa 12x10 Chief Wolf Robe Lou 3/92 75

Brown, Manneville Ellihu D.   Am 1810-1896
* See 1990 Edition . . . .

Brown, Mather   Am 1761-1831
* See 1992 Edition . . . .

Brown, Paul   Am 1893-1960
* See 1992 Edition . . . .

Brown, R. Alston   Am 1878-
O/B 21x14 Indian Couple Standing in Canyon Ilh 5/92 1,100

Brown, Roger   Am 1941-
O/C 72x48 The Coast of Maine Sby 10/91 8,800

Brown, Roy H.   Am 1879-1956
* See 1992 Edition . . . .

Brown, Thomas Austen   Br 1859-1924
O/C 30x25 Portrait of a Girl Knitting Sel 5/92 700

Brown, Walter Francis   Am 1853-1929
O/C 26x44 Seascape Skn 3/92 1,045

Brown, William Beattie   Br 1831-1909
O/M 27x18 Waterfall But 5/92 3,850

Brown, William Garl (Jr.)   Am 1823-1894
O/C 34x30 Portrait of a Mother and Son 1884 Slo 2/92 . . . 350

Brown, William Marshall   Br 1863-1936
O/C 9x12 Three Women in Interior 1899 Dum 2/92 900

Brown, William Mason   Am 1828-1898
O/C 22x36 Summer Pastures Chr 5/92 16,500
O/C/B 9x12 Champagne and Fruit Chr 5/92 9,900

Brown, William Theophilus   Am 1919-
* See 1992 Edition . . . .

Brown, Woodley   Eng 19C
O/C 20x24 River Landscape Sel 9/91 600

Browne, Byron   Am 1907-1961
O/C 48x36 Woman with Palette 1957 Chr 3/92 7,700
O/M 28x24 Flying Disc 1949 Chr 9/91 4,180
O/B 18x14 Flowers 1958 Sby 4/92 1,980
R,G&S/Pa 26x20 Head of a Woman 1953 Sby 4/92 1,320
O/C 30x24 The Bullfight Chr 6/92 1,100
O/C 14x18 Sunset, Provincetown, 1958 Yng 4/92 950
W&I/Pa 26x20 Seated Female Nude: Double 1952 Sby 4/92 . 880
O/C 20x26 View of Provincetown 1961 Dum 7/92 625

Browne, Charles Francis   Am 1859-1920
* See 1992 Edition . . . .

Browne, George Elmer   Am 1871-1946
O/Pn 10x14 Clamdiggers Chr 11/91 1,980
O/Pn 11x14 Dunes, France Chr 11/91 1,210
O/C 25x30 Red Sails at Etaples 1903 Hnd 6/92 850
O/B 11x14 Along the Beach--Douarnene Hnd 10/91 750
O/B 15x18 Poplars Chr 11/91 715
O/C 20x24 Coastal Landscape 1902 Sby 12/91 660
W/Pb 21x28 Houses on Square, Spain Chr 11/91 605
W&Pe/B 19x13 A. Rojan and F. Aigona 1922 Chr 11/91 . . . 220
W/Pa 18x23 Swirling Clouds Fre 10/91 200
W/Pa 18x23 Clouds and Landscape Ald 3/92 125

Browne, Hablot Knight (Phiz)   Br 1815-1882
* See 1991 Edition . . . .

Browne, Henriette   Fr 1829-1901
O/C 40x31 Sisters of Charity Sby 7/92 2,200

52

Browne, Joseph Archibald   Can 1862-1948
O/Pn 12x16 Landscape, Early Evening Sbt 11/91 327
Browne, Margaret Fitzhugh   Am 1884-1972
O/C 20x16 Still Life with Traveling Cases Skn 11/91 605
O/C 24x27 Still Life Yng 4/92 300
O/C 34x40 The Artist Arthur Safford Yng 2/92 150
O/B 12x10 Madonna Lilies Slo 4/92 50
Browne, Matilda   Am 1869-1947
P/B 11x13 Mother and Her Puppies Chr 3/92 1,100
O/C 16x20 Cows in a Stream Wlf 10/91 170
Brownell, Charles De Wolf   Am 1822-1909
* See 1991 Edition . . . .
Brownell, Peleg Franklin   Can 1857-1946
O/C 14x22 Beach Scene Sbt 5/92 6,779
O/C 18x24 The Hay Making 1910 Sbt 5/92 2,805
P/Pa 13x19 Autumn River, Gatineau Sbt 11/91 561
Brownscombe, Jennie   Am 1850-1936
O/C 38x28 Choirboys Sby 12/91 8,800
O/Pn 24x33 Four Maidens Spring Landscape Wlf 6/92 5,100
O/B 17x13 Woman Gazing into a Mirror But 11/91 2,750
Brozik, Wencelas Von Vacslaw   Czk 1851-1901
O/C 26x32 The Conversation Sby 2/92 13,200
O/C 18x22 Birch Forest 1901 Sby 7/92 1,320
Bruce, Edward   Am 1879-1943
O/C 15x18 Portrait of a Lady Reading Slo 2/92 2,200
O/C 11x25 The Williams Farm Slo 2/92 2,000
Bruce, Patrick Henry   Am 1881-1936
* See 1992 Edition . . . .
Bruce, William   Am 19C
* See 1991 Edition . . . .
Bruce, William Blair   Can 1859-1906
O/Pn 6x10 Harvest Time '82 Sbt 5/92 3,740
Bruck-Lajos
O/C 36x25 The Young Hunters Wlf 3/92 3,600
Bruckman, Lodewijk   Am 1913-
O/C 15x30 Chinese Dream Mys 11/91 688
Bruckner
O/B 17x21 Chess Game Dum 5/92 450
Bruckner, Henry   Am 19C
Pe/Pa 7x12 Israel Putnam Called From His Plow Wes 3/92 . . 330
Brueghel, Abraham & Courtois   Flm 1631-1690
O/C 67x101 Ceres attended by Putti Chr 5/92 242,000
Brueghel, Jan (the Elder)   Flm 1568-1625
* See 1991 Edition . . . .
Brueghel, Jan (the Younger)   Flm 1601-1678
* See 1992 Edition . . . .
Brueghel, Pieter (III)   Flm 1589-
* See 1991 Edition . . . .
Brueghel, Pieter (the Younger)   Flm 1564-1638
O/Pn 16x23 Village Wedding Dance 1625 Sby 5/92 577,500
Bruestle, Bertram G.   Am 1902-
O/B 12x16 Farm Scene Mys 6/92 412
O/B 10x14 Landscape Mys 6/92 330
Bruestle, George M.   Am 1872-1939
O/Pn 12x16 Autumn Sundown Skn 9/91 990
O/B 7x5 Landscape 1923 Mys 11/91 715
O/B 5x6 Farm Scene 1918 Mys 11/91 688
O/B 11x16 Landscape Wlf 10/91 675
O/Pn 6x8 Autumn Sundown Skn 11/91 550
Bruff, J. Goldsborough   Am 1804-1889
Pl&W/Pa 6x8 American Sailing Vessel: Two 1848 Chr 11/91 . 308
Brugairolles, Victor   Fr 1869-1936
O/B 15x19 The Seine at Dusk Wlf 3/92 1,700
Brugner, Colestin   Ger 20C
O/C 9x12 River and Fisherman '67 Fre 4/92 600
Bruls, Louis Joseph   Ger 1803-1882
O/C 29x24 The Departure 1881 But 11/91 19,800
Brun, Guillaume Charles   Fr 1825-1908
O/C 32x18 Jeune Vendeuse des Fleurs 1873 But 5/92 . . . 11,000

Brunel De Neuville, Alfred A.   Fr 1852-1941
O/C 21x26 L'Escargot 1904 Sby 5/92 5,775
O/C 22x26 Kittens at Play Sby 10/91 5,500
O/C 20x26 Kittens Playing with Yarn But 5/92 4,675
O/C 21x26 Curious Kittens with Bumble Bee Slo 2/92 4,000
O/C 25x21 Still Life with Fruit Wlf 9/91 4,000
O/C 10x13 Playful Kittens Chr 10/91 3,850
O/C 28x36 Still Life with Game Wlf 6/92 3,600
O/C 21x26 Still Life Mussels, Oysters Skn 9/91 3,300
O/C 20x24 Mischievous Kittens Hnz 10/91 3,100
O/C 15x18 Mischief Wlf 3/92 2,100
Brunery, Francois   It 1845-
* See 1992 Edition . . . .
Brunery, Marcel   Fr 20C
O/Pn 26x21 Le Myope Sby 2/92 22,000
O/C 18x15 Divine Inspiration Chr 2/92 6,600
Brush, Christine Chaplin   Am 19C
W/Pa/Pa 14x10 Apples '85 Sby 12/91 495
Brush, George De Forest   Am 1855-1941
* See 1992 Edition . . . .
Bruyere, Elise   Fr 1776-1842
* See 1991 Edition . . . .
Bruzzi, Stefano   It 1835-1911
* See 1991 Edition . . . .
Bry, Edith   Am 1898-
O/B 16x12 Still Life of Flowers Sel 12/91 100
Bryant, Everett Lloyd   Am 1864-1945
O/C Size? Still Life Mys 6/92 2,200
O/C 20x16 Still Life of Flowers Wlf 6/92 1,100
O/C 20x24 Still Life with Flowers Fre 10/91 350
O/M 22x18 Still Life Flowers in a Vase Slo 9/91 125
Bryant, Henry   Eng 19C
O/C 12x18 Ready for the Dance Wes 11/91 715
Bryant, Wallace   Am 20C
O/C 18x18 Landscape Mor 11/91 475
Brymner, William   Can 1855-1925
* See 1991 Edition . . . .
Bryson   Eng
O/C 73x58 Salon Scene 86 Dum 8/92 125
Bryson, Hope Mercereau   Am 20C
* See 1991 Edition . . . .
Bucci, ***   18C
O/C 27x41 Mountainous Landscape 1745 Sby 10/91 6,050
Buchanan, Ella   Am 20C
O/C 20x30 Estuarine Landscape Eld 7/92 275
Buchbinder, Simeon   Pol 19C
* See 1990 Edition . . . .
Buche, Joseph   Aus 1848-
O/C 24x19 Young Girl in a White Dress 1888 Sby 5/92 . . 6,600
Buchheister, Carl   Ger 1890-1964
* See 1992 Edition . . . .
Buchholz, Erich   1891-1972
O/Wd 18x12 "Der Schlussel" Var. 1 Chr 11/91 33,000
O&Gd/Wd 21x9 Abstrackte Komposition 1922 Chr 11/91 . . 33,000
Buchner, Georg   Ger 1858-1914
* See 1992 Edition . . . .
Buchta, Anthony   Am 20C
O/B 16x20 Autumn Witchery Hnz 5/92 400
Buck, Charles Claude   Am 1890-
O/Pn 31x42 Girl Reading 1931 Hnd 3/92 9,000
O/B 27x24 Allegorical Scene Mor 6/92 3,500
O/C 32x22 Woman Standing by a Pool Lou 3/92 1,350
Buck, Kirkland C.
O/B 10x12 Stream Ald 3/92 185
O/B 10x8 Mountains Ald 3/92 30
Buck, Leslie   Am 1907-
O/M 16x20 Still Life Mor 6/92 375
Buckler, Charles E.   Am 1869-
O/Ab 8x10 Stream in the Berkshires Slo 4/92 325
Buckley, Stephen   Am 1944-
* See 1992 Edition . . . .
Buckman, Katherine
W/Pa 9x8 Folk Art Watercolor Ald 5/92 200

Budd, Charles Jay   Am 1859-1926
G&W/Pa 16x20 Recounting the Story Wlf 6/92 575
Budgen   20C
P/Pa 22x12 Dance Class '59 Yng 4/92 100
Buehr, George   Am 1905-
W&I/Pa 17x23 Mountain Lake and Pagodas: Two Slo 7/92 . . 325
Buehr, Karl A.   Am 1866-1952
O/C 25x30 Autumn Landscape Hnz 5/92 1,400
O/C 24x30 Autumn Landscape Hnd 10/91 1,000
Buell, Alfred   Am 1910-
O/B 18x18 Kissing Couple Seated on the Grass Ilh 5/92 . . . 2,250
O/Cb 19x12 Woman Holding Yellow Flower 1958 Ilh 5/92 . . . 800
Buell, Marjorie Henderson   Am
PI/Pa 6x20 Comic Strip. "Little Lulu" 57 Ilh 5/92 450
Bueno, Antonio   It 1918-1984
* See 1991 Edition . . . .
Bueno, Xavier   It 1915-1979
O/C 28x20 Nina Pequena Chr 11/91 6,600
Buergerniss, Carl   Am 1877-1956
O/C 16x20 Figure in the Field Fre 4/92 325
O/C 16x20 Playing in the Fields Fre 4/92 325
O/C 16x23 Landscape Pink Flowers Fre 4/92 175
O/C 16x20 Houses in a Landscape 1927 Fre 4/92 160
Buff, Conrad   Am 1886-1975
O/C/C 20x28 Afternoon Mor 6/92 2,700
O/B 12x16 Landscape Mor 6/92 1,500
O/C 25x30 Landscape--"Sycamores" Mor 11/91 1,500
Buffet, Bernard   Fr 1928-
O/C 29x36 Nature Morte a la Boite a Sel 56 Chr 11/91 . . . 93,500
O/C 32x39 Environs de Bourges 62 Sby 11/91 88,000
O/C 26x32 Maisons au Bord du Canal 67 Sby 11/91 71,500
O/C 36x46 Vue de Cannes 60 Chr 11/91 70,000
O/C 20x29 Le Plage de Sable d'Or 68 Chr 2/92 60,500
O/B 13x16 Nature Morte au Compotier Sby 11/91 55,000
O/C 20x26 Vase de Fleurs 54 Chr 5/92 55,000
O/C 46x29 Vase de Fleurs 62 Sby 10/91 55,000
O/C 24x29 Bord de Mer 65 Sby 11/91 49,500
O/C 26x22 Pavots 65 Chr 5/92 49,500
O/C 26x22 Bouquet de Roses au Fond Jaune 63 Chr 11/91 41,800
O/C 18x26 Le Pain 1950 Sby 5/92 38,500
O&Pe/C 20x26 Homard et Bol avec courerts 48 Chr 5/92 . 33,000
WOY&I/Pa/M 20x26 Vase de Fleurs 62 Chr 11/91 30,800
G&Y/Pa/C 26x20 Le dompteur Chr 5/92 20,900
Os/Pa 28x10 Floral Still-Life '59 But 5/92 16,500
O/Cb 8x8 Insecte Chr 11/91 13,200
Buffin, Carlos   Fr 19C
* See 1991 Edition . . . .
Bugiardini, Giuliano   It 1475-1555
* See 1992 Edition . . . .
Buhler, Augustus W.   Am 1853-1920
O/C 26x20 An Old Skipper 1903 Brd 5/92 4,400
O/B 7x11 Rocky Coastline '11 Yng 2/92 200
Buhot, Felix Hilaire   Fr 1847-1898
* See 1992 Edition . . . .
Buizard, A.   Con 19C
* See 1992 Edition . . . .
Buland, Jean Eugene   Fr 1852-1927
* See 1991 Edition . . . .
Bull, Charles Livingston   Am 1874-1932
C/Pa 25x18 Bears and Bees Durn 1/92 400
C/Pa 12x9 Maniac Clung to Beast's Snout Yng 4/92 225
C/Pa 23x13 Hawk Catching Rat Yng 4/92 175
Bullard, Marion   Am 20C
O/B 12x16 Impressionist Country Road Eld 7/92 165
O/B 12x16 Impressionistic Landscape Eld 7/92 165
O/Pn 11x11 Landscape Eld 7/92 138
Bulleid, George Lawrence   Br 1858-
* See 1991 Edition . . . .
Bulmer, Lionel
* See 1992 Edition . . . .
Bunbury, Henry William   Br 1750-1811
K,Pl&S/Pa 10x8 The City Refrigerium Chr 1/92 440
Bunce, William Gedney   Am 1840-1916
O/B 15x17 Venice; Venetian Canal (2) '94 Sby 12/91 2,200

Bundy, Edgar   Br 1862-1922
O/C 22x28 Two Gentlemen Around a Table Sel 4/92 1,000
Bundy, Gilbert   Am 1911-1955
W/Pa 19x16 Waiter Dropping Dishes 1942 Ilh 11/91 550
Bunel, M.   Spa 1923-
O/C 22x18 Parisian Street Scene Sel 12/91 100
Bunker, Dennis Miller   Am 1861-1890
O/C 11x19 Fisherman's Work, Low Tide 1880 Skn 3/92 . . 67,100
Bunn, George   Br a 1887-1898
O/B 20x30 Harbour Mys 11/91 770
Bunner, Andrew Fisher   Am 1841-1897
O/C 15x30 San Nicholetto, Venice Wes 11/91 4,510
O/C 22x16 Dutch Boats on the Maas, Holland Chr 6/92 . . 1,210
W/Pa 8x15 Sailboats in Venetian Harbor Slo 2/92 350
Bunnett, Henry Richard S.   Can a 1880-
* See 1991 Edition . . . .
Bunny, Rupert Charles Wulsten   Aut 1864-1947
* See 1991 Edition . . . .
Buono, Leon Guiseppe   It 1888-
* See 1992 Edition . . . .
Burbank, Elbridge Ayer   Am 1858-1949
O/C 13x17 Wagon Trains Chr 6/92 2,200
Burchard, Pablo   Chl 1876-
* See 1990 Edition . . . .
Burchfield, Charles Ephraim   Am 1893-1967
W/Pa/Pb 26x35 July Clouds 1948 Sby 3/92 50,600
W/Pa 38x25 September Sun 1946 Sby 12/91 44,000
W,Cw&Pe/Pa 22x16 Summer Rain 1916 Chr 5/92 44,000
W&Pe/Pa 20x27 Old Tavern at Gardenville 1927 Sby 12/91 27,500
W/Pa/B 24x15 Back Alley Chr 9/91 24,200
W/Pa 20x27 Marsh Song Sby 12/91 18,700
Y&W/Pa 12x15 Old House Spring Dawn 1965 Sby 12/91 . 18,700
G&W/Pa 9x12 Mushrooms in the Rain 1916 Chr 5/92 . . . 11,000
I,WC&Pe/Pa 14x22 Old Inn Hammondsville, Ohio Chr 9/91 . 7,150
W/Pa 10x14 Shanty in the Woods Mys 6/92 3,700
Burd, Clara Miller   Am
W/Pa 14x10 Girl in Farmyard with Goats Ilh 5/92 2,600
Burdick, Horace R.   Am 1844-1942
O/Pa 14x11 Portrait Alice Burdick 1902 Yng 4/92 200
W/Pa 9x12 Pond Yng 2/92 50
Buren, Daniel   1938-
Pt/F 55x138 Untitled Sby 11/91 25,300
A/F 61x52 Blanc et Rose Chr 2/92 14,300
Burgdorff, Ferdinand   Am 1883-1975
⌕ O/B 20x24 Old Wharf, Monterey 1948 But 6/92 935
W/Pa 10x14 Lemon Sunrise on Desert 1918 Yng 4/92 600
O/Cb 20x24 San Francisco Peaks - Flagstaff Mor 6/92 300
O/Ab 24x30 Cottonwood, November Wlf 3/92 200
Burgers, Hendricus Jacobus   Dut 1834-1899
* See 1992 Edition . . . .
Burgess   20C
O/C 20x16 Lady in a Black Hat Yng 4/92 225
Burgess, Arthur James   Aut 1879-1957
* See 1992 Edition . . . .
Burgess, Emma   Am 20C
O/B 10x14 Haystacks, Autumn Slo 7/92 175
Burgess, John Bagnold   Eng 1830-1897
* See 1990 Edition . . . .
Burgin, Victor   20C
Ph/Pa 11x8 Untitled Sby 11/91 1,210
Burke, Ainslee   Am 20C
O/B 32x42 Uncharted Land But 11/91 2,475
Burkel, Heinrich   Ger 1802-1869
* See 1992 Edition . . . .
Burkhardt, Emerson C.   Am 1905-1969
O/C 27x32 In Late Afternoon Wlf 10/91 400
Burkhardt, Hans Gustav   Am 1904-
O/C 18x9 View of a Window '51 But 5/92 1,045
Burleigh, Charles H. H.   Br 1875-1956
* See 1990 Edition . . . .
Burleigh, Sidney R.   Am 1853-1931
Y/Pa Size? Figures in a Landscape Mys 11/91 715

Burlingame, Dennis Meighan   Am 1901-
* See 1992 Edition . . . .
Burliuk, David   Am 1882-1967
O/C 18x24 Bradenton, Florida 1946 Sby 12/91 5,775
O/C 48x36 Still Life Flowers and Shells 1964 Sby 12/91 . . . 5,775
O/C 35x26 Still Life Flowers 1949 Sby 12/91 5,225
O/C 20x30 Floral Still Lifes 40 Sby 12/91 3,410
O/Pn 13x5 Spring in Blue Modern #23 1907 Skn 9/91 3,080
O/C 18x22 Yacht Basin Chr 11/91 3,080
O/C 24x34 Ravello 1963 Sby 12/91 2,750
O/C 16x20 Florida Street Sby 12/91 2,310
O/C 26x20 Still Life at Water's Edge 1948 Hnd 10/91 2,200
O/B 10x14 Landscape with Figures in Carriage Sby 12/91 . . . 2,090
O/Cb 8x6 Two Peasant Girls 1950 Sby 12/91 1,980
O/B 12x12 Blue Horse Chr 11/91 1,870
O/Cb 10x14 Abstract Colors Chr 6/92 1,650
W,Pe&C/Pa 14x11 Still Life; Summer Romance: (2) Sby 4/92 1,430
W/Pa 15x13 Abstraction Chr 6/92 1,320
W/Pa 9x11 A New York Skyline Chr 11/91 990
W/Pa 15x13 Abstraction Chr 6/92 880
W&I/Pa 15x10 GW Bridge; The Ages (2) 1945 Chr 6/92 715
O/Cb 10x14 92nd Street Ferry Chr 6/92 605
O/B 8x7 Marussia, Wife of the Artist 1960 Wlf 9/91 600
O/Wd 4x5 Woman by a Window Lou 6/92 475
Pl&W/Pa 9x12 Texas Chr 11/91 462
W/Pa 11x15 Cattle Grazing in Arizona Landscape Slo 9/91 . . 400
Burmakin, Vladimir   Rus 1938-
O/C Size? Days of Easttown Fre 4/92 750
Burmann, Fritz
O/Pn 18x14 Mutter Und Kind 23 Sby 2/92 5,500
Burmester, Georg
* See 1992 Edition . . . .
Burne-Jones, Sir Edward Coley   Br
1833-1898
O/C 25x17 Little Dorothy Mattersdorf 1893 Chr 5/92 . . . 165,000
O/C 73x30 Joshua: Sketch Sby 10/91 9,900
K/Pa 15x11 Study for Mrs. Gaetano Meo Sby 10/91 4,400
Burnett, Calvin W.   Am 1921-
O/C 30x22 Boy with Balloons Skn 5/92 880
Burney, Edward Francis   Br 1760-1848
K,Pl&W/Pa 9x7 Anthony and Cleopatra Chr 1/92 1,320
Burns, James   Am 19C
O/C 48x72 Lincoln's Last Moments 1866 Chr 11/91 4,180
Burns, Maurice K.   Am 20C
O/C 17x21 Coming Ashore in Gloucester Wes 3/92 1,100
O/C 16x20 Fishing Boats in Gloucester Wes 3/92 715
O/C 20x16 Gloucester Town in Winter Wes 3/92 605
O/B 17x21 Snowy Road to Gloucester Wes 3/92 605
O/C 20x24 New England Stream in Winter Wes 3/92 550
O/C 16x20 Winter Farm Scene Wes 3/92 468
Burns, Milton J.   Am 1853-1933
O/C 9x13 Odds Against Eld 4/92 440
Pl&Pe/Pa 10x13 Lobster Eld 4/92 165
Burns, Paul   Am 1910-
O/C 24x20 Portrait Mary Lyn Galton Lou 3/92 75
Burpee, William Partridge   Am 1846-1940
O/C 10x16 Boating on a River Brd 8/92 3,190
P/Pa 14x18 Spring Thaw Brd 8/92 1,650
Burr, Alexander Hohenlohe   Br 1837-1899
* See 1990 Edition . . . .
Burr, G. G.   Am 20C
W/Pa 21x14 Figures in a Courtyard Yng 2/92 50
Burr, George Brainerd   Am 1876-1950
O/C 25x20 Portrait of Mrs. Burr Sby 12/91 1,430
Burr, George Elbert   Am 1859-1939
* See 1992 Edition . . . .
Burr, H. Saxton   Am 1889-1973
O/Cb 16x20 A Connecticut Landscape Sby 12/91 302
O/B 8x10 Cloudy Day Mys 11/91 275
Burr, John   Sco 1831-1893
O/C 48x36 Grandmother's Advice But 11/91 2,200
Burras of Leeds, Thomas   Br 19C
* See 1991 Edition . . . .

Burri, Alberto   It 1915-
O/Wd 4x5 Muffa Sby 2/92 11,000
Burrington, Arthur Alfred   Br 1856-1925
* See 1991 Edition . . . .
Burriss, R. Hal   Am 1892-
W/Pa 20x29 Drying the Nets, Mantistique, MI 1944 Eld 4/92 . 193
Burt, Charles Thomas   Br 1823-1902
* See 1992 Edition . . . .
Burton, Arthur Gibbes   1883-
G/Pa 28x17 Exhibition Poster, 1942 Yng 4/92 150
Burton, Richmond   1960-
O/L 96x60 Punctured Space 1989 Chr 5/92 17,600
O/C/Pa 17x20 Faceted Space #3 1989 Chr 2/92 6,600
Busch, J. A. H.   Dut 19C
* See 1992 Edition . . . .
Busch, Wilhelm   Ger 1832-1908
O/C 7x11 Cow and Windmill at Twilight 1863 Sby 7/92 . . . 5,720
Bush, Jack   Can 1909-1977
A/C 108x37 Tight Band 1969 Hnd 5/92 13,000
G/Pa 30x22 Untitled I Sby 10/91 6,050
O/B 9x11 Bass Lake 1949 Chr 11/91 880
Bush, Norton   Am 1834-1894
* See 1992 Edition . . . .
Bushmiller, Ernest   Am 1905-
Pl/Pa 5x19 Six Comic Strips. Nancy and Sluggo 49 Ilh 11/91 . 800
Pl/Pa 5x19 Three Comic Strips. Sluggo "Nancy" 1949 Ilh 5/92 500
Pl/Pa 15x23 Two Comic Strips. "Fritzi Ritz" 57 Ilh 5/92 450
Busquets, Jean   Fr 20C
O/C 23x28 Leaving the Cathedral Wlf 6/92 625
Bussiere, Gaston   Fr 1862-1929
* See 1991 Edition . . . .
Busson, Charles   Fr 1822-1908
* See 1992 Edition . . . .
Bustos, Hermenegildo   LA 1832-1907
* See 1992 Edition . . . .
Butcher, Laura Page   Am 20C
O/C 52x27 Portrait Mrs. Roberts Fre 4/92 1,350
Buthe, Michael
* See 1992 Edition . . . .
Butler, Edward Brugess   Am 1853-1928
O/C 25x30 Edge of the Desert 1918 Mor 6/92 1,400
Butler, Howard Russell   Am 1856-1934
O/B 16x21 Woman in Garden Night Wlf 6/92 2,000
O/B 13x16 Timid Bather 1920 Skn 5/92 825
P/Pa 7x10 Maine Coast Fre 4/92 200
Butler, Joseph   Swd 1825-1885
* See 1992 Edition . . . .
Butler, Joseph Niklaus   Ger 1822-1885
O/C 36x56 River Landscape 1866 Fre 10/91 7,000
O/C 24x36 Alpine Village 1864 Skn 5/92 2,750
Butler, Mary   Am 1865-1946
O/C 24x29 Pickering Cove Fre 12/91 1,400
O/C 24x32 Early Morning, Monhegan 1926 Slo 4/92 750
O/C 28x36 Boats Off the Rocky Coast Wes 11/91 660
O/C 28x36 Boats Anchored Off Maine Coast Wes 3/92 248
O/Cb 16x20 Mountain Study Eld 5/92 150
Butler, Rozel Oertle   Am 20C
O/C 39x30 Mexican Flower Market Lou 12/91 1,900
O/C 50x40 Boy Selling Flowers Dum 7/92 550
Butler, Theodore Earl   Am 1876-1937
* See 1992 Edition . . . .
Butler, Thomas   Br a 1750-1759
* See 1992 Edition . . . .
Butman, Frederick A.   Am 1820-1871
* See 1990 Edition . . . .
Butteri, Giovanni Maria   It -1606
* See 1991 Edition . . . .
Buttersach, Bernhard   Ger 1858-1909
* See 1992 Edition . . . .
Buttersworth, James Edward   Am
1817-1894
O/C 26x40 Racing off Sandy Hook Chr 12/91 187,000
O/C 12x16 New York Harbor Chr 5/92 41,800
O/B 10x12 Yacht Race Sby 5/92 19,800
O/C 12x16 Running Before the Wind Sby 12/91 12,100

O/B/M 9x12 Ships Approaching Port Chr 9/91 8,800

Buttersworth, Thomas   Br 1768-1842
O/C 18x24 Table Bay Sby 6/92 11,000
O/C 14x18 The Victory at Portsmouth Chr 2/92 6,600
O/C 17x21 Shipping off a Lighthouse Chr 2/92 6,050

Buttner, Werner   1954-
* See 1992 Edition

Button, A.   20C
O/B 8x10 Near the Shore Yng 4/92 175

Button, Albert Prentice   Am 1872-
O/Cb 5x6 Along the Neponset River Skn 3/92 550
P/Pa 20x16 Windmill Yng 4/92 475
O/B 8x11 Nantasket Shore Yng 4/92 400

Buzzi, A.   It 19C
W/Pa 12x9 Italian Girls: Two Fre 10/91 500

Buzzi, Achille   It 19C
O/Pn 14x11 The Greeting Chr 5/92 1,320

Bye, Arthur E.
O/B 12x16 Blossoming Chestnut Ald 5/92 130

Bye, Ranulph   Am 20C
W/Pa 22x30 Wagon in Field Ald 3/92 600
W/Pa 14x19 Harbor Scene Fre 10/91 200

Bygrave, William   Am 19C
O/C 22x34 Schooner Viola Passing Gibralter Fre 4/92 8,200

Byles, William Hounsom   Br a 1890-1916
O/C 20x30 Away From the Tape Sby 6/92 6,050

Byrd, Gibson   Am 20C
G/Pa 8x10 Tree Early Light 88 Hnd 6/92 225

Byron, *   Am 20C**
O/C 14x22 Rocky Shore Slo 7/92 100

Byron, Bourmond   Hai 1923-
O/M 24x48 Village by a River Wes 11/91 852
O/M 38x28 Figures in Haitian Landscape 1956 Slo 2/92 650
O/M 24x36 Combat de Coqs Chr 5/92 528
O/M 48x24 Paysage Haitien Chr 5/92 528
O/M 48x48 Tropical Landscape Sby 10/91 440

Byron, Michael   1954-
O/Pn 48x72 The King's Dogs 82 Chr 2/92 2,200

Byrum, Ruthven Holmes   Am 1896-
O/C 27x35 Country Road, Indiana Wlf 10/91 350

Caballero, Luis   Spa 1943-
* See 1992 Edition

Caballero, Maximo   Spa 19C
* See 1991 Edition

Cabanel, Alexandre   Fr 1824-1889
O/Pn 11x9 Andromeda '65 Sby 5/92 5,500
K/Pa 9x7 Study of a Female Head Chr 10/91 1,650

Cabie, Louis-Alexandre   Fr 1853-1939
O/C 19x33 A Beynac-Dordogne 1901 Slo 10/91 1,500
W/Pa 4x6 Riverscape with Cottage 1896 Hnd 6/92 250

Cabot, Hugh   Am 1930-
O/C 18x24 Arizona Landscape Lou 6/92 500

Cabre, Manuel   Ven 1890-
O/C 15x24 El Avila en la Florida 1932 Sby 5/92 22,000

Cabrera, Miguel   Mex 1695-1786
O/C 57x43 Coronacion de la Virgen Sby 5/92 77,000

Cacciarelli, V*   It 19C**
W/Pa/B 22x15 The Singing Cardinal Sby 1/92 2,750

Cachoud, Francois Charles   Fr 1866-1943
O/C 26x27 Clair de Lune Sby 5/92 6,600
O/C 15x18 Cottages at Moonlight Chr 5/92 2,640
O/C/B 11x15 Village Au Soir But 11/91 1,760

Cadell, Francois Campbell B.   Br 1883-
* See 1992 Edition

Cadenasso, Giuseppe   Am 1858-1918
O/C 27x22 Scene Near Mills College But 6/92 13,200
O/C 22x16 Eucalyptus in a Meadow But 2/92 7,700
P/Pa 7x9 Walk Through the Field But 10/91 3,575
O/Cb 14x10 Woman by a Pond But 6/92 3,025
O/C 18x24 Shepherd and Flock But 10/91 1,760
P/Pa 15x22 Dusk But 6/92 1,320
P/Pa 10x16 Berkeley Marsh But 6/92 1,100

Cades, Giuseppe   It 1750-1799
* See 1992 Edition

Cadmus, Paul   Am 1904-
Pl&Pe/Pa 10x14 Greenwich Village Cafeteria Chr 5/92 7,150
H&P/Pa 22x15 Male Nude Kneeling 42 Skn 9/91 7,150
Cp/Pa 12x14 Male Nude, No. MN8 Chr 3/92 4,400
H,C,K&W/Pa 24x13 Envy #1 Sby 12/91 3,410
H&P/Pa 13x16 Reclining Male Nude Skn 9/91 3,025
MM/Pa 8x11 Burt, A Still Life 1970 Skn 9/91 1,320
C/Pa 11x9 Three Drawings 1944 Sby 12/91 990
I&W/Pa 11x5 Male Nude Standing 1972 Skn 9/91 935

Cadora, E.   It 20C
W/Pa 15x9 Venetian Canal Fre 4/92 125

Cadorin, Ettore   Am 1876-1952
W/Pa 7x12 Venetian Canal Scene Wes 3/92 330

Cady, Fred   Am 1855-1960
O/C 16x20 Sunland California 33 But 2/92 1,320

Cady, Harrison   Am 1877-1970
Pl/Pa 25x20 Poor Family at Vegetable Stand 18 Ilh 11/91 . . 750

Cady, Henry   Am 1849-
O/B 5x8 Rocky Coast Mys 6/92 440

Cady, Sam
* See 1990 Edition

Caffe, Nino   It 1909-1975
O/B 28x16 Natura Morta Col Piviale Sby 10/91 6,325
O/Pn 9x11 Avvocati Sby 10/91 4,400
O/Pn 8x16 La Fomarina Wes 3/92 1,760

Caffi, Margherita   It 17C
O/C 14x17 Still Life of Flowers Sby 10/91 18,700

Caffieri, Hector   Br 1847-1932
* See 1991 Edition

Caffyn, Walter Wallor   Br -1898
* See 1992 Edition

Caggiula, M.   It 20C
G/Pa 8x13 Views of Mt. Vesuvius Slo 9/91 50

Cagnacci, Guido   It 1601-1663
* See 1992 Edition

Cagniart, Emile   Fr 1851-1911
* See 1992 Edition

Cagnoni, Amerino   It 1853-
* See 1992 Edition

Cahoon, Charles Drew   Am 1861-1951
O/Ab 9x12 Tidal Marsh, Harwich Bor 8/92 2,750
O/Pn 14x18 Evening Forest Landscape Eld 7/92 1,430

Cahoon, Martha   Am 1905-
W/Pa 15x11 Home is the Sailor Eld 8/92 1,018
O/B 8x10 The Tiger Bor 8/92 1,000

Cahoon, Ralph   Am 1910-1982
O/M 23x30 Still Life Scrimshaw Basket w/Shell Eld 8/92 . . 11,000
O/B 18x24 Nantucket Fish Co. Bor 8/92 8,500
O/M 11x15 Ship Building with Mermaids Eld 8/92 3,410
O/B 17x22 Reeling in a Mermaid But 5/92 2,090

Caillard, C.
O/C 10x8 Church Ald 5/92 60

Caille, Leon Emile   Fr 1836-1907
* See 1992 Edition

Caillebotte, Gustave   Fr 1848-1894
* See 1992 Edition

Cain, Georges-Jules-Auguste   Fr 1856-1919
O/Pn 35x45 Napoleon as First Consul 1899 Sby 2/92 30,800

Caironi, Luigi   It 19C
* See 1992 Edition

Calame, Alexander   Sws 1810-1864
O/C 32x39 La Handeck 1860 Sby 2/92 17,600

Calder, Alexander   Am 1898-1976
I&Pe/Cd 6x4 Eight Drawings of Sculpture Sby 11/91 30,800
G/Pa 43x29 Untitled (Circus Series) '74 Sby 5/92 24,200
I/Pa 22x30 Tightrope Walkers: Double 1932 Sby 5/92 16,500
G/Pa 31x23 Untitled '44 Sby 2/92 16,500
Pl/Pa 19x14 Handstand on Swing 1932 Chr 5/92 15,400
G&I/Pa 18x23 Stabile Beast Sby 11/91 12,100
I,Mk&W/Pa 22x30 Untitled 51 Sby 2/92 12,100
G/Pa 30x43 Untitled 65 Sby 6/92 12,100
G/Pa 22x30 Untitled 1975 Sby 2/92 10,450
G/Pa 29x43 Red Eagle 68 Sby 6/92 9,900

G/Pa 29x42 Figure Group 65 Sby 2/92 9,350
G/Pa 30x43 Untitled 74 Sby 10/91 8,800
G/Pa 29x39 Untitled 75 Sby 2/92 8,800
G/Pa 11x15 Composition with Spiral and Snake Sby 2/92 . 8,250
G&I/Pa 29x43 Spirals on the Rock 68 Chr 2/92 8,250
G/Pa 30x42 Umbrellas 65 Sby 6/92 8,250
G/Pa 23x31 Untitled 73 Sby 2/92 8,250
G&I/Pa 30x43 Untitled 70 Chr 5/92 8,250
G/Pa 30x42 Untitled 64 Chr 2/92 7,700
G&I/Pa 30x42 Untitled 64 Chr 2/92 7,700
G/Pa 22x31 Untitled 72 Sby 2/92 7,700
G,I&W/Pa 30x43 The Red Tube '73 Wes 11/91 7,150
G/Pa 43x29 Untitled 69 Sby 2/92 7,150
G/Pa 30x43 Carrefour 72 Sby 6/92 6,875
G&I/Pa 41x43 Pied Noir No. 2 Chr 11/91 6,600
G/Pa/B 29x50 Untitled 62 Sby 2/92 6,600
G/Pa 43x29 Spiral 70 Sby 6/92 6,050
G&I/Pa 15x43 Lighthouse and Ships 75 Chr 5/92 5,720
G/Pa 30x23 Abstract Composition 74 But 5/92 5,500
G&I/Pa 31x23 Untitled 68 Chr 2/92 5,500
G/Pa 21x30 Untitled 65 Sby 6/92 5,225
G/Pa 43x29 Untitled 71 Sby 6/92 5,225
G/Pa 29x43 Untitled 67 Sby 2/92 4,675
G/Pa 22x30 Untitled 64 Sby 6/92 4,675
G/Pa 31x23 Untitled 66 Sby 10/91 4,510
G&I/Pa 31x23 Black Zig Zag 63 Chr 2/92 4,400
G&I/Pa 23x31 Boomerang and Comma 67 Chr 11/91 4,400
G&I/Pa 23x31 Figure and Striped Profile 62 Chr 2/92 4,400
G/Pa 23x31 Sleazy Threads 71 Sby 2/92 4,400
G/Pa 30x41 Untitled 62 Sby 10/91 4,400
G/Pa 43x30 Untitled 71 Sby 10/91 4,290
G/Pa 31x23 At Last a Yellow Saucer 71 Sby 10/91 4,125
G&I/Pa 21x36 Untitled 76 Chr 5/92 3,850
G/Pa 29x22 Untitled 65 Sby 6/92 3,850
G&I/Pa 30x22 Black Stalagtites 75 Chr 11/91 3,300

Calderini, Marco It 1850-
* See 1992 Edition . . . .

Calderon, Charles-Clement Fr 20C
O/C 18x26 View of Venice Sby 1/92 6,050
O/C 22x32 Venice w/Santa Maria Della Salute Chr 10/91 . 4,620
O/Pn 13x16 The Lagoon, Venice Chr 5/92 4,400
O/Pn 7x13 Venetian Canal Scene Wes 11/91 742

Calderon, Philip Hermogenes Br 1833-1898
O/C 26x17 A Woodland Nymph 1883 Chr 5/92 22,000
O/Pn 11x16 Chronicles of the Court Sby 2/92 9,900

Calderon, William Frank Br 1865-
O/C 26x54 The Ambush 1887 Chr 2/92 7,700

Caldwell, B. Am 20C
Pe&P/Pa 20x14 Dropped Doll Fre 10/91 80

Caldwell, Edmund Br 1852-1930
* See 1992 Edition . . . .

Cale, George Viscont Eng 19C
* See 1992 Edition . . . .

Caliari, Paolo It 1528-1588
O/C 46x33 Saint Catherine of Alexandria Chr 1/92 440,000
O/C 20x16 Young Man, Bust Length Chr 5/92 176,000

Calies, R. Br 20C
O/C 16x13 Pastoral Scene Hnd 3/92 250

Califano, John Am 1864-1924
O/C 30x50 Extensive Mountain Landscape Slo 4/92 1,800
O/Ab 12x16 Fiddler on a Tree Dum 12/91 600

Caliga, Isaac Henry Am 1857-
O/Pn 5x4 Young Woman 1884 Skn 9/91 880

Calixto De Jesus, Benedito Brz 1853-1927
O/C 14x20 Chacara de Martins Chr 5/92 13,200

Callahan, Jack 20C
P/Pa 27x20 Young Girl Yng 4/92 100

Callari, Paolo It
* See 1991 Edition . . . .

Calliano, Antonio Rafaelle It 1785-1824
O/C 30x53 Scene from the Trojan War Chr 5/92 24,200

Callot, Jacques Fr 1592-1635
* See 1991 Edition . . . .

Callow, E. Br 19C
O/C 26x40 The Haywagon Chr 2/92 1,650

Callow, John Br 1822-1878
O/C 30x51 Shipping off the Coast 68 Chr 2/92 5,280
O/C 18x32 Unloading the Catch But 11/91 1,320

Callow, William Eng 1812-1908
* See 1992 Edition

Callowhill, James Am 19C
W/Pa 10x34 Sailboats on the Mediterranean Slo 10/91 200

Calogero, Jean It 1922-
O&MM/C 22x18 Lady with a Yellow Bird Slo 9/91 150

Calvaert, Dionisio Flm 1540-1619
O/Cp 11x9 Holy Family with Two Angels Sby 5/92 7,150

Calvi, Ercole It 1824-1900
* See 1992 Edition

Camacho, Jorge Cub 1934-
* See 1991 Edition

Camarasa, Hermengild Anglada Spa 1873-1959
O/Pn 21x26 Danza Gitana Chr 10/91 165,000
O/C 71x48 La de Los Ojos Verdes Chr 10/91 93,500

Camarero, J. L. Am 20C
O/C 24x20 Spanish Dancer Fre 10/91 30

Camarroque, Charles Fr 19C
O/C/B 79x35 Odalisque 1875 Sby 7/92 7,425

Cambiaso, Luca It 1527-1585
K,Pl&S/Pa 11x8 Madonna della Misericordia Chr 1/92 . . 2,420

Cambier, Guy Fr 1923-
O/B 11x9 Figures in Landscape Lou 12/91 650
O/C 16x13 Head of a Woman Lou 12/91 400

Camerarius, Adam a 1650-1689
O/C 28x22 Young Man in a Landscape Sby 10/91 10,450

Cameron, Robert Hartly Am 1909-
O/C 24x36 Playing in the Surf Fre 4/92 1,650

Caminade, Alexandre Francois Fr 1789-1862
O/C 22x18 Jeune Fille a la Poupee Lisant Sby 5/92 16,500

Camino, Guiseppe It 1818-1890
O/B 38x29 Paesaggio Verdeggianti Sby 10/91 22,000

Camoin, Charles Fr 1879-1965
O/C 21x26 Maisons a Seville Sby 5/92 68,750
O/C 21x26 Ferme a Verdelot Chr 11/91 26,400
O/C 18x22 La Petite Afrique Par Mistral Sby 6/92 11,000

Campagno, Tomas Spa 1857-
O/C 35x25 Gypsy Guitarist Hnd 10/91 1,800

Campbell, H. Am 20C
O/B 16x12 Street Scene Fre 4/92 200

Campbell, Paul Zane 20C
* See 1991 Edition . . . .

Campbell, Stephen 20C
O/C 112x112 Two Men Gesturing in Landscape Sby 10/91 . 7,700

Camphausen, Wilhelm Ger 1815-1885
* See 1992 Edition . . . .

Campigli, Massimo It 1895-1971
O/C 29x36 Donne Con Guanti 1937 Chr 11/91 330,000
O/C 35x46 Donne a Paessaggio 56 Chr 5/92 264,000
O/C 32x18 Busto di Donna Chr 11/91 143,000
Y/Pa 8x5 Figure Femminili Chr 11/91 2,200

Campio, H. It 19C
O/C 26x20 Gondola on a River Hnz 5/92 3,400

Campion, George B. Br 1796-1870
* See 1992 Edition . . . .

Camporeale, Sergio Arg 1937-
W&Pe/Pa 31x47 Retrato de Familia 1988 Chr 5/92 10,450

Campos, Florencio Molina 20C
* See 1992 Edition . . . .

Camus, Blanche Augustine Fr 19C
* See 1990 Edition . . . .

Canade, Vincent Am 1879-
O/C 16x25 Houses by an Inlet Sby 12/91 385

Canal, Giovanni Antonio It 1697-1768
O/C 26x38 Grand Canal from Palazzo Grimani Sby 5/92 . . 1.485M

Canaletto It 1697-1768
O/C 26x38 Grand Canal from Palazzo Grimani Sby 5/92 . . 1.485M

Canas, Benjamin   Brz 1933-
* See 1992 Edition ....

Canaveral Y Perez, Enrique   Spa 19C
* See 1990 Edition ....

Candia, Domingo   Arg 1896-
* See 1991 Edition ....

Candido, Peitro   Dut 1548-1628
* See 1991 Edition ....

Cane, Louis   1943-
G&H/Pa 30x22 Untitled 1977 Chr 5/92 825

Canedo, Alexander   Am 20C
O/B 20x20 Landscape Mys 6/92 330

Canella, A***   It 20C
W&Pe/Pa/B 19x14 The Connoisseur 1880 Sby 7/92 1,320
W/Pa 13x10 Young Woman by a Well Sby 7/92 770

Canevari, Carlo   It 1922-
O/Pn 24x12 Nuns with Balloons; Clown: Two Wes 3/92 .. 550
O/Pn 12x7 Flying Nuns Lou 6/92 200

Caniff, Milton   Am 1907-1988
Pl/Pa 6x20 Comic Strip. "Terry & the Pirates" 38 Ilh 11/91 ... 800

Cannella, Pizzi   1955-
* See 1992 Edition ....

Cantagallina, Remigio   It 1582-1630
* See 1992 Edition ....

Canter, Albert M.   Am 1892-
O/C 18x24 Spring Landscape 1916 Fre 4/92 250

Canton, Gustav Jakob   Ger 1813-1885
O/C 22x42 The Rest Sby 2/92 8,800

Cantu, Federico   Mex 1908-1989
O/M 22x18 Autorretrato 1934 Sby 11/91 30,800
O/B/Pn 20x24 Desnudo 33 Sby 11/91 24,200
Pl/Pa 14x10 Mujer con Alacran Sby 5/92 4,400

Canu, Yvonne   Fr 1921-
O/C 21x29 Notre Dame Sby 2/92 7,700
O/C 24x32 St. Tropez en Automne Sby 6/92 6,050
O/C 24x29 Venise, Sta. Maria de la Salut Chr 5/92 4,950
O/C 21x26 Le chemin de St. Tropez Chr 5/92 3,080
O/C 20x24 Piquenique en Touraine Chr 2/92 3,000

Caparn, Thos. J.
W/Pa 15x29 Seascape 1897 Ald 3/92 2,600
W/Pa 15x29 Seascape 1897 Ald 3/92 200

Capella, Francesco   1714-1787
* See 1992 Edition ....

Capone, Gaetano   It 1845-1920
W/Pa 15x9 Italian Courtyard Fre 10/91 1,700

Capp, Al   Am 1909-1979
l/Pa 6x22 Two Comic Strips. "Lil' Abner" 39 Ilh 11/91 600
O/C 20x22 Boat Dock 1945 Ald 3/92 375

Cappelli, Pietro   It -1924
* See 1991 Edition ....

Capron, Jean Pierre   Fr 20C
O/C 24x29 Maison aux Toits Roses 71 Hnd 3/92 800

Capuletti, Jose Manuel   20C
O/C 22x18 La Pose Sby 2/92 2,310
O/C 13x10 Le Depart; Esquisse: (2) Sby 6/92 2,090

Caputo, Ulisse   It 1872-1948
O/B 6x11 Le Jardin de Luxembourg, Paris Sby 2/92 8,250

Carabain, Jacques Francois   Bel 1834-1892
O/C 31x19 La Via Pescari, Vicenza, Italie Sby 5/92 11,000

Caracciolo, Giovanni Battista   It 19C
* See 1991 Edition ....

Caraud, Joseph   Fr 1821-1905
* See 1992 Edition ....

Caraud, R.   Fr 19C
O/Pn 23x18 Lady with Her Maidservant 97 Hnd 5/92 7,500

Caravia, Thelya Flora   It 20C
O/C 24x17 Harbour Scene Mys 6/92 385

Carballo Y Segura, Bernabe   Spa 20C
O/C 17x9 View of a Street in Summer 1915 Sby 7/92 880

Carchoune, Serge   20C
* See 1991 Edition ....

Cardenas, Juan   Col 1939-
O/C 32x38 Taller de la 94 Chr 5/92 20,900
O/L 22x28 Mujer y Piano Chr 11/91 19,800

Cardenas, Santiago   Col 1933-
O/C/Pn 28x38 Espejo y Pared 74 Chr 11/91 4,400

Cardi, Ludovico   It 1559-1613
* See 1991 Edition ....

Cardona, Juan   Spa 19C
* See 1990 Edition ....

Carelli, A***   It 19C
W/Pa/B 10x15 Naples Harbor w/Volcano 1868 Sby 1/92 .. 1,980

Carelli, Consalave   It 1818-1900
O/Pn 10x16 Bay of Naples Chr 10/91 22,000
O/Pn 8x17 Bay of Naples Chr 2/92 6,600
O/C 12x16 Coming Home Yng 2/92 4,500

Carelli, Giuseppe   It 1858-1921
O/Pn 13x19 The Bay of Naples Sby 5/92 11,000
O/Pn 7x14 A View of Amalfi Wes 11/91 4,510

Carena, Felice   It 1879-1966
O/C 52x59 The Wayfarer 1911 Sby 1/92 51,700

Cargnel, Antonio   It 20C
O/C Size? Vicele di Siena Sel 5/92 150

Cargnel, Luccio   It 20C
O/B 5x9 Fishing Boat near a Town Yng 2/92 125

Cargnell, V. Antonio   It 1872-1931
O/C 19x27 Street Scene Wlf 6/92 2,500

Cariani   It 1485-1547
O/C 29x25 Gentleman, Wearing Black Chr 5/92 63,800

Cariani, Varaldo J.
O/C 30x36 The Red Gum Hnz 10/91 1,200
O/C 30x36 Sycamore--Early October Hnz 10/91 900

Carillo, Lilla   Mex 1930-
* See 1990 Edition ....

Carlandi, Onorato   It 1848-1939
* See 1992 Edition ....

Carles, Arthur Beecher   Am 1882-1952
C/Pa 25x19 Slippers Fre 10/91 1,550
H/Pa 8x10 Cello Players Fre 4/92 250
W/Pa 13x10 Seated Nude Yng 4/92 250

Carlevarijs, Luca   It 1663-1727
* See 1992 Edition ....

Carlier, Modeste   Bel 1820-1878
O/C 40x32 Still Life Flowers in a Brass Urn Chr 2/92 ... 27,500
O/C 39x32 Still Life Assorted Flowers Violets Chr 2/92 ... 22,000
O/C 36x24 Still Life Vase of Roses and Lilacs Chr 2/92 .. 19,800
O/C 36x24 Still Life Assorted Flowers Chr 2/92 18,700
O/C 39x30 Still Life Flowers, Cherries, Pears Chr 5/92 ... 17,600
O/C 36x24 Nature Morte Aux Roses et au Homard Sby 5/92 9,075
O/C 36x24 Nature Morte Aux Fleurs et L'Orange Sby 5/92 .. 8,250
O/C 24x16 Vase of Pink and Yellow Roses Chr 2/92 6,600
O/C 36x24 Still Life with Game Dum 7/92 3,000
O/Pn 20x16 Playing with the Kittens Chr 5/92 1,650

Carlieri, Alberto   It 1672-1720
O/C 29x38 Feast in the House of Simon Chr 5/92 13,200

Carlin, James   Am 1910-
O/C 25x30 Subway Riders Sby 4/92 1,760
O/C 30x36 Checker Players 1935 Yng 4/92 1,500
W/Pa 20x26 Local Bar Yng 2/92 800
O/C 24x30 The Music Class Yng 4/92 750
W/Pa 18x24 Newark Street Scene Yng 4/92 650
W/Pa 18x24 Orchestra Yng 4/92 600
W/Pa 22x28 The Village Yng 4/92 600
O/C 24x30 Rainy Day Mys 6/92 578
W/Pa 18x24 Circus Yng 4/92 500
O/C 24x30 Ice Storm Yng 4/92 500
W/Pa 21x27 Nude and Life Class Yng 4/92 500
W/Pa 21x28 Bathers Fre 4/92 400
W/Pa 15x22 Old House in Union, New Jersey Fre 12/91 ... 110

Carlsen, Dines   Am 1901-1966
O/M 20x24 Danish Farm Hnz 10/91 1,300
O/B 20x24 Norwegian Harbour Scene Mys 11/91 440
O/M 12x15 Rapids and Rocks Hnz 5/92 425
O/M 15x12 Tree on a Cliff Hnz 5/92 375

Carlsen, Soren Emil   Am 1853-1932
O/C/B 39x45 A Freshening Breeze Chr 5/92 60,500
O/C 25x30 Along the Sound Chr 3/92 49,500
O/C 20x24 Copper Kettle and Coffee Pot Sby 12/91 24,200

O/C 12x14 Still Life Grapes, Wine and Stein '29 Durn 1/92 14,000
O/C 35x30 A Woodland Scene Chr 3/92 8,800
O/C 6x8 Still Life '92 Sby 5/92 4,950
O/C 24x38 Still Life Manta on a Table 84 Doy 12/91 4,250
O/C 27x48 Fisherman's Table 1884 Doy 12/91 4,000
O/C 21x16 Landscape Wlf 9/91 4,000
W/Pa 16x12 Woman Sewing Yng 4/92 700
O/Pn 15x18 Surf #7 Fre 10/91 475
O/Pn 6x8 Hillside Fre 10/91 300
O/C 9x12 Surf #6 Fre 10/91 275
W/Pa 9x13 Village Scene 1891 Eld 7/92 110

Carlson, Carl A. Am 1900-
W/Pa 25x19 On the Subway Mys 11/91 55

Carlson, John Fabian Am 1875-1945
O/C 25x30 February Gaiety Chr 9/91 14,300
O/Cb 12x16 Snowy Copse Chr 6/92 3,080
O/C 14x10 Portrait of William Thomson Slo 4/92 400

Carlyle, Florence Can 1864-1923
O/C 22x27 Piano Lesson Sbt 5/92 7,012

Carmichael, James Wilson Br 1800-1868
O/C 24x36 Fresh Breeze Off Whitby 1840 Sby 6/92 24,200

Carmienke, Johann Hermann Am 1810-1867
O/C 16x24 Shipwreck Along a Rocky Coast 1867 Sby 4/92 2,200

Carneo, Antonio It 1637-1692
O/C 29x47 Archimedes Chr 1/92 19,800

Carnicero, Antonio It 1748-1814
* See 1991 Edition ....

Caro-Delvaille, Henry Fr 1876-1926
* See 1991 Edition ....

Carolus, Jean Bel a 1867-1872
* See 1992 Edition ....

Carolus-Duran, Emile Auguste Fr 1838-1917
O/C 17x30 Nu Allonge Sby 5/92 5,500

Caron Fr 20C
O/Pn 14x20 Impressionistic River Landscape Sel 12/91 ... 450

Caron, Antoine Fr 1521-1599
* See 1991 Edition ....

Caron, Paul Archibald Can 1874-1941
* See 1992 Edition ....

Caroselli, Angelo It 1585-1652
* See 1992 Edition ....

Carpaccio, Vittore It 1450-1522
O&T/Pn 23x19 Madonna and Child at Parapet Sby 1/92 .. 77,000

Carpeaux, Jean-Baptiste Fr 1827-1875
O/C 32x26 La Generale de L'Espinasse Sby 5/92 38,500

Carpenter, Fred Green Am 1882-1965
* See 1992 Edition ....

Carpentier, Evariste Bel 1845-1922
O/C 28x36 Trouble Brewing 1883 Chr 2/92 17,600

Carpioni, Giulio It 1611-1674
K/Pa 13x9 Studies of Women Conversing Chr 1/92 3,080

Carr, Henry Br 1894-1970
* See 1992 Edition ....

Carr, Lyell Am 1857-
O/C 21x31 Calm After the Battle 1898 Chr 11/91 1,540

Carr, M. Emily Can 1871-1945
P/Pa 35x20 Totem Poles/Nirvana Sbt 11/91 46,750
O/Pa 32x21 Forest Interior Sbt 11/91 21,505
O/Pn 8x12 View of a Chateau Sbt 5/92 5,610

Carr, Samuel S. Am 1837-1908
O/C 12x18 Boy in Straw Hat with Calf Sby 5/92 9,900
O/C 12x16 Family Portrait Wlf 9/91 3,000
O/C 16x24 The Little Shepherdess Wes 11/91 2,750

Carra, Carlo It 1881-1966
* See 1992 Edition ....

Carracci, Annibale It 1560-1609
* See 1991 Edition ....

Carracci, Lodovico It 1555-1619
O/C 29x37 Christ Carrying the Cross Sby 5/92 71,500

Carree, Michiel Dut 1657-1747
* See 1991 Edition ....

Carreno, Mario Cub 1913-
O/C 41x31 Dialogo de las Islas 4 Sby 5/92 264,000

O/C 20x24 Sobre el Malecon 42 Chr 11/91 49,500
O/C 29x41 Sin Titulo 50 Chr 5/92 44,000
T/B 14x17 Parque Tropical 46 Sby 11/91 16,500
O/C 30x25 Plantacion 41 Chr 11/91 16,500
O/C 34x28 Poder Femenino 76 Sby 5/92 14,300
T/Pa 23x28 Mujeres 47 Sby 11/91 11,000
T&I/Pa 21x17 Figura Reclinada 48 Sby 5/92 9,900
T/Pa 11x16 Figuras con Pescado 48 Sby 5/92 8,800
I/B 20x16 Metamorfosis 47 Chr 5/92 4,400

Carrick, John Mulcaster Br a 1854-1878
O/C 40x50 The Recruiting Sergeant 1862 Sby 5/92 49,500

Carrier-Belleuse, Albert E. Fr 1824-1887
* See 1992 Edition ....

Carrier-Belleuse, Louis Robert Fr 1848-1913
O/C 21x29 A Stroll in the Park Chr 2/92 5,500
O/C 21x29 Elegant Figures Flower Garden Chr 2/92 5,500

Carrier-Belleuse, Pierre Fr 1851-1932
P/C/B 32x40 Danseuse 1895 Sby 10/91 14,850

Carriere, Eugene Fr 1849-1906
O/C 17x13 Tete de sa Femme Sby 10/91 12,100
O&R/C 17x14 Pensive Woman Sby 1/92 5,500

Carrigan, William Am 1868-1939
O/C 24x33 Side Streets Lou 6/92 1,100
O/C 24x33 Side Streets But 11/91 605

Carrington, Leonora Br 1917-
O/C 48x35 The Temptation of St. Anthony Chr 5/92 440,000
O/C 39x32 Ordeal of Owain Chr 11/91 88,000
T/Pn 23x36 Paisaje de Venus Sby 5/92 66,000
Pt&Wx/Pn 28 dia Luna Grande/Blanca 1951 Sby 11/91 .. 20,900
G,I&Pe/Pa 13x9 Figura a Caballo Chr 11/91 17,600
Pe/Pa 11x14 Figure Holding a Creature Sby 2/92 2,200

Carroll, John Am 1892-1959
O/C/B 16x13 Portrait of a Girl 1935 Dum 11/91 1,700
O/C 24x16 Nude Hnd 3/92 550

Carroll, Lawrence 1954-
MM/Wd 108x48 Greying Eyes 1989 Chr 2/92 11,000

Carse, Alexander Br 19C
O/C 20x24 Celebration in a Tavern Sby 7/92 4,400

Carson, Frank Am 1881-1962
W/Pa 12x16 Bathers Yng 4/92 150
W/Pa 18x16 Flying Flags Hnd 3/92 150

Carte, Antoine Bel 1886-1954
* See 1992 Edition ....

Carter, Clarence H. Am 1904-
O/B 13x15 Still Life Apples, Books, Pitcher 1926 Chr 12/91 6,500
O/C 22x27 Old Tree and River '41 Wlf 6/92 2,700
W/Pa 22x14 St. Mary's, Portsmouth, OH 1936 Dum 12/91 .. 600
A/C 11x15 Abstract Red and White 66 Hnd 10/91 400

Carter, Dennis Malone Am 1827-1881
* See 1990 Edition ....

Carter, Fernando A. Am 1855-1931
O/Cb 12x16 Country Path in Springtime 1925 Wes 11/91 ... 192

Carter, Gary Am 1939-
* See 1990 Edition ....

Carter, Pruett Am 1891-1955
O/C 25x36 Couple at a Picnic Ilh 11/91 2,100
O&R/C 40x30 Western Couple on Rockledge 1922 Ilh 11/91 1,800
O/C 17x24 Blonde Watching Couple Embrace Ilh 5/92 1,600
O/C 23x18 Woman Offering Drink Water Ilh 5/92 ... 1,500
O/C 19x20 Girl Writing a Letter Mor 6/92 850
W/Pa 15x18 Indian on Horseback Mor 3/92 650

Carter, Sydney Br 19C
* See 1990 Edition ....

Cartier, Jacques Fr 20C
* See 1991 Edition ....

Cartwright, Isabel Branson Am 1885-
* See 1992 Edition ....

Caruso, Bruno It 1927-
O/Cb 10x12 Composizione astratta Chr 5/92 825

Cary, William de la Montagne Am 1840-1922
O/C 11x16 Buffalo Bill Geronimo Peace Pipe Skn 11/91 ... 3,575
O/C 7x15 Death of an Elk Sby 4/92 1,045

Carzou, Jean Fr 1907-
  * See 1992 Edition . . . .
Casali, Andrea It 1720-1783
  * See 1992 Edition . . . .
Casals 20C
  O/C 26x32 Dock Scene Slo 2/92 150
Casanoday, Arcadio Spa 19C
  * See 1991 Edition . . . .
Casanova, Francois-Joseph It 1727-1802
  K&S/Pa 15x20 A Runaway Wagon Chr 1/92 6,050
  K&S/Pa 14x19 A Cavalry Skirmish Chr 1/92 4,180
  Pe&S/Pa 14x14 Carriage and Horsemen Leaving Chr 1/92 . 2,860
Casanovas, Enrique Spa 19C
  * See 1992 Edition . . . .
Casanove, Francesco Spa
  * See 1990 Edition . . . .
Cascella, Michele It 1892-
  O/C 50x30 Roses From Portofino Sby 10/91 17,600
  O/C 24x36 Fantasy of the Abruzzi But 5/92 12,100
  O/C 36x24 Yellow Tulips But 11/91 6,600
  MM/B 23x27 Still Life Flowers Doy 11/91 2,400
Cascella, Tommaso It 1890-1968
  * See 1991 Edition . . . .
Casciaro, Giuseppe It 1863-1941
  O/Pn 24x33 La Vecchia Chiesa, Capri Sby 5/92 7,700
  P&K/B 18x20 Casa di Contadini 913 Chr 2/92 1,980
  P&K/B 14x19 Sailboat on a Wooded Lake 916 Chr 2/92 . . . 1,980
Case, Edmund E. Am 1840-1919
  * See 1992 Edition . . . .
Case, Frank E. Am 20C
  O/C 47x53 Solomon's Return Wlf 10/91 650
  O/C 29x35 Hiawatha 1928 Wlf 10/91 450
  O/C 29x35 City Scenic Wlf 10/91 400
  O/C 23x35 Cairo Evening Wlf 10/91 350
  O/C 23x29 Congress Lake Wlf 10/91 350
  O/C 29x35 Arabian Market Wlf 10/91 325
  O/C 4x7 The Oregon Trail Wlf 10/91 325
  O/C 24x36 Fall Landscape Wlf 10/91 300
  O/C 23x30 Arabian Arch Wlf 10/91 225
Casenelli, Victor Am 1867-1961
  * See 1992 Edition . . . .
Casile, Alfred Fr 1847-1909
  * See 1991 Edition . . . .
Casilear, John William Am 1811-1893
  O/C/B 14x12 Mountain Cascade Chr 9/91 6,050
  O/B 6x12 The Haywagon 69 Chr 3/92 3,850
  O/C/Cd 13x19 Woodland Stream Doy 12/91 1,600
Cass, George Nelson Am -1882
  * See 1992 Edition . . . .
Cass, Rosa Bowkee
  O/C 14x12 New York Lake Scene Dum 9/91 125
Cassanova, R. Eur 19C
  O/C 21x44 Still Life of Fruit Slo 10/91 750
Cassatt, Mary Stevenson Am 1844-1926
  P/Pa 25x21 Elsie Cassatt Holding a Big Dog Chr 11/91 . . . 1.54M
  P/Pa/C 30x25 The Crochet Lesson Sby 5/92 935,000
  P/Pa 18x24 Mother Combing Sara's Hair Sby 5/92 605,000
  (CtrProof) 29x25 Simone in a Large Plumed Hat Sby 5/92 . . 88,000
Casse, John Eng 19C
  O/C 19x30 Ships at Sea Hnz 5/92 275
Cassidy, Ira Diamond Gerald Am 1879-1934
  O/C 18x24 The Scout But 4/92 22,000
Cassiga, L. Am 20C
  O/B 16x20 Seaside Villa 1934 Yng 2/92 275
Cassigneul, Jean Pierre Fr 20C
  O/C 36x26 Le Fauteuil de Rotin Sby 10/91 28,600
Casson, Alfred Joseph Can 1898-1992
  O/C 30x39 The Bowden Refinery Sbt 5/92 28,050
  O/B 9x11 October, Poverty Lake, 1950 Sbt 11/91 14,960
  W/Pa 10x10 The New Subdivision 1921 Sbt 5/92 6,311
Castagnola, Gabriele It 1828-1883
  O/C 44x28 The Kind Gesture 1876 Sby 5/92 9,900
  O/C 35x28 Faust and Marguerite 1870 Sby 2/92 5,775

Castaigne, J. Andre Fr 1861-
  O&R/C 31x21 Ship in Ancient Egyptian Port 1906 llh 11/91 . 2,500
  C/Pa 12x8 Two Women, One Swooning llh 11/91 600
Castan, Pierre Jean Edmond Fr 1817-1892
  O/Pn 11x9 Good News 1869 Chr 2/92 15,400
  O/Wd 10x8 Disturbing News 1876 Dum 2/92 2,500
Castaneda, Alfredo Spa 1938-
  O/C 47x47 ¿Que Tanto Me Conoces? 79 Sby 11/91 132,000
  MM/Pn 27x36 El Timonel 76 Sby 11/91 22,000
Castano, G.
  O/C 30x39 The Procession Dum 7/92 150
Casteels, Peeter (III) Flm 1684-1749
  * See 1992 Edition . . . .
Castegnaro, Felice It 1872-
  O/C 14x20 Venezia But 5/92 1,870
Castellano, S.
  O/C 9x7 Girl's Head Dum 4/92 250
Castelli, Bartolomeo It 18C
  * See 1991 Edition . . . .
Castelli, Giovanni Paolo It 1659-1731
  O/C 13x22 Grapes, Apples, Peaches Chr 5/92 24,200
Castelli, Luciano
  * See 1992 Edition . . . .
Castello, Battista It 1545-1639
  G&Gd/V/B 18x14 Adoration of the Kings 1613 Sby 1/92 . . 71,500
Castello, Valerio It 1625-1659
  * See 1991 Edition . . . .
Castellon, Federico Am 1914-1971
  O/B 22x23 The Gathering Wlf 9/91 3,400
  O/B/B 7x4 Neo-Classical Figures '48 Sby 6/92 1,870
Castelucho, Claudio Spa 1870-1927
  * See 1992 Edition . . . .
Castex-Degrange, Adolphe Louis Fr 1840-
  * See 1992 Edition . . . .
Castiagni, A. Am 19C
  O/C 20x24 Working Late into the Night '93 Fre 12/91 170
Castiglione, Giovanni Benedett It 1609-1665
  * See 1992 Edition . . . .
Castillo Y Saavedra, Antonio Spa 1603-1668
  * See 1992 Edition . . . .
Castillo, Jorge 1933-
  O/C 48x60 Two Characters 86 Chr 5/92 19,800
  A&O/C 60x48 El Estudiante 1986 Chr 5/92 16,500
Castino, A. 20C
  O/C 16x20 La Mietitura Yng 4/92 225
Castoldi, Guglieimo It 1852-
  * See 1991 Edition . . . .
Castres, Edouard Sws 1838-1902
  O/Pn 10x14 Highway Robbery 1874 Sby 1/92 4,400
Castro Y Velasco, Antonio A. Spa 1655-1726
  * See 1992 Edition . . . .
Caswall, Anna Maria Br a 1870-1874
  W&G/Pa/B 5x5 Portrait of a Chick Skn 3/92 715
Catala, Luis Alvarez Spa 1836-1901
  O/C 29x49 Princess Borghese Bestowing 1879 Sby 10/91 104,500
  O/C 18x26 An Unexpected Visitor 1879 Sby 2/92 38,500
  O/C 13x19 The Mountain Pass Sby 5/92 24,200
  O/Pn 14x9 In the Boudoir 1878 Sby 10/91 17,600
Catalan, Ramos Chl 20C
  O/C 18x16 Mountain Landscape Lou 3/92 200
Cathelin, Bernard Fr 1919-
  O/C 51x35 Marche aux Grands Arbres 1965 Chr 11/91 . . . 26,400
  O/C 46x32 Premiere Neige 67 Doy 11/91 14,000
  O/C 46x32 Bouquet d'Arums 1962 Doy 11/91 12,500
  O/C 20x26 View of Marbella 59 Sby 10/91 7,700
Cathell, Edna S. Am 1867-
  O/C 26x22 Bouquet Hnd 5/92 950
Catlin, George Am 1796-1872
  * See 1992 Edition . . . .

Catti, Michele   It 1855-1914
O/Pn 6x12 Street Scene Wlf 9/91   3,000
O/Pn 6x12 Street Scene Wlf 9/91   3,000
O/C Size? Shoreline with Fishing Boats Dum 8/92   450
Cauchois, Eugene Henri   Fr 1850-1911
O/C 28x42 Still Life Flowers and Cherries Chr 10/91   17,050
O/C 42x28 Flowers Oranges Overturned Pitcher Chr 5/92 . .   11,000
O/C 22x26 Still Life with Peaches, Grapes Chr 2/92   8,250
O/B 15x20 Jardin De Fleurs Sby 5/92   7,150
O/C/M 25x21 Still Life with Zinnias Chr 2/92   6,600
O/C 26x22 Still Life Pansies and Geraniums Sby 1/92   6,050
O/C 11x18 Yellow and Red Roses Chr 2/92   4,400
O/C/M 25x20 Peaches and Flowers Chr 2/92   3,300
O/C 19x25 Blooming Fields Skn 11/91   1,100
Caula, Sigismondo   1637-1713
* See 1992 Edition
Cavailles, Jean Jules Louis   Fr 1901-1977
O/C 32x21 Les Tulipes Sby 10/91   9,350
Cavaliere D'Arpino   It 1560-1640
* See 1992 Edition
Cavalieri, Luigi   It 19C
* See 1992 Edition
Cavallino, Bernardo   It 1616-1656
* See 1990 Edition
Cavallon, Giorgio   Am 1904-
O/C 52x38 Untitled 1962 Chr 11/91   24,200
O/C 24x20 Untitled 54 Chr 11/91   18,700
Cave, Jules Cyrille   Fr 1859-
O/C/M 36x28 Fleur Eclose 1903 Sby 10/91   29,700
Cavedone, Giacomo   It 1677-1640
K/Pa 15x11 Saint Stephen Looking Upwards Chr 1/92   3,850
Cavilles, Jules   Fr 1901-
* See 1991 Edition
Cawthorne, Neil   Br 1936-
O/C 20x20 Coming Into Line Sby 6/92   4,180
O/C 20x30 Saddling at Cheltenham Sby 6/92   3,575
O/C 20x30 Saddling Paddock, Goodward Sby 6/92   2,860
O/C 20x26 At the Start, Newmarket '84 Sby 6/92   2,090
O/C 18x24 Also Ran, Lingfield 84 Sby 6/92   1,320
Cay, R. H.   Con 18C
I&S/Pa 7x5 Soldier with Bayonnet 1775 Sby 1/92   330
Cazes, Romain   Fr 1810-1881
* See 1992 Edition
Cazin, Jean Charles   Fr 1841-1901
O/C 32x39 French Village on a River Chr 5/92   22,000
O/C 20x25 The Road to the Village Chr 2/92   8,800
O/C 24x28 River Landscape at Sunset Chr 2/92   6,050
O/C 22x18 A Road by the Sea Chr 5/92   3,500
O/C 24x20 Portrait of a Man Hnd 5/92   750
Ceccarelli, Naddo   It 14C
* See 1991 Edition
Cecchi, Adriano   It 1850-
W/Pa 22x16 Mediterranean Villa Slo 7/92   1,500
Cecco Bravo   It 1601-1661
O/C 38x57 Allegory of Autumn/Summer: Two Chr 5/92 . . .   71,500
Ceccobelli, Bruno   1952-
O/Wd 48x97 Ape 1985 Sby 10/91   11,000
Cecconi, Alberto   It 1897-
O/C 20x28 Children in a Flowery Meadow Hnd 10/91   1,900
Cecconi, Eugenio   It 1842-1903
O/C 6x6 Two Dogs Mys 6/92   2,530
Cecconi, Lorenzo   It 1867-
O/C 23x39 An Afternoon Idyll Wlf 9/91   20,000
Cedor, D. L.   Hai 20C
O/Pn 30x25 Exorcisme 50 Fre 4/92   1,500
Celesti, Andrea   It 1637-1712
O/C 40x42 Pharoah's Daughter Finding Moses Sby 10/91 . .   8,250
Celis, Perez   20C
* See 1992 Edition
Cellardo, John   Am 1918-
Pl/Pa 15x22 Comic Strips. "Tarzan" Ih 5/92   450
Celmins, Vija   20C
* See 1991 Edition
Celommi, Pasquale   It 1860-
O/C 21x32 Prize of the Sea Chr 2/92   8,250

Celommi, Raffaello   It 1883-
O/C 18x26 Bringing Home the Catch Chr 10/91   2,860
Celoni, A.   Con 19C
* See 1992 Edition
Celos, Julien   Bel 1884-
O/C 22x26 View of Bruges Sel 4/92   1,550
Cemin, Saint Clair   1951-
W&H/Pa 18x24 Study for Bronze Table 1987 Chr 5/92 . . .   1,210
W&H/Pa 18x24 Untitled 1990 Chr 2/92   550
Centurion, Emilio   Arg 1894-1970
O/Pn 22x27 Paisaje 1930 Sby 5/92   16,500
Ceramano, Charles Ferdinand   Bel
1829-1909
O/C 28x40 Shepherdess at Rest w/Flock 1881 Chr 2/92 . . .   8,250
Cercone, Ettore   It 1850-1896
* See 1990 Edition
Cerny, Charles
O/C 15x19 Trompe L'Oeil Still Life Wlf 11/91   625
Ceruti, Giacomo   It 18C
* See 1991 Edition
Cesari, Giuseppe   It 1560-1640
* See 1992 Edition
Cezanne, Paul   Fr 1839-1906
WG&Pe/Pa 7x9 L'Eternel Feminin; Chapeau: Dbl Sby 11/91 495,000
W/Pa 13x20 Arbres au Bord; Paysage: Double Chr 11/91   440,000
W/Pa 12x18 Vue Prise de L'Atelier Chr 11/91   220,000
Pe/Pa 5x9 Livre Sur Une Table Sby 5/92   60,500
Pe/Pa 7x5 Portrait Madame Cezanne Sby 5/92   55,000
Pe/Pa 4x4 Femme Nue Assise Chr 11/91   13,200
Chab, Victor   Arg 1930-
* See 1990 Edition
Chabaud, Auguste
O/C 21x29 Le Troupeau Dans le Ravin Sby 6/92   5,225
Chabellard, J. Charles   Fr 19C
* See 1991 Edition
Chadeayne, Robert Osbourne   Am 1897-
* See 1992 Edition
Chadwick, Edith Clark   20C
O/C 18x24 Snow Day Yng 4/92   150
Chadwick, Lynn   Br 1914-
* See 1992 Edition
Chadwick, William   Am 1879-1962
O/C 15x19 Connecticut Laurel Brd 8/92   688
O/C 14x18 Adriatic Villa Brd 8/92   605
O/C 14x18 Italian Village, Sunday Brd 8/92   578
Chaffee, Gertrude   Am 20C
O/B 18x22 California Mission Lou 12/91   150
Chaffee, Samuel R.   Am 20C
W/Pa 16x25 Sunset Over the Marshes Mys 6/92   550
W/Pa 12x19 Autumn Beach Scene Mys 11/91   522
W/Pa 16x25 Snowscene Mys 6/92   412
Chagall, Marc   Fr 1887-1985
O/C 39x28 Bouquet de fleurs 937 Chr 5/92 . . . .   2.86M
O/C 58x45 La Muse 1978 Sby 5/92 . . . .   1.1M
O/C 32x21 Couple avec bouquet de fleurs Chr 5/92   770,000
O/C 32x26 Reve de Joie Sby 5/92   605,000
G/Pa 23x31 Les Amoureux au Cap Ferrat 1949 Sby 11/91   495,000
G&Y/Pa 26x20 Arlequin a la Lune Jaune Sby 5/92   385,000
G,Br&I/Pa 11x8 Le Violiniste Dans la Neige 912 Sby 5/92   308,000
O/C 19x15 Bouquet de Bleuets Sby 2/92   286,000
G,W&P/Pa 25x19 Figures a l'Ane Vert Sby 5/92   198,000
WG&S/Pa 17x16 Two Lovers/Moonlight 1952 Sby 11/91   198,000
G/Pa 22x20 Les Amoureux au Bouquet Chr 11/91   154,000
W&Pe/Pa/B 10x12 Violoniste Chr 11/91   143,000
W,G&K/Pa 13x10 Le Jupon 913 Chr 11/91   132,000
O&G/Pa/C 16x13 Les Deux Amants 1959 Sby 5/92   132,000
G,I&Y/Pa 13x10 Lovers w/Flowers & Still Life Sby 5/92 .   121,000
Pl&W/Pa 13x10 Le Coq et la Fille Sby 11/91   79,750
I&Pe/Pa 9x8 Eiffel Tower with Lovers 1949 Sby 11/91 . . .   31,900
Pl/Pa 4x6 Maternite Chr 11/91   6,050
Chale, Gertrudis
O/B 14x20 Mujeres Sentadas Chr 5/92   1,650
Chaleye, Joannes   Fr 1878-1960
O/B 29x21 Mountainous Landscape Sel 12/91   550

Chalfant, Jefferson David Am 1856-1931
* See 1990 Edition . . . .
Challener, Frederick Sproston Can 1869-1959
* See 1992 Edition . . . .
Chalon, Henry Bernard Br 1770-1849
O/Pn 7x10 Bichon Maltais 1819 Sby 6/92 4,125
O/C 18x24 Dapple Grey Pony 1833 Sby 6/92 2,860
Chaloner, H. W. Am 19C
MM/Pa 19x26 Shipwreck Off Minot's Light 1849 Bor 8/92 . . 200
Chaloner, Walter Am 19C
W/Pa 11x21 Title? Mys 6/92 110
Chamberlain, Norman Stiles Am 1887-1961
* See 1991 Edition . . . .
Chamberlin, Frank Tolles Am 1873-1961
O/C/C 16x19 Landscape Mor 3/92 950
W/Pa 13x12 Fruit in a Green Bowl 1940 Mor 3/92 650
Chambers Am
O/C 42x32 Refreshed Woman Holding Glass Ih 5/92 750
Chambers, C. Bosseron Am 1883-
W/Pa 14x10 Guardian of the Tomb 1905 Slo 2/92 200
Chambers, Charles E. Am 1883-1941
O/C 21x30 Man on Couch, Woman Ih 11/91 2,750
Chambers, George W. Eng 19C
* See 1990 Edition . . . .
Chambers, Richard E. E. Am 1863-1944
W/Pa 10x14 Horse Ranch, Mountains: Two 1890 Chr 3/92 . 3,300
Pe/Pa 5x9 H.G.S. in Bed 1891 Wes 11/91 220
Chambers, Winifred V.
O/C 26x34 Bear and Eagle Fishing Ald 3/92 200
Champagne, Horace Can 1937-
P/Pa 21x29 Firey Sunset, B.C. Sbt 5/92 748
Champney, Benjamin Am 1817-1907
O/C 10x8 Haying 67 Chr 5/92 5,280
O/C 10x14 Bowl/Still Life with Cherries 1905 Skn 3/92 . . . 2,200
O/C 14x10 Jar of Mountain Laurel 1905 Skn 9/91 990
O/B 10x7 Mountain Laurel Skn 9/91 468
Champney, James Wells Am 1843-1903
P/B 23x20 Portrait of a Young Woman Sby 12/91 2,970
O/C 12x20 Nature's Poetry Chr 6/92 2,640
O/C 10x14 Pond at the Edge of the Wood Skn 9/91 275
Chandler
P/Pa 18x40 Fisherman Ald 3/92 575
Chaney, Al Am 20C
O/C 25x30 Seascape 37 Hnd 12/91 100
Chapelain-Midy, Roger Fr 1904-
* See 1992 Edition . . . .
Chaperon, Eugene Fr 1857-
O/C 29x40 Fete Garde de la Nationale 1927 Sby 5/92 3,300
Chapin, Bryant Am 1859-1927
O/C 12x16 Still Life Peaches Skn 5/92 1,870
O/C 12x16 Still Life Plums 1919 Skn 5/92 1,650
O/C 9x12 Still Life Apples '10 Skn 5/92 1,320
O/C 18x30 Landscape Mys 11/91 605
Chapin, C. H. Am 19C
W/Pa 30x50 Autumn Lake Scene Chr 11/91 2,200
Chapin, Charles C. Am 19C
W/Pa Size? Landscape Hnd 3/92 250
Chapin, Francis Am 1899-1965
W&I/Pa 14x10 Sailboats on the Water Wlf 3/92 50
Chapin, James Ormsbee Am 1887-1975
O/C 33x21 Studio Window Chr 9/91 4,950
Chaplin, Arthur Fr 1869-
* See 1992 Edition . . . .
Chaplin, Charles Fr 1825-1891
O/C 40x50 Personification of the Arts Chr 5/92 22,000
O/C 40x50 Personification of the Sciences Chr 5/92 22,000
Chapman, Carlton Theodore Am 1860-1926
W/Pa 6x6 Yacht Race Mys 11/91 138
Chapman, Conrad Wise Am 1842-1910
O/C 17x24 Naturaleza Muerta Fruta y Flores 1908 Sby 5/92 71,500
O/C 17x24 Naturaleza Muerta con Pinas 1908 Sby 5/92 . . 68,750

Chapman, John Gadsby Am 1808-1889
O/C 27x43 Lake of Albano 1873 Chr 11/91 2,860
O/C 18x14 Roman Vintage 1856 Slo 7/92 2,250
O/Ab 10x10 Shepherd of the Campagna 1867 Slo 4/92 900
Chapman, John Linton Am 1839-1905
O/C 30x72 Appian Way 1870 Chr 9/91 28,600
Chappel, Alonzo Am 1828-1887
* See 1991 Edition . . . .
Charbot Fr 19C
O/C 19x24 Washerwoman by a Mill But 5/92 1,980
Charchoune, Serge Rus 1888-1975
P&O/Pa 21x17 Cubist Figure Wlf 6/92 1,100
Chardin, Jean-Baptiste-Simeon Fr 1699-1779
O/C 15x18 Still Life Glass Mug, 3 Walnuts Sby 1/92 . . . . . 2.2M
Charlemont, Eduard Aus 1848-1906
* See 1991 Edition . . . .
Charlet, Emile Bel 1851-
O/C 35x28 Stag in a Snowy Landscape Sel 9/91 1,400
Charlet, Frantz Bel 1862-1928
W/Pa/B 17x27 Three Children Picking Flowers Sby 1/92 . . . 3,850
Charlet, Nicholas Toussaint Fr 1792-1845
W/Pa 7x6 Tireuse de Cartes Sby 7/92 2,200
Charlot, Jean Fr 1898-1979
O/C 30x40 Ninos Desamparados 38 Chr 5/92 20,900
O/C 15x20 Lavanderas 37 Chr 11/91 8,800
O/C 20x16 Mexican Figures Wlf 9/91 5,000
O/C 19x15 El Sacrificio de Isaac 32 Chr 5/92 4,400
W/Pa/B 16x23 Dancing Children Sby 6/92 4,125
W/Pa 30x22 Huida a Egipto 52 Sby 5/92 3,300
P&Cp/Pa 15x11 Mujer Sentada 24 Sby 5/92 1,760
O/C 10x8 Female Draped in Blue 1940 Slo 2/92 900
Charnay, Armand Fr 1844-1916
* See 1991 Edition . . . .
Charpentier, Georges Fr 20C
O/C 26x32 Dans Le Port de la Rochelle Sby 5/92 14,300
O/C 26x32 Port Scene with Fishing Boats Hnd 10/91 5,400
Charpentier, Jean-Baptiste Fr 1728-1806
* See 1991 Edition . . . .
Charreton, Victor Fr 1864-1936
O/C 21x26 Un Chateau avec des Fleurs But 5/92 33,000
O/C 18x22 Jardin de Ville en Printemps Sby 2/92 29,700
O/C 29x36 Printemps Chr 2/92 19,800
O/C 24x29 Fauteuil dans le Jardin Sby 2/92 18,700
Charton, Ernest Fr 1813-1905
O/C 28x44 Valparaiso 1862 Chr 5/92 46,200
Chartrand, Esteban Spa 1825-1889
* See 1992 Edition . . . .
Chase, Adelaide Cole Am 1868-1944
O/C 29x21 Still Life Brd 5/92 3,630
O/C 22x18 Flowers & Figurine Mys 11/91 1,595
Chase, Frank Swift Am 1886-1958
* See 1991 Edition . . . .
Chase, Henry (Harry) Am 1853-1889
* See 1992 Edition . . . .
Chase, Louisa Am 20C
A/C 78x72 Rose 1979 Sby 10/91 3,300
Chase, Sidney M. Am
* See 1990 Edition . . . .
Chase, Susan Miller 20C
O/B 8x10 Children on the Beach Yng 4/92 450
Chase, William Merritt Am 1849-1916
P/Pa 16x20 Shinnecock Studio Interior Sby 12/91 693,000
O/C 17x15 Ordering Lunch by Seaside 1893 Sby 12/91 . . 220,000
O/Pn 16x12 Portrait Woman: The White Dress Sby 12/91 198,000
O/Pn 8x12 Gondolas Along Venetian Canal Sby 3/92 25,300
O/C 18x24 Still Life with Pepper and Carrot Chr 5/92 24,200
O/C 16x20 Still Life China Vase, Copper Pot Sby 5/92 22,000
O/Pn 8x12 Venice (View of Navy Arsenal) 1913 Chr 5/92 . . 22,000
O/Pn 13x16 Sketch of My Hound, "Kuttie" Sby 5/92 20,900
O/Pn 13x9 Along the Stream 1876 Chr 5/92 16,500
O/C 15x10 Sketch of a Woman Holding a Fan Sby 5/92 . . . 16,500
O/C 24x20 Portrait of a Woman 1894 Sby 5/92 8,800
O/C 39x31 Portrait of a Woman Wes 5/92 3,080

Chasseriau, Theodore Fr 1819-1856
* See 1992 Edition . . . .
Chat, A. A. Am a 1890-1910
O/C 24x16 In the Farmyard 1902 But 6/92 2,750
Chat, John Alonzo Am 1869-
W/Pa 17x11 A Quiet Chat Fre 10/91 100
Chataud, Marc-Alfred Fr 1833-1908
* See 1992 Edition . . . .
Chateaux, R* Fr 19C**
O/C 47x59 Portrait of a Lion 1894 Sby 1/92 4,400
Chateignon, Ernest Fr 19C
O/C 10x14 The Gleeners Fre 10/91 1,800
Chatelet, Claude-Louis Fr 1753-1794
* See 1991 Edition . . . .
Chatterton, Clarence K. Am 1880-1973
* See 1992 Edition . . . .
Chaultse, J. W. F. Am 20C
O/C 32x43 Coastal Scene Wlf 10/91 200
Chaves Y Ortiz, Jose Spa 19C
O/C 11x18 Spanish Horsemen Hnz 5/92 8,250
Chavez, Gerardo Per 1937-
O/C 24x32 Feu et Lumiere 90 Chr 11/91 5,280
Chavignaud, Georges Can 1865-1944
O/Pn 13x16 Dutch Interior 1910 Sbt 5/92 654
Checa Y Sanz, Ulpiano Spa 1860-1916
* See 1991 Edition . . . .
Chee, Robert Am 1937-
G/Pa 6x7 Indians on Horseback Hnz 5/92 100
Chelminski, Jan Van Pol 1851-1925
* See 1990 Edition . . . .
Chelmonski, Josef Pol 1849-1914
* See 1991 Edition . . . .
Chemetou, Boris Fr 1908-1982
O/C 26x32 La Porte But 5/92 2,750
O/C 18x22 Personnage dans la Ville But 5/92 1,980
Chemiakine, Mikhail Rus 1943-
* See 1992 Edition . . . .
Chemielinski, W. T.
O/B 7x10 Street Scene (4) Chr 5/92 1,430
Chen, Hilo Am 1942-
A/C 72x72 Beach-35 Chr 5/92 6,600
A/C 56x61 Bathroom 35 88 Sby 10/91 4,950
A/C 30x40 Beach-2 Chr 11/91 2,750
Cheney, Russell Am 1881-1945
* See 1992 Edition . . . .
Cheret, Jules Fr 1836-1932
H&Cp/Pa 12x10 Grands Magasins Louvre Sby 10/91 990
Cherkes, Constantine Am 1919-
* See 1992 Edition . . . .
Chery, Jean Rene Hai
O/M 20x24 Fruits d'Haiti Chr 5/92 715
Chestnut, Billy Dohlman Am 20C
* See 1992 Edition . . . .
Chevalier, Peter 1953-
* See 1992 Edition . . . .
Cheviot, Lillian Br 20C
* See 1991 Edition . . . .
Chevolleau, Jean Fr 1924-
O/C 18x13 Le Fregate, No. 196 Lou 6/92 425
Chia, Sandro 1946-
O/C 78x75 Horseman in Front of the Sea 84 Sby 5/92 . . . 77,000
O/C 66x59 Bumble Bee Hunter Sby 2/92 74,250
O/C 90x100 Most Short Post 87 Chr 5/92 66,000
O/Pa/C 58x48 Untitled 1980 Sby 10/91 55,000
O&H/C 64x64 Untitled 79 Chr 2/92 38,500
MM/Pa 39x42 Three Men on a Raft 1982 Chr 5/92 35,200
W,C&G/Pa 29x20 Untitled Chr 2/92 20,900
O&L/C 32x32 Kangaroo Boxing Match 1976 Sby 2/92 . . . 16,500
W,Fp&C/Pa 56x82 Philosophers/Ballerinas 84 Chr 11/91 . . 16,500
O,Y&C/Pa 30x27 Untitled 89 Sby 6/92 4,950
H,Cp&l/Pa 12x9 Two Drawings 83 Chr 11/91 3,960
Chiapory, Bernard Charles Fr 19C
P/Pa/C 36x29 A Spring Nymph 54 Chr 2/92 6,600
P/Pa 34x29 Flora 54 Hnd 10/91 4,400

Chiari, Guiseppe It 1654-1727
* See 1992 Edition . . . .
Chichester, Cecil Am 1891-1963
* See 1992 Edition . . . .
Chierici, Gaetano It 1838-1920
O/C 28x21 Warming Dolly's Hands 1878 Sby 10/91 198,000
O/C 26x18 The Pet Chick 1885 Sby 10/91 93,500
O/C 22x32 First Steps 1876 Sby 10/91 77,000
O/C 22x30 Dinner Time 1871 Sby 10/91 71,500
Child, Carroll Colby Am 20C
W/Pa 9x12 Wooded River Landscape 1906 Sel 9/91 160
Child, Charles
O/B 17x26 Racing Day Ald 5/92 50
O/B 32x16 Looking Over Bluehill Bay Ald 5/92 25
Chillida, Eduardo
* See 1992 Edition . . . .
Chinnery, George Br 1774-1852
O/C 17x14 Inner Harbor, Macao Hnz 5/92 105,000
O/C 13x16 Parnoen's Grotto, Macao Hnz 5/92 53,000
O/C 10x8 A Young Gentleman Bor 8/92 5,000
Chintreuil, Antoine Fr 1816-1873
* See 1991 Edition . . . .
Chiriacka, Ernest Am 1920-
O/C 16x20 Sand Dunes; Noontime Slo 7/92 850
Chittenden, Alice Brown Am 1859-1944
O/C 18x24 Rose Arrangement But 2/92 2,750
Chocarne-Moreau, Paul Charles Fr 1855-1931
O/C 46x36 Boys and Their Sailboats Chr 2/92 46,200
O/C 37x47 Cache Cache Sel 4/92 5,100
Chochon, Andre
O/C 15x22 Place de la Concorde, Paris Sby 10/91 1,320
Choffard, Pierre Phillipe 1730-1809
K/Pa 9x7 Portrait Marie S. V. Carlier 1764 Sby 7/92 715
Choultse, Ivan F. Rus 20C
O/C 20x28 Strelnya Palace, St. Petersburg 16 Sby 10/91 . 12,100
O/Pn 15x18 An Orchard in Spring Sby 10/91 6,600
Chouquet, Rene 20C
* See 1991 Edition . . . .
Christensen, Dan Am 1942-
* See 1992 Edition . . . .
Christensen, Florence Am 20C
O/C 24x16 Lady with Lilacs 1912 Wlf 9/91 2,400
Christiansen, Nils H. Dan 1876-1903
O/B 6x9 Two Winter Fjord Scenes Slo 9/91 1,200
Christie, James Elder Br 1847-1914
O/C 10x14 Girvan, Scotland Lou 6/92 600
Christmas, Ernst William Am 1856-1918
O/B 15x11 Evening Reflections But 6/92 1,045
Christo Bul 1935-
MM/Pb 43x65 Umbrellas (Japan & USA) 1990 Sby 11/91 220,000
MM/B 58x97 Umbrellas (Japan & U.S.) 1989 Chr 5/92 . . 110,000
MM/Pb 28x22 300 Wrapped Trees (Paris) 1969 Sby 11/91 55,000
MM/B 28x22 The Pont Neuf, Wrapped 1975 Chr 5/92 . . 55,000
MM/B 28x22 Valley Curtain (Colorado) 1972 Chr 11/91 . . 41,800
MM/B 28x22 Puerta de Alcala Wrapped 1976 Chr 2/92 . . 33,000
MM/B 28x22 Project Murdoch Ct Melbourne 1969 Chr 5/92 25,300
MM/B 28x22 Wrapped Trees Paris 1969 Chr 2/92 24,200
MM/Cd 22x28 Surrounded Islands, Miami 1983 Doy 11/91 24,000
MM/Pb 28x22 Packed Coast (N.S. Wales) 1969 Sby 11/91 22,000
MM 28x22 Packed Coast (near Sydney) 1969 Sby 5/92 . . 20,900
Pe&l/Pa 22x28 Running Fence, Marin Co 1973 Sby 10/91 16,500
Christy, Howard Chandler Am 1873-1952
O/C 72x83 Three Bathers Sby 3/92 16,500
O/B 54x40 Dazed Man at Train Wreck 09 Ih 11/91 7,500
W/Pa 11x14 Woman Wearing Winged Tiara Ih 11/91 6,750
O/M 24x18 A Point of Contention Sby 12/91 2,860
C,Y&W/Pa 20x13 Fashion Illustration Wes 5/92 1,100
Chryssa
G/Pa 30x22 Three Works 1967 Sby 6/92 990
Church, F. J. Am 20C
W/Pa 20x10 Pilgrim Woman 83 Dum 10/91 2,500
Church, Frederic Edwin Am 1826-1900
* See 1992 Edition . . . .

Church, Frederick Stuart   Am 1842-1923
O/C 32x54 Stonehenge 1907 Sby 12/91 3,080
W&G/Pn 12x22 Woman with Two Lions '94 Lou 12/91 . . 2,300
O/C/B 32x16 Woman and Child on Beach 1907 Dum 6/92 . 1,800
Pl/Pa 12x15 New Hippopotamus in Central Park But 11/91 . 1,650
O/C 26x41 Birds and Blossoms Dum 6/92 950
O/B 25x19 Wildflowers 1912 Chr 6/92 550
R&G&l/Pa/B 18x11 Feeding the Swan Chr 11/91 88
Chwala, Adolf   Czk 1836-1900
O/C 22x34 Moonlit Lake Scene Chr 5/92 3,740
Ciampanti, Ansano   It 16C
* See 1992 Edition . . . .
Ciappa, Carlo   It 19C
O/C 23x25 Extensive Harbor View Chr 2/92 3,080
Ciappa, F. A.   It 19C
* See 1992 Edition . . . .
Ciardi, Beppe   It 1875-1932
O/C 28x36 At the Fountain Sby 2/92 71,500
Ciardi, Emma   It 1879-1933
O/Pn 11x16 Il Colleoni 1926 Sby 2/92 17,600
O/Pn 16x24 San Giorgio Maggiore 1914 Skn 11/91 6,600
Ciardiello, Michel   It 1839-
* See 1991 Edition . . . .
Ciceri, Eugene   Fr 1813-1890
* See 1992 Edition . . . .
Cignaroli, Gianbettino   It 1706-1772
O/C 53x71 The Finding of Moses Chr 10/91 66,000
Cikovsky, Nicolai   Am 1894-1934
O/C 16x20 The Tradewinds Sby 12/91 2,530
O/C 12x16 Dock Scene Wes 3/92 880
Pl&S/Pa 13x21 Bridge in Downtown Manhattan Wes 11/91 . . 330
G/Pa 15x18 Head of a Girl Hnd 6/92 300
W/Pa 17x22 Horses Watering Chr 6/92 275
P&C/Pa 11x17 View of Houses from a Hilltop 30 Chr 6/92 . . 242
Cillis, S.
O/C 18x21 Still Life Peaches, Flowers, Bottle Wlf 6/92 275
Cimaroli, Giambattista   It 1687-1757
O/C 22x28 Landscapes Along a Canal: Four Sby 5/92 . . 319,000
Cimiotti, Gustave   Am 1875-1934
O/Cb 16x20 Harbor at Balboa, California Sby 4/92 1,320
O/Cb 20x24 San Gorgonia from Palm Springs 51 Sby 4/92 . . 1,320
O/Pn 5x9 Crashing Surf Skn 9/91 338
O/C 18x15 The Purple Hills Skn 11/91 330
O/B 8x11 Bagneux, France Hnd 6/92 200
O/C 22x24 New York Empress Tree Slo 12/91 200
Cipolla, Fabius   It 1854-
W/Pa 25x17 The Recital Slo 9/91 3,250
Cipriani, Giovanni Battista   It 1727-1785
I&S/Pa 3x3 Socrates with Mourning Figures Slo 7/92 350
Cirino, Antonio   Am 1889-1983
O/C 20x24 Mother and Child by Their Home Mys 11/91 . . 3,300
O/Cb 8x10 Antique Shoppe Skn 5/92 1,430
O/Cb 8x10 Snowy Village Skn 5/92 825
Cirocco, G.   20C
O/C 24x36 Children on a Beach Sel 4/92 425
Ciry, Michel   Fr 1919-
* See 1992 Edition . . . .
Cisilia, Jose Maria   20C
* See 1990 Edition . . . .
Civetta
* See 1991 Edition . . . .
Civita, Vincenzo   It 19C
* See 1991 Edition . . . .
Claeissins, Anthonie   Flm 1536-1613
O/Pn 16x10 Nobleman; Noblewoman (2) 1576 Chr 1/92 . . 71,500
Claes, Constant Guillaume   Bel 1826-1905
O/C 25x35 The Young Miscreant 1871 Chr 5/92 6,050
Claesz., Aert   Dut 1498-1564
* See 1991 Edition . . . .
Claesz., Anthony   Dut 1592-1635
* See 1990 Edition . . . .
Claesz., Pieter   Dut 1597-1661
O/Pn 23x33 Silver Wine Jar, 3 Roemers 1651 Chr 1/92 . . 60,500

Claghorn, Joseph C.   Am 1869-1947
W/Pa 18x28 Meeting on the Road 1900 But 11/91 935
O/C 18x26 Red Garage: 3 Works Fre 4/92 250
Clair, Charles   Fr 1860-1930
* See 1991 Edition . . . .
Claire, Marie   Can 1939-
* See 1991 Edition . . . .
Clairin, Georges Jules Victor   Fr 1843-1919
O/C 43x40 Opium Smokers 1872 Sby 2/92 33,000
Clapp, Clinton W.   Am 19C
* See 1992 Edition . . . .
Clapp, William Henry   Am 1879-1954
O/M 22x26 Reclining Nude 39 But 10/91 16,500
O/B 16x19 Sunny Brook Hills 42 But 6/92 7,150
O/B 12x10 House Around the Bend But 10/91 1,650
O/B 10x12 Tree Shadows But 6/92 1,650
Clare, E. D.   Eng 19C
O/C 10x14 Still Life of Pineapple, Plum Slo 10/91 160
Clare, George   Br a 1860-1900
O/C 12x10 Primroses and Hawthorne Sby 7/92 3,025
O/C 6x9 Still Life with Fruits: Pair Sby 7/92 1,760
Clare, Oliver   Eng 1853-1927
O/C 12x10 Still Life w/Fruit; Flowers: Pair But 5/92 6,600
O/B 10x8 Still Life with Apples, Grapes Chr 10/91 3,850
O/C 18x14 Still Life with Fruit 90 Sby 7/92 3,575
O/C/M 6x8 Fruit on a Mossy Ground 91 Chr 2/92 1,980
O/C 10x8 Plums and Gooseberries Chr 2/92 1,650
Clare, Vincent   Eng 1855-1930
O/C 16x24 Flowers and Birds' Nests: Pair Sby 5/92 6,600
O/B 7x9 Flowers and Bird's Nest Chr 2/92 3,080
W/Pa 6x9 Flowers; Fruit in Landscape: Pair Slo 9/91 1,400
Clark, *   20C**
O/B 5x12 Roosters Feeding in Barnyard Slo 7/92 275
Clark, Benton   Am 1876-1949
O/C/B 22x18 Interior (Artist's Dining Room) But 2/92 . . . 13,200
O/C 15x18 State Street Bridge But 10/91 7,150
O/C 15x18 On the Deck But 2/92 5,500
O/C 26x32 LaJolla Hills But 2/92 5,225
O/C 26x32 Coronado 22 But 2/92 4,950
W/Pa 16x21 Artist's Studio But 2/92 4,400
O/C 20x24 Gateway, Brittany '01 But 2/92 4,125
O/C 26x32 LaJolla Cove But 2/92 3,850
O/C 36x29 Beachscape Wlf 6/92 3,700
O/C 13x16 Houses in Landscape '09 Mor 6/92 2,750
Clark, C. Myron   Am 1876-1925
O/C 16x24 Grand Canal, Venice Slo 7/92 1,400
O/C 13x19 Golfo di Napoli 1906 Slo 7/92 850
O/C 24x36 Speckled Trout Mys 6/92 605
O/C 32x48 Ocean Scene 1910 Eld 7/92 523
Clark, Dane   Am 20C
O/C 30x36 Aspen in the Morning Slo 4/92 1,800
Clark, Eliot Candee   Am 1883-1980
O/B 16x20 Desert Scene But 10/91 1,430
O/Pn 18x20 Hillside in Kent, Connecticut 1924 Lou 6/92 . . 1,200
O/C 14x20 Long Island, 1912 Lou 6/92 1,200
O/C 20x16 Birches Hnd 10/91 1,100
O/Cb 14x20 Summer Heat Lou 12/91 950
O/C 16x20 Chad's Ford 1916 Lou 12/91 900
O/B 20x24 Autumn Fire Music 1918 Lou 3/92 800
O/B 16x20 Summer 1945 Lou 3/92 800
O/C 30x45 Connecticut Meadows and Hills Slo 12/91 500
O/C 12x9 Venice 1904 Lou 3/92 500
O/C 10x14 Valley Crucis, NC Wes 5/92 468
O/Pn 14x11 Path at the Edge of the Wood 1938 Skn 11/91 . . 412
O/C 11x15 Dune Landscape 31 Hnd 6/92 325
W/Pa 8x11 Mountain Yng 4/92 300
P/Pa 6x10 Castle, Jaipur, India 1937 Slo 9/91 225
O/Cb 12x12 Provincetown 1943 Lou 3/92 200
O/C 10x15 Rural Country, Virginia 1935 Wlf 10/91 200
Clark, James   Br 1858-1943
O/C 39x29 By the Harem Window Sby 10/91 17,050
O/C 18x27 The Meet Sby 6/92 4,125
Clark, Matt   Am 1903-
O/C 24x36 Mining Camp But 11/91 1,100

Clark, Myron Am 1858-1923
W/Pa 10x13 Winter Landscape 1889 Wes 11/91 330
Clark, Paraskeva   Can 1898-1986
W/Pa 12x16 Woodland Still Life Sbt 11/91 1,870
Clark, Roland   Am 1874-1957
O/C 14x16 Geese Landing; Ducks Flying: Pair Doy 12/91 . . 4,750
Clark, S. J.   Br 19C
O/C 20x30 South Church, Essex Skn 9/91 1,320
Clark, W.   Br 19C
* See 1992 Edition . . . .
Clark, Walter   Am 1848-1917
O/C 11x17 Pony Express 1905 Sel 9/91 800
Clark, Walter A.
I/Pa 13x9 Patriotic Symbols Eld 8/92 110
Clark, William   Br a 1827-1841
* See 1990 Edition . . . .
Clarke, John Clem   Am 1937-
O/C 40x44 Chardin--Still Life with Plums 70 Chr 2/92 1,540
O/C 38x18 Bathing Woman II 70 Sby 6/92 880
Clary-Baroux, Adolphe   1865-1933
O/C 14x18 Le Naumachie du Parc Monceau Chr 11/91 . . . 2,200
Claude, Eugene   Fr 1841-1923
* See 1991 Edition . . . .
Claus, Emile   Bel 1849-1924
O/C 46x33 Afternoon Along the River Sby 5/92 159,500
O/C 24x29 Cottage Among Apple Trees Doy 11/91 67,500
O/C 36x29 January Doy 11/91 62,500
Clausell, Joaquin   Mex 1866-1935
O/C/B 25x30 Homenaje a Vincent Van Gogh Chr 5/92 . . . 77,000
O/C 10x13 Paisaje Marino Nocturno Chr 5/92 28,600
O/B 11x6 Vista de Yxtacalco Chr 11/91 19,800
O/Pn 6x11 Paisaje Sby 5/92 17,600
O/B 13x18 Paisaje Fuentes Brotantes Sby 11/91 17,600
O/C/B 9x14 Paisaje Sby 11/91 12,100
Clausen, Franciska   20C
G&Y/Pa 11x8 Abstract Composition Sby 6/92 1,650
Clausen, Sir George   Br 1852-1944
* See 1991 Edition . . . .
Clave, Antoni   Spa 1913-
O/C 46x32 Homme Au Pasteque Sby 11/91 143,000
O/C 35x46 Femme Aux Pasteques 1950 Sby 11/91 137,500
O,L&C/F 57x45 Guerrier au fond rouge 60 Chr 5/92 . . . 137,500
O/C 32x40 Pasteque Noire Chr 11/91 121,000
O/Pa/B 30x22 Roi d'epee Chr 5/92 110,000
O,I,G&Y/Pa 36x29 Le Roi 57 Sby 11/91 88,000
G,O&L/B 28x40 Susanna and Barber Sby 11/91 46,750
O/B 18x13 Femme peintre Chr 5/92 41,800
G,S,K&L/Pa 20x13 Revenge: Costume Design Sby 11/91 . . 28,600
G,S,K&L/Pa 20x13 Costume Design for a Gypsy Sby 11/91 24,200
G,S,K&L/Pa 20x13 Costume Design for Manrico Sby 11/91 24,200
GSK&Pe/Pa 19x38 Susanna & Barber: 3 Costume Sby 11/91 18,700
GW&Pe/Pa 20x43 Susanna & Barber: 3 Costume Sby 11/91 13,200
G&I/Pa 19x25 Susanna & Barber: 2 Costume Sby 11/91 . . 10,450
GSPe&K/Pa 20x25 Susanna & Barber: 2 Costume Sby 11/91 8,800
GS&Pe/Pa 20x14 Susanna & Barber: Costume Sby 11/91 . . 8,800
G&Pe/Pa/B 20x14 Susanna & Barber: Costume Sby 11/91 . . 8,800
G&Pe/Pa/B 19x12 Susanna & Barber: Costume Sby 11/91 . . 8,800
G&K/Pa/B 20x13 Costume Design, Count Luna Sby 11/91 . . 7,700
G,I&Pe/Pa 19x13 Susanna & Barber: Costume Sby 11/91 . . 7,700
G&Pe/Pa 20x14 Susanna & Barber: Costume Sby 11/91 . . 7,700
G&K/Pa/B 20x13 Susanna & Barber: Costume Sby 11/91 . . 6,600
G,W&Pe/Pa 22x15 Susanna & Barber: Costume Sby 11/91 . . 6,600
G&S/Pa 19x13 Susanna & Barber: Costume Sby 11/91 . . . 3,300
Clays, Paul Jean   Bel 1819-1900
O/C 30x44 Marine 1897 Sby 2/92 7,150
O/C 24x23 Ships on the Sea Wes 3/92 2,640
Clayton, Harold   Br 1896-1979
O/C 24x20 Floral Still Life Slo 4/92 3,750
Cleary, W. P.   Eng 20C
O/C 16x22 Portrait of a Hunter 1933 Sel 4/92 175
Clegg and Guttman
* See 1992 Edition . . . .
Clemens, Paul   Fr 20C
* See 1992 Edition . . . .

Clemens, Paul Lewis   Am 1911-
* See 1992 Edition . . . .
Clement, H.
O/C 20x32 Antelope Shooting 1897 Eld 7/92 880
Clement, Marie-Louise   Fr 20C
* See 1991 Edition . . . .
Clement-Serveau   Fr 1886-1972
O/C 10x8 Figure and Still Life 50 Wlf 9/91 2,200
O/Pn 8x10 Still Life with Fruit 60 Wlf 9/91 1,200
Clemente, Francesco   1952-
O/C 79x99 The Midnight Sun IX Chr 5/92 264,000
O/C 66x43 Untitled (Self-Portrait) Chr 11/91 132,000
Pg/L 84x95 Three Out of Nine Chr 5/92 99,000
O/C 59x59 Funerale 1982 Sby 11/91 60,500
O&H/Pn 36x51 Well Known Tree Chr 2/92 46,200
K/Pa 24x18 Untitled Chr 5/92 41,800
P/Pa 24x18 Daughter Sby 11/91 37,400
I&Pg/Pa/L 82x103 Autoritratto 1978 Sby 10/91 28,600
K/Pa 12x12 Untitled Chr 2/92 19,800
Ph/Wd 49x28 Untitled Chr 11/91 16,500
W/Pa 21x27 Untitled Chr 5/92 2,860
Clements, Grace   Am 1905-1969
* See 1992 Edition . . . .
Clemins, Vija
* See 1990 Edition . . . .
Cleminson, R.   Eng 19C
O/C 29x44 Scottish Hunting Scene Dum 11/91 1,100
Cleminson, Robert   Br 19C
O/C 30x50 Stag and Family in a Landscape Sby 1/92 1,870
O/C 12x16 The Day's Bag Chr 2/92 1,650
O/C 12x16 Two Spaniels and Ducks Dum 12/91 1,300
Clerisseau, Jacques-Louis   Fr 1722-1820
* See 1991 Edition . . . .
Clevanot, Ph.   Fr 19C
O/C 32x20 Fisherman's Flirt Hnd 12/91 800
Clime, Winfield Scott   Am 1881-1958
O/B 12x16 Morning At the Dock Skn 11/91 1,760
Clint, Alfred   Br 1807-1883
O/C 16x25 Fishing on a Lake But 5/92 1,210
Clopath, Henriette   Am 1862-1936
O/Cd 10x8 Lady in Interior Slo 7/92 275
Close, Chuck   Am 20C
* See 1992 Edition . . . .
Closson, William Baxter   Am 1848-1926
O/C 30x30 Autumn River Scene Hnd 10/91 850
O/B 10x8 Ladies in the Park Wes 11/91 825
W/Pa 21x15 Ice Storm and Pines 1926 Hnd 10/91 200
Clough, George L.   Am 1824-1901
O/C 8x12 Storm Over the Hudson Chr 3/92 5,280
O/C 24x36 Figures on a Country Road Mys 11/91 2,695
O/C 19x14 The Bath Wlf 6/92 2,000
O/C 24x36 Cows Watering by a Stream Sby 4/92 1,210
Cloveras   Am 20C
O/C 45x18 Chicago and New York: Pair Sel 4/92 175
Cluhade
O/B 16x20 Floral Still Life Dum 1/92 30
Clusmann, William   Am 1859-1927
W/Pa 8x13 Landscape with Windmill Hnz 5/92 100
Clymer, John   Br 20C
O/C 9x7 Harbor Scene Ald 3/92 650
O/C 24x36 Village Scene Lou 12/91 325
Clymer, John Ford   Am 1907-1989
O/B 20x30 Winter Slopes But 4/92 17,600
O/C 35x26 Children Running Through Valley 1960 Ilh 11/91 11,000
O/C 24x34 Inuit Family Sby 4/92 5,500
O/C 25x30 Sailing in the Caribbean Sby 4/92 2,200
C/Pa 11x11 Boy, Grandfather, Dog on Wharf 1961 Ilh 5/92 . . 450
Coale, Donald   Am 1906-
O/M 23x18 Old Fashioned Dress Hnd 5/92 300
Coale, Griffith Baily   Am 1890-1950
O/C 14x50 U.S.S. San Fran. Night Action 1942 Chr 11/91 . . 2,860
Coates, Edmond C.   Am 1816-1871
* See 1992 Edition . . . .
Cobb, Darius   Am 1834-1919
* See 1991 Edition . . . .

Cobb, Henry Ives   Am 1859-1931
G/Pa 14x19 Children Playing in a Park: Pair 56 Slo 9/91 325
O/C 10x14 Still Life Lou 3/92 125
Cobb, Ruth   Am 20C
W/Pa 23x18 The Telephone Skn 5/92 412
Cobbe, Bernard   Br 19C
O/C 26x36 The Pretty Miscreant Hnd 10/91 2,100
Cobbett, Edward John   Eng 1815-1899
O/Pn 18x22 Mother & Child in an Interior 1858 But 5/92 ... 2,750
Cobelle, Charles   Fr 1902-
O/C 24x30 La Tour Eiffel But 5/92 1,650
O/C 24x30 Le Parc Pres de Musee Jeu de Paume But 5/92 1,100
O/C 24x30 Paris, La Tour Eiffel Hnd 10/91 800
O/C 20x24 Village Street Scene Wlf 9/91 800
O/C 10x8 Circus Scene Dum 4/92 450
Cobo, Chema   1952-
O/C 83x78 Art Coining Authenticity 1990 Chr 2/92 4,620
Coburn, Barbara
W/Pa 22x30 Abstract Dum 4/92 125
Coburn, Frederick Simpson   Can 1871-1960
O/C 25x32 Two Horse-Drawn Sleighs '47 Sbt 5/92 26,180
O/C 24x28 The Last Load '22 Sbt 11/91 22,440
O/C 22x28 Logging Road in Winter '29 Sbt 11/91 10,285
Coccapani, Sigismondo   It 1583-1642
* See 1992 Edition ....
Cocco, Gino   It 1933-
O/M 20x30 Roses Lou 3/92 200
Coccorante, Leonardo   It 1700-1750
* See 1992 Edition ....
Cochin, Charles-N (the Younger) 1715-1790
* See 1992 Edition ....
Cochran, Allen Dean   Am 1888-1935
* See 1992 Edition ....
Cockburn, James Pattison   Can 1778-1848
* See 1991 Edition ....
Cockerll, Jon   Am -1991
Ph 12x13 Untitled (#19) Hnd 5/92 50
Cocteau, Jean   Fr 1889-1963
Fp/Pa/B 16x11 Les Amants Sby 6/92 2,970
I/Pa 12x9 Les Rapports Homosexuels Sby 6/92 2,860
Fp&Pe/Pa 10x8 Visage 1960 But 5/92 2,475
I/Pa 7x5 Autoportrait Sby 6/92 2,090
PI/Pa 8x10 Deux Visages 1960 But 5/92 2,090
I/Pa 14x10 Two Figures Dancing Wlf 10/91 2,000
W/Pa 26x20 Profil de Faune a la Brindille 1959 Sby 6/92 . 1,760
I&S/Pa 8x6 Tete D'Homme de Face: Pair 1951 Sby 6/92 .. 1,760
Y/Pa 13x8 Le Tour Eiffel 1961 Chr 11/91 1,540
I/Pa/B 12x10 Tete de Faune 1950 Sby 6/92 1,320
Codaro, V.   It 19C
O/C 23x18 Feline Fancy Chr 2/92 14,300
Codazzi, Niccolo Viviano   It 1648-1693
* See 1992 Edition ....
Codazzi, Viviano   It 1603-1672
O/C 28x52 Capriccio of Mediterranean Harbor Sby 5/92 . 13,750
Codazzi, Viviano & Cerquozzi   It 1603-1672
* See 1992 Edition ....
Codazzi, Viviano & Gargiulio   It 1603-1672
O/C 48x71 Figures in Baroque Loggia Sby 5/92 38,500
Codde, Pieter Jacobsz   Dut 1599-1678
* See 1992 Edition ....
Codino Y Langlin, Victoriano   Spa 19C
* See 1990 Edition ....
Codman, Charles   Am 1800-1842
O/C 15x20 Diamond Cove Brd 8/92 15,400
O/Pn 10x13 River Sunset Brd 8/92 3,080
O/C 12x16 Appeal to the Spirits Brd 8/92 2,970
Codman, Susan   a 1890-1899
W/C 9x12 Scenes Near Ogunquit (6) Yng 4/92 300
Codron, Jef   Fr 19C
* See 1990 Edition ....

Coedes, Louis Eugene   Fr 1810-1906
O/C 25x21 A Day in the Country 1832 Sby 2/92 18,700
Coen, Eleanor
O/C 26x36 The White Cliff Hnz 10/91 600
Coene, Jean Henri   Flm 1798-1866
* See 1991 Edition ....
Coene, Jean-Baptiste   Bel 1805-
O/C 52x30 Library with Two Monks '89 Sel 4/92 5,000
O/B 27x22 European Street in Winter Wlf 9/91 1,700
Coessin De La Fosse, Charles A   Fr 1829-1900
* See 1990 Edition ....
Coeylas, Henri   Fr 20C
O/C 26x32 Young Girl Traveling w/Grandparents Sel 4/92 . 2,000
Coffermans, Marcellus   Flm 1535-1575
O/Pn 9x6 Madonna & Child w/Angel Sby 1/92 36,300
Coffin, William Anderson   Am 1855-1925
O/C 30x40 Sunrise in January 1896 Wes 11/91 2,750
O/C 14x20 Moonrise on the Lake Ald 5/92 475
Coffin, William Haskell   Am 1878-1941
P/Pa 19x15 Smiling Woman, Blue Background Ih 11/91 ... 800
O/C 10x14 Morning 1912 Skn 11/91 440
Coggeshall-Wilson, J.   Br 20C
O/C 35x35 Pont-Aven But 11/91 3,300
Cogniet, Leon   Fr 1794-1880
* See 1990 Edition ....
Cohen
O/C 25x36 Dock with Tug Boats Dum 1/92 30
Cohen, Frederick E.   Am -1858
O/C 31x38 Coming to the New World 1851 But 11/91 ... 2,200
Cohen, Lois   Am 20C
O/Cb 24x30 Fishermen of San Pedro But 6/92 2,200
Cohn, Harold   Am 1908-
O/C 36x33 Woman Seated Face in Hands Wlf 6/92 2,000
O/Pa 17x9 Nude (3) Lou 6/92 200
Cohn, Max Arthur   Am 1903-
O/C 20x24 Washington Square Chr 9/91 3,520
Coignard, James   Fr 1925-
O,Sd&L/C 22x18 Univers Carceral et Noir Chr 5/92 ... 3,850
Coignard, Louis & Boulanger, L   Fr 1810-1867
O/Pn 17x24 Le Berger et Ses Vaches Hnd 5/92 1,600
Col, Jan David   Bel 1822-1900
* See 1992 Edition ....
Colacicco, Salvatore   Am 20C
O/B 26x32 America's Cup Yacht Susannah Sby 12/91 . 3,575
O/Pn 20x30 Sailing Ship Hudson Slo 12/91 850
O/Pn 20x30 Sailing Ship Minerva Slo 12/91 850
Colahan, Colin
O/C 30x25 Trafalgar Square World War II Sby 10/91 .. 5,500
O/C 20x24 View of the Seine Sby 10/91 1,320
Colburn, Eleanor   Am 1866-1939
O/Cb 8x10 Corral Lou 3/92 100
Colburn, Francis Peabody   Am 1909-
O/C 16x22 Still Life Apples and Pitcher Skn 9/91 605
Colburn, L. W.   Am 20C
O/C 24x20 Woman in Green Dress 1917 Yng 2/92 100
Colby, George Ernest   Am 1859-1913
W/Pa 7x14 Country Path Slo 9/91 125
W/Pa 23x15 Birch Lined Path Dum 10/91 100
Cole, Alphaeus Philemon   Am 1876-1900
O/C 12x16 The Early Bird Skn 11/91 385
O/C 12x16 Basket of Peaches Eld 7/92 330
Cole, Charles Octavius   Am 1814-
O/C 48x39 The Shell Gatherer 1856 Chr 3/92 13,750
Cole, George Vicat   Br 1810-1883
O/C 38x60 Richmond Hill 76 Chr 2/92 49,500
Cole, Joseph Foxcroft   Am 1837-1892
O/C 23x36 Farm Scene Brd 8/92 1,540
O/C 18x26 Pastoral Landscape 1871 Brd 8/92 1,210
O/C 11x17 A Twilight Farm View, Autumn Skn 9/91 825
Cole, L. E.   Am 19C
O/C 23x19 Portrait Young Gentleman 1888 Brd 8/92 231
Cole, Solomon   Eng 19C
O/C 36x28 Portrait of Gentleman Fre 4/92 1,550

Cole, Thomas   Am 1801-1848
O/C 25x36 Landscape with Manfred Fre 10/91 40,000
Cole, Walter   Am 20C
O/B 16x20 Dock Scene Yng 2/92 275
Coleman, Blanche E.   Am 19C
O/C 30x36 Rocky Seascape, Rockport Eld 7/92 330
Coleman, Charles Caryl   Am 1840-1928
O/C 10x15 Venetian Scene Mys 6/92 2,310
Coleman, Enrico   It 1846-1911
W/Pa 14x21 Leading the Horses Sby 5/92 16,500
W/Pa/B 14x19 Greek Theater at Tusculum Skn 3/92 4,620
W/Pa 14x20 Leading Horses to Water Slo 2/92 2,750
Coleman, Francesco   It 1851-
W/B 21x15 Artist and Model Chr 10/91 1,320
Coleman, Glenn O.   Am 1887-1932
O/C 24x36 Manhattan Beach Amphitheatre Night Slo 12/91 . 6,000
Coleman, Harvey B.   Am 1884-1959
O/B 25x30 Autumn Landscape Mor 11/91 475
Coleman, Marion   Am -1925
O/C 25x36 The Rose Garden But 2/92 3,025
Coleman, Mary Darter   Am 1894-1956
O/M 16x20 Landscape Mor 11/91 650
O/C 25x30 Winter Landscape Mor 6/92 600
Coleman, Michael   Am 1946-
O/C/M 24x30 On the Nunga River Sby 3/92 5,225
O/Pn 16x26 Landscape with Sunset 1968 Sby 12/91 1,650
Coleman, Ralph P.   Am 1892-1968
O/C 22x36 Couple in an Interior 1935 Ilh 11/91 2,500
Coleman, William Stephen   Br 1829-1904
O/C 26x17 Sibling Affection Chr 2/92 6,050
W/Pa 9x7 A Summer Afternoon Wlf 9/91 1,500
Colfer, John Thomas   Am 20C
O/C 25x36 High Sierras in Summer Mor 3/92 600
Colini, F.   It 19C
O/C 13x31 Venetian Canal Slo 9/91 325
Coll, Giovanni   It 1636-1681
* See 1991 Edition . . . .
Colle, Michel-Auguste   Fr 1872-1949
* See 1990 Edition . . . .
Collier, Alan Caswell   Can 1911-1990
O/B 12x16 Fog Over Yukon River Sbt 11/91 1,309
O/B 11x16 Hilly Road, Saskatchewan Sbt 11/91 1,309
Collier, Charles Myles   Am 1836-1908
O/C 20x14 Gloucester Harbor Yng 4/92 250
Collier, Evert   Dut -1702
* See 1992 Edition . . . .
Collier, John   Br 1708-1786
* See 1991 Edition . . . .
Collier, The Hon. John   Br 1850-1934
O/C 56x44 Ad Libitum 1924 Wes 5/92 15,400
Collignon   a 1762-
* See 1992 Edition . . . .
Collin, Raphael   Fr 1850-1916
O/C 18x15 An Arcadian Concert But 11/91 8,800
Collins, Arthur G.   1866-
O/B 11x8 Breton Girl Yng 4/92 275
Collins, Charles   Eng 1851-1921
* See 1992 Edition . . . .
Collins, Earl   Am 1925-
* See 1992 Edition . . . .
Collins, Hugh   Br 19C
O/C 34x44 A Musical Family 1878 Sby 10/91 8,250
Collins, Kreigh   Am 1908-1974
O/C 20x30 Men w/Lantern Around Opened Chest Ilh 11/91 . . 500
Collins, William   Br 1788-1847
* See 1992 Edition . . . .
Collinson, James   Con 19C
* See 1991 Edition . . . .
Collman, Daniel   Br 20C
O/C 30x40 Isle of Wight Doy 11/91 1,700
Collomb, Paul   1921-
* See 1992 Edition . . . .
Colman, Roi Clarkson   Am 1884-1945
O/C 20x30 Laguna Sunset But 2/92 4,400
O/C 22x30 Laguna Coast But 2/92 1,430

Colman, Samuel   Am 1832-1920
O/C 25x42 Cattle Watering Slo 12/91 10,000
O/B 3x4 Nine Paintings Wes 11/91 4,180
P/Pa 8x18 A Misty Afternoon, Venice Brd 5/92 2,200
P&G/Pa 9x11 Ship Unloading Chr 6/92 1,210
W&Pe/Pa 8x14 Town Scene in txtrcholeo, Mexico Chr 6/92 . . 990
Cologna, A.   20C
O/C 18x12 Woman with Chickens Hnd 12/91 550
Colonelli-Sciarra, Salvatore   It a 1729-1736
* See 1991 Edition . . . .
Colt, James   Am 20C
O/B 20x24 Cowboys on Horseback Mor 11/91 400
O/B 20x24 Cowboys on Horseback Mor 11/91 400
Colucci, Gio   It 20C
* See 1992 Edition . . . .
Colunga, Alejandro   Mex 1948-
O,Sd&Os/C 77x55 Bailarin 78 Sby 5/92 19,250
Colville, Alexander   Can 1920-
W&G/Pa/B 19x12 Three Weeds '58 Sbt 5/92 6,545
Coman, Charlotte Buell   Am 1833-1924
W/Pa 13x19 French River Landscape Lou 3/92 200
Combas, Robert   1957-
A/L 79x96 E'Enlevement des Sabines 1985 Chr 11/91 28,600
A/C 85x60 Le Mage Fromage 1985 Chr 5/92 8,250
Comerre, Leon Francois   Fr 1850-1934
O/C 52x79 Cassandre Tuee/Clytemnestre 1875 But 5/92 . . 99,000
O/C 30x24 Ballerina Rosita Mauri Sby 5/92 19,800
Comerre-Paton, Jaqueline   Fr 1859-
O/C 50x72 Young Girl Reclining on a Riverbank Sel 4/92 . . 7,500
Comfort, Charles Fraser   Can 1900-
O/Pn 12x16 Pine Wrack '63 Sbt 5/92 1,590
Pe/Pa 16x10 Nude 1937 Sbt 5/92 468
Compte-Calix, Francois C.   Fr 1813-1880
O/C 29x22 The Broken Engagement Sby 1/92 7,700
Compton, Edward Harrison   Br 1881-1960
O/C 24x32 Ancient Ruins Sby 7/92 6,050
W/Pa 13x9 Village Landscape Wes 11/91 880
Comte De Grimberghe, Edmond   Ger 1865-1920
* See 1990 Edition . . . .
Conca, Sebastiano   It 1680-1764
* See 1992 Edition . . . .
Conconi, Luigi   It 1852-1917
O/C 42x41 Courtly Lovers 10 Sby 10/91 30,800
Condi, N.
O/B 5x7 Portrait of British Bark Eld 7/92 660
Condo, George   1957-
O/C 79x63 Nude with Reflection 89 Sby 2/92 66,000
O&Pe/C 79x71 Separated by Life Sby 11/91 60,500
O/C 75x60 Untitled 86 Sby 5/92 45,100
O/C 38x77 Nude on Table 1990 Chr 5/92 33,000
O/C 109x61 Still Life with Landscape 87 Sby 10/91 33,000
O/C 66x50 Woman is the Sum of Her Parts Chr 5/92 27,500
O&Y/C 77x43 Sunday Painting 87 Chr 2/92 24,200
O/C 32x26 Funny Landscape 85 Chr 5/92 22,000
A/C 29x24 Rebirth 89 Chr 11/91 11,000
O/C 33x25 Untitled 83 Sby 5/92 11,000
O/C 13x10 Untitled 85 Chr 5/92 7,150
O/L 24x19 Red Portrait Sby 5/92 6,050
O/C 22x15 Ecstatic Purple + Green Painting 74 Chr 5/92 . . 3,300
O/C 14x13 Portrait de Female Manager Chr 2/92 2,860
O/C 9x7 Accumulated Head 1990 Chr 5/92 2,200
O/C 11x8 They Have Names 85 Chr 5/92 1,980
C&S/Pa 21x22 Still Life 88 Chr 2/92 1,760
C&S/Pa 28x17 Untitled Chr 5/92 1,430
O&W/Pa 22x30 Untitled Chr 2/92 1,100
Y/C 15x11 Untitled Chr 2/92 1,100
Cone, Marvin D.   Am 1891-1964
O/C 22x24 Still Life with Mask Chr 3/92 17,600
Congdon, Thomas Raphael   Am 1862-1917
* See 1992 Edition . . . .
Conger, B. F.   Am 20C
W/Pa 19x26 Winter Landscape 1939 Fre 10/91 125

Connard, Philip   Br 1875-1958
* See 1991 Edition . . . .
Connaway, Jay Hall   Am 1893-1970
O/C 24x40 Fall Along the Coast '41 Skn 3/92   2,860
Connelly, Chuck   1955-
O/C 66x78 Collision 1984 Chr 11/91   4,950
G&Y/Pa 11x9 Untitled 1986 Sby 10/91   660
Conner, Bruce   20C
* See 1991 Edition . . . .
Conner, John Anthony   Am 1892-1971
O/B 26x36 Trees by a Stream Yng 4/92   250
Conner, John Ramsey   Am 1869-1952
O/C 25x30 Christ Before Pilate Slo 7/92   800
Conner, Paul   Am 1881-1968
O/B 7x5 Alta Dena Eucaly Mor 11/91   450
O/C 16x20 San Juan Capistrano Arches 1936 Mor 3/92   325
O/B 8x10 California Landscape Mor 11/91   250
Connor, Charles   20C
* See 1991 Edition . . . .
Conover   Am 20C
W/Pa/B 14x24 Reclining Nude Wlf 10/91   200
Conrady, E. V.   Con 19C
O/C 22x38 Venetian Canal Scene Hnd 3/92   325
Conrey, Lee F.   Am 1883-
Pl&S/Pa 19x22 Visitors to a Mayan Temple Ihh 5/92   700
Conroy, George T.   Am 19C
O/C 20x30 Landscape at Dusk Hnd 3/92   275
Constable, John   Eng 1776-1837
* See 1990 Edition . . . .
Constable, William   Am 1783-1861
* See 1991 Edition . . . .
Constant, Benjamin   Fr 1845-1902
O/C 40x29 Throne Room in Byzantium Sby 7/92   6,050
O/C 56x30 Woman and Winged Victory Hnz 5/92   4,750
O/C 22x27 A Gypsy Chr 10/91   1,650
Constantin   Con 19C
O/C 23x32 End of the Day Chr 2/92   1,650
Constantin, Jean-Antoine   Fr 1756-1844
K/Pa 6x11 Studies of Heads of Young Ladies Slo 7/92   950
I&K/Pa 8x10 Studies of Neoclassical Women Slo 7/92   950
Content, Dan   Am 1902-1990
O&R/C 36x28 French Soldier, Girl Under Tree 1931 Ihh 5/92 .   800
Conti, Primo   20C
* See 1991 Edition . . . .
Conti, Tito   It 1842-1924
O/C 23x17 Flirtation Chr 10/91   6,050
Conway, Fred   Am 1900-1972
O/M 11x13 Slow Putter Sel 12/91   275
Conway, John S.   Am 1852-1925
C/Pa/B 19x25 Michelangelo's Night Chr 3/92   4,400
Cook, Ebenezer Wake   Br 1843-1926
* See 1991 Edition . . . .
Cook, George E.   Am -1930
O/C 10x16 Landscape with River Wlf 9/91   350
Cook, Howard   Am 1901-1980
* See 1992 Edition . . . .
Cook, John A.   Am 1870-1936
W/Pa 8x17 New England Surf Slo 2/92   200
Cook, Otis   Am 20C
O/C 18x22 Countryside, Cape Anne But 4/92   3,300
O/C 25x30 Fishing Vessels at Dockside Eld 7/92   770
O/C Size? Dockside Scene Eld 7/92   330
O/C 18x20 Schooner Drying Sails at Dockside Eld 7/92   303
Cook, Peter
O/C 16x24 Farm by the Sea Ald 5/92   275
Cooke, Edward William   Eng 1811-1880
* See 1991 Edition . . . .
Cooke, George   Am 1793-1849
* See 1991 Edition . . . .
Cooke, John   Br a 1887-1903
* See 1991 Edition . . . .
Cookesley, Margaret Murray   Eng 19C
* See 1991 Edition . . . .
Cooley   Am 19C
O/C 30x18 Bird House Mys 6/92   220

Cooley, Ben   Am 19C
O/C 52x37 Portrait Stephen Douglas 1867 Chr 11/91   9,900
Coolidge, Cassius Marcellus   Am 1844-1934
* See 1992 Edition . . . .
Coomans, Diana   Con 19C
O/C 24x36 Still Life Architectural Setting Chr 2/92   4,400
Coomans, Pierre Olivier Joseph   Bel 1816-1889
O/Pn 26x20 Harem Beauty Slo 9/91   6,000
Coombs, Delbert Dana   Am 1850-1938
O/C 16x30 R.R. Bridge & Falls, Lewiston 1890 Brd 8/92 . .   11,000
O/C 16x30 Picnic - Lake Grove, Auburn, ME 1885 Brd 8/92   5,720
O/C 16x30 Sailing on Lake Auburn 1888 Brd 8/92   3,300
O/C 14x20 Still Life Apples and Moxie Bottle 1898 Brd 8/92   3,300
O/C 20x35 New Gloucester Meadows 1909 Skn 11/91   1,760
O/C 10x16 View of Turner 1894 Brd 8/92   1,430
O/C 14x9 Imagining Brook Trout 1890 Yng 4/92   500
O/C 14x11 In Paul's Woods Skn 5/92   385
Cooper, Abraham   Br 1787-1868
O/C 31x36 Mr. T. H. Holt's Chestnut Colt 1847 Sby 6/92 .   18,700
Cooper, Alexander Davis   Am 1837-1888
O/C 40x63 Indian Attack 1881 Slo 12/91   1,900
Cooper, Astley D. M.   Am 1856-1924
O/C 18x22 War Party on the Trail 1920 Chr 6/92   3,300
O/C 48x30 Rocky Mountains But 6/92   3,025
Cooper, Colin Campbell   Am 1856-1937
O/C 16x20 A Spring Day, Boston Chr 5/92   12,100
O/C 21x30 Court of the Universe 1915 But 2/92   5,500
O/C 32x20 Floral Still Life But 4/92   5,500
G/Pa 10x12 Entrance to the Exposition But 2/92   4,950
O/C 9x28 Middle Eastern Market 1904 But 11/91   3,850
G/Pa 10x7 Gateway, Santa Barbara 1925 But 6/92   3,300
O/B 12x16 Sunset But 2/92   3,300
O/C/B 28x20 Interior Church of the Nativity But 6/92   3,025
O/C 30x38 Riders in the Clouds Lou 3/92   3,000
O/C 15x27 La Rochelle 1901 Chr 6/92   2,200
O/C 22x17 Harbor Scene, Amsterdam 1896 Chr 3/92   1,650
W/Pa 25x20 Path Through the Woods But 10/91   1,650
O/C 30x40 Arriving at the Pantheon Lou 3/92   1,600
G/Pa 5x7 New York Skyline But 11/91   1,100
O/B 11x14 Homes Near Florence But 6/92   1,045
W/Pa 7x11 Brooklyn Bridge Mor 11/91   900
W/Pa 18x24 Winchester 1902 Wlf 6/92   800
W/Pa 5x7 Carcassonne from the River '29 Mor 11/91   700
Cooper, Edwin   Br 1785-1833
Pl&W/Pa 11x19 Racing Scenes: Four 1818 Sby 6/92   3,960
Cooper, Emma Lampert   Am 1860-1920
* See 1990 Edition . . . .
Cooper, J. D.
* See 1992 Edition . . . .
Cooper, Rita   Am 20C
O/C 24x32 Flowering Gate Lou 3/92   150
Cooper, Thomas Sidney   Br 1803-1902
O/Pn 22x17 Canterbury Meadows 1865 Chr 2/92   7,700
O/Pn 17x13 Cows in a Landscape 1891 Sby 1/92   3,520
O/C 10x18 Sheep on the Moors 1861 But 11/91   1,100
Coopse, Pieter   Dut 17C
* See 1991 Edition . . . .
Coosemans, Alexander   Flm 1627-1689
* See 1992 Edition . . . .
Cope, Gordon Nicholson   Am 1906-1970
* See 1992 Edition . . . .
Copeland, J. Frank   Am 1872-
W/Pa 15x20 The Cove, Orr's Island Ald 5/92   100
Copley, John Singleton   Am 1737-1815
* See 1992 Edition . . . .
Copley, Robert   20C
* See 1991 Edition . . . .
Copley, William   Am 1919-
* See 1992 Edition . . . .
Coppedge, Fern Isabel   Am 1883-1951
O/C 18x20 Mill with Pond Ald 5/92   29,000
O/C 25x30 December Afternoon Chr 5/92   28,600
O/C 24x24 The Canal in New Hope 1919 Ald 5/92   17,000

O/B 10x12 The Mill Brook Ald 5/92 12,500
O/B 10x8 Winter Woods with Houses Ald 5/92 7,000
O/C 25x30 Mill Pond But 4/92 6,050
O/C 12x14 Fall Landscape Ald 3/92 3,250
O/C/B 34x30 Houses by a River Sby 12/91 2,200
O/B 10x8 Fall Trees Ald 5/92 1,850

Copperman, Mildred Tuner Am 20C
 * See 1992 Edition

Coppin, John A. Am 1904-
O/C 27x28 Standing Nude Durn 1/92 3,000
W/Pa 9x21 Chef Serving a Meal Durn 1/92 850
O/B 26x22 Cowboy on Galloping Horse Durn 1/92 800

Coppin, John Stevens Am 1904-
O/C 24x22 Couple in Car Speeding 1952 Ilh 5/92 1,700

Coques, Gonzales Flm 1614-1684
O/C 26x32 Portrait the De Meer Family Sby 1/92 23,100

Corbellini, Luigi It 1901-1968
O/C 26x21 Portrait of a Young Woman Sby 10/91 2,530
O/C 14x11 Kathy and her Parrot Sby 10/91 2,200
O/C Size? Young Girls Mys 6/92 495

Corbino, Jon Am 1905-1964
O/C 20x16 The Native Hnz 10/91 1,700
O/Cd 25x31 Study for the Flood But 11/91 1,100
PVB 16x11 Head of a Woman Hnz 5/92 300

Corbit, George Cecil Am 1892-1944
O/C 25x30 Dusky Fisherman But 2/92 8,250

Corbould, A. C.
S&G/Pa 6x9 Four Illustrations 1896 Durn 1/92 105

Corchon Y Diaque, Federico Spa 19C
O/Pn 16x13 Place de la Madeleine, Paris Sby 2/92 49,500
W&G/Pa 19x13 Elegantes au Bord de la Mer: Pair Sby 2/92 5,500

Corcos, Vittorio Matteo It 1859-1933
O/C 40x21 Without Song Chr 2/92 49,500

Cordain, Jean Fr 29C
O/C 12x16 Still Life of Fruit Slo 7/92 250

Cordero, Francisco Mex 19C
 * See 1991 Edition

Cordrey, John Br 1765-1825
O/C 17x24 Abingdon and London Coach 1808 Chr 10/91 . . . 715

Corinth, Lovis Ger 1858-1925
O/C 20x16 Portrait Mr. Eduard Kruger 1912 Chr 2/92 52,800
C/Pa 13x10 Portrait of a Man Sby 10/91 4,400
O/Pn 18x15 Church Steeple Hnz 5/92 1,500

Corneille (C. G. Van Beverloo) Spa 1922-
G&V/Pa 9x12 Untitled '66 Sby 10/91 2,640

Corneille, Michel Fr 1642-1708
K,Pl&S/Pa 6x10 Christ in the House of Mary Chr 1/92 6,600
O/C 26x21 Portia Chr 5/92 5,500
K,Pl&S/Pa 11x17 A Bacchanal Chr 1/92 1,100

Cornell, Joseph Am 1903-1972
 * See 1992 Edition

Corner, Thomas C. Am 1865-1938
 * See 1992 Edition

Cornil, Gaston Fr 1883-
 * See 1990 Edition

Cornoyer, Paul Am 1864-1923
O/Cb 8x10 Madison Square Winter Sby 4/92 5,775
O/Cb 8x10 Italian Harbor Scene Sel 2/92 1,900
O/B 8x10 Two: Nocturnal Urban Street Scenes Sel 2/92 . . 1,250

Cornwell, Dean Am 1892-1960
O/C 36x27 Distraught Mountie/Woman 1919 Ilh 5/92 16,000
O/C 33x58 Reclining Nude Sby 12/91 8,800
O/C 30x40 Man Meeting Japanese Woman 1923 Ilh 5/92 . . 7,500
O/C 21x51 Capturing the Gang Sby 12/91 6,600
O/C 30x28 Man in Chair of Spanish Home 1921 Ilh 11/91 . . 4,500
O&C/Pa/M 25x38 Wreck of Rough and Tumble 38 Sby 4/92 3,850
P/Pa 25x19 Captain Blood with Flintlock 1930 Ilh 5/92 . . . 1,500

Coronado, J* Con 19C**
O/Pn 8x10 Two Friends 62 Sby 7/92 2,200

Coronel, Pedro Mex 1923-1985
O&Sd/C 79x98 La Oquedad de Espacio 1980 Chr 11/91 . 104,500
O/C 59x43 Llanto Socavado Sby 5/92 66,000
O/C 51x36 Retrato de Pilar 1977 Chr 5/92 44,000
O/C 31x24 Bodegon Abstracto 1971 Sby 11/91 31,900
O/C 39x39 Untitled 65 Sby 5/92 27,500

O/C 38x32 Llanto Desolado 1962 Chr 11/91 19,800
Coronel, Rafael Mex 1932-
O/C 49x40 Leonardo Con Fondo Rojo Sby 11/91 77,000
O/C 40x50 Tres Figuras Sby 5/92 34,100
A/C 40x50 Alfredo de la Carpa Chr 11/91 28,600
O/C 31x24 Figura de Perfil Chr 5/92 19,800
O/C 26x22 Perfil Sby 5/92 19,800
O/C 24x30 Cabeza Sby 5/92 16,500
P&P/Pa 18x24 El Pintor 42 Chr 5/92 4,180

Corot, Jean Baptiste Camille Fr 1796-1875
O/C 21x25 Saint-Nicolas-Lez-Arras. 1872 Hnd 10/91 . . . 320,000
O/C 21x17 Souvenir d'Italie Chr 10/91 242,000
O/C 9x16 Fontainebleau Chr 5/92 198,000
O/C 14x21 Pecheurs Tendant Leurs Filets Sby 5/92 187,000
O/C 20x14 Paysan en Priere Chr 5/92 143,000
O/C 21x15 Le Patre Au Repos Sby 10/91 110,000
O/C 11x14 Grez-sur-Loing Chr 5/92 66,000
O/C 10x14 Etang avec Clocher Hnd 10/91 55,000

Corpora, Antonio It 1919-
O/C 32x26 Appunta Corre Ricordi 66 Sby 2/92 5,500

Correa, Benito Rebolledo Chl 1880-1964
 * See 1991 Edition

Correa, Juan
 * See 1990 Edition

Corrodi, Hermann David Salomon It 1844-1905
O/C 65x34 Venetian Lagoon by Moonlight But 11/91 24,750
O/C 39x25 Arab Rug Merchants 1879 Wes 11/91 17,600
O/C 16x27 Bringing in the Catch 1871 Chr 10/91 12,100
O/C 15x29 Along the Nile Sby 2/92 7,700
O/C 28x18 The Roman Campagna Chr 5/92 5,500

Corrodi, Salomon Sws 1810-1892
W/Pb 20x28 Italianate Village on a Hilltop Chr 5/92 8,250

Corruti, Domenico Maria It 1620-1684
P/Pa 4x2 Mercury Slo 7/92 750

Corsi, Sante It 19C
 * See 1990 Edition

Corsini, Raffaele It 19C
S,W&P/Pa 18x26 Bank Western Sea 1855 Chr 6/92 935

Cortes, Edouard-Leon Fr 1882-1969
O/C 26x37 Place de la Republique Chr 10/91 41,800
O/C 19x22 Parisian Fountain Sby 10/91 39,600
O/C 13x18 L'Arc De Triomphe Sby 10/91 28,600
O/C 13x18 Rue Royal Sby 10/91 28,600
O/C 13x18 Bouquinistes au Bord de la Seine Sby 10/91 . . 27,500
O/C 21x29 Rue de la Madeleine But 5/92 27,500
O/C 13x18 Le Boulevard Sby 10/91 26,400
O/C 18x24 Porte Saint Denis Chr 2/92 22,000
O/C 13x18 Snowy Evening, Place de la Bastille Sby 10/91 22,000
O/C 13x18 Le Pantheon But 11/91 20,900
O/C 13x18 Place de la Concorde Sby 10/91 19,800
O/C 20x26 La Madeleine Sby 5/92 18,700
O/C 13x18 Boulevard Haussmann Chr 5/92 18,150
O/C 18x22 The Vendome Column Hnd 5/92 18,000
O/C 13x18 Horse and Carriages on Paris Street Chr 5/92 . 16,500
O/C 13x18 Marche Aux Fleurs Sby 5/92 16,500
O/C 13x18 L'Opera Hnd 5/92 16,500
O/C 13x18 Place de l'Opera Hnd 10/91 15,500
O/C 13x18 Le Trois Quartiers Chr 2/92 15,400
O/C 13x18 Place de la Madelaine Sby 2/92 15,400
O/C 13x18 Marchande De Fleurs Sby 5/92 13,200
O/C 13x18 View of Notre Dame Sby 10/91 13,200
O/C 13x18 Winter in Paris Sby 2/92 12,650
O/C 13x18 Place de la Concorde Sby 6/92 12,100
O/C 13x18 An Evening in Paris Sby 2/92 11,000
O/C 13x18 Boulevard Malesherbes Hnd 10/91 11,000
O/C 13x18 L'Arc de Triomphe Sby 2/92 11,000
O/C 13x18 Paris Street Scene Hnd 10/91 11,000
O/Pn 15x18 View of the Madeleine Chr 5/92 9,900
O/Pa/B 13x18 Porte St. Denis Sby 6/92 8,250

Cortez, Jenness Am 1945-
O/C 16x20 Horse and Terrier in Stall 1981 Sby 12/91 . . . 3,190

69

Corwin, Charles Abel Am 1857-1938
* See 1992 Edition . . . .
Corzas, Francisco   Mex 1936-
O/C 81x71 Untitled 72 Sby 5/92 121,000
O/C 66x51 El Peregrino 90 Chr 5/92 77,000
O/C 57x47 Figuras 69 Chr 11/91 41,800
G&I/Pa 8x10 Dancing Figures: Two 61 Sby 10/91 1,870
Cosenza, Guiseppe   It 1847-
* See 1992 Edition . . . .
Cosgrove, Stanley Morel   Can 1911-
O/C 32x27 Trees in Autumn Sbt 11/91 8,415
O/C 24x20 Summer Landscape Sbt 5/92 7,012
O/C 23x19 Trees, Hudson Heights Sbt 11/91 5,376
Cosson, Marcel   Fr 1878-1956
O/Pn 18x22 Champ de Courses, Longchamps Sby 10/91 . 18,700
O/C 18x22 Au Bar Sby 10/91 7,700
O/Pn 9x8 Two Paintings Chr 11/91 2,420
Costa, Giovanni   It 1833-1903
O/C 25x20 Before the Masked Ball Chr 10/91 5,060
Costa, Olga   Mex 1913-
O/C 34x28 Nina con Sandalias 1950 Chr 11/91 60,500
G/Pa 24x19 Tehuana Sentada 49 Sby 5/92 23,100
O/M 10x17 Triangulos 56 Chr 5/92 5,500
Costa, Oreste   It 1851-1901
O/C 46x20 Young Beauty in a Garden Chr 10/91 14,300
Costanzi, Placido   It a 1590-1659
* See 1991 Edition . . . .
Coster   17C
O/Cp 20x15 Still Life Peaches, Grapes, Oysters Sby 10/91 99,000
Costigan, John E.   Am 1888-1972
* See 1992 Edition . . . .
Cosway, Richard   Br 1742-1841
* See 1990 Edition . . . .
Cot, Pierre Auguste   Fr 1837-1883
O/C 12x10 Smiling Girl Sby 7/92 1,980
Cotanda, Vicente Nicolau   Spa 1852-1899
O/C 28x12 Figures on a Country Lane Sby 2/92 3,850
Cotes, Francis   Eng 1725-1770
O/C 48x36 Colonel William Phillips Sby 10/91 18,700
Cottavoz, Andre   Fr 1922-
O/C 15x22 Vue de Golfejuan 1965 Sby 2/92 6,325
Cottingham, Robert   Am 1935-
* See 1992 Edition . . . .
Cotton, William   Am 1880-1958
* See 1991 Edition . . . .
Coubine, Otakar
* See 1992 Edition . . . .
Couch, Frank   Am 20C
O/C 20x32 Fall Landscape Lou 12/91 300
Couldery, Horatio H.   Br 1832-1893
O/B 8x12 The Hunters 1890 Sby 7/92 4,675
O/C 14x18 Cat and Mouse Chr 2/92 3,300
Coulter, Mary   Am 1880-1966
* See 1992 Edition . . . .
Coulter, William Alexander   Am 1849-1936
O/C 26x42 Clipper Ship Under Moonlit Skies 1908 But 2/92 13,200
O/C 24x36 Colusa Trimmed for Storm 1906 But 10/91 8,800
O/B 13x20 Off the Monterey Coast Wes 11/91 3,300
Courant, Maurice Francois A.   Fr 1847-1925
O/C 22x26 Port au Matin 1908 Wes 5/92 2,200
Courbet, Gustave   Fr 1819-1877
O/C 28x43 Flowers on a Bench 62 Chr 5/92 . . . . 1.54M
O/C 36x26 Woman with a Fan 61 Chr 5/92 253,000
O/C 22x29 Marine, Les Vagues Sby 5/92 198,000
O/C 28x21 Monsieur Louis-Auguste Auguin 1862 Chr 5/92 44,000
Courbet, Gustave & Ordinaire,M   Fr 1819-1877
* See 1992 Edition . . . .
Courbet, Gustave & Pata, C.   Fr 1819-1877
* See 1992 Edition . . . .
Courtat, Louis   Fr -1909
O/C 15x24 Reclining Nude Chr 10/91 9,350

Courtens, Hermann   Bel 1884-1956
* See 1992 Edition . . . .
Courtice, Rody Kenny   Can 1895-1973
O/C 34x40 Kingston Road Village Sbt 11/91 1,402
Courtois, Guillaume & Brueghel   Fr 1628-1679
O/C 67x101 Ceres attended by Putti Chr 5/92 242,000
Courtois, Gustave Claude Etien   Fr 1853-1924
* See 1990 Edition . . . .
Couse, Eanger Irving   Am 1866-1936
O/C 46x35 Moonlit Scene Woman and Child Sel 9/91 . . . 70,000
O/C 24x29 Medicine Fire Sby 5/92 30,800
O/C 24x29 Sacred Deer Bowl Ritual Sby 12/91 29,700
O/C 7x9 Landscapes (Five) But 11/91 4,400
R&O/C 18x24 Fisherfolk Sel 9/91 3,500
Pe/Pa 5x6 Sketches Depicting Indian Life (7) But 11/91 . . . 2,750
Coutaud, Lucien   Fr 1904-
O/C 39x32 Elles Aiment le Vent 59 But 5/92 5,225
Coutts, Alice   Am 1880-1973
O/C 12x10 Indian Girl, Cat and Dog But 6/92 4,125
O/B 11x9 Indian Child Playing But 6/92 2,475
Coutts, Gordon   Am 1880-1937
O/C 30x35 The Artist's Wife, Alice - Paris Mor 3/92 25,000
O/C 20x30 End of the Day But 2/92 6,600
O/C 30x40 Oaks at Piedmont But 2/92 4,675
O/C 30x22 Seated Nude "Sara" Mor 3/92 4,500
O/C/B 30x40 Watching the Sunset But 10/91 2,200
O/C 27x35 Marin County Landscape But 10/91 1,760
O/C 30x40 Harvesting Hay Wlf 6/92 1,000
O/C 21x17 Portrait of a Negro Woman Slo 12/91 800
O/C 18x27 Landscape Mor 6/92 750
O/C 20x30 Landscape Mys 11/91 495
Couture, Thomas   Fr 1815-1879
* See 1991 Edition . . . .
Couturier, Leon   Fr 1842-1935
O/Pn 12x8 Portrait of a Woman Hnd 5/92 650
Couturier, Philibert Leon   Fr 1823-1901
O/Pn 15x24 Poultry Grazing Chr 5/92 3,850
O/Pn 10x21 Feeding Time Chr 2/92 2,640
Covarrubias, Miguel   Mex 1904-1957
O/C 30x24 Tehuana Chr 5/92 38,500
G/Pa 12x9 Mujera Sentada Sby 6/92 4,125
W,G&Pe/Pa 15x10 Bailarina Balinesa Chr 5/92 3,850
I&S/Pa 13x11 Millonario Sby 5/92 3,850
I&Pe/Pa 11x8 Mestiza Sby 2/92 2,750
Pe/Pa 11x8 Young Woman with Bow Sby 2/92 2,090
C&I/Pa 11x9 Man Dancing Sby 2/92 1,760
P/Pa 24x16 Sea Creature 54 Slo 9/91 1,300
W/Pa 15x13 The Cockfight 56 Slo 9/91 1,200
I/Pa 11x8 Woman with Fan Sby 2/92 1,100
PI/Pa 12x9 Start all over Tomorrow Chr 5/92 990
I/Pa 10x7 African Rhythms: Two Skn 9/91 935
W&Br/Pa 11x9 Balinesa Chr 5/92 880
Coward, Sir Noel   Br
O/B 14x10 Caribbean Fisherman Sby 6/92 880
Cowles, Fleur
* See 1992 Edition . . . .
Cowles, Russell   Am 1887-1979
O/C 45x48 The Romantics Skn 11/91 2,750
O/C/B 41 dia The Watchful Sheperd But 11/91 1,100
Cowper, Frank Cadogan   Br 1877-1958
O/C 41x32 Lancelot Slays Knight Sir Tarquin Sby 10/91 . . 37,400
Cox, *   Br 19C
O/C 26x32 Horse: Jewel But 5/92 10,450
Cox, Albert Scott   1863-1920
O/C 14x20 Girl Near a Cottage Yng 4/92 425
Cox, David   Br 1783-1859
W&C/Pa 9x12 The Blasted Oak Chr 5/92 650
O/C 11x15 Figures Pulling a Wagon Up a Hill Hnz 5/92 . . . 550
Cox, Kenyon   Am 1856-1919
* See 1992 Edition . . . .
Cox, Martha Sterling   Am 20C
W/Pa 10x8 Gothic Knocker Fre 4/92 175

Coypel, Charles Antoine   Fr 1694-1752
   * See 1991 Edition . . . .
Cozza, Francesco   It 1605-1682
   * See 1991 Edition . . . .
**Cozzens, Frederick Schiller   Am
1856-1928**
   W/Pa 14x22 A Decided Coolness Between Them Mys 11/91 . 990
   W/Pa 12x18 Three Masted Schooner '05 Yng 2/92 475
Crabeels, Florent Nicolas   Bel 1829-1896
   O/Pn 27x33 Lakermesse 1851 Sby 10/91 36,300
Crabeth, Wouter (II)   Flm 1595-1644
   O/Pn 31x43 The Card Sharps Sby 1/92 44,000
Crafty, Victor   Fr 1840-1906
   W/Pa/B 10x14 Carriages on Sunday Ride 1891 Sby 1/92 . . 2,420
Craig, Frank   Br 1874-1918
   O/B 10x14 Letter from Home 1901 Chr 10/91 660
Craig, Henry Robertson   Irs 1916-1984
   O/C 45x40 Moroccan Tablecloth Sby 10/91 6,875
   O/C 50x70 Morning Mist, Chantilly Sby 10/91 6,600
   O/C 25x30 "At the Races", Curragh, Dublin Sby 6/92 . . . 3,300
Craig, Thomas Bigelow   Am 1849-1924
   O/C 20x30 Leading the Herd Home 1886 Sby 12/91 3,410
   O/C 10x14 Noonday in Summer 1901 Slo 9/91 1,900
   O/C 10x14 Cows Watering Dum 5/92 1,700
   O/C 18x26 Cloud Shadows Wes 11/91 1,100
   W/Pa 9x13 A Straw Hut Chr 6/92 550
Craig, William Marshall   Br 1788-1828
   * See 1992 Edition . . . .
Cram, Allen Gilbert   Am 1886-1947
   * See 1992 Edition . . . .
Cramer, Florence Ballin   1884-
   O/B 16x12 Flowers in a Vase 1926 Yng 4/92 80
Cramer, Helene   Ger 1844-
   * See 1991 Edition . . . .
Crampton, Rollin McNeil   Am 1886-1970
   A/C 36x50 Blue Circles 1968 Slo 10/91 50
**Cranach, Lucas (the Elder)   Ger
1472-1553**
   * See 1990 Edition . . . .
**Cranach, Lucas (the Younger)   Ger
1515-1586**
   * See 1992 Edition . . . .
**Cranch, Christopher Pearse   Am
1813-1892**
   O/C 20x36 International Harbor Skn 3/92 1,760
Crandell, Bradshaw   Am 1896-1966
   O/C 36x27 Ice Skating Woman Ilh 5/92 3,250
   P/Pa 29x20 Hoisting a Flag 1935 Ilh 11/91 1,400
Crane, Bruce   Am 1857-1937
   O/C 28x36 Fall Afternoon Lou 9/91 9,000
   O/C 22x30 Late Autumn Chr 3/92 6,600
   O/C 14x20 The Afternoon Sun Sby 12/91 6,600
   O/C 18x24 Morning Haze Chr 9/91 6,380
   O/C 16x20 Sunlit Meadow Brd 8/92 5,500
   O/C 18x25 The Old Fence But 11/91 5,500
   O/C 18x32 Cottage on a River Delta Sby 4/92 3,300
   O/C 12x16 Golden Glow Doy 12/91 1,200
   W&G/Pa 12x18 Geese and Ducks Feeding Skn 11/91 . . . 990
   O&R/C/B 13x21 Landscape with Stream Sby 12/91 990
   O/Wd 10x13 Early Spring Landscape Bor 8/92 625
   O/Cd 5x9 Landscape Wlf 10/91 275
Crane, Frederick   Am 1847-1915
   * See 1992 Edition . . . .
Crane, Walter   Br 1845-1915
   Pl/Pa 14x10 Paris and Helen Ilh 5/92 1,300
Craumer, Elda
   O/B 20x24 Along Water St. Ald 3/92 150
Craustoun, James H.
   W/Pa 14x19 The Vale of Melrose 1873 Hnz 10/91 275
Crawford, Esther Mabel   Am 1872-1958
   * See 1992 Edition . . . .
Crawford, John   Am a 1850-
   O/C 26x36 Wyoming Valley, Pennsylvania 1860 Chr 3/92 . 8,800
Crawford, Ralston   Am 1906-1978
   G&Pe/Pa/L 11x15 Nacelles Under Construction Chr 5/92 . . 6,600

Creamer, Mary   Am 20C
   O/C 20x24 Cup of Gold Sel 2/92 50
Cree, ***
   W&G/Pa 14x10 Miscellaneous Costume Designs Sby 2/92 . . 605
Creifelds, Richard   Am 19C
   O/C 21x17 Looking in the Mirror Chr 11/91 176
Creighton, Maxwell B.   Am 20C
   O/B 24x36 Boom Town 1964 Slo 10/91 130
Creixams, Pierre   Spa 1893-1965
   * See 1992 Edition . . . .
Cremonini, Leonardo   It 1925-
   O/C 32x40 I Gatti 55 Chr 11/91 14,300
Crespi, Enrico   It 1854-1929
   O/C 32x22 Woman Playing a Guitar 1896 Sby 1/92 660
Crespi, Giuseppe Maria   It 1665-1747
   * See 1990 Edition . . . .
Cresswell, William Nicoll   Can 1818-1888
   W/Pa 14x21 Mountain Landscape 1882 Sbt 11/91 1,215
Cressy, Susan   Am -1942
   O/C 17x14 Girl Holding Rabbit Mys 6/92 2,420
Creswick, Thomas   Br 1811-1869
   * See 1992 Edition . . . .
Cretan, Veneto   17C
   O&Gd/C 26x20 Madonna and Child Sby 7/92 1,320
Creti, Donato   It 1671-1749
   * See 1992 Edition . . . .
Crews, Monte   Am 20C
   O/C 36x28 Children's Circus Sel 4/92 550
Criley, Theodore   Am 1880-1930
   O/C 32x42 Windblown Cypresses, Carmel But 6/92 6,600
Crippa, Roberto   It 1921-1972
   * See 1992 Edition . . . .
Crisp, G.   Eng 19C
   O/C 12x18 Still Life of Apples, Grapes Slo 10/91 375
Criss, Francis   Am 1901-1975
   O/C 33x45 Alma Sewing Sby 5/92 23,100
   O/M 18x22 New York Roof Tops Sby 5/92 15,400
   O/Cb 18x24 A Sunset Chr 6/92 3,850
Crite, Allan Rohan   Am 1910-
   O/Cb 18x24 Romance on Hubert Street 1937 Sby 9/91 . . . 8,800
Critten, Lillian H.   Am 20C
   P/B 12x11 Inlet Peconich Slo 12/91 150
Critz, Carl   Am 20C
   O/C 38x30 Figural Mor 11/91 275
Crivelli, Angelo Maria   It -1760
   * See 1992 Edition . . . .
Crivelli, Vittorio   It a 1481-1501
   * See 1990 Edition . . . .
Croato, Bruno   1875-1948
   O/Pn 20x18 Vaso di Fiori 1943 Chr 2/92 2,420
Crochepierre, Andre-Antoine   Fr 1860-
   O/C/B 21x18 Lady with Knitting Needles 1887 Hnd 5/92 . . 3,600
Crocker, John Denison   Am 1823-1879
   O/C 24x44 Morning in the Wilds Mys 11/91 1,650
   O/C 24x44 Landscape With Deer 1885 Fre 10/91 1,300
**Crockwell, Spencer Douglass   Am
1904-1968**
   O/M 23x26 Women Wrap Christmas Gifts Ilh 11/91 2,250
   O/B 20x24 Couple Skating Ilh 11/91 1,600
   O/B 23x26 Six People Around New Boat Ilh 5/92 800
Croegaert, Georges   Fr 1848-1923
   O/Pn 8x8 Taking Aim Chr 10/91 5,500
   O/Pn 14x11 Thoughts of the Orient 1887 Chr 5/92 5,500
   O/Pn 14x11 La Lectrice 1887 But 11/91 3,300
Croft, Arthur   Eng 1828-
   W/Pa 21x15 Ducks on the River Mys 6/92 165
Cromwell, Joane   Am -1966
   * See 1992 Edition . . . .
Cropsey, Jasper Francis   Am 1823-1900
   O/C 16x23 A Pastoral Vision 1865 Chr 3/92 44,000
   O/C 9x16 Cabin on Greenwood Lake 1879 Chr 12/91 . . 28,600
   O&Pe/C 14x24 Farm Along the River 1889 Chr 12/91 . . . 22,000
   O/C 10 dia Spring and Summer: Pair 1859 Chr 12/91 . . 19,800
   O/C 13x10 Hudson River, Autumn 1897 Sby 9/91 16,500
   O/C 9x14 Boats Along the Hudson 1890 Sby 3/92 14,850

W&Pe/Pa 16x22 O'er the Hills and Far Away 1892 Chr 5/92 14,300
W&Pe/Pa 16x26 Mellow Autumn Time Sby 12/91 13,200
W/Pa/B 12x19 Inlet Off the Hudson 1891 Chr 5/92 12,100
O/C 5x8 Church at Stoke Poges 1860 Sby 9/91 10,725
O/C 10x20 Sunset 1894 Chr 9/91 8,800
Crosby, Frederick Gordon   Br 1885-
O/C 18x13 Still Life Brd 8/92 82
Crosby, Raymond Moreau   Am 1876-1945
Pe/Pa 9x6 Ten Drawings Chr 9/91 220
Crosby, William   Br 19C
* See 1992 Edition . . . .
Crosio, Luigi   It 1835-1915
* See 1991 Edition . . . .
Crosland, Enoch   Eng 19C
* See 1992 Edition . . . .
Cross, Anson Kent   1862-1944
O/B 7x10 Sunrise Along the Shore Yng 4/92 150
Cross, Henri-Edmond   Fr 1856-1910
O/C 16x13 Portrait of Paul Signac Wes 11/91 7,480
Pe/Pa 12x9 Madame Cross Sewing Sby 2/92 3,575
C/Pa 17x11 Seated Gentleman Sby 6/92 1,320
O/B 10x8 Coastal Scene Wlf 6/92 300
Cross, Henry H.   Am 1837-1918
O/C 24x20 Civil War Cavalry Officer Dum 11/91 550
O/C 36x31 Horse Portrait 1881 Mys 11/91 495
O/C 17x21 Landscape Dum 11/91 200
Cross, John   Eng 1819-1861
O/C 31x48 Thatched House Wlf 9/91 750
Cross, Watson (Jr.)   Am 1918-
W/Pa 18x23 Alaska Street Scene Mor 3/92 900
Crow, Gonzalo Endara   Ecu 1936-
A/C 32x36 Con el Resplandor de la Aurora 87 Chr 11/91 . 18,700
A/C 32x47 Untitled 88 Chr 5/92 14,300
Crowe, Eyre   Br 1824-1910
* See 1992 Edition . . . .
Crowell, Lucius   Am 1911-1988
O/C 24x36 Dock Scene Hnd 3/92 600
O/C 30x44 Beach Scene Hnd 5/92 400
Crowther, H   Eng 20C**
O/C 30x22 Still Life Brass Charger, Vases 1917 Wes 3/92 . . 330
Crufield, R.
O/C 10x13 Field at Sunset Dum 7/92 250
Cruikshank
O/C 16x12 Dutch City Scene Hnz 10/91 275
Cruikshank, George   Br 1792-1878
O/C 19x20 Queen Mab 1860 Sby 5/92 4,675
Cruikshank, Isaac Robert   Br 1789-1856
W&Pe/Pa 7x6 Midnight Hour; All's Well: Pair Sby 1/92 550
Cruikshank, William   Eng 1848-1922
W&G/Pa 7x9 Goldfinch with Nest of Eggs Slo 10/91 625
W&G/Pa 7x9 Robin with Nest of Eggs Slo 9/91 600
Cruys, Cornelis   dut a 1644-1660
* See 1990 Edition . . . .
Cruz-Diez, Carlos   Ven 1923-
* See 1992 Edition . . . .
Csot   Hun 1930-
* See 1992 Edition . . . .
Cuartas, Gregorio   Col 1938-
O/C 29x29 Autorretrato 74 Chr 5/92 4,400
Cubells Y Ruiz, Enrique M.   Spa 1874-1917
* See 1992 Edition . . . .
Cucaro, Pat (Pablo)   Am 1915-
O/C 12x16 Girl Lou 6/92 125
O/C 12x16 Floral Lou 6/92 100
O/C 16x20 Mysterious Maiden Lou 6/92 75
Cucchi, Enzo   1950-
O&MM/C 106x127 Rimbaud a Harrar 1985 Chr 5/92 88,000
L/Pa/C 108x132 Medio Evo 1982 Chr 2/92 73,700
O/C 25x38 Palla Santa 1979 Sby 2/92 22,000
W,Fp&H/Pa 16x12 Le Montagne/Palazzo 1982 Chr 11/91 . . 11,000
H,C&Pl/Pa 10x11 Untitled Chr 2/92 6,600
Y&H/Pa 14x7 Untitled Chr 2/92 5,280
Br&Bp/Pa 8x12 Untitled 1982 Chr 5/92 4,400
Y/Pa 11x8 Untitled 1983 Chr 5/92 3,500

Cucuel, Edward   Am 1875-1951
O/C 31x26 Shades of Autumn Chr 12/91 18,700
O/C 32x32 Ships in the Harbor Sby 4/92 2,420
O/C 30x25 Portrait of Aileen Carlyle Mor 3/92 600
Cuevas, Jose Luis   Mex 1934-
W,I&Y/Pa 23x15 Pareja en la Sinagoga 1981 Chr 11/91 . . . 5,280
H,P&S/Pa 47x31 Los Hambrientos 86 Sby 2/92 5,225
S,W&Pl/Pa 11x14 Political Demogogy 68 Chr 5/92 3,080
W&Pl/Pa 20x10 La Feria de Oklahoma Chr 5/92 2,750
I&S/Pa 17x22 La Escuela Del Crimen 68 Sby 10/91 2,310
Pl,S&W/Pa 14x10 Catalogo de las Torturas Chr 5/92 2,200
I&W/Pa 9x13 Autoretrato como Durer 1969 Hnd 10/91 . . . 1,600
W&Pl/Pa 8x9 Crouching Figure But 5/92 935
I&S/Pa 8x11 From the Diaries of Kafka Sby 6/92 935
W&Pl/Pa 9x7 Figure Study But 5/92 880
Cugat, Delia   Arg 1935-
O/C 38x51 Hacia el Este Chr 5/92 10,450
Cuixart, Modesto   20C
G&I/Pa 21x40 Untitled 1955 Sby 6/92 3,300
Culbertson, Josephine M.   Am 1852-1939
O/B 12x16 Coastals (2) Mor 11/91 150
Cullen, Maurice Galbraith   Can 1866-1934
O/C 21x29 Vue de Moret Sur Loing '93 Sbt 5/92 30,855
O/C 16x22 View of Quebec From Levis 1904 Sbt 11/91 . . 28,050
O/C 31x21 Le Soir Sbt 5/92 23,375
O/C 18x24 Little River, Chicoutimi Sbt 11/91 21,505
O/Pn 10x14 The Double Road 1903 Sbt 5/92 11,220
O/C 18x24 Sunset '96 Sbt 5/92 8,415
O/C 20x24 In the Foothills Sbt 11/91 4,441
Cullin, Isaac J.
* See 1991 Edition . . . .
Culver, Charles   Am 1908-1967
P/Pa 25x20 Canadian Geese 1967 Dum 11/91 1,800
O/M 12x18 November Flowers 1940 Dum 12/91 850
Culverhouse, Johann Mongels   Am 1820-1891
O/C/B 39x54 Skating by Moonlight 1853 Sby 2/92 14,850
O/C 28x44 Blacksmith Shop at Twilight 1867 Skn 5/92 3,520
Cuneo, Jose   Uru 1889-1977
O/Bu/Pn 57x38 Luna Y Ranchos 1942 Sby 11/91 27,500
Cuneo, Rinaldo   Am 1877-1939
O/C 30x36 View of the Embarcadero But 2/92 8,800
O/C 20x24 Rolling Hills and Farm But 6/92 4,400
O/B 11x13 Horses Beside the Barn But 6/92 2,750
O/Pn 13x16 Barges Along the Seine But 2/92 2,475
O/B 12x17 Haystacks Beside Woods But 6/92 1,540
O/B 12x16 St. Francis of Assisi But 6/92 1,100
Cuningham, Oswald Hamilton   Eng 1883-
O/C 20x16 English Charwoman with Kerchief Slo 2/92 250
Cunliff   Eng 20C
O/M 16x12 Floral Still Life in a Niche Slo 12/91 275
Cunningham, John Wilton   Am -1903
O/C 60x41 Portrait of a Woman 1902 Sel 9/91 275
Cuprien, Frank W.   Am 1871-1948
O/C 20x39 Wind Swept Oaks & Poppies Mor 3/92 2,750
O/B 12x18 Coastal Mor 11/91 1,600
O/M 16x21 Silvery Light, Monterey Mor 11/91 1,300
O/Cb 12x16 Coastal Mor 11/91 1,100
O/B 12x18 Coastal Mor 6/92 800
Curran, Charles Courtney   Am 1861-1942
O/C 12x18 Among the Wildflowers Chr 3/92 24,200
O/C/B 6x9 Old Violinist Sby 12/91 1,870
O/C/M 18x22 The Supreme Temple 1936 Skn 9/91 1,430
O/B 10x12 Eagle and Fox Cragsmoor Yng 4/92 1,400
O/C/B 22x18 Princess Among Rhododen. 1920 Skn 9/91 . . 1,100
O/Cb 12x9 Presage of Storm 1930 Sby 4/92 1,045
O/Cb 12x7 The Deer Hunter Skn 9/91 550
Currie, Sidney   Eng 19C
O/C 15x12 Eighty Years Ago 1878 Sel 12/91 650
Currier, Joseph Frank   Am 1843-1909
O/C 18x23 Still Life Copper Pitcher Fre 10/91 1,050
Currier, Mary Ann   Am 20C
* See 1991 Edition . . . .
Currier, Walter Barron   Am 1879-1934
O/C 10x12 New Hampshire Meadow 1916 Mor 3/92 150

Curry, John Steuart   Am 1897-1946
W/Pa 19x24 The Carnival Chr 11/91 3,300
Pl/Pa 9x6 Pawnee Chief 1942 Hnd 3/92 1,000
Curtis, Calvin   Am 1822-1893
O/C 18x24 Farm Along the Housatonic 1854 Sby 4/92 . . 2,970
Curtis, George   Am 1826-1881
* See 1992 Edition . . . .
Curtis, Jenny C.   Am
* See 1992 Edition . . . .
Curtis, Leland   Am 1897-
O/C 28x38 High Sierra Mountain Lake But 2/92 3,850
O/C 28x38 Snow Covered Peaks But 10/91 1,650
G/B 5x6 Kein Kaweah Divide, Sierra Nevada 1931 But 6/92 . 1,210
Curtis, Philip Campbell   Am 1907-
O/B 28x24 Quintet 1958 Doy 12/91 1,800
Curtis, William Fuller   Am 1873-
W/Pa 18x14 Tulips 1916 Yng 2/92 60
Cusachs Y Cusachs, Jose   Spa 1851-1908
O/C 12x20 Mounted Cavalry Sby 2/92 25,300
Cushman, Alice   Am 1854-
W/Pa 3x5 Gloucester Harbor Yng 4/92 125
Custis, Eleanor Parke   Am 1897-1983
G/Pa 20x26 Albanian Market Slo 7/92 3,250
G/Pa 10x10 Walking the Dog Mys 11/91 715
G/Pa 12x9 Women on a Hillside Mys 11/91 715
Cuthbert, B.   Eng 19C
O/C 20x15 Landscape with Waterfall Sel 9/91 100
Cuthbert, Virginia   Am 1908-
O/C 19x14 Young Girl by the Lake Fre 10/91 275
Cutler, Carl Gordon   Am 1873-1945
O/C 28x27 Dutch Girl Planting Eld 7/92 660
Cutone, Gianni   Am 20C
O/Cb 16x20 Vermont Winter Landscape Sel 12/91 125
Cutrone, Ronnie
* See 1992 Edition . . . .
Cutting, Francis H.   Am 1872-1964
O/C 16x20 Landscape 1944 Mor 11/91 375
O/C 7x9 Sand Dunes Mor 11/91 350
Cuyp, Aelbert   Dut 1620-1691
O/Pn 19x29 Figures by the Banks of a River Sby 10/91 . . 40,700
O/C 31x25 Dutch Harbour Mys 6/92 2,640
Cuyp, Benjamin Gerritsz.   Dut 1612-1652
O/C 65x104 Conversion of Saint Paul Chr 10/91 24,200
Cyndo, Jose Rico   Spa 1864-
* See 1992 Edition . . . .
Cyr, Henri De Gouvion Saint   Fr 1888-
O/C 84x56 Ophelia Chr 2/92 17,600
Czelsikowna, J.
O/B 14x19 Yachts, 1930 Yng 4/92 150
Czernus, Tibor
* See 1992 Edition . . . .
Czypka, Alfred   Ger 20C
O/B 8x7 Sitzende mit Scheuenblume 1967 Hnz 5/92 360
D'Acosta, Hy. Walker   Spa 19C
* See 1990 Edition . . . .
D'Aguilar, M.
O/C 24x36 Les Bords De La Riviere '77 Hnz 10/91 500
D'Anty, Henry   Fr 1910-
O/C 18x21 Nature Morte Wlf 9/91 1,200
D'Anville, Hubert-Francois
* See 1991 Edition . . . .
D'Arcangelo, Alan   Am 1930-
* See 1992 Edition . . . .
D'Arthois, Jacques   Flm 1613-1686
* See 1992 Edition . . . .
D'Ascenzo, Nicola   Am 1871-1954
Medium? 44x23 Celestory Window, St. Thomas Slo 2/92 . . . 650
O/C 20x24 Venetians Canal Scene Hnd 12/91 475
D'Avino
O/C 24x31 Family in Interior Setting Dum 1/92 2,750
D'Entraygues, Charles Bertrand   Fr 1851-
* See 1992 Edition . . . .
D'Espagnat, Georges   Fr 1870-1950
O/C 24x29 Maison a Saint-Veran Chr 2/92 33,000
O/C 36x70 La Cueillette des Fruits Sby 10/91 23,100

O/C 32x26 Mere et Ses Deux Enfants Chr 11/91 16,500
O/C 22x15 Femme Nue Debout Chr 11/91 9,900
D'Espic, Christian
* See 1992 Edition . . . .
D'Esposito, Vincenzo   a 1890-1920
W/Pa 9x14 Night Scene--Grand Harbor Slo 9/91 850
W/Pa 10x13 Warship Visit Slo 9/91 850
W/Pa 4x9 Grand Harbor, Valletta Slo 9/91 750
W/Pa 4x11 Grand Harbor, Valletta Slo 9/91 750
W/Pa 6x10 Italian Harbor Scene Slo 10/91 300
D'Este, N.   Con 19C
* See 1992 Edition . . . .
D'Hondecoeter, Gillis Claesz.   Dut 1575-1638
* See 1991 Edition . . . .
D'Leon, Omar   20C
O&Wx/C 16x20 Les Gordas de Pochomil 1986 Chr 5/92 . . . 2,750
O&Wx/C 24x20 Bodegon de Seis Frutas 1987 Chr 5/92 . . . 2,200
Da *, Livinio   a 1596-**
* See 1992 Edition . . . .
Da Carussi, Jacopo   It 1494-1556
* See 1990 Edition . . . .
Da Costa, Milton   20C
* See 1991 Edition . . . .
Da Cotignola, Francesco Z.   It 1470-1532
O&T/Pn 20x16 Madonna and Child at Parapet Sby 1/92 . . 39,600
Da Lodi, Calisto Piazza   It 1500-1562
O/Pn 103x53 The Coronation of the Virgin Chr 1/92 121,000
Da Lugano, Zoppo   1590-1660
* See 1992 Edition . . . .
Da Molin, Oreste   It 1856-1912
* See 1992 Edition . . . .
Da Perugia, Benedetto Di Bonf.   It a 1445-1496
* See 1992 Edition . . . .
Da Ponte, Francesco   It 1549-1592
O/C 32x45 Return of the Prodigal Son Sby 10/91 33,000
O/Cp 37x35 Hercules and Cerberus Chr 5/92 20,900
Da Ponte, Jacopo   It 1510-1592
* See 1992 Edition . . . .
Da Ponte, Leandro   It 1557-1622
* See 1992 Edition . . . .
Da Rios, Luigi   It 1844-1892
W&Bc/Pa 19x25 Venetian Side Canal 1881 Sby 2/92 12,100
Da Salerno, Sabbatini   It 1487-1530
* See 1991 Edition . . . .
Da Santa Croce, Girolamo
* See 1991 Edition . . . .
Da Tivoli, Rosa   Ger 1657-1706
O/C 38x53 Landscape with Herdsman and Flock Sby 5/92   12,100
O/C 37x58 Shepherd with his Horse Chr 5/92 8,800
O/C 38x53 Landscape with Sleeping Herdsman Sby 5/92 . . 7,425
Da Visso, Paolo   It
* See 1990 Edition . . . .
Dabel, E.
O/C 16x24 Landscape Eld 4/92 132
Dabo, Leon   Am 1868-1960
* See 1992 Edition . . . .
Dabos, Laurent   1761-1835
O/C 19x15 Putti Glorifying a Bust 181* Chr 10/91 3,080
Dabourr   19C
O/C 24x31 Six Figures on Barge 1864 Dum 12/91 1,100
Dabudie, Henri   Fr 19C
O/C 26x32 A Cottage by the Bay Chr 5/92 1,800
Dado (Miodrag Djuric)   1933-
O/C 51x38 Composition Fantastique 64 Chr 11/91 6,600
Daggiu   1714-1787
* See 1992 Edition . . . .
Dagnan-Bouveret, Pascal A.   Fr 1852-1929
O/C 40x34 Hamlet et les Fossoyeurs 1884 Sby 2/92 14,300
O/Pn 16x11 Child Feeding Grapes to Bird Sby 7/92 1,650
Dagnaux, Albert Marie Adolphe   Fr 1861-1933
* See 1990 Edition . . . .

Dahl, Hans Nor 1849-1937
O/C 38x62 Sailing in a Sunlit Fjord Sby 10/91 18,700
Dahl, Michael Swd 1656-1743
O/C 50x40 Portrait of a Gentleman Chr 5/92 4,400
Dahlager, Jules Am 20C
* See 1990 Edition . . . .
Dahlgreen, Charles W. Am 1864-1955
O/B 18x22 A By Road But 11/91 1,100
O/M 24x30 Down the Road, Brown County Hnd 12/91 750
Dahlgren, Carl Am 1841-1920
* See 1992 Edition . . . .
Dahn, Walter 1954-
A/C 75x63 Pink Ball & Candle 1982 Chr 11/91 19,800
A/C 63x59 Man in a Boat 1981 Chr 5/92 18,700
A/C 98x59 Untitled Chr 11/91 14,300
A/C 98x63 Untitled 85 Chr 2/92 14,300
O/C 75x63 Dunce Cap 83 Chr 5/92 13,200
A/C 91x91 Untitled (Ex Voto) 87 Chr 11/91 13,200
Daingerfield, Eliott Am 1859-1932
O/C 40x32 Edge of the Forest Sby 12/91 7,150
Daini, Augusto It 19C
W/Pa 19x28 Woman Listening to a Monk Sel 4/92 450
Daiwaille, Alexander Joseph Dut 1818-1888
O/B 17x22 Peasants Leading Their Herds Doy 11/91 10,500
Daken, Sydney Tilden Am 1876-1935
* See 1992 Edition . . . .
Dal Friso, Alvise It 1550-1609
O/C 56x74 The Nativity Chr 1/92 16,500
Dal Sole, Giovanni Gioseffo It 1654-1719
* See 1992 Edition . . . .
Dalby of York, David Br 1794-1836
* See 1991 Edition . . . .
Dalby, John Br a 1838-1853
* See 1991 Edition . . . .
Dalby, Joshua Br a 1838-1893
* See 1991 Edition . . . .
Dalens, Dirck (the Elder) Dut 1600-1677
O/Pn 15x22 Landscape with Shepherds 1642 Sby 5/92 . . 23,100
Dali, Louis Fr 20C
O/C 20x24 La Seine Hnd 3/92 1,000
O/C 20x24 Parisian Flower Market Hnz 10/91 525
O/C 9x11 City in the Snow Hnd 12/91 500
Dali, Salvador Spa 1904-1989
O/C 22x18 Les Sources Mysterieuses Sby 5/92 467,500
O/C 10x18 Psychoanalysis & Morphology 1939 Chr 11/91 242,000
W&Pl/B 40x30 Vase de Fleurs 1956 Chr 11/91 121,000
L,Pl&Br/Pa 13x10 Composition a la jambe Chr 5/92 71,500
W/Ab 19x25 St. Sebastian 1943 Sby 11/91 57,750
Br&S/Pa 31x23 Condottiere 1943 Sby 11/91 52,250
O/B 8x9 Trombone Fashioned Out of Saliva 1936 But 5/92 35,750
W,G&Y/Pa 29x22 Le Songe d'un Alchimiste Sby 10/91 . . 30,800
Pl&S/Pa/B 29x23 Projet de Cour Interieure 1943 Sby 11/91 29,700
A,W&L/Pa 21x16 Breathing Armchair 1925 Sby 11/91 . . . 27,500
Fp/B 30x40 Figure du Grand Masturbateur Chr 11/91 22,000
Pl/Fp&Pe/Pa 10x12 L'Atelier de L'Artiste Chr 11/91 22,000
Pl/Pa 10x8 Secret Life of Salvador Dali: (3) 1942 Sby 2/92 22,000
W&Pl/Pa 9x12 Design for the Decor 1941 Sby 11/91 20,900
W&l/Pa 15x21 Plaza Espanol 1958 Sby 2/92 17,050
W&l/Pa 9x9 Tete de Saint Jean Baptiste Sby 10/91 15,400
Pl&S/Pa 8x12 Tristan Fou 1960 Sby 11/91 15,400
Pl/Pa 14x21 Trois Danseurs 1940 Sby 2/92 14,850
l&Pe/Pa 9x6 Eleanor Holm in Costume Sby 10/91 12,100
l/Pa 10x14 La Madone et l'Enfant Sby 2/92 12,100
Pe/Pa 7x10 Untitled Sby 5/92 11,000
Br&S/Pa 15x21 Femme Nue Allongee Sby 2/92 8,800
Pl&Pe/Pa 6x8 La Madona de los Pajaros Sby 2/92 3,850
Pl&S/Pa 8x10 Etude Pour Une Madone Sby 2/92 3,300
Dallaire, Jean Philippe Can 1916-1965
G/Pa 6x6 Detente-Nice '49 Sbt 11/91 4,441
Dalloni, Emma Segur Fr 1890-1968
W&G/Pa 14x11 Latelier de Chevel 1954 Slo 9/91 775
Damartin, Jose Miralles Spa 1851-
O/Pn 13x16 A Spanish Fiesta 1876 Sby 10/91 19,800

Dameron, Emile Charles Fr 1848-1908
O/C 22x32 Landscape in Brittany Chr 5/92 12,100
O/C 20x26 Crossing the River Sby 7/92 4,400
Damian, Horia 20C
O/Pl 39x35 Petite Composition Ronde Jaune 59 Sby 6/92 . . 990
Damien Con 20C
O/C/B 13x16 Wooded Landscape with Fisherman Sel 2/92 . . 200
Damm, Johan Frederik Dan 1820-1894
* See 1991 Edition . . . .
Damoye, Pierre Emmanuel Fr 1847-1916
O/C 36x61 Vallee de la Forge, Longny Chr 10/91 26,400
Damron, J. C. Am 1903-1989
G/Pa 10x12 Green Jell-O with Fruit Ih 11/91 600
Damrow, Charles Am 1916-
O/M 36x48 The Roundup Slo 2/92 1,750
Damschroder, Jan Jac Matthys Ger 1825-1905
O/C 22x27 The Little Housekeeper Bor 8/92 3,500
O/C/M 15x18 The Cooking Lesson Sby 7/92 1,650
O/C/M 18x14 Gentleman Smoking a Pipe Fre 12/91 900
Damsgaard, P. R. Scn 20C
W/Pa 8x16 Seascape Sel 2/92 90
Dan-Hoai-Ngoc Jap 20C
W/S 25x21 Washing Clothes 1933 Slo 9/91 450
Dana, Charles Edmund Am 1843-1914
W/Pa 27x15 Bruges Fre 12/91 325
W/Pa 27x15 Rio Terra Dea Catecumeni 1894 Fre 12/91 . . . 325
Dana, Edmund T. Am 19C
O/C 27x31 Ship on Stormy Seas 1827 Chr 11/91 2,750
Danby, James Francis Br 1816-1875
* See 1991 Edition . . . .
Danby, Kenneth Edison Can 1940-
Et/B 32x24 Boy on a Culvert '66 Sbt 11/91 7,480
W/Pa 21x27 Late Summer Light '79 Sbt 11/91 7,012
W/Pa 19x27 Neil '69 Sbt 5/92 5,610
W/Pa 19x27 At Milford Haven '67 Sbt 11/91 4,400
Dandini, Cesare It 1595-1658
* See 1992 Edition . . . .
Daneri, Eugenio Arg 1891-1970
* See 1990 Edition . . . .
Dangon, Jeanne Fr 1873-
O/C 30x25 Still Life Chrysanthemums Sby 1/92 2,200
Danhauser, Joseph Aus 1805-1845
* See 1992 Edition . . . .
Daniell, Thomas Br 1749-1840
Pe&S/Pa 13x21 Travellers Observing Temple 1789 Chr 1/92 2,640
Pl,S&W/Pa 15x21 View of Amrooah Gate 1789 Chr 1/92 . . 1,320
Danloux, Henri-Pierre Fr 1753-1809
* See 1992 Edition . . . .
Dann, Frode N. 20C
* See 1991 Edition . . . .
Dannenberg, Alice Fr 1861-
O/C 18x24 Fillettes Faisant du Patin a Glace Sby 2/92 9,625
Danner, Sara Kolb Am 1894-1969
O/Cb 20x24 House at the Crossroads But 10/91 990
O/C 24x20 Narcissus in Oriental Vase Mor 11/91 325
Dansaert, Leon Bel 1830-1909
* See 1992 Edition . . . .
Danton, F. (Jr.) Am 19C
* See 1991 Edition . . . .
Danz, Robert Ger 1841-
* See 1991 Edition . . . .
Darboven, Hanna 20C
l/Pa 29x30 Untitled Sby 11/91 7,700
Dargelas, Andre Henri Fr 1828-1906
O/C 36x28 Chasing the Rat 1864 Sby 2/92 7,700
Darley, Felix Octavius Carr Am 1822-1888
W/Pa 8x11 Praying for Safety from Indians Fre 4/92 750
Darling, Wilder M. Am 1856-1933
O/B 11x16 Fall Landscape Wlf 6/92 475
O/Ab 10x14 The Inlet Bor 8/92 200
Darling, William S. Am 1882-1963
O/C/B 18x20 Riders, Thunderbird Ranch But 2/92 2,475
O/B 16x20 Tide Pools But 2/92 2,200

O/C 20x24 Coastal Mor 11/91 1,000
O/M 24x30 Landscape Mor 6/92 950
O/C 14x18 House in Landscape Mor 11/91 375
Darmanin, Jose Miralles   Spa 1851-
O/C 22x14 Felicitations Apres le Ballet Sby 2/92 7,700
Darrieux, Charles Rene   Fr 1879-1958
* See 1992 Edition . . . .
Dasburg, Andrew Michael   Am 1887-1979
Y/Pa/B 23x19 Trees 1933 Chr 5/92 2,200
Daubigny, Charles Francois   Fr 1817-1878
O/C 35x75 Paysage a Villerville 1859 Sby 5/92 126,500
O/Pn 16x27 Les Bords de l'Oise 1877 Sby 10/91 45,100
O/C 14x23 Lavandieres au Bord de l'Oise 72 Hnd 10/91 . . 45,000
O/Pn 15x27 Village on a River 1868 Chr 2/92 41,800
O/Pn 15x26 Les Canards 1875 Sby 5/92 31,900
O/Pn 11x21 River Landscape Twilight Chr 10/91 30,800
O/Pn 13x23 Bords de Seine, Triel Sby 2/92 26,400
O/B 9x13 Harvesters Resting Chr 10/91 5,060
O/Pn 7x12 Effet de Soir, Valmondois Chr 5/92 4,950
O/Pn 9x16 River Landscape Lou 6/92 3,500
Y/Pa 13x19 Boats on the Shore, Villerville Hnd 10/91 3,400
O/Pa 3x7 Cows Grazing Beside a River Chr 10/91 3,300
Daubigny, Karl-Pierre   Fr 1846-1886
O/Pn 14x23 Punt in a River Landscape 1873 Chr 10/91 . . 17,600
Dauchot, Gabriel   Fr 1927-
O/C 39x20 The Clown Sby 2/92 1,760
Daufin, Jacques
* See 1992 Edition . . . .
Daugherty, James Henry   Am 1889-1974
Pe/Pa 15x5 Nude Woman Wlf 10/91 50
Daumier, Honore   Fr 1808-1879
O/Pn 13x10 Baigneurs Chr 11/91 132,000
Pl,S&C/Pa 9x13 Interieur D'Un Omnibus Sby 11/91 77,000
Pe&Y/Pa 3 dia Tete d'Expression Sby 5/92 18,700
Daux, Charles Edmond   Fr 19C
* See 1990 Edition . . . .
Dauzats, Adrien   Fr 1804-1868
* See 1992 Edition . . . .
Davenport, Henry   Am 1882-
O/C Size? Afternoon Sun Brd 5/92 4,950
Davey, Randall   Am 1887-1964
O/C 20x24 On the Day 1917 Wes 11/91 8,800
David, Gerard
* See 1990 Edition . . . .
David, Hermine   Fr 1886-1970
O/B 29x24 Rue de ville Chr 5/92 4,620
David, Jacques Louis   Fr 1748-1825
* See 1991 Edition . . . .
David, Jean   Fr 20C
T/Pn 25x39 Cityscape Wes 3/92 440
G/Pa 13x10 Portrait of a Man Wes 3/92 275
David, Michael   1954-
MM/Pn 52x99 Invisible Cities IX 1987 Chr 2/92 7,920
O&Wx/Pn 36x34 Untitled No. 61 87 Chr 11/91 2,750
David, Stanley S.   Am 1847-1898
* See 1991 Edition . . . .
Davidson, Alexander   Sco 1838-1887
* See 1992 Edition . . . .
Davidson, Charles Grant   Am 1866-1945
O/C 14x20 Seascape '94 Dum 9/91 400
W/Pa 9x13 Rocky Coast Lou 6/92 300
Davidson, Charles Grant   Eng 1824-1902
W/Pa 10x18 Coastal Scene with a Lighthouse 1890 Wes 3/92 605
Davie, Alan   Br 1920-
O/Wd 15x23 Cats Claw No. 6 68 Sby 2/92 6,050
W/B 22x33 Frogs Idea on a Branch No. 2 1963 Sby 6/92 . . 3,300
Davies, Arthur Bowen   Am 1862-1928
O/B 12x16 The Bathers Chr 11/91 4,180
O/C 26x40 The Hills of Fiesole Chr 11/91 3,850
O/C 18x30 A Fording Song Wes 3/92 3,300
W/Pa 22x17 Six Figures in a Landscape Sby 12/91 2,310
O/C 14x16 Five Nudes in a Landscape Sby 12/91 2,200
O/C 36x27 Nymphs Reposing Chr 11/91 1,540
O/C 8x6 Seated Nude Hnd 12/91 1,000
O/C 20x43 Female Figures Skn 11/91 935

Pe/Pa 14x10 Lady Seated at a Window Hnd 3/92 750
W/Pa Var Figural Studies (3) Wlf 10/91 700
O/Pn 6x10 Hudson Landscape But 4/92 660
W/Pa 7x9 Figures in an Interior Hnd 10/91 650
O/C 16x12 Leda and the Swan Hnd 12/91 650
Y&G/Pa Var Figural Studies (3) Wlf 10/91 550
W/Pa 11x9 Dancing Figures; Reclining: Two Wlf 10/91 . . . 400
W/Pa Var Figural Studies (3) Wlf 10/91 400
Y/Pa 6x7 Theater Scene Lou 12/91 350
C/Pa 15x12 Landscape Sel 9/91 200
Davies, Harold Christopher   Am 1891-1976
A/Pa 23x18 Inverness, 1971 But 5/92 1,650
Davies, James Hey   Br 1848-1901
O/C 24x20 A Country Cottage But 11/91 1,100
Davies, Kenneth Southworth   Am 1925-
O/M 18x38 Four Thirty P.M. Wes 3/92 6,050
Pe/Pa 5x7 Study from Canadian Goose Decoy Wes 3/92 . . 138
Davila, Fernando   20C
* See 1992 Edition . . . .
Davila, Jose Antonio   Am 1935-
* See 1992 Edition . . . .
Davis, A.   Eng 20C
O/C 20x24 Horse and Dog Lou 6/92 150
O/C 12x18 Two Cows in Landscape 1925 Slo 2/92 80
Davis, Alice W.   Am 20C
O/C 20x24 Wychmere Harbor Bor 8/92 400
Davis, B.   Br 20C
O/C 20x30 Landscape with Pond Hnd 5/92 900
Davis, Charles Howard   Am 1856-1933
O/C 17x21 Sunlight and Shadow Skn 9/91 11,000
Davis, Cornelia Cassady   Am 1870-1920
* See 1992 Edition . . . .
Davis, Floyd M.   Am 1896-1966
W/Pa 17x26 Spying on Men Cockfighting 39 Ilh 5/92 2,000
Davis, Gene   Am 1920-
O/C 62x77 Prince William 1976 Chr 11/91 4,950
Davis, Gladys Rockmore   Am 1901-1967
* See 1992 Edition . . . .
Davis, Jack   Am 1926-
W&I/Pa 15x9 Navy Comedy--Peanut Butter Salute Ilh 5/92 . . 700
Davis, John Scarlett   Br 1804-1845
* See 1991 Edition . . . .
Davis, Leonard
O/B 6x10 Pair: Caribou Panorama Eld 7/92 660
Davis, M. E.
O/C 24x18 Flowers Dum 9/91 175
Davis, Miss Miriam J.   Eng a 1884-1893
O/Pn 9x5 Fail Not 1885 Sel 4/92 200
Davis, Richard Barrett   Eng 1782-1854
* See 1992 Edition . . . .
Davis, Ronald   Am 1937-
* See 1992 Edition . . . .
Davis, Stark   Am 1885-
* See 1992 Edition . . . .
Davis, Stuart   Am 1894-1964
O/C 34x23 Jefferson Market Sby 3/92 275,000
G/Pa 22x30 Composition 1863 (Factory by Sea) Chr 12/91 148,500
O/C 15x22 Landscape in Colors of Pear 1940 Sby 12/91 . . 110,000
G&Pe/Pa 7x10 Still Chr 5/92 26,400
I&Pe/Pa 11x17 Study Men Without Women 1932 Sby 3/92 22,000
Pe/Pa 13x18 Gloucester Landscape Sby 4/92 2,200
Davis, Theodore Russell   Am 1840-1894
* See 1992 Edition . . . .
Davis, Warren B.   Am 1865-1928
O/C 24x32 Nude on a Rock Chr 3/92 6,600
O/C/B 14x10 A Nude Draped Female Chr 11/91 935
Davis, Wayne   Am 20C
O/B 18x24 Woman at Window Mys 11/91 165
Davis, William M.   Am 1829-1920
* See 1991 Edition . . . .
Davis, William R.   Am 20C
O/C 18x28 Fishing on Saco River Eld 4/92 1,650
Davisson, Homer Gordon   Am 1866-
O/C 25x30 Houses along River, Indiana Slo 4/92 550

O/Ab 25x30 October on Salt Creek, Fort Wayne Slo 4/92 ... 550
Dawbarn, Joseph Yelverton   Eng a
1890-1930
W/Pa 6x10 Clamdiggers on Shore 1918 Wes 11/91 1,100
Dawes, Edwin M.   Am 1872-1945
* See 1992 Edition ....
Dawson, Manierre   Am 1887-1969
O/C 16x20 Untitled '20 Sby 12/91 5,500
Dawson, Montague   Br 1895-1973
O/C 24x36 The Gallant Hotspur Doy 11/91 30,000
O/C 25x36 Racing Dragons Durn 11/91 27,500
O/C 28x42 Cutty Sark Chr 2/92 19,800
O/C 24x36 The Sunny Solent Hnd 3/92 19,000
O/C 28x43 On the Breath of the Foam Sby 6/92 17,600
O/C 20x31 The Umpire's Boat Sby 6/92 17,600
O/C 20x30 The Call of the Running Tide Hnd 5/92 12,000
G/Pa 20x29 The Thermopylae Sby 6/92 11,000
O&R/B 10x15 U.S. Destroyer Gridley Sby 6/92 6,050
O&R/B 10x15 U.S. Battleship Washington Sby 6/92 4,950
O&R/B 23x15 Signalling at Sea Sby 6/92 4,400
O&R/B 14x21 Bomber Returning Home 1940 Sby 6/92 3,300
G&R/B 15x21 Invasion of Sicily, 1943 Sby 6/92 2,750
MM/B 15x21 Refuelling a British Cruiser Sby 6/92 2,750
Dawson-Watson, Dawson   Am 1864-1939
O/C 67x52 The Hunter 1891 Sby 12/91 2,420
Day, * a 19C**
* See 1992 Edition ....
Day, Bill
Pe/Pa 7x10 Caricature People Mover Problems 85 Durn 1/92 .. 55
Day, James Francis   Am 1863-1942
O/C 34x28 The Marriage Contract Chr 12/91 8,800
Day, Larry   Am 20C
O/C 24x30 Abstract Fre 10/91 500
Dayez, Georges   Fr 1907-
O/C 15x22 La Pianiste 50 Sby 2/92 5,500
O/C 11x14 Neso Del Valle '65 Durn 5/92 2,500
Daynes-Grassot-Solin, Suzanne   Fr 1884-
* See 1990 Edition ....
De Albertis, Sebastiano   It 1828-1897
W/Pa 14x10 Roman Campagna at Dusk Slo 7/92 1,200
De Alcibar, Jose   1751-1803
* See 1992 Edition ....
De Andreis, Alex   Bel 19C
O/C 20x24 Chasseur Avec Son Arquebuse But 5/92 5,500
O/C 29x24 Seated Musketeer with Pistol But 5/92 4,125
O/C 32x26 Portrait of a Cavalier Hnd 6/92 1,500
O/C 22x15 A Muskateer Hnd 5/92 700
O/C 32x25 Portrait of a Cavalier Wlf 11/91 500
De Angeus, Leonid
W/Pa 6x7 Trompe de L'Oeil Print Wlf 3/92 75
De Arellano, Juan   Spa 1614-1676
* See 1991 Edition ....
De Arrieta, Pedro
* See 1992 Edition ....
De Backer, Franois Joseph Thom   Flm
1812-1872
* See 1991 Edition ....
De Backer, Jacob (the Elder)   1560-1589
* See 1992 Edition ....
De Baen, Jan   Dut 1633-1702
* See 1992 Edition ....
De Bar, Alexandre   Fr 1821-1901
* See 1992 Edition ....
De Beauce, Pierre   Fr 19C
O/C 17x24 Travelers/Shepherd Near Castle 1866 Wes 3/92 .. 688
De Beaumont, Charles Edouard   Fr
1812-1888
O/C 23x37 Les Femmes Sont Cheres! Sby 10/91 93,500
De Becker, Jan   Dut 19C
O/Pn 8x12 Rural Farm Village 1891 Wes 11/91 468
De Belay, Pierre
G/Pa 18x24 Le Souper Chez Maxime 1932 Sby 10/91 7,150
De Berg, Louis   Con 19C
O/C 20x36 Fishing Village Slo 10/91 850

De Bergue, Tony Francois   Fr 1820-
* See 1992 Edition ....
De Beul, Franz   Bel 1849-1919
O/C 26x32 Returning from the Fields Chr 10/91 2,420
O/Pn 9x13 Goats Feeding Skn 9/91 440
De Beul, Henri   Bel 1845-1900
O/Pn 33x23 Young Woman with Sheep 1871 Sby 7/92 ... 5,225
De Bie, Cornelis   Dut 1621-1654
O/Pn 24x29 Abraham and Three Angels 1651 Sby 10/91 .. 6,600
De Bievre, Marie   Bel 1865-
O/C 29x37 Still Life Peaches, Plums Chr 2/92 60,500
O/C 28x20 Still Life Flowers and Peaches Chr 10/91 8,800
O/C 24x18 Still Life Flowers and Plums '82 Hnd 6/92 2,800
De Blaas, Eugene   Aus 1843-1931
O/C 43x26 A Token of Love 1891 Sby 10/91 50,000
O/C 39x29 The Pink Rose Chr 10/91 28,600
O/Pn 11x9 A Venetian Beauty 1882 Sby 5/92 10,450
O/Pn 11x8 The Gypsy Girl Chr 10/91 8,800
De Bles, Herri Met   Flm 1480-1550
* See 1991 Edition ....
De Bloot, Pieter   Dut 1602-1658
O/Pn 10x10 Peasants Standing at an Inn Sby 1/92 18,700
O/Pn 15x30 Interior of a Cottage Chr 5/92 17,600
De Bock, Theophile Emile A.   Dut
1851-1904
O/Pn 15x23 The Oaks Sby 5/92 4,950
O/C 30x20 Walk along a Wooded Path Chr 5/92 4,180
O/C 15x24 Cows and Farmhouse But 5/92 3,575
De Bondt, Jan   Fr a 17C
O/C 25x30 Fish in a Wooden Tub 1651 Chr 1/92 12,100
De Bonnemaison, Jules   Fr 1809-
* See 1991 Edition ....
De Botton, Jean   Fr 1898-1978
O/C 10x16 Regatta Mys 11/91 1,100
O/C 32x13 Irises Hnz 10/91 450
O/C 12x9 Vase de Fleurs 1939 Hnd 5/92 225
De Boullogne, Louis   Fr
* See 1991 Edition ....
De Boulogne, Valentin   1591-1632
O/C 55x41 David with the Head of Goliath Chr 10/91 88,000
De Braekeleer, Adrien F.   Bel 1818-1904
* See 1992 Edition ....
De Braekeleer, Ferdinand   Bel 1792-1883
* See 1992 Edition ....
De Braekeleer, Henri   Br 1840-1888
* See 1992 Edition ....
De Brantz, A.   19C
* See 1992 Edition ....
De Breanski, Alfred   Br 19C
O/C 20x30 Loch Lohmon, Scotland Chr 10/91 1,320
De Breanski, Alfred (Jr.)   Br 1877-1945
O/C 16x12 A Riverside Garden Chr 2/92 4,180
O/C 16x12 The Garden Path Chr 2/92 4,180
O/C 24x36 The Seath-Waite Fells Durn 4/92 2,500
O/C 24x16 A Flowering Trellis Chr 5/92 1,800
O/C 24x16 The Open Gate Chr 5/92 1,800
W/Pa 5x9 Highland Landscape Slo 2/92 300
De Breanski, Alfred (Sr.)   Br 1852-1928
O/C 32x48 A Highland Stream Sby 10/91 24,200
O/C/M 24x36 Watering the Cattle at Sunset Sby 5/92 10,450
O/C 24x36 Cattle Watering Mount Snowdon But 5/92 7,150
O/C 24x40 Medrnenham Abbey Sby 1/92 6,050
O/C 24x36 Derwentwater Sby 2/92 5,500
O/C 24x36 Derwent Water Sel 12/91 2,900
O/C 20x30 Near Beddgelert, North Wales Hnd 6/92 2,500
De Breanski, Alfred Fontville   Br 19C
O/C 24x36 Cows Watering in a Lake But 5/92 3,850
De Breanski, Gustave   Br 1856-1898
* See 1992 Edition ....
De Bree, Anthony   Eng 19C
* See 1991 Edition ....
De Bride, B* 18C**
O/C 27x21 Still Life Rabbit and Game Sby 1/92 3,850
De Brinant, Jules Ruinart   Fr 1838-1898
O/C 20x32 Still Life 76 Sby 5/92 14,300

De Broczik, Wenceslas Ger 1851-1901
* See 1990 Edition . . . .
De Bruyn, Cornelis-Johannes Dut a 1763-1828
* See 1990 Edition . . . .
De Burgos, Ralph Am 20C
O/M 18x12 Still Life of Sunflowers 52 Slo 9/91 90
De Caceres, Ruiz Spa 19C
O/Pn 13x10 Afternoon Rest in the Garden 1875 Wlf 3/92 . . 4,600
De Camp, Joseph Am 1858-1923
* See 1990 Edition . . . .
De Carolis, Jacopo It a 15C
T&Gd/Pn 71x43 Madonna and Child Chr 1/92 77,000
De Carrera
O/C 14x18 Spanish Countryside Dum 5/92 90
De Carruci, Jacopo It 1493-1558
* See 1992 Edition . . . .
De Casorati, V. P. It 19C
O/C 50x29 I Parasole Rosso 1898 Sby 10/91 7,700
De Caullery, Louis Flm a 1594-1620
* See 1992 Edition . . . .
De Cavalcanti, Emiliano Brz 1897-1967
* See 1990 Edition . . . .
De Caviedes, Hipolito Hidalgo 1902-
O/C 24x20 Mujer Sentada Chr 11/91 1,650
De Chamaillard, Ernest Ponth. Fr 1862-1930
O/Pn 16x20 Warned Out of Danger Skn 5/92 4,400
De Chatillon, Charles 1777-1844
* See 1992 Edition . . . .
De Chavez, Jose Spa 19C
* See 1991 Edition . . . .
De Chirico, Giorgio It 1888-1978
O/C 27x34 Delights of the Poet Sby 11/91 . . . . 2.42M
O/C 32x24 Mannequins au bord de la mer 1926 Chr 5/92 660,000
O/C 32x24 I Trovatore Sby 5/92 385,000
O/C 31x24 Interno Metafisica con Officina Sby 5/92 . . 352,000
O/C 18x22 Lottatori 1928 Chr 5/92 187,000
O/C 16x20 Piazza d'Italia Sby 5/92 143,000
O/C 16x20 Via Appia 1950 Wes 11/91 81,400
G/Pa/B 11x14 Cavalli Sulla Spiaggia Chr 11/91 51,700
G/Pa/B 12x10 Cavalli e Bagnanti Chr 11/91 49,500
Pe/Pa 15x11 II Bagnante Solitario Sby 5/92 24,750
Pl/Pa 12x10 I Palazzo di Melchiorre Chr 2/92 14,850
De Clausades, Pierre
O/C 21x25 Snow Scene Dum 11/91 800
De Cock, Cesar Flm 1823-1904
O/C 32x47 La Peche a la Ligne 1873 Sby 10/91 15,400
O/C 19x27 Deer in the Forest 1881 Sby 5/92 12,100
De Cool, Delphine Fr 1830-
* See 1990 Edition . . . .
De Corsi, Nicolas It 1882-1956
O/C 13x13 A Busy Harbor Chr 10/91 3,300
De Coster, Adam Flm 1586-1643
O/C 52x37 Young Woman Holding Distaff Sby 1/92 . . . 418,000
O/C 37x27 Young Boy Holding a Candle Sby 10/91 9,900
De Crayer, Gaspas Flm 1584-1669
* See 1991 Edition . . . .
De Curzon, Paul Alfred Fr 1820-1895
* See 1991 Edition . . . .
De Czachorski, Ladislas Pol 1850-1911
* See 1990 Edition . . . .
De Dominicis, Achille It a 1881-1884
O/C 41x29 Girl with Wildflowers & Butterflies Sel 4/92 . . . 4,000
De Dramard, Georges Fr 1839-1900
O/C 18x13 Les Oiseaux Exotiques Sby 7/92 3,025
De Dreux, Alfred Fr 1810-1860
O/C 13x16 Cheval Noir Faisant le Paiffer Sby 6/92 49,500
De Egusquiza, Rogelio Spa 1845-
* See 1991 Edition . . . .
De Espinosa, Jeronimo Jacinto 16C
* See 1991 Edition . . . .
De Fleury, J. Vivien Br a 1845-1870
O/C/B 24x42 Flemish Harbor Scene 1865 Slo 2/92 4,225

De Forest, Lockwood Am 1850-1932
O/C 14x10 Santa Barbara Mission But 6/92 1,320
O/C 10x14 Landscape 12 Mor 6/92 1,300
O/B 9x14 Coastal 1920 Mor 6/92 750
O/B 10x14 Monterey Coastal Mor 3/92 750
O/B 10x14 Cypress Point 1920 Mor 11/91 600
O/B 10x14 Coastal Landscape Mor 11/91 450
De Forest, Roy Am 20C
* See 1992 Edition . . . .
De Franceschi, Mariano It 1849-1896
* See 1992 Edition . . . .
De Fromantiou, Hendrik Dut 1633-1694
* See 1990 Edition . . . .
De Gelder, Aert Dut 1645-1727
* See 1991 Edition . . . .
De Gempt, Bernard
* See 1991 Edition . . . .
De Gerville, A. Fr 19C
O/C 13x18 Haystacks Hnd 6/92 800
De Gheyn, Jacob (II) Flm 1565-1629
K,Pl&S/Pa 5x7 Saint Lucy Chr 1/92 38,500
De Glehn, Wilfrid Gabriel Br 1870-1951
O/C 28x36 The Olive Grove 1907 Chr 10/91 29,700
De Gobbis, Giuseppe It a 1772-1783
* See 1992 Edition . . . .
De Graef, Jan Dut 20C
O/Pn 15x16 Cottage Slo 10/91 250
De Grandmaison, Nicholas Can 1892-1978
* See 1992 Edition . . . .
De Grimm, C.
Pl/Pa 10x10 Cut Short Wlf 3/92 1,100
Pl/Pa 17x13 Three Political Cartoons Ilh 11/91 225
De Groot Am 19C
O/C 8x6 Figures and Shadows 1930 Hnz 5/92 240
De Groot, Frans Arnold Breuhau Dut 1824-1872
* See 1990 Edition . . . .
De Gros, Baron Jean Louis Fr 1793-1879
* See 1991 Edition . . . .
De Guastavino, Clement Pujol Fr 19C
* See 1991 Edition . . . .
De Gyselaer, Nicolaes 1590-1654
* See 1992 Edition . . . .
De Haas, Mauritz F. H. Am 1832-1895
O/C 24x40 Shipping off the Coast 1875 Chr 9/91 30,800
O/C 24x40 Steamships and Sailboats 1874 Chr 3/92 17,600
O/C 27x36 Ships in a Dutch Harbor Skn 11/91 15,400
O/C 18x14 Moonlit Marine Scene Hnd 3/92 3,200
O/C 10x17 High Winds Brd 8/92 2,310
W/Pb 9x14 Ships Off a Rocky Coast Chr 11/91 1,760
De Haes, Carlos Spa 1829-1898
O/B 14x20 Fishing in an Estuary 1875 Chr 10/91 6,380
De Hamilton, Karl-Wilhelm
* See 1991 Edition . . . .
De Haven, Franklin Am 1856-1934
O/C 38x50 Hemlock Shade But 11/91 5,500
O/C 24x20 Woman at a Kettle 1887 Hnz 10/91 1,200
O/C 14x20 Figure Among Dunes 1888 Skn 9/91 825
De Heem, Cornelis Dut 1631-1695
* See 1991 Edition . . . .
De Heem, David Davidsz. Dut a 1610-1669
* See 1990 Edition . . . .
De Heem, Jan Davidsz Dut 1606-1684
* See 1992 Edition . . . .
De Heere, Lukas Dut 1534-1584
* See 1992 Edition . . . .
De Heusch, Jacob Dut 1657-1701
* See 1991 Edition . . . .
De Heuvel, Theodore Bernard Flm 1817-1906
* See 1992 Edition . . . .

De Hondecoeter, Gillis Claesz. Dut 1604-1653
* See 1992 Edition . . . .

De Hondecoeter, Melchior Dut 1639-1695
* See 1991 Edition . . . .

De Hooch, David Dut a 1650-
* See 1991 Edition . . . .

De Hooch, Pieter Dut 20C
W/Pa 17x24 Mother and Child on Beach Hnd 3/92 575

De Hooch, Pieter Dut 1629-1681
* See 1990 Edition . . . .

De Hoog, Bernard Dut 1867-1943
O/C 24x30 Helping Mother Sby 2/92 10,450
O/C 36x47 A Family in an Interior Chr 10/91 7,150
O/C 31x41 Nursing the Baby Chr 2/92 6,600
O/C 16x12 Girl with Cat Dum 12/91 2,100
O/C 39x29 Dinner 87 Hnd 5/92 2,000
O/C 20x16 Two Women in a Kitchen Wes 11/91 688

De Hory, Elmyr Hun 20C
O/C 24x30 Two Women at a Table Hnd 10/91 3,000
O/C 24x32 Boating on the Seine 1968 But 5/92 2,750
O/C 16x20 Danseuses But 5/92 2,475

De Iturria, Ignacio It
* See 1992 Edition . . . .

De Ivanowski, Sigismund Pol 1875-1944
O/C 35x55 Picking Wildflowers 1914 Skn 5/92 4,950
O/C 32x28 Pensive Arab Scholar Ald 5/92 500

De Jankowski, Cheslas Bois
* See 1991 Edition . . . .

De Jode, Pieter (I) 1570-1634
K,Pl&S/Pa 8x11 Elijah in the Fiery Chariot Chr 1/92 5,280

De Johs, Pieter Josselin Dut 1861-1906
O/C 21x26 Still Life Flowers Overturned Basket Chr 10/91 . . 1,540

De Joncieres, Leonce J. V. Fr 1871-
* See 1992 Edition . . . .

De Jong, Betty Fr 1881-1916
O/C 32x26 Paysanne Hollandaise Sby 7/92 1,100

De Jong, Jacobus S. Sterre Dut 1863-1901
O/C 19x15 Interior with Mother and Child Sel 12/91 1,200

De Jonghe, Gustave Leonhard Bel 1829-1893
O/Pn 22x18 Peek-a-Boo Chr 5/92 17,600
O/Pn 29x24 After the Ball; Dreams & Memories Slo 9/91 . 17,000

De Jouderville, Isaac 1613-1648
* See 1992 Edition . . . .

De Kerdrouet, Gustave Edouard Fr 1802-
* See 1992 Edition . . . .

De Koninck, Andries Dut 17C
* See 1991 Edition . . . .

De Kooning, Elaine Am 1920-
O/M 10x8 Untitled '49 Chr 2/92 3,080

De Kooning, Willem Dut 1904-
O/Pa/C 31x22 Woman Sby 11/91 . . . . 3.41M
O/C 80x70 Villa Borghese Chr 11/91 . . . . 2.09M
O/C 59x55 Untitled X Chr 11/91 880,000
O/Pa/C 23x19 Woman Sby 5/92 440,000
O/Pa/B 21x18 Oil Painting on Paper I Sby 11/91 159,500
O/Pa 29x23 Untitled Chr 5/92 71,500
O/Pa 29x23 Untitled Chr 5/92 60,500
O/Pa/B 29x23 Untitled Chr 5/92 35,200
O/B/C 19x24 Untitled Chr 11/91 22,000
C/Pa 18x24 Untitled (Woman) Sby 5/92 13,200

De L'Abadia, Juan a 1473-1500
* See 1992 Edition . . . .

De L'Ain, Helene Girard
O/C 28x20 Micheline et Freya Dum 7/92 400

De La Bastida, Jose Marie a 1783-
* See 1992 Edition . . . .

De La Brely, August Fr 1838-1906
O/Pn 22x14 Lovers Walking in Autumn 1874 Chr 5/92 . 16,500

De La Corte, Gabriel 1648-1694
* See 1991 Edition . . . .

De La Fosse, Charles 1636-1716
O/Pa/C 32x25 God the Father Supported by Angels Chr 5/92 16,500

De La Fosse, Charles Alexander Fr 1829-
* See 1991 Edition . . . .

De La Fresnaye, Roger Fr 1885-1925
K&Pe/Pa 19x13 La Ruche 1912 Sby 5/92 15,400
Pl/Pa 10x8 Figure Studies Sby 10/91 825

De La Fuente, Virgilio Mattoni Spa 1842-
* See 1992 Edition . . . .

De La Gourdaine, Jean-Pierre Fr 1745-1830
Pe&S/Pa 6x7 Paris and Helen 1822 Chr 1/92 1,870

De La Haye, Reinier 1640-1695
* See 1991 Edition . . . .

De La Patelliere, Amedee Fr 1890-1932
* See 1991 Edition . . . .

De La Porte, Henri-Horace R. 1725-1793
O/C 14x17 Still Lifes Peaches, Bread: Four Sby 1/92 . . 231,000

De La Serna, Ismael Spa 1887-1968
O/M 32x26 Still Life -50- Sby 10/91 20,350

De La Torre, Martin Fernandez Spa 1888-1938
* See 1990 Edition . . . .

De La Tour, Maurice Quentin Fr
* See 1991 Edition . . . .

De La Vega, Jorge Arg 1930-1971
O/C 58x45 Los Ritos 61 Chr 11/91 15,400

De La Villeon, Emmanuel Fr 1858-1944
O/Pn 10x9 Paysage D'Automne Wes 11/91 3,740
O/Pn 12x16 Barque sur la Riviere Chr 11/91 3,300

De Lacroix, Charles Fr 1720-1982
O/C 22x32 Waterfall Landscape Sby 5/92 12,650

De Lairesse, Gerard Flm 1641-1711
O/C 36x46 Mercury Ordering Calypso Chr 10/91 126,500
O/C 37x51 Queen Esther Accusing Haman Sby 1/92 . . . 14,300

De Lajoue, Jacques Fr 1687-1761
* See 1991 Edition . . . .

De Lall, Oscar Can 1903-1971
O/C 19x24 Abstract Sel 9/91 150

De Largillierre, Nicolas Fr 1656-1746
* See 1992 Edition . . . .

De Laszlo De Lombos, Philip A. Br 1869-1937
* See 1991 Edition . . . .

De Latoix, Gaspard Am a 19C
* See 1992 Edition . . . .

De Latouche, Gaston Fr 1854-1913
* See 1992 Edition . . . .

De Lavigerie, Samuel Marie C. Fr 19C
* See 1992 Edition . . . .

De Leeuw, Alexis Bel 19C
O/C 36x47 Snowy Winter Landscape Sel 4/92 4,300

De Lempicka, Tamara Pol 1898-1980
O/C 36x18 Portrait Mademoiselle Poum Rachou Sby 5/92 418,000
O/C 37x24 Portrait de la Belle M. Chr 2/92 20,900
O/C 34x42 L'Automne Chr 2/92 19,800
O/C 34x42 Composition Abstraite Chr 2/92 16,500
O/C 29x19 Femme Nue Sby 2/92 14,300
O/C 17x13 Femme au Turban Chr 11/91 12,100
W&Pe/Pa 5x6 Femme Nue Assise Chr 11/91 4,620
O/C 12x16 Le Fruit Chr 11/91 4,400
O/C 16x13 Vase de Fleurs Chr 11/91 4,400
Pe/Pa/Pa 15x12 Femme assise Chr 5/92 4,180
G&W/B 15x10 Femme au chapeau a voile 1925 Chr 5/92 . . 3,300
O/C 20x16 Composition in blue No. 2 Chr 5/92 3,080
O/C 16x12 Composition Abstraite 1960 Chr 11/91 2,420
O/C 16x12 Composition abstraite Chr 11/91 2,200
Pe/Pa 6x4 Three Drawings Chr 11/91 1,210
Pe/Pa 18x13 Two Drawings Chr 11/91 935

De Leon Y Escosura, Ignacio Spa 19C
* See 1992 Edition . . . .

De Leon, Francisco Diaz 20C
* See 1991 Edition . . . .

De Leon, Omar 20C
O/M 29x36 Naturaleza Muerta con Melon 1957 Sby 10/91 . 2,200

De Lette, G. It 19C
W/Pb 19x14 Venezia, Canal Grande Chr 2/92 770

De Lieto, A.   It 20C
O/C Size? View of Cannes Hnd 10/91 950
De Lilie, Watteau   Fr 1731-1798
* See 1991 Edition . . . .
De Lisio, Arnaldo   It 1869-
O/C 34x24 Young Maiden Hnz 5/92 1,000
W/Pa 28x20 The Fisherboy Slo 10/91 650
De Longpre, Paul   Am 1855-1911
O/C 30x24 Still Life Pink Peonies 1884 Sby 1/92 . . . 8,250
W/Pa 19x12 Roses and Bumblebees 1908 But 2/92 5,225
O/C 42x31 Floral Still Life Eld 8/92 3,410
O/C 30x25 Still Life with Roses But 10/91 3,300
W&MM/Pa 18x13 Bunch of Cherries 1903 Mor 11/91 2,250
W/Pa 11x29 Still: Roses & Apple Blossoms 1897 Skn 5/92 . 2,200
De Longpre, Raoul M.   Am 19C
G/Pa 20x25 Daisies But 2/92 4,950
G/Pa 21x28 Roses and Lilacs But 10/91 4,400
G/Pa 27x16 White and Red Roses Sby 4/92 3,300
G/Pa 27x20 Still Life White Roses and Lilacs Wes 5/92 . . 2,200
G/B/B 28x20 Bouquet Lavender and White Lilacs Sby 12/91 . 1,540
G/Pb 20x14 Still Life Roses and White Lilacs Skn 5/92 . . . 880
De Loose, Basile   Dut 1809-1885
O/Pn 25x29 Learning Their Lessons 1864 Doy 11/91 . . . 25,000
O/C 32x27 The Pranksters Sby 1/92 9,350
De Loutherbourg, Philippe   Fr 1740-1812
O/C 27x41 Shepherd and Shepherdess 175? Sby 5/92 . . 25,300
De Luce, Percival   Am 1847-1914
* See 1992 Edition . . . .
De Lummen, Emile Van Marcke   Fr 1827-1890
O/Pn 13x18 Cows Grazing in a Pasture Sby 7/92 3,025
O/C 18x26 Cattle Watering in a Pond But 5/92 2,475
De Lutero, Giovanni-Dosso Dos   It
* See 1990 Edition . . . .
De Lyon, Corneille
* See 1990 Edition . . . .
De Madrazo Y Garreta, Raimundo   Spa 1841-1920
O/C 40x32 Portrait Mrs. Edwin C. Post 1901 Chr 10/91 . . 33,000
De Madrazo Y Garreta, Ricardo   Spa 1852-1917
* See 1992 Edition . . . .
De Maghellen, Alfred   Fr 1871-
* See 1992 Edition . . . .
De Magrath, Georges Achilles   Fr 19C
W/Pa 13x20 A Stop along the Way Chr 5/92 1,320
De Maine, Harry   Am 1880-
O/Cb 8x10 Dusk Slo 2/92 200
De Maria, Nicola   1954-
A/C 75x91 Giorni Del Secolo Nuovo 1981 Chr 5/92 38,500
O/C 45x34 AAA Testa-Polline I Dipinti 1982 Chr 2/92 . . . 35,200
O,H&L/C 20x16 La Testa Allegra Chr 5/92 25,300
MM/C 12x16 Angeli + Mare + Azzurri 1985 Chr 11/91 . . 16,500
De Maria, Walter   Am 1935-
* See 1992 Edition . . . .
De Marseille, Lacroix   Fr 1720-1782
O/C 22x32 Waterfall Landscape Sby 5/92 12,650
De Martini, Joseph   Am 1896-
O/B 20x30 Barges on a River Sby 4/92 1,540
De Matteis, Paolo   It 1662-1728
O/C 49x70 The Journey of Rebecca Chr 5/92 132,000
O/C 51x60 Goddess Iris Appearing Sby 1/92 46,750
O/C 21x45 Erminia Seeking Refuge Sby 1/92 19,800
De Metz, F. Louis Lanfant   Fr 1841-1892
* See 1992 Edition . . . .
De Meyer, Baron Adolphe
Ph 10x6 Portfolio Thirty-Three Photographs Sby 2/92 . . . 2,420
De Meza, William   Am 19C
O/C/B 36x24 Mother and Child 1885 Doy 12/91 2,000
De Molijn, Pieter   Dut 1595-1661
O/Pn 13x20 Dune Landscape with Figures Sby 10/91 . . . 12,100
De Momper, Frans   Flm 1603-1660
O/Pn 24x41 Travellers on a Path Chr 1/92 11,000

De Momper, Frans & Vrancx, S.   Flm 1603-1660
O/C 25x34 Village w/Two Men Fixing Wheel Sby 5/92 . . . 24,200
De Momper, Joos   Flm 1564-1635
O/C 43x65 Alpine Landscape w/Story of Wm Tell Chr 1/92 . 88,000
De Momper, Phillip (I)   Flm
* See 1990 Edition . . . .
De Monfreid, Georges Daniel   Fr 1856-1929
O/B 32x25 Femme a Tasse de The 1906 Sby 10/91 15,950
De Montalant, I. O.   Fr 19C
O/C 35x60 View, Rome w/Colosseum 1878 Sby 1/92 . . . 27,500
O/C 11x21 Figures Dancing Beneath Arbor 1861 Sby 1/92 . 2,090
De Nagy, Ernest   Ger 20C
O/C 30x24 The Young Musician Wes 11/91 962
De Neuville, Alphonse Marie   Fr 1835-1885
O/C 20x16 Vedette de Dragons 1879 Sby 1/92 6,600
De Neuville, Brunel   Fr 20C
* See 1992 Edition . . . .
De Neyn, Pieter   Dut 1597-1639
O/Pn 18x27 River Landscape with a Ferryboat Chr 10/91 . 26,400
De Niccolo, Lorenzo   It
* See 1990 Edition . . . .
De Niro, Robert   Am 1922-
K/Pa 12x16 Gravigny Landscape '62 Skn 11/91 220
P/Pa 15x19 Gravigny '62 Skn 5/92 165
De Nittis, Giuseppe   It 1846-1884
O/Pn 13x9 Place des Pyramides Chr 10/91 165,000
De Nome, Francois   It 17C
O/C 20x30 The Destruction of Sodom Sby 1/92 44,000
De Noter, David Emil Joseph   Bel 1825-1912
O/Pn 24x21 Les Lettres D'Amour 1843 Sby 5/92 22,000
O/Pn 32x25 Un Bon Livre Sby 2/92 11,000
O/Pn 13x10 Still Life Game, Fruit and Pie Sby 7/92 4,950
De Paez, Jose   Mex 1715-
O/Cp 17x13 San Ignacio Chr 11/91 13,200
De Paredes, Vincenta   Spa 19C
O/C 25x45 The Hunting Party Sby 10/91 24,200
O/C 17x27 Tales from the Front Sby 10/91 8,250
De Penne, Charles Olivier   Fr 1831-1897
O/Pn 16x11 Hounds at Rest Fre 4/92 6,000
O/Pn 13x10 Apres La Chasse Sby 6/92 2,200
De Pietro, Giovanni   It a 1432-1479
T/Pn 11x14 Subject from Sienese History Chr 5/92 17,600
De Pietro, Sano   It 1406-1481
* See 1990 Edition . . . .
De Pisis, Filippo   It 1896-1956
* See 1992 Edition . . . .
De Pitati, Bonifazio   It 1487-1553
O/Pn 18 dia The Crowning of the Poet Chr 5/92 28,600
De Poorter, Willem   Dut 1608-1648
* See 1992 Edition . . . .
De Porcia, Francesco   It 16C
* See 1990 Edition . . . .
De Prades, Alfred F.   Br a 1844-1883
O/B 11x16 Two Gentlemen Driving a Pony Sby 6/92 8,800
O/C 15x25 Coaching Scenes: Two Hnz 5/92 5,000
De Pratere, Edmond Joseph   Bel 1826-1888
O/C 22x28 Cows by a Ruin Sby 7/92 5,225
De Puigaudeau, Fernand Loyen   Fr 1866-1930
C&P/Pa 13x11 Parisian Street Scene Wes 5/92 1,540
De Renault, Lex   Fr 20C
O/C Size? Saint Patrick's Cathedral 1900 Mys 6/92 880
De Ribcowski, Dey   Am 1880-1936
O/C 18x28 Sailboat Off the Coast, Marin But 10/91 1,650
O/C 22x38 California Coast in Moonlight Slo 4/92 900
O/C 20x30 Spring Landscape Sel 12/91 600
O/C 20x30 Seascape with Waves Breaking Sel 2/92 450
De Ribera, Jusepe   Spa 1588-1656
* See 1992 Edition . . . .

De Ring, Pieter   Dut 1615-1660
* See 1990 Edition . . . .
De Rosa, Francesco   It 1600-1654
O/C 35x27 Madonna and Child Wlf 6/92 1,700
De Rosa, Pacecco   It 1600-1654
O/C 35x27 Madonna and Child Wlf 6/92 1,700
De Rose, Anthony Lewis   Am 1803-1839
* See 1992 Edition . . . .
De Rudder, Louis Henri   Fr 1807-1881
K/Pa 20x16 Study of an Evangelist Sby 7/92 275
De Ruth, Jan   Fr 20C
O/C 24x19 A Nude Model Sel 4/92 650
**De Saint-Andre, Simon Renard   Fr
1613-1677**
* See 1990 Edition . . . .
De Saint-Aubin, Augustin   Fr 1736-1807
Pe&Cw/Pa 3x2 Presumed Artist & Wife (2) 1767 Chr 1/92 . 5,500
K/Pa 5x3 18th Century Peasant Man Slo 7/92 700
K/Pa 5x3 18th Century Peasant Woman Slo 7/92 700
De Saint-Aubin, Gabriel-J.   Fr 1724-1780
* See 1992 Edition . . . .
**De Saint-Martin, Francisque M.   Fr
1793-1867**
O/C 12x10 Napoleon Receiving a Letter 1824 But 11/91 . . . 3,850
**De Saint-Memin, Charles B. F.   Am
1770-1852**
* See 1992 Edition . . . .
De Santa Maria, Andres   Col 1869-1945
* See 1992 Edition . . . .
De Schryver, Louis Marie   Fr 1862-1942
O/C 41x62 Summer Flowers 1888 Chr 5/92 165,000
O/C 22x26 Le Marche de Fleurs 1891 Chr 10/91 114,400
O/C 27x39 Marchande de Fleurs 1891 Sby 5/92 104,500
De Severinses, Count Charles   20C
O/C 24x28 Landscape with Castle 1917 Hnz 5/92 170
De Silvestre, Louis (II)   Fr 1675-1760
O/C 58x44 Portrait Maria Josepha Queen Poland Chr 1/92   46,200
De Simone, Tommaso   It 19C
G/Pa 14x22 U.S.S. North Carolina Mys 11/91 302
De Smet, Gustave   Bel 1877-1943
* See 1991 Edition . . . .
De Smet, Henri   Bel 1865-1940
* See 1992 Edition . . . .
De Smet, Leon   Bel 1881-
* See 1991 Edition . . . .
De Soria, Martin   It a 1475-
T/Pn 58x28 Adoration of Shepherds & Magi: Pair Sby 1/92   28,600
**De Spinny, Guillaume Jean Jos.
1721-1785**
O/C 37x31 Lady Holding a Gold Cup Sby 1/92 1,650
De Stael, Nicolas   Fr 1913-1955
L/Pa 12x9 Le Picador Chr 5/92 18,700
**De Stomme, Maerten Boelema   Dut a
1642-1664**
* See 1991 Edition . . . .
De Szyszlo, Fernando   Per 1925-
A/C 59x47 Mar de Lurin 88 Chr 5/92 26,400
A/Pn 60x48 Puka Wamani 68 Sby 11/91 20,900
A/C 59x59 Recinto Chr 11/91 19,800
A/Pn 47x47 Inkarri 68 Sby 5/92 17,600
A/C 47x47 Pasajeros 78 Chr 5/92 17,600
A/C 59x59 Mar de Lurin 1987 Chr 11/91 16,500
A/C 40x40 Mar de Lurin Chr 5/92 16,500
De Thulstrup, Thure   Am 1848-1930
* See 1992 Edition . . . .
De Tirtoff, Romain (Erte)   Fr 1892-1990
G/Pa 14x11 Costume Design: Le Toffee Hnd 10/91 1,900
G/Pa 11x8 La Mer Arctique 1928 Hnd 10/91 1,800
De Torres, Antonio   Mex 1666-1754
O/C 77x52 Virgen De Guadalupe 1729 Sby 11/91 38,500
De Troy, Jean-Francois   Fr 1679-1752
* See 1991 Edition . . . .
De Vadder, Lodewyk   Flm 1605-1655
* See 1991 Edition . . . .

De Valira, C.   Con 19C
O/C 21x41 On the Mediterranean 1873 Chr 2/92 3,080
De Valk, Kendrik   Dut 17C
O/C 28x40 Rowdy Schoolchildren at Lessons Sby 10/91 . . 28,600
De Vannes, Albert   Am 1881-1962
O/C 25x30 Autumn Landscape Slo 7/92 600
**De Vaucorbeil, Maurice Romberg   Fr
1862-1943**
W/Pa 15x22 Figures in Marketplace Jerusalem Wlf 6/92 . . . 900
De Vileger, Simon   Dut 1500-
* See 1991 Edition . . . .
De Vito, Michele   It 19C
W/Pa/B 8x6 Costume di Civita Vecchia Chr 5/92 770
De Vity, Antonio   It 1901-
O/C 24x48 Afternoon Street Scene Slo 9/91 150
De Vlaminck, Maurice   Fr 1876-1958
O/C 32x46 La Table de Cuisine 1932 Dum 3/92 170,000
O/C 32x40 Paysage en Neige Sby 5/92 148,500
O/C 22x26 Nature Morte aux Fleurs Sby 5/92 96,250
O/C 21x26 Paysage d'Automne Chr 11/91 88,000
O/C 26x20 Portrait de Femme au Chapeau Sby 11/91 . . . 77,000
O/C 13x17 Maison au Bord de Riviere Sby 2/92 66,000
O/C 18x15 Vase de Fleurs Chr 11/91 62,700
O/C 24x29 Falaises au Bord de la Mer Chr 11/91 41,800
O/C 14x18 Rue de Village Chr 11/91 41,800
W/Pa 12x16 Le Village Chr 11/91 19,800
Br&I/Pa/Pa 15x18 Rue de Valmondois Chr 5/92 8,250
De Vletter, Samuel   Dut 1816-1844
W/Pa 11x9 Preparing the Mid-Day Meal But 5/92 1,210
De Voll, F. Usher   Am 1873-1941
* See 1992 Edition . . . .
De Vos, Florence Marie   Am 1892-
Pe&C/Pa/B 32x25 Manhattan Night Chr 3/92 4,620
De Vos, Marten   Flm 1532-1603
* See 1992 Edition . . . .
De Vos, Vincent   Bel 1829-1875
O/C 20x28 The Wicker Basket 68 Sby 6/92 7,700
O/Pn 10x7 La Toilette du Chien 74 Sby 7/92 2,200
O/Pn 7x10 Monkey Riding a Dog Mys 6/92 1,210
De Vries, Dirck   Dut a 1590-1592
* See 1992 Edition . . . .
**De Vries, Paul Vredemann   Dut a
1567-1630**
* See 1990 Edition . . . .
De Wael, Cornelis   Flm 1592-1667
* See 1992 Edition . . . .
De Waroquier, Henry   Fr 1881-1970
O/C 26x32 Venice Sby 2/92 3,850
**De Warville, Felix-Saturnin B.   Fr
1818-1892**
* See 1992 Edition . . . .
De Wet, Jacob Willemsz.   Dut 1610-1671
O/C 24x33 Joseph Greeting His Father Jacob Sby 10/91 . . 6,050
De Wilde, Frans   Bel 1840-1918
O/C 40x28 Winterpret 1884 Sby 10/91 14,850
O/C 40x28 Bloemenruil 1884 Sby 10/91 14,300
De Witte, Emanuel   Dut 1617-1692
* See 1992 Edition . . . .
De Zubiaurre, Valentin   Spa 1879-
* See 1992 Edition . . . .
De Zubiaurre, Ramon   Spa 1882-
* See 1991 Edition . . . .
De Zurbaran, Francisco   Spa 1598-1664
* See 1992 Edition . . . .
De'Busi, Giovanni   It 1485-1547
O/C 29x25 Gentleman, Wearing Black Chr 5/92 63,800
De'Ferrari, Lorenzo   It 1644-1726
* See 1990 Edition . . . .
De'Rossi, Francesco   It 1510-1563
* See 1990 Edition . . . .
Deakin, Edwin   Am 1838-1923
O/Pn 14x55 Salt Lake Belles, Grapes 1904 Chr 6/92 4,620
Dean, Walter Lofthouse   Am 1854-1912
O/C 16x24 Road to the Beach 97 Skn 11/91 1,980
O/C 20x24 Gloucester Harbor Skn 5/92 1,210

W&G/Pa 15x10 Off Cape Ann 1892 Skn 9/91 935
O/C 14x18 Old Pier, Gloucester Skn 11/91 825
O/C 10x14 Gloucester Harbor Eld 7/92 495

Deandries, A.
O/C 14x10 Cavalier Dum 8/92 850

Deane, William Wood   Br 1825-1873
* See 1992 Edition . . . .

Dearn, W.   Eng 19C
O/Ab 22x27 North Wales Cottage Dum 2/92 400

Dearth, Henry Golden   Am 1864-1918
* See 1992 Edition . . . .

Deas, Charles   Am 1818-1867
* See 1992 Edition . . . .

Deavy, E. J.   Am 20C
O/C 33x40 Brigadier-Trails Luxembourg, 1918 1932 Wes 5/92 468

**Debat-Ponson, Edouard Bernard   Fr
1847-1913**
* See 1992 Edition . . . .

Debertiz, Per   Nor 1880-1945
* See 1992 Edition . . . .

Deblois, Francois B.   Can 1829-1913
O/C 17x31 Road Through the Fields 1877 Skn 9/91 935
O/C 16x31 Sawmill on the St. Croix River 1870 Skn 11/91 . . 935
O/C 12x20 Winter/A Boston Landscape Skn 3/92 935
O/C 12x19 The Hay Wagon 1878 Skn 9/91 880
O/C 20x30 Town by the River Mys 6/92 495

Debre, Olivier   Fr 1920-
* See 1992 Edition . . . .

Debucourt, Philibert-Louis   Fr 1755-1832
O/Pn 6x8 Le Charlatan Chr 5/92 20,900

Decamps, Albert   Fr 1862-1908
O/C 46x26 Woman in a Cottage Interior Wes 5/92 2,200

**Decamps, Gabriel Alexandre   Fr
1803-1860**
* See 1992 Edition . . . .

Dechar, Peter
* See 1992 Edition . . . .

Decker, Joseph   Am 1853-1924
* See 1991 Edition . . . .

**Decorchemont, Francois-Emile   Fr
1880-1971**
* See 1992 Edition . . . .

Dedina, Jean   Czk 1870-
G/B 20x14 Elegant Boating Party 1906 Chr 10/91 6,600

Dedual, Lucien F.   Can 20C
O/C 24x36 Summer Morning, Quebec 1946 Slo 12/91 225

Dedyk, Nanko Johann   Dut 20C
O/C 20x16 The Shoemaker Fre 10/91 90

DeFarthorn, A.   Dut 20C
O/C 25x20 Woman Leaning on a Fence Fre 4/92 2,000

Defaux, Alexandre   Fr 1826-1900
O/C 21x29 A Village Square 1879 Chr 2/92 4,400
O/C 29x24 Figures in a Street, Midday 1858 Slo 7/92 . . . 2,750

Defrees, T.   19C
O/C 12x20 Venice Canal Scene 1882 Eld 7/92 440

Degas, Edgar   Fr 1834-1917
P/Pa 16x10 Danseuse Sby 11/91 . . . . 1.65M
G&P/Pa/B 20x20 Danseuses aux repos Chr 5/92 935,000
P&C/Pa/B 26x22 La Danseuse Russe Sby 5/92 715,000
P/Pa/B 24x18 Danseuse Debout, De Profil Chr 11/91 . . . 385,000
P/Pa/B 20x20 Buste de femme Chr 5/92 352,000
Pe/Pa 12x8 Etudes Pour Danseuses a la Barre Sby 5/92 . . 71,500
P&K/Pa 13x10 Danseuse Sby 5/92 55,000
P/Pa 19x12 La Danseuse Chr 11/91 49,500
C/Pa 16x14 Le Bain Sby 5/92 49,500
Pe/Pa 9x13 Jockey a Cheval Sby 10/91 27,500
C/Pa/B 12x15 Etude de Cheval Sby 11/91 23,100
K/Pa 13x9 Amazone Chr 2/92 7,700
P/Pa 9x11 Two Drawings Chr 2/92 7,700
Pe/Pa 18x12 Etude D'Homme Slo 10/91 4,950
Pe/Pa 8x12 Study of Horses Sby 6/92 4,675
Pe/Pa 6x8 Two Drawings Chr 2/92 3,850
Pa/Pa 14x12 Two Drawings Chr 2/92 3,300

Deglar, A. E.   Am 19C
Pe/Pa 29x22 Two Standing Stags Sel 12/91 25

Degottex, Jean   1918-1988
O/C 51x91 Untitled 58 Chr 11/91 34,100

Dehn, Adolf Arthur   Am 1895-1968
W/Pa 16x22 Bountiful Farm Chr 6/92 2,860
W/Pa 20x28 Park Silhouette 1956 Doy 12/91 1,500
W&H/Pa 17x24 Tropical Village Scene 42 Skn 11/91 1,320
W&H/Pb 18x24 Beauty is Where You Find It '40 Skn 9/91 . 1,265
W/Pa 17x14 The Fruit Carriers Wlf 9/91 800
W/Pa 14x21 Midwestern Farm 1956 Slo 12/91 650
W/Pa 8x6 Haitian Women Wlf 9/91 600
W/Pa 14x20 Farm Landscape 1944 Wlf 3/92 375
G/Pa 7x6 Carribean Woman Wlf 10/91 250

Dehner, Walt   Am 20C
* See 1992 Edition . . . .

Dei Crocifissi, Simone   It a 1330-1339
* See 1990 Edition . . . .

Dei Fiori, Carlo   It 1653-1695
* See 1992 Edition . . . .

Dei Fiori, Gasparo   It 1650-1732
O/C 29x19 Still Life Urn and Basket w/Flowers Sby 5/92 . 13,200

Dei Pietri, Pietro Antonio   It 1663-1716
* See 1992 Edition . . . .

Deike, Clara   Am 20C
G/Pa 22x17 Portrait of a Woman Wlf 3/92 4,500
O/C 30x32 Still Life Pineapples '31 Wlf 9/91 2,750

Deiker, Carl F.   Ger 1836-1892
O/Pn 13x9 Wild Life Scenes (2) Mys 6/92 770

**Deiker, Johannes Christian   Ger
1822-1895**
O/C 44x54 Setter with Hare in Winter Sby 6/92 7,700

Dejuinne, Francois Louis   Fr 1786-1844
* See 1991 Edition . . . .

Del Blondo, Giovanni   It 15C
* See 1991 Edition . . . .

Del Brina, Francesco   1540-1586
O/Pn 36x29 Madonna & Child w/Infant St. John Sby 5/92 . 49,500

Del Buono, Vincent   It 19C
O/B 10x8 Flying Beauty Mys 6/92 138

Del Campo, Federico   Per a 1881-1889
O/C 19x28 Canal de Tintori Sby 2/92 66,000
O/Pn 9x15 After the Concert 1877 Sby 2/92 22,000
O/Pn 7x11 Faggot Gatherers Sby 2/92 6,600
O/Pn 11x7 Torre del Greco, Capri 1887 Chr 10/91 6,600
O/Pn 5x8 Goatherd Sby 2/92 3,300

**Del Campo, Francisco Peralta   Spa
1837-1897**
* See 1992 Edition . . . .

Del Casentino, Jacopo   It 1297-1358
T&Gd/Pn 17x13 Madonna and Child Sby 5/92 187,000

Del Drago, Antonio   It a 18C
W&Cw/Pa/C 24x33 Temple of Sybil, Tivoli 1790 Chr 1/92 . 3,300

Del Fiore, Jacobello   It a 1370-1439
T&Gd/Pn 25x17 The Madonna of Humility Chr 5/92 77,000

Del Garbo, Raffaelino   It 1466-1524
* See 1991 Edition . . . .

Del Landini, Jacopo   It 1297-1358
T&Gd/Pn 17x13 Madonna and Child Sby 5/92 187,000

Del Moro, Battista   It 1514-1575
* See 1992 Edition . . . .

Del Mue, Maurice A.   Am 1875-1955
O/C 20x30 Coastal '09 Mor 3/92 700
O/C 14x20 Mountain Landscape '23 Mor 3/92 550

Del Po, Giacomo   It 1652-1726
* See 1992 Edition . . . .

Del Sellaio, Jacopo   It 1441-1493
O/Pn 27 dia A Tondo: Holy Family Chr 5/92 82,500

Del Torre, Giulio   It 1856-1932
O/Pn 8x11 Dressing the Doll 04 Chr 2/92 3,520

Delachaux, Leon   Sws 1850-1919
O/C 32x15 Warm and Friendly Fire 1884 Sby 7/92 2,310

Delacroix   Fr 20C
O/B 14x16 Village on River Hnd 12/91 700
O/B 14x16 Monte Carlo Hnd 12/91 300

Delacroix, Eugene   Fr 1798-1863
S&Pe/Pa 9x14 Cinq Etudes de lions Hnd 10/91 5,000

81

Pe/Pa 9x5 Figures and Heads Hnd 5/92 950
Delacroix-Garnier, Pauline Fr 1863-1912
* See 1992 Edition . . . .
Delahaye, Ernest Jean Fr 1855-
* See 1992 Edition . . . .
Delamain, Paul Fr 1821-1882
K/Pa 10x18 An Arab Camp Hnd 10/91 600
K/Pa 9x12 Arabs Outside a Tent Hnd 10/91 600
K/Pa 13x12 Group of Mounted Arabs Hnd 10/91 400
Pe/Pa 8x9 Seated Arab with his Horse Hnd 10/91 225
Delance, Paul Louis Fr 1848-1924
* See 1991 Edition . . . .
Delanoy, Jacques Fr 1820-1890
* See 1991 Edition . . . .
Delaroche, Paul Fr 1797-1856
P,W&G/Pa 16x12 Lady in a Blue Dress 1827 Sby 7/92 715
Delarue
O/C 29x23 Les Toits du Vieux Montmartre Dum 8/92 1,700
Delattre, Henri Fr 1801-1876
O/C 14x17 Grey Hunter in His Stall 1850 Doy 11/91 1,900
Delaunay, Jules Elie Fr 1828-1891
K&Cw/Pa 12x7 Standing Female Nude Sby 7/92 440
Delaunay, Robert Fr 1885-1941
O/C 53 dia Premier Disque Chr 11/91 . . . . 5.17M
G&Pe/B 23x18 Helice 1923 Chr 11/91 154,000
W/Pa 19x24 Arc-en-ciel 1913 Sby 5/92 60,500
G/Pa 8x5 Rythme I Chr 5/92 17,600
G/Pa 8x5 Rythme II Chr 5/92 17,600
G/Pa 8x5 Rythme IV Chr 5/92 16,500
G/Pa 8x5 Rythme III Chr 5/92 13,200
Delaunay, Sonia Fr 1885-1979
G,Y&Pe/Pa 7x9 Rythme Colore 1942 Chr 2/92 36,300
W&H/Pa/Pa 12x9 Robe de Nuit 1924 Sby 2/92 3,850
W/Pa 25x19 Composition Chr 11/91 2,750
G&W/Pa 14x20 Composition Chr 11/91 2,640
Delbos, Julius Am 1879-1970
O/C 30x40 Southwest Mission Wes 11/91 1,650
W/Pa 11x15 Semur en Auxois, France Slo 9/91 225
W/Pa 16x13 Barnyard Fre 4/92 80
Delcour, Pierre Fr 19C
O/C 16x12 Courtyard Wes 11/91 688
Delcroix, *** 20C
O/C 15x20 Italian Vista Slo 7/92 575
Delfau, Andre 20C
W&Pl/Pa 13x17 Catulli Carmina Sby 11/91 715
G&I/Pa 11x15 Serenade: Design Sby 11/91 550
W,I&Pe/Pa 14x17 La Reine Morte Sby 11/91 440
GPtl&Pe/Pa 12x29 The Nutcracker: Project for Decor Sby 11/91 440
G&I/Pa 18x12 Alice in Wonderland: Costume Design Sby 11/91 385
Delff, Willem Jacobsz. 1580-1638
O/Pn 19x15 Portrait of Maria Jacob van de Woot Chr 10/91 7,700
Delft, Cornelis Jacobsz. Dut
* See 1990 Edition . . . .
Delhogue, A Lexis-Aguste Fr 1867-1930
O/C 10x8 Washerwoman; Arabs Conversing: Pair Slo 9/91 . 2,500
Dell'Abbate, Niccolo It 1509-1571
* See 1990 Edition . . . .
**Dell'Acqua, Cesare-Felix-G. Aus
1821-1904**
* See 1992 Edition . . . .
**Della Rovere, Giovanni Mauro It
1575-1640**
* See 1992 Edition . . . .
Della Vecchia, Pietro It 1605-1678
O/C 32x56 The Feast of Esther Chr 5/92 46,200
**Dellenbaugh, Frederick Samuel Am
1853-1935**
* See 1990 Edition . . . .
Delmotte, Marcel Bel 1901-1984
O/M 27x20 Seated Nude 1965 Wes 3/92 4,180
O/M 36x48 Le Soleil se Couche 1964 Wes 3/92 1,100
O/M 27x36 Solitude 1969 Wes 3/92 1,100
Delobbe, Francois Alfred Fr 1835-1920
O/C 32x26 La Petite Jardiniere Sby 2/92 18,700

**Delobre, Emile Victor Augustin Fr
1873-1956**
O/Pn 13x16 River and Willow But 5/92 6,050
O/C 16x14 The Newspaper But 5/92 6,050
O/B 13x16 The Rocky Shore But 5/92 6,050
O/Pn 13x16 Vue de Menton 1930 Chr 5/92 5,280
O/B 16x13 Village Pres de la Mer Chr 2/92 4,950
O/Pn 13x16 Harbor with Sailboats 1930 Sby 10/91 4,675
O/B 13x16 Les Hortensias Sby 10/91 4,675
O/B 13x16 Vue de la Mer Chr 2/92 4,620
O/B 13x17 Italian Landscape But 11/91 3,850
O/B 13x9 Marthe in a Shawl But 11/91 3,575
Delooper, William Am 1932-
* See 1992 Edition . . . .
Delort, Charles Edouard Fr 1841-1895
O/C 16x13 Along the Seine Chr 2/92 6,600
O/Pn 8x6 Soldier and Prior Sby 1/92 2,530
Delpy, Hippolyte Camille Fr 1842-1910
O/C 18x22 La Chaumiere A Berneval 85 Sby 5/92 27,500
O/Pn 16x28 Les Bords de L'Yonne 1900 Sby 5/92 16,500
Delpy, Jacques-Henry Fr 1877-1957
O/Pn 17x26 River Landscape with Washerwomen Chr 10/91 1,540
Deluermoz, Henri Fr 1876-1943
* See 1990 Edition . . . .
Delval, Robert Fr 20C
O/C 13x10 Paris Street Scene Wes 5/92 192
Delvaux, Paul Bel 1897-
O/C 36x48 Le Salut (La Rencontre) 38 Sby 5/92 . . . . . . 1.265M
Pl/Pa 7x5 Femme et Homme avec Chapeau Sby 5/92 13,200
Delville, Jean Bel 1867-1953
* See 1990 Edition . . . .
Demachy, Pierre-Antoine Fr 1723-1807
* See 1991 Edition . . . .
Demarest, Suzanne Fr -1981
O/C 10x16 Sur la Plage Doy 11/91 2,000
Demarne, Jean-Louis Fr 1744-1829
O/C 14x19 Landscape with Figures Sby 10/91 7,150
Demarnette Fr 1744-1829
O/C 14x19 Landscape with Figures Sby 10/91 7,150
Deming, Edwin Willard Am 1860-1942
O/C 28x22 Deer in Mountain Mist Slo 9/91 3,250
Demont-Breton, Virginie Fr 1859-1935
* See 1992 Edition . . . .
Demoussey
W&G/Pa 11x8 Pair, Portrait 1851 Dum 10/91 1,500
Demuth, Charles Henry Am 1883-1935
W/Pa 10x14 Plums in Chinese Bowl 1923 Sby 12/91 . . . 181,500
W&Pe/Pb 20x15 Prince's Feathers 1918 Sby 3/92 30,800
W&Pe/Pa 8x5 The Conversation 12 Chr 5/92 16,500
Pe/Pa 9x11 Four Drawings Chr 11/91 1,320
Denes, Agnes 20C
* See 1991 Edition . . . .
Denis, H. Con 19C
* See 1992 Edition . . . .
Denis, Maurice Fr 1870-1943
O/C 59x79 Procession de Fete Dieu 1904 Sby 2/92 55,000
Denisoff-Uralsky, A. K. Rus 20C
O/B 18x24 Fisherman with Boat by a Dock Yng 4/92 400
Denninger, Mary Am 20C
O/B 24x20 Floral Still Life Slo 2/92 110
Dennis, James Morgan Am 1891-
O/B 12x16 Ascending Country Path, Summer Slo 7/92 225
Dennis, Roger Wilson Am 1902-
* See 1991 Edition . . . .
Dentz, T. Am 20C
O/B 6x7 By the River, New York Skn 9/91 220
Depero, Fortunato It 1892-1960
T/B 16x20 Nitrito in Velocita Sby 2/92 38,500
C/Pa 20x20 Due pagliacci Chr 5/92 4,950
O&R/B 14x13 Man Smoking Pipe 1956 Sby 6/92 3,850
Depeul, Frans Fr 20C
O/B 8x5 Lady in a Garden Hnd 12/91 400
Derain, Andre Fr 1880-1954
O/C 26x32 Vue de Cagnes Sby 11/91 231,000
O/C 36x29 Buste a la Draperie Rose Chr 11/91 60,500

K/Pa/C 69x23 Nu Debout Chr 11/91 26,400
O/C 9x10 Nature Morte a la Bouteille Sby 5/92 20,900
O/C 6x10 Deux Pommes Sby 2/92 19,800
O/C 17x14 Buste de Femme Sby 2/92 18,700
O/C 16x14 Portrait de jeune fille Chr 5/92 13,200
O/Pn 13x11 Portrait de Femme Chr 11/91 8,800
PVPa 9x25 Female Nude But 5/92 3,300
C/Pa/B 21x17 Tete de Femme Chr 2/92 2,860
PVPa 12x16 Study Roman Story But 5/92 2,200
K/Pa 16x12 Femme Debout au Rocher Chr 11/91 1,980

Dergonov, Dmitri V.   Rus 1961-
O/M 20x18 White Still Life 1987 Skn 5/92 825

Deri, A*
O/C 21x26 Abstract Composition Sby 2/92 1,980

Dericks, Louis   Fr 19C
* See 1990 Edition . . . .

DeRome, Albert Thomas   Am 1885-1959
O/C 18x24 Monterey Cypress, 1955 But 10/91 3,025
O/Cb 18x24 Santa Cruz Mts. Mor 11/91 2,250
O/C 6x8 Afternoon--Pacific Grove 40 Mor 11/91 1,400
O/C 6x8 Pinos Light--Monterey Bay '46 Mor 11/91 1,300
O/C 6x8 Sandstone Ledges, Carmel Beach - 39 Mor 3/92 . . . 1,000
O/C 6x8 Castroville-Monterey Mor 6/92 900
O/C 6x8 Nun Rock, Pacific Grove 1940 Mor 3/92 900
O/C 6x8 Granite Beach, Carmel, 1938 Mor 11/91 800
O/C 6x8 Granite Shore Pt. Pinos Lighthouse 44 Mor 3/92 . . . 700

Derrick, William Rowell   Am -1941
O/C 27x36 Wooded Landscape Durn 1/92 2,000

Deruth, Jan   20C
O/C 37x21 Adolescent Eld 7/92 330

Des Clayes, Berthe   Can 1887-1968
O/C 15x17 Tending the Flock Sbt 11/91 4,208
O/C 18x24 Horse and Red Sleigh Sbt 11/91 3,740
O/Pn 14x16 Homewards Sbt 11/91 1,870

Des Fontaines, Andre   Fr 1869-
* See 1990 Edition . . . .

Des Gachons, Andre   Fr 1871-
W/Pa 13x19 Matinee de Mai, Cote d'Azur 1902 Wlf 3/92 . . . 200

Des Gobelins, LeClerc   1734-1785
* See 1992 Edition . . . .

Des Jeux, Le Maitre   Fr 17C
* See 1992 Edition . . . .

Desboutin, Marcelin Gilbert   Fr 1823-1902
O/C 15x18 La Bonne a la Voiture D'Enfant Sby 1/92 1,980

Desch, Frank H.   Am 1873-1934
C/Pa 30x22 Man Looming Above Woman Ih 5/92 950

Deschamps, Gabriel   Fr 1919-
O/C 18x22 Vue de Cap Ferat Chr 5/92 1,320

Descubes, A*   Fr 20C**
W&Pe/Pa 18x11 Botanical: 51 Watercolors Sby 7/92 8,250
W/Pa 18x11 Botanical Studies: 49 Watercolors Sby 1/92 . . 5,225

Desflaches, Con 19C
* See 1992 Edition . . . .

Desgoffe, Alexandre   Fr
* See 1991 Edition . . . .

Desgoffe, Blaise   Fr 1830-1901
O/C 39x32 Nature Morte Avec Bibelots Sby 10/91 6,600
O/C 20x14 Still Life Ojbets d'arts Chr 10/91 5,500

Deshayes, Charles Felix E.   Fr 1831-1895
O/C 10x8 Dans Le Foret 1875 Chr 2/92 1,650
O/Pn 18x12 Woods at the Pasture's Edge 1870 Skn 5/92 . . . 550

Deshayes, Eugene   Fr 1828-1890
* See 1992 Edition . . . .

Deshays, Jean-Baptiste   Fr 1729-1756
* See 1991 Edition . . . .

Desir, G.   Hai 20C
O/B 30x41 Landscape with Birds Fre 4/92 500

Desliens, Cecile & Marie   Fr 19C
O/C/B 21x17 Repairing the Umbrella Wlf 9/91 1,500

Despallargues, Pedro   Spa 15C
* See 1991 Edition . . . .

Despeaux, Howard   Am 20C
* See 1992 Edition . . . .

Desportes, Alexandre-Francois   Fr 1661-1743
O/C 28x50 Black & White Hunting Dog 1724 Sby 1/92 . . 231,000
O/C 43x47 Hunting Dogs Chasing Hare 1723 Sby 1/92 . . . 93,500

Desprez, Louis Jean   Fr 1743-1804
Pl&W/Pa 9x14 Festival in a Grotto Hnd 10/91 1,100

Dessar, Louis Paul   Am 1867-1952
O/C 24x30 Returning Home Mys 6/92 1,870

Dessau, Paul-Lucien   Eng 1909-
O/Pn 4x3 Jester Hnz 5/92 50

Dessoulavy, Thomas   Br a 1829-1848
* See 1992 Edition . . . .

Desubleo, Michele Di Giovanni   It 1601-1676
O/C 62x79 The Rape of Europa Chr 1/92 50,600

Desvarreux, Raymond   Fr 1876-1963
O/C 16x13 A French Soldier 1917 Chr 2/92 600
O/C 24x15 The Soldier A. Dallet 1914 Chr 2/92 600

Detaille, Jean Baptiste E.   Fr 1848-1912
O/C 83x111 Soldiers at a Water Pump Sby 10/91 33,000
O/C 40x32 Cossacks Attacked by Guard 1870 Sby 5/92 . . 27,500
W/Pa 14x20 Les Eclaireurs 1893 Chr 5/92 8,800
O/C 27x19 The Enemy Sighted 1899 Sby 10/91 7,700
O/C 30x18 Le Soldat 1883 Sby 5/92 6,600
W&G/Pa 14x11 A Mounted Caribineer 1877 Sby 10/91 . . . 5,500
I,S&G/Pa 8x13 La Musique 1809 Sby 7/92 3,025

Deterelle   Fr 19C
O/C 27x35 Pastoral Scene Fre 10/91 425

Detouche, Henri   Fr 1854-1913
Y/Pa 14x10 Seated Nude Hnd 6/92 275

Detti, Cesare Auguste   It 1847-1914
O/C 19x29 Odalisque 72 Sby 10/91 19,800
O/Pn 13x17 The Hawking Party But 5/92 7,700
O/Pn 14x21 The Recital Sby 10/91 7,700
O/C 13x16 The Young Master Chr 10/91 7,150
O/C 20x16 Discussing a Fine Vintage Hnz 10/91 7,000
O/C 22x15 Faraway Thoughts Chr 10/91 6,600
O/C 19x14 The Printseller's Visit Hnz 10/91 6,000
O/C 30x26 Portrait of a Cavalier Eld 7/92 5,720
O/Pn 14x11 An Explanation Chr 2/92 2,750

Deturck, Henri   Fr 1858-1898
O/B 10x13 Indiscretion Sby 1/92 6,325

Deully, Eugene   Fr 1860-
O/C 20x28 The Letter Wlf 9/91 25,000

Deutsch, Boris   Rus 1892-1978
* See 1990 Edition . . . .

Deutsch, David   20C
* See 1991 Edition . . . .

Deutsch, Ludwig   Aus 1855-1935
O/C 20x24 Still Life of Armor 1880 Sby 1/92 1,760

Devaux, Jules Ernest   Fr 1837-
* See 1991 Edition . . . .

Devis, Arthur   Br 1711-1787
* See 1992 Edition . . . .

Devis, Arthur William   1763-1822
O/C 78x90 Portrait of Peter Denys Chr 10/91 11,000

Dewasne, Jean   Fr 1921-
E/Pn 25x44 Expo 1972 Fre 10/91 4,600

Dewing, Thomas Wilmer   Am 1851-1938
O/C 29x12 Morning But 4/92 143,000
P/B 11x7 Seated Woman Chr 9/91 4,400

DeWolf, Wallace L.   Am 1854-1930
O/C 26x40 Mt. Shasta '15 Mor 3/92 300

Deyrolle, Theophile Louis   Fr -1923
O/C 36x51 Printemps en Bretagne Sby 10/91 31,900

Dezerega, Andrea Pietro   Am 20C
O/M 8x15 On the Bench Slo 7/92 350

Di Bartolo, Andrea   It a 1389-1428
* See 1990 Edition . . . .

Di Benedetto, Steve   1958-
A/C 72x60 What Makes a Man Start Fires? 1987 Chr 5/92 . 3,300

Di Bicci, Neri   It 1419-1491
T/Pn 22x15 Christ on the Road to Calvary Sby 1/92 35,200

Di Bindo, Benedetto   It a 1411-1417
T&Gd/Pn 57x22 Madonna and Child with a Donor Chr 1/92 44,000

Di Bonaiuto, Andrea   It -1377
  * See 1992 Edition . . . .
Di Bonaventura, Segna   It a 1298-1327
  * See 1992 Edition . . . .
Di Cavalcanti, Emiliano   Brz 1897-
  O/C 25x18 Menina com Passaro Chr 5/92 46,200
  O/C 22x18 Carnaval 46 Chr 11/91 38,500
  O/C 18x24 Mulheres Sentadas 50 Chr 5/92 20,900
  I,W&Pe/Pa 8x11 Carinho de Bebe 60 Chr 11/91 8,800
Di Cola Da Camerino, Arcangelo   It a 1416-1429
  * See 1990 Edition . . . .
Di Costa, S.   It 19C
  W/Pa 15x10 The Wine Merchant Slo 9/91 450
Di Cristofano, Mariotto   It 1393-1457
  T/Pn 45x40 The Annunciation Sby 5/92 27,500
Di Francesco, Domenico   It 1417-1491
  T/Pn 39x20 Madonna and Child with Angels Sby 5/92 . . 88,000
Di Fredi, Bartolo   It
  * See 1990 Edition . . . .
Di Ghese Vanni, Arcangelo   It a 1416-1429
  * See 1991 Edition . . . .
Di Giovanni Del Guasta, Girola   It
  * See 1990 Edition . . . .
Di Giovanni, Bartolommeo   It a 1487-1511
  * See 1991 Edition . . . .
Di Giovanni, Benvenuto   It 1436-1518
  T/Pa 22x16 The Nativity Chr 5/92 93,500
Di Giuseppe, Mose Bianchi   It 1836-1900
  W/Pa 17x11 On the Hile of Gignese Over Stresa Sby 2/92 . 6,600
  W/Pa 7x11 Street Scene Sby 2/92 2,750
Di Jacopo, Zenobio   1418-1479
  * See 1992 Edition . . . .
Di Leone, Andrea   It 1610-1685
  * See 1992 Edition . . . .
Di Marino, Francesco   It 19C
  O/Pn 10x14 Panni al Sole: Pair But 5/92 1,540
Di Michelino, Domenico   It 1417-1491
  T/Pn 39x20 Madonna and Child with Angels Sby 5/92 . . . 88,000
  T/Pn 8x19 The Triumph of Eternity Chr 5/92 44,000
Di Nardo, Mariotto   It a 1394-1424
  T/Pn 36x19 Madonna and Child Sby 5/92 63,250
Di Nerio, Ugolino   It a 1317-1349
  T&Gd/Pn 28x16 Saint Andrew Chr 5/92 93,500
Di Niccolo, Andrea   It a 1470-1512
  * See 1992 Edition . . . .
Di Parma, F. Cossio   Per 20C
  O/C 37x29 El Cholo Slo 7/92 240
Di Piero, Alvaro   It
  * See 1990 Edition . . . .
Di Pietro, Sano   It 1406-1481
  * See 1992 Edition . . . .
Di Ridolfo, Michele   It 1503-1577
  * See 1991 Edition . . . .
Di Rosa, Herve   20C
  A/C 73x55 Untitled 83 Chr 5/92 3,080
Di Rosselli, Bernardo Di S.   It 1450-1526
  O/Pn 52x29 The Madonna of the Girdle Chr 1/92 44,000
Di San Marzano, Pasquale R.   It 1851-1916
  O/C 19x14 The Letter 79 Sby 7/92 7,150
Di Simone, Giovanni di Ser G.   It 1407-1486
  T/Pn 34x19 Madonna and Child with Angels Sby 5/92 . . . 71,500
Di Suvero, Mark   Am 1933-
  O/C 17x14 Artist's Workbench But 5/92 1,650
Di Tomme, Luca   It 1330-1389
  * See 1992 Edition . . . .
Diago, Roberto   Cub 1920-1957
  I/Pa 28x22 Leda Sby 5/92 5,500
Diamant, L.   Am 20C
  O/C 20x24 Cove Scene Mys 11/91 220
Diaque, L. C.   Fr 19C
  O/Pn 7x14 Barbizon Landscape Wes 11/91 330

Diaz De La Pena, Narcisse V.   Fr 1807-1876
  O/C 24x17 Venus and Cupids 56 Sby 5/92 33,000
  O/C 22x18 Lutte D'Amours Sby 10/91 15,400
  O/Pn 19x25 Shepherd and a Dog 73 Chr 5/92 12,100
  O/Pn 18x10 Study The Last Tears Chr 2/92 12,100
  O/Pn 16x13 Two Women Conversing 35 Lou 3/92 11,000
  O/Pn 11x14 Enfants Turcs 1835 Sby 10/91 8,800
  O/C 26x35 Stormy Wooded Landscape Chr 5/92 8,250
  O/Pn 15x10 Turkish Mother and Daughter Chr 5/92 8,250
  O/Pn 11x8 Floral Still Life Chr 5/92 6,600
  O/Pn 7x10 Figures Resting in Wooded Clearing Chr 2/92 . . 6,050
  O/Pn 12x9 Gypsies Picking Fruit 51 Doy 11/91 5,250
  O/C 14x17 Faggot Gatherer and Cows Lou 6/92 4,500
  O/C 18x15 Flora and Cupids Skn 11/91 4,400
  O/Pn 21x16 Family in Forest Clearing Hnz 5/92 4,000
  O/Pn 9x13 Landscape with Sunset Sby 1/92 3,850
  O/Pn 13x17 In the Forest Sby 7/92 3,080
  O/C 11x14 Figure in an Autumn Landscape Sby 1/92 1,650
  O/C 17x28 Faggot Gatherer Wlf 9/91 1,600
Diaz, Jose
  O/Pn 36x29 The Annunciation Hnz 10/91 525
Dibbets, Jan   20C
  Ph,Pe&I/Pa 28x39 Triangle Sea 1973 Sby 5/92 6,600
Dickey, Dan   Am 1910-1961
  O/C/B 40x32 By the Sea 42 But 2/92 3,300
Dickinson, Edwin W.   Am 1891-1978
  * See 1992 Edition . . . .
Dickinson, Preston   Am 1891-1930
  O,C&W/Pa 15x22 Spring in the Village '20 Chr 9/91 11,550
  G/Pa 15x19 A View of Quebec Brd 5/92 8,250
  O/C 18x24 Out to Pasture Brd 8/92 3,300
Dickman, Charles   Am 1863-1943
  O/C 26x32 Harbor Scene at Dusk But 2/92 2,750
Dicksee, Herbert Thomas   Br 1862-
  * See 1991 Edition . . . .
Dicksee, Thomas Francis   Br 1819-1895
  O/C 60x33 Miranda 1881 Sby 2/92 27,500
  O/C 30x25 Waiting 1860 Chr 10/91 26,400
Dickson, Jane   20C
  * See 1991 Edition . . . .
Didier, Jules   Fr 1831-1892
  * See 1991 Edition . . . .
Didier-Pouget, William   Fr 1864-1959
  O/C 26x32 Brume du Matin But 11/91 3,300
  O/C 19x28 Le Matin Dans La Coreze 99 Sby 10/91 3,300
Diebenkorn, Richard   Am 1922-
  O/C 93x81 Ocean Park No. 42 1971 Sby 5/92 473,000
  O/C 29x39 Still Life Black Table '62 Sby 5/92 121,000
  G&Y/Pa 25x28 Untitled #52 81 Sby 11/91 99,000
  W/Pa 10x10 Berkeley 52 Sby 5/92 22,000
Diefenbach, Anton Heinrich   Ger 1831-1914
  O/C 16x14 Spoonful for Baby 1865 Skn 9/91 4,950
  O/C 14x20 Reclining Nude Hnd 3/92 1,200
Dieffenbach, P.   Am 19C
  O/C 29x20 Young Woman by a Stream 1887 Fre 4/92 300
Diehl, Arthur Vidal   Am 1870-1929
  O/B 20x40 Mount Monadnock, Winter Skn 3/92 2,750
  O/B 11x31 Still Life 1917 Wlf 9/91 1,200
  O/C 12x18 Venetian Harbor Scene Lou 3/92 725
  O/B 19x21 Dutch Harbour Scene Mys 6/92 715
  O/C 19x29 Seascape with Steamship Dum 7/92 700
  O/C 12x24 Dunes and Distant Sea Skn 9/91 550
  O/C 6x12 Provincetown Dune Skn 11/91 550
  O/C 8x10 Two Marine Scenes Skn 9/91 550
  O/C 12x24 Path Through the Dunes Skn 11/91 522
  O/B 20x29 North African Market Scene 1922 Bor 8/92 500
  O/B 18x21 The Plowman Bor 8/92 500
  O/Pn 16x9 Street and Venetian Canal: Pair Wes 11/91 385
  O/B 9x7 Street Scene Mys 6/92 302
  O/B 20x26 Tending the Sheep Wlf 10/91 300
  O/C 16x24 Sheep Leaving a Barn Eld 7/92 275
Diem, Peter Karl   Am 1890-1956
  * See 1992 Edition . . . .

Dieterle, Marie Fr 1856-1935
O/C 51x65 Troupeau de Vaches Sel 4/92 12,500
O/C 22x18 Landscape with Cows Sby 7/92 3,850
Dietrich, Adelheid Am 1827-
O/C 13x10 Morning Glories 1867 Sby 12/91 30,800
O/Pn 6x5 Still Life with Flowers in a Vase '64 Sby 5/92 . . 14,850
Dietrich, Adolf
* See 1991 Edition
**Dietrich, Christian Wilhelm E. Ger
1712-1774**
* See 1991 Edition . . . .
Dietz, H. R. Am 1860-
* See 1990 Edition . . . .
Dietzsch, Barbara Regina Ger 1706-1783
* See 1990 Edition . . . .
Diez, Carlos Cruz Ven 1923-
Pt/Me 39x39 Physichromie No. 2073 1982 Sby 11/91 9,900
Dike, Phil Am 1906-
W/Pa 14x20 Balboa Harbor But 6/92 3,300
Dill, Laddie John Am 1943-
* See 1992 Edition . . . .
Dill, Otto Ger 1884-1957
* See 1990 Edition . . . .
**Dillens, Adolphe Alexandre Bel
1821-1877**
* See 1990 Edition . . . .
Diller, Burgoyne Am 1906-1964
L/M 11x14 Untitled Sby 11/91 4,950
P,Pe&H/Pa 14x11 First Theme #82-113 62 Sby 2/92 3,850
Dinckel, George W. Am
G/Pb 9x12 Boat in the Ocean Ald 5/92 150
Dine, Jim Am 1935-
A/C 83x54 Pappas Heart #1 1988 Sby 11/91 125,500
A/C 95x58 Smiling & Walking Rue de Seine 1973 Sby 5/92 44,000
E&C/Cd 57x47 Study for a Color Chart 63 Sby 11/91 41,250
O&MM/Wd 6x6 Scissors, Screwdriver 1962 Chr 11/91 35,200
E/Pa 30x31 Hearts 1968 Sby 2/92 24,200
W&L/Pa 27x26 Untitled 1972 Chr 2/92 24,200
E&Pe/Pa 24x36 Untitled 1970 Sby 10/91 19,800
MM/Pa 30x36 Untitled (Left Right) VI 1970 Sby 11/91 19,800
S,C&L/Pa 28x21 Self Portrait with Dayglow 1964 Sby 11/91 16,500
Pe&S/Pa 26x22 After Poussin 1980 Sby 6/92 4,400
H/Pa 25x36 Winter Landscape Wlf 3/92 1,900
O/C 18x17 Untitled Wlf 3/92 1,000
Dinet, Etienne Fr 1861-1929
* See 1992 Edition . . . .
**Dingle, John Darley (Adrian) Can
1911-1974**
O/B 16x20 Bronte Harbour Sbt 5/92 654
Diranian, Serkis Tur 19C
* See 1991 Edition . . . .
Discart, Jean
* See 1991 Edition . . . .
Discepoli, Giovanni Battista 1590-1660
* See 1992 Edition . . . .
Disler, Martin 1949-
O/C 81x130 Untitled 83 Chr 2/92 17,600
A/C 53x82 Untitled 1984 Chr 11/91 14,300
K&Os/Pa 99x59 Dessin 2 84 Chr 5/92 4,180
H/Pa 12x17 Five Drawings 84 Chr 2/92 4,180
W/Pa 42x30 Untitled 85 Chr 2/92 1,980
W/Pa 30x42 Untitled 85 Chr 5/92 1,100
Disney Studios Am 20C
G/Cel 6x8 Seven Dwarfs 1937 Wlf 10/91 2,700
G/Cel 8x9 Wynken, Blynken and Nod 1938 Skn 9/91 2,420
Cel 9x11 Man is Always the Master Dum 2/92 2,250
Cel 8x10 Mowgli & Baloo Dum 12/91 2,000
Cel 8x7 Goofy-How to Play Football 1944 Dum 12/91 1,900
G/Cel 7x6 Dopey from Snow White 1937 Skn 5/92 1,870
Cel 8x14 Snow White - Doc & Grumpy Dum 7/92 1,800
Cel 9x12 Lady and the Tramp 1955 Wlf 10/91 1,700
G/Cel 9x11 Temptations from Pinocchio 1940 Skn 11/91 . . 1,210
Cel 7x9 Deer from Snow White Dum 7/92 1,100
Cel 9x12 Lady and the Tramp 1955 Wlf 10/91 1,100
G/Cel 8x11 Lady and the Tramp 1955 Skn 5/92 1,100

Cel 8x7 Donald Duck 1944 Dum 12/91 1,000
Cel 9x7 Fantasia Dum 7/92 1,000
G/Cel 7x7 Wynken, Blynken and Nod 1938 Skn 11/91 990
G/Cel 7x7 Figaro from Pinocchio 1940 Skn 11/91 935
Cel 8x10 Mowgli & Monkeys Dum 12/91 850
Cel 9x7 Snow White-Sleeping Deer in Forest Dum 7/92 . . . 800
G/Cel 7x5 Dopey Hnd 10/91 750
PI/Pa 10x9 Graduating Mickey Mouse Ih 11/91 650
Cel 5x7 Jiminy Cricket Dum 12/91 650
Cel 10x8 Shere Khan-Jungle Book Dum 12/91 650
Cel 8x10 The Aristocats Dum 1/92 650
G/Cel 10x8 Jiminy Cricket 1940 Skn 5/92 605
G/Cel 9x12 Jiminy Cricket from Pinocchio 1940 Skn 11/91 . 605
Cel 8x10 Baloo & Monkey Dum 1/92 550
Cel 8x10 Donald Duck Dum 12/91 550
G/Cel 8x8 The Ugly Duckling 1938 Skn 5/92 550
Cel 5x7 Two Fish & Bubbles Dum 12/91 550
G/Cel 8x10 Dumbo's Bath 1941 Skn 5/92 522
G/Cel 8x10 Marching Camels from Dumbo 1941 Skn 5/92 . . 495
W&I/Pa 14x4 Mickey Mouse Holding Slice of Bread Ih 5/92 425
Cel 5x7 Chip from Chip An'Dale Dum 12/91 350
G/Cel 8x11 Huey, Dewey and Louie Hnd 3/92 350
Cel 5x7 Pongo, Perdita & Puppies Dum 12/91 350
Cel 8x10 The Aristocats Hnd 12/91 350
W/Cel 9x12 The Practical Pig 1939 Hnz 5/92 350
Cel 8x10 Witch Hazel Dum 1/92 350
G/Cel 9x12 Donald & Goofy Walking Across Plate Lou 3/92 325
G/Cel 8x11 Huey, Dewey and Louie Hnd 3/92 300
G/Cel 8x10 Roquefort the Mouse Hnd 3/92 300
Cel 5x7 Briar Rose & Prince Phillip Dum 2/92 250
G/Cel 6x3 Rabbits: Two Hnd 10/91 200
G/Cel 6x5 Sheriff of Nottingham Hnd 3/92 200
Distelboom 1653-1695
* See 1992 Edition . . . .
Ditscheiner, Adolf Gustav Ger 1846-1904
* See 1990 Edition . . . .
Ditzler, Hugh W. Am 20C
O/B 15x11 Edward's Embarkation at Dover 1899 Slo 4/92 . . 375
Diulgheroff, Nicholay It 1901-1982
G/Pa 36x29 Duplicata Wlf 6/92 1,900
Dix, Otto Ger 1891-1969
* See 1992 Edition . . . .
Dixon, A. P.
O/C 19x15 Prayer Meeting Dum 1/92 750
Dixon, Charles Edward Eng 1872-1934
W&G/Pa/B 11x31 Below Blackwell '02 Sby 1/92 1,760
Dixon, Francis Stillwell Am 1879-1967
O/C 25x30 Autumn Hillside Wes 11/91 1,100
O/B Var Sailing Ships (3) Mys 11/91 330
O/C 12x16 Ship at Full Sail Mys 11/91 330
Dixon, Maynard Am 1875-1946
O/B 22x45 Road to the Ranch 1945 Sby 12/91 63,250
O/C 12x14 House and Fence 1919 But 2/92 7,700
W/Pa 11x15 Mural Sketch: Dragoon Leaut. 1936 But 2/92 . . 3,850
Pe/Pa 8x11 Wild Horses, Nevada 1927 But 6/92 3,300
Pe/Pa 5x6 Cowboy with Lariet 1944 But 2/92 1,210
Pe,I&Cw/Pa 16x10 A Serious Discussion But 10/91 880
Pe/Pa 6x4 San Francisco Man 1902 But 2/92 550
Pe/Pa 7x11 Wild Horses of Nevada 1927 Dum 12/91 500
Dixon, R. L. Am 20C
O/C 14x25 Ship at Sea Fre 10/91 110
Diziani, Antonio It 1737-1797
* See 1992 Edition . . . .
Diziani, Gaspare It 1689-1767
I&S/Pa 3x3 An Angel Slo 7/92 850
I&S/Pa 3x3 An Angel Slo 7/92 650
I&S/Pa 2x3 Angels Amongst Clouds Slo 7/92 600
Do Valle, Rosina Becker 20C
O/C 24x15 Eva Tentando Adao 1967 Chr 5/92 1,650
Do, Giovanni It 17C
* See 1990 Edition . . . .
Doane, Henry W. Am 1905-
W/Pa 16x19 Street Scenes - Virginia City (2) Mor 3/92 . . . 3,750
Dobkin, Alexander Am 1908-
O/C 25x30 Bathsheba Mys 6/92 55

Doboujinski, Mstislav
W/Pa 9x12 Design for the Decor 41 Sby 2/92 3,080
Dobrotka, Anna-Jean   Am 20C
W/Pa 12x18 Old Homestead 1944 Wlf 6/92 250
Dobrotka, Edward   Am 20C
O/C 30x40 Elysian Field Wlf 3/92 4,500
O/C 40x30 Variation on a Theme 40 Wlf 3/92 3,800
O/C 30x28 Bryant Park Chorus 1940 Wlf 3/92 3,600
O/C 30x40 Sar Gosso Sea - Ohio 1939 Wlf 3/92 2,600
W/Cd 16x20 The Fruit Stand Wlf 3/92 1,500
W/Pa 24x36 Death on a Palehouse '34 Wlf 3/92 1,300
W/Pa 14x18 One-Way Wlf 3/92 650
W/Pa 11x16 Steel Mill Wlf 3/92 625
W/Cd 16x20 At the Station Wlf 3/92 550
W/Pa 12x18 Returning Home 1938 Wlf 3/92 550
W/Pa 15x21 Building Under Construction Wlf 3/92 500
W/Pa 17x17 Requiem Wlf 3/92 500
W/Cd 14x22 Houses in Winter Wlf 3/92 400
O/Pa 13x8 Couple at the Street Corner Wlf 3/92 325
W/Cd 15x22 Chevrolet Wlf 3/92 300
W/Cd 14x21 Arcady 1942 Wlf 6/92 225
W/Pa 13x21 Breaking up of the Penelope Wlf 6/92 225
W/Cd 17x30 Downtown Buildings Wlf 3/92 200
O/Ab 18x24 Warehouse at Night Wlf 3/92 200
W/Ab 12x8 Evangeline Gift Shop Wlf 6/92 150
W/Pa 18x23 River Houses in Winter Wlf 6/92 150
W/B 11x15 Miami Beach; Palm Trees: Two '45 Wlf 6/92 . . 100
W/Pa 5x5 Teapot Wlf 6/92 100
W/Pa 11x17 Home in the Country '47 Wlf 6/92 90
W/Ab 14x15 Shipyard with Seagulls Wlf 6/92 90
W/Pa 11x17 Irish Sea '47 Wlf 6/92 80
W/B 15x20 Outside the Monastary Walls Wlf 6/92 80
O/C 24x30 Dwellings on the Canal Wlf 6/92 60
O/B 15x20 Nude Women Sitting on Couch Wlf 6/92 60
Dobrowsky, Josef   Aut 1889-1962
* See 1991 Edition
Dobson, Margaret A.   Am 1888-1981
O/M 36x30 Girl in White Dress 1938 Mor 11/91 375
**Dobson, William Charles Thomas   Br
1817-1898**
* See 1991 Edition . . . .
Dockree, Mark Edwin   Br 19C
* See 1992 Edition . . . .
Dodds, Peggy   Am 1900-1989
O/C 31x22 Surreal Still Life Lou 12/91 300
Dodds, Robert Elihu   Am 1903-
G/Pa/B 16x23 Abstraction Skn 9/91 715
Dodge, Chester L.   Am 1880-
O/B 8x11 October View of the Sakonnet River Slo 4/92 140
Dodge, Ozias   Am 1868-1925
O/B 20x24 Early Spring 1908 Mys 6/92 165
**Dodge, William DeLeftwich   Am
1867-1935**
O/C 47x32 Woman by the Sea 1925 Sby 5/92 12,100
O/C 15x22 Sunset Near Paris 1888 Chr 11/91 2,860
O/C 12x16 In the Garden Wlf 11/91 800
W/Pa 14x10 Figures in a Cathedral '95 Lou 3/92 500
Doe, V.
O/Wd 16x24 Still Life with Fruit and Flowers Dum 1/92 85
Doggett, Frederick G.   Eng 20C
O/C 12x24 H.M.S. Iron Duke 1918 Slo 9/91 225
Dohanos, Stevan   Am 1907-
W,H&T/B 25x20 Mail Early Skn 9/91 1,760
W/Pa 12x19 Northeast Landscape Wlf 10/91 450
**Dohlmann, Augusta Johanne H.   Dan
1847-1914**
O/C 40x27 Foxglove 96 Sby 2/92 10,450
Dokoupil, Jiri Georg   1954-
O/C 81x243 Die Theoretischen Bilder 83 Sby 5/92 45,100
O/C 87x87 Blue Songs About Love 1982 Chr 2/92 18,700
A&K/V&Wd 41x148 Victory Mankind Over Nature Chr 5/92 14,300
MM 92x92 Untitled 1984 Chr 5/92 12,100
A/L 40x40 Man Eating Orange 1985 Chr 11/91 9,900
A/C 40x39 Man Reading Newspaper Chr 2/92 6,600

Dolci, Carlo   It 1616-1686
* See 1990 Edition . . . .
Dolinsky, Nathan   Am 1889-
O/C 25x30 The Porch Dance But 4/92 1,980
O/C 20x16 House in Garden Landscape Mor 3/92 475
Doll, Anton   Ger 1826-1887
O/C 19x33 Skaters on the Bodensee Near Lindau Wes 3/92 11,550
Dolph, John Henry   Am 1835-1903
O/C 14x18 Cat, Dogs and Mouse Skn 3/92 4,950
O/B 10x8 Unexpected Visitor Dum 7/92 1,500
O/C 10x30 Autumn View 1863 Slo 12/91 1,000
Domergue, Jean-Gabriel   Fr 1889-1962
O/C 22x18 Ballerina in Costume Sel 9/91 13,500
O/C 16x13 Seated Nude Sby 2/92 6,325
O/C 16x13 Portrait of a Lady Sby 10/91 5,775
O/B 13x10 L'Enthousiaste Sby 2/92 4,675
O/B 13x9 Kira la Blonde Sby 2/92 3,575
O/B 9x6 Le Dos D'Isabel Sby 2/92 3,575
O/C 20x24 Le Bouquet du Jardin Chr 2/92 1,980
**Domingo Y Marques, Francisco   Spa
1842-1920**
O/Pn 26x21 An Afternoon of Sport 1891 Chr 2/92 49,500
P/B 15x20 Gruppo Settecentesco 1902 Sby 10/91 6,600
Dominguez, Oscar   Spa 1906-1958
O&P/C 8x10 Taureau Chr 11/91 16,500
O/Pn 13x19 Paysage Surrealiste Sby 6/92 7,700
W&I/Pa 9x12 Figure Sby 2/92 5,500
Dominique, John A.   Am 1893-
O/Cb 10x12 Young's Beach Near Capistrano 1949 Mor 3/92 2,000
O/C 22x28 Atmospheric Landscape Mor 3/92 800
O/Cb 10x12 Henry's Beach--Santa Barbara 1956 Mor 11/91 . . . 550
Dommersen, William   Dut 1850-1927
* See 1992 Edition . . . .
**Dommershuizen, Cornelis C.   Dut
1842-1928**
O/C 15x12 A Street in Haarlem 94 Sby 5/92 4,400
**Dommerson, Pieter Christian   Dut
1834-1908**
* See 1992 Edition . . . .
Dommerson, William Raymond   Dut -1927
O/C 16x24 View of an Italian Lake Sby 7/92 1,650
O/C 20x16 La Place des Itales Slo 4/92 1,250
Domond, Wilmino   Hai
O/M 16x48 Pile Cafe 1964 Chr 5/92 2,200
Domoto, Hisao   Jap 1928-
* See 1992 Edition . . . .
Dona, Lydia   1955-
O&A/C 72x68 Typographic Codes 1986 Chr 2/92 1,100
Donadoni, Stefano   It 1844-1911
W/Pa 10x15 Roman Coliseum 1906 Wes 5/92 1,210
Donald, John Milne   Br 1819-1858
O/C 33x48 Figures by a Stream 1853 Chr 10/91 3,850
**Donaldson, Andrew Benjamin   Br
1840-1919**
* See 1991 Edition . . . .
Donati, Enrico   Am 1909-
O&MM/C 40x30 Red Reef 1965 Sby 2/92 5,500
O/C 16x50 Le Terreur Des Lias 1952 Sby 10/91 2,750
Donati, Lazzaro   It 1926-
O&Y/Pn 48x72 La Grande Salute 62 Sby 10/91 2,200
O/Pn 28x20 Figura in Turchese 1964 Chr 2/92 1,210
O/Pn 14x16 Frutta in Grigio 1960 Wes 3/92 495
O/Pn 28x20 Venue 1965 Slo 9/91 400
Donoho, Gaines Ruger   Am 1857-1916
O/C 24x20 Auratum Lilies But 4/92 4,400
**Donouy, Alexandre-Hyacinthe   Fr
1757-1841**
* See 1990 Edition . . . .
Dorazio, Piero   It 1927-
O/Wd&Me 11x17 Expectation Sby 10/91 11,000
Dore, Gustave   Fr 1832-1883
O/C 21x47 Mountain Landscape with Balloon Hnd 10/91 . . 4,000
I/Pa 16x12 Le Capitaine Fracasse Sby 7/92 770
Doret, E.   Con 19C
* See 1992 Edition . . . .

Dorgan, Thomas A.   Am 1877-1929
P/Pa 21x17 Comic Strip. "For Better or Worse" 25 lh 11/91 .   150
Dormont, Philip
Cs/C 18x15 Reaching for Telephone 1950 lh 11/91   150
Dornberger, Karl Johannes A.   Nor 1864-1940
O/Pn 15x16 Bedouin Scene 1918 Slo 9/91   1,000
Dorne, Albert   Am 1904-1965
I&W/Pa 11x17 Crowded New York City Tavern 51 lh 5/92 .   2,500
Dorset, Gerald
* See 1992 Edition . . . .
Dorsey, William   Am 20C
O/B 18x24 California Coast But 6/92   1,760
O/B 14x11 Springtime, Mount McKinley But 6/92   935
O/Cb 18x14 Point Lobos But 6/92   550
Doskow, Israel   Am 1881-
O/C 24x36 Still Life with Globe '36 Fre 10/91   525
O/C 28x30 Still Life with Squash '37 Fre 10/91   275
O/B 13x17 Landscape with Pond Fre 10/91   250
O/C 29x36 Boy Polishing Copper 1939 Fre 10/91   225
O/C 18x24 Still Life with Fruit '53 Fre 12/91   200
W/Pa 15x18 Landscape with Watertower Fre 10/91   125
O/C 20x24 Still Life Vase of Flowers '38 Fre 12/91   120
O/C 12x14 Landscape with a Hill Fre 12/91   100
Dosso Dossi   It
* See 1990 Edition . . . .
Dou, Gerrit   Dut 1613-1675
* See 1990 Edition . . . .
Doubble, Dorothy
W/Pa 15x22 House in Woods Ald 5/92   100
Dougherty, James   Am 20C
O/C 20x30 A Tea Set on a Table Chr 11/91   1,650
Dougherty, Parke Custis   Am 1867-
O/C 24x32 Winter Morning: Quai Voltaire 09 Chr 9/91 . . .   6,600
Dougherty, Paul   Am 1877-1947
O/C 27x36 A Freshening Gale Chr 3/92   5,500
O/C 26x37 Christmas Cove... 1908 Skn 5/92   4,125
O/C 18x24 Afternoon Light But 2/92   3,300
O/C 18x24 Afternoon Light Lou 9/91   2,000
Doughten, Alice B.   Am 1880-
O/B 6x7 Bridge on the King's Highway 1944 Ald 3/92   45
Doughty, Thomas   Am 1793-1856
O/C 21x29 The Fishing Party Sby 12/91   17,600
O/C 26x36 Ben Lomond 1829 Chr 12/91   14,300
O/C 14x20 Hudson River Landscape 1853 Wes 11/91 . . .   3,300
Douglas, Edward Algernon S.   Br 19C
* See 1991 Edition . . . .
Douglas, Edwin   Br 1848-1914
O/C 56x44 Fallow Deer Sby 10/91   7,700
Douglas, Haldane   Am 1893-1980
O/C 20x24 The Farm But 6/92   935
O/B 12x15 The Wash But 6/92   605
O/C 26x30 Landscape 1932 Mor 6/92   600
O/C 20x24 Farmhouses But 6/92   550
O/B 20x24 Winter Landscape But 6/92   495
Douglas, Robert   Am 20C
* See 1992 Edition . . . .
Douglass, Josephine   Am 19C
C/Pa 24x20 Portrait of a Lady Hnd 6/92   50
Doutcheer   Am 20C
O/C 26x36 Waiting Water to Boil Fre 10/91   1,050
Douven, Jan Frans   1656-1727
O/Cp 13x9 Gentleman Playing a Violin 1683 Chr 10/91 . . .   24,200
Douzette, Louis   Ger 1834-1924
O/C 9x14 Afternoon Fishing in Tenpitz But 11/91   1,540
Dove, Arthur Garfield   Am 1880-1946
O/C 22x36 Lattice and Awning Sby 5/92   198,000
Dow, Arthur Wesley   Am 1857-1922
O/Cb 13x11 Cliff at Gay Head Martha's Vineyard Skn 11/91 .   9,350
Dowalskoff, J. A.   Rus 19C
* See 1990 Edition . . . .
Dowd, Robert   Am 20C
O/C 38x48 Cancelled Fifty '64 But 5/92   12,100
MM 18x16 One and Half Dollars '68 Fre 10/91   100

Dowie
O/C 19x15 Colorado River Dum 1/92   55
Downes, Rackstraw   Am 20C
O/C 23x39 110th and Broadway Sby 5/92   14,300
Downie, John P.   Eng 1871-1945
* See 1991 Edition . . . .
Downing, Thomas   Am 1928-
* See 1991 Edition . . . .
Doyen, Gustave   Fr
O/C 50x32 Young Girl in a Garden Chr 5/92   13,200
Doyle, M. J.   Am 20C
O/Cb 20x24 Tabletop Still Life 1962 Slo 4/92   250
Drake, William H.   Am 1856-1926
W/Pa 14x10 Study of a Male Torso 79 Lou 3/92   850
Draper, Herbert James   Br 1864-1920
* See 1992 Edition . . . .
Drayton, Grace   Am 1877-
I&W/Pa 28x19 Paper Dolls of John Alden 1921 lh 11/91 . .   1,300
Drew, Clement   Am 1808-1889
O/C 14x20 Gloucester Brd 5/92   2,860
O/C 22x30 Packet Ship in Boston Harbor Eld 7/92   2,090
Drew, George W.   Am 1875-
O/C 24x36 Cherry Blossoms, Connecticut But 4/92   1,540
O/C 20x30 Old Homestead Mys 6/92   1,430
O/C 16x20 Morning Mist Skn 3/92   1,320
O/C 24x36 Sunny Day at Ronda Spain Hnd 3/92   1,300
O/C 16x12 Connecticut Winter Sunset Lou 3/92   900
O/C 24x36 Landscape with Stream Dum 11/91   800
O/C 24x36 Cherry Blossoms in Connecticut Slo 10/91 . . .   700
O/C 20x30 New England Homestead Hnd 3/92   650
O/C 16x20 Fall Landscape Hnd 3/92   350
Drewes, Werner   Am 1899-1985
O/C 4x9 Untitled 47 Sby 4/92   2,310
O/C 40x29 In the Blue Field 73 Chr 3/92   2,200
O/C 16x22 Marigolds and Dahlias 61 Hnd 3/92   700
Driel, F V**   Con 20C**
O/C 16x20 Still Life Lemons, Pewter Pitcher Wes 3/92   688
Driskell, Eleanore Johnson   Am 20C
O/C 16x20 Backstage Wlf 9/91   2,500
Drolling, Martin   Fr 1752-1817
* See 1992 Edition . . . .
Dromik, Richard   Fr 1953-
O/C 18x15 Chagrin D'Amour But 5/92   1,320
Droochsloot, Cornelisz.   Dut 1630-1673
* See 1992 Edition . . . .
Droochsloot, Joost Cornelisz.   Dut 1586-1666
* See 1992 Edition . . . .
Drost, Willem   Dut -1678
* See 1991 Edition . . . .
Drown, William Staples   Am -1915
P/Pa 23x9 Golden Gate 1877; Lake George: Pair Slo 2/92 . . .   950
O/C 14x18 Church Across River Yng 4/92   450
Druet, Antoine   Fr 1857-
O/C 40x29 Le Bain des Femmes au Harem 90 Sby 2/92 . .   44,000
Drummond, Arthur   Br 1871-1951
O/C 21x24 Feeding the Doves 1889 But 5/92   4,400
O/C 17x20 The Pet Fawn But 5/92   3,850
Drummond, J.   Eng 19C
O/C 20x30 Torchlight Dance Slo 2/92   1,400
Dryander, Johann Friedrich   1756-1812
O/C 33x26 Portrait of a Lady Chr 5/92   3,300
Dryden, Helen   Am 1887-
W&G/Pa 16x13 Woman with Dalmatian 1922 lh 11/91 . . .   5,250
Dryer, Moira
* See 1992 Edition . . . .
Drysdale, Alexander John   Am 1870-1934
P/Pa 6x20 Old Tree on the Bayou But 11/91   2,200
W/Pa 13x21 Weeping Willow 1916 Slo 2/92   1,500
G/Pa 18x30 Bayou Scene Mys 11/91   715
Du Bois, Guy Pene   Am 1884-1958
O/Pn 20x15 Sin Twisters Chr 9/91   115,500
C,PI,W&G/B 16x13 Ladies of Fashion, 14th St. Chr 5/92 . .   22,000
O/C 40x32 Portrait Patrick Henry Bruce Chr 9/91   8,250
Pe/Pa 21x14 Seated Woman and Nude: Double Chr 9/91 . .   7,150

W&I/Pa 15x13 Patience Chr 9/91 4,950
G/Pa 15x14 Nude Sby 12/91 2,640
Pe/Pa 10x8 The Garden Chr 9/91 1,540
Pe/Pa 6x7 Gentleman at the Cafe Lou 6/92 325

Du Bois, Raoul Pene   Am 1914-
Pe&I/Pa 12x21 Three Set Designs Wlf 6/92 75
I&Pe/Pa 12x21 Set Design for "Dixie" 1943 Wlf 6/92 50

Du Bois, Yvonne Pene   Am 1913-
O/C 13x22 Fisherman Lou 6/92 900

Du Frenes, Rudolf Hirth   Ger 1846-1916
O/C 37x28 The Procession Chr 2/92 3,520

Du Mont, Francois   Bel 19C
O/Pn 23x16 La Fidelite 1874 Chr 2/92 2,200

Du Paty, Leon & Poilpot, Theo.   Fr 19C
O/C 19x43 Le Siege de Paris en 1871: Four Sby 2/92 7,150

Du Pavillon, Isidore Pean   Fr 1790-1856
O/C 36x29 Portrait of an Officer 1839 Sby 7/92 2,090

Du Pulgaudeau, Ferdinand   Fr 1864-1930
O/C 20x26 La Grande Briere Sby 2/92 15,950
O/C 18x24 Le Port du Croisic Sby 2/92 15,400

Du Varges, A.   Con 20C
O/C 25x30 Misty Landscape Hnd 3/92 200

Dube, Mrs. Mattie   Am 1861-
O/C 36x24 Feeding the Kitten 1894 Chr 11/91 1,650

Dubois, Arsene   Fr 19C
* See 1991 Edition . . . .

Dubois, Gaston   Con 19C
* See 1991 Edition . . . .

Dubois, Maurice Pierre   Fr 20C
* See 1991 Edition . . . .

Dubreuil, Victor   Am a 1880-1910
* See 1992 Edition . . . .

Dubrowsky, Josef   Aus 1889-1962
G/Pa 17x22 Reflecting Pool '51 Wes 11/91 330

Dubufe, Edouard Louis   Fr 1820-1883
O/C 46x35 Le Prince Imperial Enfant Sby 10/91 8,800
O/C 52x38 Rosa Bonheur in 1849 Sel 4/92 7,000
O/C 64x48 Lending a Hand to the Poor Chr 10/91 3,300

Dubuffet, Jean   Fr 1901-1985
O/M 38x51 D'Ample Deploiement 53 Sby 11/91 363,000
O/M 26x21 Le Pere Conseille 54 Sby 11/91 319,000
O&L/C 36x22 Le Jardin de Recule et Butte 56 Sby 11/91 . . 297,000
A/C 71x55 Inspection du Territoire 74 Chr 11/91 286,000
Pls/C 77x51 Paysage Tricolore IV '74 Sby 11/91 220,000
O/C 20x25 Le Chien Mangeur de Cheveux 43 Sby 11/91 . . 198,000
O/C 22x18 Tete Constellee 52 Sby 11/91 143,000
A/Pa/C 27x39 Site Aux Promenadeurs 82 Sby 11/91 93,500
A/Pa/C 20x27 Site Avec 3 Personnages 82 Chr 11/91 . . . 77,000
A/Pa/B 27x20 Site Avec Trois Personnages 81 Sby 11/91 . . 71,500
G/Pa 13x16 La Vue sur l'Adret III 61 Sby 11/91 68,750
A/Pa/C 26x20 Site Avex 4 Personnages 81 Sby 5/92 66,000
G,Br&I/Pa 12x16 Quatre Arabes 48 Chr 11/91 60,500
A/Pa/C 26x20 Site Avec 3 Personnages 81 Sby 2/92 60,500
Y&PI/Pa/B 13x10 Bedouin, Bras Leves 48 Chr 11/91 44,000
G/Pa/B 14x11 Bum Aux Bras Leves 51 Chr 11/91 38,500
Pnc/Pa 16x13 Chamelier aux Amulettes Chr 11/91 38,500
G&O/Pa 11x14 Vagabond au Chien 51 Sby 5/92 36,300
G&I/Pa/B 10x10 Dubuffet Est Un Sale Con 44 Chr 11/91 . . 35,200
A/Pa 20x26 Site Avec 2 Personnages Chr 2/92 29,500
MM/Pa 18x24 Desert Aux Nuages 54 Sby 5/92 27,500
PI/Pa 13x10 Homme Debout 60 Chr 11/91 25,300
Cp&Mk/Pa 13x10 Paysage Avec Personnage 74 Sby 11/91 . . 25,300
I&L/Pa 14x10 Situation LXXIX (A L'Auto) 79 Sby 5/92 19,800
I/Pa/B 20x26 Air Animee 60 Sby 5/92 16,500
Fp&L/Pa 14x10 Situation XXVIII 78 Chr 11/91 16,500
Y&Mk/Pa 13x10 Paysage Urbain 74 Sby 5/92 15,400
PI,S&Y/Pa 8x7 Mangeur a la Fourchette 49 Chr 11/91 . . . 14,300
H/Pa/B 13x10 Table 51 Chr 11/91 13,200

Dubuis, George S.   Am 20C
* See 1992 Edition . . . .

Dubuisson, Alexander   Fr 1805-1870
O/C 35x52 The Hayfield 1850 But 5/92 9,900

Dubuques, Edward William   1900-
O/C 9x6 Samois-Sur-Seine, 1926 Yng 4/92 225

Ducaire-Roque, Maryse   Fr 20C
* See 1992 Edition . . . .

Ducasse, Gervais Emmanuel   Hai
G,Pe&PI/M 24x32 Revue des Troupes Chr 5/92 1,100
G,PI&Pe/M 24x32 Marche Valliere Chr 5/92 900
G,Pe&PI/M 18x24 Au Cabotage Chr 5/92 715

Duchamp, Marcel   Fr 1887-1968
* See 1992 Edition . . . .

Duchamp, Suzanne   Fr 1889-1963
O/C 22x26 La Fenaison Sous Les Oliviers Hnd 10/91 2,600
O/B 11x14 French Rural Village 1948 Slo 9/91 550

Duchatel, Frederikus Jacobus   Dut 1856-
W/Pa 10x14 Boating on a Canal Chr 5/92 1,650
W/Pa 18x13 Walk along the River Chr 2/92 825

Duck, Jacob   Dut 1600-1660
* See 1991 Edition . . . .

Duckhardt, R.   Am 20C
O/C 24x30 Sierra Landscape Mor 3/92 425

Dudley, Frank V.   Am 1868-
* See 1991 Edition . . . .

Duesberry, Joellyn   20C
* See 1991 Edition . . . .

Duessel, H. A.   20C
O/C 22x36 Forest Scene Dum 1/92 30

Dufaug, G. A.   Fr 19C
* See 1990 Edition . . . .

Duffaut, Prefete   Hai 1929-
O/M 24x29 Erzulie (Reine Titane) 1963 Chr 5/92 5,280
O/M 24x30 Terre Paradis Enfer 60 Chr 5/92 4,180
O/M 23x18 Coin de Jacmel 1963 Chr 5/92 2,640

Duffield, William   Br 1816-1863
O/C 16x29 After the Hunt 1860 Chr 2/92 1,650

Duffy, Aileen Plaskett
O/B 14x14 The Frozen Delaware Ald 3/92 700

Dufner, Edward   Am 1872-1957
O/C 30x25 Early Morning Light Chr 3/92 9,900
W&G/Pa/B 25x30 Summer Noon Skn 3/92 8,250

Dufour, P.   Con 20C
* See 1992 Edition . . . .

Dufresne, Charles   Fr 1876-1934
* See 1992 Edition . . . .

Dufy, Jean   Fr 1888-1964
O/C 21x32 L'Orchestre 27 Chr 11/91 52,800
O/C 24x29 Dans le Bois 29 Sby 5/92 38,500
O/C 15x24 Paysage 1920 Chr 5/92 38,500
O/C 18x22 La Seine, Paris Sby 5/92 35,750
O/C 20x24 Nature Morte sur la Terrasse Chr 2/92 35,200
O/C 21x28 Au Cirque, Cavaliers et Acrobates 25 Sby 5/92 . . 30,800
O/C 18x15 La Chasse a Courre 29 Sby 5/92 27,500
G/Pa/C 18x25 L'Orchestre Sby 5/92 24,200
O/C 32x40 Marche a Bussiere-Haute Vienne Chr 2/92 . . 24,200
O/C 18x22 Paris, Place de la Concorde Chr 2/92 24,200
O/C 14x11 L'Orchestre Sby 2/92 22,000
O/C 14x17 Au Cabaret Sby 5/92 20,900
O/C 15x18 Orchestre et Clowns Musiciens Sby 2/92 . . . 19,800
G/Pa/B 18x23 Paris, Caleches Place Clichy Chr 2/92 . . . 19,800
O/C 15x18 Paris, Montmartre Sby 5/92 19,800
O/C 20x26 Paris, la Seine 26 Chr 11/91 18,000
G/Pa 20x24 Cavaliers et Caleches Vers le Bois Sby 10/91 . . 16,500
O/C 13x16 View of Sacre Coeur Wes 3/92 16,500
W&G/Pa/B 20x26 Le Village Chr 11/91 15,400
O/C 15x18 Quai de la Monnaie Sby 10/91 15,400
O/C 15x16 Les Toits de Paris Hnd 12/91 13,500
W&G/Pa 21x27 Le Paddock Sby 5/92 13,200
W/Pa 18x24 Les Champs Elysee Lou 12/91 11,000
O/C 12x18 Nature Morte Sel 12/91 10,500
O/C 11x18 La ferme 27 Chr 5/92 9,900
W&G/Pa 19x25 Le Port Chr 11/91 9,350
W&G/Pa 19x24 Promenade Along the Seine Yng 2/92 . . . 7,000
O/C 9x22 Voiliers Chr 2/92 6,000
O/C 6x10 Sailboats in a Harbor But 5/92 4,950
W&H/Pa 21x17 House Among The Trees Sby 10/91 . . . 4,400
G,W&Pe/Pa 11x8 Fleurs 1916 Sby 2/92 3,575
W/Pa 12x14 Paris Street Scene Wes 5/92 2,970
W&PI/Pa 5x9 Cafe de Pont Neuf Lou 3/92 2,100

W/Pa 13x9 Floral Mys 6/92 1,650
Pe/Pa 10x18 The Farm; Harvester: Pair Sby 2/92 1,100

Dufy, Raoul   Fr 1877-1953
O/C 26x32 Barques Aux Martigues Sby 11/91 687,500
G&W/Pa 20x26 Cannes 1940 Sby 5/92 49,500
W/Pa 19x24 Le Conseil De Revision Sby 5/92 46,750
W&Y/Pa 20x26 Vence, Le Village Sby 11/91 45,100
W/Pa 20x26 La Mare aux Canards Sby 2/92 44,000
G/Pa/C 20x26 Chateau d'Usse Chr 5/92 38,500
O/C 13x16 Le Retour de Chasse Sby 5/92 33,000
W&G/Pa 19x25 Les Chevaux Rouges Sby 5/92 30,250
W&G/Pa 20x26 Golfe Juan, La Petite Chapelle Sby 5/92 . . 28,600
G/Pa/Pa 26x20 Grand Bouquet 1922 Chr 5/92 28,600
O/Pa/Pn 10x18 Instruments a Cordes Chr 11/91 28,600
G&W/Pa 20x25 Les Courses 1929 Chr 5/92 22,000
Pl/Pa 19x26 Jeune Fille a Cheval Sby 10/91 5,500
W&Y/Pa 13x16 Nature Morte Aux Figues Chr 5/92 5,280
Pe/B 21x17 Portrait de Femme Chr 11/91 2,860
Pl/Pa 23x16 Nue Assis But 11/91 2,750
Pl/Pa 18x22 Nu a la coquille Chr 5/92 2,420

Dughet, Gaspard   Fr 1615-1675
* See 1992 Edition . . . .

Dujardin, Karel   Dut 1622-1678
* See 1991 Edition . . . .

Dujardin, Rene Maire   Am 20C
W/Pa 5x6 Two: Harbor Scenes with Skyline Sel 12/91 50

Duke Y Ferrer, Salvatore   20C
O/C 24x30 Still w/Apple Blossoms & Bowl '86 Sby 10/91 . . 1,100

Duke, Alfred   Br 19C
O/C 36x28 In Cover (The Hunt) Fre 10/91 6,100

Dulac, Edmund   Br 1882-1953
G/B 13x12 Queen Isabella of Bavaria Chr 5/92 17,600
W&G/Pb 17x14 Fairyland Lovers Skn 9/91 5,500

Dull, Christian L.   Am 1902-
O/C 24x30 Surf Breaking Slo 2/92 350
O/C 24x30 Surf Breaking Along the Coast Fre 12/91 300

Dull, John J.   Am 1862-
W/Pa 16x21 Landscape Ald 5/92 85

Duluard, Hippolyte Francois L.   Fr 1871-
* See 1992 Edition . . . .

Dummer, Joseph Owen   Am 1844-1935
W/Pa 17x20 Mountain Brook 1902 Brd 8/92 742

Dumond, Frank Vincent   Am 1865-1951
O/C 24x30 Margaree River Valley Skn 11/91 1,320
Pl/Pa 7x10 Townscape 1892 Ih 11/91 750

Dumont, Francois   Fr 19C
* See 1992 Edition . . . .

Dumont, Pierre   Fr 1884-1936
* See 1992 Edition . . . .

Dumont, R.   Con 19C
* See 1992 Edition . . . .

Dunbar, Harold C.   Am 1882-1953
O/C 29x22 Path Through Winter Woods 1919 Skn 3/92 880
O/C 24x30 Still Life of Roses in a Vase 1937 Wes 11/91 . . . 578
O/C 16x16 Autumn, Hamburg Connecticut Wtf 3/92 450
O/C 11x14 Coastal Scene 1924 Eld 7/92 330

Duncan, Audrey
* See 1992 Edition . . . .

Duncan, Darwin   Am 1905-
O/M 18x24 Landscape Mor 6/92 600

Duncan, James D.   Can 1805-1881
* See 1992 Edition . . . .

Duncanson, Robert S.   Am 1821-1872
O/C 21x40 Thatched Cottage in Winter 1870 Wtf 9/91 . . . 12,000
O/C 31x26 Seated Man Holding a Cane 1845 Eld 8/92 . . . 6,050

Dunham, Carroll   1949-
CsPgC&H/Pn 72x48 Wild Grain 1983 Chr 5/92 46,200
A&H/Wd 56x32 Untitled 1987 Chr 11/91 28,600
A&H/Wd 41x29 Violet Stain 1986 Chr 5/92 15,950
O&I/Wd 29x24 Purple and Blue 1986 Chr 2/92 12,150
MM/Wd 34x18 K 85 Chr 5/92 11,000
C,H&Y/Pa 17x24 Untitled 88 Chr 11/91 5,500
G,Pl&C/Wd 12x10 Untitled 84 Chr 5/92 1,980
WHOs&Fp/Pa 9x6 Two Untitled Drawings 85 Chr 2/92 . . . 1,650
H/Pa 11x14 Untitled 89 Chr 5/92 1,100

Dunlap, Helena   Am 1876-1955
* See 1991 Edition . . . .

Dunlay, Thomas R.   Am
O/C 18x24 Still Life Staffordshire Bowl Sby 12/91 935

Dunn, Harvey T.   Am 1884-1952
O/C 30x82 Logging Camp 1951 Ih 11/91 22,500

Dunning, Lois   Am 19C
P/Pa 41x28 Young Girl 1881 Wtf 10/91 2,000

Dunning, Robert Spear   Am 1829-1905
* See 1992 Edition . . . .

Dunoyer De Segonzac, Andre   Fr 1884-1974
W&I/Pa 23x31 Nature Morte au Tapis Rouge Sby 5/92 . . . 57,750
W&I/Pa 23x31 Nature Morte Vase D'Anemones Sby 5/92 . 49,500
O/C 20x44 Jardin en Ete Sby 5/92 38,500
W&I/Pa 23x31 Environs de St. Tropez Sby 5/92 24,750
O/C 26x32 Harmonie en Rouge Chr 5/92 23,100
W&I/Pa 23x31 L'Eglise D'Auxerre Sby 5/92 19,800
O/C 32x24 Le Vieux Moulin Chr 2/92 19,800
W&I/Pa 23x31 Nature Morte Avec Bouteille Sby 5/92 . . . 17,600
O/C 20x43 Paysage de Saint-Tropez Chr 2/92 15,400
W&Pl/Pa 19x26 Nature Morte au Parapluie Chr 11/91 . . . 14,300
O/C 21x32 Paysage Sby 5/92 8,800
O/Pn 9x13 Nature Morte Doy 11/91 5,000
Pl&S/Pa/B 16x23 Saint-Tropez Chr 11/91 3,850
Pl,Br&S/Pa 15x23 Paysage Chr 2/92 3,080
Pl/Pa 9x13 Reclining Nude; Couple: Two 6/92 1,980
I&C/Pa 14x19 River's Edge Sby 6/92 1,320

Dunoyer, Pierre   1949-
A/C 70x60 Yellow '82 Chr 11/91 19,800
A/C 38x77 Branche de Saule 1979 Chr 5/92 8,250

Dunphy, C.
O/C 16x20 Alone 1966 Ald 5/92 120

Dunstan, Bernard   Br 1920-
P/Pa 20x18 The Phone Call Sby 10/91 2,200

Dunton, William Herbert   Am 1878-1936
O/C 39x26 Sentinel of the Plains 1906 Sby 5/92 38,500

Duntze, Johannes Bertholomaus   Ger 1823-1895
* See 1990 Edition . . . .

Dupain, Edmond Louis   Fr 1847-
* See 1991 Edition . . . .

Dupont, Gainsborough   Br 1754-1797
* See 1992 Edition . . . .

Dupray, Henri Louis   Fr 1841-1909
O/C 21x32 Cavalry Charge Hnd 5/92 4,600

Dupre, Jules   Fr 1811-1889
O/C 19x25 Interior de ferme dans le Berry 1833 Chr 5/92 . 93,500
O/C 38x30 Sous-Bois--Matinee d'Ete Chr 5/92 60,500
O/C 12x18 French River Landscape Chr 2/92 22,000
O/Pn 19x29 Punt on a River by a Village Chr 2/92 17,600
O/C 18x21 Le Pecheur Solitaire Chr 5/92 15,400
O/Pn 11x16 Paturage pres de L'Isle Adam Chr 5/92 11,000
O/Pa/B 7x11 Route en lisiere de foret Chr 5/92 10,450
O/C 10x13 Ferme au Bords d'une Riviere Chr 5/92 8,250
O/C 7x9 Cows Grazing by a Pond Chr 5/92 4,400

Dupre, Julien   Fr 1851-1910
O/C 15x18 The Reapers Chr 10/91 50,600
O/C 24x32 Shepherdess with Cows and Goats Chr 5/92 . . 38,500
O/C/B 26x22 The Milkmaid Chr 5/92 38,500
O/C 55x36 Peasant Woman leaning on Pitchfork Chr 5/92   28,600
O/C 15x22 The Milkmaid Chr 10/91 24,200
O/C 20x26 Tending the Cows Chr 5/92 20,900
O/Pn 15x22 Milkmaid with her Cow Chr 5/92 18,700
O/C 19x26 La Vachere Sby 2/92 17,600
O/C 18x24 Cows at Pasture Chr 5/92 15,400
O/C 19x24 The Milk-Maid But 11/91 12,100
O/Pn 15x22 Milkmaid with Cow Hnd 10/91 12,000

Dupre, Leon Victor   Fr 1816-1879
* See 1992 Edition . . . .

Dupre, Louis   Fr 1789-1837
* See 1992 Edition . . . .

Dupuis, Pierre   Fr 1610-1682
* See 1992 Edition . . . .

Dupuy, Paul Michel   Fr 1869-1949
O/C 32x22 Ete au Bord du Lac 1911 Sby 5/92 9,900
Dura, G.   It 19C
G/B 12x18 View of Capri Sby 7/92 2,200
Dura, Gaetano   It 19C
* See 1992 Edition . . . .
Duran, A.   Am a 1886-1900
* See 1992 Edition . . . .
Duran, Charles Emile Carolus   Fr 19C
* See 1992 Edition . . . .
Durand, Asher B.   Am 1796-1886
O/C 18x24 Study Near Factory Point, Vermont Chr 12/91 . 24,200
Duranti, Fortunato   It 1787-1851
K,Pl&S/Pa 11x8 Four Religious Studies Chr 1/92 1,980
Pl&S/Pa 11x8 Three Women Holding Babies Chr 1/92 . . . 1,870
Pe/Pa 6x8 Suffer the Little Children Chr 1/92 1,650
Durck, Frederich   Ger 1809-1884
* See 1991 Edition . . . .
Durenne, Eugene Antoine   Fr 1860-1944
* See 1992 Edition . . . .
Durfee, Bradford V.   Am a 1879-1887
O/C 20x36 American Whaleship in New Bedford Eld 7/92 . . 3,080
Durieux, Rene-Auguste   Fr 1892-1982
O/C 24x20 Institute de France Hnz 5/92 650
Durrie, George Henry   Am 1820-1863
O/C 27x36 Winter at Jones Inn 1854 Doy 12/91 150,000
O/C 6x9 Sleigh in the Snow Chr 3/92 7,150
Durrie, John
* See 1990 Edition . . . .
Durston, Arthur   Am 1897-1938
* See 1992 Edition . . . .
Duru, Jean-Baptiste   Fr 18C
* See 1991 Edition . . . .
Dusart, Cornelis   Dut 1660-1704
* See 1992 Edition . . . .
Dusi, Cosroe   It 1808-1859
* See 1992 Edition . . . .
Duteurtre, Pierre Eugene   Fr 1911-
O/C 20x16 Woman Arranging Flowers Lou 3/92 600
Duvall, Fannie Eliza   Am 1861-1934
O/C 15x22 River Landscape Mor 6/92 700
Duvall, Uckell   a 1910-1930
P/Pa 13x11 Central Park Dum 11/91 250
Duveneck, Frank   Am 1848-1919
O/C/B 18x15 Head of a Man Doy 12/91 2,800
Duvent, Charles Jules   Fr 1867-1940
* See 1990 Edition . . . .
Duverger, Theophile Emmanuel   Fr 1821-1901
O/Pn 15x19 The Visit 1857 Skn 9/91 7,700
Duvieux, Henri   Fr a 1880-1882
O/Pn 6x10 Grand Canal Skn 5/92 1,980
Dvorak, Franz   Aus 1862-
O/C 38x45 At the Races 92 Sby 5/92 16,500
O/C 21x14 The First Kiss 1890 Chr 10/91 4,400
Dyce, William   Br 1806-1864
O/C 48x39 Lady and Her Children Sby 5/92 2,200
Dye, Charlie   Am 1906-1973
O/M 18x24 Brush Popping Sby 9/91 19,800
Dye, Clarkson   Am 1869-1955
* See 1992 Edition . . . .
Dyer, Carlos   Am 1917-
O/C 18x22 Atmospheric Landscape Mor 3/92 1,000
Dyer, Clara L.   Am a 1893-1913
O/C/B 11x18 Meadows Brd 8/92 495
Dyer, Frank   Am 20C
O/C 26x30 The Bathers 1946 Wlf 10/91 400
Dyer, Hezekiah Anthony   Am 1872-1943
* See 1992 Edition . . . .
Dyf, Marcel   Fr 1899-1985
O/C 27x23 Stoneware Jug with Flowers Wlf 3/92 12,500
O/C 26x22 Fleurs But 11/91 12,100
O/C 29x24 Claudine Avec un Vase de Fleurs Sby 10/91 . . 11,000
O/C 22x18 Bouquet de Fleurs Chr 2/92 8,800
O/C 29x24 Femme Lisant Une Lettre Sby 10/91 8,800

O/C 24x29 Ramparts D'Aigues-Mortes Sby 10/91 7,150
O/C 24x29 Avant le Concours Hippique Sby 10/91 6,600
O/C 22x18 Still Life with Roses & Marguerites Wlf 11/91 . . 6,200
O/C 22x18 Dahlias et Mufliers Chr 2/92 6,050
O/C 29x24 Femme Nue Chr 11/91 6,050
O/C 29x36 Spring Landscape Sby 6/92 5,500
O/C 18x23 Aux Courses Chr 11/91 4,950
O/C 29x24 Avant le Bal But 11/91 4,400
O/C 24x29 Paysage Chr 2/92 4,400
O/C 18x22 Sailboats on a Lake Doy 11/91 4,000
O/C 26x21 Girl with Red Hair Sel 4/92 3,700
O/C 22x18 Portrait of a Young Woman Sby 10/91 3,300
O/C 18x22 Trouville Hnd 3/92 3,000
O/C 26x21 Chaise et Cruche Chr 2/92 1,320
Dyke, Samuel P.   Am a 1855-1870
* See 1992 Edition . . . .
Dykman, Charles   Dut 19C
O/C 23x30 Dutch Canal Scene Wlf 9/91 1,800
Dzigurski, Alexander   Am 1910-
O/C 24x36 Seascape at Sunset Dum 10/91 2,100
O/C 30x26 Seascape Dum 10/91 1,600
O/C 24x36 Seascape Sby 12/91 1,320
O/C 26x30 Crashing Waves Hnd 5/92 1,100
O/C 20x30 Seascape Hnd 5/92 1,000
O/C 24x36 Seascape Hnd 6/92 700
O/C 24x36 Glacier National Park Mor 11/91 600
O/C 16x20 Coastal Mor 6/92 . . . . * . . . 450
Dzubas, Friedel   Am 1915-
A/C 72x106 Gateway 1974 Sby 10/91 27,500
A/C 72x72 Sangre de Christo Sby 5/92 26,400
O/C 39x39 Cold Hedge 73 Sby 2/92 16,500
A/C 57x132 Viking Voyage 1975 Chr 11/91 14,300
A/C 10x73 High Orange 68 Sby 10/91 3,850
O/C 56x46 Distant 63 Chr 5/92 3,520
MM/Pa 42x28 Untitled 1984 Sby 10/91 1,650
E., Josep Antonio   18C
O/C 88x127 Devocion: Don Antonio 1741 Sby 5/92 68,750
Eakins, Thomas   Am 1844-1916
* See 1992 Edition . . . .
Eanes, Fanny S.   Am 1885-1974
O/C 20x24 Still Life Cherry Blossoms Wes 11/91 358
Earl, George   Br a 1856-1883
O/Pn 11 dia "Queeny," a Pet Pug Sby 6/92 11,000
Earl, Maud   Br 1864-1943
O/C 16x16 Terrier and Water Spaniel: Pair 90 Sby 6/92 . 15,400
O/Cd 40x27 Spaniel; Labrador: Pair 1924 Chr 10/91 13,200
O/C 18x24 The Pose Chr 2/92 8,800
Earl, Percy   Br a 1900-1930
O/C 27x34 "Jason", a Bay Gelding 1913 Sby 6/92 7,975
Earl, Thomas P.   Br a 1900-1935
* See 1992 Edition . . . .
Earle, Eyvind   Am 1916-
* See 1992 Edition . . . .
Earle, Lawrence Carmichael   Am 1845-1921
O/B 11x8 The Wooded Shore Skn 3/92 358
Eason, T.   Eng 19C
G/Pa 17x28 Figures Approaching the Citadel Slo 4/92 . . . 425
East, Sir Alfred   Br 1849-1913
* See 1992 Edition . . . .
Eastman, Seth   Am 1808-1875
* See 1992 Edition . . . .
Eastman, William Joseph   Am 1881-1950
O/C 36x26 Floral Still Life Wlf 10/91 200
Eaton, Charles Harry   Am 1850-1901
* See 1992 Edition . . . .
Eaton, Charles Warren   Am 1857-1937
P/Pa/B 30x20 Cedar Trees, Evening Chr 9/91 3,520
O/C 16x22 Twilight 1892 Slo 9/91 1,250
O/C 16x22 Landscape with Church Sby 4/92 1,210
O/B 12x16 Landscape Hnz 10/91 875
O/B 10x8 The Valley-Bellagio Brd 5/92 253
Eaton, Dorothy   Am
* See 1992 Edition . . . .

Eaton, J. Eng 19C
O/C 14x19 River Landscape Fre 4/92 300
Eberhard, Heinrich 20C
O/B 9x12 Three Paintings 1914 Sby 2/92 4,950
O/B 22x26 Street Scene; Crucifixion: Pair 1923 Sby 2/92 . . 2,420
Eberle, Adolf Ger 1843-1914
O/C 19x23 The Newborn Lamb Chr 5/92 41,800
O/Pn 16x19 In the Huntsman's Lodge Sby 2/92 29,700
Eberstadt, E. Weis Ger 1930-
O/B 30x25 Floral Still Life Hnz 5/92 200
Ebert, Anton Aus 1845-1896
O/C 42x29 The Broken Pitcher But 11/91 9,900
Ebert, Carl Ger 1821-1885
O/C 21x16 Artist's Grand-Daughter 1883 Lou 9/91 1,250
Ebert, Charles H. Am 1873-1959
O/C 25x30 Horn Hill, Monhegan Island Skn 5/92 6,600
P/Pa 24x27 Snow Scene Mys 6/92 275
Ebert, Mary Roberts Am 1873-1956
O/C 25x30 Mohegan Island, Maine Chr 11/91 9,900
Eby, Kerr Am 1889-1946
W/Pa 14x20 Hatchet Cove Brd 8/92 550
Eck, Jacques Fr 1812-1887
O/C 36x29 Portrait of a Composer Sby 7/92 3,300
Eckart, Christian 1959-
Gd/Pn 26x28 Detail Painting #516 1987 Chr 5/92 3,850
Eckart, Christian Dan 1832-1914
* See 1992 Edition
Eckersberg, Christoffer W. Dan 1783-1853
* See 1992 Edition
Eckert, Henri-Ambrose Ger 1807-1840
* See 1991 Edition
Eddis, Eden Upton Br 1812-1901
* See 1992 Edition
Eddy, Don Am 20C
* See 1991 Edition
Eddy, Henry B. Am 1872-1935
Br&/Pa 12x8 Woman in Cafe, Waiter 1899 Ih 5/92 350
Eddy, Henry Stephens Am 1878-1944
O/Cb 12x16 Nantucket Harbor View Skn 3/92 880
Ede, Frederic Am 1865-1909
O/C 24x30 House by a Snowy Stream Chr 6/92 3,080
O/C 22x27 Cottages and Stream 18 Hnd 3/92 1,600
Edgerly, Beatrice E. Am 20C
* See 1991 Edition
Edlich, Stephen Am 1944-
* See 1991 Edition
Edmonds, Francis William Am 1806-1863
* See 1991 Edition
Edmonson, William J. Am 1868-1951
O/C 28x25 Arab Warrior Wlf 10/91 600
Edmunds, J. Br 19C
O/C 30x50 The Harbour Hnd 5/92 1,800
Edson, Aaron Allan Can 1846-1888
O/C 17x28 Harvest Time Sbt 11/91 3,039
Eduardo, Jorge Brz 1936-
* See 1992 Edition
Edward, J. Eng 19C
O/C 20x30 Winter Landscape with Cottage 1891 Sel 12/91 . . 800
Edwards, George Wharton Am 1869-1950
C&O/C 25x19 Ile de la Cite, Paris 1936 Chr 5/92 12,100
O/B 18x24 Round Hills Mys 6/92 1,650
C/Pa 16x11 Fisherman Mys 6/92 715
C/Pa 17x10 Blind Musicians and Great Hall (2) Mys 6/92 . . . 165
C/Pa 21x15 Church in Istanbul (2) Mys 6/92 110
C/Pa 18x12 Grand Bazaar and Istanbul (2) Mys 6/92 110
C/Pa 18x12 Mansion House & Guild Hall (2) Mys 6/92 110
C/Pa 18x12 Perra & St. Paul's (2) Mys 6/92 55
Edwards, Lionel Am 1874-1954
O/C 24x26 Poverty Flats--Pueblo Mor 11/91 550
O/C 26x24 Cabin in a Landscape Mor 11/91 150
Edwards, Lionel Br 1878-1966
W/Pa 15x11 Second Whip; Terrier Man: Pair Sby 6/92 3,575
Edwards, Marjorie
O/B 24x20 Horse and Jockey Wlf 3/92 500

Edzard, Dietz Ger 1893-1963
O/C 24x20 Femme Assise Doy 11/91 5,250
O/M 30x42 Nu Allonge '45 Sel 12/91 5,000
O/C 29x24 Femme au Cafe Chr 11/91 3,300
O/C 36x29 Femme a l'Eventail Chr 2/92 2,860
O/C 13x19 Fleurs et Musique But 5/92 2,750
O/C 24x18 Jeune Fille Chr 11/91 2,420
O/Pn 13x10 Bouquet de fleurs Chr 5/92 1,320
Eeckhout, Jakob Joseph Flm 1793-1861
O/C 58x49 Portrait of Mr. Chesnaye 1845 Sby 6/92 15,950
Eerelman, Otto Dut 1839-1926
* See 1991 Edition
Egan, Eloise Am 20C
O/C 30x24 City Scape Mys 6/92 825
Egeli, Cedric B. Am 20C
O/C 50x103 Setting off on the Chesapeake 1973 Slo 9/91 . . 800
Egg, M. Eng 19C
O/C 11x16 Alpine Lake Scene Slo 12/91 100
Eggenhofer, Nick Am 1897-1985
T/B 22x30 Custer's Last Stand Sby 5/92 28,600
W&G/Pa 10x13 Riders of the Purple Sage But 11/91 3,850
W&G/B 19x15 Mounted Brave Sby 4/92 2,200
Br/Pa 9x15 Cowboys Roping Cows Ih 5/92 1,800
G/Pa 10x14 Stage Coach 1976 Lou 9/91 1,300
G/Pa 11x9 Indian Scouts Lou 9/91 1,200
Pl/Pa 10x10 Puttin' Out the Fire Lou 9/91 400
Pl/Pa 8x8 Panning for Gold Lou 9/91 350
Eggers, Peter Scn 20C
O/Pn 24x18 North Sea Sailing Craft 1888 Slo 9/91 850
Egginton, Frank J. Eng 1908-
W/Pa 15x21 Sandpipers on the Shore Slo 9/91 500
Eggleston, Edward Mason Am 1885-
O/C 36x27 Peter Pan Attracting Seagulls 1935 Ih 5/92 800
Egner, Marie Aus 1850-1940
O/C 18x28 The Cabbage Patch Chr 2/92 26,400
Eichens, Friedrich Eduard Dut 1804-1877
* See 1992 Edition
Eichinger, Otto Aus 1922-
O/Pn/Pn 10x8 Rabbis: Pair Sby 1/92 4,125
Eichinger, Ulrich Aus 20C
O/Pn 11x8 Rabbis: Pair Sby 7/92 3,850
O/Pn 11x8 Portrait of a Rabbi Sby 7/92 1,650
Eickelberg, William Hendrik 1845-1920
O/B 12x18 Amsterdam Harbour Scene Dum 11/91 2,750
Eilshemius, Louis Michel Am 1864-1941
O/B 13x9 Nude in Landscape Dum 5/92 1,200
O/Wd 22x28 Early Spring Chr 11/91 990
O/M 9x16 Fishergirl Along the Shore 1920 Slo 2/92 900
W/Pa 10x14 Girl Drying Hair Chr 11/91 825
O/Pb 12x14 Bushwacker (Horseman) 1919 Chr 11/91 660
O/B 10x13 Calm Day Slo 12/91 600
O/B 11x12 Seascape Mys 6/92 55
Eisen, Charles-Dominique-J. Fr 1720-1778
K,Pl&S/Pa 8x5 Bacchanal w/Two Nymphs 1760 Chr 1/92 . . 1,430
Eisen, Francois Flm 1695-1778
O/Pn 15x21 Peasants Merry-Making 177* Chr 10/91 3,850
Eisendieck, Suzanne Ger 1908-
O/C 24x29 Le rappel Chr 5/92 3,740
O/C 24x29 L'ete a Juvisy Chr 2/92 3,520
O/C 29x24 Les Beaux Dimanches Sby 2/92 3,520
O/C 15x18 Les Etangs d'Arques Chr 11/91 3,080
O/C 24x29 Terrasse Avant la Soiree Sby 2/92 3,080
O/C 20x24 Plage a Numana Doy 11/91 3,000
O/C 20x26 La Loge Doy 11/91 2,970
O/C 20x24 Terrace a Ramatuelle Doy 11/91 2,800
O/C 24x20 Dimanche Sur Tuilleries Sby 6/92 2,420
O/C 21x26 Le Grand Bassin Chr 2/92 2,000
O/C 14x11 Woman Wearing a Hat Sel 2/92 1,800
O/C 20x14 La Loge Doy 11/91 1,700
O/C 21x29 Aux Bords de la Riviere Chr 2/92 1,320
O/C 15x24 Plage du Gros Cagnes Sby 6/92 1,320
O/C 24x29 Promenade en Bateau Sby 2/92 1,320
O/C 7x10 Oeillets et Roses; Souvenir: Pair Sby 6/92 1,100

Eisenhut, Ferencz   Hun 1857-1903
  * See 1991 Edition . . . .
Eisenschitz, Willy   Fr 1889-1974
  * See 1992 Edition . . . .
Ekenaes, Jahn   Nor 1847-1920
  * See 1991 Edition . . . .
Ekvall, Knut   Swd 1843-1912
  * See 1991 Edition . . . .
El Greco   Spa 1540-1614
  * See 1992 Edition . . . .
Eldred, Lemuel D.   Am 1848-1921
  O/C 12x20 Sea Cliffs, Monhegan Island 01 Bor 8/92 1,100
Eling, C.   20C
  O/C/B 9x13 Still Life of Flowers Slo 2/92 60
Elkins, Henry A.   Am 1847-1884
  O/C/B 28x42 Mountainous Landscape 1874 Wlf 10/91 400
Ellaerts, Jean-Francois   1761-1848
  * See 1990 Edition . . . .
Ellasoph, Paula   Am 1895-1983
  * See 1990 Edition . . . .
Ellenshaw, Peter   Am 20C
  * See 1991 Edition . . . .
Elliot, Captain Thomas   Br a 1790-1800
  * See 1992 Edition . . . .
Elliott, Charles Loring   Am 1812-1868
  O/C 31x26 Man in a Cloak 1863 Chr 11/91 440
Ellis, Doan   Am 20C
  O/Pn 34x16 Night in a Mexican Garden 1953 Wlf 11/91 900
Ellis, Freemont F.   Am 1897-1985
  O/C 30x25 Beaver Pools in Spring 1963 Chr 11/91 4,620
  P/Pa 10x8 Campers - Santa Fe Mor 6/92 500
Ellsworth, E.   Am 20C
  O/B 8x10 By a River, 1927 Yng 2/92 70
Elmore, Alfred   Br 1815-1881
  * See 1992 Edition . . . .
Elouis, Jean Pierre Henri   Am 1755-1840
  O/C 18x14 General Anthony Wayne Sby 3/92 88,000
Elsley, Arthur John   Br 1861-
  O/C 39x29 Goodnight 1911 Chr 2/92 176,000
  O/C 36x27 Home at Last Sby 2/92 71,500
Elwell, D. Jerome   Am 1857-1912
  O/Pn 11x21 Landscape Mys 11/91 495
  O/C 10x14 Venetian Sunset 1900 Skn 9/91 330
Emerson, Arthur Webster   Am 1885-
  O/C 28x22 Gloucester Harbor 37 Skn 9/91 440
Emerson, Charles Chase   Am -1922
  G&R/Pa 18x27 Family Gathering Ih 5/92 600
Emerson, Edith   Am 1888-
  O/C Size? Underground Railroad Fre 10/91 175
Emerson, W. C.   Am 20C
  O/C 12x19 Mountain Landscape with Cattle Eld 7/92 248
Emery, James   Am 1819-1899
  O/C 14x20 Autumn on a Maine River Brd 8/92 1,540
Emery, John   Eng 1777-1822
  W/Pa 6x7 Ships at Sea Yng 2/92 475
Emezg, T.
  O/Wd 5x7 Harbor Scene with Two Sailboats 1869 Durn 2/92   200
Emmons, Dorothy Stanley   1891-
  O/B 9x11 Lower Town, Quebec Yng 4/92 1,100
Emms, John   Br 1843-1912
  O/C 16x20 Lairg Sby 6/92 5,500
  O/C 16x20 Lochy 1901 Sby 6/92 5,500
  O/C 9x12 Spring Flowers '83 Durn 5/92 1,300
  O/C 9x12 Mixed Flowers '83 Durn 5/92 800
Ende, Edgar
  * See 1992 Edition . . . .
Enders, F.   Ger 19C
  O/C 19x15 A Bearded Man Hnz 5/92 325
Enfield, Henry   Eng 1849-
  O/C 21x34 Soynefjord Slo 2/92 525
Engard, Robert Oliver   Am 1915-
  * See 1992 Edition . . . .
Engel, Johann Friedrich   Ger 1844-
  O/C 20x14 The Little Fisherman 1877 Sby 1/92 3,520

Engel, Nissen
  O/Pn 32x39 Four Musicians Sby 2/92 660
Engelhardt, George   Ger 1823-1883
  O/C 27x39 Mountain Torrent Sby 5/92 6,600
Engilberts, Jon   20C
  O/Pa/M 40x28 Magie D'Iceland Wes 3/92 110
Englehardt, Edna Palmer   Am 20C
  * See 1992 Edition . . . .
English, Frank F.   Am 1854-1922
  W/Pa 23x39 Figures and Horse Cart Fre 4/92 3,900
  W/Pa 23x39 Along a Country Lane Wlf 9/91 3,400
  W/Pa 16x32 Horse and Wagon Durn 12/91 2,000
  W/Pa/B 21x30 A Stop along the Way Chr 6/92 1,870
  W/Pa 13x19 Young Lady and Ducks Fre 10/91 1,250
  W/Pa 10x21 Lady on Bridge 1892 Fre 10/91 1,050
  W/Pa 14x23 Fishing Village Yng 2/92 1,000
  W/Pa 11x19 Country Road Fre 10/91 700
English, H. J.   19C
  O/C 12x10 Girl with Flowers Sel 9/91 175
Enjolras, Delphin   Fr 1857-
  * See 1992 Edition . . . .
Enneking, John Joseph   Am 1841-1916
  O/C 12x18 Pears 77 Chr 12/91 35,200
  O/C 22x34 A Summer Afternoon 95 Chr 5/92 30,800
  O/C 20x24 Twilight, Autumn, Rocky Brook 15 Brd 8/92 . . 13,750
  O/C 28x40 Late Afternoon, Autumn Chr 5/92 13,200
  O/C 18x24 Spring Blossoms 05 Chr 9/91 11,000
  O/C 12x18 Landscape w/Two Boys in a Boat 81 Sby 12/91 8,800
  O/C 22x30 Blue Hills Twilight '00 Skn 11/91 6,600
  O/C 22x30 Storm Clouds Approaching 97 Sby 12/91 . . . 3,850
  O/C 20x24 The Green Hillside Skn 9/91 3,850
  O/C 42x63 Piazza San Marco at Night 88 Chr 6/92 3,520
  O/C 12x20 Autumn's Glow Chr 3/92 3,300
  O/Pn 8x12 River Sunset 94 Chr 3/92 3,300
  O/B 8x12 Sunset Mys 6/92 2,530
  O/B 24x30 Mountain Side Eld 7/92 1,870
  O/B 13x16 Winter Mood Skn 9/91 1,870
  O/C 8x11 A Pasture Scene 82 Skn 3/92 1,760
  O/B 14x18 Sunset Through the Trees Yng 4/92 1,700
  O/B 10x14 Rocky Hillside Lou 3/92 1,500
  O/Pn 10x14 Trees Around a Boulder But 11/91 1,100
  O/C 12x18 Forest Scene Hnd 12/91 1,000
  O/C 24x30 Tuckerman's Ravine Yng 4/92 800
  O/C 10x12 Landscape at Dusk 1883 Slo 7/92 675
Enneking, Joseph Eliot   Am -1946
  O/Cb 8x10 The Harbor, Gloucester Skn 11/91 660
Ennis, George Pearce   Am 1884-1936
  O/C 24x29 A Rising Fog Ald 3/92 1,650
Enriquez, Carlos   Cub 1901-1957
  O/C 48x35 Bandolero Criollo 43 Sby 11/91 68,750
  O/C 24x20 Desnudo 49 Sby 5/92 18,700
  O/C 20x16 Desnudo Sby 5/92 17,600
Enriquez, Nicolas   1738-1770
  O/Cp 15x11 Female Saint; Christ: Double Sby 7/92 1,210
Ensor, James   Bel 1860-1949
  Y/Pa 13x9 La Vierge Salvatrice Sby 10/91 11,000
  Pe/Pa 8x6 Portrait of the Artist's Aunt '80 Hnd 3/92 1,300
Ensrud, Wayne
  G&W/Pa 15x22 French City Scenes: Two 1987 Durn 1/92 . . . 600
Enwright, J. J.   Eng 20C
  O/C 28x36 Gloucester Fishing Boats Durn 9/91 1,000
Epes, Paul T.   Am 20C
  W/Pa 13x10 Cottage with Stream in Landscape 1914 Slo 10/91 85
Epp, Rudolf   Ger 1834-1910
  O/C 40x26 Baby's Mealtime Chr 10/91 20,900
  O/C 34x27 Feeding the Chickens Sby 5/92 16,500
  O/C 35x26 The Bather 04 Sby 2/92 5,500
  O/C/M 22x16 Woman Wearing Green Shawl 1909 Chr 2/92 3,420
Eppink, Norman   Am 1906-
  * See 1991 Edition . . . .
Epstein, Henri   Pol 1892-1944
  O/C 22x26 Cocheral au Printemps 1934 But 5/92 3,300
  O/C 18x24 Bord de la Drouette Sby 6/92 1,980
Epstein, Jacob
  W/Pa/B 23x18 Dahlias and Sunflowers Sby 2/92 8,800

Epstein, Jehudo   Pol 1870-1946
Pe/Pa 23x18 Illustration "Les Fleurs Du Mal", 1940 Sby 2/92 . 550
* See 1992 Edition . . . .
Epstein, Sir Jacob   Eng 1880-1959
Pe/Pa 22x18 Portrait of Jackie Jean Doy 11/91 1,600
Erdman, Otto   Ger 1834-1905
O/C 36x48 Bridegroom's Health-Betrothal 1883 Sby 5/92 . 20,900
O/C 25x20 The Apology 1869 Chr 5/92 5,280
Eremina, Natalya Alekseevna   Rus 20C
O/C 27x31 Still Life Candlestick 76 Skn 3/92 330
Erfmann, Ferdinand
* See 1992 Edition . . . .
Erhardt, Georg Friedrich   Ger 1825-1881
O/C 19x14 A Young Officer Sby 7/92 990
Erichsen, Thorvald   Nor 1868-1939
* See 1992 Edition . . . .
Ericson, David   Am 1870-
O/C 21x26 Harbor Scene Lou 9/91 800
Ermels, Johann-Franciscus   Dut 17C
* See 1991 Edition . . . .
Erni, Hans   Sws 1909-
T/Pa 19x14 Sich Begegnendes 74 Chr 11/91 4,950
Ernst, Jimmy   Am 1920-1984
T/C 40x50 Morning Thought 57 Sby 2/92 10,450
O/C 42x32 Countenance 67 Sby 2/92 4,400
I/B 30x40 Thirty Days 65 Sby 6/92 3,850
O/C 20x24 Cirque D'Hiver II 52 Sby 2/92 3,575
MM 25x25 Quasars II '67 Sby 10/91 1,760
O/C 12x9 Le Petit Dejeuner 60 Chr 6/92 1,430
O/B 8x10 Red-Blue-Sound 67 Chr 6/92 1,320
Ernst, Max   Fr 1891-1976
O/C 29x24 Le mardi la lune s'endimanche 1964 Chr 5/92 220,000
O/Pn 13x10 The Sun as Seen from Venus Chr 5/92 99,000
Ernst, Rudolf   Aus 1854-1920
O/Pn 23x19 Le Gardien Nubien Sby 5/92 55,000
O/Pn 15x11 Le Guardien du Harem But 11/91 8,250
W/Pa/B 18x12 The Arabian Cobbler Wlf 11/91 7,000
Erol
O/C 70x48 Abstract '57 Wlf 3/92 375
Eroli, Erulo   It 1854-1916
W/Pa 21x31 The Fishing Party 1907 Slo 9/91 3,500
Erpikum, Leon Vuilleminot   Fr 19C
O/C 13x9 Nude in a Landscape Sby 7/92 990
Erte   Fr 1892-1990
G/Pa 14x11 Costume Design: Le Toffee Hnd 10/91 1,900
G/Pa 11x8 La Mer Arctique 1928 Hnd 10/91 1,800
Erubellin, J.   Fr 19C
* See 1990 Edition . . . .
Escobar, Vincente
* See 1992 Edition . . . .
Escobedo, Eberto   Cub 1919-
O/C 24x30 Paisaje Cubano 1954 Sby 5/92 4,950
Escudi
O/C 31x16 Maisons de Pecheurs Dum 2/92 100
Esner, Arthur L.   Am 1902-
O/C 29x36 Music Makers/Cafe Scene 1932 Skn 3/92 1,320
Esposito, Gaetano   It 1858-1911
* See 1991 Edition . . . .
Espoy, Angel   Am 1869-1962
O/C 30x40 Flowered Hillside Mor 6/92 5,000
O/C 24x30 Poppies and Lupines But 10/91 4,400
O/C 16x24 Flowered Hillside Mor 3/92 3,750
O/C 19x27 Two Boys Fishing But 6/92 3,575
O/C 30x40 Evening Waves But 6/92 1,540
O/C/B 11x16 Palace of Fine Arts But 6/92 1,540
O/C 28x40 Seascape Mor 11/91 650
Essig, George Emerick   Am 1838-1926
W/Pa 7x16 Country Lane at Sunset Fre 4/92 700
W/Pa 12x20 Sailboats in Port Fre 10/91 400
W/Pa 10x19 House on the Lake Slo 10/91 300
Estes, Richard   Am 1936-
* See 1991 Edition . . . .
Esteve, Augustin   Spa 1753-1809
* See 1990 Edition . . . .

Estorach, Antonio Salvador C.   Spa 1847-1896
O/Pn 13x9 Treasured Letters Sby 2/92 8,800
Etcheverry, Hubert-Denis   Fr 1867-1950
O/Pn 9x6 Hors Concours 1886 Sby 7/92 2,860
Etnier, Stephen   Am 1903-1984
O/M 24x36 Buoys on the Dock Brd 5/92 1,980
O/C 16x24 Along the Eastern Shore Brd 5/92 688
O/C 12x20 Pot Buoys, Harpswell '59 Yng 2/92 600
Etting, Emlen   Am 1905-
O/B 21x29 The Fortune Teller Sby 12/91 4,950
O/C 18x28 Wartime Twilight '44 Sby 4/92 2,200
O/B 17x22 The Water Boy Sby 4/92 1,430
O/C 16x20 Zizi at Dunedin Sby 12/91 990
O/B 16x12 Gentleman Standing with Nude Sby 12/91 715
O/C 22x18 Portrait of Patty Denikla 1932 Sby 4/92 660
O/B 10x15 Seated Woman with Champagne Sby 12/91 . . . 495
Ettore, L.   It 19C
W/Pa 15x9 Italian Man with Pipe Slo 9/91 300
Etty, William   Br 1787-1849
O/B/C 17x24 Male Nude with Laurel Wreath Skn 9/91 . . . 2,200
Eugen, Prins   Swd 1865-1947
* See 1992 Edition . . . .
Euston, Jacob Howard   Am 1892-
O/C 20x24 Desert Landscape Mys 11/91 220
Evan, Joseph   Am a 1857-1898
O/C 16x22 Shade Tree and Distant Fields 1891 Skn 11/91 18,700
Evans, Bruce   Am 20C
* See 1992 Edition . . . .
Evans, De Scott   Am 1847-1898
O/C 20x16 Artist and Her Model '91 Chr 3/92 6,600
Evans, Donald   Am 20C
* See 1992 Edition . . . .
Evans, Jessie Benton   Am 1866-1954
O/C 32x18 Statue in the Park Mys 11/91 550
O/C 14x14 Western Landscape Yng 2/92 450
O/C 14x14 Road Through the Desert Skn 9/91 165
Evans, Minnie   Am 1892-1987
O/Crd 22x18 The Crucifixion 1938 Wlf 10/91 450
Evans, Tim   Am 20C
W/Pa 19x29 Field with Wheatshucks Hnd 3/92 150
Eve, Jean   Fr 1900-1968
O/C 18x22 Printemps: Vincelles (Yonne) But 11/91 3,850
Evergood, Philip   Am 1901-1973
O/C 24x18 Susanna and the Elders 1958 Skn 9/91 3,575
O/C 24x20 Classicism 1929 Skn 5/92 2,200
O/M 11x12 Western Landscape 47 Sby 12/91 1,650
Pl/Pa 22x17 Charming Plump Woman Wes 3/92 550
Eversen, Adrianus   Dut 1818-1897
O/C 18x23 Dutch Street Scene Chr 10/91 22,000
O/B 6x8 Dutch Street Scene Dum 12/91 4,500
O/Pn 14x10 Dutch City Scene Hnz 10/91 1,800
O/Pn 16x12 Village Market Scene Lou 6/92 1,650
Evrard, Paula   Bel 1876-1927
* See 1990 Edition . . . .
Ewen, William Paterson   Can 1925-
P/Pa 18x24 Abstract Composition Sbt 5/92 468
Exter, Alexandra   Rus 1884-1949
G/Pa 13x10 Woman with Harp Sby 10/91 2,200
G/Pa 13x10 Abstract Woman Sby 10/91 1,650
G/Pa 13x20 Merchant of Venice: 2 Decor Designs Sby 6/92 1,320
G/Pa 13x20 Opera: 2 Decor Designs Sby 6/92 1,320
Exume   Hai 20C
O/B 21x16 Uncouple Fre 4/92 450
Exume, R.   Hai 20C
O/M 24x20 Game of Cards 50 Fre 4/92 1,300
Eybl, Franz   Aus 1806-1880
O/C/Pn 30x25 Helping Grandfather Slo 2/92 1,500
Eyden, William
O/C 14x22 Autumn Landscape Dum 9/91 750
Eytel, Carl   Am 1862-1925
* See 1992 Edition . . . .
Ezdorf, Christian   Ger 1801-1851
O/C 40x54 Figures with Approaching Storm 1831 Chr 10/91 8,250

Fa Presto It 1634-1705
O/C 79x102 Apollo and Marsyas Sby 5/92 99,000
Fabbi, Alberto It 1858-1906
* See 1990 Edition . . . .
Fabbi, Fabbio It 1861-1946
O/C 29x42 The Harem Dancers Sby 2/92 18,150
O/C 16x22 Harem Girls by a Quiet Pool Chr 5/92 5,280
O/C 30x19 The Slave Market But 11/91 3,300
W&G/Pb 16x10 The Harem Dance Chr 5/92 1,650
W/Pa 17x11 Harem Dancer Dum 5/92 800
Faber, Jean 20C
O/C 9x11 Place du Tertre; Montmartre Slo 7/92 275
Fabian, Lydia Dunham
O/C 20x24 Figures Outside Adobe House Hnz 10/91 350
Fabien, Louis Fr 1925-
O/C 23x14 Sunbathers on a Beach 1976 Dum 11/91 800
O/C 16x13 Female Nude 67 Sby 6/92 330
Fabre, Auguste-Victor Fr 1882-1939
O/C 24x30 Ladies Admiring a Bird Chr 5/92 1,980
Fabres y Costa, Antonio Spa 19C
O/Pn 26x16 Standing Cavalier Chr 2/92 13,200
Fabri-Canti, Jose Fr 20C
O/C 7x5 Ruelle De Montmartre Wes 3/92 990
Fabris, Pietro It 19C
* See 1990 Edition . . . .
Fabris, Pietro It a 1754-1792
O/C 41x62 Peasants Merry-Making 1777 Chr 1/92 495,000
O/C 50x71 Neapolitans Cooking Fish 1772 Chr 5/92 . . . 242,000
Faccini, Pietro It
* See 1991 Edition . . . .
Facciola, Giovanni It 1729-1809
W/Pa 6x8 Via Appia Antica Slo 7/92 200
Faccioli, Silvio It 19C
O/C/B 23x16 An Unrequited Proposal Slo 2/92 1,900
Fader, Fernando Arg 1882-1935
O/C 16x24 Despues de la Lluvia 06 Chr 11/91 22,000
Faed, John Br 1820-1902
O/Pn 12x9 The Brocade Chr 2/92 4,180
Faed, Thomas Br 1826-1900
O/C 28x45 The Valentine Chr 2/92 3,520
Faggi, A. It 20C
P/Pa 16x11 Portrait of Toscanini 1955 Sel 4/92 100
Fairchild, G. M.
W/Pa 9x11 Harvard Boathouse 1855 Eld 7/92 193
Fairley, Barker Can 1887-1986
O/B 11x14 High Park 1959 Sbt 5/92 935
Fairman, Frances Br 1836-1923
Pe&W/Pa 20x15 Impudence 1893 Sby 7/92 880
Fairman, James Am 1826-1904
O/C 32x45 Stormy Skies Above Echo Lake Chr 5/92 15,400
Faivre, Justin Am 1902-
O/C/B 25x34 Andy's Snug Harbor 46 But 6/92 3,025
O/B 24x26 Boats at Dock Mor 6/92 1,200
W/Pa 7x10 Figure Andy's Snug Harbor 38 But 6/92 385
Fajon, Rose Jeanne Fr 1789-
O/C 18x22 Floral Bouquet 1843 Doy 11/91 3,250
Falciatore, Filippo It a 1728-1768
O/C/B 25x19 Elegant Figures: Four Sby 1/92 165,000
Falcone, Aniello It 1600-1658
O/C 59x59 Battle Scene Sby 10/91 77,000
O/C 35x45 Cleopatra Fleeing the Battle Sby 1/92 27,500
Falconer, Ian
* See 1992 Edition . . . .
Falconer, John M. Am 1820-1903
* See 1992 Edition . . . .
Falconet, Pierre Etienne Fr 1741-1791
* See 1991 Edition . . . .
Falero, Luis Riccardo Spa 1851-1896
* See 1991 Edition . . . .
Falk, Max Eng 19C
O/Pn 13x9 The Inn Keeper '85 Wlf 9/91 1,100
Faller, Louis Clement Fr 1819-1901
O/C 9x13 French River Landscape 79 Chr 5/92 1,320
Falls, Charles B. Am 1874-1960
I&W/Pa 12x7 Christmas Card Design Caroling Boys Ih 11/91 400

Falter, John Philip Am 1910-1982
* See 1992 Edition . . . .
Fancher, Louis Am 1884-1944
C&G/Pa 11x7 Wandering Minstrel Ih 5/92 600
Fanfani, Enrico It 19C
O/C 32x25 Flora Slo 12/91 2,000
O/C 32x25 Bacchante Slo 12/91 1,500
O/C 32x25 Ceres Slo 12/91 1,500
O/C 26x20 In Chiesa Slo 12/91 625
Fangor, Wojciech 20C
O/C 52x52 M31-1967 1967 Sby 10/91 1,540
Fantin-Latour, Henri Fr 1836-1904
O/C 22x22 Fleurs et Fruits 68 Sby 11/91 . . . . 1.54M
O/C 20x24 Bouquet de fleurs diverses 81 Chr 5/92 990,000
O/C 18x16 Fleurs--Reines Marguerites Sby 5/92 495,000
O/C 13x15 Roses Foncees Sur Fond Clair 91 Chr 11/91 . . . 258,500
O/C 10x13 Nature Morte (Peches) Sby 5/92 132,000
O/C 8x9 Roses et Capucines Chr 11/91 77,000
O/C 7x8 Toilette Sby 10/91 11,000
C/Pa 7x5 Nude Study Sby 1/92 990
Fantin-Latour, Ignace Henri J. Fr 1836-1904
* See 1992 Edition . . . .
Fantin-Latour, Victoria Dubour Fr 1840-
W/Pa 16x20 Floral Still Life Ald 5/92 4,250
Farasyn, Edgard Bel 1858-1938
* See 1990 Edition . . . .
Farasyn, L. Bel 1822-1899
* See 1992 Edition . . . .
Farber, Henry Am 1843-1903
W&Pe/Pa/Pa 25x38 Sunset, NY Harbor 1880 Chr 5/92 . . . 20,900
Farber, Manny Am 20C
* See 1992 Edition . . . .
Farenghi, G. It 19C
* See 1992 Edition . . . .
Fargiullo, C. Con 19C
W/Pb 30x21 Praying in the Mosque Chr 10/91 1,760
Farina, Armando 20C
O/C 23x31 Pincio Dum 4/92 325
Farina, Isidoro It 19C
* See 1991 Edition . . . .
Farinato, Paolo It 1524-1606
* See 1992 Edition . . . .
Faris, Edgar F. Am 1881-1945
O/C 18x24 Moonlit Venetian Canal Slo 4/92 500
Farley, Richard Blossom Am 1875-
O/B 16x12 Woman and Child on the Beach Brd 8/92 1,210
Farm, Gerald Am 1935-
* See 1990 Edition . . . .
Farmer, Alice Eng 1865-1930
O/C 20x12 Aristocratic Woman 1901 Wlf 6/92 375
Farndon, Walter Am 1876-1964
O/M 14x18 Beached Dinghy Skn 5/92 1,760
Farnham, Ammi Merchant Am 1846-1922
O/C 20x16 Santa Barbara Meadow '84 But 2/92 3,025
Farnsworth, Alfred V. Am 1858-1908
W/Pa 11x19 Bolinas Bay 1907 But 6/92 2,200
Farnsworth, Jerry Am 1895-1983
* See 1992 Edition . . . .
Farny, Henry F. Am 1847-1916
O/C 16x24 The Trail Over the Pass 1910 Chr 5/92 165,000
G/Pa 9x14 Indian Encampment '92 Chr 12/91 148,500
G/Pa/B 8x16 Saddling Up '95 Chr 5/92 132,000
G/Ab 10x6 Moonlit Indian Encampment 1911 Sby 5/92 . . . 55,000
Pe,Br&S/B 12x9 A Mandan Indian 97 Chr 5/92 24,200
G/B 16x9 Deer in Snow Covered Hills Sby 12/91 5,500
Farquharson, David Eng 1839-1907
O/Pn 8x14 Canty Bay, Sunrise 83 Sby 7/92 2,200
Farquharson, Joseph Eng 1846-1935
* See 1992 Edition . . . .
Farre, Henri Am 1871-1934
* See 1992 Edition . . . .
Farrer, Henry Am 1843-1903
* See 1992 Edition . . . .

94

Farrer, Thomas Charles   Am 1840-1891
* See 1992 Edition . . . .
Farrio, G.   It 20C
O/C 14x22 Pair: Neopolitan Harbor Scene Sel 12/91 450
Farry, P.   Fr 20C
* See 1992 Edition . . . .
Farsky, Otto   Am 20C
O/Pn 12x9 Cardinal in Interior Slo 7/92 1,500
O/Pn 15x10 Portrait of a Soldier Skn 9/91 825
Fartan, M. L.
W/Pa 11x15 European Seascape Dum 2/92 55
Fasce, F.   It 19C
* See 1990 Edition . . . .
Fassett, Truman E.   Am 1885-
* See 1990 Edition . . . .
Fat, Dulcie Foo   Can 1946-
* See 1992 Edition . . . .
Faugeron, Adolphe   Fr 1866-
* See 1991 Edition . . . .
Faulkner, Charles   Br a 1890-1500
O/C 30x50 "Persimmon", with J. Watts Up 1896 Sby 6/92   12,100
Faulkner, Frank   Br 20C
* See 1992 Edition . . . .
Faulkner, John   Irs 1803-1888
W&G/Pa 30x46 Cliffs Brd 8/92 1,980
W/Pa 18x30 Turk Mountain Hnd 10/91 1,100
W/Pa 14x26 Wichlom Castle Slo 9/91 1,000
Faure, Elisabeth
* See 1992 Edition . . . .
Fausett, Dean
O/C 21x35 View over the Valley Wlf 3/92 950
Fautrier, Jean   20C
G&S/Pa 20x26 Nu Dessin 1957 Sby 6/92 7,150
Favai, Gennaro   It 1882-1958
O/Pn 29x53 Piazza San Marco Chr 5/92 7,700
O/C 50x40 A Canal in Venice Chr 5/92 3,300
O/C/Pn 22x28 The Shadows Chr 2/92 2,200
Favard, L.   Fr 20C
O/C 28x36 Early Morning Sail But 11/91 2,475
Fave, Paul   Fr 20C
O/C 32x26 The House Barge Sel 4/92 3,000
Favory, Andre   Fr 1888-1937
* See 1991 Edition . . . .
Favretto, Giacomo   It 1849-1887
Pl/Pa 12x9 Two Male Nudes Hnd 6/92 550
Fawcett, Robert   Am 1903-1967
Br&I/Pa 17x25 King Reading to Knights Ih 11/91 850
Fay, Joseph   Ger 1813-1875
* See 1992 Edition . . . .
Fayard, R.   Fr 20C
* See 1992 Edition . . . .
Faysash, Julius   Am 1904-
O/Ab 8x10 Sunlit Waters Wlf 3/92 275
O/B 8x10 Call of the Sea Wlf 3/92 250
W/Pa 14x21 Farmer in Landscape Wlf 6/92 100
Febvre, Edouard   Fr 20C
* See 1992 Edition . . . .
Fechin, Nicolai   Am 1881-1955
O/C 25x30 Relics Chr 12/91 143,000
O/C 24x20 Masha But 4/92 77,000
Fedders, Julius   Rus 1838-1909
O/C 14x21 Tranquil Pond Slo 10/91 3,000
Federico, Cavalier Michele   It 1884-
O/C 21x28 Blue Calm at Sunset Chr 5/92 2,750
O/C 12x16 Sunlit Rocky Coast Chr 5/92 1,430
Federle, Helmut   1944-
O/L 108x73 The Great Wall Chr 5/92 26,400
Feeley, Paul   Am 1913-1966
* See 1992 Edition . . . .
Fei, Paolo Di Giovanni   It a 14C
T&Gd/Pn 28x17 The Madonna of Humility Chr 5/92 253,000
Feiertag, Karl   Ger 20C
* See 1992 Edition . . . .
Feininger, Lyonel   Am 1871-1956
O&Pe/C 29x26 Glasscherbenbild Chr 5/92 209,000

W&Pl/Pa 12x16 Heiligenhafen 1936 Sby 11/91 42,900
W&Pl/Pa 9x12 Gelbe Brucke 1921 Sby 11/91 34,100
W&Pl/Pa 13x10 Manhattan I 37 Chr 5/92 28,600
Y/Pa 7x8 Study for Street, Dusk, 1910 Sby 10/91 28,600
W&Pl/Pa 10x15 Sailing Vessel and Island 1941 Sby 11/91   25,300
Y&I/Pa 7x8 The Little Town 09 Sby 11/91 25,300
Y,Pe&Pl/Pa 8x7 Workmen Sby 5/92 25,300
W&Pl/Pa 11x15 Misdroy 23 Sby 11/91 22,000
Y/Pa 6x8 Side-Wheeler 13 Sby 11/91 19,800
Y&I/Pa 9x7 Encounter Sby 11/91 18,700
W&I/Pa 11x18 Village '42 Sby 11/91 18,700
W&Pl/Pa 12x19 Ostsee 31 Sby 11/91 17,600
W,Pl&Gd/Pa 12x18 Untitled: Ships at Sea 1948 Sby 11/91   17,600
W&I/Pa 11x15 Desolation 1941 Sby 11/91 16,500
Y,Pe&Pl/Pa 10x8 Farcical Scene with a Widow Sby 5/92 .   13,200
Pl,Br&C/Pa 25x19 Skyscrapers, New York 1942 Chr 2/92 .   13,200
W&Pl/Pa 9x11 Topaz Sun II 47 Sby 11/91 13,200
Pl/Pa 6x4 Self-Portrait with Hat 1910 Sby 10/91 11,550
Y/Pa 6x4 Person Leaning Out of Window 08 Sby 5/92 . . . 11,000
Y,Pe&Pl/Pa 6x4 Church/Clown Sby 5/92 9,350
W&Pl/Pa 9x13 Untitled: Fishing Cutter 1954 Sby 10/91 . . . 9,350
Y&Pl/Pa 9x11 Stehender Blauer Zug Sby 10/91 8,800
Y/Pa 4x6 Study for Velocipedists Sby 10/91 8,800
Y/Pa 4x6 Village 09 Sby 5/92 8,800
Pl,Y&Pe/Pa 9x11 Railroad Conductors Sby 10/91 7,700
Y&I/Pa 5x4 Two Figures Sby 10/91 7,700
Y&Pe/Pa 8x6 Study Newspaper Readers II, 1916 Sby 5/92 . 7,150
Pl/Pa 8x11 Harbor Scene 42 Chr 2/92 6,600
Y&Pl/Pa 8x10 Street Scene/Feeding Swans Sby 5/92 6,600
Y&I/Pa 5x4 Street Scene Sby 10/91 6,050
Pl&Y/Pa 8x10 Altmodische Lokomotive Sby 2/92 4,950
Pe/Pa 6x4 Study for Jesuit & Jesuits I: Pair 08 Sby 10/91 . 4,675
Y/Pa 8x10 Ruckwartsfahrende Lokomotive Sby 10/91 3,300
I/Pa 10x8 Family Sby 5/92 3,025
Felber, Carl   Sws 1880-1932
O/C 25x35 A View of Celerina Chr 10/91 1,210
Felgentreff, Paul   Ger 1854-1933
O/C 8x7 Young Girl's Lesson But 11/91 2,200
Felguerez, Manuel   Mex 1929-
ORsWx&Gd/C 45x53 Entranas de Piedra 89 Chr 5/92 . .   16,500
Fenn, Harry   Am 1845-1911
* See 1992 Edition . . . .
Fenton, John William   Am 1875-1939
O/C 20x24 Spring Landscape Fre 10/91 325
Fenyes, Adolphe   Hun 1867-1945
* See 1990 Edition . . . .
Ferat, Serge   Fr 1881-1958
G/Pa 8x2 Pair of Gouaches 1929 Sby 10/91 3,575
G/B 11x8 Three Gouaches Sby 6/92 2,200
Ferber, Herbert   1906-1991
H/Pa 7x11 Three Drawings 46 Chr 11/91 2,200
Ferera, F.   Con 19C
* See 1992 Edition . . . .
Ferg, Franz De Paula   Aus 1689-1740
* See 1992 Edition . . . .
Ferguson, Henry Augustus   Am 1845-1911
O/C 24x42 Mountain Lake in Autumn 1867 Sby 5/92 14,300
O/C 7x11 Ships in Harbor Wlf 10/91 700
Fernand, Pierre & Gesner, A.   Hai
O/Pn 72x79 Bird Nests and Colonial Houses Chr 5/92 8,800
Fernandez Y Rodriguez, Silvio   Spa 1850-
O/C 40x30 A Good Smoke 1889 Chr 2/92 4,950
Fernandez, Aristides   Cub 1904-1934
Pl,HC&W/Pa 14x17 Untitled Sby 11/91 20,900
Pl,Br&W/Pa 9x13 Untitled Sby 5/92 17,600
Fernandez, Eduardo Pelayo   Spa 1850-
* See 1991 Edition . . . .
Ferneley, Claude Lorraine   Br 1822-1892
* See 1992 Edition . . . .
Ferneley, John (Jr.)   Br 1815-1862
O/C 18x40 The Start and The Finish: Pair Chr 10/91 41,800
Ferneley, John E. (Sr.)   Br 1782-1860
O/C 28x36 A Bay in a Landscape 1836 Sby 6/92 17,600
Feron, Julien Hippolyte   Fr 1864-
O/C 32x39 Vase de Fleurs et Pommes 1898 Sby 5/92 . . . 11,000

Ferranini
W/Pa 10x16 Butterflies: Two Hnz 10/91 1,800
W/Pa 10x16 Butterflies Hnz 10/91 1,000

Ferranti, C. It 20C
O/C 22x34 Harbour Scene Mys 6/92 1,980

Ferranti, Carlo It 19C
* See 1992 Edition . . . .

Ferrari, Carlo It 1813-1871
W/Pa 11x18 Peasants with Haywagon Slo 2/92 200

Ferrari, E. It 19C
* See 1990 Edition . . . .

Ferren, John Am 1905-1970
O&Sd/C 12x24 Untitled Sby 4/92 5,775
O/C 24x20 Untitled Sby 4/92 3,300
O/C 36x36 Yellow Field 60 Sby 12/91 1,980
G/Pa 13x19 Abstract in Green 33 Chr 6/92 1,540
G/B 9x11 Design for Rug Chr 11/91 1,100

Ferrer-Comas, Edouard Spa 19C
* See 1991 Edition . . . .

Ferrigno, Antonio It 1863-
O/C 30x30 Visitors to an Italianate Garden Sby 7/92 4,950
O/C 30x30 The Flower Market Wlf 9/91 2,800
O/C 30x30 The Flower Market Wlf 3/92 2,200

Ferris, Edith Am 20C
O/Pn 12x12 Four Depictions of the Lord Fre 10/91 40

Ferris, Jean Leon Gerome Am 1863-1930
O/B 16x20 The Courtship Sby 4/92 2,750
O/Ab 14x10 Conferring Knighthood Slo 4/92 1,000
O/Ab 13x9 An Elderly Gentleman's Request Slo 4/92 600
O/Ab 13x9 The Arrival of the Stagecoach Slo 4/92 550
O/Ab 14x10 Keeping an Opponent at Bay Slo 4/92 425

Ferriter, Clare Am 20C
L/M 24x32 Three Collages Slo 4/92 50

Ferroni, Alberto
O/C 20x27 Uccelli Nel Bosco '60 Sby 2/92 495

Ferroni, Egisto It 1835-1912
O/C 36x54 Maternity 1897 Sby 2/92 17,600

Ferroni, Gian Franco It
O/C 24x28 Ricordo di Sicilia 57 Sby 6/92 990

Fery, John Am 1865-1934
O/C 28x45 Moose at a River Wlf 3/92 3,000

Fette, Heinr. Ger 1802-1872
O/C 13x17 Battle Scene 1870 Sby 1/92 1,980

Fetting, Rainer 1949-
A/C 86x59 2 Figures I 81 Sby 11/91 25,300
A/C 90x97 Die Ziege (The Goat) 86 Sby 5/92 23,100
Pt/Cot 87x63 Sleep III 81 Sby 10/91 22,000
A/C 99x79 Indianer I 82 Chr 5/92 15,400
A/C 87x63 Schlaf-Traum 81 Chr 5/92 12,100
O/C 69x47 Susanne (weiss-rot) III 80 Chr 2/92 12,100

Feudel, Arthur Am 1857-1929
O/B 9x12 Forest at Dawn '86 Yng 2/92 50

Feyen, Jacques Eugene Fr 1815-1908
O/Pn 8x10 Sleeping Street Musicians Chr 10/91 3,080
O/Pn 7x10 French Street Scene Fre 4/92 475

Feyen-Perrin, Francois Nicolas Fr 1826-1888
O/C 17x24 Return from Fishing 1877 Sby 10/91 6,600

Fiammingo, Michele It 1601-1676
O/C 62x79 The Rape of Europa Chr 1/92 50,600

Fiasella, Domenico It 1589-1669
* See 1992 Edition . . . .

Fidler, Anton Aus a 1825-1855
* See 1990 Edition . . . .

Fidler, Harry Eng 20C
* See 1992 Edition . . . .

Fiedler, W. a 19C
K&Bc/Pa 17x18 Mountain Landscape w/Artist 1834 Chr 1/92 660

Field, Edward Loyal Am 1856-1914
O/C 20x29 Autumn Landscape Dum 7/92 2,500
O/C 12x16 House in Landscape Mor 3/92 1,000

Field, Freke Br a 1890-1894
* See 1990 Edition . . . .

Field, Robert Am 1769-1819
W/Iv 3x0 Portrait of a Washington Gentleman 1801 Slo 2/92 3,000

Fielding, Anthony-VanDyke C. Br 1787-1855
O/C 23x30 Mount Snowdon But 5/92 2,750

Fiene, Ernest Am 1894-1965
O/B 15x30 East River Night Chr 12/91 8,800
O/C 34x32 Lilacs in Victorian Vase Lou 6/92 1,600
O/C 30x22 White Lilacs in Japanese Vase Skn 9/91 1,430
O/C 10x19 Hunter and his Dog Chr 11/91 1,320
O/C 16x20 Purple Mountains 1923 Fre 10/91 1,000
O/C 13x16 The Harbor of Curea, Maine Lou 6/92 700

Fieravino, Francesco It a 1650-1680
O/C 36x50 Still Life Sweetmeats in Gilt Dish Sby 1/92 . . . 42,900

Figari, Pedro Uru 1861-1938
O/B 16x24 De Paseo Chr 11/91 33,000
O/B 14x20 Autoritarismo Sby 11/91 20,900
O/B 19x24 Piedad Chr 5/92 19,800
O/B 14x20 La Novia Chr 11/91 17,600
O/B 16x23 La Noticia Sby 5/92 13,200
O/B 14x20 Gaucho de la Pampa Chr 11/91 9,900
O/B 11x9 La Presentacion Sby 5/92 5,500

Filipepi, Alessandro It 1445-1510
O/Pn 19x15 Madonna & Child w/Yng St. John Chr 5/92 . 440,000

Filleau, Emery A. Am 19C
* See 1992 Edition . . . .

Fillon, Arthur 1900-
O/C 18x15 Vase de Fleurs Chr 2/92 1,320

Filmus, Tully Am 1903-
O/C 30x40 In the Rabbi's Study Chr 6/92 3,300
P/Pa 24x18 Joyous Dance Hnz 10/91 750

Filosa, Giovanni Battista It 1850-1935
O/C 26x20 Indolence Sby 10/91 10,450
W/Pa 36x24 The Love Letter Slo 7/92 3,500

Finck, Hazel Am 1894-1977
O/C 25x30 Band Concert Sby 9/91 22,000
O/C 16x21 Rendezvous on the Bridge Sby 12/91 2,860

Fini, Leonor It 1918-
W/Pa 15x12 Portrait of a Young Girl But 5/92 2,090
W/Pa/B 13x9 Ephebe Chr 5/92 990
Pl/Pa 6x3 Study of a Head Sby 10/91 990

Fink, A. Am 19C
O/C 10x15 Two Figures on a Road Hnd 10/91 250

Fink, Aaron Am 1955-
* See 1992 Edition . . . .

Finkelnberg, Augusta Am 20C
O/Cb 14x15 Two Landscapes Sel 9/91 275

Finlay, H.
W/Pa 3x7 The Everglades Eld 8/92 33

Finster, Howard Am 1916-
E/Pn 20x39 Sneakers Chr 5/92 2,200
A/B 19x19 Monsters; Last Sun Set: (2) 1986 Chr 11/91 . . . 1,980
A/B 15x6 Two Paintings 1988 Chr 2/92 1,430
MM/Pn 34x11 Coca-Cola Bottle 1990 Skn 9/91 605
O/B 23x23 Uncle Sam Mys 6/92 220
Pt/Pw Size? Uncle Sam, Peace on Earth 1991 Fre 4/92 . . . 200
O/B 11x11 Coyote in Heat Mys 6/92 82

Fioravanti, Vincenzo It 20C
O/Pn 18x24 Terraced Landscape Wes 3/92 330

Fiorendino, S.
W/Pa 21x13 Neopolitan Boy Onion Seller Dum 5/92 500

Fiorentino, E.
W/Pa 13x10 Italian Peasant Subjects: Two Dum 6/92 400

Fiorentino, Pseudo Pier Franc. It 15C
* See 1992 Edition . . . .

Fiori, H. L. Am 19C
W/Pa 9x13 Rescue from Shipwreck 1891 Yng 2/92 175

Firmin, Claude Fr 1864-1944
* See 1992 Edition . . . .

Firmin-Girard, Marie Francois Fr 1838-1921
O/C 18x25 La Place Pigalle Sby 2/92 57,750
O/C 29x39 A Country Path 1880 Sby 2/92 44,000
O/C 18x24 Marche aux Fleurs Chr 2/92 24,200
O/C 11x8 Le Jardin de la Marraine 1875 Chr 10/91 15,400
O/Pn 6x5 Walk in the Country Sby 2/92 12,100
O/C 18x24 A Busy Farm Chr 2/92 9,900

O/C 28x40 La Kermesse Sel 4/92 6,500
Fischbeck, Ludwig   Ger 1866-
O/C 38x60 Field of Lavender 1912 Hnd 12/91 1,900
Fischer, Anton Otto   Am 1882-1962
O/C 26x36 America Delivers the Goods 1942 Sby 4/92 . . . 6,325
O/C 26x31 Captain with Ghostly Crew 20 Hnd 10/91 1,500
O/C 24x36 Going Ashore Mys 11/91 1,485
O/C 12x16 Liner in a Stormy Sea Fre 4/92 500
Fischer, August   Dan 1854-1921
O/C 15x11 Piazza Erbe, Verona Chr 10/91 1,980
Fischer, Carl Holger   Dan 20C
O/C 31x40 Roses on a Tabletop Wes 11/91 908
O/C 28x40 Still Life of Roses Sel 4/92 750
Fischer, Leopold   Ger 1813-1864
W/Pa 8x7 Portrait Lord Loftus Slo 10/91 375
Fischer, Mark   Am 20C
 * See 1992 Edition . . . .
Fischer, Paul   Dan 1860-1934
 * See 1990 Edition . . . .
Fischl, Eric   Am 1948-
O/C 98x114 Cattle Auction 1990 Chr 5/92 286,000
O/C 84x108 The Brat II 1984 Sby 11/91 242,000
O/C 118x292 Life of Pigeons 1987 Sby 5/92 187,000
C/Pa 78x113 Untitled 86 Sby 11/91 82,500
O/L 58x54 First Time in Japan 1988 Sby 5/92 77,000
O/Pls 75x74 Study for Sleepwalker Sby 5/92 68,750
O/Pa 75x90 Queen Sby 5/92 46,750
O/Pa 77x73 Bathroom I Sby 11/91 44,000
O/Pa 46x35 Untitled 86 Chr 5/92 44,000
O/Pls 47x106 Untitled Sby 2/92 30,250
O/Pa 16x13 Untitled 84 Sby 11/91 28,600
O/Pa 24x16 Untitled 85 Chr 11/91 19,800
O/Pa 35x25 Dancing Man 87 Chr 11/91 14,300
C/Pa 24x18 Untitled '86 Chr 2/92 8,250
I/Pa 11x14 Triptych Sel 9/91 4,500
Fish, Janet   Am 1938-
O/C 64x40 Glasses Sby 5/92 44,000
Fisher, Albert   Am 20C
O/C/B 28x22 Pour a Free State Wlf 10/91 500
Fisher, Alvan   Am 1792-1863
O/C/Al 30x25 After the Shoot 1840 Chr 12/91 17,600
O/C 25x30 Notch of White Mountains 1834 Skn 11/91 . . . 4,400
Fisher, Anna S.   Am 1873-1942
O/C 30x25 White Petunias Skn 3/92 2,640
Fisher, Charles   Br 19C
O/C 20x30 Seascape with Rocky Coast 1881 Hnd 5/92 . . . 600
Fisher, Harrison   Am 1875-1934
W&G/Pa 29x21 Romantic Supper 1911 Slo 12/91 13,500
Fisher, Horace   Br -1893
 * See 1992 Edition . . . .
Fisher, Hugo Antoine   Am 1854-1916
W/Pa 26x35 Shepherd and Flock But 11/91 550
W/Pa 16x30 Cattle in a Landscape Yng 2/92 350
Fisher, Hugo Melville   Am 1878-1946
O/C 29x26 French Mountain Village Lou 6/92 600
Fisher, Lillie   Am 20C
O/C 23x29 Still Life Violin, Sheet Music 1883 Slo 12/91 . . 225
Fisher, Rowland   Eng 1885-1969
O/B 13x15 West Quay Mevagissey Slo 7/92 425
Fisher, Samuel Melton   Br 1859-1939
 * See 1991 Edition . . . .
Fisher, Vernon   20C
 * See 1992 Edition . . . .
Fisher, William Mark   Am 1841-1923
O/C 23x30 A Summer's Day Sby 5/92 4,675
Fisk, Lillian
O/B 8x10 Woman Ald 3/92 150
Fiske, Gertrude   Am 1879-1961
O/Cb 10x8 Old Seated Woman But 11/91 1,210
O/B 16x12 Floral Hnz 10/91 200
Fiske, Jane L.   Am 1900-
O/C 18x24 Portrait of a Woman Lou 9/91 400
Fitger, Arthur Heinrich   Ger 1840-1909
 * See 1991 Edition . . . .

Fitler, William Crothers   Am 1857-1915
 * See 1992 Edition . . . .
Fitzgerald, Frederick R.   Eng 20C
W/Pa 11x15 Hardanger Fjord Slo 9/91 250
Fix-Masseau, Pierre Felix   Fr 1869-1937
 * See 1992 Edition . . . .
Fjaestad, Gustav Edolf   Swd 1868-1948
 * See 1990 Edition . . . .
Fjellboe, Paul   Am 20C
O/Cb 12x18 River--Salt Lake City Mor 11/91 175
Flack, Audrey   1931-
O/C 80x64 Time to Save Chr 11/91 253,000
Flagg, H. Peabody   Am 1859-1937
O/C 12x16 Scene in Normandy, Autumn 1921 Wes 3/92 . . . 605
Flagg, James Montgomery   Am 1877-1960
W&G/Pa 24x12 Couple Under an Umbrella 14 Ih 11/91 . . 4,250
O/C 40x30 Gentleman in Morris Chair 1903 Slo 7/92 . . . 2,500
C/Pa 13x9 Bust of Woman with Necklace 1928 Ih 5/92 . . 1,500
C/Pa 15x13 Erroll Flynn as General Custer Ih 11/91 . . . 1,500
I/Pa 22x27 Actress, Manager and Admirer 1935 Ih 11/91 . . 1,300
W/Pa 21x25 Man Sitting on Another Ih 5/92 1,100
C/Pa 19x15 Bust of Man Holding Binoculars Ih 5/92 . . . 650
O/C 20x16 Rose Bouquet Skn 11/91 522
Pe&S/Pa 14x18 Meeting of the Minds Fre 12/91 140
Flaherty, James Thorp   Am 19C
O/C 9x12 Fishermen in Mountain Landscape 1867 Lou 6/92 . 500
Flameng, Francois   Fr 1856-1923
O/C 32x26 Young Lady Seated 1907 Sby 2/92 19,800
Flamm, Albert   Ger 1823-1906
 * See 1991 Edition . . . .
Flandrin, Hippolyte Jean   Fr 1809-1864
 * See 1992 Edition . . . .
Flaurent   Fr 19C
O/C 20x26 Cattle Watering But 5/92 2,475
Flavell, Thomas
O/B 14x18 Winter Scene of Red Barn Ald 5/92 225
Flavelle, G. H.   Eur 20C
W/Pa 14x28 Marshy Inlet Slo 2/92 75
Flavin, Dan   Am 1933-
 * See 1991 Edition . . . .
Flechemuller, Jacques   1945-
 * See 1992 Edition . . . .
Fleck, Joseph A.   Am 1893-1977
 * See 1990 Edition . . . .
Flegel, Georg   Ger 1563-1638
 * See 1992 Edition . . . .
Fleming, A. M.   Can 20C
O/C 17x13 Coastal Scenes: Pair 1900 Dum 12/91 500
Flieher, Karl   Aus 1881-1958
G/Pa 18x14 Aus Wien's Vorort Wes 11/91 495
Flink, Govaert   Dut 1615-1660
 * See 1991 Edition . . . .
Flint, Sir William Russell   Br 1880-1969
W/Pa 8x9 Ray 1963 Sby 5/92 22,000
Flipart, Giuseppe   1721-1797
O/C 17x14 Lady Playing a Harpsichord Chr 10/91 8,250
Floch, Joseph   Am 1894-1977
O/C 32x26 Zwei Frauen Mit Stilleben Doy 11/91 8,500
O/C 22x15 In My Studio Sby 12/91 2,090
C/Pa 14x10 Pensive Woman Yng 4/92 200
Flores   Spa 19C
O/Pn 12x7 Portrait of Male Moroccan Dum 9/91 275
Floris, Frans   Dut 1519-1570
O/Pn 70x57 Adam and Eve Sby 5/92 49,500
Flouest   Fr a 1789-1791
K,Pl&S/Pa 14x5 The Tennis Court Oath 1789 Chr 1/92 . . . 35,200
Focardi, Ruggero   It 1864-1934
O/Pn 16x12 Querciato Di Sesto Fiorentino 1924 Slo 10/91 . . 900
Foerster, Emil   Am 1822-1906
 * See 1992 Edition . . . .
Foerster, Herbert   Am 20C
O/C 16x24 Incoming Tide near Marblehead Fre 4/92 300
O/B 17x24 October Skies Near Hartford Fre 12/91 110
Fogarty, Thomas   Am 1873-1938
Pl/Pa 14x11 Man with Pipe in Front of House Ih 5/92 . . . 550

97

Pe/Pa 9x12 Barnyard with Horse Dum 11/91 70

Folchi, Ferdinand   It 19C
O/C 12x20 Courtyard View Slo 9/91 100

Foley, H.   Br 19C
O/C 15x10 The Village Hnz 5/92 500

Folinsbee, John Fulton   Am 1892-1972
O/C 24x30 The West Shore Sby 4/92 17,600
O/C 16x20 Mill Dam Chr 5/92 4,400
O/C 20x24 Bath Waterfront Sby 3/92 3,300
O/B 8x10 City by a River Ald 5/92 2,700
O/C 26x40 Maine Shoreline Ald 5/92 2,700
O/B 11x14 March Snow Along the Delaware Fre 12/91 2,600
O/C 20x30 Island Ald 3/92 2,300
O/C 20x30 Frozen Delaware River Chr 11/91 2,090
O/B 10x14 Westport Ald 5/92 1,000
O/B 10x14 Leeward Tacking; Wharf Scene: Pair Ald 5/92 . . . 925
O/C 20x24 Griselda Jackson Portrait Ald 5/92 450
O/C 20x16 Portrait (2) Ald 3/92 275
O/C 20x16 Boy in Blue Ald 5/92 225
O/C 20x16 Portrait Ald 5/92 50
Pe/Pa 9x12 Sketchbook Ald 3/92 25

Fon, Jade   Am 1911-1983
W/Pa 21x29 Mining But 10/91 1,650
W/Pa 21x28 Ponies at Play But 6/92 935

Fonda, Harry Stuart   Am 1864-1942
* See 1992 Edition

Fong, Lai   Chi 19C
* See 1990 Edition

Fonseca, Gonzalo   Uru 1922-
O/B 14x10 Pintura Constructiva 52 Sby 11/91 11,000

Fonseca, Reynaldo   Brz 1925-
* See 1992 Edition

Font, Constantin   Fr 1890-
O/C 58x46 Pastorale 1919 Sel 4/92 3,000

Fontaine, Gustave   Fr 19C
O/C 24x20 The Courtship But 11/91 2,200

Fontaine, Pierre-Francois-Leo.   Fr 1762-1853
* See 1992 Edition . . . .

Fontana, Lavinia   1552-1614
O/Pn 34x26 Holy Family w/Infant Saint John Chr 10/91 . . 99,000

Fontana, Lucio   It 1899-1968
O/C 26x21 Concetto Spaziale-Attese Sby 2/92 71,500
W&L 23x19 Composition in Green Sby 2/92 20,900

Fontana, Prospero   It 1512-1597
* See 1992 Edition

Fontanarosa, Lucien
O/C 11x18 Still Life with Apples Sby 6/92 1,210

Fonte, P.   Eur 19C
O/C 22x28 Milkmaids with Cows Slo 12/91 775

Fontebasso, Francesco   It 1709-1769
* See 1991 Edition

Foote, Mary Hallock   Am 1847-1938
* See 1991 Edition

Foote, Will Howe   Am 1874-1965
O/B 16x12 Head of a Woman Yng 2/92 200

Foppiani, Gustavo   It 20C
O/B 27x18 Maschere Che Suonano 60 But 11/91 3,025

Forain, Jean Louis   Fr 1852-1931
O/C 15x11 Woman Consulting with Her Lawyer Sby 10/91 . 5,500
W,Pe&C/Pa 12x9 A Gentleman Caller Sby 10/91 5,225
W&Y/Pa 12x9 L'Echo De Paris Sby 10/91 825
Pl&S/Pa 10x6 Standing Figure Hnd 6/92 350
C/Pa 11x16 Man Seated in Armchair Sby 6/92 330

Forbes, Charles Stuart   Am 1860-1926
* See 1992 Edition

Forbes, Edwin   Am 1839-1895
O/C 10x12 Mother and Calf Mys 11/91 660

Forbes, Helen K.   Am 1891-1945
O/C 34x40 Mountains and Miners Shack But 2/92 4,125
O/C 26x22 Myoshi But 10/91 1,870
O/C 30x32 Mine Dumps, Gold Valley But 6/92 1,540
O/C 40x34 Gunnajuato, Mexico But 2/92 1,430
O/C 47x28 Tropical Foliage But 10/91 1,320
O/C 34x40 La Parroquia But 6/92 660

Forbes, John Colin   Can 1846-1925
O/C 14x18 Autumn Storm Threatening Sbt 5/92 935
O/B 13x18 Sunset Sbt 11/91 748

Forbes, Kenneth Keith   Can 1892-1980
O/C 12x14 Fishing From the Dock Sbt 11/91 748

Forbes, Stanhope   Irs 1857-1947
O/C 30x24 Santa Maria della Salute Chr 10/91 9,900

Ford, Elise   Am 20C
O/C 24x20 Picking Flowers in the Meadow Slo 2/92 750

Ford, Elizabeth Merrill
O/C 26x22 Floral Hnz 10/91 180

Ford, Henry Chapman   Am 1828-1894
* See 1992 Edition

Foreau, Henri   Fr 1866-1938
W&C/Pa 11x15 Versailles in Autumn and Spring (2) Chr 5/92 495

Forg, Gunther   1952-
A/Me/B 95x63 Bleibild 88 Chr 11/91 35,200
O/Me 95x63 Untitled (177/88) Sby 11/91 33,000
A&Pe/Pa 95x63 Untitled Chr 5/92 20,900
O/Pn 28x22 Untitled 88 Chr 2/92 19,800
Ph 111x52 Treppenhaus 86 Chr 11/91 12,100
A/Wd 24x79 Farbfeld 1986 Chr 11/91 11,000
Ph/Wd 111x52 Untitled 94/88 Sby 11/91 9,900
A/Pa 103x58 Untitled 89 Chr 5/92 7,150

Forkner, Edgar   Am 1945-
W/Pa 11x10 Harbor Scene Hnz 5/92 250

Formis, Achille B.   It 1832-1906
O/C 25x49 On the Banks of the Bosporus Chr 10/91 . . . 44,000

Forrest
O/C/B 8x10 Harbor Yng 2/92 50

Forrester, Herbert   Am 20C
O/C 21x24 Sand Dunes Padre Island Fre 10/91 50
O/C 12x16 Long Island Sand Dunes Fre 10/91 25

Forry, B.   Am 20C
O/C 17x22 Still Life of Pansies in Basket Slo 12/91 425

Forsner, Leopold   Con 19C
O/C 48x36 Pink and White Flowers Chr 2/92 18,700

Forster, D. K.   Am 20C
O/C 20x14 After the Hunt Wes 11/91 578

Forster, George   Am a 1860-1890
O/C 27x21 Still Life Grapes and Butterfly 1888 Chr 3/92 . . . 5,500

Forster, John Wycliffe Lowes   Can 1850-1938
O/C 26x22 Portrait Boy in a Sailor Suit Sbt 5/92 1,683

Forster, Mary   Br 1853-1885
W/Pa 16x24 Richmond Castle, Yorkshire 1881 Sby 1/92 . . . 1,100

Forsythe, Clyde   Am 1885-1962
O/B 12x16 Landscape--Nevada Mor 11/91 1,700
O/M 12x16 The Cliffs--Catalina Mor 11/91 1,600
O/B 16x12 Bear Valley Mor 11/91 1,200
O/Cb 12x16 Landscape/Lake Mor 6/92 450
O/Cb 12x16 Landscape Mor 6/92 425

Forte, Luca   It 18C
* See 1991 Edition

Forte, Vicente   Arg 1912-
O/C 18x24 El Pajaro (The Bird) '62 Wes 11/91 770

Fortescue-Brickdale, Eleanor   Br 1871-1945
* See 1992 Edition . . . .

Forti, Eduardo   It 19C
* See 1991 Edition

Forti, Ettore   It 19C
* See 1992 Edition

Fortier, * 20C**
O/C 13x16 Forest Fire Slo 9/91 100

Fortin, Besnard
W&Pe/Pa 8x11 Four Nude Figures Eld 8/92 121

Fortin, Marc-Aurele   Can 1888-1970
O/B 18x20 Paysage D'Hiver Sbt 11/91 29,920

Fortunati, * It 19C**
W/Pa 21x15 A Moor Slo 7/92 650

Fortunati, G.   It 19C
W/Pa 20x13 Peasant Water Carrier Mys 11/91 165

Fortune, Euphemia Charlton   Am 1885-1969
O/C 32x40 Afternoon Shadows But 2/92 33,000

Fortuny Y Carbo, Mariano   Spa 1838-1874
W/Pa 15x7 Street Scene Market: Pair Wes 11/91 1,650

Fortuny Y De Madrazo, Mariano   Spa 1871-1949
   * See 1990 Edition ....

Foschi, Francesco   It 1502-1567
   * See 1991 Edition ....

Foss, O.   Fr 20C
O/C 48x32 Cubistic Composition Hnz 5/92 300

Foss, Olivier   Am 1920-
O/C 22x18 Crane by a River Fre 4/92 300

Foster, Alice C.   Am 1873-
O/C 26x18 Lady Arranging Flowers 1892 Slo 7/92 1,400

Foster, Ben   Am 1852-1926
O/C 30x30 Waining Day Chr 6/92 3,300
O/C 24x24 Landscape and Stream But 11/91 2,750
O/C 24x36 Flirtation But 4/92 1,540
O/C 32x41 Rolling Hills Fre 10/91 800
O/C 22x18 Flowers in a China Vase Yng 4/92 700

Foster, Ethel E.   Am 20C
W/Pa 15x21 Three Watercolors Slo 10/91 85

Foster, G. H.   Am 19C
O/C 16x22 Boy with Cattle by a Stream Chr 6/92 1,430

Foster, Hal   Am 1892-1982
PVPa 34x23 Sir Gawain and Prince Valiant 59 Ilh 5/92 .. 4,750
PVPa 11x8 Comic Strip. Prince Valiant 46 Ilh 11/91 ... 600

Foster, Miles Birket   Br 1825-1899
W/Pa 4x7 Italian Coastal Views Hnz 5/92 375

Foster, Will   Am 1882-1953
O/C 28x22 Odalisque But 2/92 2,090
O/C 27x22 Seated Nude But 2/92 1,210

Foubert, Emile   Fr -1910
   * See 1991 Edition ....

Foujita, Tsuguharu   Jap 1886-1968
O/C 13x10 Jeune Fille au Chat 1952 Chr 5/92 165,000
O/C 9x6 Jeune Fille 1953 Sby 5/92 115,500
G,Gd&PVPa 13x18 Adam et Eve Chr 11/91 60,500
O/C 14x15 Vase de Tulipes Sby 5/92 60,500
W&PVPa 10x7 Jeune Femme Sby 5/92 49,500
PI,W&H/Pa 16x20 Le Chat Chr 11/91 46,200
PI&S/Pa 9x7 Femme au Chat Hnz 5/92 16,000

Fould, Consuelo   Fr 1862-1927
   * See 1992 Edition ....

Foulkes, Liyn   Am 1934-
   * See 1991 Edition ....

Foullon, Lucille   1775-1865
O/C 40x32 Portrait of a Lady 1807 Chr 10/91 7,150

Fouqueray, Charles   Fr 1872-1956
P&Y/Pa 11x18 After the Battle 1915 Chr 2/92 242

Fourie, Albert Auguste   Fr 1854-
O/C 15x18 Afternoon Tea in the Garden But 11/91 6,050

Fournier, Alexis Jean   Am 1865-1948
O/B 18x20 October Sunshine Mor 11/91 1,800

Fous, Jean   Fr 1901-1971
O/B 9x7 Cityscape Hnz 5/92 250
O/Pn 9x7 Street Scene Hnz 5/92 250

Fowler, Daniel   Can 1810-1894
W/Pa 13x9 Bridge Over a Gorge 1865 Sbt 5/92 1,028

Fowler, Frank   Am 1852-1910
   * See 1991 Edition ....

Fowler, Robert   Br 1853-1926
   * See 1992 Edition ....

Fowler, Trevor Thomas   Am 1830-1871
   * See 1991 Edition ....

Fowler, William   Am
   * See 1992 Edition ....

Fowles, J.
O/C Size? Portrait of John Adams Eld 8/92 1,760

Fox, Charles Lewis   Am 1854-1927
O/C 17x14 Little Dutch Girl, a Prayer 1885 Slo 2/92 800

Fox, Edwin M.   Eng a 1830-1870
   * See 1992 Edition ....

Fox, Henry Charles   Br 1860-
W/Pa 14x21 Return from the Hunt Chr 10/91 550

Fox, John   Can 1927-
O/C 30x24 Quebec Hnz 5/92 625

Fox, R. Atkinson   Am 1860-1927
   * See 1992 Edition ....

Foyster, W.   Eng 20C
O/C 22x16 River Landscapes: Pair Slo 9/91 300

Fradin, Carl   Fr 19C
O/C 21x15 He Loves Me, He Loves Me Not 96 Hnd 3/92 ... 300

Fragiacomo, Pietro   It 1856-1922
O/Pn 15x8 Bridge over a Canal Chr 10/91 4,950

Fragonard, Alexandre Evariste   Fr 1780-1850
   * See 1990 Edition ....

Fragonard, Jean-Honore   Fr 1732-1806
K/Pa 14x19 Cascade at the Villa Aldobrandi Chr 1/92 ... 110,000
K&Cw/Pa 7x9 Child's First Steps Chr 1/92 19,800

Fragonard, Theophile-Evariste   Fr 1806-1876
Pe,I&W/Pa 6x11 Design for Sevres Porcelain Hnd 3/92 1,400

Frampton, Edward Reginald   Br 19C
   * See 1990 Edition ....

France, Jesse Leach   Am 1862-1926
O/C Size? Water's Edge Hnd 12/91 375

Frances Y Pascual, Placido   Spa 1840-
   * See 1990 Edition ....

Frances, Esteban   20C
   * See 1992 Edition ....

Franceschini, Marcantonio   It 1648-1729
   * See 1992 Edition ....

Franchere, Joseph Charles   Can 1866-1921
O/C 33x41 After Supper 1906 Sbt 5/92 24,310

Franchi, T*   It 19C**
O/C 38x26 Woman Holding a Yellow Rose Sby 7/92 4,400

Francia, Alexandre T.   Fr 1820-1844
W/Pb 17x27 A Midday Rest Chr 10/91 880

Francia, Giacomo   It 1486-1557
O/Pn 26x22 Mystic Marriage of Saint Catherine Chr 1/92   104,500

Francini, Mauro
   * See 1992 Edition ....

Francis, John F.   Am 1808-1886
O/C 25x30 Still Life Apples and Chestnuts Chr 5/92 ... 22,000
O/Ab 8x6 Sharpening the Scythe '81 Wlf 9/91 1,000

Francis, Sam   Am 1923-
O/C 26x24 Deux Magots Sby 5/92 148,500
A/C 36x72 Untitled Sby 2/92 115,500
O/C 60x48 Untitled Sby 11/91 93,500
O/Pa/C 73x37 Untitled Sby 11/91 88,000
A/Pa 72x36 A Firing of the Eye Sby 5/92 74,250
A/C 55x21 Untitled 1984 Sby 2/92 71,500
A/Pa 38x72 Untitled 1974 Chr 11/91 70,400
G/Pa 40x27 Untitled 1977 Sby 5/92 60,500
A/Pa 10x11 Untitled (Santa Barbara) 1961 Chr 5/92 44,000
A/Pa 22x30 Basic Insight 1987 Chr 5/92 41,800
A/Pa/L 30x22 Passing Through Sby 11/91 41,250
A/Pb 20x30 Nike Chr 5/92 38,500
G/Pa/B 17x13 Composition in Rouge 1960 Chr 5/92 18,700
A/Pa 12x16 Untitled 1978 Sby 2/92 15,400

Francisco, John Bond   Am 1863-1931
O/C 14x20 Purple Mountain But 2/92 2,750
O/C 16x20 Valley Sunset But 10/91 2,090
O/C 20x16 Artist's Studio But 2/92 1,870
O/C 16x20 Clear Spring Mountain But 2/92 1,430
O/C 25x30 Sunset Over a Marsh But 2/92 1,100
O/C 16x20 Squirrel Inn But 2/92 825
O/C 8x11 Shady Path Mor 6/92 650

Franck, Albert Jacques   Can 1899-1973
O/B 16x20 John St. and Grange Ave. '50 Sbt 11/91 4,441
O/B 12x10 Nassau at Bellevue '67 Sbt 11/91 2,571
PV/Pa 5x5 On Winchester Avenue '65 Sbt 11/91 374

Francken, Frans (the Younger)   Flm 1581-1642
O/Pn 10x13 Daniel Feeding Babylonian Dragon Chr 1/92 . 12,100

O/Cp 13x11 Madonna and Child Sby 10/91 10,450
Franco, Giovanni Battista It 1510-1580
  * See 1992 Edition . . . .
Franco, Siron Brz 1947-
  O/C 53x53 Skin--Be Careful, Glass Chr 5/92 12,100
Francois, Guy Fr 1578-1650
  * See 1992 Edition . . . .
Francois, Pierre Joseph Bel 1759-1851
  * See 1991 Edition . . . .
Frandzen, Eugene M. Am 1893-1950
  G/Pa 11x13 Coastal Mor 6/92 650
  G/Pa 10x12 Atmospheric Coastal Mor 11/91 275
Frangiamore, Salvatore Br 20C
  O/C/B 25x20 The Unveiling Chr 2/92 14,300
Frank, Gerald A. Am 1888-
  O/Cb 36x30 Still Life of Flowers Lou 12/91 1,500
  O/B 39x49 Song of Spring Hnd 6/92 1,400
  O/M 30x30 Floral Still Life 23 Hnd 10/91 1,000
Frank, Joseph Ger 20C
  O/C 15x19 The Deputation Durn 6/92 1,000
Frank, Leo E. Am 20C
  * See 1992 Edition . . . .
Frank-Will Fr 1900-1951
  O/C 15x18 Vue de Honfleur Chr 11/91 4,400
  G,W&K/Pa 18x24 French Cancan a Tabarin Chr 2/92 3,520
  O/C 23x19 Chartres Hnz 10/91 3,500
  W&Pe/Pa 9x10 Montmartre Chr 11/91 2,420
Franke, Albert Ger 1860-1924
  * See 1992 Edition . . . .
Frankenstein, Godfrey N. Am 1820-1873
  O/C 18x24 Niagara Falls Canadian Side 1852 Chr 11/91 . . . 1,210
Frankenthaler, Helen Am 1928-
  O/C 81x69 Yellow Crater 63 Sby 2/92 159,500
  O/C/M 16x14 Untitled '59 Chr 2/92 17,600
  MM/Pa 27x20 Untitled '85 Sby 5/92 9,900
  I&S/Pa 5x3 Untitled 1960 Sby 6/92 1,650
Frankfurter, Jack Am 20C
  O/C 16x24 Capodanno Cinese, Frammento #2 Wes 3/92 . . . 220
Frankl, Franz Ger 1881-
  * See 1992 Edition . . . .
Franquelin, Jean Augustin Fr 1798-1839
  * See 1990 Edition . . . .
Franquinet, Eugene Am 1875-1940
  O/M 8x10 Landscape Mor 6/92 1,200
  O/B 16x20 Goats in Landscape Mor 3/92 500
  O/C/B 8x11 Country Road, Autumn Slo 7/92 95
Fransioli, Thomas Adrian Am 1906-
  O/Pn 12x23 The Quest 1947 Sby 12/91 770
Franz, Ettore R. It 1845-1907
  W/Pb 27x40 Oaks of San Gregorio 1886 Chr 5/92 18,700
  W/Pa 14x20 A Scenic Idyll Wlf 9/91 5,000
Franz, Sali Am 1893-1967
  G/Pa 16x20 Hour Glass Durn 11/91 175
Franz, W. A. Con 20C
  O/C 22x30 Landscape at Sunset 1930 Fre 10/91 550
Franzen, August Am 1863-1938
  * See 1990 Edition . . . .
Frappa, Jose Fr 1854-1904
  O/C 82x44 Elegant Lady Seated 1909 Chr 5/92 4,000
Fraser, Alex (the Senior) Br 1786-1865
  * See 1990 Edition . . . .
Fraser, Charles Am 1782-1860
  O/C 23x31 Trenton Falls, New York Chr 11/91 4,400
Fraser, Don Am 20C
  O/C 20x24 Salem, CT Landscape Mys 6/92 110
Fraser, Thomas Douglass Am 1883-1955
  * See 1992 Edition . . . .
Fraye, Andre
  O/C 26x32 Harbor at Sanary-Sur-Mer Sby 6/92 1,650
Frazer, Samuel W. Am 20C
  O/C 30x25 Fishing Boats at Dock Bor 8/92 450
Freddie, Frederik Wilhelm C. Dan 1909-
  O/M 22x18 Nude 1947 Wes 3/92 10,450
  O/C 23x17 Dronningens Elsker 1944 Wes 3/92 9,350

Fredenthal, David Am 1914-1958
  W&Pe/Pa 22x30 Snow in the Village Sby 4/92 715
Frederick, A. Am 20C
  O/C 24x30 Marine Scene Sel 5/92 150
Fredericks, Ernest Am 1877-1927
  O/C 16x20 Birch Trees Ald 3/92 2,150
  O/C 16x20 Autumn Landscape Hnz 10/91 700
  O/C 16x20 Forest Landscape Hnz 10/91 250
  O/C 24x30 Autumn Landscape Wlf 10/91 50
Fredriks, Jan Hendrik 1751-1822
  O/Pn 23x18 Irises Peonies Morning Glory 1774 Chr 5/92 . 88,000
Freeman, Don Am 1908-1978
  * See 1992 Edition . . . .
Freeman, James Edward Am 1808-1884
  O/Cb 22x15 The Knight Chr 6/92 110
Freer, Frederick Warren Am 1849-1908
  O/C 27x22 Bearded Gentleman '73 Hnz 5/92 225
Freezor, George-Augustus Br a 1861-1879
  * See 1990 Edition . . . .
Freilicher, Jane 1924-
  O/C 80x70 Bluish Horizon Chr 2/92 15,400
Freiman, Lillian Can 1908-1986
  * See 1992 Edition . . . .
Freminet, Martin Fr 1567-1619
  * See 1991 Edition . . . .
Fremy, Antoine Alexandre A. Fr 1816-1885
  Pe/Pa/B 12x18 Harbor of Rio de Janeiro 1857 Chr 2/92 . . . 1,650
French, G. A. Am 20C
  O/C 22x36 Landscape with Figures Yng 2/92 300
French, Jared Am 1905-
  I&S/Pa 8x8 One Man, Three Views Sby 12/91 2,530
Frequenez, Paul Leon Fr 1876-
  * See 1991 Edition . . . .
Frere, Charles Theodore Fr 1814-1888
  O/Pn 7x16 View of the Nile Sby 1/92 7,150
  O/Pn 10x14 Le Couche Du Soleil a l'Oasis Sby 10/91 6,600
  O/Pn 10x16 An Arab Encampment Chr 5/92 5,940
  O/Pn 7x12 Arab Encampment But 11/91 2,750
  O/Pn 7x5 Caravan Entering an Oasis Skn 11/91 1,430
Frere, Edouard Fr 1819-1886
  * See 1992 Edition . . . .
Frerichs, William Charles A. Am 1829-1905
  O/C 36x29 Portrait of a Naval Officer Chr 5/92 9,900
Frey Ger 19C
  O/C 46x40 Portrait of a Young Woman 1854 Slo 4/92 1,800
Frey, Johann Jakob Sws 1813-1865
  O/C 25x33 On the Banks of the Nile 1856 Sby 10/91 24,200
Frey, Joseph F. Am 1892-1977
  O/C 24x30 Sierra Grandeur Mor 6/92 700
Frey, Max Ger 20C
  O/B 26x26 Ulm Cathedral Munchen 1942 Slo 7/92 600
Freyberg, Conrad Ger 1842-
  * See 1991 Edition . . . .
Friberg, Arnold Am 1913-
  O/C 32x26 Land of The Shining Mountains Skn 9/91 3,300
Fried, Pal Hun 1893-1976
  O/C 23x31 African Warriors Wlf 3/92 2,900
  O/C 24x30 Cowboy Roping Steer Wlf 3/92 2,200
  O/C 30x24 Madeleine Wlf 3/92 1,500
  O/C 25x30 The Rodeo Wlf 3/92 1,400
  O/C 30x24 Gypsy Wlf 3/92 1,000
  O/C 24x30 Woman Wearing a Red Coat Sel 4/92 800
  O/C 24x30 Ballerina Seated Sel 4/92 450
Friedeberg, Pedro It 1937-
  O&I/B 24x24 Chairs and Moons 1969 Hnd 3/92 1,400
  O&I/B 24x24 Chairs and Moons 1969 Hnd 10/91 550
Friedenson, Arthur A. Br 1872-1955
  O/Pn 12x16 On the Road from...Dorset 1920 Skn 5/92 935
Friedlander, Camilla Aus 1856-1928
  O/Pn 14x10 Before the Meal Chr 2/92 1,980
Friedman, Arnold Am 1879-1946
  O/C 17x21 Abstraction Sby 5/92 18,700

Pe/Pa 19x14 Four Works Chr 9/91 4,180

Friedman, Martin   Am 1896-
P,Pe&S/Pa 8x9 Reclining Nude Slo 10/91 160
W&Fp/Pa 20x13 Two Woman Slo 12/91 90

Frielicher, Jane   Am 1924-
* See 1990 Edition . . . .

Frier, Harry   Br 1849-1919
O/C 28x45 Family at Dinner 1889 Hnd 5/92 4,000

Fries, Charles Arthur   Am 1854-1940
O/C 27x35 Unsettled Weather Lou 3/92 1,700
O/C 24x36 Naked Grandeur But 2/92 1,650
O/C 18x12 Eucalyptus in Mission Valley Mor 11/91 . . . 1,600
O/C 9x11 Eucalyptus Near Alpine Mor 6/92 1,300

Frieseke, Frederick Carl   Am 1874-1939
O/Pn 14x11 Woman Tying Her Shoe Sby 5/92 44,000
O/C 20x16 The Breakfast Table '21 But 4/92 38,500
W/Pa 12x9 After the Bath Sel 12/91 4,500

Friesz, Emile-Othon   Fr 1879-1949
O/C 24x29 Le Port de Toulon 27 Sby 5/92 28,600
O/C 18x15 Trois Femmes Chr 2/92 19,800
W&G/Pa 13x16 Paysage 25 Chr 11/91 3,300
O/C 8x10 Main Aux Fruits Chr 11/91 3,080

Friis, Frederick Trap   Am 1865-1909
O/C 21x21 Santa Maria Novella Chr 9/91 6,050
O/C 18x17 Male Life Class Arts League 1890 Chr 3/92 . . 5,500
O/B 14x10 Man Reading Mys 6/92 770

Frind, August   Aus 1852-1924
* See 1990 Edition . . . .

Frisch, J. C.   Ger 19C
O/C 20x30 Middle Eastern Town Sby 1/92 1,760

Fristrup, Niels   Dan 1837-1909
* See 1991 Edition . . . .

Frith, William Powell   Br 1819-1909
O/C 25x25 The Family Lawyer Durn 9/91 12,000

Fritzel, Wilhelm   Ger 1870-
* See 1991 Edition . . . .

Fromentin, Eugene   Fr 1820-1876
O/Pn 14x21 Audience Chez Un Khalifat Sby 10/91 . . . 27,500
O/Pn 11x15 On the Nile Sby 5/92 20,900
O/C 19x27 An Arab Encampment Sby 10/91 18,700

Fromkes, Maurice   Am 1872-1931
O/C 25x20 Little Carmen of the Hills 1923 Sby 12/91 . . 825

Froschl, Carl   Aus 1848-1934
P/Pa 29x23 Seated Girl with Bouquet Slo 10/91 4,750

Frost, Arthur Burdett   Am 1851-1928
Pl/Pa 9x10 The Chicken Thief Ih 5/92 1,900
W&R/Pa 11x6 Man Holding Umbrella Ih 11/91 950
W/Pa 9x14 Mohawk Valley Fre 10/91 425

Frost, Francis Shedd   Am 1825-1902
O/C 20x30 The White Mountains 1857 Skn 9/91 2,475

Frost, John (Jack)   Am 1890-1937
O/C 30x40 Superstition Mountains, Arizona 1930 But 10/91 17,600

Frost, William Edward   Br 1810-1877
O/Pn 5x8 The Sirens Chr 5/92 1,760
O/B 9x7 Portrait of a Girl Hnd 12/91 1,600

Fruitier, M   Hai 20C**
O/C 21x26 Still Life Statue and Flowers Wes 11/91 . . . 138

Fry, Guy Edgar   Am 1903-
G/Pa 10x9 Model Sailboat on Desk 1929 Ih 5/92 225

Fry, John H.   Am 1861-1946
* See 1992 Edition . . . .

Fry, Rowena   Am 20C
* See 1992 Edition . . . .

Fryda, G.
O/C 15x24 Muting a Putenil Dum 10/91 150

Fuchs, Bernard   Am 1932-
O/C 34x24 Drug Episode Ih 11/91 700

Fuechsel, Herman   Am 1833-1915
O/C 24x40 In the White Mountains Sby 9/91 8,800

Fuertes, Louis Agassiz   Am 1874-1927
G&W/Cd 22x17 Quail/Snowy Landscape 1913 Doy 12/91 . 16,000
G&W/Cd 21x27 Woodcock in Flight 1912 Doy 12/91 . . 11,500
W/Pa 12x20 Snowy Owl Hnd 5/92 8,500
W/Pa/Cd 8x11 Snow Doves 1905 Doy 12/91 4,250

Fuger, Friedrich Heinrich   1751-1818
O/C 44x35 Portrait of a Lady Chr 10/91 11,000

Fuller, Arthur D.   Am 1889-1966
O/C 40x30 Landing Mallards Sby 6/92 5,500

Fuller, Charles B.   Am 1821-1893
O/C 11x15 Hammock, Gorham, Maine 1878 Brd 8/92 . . . 1,980

Fuller, George   Am 1822-1884
O/C 16x14 John Quincy Adams Ward 1868 Chr 11/91 . . 1,760

Fuller, J. A.   Am 19C
W&V/Pa 7x9 Walrus Hunting Sketch Eld 7/92 77

Fuller, Richard Henry   Am 1822-1871
O/C 15x26 Cows Watering by a Stream 1865 Chr 6/92 . . 1,980

Fuller, Samuel W.   Am 19C
O/B 8x9 Peaches and a Glass of Cognac 1890 Chr 11/91 . . 935

Fulleylove, John   Br 1845-1908
O/B 10x14 Friars on the Steps of a Church 1875 Sby 1/92 . 1,980
G,W&S/Pa 9x14 Figures in Garden at Nimes Slo 2/92 . . . 550

Fulop, Karoly   Am 1898-1963
* See 1992 Edition . . . .

Fulp, *   20C**
W&G/Pa 21x17 Roman Warrior on Horseback Slo 7/92 . . 110

Fulton, David   Br 1850-
* See 1992 Edition . . . .

Fungai, Bernardino   It 1460-1516
* See 1992 Edition . . . .

Furini, Francesco   It 1604-1646
* See 1991 Edition . . . .

Fusaro, Jean   1925-
O/C 15x18 Regata au drapeau Chr 5/92 2,860

Fussell, Charles Lewis   Am 1840-1909
* See 1992 Edition . . . .

Fyt, Jan   Flm 1609-1661
O/C 23x29 A Hare, a Partridge, Song Birds Chr 1/92 . . . 24,200

Gaal, Ferenc   Hun 1891-
O/Cb 13x17 Women Washing Clothes Lou 6/92 625

Gabani, Giuseppe   It 1849-1899
W/Pa 15x21 Peasant on Horseback Slo 2/92 2,100
W/Pa 29x20 Arab Warriors Wtf 11/91 1,700

Gabeblicky, E   Con 20C**
O/C 11x9 San Marco & Santa Maria Della: Two Wes 3/92 . . 605

Gabriel
O/B 33x33 Forest Scene Dum 5/92 350

Gabriel, F.   Fr 20C
O/Pn 20x16 Still Life with Flowers Sby 1/92 4,675
O/Pn 20x16 Still Life with Roses Sby 1/92 3,575
O/Pn 20x16 Still Life Flowers in a Vase Sby 7/92 . . . 2,750
O/Pn 16x12 Still Life Flowers Sby 7/92 2,530
O/Pn 16x12 Floral Still Life Slo 12/91 900

Gabrini, Pietro   It 1856-1926
O/C 26x40 Workers on a Wagon Ald 5/92 10,000

Gael, Barent   Dut 1620-1703
O/C 26x32 Catching the Herring But 11/91 15,400

Gaertner, Carl Frederick   Am 1898-1952
O/C 40x40 The Ladle 1929 Chr 9/91 4,950
W/Pa 10x13 The Tug Wtf 3/92 475
O/C 18x22 Gates Mill-Fall Mor 6/92 175

Gage, George William   Am 1887-1957
O&R/C 30x21 Fleeing an Angry Bear Ih 5/92 600

Gagen, Robert Ford   Can 1847-1926
* See 1991 Edition . . . .

Gagiliardini, Julien Gustave   Fr 1846-1927
O/Pn 10x14 Women Mending the Nets Sby 7/92 1,650

Gagni, P.   Fr 20C
O/Cb 9x12 Porte St. Denis; Quai: Pair Sby 6/92 605

Gagnon, Clarence Alphonse   Can 1881-1942
* See 1992 Edition . . . .

Gaines, Charles   20C
* See 1992 Edition . . . .

Gainsborough, Thomas   Eng 1727-1788
O/C 29x24 Portrait of a Lady Sby 5/92 16,500
O/C 29x23 Portrait Sir John Sebright, Bt. Sby 1/92 . . . 7,590

Gaiper, T. E.   Con 19C
* See 1992 Edition . . . .

Gaisser, Jacob Emmanuel Ger 1825-1899
O/Pn 9x7 First Communion But 5/92 2,090
Gaisser, Max Ger 1857-1922
* See 1991 Edition
Galan, Julio LA 20C
* See 1992 Edition . . . .
Galantiere, Nancy Fr 20C
* See 1992 Edition . . . .
Galer, Ethel Caroline Hughes Br 20C
O/C 58x18 Blossoms Chr 5/92 3,850
Galien-Laloue, Eugene Fr 1854-1941
G/Pa 13x20 Le Boulevard de Montmartre Chr 10/91 18,700
G/Pa 8x13 La Madeleine Sby 10/91 17,600
W,Pe&G/Pa 11x16 Place de L'Opera/La Neige Sby 2/92 . . 16,500
W&G/Pa 10x18 La Seine a Paris Sby 10/91 15,400
G/Pa 8x13 La Porte St. Denis, Paris Sby 2/92 14,300
G/Pa 8x13 Place Saint Augustin Sby 10/91 14,300
W&G/Pa 8x12 Crossing a Parisian Avenue Sby 2/92 13,200
Pe&G/Pa 8x12 St. Sulpice, Paris Sby 2/92 13,200
W&G/Pa 8x12 La Place du Chatelet, Paris Sby 2/92 9,900
W&G/Pa 10x15 La Place du Chatelet, Paris Sby 2/92 9,350
G/Pa 8x12 Le Boulevard Haussmann Chr 2/92 9,350
G/Pa/B 8x12 Outside a Theatre, Paris Chr 5/92 9,020
G/Pa 8x12 Les Grands Boulevards Chr 2/92 8,800
G/Pa 8x12 Quais et Notre-Dame sous la neige Chr 2/92 . . 8,800
O/C 20x26 Paysage D'Automne Sby 2/92 8,250
O/C 19x26 Au Bord de la Riviere Sby 2/92 7,975
W&G/Pa 8x12 Sur le boulevard, Paris Skn 5/92 7,700
O/C 18x24 Village Scene But 5/92 7,700
O/C 14x18 Soleil Couchant sur un Port Sby 5/92 4,400
Gall, Francois Fr 1912-1945
O/C 50x50 Les Dames d'Auteuil Doy 11/91 17,000
O/C 18x15 Derriere Les Coulisses Chr 11/91 10,450
O/C 18x24 Baigneurs a Trouville Chr 2/92 8,800
O/C 11x18 A la plage Chr 5/92 7,700
O/C 22x18 Ballerina at the Piano Sby 6/92 6,050
O/C 11x9 Femme en robe rouge Chr 5/92 6,050
O/C 10x18 Au Pont Neuf Chr 2/92 5,500
O/C 11x9 La Lecon de Piano Chr 11/91 5,500
O/C 26x22 Floral Still Life Sby 10/91 4,840
O/C 11x9 Jeune femme en robe bleu Chr 5/92 4,400
O/M 11x9 Femme a sa Toilette Chr 11/91 4,180
O/C 11x9 Femme a sa toilette Chr 5/92 4,180
O/C 11x9 Au cafe Chr 5/92 3,960
O/C 20x24 Young Woman in Pink Sby 10/91 3,960
O/C 10x13 Aux Courses Chr 11/91 3,850
O/B 15x20 Les Bouqinistes a Paris Chr 2/92 3,850
O/C 18x11 The Bather Sby 10/91 3,850
O/C 20x24 Promenade Dans Un Village Sby 2/92 3,575
O/C 9x11 La ballerine Chr 5/92 3,520
O/C 11x9 Woman in an Outdoor Cafe Dum 2/92 3,500
O/C 9x11 Riviera Scene Dum 2/92 3,000
O/C 9x11 Derriere les coulisses Chr 5/92 2,860
O/C 9x11 Outing at the Beach Sby 2/92 2,860
O/C 13x10 The Bather Sby 10/91 2,420
O/C 9x11 Vue D'Une Ferme Sby 2/92 1,650
O/C 20x13 Outside Markets Wlf 3/92 1,300
Gallagher, Michael Am 20C
* See 1992 Edition . . . .
Gallagher, Sears Am 1869-1955
W/Pa 10x14 Monhegan I Bor 8/92 450
Gallait, Louis Bel 1810-1887
* See 1992 Edition . . . .
Galland, Pierre Victor Fr 1822-1892
* See 1992 Edition . . . .
Gallard-Lepinay, Paul Char E. Fr 1842-1885
O/C 21x36 Grand Canal, Venice Chr 5/92 4,400
Gallatin, Albert Eugene Am 1882-1952
O/C 14x12 Classical Abstraction 1940 Chr 5/92 5,500
O/C 32x26 Nude in an Interior 1945 Wes 3/92 2,860
Gallegos Y Arnosa, Jose Spa 1859-1902
* See 1992 Edition

Galli, Giuseppe It 1866-1953
O/C/B 23x16 The Secret 1896 Chr 10/91 6,600
O/C 16x24 Party in the Wine Cellar 1896 Sby 1/92 4,290
Galliani, Omar
* See 1992 Edition . . . .
Galliari, Gasparo It 1760-1818
K,Pl&S/Pa 8x12 View of the Quay from an Arcade Chr 1/92 3,520
Gallis, Pieter a 1661-1683
O/C 26x21 Swag of Grapes, Peaches, Plums Chr 10/91 . . 18,700
Gallo, Giuseppe 20C
O&Pe/Wd 4x19 Narcissi Sby 6/92 1,210
Gallo, Vincent 1961-
O&H/St 24x36 Marriage of Two Families 84 Chr 11/91 . . . 2,200
O&H/St 48x30 Yes I'm Lonely 1985 Chr 11/91 2,200
Gallon, Robert Br 1845-1925
* See 1991 Edition . . . .
Galofre Y Gimenez, Baldomero Spa 1849-1902
O/Pn 8x13 The Encampment Sby 5/92 6,600
W/Pa/B 18x27 Beached Boats Chr 5/92 1,430
Galvan, Jesus Guerrero Mex 1910-1970
O/C 32x28 Nina 1966 Sby 11/91 19,800
Gamarra, Jose Urg 1934-
O/C 59x79 La Risa del Chaja 1986 Sby 5/92 29,700
Gamba, Enrico It 1831-1883
O/Cb 19x13 Elegant Lady Wearing White Fur Chr 2/92 . . . 3,800
Gambartes, Leonidas Arg 1909-1963
Cg/B 16x24 Litoral Chr 5/92 8,800
Gamble, John Marshall Am 1863-1957
O/C 20x30 Poppies and Lupine But 10/91 11,000
O/Cb 9x12 California Landscape Mor 11/91 2,500
Gamble, Roy C. Am 1887-1972
O/C 24x19 Woman Hanging Wash '11 Dum 4/92 950
O/C 36x31 Portrait of Seated Girl 1916 Dum 5/92 650
O/C 24x28 View of Detroit Dum 9/91 650
O/C 20x16 Portrait of a Woman Lou 6/92 50
Gamble, William Br 19C
O/Pn 16x20 Lost Ruins Fre 10/91 100
Gammell, Robert Hale Ives Am 1893-
O/C 22x32 Wellfleet Bay 1962 Skn 11/91 2,420
O/Pa/B 11x15 Pilgrim Heights, Truro 1952 Yng 4/92 550
Gampenrieder, Karl Ger 1860-
* See 1990 Edition . . . .
Ganbault, Alfred-Emile Fr 19C
O/C 25x32 French Soldiers Resting Hnd 10/91 7,000
Gandolfi, Gaetano It 1734-1802
* See 1992 Edition . . . .
Gandolfi, Ubaldo It 1728-1781
* See 1992 Edition . . . .
Gannam, John Am 1897-1965
* See 1990 Edition . . . .
Ganne, Yves Fr 20C
O/C 12x16 Fruit Still Life 1969 Hnz 5/92 100
Ganso, Emil Am 1895-1941
O/C 37x40 Two Nudes Doy 12/91 3,750
O/C 26x40 Harbor Scene Sby 4/92 1,760
P&Pe/Pa 16x22 Female Nudes: Two Sby 12/91 880
W/Pa 15x22 Winter Farm Scene Hnz 10/91 150
Gantner, Bernard
G&I/Pa 9x10 Ciel du Soir Sby 6/92 1,650
Ganz, Edwin Sws 1871-
O/C 40x29 Mounted Military Officer Sel 4/92 3,600
Garabedian, Charles 20C
* See 1990 Edition . . . .
Garay Y Arevalo, Manuel Spa 19C
* See 1991 Edition . . . .
Garbell, Alexandre Fr 1903-1970
* See 1992 Edition . . . .
Garber, Daniel Am 1880-1958
O/Pn 18x22 Grey Day, April Chr 12/91 39,600
O/B 13x9 Clearing 1913 Sby 12/91 8,250
Garceau, Harry Joseph 1876-1954
O/C 16x20 White River, Near Muncie, 1935 Yng 4/92 . . . 800
Garces, Luis Spa 20C
O/C 25x33 Still Life on a Table Hnd 10/91 500

Garcia Y Ramos, Jose   Spa 1852-1912
* See 1990 Edition . . . .
Garcia Y Rodriguez, Manuel   Spa 1863-1925
O/C 12x10 The Terrace 1919 Sby 2/92 11,000
O/C 22x16 Le Jardin de Dr. Maria 1922 Sby 10/91 7,150
Garcia, Domingo   PR 1920-
O/B 36x23 El Santo 63 Chr 5/92 15,400
Garcia, Joaquin Torres   Uru 1874-1949
O/M 20x16 Objetos Deformados 37 Chr 11/91 132,000
T/Pn 17x22 Composicion Constructiva 31 Chr 5/92 121,000
O/B 16x21 Dos Figuras Constructivas 46 Chr 11/91 82,500
O/B 15x16 Hombre con Sombrero 40 Chr 5/92 33,000
Garcia, Pro
G/Pa 16x23 Haitian Scene 1973 Wlf 3/92 100
Garcia-Sevilla, Ferran
* See 1992 Edition . . . .
Gardiner, Francis
W/Pa 11x15 The Bark "Canton" 1973 Eld 7/92 55
Gardiner, Frank Joseph Henry   Eng 1942-
* See 1992 Edition . . . .
Gardner, Charles   Am 1901-
W/Pa 16x23 Landscape with Brown House '48 Fre 10/91 . . 50
Garet, Jedd   Am 1955-
A/C 73x57 Black Vase 1985 Chr 5/92 1,980
O/C 42 dia The Next Room 1980 Chr 2/92 825
Garf
O/C 25x20 Dutch Interior Hnz 10/91 1,200
Gargiollo, A.   It 19C
W/Pa 21x14 Seated Smoker and Harem Girl Hnd 10/91 . . . 2,600
Gargiulio, Domenico & Codazzi   It 1612-1679
O/C 48x71 Figures in Baroque Loggia Sby 5/92 38,500
Gargiulo, Domenico   It 1609-1675
* See 1992 Edition . . . .
Garibaldi, Joseph   Fr 1863-
* See 1991 Edition . . . .
Gariot, Paul Cesaire   Fr 1811-
* See 1992 Edition . . . .
Garland, Charles Trevor   Br a 1874-1901
* See 1991 Edition . . . .
Garman, Ed   Am 1914-
* See 1992 Edition . . . .
Garnier, Jules Arsene   Fr 1847-1889
* See 1992 Edition . . . .
Garrido, Eduardo Leon   Spa 1856-1906
O/Pn 32x40 La Farandula Sby 2/92 71,500
O/Pn 28x36 The Minuet Sby 10/91 47,300
O/Pn 21x26 The Secret Sby 5/92 33,000
O/Pn 26x21 Lady in an Interior Chr 10/91 28,600
O/C 32x37 Return from the Lido Sby 2/92 27,500
O/Pn 10x13 A Sleeping Nude Chr 10/91 3,080
Gascars, Henri   Fr 1634-1701
* See 1992 Edition . . . .
Gaskell, George Arthur   Br a 1871-1900
O/C 51x34 Rising Spring 1897 Sby 5/92 11,000
Gaspard, Leon   Am 1882-1964
O&Pe/C 24x29 Russian Peasant Parade 1911 Chr 12/91 . 115,500
O/C 21x30 The Wedding Chair, Peking 1921 Sby 5/92 . . . 41,250
O/B 22x18 Ergeyevsky Lavore, Monastery But 11/91 . . . 24,750
O/C/B 8x22 Mule and Cactus 1919 Chr 12/91 17,600
O/B 9x13 Village Street Sby 4/92 5,170
O/B 15x12 Snow and Aspens Sby 4/92 4,950
Gaspari, Antonio
* See 1991 Edition . . . .
Gasser, Henry Martin   Am 1909-1981
W/Pb 20x25 Turner's Grocery Chr 6/92 3,080
W/Pa 16x23 House and Winter: Two Sby 12/91 2,860
O/C/M 23x37 Hoboken, New Jersey Chr 11/91 2,750
O/C/M 20x24 The Yellow House Wes 11/91 2,530
O/C 20x24 Feeding the Chickens Sby 12/91 2,310
O/Cb 12x17 Harlem Palladium Chr 6/92 1,980
O/C 20x28 Gloucester Harbor Scene Sby 12/91 1,870
O/B 9x12 Mountain Road Chr 11/91 1,760
W/Pa 15x21 Winter Trestle Chr 11/91 1,760

W/Pa 22x31 Mining Town Eld 7/92 1,430
W/Pa/B 24x32 After the Storm Sby 12/91 1,320
W&G/Pb 19x24 Winter Harbor Skn 11/91 1,182
W/Pa 15x22 House by the Tracks Sby 12/91 1,045
W/Pa 15x9 A Side Balcony Chr 11/91 880
W/Pa 8x10 The Repair Dock Sby 4/92 770
W/Pa 10x19 Houses Ald 5/92 210
W/Pa 9x14 Barn in a Landscape Fre 4/92 200
W/Pa 8x10 Seascape Mys 11/91 55
Gasser, Howard
I&W/Pa 8x9 Parisian Scene Wlf 6/92 200
Gassies, Jean Bruno   Fr 1786-1832
* See 1992 Edition . . . .
Gassner, L.   Am 19C
O/C 28x13 Young Girl with Kittens Wlf 9/91 1,600
Gast, John   Am a 1870-1879
O/C 13x17 American Progress 1872 Chr 5/92 77,000
Gaston, L.   Con 19C
O/C 20x16 A Pink Rose Chr 5/92 1,320
Gatch, Lee   Am 1902-1966
O&C/C 22x40 Easter Morning Chr 3/92 5,500
Gatewood, C.
W/Pa 14x21 Old Locomotive 1967 Dum 9/91 200
Gatta, Saverio Della   It -1829
W&PI/Pa 8x10 A Neapolitan Song 1822 Chr 5/92 6,050
Gaubault, Alfred Emile   Fr -1895
O/Pn 13x16 Three Soldiers Having a Drink Wes 3/92 . . . 1,870
Gaudelt, B.   Fr 19C
O/C 20x41 A Forest Clearing Chr 10/91 1,980
Gaudfroy, Fernand   Bel 1885-1964
O/C 45x38 The New Tutu Chr 10/91 4,400
Gauermann, Friedrich   Aus 1807-1862
O/Pn 18x22 Baeummadchen Mit Schafherde Sby 2/92 . . 104,500
Gauffier, Louis   Fr 1761-1801
* See 1991 Edition . . . .
Gaugengigl, Ignaz-Marcel   Am 1855-1932
O/Pn 8x6 The Painter Chr 5/92 14,300
O/Pn 7x10 Travellers on Horseback 1876 Hnz 5/92 1,900
Gaugler, Joseph P.   Am 1896-
O/Cb 20x24 Harbor of Rockport 1943 Lou 6/92 300
Gauguin, Paul   Fr 1848-1903
O/C 13x9 Tete de Bretonne Sby 5/92 198,000
P/Pa 17x14 D'Enfant (Jean Gauguin) Sby 5/92 20,900
K/Pa 9x11 Tete de Femme Chr 11/91 17,600
C&S/Pa 11x8 Seated Man Sby 10/91 6,325
Pe/Pa 5x3 Etude D'Enfant Sby 6/92 2,090
Gaul, Gilbert   Am 1855-1919
O/C 20x25 Mohawk Indian Encampment Sby 5/92 16,500
O/C 40x24 The Sentinel But 4/92 16,500
O/C 17x24 Conversation in a Field Wlf 3/92 2,400
O/B 11x16 Wading in the River Fre 4/92 1,050
O/C/B 16x12 Cabin and Stone Fence Hnd 3/92 1,000
Gauley, Robert David   Am 1875-1943
O/C 37x30 Helene and Blanquito 1919 Wes 11/91 1,320
O/C 10x13 Venice Nocturne 1896 Skn 11/91 660
Gaume, Henri Rene   Fr 1834-
* See 1990 Edition . . . .
Gauthier-D'Agoty, Jacques-F.   Fr 1710-1781
* See 1992 Edition . . . .
Gauvreau, Pierre   Can 1922-
* See 1992 Edition . . . .
Gavagnin, Giuseppe   It 19C
* See 1990 Edition . . . .
Gavarni, Paul Sulpice G.   Fr 1804-1866
* See 1992 Edition . . . .
Gavencky, Frank
O/B 34x30 Harbor Scene Hnz 10/91 1,800
Gaw, William Alexander   Am 1891-1973
O/C 16x20 Landscape Mor 3/92 2,500
O/C 22x18 Arrangement in Blue But 2/92 1,100
Gawell, Oskar   Am 1888-1928
W/Pa 18x25 The Beached Rowboat Wes 11/91 330
Gay, August   Am 1890-1949
O/B 12x16 Monterey Harbor But 10/91 14,300

O/B 8x9 Mesa Road But 10/91 8,800
C/Pa 36x42 Montmarte But 6/92 6,600

Gay, Edward B.   Am 1837-1928
O/C 18x36 The Lakeside Camp 1875 Chr 3/92 11,000
O/C 24x36 Grain Field Chr 3/92 5,280
O/C 12x10 Landscape with Stream Wlf 3/92 625
O/C 28x22 Grazing Cattle Wlf 10/91 600

Gay, George Howell   Am 1858-1931
W&G/Pa 24x39 Breaking Waves But 4/92 2,090
W/Pa 14x23 Waves on the Shore But 11/91 1,100
W/Pa 24x36 Dawn Over the Sea Yng 4/92 900
O/C 26x20 Plank Bridge/Autumnal View 1916 Skn 3/92 880
W/Pa 17x38 Seascape Lou 3/92 850
W/Pa 10x20 Coastal Surf Brd 8/92 578
W/Pa 13x22 Eventide 1890 Slo 12/91 550
O/C 25x30 Rocky Coast Bor 8/92 550
O/C 16x28 Surf Breaking on a Rocky Coastline Sel 2/92 550
W/Pa 12x18 Afterglow in Winter Slo 2/92 475
W/Pa 17x27 Crashing Surf, Sailboat in Distance Slo 4/92 . . . 400
W/Pa 10x20 Sailboats Off Rocky Coastline Slo 12/91 400
W/Pa 11x27 Seascape Brd 8/92 308
W/Pa 13x20 Off Cape Ann Yng 4/92 300
W/Pa 14x26 Landscape Wlf 10/91 250
W/Pa 14x26 Sunset 1890 Yng 4/92 225
W/Pa 21x15 Country House Wlf 6/92 200

Gay, Walter   Am 1856-1937
O/C 18x22 The Front Parlor Chr 12/91 16,500
O/C 18x15 The Recital Sby 12/91 3,960

Gay, Winkworth Allen   Am 1821-1910
O/B 8x12 Tree Study Hnd 6/92 500
O/B 8x12 Rocks Hnd 6/92 325
O/B 8x12 Little Valley Hnd 6/92 300

Gaye, Howard   Eng 1880-1891
W/Pa 10x14 Landscape with Deer Wlf 11/91 400

Gazzera, Romano
* See 1992 Edition . . . .

Gear, William   1915-
V/Pa 22x31 Garden '63 Chr 11/91 1,100

Gebhardt, Wolfgang Magnus   a 1730-1750
* See 1992 Edition . . . .

Gebler, Friedrich Otto   Ger 1838-1917
* See 1990 Edition . . . .

Gechtoff, Leonid   Am 20C
O/C 26x31 Dutch Ship 1940 Fre 12/91 210
O/M 16x20 Seascape Fre 4/92 175
P/Pa 16x18 Indian Summer Yng 2/92 150

Gechtoff, Sonia
A&Pe/Pa 46x40 Lizard Rock, 1985 '84 Sby 2/92 1,210

Gedlek, Ludwig   Aus 1847-
* See 1991 Edition . . . .

Geery, Samuel Lancaster   Am 1813-1891
* See 1992 Edition . . . .

Geets, Willem   Bel 1838-
* See 1990 Edition . . . .

Geiger, Richard   Aus 1870-1945
O/C 40x30 Woman in Costume of a Jester Lou 3/92 3,500
O/C 23x31 Slave Market Chr 10/91 2,860

Geisel, Theodor "Dr. Seuss"   Am 1904-1991
I&W/Pa 13x12 Neptune on Sea Serpent 1940 Ilh 5/92 8,000

Gelb, C. E.
O/B 5x7 Fruit Still Life Hnz 5/92 50

Geibel, Casimir   Ger 1839-1896
* See 1991 Edition . . . .

Gelerdts, Flore   Bel 19C
* See 1991 Edition . . . .

Gelff, A.   Eur 20C
O/C 32x41 Gypsy Encampment Sel 9/91 325

Gelhaar, Emil   Am 1862-1934
O/C 26x39 Venetian Scene Wes 11/91 715

Gelibert, Gaston   Fr 1850-
O/C 37x68 Pack of Dogs and Wolf Dum 4/92 4,000

Gelibert, Jules-Bertrand   Fr 1834-1916
O/C 25x21 Chiens Attrapant Un Lievre Sby 6/92 6,325

Gellard, Andre   Fr 20C
O/C 17x12 Figures Along Riverbank Slo 7/92 250

Gellee, Claude   Fr 1600-1682
* See 1992 Edition . . . .

Gemito, Vincenzo   It 1852-1929
* See 1992 Edition . . . .

Gen-Paul   Fr 1895-1975
O/C 21x25 Le Pont Neuf a Paris Chr 5/92 8,800
G/Pa 20x26 Three Jockeys on Their Mounts Sby 2/92 5,775
O/C 22x13 Portrait of a Clown Sby 2/92 4,400
O/C 18x15 Two Dancers Hnz 5/92 4,000
C&S/Pa 25x19 Portrait de Femme 67 Chr 11/91 715

Gendrot, Felix Albert   Am 1866-
O/C 18x24 Sevres Porcelain Factory Hnd 3/92 800

Generalic, Josip   Yug 1936-
O/Gl 11x14 Kanteulegerin Hnd 5/92 400

Genesio, R.   It 19C
W/Pa 12x15 Il Ponte Vecchio Brd 5/92 385

Genin, Lucien   Fr 1894-1958
W,G&K/Pa 8x9 Three watercolours Chr 5/92 3,300
G&K/Pa/B 13x17 Montmartre Chr 2/92 2,860

Genis, Rene   1922-
O/C 32x26 Ruelle au Linge a Murano Chr 11/91 2,750
O/C 39x39 Composition aux fruits Chr 5/92 2,090

Genisson, Jules Victor   Bel 1805-1860
* See 1991 Edition . . . .

Gennari, Benedetto   It 1633-1715
O/C 74x54 Venus Embracing Cupid Sby 1/92 74,250

Genoves, Juan   1930-
W&H/Pa 23x30 Four Watercolors 79 Chr 11/91 2,200
W&H/Pa 28x39 Three Watercolors 80 Chr 11/91 1,760

Genth, Lillian   Am 1876-1953
O/C 50x38 Reflections Sby 9/91 11,000
O/C 29x35 In a Spanish Garden But 11/91 9,350
O/C 39x30 Narcissus Slo 4/92 6,500
O/C 24x32 Venice Chr 11/91 4,180
O/C 39x50 Springtime Chr 11/91 3,300
O/C 20x23 The Tailor Shop Chr 6/92 2,200

Gentilini, Franco
* See 1992 Edition . . . .

Gentz, Karl Wilhelm   Ger 1822-1890
O/C 24x37 The Snake Charmer 1872 Sby 10/91 27,500

Geoffroy, Henry Jules Jean   Fr 1853-1924
* See 1992 Edition . . . .

George, A. C.   20C
W/Pa 15x18 Fruit on a Table: Two Yng 4/92 125

George, Eric   Br 19C
K/Pa 21x15 Study of a Male Torso Sby 7/92 880
K/Pa 19x12 Study of a Male Torso Sby 7/92 770

George, Ernest   Eng 1839-
W/Pa 15x10 St. Germain L'Auxeroire 1878 Slo 7/92 275

Georges, Jean Louis   Fr -1893
O/C 40x32 Still Life with Fruit 82 Sby 2/92 30,800

Georges-Michel, Michel   Fr
* See 1992 Edition . . . .

Georgi, Friedrich Otto   Ger 1819-1874
* See 1991 Edition . . . .

Georgiodiz, D.   Grk 20C
O/M 32x24 Piraeus Port Scene Slo 10/91 75

Gerard, Marguerite   Fr 1761-1837
O/C 26x21 La Correspondance Familiale Sby 1/92 143,000
O/C 18x15 The Young Mother Sby 10/91 7,700

Gerard, Theodore   Bel 1829-1895
O/Pn 24x19 The Bird's Nest 1872 Slo 9/91 4,500

Gericault, Theodore   Fr 1791-1824
* See 1991 Edition . . . .

Germain, Jacques   Fr 20C
* See 1991 Edition . . . .

Germane, F.   Fr 20C
O/C 24x30 Parisian Woman with Dog Hnd 3/92 300

Gernand, John   Am 20C
O/C 18x32 Books and Music '47 Wes 11/91 412
O/C 18x24 Vermont Barns Slo 7/92 300

Gernard, John   Am 1913-1990
W&G/Pa 10x15 Landscapes: Pair Slo 7/92 125

Gerome, Francois Fr 20C
O/C 20x24 Un Cafe Dans St. Germain Des Pres But 11/91 . 3,575
O/C 20x24 Le Place de L'Opera Slo 9/91 400
O/B 24x30 La Place De L'Opera, Paris Hnz 10/91 350
O/C 12x16 Parisian Lady Slo 2/92 350
Gerome, Jean-Leon Fr 1824-1904
O/C 29x22 Un Mufti Lisant Sby 10/91 39,600
O/Pn 16x11 Achat D'Une Esclave 1857 Sby 5/92 38,500
Gerrer, Robert-Gregory Am 1867-
O/C 22x30 Landscape Wlf 6/92 675
Gerry, Samuel Lancaster Am 1813-1891
O/C 19x13 Figures and Sheep Skn 11/91 1,540
O/C 22x18 Feeding the Sheep Yng 2/92 700
W/Pa 13x19 View of a Sailboat Fre 10/91 450
O/B 10x12 Mountain Village Lou 6/92 400
W/Pa 13x19 Sailboat Fre 4/92 350
Gervais, Lise Can 1933-
* See 1992 Edition . . . .
Gervais, Paul Jean Fr 1859-1936
* See 1990 Edition . . . .
Gervex, Henri Fr 1852-1929
* See 1992 Edition . . . .
Gerzso, Gunther Mex 1915-
O/C 39x26 Abstraccion en Azul 59 Chr 5/92 46,200
Medium? 26x20 Rojo-Azul-Verde 69 Chr 11/91 28,600
O/C 26x34 Composicion No. 5 Chr 5/92 24,200
G,P&I/Pa 14x22 Lugar Arcaico 50 Chr 11/91 22,000
O/M 28x17 Estela Azul 1959 Hnd 10/91 9,400
Gesner, Abelard & Fernand, P. Hai
O/Pn 72x79 Bird Nests and Colonial Houses Chr 5/92 . . . 8,800
Gessi, Francesco-Giovanni It 1588-1649
* See 1992 Edition . . . .
Gestel, Leo
W/Pa 4x11 Landscape Hnz 10/91 50
Gevers, Rene Fr 1869-1944
O/C 21x30 On the Street But 5/92 5,500
Ghent, Peter Br 1856-1911
Pe/Pa 12x14 Workers Building a Cathedral 1905 Eld 7/92 . 385
Gherardini, Alessandro It 1655-1726
O/C 68x48 Virgin Before God the Father Sby 1/92 27,500
Gherardini, Giovanni It 1654-1725
* See 1992 Edition . . . .
Ghezzi, Pier-Leone It 1674-1755
I/Pa 4x3 An Ecclesiastic Slo 7/92 475
PI/Pa 4x3 Masons Constructing a Stone Wall Slo 7/92 475
Ghiglion-Green, Maurice
* See 1992 Edition . . . .
Ghisolfi, Giovanni It 1632-1683
O/C 47x67 Landscape with Figures by Ruins Sby 5/92 . . 121,000
O/C 39x54 Alexander Opening Tomb of Achilles Chr 5/92 . 25,300
Giacomelli, Vincenzo It 1841-1890
O/C 59x83 Venetian Festival Scene 1880 Wes 5/92 7,480
Giacometti, Alberto Sws 1901-1966
O/Cb 9x6 Tete De Femme 1946 Sby 10/91 74,250
O/C 11x5 Tete d'Homme Chr 11/91 38,500
Pe/Pa 10x12 L'Atelier and Portrait: Double 50 Sby 11/91 . 28,600
Pe/Pa 17x13 Portrait d'une Femme 1922 Sby 11/91 23,100
W&Pe/Pa 8x11 View of Maloja Sby 5/92 15,950
Bp/Pa 8x4 Tete d'homme Chr 5/92 8,800
P/Pa 20x13 Person Looking Into Infinity 1963 Sby 5/92 . . . 5,225
Bp/Pa 9x6 Studies of Heads and Nude 1958 Sby 2/92 . . . 4,950
Bp/Pa 9x8 Untitled Sby 6/92 2,860
Giacometti, Giovanni It 1868-1934
O/C 37x26 The Flower Seller Sby 2/92 4,400
Giacomotti, Felix Henri Fr 1828-1909
* See 1992 Edition . . . .
Giallino, Angelos It 1857-
* See 1991 Edition . . . .
Giambono, Michele It 1420-1462
T/Pn 37x23 Madonna and Child Enthroned Chr 5/92 . . . 165,000
Giampetrino It 19C
* See 1990 Edition . . . .
Giani, Felice It 1760-1823
K,PI&S/Pa 4x10 Nymphs and Satyrs by a Stream Chr 1/92 . 1,100

Giani, Hugo It 20C
* See 1992 Edition . . . .
Giannaccini, Ilio It 1897-1968
O/C 27x19 Naples Street Scene Wlf 11/91 400
Giannetti, Raffaele It 1837-1915
O/Pn 14x21 Reclining Classical Maiden Chr 10/91 4,620
Gianni, G. It 1829-1885
* See 1992 Edition . . . .
Gianni, Gerolamo It 1837-
O/B 7x15 Extensive View of Valletta, Malta 1878 Chr 2/92 . . 3,300
Gianni, Gian It 19C
O/C 20x31 The Catch; Homecoming: Pair 1867 Sby 5/92 . 12,650
Gianni, M. It 19C
G/Pa 5x12 Boaters in a Grotto Yng 2/92 250
Gianni, Y. It 20C
G/Pa 4x13 Italian Ruins Slo 9/91 225
Gianpetrino It a 1520-1540
O/Pn 24x20 Virgin and Child w/Infant St. John Sby 1/92 . . 55,000
Giaquinto, Corrado It 1703-1765
* See 1991 Edition . . . .
Giardiello, Giovanni It 19C
O/C 24x58 Off the Shore Sby 7/92 1,760
Giardiello, Giuseppe It 20C
O/C 30x24 Goatherd Playing a Flute Hnd 10/91 4,400
Gibbs, E. T. Am 19C
P/Pa 17x27 Lifeboat Crew Eld 7/92 385
Gibbs, George Am 1870-1942
G/Pa 17x21 At the Cafe Wlf 10/91 400
O/B 16x20 Western Landscape Mys 6/92 220
Gibbs, James W. Eng 19C
O/C 20x30 River Landscape Fre 4/92 250
Gibran, Kahlil Am 1883-1931
* See 1992 Edition . . . .
Gibson, Charles Dana Am 1867-1944
PI/Pa 11x19 Two Portraits of Gibson Girls Lou 3/92 1,700
I&H/Pa 22x16 Quietude/Gibson Girl Skn 5/92 605
Gibson, M. E. Am 19C
O/C 19x16 Basket of Apples Slo 10/91 325
O/C 19x16 Basket of Apples Slo 9/91 230
Gibson, Thomas Br 1680-1751
* See 1991 Edition . . . .
Gide, Francois Theophile E. Fr 1822-1890
O/C 16x13 Portrait of an Arab Sby 7/92 5,500
Gies, Joseph W. Am 1860-1935
O/B 15x11 California Lagoon Dum 10/91 500
O/C/Cd 12x8 Smoking Cavalier Wlf 11/91 425
O/B 7x9 Sheep in Barnyard Dum 11/91 200
O/C 13x15 Fishing Village Dum 2/92 175
Giet, Alfred Bel 20C
O/B 25x21 Summer Landscape Sel 12/91 700
Gifford, Charles Henry Am 1839-1904
O/C 7x11 Fishing Weirs Bor 8/92 5,250
O/C 8x11 New Bedford Fishermen 86 Bor 8/92 4,700
O/Ab 5x10 Sunset Off the Coast Bor 8/92 1,000
Gifford, James Eng 19C
* See 1991 Edition . . . .
Gifford, John Br 19C
O/C 12x18 The Day's Bag Chr 10/91 2,420
Gifford, N. Roswell Am 20C
W/Pa 9x19 Caravan Yng 2/92 100
Gifford, Robert Swain Am 1840-1905
O/C 12x18 On the Coast Chr 12/91 7,150
O/C 24x30 Sunset Over a Pond Yng 2/92 900
O/C 7x13 Palms at Biskra 1880 But 11/91 770
Gifford, Sanford Robinson Am 1823-1880
O/C 10x15 Shrine of Shakespeare 1858 Sby 5/92 17,600
O/C 7x11 Sunset in the Wilderness Sby 5/92 16,500
Gigli, R. It 19C
W/Pa 15x10 Italian Courtyard Dum 11/91 350
Gignon, Louis Fr
* See 1992 Edition . . . .
Gignoux, Francois Regis Am 1816-1882
O/C 14x20 Hudson River Sunset 1858 Skn 9/91 14,300
Gilbert & George Am 20C
Ph 71x99 Nationalism 1980 Sby 10/91 55,000

Ph 119x99 Fruit, God, Fear 1982 Sby 11/91 44,000
Ph 95x79 The Queue 1978 Sby 10/91 39,600
L/B 44x32 Silver Government 1981 Chr 2/92 15,400

Gilbert, Arthur Hill   Am 1894-1970
O/C 30x29 Pebble Beach But 10/91 8,800
O/C 25x30 Along the Riverbank But 2/92 3,850
O/C 25x30 Sand Dunes But 6/92 3,300
O/C 25x30 Oak Trees in Atmospheric Landscape Mor 3/92 . 2,500
O/C 24x29 Carmel Valley But 10/91 1,980
O/C 12x16 Mountain Valley But 10/91 1,540

Gilbert, Sir John   Br 1817-1897
W&G/Pa 19x15 Cavalier and His Horse 1868 But 5/92 2,200

Gilbert, Terence J.   20C
* See 1991 Edition

Gilbert, Victor Gabriel   Fr 1847-1933
O/C 21x21 La Bonne Gourmande Sby 10/91 15,400
O/Pn 12x15 Les Bouquets de Violettes Sby 5/92 8,800
O/Pn 18x15 Flowers for Little Sister Chr 5/92 7,700
O/B 20x16 Two Children in a Field Hnd 12/91 4,200
G/Pa 12x14 Le Boulevard Sby 7/92 2,475

Gilbert, W. J.   Eng 19C
O/C 16x20 Bay Hunter Standing 1854 Sel 9/91 1,100

Gilchrist, William Wallace   Am 1879-1926
* See 1990 Edition

Gilder, Robert Fletcher   Am 1856-1940
O/B 10x14 Trees and Lake Ald 3/92 125

Gildor, Jacob   Isr 20C
G&O/Pa/C 28x31 Scene de Cafe But 11/91 1,650

Gile, Selden Connor   Am 1877-1947
O/B 16x24 Seascape, Northern California 15 But 2/92 6,600
O/B 10x15 The Barn (Double) 28 But 6/92 4,950
O/C 13x18 The Homestead '15 Mor 6/92 3,750
O/C 9x12 Deserted Barn, Pink Hill '10 But 10/91 1,100
O/C 9x12 Marin County near Inverness Lou 3/92 550

Giles, Howard   Am 1876-1955
* See 1992 Edition

Gilfone, Gianni   Am 20C
O/B 12x20 Village Church, Cuba City Wisconsin Hnz 5/92 . . 125

Gill, Frederick James   Am 1906-1974
O/C 28x36 Merry Go Round Fre 10/91 825
O/C 17x22 Farmhouse and Horse Fre 10/91 725
O/C 16x10 Quiet Sunday '42 Fre 10/91 425
O/C 21x28 Farmhouse and Horse '48 Fre 10/91 350
O/C 19x26 Winter Landscape '47 Fre 12/91 225
O/C 16x20 Dog Fre 12/91 120

Gill, Paul L.
W/Pa 14x18 The Dredge Ald 3/92 325

Gillemans, Jan Pauw (the Elder)   Dut 1618-1675
O/C 22x16 Still Life Peaches Fig Blue Bowl Sby 1/92 17,600

Gillemans, Jan Pauw (the Younger)   Flm 1651-1704
O/C 16x20 Still Life Baskets Filled w/Grapes Sby 5/92 7,150

Gillen, Albert P.
O/C 32x30 Autumn Landscape Hnz 10/91 275
O/M 20x24 Autumn Landscape Hnz 10/91 200

Gillespie, Gregory   Am 1936-
* See 1992 Edition

Gillig, Jacob   Dut 1636-1701
* See 1990 Edition

Gilligan, Ollie   Am 19C
O/C 16x24 The Bathers 1882 Wlf 10/91 250

Gillis, Marcel
* See 1992 Edition

Gilot, Francoise   Fr 1921-1986
O/C 10x9 Violets Wes 3/92 1,100

Gilpin, Sawrey   Br 1733-1807
O/C 25x30 Chestnut Hunter in a Landscape 1777 Sby 6/92   4,950

Gilsoul, Victor Olivier   Bel 1867-
O/C 41x59 The Canal Sby 5/92 10,450

Gimignani, Giacinto   It 1611-1681
* See 1992 Edition

Gioobbi, Edward   Am 1926-
A&Pg/Cb 19x27 Study for a Large Painting VI '73 Chr 5/92 . . 935

Gioja, Belisario   It 1829-1906
W/Pa 21x15 The Christening Sby 7/92 2,750
W&Cw/Pa/B 21x30 Chess with the Cardinal Chr 5/92 2,420
W/Pa 20x14 The Artist's Studio Slo 2/92 1,400
W/Pa 17x11 Moment's Repose Slo 2/92 1,300

Giordano, Felice   It 1880-1964
O/C 20x31 Italian Coastal Village Chr 10/91 4,180
O/C 36x27 Mediterranean Village Chr 10/91 3,300
O/C 23x32 Fishing Boats off Amalfi Chr 10/91 3,080
O/C 29x40 Coastal Fishing Village Sby 7/92 2,750
O/C 16x20 Marina Grande, Capri Chr 5/92 2,640

Giordano, Luca   It 1634-1705
O/C 79x102 Apollo and Marsyas Sby 5/92 99,000
O/C 41x29 Sacrifice of Isaac; & Elijah: Two Chr 5/92 82,500
O/C 45x62 The Flight into Egypt Chr 1/92 49,500

Giorgiades, Nicholas
G&S/Pa/B 21x15 Costume Design '72 Sby 2/92 220

Giovannini, Vancenzo   It 1816-1868
O/C 28x55 Stream in the Roman Campagna Sby 10/91 . . . 19,800

Giradin, E. J.
O/C 20x30 Forest Landscape Hnz 10/91 475

Girardet, Eugene Alexis   Fr 1853-1907
* See 1991 Edition

Girardet, Jules   Fr 1856-
O/C 38x27 A Moorish Courtyard 1878 Chr 2/92 27,500

Girardet, Karl   Sws 1813-1871
O/C 13x18 Cattle Watering 1859 Chr 10/91 6,600

Girardet, Leon   Fr 1857-1895
W/Pb 20x14 The Serenade Chr 10/91 660

Girardin   Hai 20C
* See 1992 Edition

Girardin, Frank J.   Am 1856-1945
O/B 20x30 Topanga Canyon But 2/92 2,090
O/C 20x30 Autumn Landscape Mor 6/92 400

Giraud, Pierre Francois Eugene   Fr 1806-1881
O/C 27x20 Le Lettre Sby 5/92 18,700

Girodet-Trioson, Anne Louis De   Fr 1767-1824
K/Pa 14x10 Portrait of a Man Chr 5/92 440

Girona, Julio   Cub 1914-
O/C 36x27 Muchacha En El Balcon Sby 11/91 6,325

Gironella, Alberto   Mex 1929-
O/C 24x20 Mariana De Austria 68 Sby 11/91 17,600

Girones, Ramon Antonio Pichot   Spa 1872-1925
O/B 16x13 Lady in her Dressing Room Chr 5/92 6,600

Giroud, P.   Fr 19C
* See 1992 Edition

Gisbert, Antonio   Spa 1835-1901
O/Pn 18x15 Figures in an Interior Chr 10/91 35,200
O/Pn 15x18 The Heir Apparent Sby 2/92 31,900
O/Pn 16x13 Elegant Lady Wearing a Pink Hat Chr 10/91 . . 7,700

Gisson, Andre   Fr 1910-
O/C 24x30 Two Nudes in a Landscape '72 Sby 10/91 4,675
O/C 24x36 Parisian Street Scene Wlf 9/91 4,000
O/C 16x20 Still Life Flowers in a Vase Sby 2/92 3,850
O/C 24x36 View of Notre Dame Sby 6/92 3,575
O/C 24x30 Parisian Street Scene Wlf 6/92 3,300
O/C 24x30 Mother and Child in Park Fre 10/91 3,100
O/C 24x36 Summer Day Doy 11/91 3,000
O/C 24x30 Summertime Sby 6/92 2,970
O/C 24x30 Dans le Jardin Chr 11/91 2,800
O/C 24x36 Landscape Scene Dum 4/92 2,750
O/C 24x12 Women Walking in a Meadow Sby 10/91 2,750
O/C 24x12 Floral Still Lifes: Pair Slo 9/91 2,600
O/C 9x12 Jeune Fille au Ruban Rose Chr 11/91 2,420
O/C 16x20 Mother and Child Sby 10/91 2,310
O/C 16x20 The Carousel in the Park Sby 2/92 2,310
O/C 24x36 Spring Landscape Sel 9/91 2,250
O/C 24x36 Rue de Paris Chr 11/91 2,200
O/C 24x36 Picnic in a Riverbank Skn 5/92 1,980
O/C 7x13 Profile of a Young Girl Wes 3/92 1,870
O/C 20x24 Paysage Chr 11/91 1,760
O/C 20x16 Still Life Petunias, Poppies Skn 3/92 1,760

O/C 16x20 Au Bord de la Riviere Chr 11/91 1,650
O/C 9x12 Portrait of a Young Girl Skn 3/92 1,650
O/C 20x24 Evening Scene Wes 11/91 1,540
O/C 9x12 Jeune fille au ruban blanc Chr 5/92 1,540
O/C 24x36 Along the Riverbank Hnd 12/91 1,500
O/C 11x14 Paris Street Dum 12/91 1,500
O/C 12x16 Parisian Street Dum 9/91 1,500
O/C 24x30 Figures on the Beach '63 But 5/92 1,320
O/C 16x20 Mother and Child Sby 2/92 1,320
O/C 24x36 Carousel in the Park Hnz 5/92 1,200
O/C 16x20 Figures on a Beach Sby 2/92 1,100
O/C 9x12 Jeune Fille Chr 2/92 1,100
O/C 12x9 Vase of Flowers; In the Park: Two Sby 6/92 ... 1,100
O/C 12x9 Vase de Fleurs Chr 2/92 935
O/C 24x30 Portrait de Jeune Fille '72 Chr 2/92 880
O/C 20x16 Bouquet of Daisies Hnd 3/92 800
O/C 12x9 Tabletop Still Life Slo 9/91 800
O/C 12x16 Parisian Street Scene Sel 4/92 500
O/C 9x12 Vendors Mys 6/92 495

Giunta, Marc   Am 20C
O/C 52x44 Cabanas Wlf 3/92 175

Giusto, Faust   It 19C
* See 1991 Edition ....

Glackens, William James   Am 1870-1938
O/C 26x31 Summer Hotel 1909 Chr 5/92 330,000
O/C 18x24 Early Spring, Washington Square Chr 12/91 187,000
O/C 21x32 A Riviera Hillside Chr 12/91 88,000
O/Cb 16x13 Vase of Flowers Chr 12/91 41,800
O/C 11x9 Portrait Study of Artist's Model Chr 12/91 30,800
O/Cb 13x16 Bound Brook, New Jersey Sby 12/91 22,000
P/Pa/B 12x16 The Gazebo--Hartford Chr 12/91 16,500
Y/Pa 13x10 The Princess Chr 9/91 2,200
Pl,S&Cw/Pa 17x13 Attack of the Blockhouse Chr 11/91 ... 2,090
Pe/Pa 12x16 Colonel Roosevelt Rough Riders Chr 11/91 .. 1,430
H/Pa 6x9 Seaside Outing Sby 4/92 990

Glandin, Alexei   Rus 1922-1983
O/C 16x24 Still Life Strawberries But 5/92 1,650

Glarner, Fritz   Am 1899-1972
O/B 49 dia Tondo #52 1958 Chr 11/91 264,000
O/C 38x32 Der Rosa Schal 1929 But 11/91 8,250

Glasco, Joseph   1925-
O&L/C 72x106 Portrait Heads 63 Chr 11/91 2,750
O&MM/C 68x38 Male Head 1950 Chr 11/91 1,210

Glass, Jonathan   Eng 20C
W/Pa 14x20 Coastal Scene and Mountain: Two Wes 5/92 ... 550

Glasser, Charles   Eur 19C
O/C 12x16 Mischievous Kittens Slo 12/91 275

Glauber, Jan   Dut 17C
* See 1991 Edition ....

Glauber, Johannes   Dut 1646-1726
* See 1991 Edition ....

Gleason, Joe Duncan   Am 1881-1959
O/Cb 12x16 Schooner 'Lottie Carson' Mor 11/91 3,750

Gleerup, Knud   Dan 1884-
O/C 26x34 Lolland Landscape 1930 Slo 9/91 700

Gleich, John   Ger 1879-
O/C 28x47 Sailing thru Straits of Gibralter But 5/92 3,575

Gleitsman, Raphael   Am 1910-
W&l/Pa 22x30 Church on a Cliff 1948 Wlf 10/91 500
I&W/Pa 16x20 Cathedral 1950 Wlf 3/92 350
Pl&S/Pa Size? City View with Cathedral 1950 Lou 6/92 ... 35

Gleizes, Albert   Fr 1881-1953
O/B 39x29 Danseuse 1917 Sby 5/92 154,000
G/Pa/B 11x9 Composition avec deux nus 20 Chr 5/92 26,400
G/B/B 15x9 L'Homme dans les Buildings 1920 Sby 2/92 . 24,200
G/Pa 12x8 Composition 30 Sby 10/91 11,000

Glendening, Alfred A. (Jr.)   Eng -1907
* See 1991 Edition ....

Glendening, Alfred Augustus   Br a 1861-1903
O/C 24x20 Figures and Cattle: Two Hnz 5/92 4,750

Glindoni, Henry Gillard   Br 1852-1913
O/C 37x28 The Lover's Tryst 1901 Sby 10/91 11,000
O/B 40x13 Spring 1896 Sby 10/91 3,300

Gloutchenko, Nicholai P.   0
O/C 24x28 The Card Players 23 Sby 10/91 19,800

Glover, H.   Eng 20C
O/C 27x20 Highland River Landscape Sel 5/92 50

Gluckmann, Grigory   Rus 1898-
O/B 22x28 Opening Night But 10/91 9,350
O/Pn 28x22 Waiting Sby 6/92 9,075
O/B 28x30 Story's End But 6/92 8,800
O/C 47x59 Rooftops in Southern France 1930 Sby 2/92 ... 3,850
O/B 16x12 Sortie Du Theatre But 2/92 3,850

Glura, Maes   Con 19C
O/C 39x30 Roman Mother and Child 1854 Hnd 10/91 2,800

Glushakow, Jacob   Am 1914-
O/B 9x17 Baltimore Waterfront 47 Chr 6/92 935

Glusing, Francis   Eur 20C
O/C 28x40 Schooner on Open Sea Slo 10/91 750

Gnoli, Domenico   It 1933-1970
* See 1992 Edition ....

Gober, Robert   1954-
MM 13x19 Untitled Sleepers 89 Sby 5/92 29,700
H/Pa 14x11 Untitled 1984 Chr 2/92 11,000
H/Pa 11x14 Untitled (RG 33D) 1985 Chr 5/92 7,150
H/Pa 14x11 Untitled (RG31D) 1985 Chr 5/92 5,500

Gobis, Giuseppe   It 18C
* See 1991 Edition ....

Godard, Gabriel   Fr 1933-
* See 1992 Edition ....

Godbold, Samuel Berry   Br a 1842-1875
O/C 45x35 Spring Flowers But 5/92 7,150

Godchaux   Con 19C
* See 1991 Edition ....

Godchaux, Roger   Fr 1878-
* See 1990 Edition ....

Godefroy, Felix   Fr -1848
W/Pa 9x13 Seascape with Ships Wlf 11/91 550

Godward, John William   Eng 1858-1922
O/C 24x32 Songs Without Words 1918 Sby 10/91 121,000
O/C 25x30 Roman Lovers on a Balcony 1901 Sby 2/92 .. 27,500
O/C 24x14 Waiting for an Answer 1889 But 5/92 27,500

Goebel, Carl   Aus 1824-1899
* See 1992 Edition ....

Goebel, Rod   Am 20C
* See 1992 Edition ....

Goeller, Emily Shotwell   Am 1887-1965
O/C 20x28 Still Life - Pears, Porcelain 1938 Mor 6/92 ... 900

Goenuette, Norbert   Fr 1854-1894
* See 1991 Edition ....

Goerg, Edouard Joseph   Fr 1893-1969
* See 1992 Edition ....

Goetsch, Gustaf   Am 1877-1969
O/C 20x16 Still Life of Flowers in a Vase 1949 Sel 2/92 .. 500
O/Cb 19x16 Harvester Sel 9/91 325
P&Pe/Pa 13x17 Marine Scene '48 Sel 2/92 200
O/C/M 30x23 Portrait of a Woman 1931 Sel 9/91 180

Goetz, Henri   Fr 1908-
P/Pa 18x10 Helmeted Head Wes 3/92 1,100

Goff, Lloyd Lozes   Am 1917-1983
O/C 30x24 The Sensational Lady Godiva Sby 4/92 6,600

Goings, Ralph   Am 1928-
* See 1990 Edition ....

Gold, Albert   Am 1906-
* See 1990 Edition ....

Goldberg, Fred F.   Am 20C
* See 1992 Edition ....

Goldberg, Glenn   Am 20C
* See 1991 Edition ....

Goldberg, Michael   Am 1924-
A&O/Pn 24x24 Earth Rhythms No. 17 1974 Wlf 6/92 400
A&O/Pn 23x26 Earth Rhythms No. 9 1974 Wlf 6/92 325
T/Pa 25x20 Untitled 1974 Wlf 6/92 300

Goldberg, Reuben Lucious   Am 1883-1970
Pl/Pa 8x17 Squeezing the U.S. Taxpayer 50 Ilh 5/92 1,400
Pl/Pa 9x16 Men Calling Election in Retrospect Ilh 11/91 ... 600

Golder, Charles H.
O/C 18x30 Winter Sunset in Green Mountains 1875 Ald 5/92 500

Goldstein, Jack   Am 1945-
A/C 48x48 Untitled '83 Chr 11/91 2,750
Gollings, William Elling   Am 1878-1932
* See 1992 Edition
Golts, M. V. D.   Dut 20C
O/C 18x27 Young Girls and a Mother Hnd 3/92 300
Golub, Leon   Am 1922-
A/L 120x166 Mercenaries I Sby 11/91 41,250
Golubov, Maurice
* See 1992 Edition
Gomez Y Gil, Guillermo   Spa 19C
* See 1992 Edition
Gomez, I. Hernandez   Spa 20C
W/Pa 21x16 Moorish Courtyard Sby 1/92 2,090
Gomez, Paul Pierre   Fr 19C
* See 1992 Edition
Gonne, Christian Friedrich   Ger 1813-1906
* See 1992 Edition
Gontard, J.   It 19C
O/C 19x24 L'Amore Slo 12/91 950
Gontcharova, Nathalie   Rus 1881-1962
O/C 11x8 Roses Blanches Sby 2/92 3,300
G/Pa 30x22 Costume Design for a Cherubim Sby 2/92 . . . 2,420
W&G/Pa 11x15 The Flamenco Dancer Sby 2/92 2,420
Gonzales, B.   Am 20C
W/Pa 9x11 Mountain Peak Yng 2/92 60
Gonzales, Eva   20C
* See 1990 Edition
Gonzales, Jeanne Guerard   Fr 1868-1908
* See 1992 Edition
Gonzalez, Carmelo   Cub 1920-
O/C 16x14 El Centinela Sby 11/91 4,950
Gonzalez, Juan Antonio   Spa 1842-
* See 1992 Edition
Gonzalez, Julio   Spa 1876-1942
* See 1992 Edition
Gonzalez, Xavier   Am 20C
MM/Pa 22x29 Blessing of the Fleet Bor 8/92 700
W/Pa 30x22 Jungle Bor 8/92 100
Good, Samuel S.   Am 1808-1885
O/C 50x40 Venus Stealing Cupid's Arrow Chr 6/92 2,750
Goodall, Frederick   Br 1822-1904
* See 1992 Edition
Goode, Joe   1937-
H&Pe/Pa 20x25 Bed '67 Chr 2/92 4,400
Goodell, Anne
O/C 10x14 Mano Resting Ald 5/92 90
Goodman, Bertram   Am 1904-
* See 1992 Edition
Goodman, Sidney   Am 1936-
* See 1992 Edition
Goodnough, Robert   Am 1917-
A&O/C 34x68 HJC 1987 Chr 11/91 3,300
A&O/C 32x64 J 1987 Chr 11/91 2,860
A/C 78x78 Process GL 1970 Sby 2/92 2,200
A&O/C 68x78 Silver Gray Development, 1971 Skn 3/92 . . . 2,090
A/C 78x78 Development KRL White 1970 Sby 2/92 1,540
A/C 28x44 Movement of Horses 1970 Dum 1/92 1,500
O&L/C 4x5 Black and White: Three Collages 53 Sby 6/92 . . 1,430
Goodridge, Sarah   Am 1788-1853
W/Iv 4x3 Portrait of a Lady Brd 5/92 495
Goodwin, Albert   Br 1845-1932
W&H/Pa 12x18 Clovelly 1921 But 5/92 6,600
Goodwin, Arthur Clifton   Am 1864-1929
O/C 30x36 Public Garden, Boston Chr 5/92 16,500
O/C 33x40 Park Street Church Brd 8/92 15,400
O/C 25x30 Fifth Avenue, New York Chr 12/91 9,350
O/C 19x24 New York Street Scene Dum 4/92 7,000
P/Pb 11x18 City Point, Boston Skn 5/92 4,675
O/C 19x24 Wharf Scene Dum 4/92 4,000
O/C 14x18 Park Street Church, Boston Chr 9/91 3,080
O/C 14x18 Park Street Church, Boston Lou 3/92 3,000
O/C 34x39 Harbor Scene Sel 12/91 1,750
P/Pa 13x18 Charles River and Bridge Skn 11/91 1,650

Goodwin, Philip Russell   Am 1882-1935
O/C 24x36 Taking Aim Chr 12/91 15,400
O/C 35x18 Shooting Mountain Goats 1909 Chr 11/91 9,900
Goodwin, Richard Labarre   Am 1840-1910
W&G/Pa 11x15 Strawberries 1887 Brd 8/92 550
Goosey, George Turland   Am 20C
O/B 8x10 Harbour Scene Mys 6/92 248
Goossens, Josse   Ger 1876-1929
O/C 82x102 Dancing Shiva But 5/92 4,675
Gorbatoff, Constantin   Rus 1876-
* See 1991 Edition
Gorder, Levon   Am 20C
* See 1992 Edition
Gordon, Hortense Mattice   Can 1887-1971
O/C 30x25 Feathers from the Sudan 1937 Sbt 5/92 1,402
Gordon, Sir John Watson   Sco 1788-1864
O/C 30x25 Portrait Sir Hector McNeill Wes 11/91 2,310
Gore, William Henry   Br 20C
* See 1990 Edition
Gori, Alessandro   17C
* See 1992 Edition
Gorka, Paul   Am 20C
O/C 24x34 Still Life with Onions Fre 12/91 210
O/C 30x20 Woman in Green; Figure (2) Fre 12/91 210
C&P/Pa 10x24 Reclining Nude Fre 12/91 60
Gorky, Arshile   Am 1904-1948
Pe,I&Y/Pa 19x25 Untitled 46 Sby 11/91 165,000
O/C 21x21 Still Life with Horse Chr 5/92 24,200
O/B 9x12 Abstract Composition Chr 11/91 15,400
H/Pa Var Three Drawings 1935 Chr 11/91 6,820
I/Pa 17x11 Untitled Sby 2/92 4,125
Gorman, R. C.   Am 1933-
O/C 32x36 Woman and Navajo Rug 1966 Sby 4/92 6,600
Gorson, Aaron Henry   Am 1872-1933
O/C 43x48 Pittsburgh Mills at Night Sby 12/91 8,250
Gorter, Arnold Marc   Dut 1866-1933
O/C 15x19 A Cottage by a River Chr 5/92 1,100
O/C 22x29 Cows in an Autumn Landscape Wlf 6/92 1,100
Gortzius, Geldorp   Dut 17C
* See 1990 Edition
Gosse, Nicolas Louis Francois   Fr 1787-1878
O/C 24x20 Bacchus et Ariane 1829 Sby 2/92 19,800
Gosselin, Ferdinand Jules A.   Fr 1862-
O/C 24x32 Cottages by a Wooded Stream Chr 2/92 6,600
Gottlieb, Adolph   Am 1903-1974
O/C 72x60 Green Expanding 1960 Sby 11/91 220,000
O/C 30x24 India 1971 Sby 10/91 93,500
O/C 38x30 House of Magician 1946 Sby 11/91 55,000
O/C 30x24 Whirling 1969 Sby 11/91 55,000
O/C 24x30 Black Light 1965 Chr 11/91 33,000
A/Pa 19x24 Untitled #57 1967 Chr 2/92 28,600
P/Pa 25x20 Untitled Sby 10/91 8,800
G/Pa 23x31 No. 7 Sby 10/91 6,600
Gottlieb, Harry   Am 1895-
* See 1992 Edition
Gottlieb, Leopold   Pol 1833-1934
* See 1992 Edition
Gottlieb, Michael (Aram)   Rus 1908-
O/B 6x5 Middle Eastern Scene Skn 9/91 55
Gottschalk, Max   Am 20C
O/C 25x30 Courthouse in St. Louis Sel 12/91 100
Gottwald, Frederick Carl   Am 1860-1941
O/C 22x26 Piazza Apostino Taormina Wlf 9/91 1,800
Gotuzzo, Leopoldo   Brz 1887-1983
O/C 35x27 Baiana 1934 Sby 5/92 5,500
Gotzloff, Carl   Ger 1799-1866
O/C 27x23 Alpine Rapids Chr 5/92 4,950

Goubaud, Innocent-Louis Fr 1780-1847
K/Pa 28x23 Portrait of Napoleon Bonaparte 1811 Chr 1/92 . 22,000
Goubie, Jean Richard Fr 1842-1899
O/C 14x12 L'Artiste et Ses Amis 1890 Sby 10/91 23,100
O/Pn 13x16 An Afternoon Ride 1882 Chr 5/92 12,100
O/C 13x16 The Morning Ride But 5/92 9,000
Gould, Alexander Carruthers Eng 1870-1948
W/Pa 9x14 Coastal Village Scenes Slo 12/91 300
Goupil, Jules Adolphe Fr 1834-1890
O/C 32x25 Confidences 1867 Chr 10/91 15,400
Gourgue, Jacques Enguerrand Hai 1930-
O/M 40x18 Village Scene Chr 5/92 2,090
Gourgue, Jean Enguerrand Hai 20C
O/M 30x24 Calling Forth a Zombie Chr 5/92 7,700
O/Pn 23x17 Returning from the Fields Wlf 9/91 2,000
Gourley
O/C 24x36 Destroyer Escort Hnz 10/91 325
Goutman, Dolya Am 20C
O/C 24x50 Animated Landscape 1961 Fre 10/91 575
Gouvrant, Gerard Fr 1946-
* See 1992 Edition
Gow, Mary L. Br 1851-1929
* See 1991 Edition
Goya Y Lucientes, Francisco J. Spa 1746-1828
* See 1992 Edition
Grabach, John R. Am 1880-1981
O/C 26x30 Back Fence, Newark Chr 5/92 8,800
O/C 26x30 Backyards in Snowcover Skn 3/92 6,600
O/C 27x33 The Stream Through the Ice Sby 12/91 4,675
O/Pn 16x12 The Cabby Wes 11/91 2,750
O/C 20x26 A Cobbler Sby 4/92 1,650
O/C 16x12 Portrait of an Artist Sby 4/92 1,650
O/C 16x20 Gloucester Fishing Boats Sby 4/92 1,320
W/Pa 16x22 New York Street Scene Hnd 10/91 1,000
Grabar, Ygor Rus 1872-
O/Pn 14x15 Still Life 1910 Chr 10/91 8,800
Grabwinkler, Paul Aus 1880-
* See 1990 Edition
Grace, Gerald Am 1918-
O/C 26x22 Interlude But 11/91 660
Graeb, Karl George Ger 1816-1884
* See 1990 Edition
Graf, Carl C. Am
* See 1990 Edition
Graffione 1455-1527
* See 1992 Edition
Grafton, Robert Wadsworth Am 1876-
O/C 20x15 Venetian Canal Scene Hnd 5/92 375
Graham, C. Br 20C
O/C 14x21 Dutch River Scene 1900 Hnd 12/91 800
Graham, Charles Am 1852-1911
* See 1991 Edition
Graham, Dan
* See 1992 Edition
Graham, Donald Am 20C
* See 1990 Edition
Graham, John Am 1881-1961
O/C 45x32 Untitled 30 Sby 5/92 44,000
O/C 24x20 Sophie Chr 5/92 35,200
O/C 12x22 Repast Sby 6/92 3,300
Graham, Peter Br 1836-1921
* See 1991 Edition
Graham, Robert Alexander Am 1873-1946
O/C 16x20 Woman with a Vase But 6/92 1,210
Graham, Robert Macdonald 20C
* See 1990 Edition
Graham, T. K. Am 20C
O/C 36x42 New Jersey Coast Fre 10/91 300
Graham, William Am 1841-1910
O/C 17x12 Church Interior Mys 11/91 440
Granacci, Francesco It 1477-1543
* See 1991 Edition

Grand-Carteret, J. Albert Fr 1901-
P/Pa 20x26 Portrait of a White Dog 1929 Sby 1/92 1,540
Graner Y Arrufi, Luis Spa 1867-1929
O/C 25x30 Port Scene Chr 10/91 20,900
O/C 25x30 Feast of the Lanterns, Naples Sby 2/92 10,450
O/Pn 70x60 Parrot Perched: 3-Part Screen 1927 Sby 5/92 . 7,975
Granet, Francois Marius Fr 1775-1849
W/Pa 32x26 Interior of Cathedral 1831 Wlf 3/92 900
Grant, Blanche Chloe Am 1874-1948
* See 1992 Edition
Grant, Catherine Am 20C
O/C 18x14 Laundry in the Wind Fre 10/91 150
Grant, Charles Henry Am 1866-1939
O/C 16x12 Clipper Ship Slo 10/91 150
Grant, Clement Rollins Am 1849-1893
O/C 28x48 Gathering on the Beach Chr 5/92 9,350
O/C 14x10 Waiting for the Ship Brd 8/92 3,080
O/Pn 11x6 Seated Woman 1891 Skn 11/91 522
Grant, Duncan
O/C 19x25 Wrestlers Sby 6/92 13,200
W&G/Pa 22x29 Stage Design Sby 2/92 2,750
Grant, Dwinnell Am 1912-
* See 1992 Edition
Grant, Frederic M. Am 1886-1959
O/C 32x46 Interlude Hnd 12/91 1,300
O/C 36x26 Venice 1913 Sby 12/91 880
O/C 32x40 Fete Among Ruins Hnz 5/92 850
G/Pa 13x17 P-38's Returning Home Slo 9/91 350
Grant, Gordon Am 1875-1962
O/C 40x50 Fleeting Shadows Skn 5/92 5,500
O/C 28x36 Clipper Ship Sby 12/91 5,225
O/B 18x24 Fore and Aft Mys 6/92 2,860
O/C 22x36 The High Seas 1943 Hnz 10/91 2,800
O/M 18x20 Schooner and Tugboat Slo 2/92 1,800
W/Pa 15x22 Maine Fisherman Lou 9/91 1,300
W/Pa 12x15 Pier Head Gossip Hnd 10/91 700
W&Pe/B 11x10 Politics Chr 11/91 330
Grant, J. Jeffrey Am 1883-1960
O/C 22x24 Street Scene Hnd 6/92 550
Grant, Sir Francis Eng 1803-1878
O/C 36x28 Young Gentleman on Pony Slo 2/92 2,250
Grant, Vernon Am 1902-1990
G/Pa 28x22 Elf Dipping Candles 1935 Ih 5/92 4,500
Grant, William James Br 1829-1866
* See 1990 Edition
Gras, Francisco Spa 20C
* See 1992 Edition
Grasdorp, Willem Dut 1678-1723
* See 1990 Edition
Grass, Carl Gotthard 1767-1814
O/C 19x24 Shepherd Family Driving Flock 1810 Sby 10/91 . 24,200
Grasset, Eugene Fr 1841-1917
Pl,G&W/Pa 21x16 La Poesie Hnd 10/91 800
Grau, Enrique Col 1920-
* See 1992 Edition
Grau-Sala, Emile Spa 1911-1975
O/C 31x39 Young Girl with Floral Still Life 1966 Sby 10/91 . 40,700
O/C 26x32 Jumping 69 Chr 5/92 30,800
O/C 21x26 Mere et Enfant Aux Fleurs 1969 Chr 11/91 . . . 30,800
O/C 24x29 Le Paddok a Deauville Sby 2/92 28,600
O/C 21x26 Au cirque 1959 Chr 5/92 26,400
O/C 18x22 La Lecon 1967 Chr 2/92 26,400
O/C 24x29 Au Balcon 1969 Sby 10/91 25,300
O/C 21x26 Mere et Jeune Fille Chr 11/91 24,200
O/C 24x29 Foire, Barcelona 1964 Sby 2/92 20,900
O/C 18x18 Au Balcon 38 Chr 2/92 18,700
O/C 21x26 Ballerinas 1968 Sby 2/92 17,600
O/B 16x13 Au paddok 1966 Chr 5/92 10,450
G&Pl/Pa/B 25x20 Femme a sa Toilette 66 Chr 11/91 2,090
Grauer, William C. Am 1896-
O/B 42x30 Abstract Wlf 6/92 250
Gravelot, Hubert-Francois Fr 1699-1773
* See 1992 Edition
Graves, Abbott Fuller Am 1859-1936
O/C 25x30 Gathering Lilies (Pasture Pond) Brd 5/92 . . . 137,500

O/C 20x16 Woman in a Garden Brd 5/92 37,400
O/C 22x27 Bouquet of Roses Chr 5/92 30,800
O/C 24x20 Doorway Brd 5/92 22,000
O/C 22x27 Bouquet of Roses Skn 3/92 16,500
O/C 20x25 Jack-O-Lantern Chr 12/91 16,500
O/C 24x20 Visitors in the Kitchen Brd 5/92 13,200
O/C 25x30 Kingsbury House, Kennebunk Sby 12/91 11,000
O/Pn 9x7 Potted Peonies Chr 3/92 6,600
O/C 13x21 Carnations in a Basket Yng 4/92 4,250
O/C 16x13 New England Greek Revival Building Brd 8/92 . . 3,960
O/C 24x20 The Connoisseur Slo 10/91 3,750
O/C 14x10 Snow Along the Coast Brd 8/92 3,740
O/C 18x12 Dockyard, Valendam, Holland Brd 8/92 3,410
O/C 24x20 The Collector Skn 3/92 3,300
O/C 22x16 The Fountain Brd 5/92 3,300
O/B 6x10 The Red Boathouse Brd 5/92 798

Graves, Morris Am 1910-
T/Pa/C 26x50 Oh, Where Are the Bright Birds? 44 Skn 9/91 41,800
T/Pa 14x9 Winter Bouquet 73 Chr 9/91 9,350
G&Mk/Pa 10x11 Pansy in Pitcher Sby 12/91 2,310
I/Pa 12x10 Swan and The Pelicans Chr 11/91 2,200

Graves, Nancy Am 1940-
O/C 100x64 Gravure '80 Chr 5/92 18,700
O/C 64x64 Balus (L. O. Series) 76 Chr 5/92 8,800

Gray, Cleve Am 1918-
O/C 16x12 Untitled 64 Chr 2/92 385

Gray, Eileen Am 20C
* See 1990 Edition . . . .

Gray, George Eng 1880-1943
O/C 18x30 Linlithgow Palace, Edinburgh Slo 12/91 625

Gray, Henry Percy Am 1869-1952
O/C 24x30 Aetna Springs Landscape But 10/91 15,400
W/Pb 20x28 Eucalyptus by the Footpath But 2/92 13,200
W/Pa 22x15 Grove of Eucalyptus But 6/92 13,200
W/Pa 16x20 Wildflowers, Marin County But 10/91 9,900
W/Pa 15x22 Eucalyptus Grove 1920 But 2/92 8,800
O/C/B 16x20 Oak Tree, Marin But 10/91 7,700
W/Pa 12x16 Monterey Sand Dunes Mor 11/91 7,500
W/Pa 10x14 Marin County Hills But 6/92 7,150
W/Pa 8x10 Valley Landscape But 6/92 7,150
W/Pa 12x14 Farmyard But 6/92 6,600
W/Pa 15x20 Oaks Near Monterey But 6/92 6,600
O/Cb 10x14 Sand Brush But 6/92 4,950
W/Pa 11x14 By the River Bank But 6/92 3,300
W/Pb 8x10 Oak Trees and Shadows But 10/91 3,300
W&Cw/Pa 14x11 Percy and Alfred Gray But 6/92 3,025
W/Pa 4x5 View Across the Valley But 2/92 2,750
W/Pa 5x7 Misty Shoreline 1910 But 6/92 2,200
W/Pa 10x14 Harbour Scene But 6/92 825

Gray, Henry Peters Am 1819-1877
* See 1991 Edition . . . .

Gray, Jack L. Can 1927-1981
O/C 30x40 Fishing Boat Doy 12/91 7,500
O/C 26x36 The Watch Skn 5/92 4,950

Gray, John Br 19C
* See 1992 Edition . . . .

Graziani, Ercole (the Younger) It 1651-1726
I&S/Pa 8x6 Virgin Appearing to a Peasant Chr 1/92 1,100

Graziano, Sante Am 1920-
O/C 29x24 Angela and White Tablecloth 1939 Wlf 3/92 275

Greacen, Edmund William Am 1877-1949
O/C 30x40 Point Pleasant Beach 1925 Sby 9/91 22,000
O/C 30x25 The Green Vase Lou 12/91 5,500
O/C 30x25 Spring Flowers in a Blue Vase Sby 4/92 3,575

Greacen, Nan Am 1909-
O/C 28x22 Floral Still Life Wlf 10/91 2,800

Greason, William Am 1884-
* See 1992 Edition . . . .

Greatorex, Eliza Pratt Am 1820-1897
O/C 14x23 Farmhouse by the Road 1868 Hnd 6/92 1,100

Greatorex, Katherine Honora Am 1851-
* See 1990 Edition . . . .

Greaves, Walter Br 1846-1930
O/C 18x24 Battersea Bridge Chr 10/91 4,180

Greco, Gennaro It 1663-1714
O/C 14x18 Figures Among Roman Ruins Sby 10/91 44,000

Green, Albert Van Nesse Am 20C
* See 1992 Edition . . . .

Green, Charles Br 1840-1898
* See 1991 Edition . . . .

Green, Charles Edwin Lewis Am 1844-
O/C 8x12 Heading Home 90 Skn 5/92 2,750
O/C 10x14 The Dingy Skn 5/92 1,980
O/C 6x8 North African Street Scene Yng 4/92 1,400

Green, E* F*** Br 19C**
O/C 28x36 Moroccan Courtship Sby 1/92 3,850

Green, Elizabeth Sheppen Am 1871-1954
C/Pa 24x15 Girl Watching Butterflies 1909 Ih 11/91 2,200

Green, Frank Russell Am 1856-1949
O/C 18x30 Haying in August 1886 Chr 12/91 11,000
O/C 10x16 Milking the Cow Chr 6/92 770

Green, George 20C
* See 1991 Edition . . . .

Green, Nathaniel D. Am 20C
O/B 11x14 Still Life of Violets Slo 2/92 90

Green, Roland Br 1896-1972
* See 1992 Edition . . . .

Green, William Bradford Am 1871-1945
O/C 18x22 Seascape Mys 11/91 192

Greenaway, Kate Br 1846-1901
* See 1992 Edition . . . .

Greenbaum, Joseph Am 1864-1940
O/C 36x40 Atmospheric Landscape Mor 3/92 3,500

Greenberg, Maurice Am 1893-
O/B 24x19 The Opera Club Wlf 10/91 225

Greenblat, Rodney Alan Am 20C
Pe/Pa 11x11 Milo and the Fish Sby 6/92 1,430

Greene, Albert Van Nesse
P/Pa 9x13 House in a Cove Ald 5/92 200

Greene, Balcomb Am 1904-
* See 1992 Edition . . . .

Greene, Gertrude Am 1911-1956
* See 1992 Edition . . . .

Greene, J. Barry Am 1895-1966
O/C 17x30 Pepe Lou 6/92 100

Greene, Walter L. 20C
O/B 10x19 Sunset on the Marsh Yng 4/92 400

Greenleaf, Jacob I. Am 1887-1968
O/B 12x16 Gloucester Street Scene Lou 6/92 750
O/C 20x24 Danvers Flats Mys 6/92 385
O/B 10x8 Phlox and Carnations Yng 4/92 375

Greenman, Frances Am 1890-1982
* See 1992 Edition . . . .

Greenwood Br 20C
O/C 28x24 Floral Still Life Fre 12/91 425

Greenwood, Joseph H. Am 1857-1927
O/C 28x38 Fields, Early Autumn '07 Skn 5/92 3,575
O/C 23x32 Signs of Spring '21 Skn 3/92 3,300
O/C 30x50 Redemption Road, Princeton 92 Skn 5/92 2,420
O/C 21x28 Path through the Fields '24 Skn 5/92 2,200
O/Cb 11x15 Two Mountain Views '21 Skn 3/92 2,090
O/C 26x32 Fields and Distant Trees 12 Skn 9/91 1,760
O/C 16x24 Autumn Fields 02 Skn 5/92 1,650
O/Pn 8x12 Afternoon Sun Skn 5/92 385
O/Cb 11x15 Shrewsbury, Indian Summer '22 Skn 5/92 330
O/Cb 11x14 Autumn Oaks Skn 5/92 275

Greer, J. T. Am 19C
* See 1992 Edition . . . .

Gregoire, Alexandre Hai 20C
O/M 20x24 Fete de Morts Chr 5/92 825

Gregor, Harold Am 1929-
A/C 60x67 Illinois Flatscape No. 2 1977 Hnd 3/92 550

Gregorief, K. M. Rus 20C
O/C 17x18 Forest Passage 1989 Slo 4/92 110

Gregory, C. F. Aut 1815-1885
* See 1992 Edition . . . .

Gregory, Charles Br 19C
* See 1991 Edition . . . .

Gregory, George   Br 1849-1938
W/Pa 21x14 Village Scenes 1898 Wtf 11/91 800

Greil, Alois   Aus 1841-1902
W/Pa/B 14x20 Victory Celebration 1870 Chr 5/92 2,640
O/Tn 9x10 At a Well, Naples Slo 2/92 450
O/Tn 9x10 Fruit Vendor, Naples Slo 2/92 450

Greiner, Otto   Ger 1869-1916
P&Pe/Pa 26x19 Study of a Young Child 1916 Sby 7/92 . . . 3,190

Greitzer, Jack   Am 1910-
* See 1990 Edition . . . .

Grel, Schmit
* See 1992 Edition . . . .

Grell, Louis   Am 1887-
* See 1992 Edition . . . .

Gremke, Henry Diedrich   Am 1860-1939
O/C 18x24 Mountain Landscape But 6/92 2,750

Gresly, Gabriel   Fr 1712-1756
* See 1992 Edition . . . .

Gretzner, Harold   Am 1902-1977
W/Pa 22x28 Club San Pablo - Oakland, CA Mor 3/92 1,300
W/Pa 21x29 Boat & Houses-Oakland Mor 6/92 800

Greuvenbroeck, Alessandro   a 1717-1724
* See 1991 Edition . . . .

Greuze, Jean-Baptiste   Fr 1725-1805
O/Pn 18x15 L'Effroi Chr 5/92 66,000

Grevenbroeck, Orazio   1678-
O/Cp 7x12 Sunset Mediterranean Harbor: Pair Sby 5/92 . . 38,500

Grey, John   20C
O/C 20x23 Genre Scene Dum 10/91 450

Grey, Steve   Am 20C
O/C 16x20 Night in Tunisia Lou 9/91 1,000

Gribble, Bernard Finegan   Br 1873-1962
O/B 11x17 Naval Battle Skn 3/92 770

Gridland, H.   Con 19C
O/C 20x30 Portrait of Two Terriers 1891 Sby 6/92 5,500

Griffier Theelder, Jan   Dut 1652-1718
* See 1992 Edition . . . .

Griffin, Thomas B.   Am 1858-
O/C 20x30 Storm Over the Ramapos River Sby 4/92 2,310
O/C 12x6 Autumn Landscape Fre 4/92 950
O/C 10x14 Landscape with Houses Lou 12/91 775

Griffin, W. Abbott
O/B 18x24 Mountain Scene Ald 3/92 105

Griffin, Walter   Am 1861-1935
O&Pe/C 9x13 Landscape in Fleury, France 1898 Chr 3/92 . . 5,500
O/C 15x19 Maine Hillside Sby 12/91 2,475
Pe/Pa 5x8 Griffin, Hudson, Fuller at Easels 1880 Brd 8/92 . 1,430
P/Pa 12x14 Poplars - France Skn 9/91 550

Griffin, William Davenport   Am 1894-
O/C 36x40 Wet Paint 1926 Chr 6/92 2,750

Griffith, Grace Allison   Am 1885-1955
W/Pa 15x17 The Lei Women '26 But 6/92 2,090

Griffith, William Alexander   Am 1866-1940
O/C/Pn 16x20 Laguna Hills 1930 But 10/91 4,950
P/Pa 20x24 Mountains Edge But 2/92 1,320

Griggs, Samuel W.   Am 1827-1898
* See 1992 Edition . . . .

Grigoriev, Boris   Rus 1886-1939
O/C 36x29 Woman with Rooster Chr 11/91 1,980
G/Pa 15x21 Isle de Paqueta, Bresil Sby 6/92 825

Grillon, Roger
* See 1992 Edition . . . .

Grimaldi, Giovanni Francesco   It 1606-1680
* See 1992 Edition . . . .

Grimelund, Johannes Martin   Nor 1842-1917
O/C 15x24 Anvers, Vue de L'Escaut 1885 Chr 2/92 9,350
O/C 15x22 The Wetlands 1888 Skn 5/92 1,540

Grimelvad, J. M.   Nor 19C
O/C 15x22 Coastal Scene 1878 Sel 4/92 350

Grimm, Paul   Am 1892-1974
O/C 26x40 Natures Charm But 6/92 7,150
O/C 24x36 Desert Glory But 2/92 5,225
O/C 24x30 Desert Expanse But 6/92 1,650

O/B 8x10 The Flowering Desert But 6/92 1,650
O/C 9x12 California Rolling Hills But 6/92 1,430
O/Cb 9x12 Landscape Mor 3/92 1,300
O/Cb 12x16 Glacier Lodge - High Sierras 1939 Mor 3/92 . . 1,100
O/Cb 9x12 Landscape Mor 3/92 1,100
O/Cb 12x9 Lake Tahoe Mor 3/92 1,000
O/M 18x24 Where Cares are Forgotten 1939 Hnd 10/91 . . 1,000
O/C 24x30 Colorful Forms Mor 6/92 950
O/M 16x20 Smoke Tree Forest - Palm Springs Mor 3/92 . . . 950
O/M 18x24 Approaching Sunset 1938 Mor 6/92 900
O/B 16x20 Garden of the Desert Mor 6/92 900
O/B 11x14 California Landscape Mys 6/92 770
O/M 12x16 Devils Garden Mor 6/92 650
O/Cb 12x9 High Sierras Mor 3/92 600
O/C/B 6x8 Desert Bloom But 6/92 550
O/Cb 9x12 Landscape Mor 3/92 550
O/Cb 10x16 Landscape Mor 6/92 500

Grimm, Samuel Hieronymous   Sws 1733-1794
W/Pa 6x8 Ships and Old Fort 1785 Wes 11/91 715

Grimmer, Abel   Flm a 1592-1614
* See 1992 Edition . . . .

Grimshaw, Arthur F.   Br 1868-1913
O/C 11x19 Thames/Tower Bridge Moonlight 1887 But 5/92 . 2,750

Grimshaw, John Atkinson   Br 1836-1893
O/C 20x30 Autumn Morning Sby 5/92 52,250
O/C 18x30 Humber Dock Side, Hull 1884 Sby 2/92 44,000
O/B 7x15 Liverpool Customs House 93 Sby 5/92 20,900

Grinnell, G. Victor   Am -1934
O/B Size? Landscape Mys 6/92 248

Grinnell, Roy   Am 1934-
O/C 22x38 Defiant Warriors But 4/92 4,950

Grips, Charles Joseph   Bel 1852-1920
O/Pn 14x12 Woman at a Spinning Wheel 1869 Skn 3/92 . . 8,250

Grips, Jean Charles   Bel 19C
O/Pn 18x14 Domestic Tasks 1882 Sby 5/92 12,650

Gris, Juan   Spa 1887-1927
O/C 22x29 Poires et Raisins Sur Une Table 13 Chr 11/91 . . . 3.3M
O/C 36x24 Guitare sur une table 1916 Chr 5/92 . . . . 1.485M
O/C 13x22 La Mandoline 21 Chr 5/92 462,000
GPL&PV/Pa 19x12 Bouteille et cigares Chr 5/92 308,000
O/C 14x10 Tete d'Arlequin Chr 5/92 77,000
Pe/Pa 9x9 Portrait Madame Cezanne Chr 5/92 60,500
Pe/Pa 14x11 Portrait Louis Guillaume Chr 5/92 55,000
I&G/Pa/B 10x12 Les Chasseurs Sby 10/91 6,050

Grison, Francois Adolphe   Fr 1845-1914
O/Pn 8x6 At the Antiquarian's 89 Chr 5/92 1,500

Griswold, Casmir Clayton   Am 1834-1918
O/C 12x20 Lake Albano Fre 10/91 1,850

Gritchenko, Alexis   Rus 1883-1977
* See 1990 Edition . . . .

Grob, Conrad   Sws 1828-1904
* See 1990 Edition . . . .

Grodensky, * *   Am 20C
O/C 42x36 The Symphony 62 Slo 9/91 150

Grodff, Orsylla Ann   Am 20C
O/C 26x20 Cows in the Forest Hnd 3/92 140

Groenewegen, Adrianus Johannes   Dut 1874-1963
O/Pn 10x20 Cattle and Sheep Watering Sby 7/92 1,650
O/Pn 10x20 Shepherdess with Sheep and Cattle Wtf 3/92 . . . 700

Groll, Albert Lorey   Am 1866-1952
O/C 25x31 Dessert Clouds Hnz 5/92 1,800
O/C 10x14 Home to the Village 1928 Skn 9/91 935

Groll, C.   Eur 19C
O/C 14x17 Farmyard with Cows, Boater Slo 2/92 700

Grolleron, Paul Louis Narcisse   Fr 1848-1901
O/C 24x29 The Advance Guard Sby 10/91 7,700
O/C 16x13 The Courtship Sby 7/92 2,530

Gromaire, Marcel   Fr 1892-1971
I&S/Pa 11x8 Jeune Fille Lisant 1921 Hnd 6/92 850

Gronland, Theude   Ger 1817-1876
* See 1990 Edition . . . .

Grooms, Red   Am 1937-
Fp/Pa 47x80 Rodeo Arena 1975 Chr 5/92 26,400
Os/Pa 23x35 Beach Scene Chr 11/91 5,940
G/Pa 15x19 Hi! Uncle Morton '86 Chr 5/92 4,950
W&L/B 11x14 Fat Feet 66 Sby 6/92 3,520
Mk/Pa 12x18 Cowboy and Native American: Pair Sby 10/91 2,860
O&L/Pls 28x21 The Kiss Chr 11/91 2,860
W&C/Pa 11x15 Dining Out, St. Thomas 1978 Chr 11/91 . . . 2,750

Grootenvorst, D.   Dut 20C
O/C 16x24 Canal Scene 24 Hnd 10/91 325

Gropper, William   Am 1897-1977
O/C 40x30 Tycoon Sby 5/92 22,000
O/C 16x20 The Peddlars Chr 11/91 4,400
O/C 15x18 Harvest Hayride Sby 12/91 2,860
G,Br&I/Pa 19x27 The Power Chr 9/91 2,420
O/C 10x8 Senate Series #100 Chr 11/91 2,420
P/Pa/B 17x13 Man and Two Horses Sby 4/92 825
Pl/Pa 9x12 Variations on a Rococo Theme Slo 2/92 400
Pl/Pa 10x13 Appeal to Reason Slo 2/92 375
Pe/Pa 8x11 Untitled Chr 6/92 308

Gros, Baron Jean Louis   Fr 1793-1879
* See 1990 Edition . . . . -

Grose, Captain Francis   Eng 1731-1791
W/Pa 11x15 Richmond from Twickenham Slo 4/92 100

Grose, Daniel C.   Am a 1860-1890
O/C 17x30 Royal House of the City, Lucknow 1887 Sby 4/92 1,760

Gross, Chaim   Am 1904-1991
W&I/Pa/B 7x22 The Lute Player 1963 Sby 12/91 2,310
W&I/Pa 8x21 The Hasidim/Triptych '64 Skn 5/92 1,100
W/Pa Size? Conversation '63 Fre 10/91 400
Y&W/Pa 18x11 Dancing Woman Skn 3/92 385
I&W/Pa 6x11 Mother and Child Skn 5/92 248

Gross, Peter Alfred   Am 1849-1914
O/Pn 15x24 Down by the River Bank 86 Hnd 5/92 550

Grossi, G.   It 20C
O/B 9x8 Piazza San Marco Slo 9/91 225

Grossman, Joseph B.   Am 1889-
O/C 25x30 Along the Wissahickon Fre 12/91 800

Grossman, Milton
O/C 26x36 Girl Picnicing with a Rabbit Ald 5/92 200

Grosvenor, Robert   20C
* See 1991 Edition . . . . -

Grosz, George   Am 1893-1959
W&Pl/Pa 24x18 Berlin Cafe Chr 11/91 44,000
W,G&I/Pa 26x21 Keine Hast 1923 Chr 11/91 40,700
W,G&Pl/Pa 18x24 Snakeskin and Clogs 1927 Chr 2/92 . . 38,500
W&Pl/Pa 27x19 Mann und Frau Chr 11/91 27,500
W,G&Pl/Pa 19x24 Nach der Befragung 1935 Chr 11/91 . . 15,400
W/Pa 26x19 Zwei Schwestern Chr 5/92 13,200
O/Cb 16x20 Two Female Nudes 1941 Sby 10/91 12,650
Pl&Br/Pa/B 23x17 Can you spare a dime? 33 Chr 11/91 . . . 9,350
W/Pa 26x19 Fight Between Palettes & Brushes Chr 9/91 . . . 8,250
Pl,Br&S/Pa 8x11 Spaziergang mit Hund 12 Chr 5/92 8,250
Pl/Pa 20x25 Meeting Chr 5/92 6,050
O/Pa/B 25x19 Stehender Weiblicher Akt Chr 11/91 6,000
W/Pa 20x16 New York City Sby 3/92 5,500
W&Pl/Pa 15x19 Dunes, Cape Cod 39 Chr 9/91 5,280
L/B 20x15 Bride Chr 2/92 4,620
Pl/Pa 11x9 Celebration Chr 11/91 3,300
W&O/Pa 20x14 Moonrise Over Reeds 36 Chr 6/92 2,860
O&G/C 25x18 Dunes 1945 Chr 6/92 2,200
Y/Pa 11x9 The Wounded Officer Sby 10/91 1,650

Groth, John   Am 1908-
I&W/Pa 29x21 Three Watercolors Sby 12/91 715

Grove, Maria   Dan 19C
* See 1990 Edition . . . . -

Grover, Dorothy   Am 1908-1975
* See 1991 Edition . . . . -

Grover, Oliver Dennet   Am 1861-1927
O/C 24x30 Lake Moraine 1926 Wes 11/91 1,100
O/Cb 11x15 Blue Mesa Hnd 10/91 400

Groves, Hannah C.   Am 1868-1952
O/C 20x24 Cooper Pond Fre 4/92 700

Grubacs, Carlo   Ger 19C
* See 1992 Edition . . . . -

Gruber, F. R.   Am 20C
Pe&Cw/Pa 7x10 Wake Up Call Fre 10/91 30

Gruber, Francis   Fr 1912-1948
* See 1991 Edition . . . . -

Gruger, Frederic R.   Am 1871-1953
Pe&S/Pa 27x11 Man and Child Overlooking Valley Ih 5/92 . 2,500

Grun, Jules Alexandre   Fr 1868-1934
* See 1991 Edition . . . . -

Grunenwald, Jakob   Ger 1822-1896
* See 1990 Edition . . . . -

Grunewald, Isaac   Swd 1889-1946
O/C 29x23 Nude Female in Landscape Wlf 9/91 3,000

Gruppe, Charles Paul   Am 1860-1940
O/C 18x24 Going to Pasture Skn 9/91 2,640
O/C 18x24 Old Homestead, Lakeville 1930 Chr 3/92 2,420
O/C 24x31 Landscape with Sheep Hnd 3/92 2,400
O/C 18x13 Mother Nursing But 4/92 1,980
O/Cb 12x16 Figures in a Summer Landscape Skn 11/91 . . . 1,320
O/C 6x9 View Upriver, Cloud Cover Skn 9/91 1,210
O/C 16x24 Fisherfolk on the Beach Yng 4/92 1,200
O/Cb 12x16 Landscape Hnd 10/91 1,200
O/C 33x26 Dutch Canal Skn 9/91 1,100
W&G/Pa 22x17 Sentier Dans Les Dunes, Hollande Skn 9/91 1,100
O/C 9x12 Barnyard with Chickens Lou 3/92 1,000
O/Cb 12x16 The Water Tub Skn 11/91 990
O/C 9x12 Farm Scene with Chickens Lou 12/91 800
W/Pa 8x11 Pond and Boatman Hnd 5/92 550

Gruppe, Emile Albert   Am 1896-1978
O/C 30x36 Gloucester Harbor Lou 12/91 5,500
O/C 10x12 Mountain Landscape Fre 4/92 5,500
O/C 30x36 Sugaring Vermont 1969 Ald 3/92 3,600
O/C 24x20 Harbor Scene Sby 12/91 3,300
O/C 20x18 Morning--Gloucester Fre 4/92 3,300
O/C 30x36 Vermont Landscape Sby 12/91 3,300
O/C 24x20 Morning Along the Docks Lou 3/92 3,000
O/C 20x18 Birch Trees Chr 6/92 2,750
O/C 20x24 Gloucester in Winter Bor 8/92 2,750
O/M 24x30 Street Scene 1931 Sby 12/91 2,750
O/C 20x24 Rockport Pier in Winter Doy 12/91 2,700
O/C 25x30 Pulling the Nets Sby 12/91 2,640
O/Cb 16x20 The Boathouse Chr 11/91 2,640
O/C 20x23 Gloucester Port Fre 4/92 2,400
O/C 18x20 Fishing Boats at Dock Sby 12/91 2,310
O/C 24x20 Harbor from a Wooded Promontory Sel 12/91 . . 2,300
O/C 20x24 Evening Light, Gloucester Harbor Slo 2/92 . . . 1,900
O/C 20x16 The Bait Diggers Skn 3/92 1,870
O/C 20x24 Sun Bathing Skn 5/92 1,760
O/B 20x16 Thatchers Island Wes 11/91 1,650
O/C 20x24 Rainy Day, Vermont Slo 2/92 1,600
O/C 24x20 A Winter Stream Chr 6/92 1,540
O/Cb 10x12 Smith's Cove, Gloucester 1945 Skn 9/91 1,540
O/Cb 16x20 Surf Fisherman Skn 11/91 1,540
O/C 20x18 Tree Trunk on a Snowy Bank Chr 6/92 1,320
O/C 24x20 Unloading the Nets Fre 4/92 1,100
O/C 12x16 Church Scene Mys 11/91 770
O/C 24x30 Fisherman and His Wife Fre 12/91 650
O/B 9x12 Coastal Scene Hnz 5/92 575
O/Cb 10x14 Crashing Waves Chr 6/92 440

Grust, F. G.   Dut 20C
* See 1992 Edition . . . . -

Grust, Theodor   Ger 1859-
* See 1992 Edition . . . . -

Grutzner, Eduard   Ger 1846-1925
* See 1992 Edition . . . . -

Gsell, Laurent   Fr 1860-1944
* See 1992 Edition . . . . -

Guaccimani, Vittorio   It 1859-1938
W/Pa 30x21 The Guardsman 1900 Slo 12/91 3,000
W/Pa 18x14 Seamstress Slo 9/91 425

Guaccimanni, Alessandro   It 1864-1927
W/Pb 25x18 A View of Venice Chr 10/91 660

Guardabassi, Guerrino   It 1848-
O/C 35x25 The Lamp Lighter Sby 2/92 3,300

Guardi, Antonio & Guardi, F.   It 1698-1730
* See 1992 Edition . . . . -

112

Guardi, Francesco   It 1712-1793
O/C 16x20 Church of San Giorgio Maggiore Sby 5/92 ... 1.265M
O/C 19x30 View of Grand Canal, Venice Sby 5/92 880,000
O/C 13x22 View of the Punta Di Dogana Sby 5/92 605,000
O/C 20x30 View of Rio Dei Mendicanti Sby 5/92 577,500
O/C 19x14 Capricci of a Landscape: Pair Sby 5/92 495,000
O/C 13x22 View of the Piazzetta, Venice Sby 5/92 407,000
O/C 5x8 Grand Canal w/Church of San Simeone Sby 5/92 176,000

Guardi, Francesco & Guardi, A.   It 1712-1793
* See 1992 Edition ....

Guardi, Giacomo   It 1764-1835
O/C 14x19 Grand Canal Looking East, Venice Sby 10/91 . 68,750
O/Pn 10x7 Fire in the San Marcuola, Venice Chr 5/92 41,800

Guardi, Giovanni Antonio   It 1698-1760
O/C 19x15 Fire in a Kitchen Interior Chr 1/92 46,200

Guarino   It 20C
O/C 20x15 Man with Pipe in Interior Slo 4/92 475

Guarino, Salvatore Anthony   Am 1882-
O/C 25x30 The Tiber, Rome Sby 2/92 2,530
O/Pn 12x16 Sicilian Port View Slo 9/91 275

Guayasamin, Oswaldo   Ecu 1919-
O/C 51x22 Angustia Sby 5/92 26,400
O/C 24x24 Cabeza de Nino Chr 11/91 6,600

Guba, R.
O/B 21x20 The Flower Seller 35 Chr 10/91 2,750

Gubsky, Igor
O/C 50x25 The Man in a Blue Beret Hnz 10/91 650

Gudin, Jean Antoine Theodore   Fr 1802-1880
O/C 9x14 Sailboats on a Lake Chr 10/91 1,430

Gue, David John   Am 1836-1917
W/Pa 13x21 Crashing Waves Mys 11/91 302

Gueldry, Ferdinand Joseph   Fr 1858-
* See 1991 Edition ....

Guerin, Armand   Fr 1913-
O/M 11x14 Montmartre; Place de Concorde: Pair Sby 2/92 .. 660
O/M 25x30 Voisinage de Paris Sby 10/91 660
O/M 18x22 Paris Street in Winter Sby 2/92 550

Guerin, Jules   Am 1866-1946
W&G/L 30x20 Road of Jericho, Palestine Slo 2/92 700

Guerrero, Luis Garcia   20C
* See 1991 Edition ....

Guerreschi, Giuseppe   1929-1985
Pl,S&G/Pa 12x9 Testa di un uomo 1954 Chr 5/92 440

Gues, Alfred Francois   Fr 1937-
O/C 19x12 Portrait of a Musketeer Wes 3/92 1,650

Guey, Fernand   Fr 1877-
O/C 61x85 Cascade Bois de Boulogne 1910 Sby 5/92 ... 55,000

Guglielmi, O. Louis   Am 1906-1956
G&PV/B 20x15 Minetta Lane Chr 12/91 16,500
G/B 12x10 Head Sby 4/92 6,050

Guichard, L.   Fr 19C
O/C 24x20 Young Lady with Dog 1877 Lou 12/91 225

Guidi, Giuseppe   It 1881-1931
* See 1991 Edition ....

Guidi, J*   Con 19C**
O/C 36x55 Ancient Roman Road 1899 Sby 1/92 2,970

Guigou, Paul   Fr 1834-1871
O/Pn 10x6 Route Bordee de Peupliers 69 Sby 10/91 4,950
O/B 6x11 Le Petit Montagne Sby 10/91 1,320

Guillaume, Albert   Fr 1873-1942
O/Pn 16x13 A Reclining Nude Chr 10/91 2,750

Guillaume, Francois Gabriel   Fr 1804-1886
W/Pa 12x15 A Litter of Pups 1832 Slo 9/91 300

Guillaume, Louis Mathieu D.   Am 1816-1892
O/C 24x18 Still Life of Tulips Slo 7/92 1,300

Guillaumet, Gustave   Fr 1840-1887
Sg/Pa/B 9x11 Moorish Woman, Seated But 11/91 1,100

Guillaumin, Armand   Fr 1841-1927
O/C 23x29 Le Pont Marie, Quai Sully Chr 11/91 110,000
O/C 26x32 La Roche de L'Echo, Crozant Chr 11/91 53,900
O/C 24x29 Paysage de Crozant 95 Sby 5/92 38,500

O/C 24x29 La Baie d'Agay Chr 2/92 33,000
O/C 24x29 Ravin de la Sedelle 16 Chr 2/92 30,800
P/Pa 20x26 Damiette 84 Chr 11/91 24,200
O/C 24x29 Bord de la Creuse Doy 11/91 24,000
O/C 16x13 Jeune Femme a la Cape Chr 11/91 19,800

Guilleminet, Claude   Fr 1821-1860
O/C 15x18 Poultry in a Barnyard Fre 10/91 2,800

Guillermo, Juan   Spa 1916-1968
O/C 46x58 Viejas Reparando Redes Wlf 6/92 2,600

Guillot-Saguez, A.   Fr 19C
* See 1992 Edition ....

Guinart, Francisco   Spa 20C
O/C 36x51 Zambra Gitana Sby 2/92 9,350

Guiramand, Paul   Fr 1926-
O/C 10x12 Cheval Chr 11/91 1,430

Guislain, J. M.   Am 1882-
O/B 10x13 Boats at Dock Yng 2/92 325

Gumery, Adolphe-Ernest   Fr 1861-
* See 1992 Edition ....

Gunn, Archie   Am 1863-1930
O/B 28x14 Woman at Vanity 1912 Ih 11/91 3,000
W/Pa 23x14 Woman Singing Ih 5/92 325

Gunther, Max   Swd 1934-
O/C 26x21 Three Works Wes 3/92 578
O/C 63x40 On Distant Shores Wes 3/92 550

Gursky, Andreas   1955-
Ph 20x24 Giordano Bruno 1989 Chr 2/92 1,760

Gurvich, Jose   Uru 1927-1974
O/C 40x49 Untitled 1973 Sby 11/91 18,700

Gussoni, Vittorio   It 20C
O/C 25x21 La Figlia Del Pescetore Wes 11/91 1,540

Gussow, Bernard   Am 1881-1957
P/Pa 11x15 New York Street Scene Slo 7/92 275

Gussow, Karl   Ger 1843-1907
O/Pn 21x18 A Good Brew 1874 Chr 5/92 1,000

Gustafson, Frank   Am 1863-
O/C 30x27 A Gentleman's Agreement Hnd 5/92 150

Gustafson, Sven
* See 1992 Edition ....

Guston, Philip   Am 1912-1980
O/C 69x110 Rug III 1976 Sby 5/92 577,500
O/C 67x129 Courtroom 1970 Sby 11/91 495,000
O/C 68x80 The Magnet 1975 Sby 11/91 363,000
O/M 30x40 Painter and Model 1969 Sby 2/92 209,000
O/C 32x36 Summer Kitchen Still Life 1978 Chr 11/91 ... 187,000
Br&I/Pa 18x24 Untitled 1953 Chr 5/92 38,500
O/M 12x14 Untitled 69 Sby 5/92 28,600

Gute, Herbert Jacob   Am 1908-1977
O/B 24x20 The Blacksmith 1939 But 11/91 2,200
W&I/Pb 14x20 Virginia Cabin Skn 5/92 275

Gutierrez, Jose L.
* See 1992 Edition ....

Gutierrez, Oswaldo   Cub 1917-
G/Pa 28x22 Bodegon Sby 5/92 3,850
O/C/B 22x28 Encrucijada Sby 5/92 3,300

Gutman, Nathan
* See 1992 Edition ....

Gutmann, Bernhard   Am 1869-1936
O/C 45x35 Seated Female Nude 19 Chr 6/92 3,850

Guttuso, Renato   It 1912-
MM&L/B 36x20 Standing Man Sby 10/91 8,800

Guy, Francis   Am 1760-1820
O/C 39x49 Brooklyn in Winter Chr 5/92 44,000

Guy, Seymour Joseph   Am 1824-1910
* See 1992 Edition ....

Guyei, A. V.
O/C 19x25 Landscape 1908 Dum 11/91 450

Guyp, Benjamin Gerritsz.   Dut 1612-1652
* See 1990 Edition ....

Gwathmey, Robert   Am 1903-1988
O/C 24x20 Man Drinking Chr 3/92 15,400
O/C 26x32 Reflections Chr 3/92 14,850
O/C 10x16 Study for Muse, 1967 Chr 11/91 8,800
O/C 24x20 Parade Chr 12/91 7,700
O/C 16x20 Girl with a Guitar Chr 11/91 5,280

O/C 15x10 Playing Chr 3/92 4,950
Pe/Pa 19x15 Stacking Wood Chr 6/92 1,650

Gwilt-Jolley, Martin
O/C 32x24 Dans le Bois a Trepied Sby 6/92 1,980

Gysbrechts, Cornelis Norbertus   Dut a 17C
* See 1992 Edition . . . .

Gysbrechts, Franciscus   Dut a 1674-
* See 1992 Edition . . . .

Gyselinckx, Joseph   Bel 19C
O/Pn 19x16 Reading Time 1866 Chr 2/92 3,200

Gysels, Pieter   Flm 1621-1690
* See 1991 Edition . . . .

Gysis, Nicholas   Gr 1842-1901
C/Pa 12x10 Bearded Man Wearing a Turban Chr 5/92 5,500
C/Pa 11x9 Head of Man in Turban Hnd 3/92 350

Haacke, Hans   20C
Bp&Mk/Pa 21x18 Map of Manhattan 1969 Sby 11/91 3,850

Haag, Carl   Ger 1820-1915
* See 1992 Edition . . . .

Haag, Jean Paul   Fr 19C
O/C 29x23 The Spinning Wheel Chr 5/92 7,150

Haanen, Casparis   Dut 1778-1849
* See 1990 Edition . . . .

Haapanen, John Nichols   Am 1891-
O/C 20x16 Winter Landscape with Stream 1922 Fre 10/91 . . 650
O/C 24x20 Early Autumn Maple 17 Skn 3/92 358
O/B 11x14 Seascape Yng 4/92 60

Haas, Johannes   Dut 1832-1908
W/Pa 14x21 Floral Composition Dum 4/92 250

Haas, Richard
* See 1992 Edition . . . .

Haas, Siegfried   Am 20C
O/C 14x19 Rocky Coast Mys 6/92 1,485

Haberle, John   Am 1856-1933
Pe/Pa 7x5 At the Breakfast Table Wes 3/92 220

Hacker, Arthur   Eng 1858-1919
O/C 24x25 Boy Playing with Kitten But 5/92 3,300

Hacker, Dieter   Ger 20C
* See 1992 Edition . . . .

Hacker, Horst   Ger 1842-1906
* See 1992 Edition . . . .

Hackett, Malcolm   Am 1903-
O/C 30x24 Girl with Bouquet Hnd 12/91 200

Haddock, Arthur E.   Am 1895-1980
W/Pa 12x18 Landscape '46 Mor 11/91 550

Haddon, Arthur Trevor   Eng 1864-1941
O/C/B 14x28 Terrasse Andalouse But 5/92 3,300
O/C 28x36 Spanish Dancers Sby 7/92 2,200

Haelszel, Johann-Baptist   Ger 1712-1777
* See 1990 Edition . . . .

Haenigsen, Harry   Am 1900-1991
Pl/Pa 12x18 Caught and Eaten by a Bear Ih 5/92 325

Haessler, George   Am 20C
Pe/Pa 10x13 Walt Disney Dum 12/91 275
Pe/Pa 10x13 Harry S. Truman Dum 12/91 70
Pe/Pa 10x13 Laurence Olivier 1952 Dum 12/91 70
Pe/Pa 10x13 Sidney Poitier 59 Dum 12/91 55
l/Pa 17x14 Jack Benny 1959 Dum 12/91 50
Pe/Pa 10x13 Henry Fonda Dum 12/91 27
Pe/Pa 10x13 Bob Hope Dum 12/91 20
Pe/Pa 10x13 Kim Novak Dum 12/91 15

Haffenrichter, Hans   Ger 1897-
W/Pa 23x17 Portrait (Pair) Lou 3/92 500

Hafner, Carl   Ger 1814-1873
O/C 11x15 Landscapes with Distant Towns: Pair Sby 1/92 . 3,850

Hagarty, Clara Sophia   Can 1871-1958
O/B 10x14 Luxembourg Gardens '11 Sbt 5/92 12,155

Hagarty, James   Br a 1762-1783
* See 1991 Edition . . . .

Hagborg, August Wilhelm N.   Swd 1852-1925
* See 1992 Edition . . . .

Hagerup, Nels   Am 1864-1922
O/C 12x24 Sunset Off the Coast But 6/92 1,430

O/C 12x24 Moonlight Across San Francisco Bay But 6/92 . . 1,320
O/C 13x30 Dawn; San Francisco Bay 1906 Slo 12/91 475

Haghe, Louis   Bel 1806-1885
O/Pn 7x11 The Connoisseurs Chr 10/91 2,200

Hagny, J.   Am 19C
O/C 42x32 Young Girl Holding Bonnet 1871 Slo 9/91 1,700

Hahn, Georg   Ger 1841-1889
* See 1990 Edition . . . .

Hahn, William   Am 1829-1887
O/C 25x37 Cattle and Rider 1876 But 10/91 5,500

Haig, Axel Herman   Eng 1835-1921
* See 1992 Edition . . . .

Haigh-Wood, Charles   Br 1856-1927
O/C 20x14 Young Woman with Fan 09 Sby 1/92 3,850

Haile, E.   Am 20C
O/C/B 22x18 Still Life of Flowers Lou 12/91 175

Haines, Frederick Stanley   Can 1897-1960
O/Al 14x17 Haliburton Trees 1948 Sbt 11/91 1,590
O/B 5x6 Milk Cart Sbt 11/91 1,496

Haines, Richard   Am 1906-
O/C 31x20 Reverie But 4/92 825

Hake, Otto   Am 1876-
O/C 37x33 The Mandarin But 4/92 16,500

Halauska, Ludwig   Ger 1827-1882
* See 1990 Edition . . . .

Hale, Ellen Day   Am 1855-1940
O/B 9x6 Cattle in Landscape Lou 3/92 300

Hale, Lillian Westcott   Am 1881-1953
Pe/Pa 19x15 Moment of Reflection Sby 9/91 11,000

Hale, Philip Leslie   Am 1865-1931
* See 1991 Edition . . . .

Haley, Robert Duane   Am 1892-1959
* See 1990 Edition . . . .

Hall, Frederick   Br 1860-1948
* See 1990 Edition . . . .

Hall, Frederick Garrison   Am 1879-
T/C 16x13 Eastern Mysticism/Still Life 1910 Skn 3/92 605

Hall, George Henry   Am 1825-1913
O/C 6x5 Still Life with Cherries 1870 Skn 11/91 4,070

Hall, Harry   Br 1814-1882
O/B 9x12 Gladiateur: A Bay Hunter 1865 But 11/91 4,400

Hall, Henry   Br 19C
* See 1992 Edition . . . .

Hall, John Alexander   Can 1914-
O/Pn 10x11 Spruce-Rimmed, Haliburton '47 Sbt 11/91 374

Hall, R.   Am 19C
O/C 18x14 Two Young Girls '99 Sel 4/92 850

Hall, S.   Eng 19C
O/C 18x12 Country Church by River Slo 10/91 75

Halle, Noel   Fr 1711-1781
O/C/B 21x26 Schoolmaster with his Pupils 1801 Chr 10/91 . 7,150

Halle, Samuel Baruch   Fr 1824-1889
* See 1992 Edition . . . .

Haller, G.
O/C 21x12 Landscape with Stream Dum 1/92 600

Hallett, Hendricks A.   Am 1847-1921
O/C 15x30 Marsh on a Cloudy Day 80 Sby 12/91 1,650
W/Pa 20x30 Apple Blossom Time Yng 4/92 600
W/Pa 19x33 Marblehead Harbor Eld 4/92 330

Halley, Peter   1953-
A/C 63x70 Black Cell 1986 Chr 5/92 63,800
A/C 60x128 Before and After 1986 Sby 11/91 55,000
A/C 49x63 Blue Cell with Smokestack 1984 Sby 11/91 . . . 55,000
A/C 85x126 Cell with Double Chamber Sby 5/92 55,000
A/C 65x66 Conduit Without Cell 1986 Sby 5/92 55,000
A/C 54x54 Pain and Pleasure 1982 Chr 11/91 49,500
A/C 60x80 Untitled 1983 Chr 5/92 38,500

Hallot, Hendricks A.   Am 20C
W/Pa 13x18 New England Landscape Fre 12/91 160

Hallowell, George   Am 1871-1926
O/Ab 6x8 Purple Mountains Brd 5/92 385
O/Ab 6x9 Sky Feathers Brd 5/92 330

Hallowell, Robert   Am 1886-1939
W/B/Pn 13x10 Still Life with Flowers '26 Sby 12/91 440

O/C 16x12 The Tower Lou 3/92 225
W/Pa 8x9 In the Clouds Lou 3/92 75
W/Pa 9x15 Mosque '25 Lou 3/92 75

Halpert, Samuel   Am 1884-1930
W&Pe/Pa 14x20 Interior 24 Chr 3/92 3,300

Hals, Dirck   Dut 1591-1656
* See 1991 Edition ....

Hals, Frans   Dut 1580-1666
* See 1992 Edition ....

Hals, Harmen-Franz   Dut 1611-1669
* See 1990 Edition ....

Halsall, William Formby   Am 1841-1919
* See 1992 Edition ....

Hambler, Richard   20C
O/B 11x14 Seascape Yng 4/92 425

Hambleton, Richard
* See 1992 Edition ....

Hamblin, Rosalie   Am 20C
O/B 18x14 Dock Scene Slo 4/92 55

Hambourg, Andre   Fr 1909-
O/C 20x29 Les petits parasols sur la plage 1964 Chr 5/92 . 18,700
O/C 11x14 Deauville Chr 2/92 10,450
O/C 9x14 Brume Legere, Beau Temps 1962 Chr 11/91 ... 9,900
O/C 9x14 Temps couvert a Deauville Chr 5/92 9,900
O/C 9x14 Fin de Jour Doy 11/91 7,000
O/C 9x14 La Campagne, Le Soir Doy 11/91 6,000
O/C 5x9 Soleil dans Brume Legere Hnd 5/92 2,000
O/C 4x9 Trois Chalutids au Large Hnd 12/91 2,000
Pl&S/Pa 6x8 Two Drawings: Venise 1961 Chr 11/91 ... 1,760
Pl&S/Pa 6x8 Three Drawings: Venise 62 Chr 11/91 1,045

Hamel, Adolphe   Ger 1820-
O/C 28x34 Paris Interior But 5/92 3,300

Hamellruser, H.   Am 19C
O/C 30x25 Portrait Henry Davis Fre 4/92 75

Hamilton, Edward Wilbur Dean   Am 1862-
* See 1991 Edition ....

Hamilton, Frank   Am 20C
W/Pa 15x17 Suzie Q & Freighter Mor 11/91 300

Hamilton, Gawen   Br 1697-1773
* See 1990 Edition ....

Hamilton, Hamilton   Am 1847-1928
O/C 24x36 Gathering Water Chr 3/92 26,400
O/C 18x30 Landscape with Hunter and Dog 1879 Skn 9/91 3,850
O/C 30x36 Woman Feeding Sheep Dum 10/91 3,500
O/C 20x37 Mist Rising Over the Mountains 1879 Sby 4/92 . 1,320
O/C 24x30 Valley Vista But 11/91 1,100
O/C 18x15 A Fishing Village Chr 6/92 495

Hamilton, Hildegard   Am 1906-
O/C 15x18 Caribbean Village Dum 6/92 200

Hamilton, James   Am 1819-1878
O/C 24x36 Shipwreck Sby 12/91 4,400
O/C 20x30 Arctic Expedition Hnz 10/91 2,600
O/C 14x20 Steamer by Moonlight 1877 Slo 12/91 900
O/C 8x16 Shipwreck 1862 Sby 12/91 792

Hamilton, John McClure   Am 1853-1939
O/Pn 10x7 Reveries in a Chair Skn 9/91 660
P/Pa 28x21 Elegant Lady 1910 Slo 7/92 600

Hamilton, Karl William   Aus 1668-1754
* See 1991 Edition ....

Hamilton, Lady Henrietta M.   Can 1780-1857
W/Wd 6x9 Birch Bark, Newfoundland Sbt 11/91 1,122

Hamilton, R.
W/Pa 13x17 A Council of War 1902 Dum 8/92 100

Hamilton, Rupert
W/Pa 5x9 Two Setters in a Field Eld 4/92 121
W/Pa 7x10 Listening - Deer in Landscape Eld 4/92 88
W/Pa 7x10 Moose Family Eld 4/92 88

Hamm, Emma   Am 20C
O/B 31x19 Lilacs Hnd 3/92 200

Hammer, Hans Jorgen   Dan 1815-1882
* See 1992 Edition ....

Hammer, Johann J.   Am 1842-1906
O/C 29x47 In the Garden 1880 Chr 3/92 7,700

Hammeras, Ralph   Am 1894-1970
O/C 30x24 Desert Spring Mor 6/92 500

Hammershol, Vilhelm   Dan 1846-1916
* See 1991 Edition ....

Hammerstad, John H.   Am 19C
O/C 14x20 Marine Mor 6/92 225

Hammond, Arthur J.   Am 1875-1947
O/B 11x14 Mother of Liberty, Gloucester Brd 5/92 660
O/C 12x20 New England Homestead Eld 8/92 468
O/B 20x24 Western Landscape Lou 12/91 200

Hammond, George F.   Am 1855-
O/Cb 25x31 Seascape Slo 7/92 150

Hammond, H.   Br 19C
W/Pa 7x10 Feeding Time Hnd 3/92 160

Hammond, John A.   Can 1843-1939
O/B 10x13 Whitby Harbour 1926 Sbt 11/91 1,122

Hamon, Jean-Louis   Fr 1821-1874
* See 1990 Edition ....

Hampton, John W.   Am 1918-
O/C 24x30 Learning the Ropes 1955 Dum 1/92 2,000

Hamza, Johann   Ger 1850-1927
O/Pn 16x12 In the Library Chr 10/91 9,900

Hancock, John   Br 1808-1890
W/Pa 7x9 Songbirds on a Branch 1836 Yng 2/92 450

Hand, I.   Eng 19C
* See 1992 Edition ....

Hane, Roger   Am 1938-1974
A/C 23x34 "Double Header" Ih 11/91 600

Hangell
O/C 12x14 Figures in Foreground with Donkey Dum 12/91 . 1,000

Hanke, August   Aus 20C
* See 1991 Edition ....

Hankey, William Lee   Br 1869-1950
O/C 25x30 Montreuil Sur Mer But 11/91 5,500
O/C 20x24 Hill Town in Var Hnd 3/92 5,200

Hankins, Abraham   Am 20C
O/C 30x24 Topreros Fre 4/92 525
O/B 16x20 The Parade 1943 Ald 5/92 200

Hanna, David   Am 1941-1981
W/Pa 40x24 David, artist's son Slo 4/92 1,000

Hanna, Thomas King   Am -1916
* See 1991 Edition ....

Hannah, Duncan   20C
* See 1991 Edition ....

Hanneman, Adriaen   Dut 1601-1671
* See 1991 Edition ....

Hannot, Jan   Dut 17C
* See 1991 Edition ....

Hanriot, Jules Armand   Fr 1853-1877
O/Pn 13x16 Afternoon by the Lake Chr 2/92 3,300

Hanscom, Trude   Am 1898-
O/C 20x24 Back Country Mor 3/92 200

Hansen, Armin   Am 1886-1957
O/B 16x20 Iceland Fishing Boat/Landscape: Dbl But 2/92 . 33,000
O/C 27x36 Wanderer of the Past But 2/92 30,250
O/C 24x35 Empire Builders But 10/91 14,300
O/C 14x12 Man with a Pipe Wlf 6/92 1,300

Hansen, C. L.   Con 20C
O/Pn 14x10 Mediterranean Light Fre 10/91 90

Hansen, Ejnar   Am 1884-1965
O/Cb 16x20 American Farm Scene Dum 4/92 225

Hansen, Hans Peter   Am 1881-1967
O/Pa 9x7 Still Life 1898 Lou 6/92 200

Hansen, Herman Wendelborg   Am 1854-1924
W/Pa/B 16x12 The Pass; The Alarm: Pair 1921 Sby 9/91 . 22,000
W/Pa/Pa 30x20 Short Cut Chr 9/91 7,700
W&G/Pa 10x14 Cowboy Shooting Sby 3/92 6,050

Hansen, John F.   Dan a 1900-1920
* See 1992 Edition ....

Hansen, Ole Peter   Nor 1823-1906
O/C 14x22 Mexican Potters at Work '94 But 11/91 1,100

Hanson, Peter   Am 1821-1887
O/C 30x46 Streams and Woodlands, New York Skn 11/91 . 4,950

Hanson, R.   Con 20C
  * See 1992 Edition . . . .
**Hansteen, Nils Severin Lynge   Nor
1855-1912**
  * See 1992 Edition . . . .
Hantai, Simon   1922-
  O/C 59x85 Untitled 57 Chr 11/91 36,300
**Haquette, Georges Jean Marie   Fr
1854-1906**
  O/Pn 9x6 Fisherwoman and Boy on a Bridge Skn 5/92 1,045
Hardenbergh, Elizabeth R.   20C
  W/Pa 12x12 Flowers in a Bowl Yng 4/92 125
Hardenbergh, Gerard R.   19C
  W/Pa 7 dia 11 Watercolors (Ducks) 84 Brd 5/92 2,750
  W/Pa 10 dia Woodcocks (2) 1889 Brd 5/92 578
Hardie, Robert Gordon   Am 1854-1904
  * See 1992 Edition . . . .
Hardime, Pieter   Flm 1677-1758
  O/C 32x47 Still Life Flowers in a Basket Sby 1/92 38,500
Hardman, John   Eng 19C
  O/C 25x30 Hunter in a Landscape 1816 Wlf 6/92 2,400
Hardwick, Melbourne H.   Am 1857-1916
  W/Pa 13x19 Women in a Countyard Yng 2/92 525
  W/Pa 17x20 Spring Landscape Mys 11/91 192
Hardy, Anna Elizabeth   Am 1839-1934
  O/C 24x18 Still Life 78 Brd 5/92 1,320
Hardy, Dudley   Br 1865-1922
  O/Pn 14x12 Market Scene Wes 11/91 1,430
  O/C 9x13 Figure in Red Near Buildings Wes 11/91 1,210
  O/C 28x24 Arab Market Scene Sby 7/92 990
Hardy, Frederick Daniel   Br 1826-1911
  O/C 40x51 An Evening of Mozart 1881 Chr 10/91 13,200
  O/C 8x7 The Evening's Pursuits Skn 11/91 1,870
  P/Pa 13x8 Little Girl Admiring the Bird Chr 5/92 550
Hardy, Heywood   Br 1843-1933
  O/C 28x36 The Meet; The Kill: Pair Chr 10/91 60,500
  O/C/B 20x30 Where Did He Go? Sby 6/92 15,400
  O/C 28x32 Returning to the Fox's Lair 1896 Chr 10/91 . . . 3,300
Hardy, James (Jr.)   Br 1832-1889
  O/C 20x16 Feeding Time 87 Chr 5/92 3,250
Hardy, Jeremiah P.   Am 1800-1887
  O/C 27x39 Maine Life, 1852 Brd 8/92 3,300
Hardy, Thomas   Br a 18C
  O/C 30x25 Portrait of a Gentleman Chr 5/92 4,400
Hardy, Thomas Bush   Br 1842-1897
  W/B 15x22 Sailing in a Stiff Breeze: Pair Sby 1/92 2,860
  W/Pa 9x12 Boats at Sea 1892 Fre 12/91 600
Hardy, Walter Manly   Am 1877-1933
  O/B 10x8 End of the Hunt/Snowy Landscape Brd 8/92 412
Hare, David
  * See 1992 Edition . . . .
Hare, John Knowles   Am 1882-1947
  P/Pa 40x30 Mother with Infant Sel 2/92 500
Hare, Julius   Br 1859-1932
  * See 1992 Edition . . . .
Hare, Richard Clark   Am 1906-
  W/Pa 11x15 Three Works Wes 3/92 385
Hare, St. George   Br 1857-
  * See 1990 Edition . . . .
Harer, F. W.
  O/B 12x16 Landscape 1911 Ald 5/92 400
Haria, Josef   Con 20C
  O/C 62x36 St. Nicholas' Cathedral, Prague 1946 Wes 3/92 . 1,210
Haring, Keith   Am 1958-1990
  A/C 117x143 Untitled (M. Mouse) 1985 Chr 5/92 104,500
  A/C 48x48 Untitled 1985 Chr 2/92 62,700
  A/Pa 83x217 Untitled (Brightheart) 82 But 5/92 41,250
  E/Me 48x48 Untitled 1981 Chr 5/92 38,500
  Br&I/Pa 38x50 Untitled '82 Chr 5/92 34,100
  Br&I/Pa 38x50 Men 1981 Chr 2/92 16,500
  A&L/Pa 38x38 Untitled 89 Chr 11/91 13,200
  Br,I&A/Pa 25x29 Untitled 89 Chr 11/91 7,700
  Fp/Pn 9x13 Untitled 1983 Chr 2/92 7,150
  Br&I/Pa 30x25 Untitled 89 Chr 11/91 4,620

  Br&I/Pa 30x25 Untitled 89 Chr 11/91 3,850
  Mk/Pa 5x5 Wolf Figure and Bee: Two 87 Sby 10/91 1,348
  Mk/Pa 6x4 Dancing Figures: Pair Sby 10/91 1,210
Haring, Keith & Martin Roy   Am 20C
  Fp&Ph 20x16 King Kong for a Day 89 Chr 5/92 3,520
Harlamoff, Alexei Alexeiewitsc   Rus 1842-
  * See 1991 Edition . . . .
Harles, Victor J.   Am 1894-1975
  O/Cb 9x12 Rocks and Surf Hnd 5/92 325
  O/Cb 12x14 Winter Landscape Hnd 5/92 300
  O/Cb 10x12 Mountain Lake Hnd 5/92 100
  O/Cb 8x10 Mountain Scene Hnd 5/92 70
Harlor, Joseph   Eng 19C
  O/C 20x24 Fisherman with Onlookers Slo 7/92 2,000
Harlow, George Henry   Eng 1787-1819
  O/C 36x28 Duchess of Bordon But 11/91 2,200
Harlow, Louis Kenney   Am 1850-1913
  W/Pa 15x19 Dutch Canal Scene Yng 4/92 90
  W/Pa 6x18 Riverscape Eld 7/92 66
Harmer, Alexander F.   Am 1856-1925
  O/C 18x30 Braves Hunting on Horseback Sby 4/92 7,700
Harmon, Annie   Am 1855-1930
  * See 1992 Edition . . . .
Harmon, Charles H.   Am 1859-1936
  O/C 18x22 Yosemite Landscape Mor 11/91 600
Harmon, Fred   Am 1902-1982
  * See 1991 Edition . . . .
Harnden, William   Am 1920-1983
  O/M 16x20 After Dinner Music Fre 10/91 300
Harnett, William Michael   Am 1848-1892
  O/C 10x8 Still: Lobster Fruit Champagne 1882 Sby 12/91 110,000
Harney, Paul E.   Am 1850-1915
  * See 1992 Edition . . . .
Harper, William   Br 19C
  O/C 27x22 The Rose Chr 10/91 2,420
Harper, William St. John   Am 1851-1910
  * See 1991 Edition . . . .
Harpignies, Henri Joseph   Fr 1819-1916
  O/C 21x32 View through the Trees 1882 Chr 5/92 28,600
  W/Pa 10x13 The Artist's Studio 1878 Sby 10/91 25,300
  O/C 13x17 Autumn at St. Prire 90 Chr 5/92 24,200
  O/C 26x32 Fisherman in a Punt 1898 Chr 2/92 13,200
  O/C 26x32 Parc de St. Fargeau 1910 Sby 2/92 12,100
  O/C/B 10x13 The River 1870 Chr 5/92 11,000
  O/C 21x26 Coucher du Soleil sur le Lac Sby 10/91 9,350
  W/Pa 8x11 Pins Dans L'Ile St. Honorat 88 Sby 5/92 6,875
  W/Pa/B 5x7 View of Raincy 1875 Sby 1/92 3,300
  W/Pa/B 8x5 Hunting on the Castle Grounds But 11/91 . . . 2,750
  S/Pa 6x9 A Hilly Landscape Chr 5/92 1,100
Harrer, Hugo Paul   Ger 1836-1876
  * See 1992 Edition . . . .
Harriet, Fulchran Jean   Fr 1778-1805
  * See 1991 Edition . . . .
Harris, Alice   Am 20C
  O/C 20x35 Eating Watermelon Wlf 10/91 275
Harris, Ben Jorj   Am 1904-1957
  G/Pa 18x12 Woman and Camera Ih 11/91 90
Harris, E. M.   Am 19C
  O/C 16x29 Stormy Seas Mys 6/92 358
Harris, Edwin   Br 1901-
  * See 1991 Edition . . . .
Harris, Lawren Stewart   Can 1885-1970
  O/C 24x26 Houses, Richmond Street '11 Sbt 5/92 327,250
  O/Pn 10x14 Algoma Sketch LII Sbt 5/92 21,505
  O/B 11x12 Pine Trees, Muskoka Sbt 11/91 14,025
Harris, Marion D.   Am 1904-
  O/C 16x20 Dock Scene Ald 3/92 215
Harris, Robert   Can 1849-1919
  * See 1992 Edition . . . .
Harris, Sam Hyde   Am 1889-1977
  O/C 18x24 Carlsbad Station But 2/92 6,050
  O/C/B 16x20 Coast Guardian But 2/92 6,050
  O/C 20x23 Todd Shipyards But 2/92 5,225
  O/C/B 16x20 Sunshine and Shadows But 2/92 3,850
  O/Cb 16x20 Laguna Memories But 2/92 3,300

O/C 16x20 House on the Hill But 10/91 2,750
O/Cb 16x20 Unfurled Sail Mor 3/92 2,000
O/B 16x20 Star of India But 2/92 1,980
O/Cb 16x20 Star of India #3 But 6/92 1,760
O/Cb 18x24 Off Beaten Path Mor 6/92 1,700
O/C/C 16x20 Ranch Shelter Mor 3/92 1,600
O/M 12x16 Mountain Landscape Mor 11/91 1,000
O/Cb 16x20 Utah Sand Mor 6/92 1,000
O/M 16x20 Mrs. Burnett's Garden Mor 11/91 950
O/Cb 10x14 Mt. Baldy Mor 6/92 750
O/B 16x18 Landscape Mor 11/91 475

Harrison, Birge   Am 1854-1929
O/C 31x40 A Frosty Morning Chr 6/92 5,500
O/C 18x30 Harvest Moonlight Reflection Skn 3/92 ... 1,320
O/B 12x16 Summer Landscape Skn 3/92 770

Harrison, Grace Earle   Am 1853-1945
W/Pa 10x7 Chinatown: Two Lou 12/91 225

Harrison, John Cyril   Br 1898-1985
* See 1992 Edition ....

Harrison, Lowell Birge   Am 1854-1929
* See 1992 Edition ....

**Harrison, Thomas Alexander   Am
1853-1930**
O/C 12x40 Crepuscule/Moonlit Seascape Skn 5/92 2,640
O/C 20x30 The Tide Coming In Chr 6/92 1,540
O/C 20x40 Seascape Hnz 5/92 1,300

Harrowing, Walter   Br a 1877-1904
O/C 23x28 Stallion in a Loose Box Sby 5/92 4,400
O/C 28x36 A Bay in a Landscape Sby 6/92 2,090

Harsh, A. Dale   Am 20C
W/Pa 14x21 Abandoned Slo 7/92 80

Harsh, Fred Dana   Am
* See 1992 Edition ....

Harshe, Robert Bartholow   Am 1879-
* See 1992 Edition ....

Hart   Br 20C
O/C 12x16 Chickens Hnd 12/91 1,100

Hart, James MacDougal   Am 1828-1901
O/B 4x7 A Bridge over a Stream Chr 6/92 1,540
O/C 54x21 Monarch of the Forest Skn 3/92 1,210
O/C/B 15x21 Cattle Watering Mor 6/92 1,100

Hart, William Howard   Am 1863-1964
O/C 18x32 Landscape Dum 5/92 7,000

Hart, William M.   Am 1823-1894
O/C 14x26 Cows Wading 64 Chr 11/91 4,950
O/C 10x9 Cattle by a Stream 1886 Fre 4/92 3,100
O/C 18x14 Landscape with Grazing Cattle Slo 10/91 .. 2,600
O/Pn 6x10 Cows Watering 1876 Sby 4/92 2,200
O/B 8x8 Wooded Landscape 1876 Hnd 6/92 1,800
O/C/Pn 25x20 Cows in a Country Landscape Wes 11/91 .. 1,485
O/C 18x32 Cows in a Landscape 1884 Hnd 3/92 1,400
O/C 10x8 Landscape With Cows 1877 Wes 11/91 1,100

Hartell, Joann   Am 20C
T/B 10x8 Meditation 49 Skn 5/92 275

Hartigan, Grace   Am 1922-
* See 1992 Edition ....

Hartinger, Anton   Aus 1806-1890
O/B 31x25 Floral Still Life with Fruit 1867 Sby 2/92 55,000
O/Pn 14x12 Roses in a Vase on a Tiled Ledge Sby 5/92 .. 27,500

Hartley, Marsden   Am 1878-1943
O/C 24x20 Flowers Sby 12/91 40,700
O/B 12x16 Autumn, Dogtown Common 1934 Brd 8/92 .. 29,700
Sv/Pa 11x15 Houses by a Hill Chr 11/91 1,650
Pl/Pa 11x14 The Alps 1933 Sby 12/91 1,210

Hartley, Rachel   Am 1884-
W/Pa 13x9 Three Little Black Girls Lou 3/92 175

Hartman, Bertram   Am 1882-1960
W/Pa 26x19 St. Tropez 1924 Chr 6/92 1,760
W/Pa 14x19 Vase of Flowers 1944 Lou 6/92 1,300
O/C/M 20x27 Flowers & Porcelain Figure 1943 Sby 4/92 ... 660
W/Pa 24x19 The El 1942 Hnz 10/91 325
W/Pa 26x19 Nude in Rocker Mys 11/91 82

Hartmann, Ludwig   Ger 1835-1902
O/Pn 9x14 At the Blacksmith's Sby 10/91 22,000

**Hartmann, Mathias Christoph   Ger
1791-1839**
G/Pa 12x10 The Betrothal But 11/91 990

Hartrath, Lucie   Am 19C
* See 1990 Edition ....

Hartsell, P.   Am 19C
O/C 30x42 Landscape with Trees Dum 5/92 900

Hartshorne, Howard Morton   Am 20C
O/B 9x11 French Village Mys 11/91 412

Hartson, Walter C.   Am 1866-
O/C 20x28 A Day in June 1912 Fre 4/92 2,100

Hartung, Hans   Ger 1904-1989
C,H&Y/Pa 20x26 Untitled 59 Sby 5/92 14,300
W&I/Pa 12x12 Untitled 73 Sby 2/92 5,500
H&Os/B 8x12 Untitled '80 Chr 5/92 4,400

Hartung, Johann   Ger a 1846-1854
O/C 12x8 Aristocrat and his Friend Sby 6/92 1,870

Hartwell, Nina Rosabel   Am 19C
* See 1992 Edition ....

Hartwich, Herman   Am 1853-1926
* See 1992 Edition ....

**Hartwick, George Gunther   Am a
1845-1860**
O/C 22x36 Yosemite Valley Wes 3/92 2,750

Hartz, Lauritz Dan   Dan 1903-
O/C/B 14x22 Landscape 1928 Hnd 10/91 400

Harvey   Am 20C
* See 1992 Edition ....

Harvey, George   Am 1800-1878
O/C/B 15x19 Twilight by the Docks 1851 But 11/91 13,200
O/Ab 8x11 Break in the Clouds Slo 10/91 1,600

Harvey, George W.   Am 1836-1920
W/Pa 13x23 Venetian Harbor Scene '87 Hnz 5/92 300
C/Pa 11x18 Dutch Farmhouse Yng 4/92 80

Harvey, George Wainwright   Am 1855-
O/B 10x13 Dutch Women on Beach 1885 Skn 9/91 660

Harvey, Gerald   Am 1933-
* See 1990 Edition ....

Harvey, Henry T.   Am 19C
O/C 24x36 The Old Mill Hnd 6/92 200

Harwood, James Taylor   Am 1860-1940
* See 1990 Edition ....

Has, H.   a 1517-1548
O/Pn 64x57 The Crucifixion Chr 1/92 46,200

**Hasbrouck, DuBois Fenelon   Am
1860-1934**
* See 1992 Edition ....

Hasch, Carl   Aus 1834-1897
O/C 17x15 Tyrolean Landscape Dum 4/92 2,500

Hasegawa, Kiyoshi   Jap 1891-
* See 1991 Edition ....

Haseltine, William Stanley   Am 1835-1900
O/C 14x25 Coastal View with Sunset Dum 12/91 2,200

Haslehurst, E. W.   Sco 20C
W/Pa/Cd 14x9 Tudor Courtyard Summer Wlf 6/92 575

Hassall, John   Am 1868-1948
Pl/Pa 11x8 Girl and Owl in Mill Ih 5/92 500

Hassam, Frederick Childe   Am 1859-1935
O/C 23x20 The Fishermen, Cos Cob 1907 Sby 12/91 ... 198,000
P/Pa 18x22 Mill Dam, Cos Cob 1903 Chr 5/92 77,000
O/Pn 9x5 At the Writing Desk 1910 Chr 3/92 52,800
Pe&P/Pa 10x11 Harbor of Thousand Masts 1919 Sby 5/92 33,000
O/Pn 11x8 View of a Town, Massachusetts 1878 Chr 3/92 15,400
O/Pn 7x8 The Three Bathers 1924 Sby 9/91 9,350

Hasselbach, Wilhelm   Ger 1846-
* See 1992 Edition ....

Hassell, Hilton McDonald   Can 1910-1980
O/B 13x23 Last Ice, Old Woman River Sbt 11/91 748

Hastings, M.
O/C 34x27 Portrait of Mary Owings Hunt Sel 12/91 350

Hastings, T. Mitchell   Am 20C
* See 1992 Edition ....

Hatch, Emily Nicholas   Am -1960
O/B 7x9 View of the Cathedral Fre 12/91 250

Hatfield, Joseph Henry   Am 1863-1928
* See 1990 Edition . . . .
Hathaway, George M.   Am 1852-1903
O/Ab 14x22 Portland Harbor Brd 8/92 5,720
O/Ab 6x11 Pearl of Orr's Island Brd 8/92 2,310
O/B 6x10 Seascape with Ships Yng 4/92 150
Hattner, L.
G/Pa 17x13 Pair: Depicting Steins Eld 8/92 193
Hau, Eva   Rus 19C
* See 1991 Edition . . . .
Haubtman, Michael   Ger 1843-1921
O/C 33x43 Hillside Overlooking the Sea Wes 11/91 2,090
Hauenstein, Oskar   Am 1883-
O/B 28x22 Lady Reading Yng 2/92 50
G/Pa 20x27 Landscape 1914 Yng 2/92 50
Haughton, Moses   Br 1734-1804
O/C 50x40 Sigismunda 1784 But 5/92 10,450
Hausch, Alexander Fiodorovich   Rus 1873-
* See 1990 Edition . . . .
Hauser, C. H.   Am 20C
O/C 25x30 Hurricane Off the Coast Slo 4/92 375
Hauser, John   Am 1858-1913
G,W&H/Pb 18x12 Toilers of the Pueblos 1904 Skn 5/92 . . . 4,675
Hauser, K. Rex   Ger 19C
O/B 18x14 Seated Tyrolian Peasant Chr 2/92 1,650
Hausmann, Gustav   Ger 1827-1899
* See 1992 Edition . . . .
Hausrof, George
O/B 27x33 On the Curb Wtf 3/92 1,000
Havard, James   Am 1937-
A&C/C 72x84 Inca Ground 78 Chr 11/91 19,800
A/C 46x126 Open Sea Tableta--New Paint 83 Chr 11/91 . . 13,200
A,Os&L/C 28x24 Flamenco Knees 89 Chr 11/91 3,850
A,K&H/B 32x40 Untitled 77 Chr 11/91 3,300
Pe&P/Pa 20x16 Soho Stripper 1966 Fre 10/91 325
Havell, Robert (Jr.)   Am 1793-1878
* See 1990 Edition . . . .
Havenith, Hugo   Eng 1853-
* See 1992 Edition . . . .
Hawkins, J.   Br 19C
O/C 27x40 Harbor Hnd 6/92 200
Hawkins, John   Am 20C
O/B 19x24 Seascape, 1920 Wtf 10/91 100
Hawksley, Dorothy   Am 20C
W&Pe/Pa 24x20 The Dreamers Wtf 6/92 2,000
Hawley, Hughson   Am 1850-1936
* See 1992 Edition . . . .
Haworth, Bobs Cogill   Can 1900-1988
W&I/Pa 20x24 Quebec Village Sbt 5/92 1,683
W/Pa 21x15 Repair (Torpedo Boat) 1944 Sbt 5/92 1,496
Hawthorne, Charles Webster   Am 1872-1930
O/M 24x20 Blue Boy Sby 3/92 7,150
O/C 26x22 Lady in a White Hat Chr 11/91 2,200
Hay, DeWitt Clinton   Am 1819-
Pe&S/Pa 2x4 Lake George Slo 4/92 325
Pe&S/Pa 7x9 Lake George 1850 Slo 7/92 200
Hay, Peter Alexander   Br 20C
* See 1992 Edition . . . .
Hayden, Charles H.   Am 1856-1901
* See 1990 Edition . . . .
Hayden, Henri   Fr 1883-1970
O/C 37x29 Scene de rue, Montparnasse 1914 Chr 5/92 . . 29,700
O/C 21x28 Green Landscape 59 Sby 2/92 5,500
G/Pa 15x22 Nature Morte en Violet Sby 2/92 1,980
Hayes, Edwin   Irs 1819-1904
O/C 14x19 French Boats Out at Sea 1860 Sby 7/92 1,650
Hayllar, Edith   Br 1860-1948
* See 1990 Edition . . . .
Hayllar, James   Br 1829-1920
* See 1992 Edition . . . .
Hayllar, Jessica   Br 1858-1940
* See 1992 Edition . . . .

Hayman, Francis   1708-1776
* See 1992 Edition . . . .
Haynes, John William   Br 1836-1908
O/C 24x20 The Interruption Chr 10/91 990
Hays, Barton S.   Am 1826-1914
* See 1992 Edition . . . .
Hays, George Arthur   Am 1854-
O/B 16x24 Herding a Flock of Sheep Mys 11/91 935
O/C/B 7x9 Afternoon (Cows in Pasture) Slo 2/92 400
Hays, William Jacob   Am 1830-1875
* See 1991 Edition . . . .
Hayter, Stanley William   Br 1901-1988
O/C 79x111 Summer Chr 2/92 16,500
O/C 28x23 Fluid Orange 58 Sby 2/92 3,300
O/C 39x25 Light Wave 65 Sby 6/92 3,300
G&H/Pa/B 12x18 Composition 1960 Chr 5/92 3,080
W&I/Pa 13x11 Airport 45 Sby 2/92 1,870
W&I/Pa 25x30 The Fly 45 Sby 2/92 1,540
Hayward, Gerald S.   Eng 19C
W/Iv 3x3 Lady with Pearl Necklace 83 Slo 4/92 160
Hayward, Joshua Henshaw   Am 19C
* See 1992 Edition . . . .
Haywood, Carolyn   Am 1898-1989
PI/Pa 8x12 Christmas Greetings Fre 10/91 100
Hazard, Arthur Merton   Am 1872-1930
O/C 36x30 Portrait Mrs. Charles Bedell Hervey 24 Sby 12/91 . 935
O/C 30x44 View from the Terrace Mor 6/92 400
Hazard, Garnet   Am 1903-
W/Pa 16x22 Fallbrook, Ontario: Pair Sbt 11/91 2,571
Hazard, James   Eng 1748-1787
O/C 19x15 Selbstportrait Dum 7/92 2,750
Hazelton, Mary Brewster   Am 1868-1953
* See 1991 Edition . . . .
Heade, Martin Johnson   Am 1819-1904
O/C 16x14 Still Life Orchid and Hummingbirds Chr 5/92 . 286,000
O/C 14x28 Boston Harbor Chr 12/91 121,000
O/C 13x26 Evening, Lake Alto, Florida Sby 12/91 115,500
O/C 16x28 Marshes Chr 5/92 71,500
O/C 9x16 Florida Sunset Chr 5/92 66,000
O/B 9x19 Harbor in Brazil '65 Sby 5/92 63,250
O/C 22x14 Glass of Roses on Gold Cloth Sby 12/91 . . . 44,000
Pe/Pa 5x7 The Jamaican Sketchbook Sby 5/92 41,250
O/C 14x22 Roses on a Palette Chr 12/91 38,500
O/C 9x17 The Cherokee Rose 1889 Chr 5/92 38,500
I&Pe/Pa 7x4 Brazil: An Autograph Journal 1865 Sby 5/92 . 30,800
O/C 16x10 Pink Rose 1878 Chr 12/91 13,200
O/Pa/C/Al 9x22 Flatlands and Haystacks Chr 9/91 12,100
Healy, Frances D.   Am -1948
O/C 20x30 Southwestern Landscape '36 Sel 12/91 325
O/C 16x24 Western American Landscape 1932 Sel 12/91 . . 275
Healy, George Peter Alexander   Am 1813-1894
O/C 23x18 Portrait of Isabel W. Carter 1872 Wes 11/91 . . . 1,430
Heard, Joseph   Br 19C
* See 1992 Edition . . . .
Heaton, Augustus G.   Am 1844-1931
* See 1991 Edition . . . .
Heaton, E.   Eng 19C
O/C 20x30 Landscape with Figure Sel 9/91 475
Hebert, Antoine Auguste Ernest   Fr 1817-1908
* See 1992 Edition . . . .
Hecht, Victor David   Am 1873-1931
* See 1990 Edition . . . .
Heckel, Erich   Ger 1883-1970
G&W/B 18x24 Landschaft 21 Chr 2/92 7,150
Heda, Gerrit Willemsz.   Dut 1642-1702
* See 1991 Edition . . . .
Heda, Willem Claesz.   Dut 1594-1680
* See 1992 Edition . . . .
Heeremans, Thomas   Dut 1641-1699
O/C 24x33 Village on Estuary w/Ferryboats 1673 Chr 1/92 35,200
Heerich, Erwin   20C
I/Pb 39x25 Untitled Sby 11/91 550

Heffner, Karl   Ger 1849-1925
O/C/M 32x47 On the Norfolk Broads Sby 2/92 11,550
O/C 26x36 Dutch River Village Chr 2/92 6,050
O/Pn 15x18 Cottages on a Marshy Plain But 5/92 5,500
Hegarty, John   Am
Pe/Pa 21x14 Female Study Durn 12/91 275
Hegstrom
O/C 9x11 European River Scene Eld 7/92 55
Heicke, Joseph   Aus 1811-1861
O/C 25x31 Berger et Bergere Gardant 1838 Sby 2/92 . . . 11,000
Heilbuth, Ferdinand   Ger 1826-1889
* See 1992 Edition . . . .
Heilmann, Mary   1940-
O/C 60x42 Untitled Chr 2/92 3,080
Heilmayer, Karl
O/C 12x21 Venetian Harbor Scene Hnz 10/91 425
Heim, *   Ger 19C**
O/Pn 6x10 Tabletop Still Life Slo 7/92 900
Heimbach, Wolfgang   Ger 1615-1678
* See 1992 Edition . . . .
Heinen, Hans   Ger 1860-
O/C 17x24 Fields in Winter Skn 11/91 660
Heinisch, Karl Adam   Ger 1847-1923
O/C 12x19 Timbermill by a Lake 94 Chr 10/91 13,200
Heinz, F*   Ger 20C**
O/C/M 19x12 Courtship; A Toast: Pair Sby 7/92 5,500
Heinze, Adolph   Am 1887-
O/B 25x30 Autumn Landscape Hnz 5/92 475
Heinzman, Louis   Am 1905-1982
O/C 20x16 Landscape--Red Limb Mor 11/91 950
Heise, Wilhelm
O/Pn 11x15 The Morning 1921 Sby 2/92 4,400
Heiss, Johann   Ger 1640-1704
O/C 13x17 Venus & Adonis: Venus & Mars: Pair Chr 10/91 14,300
Heitland, Wilmont Emerton   Am 20C
* See 1990 Edition . . . .
Heitmuller, Louis   Am 1863-
* See 1992 Edition . . . .
Heizer, Michael   Am 20C
Bp&Pe/Pa 18x24 Untitled 1969 Sby 11/91 880
Hekking, Joseph Antonio   Am a 1859-1885
* See 1992 Edition . . . .
Hekking, Willem   Dut 1796-1862
* See 1992 Edition . . . .
Helck, Clarence Peter   Am 1897-
O/B 16x13 Night Construction Skn 11/91 2,420
O/Ab 15x20 Out of Gas Slo 12/91 900
Pe/Pa 8x15 Racing Scene Mys 6/92 660
Pe/Pa 6x10 Racing Scene Mys 6/92 660
O/B 12x16 Thames Docks Yng 2/92 425
Held, Al   Am 1928-
A/C 60x48 Brughes IV 81 Chr 5/92 52,800
A/C 72x72 Pan North VII 85 Chr 11/91 49,500
A/C 84x84 Florentine Two 80 Chr 5/92 38,500
A/L 36x36 Fathom Mark III 88 Sby 11/91 30,250
Cp/Pa 27x40 76 C-14 Sby 10/91 11,000
H/Pa 27x40 75.5 75 Chr 5/92 4,620
Heldner, Knute   Am 1884-1952
O/C 24x30 Birch Trees Lou 3/92 2,200
Helfferich, Willem   Dut 20C
* See 1991 Edition . . . .
Heliker, John Edward   Am 1909-
O/C 20x16 Still Life Flowers and Vase But 11/91 2,200
O/C 20x17 Blue Still Life Chr 9/91 1,650
Helion, Jean   Fr 1904-1987
O/C 15x24 Nature Morte 28 Chr 2/92 3,850
Heller, Eugenie M.   Am 19C
* See 1991 Edition . . . .
Helleu, Paul Cesar   Fr 1859-1927
P/Pa 32x26 Lady with a Fur Wrap Sby 10/91 38,500
K&Cw/Pa 17x24 Studies of Madame Helleu Sby 10/91 . . . 13,200
K/Pa 17x21 Lady Wearing a Hat Sby 7/92 5,775
K/Pa 14x19 Mme. Helleu and her Daughters Chr 5/92 . . . 5,500
K/Pa 26x18 Lady Wearing a Black Hat Chr 10/91 4,950

Hellwag, Rudolf   Ger 1867-1942
O/C 17x22 White Caps, Green Sea Fre 10/91 900
O/C 29x38 German Village Scene Eld 7/92 550
Helsby, Alfredo   Chl 1862-1936
O/C 44x56 Chilean Farm Sby 2/92 8,250
O/C 25x35 Landscape Sby 6/92 3,300
Heming, Arthur Henry Howard   Can 1870-1940
O/C 24x22 In the Calumat Rapids '25 Sbt 11/91 3,506
O/B 12x17 Buffalo and Hunter '03 Sbt 11/91 1,402
Hemrengerg   Ger 19C
O/Pn 15x14 Landscape Hnd 6/92 325
Hemsley, William   Eng 1819-1893
O/C 14x23 Children's Game 1874 Sby 5/92 7,700
O/C 17x23 Majestic Drive 1874 Slo 12/91 6,000
Henard, *   Fr 19C**
Pl&S/Pa 18x20 Projet de Villa Facade 1854 Sby 7/92 165
Henderson, Charles Cooper   Eng 1803-1877
O/B 12x19 Passing Coaches 1865 Sby 6/92 1,210
Henderson, Joseph Morris   Sco 1863-1936
* See 1990 Edition . . . .
Henderson, Leslie   Am 1895-
O/B 20x24 Autumn Landscapes Hnz 5/92 70
O/B 16x20 Landscape with Beach Hnz 5/92 50
Henderson, W.   Eng 20C
O/C 24x36 Winter Coaching Scene Sel 12/91 425
Henderson, W. S. P.   Br 19C
* See 1992 Edition . . . .
Henderson, William Penhallow   Am 1877-1943
* See 1992 Edition . . . .
Hendriks, Gerardus   Dut 19C
* See 1991 Edition . . . .
Hendriks, Willem   Dut 1828-1891
O/C 12x16 Blossom Time, North Holland Chr 5/92 1,870
Hennah, Joseph Edward   Br 1897-
O/B 11x16 View of Mavagissey Durn 10/91 115
Hennecy, G.
O/C 21x31 The Chess Game Hnz 10/91 425
Henner, Jean Jacques   Fr 1825-1905
O/C 38x53 Madeleine au desert Chr 2/92 33,000
O/C 45x27 La Liseuse Sby 5/92 15,400
O/Pn 14x11 Seated Nude in a Forest Chr 5/92 4,950
O/C 18x13 Ideal Head Sby 2/92 4,400
O/C 11x9 Une Jeune Femme En Profil But 11/91 4,400
O/C 16x13 Red Haired Beauty in a Red Cape Chr 5/92 . . . 4,180
O/C 15x22 Reclining Nude Sby 1/92 4,125
O/Pn 11x8 Profile of a Young Woman Sby 1/92 3,300
O/C 18x14 A Red Haired Beauty Chr 5/92 2,750
O/B 12x21 Reclining Nude Sby 7/92 2,200
C&K/Pa 17x12 Portrait of a Man 1891 Sby 7/92 605
Hennessey, Frank Charles   Am 1894-1941
* See 1992 Edition . . . .
Hennessy, Patrick
O/Pn 15x16 Sunlight on the Floor Sby 10/91 1,760
Hennessy, William John   Irs 1839-1917
O/C 20x13 Apple Blossoms 1874 Wes 3/92 110
Henning
O/C 18x14 Mountain Scene Durn 4/92 125
Hennings, Ernest Martin   Am 1886-1956
O/C 30x25 Autumn Trees But 11/91 17,600
O/C 25x30 Aspen Grove Chr 12/91 16,500
Henningsen, Frants Peter   Dan 1850-1908
* See 1991 Edition . . . .
Henri
O/Pn 16x23 Dutch Still Life Durn 1/92 30
Henri, Florence   20C
* See 1991 Edition . . . .
Henri, Robert   Am 1865-1929
O/C 32x40 Spanish Girl 1912 Sby 12/91 104,500
O/C 82x40 Colonel David Perry, 9th US Cavalry Chr 5/92 . 28,600
O/Pn/B 4x6 Au Champs de Mars, Paris Chr 9/91 12,100
O/Pn 4x6 Luxembourg Garden Chr 12/91 11,000

O/Pn 8x10 Sea and Cliffs Chr 3/92 6,050
Pe/Pa 12x16 Final Touches 1925 Chr 3/92 3,850
Pe/Pa 6x9 Rowing on the River But 11/91 3,300
P&S/Pa 17x12 Gypsy Girl with Orange Shawl Sby 12/91 . . 2,530
C/Pa 10x8 Seated Girl Sby 4/92 2,530
Pe/Pa 7x10 Reclining Nude But 11/91 2,475
Pe/Pa 6x9 In the Park Chr 3/92 1,320
Pl,C&W/Pa 11x13 Portrait Marjorie Organ Wes 11/91 1,045
Pl/Pa 6x9 Three Works 1910 Wes 3/92 825
Pl&Y/Pa 11x9 Three Drawings Wes 11/91 385
Y/Pa 9x11 Peasant Lady; Standing Woman: Two Wes 3/92 . . 330
H/Pa 8x11 Reclining Nude 1926 Wlf 10/91 325
Pl/Pa 10x8 Woman in Madrid Lou 3/92 300
Pe/Pa 8x6 Portrait Mys 6/92 275
H/Pa 14x10 Three Studies Wlf 10/91 230

Henrici, John H.   Am 1839-
O/C 12x8 Boy With a Satchel But 11/91 1,650

Henrion, Armand Francois Jos.   Fr 1875-
O/Pn 9x6 Winking Clown Sby 1/92 4,675

Henry, D. M.   Br 19C
O/C 54x36 Startled Pheasants Sby 6/92 8,800

Henry, Edward Lamson   Am 1841-1919
O/C 26x43 News of the War of 1812 1913 Chr 12/91 93,500
O/C 17x25 Lastest Village Scandal 85 Chr 5/92 38,500
W&Pe/Pa 19x15 Greeting Their Guest 1891 Chr 12/91 . . . 26,400
O/Pn 7x10 The Country Store '93 Sby 5/92 13,200
O/B 19x25 Commentary on Women's Hats 1895 Chr 5/92 . . 11,000
W/Pa 9x10 The Toll Booth '95 Sby 5/92 5,500
W&Pe/Pa 7x12 Wash Day 90 Chr 5/92 4,400

Henry, Edwin   Am 1900-
O&R/C 30x24 Girl on Telephone in Bedroom Ih 11/91 600

Henry, Harry Raymond   Am 1882-1974
O/C 24x30 Hondo Canyon But 2/92 5,225

Henry, Michel   Fr 1928-
O/C 26x30 Still Life Fruit and Flowers Wes 3/92 1,430

Henry, Paul   Irs 1877-1958
O/C 23x27 Cottages by a Mountain Mys 11/91 11,000

Henry, William H.   Eng 19C
Pe/Pa 13x12 Girl Praying; Rural: Two 1870 Wlf 6/92 100

Henseler, Ernst   Ger 1852-
O/C 39x60 The Benefactor 1887 Sel 4/92 18,500

Henshall, John Henry   Br 1856-
* See 1990 Edition

Henshaw, Glenn Cooper   Am 1881-1946
P&C/Pa 11x14 Street Scene, Baltimore Wes 3/92 715
P/Pa 14x10 Baltimore Sky Line Yng 4/92 550
K/Pa 14x10 Portrait of a Boy 1912 Slo 10/91 110

Hensley, Jackson   Am 20C
O/C 28x38 Cecil's Place But 11/91 5,500

Henstenburgh, Herman   1667-1726
* See 1992 Edition

Henwood, Thomas   Br a 1842-1859
* See 1991 Edition

Hepworth, Barbara   Br 1903-1975
* See 1992 Edition

Herberer, Charles   Am 19C
* See 1990 Edition

Herberte, Edward Benjamin   Br 1857-1893
O/C 16x24 Picking up Scent; A Ditch: (2) 1887 Sby 6/92 . . 6,050

Herbin, Auguste   Fr 1882-1960
O/C 36x28 Dimanche 50 Sby 5/92 60,500
O/C 26x21 Nature Morte aux Fleurs Sby 11/91 34,100
O/C 18x22 Le Pont Des Arts 1903 Sby 11/91 30,800
G&W/Pa 13x10 Composition sur fond rouge 1940 Chr 5/92 17,600

Herbo, Leon   Bel 1850-1907
* See 1992 Edition

Herbst, Frank C.   Am 20C
* See 1992 Edition

Hereau, Jules   Fr 1839-1879
O/C 15x23 Shepherdess with her Flock Chr 5/92 1,320

Herkomer   Br 19C
* See 1992 Edition

Herland, Emma   Fr 1856-1947
* See 1990 Edition

Herman, Sali   Sws 1898-
O/C 20x24 The Barn 63 Hnd 10/91 7,400

Hermann, Ida
O/C 17x21 Moonlit Coastal Scene 1905 Sel 5/92 150

Hermann, Leo   Fr 1853-1927
O/C 14x11 A Break for Dessert Chr 2/92 2,420
W/B 10x8 A Sip of Tea Chr 5/92 800

Hermann, Ludwig   Ger 1812-1881
* See 1991 Edition

Hermanns, Heinrich   Ger 1862-1942
* See 1991 Edition

Hermans, Charles   Bel 1839-1924
O/C 127x158 Bal Masque Sby 2/92 715,000

Hermansen, Olaf August   Dan 1849-1897
* See 1992 Edition

Hernandez, Daniel   Per 1856-1932
O/Pn 17x13 Corso Mascherato a Roma Chr 5/92 12,100
O/Pn 20x14 Putting on the Skates Sby 2/92 9,350
W/Pa 28x20 La Gardeuse D'Oies 1882 Sby 2/92 5,500
O/Pn 5x8 The Rocky Beach Sby 2/92 4,950
O/C 14x11 The Red Velvet Berret Chr 2/92 3,850

Hernandez, Manuel   1928-
* See 1991 Edition

Hernandez, Sergio   Mex 1957-
O&I/Pa/Pn 76x32 Tzompantli: Three-Panel Screen Sby 5/92 17,600

Herold, Georg   20C
MM 110x87 G.O.E.L.R.O. Sby 5/92 23,100
MM/C 60x48 Russian Cocaine Sby 2/92 12,100
A/C 48x24 Kaviarbild Inamorato Sby 5/92 4,400

Herole, George Linton   Am 1868-1922
W/Pa 20x12 Along the Riverbank Slo 7/92 150

Herpfer, Carl   Ger 1836-1897
O/C 42x35 A Game of Chess Chr 5/92 35,200

Herpin, Leon Pierre   Fr 1841-1880
* See 1990 Edition

Herran, Saturnino   Mex 1887-1918
* See 1992 Edition

Herrera, Francisc (the Younger)   Spa 1622-1685
* See 1990 Edition

Herrick, Arthur R.   Am 1897-1970
O/C/M 25x30 Deerfield Ballhouse Skn 5/92 412
O/C 20x24 Concord River Skn 11/91 358
O/C 20x24 Paul Revere Road Skn 3/92 192

Herriman, George   Am 1880-1944
Pl/Pa 5x20 Comic Strip. "Krazy Kat" 41 Ih 11/91 1,600

Herring, Benjamin (Jr.)   Br 1830-1871
O/C 12x10 Ride in the Park 1871 Sby 6/92 1,210

Herring, John Frederick (Jr.)   Br 1815-1907
O/C 24x36 Horses, Pigs and Chickens Feeding Sby 6/92 . 16,500
O/C 16x16 Feeding Time in the Farmyard 1851 Sby 6/92 . . 6,600
O/C 20x30 Mallard, Ducks and Ducklings Sby 6/92 6,600
O/C 16x16 The Stableyard 1851 Sby 6/92 6,600
O/C 13x16 A Dog's Life 1835 Sby 6/92 1,320

Herring, John Frederick (Sr.)   Br 1795-1865
O/C 22x30 Horses, Pigs & Poultry/Farm 1852 But 5/92 . . 99,000
O/C 28x36 The Farmer's Stable 1844 But 5/92 93,500
O/C 33x43 Conversation in a Stable 1856 But 5/92 77,000
O/C 13x18 Lord Bentinck's Colt, Grey 1838 But 5/92 35,750
O/Pn 14x18 Mr. Wilson's Chestnut, Comus 1823 But 5/92 24,750
O/Pn 9x12 The Red Fox 1849 Sby 6/92 16,500
O/C 11x15 Ducks and Ducklings 1863 Sel 9/91 7,000

Herrmann, Hans   Ger 1858-1942
O/C 26x38 Venetian Canal Scene Sel 4/92 7,000
O/C 23x21 Canal Scene Hnd 12/91 4,200

Herrmann, L.   Ger 19C
O/C/M 50x30 Hunter with his Hunting Dogs Chr 10/91 . . . 1,320

Herschel, Philip
O/C 21x28 Paradise Ald 5/92 475

Herschend, Oscar   Ger 1871-1937
O/C 17x27 Returning Home Mys 6/92 275

Herter, Adele   Am 1869-1946
P/Pa 36x26 Table Arrangement Mys 6/92 550

Herter, Albert   Am 1871-1950
O&Pe/C 27x99 Mural Study--Greek Philosophers Chr 12/91 15,400
P/C 32x26 Tea Time Lou 9/91 5,000
O/B 24x20 Flowers Yng 2/92 90
Herve, Jules Rene   Fr 1887-1981
O/C 25x31 La Place de la Concorde in Snow Hnd 5/92 ... 8,000
O/C 26x32 Arc de Triomphe Chr 2/92 7,150
O/C 18x22 Les Tuileries Chr 2/92 5,500
O/C 18x22 Bouquinistes a Paris Chr 11/91 4,950
O/M 15x18 Ballerines au Foyer Chr 2/92 4,400
O/C 15x18 Les Tuileries Chr 5/92 4,400
O/C 18x15 Distant View Place Vendome Sby 2/92 4,125
O/B 9x11 Place de L'Opera Sby 2/92 4,125
O/C 9x11 The Book Seller; Cafe: Pair Sby 2/92 4,125
O/C 9x11 Young Sailors in the Tuilleries Sby 10/91 4,070
O/M 15x18 Ballerines dans le Salon Chr 2/92 3,850
O/C 9x11 Le Grand Basin Sby 10/91 3,410
O/C 13x16 The Diligent Student Sby 10/91 3,300
O/B 9x11 Jardin des Tuileries Chr 2/92 2,860
O/C 18x22 Paris Fountain Scene But 5/92 2,750
O/C 9x11 Les Bouquinistes et Notre Dame Chr 2/92 2,200
O/C 9x11 Path in Langres Sby 10/91 2,200
O/C 15x18 Place de la Concorde But 5/92 2,200
O/C 9x11 Au Parc Chr 2/92 2,090
O/B 9x11 Children at a Bureau Wes 5/92 1,650
O/C 9x11 Les Tuilleries Hnd 12/91 1,500
O/C 9x11 Along the Quai Sby 2/92 1,320
O/C 9x11 Megeve Sby 2/92 1,320
Herzog, Hermann   Am 1832-1932
O/C 25x35 The Waterfall Sby 5/92 29,700
O/C 22x27 The Catch Chr 12/91 22,000
O/C/Pn 22x30 American Waterfall But 4/92 13,200
O/C 26x36 Stormy Seas Chr 3/92 10,450
O/C 41x32 Swiss Mountain Landscape Dum 9/91 8,500
O/C 13x18 Sailing Party Brd 5/92 7,975
O/C 27x22 Home with Flock of Sheep Sby 9/91 7,700
O/C 22x33 Moonlit Fishing Scene 1878 Sby 3/92 7,425
O/C 15x18 Harbor at Sunset Sby 12/91 4,400
O/C 18x24 Campsight at Twilight Sby 12/91 4,125
O/C 17x23 Landscape with Deer Sby 12/91 2,750
O/C 16x23 A Norwegian Fjord Sby 12/91 2,200
O/C 17x22 The Haywagon Chr 6/92 1,540
Hess, B.   19C
O/C 19x27 Western Landscape Dum 5/92 3,000
Hess, Jaro J.   Am
W/Pa 19x15 Man Approaching Sleeping Princess Ih 5/92 ... 500
Hess, Marcel   Bel 1878-
O/C 29x24 Pink Roses in a Porcelain Vase Chr 2/92 4,620
Hesse, Eva   Am 1936-1970
MM/M 42x18 An Ear in a Pond 1965 Chr 5/92 93,500
Hesselius, John   Am 1725-1778
* See 1990 Edition ....
Hetzel, George   Am 1826-1906
* See 1992 Edition ....
Heubler, Douglas   20C
Ph Var Alternative Piece I Sby 11/91 8,800
Heuliant, Felix Armand   Fr 1834-
* See 1990 Edition ....
Heuser, C*, A***   Can 19C**
O/B 7x9 Collingwood Harbour '78 Sbt 11/91 841
Hewil, N.   Am 20C
W&G/Pa 15x19 The Grey Eagle Chr 6/92 1,320
Hewins, Amasa   Am 19C
* See 1992 Edition ....
Hewins, Philip   Am 1806-1850
O/C 32x25 Portrait of a Young Lady 1836 Bor 8/92 1,500
O/C 35x29 Jane A. Bigelow at 22 Years Bor 8/92 800
Hewitt, Charles   1946-
O/C 60x78 Artist's House is Burning Fire 1986 Chr 11/91 ... 220
Hewton, Randolph Stanley   Can 1888-1960
* See 1992 Edition ....
Hey, Paul   Ger 1867-1952
W&G/Pa 10x9 Rural Landscapes: Pair Sby 7/92 4,950
W&G/B 9x17 A Morning Walk Chr 2/92 2,750

W&G/Pb 13x27 Feeding Pigeons 08 Chr 10/91 2,420
O/C 26x26 Marsh in a Wintry Light But 11/91 1,540
Heyden, **   Ger 1907-
O/C 28x24 Picking Up the Scent But 11/91 1,540
Heydendahl, Friederich Joseph   Ger 1844-1906
O/B 10x16 Winter Landscapes: Pair Sby 7/92 3,575
Heyer, Arthur   Ger 1872-1931
O/C 31x40 Cottage Near a Pond But 11/91 880
Heyl, Marinus   Dut 1836-1931
* See 1992 Edition ....
Heyligers, Gustaaf A. F.   Dut 1828-1897
* See 1992 Edition ....
Heyligers, Hendrik   Dut 1877-1915
O/C 22x18 The Reading Lesson Sby 1/92 5,500
Heyn, August   Ger 1837-
* See 1990 Edition ....
Heywood, Tom   Br a 1882-1913
* See 1992 Edition ....
Hibbard, Aldro Thompson   Am 1886-1972
O/B 18x25 Vermont in Winter Yng 2/92 3,750
O/C 22x30 Early Fall Sby 12/91 2,970
O/Cb 17x21 Vermont Winter Skn 9/91 2,090
O/C/B 15x18 Winter Stream, Sunset Skn 11/91 1,980
O/C 28x36 Cabin in Vermont Sel 12/91 1,900
O/C 18x24 Rocky Coast Dum 6/92 1,500
O/C/B 18x24 Winter Landscape with Creek Hnd 3/92 ... 1,500
O/C 16x20 Fishing Village Dum 6/92 1,100
O/Cb 9x10 Harbor View, Buzzards Bay 1910 Skn 9/91 ... 1,045
O/B 18x26 Monhegan Island Yng 2/92 1,000
O/C 16x20 A Snowy Farm Chr 6/92 660
Hibbert, E.   Ger 19C
O/C 27x21 Bit of Scandal Chr 2/92 2,420
Hibel, Edna   Am 1917-
O/S/M 30x40 Three Women Wes 11/91 2,860
O/B 13x11 Portuguese Woman and Child Slo 9/91 1,400
T/Pn 11x8 Portrait of a Girl Slo 2/92 600
T/Pn 8x5 Bretton Lady Slo 2/92 400
O/Pn 10x8 Head of a Man; Head of a Woman: Two Wes 3/92 385
C/C/M 10x8 Head of a Young Girl Wes 3/92 165
Hickey, R. S.
O/B 12x16 Autumn Landscape Hnz 10/91 60
Hicks, Edward   Am 1780-1849
* See 1992 Edition ....
Hicks, George Elgar   Br 1824-1914
* See 1991 Edition ....
Hicks, Thomas   Am 1823-1890
* See 1990 Edition ....
Hidley, Joseph   Am 1830-1872
* See 1992 Edition ....
Hierle, Louis   Fr 19C
O/C 48x79 Diane au Repos 87 Sby 2/92 13,200
Higgins, Cardwell Spencer   Am 1902-1983
Pe&S/Pa 13x19 Churchill and Cabinet Wlf 10/91 150
Pe&S/Pa 11x8 Oriental Nude '71 Wlf 10/91 40
C&S/Pa 14x7 Oriental Nude Wlf 10/91 25
Higgins, Eugene   Am 1874-1958
G/Pa 21x14 Hard Times Chr 6/92 4,400
C/Pa 12x16 Beggers Chr 11/91 660
O/C 16x19 Two Adults and Two Children Eld 7/92 468
O/B 7x7 Conestoga Wagon Eld 7/92 440
O/C 14x18 Oxen and Cart Eld 7/92 440
Higgins, George Frank   Am a 1855-1885
O/C 12x20 Haystacks at Sunset Sby 12/91 1,650
O/C 20x28 Still Life Mys 11/91 660
O/C 20x14 Road to the Pasture Skn 9/91 605
Higgins, Victor   Am 1884-1949
* See 1991 Edition ....
Highmore, Joseph   Br 1692-1780
* See 1992 Edition ....
Hilaer, R.   Con 19C
* See 1992 Edition ....
Hilaire, Camille   Fr 1916-
O/C 15x22 Venise Chr 11/91 2,420

O/C 12x24 Nu au canape Chr 5/92 1,980
W&G/Pa/B 15x21 Voiliers 48 Chr 11/91 770

Hilbert, Robert
G/B 11x12 Your Love's Showing 1952 Ih 11/91 550

Hildebrand, Ernst   Ger 1833-1894
O/C 23x16 Young Girls With Chicks Hnz 10/91 1,800
O/C 24x31 Her Favorite Toys Sby 7/92 1,650

Hildebrandt, Eduard   Ger 1818-1969
* See 1991 Edition . . . .

Hildebrandt, Howard Logan   Am 1872-1958
O/Cb 10x8 Sailboats in the Harbor '29 Wlf 3/92 600

Hiler, Hilaire   Am 1898-
* See 1990 Edition . . . .

Hilgers, Carl   Ger 1818-1890
O/Pn 5x6 Winter Hunt and Harvest: Two 1882 Wes 5/92 . . 2,640

Hill, Arthur T.   Am 1868-1929
O/C 30x45 Sunset, East Hampton Sby 12/91 1,650

Hill, David Octavius   Br 1802-1870
O/C 19x31 Coastal Scene 1856 Hnd 5/92 1,000

Hill, Derek   Br 1916-
O/C 17x26 Demolition of Tate Bridge Hnd 10/91 1,300

Hill, Draper
Pe/Pa 12x10 Do it in Detroit 1984 Dum 1/92 130

Hill, Howard   Am a 1860-1870
* See 1992 Edition . . . .

Hill, James John   Br 1811-1882
* See 1991 Edition . . . .

Hill, Jan
W/Pa 10x14 Sailboats in Venice Dum 10/91 150

Hill, John Henry   Am 1839-1922
W/Pa 10x8 Landscape in the Catskills Eld 7/92 165

Hill, John William   Am 1812-1879
W&G/Pa/B 8x14 Still Life Grapes, Cherries Skn 3/92 12,100

Hill, Roswell S.   Am 1861-1907
O/C 21x21 Provincetown View Skn 11/91 1,100

Hill, Thomas   Am 1829-1908
O/C 20x30 Hunter and His Pointers 1861 Chr 9/91 18,700
O/B 18x25 View into the Valley But 10/91 12,100
O/C 25x20 Fishing in a Woodland Stream 1879 Skn 11/91 10,450
O/C 14x13 Hunter with Two Setters Sby 4/92 9,350
O/B 14x21 Mount Rainier But 10/91 7,700
O/Pn 42x7 Grizzly, Wawona; Pair But 10/91 7,150
O/B 21x16 Marble Canyon 1870 Mys 11/91 4,950
O/Pn 9x7 Yosemite Sby 12/91 4,125
O/B 24x34 Landscape Wlf 6/92 550

Hilliard, William Henry   Am 1836-1905
O/C 29x24 Feeding the Chickens 1882 Skn 5/92 2,420

Hillier, H. B.   Br 19C
O/C 22x18 Kilchurn Castle Hnd 10/91 1,200

Hillingford, Robert Alexander   Br 1825-1904
O/C 19x26 Tavern in the Roman Campagna 1861 Sby 2/92   5,225
O/C 19x24 Rest along the Way Chr 10/91 3,300
O/C 30x20 The Elopement Sby 1/92 2,310

Hills, Anna Althea   Am 1882-1930
O/C 14x18 Lupine on the Dunes But 10/91 2,750
O/B 7x10 The Arch But 2/92 2,475
O/Cb 11x8 Shop & Old Horses (2) 1910 Mor 6/92 1,000
O/B 8x11 Landscape Mor 3/92 700
O/Cb 11x8 Windmill--Holland 1911 Mor 11/91 650
W/Pa 10x8 Woman Sewing Mor 3/92 350

Hills, Laura Coombs   Am 1859-1952
P/Pb 22x16 Pink and Red and Apricot Zinnias Skn 9/91 . . 12,100
P/Pb 27x23 Still Life Foxglove and Larkspur Skn 11/91 . . . 8,250
P/Pa 21x17 Still Life with Anemones Skn 11/91 8,250
P/Pa 10x11 Pond Lily Skn 11/91 3,410
W,G&I/Iv 4x3 Emma Wilder Parkhurst Skn 3/92 468

Hillsmith, Fannie   Am 1911-
* See 1991 Edition . . . .

Hilton, John W.   Am 1904-1983
* See 1992 Edition . . . .

Hinckley, B. B.
O&R/B 25x19 Full-Rigged Ship Approaching 1900 Eld 4/92 . . 110

Hinckley, Thomas Hewes   Am 1813-1896
O/C/B 38x48 Mingo 1843 Wlf 3/92 3,300

Hindley, Edna   Am 20C
O/Cb 16x20 Glendale Hilltop Mor 6/92 325

Hine, Charles   Am 1821-1871
* See 1991 Edition

Hinkle, Clarence K.   Am 1880-1960
O/C 30x40 Clearing in the Woods But 6/92 4,950
O/B 11x14 Luxembourg Gardens But 10/91 1,980
O/Pn 11x14 Fisherman's Houses--Rockport Mor 11/91 . . . 1,400
W/Pa 12x16 Still Life Blue Pitcher But 6/92 1,210
W/Pa 15x21 Santa Barbara Hills But 10/91 1,100
O/C 12x16 Boat in Harbor Lou 6/92 600
W/Pa 16x12 Floral Still Life Mor 3/92 500

Hinman, Charles   Am 1932-
A/C 21x33 Untitled 66 Sby 2/92 2,750

Hinman, Helen Y.   Am 20C
O/C 15x18 Summer Landscape Drying Clothes Wlf 6/92 . . . 200

Hintermeister, Henry   Am 1897-
* See 1992 Edition . . . .

Hintermeister, Hy   Am 1897-1972
O/C 31x25 Granny at the Bat Ih 5/92 2,750
O/C 22x28 Fisherman Meeting Bear and Cubs Ih 5/92 . . . 2,100

Hinterreiter, Hans   Sws 1902-
G/Pa 6x9 Studie 138 1933 Chr 5/92 3,080

Hippolyte-Lucas, Marie Felix   Fr 1854-1925
* See 1992 Edition . . . .

Hiraga, Kamesuke   Jap 1890-1971
* See 1992 Edition . . . .

Hiremy-Hirschl, Adolph   Aus 1860-1933
* See 1991 Edition . . . .

Hirsch, Alphonse   Fr 1843-1884
* See 1990 Edition . . . .

Hirsch, Joseph   Am 1910-1981
W/Pa 11x16 Beach People Chr 11/91 660

Hirsch, Stefan   Am 1899-
* See 1991 Edition . . . .

Hirschfeld, Al   Am 1903-
W&I/Pa 17x13 Jazz Musicians Slo 7/92 1,100
PI/B 13x22 Ray Walston as the Devil Sel 9/91 1,050
PI/B 18x24 Tenderloin 1960 Sel 9/91 550

Hirshberg, Carl   Am 1854-1923
O/C 34x26 Waiting for Father Wlf 9/91 4,200
O/B 11x14 Bless This Food Wes 3/92 715

Hirshfeld, Emile Bebedicktoff   Rus 1892-1910
O/C 15x18 Docks in the Moonlight Slo 2/92 1,400

Hirst, Claude Raguet   Am 1855-1942
O/C 9x14 Still Life with Peaches But 11/91 4,400

Hirt, Heinrich   Ger 1727-1796
* See 1991 Edition . . . .

His, Rene Charles Edmond   Fr 1877-
O/C 24x32 A River Landscape Chr 5/92 2,640
O/C 20x30 River Gouche But 5/92 1,650

Hislop, Andrew   Sco 1887-1954
O/C 14x21 Canal Scene Sel 2/92 290

Hispanus, Johannes   Spa 16C
* See 1991 Edition . . . .

Hiss, Dr. John Martin   Am 1891-1972
O/Cb 16x20 Landscape Mor 11/91 200

Hister, Jean J.
W/Pa 27x18 Still Life Ald 3/92 25

Hitchcock, David Howard   Am 1861-1943
* See 1991 Edition . . . .

Hitchcock, George   Am 1850-1913
* See 1992 Edition . . . .

Hitchcock, Lucius Wolcott   Am 1868-1942
O/C 22x27 Two: Daughter Taking Leave Parents Ih 11/91 . . 2,500
O/C 11x19 Southport, Maine Skn 11/91 385
O/B 9x15 Snow Scene Mys 6/92 358
P/Pa 9x11 Avenue of Trees at Dusk Wlf 3/92 175

Hitchings, Henry   Am -1903
W/Pa 8x6 Selburke Brook 1892 Lou 6/92 75

Hittell, Charles J.   Am 1861-1938
O/C 16x25 Grand Canyon of The Colorado Mor 3/92   3,500
Hoban, Walter C.   Am 1890-1939
Pl/Pa 32x26 Comic Strip. "Rainbow Duffy" 30 Ih 11/91   250
Hobart, Clark   Am 1880-1948
O/C 20x24 Carmel Cove But 10/91   5,225
O/C 50x40 Helene Maxwell--San Francisco 1917 Mor 11/91   4,750
O/C 14x18 Monterey Coastal Scene But 10/91   2,200
O/Pa 10x12 Santa Clara Landscape But 10/91   1,100
Hobbs, George Thompson   Am 1846-
O/C 30x50 Delaware Water Gap Fre 12/91   1,050
Hobson, Henry E.   Eng 19C
W/Pa 5x11 Heather Girl Durn 2/92   600
Hoch, Franz Xaver   Ger 1869-1916
O/C 32x34 Village Quietude, Autumn Skn 5/92   1,760
Hoch, Hannah   Ger 1889-1979
W,G&Pl/Pa 12x14 Werdende Ordnung 27 Chr 11/91   34,100
W,G&Gd/Pa 17x19 Mutter und Tochter 33 Chr 11/91   6,600
Hockney, David   Am 1937-
--/Pa 75x86 Fall Pool Two Flat Blues Chr 11/91   418,000
A/C 24x36 Santa Monica Blvd. 1978 Chr 11/91   110,000
Y/Pa 19x24 Curtains with Square Stage 79 Chr 5/92   30,800
Y/Pa 20x13 Landscape 64 Sby 5/92   17,600
Cp&H/Pa 17x14 Portrait of Douglas Cooper 74 Chr 5/92 . .   17,600
I/Pa 14x17 Henry & Eugene 78 Sby 5/92   15,400
C/Pa 30x22 J. Sohn VI 84 Chr 5/92   13,200
I/Pa 12x10 La Plaza Hotel Chr 11/91   13,200
Pe/Pa 15x11 Don Cribb 1976 But 5/92   8,800
W/Pa 24x18 Van Gogh 1979 Sby 6/92   7,040
Hode, Pierre   Fr 1889-1942
  * See 1992 Edition . . . .
Hodel, Ernst   Sws 1881-1955
O/B 22x32 Goats and a Goatherd But 11/91   1,540
O/C 24x33 Snow-Covered Swiss Chalet But 11/91   1,430
Hodgdon, Sylvester Phelps   Am 1830-1906
  * See 1991 Edition . . . .
Hodgin, Marston Dean   Am 1903-
Pe/Pa 24x17 Lost Child Slo 9/91   150
Hodgkin, Howard   Am 1932-
O/Wd 49x56 Interior with Figures Sby 11/91   165,000
O/Wd 22x36 Clean Sheets Sby 11/91   99,000
O/B 36x36 Electric Light 1960 Sby 10/91   66,000
O/Wd 33x78 View Sby 5/92   38,500
Ph&O/B 72x48 Untitled 1984 Sby 10/91   9,900
Hodgson, Thomas Sherlock   Can 1924-
  * See 1991 Edition . . . .
Hodicke, K. H.   20C
  * See 1991 Edition . . . .
Hoeber, Arthur   Am 1854-1915
O/C 17x14 Country Landscape Wes 3/92   1,760
Hoeffler, Adolf   Ger 1825-1898
  * See 1990 Edition . . . .
Hoeniger, Paul   Ger 1865-1924
  * See 1991 Edition . . . .
Hoerman, Carl   Am 1885-1955
O/B 24x26 Faraglioni Rocks, Capri Wes 11/91   220
Hoet, Gerard   Dut 1648-1733
O/Cp 14x17 Diana and Callisto Sby 1/92   41,800
O/C 19x23 The Judgement of Solomon Chr 5/92   2,860
Hofbauer, Ferdinand   Aus 1801-1864
  * See 1991 Edition . . . .
Hofel, Johann Nepomuk   Ger 1786-1864
  * See 1990 Edition . . . .
Hofer, Carl   Ger 1878-1955
  * See 1992 Edition . . . .
Hoff, Margo   Am 1912-
G/Pa 10x12 Vermont Homestead Hnd 5/92   170
Cs/Pa 33x10 Red Kite Hnz 10/91   130
Hoffbauer, Charles   Am 1875-1957
W&C/Pa 12x12 Three Soldiers Resting Chr 11/91   660
W/Pa 11x14 German Prisoners 1911 Chr 11/91   440
C&K/Pa 14x18 Soldiers Marching Chr 11/91   440
Pe/Pa 9x12 Studies Young Woman in a Hat Wlf 3/92   275
O/C 12x9 Italian Garden Wes 5/92   138

Pe/Pa 6x4 Three Drawings Yng 2/92   100
Hoffman, C. A.   20C
W/Pa 10x14 View in Cairo Slo 4/92   350
Hoffman, Frank B.   Am 1888-1958
W&G/Pa 16x30 Bear Rears as Man Prepares Meal Ih 11/91   6,500
O&R/C 27x23 Fisherman with Fly Rod and Creel Ih 5/92 . .   900
Br&W/Pa 15x9 Standing Cowboy Ih 11/91   900
Hoffman, Murray   Am a 1900-1945
O/C 31x42 Petit Casino Skn 11/91   825
Hoffman, Ruth Erb   1902-
O/B 24x20 Arrangement 1950 Yng 4/92   125
Hoffmann, Harry Leslie   Am 1880-
O/C 32x30 Williams River, Vermont Slo 9/91   2,750
Hofman, Hans O.   Am 1893-
O/C 47x59 Merchant Venice: Shylock & Portia Sby 4/92 . . .   2,860
Hofman, J.   Dut 20C
O/B 10x12 Mother and Child Lou 9/91   275
Hofmann, Hans   Am 1880-1966
O/C 60x72 The Ocean 57 Chr 5/92   550,000
O/C 50x40 The Source 62 Sby 5/92   440,000
O/C 40x50 Orange Vase 55 Sby 11/91   181,500
Cs/Pw 25x30 Landscape Sby 11/91   60,500
O/B 23x21 Le Dragon Sby 2/92   49,500
O/C 30x24 Ceremonial Tools 51 Chr 11/91   44,000
Cs/Pw 28x17 Studio Table and Vase II 35 Sby 11/91   41,250
G/Pa 17x24 Untitled Sby 2/92   27,500
O/Pn 14x13 The Chair Chr 2/92   17,600
G,Y&Pl/Pa 14x17 Untitled Chr 5/92   13,200
Y&Pl/Pa 11x14 Provincetown 43 Chr 5/92   12,100
O/Pb 14x11 Zig-Zag 1960 Sby 5/92   9,900
O/Pw/B 13x11 Portrait 43 Sby 5/92   9,350
Pl/Pa/B 14x17 Provincetown 42 Chr 2/92   7,150
Hofner, J.   Ger 19C
O/B 23x18 Girl with Lambs Yng 2/92   1,600
Hofstetter, W. A.   Am 1884-
O/C 23x27 Storm Clouds Fre 12/91   275
Hoguet, Charles   Fr 1821-1870
O/C 21x40 Figures on a Cliff at Etretat Sby 10/91   11,000
Hohl, Frederick C. P.   Am 20C
O/Cb 10x11 Winter Landscape, New England Skn 9/91   82
Hohnberg, Josef Wagner   Con 1811-
  * See 1992 Edition . . . .
Hohnstedt, Peter Lanz   Am 1872-1957
O/C 35x36 Big Bend Country Lou 3/92   2,200
O/B 16x20 Eucalyptus Landscape Mor 6/92   750
O/C 25x30 Texas Landscape Lou 3/92   750
O/C 20x24 Fall Landscape Mor 6/92   500
O/C 8x10 Landscape Lou 12/91   300
Hoin, Claude Jean Baptiste   Fr 1750-1817
  * See 1990 Edition . . . .
Hoit, Albert Gallatin   Am 1809-1856
  * See 1990 Edition . . . .
Holbech, Niels Peter   Dan 1804-1889
  * See 1990 Edition . . . .
Holder, Edward Henry   Br 19C
O/C 16x26 The Cliffs of Dover But 11/91   880
Holdredge, Ransome G.   Am 1836-1899
O/C 30x50 Wasatch Mountains, Bear Lake Chr 6/92   4,400
Holdstock, Alfred Worsley   Can 1820-1901
P/Pa 13x21 River Gatineau C.E.: Pair Sbt 5/92   2,805
P/Pa 11x15 Gatineau River C.W. Sbt 5/92   935
Holfeld, Hippolyte Dominique   Fr 1804-1872
O/C 26x21 La Fillette; Le Garconnet: Pair 1863 Sby 10/91 .   22,550
Holgate, Edwin Headley   Can 1892-1977
Pe&W/Pa 10x8 Nude Study Sbt 11/91   935
C/Pa 15x13 Portrait of Barbara W. '56 Sbt 5/92   935
Holiday, Gilbert   Br 1879-1937
  * See 1991 Edition . . . .
Holiday, Henry   Br 1839-1927
Pe/Pa 18x13 Young Woman Sby 7/92   330
Holings, Clark   Am 20C
  * See 1990 Edition . . . .

Holl, Frank   Br 1845-1888
* See 1991 Edition . . . .
Hollams, F. Mabel   Br 1877-1963
O/Pn 12x16 Beeswax and Dance of Death: Pair Sby 1/92 . . 1,650
Holland, Francis Raymond   Am 20C
* See 1990 Edition . . . .
Holland, James   Br 1799-1870
* See 1992 Edition . . . .
Holland, John   Br 19C
* See 1992 Edition . . . .
Holland, Tom   Am 1936-
A/Fg 35x86 Untitled, #213, 1971 But 5/92 3,300
Holliday, Frank   20C
O/C 72x84 Pop Top 82 Chr 5/92 8,800
Holloway, Edward Stratton   Am 1939-
* See 1992 Edition . . . .
Hollyer, G.   Am 20C
O/C 24x36 Landscape Mor 3/92 175
Hollyer, Maud
W/Pa 28x20 Flower Garden Hnz 10/91 350
Hollyer, W. P.   Br 19C
O/C 30x50 Days Catch Mys 11/91 2,475
Holman, Bill   Am 1903-
PI/Pa 13x19 Comic Strip. "Smokey Stover" 35 lh 5/92 325
Holmes, A. C.   Br 20C
W&G/Pa/L 34x14 Oblivion 1887 Sby 7/92 3,300
Holmes, Dwight C.   Am 1900-
* See 1992 Edition . . . .
Holmes, Philip H.   Am a 1873-1877
O/B 5x8 Lake Scene Brd 8/92 605
Holmes, Ralph William   Am 1876-1963
O/M 24x28 Desert Landscape 1946 Hnz 10/91 900
O/C 16x20 Red Mt. Mine Mor 6/92 700
O/M 18x20 Landscape Mor 11/91 650
O/C 28x32 Still Life--Green Tea Pot Mor 11/91 475
O/B 9x10 Landscape Mor 11/91 450
O/M 16x12 Landscape Mor 6/92 450
Holmes, William Henry   Am 1846-1933
W&G/Pa 14x20 Fishing Vessel Grand Canal 1880 Slo 2/92 . . 1,200
W/Pa 14x20 Hillside View, Summer 1900 Slo 2/92 1,100
W/Pa 8x11 Boats Along the Shore Slo 2/92 250
Holmgren, R. John   Am 1897-1963
G/Pa 15x22 Couple by Gate Seen Through Tree 1947 lh 5/92 225
Holsoe, Carl Vilhelm   Dan 1863-1935
* See 1992 Edition . . . .
Holsoe, Eilsa   Dan 19C
O/Pn 15x11 Still Life of Flowers 1939 Doy 11/91 3,250
Holst, Laurits   Dan 1848-1934
* See 1992 Edition . . . .
Holsteyn, Pieter (II)   Dut 1614-1687
W,PI&Bc/Pa 7x6 Bullfinch on a Branch Chr 1/92 825
Holston, Kate   20C
Pe&C/Pa 11x14 Old Curiosity Shop Slo 2/92 90
Holt, Geoffrey   Am 1882-1977
O/C 36x40 The Canyon Walls 1917 Sby 12/91 1,430
Holty, Carl Robert   Am 1900-1973
O/M 36x42 Untitled Sby 12/91 1,320
O/C 52x38 Johanni Tag Sby 12/91 1,100
Holzer, Jenny   Am 1950-
E/AI 21x23 Selection from the Living Series Chr 2/92 3,850
Holzer, Joseph   Aus 1824-1876
* See 1990 Edition . . . .
Holzlhuber, Franz   Am a 1850-
G&Pe/Pa 17x24 Four: Fort Snelling; Indians Chr 3/92 7,150
G&Pe/Pa 24x17 Five: Miss. River; Union Hotel Chr 3/92 . . . 3,520
G&Pe/Pa 25x17 Three: Lighthouse; Niagara Falls Chr 3/92 . 3,520
W&Pl/Pa 18x25 Four: Frame House; Boathouse Chr 3/92 . . 3,300
G&Pe/Pa 17x24 Five: Teepee Frames; Indian Burial Chr 3/92 3,080
G&Pe/Pa 17x24 Four: On a Ship; Harbor View Chr 3/92 . . . 3,080
G&Pe/Pa 24x17 Four: Railroad Bridge; Log Houses Chr 3/92 3,080
G&Pe/Pa 17x25 Four: Rifleman; Sailors Chr 3/92 3,080
G&Pe/Pa 17x24 Four: State House; Restaurant Chr 3/92 . . . 3,080
G&Pe/Pa 18x25 3: Steamboat Ocean; Slave Trade Chr 3/92 2,860
Homer, Winslow   Am 1836-1910
O/C 22x29 The Backrush Sby 5/92 . . . . 1.1M

O/Pn 6x10 Three Boys in a Dory 1873 Chr 5/92 935,000
W/Pa 10x13 Young Woman w/Parasol 1880 Sby 5/92 . . . 550,000
W&Pe/Pa 10x13 Girls Strolling in Orchard '79 Chr 12/91 . 110,000
Pe&W/Pa 7x13 Girls on Pebbly Beach Sby 9/91 22,000
H/Pa 4x5 Two Figures with Kegs Sby 12/91 3,575
Honda, Hiroshi   Am 20C
W/S/C 30x40 Birds in Flowering Tree Slo 2/92 350
Honegger, Gottfried   20C
O/Pn 29x29 Tableau-Relief 1962 Sby 10/91 4,400
Honigsberg, Michael   Am 20C
P/Pa 16x11 Nude Wlf 10/91 100
Hook, Richard
G/Pa 24x18 Santa Arriving at Front Door 49 lh 11/91 350
Hooper, Alfred
W/Pa 10x14 Lake St. Charles, Lower Canada Eld 4/92 66
Hooper, John Horace   Br 19C
O/C 40x60 Sunset Near Somshall, Surrey Sby 1/92 3,520
O/C 16x24 Fisherman by a Stream Sby 1/92 1,430
Hope, Thomas H.   Am -1926
* See 1991 Edition . . . .
Hopkin, Robert   Am 1832-1909
O/C 18x24 Sailboat in Water Dum 5/92 1,600
O/C 18x24 Lake Erie Dum 12/91 1,100
W/Pa 14x23 Beached Dinghies Dum 5/92 750
O/C 10x8 Sailboat Anchoring Dum 5/92 700
W/Pa/C 18x24 Small Harbor Village Dum 5/92 600
O/C 18x24 Interior Foundry Scene Dum 2/92 550
W/Pa 12x21 Rocky Shoreline '05 Dum 1/92 550
O/Pn 16x12 Tri-Masted Ship in Stormy Seas Dum 5/92 . . . 550
W/Pa Size? Sailboat on Stormy Sea Dum 5/92 500
O/Pn 6x12 Ship at Sea Dum 5/92 400
O/C/M 7x21 Landscape with Shored Boat Dum 7/92 375
Hopkins, Arthur   Eng 1848-1930
W/Pa 23x32 The Genius of the Village Chr 2/92 7,150
Hopkins, Budd   Am 1931-
O/C 47x36 Blue Night Song 1957 Sby 10/91 1,650
O/C 85x50 Strike Blue II '66 Hnd 5/92 200
Hopkins, Peter   Am 1911-
* See 1992 Edition . . . .
Hopkins, Robert   Am 20C
* See 1992 Edition . . . .
Hopkinson, Charles Sydney   Am 1869-1962
W,G&H/Pa 12x21 Rocks in Late Sunlight Skn 3/92 385
Hopper, Edward   Am 1882-1967
W/Pa 12x18 The Yellow House Chr 9/91 220,000
W&Pe/Pa 14x20 Farmhouse at Essex, MA Chr 5/92 130,000
W/Pa 4x9 South Truro Church Sby 9/91 30,800
Hoppner, Sir John   Br 1758-1810
O/C 31x25 Portrait Mrs. Sophia Fielding 1787 Sby 1/92 . . . 79,750
O/C 35x27 Portrait Sir Henry Goodricke, Bart Sby 1/92 . . . 16,500
Horacio   Mex 1912-1972
O/C 24x18 Nino con uniforme militar Chr 5/92 9,350
O/C 24x18 Nina con Bandeja de Frutas Chr 5/92 7,150
O/C 19x15 Retrato De La Nina Maria Sby 11/91 6,050
O/C 24x18 Nina con Rosas Chr 5/92 5,500
O/C 24x18 Young Girl with Cat Sby 10/91 4,675
O/C 24x18 Nina con nido Chr 5/92 4,400
O/C 24x18 Girl With a Rose But 11/91 3,300
Horemans, Jan J. (the Younger)   1714-1790
O/C 34x25 A Fete Champetre 1756 Chr 10/91 7,150
Horemans, Jan Josef   Flm 1682-1759
* See 1991 Edition . . . .
Horlor, George W.   Br a 1849-1891
O/C 16x22 Companions 1882 Chr 10/91 14,300
Hornberger, Don   Am 20C
O/B 7x9 Barn in Golden Landscape Fre 12/91 60
Hornel, Edward Atkinson   Br 1864-1933
* See 1992 Edition . . . .
Horowitz, Leopold   Hun 1838-1917
O/Pn 9x12 Studying the Talmud 1887 Sby 7/92 2,860
Horschelt, Theodore   Ger 1829-1871
* See 1990 Edition . . . .

Horsley, John Calcott Br 1817-1903
  * See 1992 Edition ....
Horst, Gerrit Willemsz. Dut 1612-1652
  * See 1992 Edition ....
Horter, Earl Am 1881-1940
  W/Pa 17x22 Still Life Cherries Apple Pear '39 Sby 12/91 . . 7,700
Horton, William Samuel Am 1865-1936
  O/B 25x30 On the Sands, Broadstairs Chr 12/91 104,500
  O/C 25x30 Beach in the Sun 1914 Chr 5/92 38,500
  O/C 25x31 La Plage a Whitby 1913 Sby 5/92 30,800
  O/B 25x30 Arc de Triomphe Chr 12/91 12,100
  P/Pa 19x25 Mountainside Village, Night Hnd 5/92 1,000
Horvath, Ferdinand H. Am 1891-
  O/C 30x24 Music and Wine Fre 10/91 325
Horvath, H.
  O/C 20x16 Elderly Man Dum 2/92 35
Hoschede-Monet, Blanche Fr 1865-1947
  * See 1990 Edition ....
Hosiasson, Phillipe Fr 1898-1978
  * See 1992 Edition ....
Hoskins, Gayle Porter Am 1887-1962
  O/C 39x27 City Slickers Chr 9/91 3,300
Hosner, Bill
  P&W/Pa 23x15 Pontchartrain Interior Dum 1/92 1,300
Hotchkis, A. M. Eng 20C
  W&G/Pa 22x14 Abbot's Tombs, China Slo 7/92 110
Houben, Henri Bel a 1885-1898
  O/C 22x27 The Toy Sailboat But 11/91 4,400
Housser, Yvonne McKague Can 1898-
  O/C 27x35 Skating by the Factory Sbt 5/92 10,285
Houston, Georges Br 1869-1947
  O/C 28x36 By the Waterfall Sby 2/92 6,875
Hovenden, Thomas Am 1840-1895
  Pe/Pa 11x8 Sketch Girl's Head Wes 11/91 348
How, Kenneth G. Am 1883-
  O/Cb 12x16 At Portsmouth Skn 9/91 330
Howard, Bertram K. Am 1872-
  O/C 26x34 Mountain Brook, Winter 1910 Skn 5/92 3,025
Howard, Clara Frances Am -1938
  W/Pa 5x4 Still Life Hnd 6/92 50
Howard, Hugh Huntington Am 1860-1927
  O/B 11x14 Landscape Lou 9/91 275
Howard, James C. Eng 20C
  O/C 16x20 Richmond, Yorkshire 1948 Slo 9/91 225
Howard, Josephine
  O/C 14x8 Grape Still Life Hnz 10/91 650
Howard, M. Maitland Br 20C
  * See 1992 Edition ....
Howard, Marion P. Am 1883-
  W&G/Pa 4x5 Four New Hampshire Scenes 1955 Skn 9/91 . . 165
Howard, W. Am 20C
  O/Pn 21x15 Outdoor Cafe Fre 4/92 150
Howe, William Henry Am 1846-1929
  O/Wd 12x16 Holstein Bull 1891 1891 Eld 7/92 770
  O/B 7x10 Cattle, Fishing Boats 1910 Skn 11/91 522
  O/Pn 11x14 Landscape with Irrigation Ditch 1884 Sel 12/91 . 150
Howell, Felicie Waldo Am 1897-1968
  * See 1992 Edition ....
Howes, Kenneth Br 1924-
  * See 1992 Edition ....
Howitt, William Samuel Br 1765-1822
  * See 1992 Edition ....
Howland, Alfred Cornelius Am 1838-1909
  O/Pn 12x14 Plantation Cabins Lou 6/92 1,750
Howland, John Dare Am 1843-1914
  O/B 15x20 Bison on the Range Chr 3/92 4,400
Hoyland, John Br 1934-
  * See 1992 Edition ....
Hoyos, Ana Mercedes Col 1942-
  A/C 20x95 Patilla 90 Chr 11/91 26,400
  O/C 39x39 Zeni Chr 11/91 15,400
Hoyt, Edith Am 1894-
  * See 1990 Edition ....
Hozendorf, Johann-Samuel 1694-1742
  O/C 30x40 Christ on the Road to Emmaus Chr 10/91 14,300

Hsu, Ti-Shan 20C
  A&MM/Wd 60x60 R.E.M. Sby 10/91 8,250
Hubacek, William Am 1866-1958
  O/C 20x24 Roses '92 But 6/92 1,320
Hubbard, Charles Daniel Am 20C
  O/B 10x13 Coastal View Brd 5/92 358
  O/B 6x9 Summer Sky Brd 5/92 33
Hubbard, Harlan
  * See 1992 Edition ....
Hubbard, L. M. B. Am 20C
  O/C 16x22 Grape Still Life Mys 6/92 825
  W/Pa 15x21 Still Life Mys 11/91 275
Hubbard, Richard William Am 1816-1888
  * See 1991 Edition ....
Hubbard, Whitney Myron Am 1875-
  O/B 9x7 In the Garden Wes 5/92 660
Hubbell, Henry Salem Am 1870-1949
  O/C 35x25 Morning But 4/92 3,025
  O/C 70x37 "Moenippus", After Velasquez 1901 Wes 3/92 . . 990
Huber, Leon Charles Fr 1858-1928
  * See 1990 Edition ....
Hudson, Charles W. Am 1871-1943
  W/Pa 9x20 Southern River/Seaside Eld 7/92 275
Hudson, Eric Am 1864-1932
  O/C 28x34 Seining off the Maine Coast Brd 5/92 5,775
  O/C 16x18 Monhegan Harbor Brd 8/92 3,520
Hudson, Gary Am 20C
  A/C 72x108 Hossu '70 Hnd 5/92 100
Hudson, Grace Carpenter Am 1865-1937
  O/B 6x8 Chi-Do-Mit 1904 But 10/91 11,000
Hudson, Henry John Br 1881-1910
  * See 1991 Edition ....
Hudson, John Bradley Am 1832-1903
  O/B 5x9 Bridge in Winter Brd 8/92 1,760
  O/B 5x9 Winter Shore, Portland Harbor Brd 8/92 1,540
  O/B 5x9 Brickyard Brd 8/92 990
  W/Pa 8x10 Artist in His Studio Brd 8/92 880
  W/Pa 10x20 Spring Landscape 1890 Brd 8/92 770
Hudson, Thomas Br 1701-1779
  O/C 30x24 At Full Sail Brd 8/92 632
Hudson, Thomas Bradford Am 20C
  * See 1991 Edition ....
Huens, Jean L. Am 1921-
  A/C 8x8 Dobermans and Man on Crutches Ih 11/91 700
Huet, Christophe Fr a 1735-1759
  O/C 120x53 La Boisson Chaude, Froide: Four Sby 1/92 . 165,000
Huet, Ernestine Am 19C
  * See 1991 Edition ....
Huet, Jean Baptiste Fr 1745-1811
  O/C 39x51 Rooster Defending His Brood Chr 1/92 17,600
  O/C 25x60 Pastoral Scene with Shepherd Sby 1/92 14,300
Hufnagel, John Am -1940
  W/Pa 16x12 Cleveland's Terminal Tower Wlf 6/92 200
Huggins, William John Br 1820-1884
  O/C 9 dia Head of a Tiger 1872 Sby 6/92 5,500
Hughes, Daisy Marguerite Am 1883-1968
  O/C 30x25 Flower Study But 10/91 880
Hughes, Edward John Can 1913-
  O/C 38x48 Post Office at Courtenay, B.C. 1949 Sbt 11/91 . 74,800
  O/C 25x30 Farm Scene, Chilliwack, B.C. 1961 Sbt 5/92 . . 16,830
Hughes, Edward Robert Br 1851-1914
  * See 1991 Edition ....
Hughes, Edwin Br 1851-1904
  O/C 27x22 After You...No, After You! 1891 But 5/92 3,025
Hughes, George H. Can a 1832-1861
  * See 1992 Edition ....
Hughes, Talbot Br 1869-1942
  * See 1992 Edition ....
Hughes, W.
  O/C 24x36 Winter Harbour Scene Sel 9/91 190
Hughes, William 20C
  O/C 60x96 Untitled 1985 Chr 11/91 55
Hughes, William Br 1842-1901
  O/C 14x18 Pair of Still Lifes with Fruit 1872 Hnd 5/92 3,400
  O/B 14x18 Plums on a Mossy Bank 1866 Chr 5/92 2,420

O/C 6x8 Pair Still Lifes of Fruit Slo 10/91 1,700

Hughto, Daryl   Am 1943-
A/C 75x56 Monkey Shines 78 Chr 5/92 770

Hugo, F.   Am 19C
O/C 29x48 American Scene Wlf 6/92 3,000

Hugo, Jean   Fr 1894-
G/Pa 2x4 Six Drawings Chr 5/92 7,150

Huguet, Victor Pierre   Fr 1835-1902
  * See 1992 Edition ....

Huilliot, Pierre-Nicolas   Fr 1674-1751
  * See 1992 Edition ....

Hulbert, Katherine Allmond   Am -1937
O/C 30x25 Still Life Chrysanthemums Skn 9/91 1,540
O/C 9x13 Small Lake Dum 12/91 200

Huldah   20C
O/B 16x20 Flowers in a Bowl Yng 4/92 600

Hulings, Clark   Am 1922-
  * See 1990 Edition ....

Hulk, Abraham (Jr.)   Eng 1851-1922
  * See 1992 Edition ....

Hulk, Abraham (Sr.)   Dut 1813-1897
O/C 22x34 Fishing Vessels Sby 10/91 13,200
O/Pn 9x12 Coming Ashore Sby 2/92 11,000
O/C 8x12 Shipping in an Estuary Chr 2/92 3,850

Hulk, Johannes Frederik   Dut 1829-1911
O/Pn 13x16 Preparing the Boat Sby 10/91 9,900

Hulk, John Frederick   Dut 1855-1913
  * See 1991 Edition ....

Hulme, Frederick William   Br 1816-1884
  * See 1991 Edition ....

Hulsman, L.   Am 20C
O/C 10x14 Country Cabins by Moonlight 1911 Hnd 6/92 ... 160

Humblot, George   Fr 20C
  * See 1992 Edition ....

Humblot, Robert   Fr 1907-1962
  * See 1992 Edition ....

Humborg, Adolf   Aus 1847-
O/C 33x48 Neuer Wein! Sby 5/92 38,500
O/C 28x43 Contributions to The Convent 87 Hnd 3/92 8,500

Humma, J. R.   Am 19C
O/C 19x16 Portrait of a Young Man Wlf 10/91 50

Humphrey, David   1955-
O/C 50x40 Dionysis 1985 Chr 11/91 2,200
O/C 66x84 Medieval Garden 1985 Chr 5/92 1,980
O/C 48x62 Portrait of a Romantic '85 Chr 2/92 1,650

Humphrey, Jack Weldon   Can 1901-1967
O/C 20x24 Apples in Comport Sbt 5/92 4,675

Humphrey, Ralph   Am 1932-1990
A/Wd/Pa 20x26 Caboose 80 Chr 11/91 7,150
Cs/Wd 14x14 Cloud 1983 Chr 11/91 5,500
A/C 60x120 Untitled Sby 10/91 5,500
O/C 71x49 Semana Santa 1957 Chr 11/91 2,860

Humphrey, Walter Beach   Am 1892-
  * See 1992 Edition ....

Hundertwasser, Friedensreich   20C
MM/Ju&C 21x28 Versaurnter Fruhling 1966 Sby 2/92 74,250

Hunnemann, A.   Ger 20C
O/C 28x32 Riverscape Fre 4/92 400

Hunt, Bryan   Am 1947-
H&MM/Pa 28x72 Limn II 79 Sby 5/92 19,800
Wx,Os&H/Pa 91x42 Untitled 87 Chr 11/91 11,000
MM/Pa 15x11 Two Drawings 84 Chr 11/91 7,150

Hunt, Charles   Br 1803-1877
O/C 25x30 Puppy's Mealtime 84 Chr 5/92 7,150

Hunt, Charles D.   Am 1840-1914
W/Pa 12x10 Great South Bay, L.I. Eld 7/92 248

Hunt, E.
O/C 10x8 Rooster and Hens Yng 4/92 175

Hunt, Edgar   Br 1876-1953
  * See 1992 Edition ....

Hunt, Edward Aubrey   Br 1855-1922
O/C 41x51 Sunlit Spanish Coastal Scene Sel 4/92 6,500

Hunt, Esther Anna   Am 1885-1951
O/B 15x20 Children in Chinatown But 10/91 1,430

Hunt, Lynn Bogue   Am 1878-1960
  * See 1992 Edition ....

Hunt, Thomas L.   Am 1882-1938
O/C 28x30 Fishing Boats But 10/91 16,500
O/C 25x30 Boats in a Harbor But 6/92 11,000
O/Pa 8x10 Ships in the Harbor: Pair Sby 4/92 3,080
O/Pa 8x10 Winter Landscape But 10/91 2,475
W/Pa 7x10 Cottage in Landscape 1919 Mor 6/92 275
O/C/B 16x20 Seagulls Over Stormy Seas 19() Slo 7/92 275

Hunt, Walter   Br 1861-1941
  * See 1992 Edition ....

Hunt, William Holman   Br 1827-1910
  * See 1991 Edition ....

Hunt, William Morris   Am 1824-1879
O/C 25x39 Summer Twilight Skn 5/92 19,800
O/B 17x12 The Cabbage Garden Chr 11/91 2,200
O/C 10x16 Amesbury 1875 Skn 5/92 1,870
C/Pa 16x11 Open Door Yng 4/92 600

Hunten, Emil   Ger 1827-1902
  * See 1992 Edition ....

Hunter, Clementine   Am 1887-1988
O/B 24x16 Washday Lou 3/92 900
O/B 8x10 Washday Lou 6/92 400

Hunter, Colin   Br 1841-1904
O/C 17x24 Fishing Boats Anchoring Chr 10/91 990

Hunter, Frances Tipton   Am 1896-1957
Cp&W/Pa 11x9 Boy's Clothes Don't Fit Ih 5/92 600

Hunter, Frederick Leo   Am 1862-1943
O/C 16x22 Glories of the Seas 1929 Skn 11/91 550

Hunter, George Leslie   Br 1877-1931
  * See 1992 Edition ....

Hunter, H. M.   Am 20C
O/C 20x32 Ships in Port 1904 Fre 4/92 275

Hunter, Isabel   Am 1878-1941
O/C 26x20 Two Ships But 2/92 3,575

Hunter, Philippa   Can 1928-
  * See 1992 Edition ....

Hunter, Robert   18C
O/C 30x25 Portrait of a Gentleman Sby 1/92 1,320

Huntington, Chris   Am 20C
O/B 16x20 Monhegan 1969 1969 Brd 8/92 962

Huntington, Daniel   Am 1816-1906
O/C 25x30 2nd Church in Jamestown Chr 12/91 26,400

Huntington, Dwight W.   Am 19C
  * See 1990 Edition ....

Huot, Charles Edouard   Can 1855-1930
  * See 1991 Edition ....

Hupe, Martial   Fr 19C
  * See 1991 Edition ....

Hurd, Michael   Am 20C
  * See 1992 Edition ....

Hurd, Peter   Am 1904-1984
T/M 25x43 Rain on the Desert Sby 9/91 12,100
W/Pa 22x27 El Ensayo Dum 1/92 4,000
I/Pa 10x14 Rodeo in the Mountains 1931 Skn 11/91 880
W/Pa 7x9 Fighting Plane Ald 3/92 500

Hurdle, A.   20C
O/Pn 14x18 Fishing Boat in River Landscape Slo 7/92 200

Hurt, Louis B.   Br 1856-1929
O/C 24x40 Glen Shiel Ross Skir Sby 10/91 15,400
O/C 24x36 Highland Castle Near Glencoe Hnz 5/92 6,000

Huszar, Vilmos
O/C 14x18 Still Life Pitcher and Bottles Sby 10/91 3,025

Hutchens, Frank Townsend   Am 1869-1937
O/C 21x30 Woman in an Interior But 4/92 11,000
O/B 30x36 A Cottage, Summer Sby 3/92 6,600
O/C 8x13 Le Rappel Des Glaneuses Wes 11/91 880
O/C 20x24 Portrait; Lake George (2) Ald 5/92 600

Hutchins, Will   Am 1878-
W/Pa 9x13 Italian Alps Slo 7/92 200

Hutchinson, Robert Gemmell   Br 1855-1936
O/C 18x14 Smelling the Rose Sby 10/91 11,000
O/C 24x20 An After Dinner Nap Chr 5/92 4,950

Hutty, Alfred   Am 1878-1954
O/C 32x40 Winter In Woodstock, New York Skn 9/91 2,750
O/C 16x20 Sunlit Snow Wtf 9/91 1,550
Huygen
O/C 24x36 Dutch Harbor Scene Ald 5/92 55
Huygens, Adriaen   Flm 1880-1941
O/Pn 10x8 Still Life with Shrimp Lou 6/92 450
Huygens, Francois Joseph   Bel 1820-1876
* See 1992 Edition . . . .
Huys, Modeste   Bel 1875-1932
* See 1992 Edition . . . .
Huysmans, Jan Baptist   Flm 1654-1716
* See 1992 Edition . . . .
Hyates, R.   20C
W/Pa 9x14 Farmhouse in Pastoral Landscape Slo 2/92 75
Hyde, Helen   Am 1868-1919
Y/Pa 8x10 Blue Mash House, Jalapa 1912 Hnd 3/92 400
Hyde, William Henry   Am 1858-1943
* See 1992 Edition . . . .
Hynd, Frederick S.   Am 1905-1964
O/B 10x16 Beach Scene Brd 5/92 880
W/Pa 19x25 Rocky Point 40 Brd 5/92 468
O/B 12x16 Monhegan Headland Brd 5/92 220
Hyneman, Herman N.   Am 1859-1907
O/C 12x9 Profile of a Woman Sel 9/91 200
Hyppolite, Hector   Hai 1889-1948
O&Pe/B 30x24 Le President Florvil Hyppolite Chr 5/92 . . . 74,800
O/M 30x23 Monument Dumarsais Estime Chr 5/92 49,500
O/B 22x28 La Dame En Vert Sby 11/91 38,500
O/B 12x28 Corn e Dannie Chr 5/92 26,400
O/M 38x28 Ange St. Francis en Priere Chr 5/92 22,000
O/B 19x26 La Cueilleuse De Fleurs Sby 11/91 22,000
O/M 24x24 Hogoun Chango Chr 11/91 16,500
Iacovleff, Alexandre   Rus 1887-1938
O/C 61x36 Bathers 1929 Sby 2/92 10,450
Y/Pa 29x20 Nude Study of Madame Suliekin Sby 2/92 4,400
G/Pa 22x32 Semiramis: Design for Curtain 1934 Sby 6/92 . 2,200
G/B 22x28 Les Courtisanes Chr 11/91 1,650
K/Pa 12x9 Study of Elephants 1938 Sby 2/92 1,320
Ianelli, Arcangelo   Brz 1922-
* See 1992 Edition . . . .
Ibanez, Manuel Ramirez   Spa 1856-1925
O/C 17x13 Feeding the Doves 81 Sby 10/91 7,700
Ibbetson, Julius Caesar   Eng 1759-1817
O/C 24x38 Extensive River Landscape Chr 10/91 12,100
O/C 9x12 Fish Monger's Cart Chr 10/91 3,300
Icart, Louis   Fr 1880-1950
* See 1991 Edition . . . .
Icaza, Ernesto   Mex 1866-1935
O/C 24x38 Charreando en el Rancho 1900 Sby 5/92 66,000
O/C 38x24 Don Juan Zaldivar en Rancho 1900 Sby 5/92 . . 66,000
Igler, Gustav   Hun 1842-
* See 1992 Edition . . . .
Il Bagnacavallo   It 1484-1542
O/Pn 26x18 Madonna and Child Sby 10/91 18,700
Il Bolognese   It 1606-1680
* See 1992 Edition . . . .
Il C. Tempesta   It 1637-1701
* See 1990 Edition . . . .
Il Canaletto   It 1697-1768
* See 1992 Edition . . . .
Il Cavaliere Calabrese   It 1613-1699
O/C 73x100 Boethius and Philosophy Sby 5/92 506,500
Il Cecco Bravo   It 1601-1661
* See 1992 Edition . . . .
Il Cigoli   It 1559-1613
* See 1991 Edition . . . .
Il Cosci   It 1560-1631
O/Cp 4x10 The First Passover Seder Sby 1/92 33,000
Il Fiammenghino   It 1575-1640
* See 1992 Edition . . . .
Il Francia   It 1450-1517
* See 1990 Edition . . . .
Il Gaetano   It 1549-1598
* See 1990 Edition . . . .

Il Garofalo   It 16C
* See 1991 Edition . . . .
Il Genovese   It 1545-1639
G&Gd/V/B 18x14 Adoration of the Kings 1613 Sby 1/92 . . 71,500
Il Giovane, Palma   It 1544-1628
* See 1992 Edition . . . .
Il Guercino   It a 1591-1666
* See 1991 Edition . . . .
Il Lissandro   It 1667-1749
O/C 25x19 Self-Portrait Sby 1/92 22,000
Il Lucchese   It 1605-1675
O/C 41x45 Judith with the Head of Holofernes Chr 5/92 . . 13,200
Il Maltese   It a 1650-1680
O/C 36x50 Still Life Sweetmeats in Gilt Dish Sby 1/92 . . . 42,900
Il Mascacotta   It 1663-1714
O/C 14x18 Figures Among Roman Ruins Sby 10/91 44,000
Il Mecarino   It 1486-1551
O/Pn 35 dia Holy Family with Infant St. John Chr 5/92 . . 308,000
Il Mercanti   It 1657-1734
* See 1992 Edition . . . .
Il Poppi   It 1544-1597
* See 1992 Edition . . . .
Il Portoghese   It 17C
* See 1990 Edition . . . .
Il Sassoferrato   It 1609-1685
* See 1992 Edition . . . .
Il Semolei   It 1510-1580
* See 1992 Edition . . . .
Il Tempesta   It 1637-1701
* See 1992 Edition . . . .
Il Tintoretto (Domenico)   It 1560-1635
O/C 57x42 An Allegory of Prudence Chr 5/92 55,000
Il Tintoretto (Jacopo)   It 1518-1594
O/C 46x41 The Toilet of Venus Chr 5/92 187,000
Il Veronese   It 1528-1588
O/C 46x33 Saint Catherine of Alexandria Chr 1/92 440,000
O/C 20x16 Young Man, Bust Length Chr 5/92 176,000
Il Viterbese   It 1610-1662
O/C 27 dia Angelica and Medoro Chr 1/92 44,000
Illies, Arthur   Ger 1870-1952
O/C 44x81 Swans 1904 Hnd 10/91 10,000
Ilsted, Peter Vilhelm   Dan 1861-1933
* See 1990 Edition . . . .
Imai, Toshimitsu   Fr 1926-
* See 1992 Edition . . . .
Imhoff, Joseph A.   Am 1871-1955
O/C 16x20 Pueblo But 11/91 3,025
O/C 24x30 Indian Tending Fire But 11/91 2,200
G/Pa 24x19 Indian With a Red Blanket But 11/91 2,200
Immendorf, Jorg   1945-
O/L 40x134 Futurologe Sby 5/92 17,600
W&I/Pa 11x9 Untitled 86 Sby 10/91 660
Imparato, Girolamo   It a 1573-1621
* See 1992 Edition . . . .
Indiana, Robert   Am 1928-
O/C 60x60 Love 74 Chr 5/92 44,000
O/C 12x12 Love Chr 5/92 41,800
Indoni, Filippo   It 19C
W/Pa/B 22x19 Flirtation at the Well Sby 1/92 4,400
W&G/Pa 22x15 Courtship in the Roman Campagna Chr 2/92 1,870
Induno, Domenico   It 1815-1878
* See 1991 Edition . . . .
Induno, Girolamo   It 1827-1890
O/C 33x48 Una Partita a Scacchi Sby 10/91 77,000
Ingalls, M. S.   Am 19C
O/B 9x14 Still Life with Fruit Wlf 10/91 50
Ingeborg   20C
O/C 20x24 Japanese Figure Yng 4/92 225
Ingelrans, Paul-Leon-Henri   Fr a 1893-1920
O/C 33x24 Artist and His Model 1893 But 11/91 13,200
Ingham, Elizabeth H.   Am 20C
* See 1992 Edition . . . .

Ingres, Jean Auguste Dominique Fr 1780-1867
Pe/Pa 8x6 Architect Charles Norry Sby 10/91 71,500
Inman, Henry Am 1801-1846
* See 1992 Edition ....
Inman, John O'Brien Am 1828-1896
O/B 11x9 Peonies and Lilacs in a Vase Chr 11/91 3,300
O/C 15x22 An Artist's Vanitas 1883 Sby 4/92 605
Innerst, Mark Am 1957-
A/Pn 20x16 Prewar Luxury 1989 Chr 11/91 27,500
A/Cb 11x13 Cherries (Blue) Chr 11/91 11,000
A/Cb 9x11 Cherries (White) Chr 11/91 11,000
A&C/Pa 10x7 Blue Pocket Watch Chr 5/92 7,700
MM/Pa 20x30 Study for Two Ships 1983 Chr 2/92 7,700
A&H/Pa 14x10 Signs on Buildings 1990 Chr 5/92 6,600
Innes, Alice Amelia Can 1890-1970
O/Pn 10x14 Hills at Burks Falls Sbt 11/91 1,309
Inness, George Am 1825-1894
O/Pn 16x26 Montclair Evening 1876 Sby 12/91 99,000
O/C 40x30 Gathering Clouds 1890 Chr 5/92 52,800
O/C 20x30 Twilight 1875 Sby 3/92 49,500
O/C 30x45 Montclair Sby 12/91 22,000
O/Pn 27x22 Woods at Montclair 1889 Sby 9/91 39,600
O/C/B 14x22 A View of the Homestead Chr 9/91 15,400
O/Pn 10x13 Monastery of Albano Sby 3/92 14,850
Inness, George (Jr.) Am 1853-1926
O/C 12x18 Angler in Pastoral Landscape Doy 12/91 ... 6,250
O/B 41x46 Forest Stream 1925 Doy 12/91 4,000
O/Pn 14x20 Early Evening by a Cottage Doy 12/91 1,600
R&O/C/B 10x16 Leading a Cow Yng 4/92 900
Innocenti, Camilio It 1871-1961
* See 1991 Edition ....
Innocenti, Guglielmo It 19C
* See 1990 Edition ....
Insley, Albert Babb Am 1842-1937
O/C 14x20 Road at Sunset Yng 4/92 2,000
O/C 12x18 Porcupine Island off Bar Harbor Chr 6/92 990
O/C 12x18 Stream by the Woods Chr 6/92 715
O/C 11x10 Woodland Stream Skn 5/92 275
O/C 15x11 Late November Ald 5/92 240
Inukai, Kyohei Am 1934-
O/C 24x30 Blue Waters Chr 3/92 6,600
Ipousteguy, Jean 20C
O&L/B 29x24 Tete 58 Sby 2/92 1,650
Ipsen, Ernest Ludwig Am 1869-1934
* See 1990 Edition ....
Iriarte Spa 1621-1685
* See 1991 Edition ....
Irolli, Vincenzo It 1860-1942
O/C 26x19 Returning from the Grove Chr 10/91 110,000
O/C 21x20 The Grape Harvest Chr 5/92 30,800
O/C 17x10 Nursing Mother Dum 11/91 3,750
Irvine, Wilson Henry Am 1869-1936
O/B 12x16 Monhegan Coast Chr 9/91 4,400
O/C 24x27 Wooded Lake in Spring Chr 11/91 3,520
O/B 24x27 Landscape with Pond Hnd 5/92 3,000
O/B 8x10 Boats Hnz 10/91 425
Irwin, Robert 20C
A/Pls 48 dia Untitled Sby 11/91 66,000
A/Al 46 dia Untitled Sby 2/92 41,250
Isabey, Louis Gabriel Eugene Fr 1803-1886
O/C/B 28x40 The Approaching Storm 64 Chr 2/92 26,400
O/C 16x21 Fisherman's Family Chr 5/92 4,620
O/C 28x36 Floundering Ship, Survivors 42 Hnd 5/92 ... 4,600
O/C 39x29 Cabestan sur le Rivage Sel 4/92 3,000
G/Pa 5x9 Ship Tossed at Sea Sby 1/92 2,970
Isembert, Emile Fr 1846-1921
* See 1990 Edition ....
Isenberger, Eric Am 1902-
* See 1992 Edition ....
Isenbrant, Adriaen Flm a 1510-1551
* See 1992 Edition ....
Isham, Samuel Am 1855-1914
O/C 40x32 The Marquise of Carabas 96 Sby 4/92 1,430

Iskowitz, Gershon Can 1921-1988
O/C 44x38 Autumn H 1978 Sbt 5/92 .... 13,20■
Isolda Brz 1924-
* See 1992 Edition ....
Israel, Daniel Aus 1859-1901
* See 1992 Edition ....
Israel, Marvin
O&S/Pa 42x35 Untitled Sby 2/92 .... 33■
Israels, Isaac Dut 1865-1934
* See 1991 Edition ....
Israels, Josef Dut 1824-1911
O/C 24x21 Children at the Seaside Sby 5/92 .... 44,00■
O/C 17x23 Woman in Cottage by Fireside But 5/92 .... 6,05■
O/Pn 10x7 Woman Sewing by a Window Chr 5/92 .... 4,62■
Medium? 11x10 Self-Portrait Before the Easel Hnz 10/91 ... 47■
Israels, R. Am 20C
O/B 16x20 Abstract Landscape But 11/91 .... 1,10■
Issupoff, Alessio Rus 1889-1957
O/Cb 20x24 The Stallion Sby 10/91 .... 14,30■
Itami, Michi 20C
* See 1991 Edition ....
Itaya, Foussa Fr 1919-
O/C 11x9 Veiled Woman with Spaniel But 11/91 ...... 1,65■
O/C 29x36 La Cite 1960 Sby 2/92 .... 1,32■
O/Pn 10x8 Young Girl Hnz 5/92 .... 55■
Iturria, Ignacio Uru 1949-
O/C 51x64 Mesa 88 Chr 5/92 .... 13,20■
A/C 47x40 Sin Titulo 88 Chr 11/91 .... 12,10■
Iverd, Eugene Am 1893-1938
O/C 36x23 The Pause that Refreshes Skn 3/92 .... 3,19■
Ives, H. S. 20C
* See 1991 Edition ....
Ives, Percy Am 1864-1928
O/C 29x21 Call of the Druid Maiden 1887 Dum 6/92 ... 2,50■
Iwill, Joseph Fr 1850-1923
* See 1992 Edition ....
Izquierdo, Maria Mex 1906-1950
G/Pa 13x11 Paisaje 47 Sby 11/91 .... 22,00■
Jackman, Oscar Theodore Am 1878-1940
* See 1992 Edition ....
Jackman, Reva Am 1892-
* See 1991 Edition ....
Jackman, Theodore Am 20C
* See 1992 Edition ....
Jackson Am 20C
O/C 24x32 Boating on the River Mys 6/92 .... 49■
Jackson, Alexander Young Can 1882-1974
O/C 20x26 Ferme en Hiver, Kamouraska Sbt 5/92 .... 42,07■
O/Pn 9x11 Street in Hull, Quebec 1928 Sbt 5/92 .... 15,89■
O/Pn 9x11 Winter, Baie St. Paul Sbt 5/92 .... 11,22■
O/Pn 11x14 Devil's Wrehse, Lake Superior 1965 Sbt 11/91 . 5,61■
O/Pn 10x13 South Pine 1956 Sbt 11/91 .... 5,61■
O/Pn 10x13 Beside the River Sbt 5/92 .... 4,67■
O/Pn 10x13 Abandoned Con Smelters Camp 1949 Sbt 5/92 . 4,20■
O/Pn 10x13 Opeongo Lake, Algonquin 1967 Sbt 11/91 .... 3,27■
Pe/Pa 9x12 Landscape Sketch Sbt 5/92 .... 74■
Jackson, Elbert McGran Am 1896-1962
O/C 28x20 Stealing the Funnies Ih 11/91 .... 2,75■
O/C 29x23 Sailor Painting Life Preserver 1930 Ih 5/92 .... 2,25■
Jackson, James Randolph Aut 1886-1975
O/Pn 14x10 Cornfield in Crowhurst 1899 But 11/91 .... 1,54■
Jackson, Lee Am 1909-
O/B 16x20 The Flower Shop Sby 12/91 .... 1,65■
O/B 7x9 The Trotters Mys 6/92 .... 44■
Jackson, Louise W. Am 20C
P/Pa 29x22 Portrait of Grace Bullock, 1917 Skn 11/91 ..... 22■
Jackson, Martin Am 20C
O/C/B 22x28 Nocturnal View of Philadelphia Fre 12/91 .... 80■
Jackson, Samuel Phillips Br 1830-1904
W/Pa 11x18 Alpine Mountains 1858 Chr 5/92 .... 55■
Jackson, William Franklin Am 1850-1936
O/C 14x20 Poppies and Lupines But 10/91 .... 4,67■

128

ackson, William Henry Am 1843-1942
O/C/B 10x14 Russian River But 6/92 9,350
I/Pa 9x14 Camp Gy-Ba-Jk Hnd 3/92 400
acob, Alexandre Fr 1876-
* See 1992 Edition . . . .
acobi, F. C. 18C
O/C 119x77 Mountainous River Landscape Chr 10/91 . . . 16,500
acobi, M. M. Eng 19C
O/C 8x16 River with a Cabin Fre 4/92 700
acobi, Otto Reinhold Can 1814-1901
O/C 26x36 Mill in Country Landscape 1862 Sbt 11/91 5,610
acobs, Adolphe Bel a 1887-1910
* See 1991 Edition . . . .
acobs, J.
O/C 22x28 Farmhouse by Lake Dum 1/92 30
acobs, Jacob Dut 19C
W/Pa Size? Mountain Scene, Riverside Cottage '53 Hnd 12/91 150
acobsen, A. Dan 1858-1930
O/C 31x50 A Wooded Stream Chr 10/91 1,100
acobsen, Antonio N. Am 1850-1921
O/C 18x22 American Yacht Flying the Flag 1887 Brd 8/92 . 14,300
O/C 22x36 Ship Margaret Fre 4/92 11,000
O/C 22x36 The Yacht, EMBLA II 1901 Slo 10/91 11,000
O/B 16x27 The Tugboat James J. McGuirl 1908 Sby 3/92 . . 9,900
O/C 22x35 The Louisiana 1881 Sby 6/92 6,600
O/B 12x20 The Dreadnought 1917 Sby 4/92 6,050
O/C 25x36 Coastwise Liner Niagara 1900 Doy 12/91 5,500
O/C 22x36 The Advance at Sea 1885 Sby 6/92 4,950
O/B 22x36 Passenger Liner Finland Doy 12/91 4,100
O/B 12x18 The Dreadnought Sby 6/92 2,640
O/B 16x28 The Jefferson 1914 Mor 3/92 2,500
acobsen, Carl Dan 20C
O/C 18x30 The Liner Antonio 1923 Sby 6/92 660
acobsen, Robert Dut 1912-
MM/B 60x48 Abstract Composition But 5/92 2,090
acobsen, Sophus Nor 1833-1912
O/C 15x23 Winter Landscape 66 Sby 7/92 2,750
acobsz., Lambert 1598-1636
* See 1992 Edition . . . .
acomin, Marie-Ferdinand Fr 1843-1902
O/C 18x24 Paysage But 11/91 1,640
**acomin-Vigny, Alfred-Louis Fr
842-1913**
* See 1991 Edition . . . .
acopo Del Casentino It a 14C
T&Gd/Pn 11x9 Ste. Reparata; St. John Baptist (2) Chr 1/92 46,200
acouvleff, Vassily 20C
O/Pn 49x56 Kitchen Interior Sby 6/92 1,430
acque, Charles Emile Fr 1813-1894
O/C 29x40 Le Troupeau Sby 5/92 33,000
O/C 17x27 Shepherdess with her Flock Chr 2/92 23,100
O/C 24x22 Tending the Flock 1881 Chr 5/92 17,600
O/Pn 15x18 La Bergere et les Moutons 15 Sby 10/91 14,850
O/C 24x20 Tending the Flock Wlf 9/91 14,300
O/Pn 18x22 Sheep in a Forest Sel 4/92 4,750
O/C 17x27 Shepherdess Wlf 9/91 4,500
O/Pn 18x12 Still Life of Fish Wlf 9/91 1,000
O/Pn 9x7 Sheep and Hens in a Manger Skn 11/91 935
acque, Emile Fr 1848-1912
O/C 10x13 Watering the Horses at Sunset Sby 1/92 1,980
O/C 10x13 Watering the Horses at Sunset Sby 7/92 1,980
O/Pn 9x11 Haying Before the Storm Sby 1/92 1,100
acquet, Gustave Jean Fr 1846-1909
O/C 24x20 La Coquette Sby 10/91 13,200
O/C 22x18 Young Girl in a Straw Hat Chr 10/91 7,700
O/C 24x20 Lady in a Plummed Hat & Fur Cape Chr 5/92 . . 4,840
O/Pn 22x17 L'Elegante Avec Son Chien Sby 2/92 4,675
acquette, Yvonne 20C
* See 1991 Edition . . . .
acquin, Victorine Fr 19C
* See 1991 Edition . . . .
aeckel, Henry Ger 19C
O/C 27x38 View of the Bay of Naples Chr 5/92 12,100
aeckel, Herman Ger 19C
O/C 32x48 View of the Rialto Bridge, Venice Chr 10/91 . . 6,050

Jakobs, Paul Emil Ger 1802-1866
* See 1991 Edition . . . .
**Jamar, Armand Gustave Gerard Bel
1870-1946**
O/C 39x28 Woman Seated at a Table 1904 Sel 2/92 2,900
Jambor, Louis Am 1884-1955
O/C 26x32 Lobster Man in his Boat Fre 10/91 3,100
James, Charles
* See 1992 Edition . . . .
James, David Br a 1881-1898
O/C 25x50 Plunging Seas 94 Sby 10/91 24,200
O/C 25x50 Manorbier Bay, South Wales 88 Sby 5/92 17,600
O/C 25x51 Rolling Surf '84 Chr 2/92 1,760
James, H. B. Am 20C
O/C 22x36 Barn with Sheep Sel 4/92 175
James, John W. Am 1873-
O/C 25x30 Old Houses 1931 Wlf 6/92 1,700
James, Richard S. Eng 19C
* See 1992 Edition . . . .
James, William Br a 1754-1771
* See 1991 Edition . . . .
Jameson, Middleton Br -1919
O/C 24x32 Encontre, Son Premier Amour 1881 Chr 10/91 . 11,000
Jamison, Philip Am 1925-
W/Pa 15x22 Chattin's House, Westchester Sby 12/91 1,320
O/Cb 8x10 Winter Landscape Fre 12/91 1,250
W/Pa 14x20 Winter Landscape Sby 12/91 1,100
W/Pa 18x29 Winter Landscape Hnd 10/91 850
W/Pa 11x15 Pennsylvania Woodyard Ald 3/92 700
O/Pa 8x19 Barnford Hills Fre 12/91 525
Jance, Paul Claude Fr 1840-
O/C 20x24 Les Petits Jardiniers Sby 7/92 5,500
Janco, Marcel Fr 1895-1984
* See 1992 Edition . . . .
Janesch, Albert Aus 1889-
* See 1990 Edition . . . .
Janet, Ange-Louis Fr 1815-1872
Pe/Pa 5x4 Portrait of Claude Villaret Chr 1/92 308
Janet-Lange Fr 1815-1872
Pe/Pa 5x4 Portrait of Claude Villaret Chr 1/92 308
Janousek, Frantisek 20C
* See 1991 Edition . . . .
Janowitz, Joel Am 20C
W&H/Pa 16x23 Cows in a Landscape 1979 Skn 3/92 1,540
O/H 16x20 Distance Between (Study) 1984 Skn 5/92 495
Jansem, Jean Fr 1920-
O/C 52x35 Chardons Bleus Sby 10/91 33,000
O/C 26x18 Les Enfants Chr 11/91 24,200
O/C 39x26 Mere et Enfant Chr 2/92 17,600
O/C 21x26 Les Filles Chr 11/91 13,200
O/C 23x32 Masques a Venise But 11/91 13,200
O/C 35x51 Seated Woman Hnz 5/92 13,000
O/C 40x20 Le Panier Doy 11/91 12,000
O/C 36x29 Deux femmes assises Chr 5/92 11,000
O/C 29x36 Femmes a la Couture Sby 2/92 10,450
O/C 19x13 Femme Nue Chr 11/91 9,350
O/C 13x18 Personnages Sur un Mur Chr 11/91 8,800
O/C 39x31 Filette a l'Enfant Sur Fond Bleu Hnd 5/92 7,000
O&G/Pa/C 20x26 Barques a la Quai Sby 2/92 6,600
G/Pa 26x20 Nature Morte Aux Pichets Sby 10/91 6,325
W&O/Pa/C 10x14 The Dancer Sby 10/91 5,500
W,P&Pe/Pa 25x19 Nature Morte, Table Peinture But 11/91 . 2,475
W/Pa 26x20 Modele Assis Hnd 5/92 2,200
O/Cd 13x10 Young Girl Wlf 10/91 1,700
Jansen, Alfred 1903-1981
O&H/B 15x18 Untitled 1959 Chr 5/92 5,500
Jansen, Joseph Ger 1829-1905
* See 1990 Edition . . . .
Jansen, Willem George F. Dut 1871-1949
O/C 16x21 Fishing Boats at Low Tide But 11/91 2,200
**Janssens, Abraham Van Nuyssen Flm
1575-1632**
* See 1992 Edition . . . .
Janssens, Hieronymous Dut 1624-1693
* See 1991 Edition . . . .

Janssens, Victor Emile   Ger 1807-1845
O/Pn 17x14 Woman Seated in a Kitchen Hnd 10/91 3,600
Jansson, Alfred   Am 1863-1931
O/C 29x37 Sun Setting in the Forest 1914 But 4/92 3,300
Jansson, Eugene   Swd 1862-1915
* See 1992 Edition . . . .
Japy, Louis Aime   Fr 1840-1916
O/C 20x26 Homeward Bound Wes 3/92 1,760
Jardines, Jose Maria   Spa 1962-
O/C 15x22 Chickens Feeding Chr 2/92 2,420
O/C 22x15 Rest from the Harvest Chr 10/91 2,420
Jarm, William   Am 20C
O/C 60x84 Diana at the Chase 1906 Hnd 3/92 1,700
Jarvis, John   Am 20C
* See 1992 Edition . . . .
Jarvis, John Wesley   Am 1780-1840
O/C 30x25 Dr. Samuel Latham Mitchell Sby 12/91 1,650
Jarvis, W. Frederick   Am 1868-
O/B 20x30 Mountain Landscape Lou 12/91 700
O/C 24x30 November Mist, Riggs Road, MD 1931 Slo 4/92 . 700
W/Pa 21x28 Cactus and Blue Bonnets Slo 12/91 200
Jaudon, Valerie   Am 1945-
* See 1992 Edition . . . .
Javier, Maximino   Mex 20C
O/C 39x32 Camino a la Feria 83 Chr 5/92 4,400
Jawlensky, Alexej   Ger 1864-1941
O/B 12x16 Kopf Sby 11/91 297,000
O/Pa/B 14x11 Sommer Abend Chr 5/92 154,000
O/B 13x10 Winterstimmung 32 Sby 2/92 132,000
O/B 19x21 Stilleben 1910 Chr 5/92 77,000
O/B 7x6 Femina Sby 5/92 60,500
Jazet, Paul Leon   Fr 1848-
O/Pn 18x24 Stationing the Outposts Sby 10/91 9,350
Jean, Nehemy   Hai
O/M 20x16 Mange Loa 49 Chr 5/92 1,760
Jean, Simon Saint   Fr 1808-1860
O/C 18x24 Still Life Roses, Carnations 1853 Sby 10/91 . 20,900
**Jeanneret, Charles Edouard   Fr
1887-1965**
O/C 39x32 Nature Morte 25 Chr 11/91 319,000
Jeantils, G.   Fr 20C
O/C 22x15 Composition 1952 Slo 12/91 240
Jeaurat, Etienne   Fr 1699-1789
O/C 24x21 Country Market Scenes: Pair Sby 1/92 22,000
H/Pa 12x10 Mythical Figures Wooded Landscape But 5/92 . 1,100
Jelinek, R. E.   Eur 20C
O/C 22x27 Interior with Children Sel 12/91 700
Jenkins, Paul   Am 1923-
A/C 78x67 Phenomena Loop the Sun 1980 Sby 10/91 . . . 14,300
O/C 115x60 Phenomena Richard's Blue 1967 Sby 6/92 . . . 8,800
A/C 39x39 Phenomena with Soundings 1965 Sby 10/91 . . 8,800
A/C 40x30 Phenomena East Guardian 1967 Chr 11/91 . . . 7,480
A/C 48x64 Phenomena Chinese Clock 1984 Sby 6/92 7,150
O/C 51x35 Untitled 55 Chr 2/92 6,600
O/C 20x26 Phenomena One to Go By 1966 Chr 5/92 5,280
W/Pa 43x31 Untitled Chr 11/91 3,520
W/Pa 42x30 Phenomena Shield for Richard 1976 Sby 10/91 3,190
W/Pa 31x44 Phenomena Blue Chalice 1977 Sby 10/91 . . . 3,080
W/Pa 31x43 Untitled Chr 11/91 3,080
W/Pa 42x30 Phenomena for Yes 1977 Sby 10/91 2,970
A/C 38x51 Phenomena Vain Gesture 1966 Sby 10/91 2,750
W/Pa 30x42 Untitled Chr 11/91 2,750
W/Pa 31x43 Untitled Chr 11/91 2,750
W/Pa 22x30 Untitled Sby 6/92 2,200
W/Pa 23x30 Phenomena Eng. Longbow 1972 Wes 11/91 . 1,320
A/C 18x13 Phenomena Black Hint 1961 Sby 6/92 1,100
W/Pa 30x22 Untitled Chr 11/91 990
Jenkins, Wilfred   Br 19C
* See 1992 Edition . . . .
Jenney, Neil   Am 1945-
A/C 60x65 Saw and Sawed 1969 Chr 5/92 198,000
A&H/C 59x77 Schmuck and Schlemiel 1969 Chr 11/91 . 170,500
A&H/C 61x63 Litter and Bin 1970 Chr 5/92 165,000
Jennings-Brown, H. W.   Br 19C
* See 1990 Edition . . . .

Jensen, Alfred   Am 1903-1981
O/C 50x46 Imagine and After Image 62 Sby 11/91 57,75
O/C 66x41 Amphitrite, Poseiden 1962 Chr 11/91 33,00
O/C 64x54 Color's Direction 1962 Chr 5/92 28,60
O/Pa/M 12x12 Untitled Chr 2/92 6,6
Jensen, Bill   Am 1945-
O/L 15x14 Dolphie 1980 Chr 11/91 13,20
Br&l/Pa 15x11 Study for Heavy Painting 1973 Chr 2/92 . 55
Jensen, George   Am 1878-
O/C 24x30 Early Evening Chr 11/91 2,75
O/C 24x36 Fall Landscape Wlf 9/91 1,50
Jensen, Holger W.   Am 1880-
G/B 12x15 In the Tennessee Smokies Hnz 5/92 16
Jensen, Johan Laurentz   Dan 1800-1856
O/Pn 18x14 Still Life Pink Roses Sby 2/92 30,80
O/C 21x26 A Garland of Roses Sby 2/92 7,70
O/Pn 11x15 Still Life Roses in a Basket But 11/91 7,70
O/C 7x9 Flowers in Bloom Chr 2/92 5,50
O/C 8x6 Yellow Tulips 1849 Doy 11/91 3,00
O/Pn 5x7 Bouquet of Flowers Doy 11/91 2,00
Jensen, Oluf   Dan 1864-1923
O/C 19x26 The Club Room But 5/92 2,75
Jensen, Thomas M.   Am 1831-1916
O/B 12x9 Blowing Smoke Rings Mys 6/92 49
Jentner   Fr 20C
O/C 24x20 Boats on the Water '62 Hnz 5/92 14
**Jerichau, Holger Hvitfeldt   Dan
1861-1900**
* See 1991 Edition . . . .
Jerzy, Richard   20C
O/Pa 14x14 Pooch 1977 Sby 10/91 30
Jespersen, Henrik Gamst   Dan 1853-1939
O/C 24x18 Mountain Village with Stream 1902 Sby 7/92 . . 1,54
Jess
* See 1991 Edition . . . .
Jettel, Eugen   Aus 1845-1901
* See 1992 Edition . . . .
Jettmar, Rudolf   Pol 1869-1939
* See 1992 Edition . . . .
Jewell, Elizabeth G.   Am 1874-1956
O/B 14x16 Fishing Boat near Gloucester Yng 4/92 35
O/B 14x18 The Dannert Homestead Eld 4/92 22
Jex, Garnet W.   Am 1895-1975
O/C 30x36 Waterton Bridge, Alberta Slo 9/91 50
O/C 24x30 Great Falls from Virginia Slo 10/91 27
Jimenez Y Aranda, Jose   Spa 1837-1903
* See 1991 Edition . . . .
Jimenez Y Aranda, Luis   Spa 1845-1928
O/C 25x39 In the Poppy Field 1895 Sby 2/92 159,50
**Jimenez Y Fernandez, Federico   Spa
1841-**
O/Pn 9x14 Mallards; Chickens: Pair Sby 5/92 8,80
Jimenez Y Martin, Juan   Spa 1858-
O/Pn 10x16 The Sultan's Favorite Chr 2/92 22,00
Jirdeux   Fr 20C
O/C 21x14 Nude '67 Hnz 5/92 5
Jirouch, Frank   Am 1878-
O/C 24x32 Harbor Scene Sel 4/92 50
Joan
O/C 36x24 Boy Feeding Ducks Dum 1/92 200
Joanovitch, Paul   Aus 1859-
* See 1991 Edition . . . .
Jochmus, Harry   Ger 1855-1915
* See 1991 Edition . . . .
Jocker, C.   Dut 20C
O/B 18x22 Fishing Boats Yng 4/92 47
Johannesen, N. A.   Swd 20C
O/C 10x14 Small White House Above the Lake Fre 12/91 . . 50
O/C 12x19 Sailboats by the Port Fre 12/91 35
Johansson, Stefan   Swd 1876-1955
* See 1992 Edition . . . .
Johfra
O/Pn 27x20 Mythological Figure Sby 2/92 2,64
John, Augustus   Br 1878-1961
Pe/Pa 16x11 Studies of Babies 1948 Brd 5/92 1,10

John, David C.   Am 20C
O/C 15x25 Homeward Bound, Chas Webster Yng 2/92 500
Johns, Jasper   Am 1930-
O&L/C 60x44 Jubilee Sby 11/91 . . . . 4.95M
N,O&L/C 40x40 Device Circle 59 Chr 11/91 . . . . 4.4M
H,C&T/Pa 20x18 No '64 Sby 5/92 220,000
W,H&I/Pa 18x17 Untitled '78 Sby 5/92 126,500
Johnson, Alex   Eur 19C
O/C 30x25 Winter Walk 1871 Slo 2/92 275
Johnson, Arthur Clark   1897-
O/C 30x25 Woman in a Kimono Yng 4/92 450
Johnson, Avery Fischer   Am 1906-
W/Pa 14x21 Mountain Lake Wes 5/92 330
Johnson, Charles Edward   Br 1832-1913
O/C 14x25 A Mosque on a Lake 1884 Chr 5/92 1,100
Johnson, Clarence   Am 1894-1981
* See 1992 Edition
Johnson, Clovis N. (Jr.)   Am a 1920-1929
O/B 12x16 La Canada Valley Mor 6/92 600
Johnson, David   Am 1827-1908
O/C 39x60 Hudson fr Ft. Montgomery 1870 Sby 5/92 . . 209,000
O/B 14x20 Looking West from Dollar Island 79 Chr 12/91 . . 60,500
O/C 16x26 Spring, Study Bronx River 1873 Chr 3/92 . . . 16,500
O/C 12x20 Essex County Scenery 1859 Sby 9/91 12,100
O/C 18x26 Weinockie River, Passaic 1879 Chr 12/91 12,100
O/C 17x13 Study, Ramapo 1874 Chr 3/92 9,900
O/Pa/Pn 8x12 Shandaken Hills, Ulster 1859 Chr 5/92 . . . 9,350
O/B 9x17 Near Noroton, Connecticut 1875 Sby 9/91 7,700
O/B 8x13 Burlington, Lake Champlain 1873 Slo 9/91 6,000
O/C 6x9 View Across the Valley 1869 Skn 9/91 880
Johnson, Edward   Am 1911-
O/C 26x20 The Ballerina But 11/91 3,025
Johnson, Frank Tenney   Am 1874-1939
O/C 24x30 Reflection 1936 Sby 5/92 46,750
O/C 24x18 A Mountain Trail 1925 But 4/92 35,750
O/C 20x16 Lone Horseman But 11/91 11,000
Pe&K/Pa 11x8 Study of Working Men 1901 But 4/92 1,100
Johnson, Guy
O/Pa/Pn 19x18 Fog Sby 10/91 935
Johnson, H.   Br 18C
O/C 42x60 Hunters in an Extensive Landscape Hnd 10/91 . . 7,500
Johnson, J. William   Am 19C
* See 1991 Edition . . . .
Johnson, Jonathan Eastman   Am 1824-1906
O/B 22x12 The Confab Chr 12/91 66,000
O/C 12x10 Warming Her Hands '62 Chr 9/91 55,000
O/C 12x9 Children Reading Sby 5/92 17,600
O/C 10x7 The Bohemian Girl Chr 3/92 8,800
O/C 9x14 Golden October, Catskill 1869 Yng 2/92 4,000
O/C 26x21 Portrait Susan Linn Sage 1884 Doy 12/91 3,000
C&K/Pa 11x8 Portrait Middle Aged Man Chr 11/91 1,100
Y&I/Pa 6x6 Sketch of a Young Girl 1847 Chr 11/91 880
K/Pa 8x7 Study of a Young Woman Sby 4/92 440
Johnson, Karl E.
O/C 30x40 Vermont Farm Scene Eld 7/92 303
Johnson, Lester   Am 1919-
O/C 28x44 Four Figures Leaning 1970 Sby 10/91 5,225
MM/Pa 29x23 Seated Man 1970 Sby 10/91 1,980
Johnson, Marshall   Am 1850-1921
O/C 30x25 Frigate 'Constitution' Skn 11/91 4,950
O/C 12x20 Off Bear River, Nova Scotia '79 Skn 11/91 . . . 2,860
O/C 12x20 Building by a Harbor Fre 4/92 1,350
O/C 10x14 Meeting at Sea Bor 8/92 1,200
O/C 10x14 Heavy Going Bor 8/92 900
Johnson, Robert   Aut 1890-1964
O/C 12x15 Morning in the Valley Brd 5/92 2,200
Johnson, Sidney Yates   Br 19C
* See 1992 Edition . . . .
Johnson, Wesley   Am 20C
O/C 30x30 Untitled 1989 Hnd 3/92 500
Johnston, Alexander   Br 1815-1891
O/C 48x36 The Elopement 1871 Chr 5/92 4,620
Johnston, Frank Hans   Can 1888-1949
T/B 40x30 Fraser River Canyon Sbt 11/91 8,415

O/B 14x20 Northern Dogs Sbt 11/91 5,142
O/B 11x15 The Snow-Fed Stream Sbt 11/91 3,740
O/B 10x12 L'Hiver Chez Nous Sbt 11/91 3,039
O/B 19x15 Men of the North Sbt 11/91 3,039
O/B 10x13 Northern Landscape Sbt 11/91 3,039
O/Pn 9x11 Haunt of the Beaver '32 Sbt 5/92 2,805
O/B 15x18 The Blue Jewel Sbt 5/92 2,712
O/B 12x14 Welcome Spring 1922 Sbt 11/91 2,571
O/C 39x49 Indian Grave, Northern Grave Sbt 5/92 1,402
W&G/Pa 7x10 Sunlit Clearing Yng 4/92 800
Johnston, John Humphreys   Am 1857-1941
O/C 24x35 Mountain Goats Eld 7/92 770
Johnston, John R.   Am 19C
O/C 29x36 Maryland River Scene 1858 Sby 9/91 4,400
Johnston, Reuben Le Grande   Am 1850-1918
O/C 20x24 Tending the Flock Sby 12/91 2,750
O/C 18x30 Desert Campsite Sby 12/91 1,210
Johnston, Ynez   Am 1920-
Pl&G/Pa 16x23 Desert Temples Sby 2/92 1,320
Johnstone, Henry James   Br 1835-1907
* See 1991 Edition
Johnstone, John Young   Can 1887-1930
O/B 10x13 Rural Landscape, Quebec Sbt 11/91 1,870
Joia, B. C.   It 19C
W/Pa 15x12 Italian Man Mys 6/92 82
Joiner, Harvey   Am 1852-1932
O&R/B 5x11 Road Through Beechwoods Wes 11/91 605
Joli, Antonio   It 1700-1777
O/C 34x51 The Thames, Looking West Chr 1/92 286,000
Jolivard, Andre   Fr 1787-1851
* See 1992 Edition
Jolyet, Philippe   Fr 1832-1908
O/Ab 16x13 Mignon 1892 But 11/91 7,150
Jones, Allan   Am 1937-
C,H&Fp/Pa 19x23 Party Games Chr 11/91 3,300
Jones, Bradley
* See 1992 Edition
Jones, C. W.   Am 20C
W/Pa 19x15 4 Watercolors 1975 Lou 3/92 200
Jones, Charles   Eng 1836-1892
O/C 24x42 Sheep Watching the Hunt 1890 Slo 2/92 7,000
Jones, Daniel Adolphe Robert   Bel 1806-1874
* See 1990 Edition . . . .
Jones, F. Eastman   Am 19C
* See 1992 Edition . . . .
Jones, Francis Coates   Am 1857-1932
O/C 27x22 An Interesting Story Chr 5/92 49,500
Jones, Hugh Bolton   Am 1848-1927
O/C 30x54 Adams County, Pennsylvania 1879 Chr 3/92 . . 33,000
O/C 16x26 The Susquehanna 1873 Chr 3/92 33,000
O/C 30x54 Cumberland Valley 1873 Chr 9/91 28,600
O/C 16x24 Autumn Reflections Chr 5/92 26,400
O/C 14x22 Spring in the Valley Brd 8/92 19,250
O/C 22x32 The Country Lane Chr 9/91 11,000
O/C 16x22 Reflections in the Pond 1879 Chr 3/92 10,450
O/C 16x24 Autumn Landscape Sby 12/91 9,900
O/C 16x24 Country Landscape with a Stream Sby 12/91 . . 9,075
O/C 16x26 River Landscape in Spring Sby 3/92 6,600
O/C 24x20 Spring Landscape Fre 10/91 5,200
O/C 24x20 Autumn Along the River 1875 Chr 6/92 3,520
O/C 30x36 Near Stockbridge Skn 3/92 3,025
O/C 30x36 Near Stockbridge Chr 11/91 2,640
Jones, Joe   Am 1909-1963
* See 1992 Edition . . . .
Jones, Paul   Br a 1856-1888
* See 1992 Edition . . . .
Jones, Robert Edmond
W&Gd/Pa/B 20x13 Decor; Costume Design: (2) Sby 2/92 . . . 660
Jones, Samuel John Egbert   Br a 1820-1849
O/C 18x24 Flushing Pheasants Sby 6/92 7,425

Jongkind, Johan Barthold   Dut 1819-1891
O/C 17x26 L'Ecluse 1863 Sby 10/91 41,250
O/Pn 10x15 Windmills 1887 Doy 11/91 2,600
Jongsma, Jacob Lucas   Dut 1893-1926
O/C 13x20 Country Cottage Lou 3/92 550
Jonnevold, Carl Henrik   Am 1856-1930
O/C 16x20 Sunset Through a Clearing But 2/92 880
O/C 12x14 Misty Landscape Fre 4/92 450
Jonniaux, Alfred   Bel 1822-
* See 1991 Edition
Jonson, Cornelis   Dut 1593-1661
* See 1990 Edition
Jonson, Raymond   Am 1891-
G/Pa 39x30 Variation on a Rhythm '37 Hnz 10/91 7,750
Joostens, Paul   20C
* See 1990 Edition
Jopling, Louise   Br 1843-
* See 1992 Edition
Jordaens, Hans   Dut 1616-1680
* See 1992 Edition
Jordaens, Jacob   Flm 1593-1678
O/C 47x32 Triumph of the Eucharist Sby 1/92 24,200
K&Pl/Pa 11x8 Head of a Bearded Man Chr 1/92 22,000
O/C 46x38 The Artist's Model But 11/91 11,000
Jordan, Henrietta A.   Am 20C
O/C 16x28 Sailing off the Coast 1902 Fre 4/92 400
Jordan, Rudolf   Ger 1810-1887
* See 1992 Edition
Jorgensen, Christian A.   Am 1860-1935
O/C 17x30 Carmel Dunes 1923 But 10/91 4,400
O/C 15x36 San Francisco Bay But 10/91 3,575
W/Pa 12x6 Minor Lake, Yosemite But 6/92 1,760
O/Cb 8x10 Yosemite Sby 4/92 1,760
W/Pa 17x11 Early Cal Figure '91 Mor 6/92 700
Joris, Pio   It 1843-1921
O/C 64x39 Il Fuso 1888 Sby 2/92 25,300
O/C/B 35x46 The First Communion But 11/91 14,300
W/Pa/B 18x13 Cavalier Reading a Letter Sby 7/92 550
MM Size? Cathedral Interior Mys 6/92 165
Jorn, Asger   Dan 1914-1973
O/C 6x9 Bird Chr 11/91 8,580
Joseph, Albert   Fr 1868-1952
* See 1992 Edition
Joseph, F.   It 20C
W/Pa 12x9 Three Women and Dancers 1964 Lou 3/92 60
Joseph, Jacques Francois   Fr
* See 1991 Edition
Joseph, Jasmin   Hai 20C
* See 1992 Edition
Joseph, Julian   Am 20C
* See 1991 Edition
Joubert, R.   20C
O/C 24x30 Fisherman Along Lakebank Slo 12/91 700
Jouffroy, Jean Pierre   Fr 1933-
O/B 20x24 Flowers in a Vase '61 Yng 2/92 50
Joullin, Amedee   Am 1862-1917
O/C 24x30 Pueblo Girl 1912 Chr 3/92 4,620
O/C 20x26 Yeong Wo Joss House But 10/91 2,750
Jourdain, Henri   Fr 1864-1931
W/L 19x24 French Country House Chr 10/91 935
W/Pa 13x18 Coastal Landscape Lou 3/92 138
Jourdain, Roger Joseph   Fr 1845-1918
O/C 38x60 La Remorque du Canot Sby 2/92 35,750
W/Pa 15x10 The Heroine Sby 10/91 2,200
Jourdan, Adolphe   Fr 1825-1889
* See 1992 Edition
Jourdeuil, Louis Marie Adrien   Fr 1849-1907
* See 1992 Edition
Journod, M*
O/C 26x22 Bouquet au Vase Espagnol Sby 10/91 990
Jousset, Claude
O/C 20x24 Harbor Scene Dum 11/91 2,000
Jouvenet, Jean   Fr 1644-1717
O/C 31x25 Saint Paul in Meditation Sby 1/92 33,000

Joy, George Williams   Eng 1844-1925
O/C 43x32 Wellington's First Encounter Wes 11/91 5,500
Joyce, Marshall   Am 20C
W/Pa 5x7 Gurnet Light, Plymouth: Two Yng 2/92 125
Juarez, Jose   Mex 1642-1698
* See 1990 Edition
Juarez, Roberto   20C
* See 1992 Edition
Judd, Donald   Am 1928-
O/Wd 21x17 Untitled Chr 5/92 13,200
Judson, Alice   Am -1948
O/B 12x16 Misty Landscape Yng 2/92 250
Judson, Charles Chapel   Am 1864-1946
O/B 8x15 Lands End-Golden Gate Wes 11/91 275
Judson, William Lees   Am 1842-1928
O/C 14x22 Oaks in the Meadow But 10/91 2,090
W/Pa 11x23 River Landscape, Alberta 1877 Sbt 11/91 1,636
O/C 20x30 In the High Sierra Mor 6/92 1,100
Jueberman, Lilia   Am 20C
O/C 35x25 Young Man Hnz 5/92 100
Juergens, Alfred   Am 1866-1934
O/C 24x32 Autumn Landscape Wlf 9/91 1,400
Jules, Mervin   Am 1912-
O/B 29x12 Mozart Wlf 9/91 1,500
O/B 16x14 Man Playing a Violin Lou 3/92 550
Julien, Joseph   Bel 19C
* See 1991 Edition
Jund, Carl Ove Julian   Dan 1857-1936
* See 1990 Edition
Jung, Charles Jacob   Am 1880-1940
* See 1992 Edition
Jungblut, Johann   Ger 1860-1912
O/C 32x46 Returning Home Hnd 10/91 3,600
O/C 32x48 Dutch Village in Winter Hnd 10/91 3,400
O/C 11x13 A Moonlite Harbor Chr 2/92 2,750
Junge, Carl Stephen
W/Pa 14x20 Buckingham Fountain Hnz 10/91 50
Jungwirth, Irene Gayas   Am
O/M 38x30 Virgin and Christ Child Dum 7/92 225
O/C 30x24 Holy Family Dum 7/92 175
Junker, Leo Helmholz   Am 1882-1974
O/C 39x27 Cubistic Interior Hnz 5/92 375
O/Pn 18x24 Autumn Landscape Hnz 5/92 190
O/C 18x24 Pelhamwood, N.Y. 1917 Hnz 5/92 160
O/C 14x20 Autumn Landscape Hnz 5/92 90
O/B 22x27 Spring Landscape 1968 Hnz 5/92 50
O/C 22x26 Winter Scene with Sled Hnz 5/92 50
O/C 10x14 View of Palisades Hnz 5/92 25
Jutsum, Henry   Br 1816-1869
* See 1992 Edition
Jutz, Carl   Ger 1838-1916
O/Pn 5x7 Ducks by a Pond Sby 2/92 27,500
O/Pn 8x10 Poultry in a Barnyard Chr 5/92 13,200
Juvin, Juliette
* See 1991 Edition
Kacere, John   Am 1920-
* See 1991 Edition
Kachedoorian, Zubel
O/C 38x45 The Cove of Zeus '65 Dum 4/92 400
Kadar, Bela   Hun 1877-1955
G/Pa 36x24 The Embrace Chr 11/91 8,800
W&G/Pa 15x11 Woman in a Fur Cap But 5/92 1,045
Kadlacsik, Laszlo   Hun 1925-1989
* See 1992 Edition
Kaelin, Charles Salis   Am 1858-1929
P/Pa 14x17 Coastal Views: Four Pastels Sby 4/92 4,510
O/C 20x21 Winter Harbor Scene Wlf 11/91 3,100
O/C 18x16 Landscape Wlf 11/91 2,800
O/C 18x16 Landscape Wlf 11/91 2,600
O/C 18x20 Spring Landscape Wlf 9/91 2,200
O/C 18x22 Shallow Pool Wlf 9/91 2,100
P/Pa 13x15 Sunday, A Harbor View Skn 11/91 1,870
O/C 18x16 Rock Study Wlf 10/91 1,800
O/Ab 11x14 Tree Orchard Wlf 11/91 1,800
P/Pa 16x17 Harbour Scene Mys 6/92 1,760

O/C 20x24 Autumn Landscape Wlf 9/91 1,600
O/C 16x18 Houses in Winter Wlf 10/91 1,600
O/C 16x18 Landscape Wlf 10/91 1,600
O/C 16x18 Houses in Winter Wlf 10/91 1,500
O/C 16x18 Houses in Winter Wlf 10/91 1,300
P/Pa 14x16 Rocky Stream in Woods Wlf 10/91 1,300
O/C 18x16 Fall Abstraction Wlf 11/91 1,250
P/Pa 16x14 Autumn Landscape with Stream Wlf 11/91 1,200
P/Pa 14x16 Rocky Coastline Wlf 9/91 1,200
O/Ab 11x14 Sailboats in a Harbor Wlf 9/91 1,050
O/C 16x18 Landscape with Stream Wlf 9/91 1,000
O/Ab 11x14 Tree Orchard Wlf 11/91 950
P/Pa 12x16 Moonlight on the Water Wlf 11/91 850
O/Ab 8x10 Rocky Coast Wlf 10/91 850
P/Pa 16x18 Rocks by the Shore Wlf 10/91 800
P/Pa 14x17 Sailboat in Harbor Wlf 11/91 800
O/C 16x18 Fall Landscape Wlf 11/91 750
O/Ab 11x14 Harbor Scene Wlf 9/91 750
P/Pa 14x16 Rocky Coastline Wlf 11/91 750
P/Pa 16x16 Creek in Woods Wlf 11/91 700
P/Pa 14x16 Shoreline Wlf 10/91 700
O/Ab 14x11 Portrait of a Man Wlf 11/91 600
O/Pn 8x10 Grey Day Wlf 11/91 500
P/Pa 14x16 Winter Landscape Wlf 10/91 425
P/Pa 14x17 Rockport Wlf 6/92 400

Kaelin, Martin   Am 1926-
* See 1992 Edition . . . .

Kaemmerer, Frederik Hendrik   Dut 1839-1902
O/C 44x30 The Fishwives Chr 2/92 17,600
C&K/Pa 21x13 Elegant Lady Standing Chr 5/92 2,200

Kaercher, Amalie   Ger 19C
* See 1992 Edition . . . .

Kahler, Carl   Aus 1855-
O/C 24x36 Four Kittens on a Plush Cushion '94 Sel 4/92 . . 6,500

Kahlo, Frida   Mex 1910-1954
O/C 16x11 Recuerdo 1937 Chr 5/92 935,000
W&P/Pa 11x9 El Salon de Belleza 32 Chr 5/92 38,500
Pe/Pa 8x6 Autorretrato Vacilando-Sol y Luna Chr 5/92 . . 19,800

Kahn, Wolf   Am 1927-
O/C 50x42 Late Afternoon Chr 9/91 13,200
O/C 53x53 Down to the Valley II Chr 9/91 10,450
O/C 52x66 Untitled Sby 10/91 6,600
O/C 22x32 Jenk's Farm Chr 3/92 2,860
O/C 16x20 Tree Sequence I 1986 Chr 6/92 1,320
P/Pa 13x16 Summer Houses 1967 Skn 11/91 1,210
P/Pa 14x16 Sea Port '57 Hnd 12/91 600

Kalla-Priechenfried, J.   Ger 19C
O/C 19x15 Gentleman with Mandolin Sby 7/92 3,300
O/Pn 18x13 The Cardinal Sby 7/92 1,760

Kallmorgen, Friedrich   Ger 1856-1924
* See 1992 Edition . . . .

Kamena, Marina   Am 1945-
A/C 41x31 Sunday Afternoon 1985 Slo 9/91 275

Kammerer, Frederik Hendrik   Dut 1839-1902
* See 1992 Edition . . . .

Kamp, Louise M.   Am 1867-1959
O/Cb 20x24 Cabin by the Stream, Winter Skn 9/91 770

Kandinsky, Wassily   Rus 1866-1944
O/B 19x14 Trois Etoiles 1942 Sby 5/92 297,000
O&P/B 28x28 Zu vier Ecken 32 Chr 5/92 275,000
W&I/Pa 19x13 Im Netz 1927 Sby 5/92 209,000
W,Br&I/Pa 9x12 Composition 19 Sby 5/92 165,000
O/Cb 9x13 Kallmunz, Blick auf die Stadt Chr 11/91 148,500
GW&P/Pa/B 20x12 Halbkreis oben (Spitze) 28 Chr 5/92 . 132,000
W&I/Pa 7x6 Composition 25 Sby 5/92 60,500
I&Pe/Pa 11x8 Composition Sby 11/91 38,500
I/Pa 6x9 Composition 30 Sby 5/92 29,700
I&Pe/Pa 7x11 Composition 40 Sby 11/91 25,300

Kane, John   Am 1860-1934
* See 1992 Edition . . . .

Kane, Theodora   Am 1906-
W/Pa 21x29 Corning, New York Slo 10/91 100

Kann, Frederick I.   Am 1886-1965
* See 1992 Edition . . . .

Kantor, Morris   Am 1896-1974
O/C 36x28 Figure Walking with a Cane 1924 Sby 3/92 6,600

Kantor, Tadeusz   Pol 1915-
* See 1992 Edition . . . .

Kapfhamer, Adolf   Ger 1867-1911
O/Pn 20x24 Mountain Landscape: After the Storm Slo 4/92 . . 200

Kaplan, Edith Jaffy   Am 20C
MM/Pa 20x16 Still Life Collage Wlf 10/91 100

Kappes, Karl   Am 1861-1943
O/B 17x13 House in a Landscape Wlf 6/92 200
O/B 11x16 Pulley and Construction Site Wlf 6/92 80

Karatsonyi, Andrew   Am 20C
O/C 16x20 Bucking Horse 1909 Mys 6/92 440

Kardin, Alexander   Aus 1917-
O/C 19x24 French Street Scene Dum 11/91 1,200

Karfiol, Bernard   Am 1866-1952
O/C 22x30 Reclining Figure, White Dress Brd 5/92 9,350
O/C 28x36 Stevens Farm, Ogunquit, Maine Brd 8/92 3,740
O/C 30x40 A River Mill Chr 6/92 2,420
O/Cb 24x20 Portrait of a Redhead Chr 6/92 385
P/Pa 8x13 Reclining Nude Chr 6/92 330
W/Pa 17x12 Floral Still Life Slo 9/91 200

Karlovszky-Berci   Hun 19C
* See 1992 Edition . . . .

Karpoff, Ivan
* See 1992 Edition . . . .

Karski, J.   Con 20C
O/C 16x23 Men in a Sleigh Hnd 6/92 120

Kasyn, John   Can 1926-
O/M 16x22 Near Kensington Market Sbt 5/92 3,506
O/B 16x12 Backyard Empire Street Sbt 11/91 1,964
O/M 12x10 Yellow House in Weston Sbt 5/92 1,683
W/Pa 5x8 Backyard on River Street Sbt 5/92 561
W/Pa 5x8 Off Eastern Avenue Sbt 11/91 467
W/Pa 5x8 Two Cottages Cabbagetown Sbt 11/91 467

Katz, Alex   Am 1927-
O/C 48x60 Pat #2 79 Chr 11/91 60,500
O/C 48x34 Portrait of Maxine Chr 11/91 22,000
O/C 49x49 Rex #1 Chr 5/92 22,000
O/M 12x17 Amanda 73 Sby 5/92 12,100
O/M 16x20 Larry Painting Jim and Gretchen Chr 5/92 9,350
O/M 12x17 Amanda 73 Doy 11/91 4,750
O/M 15x20 Summer Landscape Chr 11/91 3,300
O/M 14x12 Vincent with a Ukelele 80 Doy 11/91 1,500

Katz, Morris   Am 1932-
O/B 16x20 Flowers 1983 Yng 2/92 50

Kauffman   Con 19C
* See 1992 Edition . . . .

Kauffman, Craig
* See 1992 Edition . . . .

Kauffmann, Hugo Wilhelm   Ger 1844-1915
O/C/M 18x25 Collecting Wood in Winter But 11/91 6,600

Kaufman, Isidor   Aus 1853-1921
* See 1992 Edition . . . .

Kaufmann, Adolf   Aus 1848-1916
O/C/M 39x43 The Harbor in Genoa Chr 10/91 3,520
O/C 32x23 Shepherdess and her Flock by River Chr 2/92 . . 2,750

Kaufmann, Ferdinand   Am 1864-1942
O/B 12x16 Tujunga Mountains But 2/92 1,650
O/B 12x16 Houses in Landscape Mor 3/92 1,400
O/C 12x16 Gray Day-Rockport Mor 6/92 1,200
O/C 12x16 Boats in Harbor Mor 6/92 950

Kaufmann, Isidor   Aus 1853-1921
O/B 19x15 Young Rabbi at Prayer Sby 2/92 176,000
O/Pn 23x17 Am Sabbat Sby 2/92 170,500
O/Pn 12x14 The Study of the Talmud Sby 2/92 126,500

Kaufmann, Karl   Aus 1843-1901
* See 1992 Edition . . . .

Kaufmann, Wilhelm   Aus 1895-1945
O/Pn 20x26 Cottages Wes 11/91 330

Kaula, Lee Lufkin   Am 1865-1957
W/Pa 15x12 Eating Porridge Chr 11/91 1,320

Kaula, William Jurian   Am 1871-1953
O/C 32x39 Hills and Valleys Skn 11/91 3,850
O/B 8x10 Winter Park 1913 Wes 5/92 1,430
W/Pa 20x26 Winter Snow Scene Mys 11/91 935
W/Pa 18x22 Spring Landscape Eld 7/92 880
O/C 15x18 Landscape Mys 11/91 770
W&P/Pb 11x15 Plowing Chr 11/91 154
Kaulbach, Hermann   Ger 1846-1909
* See 1992 Edition
Kauy, M.   Am 19C
O/C 28x22 Floral Still Life Lou 12/91 100
Kavanaugh, Marion   Am 1876-1954
* See 1992 Edition
Kavel, Martin   Fr 20C
* See 1992 Edition
Kawara, On   1933-
Lq/C 10x13 June 2, 1971 Sby 11/91 35,750
L 4x6 I Got Up At... 1973 Sby 5/92 16,500
l/Cd 4x6 I Got Up At... 1970 Chr 11/91 15,400
Kayanowk, J.   Con 20C
* See 1992 Edition
Kaye, Otis   Am 1885-1974
O/Pn 5x10 How to Stamp Out Poverty Chr 5/92 19,800
O/C/Pn 13x10 Three Bills Posted Chr 9/91 13,200
Keane, Margaret   Am 20C
O/C 24x36 Yesterday's Doll House 1963 Slo 12/91 100
Kearns, Jerry   20C
* See 1990 Edition
Keelhoff, Frans & Verboeck., E   Bel 1820-1893
O/C 27x42 A Country Road 1868 Chr 2/92 20,900
O/C 27x43 Sheep and Cattle Grazing Chr 2/92 8,250
Keene, E. E.   Eng 19C
O/C 14x18 Pair: River Landscape with Cottage Sel 2/92 675
Keil, Bernardt   Dan 1624-1687
* See 1992 Edition
Keinholz, Ed   Am 1927-
* See 1992 Edition
Keirincx, Alexander   Flm 1600-1652
* See 1991 Edition
Keiserman, Franz   Sws 1765-1833
* See 1990 Edition
Keith, Castle   Am 1864-1927
O/B 10x8 Fall Landscape Dum 9/91 500
Keith, Dora Wheeler   Am 1857-1940
* See 1992 Edition
Keith, William   Am 1839-1911
O/C 23x19 Hilltop Grazing But 6/92 8,800
O/C 16x25 Pasture by the Sea But 2/92 7,700
O/C 22x28 Sunset Aglow But 2/92 3,300
O/B 20x27 Herd of Sheep, Marin County But 2/92 2,750
O/Pn 8x11 Figure on Horseback Sby 12/91 2,475
O/C 15x11 California Landscape Chr 11/91 2,420
O/C 25x17 Pastoral Landscape But 6/92 1,650
Kelderman, J.   Dut 1914-
O/B 16x24 Landscape with Canal Hnz 5/92 160
Kelleman, W.   Ger 20C
O/B 16x19 Still Life Fruit Wes 11/91 412
Keller, A.   Con 19C
O/C 11x19 Nocturnal Harbor Scene Sel 9/91 130
Keller, Adolphe   20C
* See 1990 Edition
Keller, Arthur Ignatius   Am 1866-1924
G/Pa 7x12 Child and Old Man Ih 5/92 1,700
W&G/Pa 20x14 Caught! Slo 2/92 550
O/C 24x48 The Skirmish Slo 2/92 400
Keller, Clyde Leon   Am 1872-1962
O/Cb 20x24 Autumn Breeze Mor 3/92 600
Keller, Edgar Martin   Am 1868-1932
O/B 12x16 Harbor Mor 3/92 400
Keller, Ferdinand   Ger 1842-1922
O/C 32x40 Classical Landscape 1902 Chr 10/91 17,600
O/C 16x29 Mythological Scene Sby 7/92 1,210
Keller, Henry G.   Am 1870-1949
W/Pa 14x18 Road Through a Pine Forest 1950 Wlf 3/92 . . . 100

W&Pe/Pa 5x7 Horse in Collar Wlf 3/92 40
Keller-Reutlingen, Paul W.   Ger 1854-1920
O/C 12x16 Day-Dreaming But 11/91 7,150
Kelley, Mike   1954-
Br&l/Pa 17x14 Untitled 1983 Chr 5/92 5,280
Kelly, Ellsworth   Am 1923-
A/C 100x94 Blue Panel 1986 Sby 11/91 220,000
O/C 34x38 Rogue Chr 5/92 110,000
Pe/Pa 32x39 Curve Radius of Five Feet 60 Sby 6/92 4,950
Kelly, Leon   Am 1901-
O/B 20x23 Painter and His Dog Mys 6/92 825
Kelly, Robert George Talbot   Eng 1861-1934
* See 1992 Edition
Kelly, Sir Gerald   Br 1879-1972
* See 1990 Edition
Kelpe, Paul   Am 1902-1985
* See 1991 Edition
Kemble, Edward Windsor   Am 1861-1933
* See 1992 Edition
Kemeny, Nandor   Hun 1885-
O/B 24x32 Still Life Doll on Table Dum 2/92 2,500
Kemm, Robert   Br -1885
O/C 34x44 The Fortune Teller Chr 2/92 6,050
O/B 9x7 Young Girl Hnz 10/91 625
Kemmer, Hans   Ger a 1495-1554
* See 1990 Edition
Kemp, Oliver   Am 1887-1934
O/Ab 24x18 Man and Kangaroo Dum 1/92 800
Kendall, William Sergeant   Am 1869-1938
* See 1991 Edition
Kendrick, Sydney Percy   Eng 1874-1955
O/C 30x22 Scottish Lassie and Her Dog Slo 2/92 1,600
Kennedy, Cecil   Br 1905-
* See 1992 Edition
Kennedy, David Johnston   Am 1817-1898
G/Pa 9x18 Atlantic City 1876 Chr 12/91 2,750
Kennicott, Robert   Am 1892-1983
MM/B 60x24 Aloha 57 But 2/92 825
Kennington, Thomas Benjamin   Br 1856-1916
* See 1991 Edition
Kensett, John Frederick   Am 1816-1872
O/C 14x24 Black Mountain, Lake George Sby 5/92 286,000
O/C 18x30 Bay of Newport '63 Sby 5/92 170,500
O/C 14x10 Path Through the Forest But 4/92 7,700
O/C 10x16 Colorado Landscape But 11/91 6,600
O/C 17x21 View of a Lake Sby 9/91 6,600
Kent, Rockwell   Am 1882-1971
O/C 28x38 Garden at Oak Ridge, Virginia Sby 5/92 17,600
O/C 28x35 Valley Farm Brd 5/92 14,300
W/Pa 6x11 Seaside Scene Eld 7/92 303
Pe/Pa 7x9 Monhegan Brd 5/92 248
Kenyon, Henry R.   Am -1926
O/B 10x12 Above the Rapids Skn 11/91 770
O/C 12x16 Grand Canal Skn 5/92 770
O/C 12x19 French Cottage Scene Mys 11/91 302
Keokkeok, Johannes Hermanus B.   Dut 1840-1912
* See 1992 Edition
Kepes, Gyorgy   Am 1906-
L,Sd&O/C 30x30 Consumer Collage 1976 Skn 3/92 1,650
O&Sd/C 24x24 Memory Mirror 1963 Sby 10/91 1,320
Keppel   Am 20C
P/Pa 11x14 Two Abstracts Mys 6/92 302
P/Pa 13x16 Abstract Mys 6/92 165
Kerkam, Earl   Am 1890-1965
* See 1990 Edition
Kerling, Anna E.
* See 1991 Edition
Kern, Hermann   Hun 1839-1912
O/Pn 27x19 The Caged Mouse 1891 But 11/91 8,800
O/Pn 19x27 In Der Vorratskammer Sby 2/92 8,250
O/Pn 19x12 Holding a Mug of Beer Chr 5/92 5,280

O/Pn 26x18 Old Man Glass of Wine Wlf 11/91 3,500
O/C 10x8 In the Tailor's Shop Dum 2/92 1,200

.ernan, Joseph F.   Am 1878-1958
O/C 24x20 Boy at Gas Pump Dreamy Over Girl Ih 5/92 . . 2,000
O/C 20x22 Two Hunters w/Quail & Dog 1941 Ih 11/91 . . 2,000

.err, Vernon   Am 20C
O/M 16x20 Fields Were Golden Mor 11/91 100

.errn, Hansine Sophie Joachimi   Dan
826-1860
   * See 1990 Edition . . . .

.ertesz, Istvan   Hun 20C
O/C 24x30 Gypsy Memories Dum 1/92 1,000

.etteman, Erwin
O/C 24x32 Winter Mountain Ald 3/92 425

.ettle, Tilly   Br 1735-1786
O/C 36x28 Portrait Wife of Colonel Howard Sby 1/92 2,200

.etzky, J. W.   Am 20C
O/C 16x20 Pair of Floral Still Lifes 1966 Yng 2/92 50

.eulemans, Johannes Gerardus   Dut
842-1878
   * See 1992 Edition . . . .

.ever, Jacob Simon Hendrick   Dut
854-1922
O/C 25x19 The Reading Lesson Slo 10/91 2,700
O/C 24x20 Interior with Maidservant Slo 2/92 2,250
O/C 21x19 Daffodils and Hollyhocks Doy 11/91 2,200

.ey, Adraien Thomasz   Dut 16C
   * See 1990 Edition . . . .

.ey, John Ross   Am 1832-1920
O/C 16x32 Mountain Lake '78 Wes 11/91 6,050
C/Pa 12x19 Down the River Skn 9/91 330

.ey, William   1520-1568
O/Pn 20x15 Portrait of a Gentleman Chr 1/92 19,800

.hnopff, Fernand   Bel 1858-1921
   * See 1992 Edition . . . .

.hvitia, Mikhail   Rus 20C
O/C 24x29 Still Life Conch Shell and Oranges '85 Wlf 11/91 . 170
O/C 21x33 Spring in the Mountains '89 Wlf 11/91 150
O/C 23x32 Road to the Village '88 Wlf 11/91 100

.idder, Harvey   Am 1918-
O/C 22x20 Two Steelworkers by Furnace 1954 Ih 5/92 . . . 2,000

.ieczynski, Bodhan   Pol 1850-1916
   * See 1991 Edition . . . .

.iederich, Paul Joseph   Ger 1809-1850
   * See 1991 Edition . . . .

.iefer, Anselm   Ger 1945-
O&MM/C 110x110 Saulen 83 Chr 5/92 638,000
O/C 65x61 Markische Heide 1973 Chr 5/92 242,000
O/L 52x69 Der Ritt an Die Weichel Sby 5/92 154,000
Ph,A&C/Pa 23x31 Des Mahlers Atelier Chr 2/92 49,500
W&H/Pa 20x25 Monument Chr 5/92 46,200
G&W/Pa 12x16 Heliogabal Chr 2/92 41,800
W/Pa 16x22 Margarethe Sulamith Chr 5/92 41,800
O&Ph 23x33 Your Golden Hair, Margarete Sby 5/92 27,500
W/Pa 16x12 Tannhauser Seeing Grotto of Venus Chr 5/92 . 22,000
W/Pa 16x12 Grotto of Venus Chr 5/92 14,300

.ienholz, Edward   Am 1927-
   * See 1992 Edition . . . .

.iesel, Conrad   Ger 1846-1921
   * See 1992 Edition . . . .

.ihn, W. Langdon   Am 1898-1957
W/Pa 20x15 Puebla Indian of Laguna 1921 Eld 4/92 2,420

.ikoine, Michel   Fr 1892-1968
O/C 32x26 Cottages in the Woods Sby 2/92 17,600
O/C 26x21 Paysage Avec Maisons Sby 6/92 8,800

.ilbourne, Samuel A.   Am 1836-1881
O/C 13x8 Game Bird Eld 7/92 1,100

.ilburne, George Goodwin   Br 1839-1924
O/Pn 10x7 Hunting Scene '92 Chr 2/92 2,090

.ilgour, Andrew Wilkie   Can 1868-1930
O/Pn 5x7 Black Cedars, St. Faustin: Pair Sbt 11/91 550

.illgore, Charles P.   Am 20C
   * See 1991 Edition . . . .

.ilpack, Sarah Louise   Am 1880-1909
O/B 8x4 Stormy Coast Fre 10/91 550

Kilpatrick, Aaron Edward   Am 1872-1953
O/C 18x24 Spring Flowers But 10/91 1,980
O/C 18x25 Morrow Mist 1926 But 2/92 1,870
O/C 20x24 Winter, Owens Valley 1928 But 10/91 1,320

Kimball, Alonzo   Am 1874-1923
C&P/Pa 21x16 Portrait of a Gentleman Slo 2/92 50

Kimball, Charles F.   Am 1835-1907
O/C 38x55 Portland Harbor Brd 8/92 18,700
O/C 22x36 Coal Sheds, Topsham 1882 Brd 8/92 12,100
O/C 24x30 Under the Elms 1871 Brd 8/92 3,850
O/C 10x18 Presumpscot Falls Brd 8/92 3,740
O/C 11x15 Coal Sheds, Topsham 1881 Brd 8/92 3,520
O/C 12x18 Cushing Point 1883 Brd 8/92 2,750
O/C 12x18 The Fence 1883 Brd 8/92 2,200
O/C 12x10 Respite in the Woods Brd 8/92 2,090
O/C 10x18 Portland w/View Fort Gorges 1862 Brd 8/92 . . 1,980
O/C 12x16 Old Brick Shed, Stroudwater 1894 Brd 8/92 . . 1,320
O/C 15x20 View of Cape Elizabeth Brd 8/92 1,100

Kinder, Maria Liszt   1902-
O/C 20x24 Bass Rocks Yng 4/92 250

Kinder, Milton Robert   Am 1907-
W/Pa 11x16 Three Watercolors 1970 Lou 9/91 250
W/Pa 17x23 Three Watercolors Lou 12/91 250

Kindleberger, David   Am a 1900-1905
   * See 1992 Edition . . . .

Kindon, Mary Eliva   Br a 1881-1919
O/C 24x16 A Pensive Gentleman Bor 8/92 450

King, Albert F.   Am 1854-1945
O/C 12x18 A Pail of Apples Chr 9/91 3,850
O/C/B 4x6 Still Life Watermelon and Fruit 1884 Sby 12/91 . 2,750
O/C 12x16 Still Life with Fruit Wlf 10/91 2,000
O/C 14x20 Still Life Pipe, Pretzels & Cheese Sby 4/92 . . 1,760

King, Baragwanath   Br 1864-
G/Pa 18x12 Scottish Coastline Dum 12/91 175

King, Charles Bird   Am 1786-1862
   * See 1992 Edition . . . .

King, Francis Scott   Am 1850-
   * See 1992 Edition . . . .

King, George W.   Am 1836-1922
O/Ab 9x13 Fence in a Field Wlf 3/92 175

King, Haynes   Br 1831-1904
O/C 18x14 Interesting News Chr 2/92 3,850

King, John Yeend   Br 1855-1924
O/C 32x40 Thames Water Meadow Wlf 9/91 3,200

King, M. E.   Am 19C
O/C 8x10 Ships; Sea: Two Wlf 10/91 200

King, Paul   Am 1867-1947
O/C 40x50 A Harbor Scene Chr 11/91 10,450
O/C 50x60 Wooded Winter Landscape Chr 11/91 4,620
O/C/M 25x30 Beach, Valencia, Spain Wes 3/92 4,400
O/C 25x30 Harbor View Constantinople Chr 11/91 2,420
O/Pn 11x14 Western Landscape Slo 4/92 475
Pe/Pa 8x6 Trees by a Pond Yng 4/92 175

King, William B.   Am 1880-1927
C/Pa 19x25 Couple Visiting Lawyer with Papers Ih 11/91 . . . 375

King, William J.   Br 1857-
W/Pa 11x17 Seascape 1927 Yng 2/92 125

Kingal, J.   Aus 19C
O/Pn 8x6 A Good Drink 84 Chr 10/91 2,750

Kinghan, Charles   Am 1895-
O/C 25x31 Visiting Woman in Sickbed 1937 Ih 11/91 400

Kingman, Dong   Am 1911-1985
W/Pa 13x22 Day at the Beach 48 But 6/92 5,225
MM&L/Pa/B 16x12 San Francisco 72 Sby 12/91 3,850
W/Pa 29x21 Vigilant City Doy 12/91 3,250
W/Pa 22x15 Ferry Building, San Francisco But 10/91 2,475
W/Pa 15x22 First Trains, Now Planes 40 But 6/92 1,980
W/Pa 22x29 Building on South Street, 1956 Doy 12/91 . . . 1,900
W/C 21x14 The Three Eye Doctor Doy 12/91 1,700
W/Pa 19x25 Cathedral But 10/91 1,100
W/Pa 14x20 Mountain Landscape Slo 7/92 750
Br&I/Pa 16x14 The Cathedral Skn 3/92 82

Kingman, Eduardo   20C
O/C 23x19 Nina Indigena 45 Chr 5/92 7,480

135

Kingsbury, Edward R.   Am -1940
O/C 19x26 Ogunquit Yng 4/92   700
Kinley, Peter   Br 20C
* See 1992 Edition . . . .
**Kinnaird, Frederick Gerald   Br a
1864-1881**
O/C 30x40 Waiting for the Return Sby 7/92   3,300
Kinner, D.
P/Pa 16x20 Still Life Fruit and Pitcher Eld 7/92   55
Kinson, Francois Joseph   Flm 1771-1839
* See 1992 Edition . . . .
Kinzel, Josef   Aus 1852-1925
* See 1990 Edition . . . .
Kipness, Robert   Am 1931-
* See 1992 Edition . . . .
Kippenberger, Martin   20C
O/C 59x71 She Searches for Color 84 Sby 10/91   7,150
Kirberg, Otto   Ger 1850-1926
* See 1992 Edition . . . .
Kirby, J. K.   Eng 20C
O/C 15x18 Hookers on the Street Mys 6/92   605
Kirchner, Ernst Ludwig   Ger 1880-1938
W&K/Pa 14x20 Akte im Wald Chr 11/91   27,500
Y/Pa 10x14 Roter Pavillon, Dresden Chr 11/91   16,500
I/Pa 5x9 Liegender Weiblicher Akt Sby 5/92   4,950
Kirchner, Otto   Ger 1887-1960
O/B 9x7 German Man Drinking Wine Dum 9/91   1,100
O/B 9x7 Monk Pouring Wine by Candlelight Wlf 3/92   625
Kirischke, Franz   Aus 20C
O/C 24x20 Decorative Objects on a Table Hnd 12/91   1,200
Kirk, Frank C.   Am 1889-1963
O/Cb 10x12 Down Home Skn 5/92   660
Kirk, R.   Eng 19C
O/C 19x23 The Rivals Hnz 5/92   800
Kirkeby, Per   1938-
C,G&Os/Pa 30x21 Untitled 88 Chr 11/91   5,500
Kirkpatrick, Wm. Arber-Brown   Am 1880-
O/B 30x30 Gentleman's Still Life Yng 4/92   750
Kirnbock, R.   Con 19C
O/C 13x16 Three Dachshunds Sby 6/92   4,125
Kirsch, Max E.
O/C 18x16 Village Landscape 1916 Sby 10/91   1,320
Kirshner, Otto
O/B 10x8 Man Smoking a Pipe Dum 1/92   950
Kisling, Moise   Pol 1891-1953
O/C 29x21 Portrait de Jeune Fille Sby 2/92   90,200
O/C 22x15 Jeune Fille au Corsage Bleu Sby 11/91   68,750
O/C 12x10 Vase de Fleurs Sby 5/92   38,500
O/C 16x22 Les Fruits Sby 2/92   22,000
Kitaj, Robert B.   20C
O/C 31x85 To Live in Peace (The Singers) 73 Sby 11/91 .   330,000
O/C 48x48 Rock Garden (The Nation) Sby 5/92   154,000
C&P/Pa 54x23 Paris Bather (The Art Student) Sby 11/91 .   30,250
C/Pa 44x23 Ann on Drancy Street Sby 11/91   22,000
Kitajima, Asaichi   Jap 1877-1947
* See 1992 Edition . . . .
Kitchell, Hudson Mindell   Am 1862-1944
O/C 25x30 Indians Sunset Landscape 1925 Wes 11/91 . . .   1,980
O/C 18x24 Tepee in Landscape Wlf 9/91   1,200
O/C 14x10 Forest Glow Doy 12/91   850
O/C 10x8 Landscape with Figure Dum 11/91   800
O/C 22x30 Forest Scene with Figures 1919 Dum 8/92 . . .   750
O/C 25x30 Landscape at Sunset Fre 10/91   550
O/C 25x30 Landscape Wlf 6/92   450
O/C 16x12 Moonlit Cove 1921 Skn 3/92   385
O/C 9x10 Indian Encampment at Sunset Slo 10/91   375
O/C 22x30 Forest Scene with Two Figures 1919 Hnd 6/92 . .   300
O/C 25x30 Moonlit Landscape Wlf 6/92   300
O/B 14x10 Early Fall Maine Woods Yng 2/92   275
Kitchell, Joseph Gray   Am
O/C 12x16 Indians at Campfire Dum 11/91   300
Klaerskou, Frederick   Dan 1805-1891
* See 1990 Edition . . . .
Klaus, Joseph   Bel 19C
* See 1990 Edition . . . .

Klee, Paul   Sws 1879-1940
W&G/Pa/B 7x8 Ohne Titel 1915 Sby 5/92   385,00
G&Pe/Pa 13x19 Gruppe macht Augen 1938 Chr 5/92 . . .   374,00
W&Pl/Pa/B 7x4 Kleines Bildnis 1921 Sby 11/91   264,00
T/Cot/B 8x4 Kopf Chr 11/91   220,00
G/Pa/Pa 11x9 Structural II Chr 11/91   198,00
O&Pe/C/B 20x13 Scheinbar Bescheiden 1937 Chr 11/91 .   165,00
Pl/Pa 10x12 Sommerschloss bei Beride 1927 Chr 11/91 . .   82,50
Pl/Pa 14x12 Blume und Fruchte 1927 Chr 5/92   77,00
G/Pa 11x8 Landstreicher Abendsonne 1939 Sby 11/91 . . .   77,00
Pl/Pa 13x10 Sonderling 1930 Chr 5/92   46,20
Pe/Pa/Pa 12x18 Katze Lauert Chr 11/91   44,00
Y&Pe/Pa 12x8 Tanzstunde 1940 Sby 11/91   25,30
G/Pa 7x11 Die Welle Chr 11/91   22,00
Pe/Pa/B 19x13 Somnambulatura 1934 Sby 10/91   8,25
Kleemann, Ron   Am 1937-
A/C 22x38 Sear's Point "Vettes" Chr 2/92   8,80
Kleiber, Hans
W/Pa 16x15 Mallards Flying Ald 3/92   35
Kleinschmidt, Paul   Ger 1883-1949
* See 1991 Edition . . . .
Kleitsch, Joseph   Am 1881-1931
O/C 26x32 Church in a Landscape But 2/92   4,40
O/C 12x16 Coastal Scene Sby 12/91   3,85
O/C 18x24 Parental Joys Hnd 6/92   85
Klemm, E.   Aus 19C
O/Pn 8x13 Historian in His Study Skn 11/91   99
Klever, Julius Sergius   Rus 1850-1924
O/C/B 19x14 Hyacinths in a Pitcher 1901 But 5/92   3,30
Kley, Heinrich   Ger 1863-1945
Pl/Pa 12x10 Two Cloven-Footed Man-Beasts 1908 Ih 11/91   3,80
Kleyn, Lodewyk Johannes   Dut 1817-1897
* See 1991 Edition . . . .
Klickermann, Willhelm   Ger 19C
O/C 16x20 Rocky River Mys 6/92   5
Klimley, Stan   Am
G/Pa 18x11 Group of People Drinking Coffee Ih 5/92   32
**Klimsch, Eugen Johann Georg   Ger
1839-1896**
O/C 19x14 Playtime in the Garden 1874 Doy 11/91   11,50
Klimt, Gustav   Aus 1862-1918
Y/Pa 21x14 Kniender Halbakt von Vorne Chr 11/91   12,10
Pe&W/Pa 11x9 Study of a Baby Sby 10/91   1,32
Kline, Franz   Am 1910-1962
O/C 80x60 Henry H II 59 Chr 11/91 . . . .   1.65M
O/Pa/Pa 10x12 Black and White Chr 5/92   104,50
O/Pa/B 24x18 Napoleon Robe Sby 11/91   82,50
I/Pa 15x17 Study for "Mahoning" Sby 10/91   49,50
I/Pa 9x11 Untitled Sby 11/91   49,50
Br&I/Pa 12x9 Black and White '54 Chr 11/91   22,00
Br&I/Pa 9x12 Untitled Chr 11/91   22,00
O/C 16x22 Little Red Bakery 42 Sby 10/91   14,30
Br&I/Pa 18x21 Untitled Chr 11/91   8,80
O/M 13x17 Landscape with House Sby 10/91   5,50
Pe/Pa 12x9 George and Buti: Pair Sby 10/91   1,32
Pe/Pa 10x8 Marge and S. Cohen: Double Sby 10/91   88
Klingender, Louis Henry Weston   Br 1861-
O/C 86x125 Wolf Pack and Stag 1881 But 5/92   22,00
Klinker, Orpha   Am 1891-1964
W/Pa 29x25 Zinnias in Green Vase '36 Mor 3/92   50
Klitgaard, Georgina   Am 1893-
W/Pa 20x14 Pair Floral Still Lifes Mys 11/91   11
Klitz, Anthony   Am 20C
O/C 20x24 Impressionist Street Scene Slo 4/92   10
Kloss, Gene   Am 1903-
W/Pa 28x20 Saints' Day Pilgrimage Hnz 5/92   60
Kluge, Constantine   Fr 1912-
O/C 32x40 Le Quai du Louvre Sby 2/92   4,40
O/C 26x38 Azay-Le-Rideau Eld 7/92   2,09
O/C 24x30 Parisian Street Scene Hnz 5/92   1,60
Klumpe, Anna Elisabeth   Am 1856-1942
* See 1992 Edition . . . .
Knapp, Charles R.   Am 20C
W&G/Pa 11x8 Pilgrimage Fre 4/92   30
I&W/Pa 10x7 Church of St. Nichols, Prague 1934 Slo 7/92 . .   15

Knapp, Charles Wilson   Am 1823-1900
O/C 20x36 The Valley in Autumn Chr 12/91 13,200
O/C 28x51 Raquette River, New York But 11/91 8,250
O/C 20x36 Landscape with Farm Sby 12/91 6,050
O/C 20x36 Landscape Ald 5/92 3,000
O/C 14x24 River and Mountains Hnd 3/92 2,200
O/C 10x14 Pastoral River Landscape Slo 10/91 850
Knapp, Joseph Day   Am 1875-
W/Pa 14x10 Broadbill Drake Dum 9/91 275
Knaths, Karl   Am 1891-1971
O/C 30x48 Ice Pond Mys 11/91 4,950
O/C 30x20 Green Boughs 1951 Hnz 10/91 1,000
W&Pe/Pa 8x7 Man Carrying Fish Wes 5/92 550
W&Pe/Pa 7x9 Untitled Wes 5/92 522
W&Pe/Pa 6x9 Kitchen Scene with Figure and Dog Wlf 10/91 . 500
W/Pa 7x8 Figures in Town Square Yng 4/92 300
H/Pa 6x8 Figure and Still Life Wlf 10/91 80
Knaus, Ludwig   Ger 1829-1910
O/C 26x20 A Handful of Kittens 1865 Sby 2/92 41,250
Knebel, Franz (Jr.)   Sws 1809-1877
  * See 1992 Edition
Knecht, Fern Edie   Am a 1920-
O/B 8x10 Sweet Fern Slo 9/91 300
Knee, Gina   Am 1898-
  * See 1991 Edition . . . .
Kneller, Johann-Zacharias   1644-1702
O/Pn 24x19 Still Life Hanging Game Fowl Sby 1/92 10,450
Kneller, Sir Godfrey   Eng 1648-1723
  * See 1991 Edition . . . .
Knight, Charles R.   Am 1874-1953
  * See 1991 Edition . . . .
Knight, Dame Laura   Br 1877-1970
  * See 1991 Edition . . . .
Knight, Daniel Ridgway   Am 1839-1924
O/C 72x43 A Summer's Folly Chr 5/92 52,800
O/C 35x46 Summer Blossoms Chr 10/91 41,800
O/C 23x19 Waiting Sby 5/92 23,100
W/Pa 14x10 A Peasant Girl 1867 Chr 10/91 6,600
W&G/Pa 15x11 Gathering Flowers Sby 12/91 2,640
W&G/Pa/B 15x11 The Potato Harvester Sby 12/91 2,640
Knight, Frederic   Am 1898-
W/Pa 13x16 Landscape with Two Women Lou 6/92 250
Knight, G.   Br 20C
O/Wd 12x20 Ships at Sea Hnd 5/92 250
Knight, George   Br 20C
O/C 14x10 Off Bamberg Castle 1881 Fre 10/91 450
Knight, Louis Aston   Am 1873-1948
O/C 26x40 French River Landscape Sby 3/92 18,700
O/C 30x24 Cottage Garden Chr 10/91 10,450
O/C 25x30 A Trip to Market Chr 9/91 9,350
O/C 26x32 Cottage by a River Chr 2/92 8,800
O/C 26x32 Jardins de Chantereine Chr 10/91 8,800
O/C 27x50 Cottage by a River Sby 12/91 5,500
O/C 26x33 Old Dam Below our Mill Hnd 10/91 2,800
O/C 32x26 River Scene Hnd 12/91 2,400
O/C 9x12 A Winding River Chr 10/91 2,200
O/Pn 11x14 Diane's Cottage Dum 12/91 2,000
O/Pn 14x11 Rouen Panoramo Skn 9/91 550
Knikker, Jan   Dut 1889-1957
O/C 16x20 Seaside Resort Hnd 10/91 600
O/C 16x12 Two Fishermen Lou 6/92 525
O/C 16x12 Dutch Lakescape Dum 1/92 350
Knip, William Alexander   Dut 1883-1967
O/C 20x32 Farm on the Edge of Marsh Skn 3/92 1,650
Knoebel, Imi   1940-
A/Wd 99x67 Figure Painting 87 Chr 11/91 33,000
O/M 79x68 Untitled 84 Chr 11/91 26,400
Ph 59x38 Projektion Chr 5/92 13,200
A/Wd 44x46 Untitled 86 Chr 5/92 13,200
I&Pe/Pa Size? Untitled 68 Sby 11/91 1,870
Knoebel, Robert   Czk 1874-1924
O/C 16x16 Portrait Young Woman Skn 9/91 165
Knoop, August   Ger 1856-1900
  * See 1992 Edition . . . .

Knopp, Imre   Hun 20C
  * See 1992 Edition
Knowles, Dorothy   Can 1927-
O/C 29x48 Spruce Point on Smokey Day 1981 Sbt 11/91 . . 6,545
Knowles, Elizabeth McGillivray   Can 1866-1928
O/B 7x5 Pair of Landscapes Sbt 5/92 561
Knowles, Farquhar McGillivray   Can 1859-1932
  * See 1992 Edition . . . .
Knowles, George Sheridan   Br 1863-1931
O/C 28x36 The Wedding Feast But 5/92 4,400
Knowles, Judy   Am 20C
W/Pa 15x21 Along the Surf Fre 4/92 80
Knowles, Lila   Can 20C
O/B 12x16 Snow Scene Lou 3/92 325
Knox, Frank   Am 20C
O/C 24x30 Children Feeding Swans Sel 12/91 110
Knox, James   Am 1866-
O/B 8x10 Churches Mys 11/91 660
Knox, John   Br 1778-1845
O/C 25x35 View of Dunbarton Rock & The Clyde Chr 5/92 28,600
Knox, L. Rebecca   Am 20C
  * See 1992 Edition . . . .
Knox, S. Harry   Am 19C
O/Pn 17x15 Chicken and a Rooster Eld 4/92 2,310
Knox, Susan Ricker   Am 1874-1960
O/C 36x30 Two Girls Yng 2/92 1,100
O/C 46x30 Young Girl with Blonde Hair Sel 12/91 900
O/B 20x16 Women in Shawls Eld 7/92 385
Knox, Wilfred   Br 20C
W&G/Pa 10x14 Coast of Brazil 1920 Slo 9/91 750
W&G/Pa 10x14 Running Before the Wind 1916 Slo 9/91 . . . 725
O/C 24x36 Dragon Race Off Cowes Eld 7/92 495
W/Pa 11x15 Venetian Canal View Slo 7/92 175
Kobell, Wilhelm   Ger 1766-1855
  * See 1991 Edition . . . .
Koch, John   Am 1909-1978
  * See 1992 Edition . . . .
Koch, Ludwig   Aus 1866-1934
  * See 1990 Edition . . . .
Koch, Max
O/Pn 14x20 Dutch Interior Scene Hnz 10/91 325
Kocher, Fritz   Am 1904-1973
O/B 22x18 House in L/S Mor 6/92 350
O/C 26x19 Sailing Ship at Dock '29 Mor 11/91 350
Koehler, Henry   Am 1927-
W&O/Pa 14x19 Jockey, Urbano Ratazzi Sby 6/92 3,850
Koehler, Paul R.   Am 1866-1909
P/Pa 20x30 The Bird Estuary But 11/91 935
P/Ab 7x11 House by the Beach Bor 8/92 700
P/B 16x24 A Winding Stream But 5/92 220
Koehler, Robert   Am 19C
  * See 1992 Edition . . . .
Koekkoek   Dut 20C
O/C 33x49 Dutch Canal View 1914 Slo 2/92 1,300
Koekkoek, Barend Cornelis   Dut 1803-1862
O/Pn 7x10 A Village on a River Chr 10/91 28,600
Koekkoek, Hendrik Barend   Dut 1849-1909
O/C 30x25 Figures in a Winter Landscape But 5/92 3,025
Koekkoek, Hendrik Pieter   Dut 1843-1890
O/C 26x40 The Return Home Chr 2/92 6,050
Koekkoek, Hermanus (Jr.)   Dut 1836-1909
O/Pn 7x9 On the Zuyder Zee Chr 10/91 9,350
Koekkoek, Hermanus (Sr.)   Dut 1815-1882
O/C 15x23 Shipping Scenes: Pair Sby 2/92 66,000
O/Pn 9x14 Dry Docked Sby 5/92 19,800
O/C 18x30 The Shipwreck Sby 5/92 4,400
Koekkoek, Hermanus Willem   Dut 1867-1929
O/C 35x51 Charge of the French Cuirassiers Sby 10/91 . . 12,100

Koekkoek, Jan Hermanus   Dut 1778-1851
O/C 16x22 Out to Sea Sby 2/92   25,300
O/C 15x23 Shipwreck Sby 5/92   23,100
Koekkoek, Jan Hermanus Barend   Dut 1840-1912
* See 1992 Edition . . . .
Koekkoek, Marianus Adrianus   Bel 1833-1904
O/C 17x24 Landscape with Cattle Sby 10/91   11,000
Koekkoek, Willem   Dut 1839-1895
* See 1991 Edition . . . .
Koelman, Jan   Dut 19C
W/Pa Size? Italian Girl Mys 11/91   495
Koeniger, Walter   Am 1881-1945
O/M 30x40 Winter Hnz 10/91   1,400
Koerleh
O/C 24x20 German Genre Scene Dum 4/92   350
Koerner, Henry   Am 1915-
* See 1992 Edition . . . .
Koerner, William Henry D.   Am 1878-1938
O/C 22x40 Tall in the Saddle Chr 9/91   10,450
O/C 27x55 The Bell Mare and the Mules 1933 But 4/92 . .   8,800
O&R/B 36x26 Repartee 1917 Sby 12/91   2,640
O/B 19x30 Down by the Wharf Sby 12/91   1,980
O/B 24x36 First View of the Wilderness Sby 12/91   1,980
Koester, Alexander Max   Ger 1864-1932
O/C 23x34 Enten im See Chr 10/91   121,000
O/C 21x29 Funf Enten am Bach Chr 10/91   110,000
O/C 18x30 Funf Enten lm Teich Sby 10/91   110,000
O/C 30x37 Kaffeepause Chr 2/92   110,000
O/C 20x28 Enten lm Wasser Sby 10/91   104,500
O/C 21x31 Six Ducks on the Bank Sby 10/91   82,500
O/C 21x32 Ducks on a Riverbank Chr 5/92   63,800
Koets, Roelof   Dut 1592-1655
* See 1990 Edition . . . .
Koffermans, Marcellus   Dut 16C
* See 1990 Edition . . . .
Kogan, Nina   Rus 1887-1942
* See 1991 Edition . . . .
Kogl, Benedict   Ger 1892-1969
O/C 7x10 Cats Playing in Garden: Pair Sby 7/92   5,225
Kohlmeyer, Ida   Am 1912-
* See 1991 Edition . . . .
Kohn, Irma   Am 20C
O/C 30x30 Urban Scene 18 But 4/92   2,200
Kohrl, Anton   Aus 19C
O/C 13x12 Lady in Red Gown 1881 Slo 10/91   350
Koken, Gustav   Ger 1850-1910
O/C 43x63 Return from School 74 Chr 5/92   9,350
Kokoschka, Oskar   Aus 1886-1980
G/Pa 27x19 Gypsy Girl Sby 2/92   39,600
C/Pa/B 25x17 Portrait of Niuta Kallin Sby 2/92   17,050
Pl/Pa/B 8x7 Vergewaltigung Chr 11/91   14,300
W/Pa 17x11 Portrait of Mary Merson Sby 2/92   12,100
l/Pa 4x9 Josephine 1943 Wlf 10/91   800
W/B 19x14 Floral Still Life 1965 Hnz 10/91   500
Kolar, Jiri   Czk 1914-
L/B 32x24 Untitled Sby 6/92   4,125
L/Pn 39x27 Autovenuse 73 Chr 5/92   3,740
L 10x14 The Ballroom Sby 6/92   3,300
L/B 6x10 Exhibition Hall 67 Sby 6/92   2,310
L 10x19 Untitled (Saint Sebastian) Sby 6/92   2,310
L 11x18 Untitled (Elizabethan Portrait) Sby 6/92   2,200
L 9x8 Untitled (19th Century Couple) 69 Sby 6/92   1,210
L 13x10 Seated Woman with Dog Sby 6/92   770
Kolbe, Ernst   Ger 1876-1945
* See 1992 Edition . . . .
Kolbe, Georg   Ger 1877-1947
S&H/Pa 15x20 Jeune Fille Agenouillee Sby 2/92   1,540
Pl&S/Pa 19x13 Female Nude Sel 9/91   1,400
Kolesnikoff, Sergie   Rus 1889-
O/C 49x63 Fisherman by a River 1945 Chr 2/92   1,650
Kolitz, Louis   Ger 1845-1914
* See 1991 Edition . . . .

Kollack, Mary   Am 1840-
* See 1992 Edition . . . .
Kollner, Augustus   Am 1813-
W/Pa 10x12 Rider and his Horse Chr 11/91   1,100
Kollwitz, Kathe   Ger 1867-1945
C/Pa 22x18 Verzweifelte Frau mit Kind Chr 11/91   38,500
Kolsenikoff, Sergei   Rus 1889-
* See 1990 Edition . . . .
Komar & Melamid   20C
* See 1991 Edition . . . .
Kondratienko, Gavrul P.   Rus 1854-
O/Pn 14x18 Gurzuf on the Black Sea Sby 7/92   1,320
Koninck, Philips   Dut 1619-1688
* See 1991 Edition . . . .
Koning, Roeland   Dut 19C
* See 1992 Edition . . . .
Kono, Micao   Jap 20C
* See 1991 Edition . . . .
Kontny, Pawel A.   Hun 20C
O/C 30x42 Winter Scene Wes 3/92   578
O/C 28x46 Farm in Winter Wes 3/92   440
O/C 20x30 Southern Impression Wes 3/92   220
Kool, Willem Gillesz.   Dut 1608-1666
* See 1990 Edition . . . .
Koons, Jeff   1955-
O/C 45x59 Empire State of Scotch Dewars Chr 11/91   44,000
Ph 36x22 Moses Chr 11/91   20,900
Koopman, Augustus B.   Am 1869-1914
O/Pn 18x15 Man Wearing Hat '92 Wlf 6/92   200
Kopman, Benjamin   Am 1887-1965
W&G/Pb 8x11 Walk Down Main Street Chr 6/92   55
Koppel, Gustave   Aus 1839-1905
* See 1992 Edition . . . .
Koppenol, Cornelis   Dut 1865-1946
O/Pn 19x27 Carousel Ride by the Beach Chr 10/91   3,080
O/C 18x22 Mother and Children in an Interior Hnd 12/91 . .   1,300
Koppien, I.   Ger 19C
O/C 23x34 Bringing in the Nets Fre 4/92   900
Koretsky   Eur 19C
O/C 17x27 Sailors Adrift Hnz 5/92   500
Kornbeck, Peter   Dan 1837-1894
O/C 18x33 Italian Fishing Village 1884 Chr 10/91   6,050
Korovine, Constantin   Rus 1861-1939
O/B 13x16 Paris: Three Doy 11/91   6,250
G/B 5x10 Night Fishermen Sby 6/92   1,210
O/B 13x18 Market Scene Slo 2/92   800
O/Pn 6x7 Troika Scene Hnd 3/92   500
O/Pn 6x7 Winter Sleigh Ride Hnd 3/92   400
Kosa, Emil (Jr.)   Am 1903-1968
O/C 27x38 Malibu Canyon But 10/91   11,000
O/M 24x36 Landscape Mor 11/91   7,000
W/Pa 30x36 Farm in Winter But 6/92   2,200
W/Pa 15x22 Eucalyptus Landscape Mor 11/91   1,800
O/B 20x16 Chrysanthemums But 2/92   935
C/Pa 18x24 Seated Nude Lou 3/92   400
Kosa, Emil (Sr.)   Am 1876-1955
* See 1992 Edition . . . .
Koser, Neil   Am 20C
Y&K/Pa 36x47 Reclining Woman; Seated Nude (2) Fre 12/91   200
Kossak, Jerszy   Pol 1890-1963
* See 1992 Edition . . . .
Kossoff, Leon   20C
O/B 54x66 Inside Kilburn Underground Sby 11/91   82,500
O/Wd 60x49 Portrait of Father III Sby 11/91   77,000
Kossuth, Egon Josef   Czk 1874-
* See 1992 Edition . . . .
Kostabi, Mark   Am 1961-
O/C 72x48 Angel Visited Me in My Cell 1989 Chr 5/92 . . .   4,180
O/C 48x36 Just Passing Through 1989 Chr 5/92   4,180
O/C 50x70 Control 1984 Chr 11/91   3,520
O/C 70x48 Gimme Shelter 1984 Chr 11/91   3,520
O/C 84x60 Straphangers II 1989 Chr 5/92   3,300
O/C 72x50 Cupid Holding a Telephone 84 Chr 11/91   2,750
O/C 30x40 Kostabi Joe 1990 Chr 2/92   2,420

Kostabi, Mark/S. Rockefeller
  * See 1992 Edition
Kosuth, Joseph   Am 20C
  Ph 49x49 (Art as Idea as Idea) Sby 11/91 19,800
Kotarbinski, Milosz   Pol 1854-
  O/Wd 12x16 Countryside with Sheep Dum 2/92 900
Kotschmiester, G.   Ger 20C
  * See 1992 Edition
Kounellis, Jannis   1936-
  T/Pa 28x40 Untitled Sby 11/91 20,900
Kowalski, Leopold Franz   Fr 1856-
  * See 1991 Edition
Kozjakov   Rus 20C
  O/C 31x43 Moonlit Landscape Yng 2/92 400
Kozlow, Richard   Am 20C
  A/Ab 12x12 Honduras-Dos Dum 1/92 450
Krabansky, Gustave   Fr a 1876-1897
  * See 1991 Edition
Kraemer, Peter   Ger 1857-1941
  * See 1991 Edition
Krafft, Carl R.   Am 1884-1938
  O/C 24x27 Fording the Stream Chr 6/92 2,640
  O/C 18x20 Winter Sunset Glow Hnd 5/92 1,400
  O/C 16x20 In From the Fields But 11/91 1,320
Kramer, B. Scheire   Am 19C
  O/C 14x11 Portrait of a Lady 1899 Yng 2/92 375
Kramer, Konrad   Am 1888-
  O/Cb 20x16 Dahlias with Lark Spurs 1930 Chr 11/91 . . 3,300
Kramer, Peter   Ger 1823-1907
  O/C 18x16 Mother and Child 77 Chr 2/92 750
Krantz, F.   Fr 19C
  O/C 15x22 Kittens Hnd 10/91 2,400
Krasin   Eur 20C
  O/C 24x48 Trafalgar Square Slo 4/92 35
Krasner, Lee   Am 1911-
  * See 1992 Edition
Kratochvil, Stephen   Am 1876-
  O/C 24x32 Happy Days on the Shore 1920 Wes 11/91 . . 1,650
Kraus, Georg Melchior   Ger 1737-1806
  * See 1991 Edition
Kraus, Jan   Pol 1760-
  * See 1991 Edition
Krause, August
  P/Pa 11x17 Sheep in a Pasture Hnz 10/91 300
Krause, Lina   Ger 1857-1916
  O/Pn 18x15 Still Life Flowers in a Vase Chr 5/92 935
Krawiec, Walter   Am 1889-
  O/B 16x20 Forest Scene with River Hnz 10/91 190
Kray, Wilhelm   Ger 1828-1889
  * See 1992 Edition
Krehm, William   Am 1901-1968
  O/M 20x24 Landscape Mor 6/92 350
  O/B 11x14 Mountain Desert Landscape Lou 3/92 238
  O/B 12x16 Mountain Landscape Lou 3/92 238
Kremegne, Pincus   Rus 1890-1981
  O/C 20x24 Nature Morte aux Fruit Sby 2/92 15,400
  O/C 21x25 Paysage Chr 5/92 13,750
  O/C 20x26 La Route Du Village Chr 11/91 12,100
  O/C 20x24 Nature Morte Chr 11/91 3,300
Kremelberg, Mary   Am 20C
  O/C 28x22 Seated Nude Slo 10/91 90
Kremer, Petrus   Flm 1801-1888
  O/Pn 31x25 An Outdoor Market 50 Chr 5/92 3,850
Krenn, Edmund   Aus 1846-1902
  * See 1990 Edition
Kretzinger, Clara Josephine   Am 1883-
  * See 1991 Edition
Kretzschmer, Johann-Hermann   Ger 1811-1890
  * See 1992 Edition
Kreutzer, B.   Ger 19C
  O/C 16x20 End of the Day Wlf 9/91 1,400
Kreyder, Alexis Joseph   Fr 1839-1912
  O/C 29x21 Bouquet of Roses in a Blue Vase Sby 2/92 . . 24,750
  O/C 26x34 Still Life Roses in a Monteith Bowl Sby 5/92 . . 10,450

Krieheldorf, Carl   Ger 1863-
  * See 1992 Edition
Krieghoff, Cornelius David   Can 1815-1872
  O/C 8x14 Indian Hunters: Pair Sbt 5/92 70,125
  O/C 13x18 Blizzard Scene 1856 Sbt 11/91 51,425
  O/C 15x19 Indian Hunters in a Canoe Sbt 5/92 51,425
  O/C 12x16 Three Habitants on a Sleigh Sbt 11/91 32,725
  O/B 9x6 Indian Hunter Sbt 5/92 16,830
  O/C 14x11 Indian Squaw with Berries Sbt 11/91 13,090
  W/Pa 6x8 Milk Cart at the Habitant Sbt 11/91 5,610
Kriehuber, Fritz   Aus 1800-1876
  * See 1992 Edition
Krings, Hugo   Ger 1878-
  O/B 5x7 Shepherd and Flock Yng 4/92 175
Krohg, Christian   Nor 1852-1925
  * See 1992 Edition
Kroll, Leon   Am 1884-1974
  O/C 36x59 The Road from the Cove Chr 5/92 132,000
  O/C 20x18 Aldro Hibbard's Wife Chr 6/92 1,760
  O/Pa 12x17 Portrait of the Artist's Wife Slo 7/92 900
Kronberg, Julius Johan F.   Swd 1850-1921
  W&Pe/Pa 18x22 The Bird Seller 76 Sby 7/92 1,980
Kronberg, Louis   Am 1872-1964
  P/Pa 24x18 Red Haired Beauty 1908 Chr 6/92 2,090
  O/C 20x10 Young Woman with a Parrot 1905 Skn 3/92 . . 1,650
  O/C 27x22 The Ballet Girl Lou 12/91 1,600
  O/C 18x14 The Kitten 1904 Brd 8/92 1,072
  P/Pb 25x19 Ballerina with a Fan 1953 Skn 5/92 935
  P/Pb 25x19 Dancer in Red Kneeling 1954 Skn 5/92 . . . 825
  P&H/Pa 21x14 Ballerina Skn 11/91 715
  P/Pb 23x28 The Ballet in Green Skn 11/91 715
  W/Pa 10x14 Mt. Dore 1928 Wes 3/92 330
  W/Pa 10x14 Beach Scene--Etretat 1932 Skn 11/91 . . . 248
Kronberger, Carl   Aus 1841-1921
  O/C 15x12 Boy & Girl w/Umbrellas in Snow:Pair Hnd 5/92 . 22,000
  O/Pn 14x12 The Journey Men Sby 10/91 8,800
Kroyer, Peder Severin   Dan 1851-1909
  O/C/Pn 36x47 Vintage in South Tyrol 1901 Sby 10/91 . . . 82,500
Krug, Herman
  O/B 18x14 Portrait of a German Man Dum 1/92 90
Kruger, Barbara   Am 1945-
  PhSs/Vl 108x192 Untitled (Endangered Species) Sby 11/91 35,750
  Ph 73x48 Untitled (Your Life is Insomnia) Chr 2/92 17,600
Kruger, Richard   Am 1880-
  O/C 28x36 Coastal Seascape Mor 11/91 550
  O/C 28x36 Desert Landscape Wlf 6/92 450
Kruse, Alexander Zerdini   Am 1890-
  O/Pn 16x16 Cold Root Beer Chr 6/92 2,750
Kruse, Emil   Ger 20C
  O/C 40x30 The Matterhorn Wlf 11/91 325
Kruseman, Frederik Marianus   Dut 1816-1882
  O/Pn 12x16 Skaters on a Frozen River 1863 Sby 5/92 . . . 20,900
Kruseman, J* R***   Dut 19C**
  O/C 19x25 Mother and Child Sby 1/92 1,100
Kruseman, Jan Theodor   Dut 1835-1895
  * See 1991 Edition
Krushenick, Nicholas   Am 1929-
  * See 1991 Edition
Kryzanovsky, Roman   Am 1885-1929
  O/C 25x30 Still Life with Toy Monkey Slo 9/91 750
Krzyzanowski, Konrad   Rus 1872-
  O/C 52x72 Coastal Babes Dum 1/92 1,500
Kuba, Ludvik   Czk 1863-1956
  * See 1990 Edition
Kuehne, Max   Am 1880-1968
  O/C 33x40 A Day at the Stadium 1928 Sby 9/91 18,700
  O/M 25x33 The Open Window Chr 9/91 14,300
  O&Pe/M 24x30 The Blue Gate, Rockport Chr 12/91 . . . 13,200
  O/M 24x30 Vase of Flowers in a Room Sby 5/92 11,000
  O/M 24x30 The Promontory Sby 5/92 9,900
  O/C 15x18 Brooklyn Bridge Chr 12/91 8,800

139

O/Pn 24x16 Still Life Anemones and Fruit Chr 9/91 5,500
O/C/B 20x24 Harbor View '18 Sby 3/92 4,400
O/C 30x25 A Corner of the City Chr 9/91 3,300
O/C/B 20x24 Sandy Bay Sby 4/92 3,300
O/C 30x40 Houses by a Harbor Wes 3/92 2,420
O/C 16x20 European Harbor Hnz 10/91 2,300
O/Cb 15x18 Beach at Gloucester 55 Sby 4/92 1,870

Kuenstler, G.
O/B 16x23 Winter Stream 1914 Ald 5/92 160

Kugler, T.   Con 20C
O/C 36x24 Woodland Landscape Slo 10/91 225

Kuhlmann, Edward   Am 1882-1973
O/C 30x24 Grand Philadelphia Ball Fre 4/92 1,400
O/C/B 25x30 Landscape with Lake Wlf 10/91 100

Kuhn, Walt   Am 1877-1949
O/C 32x22 Kansas (Artist as Clown) 1932 Sby 5/92 ... 286,000
O/C 20x16 Portrait of Bert Lahr 1947 Sby 5/92 39,600
O/C 20x24 Peaches on Blue Cloth 1944 Sby 5/92 27,500
O/C 24x22 Landscape with Horses by a Barn 06 Sby 12/91 5,775
O/C 13x18 Head of a Show Girl Doy 12/91 4,200
Pl/Pa 12x9 Woman in a Camisole 1928 But 4/92 1,870
l/Pa 13x9 Nude with Robe Skn 11/91 468
W/Pa 5x4 Clown Portrait Wlf 10/91 300
W/Pa 5x3 Clown with Ball Wlf 10/91 300
W/Pa 5x4 Clown with Red Hair 1941 Wlf 10/91 300

Kuhnen, Pieter Lodewyk   Bel 1812-1877
* See 1992 Edition ....

Kuhnert, Wilhelm   Ger 1865-1926
O/Pn 9x14 On the Look Out 10 Sby 2/92 28,600

Kuitca, Guillermo   Arg 1961-
A/C 43x59 Dos Noches Chr 11/91 18,700
O/C 55x98 Si Yo Fuera El Invierno Mismo Sby 11/91 .. 18,700
O/C 42x45 Artista Sobre el Piso Sby 5/92 17,600

Kulicke, Robert M.   Am 1924-
W/Pa 12x9 Still Life and Vase: Two Chr 9/91 1,980

Kulik, Karl
* See 1991 Edition ....

Kulike, Robert   Am 1924-
W/Pa 11x8 Flowers in a Vase 1960 Eld 7/92 83

Kulz, Fred   Am
G/Pa 26x20 Seated Sultan Eyeing Woman Ilh 5/92 475

Kunc, Milan   20C
* See 1992 Edition ....

Kuniyoshi, Yasuo   Am 1893-1953
* See 1992 Edition ....

Kuntz, Roger
* See 1991 Edition ....

Kupetzky, Jan   1667-1740
* See 1992 Edition ....

Kuranov, V. S.   Rus 1937-
O/C 20x26 View of Vladimir 1991 Slo 2/92 150

Kurelek, William   Can 1927-1977
O/B 23x47 One Crying in Wilderness 1964 Sbt 5/92 ... 42,075
MM/B 14x14 Winter, Hauling Hay 1972 Sbt 5/92 37,400
MM/B 24x48 On the Way to Christmas Mass '76 Sbt 11/91 26,180
MM/B 30x9 Frost Erosion-N. Thompson 1973 Sbt 5/92 ... 6,545
MM/B 5x6 Canadian Storm Trooper '74 Sbt 11/91 3,740

Kuriloff, Edna   Am 20C
O/C 30x24 Houses in the Snow Wlf 10/91 200

Kurz, F. S.   Br 20C
W&G/Pa 12x17 Venetian Canal Fre 12/91 170

Kurzwelly, M.   Am 20C
O/C 39x28 Sunlight in Woods Fre 4/92 650

Kushner, Dorothy Browdy   Am 1909-
W&G/Pa 21x27 California Prismatic Landscape But 2/92 ... 440

Kushner, Robert   1949-
A&MM/Pa 39x29 Red Earrings 85 Chr 11/91 2,750
MM/Pa 24x19 Wicked 85 Sby 6/92 2,475

Kuss, Ferdinand   Aus 1800-1886
O/C 27x22 Still Life Tiger Lilies Lilacs Chr 5/92 8,800

Kutner, Marian
O/C 30x25 Nude Ald 5/92 100

Kuwasseg, Carl Joseph   Fr 1802-1877

Kuwasseg, Charles E. (Jr.)   Fr 20C
* See 1992 Edition ....

Kuwasseg, Charles Euphrasie   Fr 1838-1904
O/C 22x39 Harbor at Dusk 1870 Chr 2/92 16,500
O/C 13x10 Alpine Lake Towns Chr 5/92 8,800
O/C 13x21 Village Along a River But 5/92 7,700
O/C 13x21 Mediterranean Port Scene Hnd 12/91 1,600
O/Pn 9x16 Hauling Up the Sails 1866 Slo 2/92 1,500
O/C 13x10 Port Scene Ald 3/92 950

Kvapil, Charles   Bel 1884-1958
O/C 22x18 Les Cineraires 1932 Chr 11/91 2,200

L'Aine, Moreau   Fr 1740-1806
O/Cp 3x16 Parc Monceau; Cours-La-Reine: Pair Sby 5/92 . 96,250

L'Engle, Lucy Brown   Am 1889-
O/C 30x40 Turtle Dance, Taos 1941 Chr 9/91 3,850

L'Engle, William   Am 1884-1957
* See 1990 Edition ....

L'Huillier, Jacques   Fr 1867-
O/C 43x82 Soleil Levant Sur La Seine Sby 5/92 11,000

L'Orbetto   It 1578-1649
O/C 74x105 Procris and Cephalus Sby 5/92 17,600

La Farge, John   Am 1835-1910
O/Pn 6x9 Camellia in a Japanese Bowl Sby 12/91 28,600
W&G/Pa 8x14 Crater of Kilauea, Sunrise 1890 Sby 12/91 . 27,500
W,G&Pe/Pa 13x10 The Harpist Chr 12/91 18,700
W/Pa/B 5x5 Apple Blossoms and Butterfly Chr 9/91 ... 8,800
W&G/Pa 28x21 Adoring Angel '87 Chr 3/92 7,700
W/Pa 8x14 The Great Pali '63 Slo 7/92 5,500
W/Pa 6x4 Moonlight over Snow Chr 9/91 4,400
G&W/Pa/B 7x4 Study for a St. Elizabeth 1883 Chr 5/92 . 3,850
C&Pe/Pa 13x10 Head of Christ Hnd 10/91 2,800
Pe&C/Pa 11x4 Virgil; Study Chr 9/91 2,200

La Fontaine, Thomas Sherwood   Br 1915-
* See 1991 Edition ....

La Forest, Wesner
* See 1992 Edition ....

La Gatta, John   Am 1894-1976
* See 1992 Edition ....

La Pira   It 20C
G/Pa/B 18x26 Fisherman at Sunset Sby 7/92 3,850

La Roche, Armand   Fr 1826-1903
O/C 18x47 Death of the Messenger Sby 1/92 1,540

La Salle, Charles   Am 1894-1958
* See 1992 Edition ....

La Thangue, Henry Herbert   Br 1859-1929
* See 1991 Edition ....

Labisse, Felix
G/Pa/B 19x25 Praying Mantisses 43 Sby 6/92 1,980

Labitte, Eugene Leon   Fr 1858-
O/C/B 15x24 Landscape Wlf 11/91 300

Labor, Charles   Fr 1813-1900
* See 1990 Edition ....

Laborne, Edme Emile   Fr 1837-1913
O/C 28x39 Place des Vosges Sby 10/91 11,000

Lach, Andreas   Aus 1817-1882
W/B 11x15 Cobblestone Street & A Winter Path Chr 10/91 . 2,420

Lachaise, Eugene A.   Am 1857-1925
* See 1991 Edition ....

Lachaise, Gaston   Am 1882-1935
Pe/Pa 23x18 An Egyptian Dancer Chr 9/91 4,180

Lachance, Georges   Am 1888-
* See 1991 Edition ....

Lachman, Harry B.   Am 1886-1974
O/C 19x24 Hillside Village in Winter 14 Chr 3/92 3,300

Lack, Stephen   Can 1946-
* See 1992 Edition ....

LaCour, Janus Andreas Barthol.   Dan 1837-1909
O/C 47x74 Sandy Beach Scene 1886 Sel 4/92 3,500
O/C 43x66 Coastal Scene with Rocky Cliffs 1875 Sel 4/92 . 3,100

Lacretelle, Jean Edouard   Fr 1817-1900
* See 1990 Edition ....

Lacroix, Charles Francois   Fr 1720-1782
* See 1991 Edition ....

140

Lacroix, Eugene   Am 19C
O/C 18x14 Hanging Fruit 63 Chr 11/91 2,200
Lacroix, H.   Con 19C
O/C 27x21 Clamdiggers Slo 12/91 1,100
Lacroix, Paul   Am a 1858-1869
* See 1992 Edition . . . .
Ladell, Edward   Br 1821-1886
O/C 54x49 Still Life Fruit and Game Sby 10/91 41,250
O/C 27x23 Still Life Rhenish Westerwald Jug Sby 5/92 . . 11,000
Lafon, Francois   Fr 19C
O/Pn 14x11 Cupid's Touch 1886 Chr 2/92 1,980
Lafon, Henri   Fr 19C
O/Pn 10x8 Reading and a Sip of Tea 1852 Chr 5/92 5,500
Lafrenson, Nicolas   Fr 1737-1807
O/Pn 11x9 Ladies in a Park Sby 5/92 11,000
Lagage, Pierre-Cesar
* See 1992 Edition . . . .
Lagar, Celso   1891-1966
O/C 13x16 Circus Performers Chr 11/91 7,700
W,G&C/Pa 19x25 Marseille Bordello with Monkey Sby 6/92 . 7,700
O/C 18x15 Clown Avec Son Chien Chr 2/92 6,820
O&I/Pa 13x17 Au Cirque Chr 2/92 4,620
G&PI/Pa/B 18x14 Circus Performers Chr 11/91 4,400
Lagarde, A. G.   Con 19C
O/Pn 17x11 Still Life Roses with Butterfly 183* Sby 1/92 . . 2,970
LaGatta, John   Am 1894-1977
C/Pa 22x16 Couple in Formal Attire 1933 Ih 11/91 1,400
Lagneau   Fr
* See 1991 Edition . . . .
Lagorio, Liev Felixovitch   Rus 1826-1905
O/C/B 10x11 Along the Crimean Coast 1888 Sby 7/92 . . . 1,100
O/C/B 10x12 Kavkas Landscape 1889 Sby 7/92 1,100
Lagrange, Jacques   Fr 1917-
* See 1992 Edition . . . .
Lagrenee, Jean Jacques   Fr 1739-1821
O/C 27x53 Minerva; Apollo Crowning: Pair 1773 Sby 1/92 33,000
O/C/B 24x19 Young Girl with her Doll Chr 2/92 3,740
Lagrenee, Louis-Jean-Francois   Fr 1725-1805
O/C 19x15 Cupid and Psyche 1778 Sby 1/92 12,100
Laissement, Henri Adolphe   Fr 1854-1921
O/Pn 16x12 A Good Book Sby 2/92 9,625
Lalauze, Alphonse   Fr 1872-
O/C 45x35 Lancetre 1902 Sby 1/92 1,430
Laloue, Eugene Galien   Fr 1854-1941
W&G/B 7x12 Flower Sellers by the Seine Chr 10/91 7,920
O/C 11x14 Marche d'Arras Chr 10/91 7,150
Lam, Wifredo   Cub 1902-1982
O/L 33x42 La Serre (El Invernadero) 1944 Chr 5/92 330,000
O/C 22x18 Foret Chr 11/91 177,000
O/C 50x44 Figure 1961 Sby 11/91 165,000
O/Pa/B 26x38 Sin Titulo Chr 5/92 121,000
G/Pa 35x25 Femme Cheval 1947 Chr 11/91 93,500
G&W/Pa/C 36x48 Dos Figuras Chr 11/91 77,000
G/W/Pa/C 30x19 Figuras Caribenas Chr 11/91 77,000
G&W/Pa/C 36x25 Autorretrato Chr 11/91 55,000
G/Pa 25x19 Untitled 1965 Sby 11/91 27,500
P/Pa 30x22 Femme Cheval 1970 Chr 5/92 19,800
C/Pa 29x20 Diablo 1947 Chr 11/91 16,500
Lama, Giulia   1681-1747
O/C 21x17 Girl Holding a Trumpet Sby 5/92 27,500
LaMantia, Paul   Am 1938-
Pe/Pa 29x41 Untitled 1978 Hnd 5/92 275
Lamasure, Edwin   Am 1866-1916
* See 1992 Edition . . . .
Lamb, Frederick Mortimer   Am 1861-1936
O/C 30x25 Still Life Iris, Poppies Skn 11/91 1,650
O/Pb 18x21 Autumn Landscape Skn 11/91 1,045
O/Pn 16x24 Crashing Surf and Ship Skn 9/91 605
O/C 10x12 Sunlight Through Clouds Skn 11/91 440
Lambdin, George Cochran   Am 1830-1896
O/Pn 24x12 Roses in Full Bloom: Pair 78 Chr 3/92 13,200
O/C 24x18 Pink and Yellow Roses Chr 11/91 12,100
O/Pn 20x12 Roses and Wild Columbine: Pair Chr 3/92 . . . 8,250
O/C 22x18 Still Life of Roses 79 Sby 12/91 2,860

O/C 17x14 Calla Lilly Eld 7/92 1,210
Lambdin, James Reid   Am 1807-1889
O/B 10x15 Mountainous River Landscape 1880 Sel 4/92 . . . 190
Lambert, C.   Bel 20C
O/C 18x26 Harbor Scene w/Foreground Figures Sel 12/91 . . 300
Lambert, Edouard   Fr 20C
O/C 20x24 Village Street Scene Wes 11/91 660
Lambert, George   Br 1710-1765
O/C 79x77 Landscape w/Travelers 1760 Hnd 10/91 65,000
Lambert, Georges   Fr 1919-
* See 1992 Edition . . . .
Lambert, L.   Fr 19C
O/C 29x31 Cats at Play Hnd 3/92 2,000
Lambert, Theodore Roosevelt   Am 1905-1960
* See 1992 Edition . . . .
Lambert-Rucki, Jean   Fr 1888-1967
* See 1992 Edition . . . .
Lambinet, Emile   Fr 1815-1877
O/Pn 17x29 Le Seine a Bougival... 1877 Skn 3/92 9,075
O/C 36x57 Picking Apples 1859 Sel 9/91 8,000
O/C 20x29 Tending the Fields Chr 5/92 7,700
O/Pn 17x29 Au Bord du Canal 1877 Sby 5/92 6,600
O/C 33x51 Au Bords de la Riviere 1875 Chr 2/92 6,050
O/B 10x13 Pres de la Ferme Wes 5/92 3,960
Lambrechts, Jan Baptist   Flm 1680-1731
* See 1992 Edition . . . .
Lambusseti, *   It 19C**
W/Pa 27x39 Jester in the Wine Cellar Sby 7/92 880
Lamme, Arie Johannes   Dut 1812-1900
O/C 14x18 Mother and Children in a Kitchen 63 Hnd 3/92 . 2,200
LaMore, Chet Harmon   Am 1908-
O/C 40x30 The Necromancer 1943 Skn 11/91 2,090
Lampi, Giovanni Battista   It 1807-1857
* See 1991 Edition . . . .
Lamplough, Augustus Osborne   Br 1877-1930
* See 1992 Edition . . . .
Lamy, Pierre Desire Eugene   Fr 1855-1919
* See 1990 Edition . . . .
Lancerotto, Egisto   It 1848-1916
O/C 44x30 The Italian Lovers Sby 10/91 19,250
O/C 59x30 Una Donna Con Fiore Sby 2/92 11,550
Lanckow, Ludwig   Ger 19C
O/B 20x16 Hunter in Winter Forest 71 Chr 10/91 1,980
Lancon, Edouard Michel   Fr 1854-
* See 1991 Edition . . . .
Lancret, Nicolas   Fr 1690-1743
O/Pn 11x9 The Sleeping Shepherdess Sby 5/92 242,000
K/Pa 6x8 Man with Outstretched Arms Chr 1/92 26,400
K/Pa 4x4 A Nobleman Slo 7/91 1,000
Landaluze, Victor Patricio   Cub 1828-1889
O/C 14x11 Mujer Fumando Sby 5/92 22,000
O/C 14x11 Vendedor de Loteria Sby 5/92 20,900
Landelle, Charles Zacharie   Fr 1812-1908
O/C 51x34 Femme Fellah 1869 Chr 10/91 22,000
Landi, Ricardo Verdugo   It 19C
* See 1990 Edition . . . .
Landini, Andrea   It 1847-
* See 1992 Edition . . . .
Landini, Jacopo   It a 14C
T&Gd/Pn 11x9 Ste. Reparata; St. John Baptist (2) Chr 1/92 46,200
Landis, John   Am 1805-
O/C 30x25 Portrait of Gentleman 1840 Fre 4/92 1,450
Landreth   20C
W/Pa 5x7 Waterfowl: Pair Yng 4/92 90
Landseer, Charles   Br 19C
* See 1990 Edition . . . .
Landseer, Sir Edwin Henry   Br 1802-1873
O/C 12x9 Dog Looking Out of a Kennel Sby 6/92 38,500
Landy, Art   Am 1904-
W/Pa 9x23 Farm Scene Lou 3/92 150

Lane, Fitz Hugh   Am 1804-1865
O/C 22x36 Camden Mtns fr Harbor 1859 Sby 12/91 742,500
O/C 16x22 Beached for Repairs, Gloucester Chr 5/92 . . . 330,000
Lane, Leonard C.   Can 20C
* See 1992 Edition . . . .
Lanfranchi, Alessandro   It 1662-1730
* See 1992 Edition . . . .
Lanfranco, Giovanni   It 1582-1647
O/C 56x43 Samson and the Lion Chr 1/92 33,000
Lang, Louis   Am 1814-1893
* See 1990 Edition . . . .
Langdon
W/Pa 8x18 Birch Trees Dum 4/92 55
Lange, E. McNeir   Am 20C
O/Cb 20x16 Stream in Winter Slo 10/91 250
Langendijk, Dirk   Dut 1748-1805
* See 1992 Edition . . . .
Langendyk, Jan Anthonie   Dut 1780-1818
K,Pl&S/Pa 12x18 Fish Mkt Rotterdam 1805 Chr 1/92 4,620
K,Pl&S/Pa 12x18 Flower Mkt Rotterdam 1804 Chr 1/92 . . 4,180
Langer, Olaf Viggo Peter   Dan 1860-1942
O/C 25x35 Blossoming Trees in Spring 1907 Hnd 10/91 . . . 4,000
Langerock, Henri   Bel 1830-1885
W&G/Pa 17x10 Mosques, Egypt Slo 7/92 800
Langeveld, Frans   Dut 1877-1939
O/C 18x32 View of Amsterdam But 5/92 5,500
Langevin, Claude   Can 1942-
* See 1992 Edition . . . .
Langlois, Jerome Martin   Fr 1779-1838
* See 1991 Edition . . . .
Langlois, Mark W.   Br 19C
O/Pn 9x6 The Toy Seller Skn 9/91 990
O/Pn 9x6 Genre Scene Monkey Vendor Skn 9/91 770
Langworthy, William H.   Am 19C
* See 1992 Edition . . . .
Lankes, Julius J.   Am 1884-1960
O/B 12x9 Boy Fishing Hnd 3/92 650
Lanman, Charles   Am 1819-1895
* See 1992 Edition . . . .
Lansil, Walter Franklin   Am 1846-1925
O/C 18x30 A Calm in Vineyard Sound 1883 Skn 11/91 5,225
O/C 18x22 Harbor Front Boston 1913 Eld 7/92 1,540
O/C 9x20 Dawn and Dusk: Pair Slo 10/91 1,400
Lanskoy, Andre   Rus 1902-1976
O/C 58x38 Sombre et Decit 58 Sby 11/91 35,750
O/C 39x50 Angle du Jardin 61 Sby 10/91 30,800
O/C 39x26 Untitled 71 Sby 2/92 26,400
O/C 30x20 Composition in Blue and Grey Sby 2/92 20,350
G&P/Pa 26x20 Abstract Composition-Blue Ground Sby 2/92 19,800
O/C 32x21 Composition Sby 10/91 14,300
G&P/Pa 26x20 Abstract Composition-Blk Ground Sby 2/92 11,000
G&P/Pa 26x20 Abstract Sby 2/92 8,800
G/Pa 5x7 Three Figures Sby 6/92 1,760
Lantz, Paul   Am 1908-
* See 1992 Edition . . . .
Lanyon, Ellen   Am 20C
O/C 49x61 Scrimmage II Hnd 3/92 475
Lanza, Giovanni   It 1827-
W&G/Pa 17x30 Paestum Slo 4/92 2,250
Lapine, Christian Andreas G.   Can 1868-1952
O/B 20x24 The Lumber Mill Sbt 11/91 1,309
Lapira   It 19C
* See 1992 Edition . . . .
Lapira, *   It 20C**
* See 1992 Edition . . . .
Laporte, George Henry   Am 1799-1873
O/C 23x31 Over the Hill Chr 2/92 3,300
Laporte, Georges   Fr 1926-
O/C 26x22 Alleyway Slo 10/91 500
Lapostolet, Charles   Fr 1824-1890
O/Pn 13x16 Le Canal de la Guidecca Chr 5/92 3,520
O/C 16x13 A French Village Chr 2/92 2,860
Lara, Edwina   Eng 19C
O/C 9x7 Lady with Letter 1862 Slo 10/91 250

Lara, Georgina   Br 19C
* See 1992 Edition . . . .
Larche, Francois Raoul   Fr 1860-1912
* See 1992 Edition . . . .
Larionov, Mikhail   Rus 1881-1964
O/C 23x17 La Chaise d'Osier Chr 2/92 14,850
I&S/Pa 8x11 Composition Sby 10/91 1,650
O/Pa/B 10x15 Fish in Motion 1906 Sby 2/92 1,650
G/Pa 11x8 Nude Sby 6/92 550
Larpenteur, J. D.   Fr 19C
O/Pn 18x15 In the Woods; Stag Hunt: Pair Sby 6/92 2,200
Larraz, Julio   Cub 1942-
O/M 30x48 Listening 83 Chr 5/92 24,200
O/C 60x40 Sinforosa's Mirrored Wall 76 Chr 11/91 22,000
Larsen, Adolf Alfred   Dan 1856-1942
O/C 37x50 Sunset Over the Marsh 1909 Sby 10/91 13,200
Larsen, Johannes
O/C 30x40 Extensive Landscape and Lake Hnz 10/91 450
O/C 20x40 Coastline and Seascape Hnz 10/91 375
Larsen, Karl
O/B 30x24 Winter Landscape Dum 6/92 400
O/B 22x24 Blue Vase with Flowers Dum 6/92 350
O/B 22x24 Fall Landscape Dum 6/92 350
O/B 22x24 Rocky Coastline Dum 6/92 325
Larsen, Oscar   Aus 1882-1972
O/C 26x30 Wheatfield 29 Hnd 10/91 850
Larson, Lars   Nor 1876-
O/C 19x25 Farmyard With Children 1916 Wes 11/91 330
Larson, Otto   Ger 1889-
O/C 26x30 Wheatfield 29 Hnd 3/92 900
Larson, W.   Am 20C
O/C 16x24 Ship in Rough Seas 1917 Slo 10/91 300
Larsson, Carl   Swd 1853-1919
* See 1992 Edition . . . .
Larwin, Hans   Aus 1873-1938
O/C 40x40 Death Directs the Bullet Sby 1/92 7,700
O/C 44x44 The Soup Kitchen Sby 1/92 2,640
O/B 14x19 Refugees 1915 Sby 1/92 2,530
O/Pa/B 14x20 Life in the Trenches 1916 Sby 1/92 2,090
O/C/B 19x24 In the Trenches 1916 Sby 1/92 1,980
O/Pa/B 13x17 Machine Gunners 1918 Sby 1/92 1,870
O/B 17x22 After the Battle 1915 Sby 1/92 1,760
O/C/B 16x22 Front Trench 1916 Sby 1/92 1,540
O/Pa/B 25x17 Cossack 1917 Sby 1/92 1,430
O/B 20x17 Hunger Sby 1/92 1,320
O/Pa/B 18x25 Taking Wounded to the Rear 1916 Sby 1/92 1,320
O/Pa/B 10x13 Shooting from the Trench 1915 Sby 1/92 . . . 660
O/B 10x19 Firing the Canons 1916 Sby 1/92 550
O/C 14x20 In Trenches; Russian Church: Two 1916 Sby 7/92 385
Lascano, Juan   Arg 1947-
O/C 51x39 Virgo 90 Chr 11/91 35,200
Lascaux, Elie   20C
O/C 18x24 La Route de Sacre-Coeur Sby 6/92 1,650
Lascelles, J.   Sco 19C
O/C 17x24 Dollaelly, North Wales Wlf 3/92 700
Lasellaz, Gustave Francois   Fr 1848-1910
O/C 10x13 Sur la Plage Sby 2/92 7,700
Lash, Lee   20C
O/B 8x10 New London Harbour Mys 11/91 302
Lasinski   20C
O/B 18x24 Country Church Dum 2/92 95
Laske, Oskar   Aus 1841-1911
* See 1992 Edition . . . .
Lasker, Jonathan   1948-
O/C 72x54 Mantra To a Distracted God 1990 Chr 2/92 . . . 33,000
O/C 60x84 Standards of Expression 1989 Chr 5/92 28,600
O/C 30x24 For a Small Country 1987 Chr 2/92 12,100
O/L 24x30 Beer Culture 1988 Chr 5/92 9,350
Lassalle, Louis   Fr 1810-
O/Pn 10x7 At the Well Dum 4/92 2,000
O/Pn 14x11 Children Gathering Twigs in Snow Chr 5/92 . . 1,800
Lassen, Hans August   Ger 1857-
O/C 25x30 Blowing Bubbles 1888 Sby 1/92 2,310
Lassonde, Omer T.   Am 1903-1980
O/B 12x9 Girl in Pink, 1925 Yng 2/92 250

Lataster, Ger
* See 1992 Edition . . . .
Latham, Barbara   Am 1896-1976
* See 1992 Edition . . . .
Lathrop, C. W.   Am 19C
P/Pa/C 24x19 A Dutch Kitchen '93 Bor 8/92 250
Lathrop, Francis Augustus   Am 1849-1909
O/C 41x34 The Little Seamstress Slo 4/92 2,800
Lathrop, Ida Paulus
O/C 23x35 Landscape American West Dum 2/92 110
Lathrop, William Langson   Am 1859-1938
O/C 16x14 Sketching near Easton 1900 Chr 9/91 1,760
O/B 16x20 In the Marshes 1934 Ald 5/92 900
O/B 16x18 Beach Scene, Montauk 1938 Ald 5/92 575
Latimer, Lorenzo Palmer   Am 1857-1941
* See 1992 Edition . . . .
Latoix, Gaspard   Am 20C
O/C 24x20 Apache Indian on Horseback Sby 12/91 8,800
W/Pa/B 20x15 Cowboy on Horseback Sby 12/91 1,760
Latortue, Franklin   Hai
O/C 40x60 Jungle Chr 5/92 4,950
Latortue, Phillipe   Hai 20C
* See 1992 Edition . . . .
Lattard, Phillip   Am 19C
* See 1990 Edition . . . .
Laubies, Rene
O/B/C 40x26 Untitled 1964 Sby 6/92 1,210
Lauder, Charles James   Br 1841-1920
* See 1991 Edition . . . .
Laudrone, G.   Con 20C
* See 1992 Edition . . . .
Laudy, Jean   Bel 20C
* See 1991 Edition . . . .
Laufman, Sidney   Am 1891-
* See 1992 Edition . . . .
Lauge, Achille   Fr 1861-1944
* See 1992 Edition . . . .
Laugee, Georges   Fr 1853-
O/C 33x23 La Moisson Sby 5/92 9,350
O/C 26x32 Wheat Field w/Peasant Woman 1883 Sel 12/91 . 6,750
Laur, Marie Yvonne   Fr 1879-
O/C 13x10 Luring the Kittens Slo 2/92 1,400
Laurence, Sydney   Am 1865-1940
O/B 12x16 Mount McKinley Chr 12/91 12,100
O/M 8x10 Indian Cache; Springtime: Two Sby 9/91 9,900
O/C 16x20 Mount McKinley Sby 9/91 9,900
O/C 21x26 Early Evening, Mount McKinley But 11/91 6,600
O/C 20x16 Moonlight, Mission Capistrano But 4/92 3,025
O/B 12x16 View of St. Ives Doy 12/91 2,000
W/Pa 17x12 Venice But 11/91 1,320
Laurencin, Marie   Fr 1883-1956
O/C 24x20 Comme un Betail Pensif Sby 11/91 198,000
O/C/B 21x18 Femme a la Guitare Sby 5/92 132,000
O/C 25x21 Vase de Fleurs Avec Lys 1933 Sby 5/92 99,000
O/C 16x13 Fille Couronnee de Feuilles Chr 2/92 88,000
O/C 16x13 Autoportrait 1946 Sby 11/91 66,000
W/Pa 13x18 La Ronde D'Enfants Chr 11/91 47,300
O/Pn 16x12 Autoportrait 1904 Chr 5/92 35,200
W/Pa 12x10 Portrait de Femme Chr 11/91 27,500
W,Br&l/Pa 8x7 Femme a L'Oiseau Chr 11/91 17,600
W/Pa 6x5 Tete de Jeune Fille Chr 2/92 11,000
Laurens, Henri   Fr 1885-1954
G,L,H&K/B 21x12 Tete 1919 Chr 5/92 154,000
Laurens, Jean Paul   Fr 1838-1921
O/C 18x15 Gentleman in a Red Velvet Coat Chr 5/92 1,320
Laurens, Jules Joseph Augustin   Fr 1825-1901
* See 1992 Edition . . . .
Laurent   Fr 19C
O/C 17x13 Hanging Foul Fre 4/92 150
Laurent, Ernest Joseph   Fr 1859-1929
O/C 12x9 Impressionist Landscape Wlf 9/91 700
Laurent, Felix   Fr 1821-1908
* See 1991 Edition . . . .

Laurent, Jean   Fr 20C
O/Pn 12x16 Ships in Distress Slo 12/91 750
Laurent, Robert   Am 20C
C&I/Pa 12x9 Nude Chr 6/92 55
Laurenti, Cesare   It 1854-
O/C 28x39 Blind Man's Bluff 1886 Chr 2/92 66,000
Laurenti, Chesevic   It 19C
W/Pa 10x7 Feeding the Canary Mys 6/92 440
Laurenty, T.   20C
O/C 14x11 Wooded Path in Autumn 1925 Slo 2/92 70
Lauret, Francois   Fr 1820-1868
O/C 26x21 Jeune Homme au Chapeau 1851 Sby 5/92 8,525
Lauritz, Paul   Am 1889-1975
O/C 46x50 Coming Summer But 10/91 14,300
O/C 25x30 California Landscape But 10/91 2,750
O/C 16x20 Boats in Boat Yard Mor 6/92 1,800
O/C 20x24 Sierra Mountains Mor 11/91 1,800
O/B 24x34 Oregon Autumn But 6/92 1,650
O/C 20x24 Spring Landscape Hnz 10/91 1,200
O/C 30x40 Winter Landscape Mor 11/91 1,200
O/B 12x15 Landscape Mor 11/91 1,100
W/Pa 13x19 Snowscape Mor 6/92 600
Laux, August   Am 1853-1921
O/C 10x14 Gooseberries Chr 9/91 6,050
O/C 14x20 Basket of Apples Chr 3/92 5,500
O/C 8x10 Still Life with Cherries in Basket Sby 4/92 1,650
O/Pn 7x5 Kitten with Red Bow Slo 12/91 850
Lavalle, John   Am 1896-
O/C 40x30 Miss Laetitia Orlandini 1928 Skn 11/91 2,200
LaValley, William   Am 20C
O/C 25x30 Forest Interior Mys 6/92 440
O/C 30x24 Forest Interior Mys 6/92 330
Laverdam, A.
O/C 6x9 Parisian Street Scene Dum 6/92 115
Lavery, Sir John   Br 1856-1941
O/C 25x30 Golf Links, North Berwick 1919 Chr 2/92 . . . 121,000
O/C 25x30 The Veranda 1912 Chr 2/92 121,000
O/C 25x30 Rain in the Distance 1919 Chr 2/92 52,800
O/C 25x30 The Sands 1917 Sby 5/92 33,000
Lavielle, Eugene Antoine S.   Fr 1820-1889
* See 1992 Edition . . . .
Laville, Joy   Br 1923-
O/C 51x63 Woman on Two Rocks 1990 Chr 11/91 15,400
P/Pa 25x19 Jarron con Flores 71 Chr 5/92 2,750
P/Pa 13x19 Desnudo 73 Sby 5/92 2,200
Lavreince, Nicolas   Fr 1737-1807
O/Pn 11x9 Ladies in a Park Sby 5/92 11,000
Law, Anthony   Can 20C
O/B 12x16 Winter in Quebec City, 1939 Yng 2/92 1,400
Law, D.   Br 1831-1901
W/Pa 20x12 Canal Scene Hnz 5/92 370
Lawes, Harold   Eng 19C
W/Pa 14x21 On the Dart Devon Wlf 11/91 300
Lawless, Carl   Am 1894-1934
O/C 30x30 Clear Winter Day Chr 3/92 6,050
O/C 15x15 Batik, A Still Life Skn 11/91 990
Lawley, John Douglas   Can 1906-1970
* See 1992 Edition . . . .
Lawley, Lisa   20C
O/L 78x96 Untitled Chr 11/91 825
O/L 76x88 The Four Pursuits 1984 Chr 11/91 55
Lawrence, Edna W.   Am 1898-
* See 1991 Edition . . . .
Lawrence, J.   Br 19C
W/Pa 9x7 Figures by a Windmill 1867 Yng 2/92 50
Lawrence, Jacob   Am 1917-
I&Pe/Pa 17x23 Underground Railroad 1948 Sby 12/91 . . . 5,225
Lawrence, Sir Thomas   Br 1769-1830
Pe/Pa 10x9 Artist's Wife But 11/91 3,575
Pe&K/Pa 15x15 Portrait Study of James, Viscount Sby 7/92 . 1,540
Lawrence, William Goadby   Br
* See 1991 Edition . . . .
Laws, Arthur J.   Am 1894-1960
* See 1992 Edition . . . .

Lawson, Ernest Am 1873-1939
O/C 30x30 River Scene in Winter Sby 12/91 93,500
O/C 21x26 Boathouses Along a River Sby 3/92 77,000
O/C 21x25 The Biltmore Hotel, Palm Beach Chr 9/91 19,800
O/C 16x20 Waterfall But 4/92 12,100
O/B 16x20 Avenue of Trees by Moonlight But 4/92 11,000
Lazare, Lucker Hai
O/C 8x14 Nature Morte avec Poissons 72 Chr 5/92 440
Lazerges, Jean Baptiste Paul Fr 1845-1902
O/C 20x26 Bedouin Camp-Tending Camels 1891 Hnd 12/91 5,000
Lazos, Paula Mex 20C
O/C 32x40 Polvo de Imagenes Disecadas '73 Sel 9/91 . . . 75
Lazzari, Pietro Am 1898-
O/C 22x22 Figures in the Park 1935 Skn 3/92 495
Lazzell, Blanche Am 1878-1956
W/Pa 14x11 Winter Landscape Church 1934 Lou 6/92 275
Le Barbier, Jean-Jacques It 1738-1826
* See 1991 Edition . . . .
Le Berger, Robert Fr 1905-
W/Pa 10x13 Along the Seine Slo 12/91 100
Le Brocquy, Louis 1916-
O/C 30x25 Spinal Form 59 Sby 6/92 5,225
W,G&PI/Pa 5x7 Regents Park 47 Chr 11/91 990
Le Brun, Charles Fr 1619-1690
I&S/Pa 6x9 Trophies for the Gallerie de Glace Slo 7/92 . . . 1,400
Le Brun, Christopher 1951-
O/C 102x144 Pillar, Banner, Fire 82 Chr 2/92 17,600
O/C 78x59 Cloud and Tree 85 Chr 2/92 9,900
O/Pa/Pa 63x43 Untitled 1985 Chr 2/92 5,280
Le Brun, Marie Louise E. V. Fr 1755-1842
* See 1992 Edition . . . .
Le Brun, Rico Am 1900-1964
PI/Pa 24x19 The Weeping Nun 1948 Chr 6/92 935
Le Corbusier Fr 1887-1965
O/C 39x32 Nature Morte 25 Chr 11/91 319,000
C,P&W/Pa 20x15 Le Moscophone Sby 10/91 6,325
Le Moine, Elisabeth Fr a 1783-
* See 1991 Edition . . . .
Le Moyne, Francois Fr 1688-1737
O/C 62x48 The Bathers Chr 5/92 451,000
Le Pelch, Jean Fr 20C
O/C 26x22 Interior with Onions 1957 Slo 12/91 50
Le Persan, Jean Raffy Fr 1920-
O/C 29x36 Montmartre 52 Chr 11/91 4,950
O/Pn 9x10 Winter, Ski Resort Wlf 9/91 1,400
Le Pho Fr 1907-
O/C 22x26 La Cueillette des Parots Sby 6/92 2,420
O/C 32x26 Vase de fleurs Chr 5/92 1,320
O/C 32x26 Femmes dans le jardin Chr 5/92 1,100
O/C 29x36 Deux Jeunes Fille Chr 2/92 880
O/C 26x32 Bouquet de Fleurs Chr 2/92 770
Le Poittevin, Eugene Modeste E Fr 1806-1870
O/C 20x24 Victory Chr 2/92 3,850
Le Roy, Paul Alexandre Alfred Fr 1860-1942
* See 1990 Edition . . . .
Le Sauteur, Claude Can 1926-
* See 1992 Edition . . . .
Le Sidaner, Henri Fr 1862-1939
O/C 31x39 Great Gate, Hampton Court Sby 2/92 110,000
O/C 11x14 Les Roses sur la Maison, Gerberoy Sby 5/92 . 29,700
Le Sueur, Eustache Fr 1616-1655
* See 1991 Edition . . . .
Le Va, Barry Am 20C
I,C&Pts/Pa 48x73 Blocked Structures #6 1981 Sby 11/91 . . 8,800
Lea, Wesley Am 20C
* See 1992 Edition . . . .
Leader, Benjamin Williams Br 1831-1923
O/C 30x52 Stream in Summer Time: North Wales Sby 2/92 29,700
O/C 24x36 Bettws-y-Coed Church 1864 Chr 5/92 16,500
O/C 24x40 English Seaport 1901 Wes 11/91 6,050
O/C 20x30 Capel Curing Hnd 10/91 5,000
O/B 13x17 River Conway at Bettws Y Coed 1899 Sby 7/92 . 4,950

Leader, E. Eng 20C
O/C 16x24 Ducks on a Pond Slo 7/92 425
Lear, Edward Br 1812-1888
* See 1991 Edition . . . .
Lear, John Am 20C
* See 1992 Edition . . . .
Leary, D. F. Am 20C
O/C 24x30 River Landscape 1918 Slo 10/91 110
Leaver, Noel H. Br 1889-1951
W/Pa 11x18 Street Scene Tunis Slo 7/92 3,000
W/Pa 14x10 Mosque in Cairo But 11/91 2,090
W/Pa 17x11 Morocco Hnd 5/92 800
W/Pa 14x10 Mideastern Bay Hnz 5/92 650
W/Pb 15x12 House of Burgessess, Williamsburg Chr 10/91 . 440
Leavers, Lucy A. Br a 1887-1898
* See 1990 Edition . . . .
Leavitt, Edward Chalmers Am 1842-1904
O/C 24x29 Still Life Pink and Yellow Roses 1895 Sby 12/91 4,400
O/C 20x17 Still Life with Dead Game 1872 Chr 11/91 2,200
O/C 24x30 Basket of Roses 1900 Skn 11/91 1,100
O/C 12x24 Still Life Raspberries and Leaf 1893 Skn 11/91 . 1,100
O/C 12x20 Off the Newport Coast Mys 6/92 935
O/C 12x20 Still Life Pink Roses 1897 Skn 3/92 770
O/C 12x20 Anchored, Low Tide 1875 Skn 3/92 715
O/C 6x12 Still Life Raspberries 1902 Skn 3/92 715
Lebadang 1922-
O/C 23x47 Deux Barques Wlf 3/92 1,100
O/C 21x26 Abstract Wlf 9/91 750
A/C 15x18 Untitled Slo 7/92 375
Lebasque, Henri Fr 1865-1937
O/C 31x55 Le Gouter Des Enfants Chr 11/91 33,000
O/C 13x22 Nu Allonge Chr 11/91 30,800
O/C 18x21 Nu au Fauteuil Sby 5/92 28,600
O/C 11x16 Scene de Plage Sby 5/92 16,500
W&Pe/Pa/B 10x14 Midinette Chr 2/92 4,950
P&Pe/Pa 9x7 Girl Reading a Book Sby 2/92 3,080
Lebduska, Lawrence H. Am 1894-1966
O/C 55x84 The Garden of Eden 62 Chr 11/91 5,500
O/C 25x30 Jungle Sunset Sby 4/92 1,540
O/B 12x16 Still Life with Banana '47 Fre 4/92 975
O/C 20x26 Primitive Farm Scene Hnz 10/91 525
Lebedev, Vladimir Rus 1891-1967
O/C 12x16 Untitled (Abstract Forms) Slo 7/92 225
O/Ab 9x12 Untitled (Abstract Landscape) Slo 7/92 225
Lebenstein, Jan
* See 1992 Edition . . . .
Lebourg, Albert Fr 1849-1928
O/C 12x23 Le Bassin a Dieppe Sby 11/91 16,500
O/C 16x29 Environs de Clermont-Ferrand Sby 10/91 14,300
O/C 18x34 Les Laveuses a Pont-Du-Chateau Sby 10/91 . . 13,200
O/C/M 18x15 Le Quai de l'Amiraute a Alger Chr 2/92 7,150
O/C 21x25 Landscape with Cabins Dum 8/92 3,000
W/Pa/B 13x9 Seascape Sby 10/91 1,760
Lebret, Frans & J. Portielje Bel 1820-1909
* See 1992 Edition . . . .
Lebrun, Christopher 1951-
O/C 105x150 Helm 85 Chr 5/92 17,600
Lebrun, Marcel Fr 19C
* See 1992 Edition . . . .
Lecamus, Jules Alexandre Fr 1814-1878
* See 1991 Edition . . . .
Leclaire, Victor Fr 1830-1885
* See 1991 Edition . . . .
LeClerc Des Gobelins Fr 1734-1784
O/C 19x23 Elegant Company Listening: Pair Sby 1/92 . . 132,000
LeClerc, Sebastien Jacques Fr 1734-1785
O/C 19x23 Elegant Company Listening: Pair Sby 1/92 . . 132,000
Lecomte Du Nouy, Jean Jules A. Fr 1842-1923
* See 1992 Edition . . . .
Lecomte, Paul Emile Fr 1877-1950
O/C 25x31 Scene de Marche Sby 2/92 14,300

Lecomte, Valentine Fr 1872-
  * See 1992 Edition . . . .
Lecomte, Victor Fr 1856-1920
  O/C 17x23 Story Time 1888 Sby 10/91 6,875
Lecomte-Vernet, Charles Emile Fr 1821-1900
  * See 1990 Edition . . . .
Leconte, * 19C**
  I,S&G/Pa 10x13 Marine Soleil: Pair 1790 Sby 1/92 2,310
Lecoque, Alois Am 1891-1981
  * See 1992 Edition . . . .
Ledesma, Gabriel Fernandez Mex 1900-1983
  O/C 36x28 La Familia 1926 Chr 11/91 16,500
  O/C 25x28 Serenata Sby 5/92 5,500
  O/C 25x28 Serenade Hnd 10/91 3,200
Leduc, Fernand Can 1916-
  O/C 25x27 Astract Composition '52 Sbt 5/92 7,480
Lee, A. T.
  W/Pa 7x10 Western Landscape w/Buffalo Herd Eld 8/92 99
Lee, Bertha Stringer Am 1873-1937
  O/C 11x15 The Mission Road Mor 3/92 300
Lee, Catherine 1950-
  * See 1992 Edition . . . .
Lee, Doris Emrick Am 1905-1983
  O/Cb 11x16 Landscape with Cows Sby 4/92 1,320
Lee, Frank Am 1908-
  O/C 24x30 Taos Landscape Lou 3/92 400
  O/C 20x24 Taos Pueblo Lou 3/92 375
Lee, Joseph Am 1827-1880
  O/C/B 29x44 Cornelius O'Connor But 10/91 24,750
Lee, Paul Am 20C
  W/Pa 11x23 Rocky Coast Slo 7/92 120
Lee, Robert E. Am 1899-
  * See 1990 Edition . . . .
Lee, Walt Am a 1930-1939
  O/C 20x24 Landscape Mor 11/91 225
Leedy, Laura A. Am 1881-
  O/C 20x24 Harbor Scene Lou 3/92 300
Leemans, Antonius Dut 1631-1673
  * See 1990 Edition . . . .
Leempoels, Jef Bel 1867-
  * See 1991 Edition . . . .
Leenders, William J.
  W/Pa 12x18 Freighter at Anchor Wlf 3/92 275
Leeteg, Edgar Am 20C
  * See 1992 Edition . . . .
Lefebvre, Jules Joseph Fr 1835-1911
  O/Pn 6x13 A Reclining Nude Sby 2/92 16,500
Lefeuvre, Jean Fr 1882-
  * See 1990 Edition . . . .
Lefevre, Jean Fr 1916-
  O/Pn 10x12 Place de la Madeleine But 5/92 2,200
Lefevre, Robert Jacques F. Fr 1755-1830
  * See 1991 Edition . . . .
Lefler, Franz Czk 1831-1898
  O/C 35x51 Putti: Three Panels Sby 10/91 15,400
  O/C 17x48 A Bacchanale Chr 2/92 2,750
Lefort, Jean Fr 1875-1954
  O&P/Pa 14x27 Gathering in the Bois de Boulogne Chr 5/92 17,600
Legacheff, Anton Rus 1798-1865
  * See 1992 Edition . . . .
Leganger, Nicolay Tysland Am 1832-1894
  * See 1992 Edition . . . .
Legat, Leon Fr 1829-
  O/C 32x52 Le Chemin au Bord de la Riviere Sby 5/92 . . . 27,500
Legeay, Jean-Laurent Fr 1710-1786
  K&S/Pa 17x13 Capriccio with Figures Chr 1/92 4,400
Legendre, M. Fr 20C
  O/B 10x13 Village Bridges: Two Yng 2/92 50
Leger, Fernand Fr 1881-1955
  O/C 38x51 Le Petit Dejeuner 21 Chr 11/91 . . . . 7.7M
  O/C 22x26 Les Deux Femmes au Vase Bleu 35 Chr 11/91 385,000
  Pe/Pa 12x17 Trois femmes 21 Chr 5/92 308,000

Pe/Pa 12x10 Deux hommes dans un escalier 24 Chr 5/92 253,000
W&S/Pa 10x13 Etude Pour le Dejeuner 21 Sby 5/92 . . . 198,000
W&I/Pa 10x13 Etude Pour le Remorqueur 18 Sby 5/92 . . 198,000
Pl&Br/Pa/B 25x19 Le Constructeur 51 Chr 5/92 198,000
O/C 20x26 Le Motif Bleu 38 Chr 11/91 198,000
G&S/Pa 11x16 Les Cyclistes 44 Sby 11/91 187,000
Pe,Cp&W/Pa 12x10 Nature morte au buste 24 Chr 5/92 . 165,000
G,Br&I/Pa 22x30 Les Constructeurs 50 Chr 11/91 143,000
W,G&S/Pa 26x20 L'Anniversaire 53 Sby 5/92 121,000
Pe,Pl&W/Pa 10x7 Le Siphon Chr 5/92 121,000
G,Br&I/Pa 19x17 Composition a l'Echiquier 26 Chr 5/92 . 104,500
W,Br&I/Pa 10x12 Nature Morte au Compotier 25 Chr 11/91 93,500
Pe/Pa 13x10 Nature morte avec cafetiere 24 Chr 5/92 . . 93,500
G,W&Pl/Pa 9x6 Les foreurs Chr 5/92 77,000
G,Br&I/Pa 20x14 Figure Polychrome Chr 2/92 52,800
Pe/Pa 19x25 La Danseuse (recto and verso) 31 Chr 11/91 50,600
G&S/Pa 17x14 Composition Murale (Masurel) Sby 5/92 . 46,200
Pl/Pa 12x8 Etude pour "Abondance" Chr 5/92 44,000
Pl/Pa 5x4 Les deux tues 16 Chr 5/92 44,000
Pl/Pa 13x10 Les gants 33 Chr 5/92 41,800
G&S/Pa 8x6 Etude Pour L'Anniversaire 50 Sby 11/91 . . . 38,500
Br&I/Pa 22x30 Composition a l'Oiseau Sby 11/91 36,300
G/Pa 13x9 Composition abstraite 37 Chr 5/92 33,000
Pl&Br/Pa 15x12 Femme Avec Main Devant 39 Chr 5/92 . 30,800
G&S/Pa 19x25 Etude Pour la Ville - La Vitrine Sby 5/92 . 28,600
G,S&Pe/Pa 14x12 Composition Sby 5/92 25,300
G/Pa 9x17 Design United Nations Mural 52 Sby 11/91 . . 24,200
G&S/Pa/B 17x13 L'Ecuyere Dans le Cirque 48 Sby 5/92 . 23,100
G&I/Pa/B 17x25 La Ville Chr 2/92 22,000
G/Pa/B 10x13 Paysage Chr 11/91 19,800
Br&I/Pa/B 16x14 Tete de Femme 40 Sby 11/91 19,800
G&Pe/Pa 13x10 Couverture d'un catalogue Chr 5/92 17,600
I&G/Pa 13x10 Couverture d'un catalogue Chr 5/92 15,400
Pl/Pa/Pa 13x10 Nu debout Chr 5/92 14,300
Pl&Br/Pa 12x9 Element Mecanique 44 Chr 11/91 7,000
Leger, P. F. Am 20C
  O/C/B 25x33 Steamboats in River Landscape Slo 4/92 50
Legge, Russell
  I/Pa 11x16 Nude Female Subjects: Two Dum 1/92 1,000
  I/Pa 8x14 Nude Female Subjects: Two Dum 1/92 800
  I/Pa 13x8 Nude Female Subjects: Two Dum 1/92 750
  I/Pa 15x9 Nude Female Dum 1/92 600
  I/Pa 15x9 Nude Female Dum 1/92 550
  Pl/Pa 18x10 8 Drawings Dum 1/92 450
  Pe/Pa 10x7 Nude Dum 8/92 150
  Pe/Pa 8x7 Nude Dum 8/92 150
Leggett, Alexander Eng 19C
  O/C 32x42 The Cuckoo Clock Slo 10/91 4,500
Legillon, Jean-Francois Fr 1739-1797
  Pe/Pa 9x7 Studies Horses' Heads and Tails 1784 Chr 1/92 . 1,650
Legout-Gerard, Fernand Marie E Fr 1856-1924
  O/C 20x24 The Marketplace Sby 10/91 13,200
  O/C 21x25 Breton Fishing Harbor at Sunset Sby 2/92 . . . 10,450
  O/Pn 11x9 A Breton Fishing Village Sby 2/92 5,775
  O/Pn 9x11 Le Port de la Rochelle 1919 Sby 5/92 5,225
  O/Pn 5x5 A Marketplace Chr 5/92 1,320
Legrain, Pierre Fr 20C
  * See 1990 Edition . . . .
Legrand, Alexandre Fr 1822-1901
  * See 1992 Edition . . . .
Legrand, Jenny Am 20C
  * See 1991 Edition . . . .
Legrand, Louis Fr 1863-1951
  W/Pa 21x15 Le Fils de Charpentier But 5/92 1,650
Lehmbruck, Wilhelm
  * See 1992 Edition . . . .
Lehr, Adam Am 1853-1924
  O/C 20x18 Dogwood Trees Hnd 6/92 700
Leibl, Wilhelm Maria Hubertus Ger 1844-1900
  * See 1991 Edition . . . .
Leibner, O. F. Am 20C
  O/C 20x15 Male Study 1907 Slo 12/91 100

Leickert, Charles Henri Joseph   Bel
1818-1907
  O/C 25x38 River Landscape in Summer 63 Sby 2/92 60,500
  O/Pn 12x16 Lorner Sby 10/91 18,700
  O/C 22x35 A Winter Landscape Sby 2/92 14,300
  O/Pn 13x10 Village Market Sby 2/92 13,200
  O/Pn 9x11 Skaters in a Winter Landscape Doy 11/91 6,250
Leigh, Howard   Am 20C
  W/Pa 18x15 Two Taxco Mexico Scenes 1945 Hnd 12/91 ... 250
  W/Pa 18x22 Morelia Market Scene Hnd 12/91 225
  W/Pa 19x15 Taxco Village Lane 1945 Hnd 12/91 160
Leigh, William Robinson   Am 1866-1955
  O/C 40x30 Ready to Shoot Chr 12/91 159,500
  O/C 28x23 Looking for Strays 1913 Chr 5/92 132,000
  O/C 36x48 Rainbow Bridge by Moonlight Chr 12/91 24,200
  O/C 22x33 The Grand Canyon Chr 5/92 22,000
  O/C 30x26 Niagara Falls Sby 3/92 19,250
  W/Pb 15x21 Horse in Desert Landscape 1937 Sby 3/92 ... 17,050
  Pe/Pa 17x20 Seated Navajo 1951 But 11/91 13,200
  O/Ab 8x12 Desert Landscape Wtf 3/92 3,600
  O/B 13x16 Desert Landscape Wtf 3/92 2,200
  G/Pa 18x13 Battle Scene Wtf 9/91 1,500
Leighner, H. S.   20C
  O/C 18x40 River Landscape Slo 2/92 60
Leighton, Edmund Blair   Br 1853-1922
  * See 1992 Edition ....
Leighton, F.   Br 19C
  O/Pn 12x8 Blowing Bubbles 92 Chr 2/92 2,090
Leighton, Kathryn W.   Am 1876-1952
  O/C 22x26 Blackfoot Indian But 4/92 3,850
  O/C/B 30x26 Cash Money But 4/92 2,475
  O/C 44x36 Old Indian Deep in Thought But 11/91 2,200
Leighton, Lord Frederic   Br 1830-1896
  Pe/Pa 9x7 Head of a Young Girl 1853 Sby 10/91 17,600
Leighton, Nicholas Winfield S.   Am
1847-1898
  O/C 32x54 Seal Skin Brigade Chr 3/92 35,200
Leighton, Scott   Am 1849-1898
  O/C 8x10 Portrait of a Horse Brd 8/92 2,310
  O/C 9x12 Chickens Feeding Mys 11/91 495
Leirner, V.   20C
  O/C 12x18 Summer Landscape at Dawn Slo 2/92 100
Leisser, Martin B.   Am 1845-
  O/B 12x21 Connright Lake 1906 Wes 5/92 330
Leistikow, Walter   Rus 1865-1908
  W&G/Pa 12x19 Wooded Pool in Spring But 11/91 7,150
Leitch
  W/Pa 6x9 Lobster Fisherman Yng 4/92 150
Leith-Ross, Harry   Am 1886-1973
  O/C 22x32 Early Spring Fre 10/91 4,750
  O/C 22x32 Horse Farm Delaware County Fre 10/91 3,400
  O/B 10x8 Through the Trees, Woodstock Skn 5/92 2,090
  O/B 18x28 College Dormitory at Night Ald 5/92 1,900
  W/Pa Dutch Woman Ald 3/92 1,900
  W/Pa 15x19 Church Ald 3/92 500
  O/B 8x10 Woodlot Ald 5/92 250
  Y/Pa 2x4 Path of the East Wind II Ald 5/92 100
Leitner, Leander
  O/B 11x14 Landscape Ald 5/92 100
Lele, Jie   Fr 20C
  C/Pa 14x12 Young Girl Hnz 5/92 25
Leleux, Adolphe Pierre   Fr 1812-1891
  O/C 39x29 Enfants Conduisant Les Oies 1855 Sby 10/91 . 15,400
Leloir, Alexandre Louis   Fr 1843-1884
  O/Pn 10x6 Cavalier But 5/92 1,870
Leloir, Jean-Baptiste Auguste   Fr
1809-1892
  * See 1990 Edition ....
Leloir, Maurice   Fr 1853-1940
  W/Pa 30x22 Les Sept Peches Capitaux 1891 Sby 2/92 6,600
Lelong, Rene   Fr 20C
  * See 1992 Edition ....
Lely, Sir Peter   Br 1618-1680
  * See 1992 Edition ....

Lemaire, Madeleine Jeanne   Fr
1845-1928
  O/Pn 22x18 Tennis Skn 5/92 19,800
  W/Pa 13x21 Still Life and Carnations: Two Sby 7/92 1,430
Lemaire, Marie Therese   Fr 1861-
  * See 1992 Edition ....
Lemaitre, Hernando
  * See 1992 Edition ....
Lembeck, Jack   Am 20C
  A/C 29x36 Toy Anatomy 1988 Chr 2/92 6,380
Lembke, R.   Am 20C
  G&W/Pa 7x8 Four Gouaches Slo 7/92 250
Lemeunier, Basile   Fr 1852-
  * See 1990 Edition ....
Lemieux, Jean-Paul   Can 1904-1990
  O/Pn 28x40 La Nativite '66 Sbt 11/91 130,900
  O/C 31x112 Le Silence Sbt 11/91 84,150
  O/C 49x20 Hommage a Katie Fusch 1971 Sbt 11/91 56,100
  O/C 25x16 La Femme au Collier Sbt 11/91 27,115
Lemmen, Georges   Bel 1865-1916
  * See 1992 Edition ....
Lemmens, Theophile Victor E.   Fr
1821-1867
  O/Pn 7x11 A Cat on the Prowl Chr 2/92 4,180
Lemmermeyer, M.   Am 20C
  O/Cb 16x20 Afternoon at the Seashore Slo 9/91 75
Lemmi, Angeola   Am 20C
  * See 1992 Edition ....
Lemmi, Angiolo   It 19C
  O/C 87x66 The Vestal Virgin 1903 Chr 2/92 22,000
LeMore, Paul   Fr 20C
  * See 1992 Edition ....
Lenepveu, Jules Eugene   Fr 1819-1898
  O/Pn 10x15 Narcissus 1869 Sby 1/92 7,150
Lengo Y Martinez, Horacio   Spa 1890-
  * See 1991 Edition ....
Lennon, Robert   Am 19C
  O/C 16x24 Mt. Shasta Wes 11/91 412
Lenoir, Charles Amable   Fr 1861-
  O/C 49x32 Contemplation Sby 10/91 27,500
Lenoir, Simon-Bernard   1729-1791
  P/Pa/C 22x18 Portrait of a Lady 1762 Sby 1/92 3,410
Lenpen, A.   Con 20C
  * See 1992 Edition ....
Lens, Bernhard (the Younger)   Dut
1682-1740
  * See 1991 Edition ....
Leon Y Escosura, Ignacio   Spa 1834-1901
  * See 1992 Edition ....
Leon, Ernesto
  * See 1992 Edition ....
Leon, Noe   Col 1907-
  * See 1991 Edition ....
Leonard, Hy   Am
  O/C 11x23 Butterfly Woman Lookng Child Flower IIh 5/92 ... 450
Leonard, J. H.   Am 19C
  O/C 24x16 Bouquet of Roses 1902 Hnd 3/92 100
Leonard, John Henry   Eng 1834-1904
  O/Pn 22x34 Highland Lake Sel 4/92 1,700
Leonardi   It 19C
  * See 1992 Edition ....
Leoni, Ottavio Maria   It 1587-1630
  * See 1991 Edition ....
Leontus, Adam   Hai 20C
  * See 1992 Edition ....
Lepere, Jean Baptiste   Fr 1761-1844
  Pe/Pa 6x7 Neoclassical Garden with Obelisk Slo 7/92 ... 500
Lepicie, Michel Nicolas B.   Fr 1735-1784
  O/C 18x15 Young Boy Carrying Portfolio Chr 10/91 ... 93,500
Lepine, Joseph
  * See 1992 Edition ....
Lepine, Stanislas   Fr 1835-1892
  O/C 18x22 Les Bords de la Mame Sby 2/92 23,100

Lepoittevin, Eugene Modeste L. Fr 1806-1870
O/Pn 11x14 Fisherman with Net Sby 1/92 1,100
Lepri, Stanislao It 1905-
O/Pn 29x11 La Tour Mysogine; Tower: Pair 1947 Sby 2/92 . 4,400
Leprin, Marcel Fr 1891-1933
* See 1992 Edition
Leprince, August-Xavier Fr 1799-1826
* See 1991 Edition
Leprince, Jean-Baptiste Fr 1734-1781
* See 1992 Edition
Leray, Prudent Louis Fr 1820-1879
* See 1992 Edition
Leroux, Gaston Veuvenot Fr 1854-
* See 1992 Edition
Leroux, Marie Guillaume C. Fr 1814-1895
O/Pn 12x14 Bridge on a Shallow River But 11/91 1,650
LeRoy, Harold Am 20C
O/B 30x36 Abstract Mys 11/91 82
Leroy, Jules Fr 1833-1865
O/C 17x19 Kittens Making Mischief But 11/91 3,300
O/C 22x18 Le Tic Tac Chr 10/91 2,750
Leroy, P. Fr 19C
* See 1992 Edition
Lersy, Roger
O/C 50x40 Untitled '64 Sby 2/92 495
Lesieur, Pierre Fr 1922-
O/C 55x55 Nu Devant la Glace 63 Sby 6/92 5,500
O/C 32x30 Coquillages 70 Chr 5/92 2,200
O/C 63x63 Lardin des Tuileries 65 Sby 6/92 2,200
Lesley, Don
W/Pa 5x4 Mountain Scenes: Two Hnz 10/91 60
Leslie, Alfred Am 1927-
O/C 68x87 Pythoness 1959 Chr 5/92 44,000
G&L/Pa 19x24 Untitled 1953 Sby 6/92 4,125
O&L/C 7x8 Collage '53 Sby 6/92 935
O&L/F 8x6 Collage Sby 6/92 880
Lesrel, Adolphe Alexandre Fr 1839-1921
O/C 34x79 Bacchante Enivree 1882 Sby 5/92 27,500
Lessing, Carl Friedrich Ger 1808-1880
* See 1990 Edition
Lesueur, Louis Fr 1746-
K/Pa 8x11 Farmhouse with a Tree Chr 1/92 1,540
Lesur, Henry Victor Fr 1863-
O/Pn 16x13 Gentleman and Flower Girl Chr 2/92 7,700
Letendre, Rita Can 1929-
* See 1992 Edition
Letuaire, Pierre Fr 1799-1884
* See 1992 Edition
Leu, August Wilhelm Ger 1819-1897
O/C 26x32 Bavarian Landscape Dum 12/91 1,750
Leullier, Felix Louis Fr 1811-1882
* See 1992 Edition
Leurs, Johannes Karel Dut 1865-1938
O/C 16x24 Landscape Windmills and Cows Sby 7/92 1,650
Leutze, Emanuel Gottlieb Am 1816-1868
* See 1990 Edition
Leuus, Jesus Mex 20C
* See 1992 Edition
Lev-Landau
O/B 22x16 Hassidic Couple Ald 5/92 110
Leve, Frederic Louis Fr 1877-
* See 1991 Edition
Levee, John Harrison Am 1924-
O/C 54x37 Composition in Earth Colors 1954 But 5/92 1,320
O/C 25x20 December II '59 But 5/92 550
Leveille, Andre Fr 1880-1963
O/Pn 16x20 Paysage au Bord de la Riviere But 11/91 3,300
Levene, Sherrie Am 20C
* See 1992 Edition
Lever, Richard Hayley Am 1876-1958
O/C 30x40 J Boats Racing Sby 9/91 23,100
O/C 25x30 Early Morning, Central Park 1933 Wes 11/91 . . . 6,050
O/C 13x16 Harbor with Moored Boats 1915 Hnd 10/91 . . . 4,600
O/B 13x16 St. Ives, Cornwall, England Chr 11/91 4,400

O/C 16x20 Drying the Laundry Chr 6/92 3,080
O/B 11x12 Woodstock, New York 1933 Sby 4/92 2,860
O/C 7x10 Fishing Boats at Anchor, Gloucester Chr 11/91 . . 2,640
O/C 10x13 Fishing Fleet, St. Ives Doy 12/91 1,400
O/C 9x13 House by a River with Tug Boat Lou 12/91 1,350
O/C 8x10 Sunday Morning, St. Ives Chr 6/92 1,320
O/B 12x16 Unloading the Deck But 4/92 1,100
O/C 16x20 Floral Still Life Fre 10/91 1,050
MM/C 10x12 Village Street Skn 3/92 990
W/Pa 14x20 Bridges of New York Hnz 10/91 900
O/B 9x12 Sunset, Porthmeor Beach, St. Ives Lou 9/91 . . . 900
W&Pe/B 8x11 View of the City 1926 Chr 6/92 825
O/B 10x14 Rocky Coast Fre 10/91 350
Levey, H. Eng 20C
W/Pa 10x16 Traveller by Lake Wes 11/91 220
Levi, Julian E. Am 1900-
O/C 9x18 Route 22, Connecticut '37 Skn 3/92 1,045
Levier, Charles Fr 1920-
O/C 40x30 Fleurs sur la Mer Chr 2/92 3,300
O/C 40x30 A la Fenetre Chr 11/91 2,420
O/C 40x30 Les Filles Sby 10/91 2,420
O/C 44x16 Saltimbanque 57 Sby 10/91 2,310
O/C 48x24 La Table Blanche Chr 2/92 2,200
O/B 21x60 Moored Sailing Boats But 11/91 2,200
O/C 30x24 Still Life Sby 10/91 2,200
O/B 15x44 Still Life with Mandolin But 11/91 2,200
O/C 30x40 Sortie du Music Hall Doy 11/91 2,000
O/C 30x40 Le Port Sby 2/92 1,980
O/C 30x44 Le Poisson Doy 11/91 1,800
O/C 30x40 Venise Doy 11/91 1,800
O/C 48x24 Fleurs Sauvages Chr 2/92 1,760
O/C 40x30 Femmes au bar Chr 5/92 1,320
O/C 40x30 Le quais Chr 5/92 1,320
O/C 30x40 Mois de mai Chr 5/92 1,320
O/C 40x30 Tournesols Chr 2/92 1,320
O/C 40x30 Fleurs, Provence Hnd 6/92 1,100
O/C 30x40 Le Refuge Chr 2/92 1,100
O/C 30x40 Le Tarn Chr 11/91 1,100
O/C 40x30 Mediterranee Sby 2/92 1,100
O/C 30x40 Port-en-Bessin Chr 2/92 1,100
O/C 15x30 Rue de Ville Chr 2/92 1,045
O/C 24x20 Personnages Chr 11/91 660
W/Pa 23x32 Four Women Lou 12/91 550
O/C 30x24 Fleurs Chr 5/92 528
O/C 15x22 Street Scenes: Two Wes 3/92 522
W/Pa 23x32 Four Women Lou 9/91 450
O/C 20x24 French Street Scene Fre 10/91 400
W&Y/Pa 30x22 Parisian Lady Hnd 6/92 400
W/Pa 23x32 Still Life with Flowers Lou 9/91 400
W/Pa 23x32 Still Life with Flowers Lou 9/91 400
O/B 15x44 Port Scene Hnd 6/92 350
W/Pa 30x22 Vase of Flowers by a Harbour Hnd 6/92 300
Levine, David Am 1926-
W&Pe/Pa 15x22 Boardwalk at Coney Island Chr 9/91 1,430
I&Pe/Pa 14x11 Portrait of Douglas Cooper 85 Chr 5/92 . . . 1,430
W/Pa 18x10 Young Man in Tied Shirt 78 Sby 6/92 1,430
Pl/Pa 13x11 Caricature of George Balanchine 78 Sby 2/92 . 1,210
O/Pn 6x9 Three Works Chr 9/91 1,210
O/Pn 12x10 Portrait of Walter Fillin Chr 9/91 715
O/C 36x29 The Contralto 1959 Chr 11/91 715
W&Pe/Pa/B 6x10 Low Tide 71 Sby 6/92 440
Levine, David Phillip Am 1910-
W&Pe/Pa 18x14 Woman in Peach Burnoose 79 Chr 11/91 . . 1,045
W/Pa 9x20 Wave Wall 79 Chr 11/91 715
Levine, Jack Am 1915-
O/C 20x16 Mardi Gras 59 Skn 5/92 1,540
Levine, Sherrie Am 1947-
Cs/Wd 24x20 Untitled (Check #2) 1985 Sby 11/91 13,200
Cs&Wx/Wd 24x20 Broad Stripe #9 1985 Sby 5/92 8,800
Ph 29x21 Untitled (aft.Walker Evans:positive Chr 5/92 . . . 7,150
Ph 10x8 After Walker Evans 1987 Chr 11/91 2,860
Levis, Maurice Fr 1860-1902
O/C 18x26 Petite Ferme a St. Leonard Sby 7/92 4,950
Levitan, Isaac Ilyitch Rus 1860-1900
O/C 18x26 The Riverbank Sby 10/91 19,800

Levoiger, A. J. P.   Dut 1853-1952
  * See 1990 Edition . . . .
Levy, Alexander O.   Am 1881-1947
  O/C 41x30 Woman in Red Dress Lou 12/91   2,800
Levy, Nat   Am 1896-1984
  W/Pa 28x35 Old Blacksmith Shop But 2/92   2,475
  W/Pa 14x20 Barns in Landscape Mor 3/92   1,500
Levy, Rudolph
  * See 1992 Edition . . . .
Levy-Dhurmer, Lucien   Fr 1865-1953
  P&C/Pa 24x16 The Embrace: Double Sby 7/92   1,100
Lew, August Wilhelm   Ger 1819-1897
  * See 1990 Edition . . . .
Lewan, Dennis   Am 20C
  O/B 12x16 Winter Scene Hnd 6/92   200
Lewandowski, Edmund D.   Am 1914-
  * See 1990 Edition . . . .
Lewis, Alonzo Victor   Am 1886-1946
  O/B 15x12 Chief Joseph's Last Camp, MT 1929 Lou 6/92 . .   225
  O/B 15x11 Bear Paw Mountain, Montana 1928 Lou 6/92 . . .   200
Lewis, Charles James   Br 1830-1892
  * See 1992 Edition . . . .
Lewis, Edmund Darch   Am 1835-1910
  O/C 36x60 Centennial Exhibition, Phila. 1876 Chr 3/92 . .   22,000
  W/Pa/B 9x21 Town by the Sea 1878 Chr 6/92   2,310
  W&G/Pb 10x20 Ships by a Lighthouse 1891 Chr 11/91 . . .   1,760
  W/Pa 10x21 View of Narragansett 1902 But 11/91   1,760
  W/Pb 10x21 Sailboat off a Rocky Coast 1884 Chr 6/92 . . .   1,650
  W/Pb 19x29 Italianate Villa 1882 Chr 11/91   1,320
  W/Pa 10x21 Coastal Scene Mys 6/92   1,045
  O/C 30x20 Vermont Landscape Brd 5/92   1,045
  W/Pa/B 9x19 Rocky Coast with Sailboats 1888 Chr 11/91 . .   935
  W/Pa 12x19 Cows by the River 1857 Mys 11/91   632
  W&G/Pa 10x21 Lowtide 1885 Chr 11/91   605
  W/Pa 15x30 Fairmount Park 1910 Fre 4/92   500
  W&G/Pa 11x29 Japanese Gardens 1910 Fre 4/92   400
  W&G/Pa 18x27 Seascape 1907 Bor 8/92   300
Lewis, Geoffrey   Am 20C
  * See 1990 Edition . . . .
Lewis, H.
  P/Pa 18x40 Teepee by a Lake Dum 10/91   450
Lewis, Harry Emerson   Am 1892-1958
  O/M 22x28 The Artists Afield-La Quinta Canyon Mor 3/92 .   1,500
  O/M 20x24 Palm Canyon Mor 3/92   1,200
  O/B 28x36 Our Coast Mor 3/92   950
Lewis, Jeanette Maxfield   Am 1894-1982
  O/B 16x20 Street Scene Sby 12/91   990
Lewis, John Frederick   Br 1805-1876
  W&H/Pa 10x14 A Halt in the Desert Sby 1/92   3,520
Lewis, L.   Eng 20C
  W/Pa 9x21 On the Shore Hnz 5/92   100
Lewis, Martin   Am 1883-1962
  W/Pa 21x28 The Lobsterman Brd 8/92   4,840
  Y/Pa 13x8 Study for Building in Babylon 29 Hnd 3/92 . . .   800
Lewis, Percy Wyndham   Br 1882-1957
  * See 1991 Edition . . . .
LeWitt, Sol   Am 1928-
  Pe/Pa 48x48 Wall Drawing No. 1: II (A & B): (2) Sby 5/92   82,500
  S/Pa 72x150 Folding Screen Chr 11/91   39,600
  Pe/Pa 48x48 Wall Drawing No. 12: (4) Sby 5/92   36,300
  Pe&I/Pa 22x22 Location of Several Lines 1974 Sby 11/91 . .   7,700
  I/Pls 18x18 Midpoint of Lines Sby 11/91   7,700
  I/Pa 22x22 Untitled 82 Chr 11/91   7,700
  PI/Pa 11x11 Four Color Drawings 1971 Chr 11/91   7,150
  I&Pe/Pa 20x20 Blue Lines From the Center 1975 Sby 5/92 .   6,050
  Br&I/Pa 22x22 Untitled 82 Chr 5/92   6,050
  Br&I/Pa 22x22 Untitled 82 Chr 5/92   6,050
  I&H/Pa 15x15 Untitled 1975 Chr 11/91   5,280
  G/Pa 10x22 Three Untitled drawings 1989 Chr 5/92   5,060
  I/Pa 14x18 Untitled 89 Sby 2/92   4,400
  G/Pa 15x22 Irregular Forms 88 Chr 11/91   4,400
  W&Pe/Pa 11x11 Untitled Sby 2/92   4,400
  I/Pa 16x16 Grid (1/8") 1971 Chr 5/92   3,300
  PI/Pa 11x11 Three drawings Chr 5/92   2,750
  S&Pe/Pa 10x10 Untitled 81 Sby 2/92   1,100

Leyendecker, Frank Xavier   Am 1877-1924
  * See 1992 Edition . . . .
Leyendecker, Joseph Christian   Am 1874-1951
  O/C 26x19 Easter (Cover Sat. Evening Post) But 4/92   8,800
  O/C 21x30 Campers Beside a River Wes 5/92   1,650
  O/C 24x32 Illustrative Studies Sby 12/91   1,650
  O/C 21x14 Men in Hats in Profile Ih 5/92   1,300
Leyendecker, Paul Joseph   Fr 1842-
  * See 1992 Edition . . . .
Leyster, Judith   Dut 1610-1660
  * See 1992 Edition . . . .
Lhermitte, Leon Augustin   Fr 1844-1925
  O/C 85x104 The Haymakers 1887 Sby 10/91   528,000
  O/C 22x16 Jeune Mere Sby 5/92   46,750
  O/C 16x13 Maternite Sby 2/92   39,600
  P/Pa 17x23 Le Soir au Jardin a Charteves 1893 Chr 5/92 .   33,000
  P/Pa/C 12x18 Paysanne dans un champ de ble Chr 10/91 .   26,400
  P/Pa 14x17 Glaneuses Sby 2/92   16,500
  Y/Pa 15x11 Fenaison Sby 2/92   14,300
  P/Pa 13x16 Le Chateau d'Armentieres Sby 10/91   13,200
  P/Pa 17x13 L'Hyevrette, Deux Pecheurs Sby 2/92   8,525
  C/Pa 16x18 Le Repas dans la Cuisine Sby 2/92   7,150
  P/Pa/B 13x10 Rue a Arcachon Chr 10/91   7,150
  P&K/Pa 12x10 Portrait of a Young Girl Chr 10/91   5,500
  P/Pa 10x13 Les Faucheurs Sby 2/92   3,850
Lhote, Andre   Fr 1885-1962
  O/C 16x24 Voilier a Bordeaux Chr 11/91   25,300
  O/Bu 21x26 Maison a Travers les Arbres Chr 2/92   22,000
  O/C 20x24 Paysage Chr 2/92   20,350
  O/Pa/B 19x24 Trois femmes dans un paysage Chr 5/92 . .   15,400
  O/C 14x20 Paysage Sby 5/92   14,300
  O/C 14x20 Village en Automne Sby 2/92   11,275
  G&W/Pa/B 12x15 Le Village Chr 11/91   4,950
  G&W/Pa/B 11x15 Paysage Chr 11/91   4,950
Liberi, Pietro   It 1614-1687
  O/C 36x31 An Allegory of Prudence Chr 5/92   44,000
  O/C 46x61 Allegory the Constancy of Love Sby 1/92   38,500
Liberman, Alexander   Am 1912-
  * See 1992 Edition . . . .
Liberte, Jean   Fr 20C
  MM/Pn 9x6 Mother and Child Slo 2/92   225
  W&G/Pa 11x17 Village Scene Slo 2/92   125
Liberti, Carlos
  * See 1992 Edition . . . .
Liberti, F.   18C
  O/C 20x23 Putti Frolicking 17*9 Chr 10/91   7,700
Libertino   It 1614-1687
  O/C 46x61 Allegory the Constancy of Love Sby 1/92   38,500
Liberts, Ludolfs   Rus 1895-1945
  O/C 35x24 Paris Street at Night But 11/91   5,500
Lichtenstein, Roy   Am 1923-
  Mg/C 56x48 Non Objective I Sby 11/91   935,000
  O&Mg/C 50x60 In Deep Thought '80 Sby 11/91   550,000
  O&Mg/C 40x50 Path Through the Forest '84 Sby 11/91 . .   220,000
  H,Fp&Cp/Pa 6x5 Study for Sweet Dreams, Baby! Chr 5/92   99,000
  Y&H/Pa 6x6 Ohh... Albright... 1964 Chr 2/92   88,000
  E/St 26x42 Brushstroke Chr 11/91   33,000
  H&Cp/Pa 4x6 Study Modern Painting w/Sun Ray Chr 5/92   28,600
  H&Cp/Pa 6x6 Study for Dawning 64 Chr 11/91   26,400
  Mg/B 28x22 Untitled Chr 11/91   22,000
  L&MM/Pa 15x20 Landscape 1965 Sby 10/91   16,500
  MM/Cd 14x21 Landscape 1965 Doy 11/91   7,000
Licinio, Bernardino   It 1489-1560
  * See 1992 Edition . . . .
Lidderdale, Charles S.   Br 1831-1895
  O/C 20x16 Girl in a Blue Floral Dress Hnd 6/92   1,500
Lie, Jonas   Am 1880-1940
  O/C 36x30 Safe Harbor Chr 3/92   7,150
  O/C 30x40 Northern Hills 22 Hnd 10/91   6,000
  O/C 12x16 At the Landing 21 Brd 5/92   3,190
  O/C 30x25 Windswept Trees But 11/91   1,650
  O/Pn 14x15 Smokey Mountain Landscape Hnz 10/91   300
  G/Pa Size? Landscape Mys 11/91   55

Liebenwein, Maximilian   Aus 1869-1926
 * See 1992 Edition ....

Lieber, Edvard   1948-
 I,G&H/Pa 16x20 John Cage Playing Chess 1980 Chr 5/92 .. 2,090

Lieber, Tom   Am 20C
 * See 1992 Edition ....

Liebermann, Max   Ger 1847-1935
 O/Pn 17x20 Konzert in Der Berliner Oper 1921 Sby 10/91 . 49,500
 W&Cw/Pa 9x12 Self-Portrait Artist in His Studio Chr 2/92 . 15,400
 P/Pa 5x7 Unter Den Baumen Sby 2/92 13,200
 W/Pa 12x14 Das Meer Sby 2/92 10,175
 W/Pa 12x14 Children Playing at the Beach Chr 2/92 8,800

Liebers, A.
 O/C 25x20 The Flowered Hat Hnz 10/91 6,000

Liebl, Hans
 O/C 24x36 Country House Ald 5/92 225
 O/B 8x11 House By Wheatfield Ald 5/92 65

Liebman, Marjorie   20C
 O/C 20x16 Flowers Yng 4/92 100

Liebmann, Gerhardt   Am 20C
 * See 1992 Edition ....

Lievens, Jan   Dut 1607-1672
 * See 1991 Edition ....

Lievre, Lucien   Fr 1878-
 O/C 57x74 Dock Scene in Holland Wes 5/92 2,860

Ligare, David
 * See 1992 Edition ....

Ligozzi, Jacopo   It 1547-1627
 O/Cp 14x10 Adoration of the Magi Sby 5/92 308,000

Liljefors, Bruno Andread   Swd 1860-1939
 * See 1990 Edition ....

Liljestrom, Gustave   Am 1882-1958
 * See 1992 Edition ....

Lilo, F. Cocu   LA 20C
 O/B 11x14 Brazilian Landscape Hnd 5/92 350

Limouse, Roger   Fr 1894-
 * See 1991 Edition ....

Lin, Hans   Dut a 17C
 O/Pn 7x9 A Cavalry Skirmish Chr 5/92 11,000

Linard, Jacques   Fr 1600-1645
 * See 1992 Edition ....

Lincoln, Ephraim F.   Am 20C
 * See 1992 Edition ....

Lindau, Dietrich Wilhelm   Ger 1799-1862
 O/C 21x28 Outdoor Revelry 1854 Chr 2/92 4,400

Lindberg, Arthur Harold   Am 20C
 * See 1991 Edition ....

Linde, Ossip E.   Am -1940
 O/C 30x30 Landscape Mor 3/92 3,500

Lindenmuth, Arlington N.   Am 1867-
 O/C/B 9x12 Old Timer Yng 2/92 150

Lindenmuth, Tod   Am 1885-1976
 O/B 18x24 Setting Out Lobster Traps Skn 11/91 880
 O/Cb 20x30 Fishing Village Skn 5/92 715
 O/B 11x14 Wellfleet Beach Ald 5/92 450
 O/B 14x15 Lobstermen Hnd 6/92 250
 O/B 14x17 Gray Houses Ald 5/92 160

Linder, Harry   Am 1886-1931
 P/Pa 16x34 Coastal Seascape Mor 6/92 275

Linder, P.   Br 19C
 O/C 19x24 Feeding the Ducks Sby 10/91 5,500
 O/C 19x24 Teatime Sby 10/91 5,500

Linder, Philippe Jacques   Fr a 1857-1880
 O/Pn 13x9 La Coquette Skn 5/92 1,430

Linderum, Richard   Ger 1851-
 * See 1991 Edition ....

Lindh, Bror   Swd 1877-1941
 * See 1992 Edition ....

Lindin, Carl Olaf Eric   Am 1869-1942
 O/C 28x20 Docked Boats at Dusk Wes 5/92 1,540

Lindner, Ernest   Can 1897-1988
 O/B 30x24 Cornucopia 1964 Sbt 11/91 5,610

Lindner, Richard   Am 1901-1978
 O/C 72x78 The Couple 1971 Chr 11/91 319,000
 W,Bp&L/Pa 23x16 Confrontation 1977 Chr 5/92 18,700

Lindsay, Thomas Corwin   Am 1839-1907
 O/C 27x34 Rocky Coastline Slo 4/92 1,350
 O/C 26x33 Stag in Wooded River Landscape Sel 9/91 ... 575

Linford, Charles   Am 1846-1897
 O/C/B 45x30 View Forest at Sunset Fre 10/92 925

Lingelbach, Johannes   Dut 1622-1674
 * See 1992 Edition ....

Lingke, Albert Muller   Ger 1844-
 * See 1991 Edition ....

Linke, Simon   20C1958-
 O/L 60x60 Jean Michel Basquiat 1987 Sby 11/91 13,200
 O/L 72x72 Ed Ruscha, October 1986 Chr 11/91 11,000
 O/C 72x72 Lee Krasner, October 1986 Sby 5/92 11,000

Linnell, John   Br 1792-1882
 W/Pa/B 13x20 Shepherd with Flock But 5/92 2,475

Linnig, Egidius   Bel 1821-1860
 O/Pn 22x31 Shipping off a Jetty 1853 Chr 2/92 8,250

Linson, Corwin Knapp   Am 1864-1934
 O/B 7x9 Jordan, Jerusalem, Bethany: Five 1898 Sby 12/91 . 6,600
 O/C/B 22x18 Autumn Glow Sby 12/91 1,980
 O/C 9x11 Pansies Ald 5/92 250

Linton, Frank Benton   Am 1871-1943
 * See 1992 Edition ....

Linton, H. A.   Br 19C
 W/Pa 7x18 Baalbek; Arab's Shelter (Pair) But 11/91 880

Lintott, Edward Bernard   Am 1875-1951
 O/C 25x30 Promenade in the Park Sby 12/91 1,870
 O/C 24x20 Tuberose Begonia Skn 9/91 880
 O/Cb 16x12 Still Life with Roses Skn 11/91 468
 O/Cb 20x16 Still Life Chrysanthemums Skn 11/91 248
 O/C 24x20 Mignonette Slo 10/91 225
 O/C 24x20 Lady with Mink Wlf 10/91 100
 O/C 24x20 Portrait of a Young Lady Wlf 10/91 100

Linzoni, P.   It 20C
 * See 1992 Edition ....

Lipchitz, Jacques   Fr 1891-1973
 G,O&Sd/Pn 11x9 Guitariste Sby 5/92 132,000
 Br,I&S/M 26x24 Study for Sculpture: The Couple Chr 2/92 . 6,600
 Pl&C/Pa 26x19 Etude Pour Mere et Enfant Chr 11/91 ... 6,050

Lippert, Leon   Am -1950
 * See 1991 Edition ....

Lippincott, William Henry   Am 1849-1920
 * See 1992 Edition ....

Lippine   Am 19C
 O/Pn 8x12 Landscape Fre 10/91 3,700

Lipps, Richard   Ger 1857-1926
 O/C 44x32 A Busy Market Square Chr 2/92 16,500
 O/C 44x32 Marketplace, Venice Skn 9/91 14,300

Lipton, Seymour   1903-1986
 H/Pa 9x11 Two Drawings 53 Chr 11/91 6,050

Lira, Pedro   Chi 19C
 O/C 55x36 Lady Jennifer 1877 Sby 10/91 12,650

Lis, Edward
 O/B 14x18 Port Scene 1953 Ald 5/92 200

Lismer, Arthur   Can 1885-1969
 O/Pn 9x12 Algoma 1922 Sbt 5/92 24,310
 O/B 13x16 Little Cove - MacGregor Bay 1930 Sbt 5/92 .. 17,765
 O/Pn 9x12 Pine Tree, Georgian Bay Sbt 11/91 12,155
 O/B 9x12 The Glacier, Moraine Lake Sbt 5/92 8,415
 O/Pn 12x17 Still Life with Pears '45 Sbt 11/91 4,675
 O/Pn 12x16 Junk on a Derelict '48 Sbt 11/91 2,805

Lissitsky, El   Rus 1890-
 * See 1991 Edition ....

Little, C. M.   Am 20C
 O/B 16x12 Eucalyptus Landscape Mor 3/92 220

Little, John Geoffrey C.   Can 1928-
 O/C 24x30 Epicerie Poulin - Quebec Sbt 5/92 5,610
 O/C 12x16 Lachine Canal, Montreal '74 Sbt 11/91 1,870

Little, Phillip   Am 1857-1942
 O/C 30x30 Rainy Night in Washington 1910 Chr 5/92 9,350
 O/C 29x36 Maine Coast Brd 8/92 3,630
 W/Pa 19x13 Tropical Lagoon 25 Skn 9/91 385
 W/Pa 15x22 Green Hills 1940 Skn 3/92 165

Littlefield, William Horace   Am 1902-1969
 L&G 19x19 Two Abstracts Yng 4/92 300

149

H/Pa 15x11 Two Drawings 1941 Skn 9/91 220
L 28x25 Two Abstracts Yng 4/92 150
O/B 8x10 Abstract 1955 Yng 4/92 80
I/Pa 16x24 Boxers 1928 Mys 6/92 55

Litzinger, Dorothea M.   Am 1889-1925
O/C 25x30 Daffodils 1925 Skn 11/91 825
MM/B 26x20 Still Life Mountain Laurel 1925 Skn 3/92 660
O/C 21x14 Still Life Laurel, Foxglove Skn 9/91 275

Livemont, Privat   Bel 1861-1936
O/Pn 9x14 The Toast & After Dinner Coffee (2) Chr 5/92 . . 4,180

Livingston, Virginia   Am 1898-
O/C 20x16 Young Woman Slo 10/91 50

Liz, Domingo   20C
* See 1991 Edition . . . .

Ljuba   20C
* See 1992 Edition . . . .

Llona, Ramiro   Per 1947-
O/C 68x80 The Still Hour of the Crysalis Chr 5/92 19,800

Llopis, Carlos Ruano   Spa 1879-
O/C/Pn 15x21 Bull Fight Wes 11/91 1,320

**Llorente, Bernardo German   Spa
1680-1759**
O/Pn 30x22 Madonna, Queen of Heaven Hnd 10/91 3,600

Lloyd, J. C.   Br 19C
* See 1992 Edition . . . .

Lloyd, Norman   Aut 1895-
O/B 13x16 Landscape Hnd 12/91 525
O/B 13x16 Landscape Hnd 10/91 425

Lloyd, Stuart   Br a 1875-1929
W/Pa 11x25 Brittany Coast at Sunset 1906 But 11/91 . . . 1,760

Lo Scheggia   It 1407-1486
T/Pn 34x19 Madonna and Child with Angels Sby 5/92 . . . 71,500

Lo Spada   It 1520-1589
O/C 64x49 Madonna and Child Enthroned Chr 5/92 93,500

Lo Spadino   It 1659-1731
O/C 13x22 Grapes, Apples, Peaches Chr 5/92 24,200

Lo Spagnoletto   It 1588-1656
* See 1992 Edition . . . .

Loates, Glen   Can 1945-
Pe/Pa 15x11 Ring-Necked Pheasant 1974 Sbt 11/91 841

**Lobbedez, Charles Auguste R.   Fr
1825-1882**
* See 1992 Edition . . . .

Lobdell, Frank
* See 1992 Edition . . . .

Lobrichon, Timoleon Marie   Fr 1831-1914
* See 1991 Edition . . . .

Locatelli, Andrea   It 1693-1741
* See 1991 Edition . . . .

Locher, Carl   Dan 1851-1915
* See 1992 Edition . . . .

Locher, Pauline
P/Pa 14x11 East Coast Lakeshore Dum 5/92 85

Lockerby, Mabel Irene   Can 1887-
O/Pn 9x12 Red Sails 1928 Sbt 5/92 3,039

Lockhead, John   Eng
O/C 6x12 By the Stream Wlf 11/91 500

Lockman, Dewitt M.   Am 1870-1957
* See 1992 Edition . . . .

Loder of Bath, James   Br a 1820-1860
* See 1991 Edition . . . .

Lodge, Reginald   Br a 1881-1892
O/C 35x30 Iceland Falcon; Atlantic Osprey: Pr Sby 6/92 . . 6,600

Lodi, Gaetano   It a 1850-
O/C 17x21 Sneaking a Smoke and Brawl (2) Chr 5/92 . . . 6,050
O/C 17x20 Pair: Genre Subjects Sel 12/91 2,300
O/C 17x21 The Quarrel Dum 10/91 500
O/C 17x21 The Smoke Dum 10/91 500

Loeb, Dorothy   Am 1887-
O/B 39x24 Curt Skn 3/92 522

Loeb, Louis   Am 1866-1909
O/Pn 14x10 Lady Standing in the Breeze Chr 6/92 4,400

Loeb, Sidney
O/C 24x30 Rooftops Hnz 10/91 150
O/C 38x34 Spring Forest Scene Hnz 10/91 110

Loeber, Lou   Dut 1894-1983
* See 1992 Edition . . . .

Loeding, Hermen   Dut 1637-1673
* See 1990 Edition . . . .

Loemans, Alexander F.   Am 19C
O/C 30x48 Monte Chimborazo Chr 11/91 13,200
O/C 48x32 Mountain Ravine Sby 12/91 2,640
O/B 12x19 Muskoko Lake Wlf 9/91 2,000

Logan, Maurice   Am 1886-1977
O/C 30x36 Mudflat Homes But 2/92 8,250
W/Pa 20x28 The Loading Dock But 6/92 1,650
W/Pa 18x22 Village Street Scene But 10/91 1,540
W/Pa 21x30 Old Storefronts But 6/92 1,430
W/Pa 21x29 Yachts in a Harbor; Rocky Coastline But 2/92 . 1,320
W/Pa 12x16 Boats in Slips Mor 3/92 1,100
W/Pa 22x29 Porta Costa Mor 11/91 900

Logan, Robert Fulton   Am 1889-1959
O/C 40x30 Hartford State House Mys 11/91 880
O/C 39x28 State House Fre 4/92 400
O/C 20x24 Sea Pines Yng 4/92 125

Logan, Robert Henry   Am 1874-1942
* See 1992 Edition . . . .

Logsdail, William   Eng 1859-
O/C 18x14 Fisherman of Venice Chr 2/92 3,850

Lohr, August   Ger 19C
O/C 23x32 Paisaje Mexicano 1914 Sby 11/91 38,500

Lohse, O.   Sws 20C
O/Ab 9x6 Pair: Floral Still Lifes Wlf 3/92 160

Loir, Luigi   Fr 1845-1916
O/Pn 6x9 Boulevard in Winter Sby 10/91 11,000
O/C 14x16 L'Ile de la Cite Sby 10/91 8,800
Pe,W&G/Pa 10x13 Scene de Peche; Navire: Two Sby 5/92 . 4,950
O/C/Pn 5x9 Village by a Stream Chr 5/92 2,420

Loiseau, Gustave   Fr 1865-1935
O/C 24x36 Gelee Blanche 1906 Sby 5/92 77,000
O/C 26x36 Tournant de Riviere 1904 Sby 11/91 74,250
O/C 26x36 Les Falaises du Cap Frehel 1905 Sby 10/91 . . 49,500
O/C 18x24 Le Quai de l'Oise Pontoise 1906 Sby 10/91 . . 35,750

Lojacono, Francesco   It 1841-1915
O/C 19x38 Gathering Sticks Sby 5/92 55,000
O/C 17x33 Pastoral Landscape Sby 5/92 18,700

Lomax, John Arthur   Br 1857-1923
O/C 23x14 Smoking by the Fireplace Hnz 10/91 1,700
O/B 12x17 Enjoying the Story Chr 5/92 1,400

Lomi, Aurelio   It 1556-1622
* See 1990 Edition . . . .

Lommen, Wilhelm   Ger 1838-1895
* See 1990 Edition . . . .

Londer, Ja.   Dut 18C
* See 1992 Edition . . . .

Londoner, Amy   Am 1878-
O/C 36x24 Woman in Red Yng 2/92 175

**Lone Wolf (James Will. Shultz)   Am
1882-1970**
* See 1991 Edition . . . .

Long, Christopher   20C
O/C 66x66 We're Off We're Off Sby 10/91 31,900

Long, Edwin   Br 1829-1891
* See 1991 Edition . . . .

Long, Richard   20C
MM/Pa 17x12 Ten Drawings Sby 11/91 38,500

Longhi, Alessandro   It 1733-1813
* See 1992 Edition . . . .

Longhi, Luca   It 1507-1580
O/C 52x37 Portrait of a Gentleman 1541 Chr 1/92 13,200

Longhi, Pietro   It 1702-1785
O/C 25x20 Young Lady Winding Wool Chr 5/92 30,800

Longo, Robert   Am 1923-
H/Pa 60x125 Men in the Cities Chr 5/92 49,500
MM/Pa 77x84 Round Heads/Square Heads 85 Chr 5/92 . . 14,300

Loomis, William Andrew   Am 1892-1959
O/C 30x32 Apple Kiss Dum 2/92 3,500

Loos, John   Con a 1880-1889
* See 1992 Edition . . . .

Loper, Edward   Am 20C
O/C 25x36 Blue Church Fre 10/91   100
Lopez Y Portana, Vincente   Spa
1772-1850
  * See 1991 Edition . . . .
Lopez, Gasparo   It 1650-1732
O/C 29x19 Still Life Urn and Basket w/Flowers Sby 5/92 . . 13,200
Lorentzen, Christian August   1749-1828
  * See 1991 Edition . . . .
Lorenz, S. E.   Am 20C
O/C 12x18 Landscape Eld 7/92   138
Loria, Vincenzo   It 1850-
O/C 22x30 Bringing in the Catch Sby 5/92   5,500
Lorjou, Bernard   Fr 1908-
  * See 1992 Edition . . . .
Lorne, Naomi   Am 1902-
O/Pn 16x12 Wildflowers in a Vase Chr 11/91   440
Lorrain, Claude   Fr 1600-1682
  * See 1992 Edition . . . .
Los, Waldemar   Pol 1849-1888
  * See 1991 Edition . . . .
Lossi, T.   It 19C
W/Pa 11x6 Lady with an Oriental Parasol 1881 Sby 1/92 . . 3,575
Lossow, Heinrich   Ger 1843-1897
  * See 1992 Edition . . . .
Loth, Johann Carl   Ger 1632-1698
  * See 1991 Edition . . . .
Lotiron, Robert
O/C 11x14 Batteuse Sby 6/92 2,530
O/C 13x18 Rural Landscape Sby 2/92 2,200
Lotti, A.   It 19C
W/Pa 7x11 The Cardinal's Scorn Slo 12/91   275
Lotto, Lorenzo   It 1480-1556
  * See 1990 Edition . . . .
Lotz, Matilda   Am 1858-1923
O/C 15x32 Friends 1890 But 2/92 5,500
O/B 8x9 Lancer; Portrait of a Dog But 6/92   550
Louderback, Walt   Am 1887-1941
O/C 30x24 Young Couple with Dog 1924 Ih 11/91 4,250
W/Pa 20x26 Man Walking Up Hill as Guards Look Ih 11/91 .   450
Lougheed, Robert Elmer   Am 1910-1982
O/B 12x16 Toclat Country - Alaska Sby 4/92 5,170
O/B 27x32 Man Racing Speed Boats Ih 5/92 3,250
Louis, Morris   Am 1912-1962
Mg/C 82x49 Number 1-70 Sby 11/91 220,000
Mg/C 16x24 The Ladder '50 Chr 2/92 8,250
Lourdes, Manuel Guillermo
  * See 1992 Edition . . . .
Loussaint, Frank   Hai 20C
O/M 29x41 Woman Carrying Grey Buckets Fre 4/92   425
Louthian, Donald   Am 20C
A/C 50x50 Taos 1968 Slo 4/92   140
Louvrier, Maurice   1878-1954
O/C 18x22 Voiliers sur la Seine Chr 5/92 3,850
Louyot, Edmond   Ger 1861-1909
O/C 32x24 Winter River Skn 5/92 1,045
Lovatti, E. Augusto   It 1816-
O/C 14x21 Children, Coast of Capri Wlf 3/92 5,700
O/C 21x13 Monk in Capri Sby 7/92 3,300
Lovatti, Matteo   It 1861-
  * See 1991 Edition . . . .
Lovell, Katherine Adams   Am 1877-1965
O/B 9x9 Village Scene with Figures Lou 3/92   125
O/Pn 9x12 American Snow Il-East Aurora Hnz 5/92   110
O/Pn 8x10 Morning Haze Hnz 5/92   110
O/C 9x12 Barn in Lyme Connecticut Hnz 5/92   100
Lovell, Tom   Am 1909-
O/B 17x21 Four People in Swimsuits Ih 11/91 3,750
O/C 23x31 Saratoga Trunk 41 But 11/91 3,300
O/M 17x25 Woman Looking in Phone Book 1949 Ih 5/92 .   3,000
Loven, Frank W.   Am 1869-1941
O/C 30x25 Winter Snow Scene Mys 11/91   412
Loveridge, Clinton   Am 1824-1902
O/C 12x16 Cows in a Pasture Mor 3/92 3,000
O/B 6x12 Two: Lake Erie; Lake George Skn 3/92 2,860

Lovell, R.   Am 19C
O/C 10x14 A Bark at Sea 1875 Bor 8/92   800
Lovick, Annie Pescud   Am 1882-
O/C 36x30 Copy of a Colonial Portrait Yng 2/92   40
Lovmand, Christine Marie   Dan 1803-1872
  * See 1991 Edition . . . .
Low, Will Hicock   Am 1853-1932
O/C 22x18 The Arched Bridge 1874 Sby 12/91 1,650
Lowell, Milton H.   Am 1848-1927
O/C 10x14 Cabin on the Banks Wes 11/91   825
O/C 16x24 Spring Landscape and House Slo 12/91   250
Lowell, Orson Byron   Am 1871-1956
Pl&G/B 24x20 Everything Else, Though Chr 11/91   715
Pl/Pa/B 22x21 Dinner with Mother Hnd 6/92   300
Lowenheim, Frederick   Am 1870-1929
O/Cb 22x17 Two Illustrations Ih 11/91   950
Lowith, Wilhelm   Aus 1861-
O/Pn 4x6 The Toast 1889 Sby 1/92 2,640
Loyd, Mell
O/C 25x45 Mountain Scene Dum 1/92   300
Loyeux, Charles Antoine Joseph   Fr
1823-1893
  * See 1992 Edition . . . .
Lozano, Manuel Rodriguez   20C
  * See 1992 Edition . . . .
Lozano, Margarita   Fr 1936-
  * See 1992 Edition . . . .
Lubbers, Holger   Dan 1855-1928
O/C 21x32 Ships Approaching the Shore Mys 6/92 1,760
Lubieniecki, Christoffel   Pol 1660-1728
  * See 1991 Edition . . . .
Lucas Y Padilla, Eugenio   Spa 1824-1870
  * See 1991 Edition . . . .
Lucas Y Villaamil, Eugenio   Spa
1858-1918
O/C/B 15x22 The Wedding Party 90 Sby 10/91 17,600
Lucas, Henry Frederick Lucas   Br
1848-1943
O/C 24x30 "Rugby" a Black Horse 1879 Sby 6/92 1,760
Lucas, L. W.   Am 20C
O/C 17x22 Buckeye 1930 Sel 4/92   350
O/C 16x26 Perfection, Revelation 1930 Sel 4/92   200
Lucas-Robiquet, Marie Almee   Fr 1864-
  * See 1991 Edition . . . .
Lucchesi, Giorgio   It 1855-1941
O/C 40x28 Still Life Dried Flowers, Apples 1904 Skn 11/91 20,900
Lucchesi, P.   It 19C
O/C 31x24 Reading the Note Wlf 6/92 1,500
Luce, Maximilien   Fr 1858-1941
O/C 32x40 Eragny, Le Verger de Pissarro 95 Sby 11/91 . 462,000
O/C 39x26 Saint Tropez, Les Pins Sby 5/92 71,500
O/B 10x16 Paysage Mediterranean Sby 5/92 52,250
O/C 24x37 La Baignade Chr 2/92 30,800
O/C 25x32 Bessy sur Cure, Le Village 1906 Sby 5/92 . . . 29,700
O/C 14x19 Paysanne sur la Route de Moulineux Sby 5/92   29,700
O/C 20x26 Les Travailleurs Sby 2/92 19,800
O/C 18x32 Chevres sur la Falaise 35 Sby 11/91 18,700
O/Pa/C 13x20 Baigneuses au Bord de la Seine 38 Sby 5/92 13,200
O/Pa/C 11x14 La Barrage sur la Seine Chr 2/92 13,200
O/Pa/B 15x7 Etude D'Homme, Pecheur Sby 10/91 7,150
Lucebert, Jean   Fr 20C
O/C 40x32 Thessaurier Baby '60 Sby 2/92 27,500
Lucioni, Luigi   It 1900-1988
O/M 6x9 House Among the Trees Skn 9/91 1,320
Luckenbach, Reuben   Am 19C
  * See 1991 Edition . . . .
Luckx, Frans Josef   Bel 1802-1849
O/C 35x46 Pleading for Justice 1836 Sby 10/91 16,500
Ludekens, Fred   Am 1900-1982
W/Pa 10x29 Incident at the Ballgame Slo 7/92 1,400
G/Pa 10x19 Buffalo Hunt 1954 Mys 6/92   248
Ludins, Eugene   Am 1904-
O/C 12x16 Figures by a Dock Slo 10/91   200

Ludovici, A. (Jr.) Br 1852-1932
* See 1992 Edition . . . .
Ludwig, Warren Am 1899-1965
O/C 34x26 Woman Wearing a White Dress 1935 Sel 12/91 . . 400
Lueg, Konrad 20C
O&Pe/C 54x40 Boxers '64 Sby 11/91 5,500
Luhrs, Henry
G/Pa 14x25 Two Illustrations Ih 5/92 550
Luini, Bernardino It 1475-1532
* See 1990 Edition . . . .
Luisi, Nicholas Am 20C
C,W&G/Pa 10x13 Train Yard Slo 7/92 60
Lukits, Theodore N. Am 1897-
* See 1992 Edition . . . .
Luks, George Benjamin Am 1867-1933
O/C 27x20 The Black Hat Chr 12/91 63,800
W&C/Pa 14x20 Country Road Chr 3/92 8,250
O/C 35x40 Summer Field Wes 11/91 3,850
Y/Pa/B 10x8 Art Students Sby 4/92 2,750
W/Pa 11x16 At the Mill Wlf 9/91 2,200
Pe/Pa 18x12 Woolworth Building Chr 9/91 1,980
W/Pa 18x7 Penta (Ponta) Delgada 1893 Slo 7/92 1,900
O/Ab 19x15 Marie Wlf 9/91 1,800
Pe/Pa 7x4 Figure Studies: Two Sby 4/92 1,430
K/Pa 10x8 Giraffes (2) Chr 11/91 1,320
Lumis, Harriet Randall Am 1870-1953
C/Pa 24x20 Study of a Young Boy Hnz 10/91 50
Lumpkins, William Am 20C
* See 1992 Edition . . . .
Lumsdaine, Leesa Sandys Am 20C
* See 1992 Edition . . . .
Luna, Antonio Rodriguez Mex 1910-
* See 1992 Edition . . . .
Luna, Justo Ruiz Spa 19C
* See 1992 Edition . . . .
Lunardi, W. It 20C
O/C 32x51 Neopolitan Harbor Scene Sel 2/92 600
Lundberg, August Frederick Am 1878-1928
O/C 24x20 Winter Morning 1924 Slo 2/92 1,100
Lundmark, Leon Am 1875-1942
O/C 25x30 Sailboats at Dusk Hnz 10/91 650
O/C 25x30 Ripples and Roar Mor 3/92 325
O/B 12x16 Seascape Hnd 6/92 325
O/C 12x16 California Seascape Slo 10/91 300
Lunetti, Tommaso Di Stefano It 1490-1564
* See 1992 Edition . . . .
Lunois, Alexandre
P&G/Pa 25x33 The Bullfight Sby 10/91 1,430
Luny, Thomas Br 1759-1837
O/C 18x28 Harbor View 1792 Skn 5/92 10,450
O/C 18x28 Putting Ashore 1792 Skn 5/92 7,700
Lupertz, Marcus 1941-
K&W/Pa 16x22 Lupolis Chr 5/92 4,620
Lurcat, Jean Fr 1892-1966
O/C 22x15 Nature Morte 25 Sby 2/92 5,775
O/C 13x24 Still Life Four Fruit Sby 2/92 4,675
O/C 11x16 Still Life Fruit on a Ledge 27 Sby 2/92 4,675
O/C 11x21 Aux Bords de la Mer Chr 11/91 1,980
Lusk, Maria Koupal Am 1862-
W&G/Pa 36x6 Morn Glories; Bach Buttons 1889 But 4/92 . . 1,430
Lussigny, L. Fr 19C
* See 1992 Edition . . . .
Luti, Benedetto It 1666-1724
* See 1990 Edition . . . .
Luttichuys, Isaac 1616-1673
O/C 50x40 Portrait of a Lady Chr 10/91 8,250
Lutz, Daniel Am 1906-1978
O/C 24x18 Grand Portal '52 But 2/92 990
O/C 24x30 Tropical Landscape Hnz 10/91 225
Luyken, Jan
* See 1992 Edition . . . .
Luzzi, Cleto It 20C
O/C 29x40 The Gondola Ride Sby 1/92 4,125

Lyall, Laura Adeline (Muntz) Can 1860-1930
O/C 27x35 Mother and Child 1895 Sbt 5/92 14,025
Lyford, Philip Am 1887-1950
* See 1991 Edition . . . .
Lyle, Byron Br 19C
* See 1991 Edition . . . .
Lyman, John Goodwin Can 1886-1967
* See 1992 Edition . . . .
Lynch, Albert Per 1851-
O/Pn 29x22 The Letter Chr 5/92 33,000
O/C 26x21 Portrait of a Girl Sby 2/92 13,750
G&W/Pb 13x25 Gathering in the Drawing Room Chr 5/92 . . 7,150
O/C 26x18 A Winter Celebration Chr 2/92 6,820
O/C 24x20 Lady Wearing Black Hat Sby 7/92 3,850
Lyne, Michael Br 1912-1989
O/C 28x42 Mme. de Rothschild's Stag Hounds Sby 6/92 . . 12,100
W&G/Pa 14x21 The Marches, Middlebury, CT 1950 Sby 6/92 . . 3,850
Lyon, Hayes Am 20C
* See 1992 Edition . . . .
Lyouns, Herbert F. Williams Eng 1863-1939
O/C 20x24 Rocky Coast 1910 Slo 12/91 525
Maar, Dora 1909-
Pe/Pa 12x10 Three Drawings 1940 Sby 11/91 11,000
W/Pa 10x13 Three Watercolors Chr 5/92 5,500
Maas, Dirk Dut 1659-1717
* See 1990 Edition . . . .
Maas, Paul Bel 1890-1962
O/C 47x32 Les Vacances Skn 5/92 2,200
Maass, David Am 20C
O/M 20x24 Winged Bullets-Canvasbacks Skn 3/92 3,960
Mabe, Manabu Brz 1910-
O/C 60x50 Yellow Abstract '65 Wes 3/92 12,100
O/C 51x39 Red, Black, Blue & White 1959 Wes 3/92 . . . 8,250
O/C 28x20 Untitled '64 Wes 3/92 5,500
Macartney, Jack Am 1893-1976
* See 1992 Edition . . . .
Maccio, Romulo Arg 1931-
O/C 40x36 Sin Titulo Chr 5/92 7,150
Maccloy, Samuel Br 1831-1904
* See 1992 Edition . . . .
Macco, George Ger 1863-1933
O/C 30x45 Winter Snow Scene 1932 Mys 11/91 1,540
MacDonald, James Edward Hervey Can 1873-1932
O/B 8x10 Logs Coming Down Narrows Sbt 5/92 7,948
O/B 6x8 Banks of the Humber Sbt 5/92 4,441
O/Pn 8x10 Barbados, Coastal Scene Sbt 5/92 4,208
O/B 9x11 Barbados '32 Sbt 11/91 3,039
Pe/Pa 9x11 Winding Stream Sbt 5/92 1,776
MacDonald, Manly Edward Can 1889-1971
O/C 24x30 Two Boys Fishing Sbt 11/91 4,909
O/C 24x30 Bridge on the Scootama Sbt 5/92 3,740
O/C 20x26 River View, Autumn Sbt 11/91 2,571
O/B 12x16 The Don Valley Sbt 11/91 2,104
O/B 9x11 Horses with Plough Sbt 11/91 1,636
O/B 16x20 Rouge River Sbt 11/91 1,496
MacDonald-Wright, Stanton Am 1890-1973
* See 1992 Edition . . . .
MacEntyre, Eduardo Arg 1929-
* See 1990 Edition . . . .
MacEwen, Walter Am 1860-1943
O/C 55x81 Stad Herberg of Nieuw Amsterdam Doy 12/91 . . 8,500
MacGilvary, Norwood Hodge Am 1874-1950
* See 1991 Edition . . . .
MacGregor, Robert Eng 1848-1922
O/C 23x35 Ship at Sea Wlf 6/92 850
Mach, P N** Isr 20C**
O/C 35x29 Abstract Village '60 Wes 3/92 330
Machelbach, * Eur 19C**
O/Pn 12x9 Jester and Barmaid Slo 7/92 2,500

152

Machen, William H.   Am 1832-1911
O/C 17x14 Two Game Birds Dum 5/92 1,000
O/C 13x24 Farmyard Wes 3/92 660
Machiavelli, Zanobi   1418-1479
* See 1992 Edition
Macilhenney, C. Morgan   Am 1858-1904
O/C 18x24 Old Willow Fre 10/91 350
Macintosh, Marian T.   Am 1871-1936
* See 1990 Edition
Mackall, Robert McGill   Am 1889-
O/C 26x32 Landscape with Figure 1929 Mys 11/91 880
MacKay, Florence   Br 19C
W/Pb 10x8 Thatched Cottage with Garden Chr 2/92 2,200
MacKenzie, D.   Eng 20C
O/C 30x25 Woman with Lace Shawl 1911 Slo 10/91 75
MacKenzie, Frank J.   Am 1867-1939
O/B 6x10 Four: Glen Echo Park; California 1930 Slo 12/91 . . 300
O/B 6x9 California Landscape Slo 12/91 275
MacKenzie, Frederick   Br 1787-1854
W/Pa 15x13 Vespers in Christ Church, Oxford Lou 3/92 . . . 2,000
Mackeprang, Adolf   Dan 1833-1911
O/C 21x28 Ducks by a Pond 1857 Chr 10/91 1,320
Mackey, H.
O/C 16x24 Scottish Fishermen Ald 5/92 110
**Mackintosh, Charles Rennie   Sco
1868-1928**
* See 1992 Edition
MacKnight, Dodge   Am 1860-1950
W/Pa 15x22 Buttes in Afternoon Sunlight Skn 11/91 1,650
W&H/Pa 15x22 Dunes in Bloom Skn 3/92 1,430
W/Pa 16x22 Marshy Landscape 1924 Chr 6/92 1,430
W/Pa 14x20 Moonlight over the Point Yng 4/92 1,300
W/Pa 16x20 Quiet Stroll Through the Village Skn 11/91 . . . 880
Macky, Eric Spencer   Am 1880-1958
* See 1990 Edition
Maclane, Jean   Am 1878-1964
* See 1992 Edition
**MacLennan, Eunice Cashion   Am
1886-1966**
W/Pa 16x20 Plowing Time Up the Valley Mor 6/92 300
MacLeod, Pegi Nicol   Can 1904-1949
O/Pn 24x26 Still Life of Flowers Sbt 11/91 3,272
O/Pn 24x19 Study of a Child Sbt 5/92 1,496
O/Pn 24x20 City Street From a Veranda Sbt 11/91 935
Maclet, Elisee   Fr 1881-1962
O/B 20x25 Paris Street Scene Dum 4/92 14,000
O/C 18x22 Le Vieux Port De Cassis Sby 10/91 11,000
O/C 18x22 Vue de la Seine et Notre Dame Sby 10/91 9,350
O/C 25x18 Moulin de la Gallette Chr 2/92 8,800
O/C 20x24 Le Port Chr 11/91 7,700
O/C 15x21 Le Pont Canal Chippillu Chr 2/92 6,050
O/C 12x16 Le Vieux moulin Chr 5/92 4,180
W/Pa 10x14 Riverboat Sby 10/91 2,530
W&Pl/Pa 8x10 Jardins a Montmartre Sby 2/92 2,090
W&Pl/Pa 8x10 Rooftops of Paris Sby 2/92 1,870
Maclise, Daniel   Br 1806-1870
O/C 40x56 Visit to the Printing House Sby 10/91 19,800
MacMorris, Daniel   Am 1893-1985
O/Cb 16x20 Missouri Landscape '46 Sel 9/91 80
Macnaughton, John H.   Can a 1876-1899
W/Pa 10x8 Habitant in Fur Coat Sbt 11/91 561
MacNeil, Ambrose (DeBarra)   Am 1852-
* See 1992 Edition
Macomber, Mary Lizzie   Am 1861-1916
* See 1992 Edition
MacRae, Elmer Livingston   Am 1875-1952
P/Pa 7x5 Clarissa, Martha's Vineyard, 1912 Yng 2/92 325
MacRae, Emma Fordyce   Am 1887-1974
O&Pe/C 31x25 A Belgian Girl Chr 9/91 4,180
O/M 26x18 Four of a Kind Sby 7/92 1,750
Macrum, George H.   Am 20C
O/B 15x18 European Street Scene Mys 6/92 550
MacWhirter, John   Br 1839-1911
O/C 20x36 The River Wye Hnd 12/91 800

Macy, William Starbuck   Am 1853-1916
O/C 10x8 Rural Landscapes: Two Yng 4/92 1,000
Madden, Jan   Eng 1884-
O/C 24x36 Village Fishing Scene Wlf 6/92 425
Maddersteeg, Michael   Dut 1658-1709
* See 1990 Edition
Madelain, Gustave   Fr 1867-1944
O/Pn 18x13 Parisian Street Scene 1867 Sby 2/92 3,300
Madeline, Paul   Fr
* See 1992 Edition
Madou, Jean Baptiste   Bel 1796-1877
O/Pn 13x8 Gentleman in a Bookshop 1873 Wes 11/91 . . . 1,650
Madsen, Otto   Am 1882-
O/C 18x21 Snowy Wooded Landscape Sel 9/91 140
Maella, Mariano Salvador   Spa 1739-1819
O/C 94x62 Esau Selling His Birthright Chr 1/92 16,500
Maes, Eugene Remy   Bel 1849-1931
O/C 34x48 Chickens and Ducks Hnd 10/91 11,000
O/C 24x36 Battle for the Corn 1869 Chr 2/92 6,600
Maes, Giacomo   It 19C
* See 1992 Edition
Maes, Nicolaes   Dut 1632-1693
O/C 27x34 Interior of a Cottage w/Young Maid Chr 5/92 . 110,000
O/C 28x25 Young Boy in Green & White Costume Chr 1/92 55,000
O/C 26x22 Portrait of Gentleman, Lady: Pair Chr 1/92 . . . 35,200
O/Pn 17x12 Portrait of a Young Man 1675 Sby 1/92 14,300
O/C 18x14 Portrait of a Gentleman But 5/92 11,000
Maestosi, F.   It 19C
* See 1990 Edition
Maestri, Michelangelo   It -1812
G/Pa 15x11 Classical Figures Chr 10/91 5,500
G/Pa 15x21 Putti Driving Chariots (2) Chr 10/91 3,740
Bc/Pa 9x13 Amor Volubile But 11/91 770
Magada, Stephen   Am 20C
O/C 30x38 Amusement Park Hnd 5/92 750
Magafan, Ethel   Am 1915-
O/M 7x27 Colorado Farm Scene 1936 Skn 3/92 1,760
**Magaud, Dominique Antoine J.B.   Fr
1817-1899**
* See 1991 Edition
Magdich, Dennis
O/C 18x16 Woman w/Lariat Smoking Cigarette Ih 11/91 600
Magee, Alan   Am 20C
* See 1992 Edition
Maggi, Cesare   20C
* See 1991 Edition
Maggs, John Charles   Br 1819-1895
O/C 34x52 Outside the White Lion Hotel 1873 Sby 6/92 . 23,100
O/C 14x26 Spead Eagle Tap 1884 Chr 5/92 5,500
O/C 14x27 London-Birmingham Run Sby 6/92 3,300
O/C 17x27 Coach in a Snowstorm Chr 2/92 2,420
Magnasco, Alessandro   It 1667-1749
O/C 25x19 Self-Portrait Sby 1/92 22,000
Magne, Desire Alfred   Fr 1855-
* See 1991 Edition
Magni, Giuseppe   It 1869-1956
O/C 22x29 Feeding the Chickens But 5/92 28,600
O/C 22x32 A Musical Afternoon Chr 2/92 24,200
O/C 21x26 Admiring the Baby Sby 10/91 13,200
Magnus, Camille   Fr 1850-
O/C 35x52 Faggot Gatherer Chr 5/92 7,700
Magnussen, Gustaf A.   Am 1890-1957
O/C 14x20 San Luis Rey Mission Mor 3/92 700
Magnussen, Gustave A.   Am 1868-1944
O/C 11x14 Boats on a Bay Mor 11/91 1,100
Magonigle, Edith   Am 20C
* See 1992 Edition
Magritte, Rene   Bel 1898-1967
O/C 26x20 L'Image en Soi 1961 Chr 11/91 715,000
O/C 23x19 Les Travaux D'Alexandre 1950 Sby 5/92 660,000
O/C 29x20 Le Montagnard 1947 Chr 11/91 214,500
Pl/Pa 11x7 Une Simple Histoire d'Amour Sby 11/91 25,300
Pe&Bp/Pa 8x11 Untitled Sby 11/91 11,000
Mahaffey, Noel   Am 1944-
* See 1991 Edition

153

Mahlknecht, Edmund   Aus 1820-1903
O/C 22x38 Farmyard Scene Sby 5/92   14,300
Maillaud, Fernand   Fr 1863-1948
O/B 28x37 La Jerinette a Toulon But 11/91   13,200
O/C 18x22 Spring Landscape with Cottage Sby 6/92   6,600
Maillol, Aristide   Fr 1861-1944
Sg&K/Pa 15x9 Jeune Femme Debout de Dos Sby 10/91 . .   9,350
C/Pa/B 13x9 Nu Debout Sby 2/92   3,575
Pe/Pa 12x9 Femme nue, vue de dos Chr 5/92   3,300
Mainardi, Sebastiano   It 1450-1513
T/Pn 32 dia Madonna, St. Joseph & Christ Sby 1/92 . . .   115,500
Mairovich, Zvi   20C
O/C 20x24 Abstract Composition Sby 10/91   1,100
O/C 10x13 Jerusalem Sby 10/91   990
Maitin, Sam   Am 20C
W/Pa 13x21 Mother and Child Fre 12/91   225
Major, B.   Am 20C
O/C 14x17 Harbor Scene Lou 3/92   350
O/Cb 11x14 Autumn Landscape Wes 11/91   192
Major, Ernest   Am 1864-
* See 1992 Edition . . . .
Makart, Hans   Aus 1840-1884
O/C 59x39 Venus and Cupids Sby 10/91   23,100
Makielski, Leon A.   Am 1885-
O/Pn 13x16 Summer in Vermont Chr 3/92   3,520
Makovsky, Constantin   Rus 1839-1915
O/C 72x78 Blind Man's Bluff Sby 2/92   110,000
Makovsky, Vladimir Yegorovich   Rus 1846-1920
* See 1991 Edition . . . .
Malaine, Joseph-Laurent   Fr 1745-1809
O/Pn 29x23 Floral Still-Life: Roses, Tulip 1807 But 5/92 .   44,000
Malavine, Philippe   Rus 1869-1939
* See 1990 Edition . . . .
Malcom, B.   Eng 19C
O/C 18x14 Cat Sel 9/91   110
Maldarelli, Federico   It 1826-1893
* See 1990 Edition . . . .
Maldura, Giovanni   It 1772-1849
O/C 38x29 The Flight into Egypt But 5/92   4,400
Maleas, Constantin
O/Pa 18x18 Assouan 1924 Sby 2/92   4,675
Malet, Albert   Fr 1905-1986
* See 1992 Edition . . . .
Malevich, Kasimir   Rus 1878-1935
* See 1992 Edition . . . .
Malfroy, Charles   Fr 1862-1940
* See 1990 Edition . . . .
Malfroy, Henry   Fr 1895-
O/Pn 11x13 Flower Sellers, Paris Slo 9/91   2,250
Malherbe, William   Am 1884-1951
O/C 41x33 Nature Morte Fruits et Fleurs Chr 11/91   6,600
Mali, Christian Friedrich   Ger 1832-1906
* See 1992 Edition . . . .
Malkine, Georges   Fr 1898-1970
O/C 29x24 Le Baiser 1927 Wes 3/92   7,700
Mallebranche, Louis-Claude   Fr 1790-1838
O/Pn 16x24 Snowy Winter Scene 1836 Sel 4/92   1,800
Mallet, Jean-Baptiste   Fr 1759-1835
O/C 15x18 Une Nymphe Au Bain Sby 5/92   28,600
Mallo, Maruja   Spa 1910-
* See 1990 Edition . . . .
Malmstrom, August   Swd 1829-1901
* See 1991 Edition . . . .
Maloney, Daniel   Am 20C
W/Pa 12x6 Floral Still Life 54 Eld 7/92   143
Malready, W.   Br 19C
O/C 17x21 Young Couple Asleep 1826 Hnz 5/92   950
Man Ray   Am 1890-1976
O/Pn 15x19 La Maree 49 Sby 11/91   110,000
O/C 10x14 Landscape with Houses 1913 Chr 12/91   22,000
W/Pa 12x16 King Lear (Shakespeare Equat.) 48 Sby 2/92 .   16,500
G,S&L/Pb 14x10 Opt. Longings & Illusions 1943 Sby 5/92   14,300
Pl/Pa 11x15 Untitled 1936 But 11/91   3,850

Mancin, Francesca   It 1830-1905
* See 1990 Edition . . . .
Mancinelli, Guiseppi   It 1817-1875
* See 1991 Edition . . . .
Mancinelli, R.   It 20C
G/Pa 12x9 House of Crescentius, Rome Hnd 12/91   150
Mancini, Antonio   It 1852-1930
W/Pa 11x9 Young Peasant Girl Wlf 6/92   2,800
Mandel, Howard   Am 1917-
G/Pa 16x12 Italian Market 1955 Slo 10/91   125
Mane-Katz   Fr 1894-1962
O/C 31x25 Vase de Fleurs 39 Chr 2/92   17,600
O/C 30x39 Nue Assise 42 Sby 10/91   14,025
O/C 30x25 Young Violinist But 5/92   12,100
O/C 29x24 Vase of Flowers But 5/92   9,350
O/C 18x12 Young Woman Sby 2/92   7,150
O/C 12x10 Mare with Foal Sby 2/92   4,675
G/Pa 12x19 A Jewish Wedding Hnd 3/92   4,400
G/Pa/B 26x20 Desert Conversation 35 Chr 11/91   3,850
Manet, Edouard   Fr 1832-1883
O/C 25x31 Les travailleurs de la mer Chr 5/92 . . . .   1.98M
P/C 22x14 Jeune fille au chapeau marron Chr 5/92   385,000
Manglard, Adrien   Fr 1695-1760
O/C 42x83 Bay of Naples with Mt. Vesuvius Sby 1/92 . .   137,500
O/C 38x51 Capriccio of Southern Port w/Ships Sby 5/92 .   19,800
Mangold, Robert   Am 1937-
A&H/Pa 30x45 Red Ellipse/Ivory Frame 1989 Chr 2/92 . .   24,200
A/Pn 14x13 Square Within a Square 1974 Chr 11/91   20,900
H/Pa 11x14 Four Drawings 1972 Chr 11/91   8,800
Cp/Pa 22x28 Rectangle Within a Triangle 1976 Sby 2/92 .   8,800
H/Pa 12x11 Three Drawings 1972 Chr 11/91   6,600
A&C/Pa 30x22 Study for Irregular #5 1986 Sby 2/92 . . .   6,050
Mangold, Sylvia Plimack   1938-
A/C 30x34 Half Window 1972 Chr 11/91   2,420
Manguin, Henri   Fr 1874-1943
O/C 29x24 Femme dans un Interieur Chr 2/92   90,200
Manigault, Edward Middleton   Am 1887-1922
* See 1990 Edition . . . .
Manley, Thomas R.   Am 1853-1938
O/B 9x14 Two Maine Landscapes Lou 9/91   1,600
O/C 9x16 Day at the Beach 187- Skn 11/91   880
Manly, Charles MacDonald   Can 1855-1924
W/Pa 11x22 The Watering Place '96 Sbt 11/91   1,028
Mann, Harrington   Am 1865-1937
O/C 40x30 Portrait of Lord Duveen 1921 Sby 12/91   2,200
Mann, Joshua Hargrave Sams   Br -1886
* See 1992 Edition . . . .
Mann, W. D.   19C
O/B 8x11 Two: Moon over a Lake Yng 4/92   80
Manners, William   Eng a 1884-1910
O/C 16x24 Timber Hauling Wes 11/91   1,650
O/C 12x17 The Harvest 1901 Wlf 11/91   800
Mannheim, Jean   Am 1863-1945
O/C 24x20 Girl with a Hand Mirror Lou 6/92   5,500
O/B 12x16 The Old Barn But 6/92   3,575
O/C 17x22 Woman Reading But 6/92   2,475
O/M 20x24 Zinnias in Blue Vase Mor 6/92   1,000
Mannucci, Cipriano A.   It 1882-1970
* See 1992 Edition . . . .
Manoir, Irving   Am 1891-1982
* See 1992 Edition . . . .
Mansfeld, Moritz   Aus 19C
O/Pn 10x8 Ornate Still Life 1883 Chr 2/92   2,420
Mansfield, Joseph
* See 1992 Edition . . . .
Mantelet-Martel, Andre   Fr 1876-
* See 1990 Edition . . . .
Manuel, Jorge
* See 1992 Edition . . . .
Manuel, Victor   Cub 1867-1969
O/C 21x16 Bohio Sby 5/92   12,100
O/C/B 18x14 Mujer con Sombrero Sby 5/92   9,350
O/C 22x19 Gitana Con Manzana Roja Sby 11/91   8,800

G,I&Cp/Pa 15x11 Mujer con Fondo Azul Sby 5/92 2,750

Manzoni, Ignazio   It 1799-1888
O/C 52x40 The Cavaliers' Repast Sby 2/92 9,900

Manzoni, Piero   Fr 1933-1963
* See 1990 Edition

Manzu, Giacomo   1908-1991
PI&S/Pa 20x24 Ninfa Chr 2/92 7,150
G&Pe/Pa 28x20 Studio Donna Chr 11/91 7,150
G&Y/Pa 12x17 Piccone Chr 2/92 6,600
Br&I/Pa 23x18 Sonia Accovacciata Chr 11/91 6,600
PI&K/Pa 15x18 Artist and Model 1967 Sby 5/92 5,775

Manzur, David   Col 1929-
MM/C 11x17 The Moon as a Flower 64 Chr 5/92 2,750

Mao   It 1575-1625
O/C 63x44 The Education of Jupiter Sby 10/91 55,000

Mapplethorpe, Robert   Am 20C
MM/Pb 20x12 Calender Guy 69 Sby 5/92 24,750

Maquette, A.
O/B 18x15 Genre Painting w/Family by Fire Ald 5/92 290

Marais-Milton, Victor   Fr 1872-
O/C 26x22 Voice of the Pope But 5/92 9,350

Marasco, Antonio   It 1886-
* See 1991 Edition

Marc, Franz   Ger 1880-1916
C&K/Pa 24x14 Kleines Madchen 1905 Chr 11/91 26,400

Marca-Relli, Conrad   Am 1913-
O&L/C 60x60 X-L-31-62 62 Chr 11/91 30,800
L/C/Pn 21x26 Untitled Sby 2/92 3,300
L 31 dia M-XL-3 64 Sby 10/91 1,650
O&L/C 26x33 Composizione Chr 5/92 1,100

Marcel-Clement, Amedee Julien   Fr 1873-
* See 1990 Edition

March Y Marco, Vincente   Spa 1859-1914
O/C 14x24 Assignation in the Garden 86 Sby 10/91 40,700

Marchand, Andre   Fr 1877-1951
O/C 32x40 Le Plein Soleil 73 Sby 10/91 8,250

Marchand, Charles   Aus 19C
O/C 27x42 Grand Canal, Venice 1880 Chr 10/91 3,300

Marchand, Jean Hippolyte   Fr 1883-1940
* See 1992 Edition

Marchesini, Alessandro   It 1664-1738
O/C 34x43 Phaethon Approaching Apollo Sby 1/92 30,250

Marchetti, Ludovico   It 1853-1909
O/Pn 12x9 The Rehearsal 1879 But 5/92 4,950

Marchioni, Elisabetta   It a 17C
O/C 42x55 Still Lifes Roses Peonies: Pair Sby 1/92 88,000

Marchisio, Andrea   It 1850-1927
O/C 17x25 The Long Journey Wlf 6/92 2,750

Marcius-Simons, Pinckney   Am 1865-1909
* See 1992 Edition

Marcon, Charles   20C
O/M 39x26 L'Homme Pour Les Oiseaux 73 Sby 10/91 14,300

Marcoussis, Louis   Fr 1883-1941
O&Sd/Gl 28x23 Objet III (recto and verso) 27 Chr 2/92 . . . 58,300
O/B/Pn 12x29 Nature Morte Chr 5/92 39,600
G,I&Pe/Pa 17x12 Nature Morte Devant la Fenetre Sby 11/91 35,200
W/Pa 7x5 Paris 1933 Sby 5/92 6,050

Marcucci, F. Massimo   It 20C
W/Pa 20x13 Lady with Coral Pearls Slo 7/92 650

Marden, Brice   Am 1938-
O&Wx/C 72x108 Grove Group II Sby 11/91 825,000
O&Wx/C 96x144 Dylan Karina Painting 1969 Sby 5/92 . . . 632,500
O&Wx/C 68x100 Nico Painting 1966 Sby 11/91 374,000
H&Wx/Pa 26x40 Untitled 69 Sby 5/92 71,500
O&H/Pa/B 30x22 Untitled Chr 5/92 20,900

Marec, Victor   Fr 1862-1920
O/Pn 24x18 Luxembourg Gardens Sel 9/92 9,000

Maresca, S.   It 19C
O/C 14x24 Lady at a Seaside Wall Hnd 6/92 400
O/C 14x24 Mount Vesuvius Hnd 6/92 375

Marescalchi, Pietro   It 1520-1589
O/C 64x49 Madonna and Child Enthroned Chr 5/92 93,500

Marevna, (Marie Vorobieff)
* See 1992 Edition

Margetson, William Henry   Br 1861-1940
* See 1991 Edition

Margotton, Rene   Fr 1915-
O/L 31x16 Fleurs au Compotier 1968 Wlf 3/92 550
O/C 18x24 Pecheurs A La Maree Basse 1967 Wes 11/91 . . 138

Margulies, Joseph   Am 1896-
* See 1992 Edition

Mariani, Carlo Maria   It 1931-
O/C 24x18 Ciparisso Chr 11/91 11,000

Mariani, Pompeo   It 1857-1927
O/C 19x27 Breaking Waves Chr 10/91 2,750

Marieschi, Michele   It 1696-1743
O/C 18x28 Capriccio w/Palladian Church: Pair Sby 5/92 . 297,000

Marilhat, Prosper Georges A.   Fr 1811-1847
O/C 18x22 Bather at Twilight Sby 7/92 3,410

Marin, John   Am 1870-1953
W,C&Pe/Pa 26x21 A Street Seeing 28 Chr 12/91 198,000
W/Pa 14x17 Berkshire Hills '12 Sby 5/92 22,000
W&Pe/Pa 8x10 Downtown New York '12 Sby 9/91 15,400
W&Pe/Pa 8x11 Sunset Chr 9/91 7,700
P/Pa 9x12 Village Scene '08 Wlf 6/92 1,700

Marin, Joseph Charles   Fr 1759-1834
* See 1991 Edition

Marinelli, Vincenzo   It 1820-1892
* See 1990 Edition

Marini   It 19C
W&G/Pa/B 18x12 A Street Scene in Cairo Chr 5/92 770

Marini   It 20C
O/C 21x18 Child with Flowers Sel 4/92 50

Marini, Antonio   It 18C
* See 1992 Edition

Marini, Leonardo   It 1730-1789
* See 1991 Edition

Marini, Marino   It 1901-1980
O/C 39x31 Cavalier Bleu 1952 But 5/92 77,000
T,G&Pl/Pa 34x25 Cavallo e Cavaliere 1955 Chr 2/92 52,800
O/Pa 37x29 Cavallo 1950 Chr 11/91 38,500
O&I/Pa/C 25x17 Uomini E Cavallo 1953 Sby 5/92 27,500
E/Pa 23x19 Cavallo 50 Chr 5/92 15,400
I&W/Pa 12x8 Heads Hnz 10/91 1,200

Marinko, George   Am 1908-1989
O/B 10x14 Abstract Yng 4/92 300

Marinus, Ferdinand Joseph B.   Bel 1808-1890
* See 1991 Edition

Maris, Jacob Henricus   Dut 1837-1899
O/Pn 12x10 Girl with Downcast Eyes But 5/92 3,025
O/C 16x20 Man in a Punt Sel 4/92 2,600
O/Pn 9x7 Italian Farm Scene Brd 5/92 1,870

Maris, Willem   Dut 1844-1910
* See 1992 Edition

Marisol   1930-
H&Cp/Pa 22x14 My Name is I Hate You 1971 Chr 11/91 . . 3,300

Marisse, Jim   Am 20C
P/C 54x58 Abstract 84 Hnd 5/92 300
C&I/Pa 24x38 Face 89 Hnd 5/92 90

Markart, Hans
O/Iv 7x2 Nudes (3) Dum 8/92 3,000

Markham, Charles Cole   Am 1837-1907
O/C 14x12 That Little German Band 1874 Chr 5/92 8,800

Markham, Kyra   Am 1891-
O/B 18x15 Interior Scene with Cat '51 Skn 11/91 440
O/B 24x19 Boss Woman Mys 11/91 330

Marko, Andreas   Aus 1824-1895
O/C 41x54 Goatherders Roman Campagna 1872 But 11/91 18,700
O/C 62x49 Shepherdess with Her Flock 1887 But 5/92 8,250

Marko, Karl   Hun 1822-1891
O/C 36x24 The Return Home Chr 10/91 2,750

Marko, Karoly (Sr.)   Hun 1791-1860
O/C 34x49 Susannah and the Elders Sby 5/92 15,400

Markowicz, Arthur   Pol 1872-1934
* See 1992 Edition

Marks, Henry Stacy   Br 1829-1898
O/C 38x25 White Stork in the Marshes Sby 2/92 11,000

Marlatt, W.   Eng 19C
W/Pa 14x20 Man and Woman Tending Field Wlf 6/92   500
W/Pa 14x20 Children Playing Wlf 6/92   300
Marno, J.   Con 19C
* See 1992 Edition
Marny, Paul   Br 1829-1914
O/C 20x36 Old Rouen Sby 2/92   4,400
W/Pb 37x27 Underneath the Bridge Chr 10/91   1,650
Marot, Francois   1666-1719
O/C 36x50 Terpsichore Chr 10/91   8,800
Marple, William L.   Am 1827-1910
O/C 12x20 On the Lake 1880 Eld 7/92   770
O/C 20x12 Nocturnal Harbor Scene Sel 9/91   375
Marquet, Albert   Fr 1875-1947
W/Pa/Pa 5x7 Terre Rouge, Algers Chr 2/92   3,520
Marquez, Roberto
* See 1992 Edition . . . .
Marrel, Jacob   Dut 1614-1681
O/Pn 25x18 Floral Still Life with Lizard 1635 But 5/92 . .   330,000
Mars, Peter   Am 20C
MM/Pa 22x18 Statue of Liberty Hnd 5/92   300
Marsano, L.   It 19C
O/C 27x41 The Grand Entrance Chr 2/92   13,200
Marsans, Luis   20C
* See 1991 Edition
Marsh, Lucille Patterson   Am 1890-
O/Cb 17x13 Blonde Haired Baby Ih 11/91   1,600
Marsh, Reginald   Am 1898-1954
Br,l&W/Pa 22x30 NY Street Scenes: Double Chr 5/92 . .   27,500
W/Pa 14x20 Skyscrapers Chr 9/91   15,400
W,C&G/Pa 21x15 Reading in Times Square 38 Chr 5/92 . .   12,100
O/M 17x13 The Boardwalk 53 Chr 12/91   11,000
O/Cb 16x12 The Shopper '48 Sby 3/92   11,000
T/B 16x12 14th Street Shopper 1950 Sby 12/91   9,350
W&Pe/Pa 14x20 Trainyards, New York 1929 Chr 3/92 . . .   9,350
S/Pa 27x40 In the Surf 1947 But 11/91   8,250
W/Pa 11x15 Beach Scene 1951 Dum 7/92   5,500
T/B 12x16 Two on a Horse Chr 3/92   5,500
W&Pe/Pa 14x20 Cityscape, New York 1931 Chr 3/92 . . .   5,280
O/M 7x6 Girl on a Carousel Horse; Nude: Two Chr 3/92 . .   4,290
O/M 10x8 On the Boardwalk Sby 12/91   4,125
W/Pa 9x7 Out for a Stroll 53 Sby 4/92   3,575
W&Pe/Pa 14x20 New York Harbor Chr 3/92   3,080
W&Pe/Pa 14x20 Summer Manse 1929 Chr 3/92   2,420
W&Pe/Pa 14x20 Tugboat at Dock 1931 Chr 3/92   2,420
O/C 24x14 Seated Nude But 11/91   2,200
I/Pa 7x4 A Sleeping Man Lou 6/92   625
Sg/Pa 12x16 Reclining Nude Hnd 6/92   600
Y/Pa 19x12 Ena Douglas Chr 6/92   550
Marshall, Ben   Br 1767-1835
O/C 29x35 Artist and Newfoundland 1811 Sby 6/92   38,500
Marshall, Charles S.   Am 20C
O/C 36x40 Marsh on a Misty Evening Wlf 3/92   600
Marshall, Don
W/Pa 11x17 Wisconsin Scenes: Two Hnz 10/91   50
Marshall, Thomas Falcon   Br 1818-1878
* See 1991 Edition . . . .
Marsini, *   Con 20C**
W&G/Pa 18x11 Arabs Bartering in Market Slo 9/91   600
Marston, Mott M.   Am 20C
W/Pa 14x10 8 Los Angeles Scenes Mor 11/91   400
W/Pa 11x15 28 Landscapes Mor 11/91   175
Martens, Ernest Edouard   Fr 1865-
O/C 24x29 Promenade en Barque Sby 10/91   12,100
Martens, John William   1794-1864
Pe/Pa 8x7 Two Drawings Yng 4/92   80
Martens, L.   Con 19C
W/Pa 10x8 Luciola Slo 2/92   170
**Martens, Willem Johannes   Dut
1838-1895**
* See 1990 Edition . . . .
Martin, Agnes   Am 1912-
Gd&O/C 72x72 Night Sea '63 Sby 11/91   352,000
O&Pe/C 72x72 Stone Sby 11/91   220,000
A,Pe&I/C 72x72 Happy Valley 1967 Sby 5/92   198,000

A&H/C 72x72 Untitled XXI, 1980 Sby 5/92   159,500
Pl/Pa 12x9 Aspiration Chr 11/91   7,150
Martin, Benito Quinquela   Arg 1890-1977
O/C 24x32 A la Orilla del Rio Chr 11/91   14,300
Martin, David   Br 1737-1798
O/C 30x25 Portrait of a Young Man 1788 Sby 10/91   5,500
Martin, Fletcher   Am 1904-1979
O/C 34x26 Snug Harbor 33 Chr 3/92   6,600
W/Pa 19x14 The Poker Players But 11/91   1,650
O/C 20x16 Porfile of a Sailor Sby 12/91   1,320
Et/B 20x15 Stormy Weather Sby 12/91   1,320
Martin, H.   Eur 19C
W/Pa 16x27 Venetian Canal Slo 9/91   1,600
Martin, Henri   Fr 1860-1943
O/C 26x32 Trois Femmes dans le Jardin Sby 5/92   74,250
O/C 32x33 Le bassin Chr 5/92   66,000
O/C 14x31 Le Port de Marseille Sby 5/92   29,700
O/C 26x18 Muse Sby 10/91   19,800
O/C 21x15 Madame Henri Martin Chr 5/92   17,600
Martin, Homer Dodge   Am 1836-1897
O/C 11x17 Canadian Landscape Wlf 9/91   1,200
Martin, Homer Roy   Am 20C
O/B 18x24 Study of a Barn '64 Bor 8/92   200
O/B 19x23 Quarry '61 Bor 8/92   175
O/B 30x40 Castaways '64 Bor 8/92   150
O/B 18x23 Industrial Evening '64 Bor 8/92   100
O/B 30x40 Renovation '64 Bor 8/92   100
O/C 50x40 Evening Hedgerow '64 Bor 8/92   50
O/B 18x24 Evening Mist '64 Bor 8/92   50
O/C 12x10 Shaftway '63 Bor 8/92   50
O/B 16x12 Thistle with Beetle '64 Bor 8/92   25
Martin, J. R.   19C
* See 1991 Edition . . . .
Martin, Jacques   Fr 1844-1919
O/C 21x30 Nature Morte Avec Fleur Dum 7/92   2,250
Martin, John   Eng 1789-1854
W/Pa 7x11 Cornfield with Distant Church 1839 Sby 1/92 . .   7,150
O/C 30x41 Venetian View 1850 Slo 9/91   1,900
Martin, John Knox   Am 1923-
* See 1992 Edition . . . .
Martin, Keith   Am 20C
* See 1992 Edition . . . .
Martin, Maurice   Sws 19C
O/C 35x40 Village in Snow Doy 11/91   5,500
O/C 22x26 Road to the Village Sby 6/92   1,980
Martin, S. R.   It 19C
W/Pa 20x28 The Forum Chr 5/92   3,080
Martin, Sue Pettey   Am 1896-
O/C 38x47 Sleeping Nude Fre 10/91   900
Martin, Sylvester   Br 1856-1906
O/B 7x13 Pheasant Shooting; Waiting: Two 1886 Slo 2/92 . .   950
Martin, Thomas Mower   Can 1838-1934
* See 1991 Edition . . . .
Martin, W.   Br 20C
O/C 10x14 Pair of Beach Scenes Hnd 6/92   800
Martin-Ferrieres, Jac   Fr 1893-1974
O/C 27x34 Collioure Chr 2/92   17,600
O/C 18x22 Chiogga 24 Chr 2/92   15,400
O/C 28x34 Collioure Hnd 10/91   8,000
O/M 18x24 Reclining Nude in a Bedroom Sby 2/92   5,225
Martin-Kavel, Francois   Fr 19C
* See 1991 Edition . . . .
Martindale, G. Thomas   Br 19C
* See 1991 Edition . . . .
Martinelli   It 1910-
O/C 24x46 Landscape Dum 11/91   100
Martinetti, Angelo   It 19C
* See 1992 Edition . . . .
Martinetti, Maria   It 1864-
W/Pa 15x22 The Game Sby 7/92   2,200
Martinez
* See 1992 Edition . . . .
Martinez, Alfredo Ramos   Mex 1872-1946
O/C 30x24 La India de las Floripondias Chr 5/92   71,500
P,C&G/Pa/B 22x17 Tres Mujeres Sby 5/92   26,400

156

G&I/Pa/B 21x17 Tres Mujeres Sby 5/92 22,000
O&G/Pa 18x18 Floral Still Life But 5/92 9,900
W&G/Pa 33x28 Floral Still Life But 10/91 9,350
MM/Pa 22x16 Woman with Flower But 5/92 7,700

Martinez, Gonzalo Martinez Spa 1860-1938
,O/C 26x33 La Cigarreras Sby 5/92 15,400

Martinez, Jose Ignacio Pinazo Spa 1879-
* See 1991 Edition . . . .

Martinez, Ricardo Mex 1918-
O/C 79x69 Pareja Antigua 68 Chr 5/92 55,000
O/L 47x31 Hombre 55 Sby 11/91 40,700
O/C 59x51 Hombre Primitivo 60 Chr 5/92 28,600
O/C 35x59 Hombre En Reposo 60 Sby 11/91 25,300
O/C 39x59 Figura con Fondo Azul 81 Sby 5/92 24,200
O/M 24x22 El Peregrino 43 Chr 11/91 18,700
O/C 32x41 Los Musicos 54 Chr 11/91 18,700
O/C 45x33 La Mujer Verde 61 Sby 5/92 16,500
O/C 27x33 Two Nude Figures '66 But 5/92 11,000
O&Pe/Pa 3x5 Reclining Female Nude 66 But 5/92 935
Pe/Pa 12x9 Mother and Child 1966 But 5/92 660

Martinez, Xavier Am 1869-1943
* See 1992 Edition . . . .

Martinez-Pedro, Luis Cub 1910-
Pe/Pa 22x20 Retrato con Paisaje Cubano 41 Chr 5/92 7,700
G/Pa 24x18 Figura 48 Sby 5/92 2,970

Martini, Alberto It 1876-1954
* See 1990 Edition . . . .

Martini, Simone It 1284-1334
* See 1992 Edition . . . .

Martino, Antonio Pietro Am 1902-1989
O/C 12x16 House and Creek 1930 Ald 3/92 7,750
O/C 25x28 The Rock 1925 Brd 5/92 4,675
O/C/M 30x36 Winter Landscape in Manayunk Fre 4/92 4,600
O/C 20x24 Houses in a Winter Landscape Fre 4/92 3,000
O/C 32x40 Winter Ald 5/92 1,500
W/Pa 21x29 Bass Rocks 1931 Ald 5/92 500

Martino, Edmund Am 1915-
O/C 22x30 Straw Flowers and Fruit '50 Fre 4/92 70
O/C 22x30 Floral and Fruit 1950 Slo 10/91 45

Martino, Giovanni Am 1908-
O/B 12x18 Grape Street Hill 1945 Ald 5/92 900
O/B 13x19 Stucco Houses Ald 5/92 850
O/B 11x16 November Snow Sby 12/91 825
W/Pa 17x26 Sailboat Ald 5/92 700
O/B 12x18 Working in Garden 1935 Skn 3/92 660

Martyl, * Am 20C**
G/M 12x16 Alley Cat Slo 9/91 140

Marx, Ernest Bernhard Ger 1864-
O/C 50x81 Reclining Nude Sby 7/92 10,725

Marx, John
O/C 22x36 Shipping Off Quebec 1886 Eld 7/92 1,100

Maryan 20C
* See 1991 Edition . . . .

Mas Y Fondevila, Arcadio Spa 1850-
* See 1992 Edition . . . .

Mascacotta 1663-1714
* See 1992 Edition . . . .

Mascart, Gustaf Fr 20C
O/C 26x37 A River Town Wes 3/92 3,300

Masillo It 1677-1743
O/C 16x26 Still Life Basket with Knitting Sby 1/92 19,800

Mason, Maud Mary Am 1867-1956
C&P/Pa 15x10 Still Life Bottle and Vegetables Lou 6/92 600

Mason, Roy M. Am 1886-1972
W/Pa 15x21 Ducks Taking Off Dum 9/91 650

Mason, William Sanford Am 1824-1864
* See 1992 Edition . . . .

Masriera Y Manovens, Francisco Spa 1842-1902
O/C 45x38 Mal des Amores: An Odalisque 1889 Sby 2/92 . . 22,000
O/C 49x24 An Exotic Beauty 1898 Chr 10/91 19,800
O/Pn 18x15 The Young Bride 1885 Sby 10/91 17,600
O/Pn 18x15 Jeune Femme Aux Mimosas 1885 Sby 2/92 . . . 7,425

Massani, Pompeo It 1850-1920
O/C/B 14x10 Il Vecchio Violinista But 11/91 2,200

Massillo It 18C
* See 1990 Edition . . . .

Masson, Andre Fr 1896-1987
O/C 45x58 Femme Paralytique Sby 11/91 484,000
O/C 14x23 Bacchanale Chr 11/91 93,500
O/C 51x64 La Chimere Domptee 1960 Chr 11/91 93,500
O/C 57x45 Necromancie 1962 Chr 11/91 82,500
C&I/Pa 15x16 Autoportrait 1944 Sby 11/91 35,750
O/C 15x11 Orphee Chr 11/91 27,500
P/Pa/C 20x26 L'Oeil du Cyclope Chr 11/91 22,000
P/Pa/C 29x24 Trophee Chr 5/92 22,000
Cp&Y/Pa 12x9 Arbre 33 Chr 5/92 2,640

Masson, Henri Leopold Can 1907-
O/Pn 12x10 Monks Sbt 11/91 3,272
O/C 18x21 Quarry, Hull, P.Q. Sbt 11/91 2,805
O/Pn 10x12 Street Scene '49 Sbt 11/91 1,496
MM/Pa 16x14 Old Houses, Venice 1957 Sbt 5/92 1,028

Mastenbroek, Johann Hendrick Dut 1875-1945
O/Pn 8x12 Sailing Boats; Canal (Pair) But 11/91 2,200

Master B B 17C
* See 1991 Edition . . . .

Master Leonardesque Female Por It 16C
* See 1991 Edition . . . .

Master of 1310 a 1310-1325
Gd&T/Pn 36x50 Scenes; Life of Martyred Female Sby 1/92 814,000

Master of 1518 It 16C
* See 1992 Edition . . . .

Master of 1540s a 1541-1551
O/Pn 16x14 Gentleman, wearing black 1541 Chr 5/92 . . . 60,500

Master of Almudevar It a 1473-1500
* See 1992 Edition . . . .

Master of Apollo & Daphne 1480-1510
O&T/Pn 27x80 King David Praying Sby 5/92 38,500

Master of Castello Nativity It 15C
* See 1992 Edition . . . .

Master of Female Half It 16C
* See 1992 Edition . . . .

Master of Frankfort a 1493-1520
O/Pn 27x9 Saint James the Greater;Female:Pair Sby 5/92 . 30,800

Master of Greenville Tondo 16C
* See 1991 Edition . . . .

Master of Incredulity St. Thom a 1505-1525
O/C 14x12 Madonna and Child in Landscape Sby 5/92 . . . 16,500

Master of Leonardesque 16C
O/Pn 24x18 Portrait Lady Wearing White Dress Chr 1/92 . 330,000

Master of Magdalene Legend It a 15C
* See 1992 Edition . . . .

Master of Naumberg Madonna 15C
* See 1991 Edition . . . .

Master of Panzano Triptych It
* See 1990 Edition . . . .

Master of Saint Ivo It a 1400-
Gd&T/Pn 27x15 Madonna and Child Enthroned Sby 1/92 . 66,000

Master of San Miniato It 15C
* See 1992 Edition . . . .

Master of Staffolo It 15C
* See 1992 Edition . . . .

Master of Stories of Helen It 1440-1470
* See 1992 Edition . . . .

Master, Johnson Nativity It 15C
* See 1990 Edition . . . .

Master, Miller Tondo It 15C
* See 1990 Edition . . . .

Masters, E. Eng 19C
O/C 32x18 Boaters on Mountain Lake Slo 2/92 850

Matania, Fortunino It 1881-1985
Pe&W/Pa 9x15 Colonial Men Meeting in Tavern Ih 5/92 . . . 225

Matcalf
MM/Pa 19x13 Boy Watching Snail Hnz 10/91 325

Matham, Theodor Dirck 1606-1676
* See 1992 Edition . . . .

Matheson, Gertrude A.   Sco 1879-1941
O/Pn 7x9 After the Hunt Slo 7/92   400
Mathews, Arthur Frank   Am 1860-1945
* See 1992 Edition
Mathews, John Chester   Br a 1884-1900
* See 1992 Edition
Mathews, Lucia Kleinhans   Am 1870-1955
W/Pa 19x23 Monterey Pines But 2/92   12,100
Mathewson, Frank Convers   Am 1862-1941
* See 1992 Edition
Mathieu, Gabriel   Fr 19C
O/C 22x32 River Landscape Fre 10/91   200
Mathieu, Georges   Fr 1921-
O/C 38x64 Untitled Chr 11/91   42,900
O/C 36x29 Athanor 67 Sby 10/91   35,750
Mathieu, Paul
O/C 20x28 En Hollande Sby 10/91   5,500
Matisse, Henri   Fr 1869-1954
O/C 18x14 Nu Debout Devant la Cheminee Sby 5/92 . . . . . .   2.2M
C/Pa 26x20 Femme Assise Blouse Roumaine 38 Sby 5/92 .   1.21M
C/Pa 24x18 Ballerine Assise 44 Sby 5/92   880,000
Pe/Pa 14x12 Le Chapeau Aux Plumes 1919 Sby 5/92 . .   495,000
O/Pn 13x10 Portrait de Femme Sby 11/91   410,000
C/Pa 21x17 Jeune Fille a la Mantilla Sby 5/92   385,000
I/Pa 21x16 Femme se Reposant 35 Sby 11/91   341,000
Pe/Pa 23x26 Antoinette Etendue Sby 5/92   302,500
PI/Pa 15x22 Nu Allonge 1935 Sby 5/92   253,000
Br&I/Pa 13x8 Profil de Femme Sby 5/92   121,000
I/Pa 15x10 Nu Au Repos Sby 5/92   110,000
Br&I/Pa 17x13 Visage 51 Sby 5/92   104,500
W/Pa/B 10x13 Collioure Chr 11/91   77,000
Pe/Pa 11x15 Femme Assise Sby 5/92   55,000
PI/Pa 10x7 Marocain Assis Sby 11/91   55,000
Pe/Pa/B 21x16 Buste de Femme 47 Sby 11/91   52,250
Pe/Pa 16x21 Tete de Femme Chr 11/91   38,500
PI/Pa 9x12 Zorah (Tete Dans les Mains) Sby 5/92   38,500
PI/Pa 17x15 Tete de Femme 1949 Chr 11/91   33,000
PI/Pa 10x8 Marocain, de Trois-Quarts 1913 Sby 11/91 . . .   28,600
PI/Pa 10x8 Marabout et Drapeau 1913 Sby 11/91   27,500
C/Pa 12x9 Denise, tete dans la main Chr 5/92   26,400
PI/Pa 10x7 La Porte de la Casbah 1913 Sby 11/91   26,400
Pe,PI&W/Pa 11x9 Costumes Rouge et Noir: Pair Sby 5/92   25,300
PI/Pa 10x8 Croises & Soldat Marocain: Pair 1913 Sby 11/91   25,300
PI/Pa 10x8 Porte and Cavaliers: Pair 1913 Sby 11/91 . . .   25,300
PI/Pa 10x8 Marocain Assis 1913 Sby 11/91   24,200
PI/Pa 10x7 Deux Vues de Tanger 1913 Sby 11/91   23,100
Pe/Pa 10x8 Marocain, Mi-Corps 1913 Sby 11/91   23,100
PI/Pa 9x11 Vue de la Medine 1912 Sby 11/91   23,100
PI&G/Pa 10x7 Vue de la Fenetre, Tanger I Sby 11/91 . . .   22,000
Pe/Pa 14x9 Nu Assis Sur Un Tabouret Sby 5/92   17,600
PI/Pa 10x8 Palais du Sultan 1913 Sby 11/91   17,600
PI/Pa 7x10 Tanger I: Pair 1912 Sby 11/91   16,500
PI/Pa 10x8 Tanger: Pair 1913 Sby 11/91   16,500
PI/Pa 10x7 Mosquee de la Casbah I 1912 Sby 11/91   14,300
I/Pa 9x7 Sketches from Collioure Sby 5/92   13,200
PI/Pa 8x10 Medine: Treillis Fleuri 1913 Sby 11/91   12,100
Pe&I/Pa 10x8 Costume Design "Rouge et Noir" Sby 10/91   11,000
Br&I/Pa 3x3 Visage d'une Jeune Femme Sby 11/91   11,000
Matson, Victor   Am 1898-1972
O/C 24x30 California Landscape Mor 3/92   750
Matta   Chl 1911-
O/C 29x37 Theorie de L'Arbre 1941 Sby 5/92   451,000
O/C 26x21 Les Pommes De Cezanne 42 Sby 11/91   187,000
O/C 81x83 Ouvre le Feu Chr 11/91   143,000
O/C 37x29 Sin Titulo Chr 11/91   71,500
O/C 33x39 Marajos Chr 5/92   66,000
O/C 19x80 Triptych Sby 11/91   55,000
O/C 24x29 Untitled Sby 11/91   55,000
O/C 38x38 Composicion Sin Titulo Chr 11/91   49,500
O/C 45x33 Le Dos du Miroir Chr 5/92   44,000
O/L 41x39 Yellow Flame 74 Chr 11/91   44,000
O/C 42x34 Untitled Composition Chr 5/92   35,200
O/C 31x25 Abstract Composition Chr 11/91   24,200

H&Y/Pa 20x26 Degrees de Solitude Sby 5/92   22,000
G&Y/Pa 10x12 Desnudo Sby 5/92   22,000
PI&Cp/Pa 8x11 Sueno Sby 5/92   22,000
Pe&Y/Pa 20x26 Composicion Sin Titulo 56 Chr 11/91 . . .   17,600
H&Y/Pa 20x26 Contre la Terreur Sacre Sby 5/92   16,500
Pe&Y/Pa 11x11 Erotic Composition Chr 11/91   16,500
Pe&Y/Pa 13x20 La Copa Negra Chr 5/92   15,400
O,G&Y/Pa 15x16 Untitled 1955 Sby 11/91   14,300
Y&Pe/Pa 20x27 Composicion Chr 11/91   11,000
Y&Pe/Pa 10x14 Baseball Pitcher Chr 11/91   8,800
H&Y/Pa 17x25 Untitled Sby 11/91   8,800
Br&I/Pa/B 15x18 Sin Titulo 57 Chr 5/92   2,750
Matta-Clark, Gordon
* See 1992 Edition
Matteis, Paolo   1662-1728
O/C 18x14 Madonna and Child Sby 1/92   3,850
Mattern, Alice L.   Am 1909-1945
O/C 42x39 Allegro '43 Skn 11/91   880
O/C 42x36 Cadence Skn 11/91   825
Matteson, Tomkins Harrison   Am 1813-1884
* See 1991 Edition
Matthew, Edward
* See 1991 Edition
Matthews, Marmaduke   Can 1837-1913
W/Pa 15x21 Noonday Rest Sbt 11/91   1,402
W/Pa 20x31 Children Tending Their Cow Sbt 5/92   842
Matthews, William F.   Am 1878-
* See 1991 Edition
Matto, Francisco   Uru 1911-
O/B 20x28 Constructivo Con Jarra Y Cabeza Sby 11/91 . .   11,000
Mattson, Henry E.   Am 1887-1971
* See 1992 Edition
Matulka, Jan   Am 1890-1972
W&Pe/Pa 15x22 Village Street Scene Chr 3/92   4,400
O/C 14x20 New York Cityscape Sby 12/91   1,760
Matzek, O   Con 20C**
O/C 25x19 Still Life of Fish, Fowl 1889 Wes 11/91   138
Matzow, F.   Am 20C
O/C Var Pair Landscapes Mys 6/92   192
Maufra, Maxime   Fr 1861-1918
O/C 24x32 La Jetee de Pontivy 1909 Sby 2/92   44,000
O/C 24x32 La Plage 1911 Sby 5/92   38,500
O/C 24x29 La Rentree Des Bateaux de Peche Sby 2/92 .   28,600
O/C 18x21 La Gabarre Anglaise 1905 Sby 5/92   23,100
O/C 26x32 La Marne a Champigny 1902 Sby 10/91   22,000
O/C 24x29 Le Torrent Bleu 1904 Sby 5/92   19,800
O/C 15x22 La Riviere d'Auray, Bretagne Chr 2/92   14,300
Maurer, Alfred Henry   Am 1868-1932
O/B/C 18x22 House in a Landscape Chr 3/92   13,200
W/Pa 22x18 Floral Still Life Wlf 9/91   5,000
Maurer, Jacob   Ger 1826-1887
O/C 18x25 The Day's Journey Skn 11/91   1,870
Maurer, Louis   Am 1832-1932
* See 1991 Edition
Maury, Georges-Sauveur   Fr 1872-
* See 1991 Edition
Mauve, Anton   Dut 1838-1888
O/C 24x32 The Potato Pickers Sby 5/92   34,100
O/Pn 10x12 Peasant Woman in a Farmyard Chr 5/92 . . .   18,700
Pe/Pa 11x16 Interior Scene Hnz 10/91   875
Max, Peter   Am 1937-
A/C 36x24 Grammy 1989 Hnd 10/91   4,600
G/Pa 17x22 Man w/Raised Fist 1961 Ih 11/91   1,900
Maxence, Edgard   Fr 1871-1954
* See 1990 Edition
Maxey, Theobold   Am 20C
O/B 18x22 Central Park Scene Wes 3/92   550
Maxfield, James Emery   Am 1848-
* See 1990 Edition
Maxim, David
* See 1992 Edition
Maxwell, Laura W.   Am 1877-1967
O/C 12x14 Flowered Landscape Mor 11/91   600
O/B 10x12 Carmel Coastal Mor 11/91   475

May, E.
O/C 72x49 Angel Playing Lyre Dum 9/91 90
May, Henrietta Mabel   Can 1884-1971
* See 1992 Edition
Mayaz, Everett   Am 20C
O/B 14x20 Spring Meadow Hnd 3/92 190
Mayer, Auguste Etienne   Fr 1805-1890
O/Pn 8x10 Idyllic Landscape But 5/92 2,200
Mayer, Constance   Fr 1775-1821
* See 1990 Edition
Mayer, Frank Blackwell   Am 1827-1899
* See 1990 Edition
Mayer, Peter Bela   Am 1888-
* See 1992 Edition
Mayer, William C.   Am 20C
* See 1991 Edition
Mayhew, H.   Am 20C
O/C 22x26 Winter Street Scene Slo 9/91 200
Mayhew, Neil Brooker   Am 1876-1940
* See 1992 Edition
Maynard, George Willoughby   Am 1843-1923
O/B 8x15 The Fort, Marblehead, Mass. 19 Chr 11/91 . . 2,420
Maynard, Richard Field   Am 20C
O/C 27x32 Young Beauty Gold Fan 1914 Doy 12/91 3,600
Maze, Paul   Fr 1887-1979
P/Pa/M 15x25 Parlor Interior But 5/92 10,450
P&Pe/Pa 13x8 Woman Bathing But 5/92 880
Pl/Pa 13x8 Study of a Female Nude But 5/92 550
Mazon, R.   Mex 20C
O/C 40x32 Abstract '84 Sel 9/91 150
Mazot, Angeline   Fr 19C
* See 1990 Edition
Mazotta, Federico   It 19C
* See 1990 Edition
Mazzanovich, Lawrence   Am 1872-1946
* See 1991 Edition
Mazzola, Filippo   It 16C
* See 1990 Edition
Mazzolini, G*   19C**
O/C 25x20 Allegory of Winter Sby 7/92 4,400
Mazzolini, Giuseppe   It 1748-1838
O/C 40x30 Rocking the Baby Asleep Chr 10/91 7,150
O/C 25x20 Maternita Sby 10/91 6,050
Mazzolini, Giuseppe   It 1806-1876
O/C 40x30 La Madre e Suo Bambino 1867 Sby 5/92 4,400
Mazzolini, Joseph   It 19C
* See 1990 Edition
Mazzotta, Federico   It 19C
O/C 32x23 Playtime Chr 10/91 9,900
McAfee, Ila   Am 1897-
O/B 12x16 Indians on Horseback But 11/91 2,200
McAuliffe, James J.   Am 1848-1921
* See 1992 Edition
McBey, James   Br 1889-1959
W/Pa 14x21 Lisbon Port 1946 Fre 12/91 1,150
W&I/Pa 14x10 Stop Along the River Bank 1930 Skn 5/92 . . 825
McBride, Eddie   Am 1889-
Pl/Pa 13x10 Baseball Park Figures 1919 Ih 11/91 325
McBurney, James Edwin   Am 1868-
O/C 22x18 The Summit--Gothic, Colorado Slo 7/92 600
McCall, James   Eng 20C
O/M 18x16 Black Sheep with Halo: Four Wlf 10/91 50
O/M 20x16 Black Sheep with Halo: Three Wlf 10/91 50
McCann, Gerald   Am 20C
* See 1992 Edition
McCarter, Henry   Am 1886-1942
* See 1991 Edition
McCarthy, Frank C.   Am 1924-
* See 1991 Edition
McCawlay, J. T.   Am 20C
O/B 12x16 Harbour Scene Mys 11/91 82
McCay, Winsor   Am 1869-1934
Pl/Pa 28x22 Comic Strip. Little Nemo 1906 Ih 11/91 12,000
Pl/Pa 19x14 Comic. "Dream Rarebit Fiend" 1907 Ih 5/92 . . 2,800

McChesney, Clara Taggart   Am 1860-1928
W&G/Pa 16x13 Mother and Child But 11/91 2,200
McCloskey, James   Am 20C
O/C 18x24 Protest Outside the White House Slo 12/91 1,400
McCloskey, William J.   Am 1859-1941
O/C 10x17 Wrapped Oranges 1901 Sby 5/92 341,000
McCollum, Allan   1944-
A&E/Stone 20x73 Colored Surrogates 1987 Chr 11/91 . . . 17,600
H/Pb 12x12 Collection of 30 Drawings Chr 2/92 11,000
McComas, Eugene Francis   Am 1886-1982
* See 1992 Edition
McComas, Francis John   Am 1874-1938
* See 1992 Edition
McConnell, George   Am 1852-1929
O/B 17x25 September Morn, Maine 1919 Brd 8/92 908
O/B 20x26 Rocky Coastal View 1920 Slo 4/92 25
McCord, George Herbert   Am 1848-1909
O/C/M 50x41 Morristown, New Jersey Chr 12/91 11,000
O/C 18x30 Fisherman's Return Chr 3/92 6,050
O/C 8x16 Landscape Near Yonkers Sby 12/91 4,950
O/C 12x20 Sunset on Lake George Chr 3/92 4,620
O/C 20x36 Fisherfolk on the Coast Chr 6/92 3,080
O/C 18x30 Harbor Scene Lou 12/91 2,600
O/C 30x25 The Approaching Storm Sby 12/91 1,540
O/C 6x8 Church Scene But 4/92 1,430
O/C 14x20 Fall Landscape Dum 6/92 950
O/C 8x12 Abandoned Mill in Moonlight Wlf 11/91 600
McCormick, Evelyn   Am 1869-1948
* See 1992 Edition
McCormick, Howard   Am 1875-1943
O/Pn 14x14 Hopi Katchina Skn 9/91 1,430
McCoy, Wilson   Am 20C
O/Cb 8x10 Mountain Landscape Wes 11/91 138
McCulloch, Horatio   Sco 1805-1867
O/Pn 14x19 The Oak Tree Chr 2/92 1,650
McDermitt, William T.   Am 1884-1961
O/Cb 16x20 Sierra Landscape Mor 3/92 300
McDermott & McGough   Am 20C
O/C 26x12 Untitled 1763 Chr 11/91 1,650
McDorman, Donald   Am 20C
O/M 16x20 Boys World (Still Life) Wes 3/92 550
McDougall, John Alexander   1810-1894
O/C 24x18 Peeling Vegetables Yng 4/92 1,900
McDowell, H. E.
O/C 20x28 Still Life '98 Dum 4/92 750
McDuff, Frederick   Am 1931-
O/C 11x18 Figures Along the Shore Slo 2/92 2,200
McEntee, Jervis   Am 1828-1891
O/B 9x7 Morning Glories Chr 3/92 5,500
O/B 12x14 A Pool in Autumn Dum 1/92 4,000
O/B 8x11 View From Sunset Rock '71 Wes 11/91 3,960
O/C 16x11 The Woods in Fall 83 Sby 12/91 3,410
Pe/Pa 15x11 Trees Slo 9/91 200
Pe/Pa 6x6 Sunset in the Mountains Sel 12/91 90
McEwan, William   Am 19C
* See 1990 Edition
McEwen, Jean Albert   Can 1923-
* See 1992 Edition
McFee, Henry Lee   Am 1886-1953
O/C 20x16 Still Life Onions and Lemons Chr 9/91 6,050
O/C 24x20 Still Life Kitchen Utensils Chr 9/91 4,950
McGeorge, Thomas   Am
O/C 31x25 Portrait of Thomas Woodward 1832 Eld 8/92 . . . 605
McGhie, John M.   Br 1867-1941
* See 1992 Edition
McGinn, Jennie
O/C 20x12 Jamaican Drum Player '61 Dum 5/92 30
McGinnis, Robert E.   Am 1926-
G/Pa 20x15 Woman with Arms Ih 5/92 3,750
O/B 16x40 Kyle Nolan's Camp Skn 9/91 1,870
McGlynn, Thomas   Am 1878-1966
O/Pn 19x21 Sacramento State Fair But 10/91 4,125

159

McGrath, Clarence Am 20C
* See 1990 Edition . . . .
McGrew, Ralph Brownell Am 20C
* See 1990 Edition . . . .
McGuiness, Bingham Br a 1882-1892
  W/B 35x21 Venetian Canal 1890 Sby 7/92 2,475
  W/Pa 14x21 English Roadside Cottage Eld 7/92 330
McIntosh, N. Can 20C
  W/Pa 7x5 Sailing Vessels Dum 4/92 40
McIntosh, Pleasant Ray Am 1897-
  O/B 22x22 In the Chinese Room Hnd 5/92 500
McIntosh, Robert Am 20C
  O/C 12x9 Stone Canyon and Belair (2) Lou 6/92 125
McIntyre, Joseph Wrightson Br 19C
  O/C 22x30 Derbyshire Trout Stream Chr 5/92 850
McKain, Bruce Am 1900-
  O/B 25x30 Fisherman Skn 3/92 990
McKay, F. H. Am 20C
  O/Ab 8x10 Country Houses Slo 4/92 50
McKay, Thomas Hill Am 1875-1941
* See 1992 Edition . . . .
McKeever, Ian 1946-
  O&L/C 87x67 Glacier III 86 Chr 5/92 6,600
  O&L/C 87x67 Through the Ice Lens 86 Chr 5/92 6,050
McKell, James
  O/Ab 20x28 Dog Attacking Bear Dum 1/92 150
McLane, Myrtle Jean Am 19C
* See 1991 Edition . . . .
McLaughlin, John Am 1898-1976
  O/C 60x44 #11-1959 1959 Chr 11/91 26,400
  O/M 32x38 Untitled #17 '54 Chr 11/91 26,400
  O/C 60x38 #20-1958 1958 Chr 2/92 22,000
  O/C 48x60 #7-1961 1961 Sby 5/92 15,400
McLean, Bruce 1944-
  A&C/C 75x59 Untitled Chr 5/92 2,750
  A&K/C 79x59 Untitled Chr 2/92 2,200
McLean, Kate
  Pe/Pa 18x14 Portrait of Black Man '61 Dum 11/91 100
McLean, Richard Am 1934-
* See 1990 Edition . . . .
McLellan, Ralph Am 20C
* See 1990 Edition . . . .
McManus, George Am 1869-1954
  Pl/Pa 21x17 Organizing a Pinochle Game 1923 Ih 5/92 . . . 1,000
  Pl&Pe/Pa 4x18 Comic Strip. "Bringing Up Father" 37 Ih 11/91 550
McMullan, James Am 1934-
  W/Pa 12x8 Jerry Lewis Leaping Through Curtain Ih 11/91 . . 350
McNeil, George 1908-
  O/C 66x66 The British Navy '57 Chr 11/91 17,600
  O/C 60x56 Shaman and Magic Birds '80 Sby 10/91 5,225
  A/C 48x44 Idle Fears 1979 Sby 10/91 3,850
  O/C 48x44 Bird Lady 1976 Sby 10/91 1,650
  O/C 68x56 Dementia Disco 1985 Sby 2/92 1,320
Mead, E. B. Am 20C
  MM 9x5 Portrait of a Woman Yng 2/92 50
Meadows, Arthur Joseph Br 1843-1907
  O/C 16x32 Peasants by a Wooded River Chr 10/91 1,100
Meadows, Edwin L. Br a 1854-1872
  O/C 20x30 Hay Wagon 1858 Wes 3/92 5,500
  O/C 30x48 View of Spofforth, Yorkshire 78 Chr 2/92 4,400
Meadows, James Edwin Br 1828-1888
* See 1992 Edition . . . .
Meakin, Lewis Henry Am 1853-1917
* See 1992 Edition . . . .
Mears, Henrietta Dunn Am a 1920-1929
  O/Cb 12x14 Spring Landscape But 2/92 1,540
Mechau, Frank Albert Am 1903-1946
* See 1992 Edition . . . .
Medard, Jules Ferdinand Fr 1855-1925
  O/C 32x39 Corbeilles de Fleurs Sby 10/91 29,700
Meeker, Joseph Rusling Am 1827-1889
  O/C 27x22 Bayou Landscape 1877 Sby 12/91 22,000
  O/C 24x14 The Swamp 85 Chr 9/91 13,200
Meeks, Eugene Am 1843-
* See 1990 Edition . . . .

Meerts, Frans Ger 1836-1896
* See 1991 Edition . . . .
Mehus, Livio Flm 1630-1691
* See 1991 Edition . . . .
Mei, Bernardino It 1615-1676
  O/C 45x61 Allegory of Justice 1636 Chr 5/92 209,000
Meidner, Ludwig Ger 1884-1966
  Y/Pa 11x8 Kneeling Figure 51 Chr 5/92 1,100
Meifren Y Roig, Eliseo Spa 1859-1940
  O/C 22x30 Boats in the Village Harbor Sby 10/91 44,000
Meigs, Walter Am 20C
  A/Pa 19x25 Journey into Morning 1961 Skn 11/91 550
Meindl, Albert Aus 1891-1967
* See 1992 Edition . . . .
Meissel, Ernst Ger 1838-1895
* See 1991 Edition . . . .
Meissner, Adolf Ernst Ger 1837-1902
* See 1992 Edition . . . .
Meissonier, Jean Charles Fr 1848-1917
  O/C 20x16 An Interesting Story Sby 2/92 6,600
Meissonier, Jean Louis Ernest Fr 1815-1891
  Pe&G/Pa 9x7 Seated Man on a Stool Sby 7/92 1,210
Melbye, Daniel Hermann Anton Dan 1818-1875
* See 1992 Edition . . . .
Melcher, George Henry Am 1881-1957
  O/C 25x30 Landscape Mor 6/92 1,200
Melchers, Frantz Bel 1868-
  O/C 39x31 Afternoon by the Sea, Cannes 14 Chr 10/91 . . . 6,600
Melchers, Julius Gari Am 1860-1932
  O/C 31x19 A Garden Party Sby 9/91 96,250
  O/B 25x30 Contemplative State Fre 4/92 6,100
  O/B 19x12 Eve Holding Apple Sby 4/92 3,520
  O/C 38x28 Lady in Plum 1927 Chr 9/91 2,860
  O/C 22x18 Portrait of Mrs. Mackall 1909 Chr 11/91 2,750
Melendez, Luis Spa 1716-1780
* See 1992 Edition . . . .
Mellen, Mary Blood Am 1817-
  O/C 13x21 Shipwreck on the Beach Sby 3/92 51,700
Mellor, J. Am 19C
  O/C 12x18 Old Mill Hnz 5/92 360
Mellor, William Br 1851-1931
  O/C 30x20 Cows & Sheep Mys 6/92 2,090
Melohs, Charles Am 20C
  O/C 30x25 Spanish Garden Fre 4/92 300
Melrose, Andrew W. Am 1836-1901
  O/C 12x18 The Palisades Chr 5/92 8,800
  O/C 11x17 The Old Homestead But 4/92 4,400
  O/C 20x16 Figure in a Landscape Mys 6/92 495
  W/Pa 19x26 Market Drayton Fre 12/91 160
Meltsner, Paul R. Am 1905-
  O/Cb 24x30 The Fisherman Skn 3/92 605
Meltzer, Arthur Am 1893-
  O/B 24x33 The Beach at Cape May Ald 3/92 4,800
  O/C 16x20 The Broken Shell Wlf 10/91 1,100
  O/C 12x22 Winter Garden Ald 5/92 975
  Pl&W/B 22x12 Among the Ruins Ald 3/92 500
Meltzoff, Stanley Am 1917-
  O/B 21x21 "Ion exchange resin" Rohm & Haas 1953 Ih 11/91 600
Menageot, Francois Guillaume Fr 1744-1816
  O/C 53x39 Le Martyre De Saint-Sebastien Sby 5/92 60,500
Menard, Marie Auguste Emile Fr 1862-1930
  P/L 35x45 Sunset, Capri Skn 5/92 2,475
Menardeau, Maurice Fr 1897-1977
  O/C 21x28 Village Scene Lou 9/91 350
Mendenhall, Emme Am 20C
  W/Pa 16x12 Church with Steeple Hnd 6/92 180
Mendenhall, John Am 1937-
* See 1991 Edition . . . .
Mendes, Samuel Henri Da Costa Con 20C
  O/C 13x10 Village Scene Lou 6/92 50

Mendez-Gonzales, Manuel   Spa 19C
* See 1992 Edition ....
Mendieta, Ana   20C
* See 1991 Edition ....
Mendjisky, Serge   Fr 1929-
O/C 24x32 Le Petit Bois Chr 2/92 2,420
O/C 32x40 Vue de Bargemont Chr 11/91 2,200
O/C 21x26 La Petite Haie Chr 11/91 1,760
O/C 26x32 Paysage Chr 11/91 1,760
O/C 18x24 Le Passage Aux Tribunes Chr 11/91 .. 1,540
O/C 10x14 Paysage de Provence Chr 2/92 1,045
O/C 26x18 Homme Assis 61 Chr 2/92 660
Menendez-Pidal, Luis   Spa 1864-
O/C 20x28 Watching Out for the Vat Sby 1/92 .. 13,750
Menkes, Sigmund Joseph   Am 1896-1986
O/C 43x29 Porch in the Summer Sby 2/92 6,875
O/C 32x26 Jeune Femme Assise Sby 10/91 6,325
O/C 22x18 Artist's Wife with Poppies Chr 5/92 . 4,180
O/C 19x15 Girl with Flowers But 5/92 2,090
O/C 16x13 Young Boy at His Desk Mys 6/92 880
Menkman, William
* See 1992 Edition ....
Menotti, V. A.   It 19C
O/C 20x32 The Lesson Chr 5/92 4,950
Menta, Edouard   Fr 1858-
O/C 32x26 La Femme aux Perroquets et Oiseaux Sby 2/92 14,300
O/C 26x17 Le Petit Cuisinier Sby 5/92 7,700
Mentor, Will   20C
O/C 81x57 There are Still Places Like This 1985 Chr 2/92 . 3,000
Menzel, Adolf Friedrich E.   Ger 1815-1905
K/Pa 12x9 Man Descending Stairway 1884 Chr 5/92 24,200
H/Pa 3x5 The Royal Coach 70 Sby 1/92 7,700
Pe/Pa 5x8 Man Picking Fruit Chr 5/92 5,500
Menzler, Wilhelm   Ger 1846-
O/C 25x17 Tatiana's Baby Sby 7/92 7,700
O/Pn 17x11 Portrait Elegant Young Woman 83 Sby 1/92 . 3,410
O/C 13x9 Lady in a Garden Chr 5/92 1,320
Menzler-Peyton, Bertha S.   Am 1871-1950
O/B 4x6 Landscape and Mesa (2) Mor 6/92 500
Merchant, Henry   Br 20C
O/C 32x24 The Cobbler Sby 1/92 1,320
Mercier, Philippe   Fr 1689-1760
O/C 63x60 Allegory: Lady Seated at Easel 1740 Chr 1/92 . 55,000
Mereiles De Lima, Vitor   LA 1832-1903
O/C 26x21 Retrato da Menina 1884 Chr 5/92 6,600
Merida, Carlos   Mex 1891-1984
O/C 39x28 Motivo Guatemalteco 1919 Chr 11/91 .. 60,500
MM/M 24x18 Los Astrologos 1959 Sby 11/91 49,500
Pls/Pn 23x21 Composicion 1964 Sby 5/92 33,000
O/Pa/B 17x13 Composicion 1977 Chr 5/92 22,000
O/C 28x20 Planes 1960 Chr 11/91 22,000
G/Pa/M 22x16 Kanek, The God of Fire 1967 Sby 5/92 . 16,500
W&G/Pa 11x15 Tres Mujeres 27 Sby 11/91 9,900
Pe&Y/Pn 10x6 Proyecto para Mural Chr 11/91 ... 4,950
Merkel, O.   Am 20C
O/Iv 5x3 Woman with Pearls Fre 4/92 550
Merle, Georges Hugues   Fr 19C
* See 1992 Edition ....
Merle, Hugues   Fr 1823-1881
O/C 57x38 Tarot Reading Hnz 5/92 7,250
Merlin, Daniel   Fr 1861-1933
* See 1992 Edition ....
Merriam, James Arthur   Am 1880-1951
* See 1992 Edition ....
Merritt, Anna Lea   Am 1844-1930
* See 1992 Edition ....
Mersfelder, Jules   Am 1865-1937
* See 1992 Edition ....
Merson, Luc-Olivier   Fr 1846-1920
* See 1991 Edition ....
Merz, Gerhard   1947-
A&Ss/C 120x187 Mountain Climber Chr 5/92 16,500
Merz, Mario   1925-
MM/B 36x56 Numero Per Pino Cono Chr 11/91 36,300
G/Pb 40x29 Fibonacci 1202 1973 Chr 5/92 13,200

C&I/Pa 40x29 Untitled Sby 11/91 10,450
Mesches, Arnold   Am 1923-
O/M 10x25 Bird Watcher Mor 6/92 375
Mesdag, Hendrik Willem   Dut 1831-1915
* See 1992 Edition ....
Mesgriny, Claude Francois A.   Fr 1836-1884
* See 1992 Edition ....
Mesples, Paul Eugene   Fr 1849-
* See 1991 Edition ....
Mess, George Jo   Am 1898-1962
O/C 42x48 Indiana Landscape Dum 9/91 1,300
O/C 26x22 Still Life of Flowers Dum 9/91 200
Mess, Gordon Benjamin   Am 1900-1959
O/C 25x30 Landscape with Church Lou 3/92 425
Messel, Oliver
W&Gd/Pa 21x13 Marriage Figaro: Costume Sby 6/92 ... 1,100
Metcalf, Conger   Am 20C
Sg/Pa 18x10 Favored Model Hnz 5/92 210
I&Sg/Pa 17x11 Street Performer Hnz 5/92 150
Metcalf, Willard Leroy   Am 1858-1925
O/C 39x36 The Golden Hour But 4/92 170,500
O/C 26x29 Buds and Blossoms '07 Sby 5/92 110,000
O/C 26x25 Sunny Brook, Chester, Vermont 1923 Chr 12/91 77,000
O/C 27x21 September Chr 12/91 71,500
O/C 9x12 A View of the Village 77 Chr 12/91 .. 24,750
O/C 13x10 The Poppy Field Chr 3/92 24,200
O/C 10x13 North African Scene Chr 3/92 16,500
O/Pn 5x7 Sunset Manchester, Massachusetts 77 Chr 3/92 . 8,800
Meteyard, Thomas Buford   Am 1865-1928
O/C 15x22 Misty Day/New England Skn 5/92 3,025
Metz, Gerry Michael   Am 1943-
G/Pa 12x16 Spring Snow Slo 9/91 500
Metzger, Edward   Ger 1807-
O/C 16x26 Mountainous Landscape But 5/92 1,100
Metzinger, Jean   Fr 1883-1956
O/C 13x16 Homme Assis au Chat Sby 11/91 30,800
O/C 19x15 Portrait Femme Divisioniste Sby 2/92 . 13,200
Pe/Pa 17x12 Femme Nue Chr 11/91 9,900
O/Pn 8x10 Nature Morte Sby 2/92 9,900
Metzmacher, Emile Pierre   Fr 19C
W/Pa 16x13 Glass of Cognac Chr 5/92 1,650
Meucci, Michelangelo   It 19C
O/Pn 16x14 Still Life of Dead Game Chr 2/92 .. 1,100
O/Pn 18x14 Hanging Game 1874 Hnd 3/92 550
O/Pn 12x9 Still Life Game Birds 1876 Skn 11/91 . 330
O/B 9x7 Two Birds 1875 Hnd 10/91 300
Meugnier, J.
* See 1992 Edition ....
Meulener, Pieter   Dut 1602-1654
* See 1992 Edition ....
Meunier, Suzanne   Fr 19C
O/B 7x9 Church with Figure Lou 9/91 175
Meurer, Charles A.   Am 1865-1955
O/C 14x24 In the Barnyard 1921 Wlf 11/91 2,400
Meuser   1947-
E/St 39x20 Untitled 78 Chr 11/91 3,300
Meyer, **   Con 20C
O/C 20x30 Stream Through a Meadow Wes 3/92 ... 220
Meyer, E.   Am 20C
O/C 20x36 Figure by a Bridge Yng 2/92 325
Meyer, Emile   Fr 19C
* See 1992 Edition ....
Meyer, Ernest Frederick   Am 1863-1961
O/B 20x16 Forest Passage in Winter Slo 4/92 .. 100
Meyer, Georges   Fr 19C
O/Pn 11x14 Jeune Femme a L'Ombrelle Sby 2/92 . 7,150
Meyer, H.   Br 19C
O/C 24x20 The Boxer, Deaf Burke Chr 2/92 4,950
Meyer, Herbert   Am 1882-1960
O/C 28x38 Winter Yng 4/92 2,500
Meyer, Johann Heinrich Louis   Dut 1806-1866
* See 1992 Edition ....

Meyer, Louis   Dut 1809-1886
O/C 18x26 The Rescue Mys 6/92 2,530
Meyer, Louise   Ger 1789-1861
* See 1990 Edition
Meyer-Wismar, Ferdinand   Ger 1833-1917
* See 1992 Edition ....
Meyerheim, Hermann   Ger 1840-1880
* See 1991 Edition ....
Meyerheim, Wilhelm Alexander   Ger 1815-1882
O/C 27x38 The Hay Barge 1872 Sby 2/92 16,500
Meyerowitz, William   Am 1898-1981
O/C 24x20 A Cubist Still Life Chr 6/92 1,760
O/C 28x14 Horseback Hnd 12/91 1,300
O/C 16x12 Isadora Brd 5/92 688
Meyers, Frank Harmon   Am 1899-1956
* See 1991 Edition ....
Meza, Guillermo   Mex 1917-
O/C 39x32 Desde la Sombra 1985 Chr 11/91 7,700
O/C 40x54 Hongos Dibolicos '64 Hnd 5/92 3,000
Y&Cw/Pa 26x36 Estudio de la Muerte Hnd 5/92 425
Mezzara, Rosa   20C
* See 1990 Edition ....
Miahle, Federico   Mex 1800-1868
O/C/M 19x32 Teatro Tacon Sby 5/92 10,450
Michalowski, Norm
O/C 24x18 Middle Eastern Woman 1902 Dum 10/91 650
Michau, Theobald   Flm 1676-1765
* See 1990 Edition ....
Michaud, Leonie   Fr 1873-
* See 1990 Edition ....
Michaux, Henri   Bel 1899-
C/Pa 42x30 Femme Avec Colombe Sby 10/91 1,320
Pe/Pa 14x9 Collection: Seven Hnz 5/92 70
O/B 10x8 Head of a Child Hnz 5/92 50
Michel, A.   Fr 20C
O/C 13x18 Flower Sellers Along Promenade Slo 7/92 500
Michel, Georges   Fr 1763-1843
O/C 24x31 Village with Stormy Skies Chr 5/92 7,425
O/B 18x23 Trees Skn 5/92 1,650
C&Cw/Pa 17x20 Moulin a Vent Hnd 10/91 700
Pe/Pa 4x7 Factory Beside a River Hnd 10/91 350
Michel, Robert   Ger 1897-
I&L/Pa 12x9 Hebel 1921 Sby 11/91 13,200
Michelet, G. C.   Fr 20C
O/Pn 51x78 Fiesta al Koran 1902 Chr 10/91 16,500
Michelson, Leo   Am 1887-1978
O/C 28x37 Cathedral Wlf 9/91 500
G&P/Pa 17x12 Floral Still Life Wlf 9/91 500
G&I/Pa/C 13x16 Three Musicians 1965 Wlf 9/91 300
Michetti, Francesco Paolo   It 1851-1929
O/C 36x26 Nella Gioia Del Sole 1876 Sby 10/91 38,500
P/Pa 21x15 Bearded Man in a Straw Hat Sby 2/92 13,200
Michon, Guy   Can 1925-1984
O/C 21x50 Three Faces Sbt 5/92 280
Michonze, Gregoire   Fr 1902-1982
G/Pa 9x10 Street Scene in Frans Stadje 54 Wlf 3/92 600
Middendorf, Helmut   Ger 1953-
A/L 86x64 Die Strasse I (The Street I) 1982 Sby 2/92 14,300
O/L 100x140 City of the Red Nights II 1982 Chr 5/92 11,000
A/C 73x101 Figure with Fire 1985 Chr 11/91 11,000
O/L 71x87 Grosstadtein Geborene 1982 Chr 5/92 7,700
Mieduch, Dan   Am 1947-
O/C 24x36 He'd Sooner Wait 'Til Spring 1979 Dum 1/92 .. 2,700
Miel, Jan   Flm 1599-1663
O/C 24x31 Carnival with Figures Dancing Chr 10/91 30,800
Mielich, Leopold Alphons   Aus 1863-1929
O/C 53x76 Market Scene Sby 7/92 14,850
Mieninger, Ludwig
* See 1992 Edition ....
Migliaro, Vincenzo   It 1858-1938
T/B 9x7 A Fishing Village Chr 2/92 2,200
Mignard, Pierre   Fr 1612-1695
K/Pa 5x5 Presumed Portrait Artist's Daughter Chr 1/92 3,850

Mignon, Abraham   Ger 1640-1679
* See 1990 Edition ....
Mignot, Louis Remy   Am 1831-1870
* See 1991 Edition ....
Mijares, Jose   Cub 1921-
G/Pa 12x18 Ensayo (Two) Chr 5/92 2,75
O/Pa 22x15 Untitled Wlf 3/92 2,60
O/C 18x13 Bambues Chr 5/92 1,43
Milder, Jay   Am 1934-
* See 1992 Edition ....
Miles, Thomas Rose   Br 1869-1900
* See 1992 Edition ....
Milesi, Alessandro   It 1856-1945
* See 1991 Edition ....
Milich, Abram Adolphe   Pol 1884-1964
* See 1992 Edition ....
Millais, Raoul   Eng -1936
O/Pn 13x18 Cowboy on Horseback 1921 Slo 2/92 27
Millais, Sir John Everett   Br 1829-1896
* See 1991 Edition ....
Millar, Addison T.   Am 1860-1913
O/C 39x32 Summer Garden Sby 12/91 4,67
O/C 18x24 Silvermine Birches Chr 6/92 1,76
O/C 12x16 Fisherfolk by the Shore Chr 11/91 1,10
O/C 24x18 Working at the Hearth Skn 11/91 66
Millard, Charles Stuart   Can 1837-1917
* See 1992 Edition ....
Millares, Manolo   Spa 1926-1972
* See 1991 Edition ....
Millart, A.   Am 20C
O/C 36x22 Spanish Woman in a Red Dress Sel 4/92 27
Miller, Alfred Jacob   Am 1810-1874
O/C 17x14 Indian Girl Swinging Chr 5/92 71,50
Miller, Barse   Am 1904-1973
* See 1992 Edition ....
Miller, Charles Henry   Am 1842-1922
O/C 19x31 Gypsy Camp at Queens 1887 Hnz 10/91 90
Miller, E. L.   Am 1889-
O/C 34x22 Seated Black Woman Fre 10/91 80
Miller, Edith M.   Am a 1920-1939
W/Pa 15x19 Industrial Scene Mor 3/92 55
Miller, Elsie
O/Cb 16x15 Two Book Covers Ih 11/91 40
Miller, Evylena Nunn   Am 1888-1966
O/C 20x24 Landscape - Sierra Approach Mor 3/92 22
Miller, F. H.   Am 19C
O/C 7x15 Seascape with Sails Bor 8/92 2,30
O/C 7x15 Seascape with Large Rocks 79 Bor 8/92 1,95
Miller, George   Br 1827-1853
O/B 12x14 Charley, a Springer Spaniel 1863 Sby 6/92 2,86
Miller, Harriette G.   Am 20C
* See 1991 Edition ....
Miller, Henry   Am 1897-1980
W&V/Pa 15x21 Kiosk along the Seine, Paris Chr 6/92 2,42
W/Pa 15x10 Standing Figure 56 But 5/92 88
W/Pa 13x10 Untitled 47 But 5/92 88
Miller, John Paul   Am 20C
W/Pa 15x22 Street Scene '44 Wlf 10/91 80
Miller, John Zollinger   Am 1867-
O/C/Wd 16x20 Manuevers at Norwood, NY Fre 10/91 40
Miller, Josef   Ger 19C
* See 1992 Edition ....
Miller, Kenneth Hayes   Am 1876-1952
* See 1992 Edition ....
Miller, Melvin   Am 1937-
O/C 12x16 Gloucester Harbour 1969 Wlf 9/91 600
O/C 8x14 Ma and Pa 1969 Wes 11/91 550
O/M 10x13 Tug Boat & Locomotive: Two 1968 Wes 5/92 495
O/M 10x13 Mammy 1968 Wes 11/91 138
Miller, Ralph Davison   Am 1859-1946
O/C 20x30 Sheep in a Barn 1907 Mor 11/91 1,700
Miller, Richard Edward   Am 1875-1943
O/C 40x32 Goldfish 1912 Sby 5/92 462,000
O/C 20x29 Cafe Society Chr 12/91 104,500
O/C 18x15 Mother and Child Chr 3/92 22,000

O/C 79x65 The Visit Sby 9/91 16,500
O/C 24x29 Harbor at Night Sby 12/91 3,025

Miller, Rod E.
O/C 9x12 Ascutney Mountain 1900 Eld 4/92 385

Miller, William Rickarby   Am 1818-1893
W&G/Pa 12x20 Jersey City w/Glimpse of NY 1854 Chr 5/92 14,300
W/Pa 14x10 The Boat Ride 1855 Skn 5/92 1,210

Milleson, Royal H.
O/C 18x24 Winter Landscape Hnz 10/91 625

Millet, Francis Davis   Am 1846-1912
O/C 20x16 After the Festival 1888 Chr 5/92 17,600
O/C 39x29 The Turkish Soldier 1878 Sby 2/92 17,600
O/C 36x26 Portrait of a Woman 1881 Sby 12/91 660

Millet, Jean Francois   Fr 1814-1875
O/C 32x40 Return from the Fields Chr 10/91 . . . . 2.145M
O/Pn 11x7 Les Peupliers Sby 5/92 176,000
K/Pa 8x6 Auvergne Goat Girl Chr 5/92 44,000
O/C/Pn 10x8 Portrait of Monsieur Fleury Chr 5/92 35,200
O/Pn 13x9 La Fuite en Egypte Hnd 10/91 28,000
Y/Pa 9x14 Team of Horses with Plow Hnd 10/91 10,500
PVPa 2x4 Four Landscape Sketches Sby 5/92 7,150
PVPa 2x2 Le becheur Hnd 10/91 6,500
C&S/Pa 11x6 Standing Nudes: Double Sby 10/91 5,500

Milliere, Maurice   Fr 1871-
* See 1991 Edition . . . .

Millner, Karl   Ger 1825-1894
* See 1992 Edition . . . .

Millvage, A.
O/B 12x8 Sailing Ship in the Moonlight Dum 2/92 175

Milne, David Brown   Can 1882-1953
O/C 18x22 Autumn, Forest Interior Sbt 11/91 23,375

Milne, John Maclaughlan   Br 1885-1957
* See 1992 Edition . . . .

Milone, Antonio   It 19C
O/Pn 9x14 Two Donkeys and a Rooster Sby 7/92 2,750

Milroy, Lisa   1959-
O/C 18x24 Untitled '83 Chr 2/92 1,980

Milton, John
* See 1991 Edition . . . .

Milton, Victor Marais   Fr 1872-
O/C 21x25 Vieille Chanson Wlf 3/92 9,000

Minaux, Andre   Fr 1923-
O/C 26x20 Still Life with Sunflower But 5/92 1,980

Mingret, Jose   Spa 20C
O/B 15x22 Bellagio 1927 Chr 5/92 528

Minor, Robert Crannel   Am 1839-1904
O/C 30x40 Landscape Hnd 10/91 1,800

Minozzi, F*
O/Pn 11x14 Sunset 1909 Sby 2/92 1,980

Mintchine, Abraham
O/C 14x18 Paysage en Provence Sby 6/92 3,850

Miotte, Jean
* See 1992 Edition . . . .

Mira, Alfred S.   Am 20C
* See 1992 Edition . . . .

Miralles, Francisco   Spa 1850-1901
O/Pn 12x16 Aires Libres Sby 2/92 35,750
W/Pa 11x15 Allongee Dans L'Herbe 1882 Sby 10/91 . . 12,650
O/C 26x20 Jealousy Hnd 5/92 3,000

Mirella
* See 1992 Edition . . . .

Mirko, Basdella   Am 1910-1969
MM/Pa/C 22x18 Iron Gate 1949 But 5/92 2,200

Miro, Joachim   Spa 20C
O/Pn 13x16 Cairo and Carabana Arabe: Pair Sby 10/91 . . . 6,600

Miro, Joan   Spa 1893-1983
O/C 18x14 Composition a la lune bleu 1949 Chr 5/92 . . 572,000
PYI&Pe/Pa 18x24 Pastorale 24 Sby 11/91 330,000
GKBr&I/Pa 29x39 Graphisme concret Chr 5/92 187,000
G/Pa 12x10 Programme, Ballets Russes 33 Chr 5/92 . . 165,000
O/Pa/C 14x11 Projet pour une tapisserie Chr 5/92 110,000
O&Pe/Pa/C 37x24 Personnage Oiseaux Sby 11/91 . . . 104,500
O&G/Pa/L 19x14 Oiseaux Sby 2/92 55,000
W,S&Y/Pa 19 dia Tete Sby 5/92 55,000
G,W&I/Pa 17x25 Sans Titre 70 Chr 5/92 52,800

I&K/Pa 9x13 Composition Sby 11/91 27,500
Y&S/Pa 16x13 Fleurs Pour des Amis: Pair Sby 10/91 22,000
Br&I/Pa 20x14 Femme et Oiseau dans la Nuit 72 Chr 2/92 19,800
Fp/Pa 11x9 Composition 69 Sby 5/92 18,700
Y/Pa 13x20 Composition Chr 2/92 13,200
Y/Pa 19x25 Composition no. 1 Chr 5/92 13,200
Y/Pa 19x25 Composition no. 3 Chr 5/92 13,200
Y/Pa 19x25 Composition no. 5 Chr 5/92 13,200
PI/Pa 8x5 Personnage Chr 5/92 13,200
W&I/Pa 11x8 Untitled: Pair of Watercolors 1963 Sby 10/91 11,550
Y/Pa 12x9 Abstract Composition 65 Sby 6/92 4,400

Mirou, Anton   Flm 1586-1661
* See 1992 Edition . . . .

Mitchell, Alfred R.   Am 1886-1972
O/B 16x20 Dorothea and Amaryllis Mor 11/91 15,000
O/B 16x20 Paradise Creek But 10/91 7,700
O/B 20x26 The Old Cherry Tree But 10/91 6,600
O/B 13x16 Dolphin Fountain Mor 11/91 4,250
O/B 13x16 Stream and Pool But 2/92 2,750
O/B 8x10 Red Church; Sunset: Two But 6/92 770

Mitchell, Arthur   Am 1864-
O/B 11x14 Evening Chores Sel 9/91 225

Mitchell, Arthur R.   Am 1886-1977
O/C 28x26 Sheriff in Pursuit Ih 11/91 2,100

Mitchell, George Bertrand   Am 1872-1966
O/C 25x30 New England Harbor Slo 2/92 2,000

Mitchell, Glen   Am 1894-1972
* See 1990 Edition . . . .

Mitchell, Joan   Am 1926-
O/C 102x63 Afternoon Chr 5/92 187,000
O/C 110x79 Grande Vallee no. XII Chr 11/91 176,000
O/C 37x36 Untitled Sby 10/91 49,500
O/C 32x40 Untitled Chr 5/92 36,300
K/Pa 23x31 Untitled Chr 5/92 18,700
O/C/B 14x13 Untitled Sby 11/91 16,500
P/Pa 19x28 Cypresses Sby 5/92 13,200

Mitchell, John Campbell   Am 1862-1922
* See 1991 Edition . . . .

Mitchell, John, of Aberdeen   Sco 1838-1926
W/Pa 17x24 On the Road to Braemar Hnz 5/92 500

Mitchell, Leon (Jr.)   Am 20C
Y&Pe/Pa 22x17 Run Along Sonny 1926 Wlf 10/91 325

Mitchell, Thomas   Can 1879-1958
O/B 12x16 Hunter Returning to Cabin Dum 9/91 375

Mitchell, Willard M.   Can 20C
W/Pa 3x2 Notre Dame, Montreal Lou 3/92 35

Mitchnick, Nancy
* See 1992 Edition . . . .

Mitsutani, Kunishiro
Pe&W/Pa 13x20 Japanese Temple Scene Sby 2/92 . . . 3,850

Mlejnek, O.
* See 1992 Edition . . . .

Modersohn, Otto   Ger 1865-1943
* See 1992 Edition . . . .

Modigliani, Amedeo   It 1884-1920
PI&Br/Pa 21x17 Caryatide Chr 5/92 110,000
Pe/Pa 19x12 L'Homme a la Pipe Sby 11/91 57,750
Pe/Pa 14x10 Donna seduta Chr 5/92 5,280

Modra, Theodore B.   Am 1873-1930
* See 1991 Edition . . . .

Moeller, Louis Charles   Am 1855-1930
O/C 12x16 One Man's Opinion Chr 3/92 7,700

Moentana, J.   It 20C
O/C 19x27 The New Wine Sel 12/91 175

Moerenhout, Joseph Jodocus   Flm 1801-1874
O/Pn 7x9 Figures in a Landscape '50 Fre 12/91 950

Moffett, Ross   Am 1888-1971
O/C 48x60 Cod Fisherman Skn 11/91 4,950
O/C 36x46 The West End, Autumn Dum 9/91 4,750

Mogan, John William   Am 20C
O/C 24x24 Wall Street on the 4th of July Lou 6/92 1,800

Mogford, John   Br 18C
* See 1991 Edition . . . .

163

Mogford, John   Br 1821-1885
W&Cw/B 10x21 Lake Landscape 1876 Chr 10/91 1,100
Mohan, James D.   Am -1987
G/Pb 20x30 The Train Yard Skn 11/91 385
Moholy-Nagy, Laszlo   Am 1895-1946
O/Al 24x20 Construction "Al 6" 33 Chr 11/91 88,000
Mohr, Karl   Ger 1922-
* See 1992 Edition
Mohrmann, John Henry   Am 1857-1916
* See 1992 Edition
Moie, M. Aquila R.   Spa 20C
O/C 16x13 Young Girl Hnz 5/92 100
Moira   20C
O/C 24x20 Still Life of Flowers Slo 12/91 160
Moisand, Marcel Emmanuel   Fr 1874-1903
* See 1992 Edition ....
Moitte, Jean Guillaume   Fr 1746-1810
* See 1992 Edition ....
Mola, Pier Francesco   It 1612-1666
O/C 37x28 Aaron, High Priest of Israelites Sby 1/92 .. 66,000
Molarsky, Abram   Am 1883-1951
O/B 24x20 Still Life with Iris Skn 9/91 1,760
Molarsky, Maurice   Am 1885-1950
O/C 16x12 Portrait of a Woman Lou 6/92 475
Mole, John Henry   Br 1814-1886
O/C 14x21 On Hampstead Heath 1885 But 5/92 2,750
Molenaer, Claes   Dut 1630-1676
* See 1991 Edition ....
Molenaer, Jan Miense   Dut 1610-1668
O/Pn 20x14 Lady Seated at a Virginal 1634 Chr 1/92 .. 286,000
O/Pn 14x13 Card Players in a Tavern Chr 10/91 7,150
Molet, Salvador   Spa 1773-1836
* See 1990 Edition ....
Molinari, Antonio   It -1648
* See 1991 Edition ....
Molinari, Antonio   It 1655-1734
O/C 49x49 Susannah and the Elders Chr 1/92 28,600
O/C 41x38 Saint Sebastian Sby 1/92 15,400
Molinari, Guido   Can 1933-
* See 1991 Edition ....
Moll, Evert   Dut 1878-1955
* See 1992 Edition ....
Mollica, Achille   It a 1870-1887
* See 1992 Edition ....
Molnari, R.
O/C 20x24 Girl with a Doll Hnz 10/91 1,300
Molne, Louis Vidal   Spa 1907-1970
O/C 15x18 Woman with Fruit and Vase But 5/92 1,650
Molsted, Christian   Dan 1862-1930
* See 1992 Edition ....
Molyn, Pieter   Dut 1595-1661
* See 1990 Edition ....
Molyneux, Edward
* See 1992 Edition ....
Mommers, Hendrick   Dut 1623-1693
O/C 28x24 Peasants and Animals Resting Sby 5/92 27,500
O/Pn 24x19 Peasant Family with Market Wares Sby 5/92 .. 4,400
Monaldi, Paolo   It a 1760-
* See 1991 Edition ....
Monamy, Peter   Br 1670-1749
* See 1991 Edition ....
Monasterio, Luis Ortiz   Mex 1906-
G,W&Pe/Pa 22x30 Vendedores de Flores 31 Chr 11/91 ... 7,700
Moncayo, C. T.   20C
O/C 13x18 Ducks on a Pond 1964 Slo 12/91 350
Moncayo, Emilio   Ecu 20C
O/Ab 21x35 Paisaje (Two) But 11/91 550
Monchablon, Jean Ferdinand   Fr 1855-1904
O/C 36x49 Le Paturage 1888 Sby 5/92 57,750
Monchot. L.   Fr 1850-1920
O/C 16x12 Flirtation in the Garden Slo 12/91 1,000

Mondriaan, Frederic Hendrik   Dut 1853-1932
W/Pa 14x21 Barbizon Landscape Wes 5/92 1,430
Mondrian, Piet   Dut 1872-1944
O/C 21x21 Comp. rouge gris bleu jaune 22 Chr 5/92 ... 2.585M
W&G/Pa 12x9 Blue Chrysanthemum Sby 5/92 132,000
Mondrus, Martin   Am 1927-
O/C 30x36 Venice Blvd., Red Car Yards '46 Mor 11/91 6,000
I&S/Pa 12x9 L.A. Smog Mor 6/92 175
I&S/Pa 12x9 Palisades in Santa Monica Mor 6/92 100
Monet, Claude   Fr 1840-1926
O/C 19x26 Le Port d'Honfleur Chr 11/91 825,000
O/C 26x32 Paysage a Port-Villez 83 Sby 5/92 825,000
O/C 26x32 Chemin 86 Sby 11/91 770,000
O/C 27x21 Nympheas Sby 5/92 198,000
P/Pa/B 8x13 Soleil Couchant Sur La Plaine Chr 11/91 .. 143,000
Money, Fred   Fr 1882-1956
O/C 18x22 Geraniums Doy 11/91 1,500
O&C/Pa/B 20x29 Le Marche Sby 2/92 880
Monfallet, Adolphe Francois   Fr 1816-1900
* See 1992 Edition ....
Monge, Jules   Fr 1855-
O/C 13x18 Prise du Bois Belleau 1918 Sby 1/92 2,750
O/C 18x24 Salute Sel 4/92 2,000
Monge, Luis   Ecu 1920-
* See 1990 Edition ....
Mongin, Antoine-Pierre   Fr 1761-1827
K/Pa 14x12 Nymphs and Putti Bathing Chr 1/92 440
Monginot, Charles   Fr 1825-1900
O/C 13x10 Genre Scene Monkey and Cat Skn 11/91 .. 1,540
Monje, Luis   Ecu 1925-
O/C 50x65 Selva Tropical 1975 Chr 11/91 16,500
O/C 67x52 Selva 1981 Chr 5/92 11,000
Monks, John Austin Sands   Am 1850-1917
* See 1991 Edition ....
Monnoyer, Antoine   Fr 1677-1735
O/C 53x38 Tulips, Peonies, Narcissus Sby 1/92 33,000
Monnoyer, Jean Baptiste   Fr 1636-1699
* See 1992 Edition ....
Monogrammist I.K.   a 16C
K,Pl&S/Pa 11x15 Scriptorium/4 Evangelists 1539 Chr 1/92 .. 35,200
Monsen, G.
O/C 22x35 Steam Yacht "Cora" Eld 7/92 440
Monsted, Peder Mork   Dan 1859-1941
O/C 37x27 Lac Leman 1887 Sby 2/92 22,000
O/C 36x59 River Landscape, Summer 1905 Chr 10/91 .. 18,700
O/C 21x33 Autumn Landscape 1903 Sby 10/91 14,850
Monsu Desiderio   It 17C
O/C 20x30 The Destruction of Sodom Sby 1/92 44,000
Montagny, Elie Honore   Fr -1864
* See 1992 Edition ....
Montague, Alfred   Br a 1832-1883
O/C 18x14 Rotterdam, Holland Sby 1/92 2,310
O/C 12x18 Figures in a Landscape Slo 7/92 1,300
Montague, Clifford   Br 19C
* See 1992 Edition ....
Montan, Anders   Swd 1846-1917
O/B 11x8 Blast Furnace Slo 12/91 850
Montelatici, Francesco   It 1601-1661
O/C 38x57 Allegory of Autumn; Summer: Two Chr 5/92 .. 71,500
Montemezzo, Antonio   Ger 1841-1898
* See 1991 Edition ....
Montenegro, Roberto   Mex 1885-1968
O/C 30x25 Autorretrato En Bola De Cristal 53 Sby 11/91 .. 79,750
H,W&G/Pa 15x22 Lex (La Ley) 66 Sby 11/91 3,850
Montezin, Pierre Eugene   Fr 1874-1946
O/C 45x35 Bouquet de Fleurs Sby 5/92 21,450
Montfort, Antoine Alphonse   Fr 1802-1884
* See 1991 Edition ....
Montgomery, Alfred   Am 1857-1922
* See 1992 Edition ....
Montgomery, Claude   Am 20C
W/Pa 20x26 Lone Tree Island, Georgetown Brd 8/92 908

Montgomery, W. Howard   Am 20C
O/B 24x24 Passing of Summer 1920 Skn 9/91 440
Monti, Francesco   1646-1712
O/C 30x40 Belshazzar's Feast Chr 10/91 18,700
Monti, Francesco   It 1685-1768
* See 1992 Edition
Monticelli   It 19C
W/Pa 17x24 View of Naples Harbor Sel 12/91 750
Monticelli, Adolphe Joseph T.   Fr 1824-1886
O/Pn 10x15 The Hay Cart Sby 10/91 13,200
O/Pn 23x18 The Wedding Chr 2/92 13,200
O/Pn 16x25 Dans le Jardin Hnd 10/91 11,000
O/Pn 12x18 Une Fete Chr 10/91 9,900
O/C 22x26 Femmes Dans Un Parc Fre 4/92 5,250
O/Pn 6x10 Columbus Before Queen Isabella Slo 7/92 1,500
Montoro   It 20C
O/C 55x44 La Perla Sel 4/92 175
Montoya, Gustavo   Mex 1905-
O/C 22x18 Girl in a Pink Dress But 11/91 4,950
O/C 22x18 Nina Con Guitarra 1966 Sby 6/92 4,125
O/C 25x19 Nina en Azul con Perro 1973 Chr 5/92 2,750
O/C 22x18 Nino con Paloma Sby 10/91 2,750
O/C 22x18 Nino en Verde con Maceta Sby 10/91 2,310
O/C 24x20 Ninas con Sombrillas 1966 But 5/92 1,650
Montrichard, Raymond   Am 1887-1937
* See 1992 Edition . . . .
Montullo, J.   It 19C
O/B 14x17 Italian Fisherfolk 1870 Slo 10/91 800
Montullo, S*   It 19C**
* See 1992 Edition . . . .
Monvoisin, Raymond Auguste Q.   Fr 1794-1870
* See 1991 Edition . . . .
Moon, Carl   Am 1879-1948
* See 1990 Edition . . . .
Moore, A.W.   Am 20C
O/C 30x35 Birches in Autumn, New York Slo 7/92 350
Moore, Albert Joseph   Br 1841-1892
* See 1992 Edition . . . .
Moore, Arthur W.   Eng 1840-1913
O/C 38x72 Autumn View with Grazing Sheep Slo 2/92 . . . 650
Moore, Benson Bond   Am 1882-1974
O/C 16x20 Georgetown in Autumn 1916 Slo 12/91 3,250
O/Cd 25x30 Near Sunset, Rock Creek Wtf 3/92 550
O/B 9x11 Farmhouses in Pastoral Landscape Slo 10/91 . . 275
Moore, Edwin Augustus   Am 1858-
O/C 24x30 Cow Wading by a Stream 1893 Chr 6/92 2,860
Moore, Frank Montague   Am 1877-1967
O/B 24x34 Moonlight Coastal Mor 3/92 2,750
O/B 20x30 Sunset on the Waves But 6/92 1,430
O/C 20x30 At Anchor, Monterey Wes 3/92 990
O/Cb 12x16 Yucca-Flinridge Mor 6/92 125
Moore, Henry   Br 1898-1986
W,Y&Pe/Pa 8x12 Reclining Figure Chr 11/91 24,200
Pl/Pa 10x7 Figures: Double 50 Chr 11/91 9,900
Moore, Henry Wadsworth   20C
O/C 33x38 Fountains and Cedars Eld 7/92 715
Moore, John   Am 20C
* See 1992 Edition . . . .
Moore, Nelson Augustus   Am 1824-1902
* See 1991 Edition . . . .
Moormans, Franciscus   Dut 1832-1884
O/Pn 10x9 Interior Scene: Mother, Child, Toy 1872 Slo 7/92 3,000
Mora, Francis Luis   Am 1874-1940
O/B 16x12 Nude with Spanish Shawl Chr 6/92 3,080
W/Pa/B 24x18 Copla Sevillana 1914 Chr 6/92 1,540
O/C 96x72 Our Christian Era Sby 12/91 1,045
Pe/Pa 12x9 Sonia and Rosemary 1919 Chr 11/91 440
W/Pa 14x7 Nude Amongst Flowers Durn 12/91 350
O/C 16x12 Figures in a Landscape Wtf 10/91 300
Pe/Pa 14x20 Tranquil Desert Chr 6/92 242
C/Pa 7x7 Indian Maiden Lou 3/92 200
Pe/Pa 10x8 Dignity Wtf 10/91 175
Pe/Pa 6x4 Man Reading Wtf 10/91 175

Br&I/Pa 8x10 Guitarist and Children 1936 Wtf 3/92 150
Pe/Pa 7x4 Standing Nude Child Yng 2/92 125
Pe/Pa 7x4 Study for "Hour of Peace" Brd 5/92 44
Mora, Joseph Jacinto   Am 1876-1947
Pl/Pa 25x18 Cantina 1943 Slo 4/92 130
Morado, Jose Chavez   Mex 1909-
O/M 24x32 Peregrinacion en la Noche 56 Chr 5/92 4,400
Moragas Y Torres, Tomas   Spa 1837-1906
* See 1990 Edition . . . .
Morales, Armando   Nic 1927-
O/C 64x51 Foresta Tropical I (Jungla) 85 Chr 5/92 . . . 176,000
O/C 39x32 Desnudos 82 Sby 5/92 82,500
O/C 80x64 Dos Figuras Sby 11/91 49,500
O/C 50x43 Woman Leaving Room II 73 Sby 5/92 44,000
O/B/Pn 24x20 Mujer y Bicicleta 78 Sby 5/92 27,500
O/C 11x15 Caballos 49 Chr 5/92 22,000
O/Pa 28x22 Mujeres con Cruce de Ferrocarril 86 Chr 11/91 22,000
O/C 10x13 Two: El Torero; Tauromaquia 89 Chr 5/92 . . . 19,800
O&Wx/C 18x14 Tres Desnudos y el Eclipse 72 Chr 11/91 . 17,600
P/Pa 19x24 Nude with Circus Animals 83 Chr 5/92 16,500
O&Wx/C 14x16 Still Life Two Grapefruit, Pear 73 Chr 11/91 11,000
Morales, Darío   Col 1944-1988
Pe/Pa 12x15 Desnudo Reclinado 81 Chr 11/91 8,800
Morales, Eduardo   Cub 1868-1938
O/C 13x17 Quitrin Y Jinete 1917 Sby 11/91 10,175
O/C 17x24 La Volanta 905 Chr 5/92 5,500
O/C 20x14 Palmeras 1919 Chr 5/92 5,500
Morales, Rodolfo   Mex 1881-1968
O/C 54x69 Retorno Al Pasado Sby 11/91 39,600
O/C 31x39 La Espera Chr 11/91 26,400
O/C 32x39 La Patria esta Primero Chr 5/92 13,200
O/C 28x39 Sonrosada Chr 11/91 13,200
O/C 32 dia Dos Mundos Chr 5/92 7,150
O/C/B 19x13 Untitled 67 Sby 5/92 6,050
Moran, Edward   Am 1829-1901
O/C 30x50 Ships at Sea 1876 Sby 5/92 31,900
O/C 30x23 Fish Pond, Orient Bay 1876 Sby 12/91 19,800
O/C 22x35 Gathering Cockles 1883 Sby 9/91 9,900
O/B/Pn 9x17 Port Hamilton, New York Sby 12/91 5,500
O/C 20x16 Passing Ambrose Lightship Wes 11/91 3,300
O/C 27x22 Merchant Ship Lighthouse Day Chr 12/91 . . . 3,200
O/C 12x16 Sailboats on a Calm Sea Chr 6/92 2,750
Moran, Edward Percy   Am 1862-1935
O/C 24x18 In the Garden Sby 12/91 7,975
O/C 30x40 Lost Drummer Boy But 4/92 7,150
O/C 28x22 George Washington & Ben Franklin Sby 12/91 . 2,750
O/C 28x22 At Fort Ticonderoga Sby 4/92 2,640
O/C 14x11 Lady in a Plumed Hat Chr 6/92 1,650
O/C 12x16 For the Marquise Wes 11/91 1,045
Moran, J.   Am 19C
O/C/B 22x18 Devil's Hole Along Wissahicken 1889 Fre 4/92 . 525
Moran, Leon   Am 1864-1941
W&G/Pa 19x13 Blue Carnation 1896 Slo 10/91 500
O/C 30x20 Dutch Girl at Shore Hnz 5/92 400
Moran, Peter   Am 1841-1914
Pl/Pa 6x10 Cows Watering and Grazing Lou 12/91 450
H/Pa 5x11 Old Hen and Chickens Island Lou 12/91 250
Moran, Thomas   Am 1837-1926
O/C 42x30 In the Teton Range 1899 Chr 12/91 572,000
O/C 20x30 Late Afternoon in Summer 1909 Chr 5/92 . . 66,000
W&G/Pa/B 13x10 Moonlight, Devil's Den 1873 Chr 5/92 . . 66,000
O/C 20x30 Venice 1901 Chr 5/92 60,500
O/Pn 14x19 Moonlight in Venice 1898 Chr 5/92 52,800
O/C 30x60 Stranded Ship/E. Hampton 1895 But 4/92 . . 41,250
W&Pe/Pa 7x9 Venice 1889 Chr 9/91 5,500
G/Pa 6x8 Boating Party Under Stormy Skies Hnd 5/92 . . 4,000
W&G/Pa 8x11 Off the Bahamas 1833 Sby 12/91 3,850
O/B 10x8 Portrait of a Man in a Hat But 11/91 3,025
Morandi, Giorgio   It 1890-1964
O/C 12x18 Natura Morta Chr 11/91 385,000
Pe/Pa 3x4 Le Conchiglie 1920 Chr 2/92 7,700
Morandini, Francesco   It 1544-1597
* See 1992 Edition . . . .
Morane, C.   Con 19C
O/Pn 13x9 A Cardinal Reading Chr 5/92 825

Morang, Dorothy   Am 1906-
O/Cb 24x20 Poised Shapes 1939 But 4/92 2,750
Moras, Walter   Ger 1856-1925
O/C 16x12 Child with a Gaggle of Geese But 11/91 3,300
Morcillo, Gabriel   Spa 20C
O/C 33x29 The Red Fez 23 Sby 10/91 22,000
More, Ramon Aguilar   1924-
O/C 32x40 Madrugada en la Ciudad 61 Chr 11/91 1,980
Moreau, Adrien   Fr 1843-1906
O/Pn 7x10 Summer Afternoon by the River Chr 5/92 7,700
O/C 40x28 Printemps '72 Sel 4/92 6,500
O/Pn 18x15 Interior Genre Scene Skn 11/91 2,970
Moreau, Charles   Fr 1830-
 * See 1990 Edition . . . .
Moreau, Chocarne   Fr 19C
 * See 1990 Edition . . . .
Moreau, Gustave   Fr 1826-1898
W&G/Pa 15x9 Le Lion Amoureux Sby 10/91 550,000
Moreau, Louis-Gabriel   Fr 1740-1806
O/Cp 3x16 Parc Monceau; Cours-La-Reine: Pair Sby 5/92 . 96,250
Moreelse, Paulus   Dut 1571-1638
O/Pn 44x31 Portrait of a Young Woman 1623 Sby 5/92 . . 17,600
Morehouse, Fred C.
O/C 17x23 Title? 1890 Ald 5/92 150
Morel, Jan E. & Van Severdonck   Dut 1835-1905
O/Pn 13x12 Shepherd Tending His Flock 187? Sby 7/92 . . 3,630
Morel, Jan Evert   Dut 1777-1808
 * See 1992 Edition . . . .
Morel, Jan Evert (II)   Dut 1835-1905
 * See 1992 Edition . . . .
Moreley, James   Irs 19C
O/C 24x36 Fisherman and Grazing Cows Wes 11/91 605
Morelli, Domenico   It 1826-1901
O/C 31x19 The Lute Player 1870 Sby 1/92 6,600
W/Pa 9x5 Madonna 1884 Yng 2/92 175
Morello, F.   It 20C
O/Pn 10x13 Interno (Stable Interior) Slo 12/91 550
O/Pn 13x18 Mercato a Napoli Slo 12/91 550
Moret, Henry   Fr 1856-1913
O/C 18x22 Les Falaises Pres de la Mer 96 Sby 5/92 55,000
O/C 21x25 La Mer Bretagne Chr 2/92 46,200
O/C 15x24 Plage de Ragnenez, Finistere 1902 Chr 2/92 . . 16,500
Moretti, Giovanni   It 19C
O/C 18x14 Pleasant Encounter Hnd 5/92 2,000
Moretti, Lucien-Philippe   Fr 1922-
O/C 11x9 Jeune fille a sa toilette Chr 5/92 1,650
Moretti, R.   It 17C
W/Pa 13x21 Maja Serenade Hnd 12/91 2,800
Moretti, R.   It 19C
W/Pa 13x20 Winding the Yarn Chr 10/91 1,320
Moretti, Raymond   It 19C
 * See 1992 Edition . . . .
Moretto, Alesandro Bonvicino   It 1498-1554
 * See 1992 Edition . . . .
Morgan, Frederick   Br 1856-1927
O/C 38x28 The Flower Cart Sby 10/91 88,000
WG&Cw/Pa/B 23x15 Gathering Flowers Chr 2/92 12,100
Morgan, Mary DeNeal   Am 1868-1948
O/Pn 25x93 Flower Garden, Carmel But 10/91 7,700
O/Cb 9x32 Triptych: Carmel Coastline But 2/92 6,600
G/B 16x12 Over the Dunes But 6/92 3,025
W&G/Pa 12x7 Sand Dune But 10/91 2,090
O/Pn 6x10 Carmel Valley by Sea Mor 11/91 1,300
G/Pa 12x16 Mountain Landscape But 6/92 880
Morgan, Mary Vernon   Br a 1871-1927
O/C 11x26 Yellow Roses 1883 Brd 8/92 990
Morgan, Wallace   Am 1873-1948
Pe&W/Pa 17x14 Crowd Looking at a Biplane IIh 5/92 750
Morgan, William   Am 1826-1900
O/C 24x34 The Visit Sby 12/91 3,080
Morgenstern, Frederick Ernst   Ger 1853-1919
O/C 16x23 Moored Sailing Boats But 11/91 2,200

Morgenstern, Harry V.   Am 20C
O/Ab 14x23 Industrial Scene Wlf 10/91 300
Morisot, Berthe   Fr 1841-1895
O/C 45x54 Venus va Demander Sby 5/92 110,000
P/Pa 12x16 Enfant au Lit Sby 11/91 44,000
P/Pa/B 18x24 Nu Couche Sby 5/92 30,800
W/Pa/Pa 6x10 Au Bord de la Seine Chr 11/91 9,900
W/Pa/C 7x10 Dans L'Ile Du Bois de Boulogne Sby 10/91 . 7,700
Morisset, Francois Henri   Fr 1870-
O/C 21x26 By the River Chr 10/91 6,050
Moritz, Louis   Dut 1773-1850
O/C 38x30 Portrait of a Gentleman But 5/92 1,100
Morland, George   Br 1763-1804
O/C 25x29 Gypsy Encampment 1795 Sel 4/92 1,300
Pe&K/Pa 18x14 Man on Horseback Receiving Drink Hnd 5/92 900
Morley, Malcolm   Am 1931-
A/C 105x87 Vermeer, Portrait Artist in Studio Sby 5/92 . . 627,000
O/C 81x60 S.S. France Sby 11/91 319,000
O/C 60x96 Age of Catastrophe Sby 5/92 308,000
O/C 67x100 Camels and Goats 80 Sby 11/91 231,000
O/C 48x66 Picasso Bridge 71 Sby 2/92 66,000
O/C 50x80 Love Boat Sby 2/92 44,000
W/Pa 22x31 Gloria 1989 Chr 5/92 33,000
W/Pa 22x30 Indian Family Sby 5/92 28,600
G&W/Pa 13x16 Study for Albatross Sby 11/91 11,000
W/Pa 15x23 Untitled Sby 11/91 8,250
W/Pa 36x24 Untitled Chr 11/91 3,080
Mormile, Gaetano   It 1839-1890
O/Pn 10x13 Donkey's at Rest Chr 10/91 4,620
O/C 16x13 Serenading Outside a Window Sby 1/92 3,520
Morot, Aime Nicolas   Fr 1850-1913
O/C 18x14 Portrait of a Peasant Woman 1876 Sby 2/92 . . 3,025
Morphesis, Jim
 * See 1992 Edition . . . .
Morreale, Frank   Am 20C
O/C 43x29 Abstract Hnd 5/92 400
O/C 28x21 Abstract Profile 87 Hnd 5/92 100
MM/Pa 23x25 Mask 88 Hnd 5/92 100
Morrell, A. W.   Am 20C
O/C 24x37 Ship at Sea Fre 10/91 100
Morrell, Wane Beam   Am 1923-
O/C 24x36 White House Fre 4/92 825
Morrell, Wayne
O/B 19x25 Girl Sitting Under an Umbrella Eld 7/92 523
Morren, Georges   Bel 1868-
 * See 1992 Edition . . . .
Morrice, James Wilson   Can 1865-1924
O/Pn 9x13 Canadian Cavalry in Flanders Sbt 11/91 7,948
Morris   Am 20C
O/C 24x18 Patience Wlf 6/92 350
Morris, C.   Eng 1861-
O/C 12x10 The Watermill Fre 4/92 475
Morris, Charles   Br a 1886-1894
O/C 18x32 Playing Boats But 5/92 1,760
Morris, E. Butler   Br 19C
O/C 25x30 The Troubled Bride 1852 Chr 5/92 1,210
Morris, George   Am
 * See 1992 Edition . . . .
Morris, George L. K.   Am 1905-1975
O/B 16x20 Indians Hunting #1 1934 Chr 9/91 13,200
L&G/Pa 12x18 Two Refrigerators Sby 4/92 2,750
G&Pe/Pa 10x8 Study for "Suspended Discs" Chr 9/91 . . . 2,640
Morris, George Spencer   Am 20C
O/B 12x18 Seascape Yng 4/92 300
Morris, H.   Br a 1840-1849
O/C 16x11 In the Reading Room Lou 3/92 2,000
O/C 15x11 The Gift Lou 3/92 1,750
Morris, J. M
O/C 15x20 English Scene Dum 4/92 140
Morris, J. W.   Br 19C
O/C 24x20 Guardian of the Fold 1881 But 11/91 1,100
Morris, John B. (Jr.)   Am 1907-1941
W/Pa 14x10 St. Helen's Church, Beaufort, SC 1939 Lou 6/92 125
W/Pa 10x14 San Luis Rey, California 1940 Lou 6/92 75

Morris, John Floyd   Am 20C
O/C 21x67 Strange Parkland Chr 11/91 1,650
Morris, Kathleen Moir   Can 1893-1986
O/Pn 11x14 Cattle at Pasture Sbt 5/92 654
Morris, Kyle   Am 1918-1979
* See 1990 Edition . . . .
Morris, Philip Richard   Eng 1833-1902
* See 1991 Edition . . . .
Morris, Robert   Am 1931-
* See 1992 Edition . . . .
Morris, William   Eng 1834-1896
O/C 30x50 Young Anglers 1883 Chr 5/92 1,980
Morrison, *   Can 19C**
O/C 12x24 Fort Henry, Kingston Sbt 11/91 561
Morrison, J. C.   Eng 19C
O/C 18x30 Awaiting the Catch Hnz 5/92 350
Morrison, Kenneth M.   Br 20C
* See 1992 Edition . . . .
Morrisroe, Mark   1959-
Ph 20x16 Three photographs Chr 5/92 715
Ph 20x16 Three Untitled photographs 86 Chr 5/92 660
Morse, George F.   Am 19C
O/B 9x13 Croquet Brd 5/92 726
O/B 9x13 Belmont 79 Brd 5/92 550
O/B 9x13 Westbrook 77 Brd 5/92 330
O/C 5x7 Skating Scene Brd 5/92 220
Morse, Henry Dutton   Am 1826-1888
O/C 20x16 Hanging Duck and Woodcock 1864 Eld 8/92 . . 825
Morse, J. B.   Am 19C
O/C 18x12 Adironack Lake Eld 8/92 440
Morse, Jay Vernon   Am 1898-1944
O/C 20x26 Abandoned Ferry Slip 1927 But 2/92 1,980
W/Pa 14x19 Suicide Bridge, Pasadena 1934 But 2/92 . . . 1,540
Morse, Samuel F. B.   Am 1791-1872
* See 1991 Edition . . . .
Morse, Vernon Jay   Am 1898-1965
O/B 14x14 Forest Interior 1926 Mor 11/91 600
Mortelmans, Frans   Bel 1865-1936
* See 1992 Edition . . . .
Morviller, Joseph   Am a 1855-1870
O/C 18x24 Morning Sun 1859 Doy 12/91 3,500
O/C 9x13 Lead Mine Bridge 186- Yng 4/92 225
Mosbacher
O/C 23x19 Rhine River Scene Dum 5/92 100
Mosca, Ivan   It 20C
O/C 26x34 Ballo in Periferia 1949 But 5/92 825
Moser, Richard   Aus 1874-
W&G/Pa 10x13 The Village Stream 1915 Chr 10/91 . . . 2,420
Moser, Wilfrid
O/C 33x26 Marina di Carrara 1959 Sby 2/92 4,400
Moses, Anna Mary R. (Grandma)   Am 1860-1961
T/M 16x24 August 1956 Sby 3/92 28,600
O/B 8x11 Church Time 1959 Sby 9/91 14,300
O/B 11x15 Old Bridge, Richmond, VT 1938 But 11/91 . . 13,200
O/B 8x9 He'll Get There 1947 But 11/91 7,150
T/B 8x10 Where Has He Gone 1947 But 11/91 5,225
O/B 9x10 Where it was Cozy 1947 But 11/91 5,225
Moses, Ed   Am 1926-
MM 25x20 Untitled 72 Sby 6/92 1,980
Moses, Forrest   Am 1893-1974
O/B 16x24 Turn of the Season But 4/92 1,430
Moses, Thomas G.   Am 1856-1934
O/C 30x40 Laguna Coast 1930 But 2/92 1,320
O/C 12x16 Mt. Shasta Mor 6/92 350
Moskowitz, Robert   Am 1935-
K&H/Pa 14x8 Untitled (Flat Iron) 80 Chr 11/91 3,850
H/Pa 18x24 Untitled 1962 Chr 5/92 2,200
Mosler, Henry   Am 1841-1920
* See 1992 Edition . . . .
Mossa, Gustave Adolf   Fr 1883-1971
W&P/Pa 11x17 L'Abbe de St. Maurice 1912 Sby 1/92 . . . 10,450
Mosset, Olivier   1944-
A/C 48x24 A Little Late in the Day 86 Chr 2/92 3,300

Mostyn, Tom   Br 1864-1930
O/C 69x93 The Never Never Land Sby 2/92 8,250
O/C 24x20 Cottage Stratford on Avon Fre 12/91 2,000
Mote, George William   Br 1832-1909
* See 1991 Edition . . . .
Motherwell, Robert   Am 1915-1991
O/C 54x72 Two Figures 1958 Sby 11/91 330,000
A/C 73x85 Summer Seaside Night 1974 Sby 11/91 99,000
O,C&L/B 40x27 The Scarlett Ring 1963 Chr 11/91 90,000
A&L/Cb 45x30 Must It Be? #2 72 Sby 11/91 82,500
O/C 72x72 The Sicilian Door 72 Sby 5/92 66,000
O/M 9x12 Spanish Elegy No. 17 1953 Chr 11/91 60,500
O/Cb 9x12 Spanish Elegy 1959 Sby 5/92 57,750
O/Cb 14x18 Seville 50 Sby 2/92 44,000
O/C 38x30 Artist (Brown Figure) 48 Sby 5/92 38,500
A/C 25x30 Open Series #48 Sby 10/91 33,000
A/C 44x61 In Plato's Cave #VII 1973 Sby 10/91 30,800
A/Cb 12x24 Wall Painting Sketch 73 Sby 11/91 27,500
O&H/Pa 20x24 Monument Jackson Pollock 1956 Sby 11/91 . 22,000
L,I&G/B 14x11 Untitled 59 Chr 11/91 22,000
A/Pa 20x23 Rough Open 75 Sby 11/91 18,700
W&I/Pa 14x11 Untitled 45 Sby 11/91 9,900
Mottet, Yvonne
O/C 29x22 Still Life Flowers in a Vase Sby 2/92 1,430
Mottez, Victor Louis   Fr 1809-1897
* See 1991 Edition . . . .
Mouchot, Ludovic   Fr 1846-1893
O/Pn 16x13 Cavalier Carousing w/Washer Woman But 5/92 . 1,870
O/C 16x12 Flirtation in the Garden Dum 8/92 1,700
Moulin, Charles Lucien   Fr 19C
O/C 68x28 Baigneuse Aux Figues Sby 5/92 8,800
O/C 68x28 Baigneuses a la Tresse Sby 5/92 8,800
Mount, Shepard Alonzo   Am 1804-1868
O/Pn 10x15 Family Homestead 1852 Sby 12/91 8,800
Mount, William Sidney   Am 1807-1868
* See 1992 Edition . . . .
Mowbray, Henry Siddons   Am 1858-1928
O/B 7x15 Angels Heralding Arrival Peace Dove 1896 Ih 11/91 850
Mower, Martin   Am 1870-1960
* See 1990 Edition . . . .
Moyaert, Nicolas   Dut 1592-1655
* See 1990 Edition . . . .
Moylan, Lloyd   Am 1893-
W&G/Pa 19x15 Road Signs Skn 9/91 440
Mucha, Alphonse Maria   Czk 1860-1939
Pe/Pa 7x6 Study of a Young Woman Sby 1/92 3,575
Pe/Pa 28x24 Maternite Sby 5/92 3,300
Muchen, William Henry   Am 1832-1911
* See 1992 Edition . . . .
Mucke, Carl Emil   Ger 1847-1923
* See 1992 Edition . . . .
Mueller, E.
O/C 28x40 Cows Near Stream Dum 8/92 225
Mueller, Otto   Ger 1874-1930
* See 1990 Edition . . . .
Mueller, Stephen   Am 20C
* See 1992 Edition . . . .
Muendel, George   Am 1871-
O/C 24x18 The Palisades fr Upper Manhattan 98 Sby 12/91 2,420
Muenier, Jules Alexis   Fr 1863-1942
* See 1991 Edition . . . .
Muhl, Roger   Fr 1929-
O/C 40x43 Alpilles le Matin Doy 11/91 4,200
O/C 51x48 La Mediterranee le Soir Sby 6/92 3,575
O/C 20x21 Bergerie Sby 10/91 3,300
O/C 43x47 Les Alpilles Chr 5/92 2,800
O/C 32x51 Montagne Ochre Sby 6/92 1,100
O/C 12x24 Bergerie Doy 11/91 1,000
Muhlenfeld, Otto   Am 1871-1907
* See 1991 Edition . . . .
Muhlig, Bernhard   Ger 1829-1910
* See 1992 Edition . . . .
Muhlstock, Louis   Can 1904-
P/Pa 21x32 Reclining Nude Sbt 11/91 1,683

Mulard, Francois Henri   Fr 1769-1850
O/C 39x32 Portrait Lady in Elegant Dress Sby 1/92 165,000
Mulhaupt, Frederick John   Am 1871-1938
O/B 8x10 Gloucester Harbor Skn 9/91 7,150
O/C 18x24 Harbor Scene with Sailboats Sel 12/91 4,750
O/B 8x10 The Piers, Gloucester Skn 11/91 3,575
O/B 8x10 Half Moon Bay, Gloucester Skn 5/92 1,540
Mulhern, Mark   1951-
O/C 78x90 Sorting It Out 84 Chr 11/91 990
O/C 68x60 Bus II 1982 Chr 11/91 275
Mulholland, Sydney A.   Br 19C
W/Pa 13x24 Fisherman on a Country Road Slo 12/91 175
Mulier, Pieter (II)   Dut 1637-1701
* See 1992 Edition
Mulier, Pieter (the Elder)   Dut 1615-1670
* See 1992 Edition
Muller, Adolf & Bayrer, Wilh.   Ger 1853-
W&G/Pa/B 12x16 Two Sporting Scenes 1900 Skn 5/92 ... 1,320
Muller, C.
O/C 8x6 Man in Library Ald 5/92 700
Muller, C.   Am 20C
O/C 18x22 Fall Scene Mys 6/92 412
Muller, Carl   Ger 20C
O/C 25x30 A Venetian View Wes 11/91 3,300
Muller, Charles Louis   Fr 1815-1892
O/C 42x30 Au Bains de Mer Sby 2/92 9,900
O/C 53x76 Giving His Daughter into Slavery Hnz 5/92 6,500
Muller, Charles Louis   Fr 1902-
O/C 38x28 Arab Woman with White Parrot Sby 7/92 3,850
Muller, Ernst   Ger 1823-1875
O/Pn 13x9 The Jolly Lute Player Wes 11/91 495
Muller, Franz   Ger 1843-1929
* See 1992 Edition
Muller, Fritz   Ger 1897-
O/B 9x7 Bavarian Gentleman and Wife Slo 7/92 875
Muller, Jan   Am 1922-1958
* See 1991 Edition
Muller, Moritz   Ger 1841-1899
* See 1992 Edition
Muller, W. Georg   Ger 18C
K,Pl&S/Pa 13x8 Apotheosis of Saints Aloysius Chr 1/92 .. 1,760
Muller, William James   Br 1812-1845
O/C 36x28 Moor Slave Carrying Tray Fre 10/91 4,500
Muller-Fraustatt, G.   Aus 20C
O/C 24x32 Fisherfolk Slo 4/92 200
Muller-Kurzwelly, Konrad A.   Ger 1855-1914
O/C 39x28 Sunlight in Woods Slo 7/92 950
Muller-Lingke, Albert   Ger 1844-
O/C 10x9 Winter Concert Trek through Snow Slo 4/92 500
Mullholland, S. A.   Eng 19C
W/Pa 9x21 A Memory of the Adriatic Slo 4/92 200
Mullholland, St. John   Br 19C
* See 1992 Edition
Mullican, Matt   Am 20C
O/C 72x48 Untitled Sby 10/91 7,700
Mullin, Willard   Am 1902-1978
Pl&H/Pa 15x14 Two Sports Cartoons 1950 Ih 5/92 450
Mullins, Burt Rubin   Am 1901-
W/Pa 20x14 Gallier Hall, New Orleans Lou 6/92 275
Mulvany, Thomas James   Irs 1779-1845
O/Pn 20x24 Grouse Shooting But 5/92 5,500
Munakata, Shiko   20C
* See 1990 Edition
Munari, Cristoforo   It 1667-1720
* See 1992 Edition
Muncey, P. W.   Am 20C
O/C 20x24 Impressionist Coastal Landscape Slo 12/91 100
Munch, Edvard   Nor 1863-1944
O/C 32x26 Portrett av Annie Stenersen 1934 Sby 11/91 .. 55,000
Munger, Gilbert Davis   Am 1836-1903
O/Pn 12x18 Reflections on a Lake Chr 11/91 4,620
Munier, Emile   Fr 1810-1885
O/C 55x38 Mother and Child 1892 Chr 5/92 85,800
O/Pn 21x14 Knitting Lesson Sby 7/92 12,100

Munkacsy, Mikaly   Hun 1844-1900
* See 1992 Edition ....
Munninger, Ludwig   Ger 20C
* See 1992 Edition ....
Munnings, Sir Alfred James   Br 1878-1959
O/B 12x24 The Start Sby 6/92 143,000
O/Pn 20x24 Going Out at Epsom Sby 6/92 110,000
O/C 20x24 Boy Leading a Pony 1912 Sby 6/92 77,000
O/Pn 10x14 Ned Osborne Up on "Grey Tick" Sby 6/92 .. 46,750
Pe&O/Pn Size? Duke of Westminster's "Angela" Sby 6/92 . 34,100
O/C 20x24 Mare and Foal: Pair But 5/92 33,000
O/B 20x24 Mrs. Robert Rankin and Daughters Sby 6/92 .. 29,700
O/C 16x20 Richmond Park Sby 6/92 9,900
Munoz Y Lucena, Tomas   Spa 1860-1942
* See 1991 Edition ....
Munoz, Godofredo Ortega
O/Pn 11x12 Still Life with Pear Sby 6/92 8,800
Munoz-Vera, Guillermo   Chl 1949-
* See 1990 Edition ....
Munro, Hugh
O/C 30x25 In the Rose Garden Sby 6/92 8,250
Munsch, Leopold   Aus 1826-1888
O/B 5x8 Woman with Ducks But 5/92 1,650
Munter, Gabriele   Ger 1877-1963
O/B 19x27 Entwurf zum Blauen See Chr 5/92 231,000
Munthe, Gerhard Arij Ludvig M.   Dut 1875-
O/Pn 9x12 Ships at Sea Wes 5/92 798
Munthe, Ludwig   Nor 1841-1896
O/Pn 18x15 Frozen River at Sunset Sby 10/91 6,875
Muntz, Johann Heinrich   1727-1798
* See 1992 Edition ....
Mura, Angelo Della   It 1867-1922
W/Pa 4x2 Coastal City Lou 9/91 150
Muray, Nickolas   Am 1892-1965
* See 1992 Edition ....
Murch, Walter Tandy   Am 1907-1967
* See 1992 Edition ....
Murillo, Bartolome Esteban   Spa 1618-1682
O/C 25x18 Saint Vincent of Ferrara But 11/91 16,500
Murphy, Catherine   Am 20C
* See 1990 Edition ....
Murphy, Herman Dudley   Am 1867-1945
O/C 24x30 Mount Monadnock Chr 9/91 6,600
O/C 20x30 Monadnock Chr 6/92 6,380
O/B 12x16 Marsh Scene Mys 11/91 2,200
Murphy, John Cullen   Am 1919-
I,W&R/Pa 20x15 Player Diving over Tackler 1948 Ih 11/91 . 500
Murphy, John Francis   Am 1853-1921
O/C 16x22 Gray Afternoon '90 Chr 3/92 6,600
O/C 12x19 Late Afternoon 89 Chr 3/92 5,500
O/C 16x22 Summer Landscape 1905 Sby 12/91 5,500
Pe/Pa 8x12 Five Landscape Drawings But 4/92 4,950
O/C 36x40 The Red Tree 1912 Doy 12/91 3,500
O/C 11x15 Pride of the Meadow Chr 3/92 2,500
O/C 5x7 Gentle Stream But 4/92 2,200
O/B 9x7 Autumn 1900 Slo 2/92 2,000
O/Pn 8x10 Autumn Hnd 10/91 1,900
O/Pn 18x12 October Skn 3/92 1,210
O/C 8x10 Autumnal Landscape 1906 Sel 9/91 1,100
Murray, Anne T.   20C
W/Pa 18x28 Venetian View 1939 Slo 10/91 95
Murray, Elizabeth   Am 1940-
O/C 89x65 New York Dawn 77 Sby 11/91 126,500
O/C 132x130 Small Town Sby 11/91 82,500
O/C 58x53 Searchin' 1977 Chr 11/91 26,400
C&K/Pa 37x38 Untitled Chr 11/91 16,500
Murray, F. Richardson   Am 20C
* See 1990 Edition ....
Murray, H.   Eng a 1850-1860
W/Pa 12x18 Hunt Scenes Wlf 3/92 3,200
W/Pa 11x18 The Meet and The Scent (2) Chr 10/91 3,080
W&G/Pa 12x18 Winter & Summer Coaching (2) Chr 5/92 .. 1,320

Murray, J. G.   Am 20C
O/C 10x13 Landscape 1905 Hnz 5/92   190
Murray, John   Am 20C
* See 1991 Edition . . . .
Murry, Jerre   Am 1904-
* See 1992 Edition . . . .
Muschamp, Francis Sydney   Br -1929
O/C 27x37 A Game of Chess 1889 But 5/92   15,400
Music, Antonio   It 1909-
O/C 18x26 Cavallo Azzurro 1950 Sby 10/91   121,000
O/C 13x16 Cavallini 1950 Chr 2/92   115,500
O/C 15x18 Motiva Dalmata 1953 Sby 2/92   93,500
O/C 13x16 Cavallini 1951 Sby 5/92   77,000
O/C 16x13 Ida 1942 Sby 2/92   49,500
O/C 16x13 Autoritratto 1950 Sby 2/92   30,800
Musin, Auguste   Bel 1852-1920
O/C 27x49 Scheveningue (Holland) 1876 Sby 10/91   6,875
O/C 17x15 Claire Matinee 1893 Sby 7/92   3,740
Muss-Arnoldt, Gustav   Am 1858-1927
* See 1991 Edition . . . .
Mussellman, M.   Am 20C
P/Pa 17x13 Lady with Red Background Fre 4/92   150
Mussini, Luigi   It 1813-1888
O/C 25x32 Figures in a Classical Courtyard Chr 5/92 . . .   7,150
W/Pa 19x14 Woman with Tambourine But 5/92   1,100
Muter, Marie-Mela   Fr 1886-1967
* See 1992 Edition . . . .
Muzzioli, Giovanni   It 1854-1894
* See 1992 Edition . . . .
Myers, Bob   Am 20C
* See 1990 Edition . . . .
Myers, D.   Am 20C
O/C 12x14 Landscape with Sheep Yng 2/92   700
Myers, Frank Harmon   Am 1899-1956
O/B 18x22 Afternoon Bathers But 6/92   6,600
O/C 25x30 Pacific Surf But 2/92   1,320
O/C/B 22x28 The Big Surge But 6/92   1,210
O/C 25x30 Seascape But 2/92   1,100
O/C 20x24 Rocks and Sea But 6/92   990
Myers, Jerome   Am 1867-1940
P/B 16x20 Ring Around the Rosie 1919 Chr 3/92   4,180
O/Pa/M 8x10 New York Street Vendor Wes 3/92   1,870
C&Pe/Pa 9x6 Woman of 1905 Chr 9/91   1,210
Myers, Marie   Am 20C
O/Cb 20x14 Lady with a Fan Hnd 12/91   500
Mygatt, Robertson K.   Am 1861-1919
O/C 16x22 Fog Lifting, Sunrise 1916 Brd 8/92   3,960
Myles, J. W.
O/Pn 24x19 Portrait of Young Girls Durn 8/92   1,400
Myrick, Frank
W/Pa 10x14 Martha's Vineyard Eld 7/92   193
Mytens, Jan   Dut 1614-1670
* See 1992 Edition . . . .
Myton, F.   Am 19C
O/C 10x14 Watering Cattle 1882 Slo 2/92   375
Nabert, Wilhelm Julius August   Ger 1830-1904
* See 1990 Edition . . . .
Nachtmann, Franz Xaver   Ger 1799-1846
G&W/Pa 9x12 Elegant Music Room 1891 Chr 10/91   9,350
Nadelman, Elie   Am 1882-1946
Pe/Pa 10x8 Head Study Sby 9/91   7,150
Pe/Pa 9x6 Clay Figure of a Nude: Two Chr 9/91   3,850
Nadin, Peter   1954-
W,O&K/Pa 14x20 Harbour Island Bahamas 1988 Chr 5/92 .   1,100
W,G&Pl/Pa 18x24 Brain Coval Foot Hand 1987 Chr 2/92 . . .   330
W&O/Pa 9x12 Harbour Island Bahamas 1987 Chr 2/92   132
Nagy, Peter   20C
A/C 36x36 Glioblastoma 1986 Chr 5/92   1,320
A/C 36x36 Totally Fantastic Voyage 86 Chr 2/92   1,320
Nahl, Charles Christian   Am 1818-1878
O/C 22x27 Mourning the Master 1867 But 10/91   25,300
Nahl, Perham Wilhelm   Am 1869-1935
O/C 20x25 Dunes by the Sea But 6/92   6,050
O/C 29x24 Manton de Manila 1913 But 6/92   1,100

Nakagawa, Hachiro   Jap 1877-1922
* See 1990 Edition . . . .
Nakamura, Kanzi   Jap 20C
O/C 27x20 Porcelain Scholars Fre 4/92   2,600
Nalsh, John George   Br 1824-1905
* See 1991 Edition . . . .
Nandor, Katona   Hun 1864-1932
O/C 13x19 Mountain Yng 4/92   150
Nanteuil, Charles Gaugiran   Fr 1811-
O/C/B 11x16 Market Place/Water Trough: Pair Sby 10/91 .   9,900
O/C 13x18 Returning from Market 1879 Chr 5/92   6,600
Napoletano, Filippo   It 18C
* See 1991 Edition . . . .
Nardi, Enrico   It 1864-
* See 1992 Edition . . . .
Nardi, F.   It
W/Pa 22x15 Seated Cardinal Durn 6/92   1,750
Nardi, Natalie   Am 20C
O/B 20x24 Street Scene of Newburyport 1940 Mys 11/91 . . .   132
Nardone, Vincent Joseph   Am 1937-
* See 1992 Edition . . . .
Narvaez, Francisco
* See 1992 Edition . . . .
Nash, Fred B.   Am 20C
O/C 22x36 Landscape '17 Lou 12/91   65
Nash, Joseph (Jr.)   Eng 20C
O/Pn 6x8 Three-Masted Schooner Wes 5/92   412
Nash, Manley K.   Am 20C
O/C 25x30 Wooded Snowy Winter Landscape Sel 12/91 . . .   450
Nash, Willard Ayer   Am 1898-1943
* See 1992 Edition . . . .
Nasmyth, Alexander   Eng 1758-1840
O/C 13x17 Thatched Cottage beyond a Field Wtf 3/92   2,600
Nasmyth, Patrick   Br 1787-1831
* See 1992 Edition . . . .
Nason, Gertrude   Am 1890-1969
* See 1992 Edition . . . .
Nast, Thomas   Am 1840-1902
S,Pl&O/Pa 14x20 Knoxville; Gen. Sherman: Two 64 Chr 9/91   4,180
S&O/Pa 29x21 Petersburg; Gen. Thomas: Two 64 Chr 9/91   3,520
Pl/Pa 7x8 Ploughing the Fields for Corruption Ih 11/91   1,100
Natkin, Robert   Am 1930-
A/C 66x50 Intimate Light: Yellow Chr 11/91   12,100
A/C 76x86 Napolian's Tryst 1970 Chr 2/92   9,900
A/C 52x52 Bern Series Chr 5/92   6,600
A/C 60x48 Festival #2 Sby 6/92   5,775
A/C 87x96 For Madame Fong Sby 10/91   5,225
A/C 20x26 Untitled 1967 Chr 2/92   3,300
A/C 34x34 Untitled Chr 5/92   3,300
A/C 90x54 Untitled 1966 Sby 6/92   2,750
A/C 25x30 Untitled Sby 5/92   1,925
A/Pa 31x24 Untitled (Bern Series) Chr 11/91   1,100
O/C/Pn 10x13 Apollo Series But 5/92   990
W/Pa 25x22 Enchanted 1965 Durn 1/92   700
Natoire, Charles-Joseph   Fr 1700-1777
O/C 40x33 Hunter & Woman; Horseback (2) Chr 1/92 . .   737,000
Nattier, Jean Marc   Fr 1685-1766
P/Pa/C 32x25 Portrait Madame Royer at Ledge Sby 5/92   297,000
O/C 54x41 Portrait of Louis Le Dauphin Sby 5/92   49,500
Nattonier, C.   Fr 20C
O/C 20x24 Polly Toasts; Communication: Pair Bor 8/92 . . .   2,000
Natullo, Sandro   It 20C
O/C 8x10 Italian Market Slo 10/91   150
Naudin, Bernard   Fr 1876-
W&G/Pa 10x21 Summer Muses Skn 11/91   220
Nauman, Bruce   Am 1941-
Pe,C&P/Pa 53x61 Violins, Violence, Silence 81 Sby 11/91 .   88,000
W,C&H/Pa 17x29 No/On 84 Chr 11/91   16,500
Ph&L/Pa 23x30 Rats Underfoot 1988 Chr 11/91   8,800
Naumann, Carl Georg   Ger 1827-1902
* See 1990 Edition . . . .
Navarro Y Llorens, Jose   Spa 1867-1923
* See 1992 Edition . . . .

Navez, Francois Joseph Navez   Bel 1787-1869
* See 1991 Edition ....

Navez, R   Bel 19C**
O/C/M 18x24 Sleeping Child With Dog '51 Wes 11/91 412

Naviet, Joseph   Fr 1821-1889
* See 1991 Edition ....

Nazaire, L.   Hai 20C
O/C 26x18 Village Scene Fre 4/92 275

Neagle, John   Am 1796-1865
O/C 20x17 Portrait of Joseph C. Neal 1867 Chr 11/91 2,200

Neale, John   Br 20C
O/C 12x16 Harbor Scene 1941 Dum 6/92 150

Neder, Johann Michael   Aus 1807-1882
* See 1992 Edition ....

Neefs, Pieter (the Elder)   Flm 1578-1656
O/Pn 17x25 Interior of a Gothic Church 1636 Sby 5/92 ... 31,900

Neel, Alice
O/C 34x45 Portrait of Edward Weiss 76 Sby 2/92 15,400

Neergaard, Hermania Sigvardine   Dan 1799-1874
O/Pn 7x6 Bird's Nest 1871 Sby 1/92 4,125

Neff, Edith   Am 20C
* See 1992 Edition ....

Nefkens, Martinus Jacobus   Dut 1866-1941
O/C 12x10 Along the Path But 11/91 1,100

Negretti, Jacopo   It 1544-1628
* See 1992 Edition ....

Nehlig, Victor   Fr 1830-1910
O/C 10x8 House to Let Skn 11/91 2,420

Neillot, Louis   Fr 1898-1973
O/C 15x18 Paysage 71 Chr 11/91 2,420

Neilson, Charles Peter   Am a 1890-1910
W/Pa 22x10 San Francisco But 10/91 1,320

Neilson, Raymond Perry Rodgers   Am 1881-1964
O/C 36x29 Before the Mirror Sby 5/92 18,700
O/C 30x25 Chelsea Lady/Sweetheart Roses 1945 Slo 2/92 . 1,200
O/C 30x25 Europa and Pinocchio Roses 1945 Slo 2/92 750

Neimann, Edmund John   Br 1813-1876
O/C 20x30 Lake Scene But 5/92 2,200

Nel-Dumouchel, Jules   Fr 19C
* See 1991 Edition ....

Nelson, Ernest Bruce   Am 1888-1952
* See 1991 Edition ....

Nelson, Ernest O.   Am 19C
* See 1991 Edition ....

Nelson, George Laurence   Am 1887-1978
* See 1992 Edition ....

Nelson, Joan   Am 1958-
O/Wd 25x20 Untitled #194 1988 Sby 5/92 13,200
ET/M 40x48 Untitled 1984 Sby 5/92 12,100
Wx&Pg/M 17x16 Untitled #66 1985 Sby 11/91 12,100
O&Wx/Pn 22x20 Untitled (#211) 1988 Chr 11/91 12,100
O&Wx/M 16x15 Untitled #86 86 Chr 11/91 9,900
Wx&Pg/Pn 16x18 Untitled 85 Chr 2/92 8,800

Nelson, Roger Laux   Am 20C
* See 1991 Edition ....

Nelson, William   Am 20C
O/C 24x18 Young Girl in the Garden 73 Slo 9/91 125

Neme, Clarel   Uru 1926-
* See 1992 Edition ....

Nemeth, Lajos   Hun 1861-
W/Pa 7x14 Grazing Cows Fre 10/91 325

Nemethy, Albert   Am
O/C 24x34 Steamboat "Alexander Hamilton" Eld 4/92 1,210
O/C 13x30 Steamboat "Confidence" Eld 4/92 715

Neogrady, Laszlo   Hun 1900-
O/C 24x31 Springtime Sby 7/92 2,200
O/C 24x32 Morning Sun in the Alps But 11/91 935
O/C 2?x29 Winter Landscape Wlf 3/92 550
O/C 24x36 Winter Forest and Mountains Hnz 5/92 500

Neogrady, Laszlo (Antal)   Hun 1861-1942
O/C 24x36 Feeding the Ducks Wlf 9/91 2,000

Nepolsky, Hermann   Eur 20C
O/C 40x34 Floral Still Life Slo 12/91 1,200

Nepote, Alexander   Am 1913-1986
* See 1992 Edition ....

Nerly, Friedrich   It 1824-1919
* See 1991 Edition ....

Nesbit, Robert H.   Am 20C
O/Ab 11x18 Landscape Wlf 10/91 400
O/Cb 11x18 Summer-Fall Wlf 10/91 400

Nesbitt, Lowell   Am 1933-
O/C 40x72 White and Yellow Japanese Iris 79 Sby 2/92 ... 7,700
O/C 63x88 Red Lily '69 Sby 10/91 4,125
A/C 77x77 Iris '65 Chr 5/92 3,300
O/C 40x40 Parrot Tulip on White 79 Sby 2/92 3,300
O/C 38x30 Amaryllis '77 Sby 10/91 3,025
A/C 64x78 Mangrove Shoots '67 Sby 10/91 2,310
O/C 70x80 Spring Forest III 1984 Sby 6/92 1,925
O/C 77x77 Grapes 66 Doy 11/91 1,900

Neshitta, Jos. Fl.
W/Pa 12x15 House in Landscape Dum 1/92 200

Nessi, Marie-Lucie
* See 1992 Edition ....

Nesterov, Mikhail Vasillevich   Rus 1862-1942
* See 1990 Edition ....

Netscher, Caspar   1635-1684
O/C 21x18 Portrait of a Lady Chr 10/91 4,180

Nettleton, Walter   Am 1861-1936
* See 1992 Edition ....

Neubauer, H.
* See 1992 Edition ....

Neuberger, Klara
* See 1992 Edition ....

Neugebauer, Hans
O/C 16x20 Still Life Ald 3/92 260

Neuhaus, Karl Eugen   Am 1879-1963
O/C 24x20 Pinnacle Rock, Carmel But 2/92 990

Neuhuys, John Albertus   Dut 1844-1914
O/B 12x9 Hide and Seek Hnd 10/91 2,600

Neuman, Carl   Am 1858-1932
O/C 34x28 Floral Still Life Fre 10/91 900

Neuman, Robert   Am 1926-
* See 1992 Edition ....

Neumann, Alexander   Ger 1831-
O/C 38x47 Rachael and Jacob at the Well 1862 Slo 10/91 . 5,750

Neumann, Johan Jens   Dan 1860-1940
* See 1990 Edition ....

Neumann, Prof. Carl   Dut 1833-1891
* See 1992 Edition ....

Neuquelman, Lucien   Fr 1909-
* See 1992 Edition ....

Neuschul, Ernest
* See 1992 Edition ....

Neustatter, Ludwig   Ger 1829-1899
* See 1990 Edition ....

Nevelson, Louise   Am 1900-1989
L/Pn 24x20 Unknown Cosmos IV Chr 5/92 4,950
L/Pb 30x20 Untitled Chr 5/92 4,950
Pl/Pa/B 8x12 Four Women Sby 6/92 1,210

Newberry, Clare T.   Am 1903-1970
W/Pa 10x15 Siamese Cat 1934 Ih 5/92 125

Newberry, Lane   Am 1930-
O/C 18x20 Pre-Emption House, Naperville Hnz 5/92 200

Newell, George Glenn   Am 1870-1947
O/C 22x27 Landscape with Figures Wlf 9/91 1,600

Newell, Henry C.   Am a 1865-1885
O/C 14x24 August Day North Shore 75 Chr 9/91 3,520

Newell, Hugh   Am 1830-1915
* See 1992 Edition ....

Newell, Peter   Am 1862-1924
O/C 21x17 The Polling Place But 4/92 1,980

Newman, Barnett   Am 1905-1970
* See 1991 Edition ....

Newman, Benjamin T.   Am
* See 1991 Edition ....

Newman, George A.
O/B 18x12 House by Canal Ald 5/92 200
Newman, Henry Roderick Am 1833-1918
W&Pe/Pa/L 40x27 Abu Simbel 1900 Chr 3/92 55,000
W/Pa/Pn 13x8 Cherry Blossoms 1898 Sby 4/92 9,900
Newman, John 1936-
H&Y/V 29x52 Untitled Chr 5/92 4,400
Newman, John 1952-
H&Y/V 49x25 Drawing for Tolled Belle Chr 2/92 5,500
Newman, Robert Loftin Am 1827-1912
O/B 11x19 Children Playing Doy 12/91 3,000
O/C 10x14 Psyche Chr 9/91 2,860
Newmarch, Strafford Br a 1866-1874
O/C 26x18 Under the Arbor Skn 5/92 825
Newton, Richard (Jr.) Am 20C
O/C 24x32 Horses Grazing Sby 12/91 990
Ney, Lloyd Raymond Am 1893-1964
G&Pe/Pa 11x15 Untitled 41 Chr 3/92 2,200
Neymark, Gustave Mardoche Fr 1850-
O/C 24x32 Bataille de Loos Sby 1/92 1,760
Neyts, Gillis Flm 1623-1687
  * See 1992 Edition . . . .
Niblett, Gary Am 1943-
  * See 1990 Edition . . . .
Nibrig, Ferdinand Hart Dut 1866-1915
  * See 1992 Edition . . . .
Nice, Don 1932-
W&H/Pa 38x89 American Predella 1975 Chr 2/92 3,080
Nicholas, Thomas Andrew Am 1934-
O/C 14x10 Chrysanthemums Wes 3/92 468
Nicholl, Charles Wynn Irs 1831-1903
  * See 1990 Edition . . . .
Nicholls, Burr H. Am 1848-1915
O/C 20x14 On the Canal But 11/91 1,650
Nicholls, Rhoda Holmes Am 1854-1930
  * See 1991 Edition . . . .
Nichols, Dale Am 1904-
O/C 24x30 Saturday Evening 1972 Dum 6/92 6,000
O/C 24x30 Man on a Wyoming Island 1970 Chr 9/91 4,400
W/Pa Size? After the Shower--Guatomala 1967 Fre 10/91 . . . 110
Nichols, Edward W. Am 19C
O/C 10x8 Mountainous Landscape Mys 6/92 688
Nichols, Harley Dewitt Am 1859-1939
O/Cb 9x12 Base of the Cliff Mor 6/92 400
Nichols, Henry Hobart Am 1869-1962
O/C 25x30 Across the Valley Chr 9/91 6,050
O/C 25x30 The Culvert, Bronxville Chr 9/91 6,050
O/C 30x36 Landscape Dum 9/91 2,500
O/C 26x32 The Housatonic Hnd 6/92 2,500
Nichols, Thomas Am 20C
O/C 10x14 Oriental Still Life Wlf 10/91 1,000
Nichols, William Am 20C
  * See 1990 Edition . . . .
Nicholson, Ben Br 1894-1982
O/M 48x84 November, 1956 (Pistoia) 56 Chr 5/92 . . . . . . 1.54M
O/Cb/B 17x20 Still Life '49 Chr 11/91 165,000
O&Pe/M 26x40 Sept 63 (Prato) 63 Chr 5/92 110,000
T&Pe/B 8x7 Still Life 47 Chr 11/91 71,500
O&Pe/Pa/M 10x7 May 53 (Tring) 53 Chr 5/92 35,200
Nicholson, Charles W. Am 1886-1965
O/C 18x27 Flowered Landscape Mor 3/92 225
Nicholson, Edward Horace Am 1901-1966
O/C 24x30 Road to Morro Bay But 10/91 6,050
O/Cb 16x22 Reclining Nude Mor 6/92 1,300
O/Cb 16x20 Coastal Landscape Mor 3/92 325
Nicholson, George Washington Am 1832-1912
O/B 23x16 Coastal Village But 11/91 2,475
O/C 20x36 Outskirts of an Arabian Village Sby 4/92 2,200
O/C 28x50 Travelers Along the Coast Fre 12/91 1,900
O/Pn 33x26 Peasants in a Village Chr 6/92 1,650
O/C 24x42 Fisherfolk Along the Shore Slo 4/92 1,600
O/Pn 16x12 Encampment Fre 10/91 1,050

Nickle, Robert
W/Pa 9x11 Boy Sitting on Porch Ald 5/92 90
Nickolaus, August Wilhelm Swd 1852-1925
  * See 1990 Edition . . . .
Nicol, Erskine Br 1825-1904
O/C 13x16 A Crow to Pluck 1856 Sby 1/92 3,850
O/C 16x25 The Bashful Suitor Sby 7/92 3,850
O/C 20x15 Notice to Quit Slo 7/92 2,500
O/C 19x15 Seaman in Stormy Weather 1870 Chr 10/91 . . . 1,650
Nicolaus, Martin Ger 1870-1945
O/C 28x37 An Afternoon Reverie Chr 2/92 1,320
Nicolina, A. It 19C
O/C 32x25 At the Tavern Chr 5/92 2,200
Nicoll, James Craig Am 1846-1918
  * See 1990 Edition . . . .
Niczky, Eduard Ger 1850-1919
  * See 1990 Edition . . . .
Niel, Robert Aus 20C
O/C 26x37 Schafstall Slo 9/91 650
Nielsen, Amaldus Clarin Nor 1838-1932
  * See 1992 Edition . . . .
Nielsen, Jack
  * See 1992 Edition . . . .
Nielson, R. Dan 20C
O/C 19x23 Deer by a Lake Fre 4/92 300
Niemann, Edmund John Br 1813-1876
O/C 20x30 View of Epsom, Surrey Sby 7/92 3,300
O/C 16x24 View of Stapleford Wlf 9/91 2,600
Niemeyer, John Henry Am 1839-1932
  * See 1990 Edition . . . .
Niepold, Frank Am 1890-
O/C 20x30 Morning, February Wes 3/92 935
Nierman, Leonardo Mex 1932-
A/B 31x23 Ciudad en Acantilado Wlf 9/91 3,000
O/M 32x24 Biblical Fire Wes 11/91 1,430
A/M 40x65 Desintegracion '59 Hnd 3/92 1,300
O/M 24x15 Influencia Solar '63 Wes 3/92 798
O/M 16x24 Abstract '66 Wes 3/92 688
Nieto, Rodolfo Mex 1936-1988
O/C 46x35 Mexico Sby 11/91 11,000
Y&Pl/Pa 14x18 Two: Sin Título Chr 5/92 4,400
O/C 22x18 El Maguey Despierta 1961 Chr 5/92 3,850
Nignet, Georges Fr 20C
O/C 30x40 Les Quai Du Seine Doy 11/91 2,600
O/C 30x40 Portofino Fre 4/92 2,300
O/C 24x36 Boulevard d'Orleans Doy 11/91 1,600
O/C 30x40 La Rivere de Loire Doy 11/91 1,600
Nikoff, Alexis Matthew Podcher Am 1886-1933
  * See 1992 Edition . . . .
Nikolaki, Z. P.
O/C 40x31 After the Ball Wlf 6/92 1,900
Nilson, Johann Esaias 1721-1788
K,Pl&S/Pa 7x10 Faith Seated Under Awning 1757 Chr 1/92 . 4,950
Ninerze-Ruiz, E* Spa 20C**
O/C 29x23 Young Woman Holding Eggs 1925 Sby 1/92 . . . 1,870
Nino, Carmelo Ven 1951-
  * See 1991 Edition . . . .
Nisbet, Robert Buchanan Br 1857-1942
W/Pa/B 22x26 Sheep Grazing '09 But 11/91 715
Nisbet, Robert Hogg Am 1879-1961
O/C 22x20 Early Fall Wlf 10/91 1,000
O/C 22x20 Landscape Wlf 6/92 650
O/B 8x12 Landscape Fre 4/92 200
Nissl, Rudolph Aus 1870-1955
  * See 1992 Edition . . . .
Noble, John Sargeant Br 1848-1906
  * See 1992 Edition . . . .
Noble, Thomas S. Am 1835-1907
O/B 18x24 The Library 1892 Sby 4/92 3,960
Noe, Luis Felipe Arg 1933-
MM/C 38x51 Cuadro del Agnostico 1963 Chr 11/91 6,600
Noel, Alexandre-Jean Fr 1752-1834
  * See 1992 Edition . . . .

Noel, Georges   Fr 1924-
  * See 1992 Edition . . . .
Noel, Jules Achille   Fr 1815-1881
  O/C 15x21 Harbor Scene Slo 10/91 14,000
  O/Pn 14x10 French Village Scene Hnd 10/91 1,500
Noguchi, Isamu   Am 1904-
  G&Pe/B 16x11 The Bells: Design for the Decor Sby 11/91 . 4,400
  W&Pe/Pa 11x9 The Bells: Six Costume Designs Sby 11/91 . 2,420
Noland, Kenneth   Am 1924-
  A/C 96x24 Keen Transit 1967 Sby 5/92 35,750
  A/C 45x45 Capella Chr 11/91 35,200
  A/C 64x64 Winged 1964 Chr 11/91 33,000
  A/C 6x102 Beauty Spot 1969 Sby 2/92 22,000
  A/C 66x45 Watch For Dawn 1986 Chr 11/91 18,700
  A/C 17x69 Via Toss 1968 Chr 5/92 16,500
  A/C 6x101 Revelet 1969 Chr 11/91 13,200
Nolde, Emil   Ger 1867-1956
  W/Pa 14x19 Grosser roter Mohn Chr 5/92 176,000
  W/Pa 11x9 Buddhakopf vor roten Blumen Chr 11/91 . . . 19,800
  W/Pa 14x9 Zwei Kostumierte Figuren Chr 11/91 12,100
Nollekens, Josef Frans   Flm 1702-1748
  * See 1992 Edition . . . .
Nolpe, Pieter   Dut 1613-1652
  * See 1991 Edition . . . .
Nonetti, A.   It 20C
  O/C 20x30 Italian Port Scene Slo 9/91 1,600
Nonnenbruch, Max   Ger 1857-1922
  * See 1991 Edition . . . .
Nonnotte, Donat   Fr 1708-1785
  * See 1990 Edition . . . .
Nooms, Reinier   Dut 1623-1664
  * See 1992 Edition . . . .
Noortig, Jan   17C
  O/Pn 18x21 Peasants Playing Jump Rope 1655 Sby 5/92 . 8,525
Nordalm, Federico   Nic 1949-
  O/C 40x36 Naturaleza Muerta con Naranjas 1991 Chr 5/92 . 9,350
  O/C 34x37 Naturaleza Muerta 1990 Chr 11/91 7,700
Nordell, Carl   Am 1885-
  O/C 24x32 Still Life Jug and Teapot But 11/91 3,850
  O/C 36x27 Portrait of a Young Woman Skn 5/92 715
Nordell, Polly   1876-1956
  W/Pa 16x20 Ducks and Chicks Yng 4/92 170
Nordenberg, Bengt   Swd 1822-1902
  * See 1990 Edition . . . .
Nordfeldt, Bror Julius Olsson   Am 1878-1955
  O/C 30x40 Minnesota Landscape 35 Sby 4/92 8,575
  O/C 25x20 Still Life Vase and Wheat Wlf 6/92 3,100
  P/Pa 11x15 Houses by the Hills Mys 11/91 632
Nordfeldt, Emily
  I/Pa 16x12 A Duck Ald 5/92 45
Nordhausen, August Henry   Am 1901-
  O/C 20x16 Daydreaming Sby 12/91 935
Nordstrom, Carl Harold   Am 1876-1934
  W&H/Pa 8x12 Harbor View of Seagulls Skn 9/91 110
Norman, Irving
  * See 1992 Edition . . . .
Normann, Adelsteen   Nor 1848-1918
  O/C 38x30 The Furies Chr 2/92 3,300
Normil, Andre   Hai 20C
  O/C 20x24 Adam and Eve 67 Chr 5/92 2,200
  O/C 20x30 Haitian Scene 66 Wlf 6/92 350
Norse, Stansbury   Am 19C
  W/Pa 8x16 Crashing Surf Slo 10/91 50
North, J. M.   Am 19C
  O/B 12x6 Landscape with Farmyard Sel 12/91 350
North, T. E.   Am 20C
  W&G/Pa 10x14 The Rivals Wlf 3/92 525
Northcote, James   Am 1822-1904
  O/C 16x24 Under the Willows 1887 Wes 11/91 1,650
Northcote, James   Eng 1746-1831
  * See 1990 Edition . . . .
Northern, Ellen Gifford
  O/B 20x14 Tree and House Ald 3/92 200
  O/C 18x24 Forest Landscape Ald 5/92 190

  O/B 16x21 Tree and Distant House Ald 3/92 150
  O/C 16x20 Stream Ald 3/92 110
Northleach, J. Miles   Eng 19C
  * See 1990 Edition . . . .
Norton, Elizabeth Sawyer   Am 1887-1985
  O/C 24x16 Young Woman in Blouse Slo 12/91 300
Norton, Lewis D.   Am 1868-1940
  P/Pa 11x17 Shipyard, Kennebunkport 1932 Brd 8/92 . . . 1,540
Norton, Louis Doyle   Am 1867-
  P/Pa 12x18 Young Grove, Autumn Skn 9/92 330
Norton, William Edward   Am 1843-1916
  O/C 20x30 Delivering a Passenger Fre 4/92 7,700
  O/C 20x30 American Two-Masted Schooner Eld 7/92 . . . 2,640
  O/C 9x13 Ship in the Harbour Mys 6/92 990
Norwell, Graham Noble   Can 1901-1967
  O/C 20x24 Landscape with a Farm Sbt 11/91 935
Noterman, Zacharias   Bel 1820-1890
  * See 1992 Edition . . . .
Nott, Raymond   Am 1888-1948
  P/Pa 19x24 Seaside Town But 6/92 1,320
  P/Pa 19x21 Eucalyptus Landscape Mor 6/92 600
  P/Pa 21x19 Eucalyptus Landscape Mor 11/91 550
Notz, Johannes   Sws 1802-1862
  C,Pe&K/Pa 14x11 Lady and Gentleman (2) 1836 Chr 5/92 . 1,760
Nourse, Elizabeth   Am 1859-1938
  W/Pa 23x16 Interior Scene w/Mother & Children Lou 12/91 . 900
Novelli, Pietro Antonio   It 1729-1804
  K&Pl/Pa 21x10 The Risen Christ Chr 1/92 1,100
Novo, Stefano   It 1862-
  O/C/M 21x30 Feeding the Cat 1900 Chr 2/92 9,350
  O/C 16x8 Flower, Produce Vendor: Pair 1899 Chr 10/91 . 5,500
  O/Pn 10x13 Outdoor Market in Venice Chr 10/91 2,860
  W/Pa 23x17 Object of His Desire Slo 12/91 450
Novotny, Elmer L.   Am 1910-
  O/Pn 34x26 In the Field 1943 Wlf 9/91 1,100
  O/Ab 19x16 Young Poet Wlf 10/91 300
Novros, David   Am 1941-
  * See 1991 Edition . . . .
Nowak, Ernst   Aus 1853-1919
  O/C 19x15 Cardinal with a Glass of Wine But 11/91 3,850
Nowak, Leo   Am 20C
  O/C 40x30 Reflections in Blue Wlf 9/91 900
  O/C 30x24 Brunette in White Wlf 9/91 600
  O/C 30x40 Conversation Wlf 9/91 550
  O/Ab 30x24 Standing Nude Wlf 9/91 300
Noyer, Denis Paul   Fr 20C
  O/C 26x21 Place du Terte 1968 Hnd 5/92 425
Noyer, Philippe-Henri   Fr 1917-
  O/C 26x20 Dejeuner dans le jardin 45 Chr 5/92 2,200
  W/Pa 19x25 Boy with Parakeet 1955 Dum 11/91 900
  O/Pn 6x11 Moonlit Seascape with Figure Wlf 9/91 700
  O/C 20x24 Canal Scene 1964 Hnd 6/92 600
  W/Pa 25x19 Seated Girl '59 Hnz 5/92 225
Noyes, George Loftus   Am 1864-1951
  O/Cb 14x15 Winter Stretch, Medfield, Mass. Sby 12/91 . . 6,050
  O/Cb 12x16 April Morning, Massachusetts 16 Sby 12/91 . 5,500
  O/Pn 5x8 Indian Genre Scene Skn 3/92 1,540
  O/Pn 7x6 Summer Shore Skn 11/91 550
  W/Pa 21x14 Venetian Canal Scene Skn 11/91 440
Nozkowski, Thomas   1944-
  O/Cb 16x20 Untitled 1987 Chr 5/92 1,650
Nuderscher, Frank B.   Am 1880-1959
  O/C 20x25 Eads Bridge with Courthouse Lou 3/92 3,750
  Pe&W/Pa 25x30 Manchester & Sutton 1825 1937 Sel 2/92 . 500
  O/B 12x16 Old Settlers Sel 5/92 475
  O/C 60x78 St. Louis Levee with Eads Bridge 1934 Sel 9/91 . 325
  O/C 16x19 Missouri River 1930 Sel 9/91 210
  O/C 58x72 Historical Scene on Mississippi 1932 Sel 9/91 . . 200
  O/M 21x24 Marine Scene Sel 12/91 125
Nunamaker, Kenneth   Am 1890-1957
  O/C 22x24 The Icy River Chr 5/92 8,800
Nunez, Armando Garcia   Mex 20C
  O/C/B 10x14 Vista del Popocatepl Chr 5/92 1,210
Nutt, Jim   Am 20C
  * See 1991 Edition . . . .

Nuvolone, Carlo Francesco   It 1608-1665
* See 1991 Edition ....
Nybo, Povl Friis   Dan 1869-
O/C 60x79 In the Studio 1914 Sby 7/92 3,850
Nye, Edgar Hewitt   Am 1879-1943
O/M 24x20 Landscape Eld 7/92 1,320
W/Pa 11x8 Three Works Wes 11/91 165
W/Pa 8x11 Farm and By the Fire: Two Wes 11/91 138
Nye, M.
* See 1992 Edition ....
Nyholm, Arvid Frederick   Scn
O/C 27x22 Our Lady in Sorrow Hnd 5/92 800
O'Brien, Lucius Richard   Can 1832-1899
W/Pa 13x21 Sailboats in a Marsh 1898 Sbt 11/91 3,740
W/Pa 9x14 Napanee, Ontario '74 Sbt 11/91 3,506
W/Pa 13x21 Meadow, 1891 1891 Sbt 11/91 3,272
W/Pa 13x9 Ship at a Dock 1883 Sbt 11/91 2,104
O'Conner, James Arthur   Irs 1792-1841
* See 1992 Edition ....
O'Connor, John   Irs 1830-1889
* See 1992 Edition ....
O'Conor, Roderick   Irs 1860-1940
* See 1991 Edition ....
O'Donnell, Hugh   20C
* See 1991 Edition ....
O'Gorman, Juan   Mex 1905-1982
T/Pn 43x49 Los Mitos Paganos 1944 Chr 11/91 330,000
O/Me 9x23 La Ciudad Podrida Sby 11/91 44,000
T&L/B 10x9 Mesa Revuelta 1947 Sby 11/91 30,800
W&G/Pa 31x43 Mosaico: Mexico Antiguo Sby 5/92 22,000
W&G/Pa 32x43 Mosaico: Nueva Espana 1952 Sby 5/92 ... 22,000
G&W/Pa/B 17x21 Los Compadres Chr 11/91 11,000
Pe/Pa/B 14x9 Boceto para El Proyecto 1966 Chr 11/91 6,600
O'Hara, Eliot   Am 1890-1969
W/Pa 30x21 Stonehenge Eld 7/92 99
W/Pa 30x21 Train at Bergen, Norway Eld 7/92 55
O'Higgins, Pablo   Mex 1904-
O/C 21x29 Paisaje Rocalloso Chr 11/91 6,050
O'Keeffe, Georgia   Am 1887-1986
O/C 58x34 Lake George Reflection 1921 Sby 5/92 632,500
O/B 16x12 Calla Lilies Sby 5/92 220,000
O/C 12x10 Blue Morning Glory 1936 Sby 12/91 110,000
O'Kelly, Aloysius   Irs 1853-
O/C 24x29 By the Hearth Doy 11/91 5,750
O/C 24x16 Young Breton Maiden Doy 11/91 4,500
O'Kelly, Mattie Lou   Am 1907-
* See 1991 Edition ....
O'Malley, Power
O/C 28x22 Terence Sby 2/92 825
O'Neil, Henry Nelson   Br 1817-1880
* See 1991 Edition ....
O'Neil, Thomas F.   Am 1852-1922
O/B 8x10 Fundy Reef, Cape Elizabeth 1910 Brd 8/92 550
O'Neill, Daniel   Br 20C
* See 1992 Edition ....
O'Neill, George Bernard   Br 1828-1917
* See 1991 Edition ....
O'Neill, Raymond Edgar   Am 1893-1962
O/M 49x39 On Trial 1935 Chr 9/91 18,700
O'Neill, Rose   Am 1875-1944
Pl/Pa 14x21 Nanny and Children 1901 Ih 11/91 700
O'Shea, John   Am 1876-1956
O/C 34x40 Down the Coast But 10/91 12,100
O/C 24x30 Birches Mor 3/92 4,250
O/B 20x24 Coastal Hills, Carmel Valley But 10/91 3,300
O/Cb 12x18 Landscape Mor 11/91 800
O/Cb 12x18 Landscape Mor 3/92 800
Oakes, Frederick   Am
* See 1991 Edition ....
Oakes, Minnie F.   Am a 1891-
O/C 24x19 Still Life Pink and White Azaleas 89 Skn 3/92 .. 2,200
Oakes, Wilbur L.   Am 1876-
* See 1991 Edition ....
Oakley, Thornton   Am 1881-1953
W/Pa 11x8 Durbar and Rajah (Pair) Hnz 5/92 200

Oakley, Violet   Am 1874-1961
P/Pa 18x13 Country Life Fre 4/92 550
C&Y/Pa 20x14 Country Life Fre 10/91 200
O/C 30x25 Wedding Reception 1941 Hnz 10/91 200
Oberhauser, Emanuel   Ger 19C
* See 1991 Edition ....
Obermuller, Franz   Aus 1869-1917
* See 1990 Edition ....
Obersteiner, Ludwig   Aus 1857-
O/Pn 6x5 Feeding Time Chr 5/92 2,750
Oberteuffer, George   Am 1878-1940
O/C 32x38 Rear View of a Cathedral Paris Chr 11/91 4,400
Obin, Antoine   Hai
O/M 16x20 Nature Morte avec Fruits Tropicaux Chr 5/92 ... 1,320
Obin, Michael   Hai 20C
O/B 20x24 Cap Haitian Road Wlf 9/91 1,000
Obin, Philome   Hai 1892-
O/M 22x28 Le Reve de l'artiste 1948 Chr 5/92 22,000
O/M 24x30 Carnaval de 1954: Cap-Haitien 56 Sby 5/92 .. 14,300
O/B 15x19 Deguisees du Carnaval 1947 Chr 11/91 10,450
O/M 20x24 Des Paysans Sby 10/91 7,150
O/M 24x30 Section du Bas-du-Limbe Sby 10/91 6,600
O/M 16x20 Hospitalisation de Philome Obin Chr 5/92 ... 4,400
O/B/M 15x20 Women Washing Clothes Sby 11/91 3,575
Obin, Seneque   Hai 1893-1977
O/M 21x24 1905 (Country Landscape) Chr 5/92 9,020
O/B 18x24 Fishing by Night Chr 5/92 6,600
O/M 20x24 A Table Sby 11/91 5,775
O/M 14x13 Nature Morte Chr 11/91 4,620
Obin, Telemaque   Hai
O&Pe/M 20x24 Two: Limbe; Fifi et sa Fille Chr 5/92 1,320
Obregon, Alejandro   Spa 1920-
O/C 29x22 Flores Sby 5/92 25,300
O/C 33x19 Condor Sby 11/91 17,600
I&S/Pa/B 22x30 Composicion Sby 5/92 3,850
Ochtervelt, Jacob   Dut 1635-1682
* See 1991 Edition ....
Ochtman, Leonard   Am 1854-1935
G/B 12x16 Rolling Hills Wes 5/92 495
O/Pn 8x11 Winter Landscape Hnz 10/91 425
Odie, Walter M.   Am 1808-1865
O/C 25x30 Fishing on a Gentle River 1858 Sby 4/92 2,200
O/C 20x25 Figure on Horseback 1852 Slo 9/91 450
Odierna, Guido   It 19C
O/C 20x24 Still Life of Flowers Sel 9/91 300
Oehlen, Albert   1954-
O&MM/C 75x95 Rock N' Roll Beerdigung 85 Chr 5/92 ... 20,900
O/C 95x79 Untitled Chr 5/92 19,800
O&Pl/C 79x78 Loves Body 85 Chr 2/92 15,400
Oehmichen, Hugo   Ger 1843-1933
O/C 24x20 The Sewing Lesson Sby 5/92 11,000
Oertel, Johannes Adam Simon   Am 1823-1909
* See 1992 Edition ....
Ogilvie, John Clinton   Am 1836-1900
O/C 16x12 Putnam Ct. Scene Mys 6/92 495
Ogilvy, Charles   Eng 1832-1890
O/C 20x30 Ship Rathfern 1874 Slo 7/92 1,500
Oguiss, Takanori   Jap 1900-
* See 1992 Edition ....
Ohlson, Doug   1936-
A/C 76x78 Cherry Chr 2/92 1,100
O/C 32x33 Untitled 1979 Chr 2/92 300
Ohtake, Tomie   Jap 1913-
* See 1990 Edition ....
Okada, Kenzo   Am 1902-
O/C 58x56 No. 8 Sby 2/92 63,250
O/C 63x51 A Grove Chr 5/92 24,200
Okubo, Mine   Am 1913-
W/Pa 14x18 New York City Buildings 39 Slo 7/92 275
Olbrich, W.   Aus 20C
O/C 32x50 Rushing Waters Hnd 10/91 750
Oldenburg, Claes   Am 1929-
C&W/Pa 19x14 Study for the Stake Hitch 83 Sby 11/91 .. 22,000
K,Y&W/Pa 24x18 Ironing Board 63 Sby 10/91 9,900

W&Y/Pa 14x17 Two Purses 63 Sby 10/91 9,900
W&Pe/Pa 9x12 Sketch for Feasible Monument 72 Sby 11/91 8,250
Y&K/Pa 22x15 Untitled '84 Chr 5/92 1,320

Oldenhave, A.   Eur 20C
O/Pn 7x9 London Street Scene Slo 4/92 140

Oldfield, Otis   Am 1890-1969
* See 1992 Edition ....

Oleson, Olaf
O/B 12x16 April Woods - Palisades 1924 Ald 5/92 225

Olinsky, Ivan G.   Am 1878-1962
O/C 36x30 Girl in Folk Blouse Lou 12/91 3,000
O/Pn 10x6 Portrait of Rosalind Marks But 4/92 2,200
Pe/Pa 19x19 Study for Farmer Roscoe Brd 8/92 231

Olinsky, Tosca   Am 1909-1984
* See 1992 Edition ....

Olitski, Jules   Am 1922-1964
A/C 80x56 Wand 1965 Sby 5/92 38,500
A/C 73x55 First Love-2 1972 Sby 5/92 11,000
A/C 56x17 V 1966 Chr 5/92 11,000
A/C 93x51 First Love--22 1972 Chr 5/92 9,350
A/C 65x19 Divine Hostage - 4 1973 Chr 11/91 6,600

Oliva, F.
O/C 32x51 Far Away Thoughts Ald 5/92 5,500

Olive, Jacinto   Spa 1896-1967
* See 1991 Edition ....

Oliveira, Nathan   Am 1928-
O/C 42x40 Seated Man 60 Sby 2/92 68,750
O/C 60x52 Seated Man '72 But 5/92 33,000
W&Pe/Pa 12x9 Head '59 Sby 2/92 3,850
W/Pa 18x14 Untitled, 1965 '65 But 5/92 2,200

Oliver, Archer James   Eng 1774-1842
O/C 30x25 Portrait of Miss Hardinge 1809 Slo 10/91 2,100

Oliver, C.   Am 20C
O/C 16x20 Forest Stream Yng 2/92 100

Oliver, Clark   Am 19C
O/C 12x18 Ships in Harbor; Sunset Slo 9/91 400

Oliver, H.   Br 19C
O/C 24x20 Snowball Time Sby 1/92 1,200

Oliver, Myron   Am 1891-1967
* See 1992 Edition ....

Oliver, Thomas Clarkson   Am 1827-1893
* See 1991 Edition ....

Oliver, William   Br 1805-1853
O/C 30x20 Young Woman in Classical Dress Sby 1/92 3,575
O/C 54x35 Portrait of a Lady Seated Sel 4/92 3,250

Olivera, Nathan   Am 1928-
* See 1992 Edition ....

Olivetti, Luigi   It 19C
W/Pa 22x15 Water Carrier by an Arched Doorway Chr 2/92 2,640
W/B 20x14 Spinning Thread 1904 Chr 5/92 1,430
W/Pa 21x15 Spinning Yarn by a Terrace Chr 2/92 1,320
W/Pb 22x15 Boy Fishing off a Rock 1913 Chr 5/92 1,100
W/Pa 21x14 Maiden Spinning Yarn Slo 9/91 1,100

Olivier, Michel-Barthelemy   Fr 1712-1784
* See 1992 Edition ....

Ollefavre   20C
O/C 20x26 Pointers Hnd 3/92 900

Oller, Francisco   Am 1833-1917
* See 1991 Edition ....

Olleros y Quintana, Blas   It 1851-1919
O/Pn 9x18 At the Beach Sby 2/92 8,250

Ollivier, Michel Barthelemy   Fr 1712-1784
O/C 17x13 Fetes Galantes: Pair Chr 5/92 57,200

**Olsen, Christian Benjamin   Dan
1873-1935**
O/C 8x12 Santa Cruz Terrirife 1923 Durn 1/92 350
O/C 9x16 Tarifa 29 Durn 1/92 350

Olsen, M.   Am 20C
O/Cb 14x18 Harvest Slo 9/91 60

Olson, Joseph Olaf   Am 1894-1979
W/Pa 16x22 Winter Landscape with Bird '62 Wlf 6/92 225

**Ommeganck, Balthasar Paul   Flm
1755-1826**
* See 1992 Edition ....

Onderdonk, Julian   Am 1882-1922
O/B 6x9 A Summer Evening 1909 Chr 9/91 4,400
O/C 16x24 Spring Blossoms Chr 9/91 4,400
O/C 9x12 Autumn Afternoon 1908 Wlf 9/91 2,600

**Onderdonk, Robert Jenkins   Am
1853-1917**
* See 1992 Edition ....

Ongania, Umberto   It 20C
W/Pa 16x11 Grand Canal Hnd 5/92 275
W/Pa 8x16 Grand Canal, Venice Slo 9/91 200

Onkley, Thornton
O/C 27x18 The Train Shed Durn 11/91 225

Onley, Toni   Can 1928-
W/Pa 11x15 4 Watercolours '86 Sbt 5/92 2,805

Onslow-Ford, Gordon   20C
* See 1992 Edition ....

Opdenhoff, George Willem   Dut 1807-1873
O/Pn 10x15 Shipping in an Estuary Chr 2/92 7,150

Operti, Albert Jasper   Am 1852-1922
* See 1992 Edition ....

Opfer, Gustav   Ger 1876-
O/C 28x19 Spring Blossoms Chr 10/91 3,850

Opie, John   Br 1761-1807
* See 1992 Edition ....

Opie, Julian   1958-
O/Me 19x13 Blues '83 Chr 2/92 1,540

Oppenheim, Dennis   Am 1938-
* See 1992 Edition ....

Oppenheimer, Josef   Ger 1876-1966
P/Pa 25x19 Portrait of a Young Woman 31 Hnd 12/91 1,000

Opper, Frederick   Am 1857-1937
Pl&W/Pa 28x22 Comic: Happy Hooligan 1908 Ilh 5/92 950

Opsomer, Isidore   Bel 1878-1967
* See 1992 Edition ....

Orange, Maurice Henri   Fr 1868-1916
* See 1991 Edition ....

Orchardson, Sir William Q.   Br 1832-1910
* See 1992 Edition ....

Ord, Joseph Blays   Am 1805-1865
* See 1990 Edition ....

**Ordinaire, Marcel & Courbet, G   Fr
1848-1896**
* See 1992 Edition ....

Ordonez, Sylvia   Mex 1957-
* See 1990 Edition ....

Ordway, Alfred T.   Am 1819-1897
O/C 24x40 Early Summer '71 Skn 5/92 2,200
O/B 12x15 Bridge Yng 4/92 150

Organ, Marjorie   Am 1886-1931
Y/Pa 14x10 Grimaces, and Lady: Two Wes 11/91 165
I/Pa 10x7 Two: Lady and Little Girl Sel 12/91 50

Orizzonte   Dut 1662-1749
* See 1991 Edition ....

Orlando, Felipe   Cub 1911-
O/C 35x24 The Lamp 50 Slo 4/92 2,000

**Orlovsky, Vladmir Donatovitch   Rus
1842-1914**
O/C/Pn 39x23 Country Scenes: Four Sby 5/92 13,200

Orozco, Jose Clemente   Mex 1883-1949
O/C 29x24 Autorretrato 1938 Sby 11/91 231,000
W&Pe/Pa 9x13 La Cortina Roja Chr 11/91 71,500
G/Pa 14x19 Parnaso Mexica Chr 5/92 44,000
O/C/B 19x15 Torso Chr 11/91 24,200
O/C/M 12x15 Estado Mayor de Bufones Chr 5/92 17,600
I&S/Pa 9x13 Untitled Sby 11/91 12,100
Br&I/Pa 15x12 La Pareja Chr 5/92 6,600

**Orpen, William Newenham Montag   Br
1878-1931**
* See 1990 Edition ....

Orr, Eric   Am 20C
* See 1992 Edition ....

Orselli, Arturo   It 19C
* See 1992 Edition ....

Ortega, Al   Am 20C
O/C 58x48 Three Figures Fre 12/91 300

Ortego   Spa 19C
O/Pn 9x7 Daydreams 1878 Slo 4/92   350
Ortkens, Aert   Dut 16C
* See 1990 Edition
Ortlieb, Friedrich   Ger 1839-1909
O/C 30x40 The Right Note Sby 2/92   9,900
Ortlip, Aimee E.   Am 1888-
* See 1992 Edition
Orwig, Louise   Am 20C
O/Ab 10x9 Concarneau, France 1926 Wlf 10/91   200
Osborne, Emily May   Br 1834-1893
W/Pa 11x9 Children in a Field 1853 Hnd 5/92   700
Osborne, S. M.   Am 19C
* See 1992 Edition
Ossorio, Alfonso   Am 1916-
MM/Pn 32x23 Maxie 68 Sby 10/91   4,950
Osterberg, E.   Am 20C
O/B 12x9 Indian Chief 1924 Sel 9/91   140
Ostersetzer, Carl   Ger 19C
* See 1992 Edition
Osthaus, Edmund Henry   Am 1858-1928
O/C 48x72 Hunting Dogs 1890 Chr 12/91   38,500
O/C 19x50 At the Rendezvous Sby 12/91   33,000
O/C 28x22 Retrieving 1891 Sby 12/91   27,500
O/C 22x36 Short-Haired Pointer Puppies 1893 Sby 6/92 .   23,100
O/C 24x30 On the Scent Sby 6/92   11,000
W/B 22x30 Three on Point Sby 6/92   11,000
O/C 14x24 Five Puppies with Quail Hnd 10/91   10,000
W/Pa 18x16 An Awkward Moment Sby 6/92   7,700
W&G/Pa/B 15x20 Hunting Dogs 98 Chr 3/92   7,700
W/Pa 18x24 On the Scent Hnd 10/91   6,000
W/Pa 11x15 Following the Scent Sby 6/92   3,850
O/C 26x54 Autumn View; Dawn Slo 9/91   3,250
W/Pa 20x15 Brood of Young Grouse Wes 11/91   2,200
O/C 30x40 Two Pointers Wlf 3/92   1,300
Pe/Pa 4x8 Two Hunting Dogs at Waters Edge Dum 7/92 . . .   600
Otero, Alejandro   Ven 1921-
Du/Wd 79x22 Tablon 55 1976 Chr 11/91   33,000
Otis, Bass   Am 1784-1861
O/Pn 46x36 Mother & Child 1838 Wlf 6/92   4,100
Otis, George Demont   Am 1879-1962
O/C 30x40 View Through the Aspen But 2/92   11,000
O/C 28x36 Muir Beach - Pacific Shores But 2/92   7,700
O/Pn 20x24 The Desert Bloom 31 Sby 4/92   4,400
O/Pn 9x12 Mexican Shack, 1930 But 10/91   3,850
O/C 16x20 The Settlement But 6/92   2,750
O/B 16x20 California Bungalow, Santa Paula Lou 6/92   2,600
O/B 9x12 Landscape - Foothills Mor 3/92   2,250
Ott, Jerry   Am 20C
* See 1992 Edition
Ott, Sabina   1955-
* See 1992 Edition
Otte, William Louis   Am 1871-1957
O/B 14x22 West Wind But 2/92   6,050
Ottesen, Otto Didrik   Dan 1816-1892
O/C 11x16 Bouquet of Spring Flowers 1869 Sby 5/92   8,800
O/Pn 8x10 Still Life with Strawberries Chr 2/92   5,500
Ottini, Pasquale   It 1580-1630
* See 1992 Edition
Ottmann, Henri   Fr 1877-1927
* See 1992 Edition
Otto, Carl   Ger 1830-1902
* See 1992 Edition
Oudinot, Achille   Fr 1820-1891
O/C 52x39 Banks of the River 1878 Skn 11/91   10,450
Oudot, Roland   Fr 1897-1981
O/C 26x36 Landscape Trees and Church Sby 2/92   4,675
O/C 23x36 Nature Morte Fleurs et Fruits Chr 11/91   4,620
O/C 9x13 Les Baigneuses Chr 11/91   2,420
O/C 9x13 Les Nymphes Chr 11/91   2,420
Oudry, Jacques-Charles   Fr 1720-1778
* See 1991 Edition
Oudry, Jean Baptiste   Fr 1686-1755
* See 1992 Edition

Oulton, Therese   1953-
O/C 30x45 Incognita IV-V '85 Chr 5/92   5,500
Ouren, Karl   Nor 1882-1943
* See 1992 Edition
Outcault, Richard F.   Am 1863-1923
I&S/Pa 15x23 Ballerina Examines Flowers 1899 Ih 5/92 . . .   4,000
Outin, Pierre   Fr 1840-1899
* See 1991 Edition
Ovens, Jurgen   Ger 1623-1678
O/C 52x67 Portrait of a Family 1659 Sby 1/92   126,500
Oviatt
C&Pe/Pa 24x20 Sculptor with Assistant Ih 11/91   900
Pe,C&G/Pa 24x20 Fishing in Bizarre Landscape Ih 5/92   500
Oviedo, Ramon   LA 1927-
O&L/C 40x50 Prisa Para Que Sby 11/91   7,150
MM/C 40x50 Colombinos Sby 5/92   6,600
MM/C 30x40 Escena en Rojo Chr 5/92   4,400
Owen, C. B.   Am 20C
O/C 16x12 Girl with Poultry Fre 4/92   550
Owen, Robert Emmett   Am 1878-1959
O/C 25x30 Winter Sun Litchfield, Connecticut Doy 12/91 . .   4,500
O/C 20x24 Farm Road in Winter Yng 4/92   2,500
O/C 30x36 Autumn Landscape Lou 12/91   2,300
O/C 16x20 Red Barn/Winter Skn 3/92   2,200
O/C 13x16 Winter Snow Scene Mys 11/91   1,375
Ozawa, Kiyoshi   Jap 20C
O/C 13x16 Untitled 47 Wlf 3/92   110
Ozenfant, Amedee   Fr 1886-1966
O/C 18x24 Trois Yachts Sby 2/92   17,600
Ozols, Vilis   Rus 1929-
O/M 22x25 Table Top Still Life Skn 3/92   990
Paalen, Wolfgang   Mex 1905-1959
* See 1991 Edition
Paap, Hans   Am 1894-1966
O/C 16x19 Landscape Mor 3/92   350
Pacecco De Rosa   It 1600-1654
* See 1992 Edition
Pachaubes
O/C 10x8 Empire Trompell Du: Pair Dum 6/92   650
Pacheco, Fernando Castro   Mex 1918-
O/C 24x19 Woman Draped with a Cloth 55 Wlf 6/92   900
Pacheco, Maria Luisa   Bol 1919-
* See 1992 Edition
Pacher, Ferdinand   Ger 1852-1911
* See 1991 Edition
Paddock, Ethel Louise   Am 1887-
O/C 24x20 Rambler Roses Lou 3/92   50
Padilla, J.
* See 1992 Edition
Pagan, Luigi   It 20C
O/C 28x40 St. Mark's Hnd 10/91   200
Page, Edward A.   Am 1850-1928
* See 1991 Edition
Page, Marie Danforth   Am 1869-1940
O/C 36x30 Her Littlest One 1915 Skn 3/92   16,500
Page, Walter Gilman   Am 1862-1934
* See 1992 Edition
Page, William   Br 1794-1872
* See 1992 Edition
Pagels, Herman J.   Ger a 1876-1935
* See 1992 Edition
Pages, Jules Eugene   Am 1867-1946
* See 1992 Edition
Pages, Jules Francois   Am 1833-1910
O/C 10x14 Still Life--Pan w/Vegetables '02 Mor 11/91 . . .   1,400
Paglaicci, Aldo   It 1913-
O/C 22x17 Donne Nude 57 Chr 11/91   1,760
Pagliei, Gioacchino   It -1896
O/C 40x27 Life Study of Standing Male Nude 1880 Slo 2/92   1,700
Paice, George   Br a 1878-1900
O/C 13x17 Royal Scots Steeplechase: Four Sby 6/92   3,025
O/C 14x18 Topper '10 Wes 11/91   550
Pail, Edouard   Fr 1851-
* See 1992 Edition

Pailier, Henri   Fr 19C
* See 1991 Edition . . . .
Pain, Robert Tucker   Eng a 1863-1877
O/C 29x35 Near Pandy Mill, North Wales 1864 Slo 12/91 . . 2,250
Pairon, A.   Fr 19C
O/C 14x26 Coastal Scene Hnd 6/92 150
Pajou, Augustin   Fr 1730-1809
* See 1992 Edition . . . .
Pal, Fried   Hun 1914-
O/C 40x30 Fishing Village But 5/92 1,540
O/C 24x30 Nanette Wes 11/91 1,045
K/Pa 11x14 Nude Hnz 5/92 160
Palacios, Alirio   Ven 1944-
MM/Pa/C 72x74 Series Magical Horses 89 Chr 11/91 19,800
MM/Pa/C 55x65 Jinete y Caballo 89 Chr 5/92 13,200
Paladino, Mimmo   It 1948-
O&Wd/C 87x159 Red Horse 1984 Chr 5/92 132,000
O&Gd/L 28x20 Poeta all'Ombra 1982 Chr 5/92 51,700
O&MM/C 63x120 Hunt, Things of House 1980 Sby 2/92 . 35,750
K&I/Pa 19x27 Untitled 1982 Chr 11/91 6,600
K&O/Pa 19x27 Untitled 1982 Chr 2/92 5,500
K&O/Pa 19x27 Untitled 1982 Chr 2/92 5,500
WPlH&L/Pa 12x16 Untitled 1984 Chr 5/92 5,500
Palaez, Antonio   Mex 1931-
O/C 55x47 Elementus Opuestos, No. 1 Hnd 5/92 275
Palamedes, Anthonie   Dut 1601-1673
O/C 31x26 Portrait Old Woman, Age 79 1659 Sby 5/92 . . 8,250
O/Pn 5x6 Elegant Couple in an Interior Sby 1/92 5,500
Palamedesz., Palamedes   Dut 1607-1638
O/Pn 18x24 Military Skirmish on a Bridge Sby 10/91 . . 14,300
Palanquinos Master   15C
O&T/Pn 49x35 Battle Scene Sby 10/91 39,600
Palanti, Giuseppe   It 1881-1946
O/Pn 13x22 Laghetto a Madonna di Campiglio Chr 5/92 . . 2,200
Palermo, Blinky   Am 20C
MM/Pb 14x11 Untitled '66 Sby 11/91 24,200
I,Mk&Pe/Pa 12x13 Plan for Mural: Two 69 Sby 11/91 . . 12,100
Fp/Pa 29x20 Untitled Sby 11/91 8,250
Palermo, Salvatore   Am 20C
W/Pa 15x22 Still Life #31 1931 Fre 10/91 30
Palicio, Fernando   Spa 1920-
O/B 10x8 Hand with Cards, Flowers: Two Hnz 5/92 160
Palin, William Mainwaring   Br 1862-1947
* See 1991 Edition . . . .
Palizzi, Filippo   It 1818-1899
* See 1992 Edition . . . .
Palizzi, Giuseppe   It 1813-1888
O/C 22x18 View of Roman Ruins Sby 10/91 19,800
Palko, Franz-Xaver-Karl   1724-1767
* See 1991 Edition . . . .
Palladino, Mimmo
* See 1992 Edition . . . .
Pallares Y Allustante, Joaquin   Spa 19C
O/C 13x18 L'Avenue de Champs Elysees Sby 10/91 7,700
O/C 11x16 La Place de la Concorde Sby 10/91 7,700
O/C 11x16 Place de la Concorde But 5/92 5,500
O/Pn 10x13 Ladies Crossing Boulevards of Paris Chr 10/91 5,280
O/Pn 10x13 Ladies Crossing Boulevards of Paris Chr 5/92 . 4,950
Pallissat, C.   Fr 19C
* See 1992 Edition . . . .
Palma II Giovane, Jacopo N.   It 1544-1628
* See 1992 Edition . . . .
Palmaroli Y Gonzalez, Vicente   Spa 1834-1896
O/Pn 23x39 Summer's Afternoon at the Beach Sby 5/92 . . 77,000
O/Pn 21x31 By the Seashore Chr 10/91 33,000
O/Pn 14x10 A Good Book Sby 7/92 6,050
Palmeiro, Jose
* See 1992 Edition . . . .
Palmer, Harry Sutton   Eng 1854-1933
* See 1992 Edition . . . .
Palmer, Herbert Sidney   Can 1881-1970
O/B 10x13 The Gravel Bank Sbt 11/91 2,571
O/B 10x13 Northern Landscape Sbt 11/91 1,590

Palmer, Lynwood   Eng 1868-1941
* See 1990 Edition . . . .
Palmer, Pauline   Am 1865-1938
O/C 36x27 Italian Village with Washerwomen Hnd 5/92 . . 11,000
O/C 46x34 Gordon & Priscilla Pike 1929 Lou 12/91 3,400
O/C/B 40x30 Flower Girl on a Garden Path Hnd 10/91 . . . 3,000
O/C 16x20 Summer Landscape Wtf 9/91 2,600
O/B 20x24 The White Church Hnd 5/92 1,400
O/B 28x22 Red-Headed Girl with Doll Wes 11/91 880
O/C 16x24 Lake Scene Mys 6/92 715
Palmer, R.   Am 20C
O/Ab 5x8 Edge of the Woods Brd 5/92 286
Palmer, R. N.
Pe/Pa 8x18 America Boat Ald 5/92 100
Palmer, Ruth F.   Am 20C
O/C 30x20 Hollyhocks Lou 3/92 150
Palmer, Walter Launt   Am 1854-1932
O/C 30x40 Ice in the Glen Chr 12/91 33,000
O/C 16x23 Twilight World's Columbian Expo. Chr 12/91 . . 22,000
O/C 13x16 Afternoon Idle '82 Chr 9/91 16,500
O/C 17x26 Moonlit Stream in Winter But 11/91 15,400
O/B 29x36 Harvest Time 1881 But 11/91 11,000
G&Pe/Pa/B 18x24 Cottage in the Snow Chr 3/92 6,600
W/Pa 14x17 Autumn Scene With Pumpkin 1884 Hnz 10/91 3,100
Palmer, William   Br 1763-1790
* See 1991 Edition . . . .
Palmer, William Charles   Am 1906-1987
* See 1992 Edition . . . .
Palmezzano, Marco   It 1458-1539
* See 1992 Edition . . . .
Palmieri
O/B 16x20 Child on Shoreline Dum 4/92 800
Paltronieri, Pietro   It 1674-1741
* See 1990 Edition . . . .
Panabaker, Frank Shirley   Can 1904-
* See 1992 Edition . . . .
Pancoast, Henry Boller   Am 1876-
* See 1992 Edition . . . .
Pancoast, Morris Hall   Am 1877-1963
O/C 25x30 Winter Scene 1924 Skn 3/92 9,900
O/Cb 8x10 On the Beach Skn 5/92 2,530
O/C 14x18 A Winter Scene Skn 11/91 1,100
Pancorvo, Alberto   Col 1956-
* See 1991 Edition . . . .
Panerai, Ruggero   It 1862-1923
O/B 7x4 Street Scene Skn 5/92 2,640
Panini, Francesco   It 1725-1794
* See 1992 Edition . . . .
Panini, Giovanni Paolo   It 1691-1765
O/C 40x50 Mediterranean Harbor w/Colonnade Chr 1/92 . 220,000
O/C 20x16 Capricci of Classical Ruins Chr 1/92 66,000
Pannini, Francesco   It a 1790-
* See 1992 Edition . . . .
Pansing, Fred   Am 1844-1916
W/Pb 5x10 A Harbor Scene Chr 11/91 1,650
Panton, Lawrence Arthur Colley   Can 1894-1954
O/B 11x14 Skeleton Lake, Muskoka '38 Sbt 11/91 841
Panza, Giovanni   It 19C
O/C 24x28 A Marketplace Chr 10/91 4,950
Paoletti, Antonio Ermolao   It 1834-1912
* See 1992 Edition . . . .
Paoletti, R.
O/C/B 20x30 Street Boys Playing Cards Dum 5/92 750
Paoletti, Silvio D.   It 1864-1921
O/C 26x38 The Sewing Song Chr 10/91 16,500
Paolilo, Luigi   It 1864-
* See 1992 Edition . . . .
Paolini, Giulio   20C
Pt&Pe/Cot 27x171 Et.Quid. Sby 11/91 33,000
Paolini, Pietro   It 1605-1682
O/C 40x53 The Concert Chr 5/92 187,000
Paolo, Giovanni   It 1691-1786
* See 1990 Edition . . . .

Papaluca, L.   It 20C
O/C 14x22 S.S. Exceller, Export Lines Wes 11/91 358
Papart, Max   Fr 1911-
G,L&l/Pa 12x8 Personnage Chr 11/91 2,420
A&L/Pa 20x25 Along the Seashore Chr 2/92 1,980
A&L/Pa 20x25 Thing of Beauty Chr 2/92 1,870
Fp/Pa 11x8 Portrait d'Homme Chr 11/91 770
Fp/Pa 11x8 Portrait d'homme Chr 5/92 550
Pape, Emile   Hun 1884-
  * See 1992 Edition
Pape, Eric   Am 1870-1938
O/C 59x46 Young Woman with an Umbrella Skn 5/92 . . . 4,125
O/Cb 37x25 The Last Soldier Skn 5/92 3,080
O/C 8x15 View Along the Nile Skn 3/92 1,760
W/Pa 30x18 Symbolic Figure: Moon and Stars 95 Hnd 5/92 . 850
Pape, Friedrich Edouard   Ger 1817-1905
  * See 1990 Edition
Papety, Dominique Louis   Fr 1815-1849
O/C 15x12 Head of a Woman Sby 1/92 1,980
Papperitz, Fritz Georg   Ger 1846-1918
  * See 1992 Edition
Papsdorf, Richard   20C
  * See 1992 Edition
Paradise, Phillip   Am 1905-
W/Pa 18x28 Morning in the Village But 2/92 3,575
W/Pa 16x22 Messengers of Mercy But 6/92 550
Parcell, Malcolm
O/B 10x8 Half-Dressed Woman Seated Wlf 6/92 1,200
Parcy, Sidney Richard   Br 1821-1886
  * See 1990 Edition
Paretto, P. W.   It 20C
O/C 29x25 Madonna and Child Sel 4/92 300
Paris, Alfred Jean Marie   Fr 1846-1908
O/C 43x32 The Return Home 1885 Chr 2/92 4,950
Paris, Walter   Am 1842-1906
  * See 1992 Edition
Parizot, Lily   Fr 1876-
W&G/Pa 11x15 Quai de la Tournelle 1928 But 5/92 468
Park, David   Am 1911-1960
H/Pa 17x14 Standing Couple 1955 Chr 11/91 6,050
G/Pa 9x6 Four Studies for Wallpaper Design But 5/92 . . . 770
Park, John Anthony   Br 1888-1962
  * See 1992 Edition
Park, Stuart   Br 1862-1933
O/C 12x15 Still Life with Daffodils But 5/92 935
Parker, Agnes Miller   Am 20C
O/C 24x18 School Projects 1927 Sby 4/92 3,960
Parker, Al   Am 1906-1985
Var. Var Four Prototype Covers 1967 Ih 11/91 650
W/Pa 16x13 Man Kissing Sleeping Woman 1943 Ih 5/92 . . . 600
Parker, Bill   Am 20C
  * See 1991 Edition
Parker, Cushman   Am 1882-1940
O/C 24x30 Family at Breakfast. Kellogg's Ih 5/92 2,750
Parker, George Waller   Am 1888-1957
  * See 1992 Edition
Parker, Henry H.   Br 1858-1930
O/C 24x36 Harvest Time on the Sussex Coast Hnd 12/91 . 10,500
O/C 25x37 Near Goreing on the Thames Dum 12/91 8,000
O/C 24x36 When the Day's Work is Done Sby 7/92 7,700
O/C 17x28 Near Great Marlow, on Thames Chr 2/92 7,150
O/C 20x30 Banks of the Thames Chr 5/92 3,500
O/C 24x36 Clearing the Meadow Chr 10/91 2,750
Parker, John Adams   Am 1829-1905
  * See 1991 Edition
Parker, Lawton S.   Am 1868-1954
O/C 26x32 Reclining Nude Mor 6/92 22,500
MM/Pa 10x7 Figure in Interior Mor 3/92 1,000
MM/Pa 7x5 Flowers in Interior Mor 11/91 800
Parker, Ray   Am 1922-
  * See 1992 Edition
Parker, Robert   Am 20C
W/Pa 18x19 World Leaders 54 Hnz 5/92 50
Parker, S.   Am 20C
O/C 42x32 Portrait of a Girl with a Kitten 1916 Hnd 10/91 . . 750

Parkhurst, Thomas   Am 1853-1923
O/C 26x30 A Summer Sea But 10/91 1,100
Parra, Carmen
  * See 1992 Edition
Parrish, David   Am 1939-
  * See 1991 Edition
Parrish, Maxfield   Am 1870-1966
O/Pa 21x16 The Dinkey-Bird 1904 Sby 9/91 126,500
O/Pn 16x20 Little Sugar River: Evening Chr 3/92 57,200
W&l/Pa 10x8 The Sign Painter 22 Hnd 3/92 2,300
Parrish, Steven Windsor   Am 1846-1938
O/C 20x30 On Annisquam River 1919 Skn 5/92 3,300
Parrocel, Charles   Fr 1688-1752
  * See 1990 Edition
Parrott, William Samuel   Am 1844-1915
  * See 1992 Edition
Parshall, Dewitt   Am 1864-1956
O/B 16x20 Moonlight Grand Canyon But 2/92 1,320
O/C 9x7 Portrait of Girl Mor 11/91 350
P&G/Pb 12x15 Gaviota Ledges 1947 Ald 5/92 160
Parsons, Beatrice   Eng 1870-1955
W/Pa 10x14 Formal Garden Slo 7/92 2,500
Parsons, Betty   1900-1982
O/C 49x40 Magic 57 Chr 11/91 1,100
Parsons, Marion Randall   Am 1878-1953
  * See 1992 Edition
Parsons, Orrin Sheldon   Am 1866-1943
O/C 12x16 Pena Blanca Dum 1/92 1,500
Partington, Richard Langtry   Am 1868-1929
O/C 8x14 Summer Beach Scene Bor 8/92 600
O/C 12x16 Swimming Hole Bor 8/92 300
O/C 52x30 Portrait of a Lady 1923 Fre 12/91 200
Parton, Arthur   Am 1842-1914
O/C 8x13 Afternoon on the Lake 1868 Chr 11/91 2,640
O/C 12x20 Landscape with Sheep 1866 Sby 12/91 2,200
O/C 12x20 Cows Grazing by a Stream Sby 4/92 2,090
Parton, Ernest   Am 1845-1933
O/Cb 10x14 The Lily Pond Chr 3/92 3,850
O/C 23x17 Deep in the Woods Skn 3/92 880
Partridge, Alfred A.   Br 20C
O/C 18x24 Black Hunter; Bay Hunter: Pair '90 But 11/91 . . 1,980
Pascal, Paul   Fr 1832-1904
G&W/Pb 18x25 An Arab Caravan 1900 Chr 5/92 1,320
W/Pa 7x9 Arab Boatmen Hnz 10/91 120
Pascal, Paul B.   Fr 1867-
G/Pa 17x25 View of the Pyramids Chr 10/91 1,430
Paschke, Ed   Am 1939-
O/C 42x80 Coupe Fairn 1985 Chr 11/91 35,200
O/L 68x80 Joeski '86 Chr 2/92 26,400
O/L 34x70 Transactionale '81 Chr 5/92 24,200
O/C 46x36 Spiro T. Agnew and Go-Go-Girl '77 Hnd 5/92 . 7,000
Pascin, Jules   Fr 1885-1930
O/Pn 14x17 Femme Couchante Sby 11/91 121,000
W&Pl/Pa 8x12 Au Cafe Chr 11/91 6,600
I&W/Pa 8x10 Femme Nue 1912 Sby 10/91 3,025
Pe/Pa 12x15 Femme assise Chr 5/92 2,860
Pl&W/Pa 9x11 Three Female Nudes Sby 2/92 2,750
Pe/Pa 19x25 Two Women on a Sofa Sby 2/92 2,750
Pe&W/Pa 8x3 Femme Orientale/Circus Figure: Pair Sby 2/92 . 1,650
Pl&S/Pa 6x5 Jeune Femme a la Fenetre Sby 2/92 1,650
W,G&Pl/Pa 6x5 Two Women Chr 5/92 1,650
W/Pa 5x9 En Attendant L'Autobus 1917 Sby 6/92 1,540
W,Pe&C/Pa 12x10 Femme Allongee Chr 11/91 1,430
Pe&W/Pa 3x4 Three Drawings Sby 2/92 1,430
C/Pa 13x17 Reclining Nude Sby 6/92 1,320
W&Pl/Pa 8x11 Three Drawings Chr 11/91 1,320
H/Pa 8x11 3 Figures--Lying Down Skn 9/91 1,100
Pl/B 5x7 At the Dance Sby 6/92 770
I/Pa 12x8 Caricature Sketches '39 Slo 7/92 350
Y/Pa 12x6 Standing Female Nude Hnd 10/91 350
Pashley, E.   Eng 19C
O/C 19x13 Peaches Fre 4/92 675
Pasini   It 19C
  * See 1992 Edition

Pasini, Alberto It 1826-1899
O/C 14x11 Marketday, Constantinople 1887 Sby 10/91 . . . 77,000
O/C 14x11 Porto Custodia della Madonna 1879 Chr 10/91 . 8,800
Pasini, V. It 19C
W/Pa/C 15x10 Young Boys on a Canal Sby 1/92 715
Paskell, William Am 1866-1951
O/B 6x10 Sunset Over the Marshes Yng 4/92 350
W/Pa 14x10 Birch Trees Yng 4/92 250
W/Pa 8x12 Winter Snow Scene Mys 11/91 121
W/Pa 8x12 Coastal Scene Mys 11/91 82
O/C 16x20 Harbour Scene Mys 6/92 82
W/Pa 10x14 Windmill Scene Mys 11/91 82
O/C 20x25 Seascape Ald 3/92 25
Pasmore, Daniel Br 1829-1891
O/C 21x26 The Trinket Box 1847 Sby 1/92 3,300
O/C 16x12 The Hurdy-Gurdy Player 1857 Sby 1/92 2,970
Pasmore, Victor Br 1908-
* See 1992 Edition
Passey, Charles H. Br a 1883-1885
* See 1992 Edition
Passot, Nicolas 1521-
O/C 49x63 Elaborate Church Interior Sby 5/92 33,000
Pastega, Luigi It 1858-1927
O/C 21x14 The Watercarrier Chr 5/92 4,400
Pasternak, Leonid Ossipovitch Rus 1862-1945
P/Pa 23x18 Portrait of Judith Spat Doy 11/91 3,000
Pastina, Ed It 19C
O/C 40x54 Nomad in Architectural Ruins 1855 Fre 10/91 . . 8,000
Pata, Cherubin Fr 19C
* See 1990 Edition
Pata, Cherubin & Courbet, G. Fr 19C
* See 1992 Edition
Patel, Pierre Antoine (II) Fr 1605-1676
Bc/V 7x10 Mountainous Landscape Chr 1/92 6,600
Pater, Jean-Baptiste Fr 1695-1736
O/C 21x26 Figures Bathing at a Fountain: Pair Sby 5/92 . 577,500
Paterson, Caroline Br a 1878-1892
W&G/Pa 14x12 The Doctor Sby 2/92 4,950
Patin, C. Con 19C
O/C 24x36 Landscape with Shepherdess Slo 10/91 250
Patin, S. Am 20C
O/C 20x15 Girl in a Meadow Dum 8/92 60
Patino, Virgilio Col 1947-
O/C 55x40 Paisaje del Valle del Cauca 1990 Chr 5/92 . . . 7,700
Patkin, Izhar 20C
* See 1992 Edition
Paton, Phil Am 20C
O/B 10x12 Monterey Coastal Mor 3/92 250
Patrois, Isidore Fr 1815-1884
* See 1991 Edition
Pattein, Cesar Fr a 1882-1914
O/C 31x46 Children Fishing 1894 Sby 2/92 8,525
Patten, George Br 1801-1865
* See 1991 Edition
Patterson, Charles Robert Am 1878-1958
* See 1992 Edition
Patterson, Howard Ashman Am 1891-
* See 1992 Edition
Patterson, Margaret Jordan Am 1867-1950
G/Pa 18x13 San Luis Obispo, Lisbon 1909 Wes 3/92 935
G/Pa 18x13 St. Louis Abispo--Lisbon 1909 Hnd 10/91 . . . 550
G/Cd 14x19 Fuenterrabia, Spain Wes 11/91 330
Patterson, Russell Am 20C
* See 1991 Edition
Pattison, Abbott Am 1916-
O/C 28x42 Abstract Composition 1950 Hnd 5/92 450
O/C 20x13 Sculpture Study Hnd 3/92 275
Pattison, James W. Am 1844-1915
* See 1992 Edition
Pattison, Robert J. Am 1898-1981
* See 1991 Edition
Patty, William Arthur Am 1889-1961
O/M 22x30 Harbor--Sailboats Mor 11/91 850

O/Cb 10x8 Fishing Boat--San Pedro, Ca Mor 11/91 400
Paul, Charles R. Am 20C
G/Pa 17x13 View of the Drake Hotel Fre 4/92 225
Paul, John Br 19C
O/C 49x74 View of Old Northumberland House Sby 5/92 . 63,250
O/C 30x50 Hampton Court Bridge, Middlesex Sby 5/92 . . . 7,150
O/C 20x24 Bay Stallion in a Stall 1872 Chr 5/92 1,650
Paul, Joseph Eng 1804-1887
O/C 30x26 Fisherman on a Bridge But 5/92 4,400
Paulman, Joseph Con 19C
* See 1992 Edition
Paulsen, N. Chr. Dan 19C
O/C 29x45 Naval Gun Battle Dum 9/91 4,750
Paulucci, Enrico
O/C 24x28 Scogli 1957 Sby 2/92 3,000
Paulus, Francis Petrus Am 1862-1933
O/Pn 15x12 Portrait of Robert Hopkin Dum 8/92 1,900
Paulus, Fritz Sws 1891-1968
O/B 35x27 Alpine Scene 1943 Hnz 5/92 100
Paulus, Josef Ger 1877-
O/C 22x31 Bringing in the Days Catch Wlf 3/92 750
Pavelic, Myfanwy Spencer Can 1916-
P/Pa 16x13 Nude 1980 Sbt 5/92 1,122
Pavesi, Pietro It 19C
* See 1992 Edition
Pavil, Elie Anatole Fr 1873-1948
O/C 15x22 Au Bord de la Seine Sby 7/92 2,640
Pavlosky, Vladmir Am 20C
O/C 25x30 Canoeing, Early Autumn Skn 11/91 715
Pawla, Frederick Alexander Am 1877-
O/C 30x35 Sailing Ship Lou 3/92 900
Pawley, James Br a 1854-1869
O/C 31x37 The Pet Cockatoo Sby 10/91 12,650
Paxson, Edgar Samuel Am 1852-1919
O/C 40x28 The War Party 1901 Sby 5/92 18,700
O/B 18x40 The Golden West 1910 Sby 3/92 10,450
Paxson, Ethel Easton Am 1885-1982
* See 1992 Edition
Paxton, Elizabeth V. O. Am 1877-1971
* See 1990 Edition
Paxton, William McGregor Am 1869-1941
O/M 20x24 The Red Mules Chr 5/92 33,000
O/C 15x18 Gloucester Harbor Yng 4/92 700
Pay, Michel Fr 19C
O/C 54x45 Scene sur le Lac Smere 1874 Sby 7/92 1,650
Payne, Charlie Johnson Br 1884-1967
* See 1990 Edition
Payne, David Br 19C
* See 1992 Edition
Payne, Edgar Alwyn Am 1882-1947
O/C 24x28 The Sierra Divide 1921 But 2/92 74,250
O/C 36x45 Hills of Altadena Chr 6/92 28,600
O/C 25x30 Morning Harbor Scene But 10/91 19,800
O/C 18x19 Tuna Boats But 2/92 19,800
O/C 34x34 Long Lake But 10/91 16,500
O/C 25x30 Mountain Lake Sby 3/92 16,500
O/C 24x28 Adriatic Ships Mor 3/92 15,000
O/C 20x24 Snowcapped Mountains Sby 3/92 13,750
O/C 18x41 Blue Hills Chr 6/92 13,200
O/C 22x26 Palisade Glacier But 2/92 13,200
O/C 16x20 Landscape - Foothills Mor 3/92 13,000
O/C 29x29 Day's End at the Harbor Chr 9/91 9,900
O/C 24x20 Reflected Sails, Chioggia But 6/92 9,900
O/C 20x24 Adriatic Fishing Boats Mor 6/92 9,000
O/C 15x19 High Sierras But 10/91 8,800
O/C 20x24 Mount Ritter Sby 9/91 7,700
O/C 16x20 Landscape Mor 3/92 7,000
O/Cb 13x15 Boats in Harbor Mor 3/92 6,500
O/C/B 12x16 Laguna Canyon Mor 3/92 6,500
O/C/B 10x12 Adriatic Fishing Boats But 2/92 6,050
O/C 12x16 Landscape/California Mor 11/91 5,000
O/B 13x11 Square Rigger Mor 6/92 5,000
O/Pn 12x16 Mount Robinson But 10/91 4,950
O/C/B 11x15 Sunny Sierra But 2/92 4,675
G/Pa 14x20 California Oaks Mor 6/92 4,500

178

O/Cb 12x16 Sierra Landscape Mor 3/92 4,250
O/C 12x16 Boats in Harbor Mor 6/92 4,000
O/Cb 10x14 Deep in the Sierras But 6/92 3,300
O/C 18x20 Misty Mountains But 10/91 3,025
O/C/Pn 10x12 Mountain View But 10/91 3,025
O/C 12x9 Boats at Dock Mor 11/91 2,500
O/C 9x14 California Mountain Landscape Dum 12/91 2,500
O/Cb 13x15 Clouds Over Sierra Lake Mor 11/91 2,000
O/Cb 12x15 Sierra Landscape Mor 11/91 2,000
MM/Pa 14x14 Boats of Sotto Marino Mor 11/91 900
O/Cb 7x7 Two Saddle Horses Mor 6/92 700
W/Pa 19x14 Mountainous Landscape Chr 6/92 495

Payne, Elsie Palmer Am 1884-1971
G/Pa 19x21 Hillside Homes But 2/92 4,400
G/Pa 12x14 Gallup; Red Cliffs: Four But 6/92 2,750
G/Pa 12x14 Lake Louise; Sierras: Three But 6/92 2,750
O/C 24x20 Giant Magnolia But 10/91 2,090
O/C 20x16 Girl in Red 46 But 10/91 2,090
G/Pa 11x14 California House #2 But 6/92 1,870
O/C 24x20 White Flowers But 10/91 1,650
G/Pa 13x15 Italian Village; Concameau: Two But 6/92 1,540
G/Pa Var Street; Market; Gateway; Chapel: 4 But 6/92 . . . 1,540
O/C 30x25 Dahlias But 10/91 1,430
G/Pa 12x15 Lake Louise But 2/92 1,430
O/C 20x24 Petunias, Fuschias, Daisies But 10/91 1,430
O/C 34x28 A Colored Gentleman But 10/91 1,320
G/Pa 11x9 Venice; Concarneau: Three But 6/92 1,320
G/Pa 12x14 House in Spuyten Duyvil, New York But 6/92 . . 1,210
W/Pa 17x15 MacArthur Park, Los Angeles But 2/92 1,100
O/C 23x18 Roma But 10/91 1,100
G/Pa 18x15 Harbor; U.S. Harbor: Two But 6/92 1,045
W/Pa 18x22 Italian Memory But 2/92 1,045
G/Pa 13x14 Old Chinatown, Los Angeles But 2/92 1,045
O/Cb 12x16 California Houses and Trees But 2/92 990
W/Pa 14x12 Covered Sidewalk, Mariposa But 6/92 990
G/Pa 12x15 Sycamores; Farmhouse: Two But 6/92 935
G/Pa 12x13 Tree: Three But 6/92 935
G/Pa 9x11 Alps; Mountain Trees: Two But 6/92 880
G/B 20x16 House in Spuyten Dayvil But 2/92 880
G/Pa 12x15 Lateen Sails But 6/92 770
O/C 24x20 Head of a Model, Rolene But 2/92 715
G/Pa 12x12 Autumn in Connecticut But 6/92 605
O/B 15x19 Flowers in White Vase Mor 11/91 500

Payzant, Charles Am 19C
W/Pa 17x23 Fisherman Lou 9/91 850

Peale, Anna Claypoole Am 1791-1878
* See 1992 Edition

Peale, Charles Willson Am 1741-1827
O/C 35x27 Portrait Mrs. Joseph Daffin 1790 Fre 10/91 . . . 10,000

Peale, Harriet Cany Am 1800-1869
O/C 30x25 Portrait of a Girl with Bonnet 1854 Chr 9/91 . . . 3,520
O/C 28x23 Portrait of Saint Joseph 1852 Fre 12/91 500

Peale, James Am 1749-1831
O/C 20x27 Still Life with Fruit Sby 3/92 49,500
W/Pa 15x21 Indians in a Canoe 1859 But 4/92 3,850

Peale, Margaretta Am 1795-1882
* See 1991 Edition

Peale, Mary Jane Am 1827-1902
* See 1991 Edition

Peale, Rembrandt Am 1778-1860
* See 1992 Edition

Peale, Rubens Am 1784-1864
O/C 10x14 Still Life Sby 12/91 5,775

Peale, Sarah Miriam Am 1800-1885
* See 1992 Edition

Peale, Titian Ramsey Am 1799-1885
* See 1991 Edition

Pearce, Charles Sprague Am 1851-1914
* See 1990 Edition

Pearlstein, Philip Am 1924-
O/C 26x30 Female Nude Lying Down 63 Sby 10/91 6,600
Br&I/Pa 29x41 Models in Hammock & Chair 75 Chr 2/92 . . 5,500
Pe/Pa 18x15 Female with Hand in Hair 1970 Wtf 3/92 950

Pearson, Cornelius Am 1805-1891
W/Pa 12x22 Perfect View of the Lake 1873 Skn 11/91 550

Pearson, John Loughborough Br 1817-1897
W/Pa 11x18 Loch Windemere Skn 5/92 330

Pearson, Marguerite Stuber Am 1898-1978
* See 1992 Edition

Pease, David Am 20C
O/C 15x15 Valentine Garden Fre 10/91 150

Pease, Ray Am 1908-
O/B 16x14 Sunday Afternoon Wtf 6/92 950
O/B 18x16 Acorn Cafe Wtf 6/92 350

Pecault, C. E. Fr 19C
* See 1992 Edition

Pechaubes, Eugene Fr 1890-1967
* See 1991 Edition

Pecheur, Emile Fr 19C
* See 1991 Edition

Pechstein, Max Ger 1881-1955
O/C 39x30 Madchen Mit Buch Sby 10/91 77,000
W/Pa 19x25 Fruhling I 1922 Chr 11/91 44,000
Y/Pa 9x12 Reusen Vor Gehoft 1927 Sby 10/91 6,600

Peck, Anne M. Am 1884-
O/C 6x7 Still Life of Currants Mys 6/92 550

Peck, Orrin M. Am 1860-1921
* See 1991 Edition

Pecrus, Charles Francois Fr 1826-1907
O/Pn 11x18 Scene du Plage, Trouville 1875 Chr 5/92 . . . 22,000
O/Pn 11x18 La Plage a Trouville Sby 10/91 9,900
O/Pn 21x15 A Sudden Thought Wtf 9/91 2,000

Pedersen, Finn 1944-
O/C 26x32 Untitled 86 Chr 2/92 935

Pedersen-Mols, Niels Dan 1859-
* See 1991 Edition

Pedrini, Giovanni Pietro Rizzo It a 1520-1540
O/Pn 24x20 Virgin and Child w/Infant St. John Sby 1/92 . . 55,000

Pedulli, Federigo It 1860-
W/B 30x21 Il Cortile Del Bargello a Firenze But 11/91 2,750

Peel, James Br 1811-1906
O/C 36x30 Travellers on a Country Path Sby 7/92 2,750
O/C 24x40 Witley, Surrey Sby 7/92 1,000

Peel, Paul Can 1860-1892
O/C 31x22 Portrait Gloria Roberts 1889 Sbt 5/92 22,440
O/C 29x22 Lady Ross Examining Passion Flower Sbt 11/91 11,220
O/C/B 13x16 Woodland Glade 1890 Sbt 11/91 7,480
O/C/B 7x5 Portrait Bearded Gentleman Sbt 5/92 2,805

Peelor, Harold Am 1856-1940
O/B 28x40 Mission San Xavier Del Bac, Tucson But 2/92 . . 2,200

Peeters, Bonaventur (the Elder) Flm 1614-1652
* See 1992 Edition

Peeters, E. Am 19C
* See 1992 Edition

Peeters, Jan Flm 1624-1680
O/C 45x73 Stormy Seascape with Shipping Chr 5/92 22,000

Peirano, * 17C**
O/C 28x34 Still Life Flowers on a Stone Ledge Sby 5/92 . 28,600

Peirce, Waldo Am 1884-1970
O/C 36x48 Clamming on the Beach Brd 8/92 3,080
W&Pe/Pa 21x25 Rural Free Delivery, Study Brd 8/92 1,430
O/C 18x14 Kathy Brd 8/92 1,100
O/C 24x30 Penobscot Valley Country Club 64 Brd 8/92 . . . 1,100
O/C 24x20 M. C. the First Brd 8/92 990
W/Pa 18x24 The Big Pine 1941 Sby 4/92 990
O/C 14x18 Penguins 58 Brd 8/92 742
O/C 20x16 Olga Olinsky, Paris, 1924 Yng 4/92 450
W/Pa 6x9 Army Hospital 43 Brd 8/92 385

Peixotto, Ernest Clifford Am 1869-1940
* See 1992 Edition

Pekarsky, Mel Am 1934-
H/Pa 30x40 Looking South 78 Skn 3/92 138

Pekin, A. G. Am 19C
P/Pa 17x11 Woman with Water Jars Hnz 5/92 50

Pelaez, Amelia Mex 1897-1968
O/C 30x38 Nocturno 1947 Sby 11/91 28,600

O/C/Pn 24x26 Naturaleza Muerta Sby 5/92 20,900

Pelham, Thomas Kent   Eng 19C
* See 1991 Edition . . . .

Pellan, Alfred   Can 1906-
VPa/Pn 8x7 Femmes au Profil Sbt 5/92 8,882

Pellegrini, Riccardo   It 1863-1934
O/B 14x19 Ritorno All'Ovile Sby 10/91 12,100
O/B 14x19 Ritorno Delle Oche Sby 10/91 12,100

Pelletier, Pierre Jacques   Fr 1869-1931
O/C 26x36 Washerwoman by a Riverbank Chr 10/91 5,280

Pellew, John   1903-
W/Pa 14x20 East Gloucester Yng 4/92 275

Pellicciotti, Tito   It 1872-1943
O/C 13x16 Young Music Makers Sby 2/92 9,350

Pellicerotti, Frederico   It 19C
* See 1992 Edition . . . .

Pelouse, Leon Germain   Fr 1838-1891
* See 1992 Edition . . . .

Pelruola, S.
W/Pa 16x30 Women Overlooking a Port City 1897 Ald 5/92 . . 60

Pels, Albert   Am 1910-
O/Pn 19x27 Three Black Musicians Chr 11/91 2,200
O/C 12x16 Waiting Room Train Station Chr 11/91 1,540
O/C 24x18 Coney Island Bather Lou 3/92 1,100
O/C 20x30 Rush Hour Chr 6/92 1,100
O/C 36x24 Towel Turban Hnd 10/91 550
O/C 24x20 Three People and a Unicorn Ald 5/92 450
O/C 20x16 Picketing for Housing and Jobs, 1947 Chr 6/92 . . 440
O/C 36x24 White Towel Turban Chr 6/92 352
O/C 19x15 Picketing for Jobs and Housing 1947 Hnd 10/91 . 250

Peltier   Con 19C
W/Pa 14x24 River Landscape Fre 12/91 170

Peltier, Marcel   Fr 20C
O/C 35x46 Le Port But 5/92 550

Pelton, Agnes   Am 1881-1961
W/Pa 35x29 Gladiolas Chr 11/91 2,860
W/Pa 21x14 Iris Wlf 6/92 1,400

Peluso, Francesco   It 1836-
* See 1991 Edition . . . .

Pena, Angel   Ven 1949-
* See 1992 Edition . . . .

Penck, A. R.   Ger 1939-
O/C 112x112 Untitled Sby 11/91 137,500
O/C 59x59 Standart 3 Chr 5/92 99,000
O/M 69x47 Konzept (First Draft) Sby 5/92 66,000
O/C 59x59 Das Rote Flugzeng 1977 Chr 5/92 38,500
A/Pa 20x33 Untitled Chr 5/92 6,600

Penfield, Anna   Am 19C
* See 1991 Edition . . . .

Penfield, Edward   Am 1866-1925
I&W/Pa 16x17 Knight on Horseback Ih 11/91 3,500
W/Pa 8x12 Horses Walking Along a Spanish Road Ih 5/92 . 1,600

Penfold, Frank C.   Am a 1880-1890
* See 1992 Edition . . . .

Penley, Aaron Edwin   Br 1807-1870
* See 1991 Edition . . . .

Penman, Edith   Am -1929
O/C 16x13 Orientalist Still Life Skn 9/91 715

Pennachini, Domenico   It 1860-
* See 1992 Edition . . . .

Pennell, Joseph   Am 1860-1926
W/Pa 9x12 New York Harbor w/Statue of Liberty Hnd 10/91 2,000
W/Pa 10x13 The Long Night Hnd 10/91 2,000
G,I&Pe/Pa 14x10 The Canongate Edinburgh 1882 Sby 12/91 1,320
PI/Pa 26x20 Mont St. Michel 1902 Dum 12/91 350
PI/Pa 14x10 New York Herald--Naval Review Yng 2/92 350

Pennoyer, Albert Sheldon   Am 1888-1957
O/C 25x30 Rocky Mountain Skiing Scene Skn 9/91 715

Penny, Edward   Br 1714-1791
* See 1991 Edition . . . .

Penny, Edwin   Br 19C
* See 1992 Edition . . . .

Peoli, Juan Jorge   Spa 19C
O/C 36x50 Family Surveying a Dam, Cuba Chr 10/91 6,600

Peploe, Samuel John   Br 1871-1935
* See 1992 Edition . . . .

Pepper, George Douglas   Can 1903-1962
O/B 12x14 Sunlight in Lumber Town Sbt 11/91 3,179

Peraire, Paul Emanuel   Fr 1829-1893
O/C 17x34 Sur la Riviere 1879 Sby 7/92 6,325

Perboyre, Paul Emile Leon   Fr 19C
O/Pn 12x9 Les Cuirassiers Sby 5/92 4,950
O/C 18x22 La Sortie de la Tranchee 1917 Sby 1/92 2,750
O/C 18x22 La Cavalerie Anglaise S'Emparant 1919 Sby 1/92 2,530
O/C 18x22 Artillerie de 75 en Batterie Sby 1/92 2,090
O/C 22x26 Combat de Cavalerie 1916 Sby 1/92 2,090
O/Pn 21x26 Artillerie Allemande 1919 Sby 1/92 1,980
O/C 20x24 Artillerie Allemande Suprise 1914 Sby 1/92 . . . 1,760
O/C 18x22 Convoi de Prisonniers en Picardie 1917 Sby 1/92 1,760
O/C 18x22 Les Allemands Rejetes 1918 Sby 1/92 1,540
O/C 18x22 Otages Delivres Sby 1/92 1,540
O/C 21x26 Prise D'Une Batterie Allemande 1919 Sby 1/92 . 1,540
O/C 18x22 Les Morocains Dans Les Combles Sby 1/92 . . . 1,430

Perceval, Don Lewis   Am 1908-1979
O/C 18x24 Prospector and Donkey Lou 3/92 800

Percival, Phyllis M.   Can 20C
O/C 24x30 Lunenberg Harbour Sbt 5/92 1,215

Percy, Sidney Richard   Br 1821-1886
O/C 36x58 Road to the Rhaiads Dam 1862 Sby 5/92 22,000
O/C 25x38 Llambries Lake, North Wales 1856 Chr 10/91 . . 16,500
O/C 23x33 Landscape with Rustic Cottage Hnd 12/91 4,800

Perehudoff, William   Can 1919-
* See 1992 Edition . . . .

Pereira, Irene Rice   20C
MM/Pn 18x17 Copper Light; Untitled (2) Sby 2/92 5,775
I/Pa 27x20 Figure Studies: Pair 64 Sby 6/92 1,100

Pereny, Madelaine   Am 1896-
O/C 40x37 Escape But 11/91 550

Perez, Alonso   Spa a 1893-1914
O/Pn 16x13 Intermission at the Opera Sby 10/91 11,550
W/Pa 7x10 A Cavalier's Banquet But 5/92 1,650

Perignon, Alexis Joseph   Fr 1806-1882
* See 1990 Edition . . . .

Perilli, Achille
* See 1992 Edition . . . .

Perillo, Gregory   Am 1932-
O/C 30x30 In Enemy Territory '85 Lou 12/91 1,500
O/C 24x30 Blackfoot Brave Sby 4/92 1,100

Perkins, Granville   Am 1830-1895
O/C 12x18 Sailing on Rough Seas 1891 Chr 6/92 5,280
O/C 22x18 Seascape and Woodland: Pair 1894 Sby 12/91 . 2,200
W&G/B 11x28 Stormy Coast 1890 Sby 4/92 935

Perkins, Mary Smyth   Am 1875-1931
O/C 30x36 Canal, New Hope Chr 5/92 15,400
O/C 30x36 Summer Day, Lake Solitude Chr 5/92 8,800

Perkins, Parker S.   Am 1862-
O/B 20x22 Turn of the Tide Mys 6/92 770

Perl, John   Am 20C
W/Pa 18x24 Boat Dock 1943 Hnz 5/92 100

Perlasca, Martino   Sws 1860-1899
O/C 45x34 Still Life Assorted Flowers Chr 5/92 11,000

Perlberg, Friedrich   Am 1848-1921
G/Pa/B 23x17 Old Faithful and Giant Geyser: Two Sby 12/91 660

Perlin, Bernard   Am 1918-
T/B 40x30 Autumn Leaves 1947 Chr 12/91 24,200
T/B 25x18 Divorce Sby 12/91 4,400
T/Pa 13x22 Gas Station 1945 Sby 4/92 1,430
T/B 18x20 Under Queensboro Bridge Skn 3/92 1,430
O/B 12x9 Flute Player Mys 6/92 1,210

Perrault, Leon Jean Basile   Fr 1832-1908
O/C 38x51 Battling Boys 1889 Chr 2/92 11,000
O/C 44x34 Young Woman Holding a Feather 1889 Chr 5/92 2,200

Perret, Aime   Fr 1847-1927
O/C 32x26 Field Labor Sel 2/92 7,250
O/C 32x26 A Day of Labor Chr 10/91 6,050
O/C 20x24 La Sieste des Faneuses 1925 Chr 2/92 2,750

Perrey, Leon Auguste   Fr 1841-1900
* See 1992 Edition . . . .

Perrie, Bertha Eversfield Am 1868-1921
O/C 20x24 Docked Boats, Gloucester Harbor Slo 4/92 650
Perrier, Emilio Sanchez Spa 1855-1907
* See 1992 Edition
Perrigard, Hal Ross Can 1891-1960
O/B 12x16 Winter Farm Scene Mys 6/92 1,210
O/B 6x8 Rocky Coast and Village (2) Mys 6/92 935
Perrin Am 19C
W/Pa 12x20 Mountain River Landscape Sel 2/92 100
**Perrin, Francois Nicolas A. F. Fr
1826-1888**
O/C 26x38 Clamming Chr 2/92 6,050
Perrine, Van Dearing Am 1869-1955
O/B 11x14 Sunset Near the Hudson Yng 2/92 1,900
Perron, Charles 1880-1935
* See 1992 Edition ....
Perron, Charles Clement F. Fr 1893-1950
* See 1990 Edition
Perroneau, Jean-Baptiste Fr 1715-1783
* See 1990 Edition
Perry, Enoch Wood Am 1831-1915
O/C 7x9 Reading Paper; Tending Fire: Pair '77 Sby 3/92 .. 7,700
O/Pa/C 13x19 Garden and Backyard Scene But 4/92 4,950
O/B 12x10 Woman Adjusting the Clock & Man (2) Mys 6/92 . 522
Perry, Lilla Cabot Am 1848-1933
O/C 10x14 Mauve Hills Skn 11/91 1,430
O/C 18x22 Winter Morning Wes 3/92 165
Pertgen, Karl Maria Ger 1881-
* See 1991 Edition
Pescheret, Leon Am 1892-1961
* See 1992 Edition ....
Peske, Jean Fr 1880-1949
* See 1992 Edition ....
Pesne, Antoine Fr 1683-1757
* See 1990 Edition ....
Peterdi, Gabor Am 1915-
O/C 36x40 Horizontal Garden '60 Hnd 5/92 1,500
Peterelle, Adolphe Fr 1874-1947
O/C 24x20 Kneeling Female Nude Sel 4/92 425
Peters, Anna Ger 1843-1926
O/C 24x20 Still Life Flowers and Lace Sby 2/92 15,950
Peters, Carl William Am 1897-1980
O/C 20x24 New England Town Sel 9/91 2,000
O/B 12x16 Landscape with Stream Lou 3/92 850
O/C 20x24 Frozen Stream Slo 2/92 800
Peters, Charles Rollo Am 1862-1928
O/C 19x26 Nighttime on the Duckblind But 10/91 7,700
Peters, G. W. Am 20C
W&G/Pa 12x16 Storm Clouds 1905 Fre 10/91 150
Peters, Matthew William Irs 1741-1814
O/C 30x25 Young Lady Holding a Bouquet But 11/91 3,300
O/C 18x16 Portrait of a Woman Hnz 5/92 300
Peters, Paul
W/Pa 8x4 Beach Scene 1946 Durn 4/92 60
Peters, Pietronella Dut 1848-1924
* See 1991 Edition
**Petersen, Edvard Frederik Dan
1841-1911**
* See 1990 Edition ....
**Petersen, John Eric Christian Am
1839-1874**
* See 1992 Edition ....
Petersen, Martin Am 1870-
O/B 28x26 Reading the Paper in Central Park Hnd 5/92 ... 3,800
Peterson, Heinrich A. Br 19C
O/C 21x31 Ship Champion Fre 4/92 10,000
Peterson, Jane Am 1876-1965
O/C 18x18 The Clock Tower, Venice Sby 3/92 20,900
G&C/Pa/B 18x12 Market Grasse, Paris Chr 3/92 18,700
O/B 18x18 Market Day at the Rialto - Venice Doy 12/91 .. 15,000
G,W&C/Pa 18x24 The Garden Pool Chr 9/91 8,800
O/Cb 30x25 Red Roses in a Vase Sby 3/92 8,250
O/C 18x12 A Neighborhood Gathering Chr 9/91 6,600
G&C/Pa 18x24 San Maggiore, Venice Sby 3/92 6,600
G&W/Pa 24x18 Brittany Street Scene Sby 3/92 5,500

O/C 30x24 Gladiolus Sby 3/92 5,500
O/B 18x18 Venetian Canal Sby 5/92 4,400
O/Cb 18x18 June Flowers Sby 12/91 3,860
O/C 24x30 7 Pansies Skn 3/92 3,850
O/B 18x18 Stage Fort Beach Lou 3/92 3,300
O/B 12x16 Fishing Boats, Italy Chr 3/92 2,860
O/C 24x18 Harbor Scene Lou 3/92 2,850
W/Pa 13x20 A Day at the Beach Wlf 9/91 2,600
O/C 18x16 Pansies Skn 5/92 2,420
O/M 11x11 Lady in a Garden Hnz 10/91 2,200
O/C 20x24 Breeze Through the Palms Wes 3/92 2,090
W&G/Pa 18x24 The Last Gleam Hnd 5/92 1,800
P/Pa 24x16 Poppies in a Vase 1939 Eld 7/92 1,760
O/C 16x20 Maine Coast, Prouts Neck Lou 3/92 1,200
W/Pa 23x19 Dogwood Bough Wlf 10/91 1,100
O/C 18x25 Pansies in a Teal Bowl Skn 5/92 1,045
O/Cd 24x23 Harbor View Wlf 10/91 900
W,G&H/Pa 18x18 Gate Napolians' (sic) Garden 1923 Skn 9/91 770
O/B 23x29 Tugboat in Harbor Wlf 10/91 750
O/Cd 17x21 Sailboats Wlf 10/91 700
O/Pa/B 19x12 Irises Wlf 3/92 425
W&I/Pa 19x19 Landscape Wlf 3/92 150
Peterson, Roland Am 1926-
* See 1992 Edition ....
Pether, Abraham Br 1756-1812
O/C 16x21 Herder with Horse, Cattle Skn 11/91 1,870
Pether, Henry Br 19C
* See 1991 Edition ....
Pether, Sebastian Br 1790-1844
O/C 28x36 Moonlight on the Thames Chr 5/92 825
Petit, Alfred Fr -1895
* See 1992 Edition ....
Petit, C. Con 19C
* See 1992 Edition ....
Petit, Eugene Fr 1839-1886
O/C/B 28x39 Still Life Flowers in a Basket Chr 5/92 3,960
O/C 19x13 Floral Still Life But 5/92 3,025
Petit, Grace Am 20C
O/B 20x24 November Chill Mys 6/92 440
Petit, L. Fr 20C
* See 1992 Edition ....
Petit-Gerard, Pierre Fr 1852-
* See 1991 Edition ....
Petite, Jean Fr 20C
O/Pn 4x9 Village Scene Wes 3/92 440
Petiti, Filiberto It 1845-1924
O/C 23x40 Wooded Landscape with Figures 1876 Sby 1/92 6,050
Petitjean, Edmond Fr 1844-1925
O/C 18x26 Village with a Washerwoman Chr 10/91 7,700
O/C 19x17 French River Village 1888 Chr 2/92 6,600
O/C 17x24 Normandy Village Chr 5/92 6,600
O/C 22x18 Sunlit Cottages by a Pond Chr 5/92 4,180
O/C 20x30 Cottage and River 1889 Hnz 5/92 3,300
Petitjean, Hippolyte Fr 1854-1929
O/B 10x14 La Maison Sur Mer Sby 10/91 3,300
O/B 5x9 Paysage Chr 11/91 2,090
Peto, John Frederick Am 1854-1907
O/B 10x8 Still Life Candle, Pipe and Books Chr 3/92 50,600
O/Pn 5x7 Still Life Mug, Pipe and Book 1899 Sby 9/91 .. 16,500
O/C 22x16 Papers Tacked on a Wall But 11/91 2,750
Petrini, Giuseppe Antonio It 1677-1759
* See 1992 Edition ....
Petroff, Andre Eur 20C
C,P&G/Pa 19x15 Porte Nice 19_8 Slo 2/92 50
Petter, Franz Xaver Aus 1791-1866
* See 1991 Edition ....
Pettit, A. Am 20C
O/Cb 16x20 Moonlit Adobes Hnd 5/92 200
Pettitt, Charles Br 19C
* See 1990 Edition ....
Pettoruti, Emilio Arg 1892-1971
O/C/C 32x24 El Cantor 934 Chr 11/91 264,000
O/C 58x45 Midi en Hiver (Farfala) 1964 Chr 5/92 132,000
O/C 20x26 Vino Rubi 945 Sby 11/91 66,000
O/C/B 10x13 Naturaleza Muerta 18 Sby 5/92 55,000

O/C 24x32 El Mantel a Cuadros 938 Chr 11/91 49,500
O/B 9x11 Ragazza 1922 Chr 11/91 49,500
O/C 32x21 Caida de Hojas 954 Chr 5/92 38,500
O/Pn 19x12 Avenida Arbolada 929 Chr 5/92 28,600

Petty, George Am 1894-1975
G&Cp/Pa 18x12 Woman Ice-Skater 1939 Ih 11/91 7,500

Pettyjohn, Jessie Steiner Am 1880-1945
W/Pa 10x14 Mountain Landscape Mor 3/92 130

Petua, Leon Jean Fr 1846-1921
* See 1990 Edition

Pevsner, Antoine 20C
MM 14x11 Fond Vert 1923 Sby 5/92 63,250

Pew, Gertrude L. Am 1876-
W/Pa 6x5 Nymph Reaching for an Apple But 4/92 2,200

Peyraud, Frank Charles Am 1858-1948
O/C 20x24 Early Autumn Wlf 3/92 650
O/B 16x20 Summer Afternoon Hnd 10/91 450
O/C 14x20 Fall Landscape Mor 11/91 400

Peyrol-Bonheur, Juliette Fr 1830-1891
O/C 27x40 Cows Grazing on Cliffs Chr 5/92 8,250

Peyton, Bertha Menzler Am 1871-1950
* See 1992 Edition

Pezzuti, P. It 19C
* See 1992 Edition

Pfaff, Judy 20C
* See 1990 Edition

Pfeiffer, Gordon Edward Can 1899-1983
O/B 18x24 Winter View of Quebec City Sbt 11/91 1,870

Pfeiffer, Wilhelm Ger 1822-1891
* See 1991 Edition

Pfister, Jean Jacques Am 1878-1949
O/C 12x16 Landscape with Mountains Yng 2/92 50

Pfleager, M.
O/C 10x14 Mountain Stream Hnz 10/91 50

Pflug, Christiane Sybille Can 1936-1972
O/C 24x30 Railroad Yard at Liquor Control 1961 Sbt 11/91 . 4,207

Pflug, Johanes Baptiste Ger 1785-1866
* See 1991 Edition

Phelan, Charles T. Am 1840-
O/C 24x37 Pastoral Landscape with Sheep Wlf 6/92 1,100
O/B 8x6 Autumn Landscapes: Pair 75 Sby 12/91 990

Phelps Am 20C
O/B 19x15 Book and Candle Yng 2/92 50

Phelps, Edith Catlin Am 1879-1961
* See 1990 Edition

Phelps, William Preston Am 1848-1923
O/C 18x30 Welch Mountain, New Hampshire But 4/92 3,300
O/C 22x40 A Farmyard Scene Skn 11/91 2,310
O/C 24x36 Autumn Woodlands, Chesham Skn 11/91 1,650

Philipp, Robert Am 1895-1981
O/C 24x30 Two Women in a Cafe Hnz 5/92 5,500
O/C 18x15 At the Theater Chr 11/91 4,400
P/Pa 22x28 Reclining Nude But 11/91 2,750
O/C 30x25 Rochelle in Red Kimono 1966 Sby 12/91 2,310
O/C 36x30 Still Life with Flowers Chr 11/91 2,200
O/C 10x12 Girl with Scarf; Hat: Two Hnz 5/92 1,500
O/C 11x14 Cocktail Time Mary 5/92 1,375
O/C 22x17 A Seated Nude Chr 6/92 825
O/C 12x16 Docked Boats Chr 6/92 440

Philippe, Auguste Salnave Hai
O/M 24x18 Nature Morte Chr 5/92 4,180

Philippeau, Karel Frans Dut 1825-1897
O/Pn 12x16 Offering Grapes 67 Chr 10/91 7,700

Philippoteaux, Paul Dominique Fr 1846-
O/C 20x24 Exotic Dancers Durn 7/92 2,750
O/C 20x24 Exotic Dancers in Court Yard Hnd 5/92 750

Phillip, John Br 1817-1867
* See 1991 Edition

Phillipe-Auguste, Salnave Hai 20C
* See 1992 Edition

Phillips, Barye Am -1969
G/Pa 14x12 Man in Red Uniform with Sabre Ih 5/92 500

Phillips, Bert Greer Am 1868-1956
O/B 12x12 The Scout Chr 5/92 18,700
O/B 7x9 Deer Hunter: Taos 1927 Sby 12/91 7,425

Phillips, Charles Br 1708-1747
O/C 15x12 Portrait Mathew Lynch of Drumcong Chr 5/92 . 24,200

Phillips, Coles Am 1880-1927
W&G/Pa 22x19 Girl Walking 21 Ih 11/91 9,000

Phillips, Dorothy Sklar Am 20C
* See 1991 Edition

Phillips, Gordon Am 1927-
O/B 23x32 A Welcome Sight '66 Sby 12/91 18,700
O/C 24x42 Chores '71 Chr 5/92 9,350
O/C 24x30 Talk of the Southern Trails '73 Chr 12/91 ... 8,800
O/C 28x24 Snowed Last Night '78 Chr 3/92 2,750

Phillips, J.
O/C 31x26 Portrait of a Gentleman 1870 Hnz 10/91 180

Phillips, Marjorie Am 1895-
O/C 30x40 Silos No. 2, 1960 Slo 10/91 450
O/C 28x34 Topographical Landscape Slo 10/91 140
O/C 32x40 Almost Spring Fre 12/91 110

Phillips, Peter 1939-
O&L/C 72x60 Wall Machine Chr 11/91 17,600

Phillips, S. George Am -1965
O/C 36x25 Riverside in Spring Yng 2/92 1,500

Phillips, Thomas Br 1770-1845
O/C 54x47 Portrait George O'Brien Wyndham Sby 5/92 .. 7,150

Phillips, W. E.
O/B 23x20 Man Walking into Town Ald 3/92 425

Phillips, Walter Joseph Can 1884-1963
G/Pn 16x20 Mount Cathedral Sbt 5/92 5,610

Philpot, Glyn Br 1884-1937
* See 1992 Edition

Philppeau, Karel Frans Dut 1825-1897
* See 1991 Edition

Phippen, George Am 1916-1966
* See 1991 Edition

Piacenza, Aldo Am 1888-
O/C 33x48 Fort Dearborn, Chicago Hnd 10/91 550

Pianch, Rius
O/C 24x20 Trompe L'Oeil Still Life Wlf 3/92 550

Piaseck, Leszek Con 20C
O/C 23x19 Soldier on Horseback Hnd 6/92 80

Piazzetta, Giovanni Battista It 1683-1754
* See 1991 Edition

Piazzoni, Gottardo Am 1872-1945
O/B 6x9 The Boathouse '02 But 2/92 1,430
O/B 9x10 Summer, Kentield, California, 1914 But 2/92 ... 990
O/C/B 9x7 Tassajara '04 But 2/92 935

Picabia, Francis Fr 1878-1953
O/C 29x24 Le Sully a Nemours 1908 Chr 11/91 38,500
O/Cb 11x14 Antibes Chr 5/92 11,000
O/Pn 9x13 Peniches sur la riviere 1902 Chr 5/92 7,700
W&Pe/Pa 10x9 Ou Sont les Armes des Betes? Chr 2/92 . 7,150
O/B 12x7 Femme Nue Debout Sby 10/91 6,600
H/Pa 11x8 Portrait of a Woman Sby 2/92 2,860

Picart, O Fr 19C
O/C 23x16 Puss and Her Family Wes 3/92 1,870

Picasso, Pablo Spa 1881-1973
O/C 38x51 Compotier et guitare 32 Chr 5/92 .... 3.85M
Sg/Pa 42x29 Femme au voile Chr 5/92 .... 1.485M
C/Pa 27x18 Homme a la Sucette 38 Chr 5/92 968,000
O/C 36x29 Femme Assise Galette des Rois 65 Chr 11/91 . 880,000
Pe/Pa 19x13 Etude Pour L'Acteur Sby 5/92 825,000
P,C&I/Pa 19x25 Bouteille de Bass et guitare Chr 5/92 .. 770,000
G,Y&Pe/Pa 20x14 Tete de Femme Sby 11/91 715,000
G/Pa/C 13x9 Study for Nude with Drapery Sby 5/92 ... 687,500
O/C 29x24 L'Enlevement des Sabines 62 Sby 11/91 ... 660,000
O/C 18x22 Bouteille et Verre Sby 11/91 577,500
O/B 10x10 Bouteille de Bass, Verre Sby 5/92 470,000
O/Pa/C 20x13 Tete de Femme Sby 11/91 462,000
G&W/Pa/C 12x10 Study of Head for Nude Sby 5/92 ... 440,000
O/C 36x28 Tete de Mousquetaire 72 Sby 5/92 412,500
G,L&I/Pa/B 10x8 Verre et bouteille de Bass Chr 5/92 .. 396,000
O/C 16x10 Tete de Femme 39 Sby 5/92 385,000
O/C 20x24 Nature morte au crane de mouton 39 Chr 5/92 . 352,000
O/Pn 26x21 Tete d'homme 69 Chr 5/92 352,000
G/Pa/B 11x8 Guitare sur un gueridon 21 Chr 5/92 286,000
C/Pa 24x19 Nu Debout Chr 11/91 275,000

PI&W/Pa 10x13 Composition Chr 5/92 242,000
Pe/Pa 11x8 Pierrot 1918 Chr 5/92 242,000
G,W&PI/Pa 20x24 Figures 67 Chr 11/91 231,000
C&H/Pa 25x19 Compotier, bouteille Chr 5/92 165,000
C&P/Pa 12x11 Femme Assise Aux "4 Gats" Sby 11/91 . . 154,000
O/C 6x10 Nature Morte, Fruit et Pichet 38 Chr 11/91 . . . 154,000
G&W/Pa 8x5 Arlequin tenant 1915 Chr 5/92 132,000
PI/Pa 9x7 Le Peintre 70 Chr 5/92 110,000
Br&I/Pa 10x6 Femme nue debout Chr 5/92 93,500
Y&PI/Pa 5x4 Jeunne Femme et Homme Age Sby 5/92 . . . 88,000
Pe/Pa/Pa 9x13 Tete de femme Chr 5/92 88,000
Pe&Y/Pa 10x13 Femme nue allongee 61 Chr 5/92 77,000
B,PI&S/Pa 20x24 Hommes; Femme: Double 67 Chr 11/91 . 77,000
Cp/Pa 10x13 Etude "Dejeuner sur l'Herbe" I 62 Chr 5/92 . 71,500
I/Pa 14x11 Les Trois Graces Sby 5/92 71,500
Y&Pe/Pa 10x13 "Dejeuner sur l'herbe" II 62 Chr 5/92 . . . 66,000
PI/Pa 14x10 Femme Nue Assise 25 Chr 2/92 66,000
Pe/Pa 12x8 Homme Debout Accoude Sby 11/91 44,000
PI/Pa 13x9 Femme Nue Drapee Sby 11/91 39,600
Pe/Pa 8x11 Cavalier 62 Chr 5/92 37,400
Y&L 27x10 Les Cravates Sby 2/92 37,400
Pe/Pa 20x26 Colombe Sby 11/91 36,300
Pe/Pa 11x14 "Dejeuner sur l'Herbe" II 62 Chr 5/92 33,000
Pe/Pa 5x7 Deux Tetes de Dora Maar Chr 5/92 33,000
Fp/B 7x10 Deux tetes d'hommes 68 Chr 5/92 30,800
Br&I/Pa 12x8 Seduction Sby 11/91 30,800
Fp/Pa 11x8 Two Drawings Chr 5/92 30,800
Pe/Pa 11x17 "Dejeuner sur l'herbe" XVI 63 Chr 5/92 . . . 26,400
Pe/Pa 11x8 Achille 62 Chr 5/92 26,400
PI/Pa 8x5 Le Fils du Peintre Ricardo Canals Chr 11/91 . . 26,400
Pe/Pa 10x6 Baigneuse au Bord d'un Ruisseau Sby 11/91 . 25,300
PI/Pa 11x9 Pour Kertesz 47 Chr 11/91 22,000
Fp&Y/B/C 12x9 Buste de Femme/Tete: Pair 71 Sby 5/92 . 19,800
Fp/Pa 11x10 Tete Masquee 67 Chr 5/92 18,700
PI/Pa 9x7 Tete d'Homme 68 Sby 2/92 17,050
Pe/Pa 14x8 La Fille de l'Artiste (Maya) 42 Sby 5/92 . . . 13,200
Br&I/Pa 9x13 Les Chevaux Sby 5/92 11,000
PI/Pa/B 8x5 Le Vieillard Chr 11/91 9,350
Pichette, James   Fr 1920-
 * See 1992 Edition . . . .
Pichler, Adolf   Hun 1835-1905
 * See 1991 Edition . . . .
Pichot, Emile Jules   Fr 1857-
O/C 32x26 Young Girl Reading Sel 4/92 3,100
Pickenoy, Nicolas Elias   Dut 1590-1656
 * See 1992 Edition . . . .
Pickering, J. L.   Am 19C
 * See 1992 Edition . . . .
**Pickersgill, Frederick Richard   Br
1820-1900**
O/C 44x77 Flight of the Pagan Deities 1856 Sby 5/92 . . . 24,200
O/C 22x36 The Three Graces Chr 2/92 8,250
Pickett, Joseph   Am 1848-1918
O/C 24x36 Primitive Farmyard Wlf 10/91 650
Picknell, William Lamb   Am 1854-1897
O/C 20x36 The River's Edge Doy 12/91 5,500
Picot, Francois Edouard   Fr 1786-1868
 * See 1990 Edition . . . .
Picou, Henri Pierre   Fr 1824-1895
 * See 1991 Edition . . . .
**Pidoux, Auguste Henri Joseph   Fr
1809-1870**
C&K/Pa 13x10 Portrait of an Artist 1853 Sby 7/92 275
Pieler, Franz Xaver   Aus 1879-1952
O/C 32x23 Still Life Flowers & Bird's Nest Sby 7/92 3,850
O/C 11x9 Flowers with Butterflies & Ladybugs Chr 10/91 . 2,750
Pierce, Charles Franklin   Am 1844-1920
O/C 15x22 Spring's Warmth/Sheep Skn 3/92 2,420
O/C 12x16 Rest in the Pasture Skn 9/91 248
Pierce, H. Winthrop   Am 1850-
O/C 27x22 Bundling the Wheat 1884 Chr 11/91 1,540
Pierce, Lucy   Am 1887-1974
O/C 30x25 Portrait of Ina Story But 2/92 1,100
Pierre, Andre   Hai 20C

Pierre, Fernand   Hai 20C
O/M 20x24 Tigers and Panthers Slo 9/91 700
Pierre, Gustave Rene   Fr 1875-
O/C 13x22 Marching Soldiers in Winter Chr 2/92 600
O/C 13x22 Refugees of War Chr 2/92 600
Pierre, Jean-Baptiste-Marie   Fr 1713-1789
 * See 1991 Edition . . . .
Pierre, Laureus   Hai 20C
 * See 1992 Edition . . . .
Pieters, Evert   Dut 1856-1932
O/C 38x32 In the Garden Sby 5/92 29,700
O/C 24x20 Children in a Field Chr 10/91 24,200
O/C 32x51 Clamming at Scheveningen Sby 5/92 16,500
O/C 31x37 The Contented Family Chr 10/91 15,400
O/C 31x36 The Toy Horse Sby 2/92 15,400
O/C 37x32 Afternoon Meal Slo 9/91 14,000
O/C 16x24 Awaiting the Ferry Sby 2/92 5,500
O/C 22x25 Coastal Scene Wlf 3/92 5,200
O/C 24x20 Interior Scene Skn 3/92 2,860
Piette, Ludovic   Fr 1826-1877
 * See 1990 Edition . . . .
Pietzsch, Richard   Am 1872-
O/C 24x30 Land and Sea 1927 Fre 10/91 75
Piffard, Harold Hume   Br a 1895-1899
 * See 1990 Edition . . . .
Pigal, Edme Jean   Fr 1798-1872
O/Pn 13x10 War Stories Skn 5/92 1,540
Pignon, Edouard   Fr 1905-
O/C 29x24 Nature Morte 44 Sby 2/92 19,800
Pignoux   Fr 19C
 * See 1992 Edition . . . .
Pigott, Marjorie   Can 1904-1990
W/Pa 22x24 Wildflowers Sbt 11/91 1,262
Piguet, Rodolphe   Sws 1840-1915
 * See 1992 Edition . . . .
Pihnnero, H.   It 19C
 * See 1992 Edition . . . .
Pike, John   Am 1911-1979
W/Pa 20x27 Passing Patrol Slo 9/91 1,000
Pikelny, Robert   1904-
O/B 28x20 Portrait of a Man 1929 Chr 11/91 660
Pillement, Jean   Fr 1728-1808
O/C 18x27 View of the Tagus, Portugal 1790 Chr 1/92 . . . 38,500
P/Pa 15x23 Coastal Landscape with Figures Chr 1/92 . . . 16,500
Pilot, Robert Wakeham   Can 1898-1967
O/C 21x28 Prince of Wales Terrace, Montreal Sbt 11/91 . . 38,335
O/C 19x24 Smelt Fishers, Quebec 1956 Sbt 5/92 28,050
O/C 15x20 Pommier en Fleurs Sbt 5/92 17,600
O/C 22x28 The Seigneur's Mill Sbt 11/91 16,830
O/Pn 8x11 After-Glow, Levis, P.Q. 1958 Sbt 11/91 2,338
**Pils, Isidore Alexandre August   Fr
1813-1875**
W&Pe/Pa 6x10 Fontainebleau 1869 Sby 7/92 660
Piltz, Otto   Ger 1846-1910
 * See 1991 Edition . . . .
Pimentel, Rodrigo Ramirez   Mex 1945-
 * See 1992 Edition . . . .
Pinal, Ferdinand   Fr 1881-1958
 * See 1992 Edition . . . .
Pincemin, Jean-Pierre   1944-
O/C 87x67 Untitled Chr 2/92 12,100
Pinchart, Emile   Fr 1842-
 * See 1992 Edition . . . .
Pinchon, Jean Antoine   Fr 1772-1850
 * See 1992 Edition . . . .
Pinchon, Robert Antoine   Fr 1886-1943
 * See 1992 Edition . . . .
Pine, Theodore E.   Am 1828-1905
O/Pn 12x16 The Missing Chr 6/92 825
Pinel, Gustave Nicolas   Fr 1842-1896
 * See 1990 Edition . . . .
Pinelli, Bartolomeo   It 1781-1835
 * See 1992 Edition . . . .
Pinggera, H.   Con 19C
 * See 1992 Edition . . . .

Pinqqera, H.   Con 19C
O/C 42x62 Romans of the Decadence Sby 2/92 25,300
Pinto, Alberto   Por 19C
O/C 24x20 Deux Femmes de Bretagnes Sel 4/92 2,600
Pinto, Biagio   Am 1911-
O/C 15x12 Sailboats Fre 4/92 900
Pinto, Jody   Am 1942-
C/Pa 29x23 Tomatos Fre 4/92 150
Piola, Domenico   It 1627-1703
O/C 61x47 Female Figure Holding Torch, Putti Sby 1/92 . 132,000
Piot, Adolphe   Fr 1850-1910
O/C/M 34x26 The Reading Lesson Sby 5/92 19,800
O/C 40x27 La Jeune Femme a la Rose Sby 5/92 13,200
O/C 33x26 Sweet Innocence Chr 10/91 7,700
O/C 14x11 L'Innocence Sby 10/91 6,050
Piotrowski, Antoni   Pol 1853-1924
  * See 1990 Edition . . . .
Piper, John   Br 1903-
G,W&I/Pa 14x20 Garn Fawr 1983 Sby 10/91 4,950
W&G/Pa 8x13 Gloriana 1953 Slo 7/92 1,800
Piper, Natt A.   Am 1886-1969
W/Pa 13x9 In Drydock Mor 11/91 150
Pipo, Emanuel Ruiz   Spa 1928-
O/C 16x12 Dancers 1959 Hnz 5/92 975
O/B 13x11 Cherubs Hnz 5/92 500
Pippel, Otto   Ger 1878-1960
  * See 1992 Edition . . . .
Pippin, Horace   Am 1888-1946
  * See 1990 Edition . . . .
Piranesi, Giovanni Battista   It 1720-1778
I/Pa 3x2 Study of a Dog Slo 7/92 950
Pirie, George   Br 1863-1946
  * See 1991 Edition . . . .
Pirtle, Pauline   Am 20C
W/Pa Size? Four Watercolors Sel 9/91 60
Pissarro, Camille   Fr 1830-1903
O/C 22x52 Les Quatre Saisons: Four 1872 Chr 11/91 . . 6.82M
O/C 32x25 Pont-Neuf, apres-midi de pluie 1901 Chr 5/92 . 1.87M
O/C 26x21 Parc Aux Charrettes, Pontoise 1878 Sby 5/92 . 1.595M
O/C 21x26 Jardin De Kew 1892 Sby 5/92 . . . . 1.1M
O/C 24x29 Paysannes Assisses, Causant 81 Chr 11/91 . . 990,000
O/C 13x16 Le Moisson 83 Sby 11/91 880,000
O/C 21x26 Moulin a Knocke, Belgique 94 Chr 5/92 550,000
O/C 18x21 Vue de la Ferme d'Osny 1883 Sby 11/91 495,000
G&Pe/S/Cd 14x10 Au bord de l'eau 81 Chr 5/92 418,000
O/C 9x11 Vue Des Bassins Duquesne 1902 Sby 11/91 . . 137,500
PI/Pa 9x7 La Lumiere de la Lampe Sby 5/92 49,500
W&G/Pa 3x5 Paysanne Sur Un Sentier Sby 5/92 49,500
Pt/Por 16x8 La Saint-Martin a Pontoise Chr 11/91 48,400
PI/Pa 9x7 Femmes Cousant Sby 5/92 46,750
P/Pa/B 10x12 Paysage Sby 11/91 46,750
Pt/Por 8x8 Paysanne Dans Un Champ Chr 11/91 46,200
W&C/Pa/B 9x11 Meule a Eragny Sur Epte Sby 5/92 44,000
W/Pa 12x9 Paysage 90 Sby 11/91 38,500
Pe,Y&K/Pa 9x13 Paysage a la Campagne Sby 2/92 14,300
PI/Pa 6x6 Rouen, Rue de Arpente But 11/91 3,850
Pissarro, H. Claude   Fr 1935-
O/C 21x25 Etude pour Les Trois Clochers Chr 5/92 10,450
O/C 18x22 La Promenade a Nice Chr 5/92 9,900
O/C 21x25 Les Trois Clochers Chr 11/91 9,350
O/C 20x24 Le Presbytere de Listrou Chr 11/91 7,700
O/C 18x22 La Femme en Rouge Sel 9/91 7,000
O/C 24x29 Villa du Haut de Septeuil Doy 11/91 6,750
O/C 20x24 Le presbytere de Listrou Chr 5/92 6,600
O/C 20x24 Les bords de l'Etang Perrey Chr 5/92 6,600
O/C 18x22 Granville, l'entree du port Chr 5/92 6,050
O/C 13x16 Les Deux Clochers Sby 10/91 6,050
O/C 20x24 Varangeville Chr 2/92 6,050
P/Pa 14x19 Bord de Riviere Doy 11/91 5,750
O/C 20x24 Le Jardin D'Amelie Sby 2/92 4,950
K/Pa 15x20 Le vieux pont a Fresnay-sur-Sarthe Chr 5/92 . 4,950
O/C 20x24 Michelle a Amelie Sby 2/92 4,950
O/C 20x24 Roses et Seringa Chr 2/92 4,950
O/C 18x22 La Plaine du Cher a Blere Sel 2/92 4,750
O&Y/Pa 32x24 Femme Dans la Campagne Chr 11/91 4,400

O/C 18x22 L'Avenue de la Gare a Rennes Sby 6/92 4,400
P/Pa 20x15 Le bouquet a la chope Chr 5/92 4,180
P/Pa 14x20 L'Avenue des Bains Sby 2/92 4,125
P/Pa 15x20 Paris - La Cathedral Notre Dame Sby 6/92 . . 3,960
K/Pa 14x20 Voiliers Chr 5/92 3,520
K/Pa 15x20 L'Esplanade des Invalides, Paris Chr 2/92 . . 2,860
P/Pa 14x20 Le Moulin de Bouche Chr 11/91 2,860
K/Pa 14x19 Les Pommiers Chr 2/92 2,500
P/Pa 10x15 Le tournant du Petit-Mesnil Chr 5/92 2,420
P/Pa 10x15 Verger a la Fillotiere Sby 2/92 2,420
K/Pa 10x15 Petits Vachers Gardant Chr 11/91 2,200
P/Pa 10x14 Les Pommiers But 5/92 1,980
P/Pa 10x15 Neige a Champigny-de-l'Ome But 5/92 1,650
Pissarro, Lucien   Fr 1863-1944
  * See 1992 Edition . . . .
Pissarro, Paul Emile   Fr 1884-1972
O/M 21x26 La Maison du Bateau Sby 2/92 4,675
O/C 21x26 Arbres Verts Sby 2/92 3,575
W&C/Pa 10x13 The Farm; La Colline: Pair Sby 2/92 . . . 3,575
O/C 20x24 Le Lac Sby 6/92 3,300
O/C 18x24 Les Moissons a Cley Chr 11/91 2,640
O/C 26x22 Le Pain de Sucre Doy 11/91 2,000
O/C 22x18 Neige au Bord de la Lievre Sby 2/92 1,870
W&PI/Pa 10x13 Two Watercolors Chr 11/91 1,210
W&G/Pa 9x12 Landscape Dum 1/92 1,000
W&G/Pa 9x12 Wheat Field Dum 1/92 1,000
W,C&H/Pa 10x12 Haystacks But 5/92 660
W&K/Pa 13x20 Au Printemps Chr 1/92 418
Pissis, Amaro   Fr a 1810-1850
S/Pa 9x11 Botafogo Sby 11/91 2,420
S&Cw/Pa 9x11 Entree De La Baie Sby 11/91 2,420
W&O/Pa 12x9 Prancha De Botanica Sby 11/91 2,090
Pistoletto, Michelangelo   It 1933-
  * See 1992 Edition . . . .
Pitt, William   Br a 1853-1890
O/C 24x36 The Mill Stream, Sussex 1880 But 5/92 3,300
Pittman, Hobson   Am 1899-1972
W/Pa 16x22 Room Interior Fre 12/91 1,700
O/Pa 24x18 Still Life with Fruit Fre 4/92 1,600
W/Pa 10x8 Orita Lido 1956 Fre 4/92 550
Pittoni, Giovanni Battista   It 1687-1767
O/C 18x12 Vision of Saint Joseph Sby 1/92 23,100
Pitz, Henry Clarence   Am 1885-1976
Pe&W/Pa 21x11 Dancer 1964 Fre 12/91 275
W/Pa 20x30 The Ravene Fre 12/91 210
Pizizelli   It
O/C 42x32 Two Seamstresses Dum 6/92 700
Pla Y Gallardo, Cecilio   Spa 1860-
O/Pn 6x10 Watching the Boats 1916 Sby 10/91 17,600
O/B 9x11 Playa Sby 2/92 16,500
Pla Y Rubio, Alberto   Spa 1867-
  * See 1992 Edition . . . .
Place, Vera Clark
O/C 40x33 Dancers Dum 1/92 600
Planas, Juan Battle   Spa 1911-1966
G/Pa 9x6 El Maestro 1945 Chr 5/92 6,600
Planquette, Felix   Fr 1873-
O/C/B 26x36 Cows at the Watering Hole Hnd 3/92 1,500
Planson, Andre   Fr 1898-
W/Pa 20x26 Reclining Nude Sby 10/91 2,640
Plaskett, Joseph Francis   Can 1918-
  * See 1992 Edition . . . .
Plassan, Antoine Emile   Fr 1817-1903
O/Pn 19x25 Family News 73 Sby 5/92 3,850
O/Pn 9x13 Une Ferme a Anvers Chr 5/92 3,080
Plathner, Hermann   Ger 1831-1902
O/C 15x12 Hungry Visitors 1863 Chr 5/92 4,950
Platt, Charles Adams   Am 1861-1933
O/C 22x36 An Inlet Chr 11/91 3,850
Player, William H.   Br a 1858-1884
O/C 16x24 Bonchurch, Isle of Wight 1852 But 11/91 . . . 3,300
Pleissner, Ogden Minton   Am 1905-1983
W&Pe/Pa 15x21 St. George's Bay, Bermuda Chr 5/92 . . 20,900
O/C 24x36 Late Afternoon, Brittany Chr 5/92 19,800
W/Pa 16x23 Fosse au Fer Chr 9/91 15,400

184

W/Pa 19x29 The Coast of Normandie Sby 5/92 11,000
W/Pa 17x11 Card Players, Luxembourg Gardens Sby 12/91 5,225
W,G&O/Pa 7x10 Netting the Salmon Sby 12/91 4,400
W/Pa 12x23 Farm in Normandy Sby 12/91 4,180
W/Pa 7x10 Vannes Sby 12/91 3,850
W/Pa 14x18 La Neige Sby 12/91 3,575
W/Pa 10x15 Moisie River, Quebec Sby 4/92 2,640
W&Pe/Pa 10x15 Upsalquitch River, New Brunswick Sby 4/92 2,640

Plisson, Henri   Am 1908-
  * See 1992 Edition . . . .

Ploll, Victor   Ger 19C
  O/Pn 10x7 Conversation at the Well Chr 10/91 1,430

Ploquin, Gaston   Fr 20C
  * See 1990 Edition . . . .

Plumb, Charlie   Am
  PI/Pa 15x23 Three Sunday Comics. "Ella Cinders" 47 Ih 5/92   250

Plummer, William H.   Am 19C
  O/C 24x18 Moonlight Sail 1890 Brd 5/92   660

Plumot, Andre   Bel 1829-1906
  * See 1992 Edition . . . .

Poag, Jim   1954-
  O/C 67x81 Pollution and Haze '84 Chr 11/91 . .   55

Podchernikoff, Alexis M.   Am 1886-1933
  O/C 32x42 Marin Landscape But 10/91 7,700
  O/C 26x46 Morning Light, Santa Inez But 6/92 4,125
  O/C 40x30 Afternoon Glow 1918 But 2/92 2,750
  O/C 30x20 California Nocturne Mor 11/91 2,000
  O/C/B 10x12 Figure and Cattle But 6/92 1,870
  O/B 12x14 The Sun's Last Glow 1929 But 10/91 1,760
  O/C 20x16 Lone Figure Beneath Moonlit Skies But 6/92 . 1,650
  O/C 30x20 Figures in a Landscape Mor 11/91 1,600
  O/B 14x18 Little Rabbit Hunter But 2/92 1,320
  O/C 18x24 River Sunrise Hnd 5/92 1,300
  O/C/B 10x12 Golden Sunset But 6/92 1,045
  O/C 22x28 Pastoral Landscape But 6/92 1,045
  O/C 20x16 Moonlight Landscape Mor 3/92 1,000
  O/C 12x16 Old Spanish Adobe Mor 6/92 1,000
  O/B 9x10 Figure in Landscape Mor 6/92   950
  O/Cb 10x12 Cows at Stream Mor 3/92   850
  O/C 10x8 Mission Santa Barbara But 6/92   825
  O/B 9x9 Figure in Autumn Mor 6/92   550
  O/M 8x10 Landscape Mor 3/92   500

Poehler, Jan (John)   Am 20C
  O/C 32x27 Portuguese Fishermans Church '45 Wes 11/91 .   138

Poerson, Charles   Dut 1653-1725
  * See 1990 Edition . . . .

Pogany, Willy   Am 1882-1955
  W/Pa 10x7 Leaping Bengal Tiger Mys 11/91   165
  W/Pa 17x26 Ship in Full Sail Mys 11/91   110

Poggioli, Marcel Dominique   Fr 1882-
  * See 1992 Edition . . . .

Pohl, Edward H.   Am 1874-1956
  O&P/C 15x19 Sierra Landscape Mor 3/92   500

Poilpot, Theophile & Du Paty,L   Fr 1848-1915
  O/C 19x43 Le Siege de Paris en 1871: Four Sby 2/92 7,150

Poiret, Paul   Fr -1844
  * See 1991 Edition . . . .

Poirier, Anne and Patrick
  * See 1992 Edition . . . .

Poisson, Louverature   Hai 1914-1985
  O/M 16x21 Crime Passionel Chr 5/92 5,500
  O/C 30x24 Fire Dance Skn 3/92   935

Poitevin, Auguste Flavien   Fr 19C
  * See 1990 Edition . . . .

Pokitonov, Ivan   Rus 1851-1924
  O/Pn 7x11 Hunter in a Marshy Landscape 1898 Chr 2/92 . . 8,250
  O/Pn 7x11 Hunter in a Winter Landscape 88 Chr 2/92 . . . 6,600

Polar, H.
  W/Pa 20x18 Mother and Children Dum 8/92   900

Polasky, R.   Eur 20C
  O/C 24x20 Boy in a Wooded Landscape Sel 2/92   400

Polderman, W.
  O/C 24x36 Landscape Dum 11/91   750

Poleo, Hector   Ven 1918-
  O/C 24x29 La Rose 1966 Chr 5/92 33,000

Poliakoff, Serge   Fr 1906-1969
  O/C 33x40 Untitled 1969 Sby 2/92 71,500
  T/Pa 26x20 Untitled Sby 11/91 38,500

Polini, A.   It 20C
  O/C 16x24 Grand Canal, Venice 1889 Slo 7/92 2,250

Polke, Sigmar   Ger 1941-
  Rs&A/F 59x71 Medallion Chr 5/92 187,000
  MM/C 98x98 Schliefe--Gebetbuch Maximilian 86 Chr 5/92 154,000
  Dis/C 53x39 Bildnis Helmut Klinker Sby 5/92 110,000
  GWGd&T/Pa 39x28 Untitled 83 Chr 5/92 38,500
  E&A/Pa 28x39 Untitled 82 Chr 5/92 30,800
  I/Pa 34x24 Untitled '66 Sby 11/91 30,250

Pollak, August   Aus 1838-
  * See 1992 Edition . . . .

Pollard, James   Br 1792-1867
  * See 1990 Edition . . . .

Pollentine, Alfred   Br 19C
  O/C 20x30 Grand Canal, Venice Slo 2/92 2,000
  O/C 17x24 Ducale Palace, Venice 55 Chr 10/91   770

Pollet, Victor Florence   Fr 1811-1882
  W&G/Pa 10x13 Repos 1875 Chr 2/92 2,860

Pollock, Jackson   Am 1912-1956
  Br&I/Pa 19x25 Untitled Sby 11/91 330,000
  O,E&Pt/C 9x13 Silver and Black 1950 Chr 11/91 165,000
  I&G/Pa 10x8 Untitled Sby 11/91 27,500

Polo, Roberto
  O/C 50x72 Untitled 68 Sby 2/92 17,600

Pon, Bruce
  O/C 28x22 After a French Masterpiece Dum 1/92   325

Ponce De Leon, Fidelio   Cub 1895-1949
  O/C 33x44 Five Women 41 Sby 11/91 104,500
  O/C 26x21 Untitled Sby 5/92 12,100
  O/B 23x19 Retrato de Mujer Chr 11/91 7,700

Pons, Fortune
  O/C 22x26 Sheep Herder Ald 5/92   525

Ponsen, Tunis   Am 20C
  O/Pn 15x18 River Scene Hnd 12/91   475
  O/C 30x26 Art Books Hnd 3/92   450

Pont, Charles Ernest   1898-
  W/Pa 20x26 Hall's Point Yng 4/92   275

Pontecorvo, Raimondo   It 19C
  W/Pa 28x20 The Looking Glass Doy 11/91 2,200

Pontormo   It 1494-1556
  * See 1990 Edition . . . .

Pooke, Marion Louise   20C
  O/C 20x16 Two Portraits Yng 4/92   400

Poole, Eugene A.   Am 1841-1912
  * See 1992 Edition . . . .

Poole, Horatio Nelson   Am 1884-1949
  * See 1992 Edition . . . .

Poole, Paul Falconer   Br 1807-1879
  * See 1992 Edition . . . .

Poons, Larry   Am 1937-
  A/C 76x100 72nd Street Dead 1973 Sby 5/92 12,100

Poor, Henry Varnum   Am 1888-1970
  * See 1992 Edition . . . .

Poore, Henry Rankin   Am 1859-1940
  * See 1992 Edition . . . .

Pope, Alexander   Am 1849-1924
  O/C 30x40 Stallion Hnz 10/91 1,700

Pope, Gustav   Br a 1852-1895
  * See 1991 Edition . . . .

Pope, Thomas Benjamin   Am -1891
  * See 1992 Edition . . . .

Popelin, Gustave Leon Antoine   Fr 1859-
  * See 1991 Edition . . . .

Popova, Liubov   Rus 1889-1924
  * See 1992 Edition . . . .

Poray, Stanislaus   Am 1888-1948
  O/C 23x28 Farm Scene But 10/91 1,980
  O/C 21x27 Nocturnal - Ca. Mission Mor 3/92 1,300
  O/C 20x24 The Jade Vase Mor 6/92 1,100
  O/C 29x36 Still Life--Brass & Glass '26 Mor 11/91   950

O/C 20x24 17 Mile Drive Mor 11/91 600
O/B 10x10 Landscape Mor 11/91 400
Porpora, Paolo It 1617-1683
O/C 20x27 Still Life Fish in a Landscape Sby 10/91 33,000
Portaels, Jean Francois Bel 1818-1895
* See 1992 Edition . . . .
Porter, Benjamin Curtis Am 1845-1908
O/Pn 24x17 Rose Skn 11/91 358
Porter, Charles Ethan Am 1850-1923
O/C 21x17 Forest Interior 1890 Lou 6/92 1,100
O/C 12x18 Still Life of Apples Slo 10/91 575
Porter, Fairfield Am 1907-1975
O/C 19x18 Autumn I '67 Sby 12/91 29,700
O/C 14x25 Wild Flowers '55 Sby 5/92 19,800
W&Pe/Pa 16x20 Country Road; Autumn: Dbl '63 Chr 9/91 . 5,500
Pe/Pa 10x13 Landscape 1958 Hnz 10/91 180
Porter, John J. Am a 1850-
O/C 30x46 Mail Call, Steamboat Wyandotte 1859 Chr 5/92 18,700
Porter, Katherine Am 1941-
G,K&H/Pa 20x20 Winter Dance Chr 11/91 2,200
G,H&Cp/Pa 17x19 Untitled Sby 6/92 1,430
W/Pa 10x12 Untitled Sby 10/91 770
O/C/Pa 16x13 Untitled 1978 Sby 10/91 660
Porter, L. Br 19C
O/Pn 7x6 Children with Looking Glass Hnz 5/92 350
Portielje, Edward Antoon Bel 1861-1949
O/C 18x15 Two Women Seated Around a Table Sel 12/91 . 5,700
O/C 18x14 Snack Time Wlf 9/91 2,600
Portielje, Gerard Bel 1856-1929
O/B 11x14 The Bird Fancier Wlf 9/91 6,500
O/Pn 9x6 The Musician But 11/91 2,090
Portielje, Jan Frederik Pieter Dut 1829-1895
O/C 28x22 An Oriental Beauty Sby 2/92 13,200
Portinari, Candido Brz 1903-1962
O/L/B 16x12 Moca 1940 Chr 5/92 52,800
O/C 29x24 Portrait Maria Sermolino 1940 Chr 5/92 22,000
O/C 18x15 Retrato de Sofia Cantalupo 1933 Chr 5/92 . . . 22,000
O/Pn 7x9 Incendio 960 Chr 11/91 19,800
O/C 18x15 Retrato de Roberto Cantalupo 1933 Chr 5/92 . . 8,800
Pl&Br/Pa/B 11x14 Estudio del "Ultimo Baluarte" Chr 5/92 . . . 3,300
Portocarrero, Rene Cub 1912-
O/B 41x31 Paisaje 1944 Sby 5/92 143,000
O/C 40x29 Catedral Sby 5/92 20,900
O/C 18x24 Ciudad 1956 Chr 5/92 16,500
G/B 28x22 Mujer Sentada 1945 Sby 5/92 7,700
G&V/B/C 16x11 Cabeza Sby 5/92 7,150
PI/Pa 19x22 Dos Figuras Sby 11/91 6,600
O/C 20x14 Catedral 63 Chr 5/92 4,950
O/C 20x16 Muneco 62 Chr 5/92 4,500
O/C 23x17 Catedral 62 Chr 5/92 3,850
P/Pa 19x13 Mujer en Azul Sby 5/92 3,850
T&I/B 15x11 Composicion Geometrica 1953 Sby 11/91 2,200
T/B 11x10 The Lovers Slo 9/91 1,200
P/Pa 23x15 Woman Seated in a Chair Doy 11/91 1,200
Posen, Steven Am 1939-
* See 1991 Edition . . . .
Possart, Felix Ger 1877-1928
O/C 49x69 Rest on the Flight into Egypt Slo 12/91 2,600
Possner, Hugo Am 20C
* See 1991 Edition . . . .
Post, Frans Dut 1612-1680
O/C 24x33 Brazilian Landscape with Procession Chr 1/92 473,000
Post, George Booth Am 1906-
W/Pa 18x24 Fishermen Mending Nets Mor 6/92 700
W/Pa 16x22 Horses in Farmyard Slo 4/92 350
Post, Pieter Jansz Dut 1608-1669
* See 1992 Edition . . . .
Post, William Merritt Am 1856-1935
O/C 12x16 Sunset on the Marshes, 1915 Lou 3/92 2,850
O/C 14x20 Fall Landscape with Stream Chr 6/92 1,650
O/C 18x24 Autumn Scene Mys 6/92 1,540
O/C 16x12 Landscape of an Old Lane Eld 7/92 770
O/Pn 6x8 Stream at Dusk Hnd 12/91 425

Postiglione, Luca It 1876-1936
O/B 6x4 Recumbent Nude Slo 9/91 250
Pothast, Bernard Dut 1882-1966
O/C 32x40 The Happy Family Chr 5/92 16,500
O/C 29x36 Playing with Baby Wlf 6/92 11,000
O/C 22x18 The Reading Lesson Sby 10/91 8,800
O/C 30x30 Family with Caged Bird Hnd 6/92 7,500
Pott, Laslett John Br 1837-1898
* See 1992 Edition . . . .
Potter, Mary J.
O/C 23x20 Long John Dunn at Taos Pueblo Dum 7/92 300
Potter, W. C.
O/C 24x36 Angling Party on Adirondack Lake 1865 Eld 8/92 1,760
Potthast, Edward Henry Am 1857-1927
O/C/B 12x16 At the Seashore Chr 5/92 99,000
O/Pm 16x12 Brighton Beach Chr 5/92 46,200
O/B 12x8 Wading at the Shore Chr 5/92 35,200
O/C 24x30 Woodland Dance Wlf 6/92 21,000
O/Pm 9x12 Bathers in a Cove Sby 5/92 20,900
O/C 24x30 The Maine Coast Chr 5/92 18,700
O/B 12x16 Golden Sunset Chr 12/91 12,100
O/B 16x20 The Grand Canyon Wlf 9/91 10,000
O/C 24x30 Pack Trip in the Rockies But 4/92 9,900
Pe&G/Pa 6x9 Woman with a Parasol 91 Chr 5/92 9,350
O/C 36x29 Kneeling Female Nude Wlf 3/92 6,200
Potucek, Eva Am 20C
* See 1992 Edition . . . .
Poucette Fr 1935-
O/C 18x26 Windsor's Doll; Vent D'Homme: Pair Slo 12/91 . . 280
Pougialis, Constantine Am 1894-
O/C 22x30 Port Scene with Lighthouse Hnd 10/91 200
Pougny, Jean Fr 1894-1956
* See 1992 Edition . . . .
Pousette-Dart, Richard Am 1916-
* See 1992 Edition . . . .
Poussin, Louverture Hai 20C
O/Pn 24x24 The Bath Wlf 9/91 500
Poveda, Carlos 1940-
* See 1990 Edition . . . .
Povesi, P. It 20C
W/Pa 16x12 Mosque Interior Hnd 5/92 325
Powell, Ace Am 1912-1978
* See 1991 Edition . . . .
Powell, Arthur James Emery Am 1864-1956
O/B 10x12 Snowscene and Autumn (2) Mys 11/91 550
Powell, Charles Martin Br -1824
* See 1990 Edition . . . .
Powell, Edna 20C
W/Pa 12x17 Winter Yng 4/92 60
Powell, Lucien Whiting Am 1846-1930
O/C 18x30 Bay of Naples Wes 11/91 1,320
W/Pa 26x19 Woodland Waterfall Wes 11/91 1,100
W/Pa 23x28 Venetian Scene 1908 Wes 11/91 468
Powers, Ralph E.
W/Pa Var Five Nautical Watercolors Hnz 10/91 650
O/C 25x30 Under Full Sail Hnz 10/91 500
P/Pa Var Two Pastel Landscapes Hnz 10/91 300
Pradier, Jean Jacques Fr 1792-1852
K/Pa 11x7 Female Nude with a Harp Sby 1/92 1,100
Pradilla Y Ortiz, Francisco Spa 1848-1921
O/C 18x24 Un Rapto Sby 10/91 23,100
Pradilla, M. Spa 19C
* See 1992 Edition . . . .
Prampolini, Enrico It 1894-1956
* See 1991 Edition . . . .
Prasad, Jaggu 20C
G/Pa 9x11 Still Lifes: Five Slo 2/92 200
Pratella, Attilio It 1856-1932
O/C 20x28 The Bay of Naples Sby 2/92 38,500
O/B 10x15 The Bay of Naples Sby 10/91 13,750
W/B 11x9 Fisherman by a Harbor Chr 10/91 3,520
Pratella, Paolo It 1892-
* See 1992 Edition . . . .

Prather, Ralph Am 1889-
W/Pa 13x9 Two Fishermen Fre 12/91 130
Pratt, Henry Cheever Am 1803-1880
O/C 24x40 Ohio River Near Marietta 1855 Chr 5/92 11,000
Pratt, John Am 20C
O/Gl 8x10 The Governess Hnd 6/92 190
Pratt, Mary Can 1935-
* See 1992 Edition
Pratt, William Br 1855-1897
O/C 14x10 The Little Gardener 1896 Sby 5/92 4,400
Prax, Valentine 1899-1981
O/Pa/B 24x20 Femme Devant Une Fenetre Chr 2/92 2,200
Prell, Hermann Ger 1854-1922
* See 1990 Edition
Prell, Walter Ger 1857-
O/C 50x76 Soir de Novembre Sby 10/91 4,400
Preller, Frederick Johann C. Ger
1804-1878
O/C 12x21 Fleets Along the Shore Slo 2/92 1,000
Prendergast, Charles Am 1868-1948
* See 1990 Edition
Prendergast, Maurice Brazil Am
1859-1924
W/Pa 12x20 Franklin Park, Boston Sby 12/91 836,000
W&Pe/Pa 15x19 Little Bridge, Venice Sby 5/92 77,000
W&Pe/Pa 14x20 The Cove Sby 12/91 77,000
W&Pe/Pa 13x9 Low Tide, Afternoon, Treport '92 Chr 5/92 38,500
Prentice, John Am 1920-
Pl/Pa 6x20 Three Comic Strips. "Rip Kirby" 1957 Ih 11/91 . . 225
Prentice, Levi Wells Am 1851-1935
O/C 16x20 Tea, Cake and Strawberries Sby 9/91 31,900
O/C 15x19 Apple Harvest Chr 9/91 26,400
O/C 16x20 Still Life with Bass Ale Oysters Sby 5/92 19,800
O/C 5x10 Still Life with Strawberries Sby 5/92 8,800
Presser, Josef Am 1907-
* See 1992 Edition
Pressmane, Joseph Fr 1904-1967
* See 1991 Edition
Preston, May Wilson Am 1873-1949
O/B 9x12 Three Children with a Kite Chr 3/92 1,760
W/Pa 9x13 Three Dancing Couples 1913 Ih 11/91 700
Pe&W/Pa 12x13 Couple in Library 1903 Ih 5/92 325
Preston, W. F.
O/C 42x62 Cows Grazing 1892 Ald 5/92 900
Preston, William Robert Am 20C
A/Pa 15x21 Milkweed Wes 11/91 138
Prestopino, Gregorio Am 1907-
* See 1990 Edition
Preti, Mattia It 1613-1699
O/C 73x100 Boethius and Philosophy Sby 5/92 506,500
O/C 67x144 The Triumph of Love Chr 5/92 275,000
Preusser, Robert Ormerod Am 1919-
O/C 24x28 Color Action Skn 3/92 4,950
Prevot-Valeri, Andre
O/C 18x22 Summer Landscape Sby 6/92 2,200
Preyer, Emilie Ger 1849-1930
O/C 13x16 Still Life Flowers, Fruits, Nuts Chr 10/91 41,800
O/C 9x11 Still Life Walnut and Fruit 1871 Sby 2/92 30,800
Preyer, Johann Wilhelm Ger 1803-1889
* See 1992 Edition
Prezzi, Wilma Maria Am 1915-1964
O/C 25x30 Still Lifes Skn 3/92 2,200
Price, Alan Am 20C
* See 1992 Edition
Price, Clayton S. Am 1874-1950
Pe/Pa 8x11 Horse But 2/92 1,210
Price, Garrett Am 1896-1979
P&W/Pa 13x9 Woman, Phone, Cat w/Kittens 51 Ih 11/91 . . 2,000
Pl&S/Pa 10x12 Golfers Hnd 6/92 130
Price, Victor Coverly Eng 1901-
O/C 24x36 London with Thames River Wlf 6/92 400
Price, William Henry Am 1864-1940
O/B 13x16 Sierra Landscape Mor 11/91 325
Prichett, Edward Br 19C
O/C 25x39 View of St. Mark's Square Sby 10/91 24,200

Priebe, Karl Am 1914-
W&G/Pb 20x16 The Seminarian '45 Skn 3/92 605
Priechenfried, Alois Ger 1867-1953
O/C 22x27 Going to Church in Czechoslovakia Hnd 10/91 . 7,000
Priestman, Bertram Br 1868-1951
O/C 14x30 The Windmill But 5/92 2,200
Priking, Franz Ger 1927-1979
O/C 22x18 Nature morte 51 Chr 5/92 4,400
O/C 22x26 Paysage Chr 5/92 3,300
Prince, H. Eng 19C
O/C 14x18 Sunday on the Farm 1897 Slo 2/92 225
Prince, Richard 1949-
Ph 20x24 Untitled 81 Chr 5/92 18,700
Ph 20x24 Untitled 1986 Chr 2/92 12,100
Ph 86x44 More Than One Time Sby 11/91 11,000
Ph 30x45 Untitled 1987 Chr 5/92 7,150
Ss&A/C 24x18 All I've Heard 1989 Chr 5/92 6,600
Ph/B 30x45 Untitled (Sunsets) Chr 11/91 4,400
Prince, William Meade Am 1893-1951
O/C 30x21 Hun Toppling Statue of Liberty Ih 5/92 2,250
O/C 20x16 Young Male Artist 1916 Ih 11/91 1,500
Princeteau, Rene Fr 1844-1914
* See 1990 Edition
Pringle, James Fulton Am 1788-1847
* See 1992 Edition
Pringle, William Br a 1834-1858
* See 1992 Edition
Prins, Johan Huibert Dut 1757-1806
* See 1992 Edition
Prins, Pierre Ernest Fr 1838-1913
* See 1990 Edition
Prinsep, Lilian Fr 19C
O/C 13x17 Summer Flowers in a Basket '91 Sby 1/92 1,430
Prinsep, Valentine Cameron Br
1836-1904
O/C 37x29 Among the Brambles Sby 10/91 22,000
Prinz, Bernhard
* See 1992 Edition
Prior, William Mathew Am 1806-1873
* See 1992 Edition
Pritchard, George Thompson Am
1878-1962
O/C 25x30 Boats at Dock But 6/92 2,475
O/C 20x29 California Landscape Wlf 9/91 2,100
O/C 20x30 Landscape with Stream Wlf 6/92 650
Pritchard, J. Ambrose Am 1858-1905
* See 1992 Edition
Pritchett, Samuel Eng 1827-1907
O/C 24x36 Venetian View Slo 9/91 5,250
Privato, Cosimo It 20C
O/C 28x40 Venice Canal Scene Hnd 10/91 325
Probst, Carl Aus 1854-
O/C 27x20 Courting in the Park Mys 11/91 880
Probst, Thorwald Am 1886-1948
O/B 16x20 Landscape Mor 3/92 1,200
O/Cb 14x18 Eucalyptus Landscape Mor 11/91 325
Prochazka, Iaro Czk 1886-1947
O/B 27x20 St. Nicolas Church, Prague Sby 1/92 1,320
Procter, Burt Am 1901-1980
O/C 16x28 Two Riders But 6/92 2,475
Prohaska, Ray Am 1901-1981
O/C 20x31 Woman Walking Past Window Ih 5/92 850
Proiss, Friedrich Anton Otto Ger 1855-
* See 1990 Edition
Prol, Rick 20C
O/C 50x42 Quantos Anos Chr 2/92 1,430
O/C 48x33 Poison Chr 2/92 220
Pron, Louis Hector Fr 1817-1902
* See 1991 Edition
Proschwitzky, Frank Br a 1883-1889
O/C 20x16 The Persian Cat 1886 Sby 6/92 2,750
Prosdocini, Albert It 1852-
W/Pa 18x10 Venetian Canal with a Gondola Chr 10/91 935
Proudfoot, William Eng 1822-1901
O/C 30x25 Sabbath Morning, Earnest Prep. 1884 Wes 3/92 . 825

O/C 30x25 Sabbath Morning 1884 Slo 7/92 300

Prout, Charles
O/C 12x18 German City Scene Dum 11/91 575
O/C 12x18 Brittany Town Dum 1/92 550

Prout, Samuel   Eng 1783-1852
W/Pa 18x12 Cathedral Interior 1836 Slo 7/92 850
W&G/Pa 12x8 Figures Amongst Ruins Wes 11/91 798
W/Pa 7x5 A Shrine Hnd 5/92 550

Prouve, Victor Emile   Fr 1858-1943
K&C/Pa 30x20 Study for Sardanapalus Sby 1/92 1,870

Provost, Jan   Dut 1462-1529
* See 1991 Edition . . . .

Prucha, Gustave   Aus 1875-
O/C 29x40 A Troika in Winter Chr 2/92 3,960
O/C 32x42 Winter Hunt Chr 2/92 1,650

Prud'hon, Pierre Paul   Fr 1758-1823
* See 1992 Edition . . . .

Pruitt-Early   Am 20C
MM 8x8 Kiss My Ass Chr 5/92 1,500

Pruna, Pedro   Spa 1904-1977
O/B 13x18 Jeune Mere 24 Chr 2/92 3,520
O/Pa/B 8x11 Les Baigneuses Chr 2/92 3,300
W,G&Pe/Pa 11x8 Costume Design for Sailor 1926 Sby 2/92 . 1,650

Pryn, Harald Julius Niels   Dan 1891-
O/C 41x54 A Snowy Path Chr 5/92 1,650

Pryor, Yvonne Le Duc   Fr 20C
W/Pa 22x26 Abstract Hnd 3/92 100
W/Pa 15x22 Abstract Compositions: Two Hnd 3/92 100
O/C 20x16 Down the Hill Hnd 3/92 100

Pseudo-Boltraffio   16C
* See 1992 Edition . . . .

Pugh, Anna   20C
T/B 13x17 Tree and Endangered Species: Two Slo 10/91 . . . 275
T/B 13x17 Endangered Species Slo 12/91 50

Puig, V.   Spa 20C
* See 1992 Edition . . . .

Puig-Roda, Gabriel   Spa 1865-1919
W/Pa 31x22 La Artista Pintando 1909 Sby 10/91 18,700
W/Pa 20x30 A Proposition 93 Sby 5/92 14,850
W/Pa 28x22 Mujer Sentada, Cosiendo 1902 Sby 5/92 13,200

Pujol   Fr 20C
O/C 24x32 French Street Scene Ald 5/92 250
O/C 20x24 Scene de Notre Dame Hnd 6/92 100

Pujol De Gustavino, Clement   Fr 19C
* See 1991 Edition . . . .

Pujol, Paul   Fr 19C
O/C 74x54 Le Palais du Justice Sby 1/92 12,100

Puligo, Domenico   It 1492-1527
* See 1990 Edition . . . .

Pulsifer, Camilla   Am 20C
O/B 9x6 Rural Landscape '48 Wlf 10/91 30

Pulzone, Scipione   It 1549-1598
* See 1990 Edition . . . .

Pummel, Robert   Am 1936-
* See 1990 Edition . . . .

Purdy, Donald   Am 1924-
O/M 24x30 The Red Umbrella 88 Chr 2/92 1,320
O/M 18x24 Sunday in the Park 89 Chr 2/92 935

Pushman, Hovsep   Am 1877-1966
O&Gd/M 28x24 An Oriental Theme Chr 5/92 29,700
O/B 28x23 Lost Illusions No. 2 Hnd 5/92 16,000
O/B 26x25 Oriental Still Life Hnd 5/92 13,000
O/C 23x17 Divine Shelter Hnd 5/92 10,000

Putative Jan De Cock   Dut 16C
* See 1991 Edition . . . .

Puthuff, Hanson   Am 1875-1972
O/C 24x30 Autumnal Bloom Mor 11/91 7,000
O/C/B 10x12 Grand Canyon But 2/92 6,600
O/C/B 8x10 Foothills in Autumn But 2/92 4,675
O/B 10x12 Malibu Lake But 2/92 3,850
O/B 7x9 Foothills in Spring But 2/92 3,025
O/Cb 12x16 Tree Study But 2/92 3,025
O/Ab 12x16 Desert Mountain Wlf 3/92 1,800
O/Cb 8x10 Landscape Mor 3/92 900

Putz, Leo   Ger 1869-1940
* See 1990 Edition . . . .

Puy, Jean   Fr 1876-1960
O/Pn 11x14 Nature Morte Aux Fruits Chr 11/91 6,050
O/Pa/C 20x29 Gros Temps a Saint Tropez Chr 2/92 5,500

Puytlinck, Christoffel   Dut 1640-1670
O/C 45x35 Dog Attacking Fowl and Other Birds Chr 1/92 . 11,000

Pycke, Francois   Bel 1890-1922
* See 1992 Edition . . . .

Pyle, Aaron G.   Am
* See 1992 Edition . . . .

Pyle, Howard   Am 1853-1911
G&R/Pa 14x15 Boy at Desk 1882 Ih 5/92 13,000
O/B 19x12 Book Illustration. Day Dreams 01 Ih 11/91 12,000
O/C 27x18 Man Entering Doorway 1909 Ih 5/92 10,000
O&R/B 18x12 Paul Revere's Ride '85 Sby 3/92 8,800

Pynacker, Adam   Dut 1622-1673
* See 1992 Edition . . . .

Pyne, James Baker   Br 1800-1870
* See 1992 Edition . . . .

Pynenburg, R.   Dut 20C
O/C 24x20 Cabin Interior But 11/91 550

Qua, Sun   Chi 19C
* See 1990 Edition . . . .

Quaedvlieg, Carl Max Gerlach   Dut 1823-1874
* See 1992 Edition . . . .

Quaglia, Carlo   It 1907-1970
* See 1992 Edition . . . .

Quaglio, Franz   Ger 1844-1920
O/Pn 6x7 Haircut and Mealtime for Everyone 1900 Chr 5/92   4,400
O/Pn 8x11 Market Scene 1900 Hnd 6/92 2,800
O/Pn 5x7 A Haywagon Chr 5/92 2,200

Quartararo, Riccardo   It 15C
O/Pn 36x26 Archangel Michael Triumphant Sby 1/92 44,000

Quartley, Arthur   Am 1839-1886
* See 1991 Edition . . . .

Quaytman, Harvey   Am 20C
* See 1991 Edition . . . .

Quellinus, Erasmus (the Younger)   Flm 1607-1678
O/C 48x38 The Madonna and Child Chr 1/92 38,500

Quentel, Holt   20C
* See 1991 Edition . . . .

Querena, Luigi   It 1860-1890
* See 1992 Edition . . . .

Querfurt, August   Ger 1696-1761
O/Pn 27x20 Couple on Horseback Falconing Sby 5/92 8,360
O/Cp 6x7 Bandits Watched by Two Horsemen Chr 5/92 . . . 2,200

Quest, Charles F.
O/C 23x33 Still Life Sculpture by Donatello Sel 9/91 350

Queverdo, Francois Marie I.   Fr 1748-1797
W/Pa 9x7 La Jarretiere 1770 But 5/92 935

Quigley, Albert D.   Am 20C
O/Cb 18x24 Monadncok, Missouri 1944 Slo 10/91 30

Quignon, Fernand Just   Fr 1854-
* See 1991 Edition . . . .

Quinaux, Joseph   Bel 1822-1895
O/Pn 12x16 Paysage en l'Ile de France But 11/91 1,100

Quincy, Edmund   Am 1903-
* See 1992 Edition . . . .

Quinn, William   Am 20C
I/Pa 11x8 Nudes Sel 4/92 200
Cs/Pa 23x18 Blue Stocking 1960 Sel 4/92 175

Quinsa, Giovanni   It a 1641-
* See 1991 Edition . . . .

Quinton, Alfred Robert   Br 20C
W/Pa 24x40 Vale of Evesham Sby 1/92 3,410

Quiroa, Marco Augusto   20C
O/C 26x27 Maquina para Cantar 79 Chr 5/92 2,200

Quirt, Walter   Am 1902-
* See 1990 Edition . . . .

Quist, E.   Am 20C
O/Pa 3x6 Western Views: Seven Sby 12/91 770

Quizet, Alphonse Fr 1885-1955
* See 1992 Edition . . . .
Raaphorst, Cornelis Dut 1875-1954
O/C 20x24 Playful Kittens Chr 10/91 9,680
O/C 15x19 Kittens at Play Mys 6/92 1,980
Rabin, Ethel Am 20C
O/C 22x17 View of City Street Hnd 12/91 200
Rabut, Paul Am 1914-1983
Cs/C 11x15 Trio Hiding Amidst Rocks Ih 5/92 550
Rachmiel, Jean Am 1871-
* See 1992 Edition . . . .
Rackham, Arthur Br 1867-1939
* See 1992 Edition . . . .
Racoff, Rotislaw Rus 20C
O/Pn 13x11 Trompe L'Oeil 1960 Hnz 5/92 825
O/B 14x11 Boats in the Bay '54 Hnz 10/91 425
Rademaker, Abraham Dut 1675-1735
Pl,W&Cw/Pa 6x8 The Ruins of Kathuyser Church Chr 1/92 . 1,100
Radin, W.
W/Pa 10x13 Marsh Dum 4/92 150
Rae, John Am 1882-
* See 1992 Edition . . . .
Raeburn, Sir Henry Sco 1756-1823
O/C 50x39 Portrait of a Lady Sby 10/91 4,400
Raffael, Joseph Am 1933-
* See 1992 Edition . . . .
Raffaelli, Jean Francois Fr 1850-1924
O/C 26x35 Menton Chr 10/91 33,000
O/Pn 17x22 House along the River Chr 10/91 19,800
O/Pn 17x22 House Along the River Chr 2/92 13,200
Raffalt, Ignaz Aus 1800-1857
* See 1992 Edition . . . .
Raffet, Auguste Fr 1804-1860
W&H/Pa 6x8 Mort De Marechal Lannes But 5/92 660
Pl&S/Pa 3x3 Five Drawings Hnd 12/91 400
Raggi, Giovanni It 1712-1794
O/C 98x62 Saint Grata Showing Father Lupus Sby 1/92 . . 66,000
Raggio, Giuseppe It 1823-1916
O/C 27x56 Rounding up the Team '78 Fre 10/91 11,500
Ragione, Raffaele It 1851-1925
O/C 13x16 Au Parc Monceau Sby 2/92 36,300
Rahon, Alice Fr 1916-1987
O/C 26x26 Scene De Chasse 42 Sby 11/91 42,900
Raibolini, Francesco Di Marco It 1450-1517
* See 1990 Edition . . . .
Rain, Charles Am 1911-
* See 1991 Edition . . . .
Rainer, Arnulf 1929-
* See 1992 Edition . . . .
Rajon, P. Br 19C
O/C 21x17 Scene with Staircase Hnz 5/92 750
Rakemann, Carl Am 1878-
O/C 16x20 Dutch Fisherwomen 1908 Slo 7/92 225
Raleigh, Charles Sidney 1830-1925
O/B 6x12 The Hospital Ship "New Haven" 1891 Eld 7/92 . 660
Ralli, Theodore Jacques Grk 1852-1909
* See 1990 Edition . . . .
Rame, E. Eur 19C
* See 1992 Edition . . . .
Ramenghi, Bartolomeo It 1484-1542
O/Pn 26x18 Madonna and Child Sby 10/91 18,700
Ramirez, Don Am 20C
Pe/pa 22x30 Study 77 Hnd 5/92 350
Ramon, A. A. Am a 1930-1939
O/Cb 12x18 Laguna 29 But 6/92 1,210
Ramos, Alvaro Delgado 1922-
O/C 36x29 Jugador de Naipes Chr 2/92 2,200
Ramos, Domingo Cub 1894-
O/C 38x48 Bahia de Cabana 1953 Chr 11/91 18,700
O/C 18x22 Paisaje Tropical 1954 Sby 5/92 12,650
Ramos, Mel Am 1935-
O/C 70x61 Life Savers 1965 Chr 11/91 82,500
O/C 26x20 Peek-a-Boo, Red Head 1964 Chr 2/92 35,200
O/C 50x100 Leta and Flycatcher 1969 Chr 11/91 5,500

Rampazo, Luciano Fr 1936-
O/C 26x35 La Madeleine Doy 11/91 1,900
Ramsay, Allan Br 1713-1784
* See 1991 Edition . . . .
Ramsey, Lewis A. Am 1873-1941
O/B 10x8 Landscape Lou 12/91 325
Ramsey, Milne Am 1847-1915
O/C 18x22 Study in Yellow 88 Chr 5/92 7,150
O/C 24x20 Still Life Orange, Almonds 80 Skn 11/91 2,750
Ramus, Aubrey Br 20C
W/Pa 10x13 Lowestoft Harbour Slo 9/91 300
O/B 11x16 Highland Landscape with Cattle Sel 12/91 225
Ranc, Jean Fr 1674-1735
* See 1991 Edition . . . .
Randall, Leyon G. Am 20C
O/C 20x24 California Landscape Lou 3/92 75
Randle, C.
W/Pa 6x10 Two: Brazil, Mt. Video 1816 Eld 7/92 88
Randolph, Lee F. Am 1880-1956
O/Cb 6x7 Lighthouse Point But 2/92 1,870
Ranft, Richard
O/C 24x29 Picnic by the Chateau 1929 Sby 2/92 1,650
Ranftl, Johann Matthias Aus 1805-1854
O/Pn 14x11 Playing with Puppies 1848 Sby 2/92 14,300
Range, Andreas Ger 1762-1828
O/C 26x20 Portrait of a Gentleman 1796 Wes 5/92 605
Ranger, Henry Ward Am 1858-1916
O/Pn 12x16 Autumn Landscape Wlf 9/91 2,250
O/C 18x26 Becalmed Sailboat, 1893 '92 Eld 7/92 1,870
O/C 12x17 Farm Landscape Lou 12/91 900
O/Pn 9x13 Figures Outside Cottage Slo 9/91 650
Ranieri, L. It 19C
W/Pa 21x15 Feeding Pigeons & At the Well (2) Chr 5/92 . 1,430
Ranney, William T. Am 1813-1857
* See 1992 Edition . . . .
Ransom, Fletcher C. Am 19C
* See 1990 Edition . . . .
Ranson, Paul Fr 1864-1909
* See 1990 Edition . . . .
Ranzoni, Gustav Aus 1826-1900
O/C/B 20x30 Shepherd Tending his Flock 875 Hnd 3/92 . . . 1,200
Raphael It 1483-1520
* See 1992 Edition . . . .
Raphael, Joseph M. Am 1872-1950
O/C 81x89 La Fete Du Bourgmestre But 11/91 41,250
O/B 30x36 Oriental Still Life 40 But 6/92 13,200
O/B 11x14 Painting in Bruges But 2/92 2,475
Raphael, Mary F. Br a 1896-1915
* See 1992 Edition . . . .
Raphael, William Br 1833-1914
O/C 24x42 Afternoon in the Woods 1870 Sbt 5/92 8,415
O/B 13x10 In the Mirror 1870 Sbt 5/92 2,571
Rapp, Joh Rudolf Sws 1827-1903
O/B 11x14 Coastal Seascape; Alpine Vista (2) Sby 1/92 . 4,125
Rasch, Heinrich Ger 1840-1913
* See 1992 Edition . . . .
Raschen, Henry Am 1854-1937
O/C 25x36 Mountain Glow, Apache But 11/91 7,700
Raser, J. Heyl Am 1824-1901
* See 1992 Edition . . . .
Raskin, Joseph Am 1897-1981
* See 1992 Edition . . . .
Raskin, Saul Isr 20C
W/Pa 18x14 Landing Point, Tel Aviv 1946 Dum 12/91 . . . 300
W/Pa 18x14 Windy-Depicting Sailors Dum 12/91 250
Rasko, Maxmilian Aurel Reinitz Hun 1883-1961
O/C 80x46 Portrait of Emma Kessler 27 Slo 4/92 1,600
Rasmussen, Georg Anton Nor 1842-1914
O/C 30x45 A Fjord Chr 2/92 3,520
Raspis, Francesco 18C
* See 1992 Edition . . . .
Rathbone, John 1750-1807
O/C 28x36 Landscape Matlock, Derbyshire Sby 1/92 . . . 5,775

Rathoud, A.   Ger 19C
O/C 18x38 Herder and Cows Slo 2/92   500
Ratkay   Am 20C
O/B 19x31 Religious Ceremony Mys 6/92   330
Ratterman, Walter G.   Am 20C
C&W/Pa 16x13 Portrait of a Young Lady Slo 12/91   110
W/Pa 11x14 Sympathy '15 Wlf 10/91   70
Rattner, Abraham   Am 1895-1978
O/C 26x32 Seine River, Paris Lou 9/91   2,000
Pl/Pa 14x11 St. Francis and Ballet: Two '29 Wes 5/92   385
Rau, Emil   Ger 1858-
O/C 31x38 The Courtship 80 Chr 10/91   16,500
O/C 36x43 A Tyrolean Family Sby 2/92   14,300
O/C 44x36 Hiking in the Alps Chr 2/92   13,200
O/C 22x18 The Green Hat 87 Sby 2/92   8,250
Rau, William   Am 1874-
O/C 18x12 Winter, Central Park 09 Chr 6/92   825
O/B 11x9 Abandoned Barn Slo 2/92   250
Rauch, Ferdinand   Aus 1834-
W&l/Pa 4x6 Two Tigers Biting a Lion Eld 8/92   132
Rauch, Johann Nepomuk   Aus 1804-1847
O/Pn 13x17 Horse, Cows, Goats Near Well 1836 Chr 10/91   6,050
Raudnitz, Albert   Ger 19C
   * See 1992 Edition . . . .
Raupp, Karl   Ger 1837-1918
   * See 1992 Edition . . . .
Rauschenberg, Robert   Am 1925-
MM 28x21 Small Red Painting Sby 11/91 . . . .   1.25M
MM/Pa 29x34 Omen 1965 Sby 11/91   121,000
SltPe&W/Pa 42x30 Allegory (Lesson I) 69 Sby 11/91   110,000
L&O/C 9x9 Untitled 1960 Chr 5/92   80,000
H&G/Pa 23x30 Close-Out 69 Sby 2/92   49,500
Slt&L/Pa 60x40 Half Acre 79 Chr 5/92   28,600
L&Slt/Pa 23x15 Untitled 79 Chr 11/91   19,800
Slt/Pa 14x10 April's Fool V Chr 5/92   9,350
O/Pa/B 11x9 Untitled 1958 Sby 6/92   2,200
Ravier, Auguste Francois   Fr 1814-1895
O/B 8x10 Landscape Lou 6/92   1,700
O/C 10x13 Two Barren Trees Wlf 3/92   500
Rawlisky
O/C 24x19 Winter Fantasy Dum 1/92   165
Raymond, Alex   Am 1909-1956
Pl/Pa 6x19 Comic Strip. "Rip Kirby" 47 Ih 5/92   450
Pl/Pa 6x20 Comic Strip. "Rip Kirby" 56 Ih 11/91   450
Raymond, H.   Am 19C
Pe/Pa 10x8 Seated Nude Yng 2/92   150
Rayner, Louise   Br 1829-1924
W&C/Pa 16x12 A Cobblestone Street Chr 2/92   2,420
Rayo, Omar   20C
   * See 1991 Edition . . . .
Rea, Louis Edward   Am 1868-
   * See 1991 Edition . . . .
Read, Samuel F.   Eng 20C
O/C 12x20 Woman on a Path Wes 5/92   110
Read, Thomas Buchanan   Am 1822-1872
O/C 30x50 Mill Creek Valley, Cincinnati Chr 3/92   9,350
Real, Mon   Fr 20C
O/C 14x11 Two Women Hnz 5/92   50
Realfonso, Tommaso   It 1677-1743
O/C 36x37 Still Life Flowers in Silver & Gold Sby 1/92 . . .   27,500
O/C 16x26 Still Life Basket with Knitting Sby 1/92   19,800
Ream, Carducius Plantagenet   Am 1837-1917
O/C 14x18 Melon, Grapes, New Bonnet: Two Chr 11/91 . . .   2,860
O/B 10x14 Grapes Chr 11/91   1,760
O/C 18x24 Peaches Chr 11/91   1,650
O/C 15x10 Still Life with Grapes Wlf 10/91   1,400
O/C 8x10 Still Life with Grapes Dum 7/92   950
O/C 8x10 Still Life Grapes and Spoon Hnd 5/92   500
Ream, Morston C.   Am 1840-1898
   * See 1992 Edition . . . .
Reardon, Foxo
Pl/Pa 17x25 Comic Pages. "Bozo and Bozann" Ih 5/92 . . .   150
Rebay, Hilla   20C
O/Pn 24x28 Composition #9 Sby 2/92   7,150

I&L/Pa 11x15 Composition No. 12 Sby 2/92   1,650
Rebeyrolle, Paul   Fr 20C
   * See 1992 Edition . . . .
Rebolledo, Benito Correa   Chl 1880-1964
   * See 1992 Edition . . . .
Rebull, Santiago   Mex 1829-1902
   * See 1992 Edition . . . .
Recco, Giuseppe   It 1634-1695
O/C 20x28 Still Life Fish and Lobster Sby 1/92   13,200
Reckless, Stanley L.   Am 1892-
   * See 1992 Edition . . . .
Redein, Alexander   Am 1912-1965
O/B 22x26 Terns 1915 Slo 2/92   175
Redelius, Frank   Am 20C
O/M 15x17 Black Lace 1951 Wlf 9/91   1,050
Roderer, Franz   Ger 20C
O/C 36x47 Salzbourg But 5/92   1,320
Redfield, Edward Willis   Am 1869-1965
O/C 32x40 Road to the Village 1908 Chr 5/92   71,500
O/C 32x40 Washington's Birthday, New Hope Sby 5/92 . . .   68,750
O/C 32x26 The Brook Sby 12/91   52,250
O/C 26x32 Winter Landscape Sunset '05 Fre 10/91   14,500
O/C 32x21 The Shepherd '93 Lou 12/91   10,000
Redig, Laurent Herman   Bel 1822-1861
O/C 39x55 A Cold Winter's Day 1860 Chr 2/92   18,700
Redin, Carl   Am 1892-1944
   * See 1992 Edition . . . .
Redmond, Granville   Am 1871-1935
O/C 21x25 California Spring But 10/91   49,500
O/C 18x32 A California Sunset Chr 9/91   16,500
O/C 16x24 A Day in the Country '08 But 10/91   15,400
O/Cb 12x9 Moonlight Landscape Mor 3/92   10,000
O/C 6x8 Country Road Mor 11/91   5,500
O/Cb 12x9 Coastal Mor 3/92   3,750
O/B 5x7 Tiburon and Belvedere But 2/92   2,475
Redmore, Henry   Br 1820-1887
O/C 13x22 Off Dover 1876 Chr 5/92   3,850
Redon, Odilon   Fr 1840-1916
O/C 26x20 Vase de Fleurs Chr 11/91   605,000
O/Pn 30x19 Le Char D'Apollon Sby 11/91   330,000
C/Pa/Pa 14x11 Tete flotante Chr 5/92   38,500
O/Pa/B 5x7 Petit Village Chr 11/91   17,600
S&Pe/Pa 8x7 Prophet Sby 10/91   7,700
Redoute, Pierre Joseph   Fr 1759-1840
   * See 1990 Edition . . . .
Redwood, Allen Carter   Am 1834-1922
   * See 1992 Edition . . . .
Reed, D. C.   Br 19C
   * See 1992 Edition . . . .
Reed, David
   * See 1992 Edition . . . .
Reed, George   Am 19C
O/C 9x12 Still Life of Peaches 1887 Dum 5/92   250
Reed, Katie   Am 20C
O/Ab 7x13 Path in Moonlight 1898 Slo 2/92   125
Reed, Marjorie   Am 1915-
O/Cb 16x20 Desert Encillias Mor 6/92   550
Reedy, Leonard H.   Am 1899-1956
W/Pa 9x12 Indian Encampment Hnd 5/92   300
Reeves, Richard Stone   Am 20C
O/C 16x28 "It's in the Air" Defeating 1979 Sby 6/92   8,800
O/C 22x36 Early Work at Saratoga Sby 6/92   8,250
O/Pn 14x17 Spectacular Bid w/Shoemaker Up 79 Sby 6/92 .   6,050
O/C 26x32 Katonka 1976 Sby 6/92   5,500
O/C 32x38 Prismatical 1982 Sby 6/92   5,500
O/C 32x38 "Barrera" 78 Sby 6/92   3,575
Reeves, Walter   Br 19C
O/C 16x24 Mill Street, Weir. Ludlow 1883 Sel 9/91   1,100
Regagnon, Albert   1874-1961
O/Pn 18x13 The Barn Sby 10/91   3,300
O/Pn 10x13 Canal de Brienne 1927 Chr 11/91   440
Reggianini, Vittorio   It 1858-1924
O/Pn 20x15 At Home Wlf 9/91   27,000
Regnard, Jean   Fr 20C
O/C 21x28 L'Apres-Midi Sur le Seine Doy 11/91   1,200

Regnault, Jean Baptiste   Fr 1754-1829
* See 1990 Edition ....
Regnier, Nicolas   Flm 1590-1667
O/C 54x42 David with the Head of Goliath Chr 5/92 ... 187,000
Rehder, Jules   Ger 20C
O/C 20x16 Blackforest Hnd 12/91 200
Rehder, Julius Christian   Am 1861-1955
Pe/Pa 11x9 Cottage Interior Slo 12/91 60
Reher, Emil Kuhlmann   Ger 1886-
O/C/B 20x24 The Bookworm Wes 3/92 605
Rehfeld, O. T.   20C
O/C 10x15 Still Life Lobster and Mushrooms Hnd 12/91 ... 140
Rehn, Frank Knox Morton   Am 1848-1914
O/C 23x36 Ships by a Foggy Coast 1881 Chr 6/92 3,520
O/C 30x50 Sunrise Over Venice Wes 11/91 3,190
O/C 22x36 Coastal View; Sunset 79 Slo 9/91 3,000
O/C 16x28 ...Long Beach, N.Y. Skn 11/91 2,310
W/Pa/B 16x28 Crescent Beach; Off the Coast: Pair Sby 4/92 1,650
O/C 24x36 Rocky Shoreline Eld 7/92 770
O/Pn 12x17 Sailboats; Harvest Time: Pair 1890 Chr 6/92 ... 605
O/C 16x28 Seascape Yng 2/92 450
O/C 16x24 House in Landscape Wlf 10/91 100
Reichardt, Ferdinand   Am 1819-1895
O/C 13x37 Niagara Falls Chr 12/91 15,400
Reichert, Carl   Aus 1836-1918
* See 1992 Edition ....
Reichert, Charles Henry   Am 1880-1974
O/Ab 8x10 House by Road; Moonlight Meadow (2) Slo 2/92 . 125
Reichratz   20C
W,C&Pe/Pa 10x10 Auction; Haymakers: (2) 1947 Slo 2/92 .. 150
Reid, Archibald   Sco 1844-1908
O/B 8x11 Eton College Hnz 5/92 50
Reid, Flora MacDonald   Br a 1879-1929
* See 1990 Edition ....
Reid, George Agnew   Can 1860-1947
* See 1992 Edition ....
Reid, J. B.   Am 20C
W/Pa 9x11 House on Cliff St. Mys 11/91 248
Reid, John T.   Am 19C
W&G/Pa 14x10 Three Landscapes 1890 Yng 2/92 200
Reid, Robert   Am 1862-1929
O/C 36x24 Portrait of a Lady Chr 6/92 3,520
O/C 36x24 Lady in White Mys 11/91 3,000
Reid, Robert O.
I&W/Pa 16x16 Girl Looking in Mirror 1942 Ih 11/91 250
Reid, Robert Payton   Br 1859-1945
O/C 30x20 Summer's Day in the Flower Garden Chr 5/92 . 19,800
Reider, Marcel   Fr 1852-
O/C 14x11 Reflections on a Wintry Night Sby 1/92 2,310
Reiffel, Charles   Am 1862-1942
P/Pa 14x14 Fall Landscape But 2/92 1,650
Reilly, Frank   Am 1906-1967
O/B 15x24 Locomotive #6200 Passing Farm Ih 5/92 450
Reiman, Gustav
W/C 15x23 Landscape Scene Dum 9/91 175
Reimer, F.   It a 1830-1835
W/Pa 23x29 Havana Packet, Havana, New York Eld 7/92 .. 1,870
Reinagle, Philip   Br 1749-1833
* See 1992 Edition ....
Reinagle, Richard Ramsay   Br 1775-1862
* See 1991 Edition ....
Reindel, Edna   Am 1900-
O/C 26x22 Still Life with Tomato, Eggplant Chr 6/92 3,850
O/M 12x16 Nudes in a Forest Hnz 10/91 210
Reindel, William G.   Am 1871-1948
* See 1992 Edition ....
Reinhardt, Ad   Am 1913-1967
O/C 60x60 Abstract Painting 1960 Chr 11/91 495,000
O/C 80x40 Abstract Painting 1955 Sby 5/92 495,000
O/C 40x32 Abstract Painting 41 Chr 11/91 198,000
O/C 10x8 Blue Composition 1959 Chr 11/91 41,800
Reinhardt, Ludwig Louis   Ger -1870
* See 1992 Edition ....
Reinhardt, Siegfried   Am 1925-1984
O/Pa 13x10 Allegory with Two Female Nudes 1952 Sel 5/92 . 325

O/M 24x13 Boy Drawing 1951 Sel 5/92 200
Reinhold, Friedri (the Younger)   Aus 1814-1881
* See 1991 Edition ....
Reisman, Philip   Am 1904-
O/M 18x24 Ship Skeleton 1947 Sby 12/91 2,970
O/M 21x14 Singing Trip 40 Sby 4/92 2,200
G/M 18x14 The Shoe Peddlar 38 Sby 12/91 1,760
Reiss, L. H.
O/B 7x10 Farm at Dusk 1924 Dum 11/91 300
Reitzel, Marques   Am 1896-1963
* See 1992 Edition ....
Relli, Conrad Marca   20C
* See 1991 Edition ....
Relyea, Charles M.   Am 1863-1932
O/B 27x18 Molly Pitcher on the Battlefield Sby 4/92 770
Rembrandt Van Rijn, Harmensz.   Dut 1606-1669
* See 1990 Edition ....
Remenick, Seymour   Am 1923-
C&P/Pa 6x10 Stormy Sky Fre 12/91 140
C&P/Pa 8x13 Horses in a Landscape Fre 12/91 110
C&P/Pa 8x11 White and Blue Sky Fre 12/91 100
I/Pa 7x11 Harbor View Fre 12/91 60
C/Pa 6x11 Birdseye View of a Dock Fre 12/91 35
Remfry, David
* See 1992 Edition ....
Remington, Edith Liesel
O/C 18x28 Organizing the Horses Ald 5/92 275
Remington, Frederic Sackrider   Am 1861-1909
W/Pa 11x15 The Couriers 85 But 4/92 88,000
O/C 19x12 A Military Bugler 1900 Hnd 12/91 34,000
O/C 14x8 Artillery Officer, Full Dress Chr 5/92 26,400
W/Pa 6x5 Bust of a Trooper Hnz 10/91 5,250
PVB 13x7 Knife Sheath From Hiawatha Sby 12/91 5,225
I/Pa 10x8 The Wolf Hnd 10/91 4,200
I/Pa 11x9 Shield-Sioux Hnd 10/91 2,600
I/Pa 10x9 Shirt-Blackfoot Hnd 10/91 2,500
I/Pa 11x8 Woman's Shirt Hnd 10/91 2,400
Remisoff, Nicolai   Am 1887-
O/C 44x28 Summer Lake Arrowhead 6/92 3,025
G/Pa/B 12x18 Soiree De Boston: Design 1920 Sby 11/91 . 1,650
G&Pe/Pa 12x9 Soiree De Boston: Ten Costume Sby 11/91 . 1,430
G/Pa 12x9 Theater Scene with Man, Stage Ih 11/91 800
Rempel, Helen H.   Am 20C
W/Pa 9x12 Sailboats at Dock Mor 11/91 70
Renard
O/C 24x19 Boys Playing Musical Instruments Dum 1/92 ... 150
Renard, Paul   Fr 20C
O/C 16x12 Rue de Rivoli at Twilight But 5/92 2,200
W/Pa 12x16 Parisian Street Scene But 5/92 1,100
Renard, Pierre   Fr 1870-1914
W/Pa/B 12x16 L'Arc du Triomphe But 11/91 1,320
Renaudin, Alfred   Fr 1866-
O/C 20x29 Vue de Fenetrange Sby 2/92 8,250
O/C 21x28 Le Moulin a Eau Sby 5/92 5,500
Renault   Fr 19C
O/Pn 5x4 Kitten with Ladle and Cheese But 5/92 2,475
Renieri, Nicola   Flm 1590-1667
O/C 54x42 David with the Head of Goliath Chr 5/92 187,000
Rennie, Helen   Am 20C
O/B 20x30 Woods Hole #2 1957 Slo 7/92 300
Renoir, Pierre-Auguste   Fr 1841-1919
O/C 22x18 L'Alphabet (Jean et Gabrielle) Chr 11/91 ..... 2.42M
O/C 16x13 Portrait de Jean Renoir Sby 5/92 .... 2.31M
O/C 21x26 Yvonne et Jean Chr 5/92 .... 2.2M
O/C 18x22 Paysage a la Roche-Guyon Sby 5/92 ...... 1.155M
P/Pa 22x17 La Loge Chr 11/91 990,000
O/C 19x22 La maison de Collette a Cagnes Chr 5/92 880,000
P/Pa/B 15x11 Portrait de fillette Chr 5/92 825,000
O/C 17x13 Mademoiselle Christine Lerolle Sby 11/91 605,000
O/C 12x16 Paysage Aux Mimosas Sby 5/92 517,000
O/C 11x10 Femme Accoudee (Gabrielle) Sby 5/92 385,000
O/C 14x11 Portrait de Femme Sby 5/92 330,000

C/Pa 20x16 Amelie Dieterle au Chapeau Sby 5/92 286,000
O/C 11x10 Portrait Jeune Fille en Rose Sby 5/92 231,000
O/C 15x12 Tama Chr 5/92 214,500
O/C 12x9 Fille avec des bas rouges Chr 5/92 198,000
O/C 15x10 Glaieuls Sby 5/92 126,500
O/C 7x17 Nature Morte Peches et Raisins Chr 11/91 . . . 126,500
O/C 9x11 L'Arrosoir Sby 5/92 121,000
O/C 8x10 Maisons Dans Les Arbres Chr 11/91 88,000
O&Pe/C 6x6 Portrait de Pierre Renoir Chr 2/92 49,500
O/C/Pn 6x4 Tete de Femme Chr 11/91 49,500
Y/Pa 14x11 Enfant a la Charlotte Sby 11/91 41,800
O/C/Pn 6x14 Composition Mythologique Chr 11/91 33,000
O/C 9 dia Decoration d'assiette Chr 2/92 33,000
S&C/Pa 10x12 Etudes Des Nus Sby 10/91 29,700
O/C 10x13 Lady in a Garden Bor 8/92 10,000
Renouard, George Am 20C
O/C Size? Landscape Mys 11/91 605
Renouf, Emile Fr 1845-1894
* See 1990 Edition . . . .
Renoux, Andre Fr
O/C 11x18 Librairie Sby 10/91 2,750
O/C 11x14 Beaute Divine Sby 10/91 2,420
Renoux, Charles Calus Fr 1795-1846
* See 1990 Edition . . . .
Repin, Ilya Efimovich Rus 1844-1930
O/C 21x17 Portrait Princess Paul Troubetosky Slo 12/91 . . 11,500
Reschi, Pandolfo Pol 1643-1699
O/C 47x67 Landscape with Huntsmen Sby 5/92 44,000
O/C 47x67 Landscape with Herdsmen Sby 5/92 44,000
Resio, Raffaele It 19C
W/Pa 22x15 A Cardinal Chr 5/92 550
Resnick, Milton Am 1917-
O/L/B 35x23 Untitled 59 Sby 10/91 8,800
Resnikoff, I.
O/C 24x20 Abstract Cubist Composition Sby 6/92 6,600
Ressler, William Am 20C
W/Pa 24x18 Mystic Harbour Mys 6/92 220
Rethel, Alfred Ger 1816-1859
* See 1990 Edition . . . .
Rettegi, S. W. Eur 20C
O/B 48x27 Still Life with Urn of Flowers 1928 Wlf 11/91 . . 4,300
Rettig, Heinrich Ger 1859-1921
* See 1992 Edition . . . .
Reusswig, William Am 1902-1978
O/C 35x35 Couple Sitting on Footbridge Ih 5/92 1,700
O/C 28x42 Three Adults Look On Ih 5/92 1,300
Reuterdahl, Henry Am 1871-1925
G&R/Pa 16x12 Two: Naval Battle at Close Quarters Ih 5/92 1,600
W&T/Pa 16x15 Men Stoking Furnace, Plant 1911 Ih 5/92 . . 1,400
Reveron, Armando Ven 1890-1954
O/C 19x24 Cocoteros En La Playa 1926 Sby 11/91 90,750
O/C 12x16 Paisaje con Arbol Sby 5/92 38,500
Reyher, Max Am 1862-1945
O/Pn 16x20 Flowers Revenge 1938 Wes 11/91 3,300
Reymond, F. Con 19C
O/C/B 17x14 At the Well Wes 3/92 220
Reyna, Antonio Spa 1859-1937
O/C 14x30 Venetian Canal Scene Chr 2/92 20,900
O/C 14x30 Piazzetta San Marco Doy 11/91 18,000
O/C 14x29 Doge's Palace, Venice Hnd 10/91 16,000
O/C 10x16 Fishing Boats Docked Chr 2/92 4,400
O/Pn 15x9 The Fruit Seller Chr 5/92 3,300
Reynolds, C. Eng 20C
MM 6x10 Dogs and Caged Mouse 1903 Mys 6/92 275
Reynolds, Charles H. Am 20C
O/B 16x20 Navajo Moving Day But 11/91 1,870
O/C 24x30 Aspen But 11/91 1,650
G/Pa 16x20 Old Sharp's Studio, Taos But 11/91 1,540
O/B 14x12 Pueblos at Night But 11/91 880
O/Cb 9x12 Southwest Landscape Mor 3/92 550
Reynolds, D. K. 20C
O/C 12x20 Sailing Ships on Windy Seas Slo 7/92 150
Reynolds, Frank
Pe/Pa 5x5 Landscape with Deer Hnz 10/91 50

Reynolds, Sir Joshua Br 1723-1792
O/C 95x59 Portrait Mary Elizabeth Grenville But 5/92 66,000
Reynolds, Wade
* See 1992 Edition . . . .
Rhinehart, M. Charles Am 20C
O/B 21x26 Landscape Sel 9/91 450
O/C 24x30 Landscape Sel 9/91 450
O/C 40x37 Eagles Sel 9/91 225
Rhodes, John Eng 1809-1842
* See 1992 Edition . . . .
Rhomberg, Hanno Ger 1820-1869
O/B 26x22 The First Smoke 1858 Sby 10/91 9,900
O/C 34x27 Portrait of a Lady 1845 Sby 2/92 6,600
Rhys, Oliver Ger 19C
* See 1992 Edition . . . .
Riba, Paul Am 1912-1977
W/Pa 10x18 Fish Hnz 5/92 50
Riba-Rovira, Francois
* See 1992 Edition . . . .
Ribak, Louis Am 1902-
* See 1992 Edition . . . .
Ribera, Pierre Fr 1867-1932
O/C 25x30 Sur le Pont de Bateau 08 Sby 5/92 22,000
Ribot, Germain Theodore Fr 1825-1893
O/B 13x16 Nature Morte Aux Fruits Sby 2/92 6,600
O/B 10x7 The Little Chef Chr 5/92 2,000
Ribot, Theodule Augustin Fr 1823-1891
O/C 26x32 Fete Gallante Chr 2/92 55,000
O/C 18x15 A Girl Reading Chr 5/92 13,200
O/C 36x21 L'Incendie au Village Sby 10/91 13,200
O/C 22x18 Old Woman Praying Chr 10/91 11,000
O/C 18x15 The Artist's Mother Sby 5/92 4,400
Ricardi, G. It 19C
* See 1992 Edition . . . .
Riccardi, Ceasar Am 20C
O/C 24x30 Port Scene '54 Fre 4/92 550
O/C 24x30 Red House '56 Fre 4/92 325
Ricchi, Pietro It 1605-1675
O/C 41x45 Judith with the Head of Holofernes Chr 5/92 . . 13,200
Ricchiardi, Giovanni -1820
O/C 34x27 Pair:Portraits Duke & Duchess Aosta Sby 5/92 . 5,500
Ricci, Arturo It 1854-
O/B 14x19 The Last Drop Sby 1/92 3,300
Ricci, F. It 19C
O/Pn 7x12 A View of Rome 1878 Chr 2/92 1,100
Ricci, Pio It 1850-1919
O/C 25x33 A Musical Trio Chr 5/92 6,380
O/Pn 9x6 Lady Embroidering Hnd 10/91 4,200
O/C 12x8 The Temptation 1875 Chr 2/92 3,960
Ricci, Sebastiano It 1659-1734
* See 1992 Edition . . . .
Ricciardi, Caesare A. Am 1892-
O/C 29x36 Al's Riding Academy 1962 Ald 3/92 275
O/C 20x24 Magnolia Trees Ald 3/92 260
P/Pa 9x12 Three Pastels '41 Fre 10/91 230
O/C 28x36 Autumnal Landscape Fre 10/91 200
O/C 24x30 Boats in Port '54 Fre 10/91 175
P/Pa 8x10 Boats in Port Fre 12/91 120
O/C 14x18 Harbor Scene with Boats Fre 10/91 110
O/C 32x24 Portrait of a Violinist 1939 Fre 12/91 60
Ricciardi, Oscar It 1864-1935
O/C 20x23 Bay of Naples with Vesuvius Chr 2/92 4,950
O/Cb 6x9 Cavaliers in a Grotto Skn 11/91 2,200
W/Pa 10x13 Porta Capuana, Napoli Chr 11/92 2,200
O/Pn 9x15 A Fishing Village Chr 5/92 1,540
O/Pn 8x12 Bringing in the Catch Chr 5/92 1,320
O/Pn 6x15 Return from Market Chr 2/92 1,210
O/Cb 10x8 Italian Flower Market Slo 12/91 375
Rich, John Hubbard Am 1876-1954
O/C 27x23 Woman with Flowers But 2/92 6,050
O/C 20x23 Floral Still Life But 6/92 1,650
O/C 16x20 Still Life--Fruit & Bottle Mor 11/91 800
O/Pa 10x12 Flowers in Oriental Bowl Mor 6/92 450
O/B 13x11 Portrait Girl Mor 6/92 450

Richard, Edna Vergon   Am 1890-1985
O/Cb 18x24 Doud's Hill, Big Sur But 2/92 2,090
Richard, P.   Fr 19C
O/C 32x46 Still Life of Roses by a Lake Chr 2/92 4,950
Richard, Rene-Jean   Can 1895-1982
O/B 18x24 Coastal Seascape Sbt 11/91 1,683
O/Pn 12x16 North Shore, Quebec Sbt 11/91 1,402
Richard, Will   Am 20C
O/C 30x24 Wild Sheep, Yukon Territory 1922 But 4/92 1,320
O/C 24x30 Elk 1922 But 4/92 1,100
O/C 24x36 Mountain Goat on a Hill But 4/92 1,100
Richard-Putz, Michel   Fr 1868-
* See 1990 Edition
Richards, Ceri   Eng 1903-1971
Pl&W/Pa 12x15 Mountainous Landscape 1946 Wes 11/91 . . 880
Richards, F. T.   Am 1864-1921
O/C 28x36 Seated Nude Woman Ih 11/91 2,750
Richards, Frederick DeBourg   Am 1822-1903
O/C 30x24 Grand Canyon of Arkansas-Colorado But 4/92 . . 2,750
Richards, Harriet Roosevelt   Am -1932
C&W/Pa 9x8 Children Building a Snowman Ih 5/92 400
Richards, Thomas Addison   Am 1820-1900
O/C 29x36 Juliet 1842 Wes 11/91 1,760
Richards, William Trost   Am 1833-1905
O/C 30x25 Forest Interior in Autumn Sby 5/92 93,500
O/C 24x20 Gathering Leaves 1876 Chr 12/91 82,500
O/C 14x26 Along the Shore 1870 Chr 5/92 30,800
O/C 22x36 Distant Sails at Dusk 90 Chr 12/91 26,400
O/Pn 5x7 Three Coastal Sketches Sby 12/91 15,400
O/C 28x44 Along the Coast 1883 Dum 10/91 15,000
O/C 28x44 Along the Coast 1883 Dum 2/92 14,000
O/C/Pn 28x44 The Cliffs of Cornwall '90 Chr 3/92 11,000
O/Pn 6x9 The Pond at Oldmixon Sby 12/91 6,600
W/Pa 11x18 New Jersey Shore 1887 Chr 3/92 6,050
W/Pa 9x14 Kynance Cove, Cornwall Sby 12/91 5,500
W&Pe/Pa 8x14 Craggy Rocks Along the Sea Chr 3/92 4,400
O/B 21x15 Seascape 87 Sby 4/92 3,850
W&G/Pa 8x14 Sea and Cliffs Chr 11/91 2,860
O/B 9x16 Rocky Coast Sby 12/91 1,980
W/B 16x25 Breaking Waves '97 Sby 12/91 1,320
Richardson, Jonathan (Sr.)   Br 1665-1745
Pe/V 5x4 Jonathan Richardson as Boy 1716 Chr 1/92 3,520
Richardson, Joshua V.   Can 20C
O/B 15x20 Farmhouse in a Forest 1911 Sbt 11/91 374
Richardson, M. W.   Am 20C
O/M 26x31 Spring Landscape 1937 Hnd 12/91 140
Richardson, Mary Curtis   Am 1848-1931
* See 1992 Edition
Richardson, Mary Neal   Am 1859-1937
O/C 31x26 Having a Conversation Brd 8/92 1,100
Pe/Pa 11x8 Woman in a Shawl 1911 Brd 8/92 770
MM/Pa 12x9 Lady with a Bun Brd 8/92 440
Pe/Pa 10x9 Young Man Looking Down 1911 Brd 8/92 440
Pe/Pa 13x9 Portrait of a Gentleman 1911 Brd 8/92 330
Richardson, Thomas Miles (Jr.)   Br 1813-1890
* See 1991 Edition
Richardson, Thomas Miles (Sr.)   Br 1784-1848
O/B 12x20 Fishing Boats, Tynemouth But 11/91 1,430
Richardson, Volney A.   Am 1880-
* See 1992 Edition
Richardt   Con 19C
O/C 24x15 A Festive Donkey Chr 5/92 2,000
Richardt, Ferdinand   Am 1819-1895
O/C 23x34 Visit of Prince of Wales 1868 Sby 2/92 26,400
Richars, W.   Eng 20C
W/Pa 10x14 Lady in Canoe 1900 Slo 2/92 200
Riche, Almery Lobel
O/C 15x12 Oxen Cart Ald 3/92 300
Richenburg, Robert   Am 1917-
A/C 45x33 The City '60 Chr 11/91 2,750
O/C 40x52 Abstract Skyline Wes 11/91 248

Richert, Charles Henry   Am 1880-1974
O/Pa 7x9 Farm Building in Pastoral Landscape Slo 4/92 325
O/C 17x14 Forest Ald 3/92 205
O/Ab 11x14 Maine Coastal View Slo 4/92 200
O/B 20x24 Garden Party Mys 11/91 192
W/Pa 9x12 Silk Mill on the Charles Yng 4/92 150
W/Pa 9x14 Road in Autumn Yng 2/92 80
Richet, Leon   Fr 1847-1907
O/C 37x29 Les Fagotieres 1882 Sby 10/91 11,000
O/C 18x26 Fishermen in River Landscape Chr 10/91 9,900
O/C 22x26 Sunlit Woodland Clearing Sby 2/92 9,350
O/C 16x24 Thatched Cottage and Figure 1881 Chr 10/91 . . 9,350
O/C 16x24 River Landscape Chr 10/91 6,600
O/C 15x22 Thatched Cottage in a Meadow Chr 10/91 5,170
O/C 11x16 Forest Clearing with Pond Hnd 12/91 4,000
Richir, Hermann Jean Joseph   Bel 1866-1942
O/C 62x43 La Femme Au Voile Sby 5/92 17,600
Richley, Rudolf
* See 1992 Edition
Richmond, Agnes M.   Am 1870-1964
O/C 22x16 Olden Times Chr 9/91 3,080
O/C 38x32 Woman Seated Along the Shore 1920 Chr 3/92 . 2,860
Richmond, Thomas (Jr.)   Br 1802-1874
O/C 24x30 "White Nose", a Dark Bay Hunter 1827 Sby 6/92 6,050
Richter, Adrian Ludwig   Ger 1803-1884
O/Pn 12x9 Maedchen Am Waldbach But 5/92 2,750
Pl&W/Pa/B 6x4 Anficht des Amseltalles Wes 5/92 880
Richter, Edouard Frederic W.   Fr 1844-1913
O/C 29x37 Teatime in the Garden Chr 2/92 23,100
Richter, Gerhard   Ger 1932-
O/C 55x58 Zwei Spanische Akte '67 Sby 11/91 473,000
O/C 35x59 Mustang-Staffel Sby 11/91 462,000
O/C 79x63 Gebirge (Himalaja) 68 Chr 11/91 385,000
O/C 103x79 Untitled (613-3) 1986 Chr 5/92 242,000
O/C 28x22 Untitled (513/3) 1982 Chr 5/92 220,000
O/C 49x59 Abstraktes Bild Chr 11/91 154,000
O/C 49x49 Stadtbild SL3 69 Chr 5/92 110,000
O/C 40x55 Untitled (595-4) 1986 Chr 2/92 110,000
O/C 36x50 Untitled 1988 Sby 11/91 99,000
O/C 41x40 Abstraktes Bild 1984 Chr 11/91 93,500
O/C 17x24 Untitled 1984 Chr 5/92 38,500
O/Pa/L 24x34 Skizzen Zu Parkstuck 1972 Chr 11/91 25,300
O/C 10x21 Untitled (#48) Sby 10/91 13,200
O/Pa 16x16 Fingermalereien 71 Chr 5/92 10,450
O&Ph/Pls 36x36 Untitled (Candle) 89 Chr 11/91 7,700
O&Ph/Plx 35x35 Untitled 1989 Sby 2/92 5,500
O/Ph/Pls 35x35 Untitled (Candle) 89 Sby 10/91 5,500
H/Pa 12x8 Untitled 85 Sby 10/91 4,125
Richter, Guido Paul   Ger 1859-1941
* See 1990 Edition
Richter, Henry L.   Am 1870-1960
O/C 20x36 California Coastline Mor 3/92 1,700
Richter, Johann   Swd 1665-1745
* See 1991 Edition
Richter, Leopoldo   20C
* See 1991 Edition
Richter, M. J.   Ger 19C
O/C 12x10 Village in Winter Hnd 12/91 475
Richter, Wilmer S.
W/Pa 18x15 Winter Houses Ald 5/92 275
O/B 12x15 Winter Farm Scene Hnz 10/91 150
Rickly, Jessie   Am
O/M 30x36 Still Life of a Vase of Flowers '31 Sel 2/92 140
O/B 28x24 Still Life of Lillies Sel 2/92 125
Rickman, Philip   Br 1891-1936
W&G/Pb 11x15 Two: Game Birds Skn 3/92 1,980
Rickman, Thomas   Br 1776-1841
W&I/Pa 19x26 Design: St. Pancras Church 1818 Sby 7/92 . . 1,100
W&I/Pa 26x19 St. Pancras New Church Sby 7/92 1,100
Rico Y Ortega, Martin   Spa 1833-1908
O/C 19x29 Grand Canal, Venice Chr 2/92 49,500
O/C 32x15 Venetian Canal Scene Chr 2/92 44,000
O/Pn 14x8 Venetian Canal Scene Chr 10/91 16,500

O/Pa/Pn 12x7 Venetian Cafe by the Lagoon Sby 10/91 . . . 15,400
O/C 14x10 A Venetian Canal Chr 2/92 6,600
W/Pa 19x12 Venetian Fisherman Doy 11/91 4,500
W&G/Pa 14x20 Canal Scene Hnz 5/92 1,600

Ridell, Annette Irwin   Am a 1920-1939
O/C 27x31 Back Bay But 6/92 7,150

Rider, Arthur Grover   Am 1886-1975
O/C 36x46 Bringing Home the Catch But 10/91 35,200
W/Pa 14x18 King's Canyon But 2/92 1,045

Rider, Henry Orne   Am 1860-
O/C 16x20 House in Autumn 1928 Brd 5/92 132
O/Cb 16x12 Autumn Landscape 1928 Brd 5/92 77
O/Cb 16x12 Autumn Landscape #2 1928 Brd 5/92 77

Ridout, Phillip H.   Br a 1897-1912
O/C 8x16 Hunt Scenes: Pair Hnd 10/91 1,500

Rieder, Marcel   Fr 1852-
O/C 24x29 Seamstress by Lamplight Sby 2/92 6,600
O/C 24x29 Teatime on a Winter Afternoon Chr 10/91 4,950

Riedi, Marcel   Fr 1852-
O/C 20x24 A Musical Soiree But 5/92 2,090

Riegen, Nicolaas   Dut 1827-1889
O/C 26x39 Hauling in the Catch 1871 Sby 5/92 11,550

Rieger, Albert   Aus 1834-1905
  * See 1992 Edition

Riemerschmied, Richard   Ger 1868-1957
O/Pn 20x18 Nude Wading in Forest Stream Sby 1/92 1,320

Riesener, Henri Francois   Fr 1767-1828
  * See 1991 Edition

Rifka, Judy   20C
  * See 1991 Edition

Rigaud, B. R.
O/C 20x30 Blackfeet Indians Encamped Dum 1/92 75

Rigaud, Hyacinthe   Fr 1659-1743
  * See 1991 Edition

Rigaud, Jean   Fr 1912-
O/Pa 13x10 Bruges Lou 12/91 225

Rigaud, John Francis   Br 1742-1810
  * See 1990 Edition

Riggs, Robert   Am 1896-1970
O/C 36x30 After the Matinee 1959 Mys 11/91 275

Rigler, Jeanette
O/C 20x24 Winter Landscape Hnz 10/91 100

Rignano, Vittorio   It 1860-1916
  * See 1990 Edition

Rigolot, Albert Gabriel   Fr 1862-1932
O/C 24x32 Fishing on a Summer Day Chr 5/92 20,900

Rikelme, Claudio   20C
  * See 1991 Edition

Riley, Bridget   Br 1931-
A/C 57x56 Tinct 1972 Sby 2/92 27,500
G/Pa 50x7 Red Enclosed by Blue and Green '73 Sby 2/92 . 2,970

Riley, John   Eng 1646-1691
  * See 1992 Edition

Riley, Nicholas   Am 1900-1944
W/Pa 18x19 Elderly Woman Outside 40 Ih 11/91 700

Rimbert, Rene   Fr 20C
  * See 1991 Edition

Rinaldi, Claudio   It 19C
  * See 1992 Edition

Rindisbacher, Peter   Am 1806-1834
W/Pa 8x12 The Chase Chr 9/91 60,500
Pl&W/Pa/B 9x17 Buffalo Hunt Chr 5/92 49,500

Ring, Ole   Dan 1902-1972
O/C 17x14 Street in Denmark, Koge 1937 Hnd 12/91 3,000

Rink, * Con 20C**
O/Pn 13x10 The Waiting Room Sby 7/92 1,210

Rinke, Klaus   20C
Ph/Pb 33x46 Kerno Park, Japan 1970 Sby 11/91 1,320

Riopelle, Jean Paul   Can 1924-
O/C 22x13 Untitled 51 Chr 11/91 71,500
O/C 14x10 Printemps 52 Chr 11/91 49,500
G/Pa 43x30 Untitled 57 Chr 11/91 20,900
A/B 44x28 Serie Ste. Marguerite Chr 5/92 16,500
O/C 13x9 Des le Matin 67 Chr 2/92 13,750
O/C 10x13 Opera des Pics Chr 11/91 13,200

K/Pa 32x24 Untitled Chr 2/92 12,100
W&G/Pa 17x20 Untitled 65 Chr 11/91 11,000
A/Pa/C 18x34 Les Ficelles Chr 2/92 9,900

Riordan, John Eric Benson   Can 1906-1948
O/B 9x16 Laurentian Winter Scene Sbt 5/92 654

Rioult, Louis Edouard   Fr 1790-1855
O/C 55x68 Jeune Baigneuse Jette de L'Eau 1831 Sby 1/92 19,800

Rip, Willem Cornelius   Dut 1856-1922
O/C 16x29 Dutch Landscape with Boats Dum 7/92 4,000
O/C 14x20 The Goose Girl Hnd 3/92 1,900

Ripley, Aiden Lassell   Am 1896-1969
W/Pa 15x21 Fishing, Early Spring Skn 3/92 7,150
W&H/Pa 18x26 Moose Hunting 1941 Skn 3/92 4,950
W/Cb 12x16 Pointing the Way Brd 8/92 3,080
W,G&H/Pb 9x7 Two Hunting Scenes Skn 9/91 550
H/Pa 6x9 Three Woodland Views Skn 9/91 440

Risher, Anna Priscilla   Am 1875-1946
O/B 12x15 Adobe But 2/92 605

Risos
  * See 1992 Edition

Rispoli, G.
O/C 16x24 Italian Market Scene Dum 9/91 625

Ritchie, John   Br a 1858-1875
O/C 18x24 Life in the Backwoods, A Letter But 11/91 2,090

Ritman, Louis   Am 1889-1963
O/C 20x26 Double Bouquet But 4/92 20,900
O/C 40x30 Nina in the Garden Lou 12/91 19,000
O/C 26x32 Red Head in White Lou 9/91 10,000
O/C 21x26 On the Riverbank Chr 9/91 7,700
O/C 32x21 The Red-Check Tablecloth Sby 9/91 7,150
O/C 21x32 Under the Trees Sby 9/91 7,150
O/C 20x26 Verdun, France Lou 12/91 5,500
O/C 20x40 Village Church Sby 12/91 4,400
O/C 15x24 Still Life Basket of Fruit & Sugar Sby 4/92 2,750
O/C 18x15 The Pink Collar Skn 9/91 2,750
W&/Pa 18x24 Gladioli Garden Sby 12/91 880

Ritschel, William P.   Am 1864-1949
O/C 36x48 Outward Bound But 2/92 33,000
O/C 30x40 Rockbound Coast Sby 12/91 12,100
O/B 9x7 Javanese Girl But 2/92 3,300
O/Pn 10x8 River Barges Mor 11/91 3,000
O/B 12x16 Sailboats & Figures 1904 Mor 11/91 2,750
O/B 13x23 Seascape But 2/92 2,750
W/Pa 10x17 Tahitian Seascape But 2/92 1,870
O/C 20x12 Waves Breaking in the Pacific Lou 6/92 1,850
O/Pn 10x8 At the Pier/A River View Skn 9/91 1,045

Rittenberg, Henry R.   Am 1879-1969
  * See 1991 Edition

Ritter, Caspar   Ger 1861-1923
  * See 1991 Edition

Ritter, Paul   Am 1829-1907
  * See 1992 Edition

Rivas, Antonio   It 19C
O/C 26x44 Fortune Tellers 85 Chr 2/92 5,500
O/Pn 8x6 Choir Boys Hnd 3/92 650

Rivera, Diego   Mex 1886-1957
O/M 48x48 Vendedora de Flores 1942 Chr 11/91 . . . . 2.97M
O/C 48x48 Mujer con Alcatraces 1945 Sby 5/92 . . . . 2.805M
O/C 20x24 Paisaje de Toledo 1913 Chr 5/92 . . . . 1.21M
O/C 32x26 Paysage D'Arcueil 18 Sby 11/91 682,000
O/C 27x21 Naturaleza Muerta Tulipanes 1916 Chr 5/92 . . 462,000
T/L 32x24 Dos Tehuanas 1934 Chr 5/92 440,000
O/C 30x24 Nino Charnula 1950 Chr 11/91 418,000
O/C/M 47x32 El Nino en la Fiesta 1955 Sby 5/92 319,000
O/C 46x37 Cazahuatl 1937 Sby 5/92 308,000
T/L/B 32x24 Retrato de Juanita 1935 Chr 11/91 308,000
O/C 11x15 Naturaleza Muerta Chr 5/92 187,000
W&H/Pa 12x16 Mujer Sentada 1914 Sby 11/91 115,500
W/Pa 15x11 Cargador de Flores 1954 Sby 5/92 104,500
W/Pa 15x11 Cargadores 37 Sby 11/91 63,250
W/Pa 15x11 Cargador 1937 Sby 11/91 52,250
C&Sg/Pa 16x11 Nina 43 Sby 11/91 46,750
H&W/Pa 15x21 Acueducto 18 Sby 5/92 44,000
C,W&Sg/Pa 15x11 Cabeza de Nino Chr 5/92 44,000

O/Pn 11x7 Calle de Vizcaya Chr 5/92 41,800
Cp/Pa 12x9 Autorretrato 27 Sby 5/92 35,750
W&C/Pa 16x13 Campesinos 28 Sby 5/92 33,000
W/Pa 11x15 Vendedora de Cocos Chr 5/92 33,000
W/Pa 15x11 Nino con Perro Sby 5/92 30,800
G/Pa 26x20 Cantinflas 53 Sby 11/91 29,700
W/Pa 16x11 Albanil Chr 5/92 28,600
C&Sg/Pa 12x9 Nina Indigena 1935 Chr 5/92 28,600
W/Pa 15x11 Hombre Con Pico Sby 11/91 27,500
W/Pa 11x15 Mercado 1941 Sby 5/92 27,500
W&I/Pa/B 19x24 Vendedor de Ollas 1940 Chr 5/92 24,200
W&C/Pa 13x17 Yucatan Sby 5/92 23,100
C/Pa 25x19 Zapatista 27 Sby 5/92 23,100
C/Pa 25x19 Boceto Para Germinacion 27 Sby 5/92 22,000
W/Pa 11x7 Campesinos Sby 11/91 22,000
C&Sg/Pa 15x11 Nino Sby 5/92 22,000
G/Pa 15x11 Bailarinas (Two Watercolors) 39 Chr 11/91 . 20,900
S/Pa 18x25 Vendedores Callejeros Chr 5/92 20,900
W/Pa 6x9 Mujeres en el Velorio 1951 Chr 11/91 17,600
C/Pa 19x24 Mercado de Flores 27 Sby 5/92 15,400
C/Pa 12x19 Boceto Para La Tierra Fecunda 25 Sby 11/91 . 14,300
Pe/Pa 4x6 Fourteen Drawings '56 Chr 11/91 12,100
Sg/Pa 14x9 Mademoiselle Vera 1921 Sby 11/91 11,000
W&Cp/Pa 7x13 Paisaje con Cactus 27 Sby 5/92 11,000
Pe/Pa 9x6 Seven Drawings 55 Chr 11/91 8,800
Br&V/Pa 13x10 El Arresto 1930 Sby 11/91 7,700
C/Pa 7x9 Three Drawings 1947 Chr 11/91 6,600
Pe/Pa 11x8 La Reconstruccion Chr 11/91 6,380
Br&V/Pa 11x15 Vendedores De Canastas 36 Sby 11/91 . . 6,050
C/Pa 15x11 Campesina 36 Sby 11/91 5,500
Pe/Pa 25x19 Michael Goodman Trabajando 31 Chr 11/91 . . 4,950
I&H/Pa 13x9 Paisaje Sby 5/92 4,950
W/Pa 6x4 Campesino 48 Chr 5/92 4,400
Pe/Pa 6x4 Sketchbook with eleven drawings 1951 Chr 5/92 3,080

Riveros, Jorge Col 1934-
* See 1991 Edition . . . .

Rivers, Larry Am 1923-
O/C 35x59 French Money I 62 Sby 11/91 137,500
O/B 30x23 Last Civil War Veteran 62 Chr 11/91 82,500
G,H,C&L/Pa 14x17 Untitled 63 Chr 11/91 30,800
O/Cb 15x16 Figures at a Table 58 Sby 11/91 28,600
O/C 36x36 Sivia Sunbathing '80 Sby 2/92 17,600
Cp/Pa 25x28 Artist's Studio (Sienna Boot) Sby 10/91 . . . 11,000
MM/Pa 28x41 Carly Simon & Mongolian 1980 Chr 11/91 . . 7,150
Pt&P/Pa 22x30 Stencil Camel Sby 2/92 6,600
H&Y/Pa 20x14 Untitled (Dreyfus Fund) '64 Chr 5/92 . . . 6,600
K,H&L/Pa 30x44 Carly Simon Chr 2/92 6,050
Cp/Pa 18x24 The Big D 1975 Sby 10/91 4,950
O,I&L/Pa 14x17 Portrait of Robert Fraser '66 Sby 6/92 . . 4,840
H/Pa 9x6 Untitled (Nude Studies): Two Sby 10/91 2,640
Cp,H&Y/Pa 8x8 Untitled Chr 11/91 2,200

Rives, Frances E. Am 1890-1968
* See 1991 Edition . . . .

Riveti, J. W.
O/C 9x16 Coaching Scene Dum 5/92 150

Riviere, Briton Eng 1840-1920
* See 1991 Edition . . . .

Riviere, Henri Fr 1864-1951
W&Pe/Pa 16x10 Pointe du Rez 1907 Chr 5/92 2,200

Rivoire, Francois Fr 1842-1919
W/Pa 20x27 Still Life with Roses Chr 2/92 4,950
W/Pa 23x19 Still Life with Roses Sby 1/92 2,860

Rix, Julian Am 1850-1903
O/B 4x6 Golden Twilight 1913 Skn 3/92 550
O/B 4x5 Setting on Distant Shores Skn 11/91 550

Rix, W. 20C
W/Pa 9x8 Leodridge Toreador Slo 9/91 200

Roader, A. Dut 20C
O/C 27x41 Flower Market Sel 5/92 225

Robaudi, Alcide Theophile Fr 19C
* See 1992 Edition . . . .

Robb, Elizabeth B. Am 20C
* See 1991 Edition . . . .

Robb, J. E. Am 19C
* See 1991 Edition . . . .

Robbe, Henri Bel 1807-1899
* See 1991 Edition . . . .

Robbe, Louis Marie Dominique Bel 1806-1887
O/C 20x28 Moutons Dans un Paysage Sby 5/92 5,500
O/C/B 22x29 Paysage en Flanders Hnd 10/91 2,400

Robbins, Bruce 1948-
GAOs&H/Pa 41x29 Bud 1987 Chr 5/92 165

Robbins, Horace Wolcott Am 1842-1904
O/C 11x18 Boating in Autumn 1870 Chr 12/91 4,400

Robert, Hubert Fr 1733-1808
O/C 39x58 Peasants Resting Among Ruins: (2) Sby 1/92 396,000
O/C 22x31 Antiquities of Provence Chr 1/92 220,000
O/C 30x34 Ruins of Roman Bath w/Figures 1796 Chr 1/92 82,500
O/C 29x23 Mother and Child Drawing Wine Chr 1/92 . . . 74,250
O/C 40x30 Capriccio with Temple of Concordia Chr 5/92 . 71,500
O/C 47x33 Capriccio of Roman Ruins Chr 1/92 55,000
O/C 30x34 Roman Ruins w/Washerwoman 1796 Chr 1/92 46,200
O/C 34x38 Fantasy View of a Gallery Coliseum Sby 1/92 . 41,250
K/Pa 14x11 Figures Outside a Cottage Chr 1/92 6,050

Robert, Marius Hubert Fr 20C
O/C 24x32 Mediterranean Harbor Scene Hnz 5/92 525

Robert-Fleury, Tony Fr 1837-1912
O/C 28x18 The Prisoner Sby 7/92 1,870

Roberts, Alice T. Am 20C
O/C 27x35 The Model Fre 4/92 1,200

Roberts, David Sco 1796-1864
* See 1992 Edition . . . .

Roberts, Edwin Thomas Br 1840-1917
O/C 28x36 Ladies First Chr 2/92 15,400
O/C 18x14 Sweetheart's Requited Affection Dum 9/91 . . 5,500
O/C 18x14 Sweetheart's Love at First Sight Dum 9/91 . . 4,500

Roberts, J. Eng 19C
O/C 21x38 Landscape with Stream Dum 11/91 1,100

Roberts, Thomas E. Eng 1820-1901
* See 1992 Edition . . . .

Roberts, Thomas Keith (Tom) Can 1909-
O/B 10x14 Scotch Bonnet Lighthouse Sbt 5/92 561

Roberts, Thomas William Aut 1856-1931
O/C/M 27x20 The Letter 1896 But 11/91 2,750

Roberts, William Goodridge Can 1904-1974
O/Pn 30x20 Still Life Roses and Apples Sbt 11/91 22,440
O/B 20x24 Summer Landscape Sbt 5/92 7,480
O/B 12x16 Still Life with Green Jug Sbt 5/92 3,506
O/B 15x18 Laurentian Hillside in Winter Sbt 5/92 3,039
O/B 15x18 Summer Landscape Sbt 11/91 2,805

Robertson, Charles Eng 1760-1820
I&S/Pa 12x15 Venus Supplicating Juno Slo 4/92 250

Robertson, Charles Eng 1844-1891
* See 1990 Edition . . . .

Robertson, Percy Br 1868-1934
W&G/Pa 7x12 High Holborn, London 1903 But 11/91 3,300

Robertson, Sarah Margaret A. Can 1891-1948
* See 1992 Edition . . . .

Robie, Jean Baptiste Bel 1821-1910
O/C 40x30 Elegant Floral Still Life 1867 Doy 11/91 50,000
O/Pn 28x20 Still Life Roses on a Mossy Bank Chr 10/91 . 33,000

Robin
O/C 9x7 Hunter on Horseback Dum 1/92 95

Robins, Thomas Sewell Br 1814-1880
* See 1991 Edition . . . .

Robinson, Albert Henry Can 1881-1956
O/C 27x33 Murray River Valley 1927 Sbt 11/91 65,450
O/C 13x16 Moonlight, Quebec City Sbt 5/92 6,545
O/Pn 9x11 Cacouna Sbt 11/91 4,675

Robinson, Alexander Charles Am 1867-1952
W/Pa 10x13 Spanish City Hnz 5/92 100
W/Pa 10x13 Afternoon-Spanish Coast Hnz 5/92 80

Robinson, Charles Dormon Am 1847-1933
O/C 22x28 Yosemite 1909 But 6/92 9,900
O/C 16x22 Ships Off Alcatraz But 6/92 9,350

O/C 24x18 Cabin Among the Redwoods But 6/92 990
O/C 12x16 Sailboats/Coastal 1909 Mor 11/91 850
O/B 6x12 Landscape, Poppies & Lupine Mor 3/92 650

Robinson, Florence Vincent Am 1874-1937
W/Pa 14x20 Garden Terrace Doy 12/91 500
W/Pa 16x12 Mediterranean Courtyard: Pair Doy 12/91 . . . 500

Robinson, Hal Am 1875-1933
O/C 25x30 Moonlit Winter Landscape Sby 12/91 2,200
O/C 16x20 Stream in Autumn Landscape Wlf 9/91 1,200
O/C 22x28 Early Fall Landscape Wlf 9/91 800
O/B 12x16 Landscape Mys 6/92 550
O/C 14x12 Twilight Slo 9/91 425

Robinson, J. M. Am 20C
O/C 22x28 Street Market Dum 1/92 750

Robinson, M. Am 20C
O/C 24x19 Children by a Cottage Hnz 5/92 850

Robinson, Theodore Am 1852-1896
W/Pa 7x10 Nantucket Windmill Sby 3/92 7,150
W&Pe/Pa/Pa 10x6 Young Man with a Scythe '77 Sby 3/92 . 7,150
O/C 10x13 Brittany Farm Hnz 5/92 5,250

Robinson, Thomas Am 1834-1888
O/C 17x26 Landscape with Cows by the Shore Sby 12/91 . 1,210

Robinson, William Heath Eng 1872-1944
* See 1992 Edition . . . .

Robinson, William S. Am 1861-1945
O/B 12x16 Boats at the Pier, Gloucester 1931 Skn 11/91 . . 1,540
O/Ab 16x12 Fishing Schooner at Anchor Bor 8/92 1,400
O/Ab 12x16 Village Scene Bor 8/92 800

Robinson, William T. Am 1852-1934
O/C 18x22 Barnyard Scene Skn 9/91 935

Robus, Hugo Am 1885-1964
* See 1992 Edition . . . .

Robusti, Domenico It 1560-1635
O/C 57x42 An Allegory of Prudence Chr 5/92 55,000
O/C 22x20 Portrait of a Man Sby 5/92 14,850

Robusti, Jacopo It 1518-1594
O/C 46x41 The Toilet of Venus Chr 5/92 187,000

Rocca, Michele It 1670-1751
* See 1992 Edition . . . .

Rochburne, Dorothea
H/Pa 30x40 Paper Folded Upon Itself 72 Sby 2/92 2,090

Rocher, Charles Fr 1890-1962
O/B 25x19 Bouquet Roses and Tea Service Hnd 3/92 1,500

Rocher, M* Fr 20C**
O/C 14x18 La Conciergerie Sby 7/92 2,310

Rock, Geoffrey Allan Can 1923-
O/B 20x30 Girl on the Beach 1982 Sbt 11/91 1,870
O/B 20x29 The Shell, Ardmore, B.C. 1989 Sbt 11/91 1,870

Rockburne, Dorothea Can 20C
* See 1992 Edition . . . .

Rockefeller, Norman Am 20C
O/Ab 14x10 Teddy 1923 Wlf 10/91 75

Rockenschaub, Gerwald 1952-
A/C 18x18 Untitled 86 Chr 5/92 1,760

Rockwell, Cleveland Am 1837-1907
O/C 12x20 Mountain Landscape 1893 Hnd 3/92 1,200

Rockwell, Norman Am 1894-1978
O/C 27x24 Meeting the Clown Sby 3/92 115,500
O/C 40x30 Merry Christmas: Concert Trio Chr 12/91 110,000
O/C 29x20 The Magician Sby 12/91 104,500
O/C 31x27 Is He Coming? Sby 5/92 77,000
O/C 30x26 Steamship Comfort Sby 3/92 38,500
O/C 28x25 Budwine Boy Sby 12/91 27,500
O&R/C 26x18 Midnight Encounter 1916 Chr 3/92 14,300
O/Pa 10x8 Mighty Proud Sby 5/92 13,200
O&R/C 18x28 The Long Trek Home 1915 Chr 5/92 11,000
Pe/Pa 17x14 Boy and as Man Punting Dum 12/91 5,500
H/Pa 13x9 Sketch for Scott Paper Ad Wlf 10/91 3,500
O&C/B 18x15 Study of an Arab Sby 12/91 3,300
O/B 18x15 Young Thai Girl Sby 12/91 2,420

Roda, Leonardo It 1868-1933
O/Ab 18x24 Peasants at Mountain Grotto Slo 10/91 800

Rodde, Michel Fr 1913-
* See 1991 Edition . . . .

Rodero, E. Spa 20C
O/C 20x24 Fish and Copper Kettle Slo 12/91 20

Rodin, Auguste Fr 1840-1917
G,Pe&Pl/Pa 8x6 Le Cercle des Amours Sby 5/92 104,500
Pl,S&G/Pa 6x4 Jeune Femme et Enfant Sby 11/91 37,400
S&G/Pa/B 6x4 Tete D'Expression Sby 11/91 29,700
Pl,S&Pe/Pa 8x4 Three Male Figures Sby 11/91 27,500
Pl,S&G/Pa/B 5x4 Tete Casquee de Profil Sby 11/91 17,600
Pe&S/Pa 18x12 Cambodian Dancer Lou 6/92 1,150
Pe&S/Pa 19x13 Dancing Figure with Arm Raised Lou 6/92 . 1,000
Pe&S/Pa 18x12 Dancing Woman Lou 6/92 700
Pe&S/Pa 18x12 Figure with Hands Over Head Lou 6/92 . . 675
Pe&S/Pa 13x8 Figure with Arms Over Forehead Lou 6/92 . 650

Rodman, H. Purcell Am 20C
W&G/Pa 16x18 Churchyard Slo 7/92 50

Rodolphe, Gustave Clarence Fr 19C
* See 1991 Edition . . . .

Rodon, Francisco 1934-
* See 1992 Edition . . . .

Rodriguez, C. N. 19C
O/Pn 14x19 La Batalla 1850 Sby 5/92 2,200

Rodriguez, Mariano Cub 1912-1990
G/Pa 35x28 Mujer con Peces 49 Sby 5/92 15,400
W/Pa 28x22 Hombre con Sombrero 48 Sby 5/92 4,400

Rodvogin, Harris Am 20C
O/C 30x40 Marilyn Monroe Slo 7/92 1,100

Roecker, H. L. Am 1865-1941
O/B 25x30 Farm Scene 24 Hnd 3/92 425

Roedig, Johannes Christian Dut 1750-1802
O/C 36x30 Tulips, Peonies, Poppies, Roses Chr 5/92 28,600

Roelofs, Willem Dut 1822-1897
* See 1991 Edition . . . .

Roepel, Coenraet Dut 1678-1748
O/C 16x13 Poppy Anemones, Auriculas Chr 1/92 39,600

Roermeeter, Gerardus Johann Dut 1844-1936
W/Pa 14x21 Dutch Cottage Hnz 10/91 200
Pe/Pa 5x4 Windmill and Cottages Hnd 6/92 40

Roesch, Kurt Am 1905-
O/C 48x34 The Star-Gazer 1936 Skn 9/91 1,980

Roesen, Severin Am a 1848-1871
O/C 30x25 Vase of Flowers Sby 12/91 60,500
O/C 30x25 Still Life Fruit and Wine Chr 3/92 35,200
O/C 26x40 Still Life Mixed Fruits, Pilsner Slo 2/92 19,000
O/C 16x20 Still Life with Strawberries Sby 9/91 13,750

Roesler, Ettore Franz It 1845-1907
* See 1991 Edition . . . .

Roessler, Walter Ger 20C
O/B 9x7 Bavarian Man with Wine Glass Dum 1/92 225
O/B 9x7 Bavarian Man with Pipe Dum 1/92 200

Roffiaen, Jean Francois Bel 1820-1898
* See 1992 Edition . . . .

Roger, Augustin Fr 19C
* See 1992 Edition . . . .

Rogers, Claude Br 1907-
O/C 12x10 Portrait of Beryl 1927 Hnd 3/92 700

Rogers, J. M. Am 20C
W/Pa 10x13 Boats at Anchor Yng 2/92 70

Rogers, Margaret Esther Am 1872-1961
O/Cb 30x35 Might and Power 1928 Slo 9/91 100

Rogers, Otto Donald Can 1935-
A/C 60x60 Hyacinths and Certitude '82 Sbt 11/91 1,776

Rogers, W. Eng 19C
W/Pa 21x28 Pointers on the Scent Slo 9/91 600

Rogers, Wendall Am 20C
O/C 36x48 Cape Cod Cottage Eld 7/92 275
O/C 36x48 Cape Cod Marsh Scene Eld 7/92 193
O/C 32x40 Cape Cod Stream Scene Eld 7/92 165
O/C 36x48 Old Brewster Mill Eld 7/92 165
O/B 16x20 Cape Cod Pond Eld 7/92 138
O/C 32x40 Cape Cod Winter Eld 7/92 110

Rogers, William Eng 19C
* See 1992 Edition . . . .

Rohlfs, Christian   Ger 1849-1938
O/C 28x18 Weiblicher Akt 16 Sby 11/91 55,000
O/C 20x40 Kohlkopfe 10 Chr 2/92 33,000
W&G/Pa 19x16 Kniender Akt Sby 5/92 29,700
G&W/Pa 25x20 Blumenstrauss 22 Chr 11/91 18,700
G/Pa 12x8 Pauliturm in Soest Sby 5/92 8,250
Rohner, George   Fr 1913-
O/C 26x40 Chemins Sous Les Arbres 49 Chr 11/91 1,760
Rojas, Elmar   LA 1938-
  * See 1992 Edition
Rolfe, Alexander F.   Br a 1839-1871
  * See 1992 Edition
Rolfe, Henry Leonidas   Br 1847-1881
  * See 1991 Edition
Rolle, August H. O.   Am 1875-1941
  * See 1992 Edition
Rollentine, V.   Eur 19C
O/C 16x24 Ducal Palace, Venice 1885 Slo 12/91 1,600
Rollin, J   Con 19C**
O/Pn 17x15 Moonrise, Flanders Wes 11/91 798
Rollins, Tim   Am 1955-
  * See 1992 Edition
Rollins, Tim & K.O.S.   20C
O,A,K&L/Pa 24x36 Red Badge of Courage XIII 86 Chr 5/92 . 7,700
O/Pa/L 21x36 Red Badge of Courage 1986 Sby 2/92 6,600
Rollins, Warren E.   Am 1861-1962
O/C 18x12 Indian Carving a Mural But 4/92 8,250
O/C 28x18 The Screen Door But 11/91 2,475
O/C 14x22 Evening Seascape But 6/92 2,200
O/C 8x19 Santa Fe Landscape But 11/91 935
Rolshoven, Julius C.   Am 1858-1930
O/C 73x40 Tunisian Dancer Sby 12/91 2,750
O/B 16x20 Italian Ruins Lou 12/91 50
Romain, E.
O/C 20x26 Venetian Canal Scene Durn 10/91 750
Romako, Anton   Aus 1832-1889
O/C 53x39 The Reaper Sby 10/91 20,900
Romanach, Leopoldo   Cub 1862-1951
O/C 14x27 Cruzando el Rio Sby 5/92 17,600
O/C 26x34 El Borracho Sby 11/91 8,250
Romanelli, Giovanni Francesco   It 1610-1662
O/C 27 dia Angelica and Medoro Chr 1/92 44,000
Romano, Umberto   Am 1905-1984
  * See 1992 Edition
Romano, V.   It 20C
O/C 14x19 Palazzo Donn'Anna Slo 10/91 80
Romanovsky, Dimitri   Am 20C
O/B 11x8 Stroll in the Garden 1909 Mys 11/91 1,045
O/Cb 11x8 Portrait Young Woman 1909 Skn 9/91 440
Romero Y Escalante, Juan De S.   Spa 1643-1695
  * See 1992 Edition
Romero, Carlos Orozco   Mex 1898-
O/C 27x22 Mujer en Blanco 1939 Chr 5/92 19,800
O/C 20x30 Paisaje Montanoso 1966 Sby 11/91 19,800
Romieu, Leon Edouard   Fr 19C
  * See 1992 Edition
Romiti, Romano   It 1906-1951
  * See 1992 Edition
Romney, George   Br 1734-1802
  * See 1992 Edition
Romo, Jose Luis   20C
O&Sd/C 16x20 La Lucha del Poder 88 Chr 5/92 2,750
Romulo, Teodulo   Mex 1943-
  * See 1990 Edition
Ronald, William Smith   Can 1926-
A/C 48x36 Maya '57 Sbt 11/91 3,974
Ronay, J. L.   Con 19C
O/C 31x25 Gypsy Fiddler Slo 9/91 2,600
O/C 31x25 Gypsy Beauty Slo 9/91 2,100
Rondel   Am 20C
O/B 7x9 River Landscape Slo 12/91 80
Rondel, Frederick   Am 1826-1892
O/B 8x10 Pine Island, New York Chr 12/91 10,450

Rondel, Henri   Fr 1857-1919
O/C 33x52 Breaking Surf with Ship in Distress Sby 12/91 . . 7,150
O/C 7x12 Swans Wading Chr 11/91 3,300
O/C 14x14 Huntsman's Companion Skn 11/91 1,650
W/Pa 22x17 Quaker Meeting House Bridge Chr 11/91 880
Rondel, Henri   Fr 1857-1919
O/C 18x15 Elegant Lady Bust-Length Chr 10/91 5,280
O/C/B 28x24 Young Red Haired Beauty Chr 10/91 3,740
O/C 23x19 An Elegant Beauty Chr 10/91 2,750
Roner, F.   Eur 19C
O/Pn 11x9 Alpine View Slo 10/91 300
Roney, Harold A.
O/C 14x16 Rural Road in Winter Hnz 10/91 325
Ronmy, Guillaume Frederic   Fr 1786-1854
  * See 1991 Edition
Ronner-Knip, Henriette   Dut 1821-1909
  * See 1991 Edition
Roos, Philipp Peter   Ger 1657-1706
O/C 38x53 Landscape with Herdsman and Flock Sby 5/92 12,100
O/C 37x58 Shepherd with his Horse Chr 5/92 8,800
O/C 38x53 Landscape with Sleeping Herdsman Sby 5/92 . . 7,425
Roosenboom, Albert   Fr a 1865-1875
O/C 10x8 Before the Party Chr 2/92 3,520
O/Pn 10x9 Still Life Flowers in an Urn Sby 1/92 1,430
Roosenboom, Margarete   Dut 1843-1896
O/Pn 10x8 Tabletop Still-Life with Flowers Wes 3/92 6,600
Roosenboom, Nicholas J.   Dut 1808-1880
  * See 1992 Edition
Roots, Tom Smith   Am 20C
W/Pa 14x21 Columbus, Ohio Freight Yard 1940 Wlf 6/92 . . 175
Rosa, Louis   Fr 20C
O/B 34x21 Bois du Lorraine Durn 10/91 500
Rosa, Salvator   It 1615-1673
  * See 1991 Edition
Rosal, Ottone   It 1895-1957
  * See 1991 Edition
Rosam, Walter Alfred   Ger 1883-1916
O/C 79x59 Aeneas and Dido Doy 11/91 5,000
Rosati, Giullio   It 1858-1917
  * See 1992 Edition
Rosati, James   20C
C/Pa 17x23 Untitled: Two 58 Sby 10/91 990
Rose, Antonio Julius Karl   Ger 1828-1911
O/C 13x16 Fisherboats Sby 7/92 1,650
Rose, Guy   Am 1867-1925
O/C 24x29 Off Mission Point Sby 5/92 85,250
Rose, Herman   Am 1909-
  * See 1991 Edition
Rose, Iver   Am 1899-1972
O/M 21x31 Vegetable Sellers '42 Lou 3/92 1,700
O/M 36x24 Standing Clown Hnz 5/92 700
Rose, Julius   Ger 1828-1911
O/C 15x23 Greek Harbor on a Blustery Day Sby 1/92 2,860
Roseland, Harry Herman   Am 1868-1950
O/C 48x30 Look Out to Sea '08 Sel 12/91 17,500
O/C 14x20 The Fortune Teller 1910 Wlf 9/91 8,000
O/C 19x30 Reading Tea Leaves 32 Chr 6/92 6,600
O/C/B 9x12 The Writing Lesson Wlf 9/91 6,000
O/Cb 12x9 Purl One, Drop Two Chr 3/92 5,280
O/Cb 12x9 Watched Pot Never Boils Chr 3/92 4,950
O/B 8x11 Her Favorite Flower Skn 5/92 3,025
O/C 10x14 The Colored Palmist Lou 12/91 3,000
O/C 14x20 The Maternal Kiss Sby 4/92 2,200
O/C 14x20 Cottage Interior Hnz 5/92 500
Rosell, Alexander   Br 19C
O/C 30x25 Allied Forces 1900 Sby 10/91 7,150
Rosen, Charles   Am 1878-1950
O/C 41x32 Morning Along the Canal Chr 5/92 30,800
Rosen, Ernest T.   Am 1877-1926
O/C 39x27 Woman Holding Cigarette Sby 4/92 2,860
Rosen, George   Am 20C
O/Cb 20x16 Cowboy at Campfire Mor 6/92 600
Rosen, Jan   19C
  * See 1991 Edition
Rosenquist, James   Am 1933-
O&A/C 96x84 Bird of Paradise/Plant Sby 5/92 159,500

O/C 30x33 Exit 1961 Chr 5/92 44,000
A&L/Pa 52x83 Drawing for Star Sack 1974 Sby 11/91 . . 23,100
I,A&L/Pa 42x31 Giselle Star Pale 1974 Sby 10/91 10,450
Pg/Pa 20x28 #18 for Time Colors Time 1980 Sby 6/92 . . 2,200
Pg/Pa 20x28 #19 for Time Colors Time 1980 Sby 6/92 . . . 1,650

Rosenthal, Albert   Am 1863-1939
* See 1992 Edition . . . .

Rosenthalis, Moshe
* See 1992 Edition . . . .

Rosenwey, Paul   Am 20C
O/B 15x19 Evening Sky Over Paris Fre 12/91 180

Rosier, Amedee   Fr 1831-
* See 1992 Edition . . . .

Rosierse, Johannes   Dut 1818-1901
* See 1992 Edition . . . .

Roslin, Alexandre   Swd 1718-1793
* See 1992 Edition . . . .

Rosner, Charles   Am 20C
* See 1992 Edition . . . .

Ross, Alvin   Am 20C
O/C 21x16 Kitchen Sink 1960 Sby 12/91 1,320

Ross, James   Am 20C
W/Pa 13x20 Art Museum and Waterworks Fre 12/91 950
W/Pa 22x30 Country Near Flemington Fre 12/91 750
W/Pa 20x28 Eastern Point Light Fre 4/92 750
W/Pa 21x30 Time for Soup and Mittens Fre 4/92 750
W/Pa 13x20 Silent Earth Fre 4/92 700
W/Pa 13x20 Covered Bridge in Winter Fre 4/92 675
W/Pa 13x20 Vintage Terrain Fre 4/92 600
W/Pa 22x30 Once Upon a Railroad Fre 12/91 550
W/Pa 21x29 Vigilant Custodian Fre 12/91 550
W/Pa 13x19 Chester County Landscape Fre 12/91 525
W/Pa 17x24 Duty Free Fre 4/92 525
W/Pa 22x30 Vintage October Fre 12/91 525
W/Pa 19x27 Lake in Season Fre 12/91 425
W/Pa 9x12 Spring a Stirring Fre 4/92 275

Ross, Joseph Halford   Br 1866-
* See 1992 Edition . . . .

Ross, Robert Thorburn   Sco 1816-1876
O/C 31x25 Portrait of a Lady and Child But 5/92 1,870

Ross, T.   Am 20C
O/C 16x20 Landscape with Creek '11 Hnd 12/91 400

Rossart, M.   Am 20C
O/C 25x30 Verdant Landscape Sel 9/91 250

Rosseau, J. J.   Eur 19C
* See 1992 Edition . . . .

Rosseau, Percival Leonard   Am 1859-1937
* See 1992 Edition . . . .

Rosselli, Bernardo   It 1450-1526
T/Pn 16x56 Scenes from Life of King David Sby 1/92 . . 473,000
T/Pn 32x17 Virgin w/Infant St. John Baptist Sby 1/92 . . 60,500

Rosselli, Cosimo   It 1439-1507
* See 1990 Edition . . . .

Rossert, Paul   Fr 1851-1918
* See 1990 Edition . . . .

Rossetti, Dante Gabriel   Br 1828-1882
* See 1992 Edition . . . .

Rossetti, Luigi   It 1881-1912
* See 1992 Edition . . . .

Rossi, Alexander M.   Br 19C
O/C 28x36 The Card Game 1873 Chr 10/91 16,500

Rossi, Lucio   Fr 1846-1913
* See 1991 Edition . . . .

Rossi, Luigi   Sws 1853-1923
W/Pa 13x9 Woman Wearing Black Seated Durn 6/92 2,000
W/Pa 13x9 Woman Wearing Red Seated Durn 6/92 2,000

Rossi, Nicola Maria   It 1699-1755
* See 1992 Edition . . . .

Rossi, Pasqualino   It 1641-1725
* See 1992 Edition . . . .

Rossier, Rudolf   Aus 1864-
* See 1991 Edition . . . .

Rossignol, Lily   Fr 20C
O/C 36x53 Castel San Angelo, Rome 91 Chr 10/91 9,350

Rossler, Rudolf   Aus 1864-
O/C 21x48 Children Singing Chr 10/91 2,750

Rotari, Pietro Antonio   It 1707-1762
O/C 17x13 Girl in Blue Dress & Cap Sby 1/92 46,750
O/C 17x13 Girl in Red Wearing White Cap Sby 1/92 13,200

Rotella, Mimmo   It 1918-
* See 1992 Edition . . . .

Roth, Andreas   Am 20C
* See 1992 Edition . . . .

Roth, Ernest David   Am 1879-
O/C/B 11x12 Boston Public Garden in Winter Wes 5/92 522

Rothaug, Alexander   Aus 1870-1946
* See 1992 Edition . . . .

Rothaug, Leopold   Am 1868-
O/C 20x28 Figure in the Forest Mys 6/92 880

Rothbort, Samuel   Am 1882-1971
* See 1992 Edition . . . .

Rothe, G. H.   20C
Gd&O/Pn 74x36 Untitled 1987 Sby 10/91 1,320
Gd&O/Pn 72x35 Untitled Sby 10/91 1,320

Rothenberg, Susan   Am 1945-
O/C 89x113 Grandmother 1983 Chr 5/92 242,000
O/C 87x117 Patches Sby 11/91 176,000
A/C 67x78 Untitled (Head) 1978 Sby 11/91 126,500
O/C 78x111 Greenfield 1980 Chr 2/92 121,000
A/C 22x36 Somebody Else's Hand 1979 Sby 2/92 44,000
C/Pa 27x40 Untitled Sby 11/91 30,250
O&C/Pa 30x44 Untitled (Head & Spine) 1983 Chr 5/92 . . 16,500
C&H/Pa 22x31 Untitled 1985 Chr 2/92 12,100
O/Pa 26x23 Untitled 85 Chr 5/92 6,600
H/Pa 17x14 Untitled Sby 2/92 2,475

Rothenstein, Sir William   Br 1872-1945
* See 1990 Edition . . . .

Rothko, Mark   Am 1903-1970
O/C 33x30 Untitled Sby 5/92 429,000
A/Pa/B 48x41 Untitled Chr 5/92 264,000
O/Pa/C 24x18 Untitled Sby 2/92 107,250

Rotier, Peter   Am 1887-1963
W&G/Pa 16x23 The Blue Bull Skn 9/91 550

Rottenhammer, Hans (the Elder)   Ger 1564-1625
* See 1992 Edition . . . .

Rottman, Mozart   Hun 1874-
* See 1990 Edition . . . .

Rottmayr, Johann Franz Michael 1654-1730
O/C 58x78 The Good Samaritan Chr 5/92 33,000

Rouan, Francois   1943-
O/C 79x67 Porta Ardeatina 1974 Chr 11/91 57,200

Rouargue, S* Fr 19C**
P/Pa/B 29x21 An Artist in Her Garden 1828 Sby 7/92 990

Rouault, Georges   Fr 1871-1958
O/Pa/C 27x20 Clown a la Grosse Caisse Sby 5/92 440,000
G/Pa/C 41x29 Acrobat XIII 1913 Chr 5/92 385,000
O/Pa/C 17x13 Christ (Passion) Sby 5/92 132,000
G,Br&V/Pa 6x9 Etoile du Soir 1932 Chr 11/91 44,000
G&Y/Pa 12x8 Sainte-Nitouche 1918 Chr 5/92 35,200
G/Pa 14x9 Paysage tropical 1918 Chr 5/92 33,000
G/Pa 15x10 Le politicard 1918 Chr 5/92 30,800
G&Y/Pa 15x10 L'administrateur colonial 1918 Chr 5/92 . . 24,200
G,Br&S/Pa 12x8 Cristal de Roche 1918 Chr 5/92 22,000
G/Pa 15x10 Fleau colon 1918 Chr 5/92 20,900
G,Pl&Y/Pa 13x8 Mademoiselle Irma 1918 Chr 5/92 16,500
G/Pa 12x8 Bon electeur 1918 Chr 5/92 15,400

Roubaud, Franz   Fr 1856-1928
* See 1990 Edition . . . .

Rouby, Alfred   Fr 1849-
* See 1990 Edition . . . .

Rouland, Orlando   Am 1871-1945
O/C 21x29 Reflections Central Park Skn 11/91 2,200

Roumegous, Auguste Francois   Fr 19C
* See 1992 Edition . . . .

Rountree, Harry   Am 1878-1950
Pl&S/Pa 12x8 Baby Bird Falling Out of Basket 24 Ih 5/92 . . . 350

Rouse, Robert William Arthur Br 20C
* See 1992 Edition . . . .

Rousse, Robert W. Arthur Eng 19C
O/C 24x36 Landscape '88 Wlf 9/91 2,000

Rousseau, Helen Am 1898-
O/B 32x36 Sailing Lesson But 2/92 5,500
O/B 24x30 Southern California Neighborhood But 10/91 4,400
O/B 24x30 Barnyard (November Haze) But 6/92 1,320

Rousseau, Henri Fr 1844-1910
* See 1991 Edition . . . .

Rousseau, Henri Emilien Fr 1875-1933
W,G&C/Pa 19x25 Course en Camargue 29 Sby 7/92 1,430

Rousseau, Marguerite Bel 1888-1948
O/B 21x29 A Regatta 13 Chr 2/92 35,200
O/Pn 15x22 French Beach Scene Dum 6/92 3,750
O/C 15x22 Afternoon at the Beach Sby 2/92 3,300
O/C/B 15x22 Beach Scene 19 Hnd 3/92 2,400

Rousseau, Maurice Con 19C
O/C 20x26 Shepherdess and Her Flock Sby 7/92 1,925

Rousseau, Phillipe Fr 1816-1887
O/C 40x47 La Chaise de Poste; Paysage 1841 Sby 2/92 . . 29,700

Rousseau, Theodore Etienne Fr
1812-1867
O/Pn 15x20 The Plains of Meudon 1844 Hnd 10/91 90,000
O/C 10x20 Soleil Couchant Chr 5/92 44,000
O/Pn 14x21 L'Etang Chr 5/92 30,800
O/Pn 9x13 L'Etude des Marais Chr 10/91 22,000
O/Pn 6x8 Le Petit Pecheur Chr 10/91 15,400
Pe/Pa 6x9 Pont de pierre Hnd 10/92 3,400
Pl&Pe/Pa 5x9 Landscape with Building Hnd 10/91 2,600
Pe&S/Pa 5x7 Two Landscapes Hnd 10/91 1,100

Roussel, Ker-Xavier Fr 1867-1944
O/B 11x15 Le Faune et Les Deux Nymphes Chr 11/91 9,350
O/Cd 11x15 Dance Pour la Nymphe Doy 11/91 7,250

Roussel, Pierre Fr 1927-
* See 1991 Edition . . . .

Rousset, Jules Fr 1840-
* See 1992 Edition . . . .

Roux, Frederic Fr 1805-1874
W/Pa 10x13 A Ship in Port 1859 Hnd 6/92 575

Roux, Paul Fr 1840-1918
O/C 35x58 Landscape Near Eole Sby 1/92 4,950

Rovello, E.
O/C 15x30 Flower Girls Dum 8/92 600

Rovello, G. It 19C
O/C 15x30 Flower Girls in a Boat Hnd 6/92 400

Rowbotham, Charles Br a 1877-1914
W/Pa 8x19 Italian Coastal Scene 1827 But 5/92 1,320

Rowbotham, Thomas Charles L. Br
1823-1875
W&G/B 10x22 Monastary on a Cliff 1867 Chr 10/91 1,870

Rowe, Ernest Arthur Br -1922
* See 1992 Edition . . . .

Rowlandson, George Derville Br 1861-
O/C 20x30 Picking Up the Scent Sby 6/92 6,325

Rowlandson, Thomas Eng 1756-1827
W/Pa 11x10 Dr. Sangado and His Patient Slo 7/92 2,250
Pl&W/Pa 8x6 Connoisseur and Hired Boy Wes 11/91 1,980
Pl&W/Pa/B 8x11 Old Bartholomews Wes 11/91 1,540
I&W/Pa 8x7 Actresses' Dressing Room Slo 12/91 675
W/Pa 9x12 Caught in the Act Slo 12/91 450

Roy, Alix Hai
O/M 24x14 Fruits and Vegetables Chr 5/92 3,960

Roy, Martin & Keith Haring Am 20C
Fp&Ph 20x16 King Kong for a Day 89 Chr 5/92 3,520

Roy, Pierre Fr 20C
* See 1992 Edition . . . .

Roybet, Ferdinand Fr 1840-1920
O/Pn 26x22 The Cavalier Sby 7/92 3,575
O/Pn 22x18 The Young Prince Dum 10/91 3,500
O/Pn 16x10 Young Shepherds Skn 5/92 2,310
O/Pn 7x10 Cavaliers: Pair Sby 1/92 770

Royle, Herbert Eng 1870-1958
* See 1992 Edition . . . .

Rozaire, Arthur D. Can 1879-1922
* See 1992 Edition . . . .

Rozen, George
O/C 20x16 Man on Horseback Being Lassoed Ih 5/92 3,250

Rozen, Jerome
O/C 28x20 Cowboy on a White Horse Ih 11/91 2,100
O/C 27x20 Glowering Man with Whip Ih 5/92 1,300

Rozier, Jules Charles Fr 1821-1882
O/C 14x11 The Garden Wall Skn 9/91 1,320

Rubbiani, Felice & Velani, F. It 1677-1752
O/C 33x56 Still Life Flowers in Vase, Grapes 34 Sby 5/92 . 37,400

Ruben, Franz Leo Aus 1843-1920
* See 1991 Edition . . . .

Rubens, Sir Peter Paul Flm 1577-1640
* See 1992 Edition . . . .

Rubin, Hy Am 1905-1960
S&C/Pa 23x13 Two Men with Lantern 39 Ih 11/91 200

Rubin, Michael Am
A/L 40x54 Solar Path '91 But 5/92 7,150

Rubin, Reuven Isr 1893-1974
O/C/M 36x25 Self-Portrait Chr 2/92 90,200
O/C 26x32 Road to Galilee Chr 5/92 46,200
O/C 34x45 Harvest Time in Nazareth Sby 10/91 44,000
O/C 32x26 Landscape with Olive Trees Chr 5/92 35,200
O/C 28x21 Yellow Daffodils Chr 5/92 33,000
O/C 36x29 Still Life with White Flowers But 11/91 23,100
O/C 9x17 Still Life with Fruit Chr 11/91 8,250
O/C 13x10 The Fisherman Sby 6/92 7,150
Pl,S&K/Pa 24x18 Mother and Child Chr 5/92 4,400

Ruckreim, Ulrich 20C
Fp/Pa 29x39 Untitled Sby 11/91 2,200

Rude, Olaf Dan 1866-1957
* See 1991 Edition . . . .

Rude, Sophie (Nee Fremlet) Fr 1797-1867
* See 1991 Edition . . . .

Ruelas, Julio Mex 1870-1907
* See 1991 Edition . . . .

Ruellan, Andree Am 1905-
O/C 11x14 Peaches Hnd 5/92 600
V/Pa 12x17 Poinsettias Hnd 5/92 100

Ruff, Thomas 1958-
Ph 102x74 17h, 36m/-34° 1989 Chr 5/92 13,200
Ph 83x65 Untitled 1989 Chr 2/92 12,100
Ph 102x73 22h 48mm-60° 1989 Chr 11/91 11,000
Ph 83x65 Untitled 1988 Chr 11/91 8,250

Rugendas, Johann Moritz Ger 1802-1858
O/C 20x16 Saliendo de la Iglesia Sby 5/92 57,750

Ruiz, Antonio Mex 1897-1964
H/Pa 10x13 Escena De Cristo 20 Sby 11/91 8,800

Ruiz, Tomasso Spa 18C
O/C 10x23 Bay of Naples, Vesuvius 1741 Chr 10/91 33,000

Ruiz, Yamero Am a 1890-1910
O/C 13x21 Woman Sitting by River But 6/92 2,090

Ruiz-Pipo, Manolo Spa 1929-
* See 1992 Edition . . . .

Rundt, Hans Hinrich 1660-1750
O/C 43x54 Christ in Garden of Gethsemane 1729 Sby 10/91 7,700

Rungius, Carl Clemens Moritz Am
1869-1959
Pe&Y/B 8x11 Siesta Wes 11/91 3,190
O/C 9x11 Rocky Mountain Landscape Wes 11/91 2,090
O/C 9x11 Wyoming Landscape Wes 11/91 2,090
O/C 9x11 Yukon Territory Wes 11/91 2,090

Runyon, Grace A. Am a 1930-1939
O/M 20x24 Landscape Mor 3/92 300

Ruocco, Franco It 20C
O/C 20x30 Sunlit Coastal Scene Sel 9/91 230

Ruolle, Lucien Fr 1925-
O/C 26x22 Ardente Declaration Dum 7/92 300

Ruoppolo, Giovanni Battisa It 1629-1693
* See 1991 Edition . . . .

Ruperti, Madja
L&S/M 47x32 Plymouth 63 Sby 2/92 880

Rupprecht, H.
O/C 24x30 Autumn Landscape Dum 9/91 450

Ruscha, Ed   Am 1937-
O/C 99x80 Not A Bad World, Is It? 1983 Chr 11/91 132,000
O/C 22x80 Days of the Week 1979 Chr 5/92 77,000
A/C 55x74 Do Az I Do 1988 Sby 11/91 71,500
MM 36x40 Various Cruelties Sby 11/91 18,700
Gp&P/Pa 23x29 Rain 1970 Sby 5/92 17,600
Pg/Pa 22x30 More Poison 1984 Sby 5/92 16,500
Gp/Pa 15x23 The Briefcase 1973 Chr 11/91 9,350
Ruschi, Francesco   It 1610-1661
* See 1992 Edition ....
Rusinol, Santiago   Spa 1861-1931
O/C 21x13 The Garden Wall Chr 10/91 25,300
Rusk, L. S.   Am 20C
O/C 45x60 A Summer Stream 1915 Wlf 9/91 1,000
Russ, C. B.   Am a 1860-1920
O/C 12x20 Upper Mississippi River 1887 Yng 4/92 1,100
O/C 18x15 Grazing By the Pool's Edge Skn 11/91 440
Russ, Robert   Aus 1847-1922
* See 1991 Edition ....
Russell, Charles Marion   Am 1864-1926
W&G/B 14x22 Campsite by the Lake 1908 Chr 5/92 ... 143,000
W/Pb 12x21 Trappers Crossing the Prairie 1901 Sby 5/92 . 74,800
W,G&R/Pb 13x18 Misplaced Confidence Sby 12/91 55,000
G&Pe/B 8x11 Deer in a Snowy Forest 1906 Chr 5/92 ... 35,200
Pl/Pa 16x23 Last of the Buffalo But 4/92 24,750
Russell, George Horne   Can 1861-1933
O/C 23x41 Harbour Scene at Dusk Sbt 11/91 3,085
O/C 12x20 Lunenburg, Nova Scotia Sbt 11/91 1,870
O/C 18x24 Scottish Landscape Sbt 5/92 1,122
Russell, Gyrth   Am 1892-1970
* See 1992 Edition ....
Russell, John   Br 19C
O/C 32x48 The Day's Catch 1871 Sby 6/92 11,550
Russell, John   Br 1745-1806
O/C 12x10 Portrait of a Young Nobleman 1788 Chr 5/92 .. 8,250
Russell, John Wentworth   Can 1879-1959
O/B 11x13 Figure Seated by a Garden 11 Sbt 11/91 1,683
Russell, Morgan   Am 1886-1953
O/C 25x32 The Quarry Doy 12/91 1,000
Pe/Pa 8x9 Study Female Nude But 5/92 550
Russell, R.   Am 20C
O/Cb 15x11 Two Indian Chiefs 1908 Chr 6/92 935
Russell, Walter   Am 1871-1963
* See 1992 Edition ....
Russman, Felix   Am 1888-
O/C 30x40 Wild Life at Sunset Hnd 12/91 400
Russo, Alexander Peter   Am 1922-
O/C 32x28 Winter Night 1949 Lou 3/92 700
Russolo, Luigi   It 20C
* See 1991 Edition ....
Rust, Johna Adolph   Dut 1828-1915
O/C 11x14 A Fishing Village Chr 2/92 2,200
Ruthenbech, Reiner   20C
I,Mk&H/Pa 16x24 Untitled Sby 11/91 1,100
Ruvolo, Felix   Am 1912-
O/B 15x11 Two Theatrical Scenes Hnz 5/92 1,100
G/Cd 23x17 Gold Fish Pond Slo 9/91 90
Ruysch, Rachel   Dut 1664-1750
* See 1990 Edition ....
Ruytinx, Alfred   Bel 1871-
* See 1992 Edition ....
Ryan, Patrick   19C
* See 1991 Edition ....
Ryan, Tom   Am 1922-
* See 1990 Edition ....
Ryback, Issachar   Rus 1897-1935
W/Pa 13x10 Yeshiva Boy Chr 5/92 2,860
Ryckaert III, David   Flm 1612-1661
O/Pn 24x32 Card Players in an Interior Sby 5/92 7,150
Ryder, Chauncey Foster   Am 1868-1949
O/C/Pn 25x30 Deep Hollow Chr 9/91 9,900
O/C/M 25x30 The Old Road Chr 5/92 8,800
O/C 25x30 The River Road Wlf 9/91 8,000
O/C/M 25x30 Autumn Hills Chr 3/92 6,600
O/C 12x16 Approaching Storm Sby 4/92 4,125

O/C 12x16 The Lane to the Pasture Sby 12/91 .... 2,31?
O/C 16x20 Up Hill on Essex Road 1908 Skn 9/91 ...... 1,98?
O/Pn 6x9 Cape Porpoise, Maine Chr 11/91 .... 1,76?
O/Ab 6x8 A Green Wave Wlf 9/91 .... 1,30?
O/B 6x9 Stream at the Foot of the Hill Skn 3/92 .... 1,04?
Ryland, Robert Knight   Am 1873-1951
O/B 16x13 No Rooms in Manhattan Chr 3/92 .... 2,20?
Ryman, Herbert D.   Am a 1930-1939
W/Pa 20x29 Circus Canvas Mender's Wagon 1949 But 6/92 . 77?
Ryman, Robert   Am 1930-
O/Fg 94x84 Director 83 Sby 11/91 .... 330,00?
O/L 13x13 Untitled 1961 Sby 10/91 .... 88,00?
O/My 18x18 Untitled 69 Sby 2/92 .... 33,00?
Fp/F/B 20x20 Bent Line Drawing 70 Chr 2/92 .... 18,70?
Ryott, J. R.   Br a 1810-1860
O/C 27x37 Prize Cow with Farmer 1839 But 5/92 ...... 13,20?
Rysh, R.   Con 19C
O/Pn 15x11 Peonies and Zinnias Fre 10/91 .... 25?
Saal, Georg Otto   Ger 1818-1870
* See 1991 Edition ....
Sabatini, I.   It 19C
* See 1991 Edition ....
Sabbatini, Andrea   It 1487-1530
* See 1991 Edition ....
Sabbatini, Lorenzo   It 1530-1576
O/C 41x33 The Annunciation Sby 10/91 .... 16,50?
Sabitini, Raphael   Am 1898-
P/Pa 19x28 Man Eating Fish Fre 12/91 .... 15?
Sabouraud, Emile   Fr 1900-
O/C 16x32 Les Bords De Larques Wes 11/91 .... 1,32?
O/C 24x29 Belle ile 1947 Skn 5/92 .... 412?
Saccaggi, Cesare   It 1868-
W/Pa 27x20 A Young Lady 1904 Hnz 5/92 .... 600?
Saccaro, John   Am 1913-1981
O/C 46x58 Composition #21 But 2/92 .... 5,225?
O/C 30x21 The Blue Lovers Lou 9/91 .... 1,200?
Sacke, W. T.
O/C 23x35 Gloucester Harbour Dum 1/92 .... 350?
Sacks, Joseph   Am 1887-1974
O/C 36x30 Mrs. Victor C. Mathers Fre 10/91 .... 2,000?
Sadee, Philippe   Dut 1837-1904
* See 1991 Edition ....
Sadler, Walter Dendy   Br 1854-1923
O/C 28x44 Always the Largest Fish That's Lost 81 Sby 2/92 8,250?
O/C 16x20 The Serenade 1895 Dum 6/92 .... 4,000?
Saenz, Antonio Lopez   Mex 1936-
O/C 51x40 Sonando un Viaje 89 Chr 5/92 .... 10,450?
Saftleven, Herman   Dut 1609-1685
O/Pn 18x25 Rhine Landscape 167* Wlf 9/91 .... 13,000?
K&S/Pa 12x7 A Man Carrying a Sack Chr 1/92 .... 10,450?
Sagrestani, Giovanni Camillo   1660-1730
O/C 46x35 Triumph of Galatea Chr 10/91 .... 12,100?
Sahlin, Carl   Am 20C
W/Pa 25x17 Three Works Wes 11/91 .... 825?
Sailmaker, Isaac   1633-1721
* See 1992 Edition ....
Sain, Edouard Alexandre   Fr 1830-1910
O/C 41x25 Rosina Sby 10/91 .... 9,900?
O/C 34x27 Kiarella 1865 Slo 2/92 .... 4,000?
Saint Andre, Berthome   Fr 1905-1977
* See 1992 Edition ....
Saint-Marcel, Emile Normand   Fr 1840-
V/Pa 5x8 Study of a Lion Sby 7/92 .... 605?
Saintin, Henri   Fr 1846-1899
O/C 26x40 Drawing Water Along the River Sby 1/92 .... 1,210?
Saintin, Jules Emile   Fr 1829-1894
* See 1991 Edition ....
Saintpierre, Gaston Casimir   Fr 1833-1916
* See 1991 Edition ....
Sakai, Kazuya   Arg 1927-
O/C 43x39 De la Serie Blanco y Negro 58 Chr 5/92 ...... 5,500?
Sala Y Frances, Emilio   Spa 1850-1910
* See 1992 Edition ....

Sala, Juan   Spa 1867-1918
O/C 20x24 Teatime by the River Chr 2/92 11,000
Sala, Paolo   It 1859-1924
W/Pa/B 39x27 Dance of Spring Chr 5/92 5,500
W/Pa 14x21 Panorama di Venezia Chr 2/92 4,620
W/Pb 9x13 St. Paul's Cathedral, London Chr 10/91 1,980
Sala, Ventura Alvarez   Spa 1871-
* See 1991 Edition
Salabet, Jean   Fr 20C
* See 1992 Edition
Salanson, Eugenie Marie   Fr a 1864-1892
O/C 53x34 The Lobster Catch 1884 Sby 5/92 11,550
O/C 44x28 The Fishing Girl Eld 8/92 1,980
Salantine, *   Ger 19C**
O/C 23x20 Schoolmaster's Discovery 1852 Sby 7/92 3,850
Salazar, Carlos   Col 1956-
* See 1992 Edition
Salazar, Ignacio   Mex 1947-
* See 1990 Edition
Salemme, Attilio   It 20C
O/C 47x59 The Assignation 52 Sby 6/92 17,600
O/C 16x42 Vintage of Uncertainties '49 Sby 2/92 12,100
Salieres, Paul Narcisse   Fr 19C
O/C 63x44 The Twin Boys Sby 10/91 22,000
Salinas Y Teruel, Augustin   Spa 1862-1915
* See 1992 Edition . . . .
Salinas, Juan Pablo   Spa 1871-1946
O/C 16x26 The Wedding Party Sby 2/92 121,000
Salinas, Porfiro   Am 1910-1972
O/Cb 9x12 Texas Hill Country Lou 6/92 1,300
Saling, Paul E.   Am 1876-1936
O/C 34x40 Congregational Church-Saybrook Mys 6/92 440
Salini, Tommaso   It 1575-1625
O/C 63x44 The Education of Jupiter Sby 10/91 55,000
Salle, David   Am 1952-
O&MM/C 84x100 A Collapsing Sheet Sby 5/92 143,000
O&A/C 88x113 Skintight World Chr 5/92 143,000
A/C 48x70 He Aspires to the Condition of the. Sby 5/92 . . 60,500
O&A/C 92x66 Swimmer Chr 11/91 55,000
A/C 43x63 B.A.I.A. Chr 5/92 38,500
O&A/C 58x85 Untitled Chr 5/92 38,500
O,A&L/C 60x42 Engagement Rings Chr 2/92 28,600
W&H/Pa 18x24 Untitled 84 Chr 11/91 19,800
W&H/Pa 18x24 Untitled 1982 Chr 5/92 17,600
W&H/Pa 14x20 Untitled 1985 Chr 2/92 11,000
W&H/Pa 20x28 Untitled 1986 Chr 11/91 7,700
Br&l/Pa 22x30 Untitled Chr 5/92 6,600
W/Pa 18x24 Untitled 84 Sby 2/92 5,500
Salles, Jules Wagner   Fr 1814-1898
* See 1992 Edition . . . .
Salmon, Robert   Am 1775-1842
O/Pn 20x31 Shipping off Greenock 1826 Chr 3/92 28,600
O/B 10x12 Cunard Lighthouse 1828 Sby 5/92 13,200
O/Pn 10x12 Ships off the Scottish Coast Fre 4/92 12,000
O/Pn 11x14 Fishing Scene 1840 Skn 3/92 8,525
Salmson, Hugo F. & Schoenfels   Swd 1843-1894
* See 1992 Edition . . . .
Salome   Ger 20C
* See 1991 Edition . . . .
Salt, John   Br 1937-
O/C 46x58 Catskill Pastoral Sby 10/91 19,800
O/C 52x77 Arrested Vehicle (Fat Seats) Chr 5/92 11,000
Salvi, Ensel   It 20C
O/C 18x28 Coastal Scene '47 Wes 11/91 220
Salvi, G.   Eng 19C
O/Pn 6x12 Country Cottage Hnz 5/92 200
Salvi, Giovanni Battista   It 1609-1685
* See 1992 Edition . . . .
Samara, Helga   Ger 1941-
O/B 12x9 Floral Still Life Dum 5/92 350
Samaras, Lucas   Am 1936-
I&S/Pa/B 97x133 Head Group #3 Sby 10/91 28,600
P/Pa 12x9 Nude by a Red Table '62 Sby 2/92 3,850

L 54x53 Reconstruction #104 Sby 10/91 3,850
P/Pa 9x12 Embracing Couple '62 Sby 6/92 2,475
I&W/Pa 11x8 Untitled 62 Sby 10/91 2,310
P/Pa 13x10 Untitled Sby 6/92 1,650
P/Pa 12x9 Untitled #3 '62 Sby 6/92 1,650
I&W/Pa 11x9 Untitled '63 Sby 10/91 990
Sambrook, Russell   Am 20C
O/C 68x32 Alka Seltzer Wlf 10/91 625
O/C 44x31 Mounty Wlf 10/91 325
Sammons, Carl   Am 1886-1968
O/C 20x26 Wildflowers, Seventeen Mile Drive But 10/91 . . . 4,125
O/C/B 12x16 Smoke Trees, Palm Springs But 2/92 2,090
O/Cb 12x16 California Coastal Mor 11/91 1,500
O/Cb 12x16 Carmel Coast Mor 11/91 1,200
O/Cb 18x24 Coastal Mor 3/92 1,200
O/C 14x20 Desert in Bloom But 10/91 1,100
O/Cb 12x16 June Lake, High Sierra Mor 3/92 750
O/C 6x8 Carmel by the Sea Mor 11/91 700
O/C 20x26 Landscape Mor 6/92 700
O/C 6x8 Carmel Coast Mor 11/91 550
O/C/B 6x8 Carmel Coastal Mor 3/92 500
O/C/B 6x8 Carmel Coast Mor 3/92 450
O/Cb 4x6 Carmel Coast (2) Mor 11/91 400
O/Cb 4x6 Gull & Twin Lakes (2) Mor 11/91 350
Samokich, Nicolai Semionovitch   Rus 1860-
W&PI/B 11x9 Village Market with Carriage Sby 7/92 1,100
Sample, Paul Starrett   Am 1896-1974
O/C 20x26 Fox by a Winter Stream Chr 6/92 5,720
O/C 16x20 Haying Sby 12/91 3,300
W/Pa 7x13 Salinas Valley - '29 '29 Mor 3/92 900
W/Pa 10x13 Back Alley But 6/92 825
G/Pa 12x18 The Boxer Hnz 5/92 750
W/Pa 15x22 Winter Landscape Yng 2/92 750
O/Cb 16x20 Mountain and Meadow Mor 6/92 700
Pe&W/Pa 16x20 Washington Park 1933 Hnd 12/91 600
W/Pa 11x15 Landscape in Winter Wlf 6/92 375
Sampson, A.   Eur 19C
O/C 36x22 Italian Girl Yng 2/92 200
Samson, Jeanne   Fr 19C
O/Pm 16x11 The Artist Sketching 1874 Hnz 5/92 700
Samuelson, Peter   Br 1912-
O/B 16x14 The Post John in Summertime '61 But 5/92 . . . 1,320
O/B 15x18 Wolfram Pichter But 5/92 550
Sanborn, Percy A.   Am 1849-1929
O/C 22x34 Glory of the Seas 1869 Sby 12/91 6,325
Sanchez, Edgar   Ven 1940-
A/C 55x67 Imagen, Vision B2000 Chr 11/91 9,900
A/C 59x59 Rostro y Piel 202 Chr 5/92 9,350
Sanchez, Emilio   Cub 1921-
O/C 55x38 Una Casita Verde Chr 11/91 6,600
O/C 48x48 Sin Titulo Chr 5/92 4,400
P/Pa 30x22 Doorway Wlf 9/91 750
Sanchez, Enrique   Mex 1940-
* See 1991 Edition . . . .
Sanchez, Tomas   Cub 1948-
A/C 43x59 Meditacion 87 Chr 5/92 66,000
O/C 43x50 La Nube y Su Sombra 88 Chr 11/91 33,000
Sanchez-Perrier, Emilio   Spa 1855-1907
O/Pn 14x22 El Rialaje (Alcala) Sby 10/91 29,700
O/Pn 9x16 River de Huelva, Near Seville Sby 2/92 25,300
O/Pn 8x11 Rower on a Quiet River Sby 2/92 17,600
O/Pn 10x13 Sevilla Sby 10/91 17,600
O/Pn 13x16 Rowing on a Lake Sby 10/91 16,500
O/Pn 11x14 Fishing Along the River Sby 2/92 14,300
O/Pn 7x12 Boating on a River Sby 1/92 13,200
Sander, J. S.   Am 19C
O/C 22x28 Mountain Lake with Figures Yng 2/92 150
Sander, Ludwig
O/C 24x20 Pensacola IV 1960 Sby 10/91 2,200
Sander-Buckholz
W/Pa 26x20 Botanical Study Hnz 10/91 100
Sanderson-Wells, John   Br 1872-1955
* See 1992 Edition . . . .

Sandham, J. Henry   Can 1842-1912
* See 1991 Edition . . . .
Sandhurst, G.   Br 19C
O/C 24x36 Street Urchins But 5/92 4,675
Sandona, Matteo   Am 1881-1964
O/B 9x11 Purse Seine Boats, San Francisco 1946 Mor 3/92 . 350
Sandorfi, Istvan   20C
* See 1991 Edition . . . .
Sandrucci, Giovanni   It 19C
* See 1991 Edition . . . .
Sandzen, Birger   Am 1871-1954
* See 1992 Edition . . . .
Sanger, Grace H. C.   Am 1881-
O/B 17x13 Woman Under Umbrella Mys 11/91 1,100
W/Pa 12x9 Woman on a Sofa Mys 6/92 220
O/C 30x25 Young Woman Mys 11/91 55
SanGiovanni, A*   It 18C**
O/C 19x24 Still Life of Flowers in Urns Sby 10/91 15,400
Sani, Alessandro   It 19C
O/C 20x26 Serving the Meal Chr 2/92 9,350
O/C 25x20 A Pleasant Serenade Hnz 5/92 6,000
Sani, David   It 19C
O/C 22x31 Blowing Bubbles for the Baby 89 Chr 5/92 6,050
Sanin, Fanny   20C
* See 1991 Edition . . . .
Sant, James   Br 1820-1916
O/C 22x18 Day Dreaming Sby 5/92 6,600
Santerre, Jean Baptiste   Fr 1658-1771
* See 1991 Edition . . . .
Santini, G.   It 20C
O/C 16x23 Neapolitan Coastal View Slo 2/92 475
Santomasso, Guiseppe   It 1907-
MM/Pa 18x14 Untitled '83 Chr 11/91 3,080
Santoro, Francesco Raffaello   It 1844-
O/C 25x38 The Flirtation Sby 1/92 3,850
O/Pn 5x11 Dirt Road Fre 4/92 275
Santoro, Rubens   It 1859-1942
O/Pn 20x16 The Wine Harvest 1883 Chr 10/91 66,000
O/Pn 13x10 Venetian Canal Scene Chr 10/91 44,000
O/Cb 8x11 A Venetian Sunset Sby 10/91 14,300
O/Pn 10x7 Portrait North African Man Chr 2/92 11,000
Santry, Daniel   Am 1867-1951
* See 1992 Edition . . . .
Sanz, Bernhard Lukas   1650-1710
O/C 27x36 Mountainous River Landscape Sby 5/92 6,600
Sanzio, Raffaello   It 1483-1520
* See 1992 Edition . . . .
Sapp, Allen   Can 1929-
A/C 24x36 Visiting Sbt 11/91 1,870
A/C 12x16 That's All for the Day Sbt 11/91 1,028
Saret, Alan   1944-
Cp/Pa 31x35 Surprise at Entrance of Varla 1988 Chr 5/92 . . 1,650
Sargeant, Geneve Rixford   Am 1868-1957
* See 1992 Edition . . . .
Sargent, Dick   Am 1911-1978
O/B 27x21 Man Struggling w/Coat Hangers 1955 Ih 11/91 . 3,250
Sargent, John Singer   Am 1856-1925
O/C 40x34 "Expectancy": Frances Winifred Hill Sby 12/91 418,000
O/C 21x25 Olive Trees in Corfu Sby 3/92 99,000
O/C 22x28 Male Model Resting Sby 5/92 66,000
W/Pa 10x14 Venetian Canal Sby 5/92 46,750
O/C 14x19 A Mosque, Cairo, 1891 Chr 12/91 29,700
W/Pa 15x21 Berles-Au-Bois, France 1919 Sby 5/92 27,500
Pe/Pa/Pa 8x11 Becalmed 1877 Sby 3/92 16,500
W/Pb 21x15 Portrait Princess Henrietta Stuart Sby 3/92 . . 15,400
Sargent, Paul Turner   Am 1880-
O/B 12x16 Landscape 1925 Sel 12/91 170
Sargent, R.   Am 20C
W/Pa 22x31 Still Life Yng 2/92 40
Sargent, Walter   Am 1868-1927
* See 1992 Edition . . . .
Sarka, Charles N.   Am 1879-1960
PVPa 12x18 Car and Dogs Chasing Ih 5/92 650
Sarkisian, Sarkis
O/B 16x16 Pineapple in Orange Circle '68 Dum 5/92 650

Sarkissian, Paul   20C
* See 1990 Edition . . . .
Sarnoff, Arthur   Am 1912-
A/B 24x30 Winter Idyll Wtf 9/91 750
O/C 24x30 Street Scene Wtf 9/91 650
G/Pa 25x14 Woman with Bouquet of Flowers Ih 11/91 650
A/B 24x36 Wooden Bridge Wtf 9/91 500
T/B 22x18 Lady in White Mink Wtf 10/91 300
O/Ab 20x24 Lion Wtf 10/91 200
Sarri, Egisto   It 1837-1901
* See 1991 Edition . . . .
Sartain, William   Am 1843-1924
O/C 14x18 Drink by the Shade Tree Skn 3/92 2,750
Sartelle, Herbert   Am 1885-1955
O/C 28x36 Spring Valley But 6/92 1,540
Sartor, A.   It 20C
W/Pa 21x12 Bridge of Sighs Slo 10/91 190
Sartorio, Giulio Aristide   It 1860-1932
O/C 20x25 Allegoria 1892 Sby 10/91 7,700
Sartorius, Francis   Br 1734-1804
O/C 25x30 Duke of Kingston's "Christophas" Sby 6/92 . . . 31,900
Sartorius, John Nost   Br 1759-1828
O/C 25x29 The Check and Full Cry: Pair 1810 Sby 6/92 . . 38,500
Saru, George   Rom 20C
O/C 24x30 Abstract 1987 Fre 10/91 200
MM 24x30 The Fall 1988 Fre 10/91 125
Sato, Key   Jap 1906-
O/C 36x29 Son de l'Eau 63 Sby 2/92 6,050
Sato, Tadashi   Am 1923-
O/C 18x23 Abstraction in Blue and Gray 1948 Chr 3/92 . . 1,320
Satterlee, Walter   Am 1844-1908
W/Pa 13x11 Moroccan Gentleman Dum 10/91 125
Sattler, Hubert   Aus 1817-1904
* See 1992 Edition . . . .
Sauer, Walter   Bel 1889-1972
* See 1991 Edition . . . .
Sauerwein, Frank Peters   Am 1871-1910
O/Cb 12x9 Chief Red Feather Chr 6/92 308
Saufelt, Leonard   Fr 19C
* See 1991 Edition . . . .
Saul, Peter   Am 1934-
* See 1991 Edition . . . .
Saunders, Charles L.   Eng a 1881-1885
O/C 24x38 Twilight on a Canal Chr 10/91 1,650
Saunders, Norman   Am 1906-1988
O/C 30x37 Roping a Bull Ih 11/91 1,300
G/Pa 4x5 Batman Confronts Villain Ih 5/92 850
Saunier, Noel   Fr 1847-1890
* See 1992 Edition . . . .
Saura, Antonio   Spa 1930-
O/C 63x51 Untitled Chr 11/91 79,200
G&I/Pa 30x40 Untitled 66 Sby 2/92 16,500
G&I/Pa 30x40 Composicion 66 Sby 2/92 13,200
Sauret
O/C 14x10 Depicting Lovers Dum 12/91 300
Sauvage, Piat Joseph   Flm 1744-1818
* See 1990 Edition . . . .
Sauzay, Adrien Jacques   Fr 1841-1928
* See 1991 Edition . . . .
Savage, Eugene Francis   Am 1883-1978
* See 1991 Edition . . . .
Savain, Petion   Hai
O/C 20x16 Mere et Infant 72 Chr 5/92 880
Savelieva, Valentina   Rus 20C
O/C 55x86 End of the Night Shift But 5/92 13,200
Savery, Jacob   Dut 1565-1603
* See 1990 Edition . . . .
Savery, Roelandt Jacobsz   Flm 1576-1639
* See 1992 Edition . . . .
Savini, Alfonso   It 1836-1908
* See 1991 Edition . . . .
Savinio, Alberto   It 1891-1952
O/C 26x21 Les collegians 1929 Chr 5/92 275,000
Sawyer, Clifton Howard   Am 1896-1966
O/C 18x22 Verbena '63 But 6/92 1,540

Sawyer, Philip Ayer   Am 1877-1949
O/C/M 18x15 Seated Nude 1933 Wes 11/91 302
Sawyier, Paul   Am 1865-1917
O/C/B 14x16 Boats in a Dock Hnd 3/92 8,500
Saxlide, Carl R.   Am 20C
  * See 1991 Edition . . . .
Sayre, Fred Grayson   Am 1879-1939
G/Pa 10x15 Eucalyptus Landscape Mor 11/91 1,000
Scaffai, Luigi   It 1837-
O/Pn 17x12 Bashful Maid Wtf 6/92 3,900
O/Pn 10x7 Figures in Interior Slo 9/91 3,000
Scahry, Saul   Am 1904-
O/C 9x13 Abstract Still Life Chr 6/92 660
Scalbert, Jules   Fr 1851-
O/C 51x66 Hommage a Louis Pasteur Sby 10/91 19,800
O/C 28x40 Les Baigneuses Sby 5/92 16,500
O/C 32x26 Satyr and Nymphs Wtf 11/91 7,000
Scalise, Nicholas Peter   Am 1932-
W/Pa 22x16 Dried Flowers Slo 10/91 160
Scamanda, *
O/C 20x16 Alice 1941 Sby 2/92 660
O/C 20x16 The Fashion Show 1941 Sby 2/92 550
Scanlan, Robert Richard   Br -1876
O/C 41x56 Donneybrooke Fair Sby 2/92 10,450
Scarlett, Rolph   Am 1889-1984
O/C 40x48 Geometric Abstraction Chr 3/92 4,950
O/C 30x48 Devided Chr 6/92 3,300
G,I&H/Pa 18x18 Abstract Composition Sby 12/91 2,420
G,I&H/B 16x19 Abstract Composition Sby 12/91 2,200
Scarsellino, Ippolito   It 1551-1620
  * See 1992 Edition . . . .
Scatizzi, Sergio   It 1918-
O/C 20x21 Landscape in Spring '56 But 5/92 880
Schaefels, Lucas   Bel 1824-1885
O/C 34x27 Chinese Vase; Bowl: Pair 1883 Sby 1/92 17,600
O/C 49x34 Still Life Fruit and Dead Hare 1871 Chr 10/91 . 3,850
Schaefer, Carl Fellman   Can 1903-
O/B 12x16 Lemon and Gourds '51 Sbt 11/91 1,870
Schaefer, H.
W/Pa 9x7 Freiburg, Baden Hnz 10/91 225
Schaeffer, August   Aus 1833-1916
  * See 1990 Edition . . . .
Schaeffer, Mead   Am 1898-1980
O/C 35x27 People Skiing 1946 Ih 11/91 13,000
Schaettle, Louis   Am -1917
O/C 96x164 Pegasus 95 Hnd 3/92 950
Schafer, Frederick   Am 1839-1927
O/C 30x50 Slate Creek, California But 6/92 3,300
O/C 30x50 Merced River, California But 6/92 2,475
O/C 30x52 John Muir's Valley But 6/92 1,760
Schafer, Henry Thomas   Br a 1873-1915
O/C 23x12 Daisy Chain; Ivy Blossoms: (2) 1886 Sby 1/92 . 6,600
W/Pb 25x18 Louviers, Normandy Chr 10/91 1,760
W/Pa 18x14 Street Scene, Normandy Wes 11/91 770
W/Pa 10x8 Mortaix, Brittany Hnz 5/92 300
Schafer, Ray A.
O/B 16x20 Fly Ald 5/92 40
Schaffer, H.   Ger 19C
  * See 1992 Edition . . . .
Schaffner, W.
O/C 40x32 Horse's Harness and Lamp Eld 4/92 743
Schall, Jean Frederic   Fr 1752-1825
O/Cp 10x9 The Lover Listened To Sby 5/92 52,250
O/C 18x15 The Courtship Wtf 6/92 5,600
Schamberg, Morton Livingston   Am 1881-1918
P&Pe/Pa 9x7 Composition Chr 5/92 14,300
Schanker, Louis   Am 1903-1981
  * See 1992 Edition . . . .
Scharf, Kenny   Am 1958-
A/C 60x96 Elroy and Leroy '82 Chr 2/92 35,200
O&E/C 96x96 Major Blast 84 Chr 5/92 33,000
A,E&O/C 88x72 Pikki Taki Chop 85 Sby 10/91 30,250
O&E/C 72x48 Tune In, Tune On, Flip Out 83 Chr 5/92 . . . 25,300
A&Pt/C 90x108 In Ecstasy '82 Sby 5/92 22,000

A&E/C 48 dia Starring the Star 85 Sby 2/92 11,000
A&O/C 37x47 Gleem 88 Chr 2/92 9,900
A&E/C 26x36 Solsu N Luis Violetch 84 Sby 2/92 9,900
A&E/Pn 23x23 The Hero, to the Rescue Chr 5/92 9,900
O/C 32x24 Greenorite Over Blupoint 84 Chr 5/92 8,250
Scharl, Josef   Ger 1896-1954
  * See 1991 Edition . . . .
Scharp, Henri   Con 19C
  * See 1992 Edition . . . .
Schary, Saul   Am 1904-1978
O/C 58x45 Pierrot '29 Chr 5/92 19,800
O/C 18x22 Along the Arno Fre 12/91 160
Schattenstein, Nikol   Am 1877-1954
  * See 1991 Edition . . . .
Schatz, Daniel Leon   Am 1908-
  * See 1992 Edition . . . .
Schauss, Ferdinand   Ger 1832-1916
O/C 62x50 Young Saint John the Baptist Sby 5/92 22,000
Schawinsky, Xanti
A/Bu 24x18 Double Profile Sby 10/91 8,800
Schedone, Bartolomeo   It 1570-1615
  * See 1992 Edition . . . .
Scheerboom, Andries   Dut 1832-1880
  * See 1992 Edition . . . .
Scheffer, Ary   Fr 1795-1858
  * See 1992 Edition . . . .
Scheffer, Robert   Aus 1859-
  * See 1992 Edition . . . .
Scheffers, Glen C.   Am 19C
  * See 1992 Edition . . . .
Scheffler, Rudolf   Am 20C
  * See 1991 Edition . . . .
Scheggini Da Larciano, Giovan.   It 1455-1527
  * See 1992 Edition . . . .
Scheibe, Egon   Am 20C
O/Ab 30x24 Charleston Dance Couple Wtf 10/91 200
Scheiber, Hugo   Hun 1873-1950
G&W/Pa 23x18 Man Leaning Against Tree Chr 11/91 2,640
G&P/Pa 28x20 Seated Man Chr 11/91 2,090
K/Pa/Pa 22x17 Village Path Chr 5/92 1,760
Schein, Eugene   Am 20C
O/C 12x18 Four Dancing Girls Wtf 10/91 50
Schelfhout, Andreas   Dut 1787-1870
O/C 14x22 Skaters in Frozen Winter Landscape Chr 2/92 . 19,800
Schell, Susan Gertrude   Am 1891-1970
  * See 1992 Edition . . . .
Schenau, Johann Eleazar Zeizig   Ger 1737-1806
O/C 13x9 Charmed/A Genre Scene Skn 5/92 6,600
Schenck, August Friedrich A.   Dan 1828-1901
O/C 52x43 Shepherd and Dog Rescuing Sheep Sel 4/92 5,000
O/C 35x48 In the Snow Storm Sby 7/92 3,025
O/C 18x24 Driving the Sheep in Snowstorm Sby 7/92 1,870
Schepansky, A.
O/C 25x36 Mill Near Stream 42 Dum 1/92 850
Scherrewitz, Johan   Dut 1868-1951
O/C 14x20 Seaweed Gatherer Returning Home Chr 2/92 . . . 6,050
Schetky, John Christian   Eng 1778-1874
O/C 24x42 Ship Talbot in Action Eld 4/92 358
Scheuerer, Julius   Ger 1859-1913
  * See 1992 Edition . . . .
Scheuerer, Otto   Ger 1862-1934
  * See 1992 Edition . . . .
Schevill, William V.   Am 1864-
O/C 34x28 Portrait of a Mother and Child 1922 Sel 12/91 . . . 350
Schiavo, Paolo   It 1397-1478
T/Pn 20x67 Venus Reclining on Pillows Chr 5/92 77,000
Schiavone, Andrea   It 1522-1563
  * See 1990 Edition . . . .
Schiele, Egon   Ger 1890-1918
W&Y/Pa 12x19 Sitzender Akt; Bildnis: Dbl 1913 Sby 11/91 264,000
W&G/Pa 18x12 Stehender Mann 1911 Chr 5/92 242,000
G/Pa 18x12 Portrait eines Knaben 10 Chr 5/92 176,000

Schier, Franz Ger 1852-1922
O/C 44x38 The Romantic Suitor Chr 10/91 3,850
Schiertz, August Ferdinand Ger 1804-1878
O/Pn 14x19 Sentries Halting Travellers 1839 Sby 7/92 3,300
Schifano, Mario It 1934-
A/C 40x31 Steam Ship Sel 12/91 250
Schilder, Andrei Nicolajevitch Rus 1861-
* See 1990 Edition . . . .
Schille, Alice Am 1869-1955
W/Pa 20x17 Figures Walking in Landscape Sby 4/92 6,600
O/C 20x24 Sled Riding Wtf 9/91 3,200
Schindler, A. Zeno Am 1813-1880
* See 1992 Edition . . . .
Schindler, Emil Jakob Aus 1842-1892
* See 1992 Edition . . . .
Schindler, Thomas 20C
* See 1990 Edition . . . .
Schiodte, Harald Valdemar I. Dan 1852-1924
* See 1990 Edition . . . .
Schirfen, Johannes Ger 20C
O/Cb 15x18 Reclining Nude Hnd 12/91 700
Schjelderup, Leis Nor 19C
O/C 46x62 See-Saw by the Sea Chr 2/92 14,300
Schleich, Robert Ger 1845-1934
O/C 9x16 The Haystacks Sby 5/92 22,000
Schleicher, Carl Aus 19C
O/B 8x6 Man Smoking a Pipe Sel 12/91 650
Schlesinger, C.
O/Tn 17x14 Young Lady Holding a Mask Hnz 10/91 1,500
Schlesinger, Felix Ger 1833-1910
O/C 12x9 Young Girl with Rabbits Sby 10/91 20,900
O/C 16x19 Visit from Grandfather Chr 5/92 9,900
Schlesinger, Henri-Guillaume Fr 1814-1893
* See 1992 Edition . . . .
Schlesinger, Karl Ger 1825-1893
O/Me 17x14 Before the Masked Ball Chr 2/92 2,200
Schluter, August Ger 1888-1928
O/C 16x20 Alpine Landscape Hnz 5/92 200
Schmidt Con 19C
O/C 35x45 The Harvesters Sby 5/92 9,625
Schmidt, Albert H. Sws 1883-1970
* See 1991 Edition . . . .
Schmidt, Carl Am 1885-1969
O/C 30x36 Moving Herd But 4/92 3,850
O/Cb 16x20 Mountain Snow But 6/92 1,650
Schmidt, Carl Am 1909-
* See 1992 Edition . . . .
Schmidt, E. Allan Ger 19C
O/Pn 5x4 Blacksmith's Shop Slo 2/92 2,250
Schmidt, E. Trier Br a 1879-1903
O/C 31x23 Still Life Peonies on a Table Sby 2/92 7,700
Schmidt, Jay Am 1929-
O/C 24x48 Landscape Mor 11/91 100
Schmidt, Karl Am 1890-1962
O/B 8x9 Summer Coastal 1913 Mor 11/91 700
O/B 7x9 Coastal Mor 3/92 325
Schmidt-Rottluff, Karl Ger 1884-
* See 1992 Edition . . . .
Schmitz, Ernst Ger 1859-1917
O/C 27x38 In Der Werkstatte Sby 2/92 18,700
Schmutzler, Leopold Aus 1864-1941
O/C 30x37 Domestic Bliss Sby 2/92 27,500
O/C 38x28 The Water Carrier Chr 2/92 6,600
Schnabel, Julian Am 1951-
O/V 108x122 Maria Callas No. 4 Sby 5/92 319,000
O&Wx/C 96x92 Against Modernism 79 Sby 11/91 143,000
O/V 108x84 Sad Vase 1983 Sby 2/92 126,500
MM/Wd 72x60 Stephen Janson Chr 5/92 93,500
O&MM/C 116x160 Stimulus for Memory Sby 11/91 88,000
O&L/Pa/C 100x80 Forms of Insanity 89 Chr 11/91 66,000
T/Pa 50x30 Journey of the Lost Tooth 82 Sby 10/91 14,300

Schnakenberg, Henry Ernest Am 1892-1970
W/B 17x22 Central Park Chr 9/91 1,210
Schneider, Arthur Am 20C
O/C 12x20 Children by Tent Dum 11/91 275
Schneider, J. M. Eur 20C
O/C 24x20 Parlor Interior Sel 9/91 170
Schneider, Otto Henry Am 1865-1950
O/M 14x17 Houses in Landscape Mor 11/91 850
Schnetz, Jean Victor Fr 1787-1870
* See 1992 Edition . . . .
Schodl, Max Aus 1834-1921
* See 1990 Edition . . . .
Schoenfeld, Flora Am 20C
* See 1991 Edition . . . .
Schofield, Walter Elmer Am 1867-1944
O/C 30x36 Midwinter Pennsylvania 1940 Ald 5/92 31,000
O/C 30x36 Cliffs Sby 5/92 8,250
O/C 25x30 Laguna Beach But 6/92 6,600
O/C 20x24 Rocky Coastline Sby 3/92 4,400
O/C 30x36 Coastal Cliffs Hnz 10/91 2,750
Scholder, Fritz Am 1937-
A/C 30x30 Indian at the Bar 1969 Sby 10/91 10,450
A/Pa 30x22 Possession with Lion 1989 Sby 10/91 3,300
Scholz, Max Ger 1855-1906
* See 1992 Edition . . . .
Schonborn, Anton Am -1871
* See 1992 Edition . . . .
Schonleber, Gustav Ger 1851-1917
* See 1991 Edition . . . .
Schoonover, Frank Earle Am 1877-1972
O/C 36x27 Ahuitzotl and the Ocelot 1917 Ih 11/91 15,000
O/C 28x38 Man and Dog in Deep Snow 1928 Ih 5/92 11,000
O&R/C 30x40 The Lion Adventure Sby 12/91 880
G/Pa 18x30 Western Shootout Wtf 11/91 800
Schopin, Frederic Henri Ger 1804-1880
* See 1991 Edition . . . .
Schotel, Jan Christianus Dut 1787-1838
* See 1992 Edition . . . .
Schott, Max Con 19C
O/C 26x22 Portrait of a Lady 1904 Sby 1/92 2,090
Schouman, Aert Dut 1710-1792
* See 1990 Edition . . . .
Schoumann, Martinus Dut 1770-1848
* See 1990 Edition . . . .
Schouten, Henri Bel 1864-1927
O/C 26x22 Interior w/Cobbler's Bench 1895 Sel 4/92 4,250
O/C 27x36 Poultry in a Landscape Sel 9/91 3,000
Schrader, Julius Friedrich Ger 1815-1900
O/C 48x68 Cupid Caught Napping 1867 Sby 10/91 11,000
Schramm, Viktor Rom 1865-1929
* See 1991 Edition . . . .
Schranz, Anton Ger 19C
* See 1991 Edition . . . .
Schreckengost, Viktor Am 1906-
W/Pa 14x29 Fish Wtf 3/92 375
Schreiber, Charles Baptiste Fr -1903
* See 1990 Edition . . . .
Schreiber, Georges Am 1904-1977
O/C 26x31 Village Landscape 28 Sby 12/91 1,980
Schreyer, Adolf Ger 1828-1899
O/C 34x47 Arab Horsemen at a Pool Chr 2/92 121,000
O/C 23x38 Halt of the Arab Chiefs Chr 10/91 48,400
O/Pn 13x20 A Haywagon Chr 5/92 7,700
O/C 19x33 The Halt Sel 4/92 7,000
O/Pn 7x18 Wallachian Horsemen Mys 11/91 3,575
Schreyer, C. W.
O/C 16x24 Fishing by a Stream Ald 5/92 140
Schreyvogel, Charles Am 1861-1912
* See 1992 Edition . . . .
Schroder, Albert Friedrich Ger 1854-1939
O/Pn 10x13 Gentleman with a Long Stem Pipe Slo 4/92 . . 1,800
Schroeder, W. W. Am 20C
O/C 15x20 Autumn Landscape Hnz 5/92 300

Schroeter, M. Am 20C
O/C 19x28 St. Louis Landscape Mys 6/92 275
Schroff, Alfred Hermann Am 1863-1939
* See 1992 Edition . . . .
Schrorer, M. Am 20C
O/C 20x14 Snowy Winter Street Sel 9/91 230
Schuessler, C. Br 19C
O/C 63x48 Guinevere and Lancelot 1859 Hnd 10/91 1,600
Schuffenecker, Claude Emile Fr 1851-1934
* See 1992 Edition . . . .
Schultz, George F. Am 1869-
O/C 24x36 River Scene with Windmill Hnd 3/92 1,000
P/Pa/C 22x30 River's Edge Hnd 3/92 600
P/Pa/C 22x30 River's Edge Hnd 10/91 550
Schultz, Gottfried Ger 1842-
* See 1992 Edition . . . .
Schultz, Harry Am 1900-
O/C 16x20 The Merry-Go-Round 30 Hnd 5/92 200
Schultzberg, Anshelm Leonhard Swd 1862-1942
O/Cb 40x43 Landscape w/Flowering Lilac Bower Sel 2/92   10,000
O/C 28x36 Winter Woodland 1922 Skn 11/91 9,900
Schulz, Adrien Fr 1851-1931
* See 1992 Edition . . . .
Schulz, Charles M. Am 1922-
Pl/Pa 5x27 Two Comic Strips. "Peanuts" 57 Ih 5/92 4,000
Pl/Pa 14x23 Comic Strip. "Peanuts" 55 Ih 5/92 1,500
Schulz, Ken Am 20C
W/Pa 18x20 The Sugarlands Durn 2/92 70
Schulze, Andreas 1955-
A/Cot 79x158 Untitled 1984 Sby 11/91 7,700
A/C 79x158 Untitled 82 Chr 5/92 6,050
A/C 83x142 Untitled Chr 2/92 5,500
Schumacher, Charles F. Am 19C
O/C 22x14 Swiss Lake Scene 1878 Mys 6/92 55
Schumacher, William Emile Am 1870-1931
* See 1992 Edition . . . .
Schumaker, S.
O/C 32x25 Rose Still Life Hnz 10/91 200
Schuman, * Ger 19C**
O/C 16x17 Two Peasant Women in a Field Sby 1/92 1,540
Schurr, Claude Fr 1921-
* See 1992 Edition . . . .
Schuster, Donna Am 1883-1953
O/C 25x30 Kitchen Still Life Mor 11/91 7,000
O/C 24x22 Self Portrait Mor 3/92 5,500
O/C 28x22 Apples and Daisies But 2/92 4,675
O/B 16x12 Boats in Harbor Mor 3/92 4,000
O/B 18x24 Hollywood Hills Mor 3/92 3,000
O/B 15x16 California Landscape Mor 6/92 2,750
O/B 13x19 Early Pasadena But 10/91 2,475
O/C 30x25 Tulips But 2/92 2,200
O/Cb 16x20 Hollywood Hills But 10/91 1,430
W/Pa 14x18 Fishing Boats at Rest Mor 11/91 1,200
O/Cb 10x14 Sierra Landscape Mor 6/92 850
O/B 7x9 Canal in Venice Mor 3/92 600
Schuster, Joseph Aus 1873-1945
* See 1992 Edition . . . .
Schuster, Karl Maria Aus 1871-1953
O/C 39x30 The New Gloves 1909 Sel 4/92 4,750
Schuster, Ludwig Aus 1820-
* See 1992 Edition . . . .
Schutz, Christian Georg Ger 1718-1791
O/C 11x15 Mountainous River Landscape Sby 10/91 19,800
Schutz, Heinrich Ger 1875-
O/B 22x29 A Load of Firewood 16 Chr 5/92 1,100
Schuyff, Peter 1958-
A/L 120x120 Untitled Chr 11/91 8,800
A/L 120x120 Master Tone Chr 11/91 7,700
A/L 75x75 Untitled 87 Chr 11/91 7,700
A/L 120x120 The Weld Sby 10/91 4,400
A/C 75x75 Untitled (Blue) Sby 2/92 4,400
A/L 42x36 Untitled 85 Sby 2/92 3,300

A/C 33x24 Mr. America #1 '84 Chr 11/91 2,640
Schuyler, Remington Am 1887-1955
* See 1992 Edition . . . .
Schwabe, Heinrich August Am 1843-1916
* See 1992 Edition . . . .
Schwanfelder, Charles Henry Br 1774-1837
O/C 23x30 A Bay Hunter 1826 Sby 6/92 4,400
Schwardt, G. F. Am 20C
O/C 18x22 New England Homestead 1902 Hnd 3/92 170
Schwartz, A. W. Am 20C
O/C 20x24 Spring Landscape Fre 10/91 175
Schwartz, Albert G. Ger 1833-
* See 1991 Edition . . . .
Schwartz, Andrew Thomas Am 1867-1942
O/C 32x36 Annisquam River Chr 3/92 9,900
O/C 25x30 Sunset on the Arroyo Wes 11/91 3,300
O/C 26x30 Purple Mountains Chr 6/92 1,430
O/C 40x30 Autumn Landscape Durn 1/92 1,300
Schwartz, Davis F. Am 1879-1969
W/Pa 12x16 Boats at Dockside Hnd 5/92 300
Schwartz, Lester Am 20C
W/Pa 31x27 Sebastian 1961 Hnz 5/92 100
Schwartz, Manfred Am 1909-1970
* See 1992 Edition . . . .
Schwartz, William S. Am 1896-1977
O/C 36x40 Hurdy-Gurdy Man 1929 Chr 3/92 13,200
O/C 30x26 Russian Village Hnz 10/91 6,600
O/C 24x20 The Brown Vase Hnd 5/92 1,900
G/B 22x30 Farm Landscape Hnz 10/91 1,100
G/Pa 11x22 Landscape with Farm Hnd 3/92 800
Schwarz, Alfred Ger 1833-
* See 1992 Edition . . . .
Schwede, Mark 20C
MM/C 87x61 Untitled 1987 Chr 11/91 66
Schweitzer, G.
W/Pa 14x21 Country Road Hnz 10/91 200
Schweninger, Karl Aus 1818-1887
* See 1992 Edition . . . .
Schweninger, Karl (Jr.) Aus 1854-1903
* See 1992 Edition . . . .
Schweninger, Rosa Aus 1849-
* See 1992 Edition . . . .
Schwitters, Kurt Ger 1887-1948
L&O/Cd 6x8 Merzbild 9A Sby 11/91 242,000
L/Pa 5x4 Merzbild Chr 11/91 93,500
O&MM/Wd 6x7 C.68 Wanteeside 1945 Sby 5/92 77,000
L/Pa 7x6 Merzbild Chr 11/91 55,000
L/Pa 7x5 Ohne Titel 1930 Chr 5/92 52,800
O/Pn 9x7 Cabin near Hotel Djupvasshytta 1938 Chr 5/92 . . 1,870
Schyf Ger 19C
O/B 9x12 Scene on a Frozen Lake Hnz 5/92 350
Scifoni, Anatolio It 1841-1884
O/Pn 26x21 The Offering Hnz 5/92 8,000
Scilla, Agostino It 1639-1700
* See 1992 Edition . . . .
Scognamiglio, E. It 19C
O/C 30x19 Gypsy Musicians Sby 7/92 3,300
O/Pn 12x8 A Gypsy Woman Chr 2/92 1,320
Scoppetta, Pietro It 1863-1920
O/B 6x8 L'Arc du Carrousel Louvre Sby 10/91 13,750
O/B 5x7 L'Arc du Carrousel Tuileries Sby 10/91 9,900
O/C 5x7 Dans le Parc Sby 10/91 4,400
Scorrano, Luigi It 1842-1924
* See 1992 Edition . . . .
Scott, Campbell Sco 20C
O/C 24x36 Sunset in the Highlands Brd 5/92 770
O/C 24x36 Landscape with Stream Wes 11/91 468
Scott, Clyde Am 1884-1959
O/C 30x40 Shimmering Sands, Laguna But 2/92 2,475
Scott, Edwin Am 20C
* See 1992 Edition . . . .

Scott, Frank Edwin   Am 1863-1929
* See 1991 Edition . . . .
Scott, Howard   Am 1902-1983
G/Pa 15x36 Holding Beer Glasses lh 5/92   800
Scott, John   Am 1907-
* See 1991 Edition . . . .
Scott, John White Allen   Am 1815-1907
O/C 14x20 Still Life Fruit on Tabletop Sby 12/91 1,045
Scott, Julian   Am 1846-1901
O/B 12x7 Union Soldier 1894 Wes 11/91 2,200
Scott, Katherine   Am 1871-
* See 1992 Edition . . . .
Scott, Michael
Pl/Pa 10x16 Palomide House 1965 Dum 11/91   125
Scott, Peter   Br 20C
O/C 15x18 A Pearly Dawn 1939 Sby 6/92 4,950
Scott, Walt   Am 20C
W/Pa 21x14 Three Witches 1926 Wtf 9/91 1,200
Scott, William   20C
* See 1992 Edition . . . .
Scull, Nina W.   Am 20C
O/B 24x30 Boats at the Pier 1937 Fre 4/92   675
Scully, Sean   Br 1946-
O/C 100x132 Darkness Here 89 Sby 11/91 176,000
O/C 60x52 Manus II 83 Chr 11/91 176,000
O/C 75x91 For Charles Choset Sby 5/92 93,500
O/C 30x30 Zembra 1985 Sby 10/91 41,800
P/Pa 30x38 Untitled 89 Sby 5/92 16,500
O/Pa 10x21 Change #1 1975 Chr 5/92 6,600
A/Pa 23x20 P7 1980 Sby 2/92 6,600
A/Pa 23x30 Untitled 90 Sby 2/92 6,600
C/Pa 31x23 #8 1981 Sby 2/92 2,970
Scutt   Am 20C
W&G/Pa 14x22 Truckstop Romance Hnd 10/91   100
Seager, Edward   Am 1809-1886
Pe/Pa 11x15 Four Drawings Chr 11/91   528
S/Pa 8x13 Castle by a Sea; Farmyard: Two Wes 3/92   522
Pl/Pa 5x7 Two Drawings; and Sketchbook Wes 11/91   220
W/Pa 8x13 Windmill Sel 12/91   100
Pe/Pa 8x11 Country Road 1848 Fre 12/91   50
Seago, Edward   Br 1910-1974
O/B 20x30 Barnyard in Norfolk Sby 10/91 13,200
Sealy, Allen Culpepper   Br 1850-1927
O/C 21x27 The Meet 1892 Sby 6/92 16,500
Searle, Ronald   Br 1920-
V/Pa 19x14 Miami Beach Skn 9/91   495
Sears, Benjamin Willard   Am 1846-1905
O/C 26x18 Sentinel Rock, Yosemite 1903 But 2/92 1,760
Sears, Taber   Am 1870-
* See 1992 Edition . . . .
Sebes, Pieter Willem   Dut 1830-1906
* See 1992 Edition . . . .
Sebire, Gaston   Fr 1920-
O/C 21x18 Bleuets et Roses But 11/91 3,025
O/C 22x15 Vase de Fleurs Chr 2/92 2,860
O/C 29x40 Campagne Normande Chr 5/92 2,420
O/C 10x6 Two Paintings Chr 2/92 1,320
O/C 16x32 L'entree du Havre Chr 5/92   660
Seboth, Josef   Aus 1814-1883
* See 1991 Edition . . . .
Secola, A.   Con 19C
* See 1992 Edition . . . .
Sedgley, Peter
* See 1992 Edition . . . .
Sedlon, Richard   Am -1992
C,I&G/Pa 34x26 Pooka Convention 1976 Wtf 3/92   250
Pl,Pe&C/Pa 34x24 Pookas Conven., Class '42 1976 Wtf 3/92   225
Seeger, Hermann   Ger 1857-
* See 1991 Edition . . . .
Seel, Adolf   Ger 1829-1907
* See 1990 Edition . . . .
Seery, John   1941-
A/C 30x29 Yankee Clipper 1976 Chr 11/91 2,200
A/C 40x78 Cliffs 1980 Chr 2/92 1,100
A/C 55x43 Soft Entry 70 Chr 11/91   900

O/V 19x23 Untitled Chr 11/91   715
Segal, George   Am 1924-
P/Pa 18x12 Seated Nude 61 Sby 2/92 1,980
Segantini, Giovanni   It 1858-1899
* See 1992 Edition . . . .
Segar, Sir William   Br 17C
* See 1990 Edition . . . .
Segner, E. B.
O/C 40x30 Newlyweds Leaving Registrar Office lh 5/92 . . . 1,300
Segovia, Andres   Spa 1929-
* See 1990 Edition . . . .
Segui, Antonio   Arg 1934-
O/C 51x64 Malos Pensamientos 84 Chr 5/92 24,200
O/C 71x51 Sin Titulo 81 Chr 5/92 24,200
O/C 29x36 El que Piensa Mucho 83 Sby 5/92 15,400
O/C 26x36 Ciegos en el Jardin 80 Chr 11/91 14,300
O/C 70x70 The Boss Sby 10/91 9,900
MM/Pa 31x23 Hombre en un Interior 1972 Chr 5/92 8,800
O/C 24x36 Sin Titulo 50 Chr 5/92 6,600
Seguin-Bertault, Paul   1869-1964
O/C 24x32 Jardin du Luxembourg Chr 2/92 1,760
Sehring, Adolf   Rus 1930-
* See 1991 Edition . . . .
Seiden, Regina   Can 1897-
O/C 21x29 Nuns with Children Sbt 11/91 1,496
Seideneck, George Joseph   Am 1885-
O/B 5x7 3 Landscapes Mys 11/91   495
Seifert, Alfred   Czk 1850-1901
O/Pn 6x4 A Young Beauty Chr 10/91 1,980
Seignac, Guillaume   Fr 1868-1926
O/C 69x38 Psyche Sby 5/92 110,000
O/C 22x18 Basket of Cherries Chr 10/91 4,400
Seignac, Paul   Fr 1826-1904
* See 1992 Edition . . . .
**Seiler, Carl Wilhelm Anton   Ger
1846-1921**
O/Pa/C 16x12 Genre Scene 1890 Lou 6/92   550
Seiler, Joseph Albert   Aus a 1848-
O/C 33x26 Christmas Morning St. Nepomuk Chr 10/91 9,900
**Seitz, Alexander Maximilian   Ger
1811-1888**
* See 1990 Edition . . . .
Seitz, Anton   Ger 1829-1900
* See 1990 Edition . . . .
Seitz, Georg   Ger 1810-1870
* See 1991 Edition . . . .
Sekine, Yoshio   20C
* See 1992 Edition . . . .
Seler, Carl   Ger 1846-1921
* See 1992 Edition . . . .
Seligmann, Kurt   Sws 1900-1961
Pl/Pa 24x19 Surrealist Figure Sby 10/91 6,325
Sell, Christian   Ger 1831-1883
O/C 21x29 The Out-Post 1860 Chr 5/92 3,850
Sellaer, Vincent   Flm a 1538-1544
O/Pn 37x43 Madonna & Child w/Saints Elizabeth Sby 1/92 31,900
Selmercheim-Desgrange, Jean   20C
* See 1991 Edition . . . .
Selous, Henry Courtney   Br 1811-1890
* See 1992 Edition . . . .
Seltzer, Olaf Carl   Am 1877-1957
O/C 20x30 Scouting the Wagon Trail But 4/92 38,500
O/C 54x35 The Angry Cow But 4/92 33,000
O/C 36x48 The King's Mirror 1904 Sby 9/91 14,300
W,G&Pe/B 13x18 Indians on the Plains Sby 12/91 9,900
W&I/Pa 7x9 Coyote But 4/92 3,300
Seltzer, William S.   Am
* See 1990 Edition . . . .
Selzer, Edgar   Am 20C
W/Pa 10x16 Coastal View with Figures Slo 4/92   50
Semenowsky, Eisman   Fr 19C
O/Pn 28x17 The Skater 1889 Sby 5/92 3,300
Semple, Joseph   Irs 19C
O/B 8x14 Ship "Countess of Dublin" 1869 Dum 11/91 3,500

Senat, Prosper Louis   Am 1852-1925
   * See 1992 Edition . . . .
Senet-Perez, Rafael   Spa 1856-1927
   O/C 21x39 View of the Grand Canal Doy 11/91   18,000
   O/C 13x21 Entrance to the Grand Canal Slo 9/91   12,000
Sennhauser, John   Am 1907-1978
   O/C 26x10 Colorforms in Space, No. 9 48 But 5/92   6,600
Sepeshy, Zolton L.   Am 1898-1934
   O/C 36x34 City Scene 1927 Dum 1/92   3,000
   W/Pa 16x22 Boathouse on Crystal Lake Dum 12/91   650
   O/Ab 14x19 Donkey and Figure on Road Dum 11/91   500
   O/C 19x24 Landscape Dum 9/91   300
Sequenz, J   Con 20C**
   O/Pn 10x12 Picking Flowers Wes 11/91   220
Serier, W.   Fr 20C
   O/C Size? Beach Party Hnd 6/92   275
Serisawa, Sueo   Am 1910-
   O/C 30x26 The Red Canna '38 But 2/92   2,750
Serpan, Iaroslav   1922-1976
   O&L/C 53x51 Dgrugi 1958 Chr 11/91   3,850
Serpell, H. D.   Sco 20C
   O/B 25x30 Out for the Summer! 1940 Hnz 5/92   375
Serpioni, Alberro
   W/Pa 21x14 The Cavalier Wlf 11/91   900
Serra Y Auque, Enrique   Spa 1859-1918
   O/C 23x37 A Shrine in a Marsh 1901 Chr 2/92   3,960
Serra, Ernesto   It 1860-
   * See 1992 Edition . . . .
Serra, Richard   Am 1938-
   Pts/Pa 60x142 Judgments on a Sheet Sby 11/91   49,500
   Os/Pa 45x81 Untitled Chr 11/91   44,000
   Pts/Pa 45x114 Untitled 74 Sby 10/91   19,800
   H/Pa 11x9 Untitled 85 Chr 2/92   500
Serrano, Manuel Gonzalez   Mex 1917-1948
   * See 1992 Edition . . . .
Serres, Dominic   Br 1722-1793
   * See 1991 Edition . . . .
Serres, John Thomas   Br 1759-1825
   O/C 20x38 Leith Harbor 1825 Sby 6/92   11,550
   K/Pa 8x11 Fishermen with Cart 1808 Chr 1/92   1,430
Serri, Alfredo   It 1897-1972
   * See 1992 Edition . . . .
Serritelli, Giovanni   It 18C
   O/C 19x33 Figures and Cattle Slo 2/92   2,100
Serrure, Auguste   Flm 1825-1903
   * See 1991 Edition . . . .
Serveau, Clement   Fr 1886-1972
   * See 1991 Edition . . . .
Sessions, James   Am 1882-1962
   G/B 20x26 End of the Trail-Old Trading Post Sby 12/91 . . .   1,980
   W/Pa 16x18 Schooner on the Beach 31 Hnd 3/92   950
   W/Pa 14x18 Two Fishing Boats 38 Hnd 3/92   850
   W/Pa 22x34 Farmer in Jeep Dum 6/92   500
   W/Pa 23x33 WWII Soldiers Celebrating Dum 6/92   500
   W/Pa 16x14 Beach Houses Yng 4/92   300
Sether, Gulbrand   Am 1869-
   O/C 27x39 Fisherman's Port in Norway Sby 7/92   1,320
Settanni, Luigi   Am 1909-1984
   O/C 16x11 Seated Nude Fre 10/91   1,800
Setterberg, Carl   Am 1897-
   W/Pa 15x21 Pueblo Church But 11/91   880
Seurat, Georges   Fr 1859-1891
   Y/Pa 26x19 Guerrier Casque, De Profil Chr 11/91   26,400
Severini, Gino   It 1883-1966
   O/C 26x18 Choses Deviennent "Peinture" 1964 Chr 11/91 .   77,000
   Pl/Pa 12x9 Pulcinella e Arlecchino Chr 2/92   8,800
   Pl/Pa 8x11 Natura morta Chr 5/92   3,850
   Pl/Pa 7x11 Natura morta 55 Chr 5/92   3,080
Sevilla, Ferran Garcia   1949-
   O/C 77x67 Pariso 22 Chr 5/92   7,150
   O/C 64x51 Pariso 13 Chr 5/92   4,400
Sewell, Amos   Am 1901-1983
   O/Cb 27x25 Halloween Wlf 9/91   5,500

Sexton, Frederick L.   Am 1889-
   O/C 24x32 Hamburg Cove Mys 6/92   935
   O/B 16x29 Pail of Water Mys 6/92   935
   O/C 20x28 Winter Snow Scene Mys 6/92   935
   O/B 20x28 Getting Water from the Well Mys 6/92   522
   O/B 20x28 Winter Scene Mys 6/92   440
   W/Pa 12x16 Winter Farm Scene Mys 6/92   248
   O/B 12x15 Boatyard Mys 6/92   165
Seydel, Eduard Gustav   Ger 1822-1881
   O/C 14x17 Coffee Time 1859 Sby 5/92   5,225
Seyfurth, F.
   O/B 31x25 Middle Eastern Man Dum 1/92   75
Seyler, Julius   Ger 1873-1958
   * See 1991 Edition . . . .
Seymour, Edouard   Aus 1894-
   O/B 20x16 Blumen Stilleben But 11/91   825
Seymour, James   Br 1702-1752
   O/C 25x30 Saddled Grey Race Horse Sby 6/92   36,300
Seymour, Samuel   Am 1797-1882
   W&l/Pa 5x6 Indian Braves & Squaw 1806 Chr 11/91 . . .   13,200
Seymour, Tom   Am 20C
   O/C 16x24 Autumn Tints Hnd 5/92   200
Seyssaud, Rene   Fr 1867-1952
   O/C 24x29 Moisson a Aurel Chr 11/91   14,300
Shabunin, H. A.   Rus 19C
   * See 1991 Edition . . . .
Shadbolt, Jack Leonard   Can 1909-
   W&Pl/Pa 30x22 Vancouver School of Art '46 Sbt 11/91 . .   6,077
   W&l/Pa/B 31x21 Dock View with Boats '62 Sbt 11/91 . . .   3,039
Shafer, S. P.   Am 19C
   O/C 16x20 Still Life with Apples Wlf 11/91   850
Shahn, Ben   Am 1898-1969
   l/Pa 17x14 Moon for the Misbegotten Sby 12/91   4,400
   l/Pa 4x6 Eyes and Nose Sby 4/92   1,320
Shalders, George   Br 1826-1873
   * See 1991 Edition . . . .
Shannon, Charles Haslewood   Br 1865-1937
   O/C 40x33 The Wounded Amazon 1922 But 11/91   2,750
   K/Pa 9x9 Figure Studies Sby 7/92   550
Shannon, Sir James Jebusa   Br 1862-1923
   O/C 45x34 Miss Annie Beebe 1886 Sby 10/91   33,000
Shapiro, Joel   Am 1941-
   C&K/Pa 60x40 Untitled 1988 Chr 5/92   42,900
   C&K/Pa 53x57 Untitled Sby 10/91   25,300
   C&K/Pa 31x23 Untitled 87 Chr 11/91   15,400
   K&C/Pa 19x14 Untitled 1987 Chr 5/92   7,700
   C&K/Pa 16x20 Untitled 1985 Chr 5/92   5,500
Shapleigh, Frank Henry   Am 1842-1906
   O/C 30x48 Quebec From Point Levi, 1883 1883 Eld 4/92 . .   8,800
   O/C 26x48 Italian Lake Scene 1868 Slo 9/91   2,900
   O/C 16x22 Farm Scene Dum 8/92   1,300
   O/Pn 8x13 Abandoned Dory 1873 Brd 5/92   1,265
   O/C 10x16 Kennebunkport/Farmyard 1882 Skn 3/92   935
   O/C 20x14 Spanish Fort, Matanzas, FL 1890 Skn 11/91   825
   O/C 10x16 The Crawford Notch 1887 Skn 9/91   825
   O/C 12x9 The Hay Wagon 1862 Skn 11/91   440
   O/C 12x25 Massachusetts Coastal View 1864 Eld 7/92 . . .   385
Share, H. Pruett   Am 1853-1925
   * See 1992 Edition . . . .
Sharp, Dorothea   Eng 1874-1955
   * See 1992 Edition . . . .
Sharp, Joseph Henry   Am 1859-1953
   O/C 12x18 Crow Reservation, Montana Chr 5/92   46,200
   O/B 18x11 Portrait of an Indian, Taos Chr 5/92   26,400
   O/C 20x30 Flagships Connecticut and Kansas Chr 12/91 .   18,700
   O/C 26x30 Aspens, Taos Canyon 1932 But 11/91   16,500
   O/C 22x27 Autumn in Taos Canyon But 11/91   15,400
   O/C 22x27 Marigolds and Asters Chr 12/91   14,850
   O/C 20x24 Still Life Snapdragons Chr 5/92   12,100
   O/Cb 10x14 Artist's Pueblo Studio Chr 5/92   9,900
   O/C/B 9x13 Fort Washakie NY Wlf 3/92   8,200
   O/B 10x14 Western Landscape Sby 12/91   7,700
   O/C 30x24 Acoma, New Mexico Chr 11/91   6,050

O/B 10x14 Ranch at Lodge Grass But 11/91 4,125
O/C 24x36 Roses and Blue Vase But 11/91 2,475
O/B 6x9 Sunset on the Pond But 11/91 1,650
I/Pa 4x6 Indian Head But 11/91 770

Sharp, Louis Hovey Am 1875-1946
O/C 20x26 The Navajo Spring 1915 But 11/91 2,750
O/C 25x30 South Point Lobos Mor 6/92 1,500
O/Cb 16x20 Monterey Coastal Mor 11/91 700

Sharpe, James Am 1936-
* See 1992 Edition . . . .

Shattuck, Aaron Draper Am 1832-1928
* See 1992 Edition . . . .

Shattuck, William Ross Am 1895-1962
O/B 29x18 Man in Blue Mor 6/92 350

Shaw, Annie Cornelia Am 1852-1887
* See 1992 Edition . . . .

Shaw, C. E. Am 20C
W/C 9x14 Beach Scene '40 Dum 11/91 275

Shaw, Charles Green Am 1892-1974
O/Cb 16x20 Abstract Composition 1941 Sby 4/92 8,250
O/C 50x40 Revolt Chr 9/91 7,150
O/C 60x40 Duet Sby 10/91 1,320
W/Pa 5x7 Now September Chr 6/92 660

Shaw, D. Eng 19C
O/C 18x14 Victorian Beauty Slo 12/91 150

Shaw, Harry Hutchinson Am 1897-1989
O/C 40x48 Southern Ohio Hills 1931 Skn 3/92 2,090
O/C 24x36 Southwestern Landscape Hnd 12/91 325
O/C 24x30 Rising Mist in The Sievers Hnd 12/91 200
O/C 24x30 Tropical Harbor #2 Hnd 12/91 200
O/C 16x20 Mountain Farm, NC; Scotland: Two Hnd 3/92 50

Shaw, John Byam Eng 1872-1919
O/Pn 12x8 The Troubadour 1899 Hnd 3/92 2,500

Shaw, Joshua Am 1777-1860
O/C 14x18 Mount Katahdin 1819 Sby 4/92 3,850

Shaw, W. R. B. Am 19C
O/B 10x12 Wildflowers 1871 Fre 10/91 850

Shawe, George 1915-
O/C 16x20 The River Path Chr 2/92 770

Shawhan, Ada Romer Am 1865-1947
O/C 12x14 By the Window But 6/92 1,430

Shayer, Charles & Shayer, H. Br 19C
O/C 12x16 English Countryside Wlf 6/92 4,000

Shayer, Henry & Shayer, C. Br 19C
O/C 12x16 English Countryside Wlf 6/92 4,000

Shayer, William (Jr.) Eng 1811-1892
* See 1992 Edition . . . .

Shayer, William (Sr.) Eng 1788-1879
O/C 28x36 The Fruit Sellers 1833 Sby 10/91 55,000
O/C 30x41 Bringing in the Catch 1837 Chr 2/92 17,600
O/C 28x36 The Harvest Chr 10/91 17,600
O/Pn 18x24 Fishing Boats at Low Tide Sby 2/92 11,000
O/C 27x32 On the South Coast Sby 2/92 7,700
O/Pn 17x24 Pair Fishing Scenes Wlf 9/91 3,400

Shearer, Christopher H. Am 1840-1926
O/C 20x30 River Landscape 1885 Fre 4/92 2,000
O/C 7x12 Moonlit Landscape 1903 Ald 3/92 1,200

Shearman, J. 20C
W/Pa 18x11 Venetian Canal 1900 Slo 4/92 180

Shed, Charles Dyer Am 1818-1893
O/C 18x32 Sailboats and Steamship But 6/92 2,200

Shee, Sir Martin Archer Irs 1769-1850
O/C 32x27 Portrait of Lady Foster But 5/92 4,400

Sheed, G. Am 20C
O/C 12x20 Harbor Scene 1911 Slo 10/91 225

Sheeler, Charles Am 1883-1965
* See 1992 Edition . . . .

Sheets, Millard Owen Am 1907-1989
W/Pa 22x30 Mission San Xavier 1937 But 10/91 7,700
W/Pa 22x30 The Tower, Alamos, Mexico 1963 But 6/92 . . . 7,700
W/Pa 22x30 Approaching Storm But 6/92 4,950
W/Pa 23x30 Ladies in the Morning, Hawaii 1950 But 6/92 . . 4,400
W/Pa 23x30 Beach Near Kailua-Kona 1950 But 6/92 4,125
W/Pa 22x30 Two Figures in a Landscape 1939 But 6/92 . . 4,125
W/Pa 22x30 Cattle Grazing But 10/91 2,090

W/Pa 12x17 Reclining Black Woman 1934 But 10/91 1,870
W&Pe/Pa 11x15 Burma '44 Wlf 6/92 950

Sheets, Nan Jane Am 1885-1976
O/C 20x15 Impressionist Landscape Wlf 3/92 450

Sheldon, Charles Am 1889-1961
Pl&S/Pa 20x16 Two Women on a Paris Street Ih 5/92 750

Sheppard, Warren W. Am 1858-1937
O/C 22x36 Schooner Choppy Seas Fre 10/91 9,300
O/C 20x30 Sails in the Sunset Dum 8/92 4,500
O/C/B 25x36 Ships Sailing by Sunset 1894 Sby 4/92 4,400
O/C 24x16 Venetian Canal Scene Chr 6/92 3,520
O/C 21x16 Sailboat in the Moonlight 88 Chr 11/91 3,300
O/C 24x18 Moonlight Sailing But 4/92 1,540
O/C 18x36 Moonlight Over the Bay of Naples Slo 4/92 800

Sheppo, B. Am 20C
W/Pa 18x22 Dock Scenes: Pair Slo 7/92 425

Sheridan, John E. Am 1880-1948
G/Pa 8x6 Four Sketches for Magazine Covers Ih 11/91 . . . 1,600

Sheridan, Joseph Marsh Am 1897-
Y/Pa 17x14 6 Works Chr 6/92 132

Sheringham, George Br 1884-
* See 1992 Edition . . . .

Sherman, Cindy Am 1954-
Ph 40x30 Untitled Film Still 38 1979 Chr 2/92 18,150
Ph 45x30 Untitled (#97) 1982 Chr 5/92 16,500
Ph 24x49 Untitled (#85) 1981 Chr 11/91 14,300
Ph 45x30 Untitled (#98) 1982 Chr 5/92 14,300
Ph 8x10 Untitled (Film Still #50) 1979 Chr 5/92 13,200
Ph 50x30 Untitled (#112) 1982 Chr 11/91 11,000
Ph 45x30 Untitled (#99) 1982 Chr 5/92 8,250
Ph 30x45 Untitled (#189) Chr 5/92 7,150
Ph 40x30 Untitled 1986 Chr 2/92 3,080
Ph 40x30 Untitled 1986 Chr 11/91 2,310

Sherman, G.
O/C 36x24 Street Scene Hnz 10/91 675

Sherman, John 1896-
O/B 16x12 Cathedral Spires, Yosemite Yng 4/92 350

Sherrin, Daniel Br a 1895-1915
O/C 33x60 Scottish Landscape Hnd 5/92 5,000
O/C/B 25x56 Seascape Hnd 10/91 3,400
O/C/B 25x56 Seascape Hnd 3/92 1,700
O/C 24x42 Cottage by the Shore 1902 Sby 7/92 1,100
O/C 20x30 Cottage Garden Wes 11/91 715
O/C 16x21 A Surrey Lane Hnd 12/91 650
O/C 24x36 The Neetfield Sel 9/91 450
O/C 16x24 Spring Landscape Wes 11/91 330

Sherwood, Vladimir Osipovich Rus 1832-1897
* See 1990 Edition . . . .

Sherwood, William A. Can 1875-1951
* See 1991 Edition . . . .

Shields, Alan Am 1944-
L&W/Pa 40x40 Collage Sel 4/92 100

Shikler, Aaron Am 1922-
O/Pn 11x15 Egg Tomatoes Chr 9/91 3,300
O/C 10x14 Jo in the Studio Chr 9/91 3,080
O/C 20x30 Provincetown '74 Wes 5/92 1,650

Shilling, Arthur Can 1941-1986
O/B 25x20 Young Indian Boy Sbt 11/91 3,740
Pe/Pa 13x17 Artist's Wife and Child 78 Sbt 11/91 468

Shinn, Everett Am 1876-1953
O/C 26x17 The Singer 1902 Chr 5/92 176,000
P/B 12x13 The Tightrope Walker 1904 Chr 12/91 88,000
P/Pa/Pa 14x18 Dewey Arch, Madison Square Chr 12/91 . . 38,500
P/Pa 22x30 Horsedrawn Bus '99 Sby 5/92 20,900
O/B 10x8 The After Dinner Turn Sby 5/92 16,500
O/Pn 10x8 Clown Antics 1944 Chr 5/92 15,400
P&C/B 12x13 Girl in a Chair 1912 Chr 12/91 8,800
P/Pa/B 18x12 The Dressing Room 1934 Skn 3/92 8,800
O/Cb 10x13 Reclining Nude Chr 12/91 6,050
W/Pa 12x16 Barefoot Man in Cloak (2) 1941 Ih 11/91 2,500
I&W/Pa 12x15 Children Playing in Snow Ih 11/91 2,500
W,Pe&G/B 13x16 The Boston Tea Party Chr 11/91 2,420
W&Pe/Pa 12x8 Two Works Chr 9/91 1,650
P/Pa 16x8 Standing Nude Hnz 5/92 625

208

C/Pa/B 20x16 Girl with Bouquet of Daisies Hnd 10/91 180
l/Pa 8x6 Illustration for "Tommy Traddles" Sel 5/92 175

Shinoda, Toko 1913-
* See 1992 Edition . . . .
Shirlaw, Walter Am 1838-1909
* See 1992 Edition . . . .
Shishkin, Ivan Ivanovitch Rus 1831-1898
O/C 9x6 In the Pine Forest Sby 7/92 1,100
Shokler, Harry Am 1896-
O/C 26x32 Duryea's Dock, Montauk Chr 5/92 8,250
Shore, H.
W/Pa 21x28 Camellias Hnz 10/91 100
Short, Frederick Golden Am 20C
* See 1991 Edition . . . .
Shotwell, Margaret Harvey Am 1873-1965
O/C 30x25 Woman Holding a Blue Bowl Wes 3/92 605
Shoup, Charles Am 20C
* See 1990 Edition . . . .
Shreve, Carl
O/C 32x29 People Around Open Fireplace Ih 11/91 1,200
Shulz, Ada Walter Am 1870-1928
O/B 26x24 A Puppy and Petunias 1927 Hnd 5/92 6,000
O/B 20x24 Homestead Hnd 5/92 4,600
Shulz, Adolph Robert Am 1869-1963
O/C 25x34 Autumn Landscape Hnd 10/91 3,200
Shurtleff, Roswell Morse Am 1838-1915
O/C 12x16 A Wooded Glen But 4/92 7,150
O/C 12x16 Autumn in Keene Valley Skn 3/92 1,045
O/C 12x16 Landscape with Cows Lou 3/92 600
O/C 24x34 Landscape with Figures Lou 12/91 275
Sieberechts, Guiellimus Jan Flm 1627-1703
* See 1992 Edition . . . .
Sicilia, Jose Maria 1954-
O/C 103x98 Tulip 6 85 Chr 5/92 55,000
A/C 119x80 Flor 13 85 Chr 11/91 33,000
A/C 40x40 Untitled 85 Sby 2/92 33,000
A/C 109x52 Frame Flower I Sby 5/92 25,300
A/C 64x32 Flower Bunch 3 Sby 11/91 17,600
A/C 36x36 Brown Flower Chr 11/91 16,500
Sickert, Walter Richard Br 1860-1942
* See 1992 Edition . . . .
Sickles, Noel Am 1910-1982
Pl/Pa 5x24 Comic Strip. "Scorchy Smith" 36 Ih 5/92 1,400
C&Y/Pa 10x15 Man on Sidewalk as Car Approaches Ih 11/91 500
Siebert, Edward Seimar Am 1856-1944
* See 1992 Edition . . . .
Siegen, August Eur 20C
O/C 31x23 Arab Street Scene Wlf 9/91 2,800
Siegert, August Ger 1786-1869
* See 1992 Edition . . . .
Siegert, August Friedrich Ger 1820-1883
* See 1992 Edition . . . .
Siegfried, Edwin Am 1889-1955
P/Pa 23x33 Alameda Estuary But 6/92 1,540
P/Pa 26x32 Sunset San Francisco Bay Mor 11/91 900
Siegriest, Louis Am 1899-1989
O/C 17x19 House Among the Trees But 2/92 8,800
O/C 16x20 Coastal Scene Hnd 5/92 2,400
Siegriest, Lundy Am 1925-
O/C 16x20 Cows in a Farmyard But 5/92 2,200
O/C 16x20 Cows in the Shade But 10/91 2,200
Siemer, Christian Am 20C
* See 1991 Edition . . . .
Sigler, Hollis Am 20C
* See 1991 Edition . . . .
Sigmund, Benjamin D. Br a 1880-1904
W/B 15x21 Summer Landscape Sby 7/92 1,430
Signac, Paul Fr 1863-1935
O/C 29x36 Antibes, le nuage rose 1916 Chr 5/92 660,000
O/C 18x22 Le Chenal de la Rochelle 1927 Sby 11/91 . . . 275,000
G,W&K/Pa/B 11x16 Landerneau 24 Chr 5/92 30,800
W&K/Pa 11x16 Le Lac D'Annecy Chr 11/91 26,400
W&K/Pa/B 11x9 Audierne 27 Chr 5/92 18,700

W&C/Pa/B 10x14 Penmarche 22 Sby 10/91 14,300
W/Pa/B 4x6 Samois 00 Sby 2/92 9,350
W&Pe/Pa/B 4x6 Honfleur Sby 2/92 8,800
W&C/Pa 4x7 Bateau de Pecheur en Port Sby 10/91 6,600
Signorelli, Luca It 1441-1523
* See 1991 Edition . . . .
Signoret, Charles Louis Eugene Fr 1867-1932
O/C 31x44 Enfants Cueillant des Fruits Sel 4/92 12,000
Signorini, Giuseppe It 1857-1932
W/Pa 35x25 The Harem Sby 10/91 22,000
W&G/B 27x37 The Discussion Sby 5/92 16,500
W&Cw/B 15x19 The Tea Party Chr 10/91 5,500
W,G&Pe/B 18x12 The Painter's Studio Chr 2/92 5,280
W/Pa 22x15 Moor on a Prayer Rug 78 Doy 11/91 3,250
W/B 15x11 The Mandolin Player '92 Chr 2/92 1,210
W/Pa 13x10 Cavalier Mys 11/91 1,100
Sigriste, Guido Sws 1864-1915
O/Pn 13x16 Arrest of Carmen Sby 1/92 1,980
Silbert, Max Fr 1871-
* See 1991 Edition . . . .
Sillens, Herman Dan 19C
* See 1992 Edition . . . .
Sillett, James Br 1764-1840
* See 1990 Edition . . . .
Silsby, Wilson Am 1883-1952
O/C 28x38 Boats at Dock .28 But 2/92 880
Silva, Benjamin Brz 1927-
O/C 39x39 Painter's Studio 1973 Chr 5/92 6,600
O/C 46x35 Platforma II But 5/92 3,025
Silva, Francis Augustus Am 1835-1886
O/C 14x24 Moonrise '72 Chr 9/91 35,200
O/C 20x36 Passing Showers Fre 4/92 17,000
O/C 14x24 Hudson River at Kingston Point Chr 3/92 . . . 12,100
Silva, William Posey Am 1859-1948
O/C 7x9 13 Assorted Field Sketches But 6/92 4,400
O/C 20x24 Windblown Cypress, Monterey But 6/92 3,025
O/Cb 8x10 Reflections--Magnolia Gardens Mor 11/91 650
O/Cb 14x18 Cypress on Cliff - Point Lobos 1949 Mor 3/92 . 550
O/Cb 8x10 Harbor--Cape Cod Mor 11/91 425
O/B 10x14 Springtime Carmel Valley Mor 6/92 400
Silvani, Ferdinando It 1823-1899
* See 1992 Edition . . . .
Silverman, * Am 20C**
O/C 40x36 Portrait of Jimi Hendrix Slo 9/91 200
Silverman, Burton Am 1928-
P/Pa 19x16 Girl Playing the Guitar Sby 4/92 264
Simbari, Nicola It 1927-
O/C 32x39 Capri 66 Sby 2/92 7,700
O/C 40x44 Elfrida a Tavola 67 Chr 11/91 6,600
O/C 28x35 Beach at Ostia Sby 6/92 5,775
O/C 24x32 Girl on a Bicycle Sby 10/91 5,720
O/C 31x39 Nostalgia del mare 62 Chr 5/92 5,500
O/C 19x27 Beachscape with Figures '67 Wlf 6/92 5,200
O/C 24x32 The Round Table 68 Sby 5/92 5,170
O/C 23x23 Figure Sulla Spiaggia Sby 10/91 4,400
O/C 36x40 Red and Gold Flowers 63 Sby 10/91 4,400
O/C 32x40 Standing Woman Hnd 6/92 3,600
O/C 32x40 Standing Woman Chr 11/91 2,860
O/C 24x32 Boats Along the Adriatic Sby 6/92 2,475
O/C 31x23 At Sea '57 Chr 11/91 2,200
G/Pa/C 28x40 Paris at 6 P.M. Sby 6/92 1,650
Simboli, Raymond Am 1894-1964
O/C 30x36 Factories, Pittsburgh Chr 3/92 5,500
Sime, Sidney Herbert Am 20C
* See 1991 Edition . . . .
Simkhovitch, Simka Am 1893-1949
O/C 44x50 The Picnic 1934 Chr 5/92 30,800
Simkin, Richard Eng 1840-1926
W/Pa 13x17 Scouting Party of 14th Hussars 1874 Wes 3/92 . 358
Simkins, Henry John Can 1906-
W/Pa 19x24 Sugar Camp (St. Janvier, Quebec) Sbt 11/91 . . . 841
Simmler, Wilhelm Ger 1840-1914
* See 1992 Edition . . . .

**Simmons, Edward Emerson   Am
1852-1931**
   * See 1992 Edition . . . .
Simmons, Laurie   1949-
   Ph 64x48 Talking Gardening Glove Chr 2/92   8,250
   Ph 60x45 Aztec Crevice Chr 5/92   6,600
Simon, A***
   O/C 24x28 The Marketplace Sby 10/91   2,200
Simon, Grant Miles
   W/Pa 11x9 Trees Ald 5/92   60
Simon, Grant W.   Am 20C
   W/Pa 22x18 Philadelphia Scene 1948 Slo 10/91   160
Simon, Hermann C.   Am 19C
   G&R/Pa 19x12 Deer Through the Brush 1893 Slo 7/92   100
Simon, John   Am -1917
   O/C 30x20 Autumn Landscape Wtf 6/92   600
Simon, Lucien   Fr 1861-1945
   O/C 22x26 Dans L'Atelier Sby 7/92   7,700
Simonelli, Giuseppe   It 1650-1710
   * See 1992 Edition . . . .
Simonet, Augustin   Fr 19C
   * See 1991 Edition . . . .
Simonetti, A**   It 19C
   W/Pa 6x10 Towards St. Mark's Square Wes 3/92   302
Simonetti, Amedeo Momo   It 1874-1922
   W/Pa 21x15 Flower Seller Hnd 10/91   2,200
   O/C 31x25 Drawing Room Scene Dum 4/92   1,500
Simonetti, Andres   It 20C
   W/Pa 21x30 Harem Scene But 5/92   5,500
Simonetti, Ettore   It 19C
   W/Pa 31x22 The Shoe Shop Sby 10/91   22,000
   W/Pa 30x22 Trying on Shoes Sby 5/92   19,800
   W&Pe/B 30x22 The Presentation 1885 Sby 7/92   4,400
Simonetti, Y**   It 19C
   G/Pa 17x27 Italian Coastal Scene Wes 11/91   742
Simoni, Cesare   It 19C
   O/C 27x36 Port Scene Lit by Moonlight Sby 1/92   4,950
Simoni, Gustavo   It 1846-
   W/Pa 14x11 A Seated Woman 1872 Chr 10/91   935
Simoni, Scipione   It a 1891-1898
   O/Pn 6x9 The Entertaining Jester 1880 But 11/91   4,400
   W/Pa 34x21 Women Conversing on Steps Sby 1/92   4,400
Simonini, Francesco   It 1686-1753
   O/C 29x39 A Battle Scene Chr 1/92   18,700
Simons, Michiel   Dut a 1648-1673
   * See 1992 Edition . . . .
Simonsen, Niels   Dan 1807-1885
   * See 1992 Edition . . . .
**Simonsen, Simon Ludvig Ditiev   Dan
1841-1928**
   O/B 9x11 Spaniel 1897 Mys 11/91   1,320
Simonson, David   Ger 1831-1896
   * See 1990 Edition . . . .
**Simonson-Castelli, Ernst Oskar   Ger
1831-1896**
   O/C 32x25 Young Girl with Flowers Sby 7/92   1,100
Simony, Stefan   Aus 1860-
   * See 1992 Edition . . . .
Simpietro, Francisco   It 1815-1892
   O/C 18x14 Italian Coastal View 1919 Slo 7/92   225
Simpkins, Ronald   Can 1942-
   * See 1992 Edition . . . .
Simpson, Charles Walter   Br 19C
   * See 1991 Edition . . . .
Simpson, David
   * See 1992 Edition . . . .
Sims, Phil   1940-
   O/C 67x60 Black Painting VI 82 82 Chr 2/92   220
Sinclair, M.   Eng 19C
   O/C 12x18 On the Rhine Fre 4/92   850
Sinclair, Olga   20C
   * See 1992 Edition . . . .
Sinet, Andre   Fr 1867-
   P/C 16x11 At the Opera 896 Chr 2/92   14,300

Singer, Burr   Am 1912-
   * See 1992 Edition . . . .
Singer, Clyde   Am 1908-
   O/B 10x20 Flower Vendors '77 Wtf 9/91   2,000
   O/B 22x28 44 St. Night Sby 12/91   1,760
   O/Pn 18x24 Two Patrons at McSorleys 1985 Wtf 9/91   1,500
   O/Cb 16x20 Courthouse Bus Stop '54 Lou 3/92   650
   O/B 12x19 On West 46th Street 1960 Wtf 10/91   400
   O/Pn 15x8 Girl Walking 1982 Wtf 10/91   325
   W/Pa 10x7 Girl on a Windy Day '57 Wtf 6/92   275
   O/Cb 11x5 Nude Rear 1983 Wtf 10/91   200
   O/Pn 9x7 Passing By 1978 Wtf 10/91   200
   O/Cb 16x12 Refreshment Break 1989 Wtf 10/91   200
Singer, Ruth   Am 20C
   O/B 14x20 Reclining Woman Mys 11/91   28
Singer, William H. (Jr.)   Am 1868-1943
   * See 1991 Edition . . . .
Singler, Gustave   Fr 1909-
   O/C 32x39 Provence-La Vielle Ville.I 59 Sby 10/91   30,800
Singleton, Henry   Br 1766-1839
   O/C 25x30 The Sewing Lesson Chr 2/92   2,200
Sinibaldi, Jean Paul   Fr 1857-1909
   O/C 18x24 The Christening Sby 2/92   6,050
Sintsov, N.   Rus 19C
   O/C 29x21 Old Man and a Boy Sel 4/92   1,750
Siqueiros, David Alfaro   Mex 1896-1974
   Du/C/M 40x26 Esclavo 1948 Sby 5/92   104,500
   O&Py/Bu 34x23 Retrato De Ione Robinson 31 Sby 11/91 .   93,500
   Px/M 32x23 Dos Cabezas 57 Chr 11/91   88,000
   O/Bu 37x27 Retrato de Blanca Luz 1931 Chr 5/92   88,000
   O&Px/Bu 39x30 Picadores de Piedra 26 Sby 5/92   82,500
   O/B 31x23 Figura 69 Chr 5/92   44,000
   Px/M 24x30 Paisaje 54 Sby 5/92   44,000
   O/M 30x21 Mujer con Rebozo Chr 5/92   33,000
   Pol/Pa/M 22x15 Mundo de Hambre y Terror 64 Chr 5/92 .   24,200
   W&G/Pa 22x17 Tres Mujeres y Uno Muchacho But 5/92 . .   6,600
   G/Pa 11x14 Mother and Child But 11/91   4,125
Siqueiros, Jose Alfaro
   * See 1991 Edition . . . .
Sironi, Mario   It 1885-1961
   O/B/C 18x15 Paesaggio Chr 2/92   35,200
   O/C 29x17 Composizione Con Figura Brd 8/92   26,950
   G,Br&l/Pa 17x17 I Filosofi Sby 10/91   18,700
   G&Pe/Pa/C 18x22 Cavallo e Cavaliere Chr 2/92   17,600
   O/C 9x11 Colloquio Sby 2/92   11,000
   G/Pa/C 10x7 L'Uomo Seduto Sby 2/92   7,150
Sisley, Alfred   Fr 1839-1899
   O/C 29x36 Printemps a Veneux Sby 11/91   797,500
   O/C 15x22 Rue de Village--Temps Gris 74 Sby 5/92   660,000
   O/C 22x29 Rue a Veneux Chr 11/91   550,000
   O/C 20x26 Chantier a Saint Mammes 80 Sby 5/92   522,500
Sisley, S**   Eng 19C
   O/C 22x16 Woodland Path Wes 3/92   495
Sisson, Laurence   Am 1928-
   O/M 22x30 Treasure Island Brd 8/92   2,530
   O/M 46x30 Tidal Pool, Autumn Skn 5/92   1,320
Sites, George   Am 20C
   O/B 20x24 Setters in the Woods Mys 11/91   275
Sitzman, Edward R.   Am 1874-
   O/C 25x30 Landscape '41 Hnd 10/91   850
   W/Pa 14x20 House in the Mountains Ald 3/92   150
   W/Pa 20x14 Autumn Landscape Hnd 12/91   50
Sjamaar, Pieter Geerard   Dut 1819-1876
   * See 1992 Edition . . . .
Sjostrom, G. J.
   * See 1992 Edition . . . .
Skarbina, Franz   Ger 1849-1910
   O/C/B 15x12 Leipzigerstrasse--Berlin 1904 Chr 10/91 . . .   19,800
Skeaping, John Rattenbury   Br 1901-1980
   O/Pn 20x30 Stallion Kenneth Rowntree Chr 5/92   1,650
   O/C 13x18 Around the Track 63 Sby 6/92   1,100
Skelton, Leslie James   1848-1929
   O/B 6x12 Horn's Peak, Sangre de Cristo 1895 Eld 7/92 . . .   605
Skelton, Red   Am 20C
   * See 1992 Edition . . . .

Skipworth, Frank Markham   Br 1854-1929
O/C 26x34 The Lesson Chr 2/92 17,600
Sklar, Dorothy   Am 20C
W/Pa 13x20 L.A. Street Scene '45 Mor 3/92 1,300
O/C 16x30 Malibu Sun Mor 6/92 475
Skou, Sigord   Am -1929
* See 1992 Edition
Skovgaard, Johan Thomas   Dan 1888-
* See 1992 Edition . . . .
Skredswig, Christian Eriksen   Dan 1854-1924
O/C 25x39 Cows Watering 1881 Chr 10/91 14,300
Slade, Caleb Arnold   Am 1882-1961
O/C 20x24 Harbor Scene Wes 3/92 935
O/C 32x40 Figures Outside Eastern Mosque Wes 3/92 358
Slee, William F.
O/C 6x9 English Fen and Two Oaks: Pair Eld 4/92 121
Sloan, John   Am 1871-1951
O/C 32x26 Nude Glancing Back Chr 12/91 60,500
O/C 32x26 Portrait of Stuart Davis Sby 3/92 23,100
Pe/Pa 12x11 Here it is, Hope You'll Like It 1926 Chr 6/92 . . 1,320
Sloan, Junius R.   Am 1827-1900
* See 1991 Edition
Sloane, Eric   Am 1910-1985
O/M 24x40 Berkshire Barn Chr 12/91 19,800
O/Cb 20x24 The Slope Chr 9/91 3,850
O/M 29x39 Ready for a Blow Dum 12/91 3,500
O/B 18x24 New Snow Dum 1/92 2,750
O/B 25x29 The Sea Fox Doy 12/91 2,600
O/M 34x46 Canvasbacks Flying Over Marsh Doy 12/91 . . . 2,400
O/M 16x20 The Huntsman/Autumn Skn 9/91 2,310
Sloane, George   Br 20C
O/Pn Size? The Charmer 1902 Slo 2/92 3,100
O/B 12x16 A Noble Pursuit 1909 Doy 11/91 1,400
Sloane, Marian Parkhurst   Am 1875-1955
P/Pa 10x14 Afternoon, Chelsea England Fre 4/92 950
O/C 17x22 Peaceville Valley, CT Mys 6/92 385
Slobodkina, Esphyr   Am 1914-
O&Pe/M 13x8 Abstract Forms in Space Chr 3/92 7,700
Slocombe, Frederick Albert   Br 1847-
* See 1990 Edition
Sloman, Joseph   Am 1883-
O/C 20x26 Veranda on Rittenhouse Fre 4/92 900
Slott-Moller, Harald   Dan 1864-1937
O/C 47x79 Poet, Holger Drachman 1911 Sby 2/92 11,000
Slusser, Jean Paul   Am 1886-
O/C 28x32 Sunbathers 1935 Wlf 9/91 3,400
O/C 26x33 Village Scene Lou 12/91 975
O/C 25x30 Still Life of Vegetables Lou 6/92 800
O/C 20x16 Three Bathers Lou 9/91 700
Pe&C/Pa Size? Four Sketchbooks Lou 12/91 575
C,Y,W&G/Pa 17x30 A Town in Maine Lou 6/92 350
W/Pa 15x23 Port Clyde, Maine, 1940 Lou 12/91 300
W/Pa 16x11 Chicago Street Scene Lou 6/92 225
Pe/Pa 10x7 Three Drawings Lou 9/91 175
Small, Frank O.   Am 1860-
O/C 22x16 The Welcoming Smile Skn 9/91 3,300
Small, Sirgay   20C
O/B 8x10 Figures on a Balcony Yng 4/92 400
Smeers, Frans   Bel 1873-
* See 1992 Edition . . . .
Smets   Dut 20C
U/C 12x18 Ice Skating Scene Mys 11/91 440
Smets, Louis   Dut 19C
* See 1990 Edition . . . .
Smillie, George Henry   Am 1840-1921
O/C 20x30 Springtime Sby 12/91 6,050
O/C 9x16 After the Rain, Cape Elizabeth 1881 Brd 8/92 . . . 3,850
O/C 16x24 Landscape at Sunset Sby 12/91 2,200
O/C 12x15 Fields Across the Stream 1914 Skn 3/92 990
O/B 12x15 Sailboats on a Lake Yng 2/92 300
Smillie, James David   Am 1833-1909
* See 1992 Edition . . . .

Smith of Chichester, George   Eng 1714-1776
O/C 26x42 View of Chichester 1750 Sby 5/92 11,000
Smith, Albert E.   Am 1862-1940
O/B Size? Cos Cob Landscape Mys 11/91 990
O/B 9x13 Sunset in Cos Cob Mys 11/91 880
O/B 9x12 Landscape 1913 Mys 6/92 660
O/B 9x12 Autumn Landscape Fre 4/92 225
Smith, Alexis   1949-
MM 16x70 Keep 'em down on the farm Chr 5/92 7,700
Smith, Alice Ravenel Huger   Am 1876-
W/Pa 10x7 Black Woman Subject Dum 5/92 900
W/Pa 10x7 Woman Subject Dum 5/92 700
W/Pa 18x12 Portrait of a Child 1910 Slo 12/91 120
Smith, Archibald Cary   Am 1837-1911
* See 1990 Edition . . . .
Smith, Carlton A.   Eng 1853-1946
O/B 13x8 Lazy Moments Wlf 3/92 5,000
Smith, Charles   Br 1857-1908
O/C/B 19x24 Peasant Woman by a Brook 81 Chr 5/92 1,320
Smith, Charles Augustus   Am 20C
O/M 24x30 Floral Still Life Fre 4/92 350
Smith, Charles L. A.   Am 1871-1937
W/Pa 20x24 Santa Maria Valley 1920 Mor 11/91 3,500
W&G/Pa 19x25 Rolling Hills But 10/91 2,475
O/C 22x27 Autumn Trees But 2/92 1,430
W/Pa 9x11 California Landscape Mor 11/91 600
Smith, Dan   Am 1865-1934
PV/Pa 17x15 Uniformed Man on Horseback Ih 5/92 1,300
Smith, David   Am 1906-1965
E/Pa 20x26 Untitled Chr 11/91 16,500
W&Br/Pa 17x25 Untitled Composition 59 Hnz 10/91 2,200
Smith, Ernest Browning   Am 1866-1951
O/C 20x17 California Cove But 6/92 1,320
O/C 16x20 Landscape Mor 3/92 1,200
O/C 24x30 Landscape Mor 3/92 800
Smith, Francis Drexel   Am 1874-1956
* See 1992 Edition . . . .
Smith, Francis Hopkinson   Am 1838-1915
G&C/Pa/B 23x36 Summer, Inn of William Conq. Chr 3/92 . . 16,500
W,G&C/Pb 18x25 Blossoms by Wishing Well Skn 5/92 6,600
WG&Pe/Pa/B 15x25 Italian Courtyard Chr 9/91 6,600
W&G/Pa 15x26 Inn of William the Conqueror Sby 3/92 . . . 5,170
W&G/Pa 13x24 The Gleaners Chr 6/92 4,400
W,C&G/Pa 14x25 Battery Park, New York City Chr 11/91 . . 3,300
W&G/Pa 26x18 Picnic by a Stream '75 Sby 12/91 2,200
Smith, Frank Vining   Am 1879-1967
O/C 24x28 South Shore Road 1918 Skn 5/92 2,420
Smith, Frederick Carl   Am 1868-1955
O/C 18x24 Field of Hollyhocks But 6/92 1,320
O/B 10x16 Sailboats at Catalina Mor 11/91 800
O/C 14x18 Landscape Mor 3/92 220
Smith, George Melville   Am 1879-
* See 1992 Edition . . . .
Smith, Gordon   Can 1937-
* See 1992 Edition . . . .
Smith, Gordon Appelby   Can 1919-
A/C 52x60 July Sea 1973 Sbt 11/91 3,272
Smith, H. L.   Am 20C
O/C 22x28 Irish Setter in Landscape Slo 12/91 325
Smith, Harry Knox   Am 1879-
C&/Pa 15x11 Jail 1929 Wes 3/92 248
Smith, Hassel   Am 1915-
* See 1992 Edition . . . .
Smith, Henry Pember   Am 1854-1907
O/C 19x29 Cottage by a Forest Clearing Chr 11/91 4,950
O/C 14x20 Guidecca Canal Sby 4/92 2,530
O/C 12x16 The Time of Sunset-River Zan Sby 12/91 2,200
W/Pb 10x14 Back Canal of Venice Chr 11/91 1,760
W&G/B 23x39 Venetian View Sby 4/92 1,320
O/C 10x14 Late Afternoon by the Pond Skn 3/92 770
Smith, Hughie Lee   Am 1910-
O/M 22x30 Man in Courtyard '53 Dum 2/92 8,000
O/B 18x24 Woman by Seashore '57 Dum 4/92 7,500
O/B 18x24 Two Figures Dancing Dum 6/92 2,250

O/B 18x24 Female Figure Atop Mountain Dum 6/92 2,200
O/B 17x21 Snow Covered Mountainscape Dum 6/92 2,000
O/B 17x21 Mountainscape Dum 6/92 800
Smith, J. G. Am
O/B 18x24 Mexican Boy Lou 6/92 75
Smith, Jack Martin
  * See 1992 Edition
Smith, Jack Wilkinson Am 1873-1949
O/C 23x31 Rocks and Surf But 2/92 19,800
O/C 20x24 Tide Pools Mor 11/91 14,000
O/C 28x36 Oregon's Gray Coast But 10/91 7,700
O/C 24x28 Seascape Mor 11/91 7,000
O/B 18x24 High Sierra Landscape Mor 3/92 3,750
O/Cb 12x16 Lakes in San Gabriel Canyon Mor 6/92 3,750
Smith, Jeremy Can 1946-
Et/Pn 68x31 Young Woman in Doorway 1982 Sbt 5/92 . . 12,155
Smith, Jerome Howard Am 1861-1941
  * See 1992 Edition
Smith, Jessie Willcox Am 1863-1935
C&W/Pa 22x15 2 Girls Looking Reflections 1905 Ih 5/92 . 14,500
Smith, John Brandon Br a 1850-1900
  * See 1990 Edition
Smith, Joseph Lindon Am 1863-1950
O/Cb 28x24 Temple Along the Nile Skn 3/92 2,750
O/C 18x14 Flowers by a Pond Yng 4/92 1,000
O/C 33x24 Egyptian Temple Interior Yng 2/92 700
W/Pa 22x15 Verdant Cliffs 25 Skn 3/92 385
Smith, Kiki 1954-
I&Pt/F 32x66 For Mr. G. Chr 5/92 2,860
Smith, Langdon Am 1870-1959
Pe/Pa 10x6 Early Westerner w/Rifle Mor 11/91 400
Pe/Pa 10x6 Cowboy with Lariat Mor 11/91 225
Smith, Lawrence Beall Am 1909-
  * See 1992 Edition
Smith, Leon Polk Am 1906-
O/C 68x43 Correspondence 1962 Sby 10/91 17,600
A/C 47x24 Constellation K 1969 Sby 10/91 9,075
O&Pt/C 25x20 Caddo 1958 Chr 2/92 4,950
L/Pa 26x20 Untitled (Blue on Black) 1960 Chr 5/92 2,200
W&I/Pa 10x12 Untitled 45 Sby 10/91 1,265
Smith, Letta Crapo Am 1862-1921
  * See 1990 Edition
Smith, Mary Am 1842-1878
  * See 1992 Edition
Smith, Miriam Tindall 20C
  * See 1991 Edition
Smith, R. Am 20C
O/C 22x30 Still Life with Fruit Hnd 6/92 1,800
Smith, Richard
  * See 1992 Edition
Smith, Rosamond Lombard Am 20C
  * See 1991 Edition
Smith, Rupert Jasen
  * See 1992 Edition
Smith, Russell Am 1812-1896
O/C 18x27 Lafayette College, Easton Chr 11/91 7,700
O/C 12x18 Valley Kishacoquillis, PA Mys 6/92 3,630
O/C 12x18 Cabin on the Wissahickin 1838 Fre 10/91 1,150
O/B 8x11 Above Catawisa, Pennsylvania 1839 Wes 11/91 . 1,100
O/B 8x11 The Rivals Wes 11/91 880
Smith, S. Catterson 1806-1872
O/B 7x5 An Irish Colleen Dum 11/91 450
Smith, Stephen C. (the Elder) Br 1806-1872
  * See 1991 Edition
Smith, T. Eng 19C
O/C 11x18 Girls Resting by Path Slo 10/91 350
Smith, Thomas Lochlan Am 1835-1884
  * See 1992 Edition
Smith, Vernon B. Am 1894-
O/M 18x24 Willows Skn 3/92 440
Smith, Wallace Herndon Am 1901-
O/M 21x29 St. Mark's Square Sel 9/91 850
O/C 23x19 Still Life Vase of Flowers Sel 9/91 400

Smith, Walter Granville Am 1870-1938
O/C 30x22 Portrait of the Artist's Wife Brd 5/92 6,050
O/C 30x40 Skating by the Mill 1938 Chr 3/92 5,500
W/Pa 18x29 En Voyage Brd 8/92 5,280
O/C 5x12 Fishing off the Coast Chr 6/92 2,200
Smith, William A. Am 1918-1989
G/Pa 19x18 Man Abducting Woman 1951 Ih 11/91 350
Smith, William Brooke Am 20C
O/B 30x24 Portrait of a Black Man '68 Lou 12/91 50
Smith, William H. 19C
O/C 14x12 Grape Still Life 1878 Hnz 10/91 950
Smith, Xanthus Russell Am 1839-1929
O/C 20x30 Abandoned 1880 Chr 12/91 12,100
O/C 15x23 Lizzie Driscoll at Dock 1878 Chr 3/92 6,600
O/C 14x22 Clipper Ship Eld 4/92 2,750
O/C/M 8x12 The American Falls 1879 Sby 12/91 2,475
W/Pa 4x8 Fisherman by a Bridge 1913 Yng 4/92 150
Smithers, Collier Br 20C
O/C 55x47 Angel of Fortune 1901 Sby 10/91 18,700
Smithson, Robert Am 1938-1973
Mk&Pe/Pa 12x15 Asphalt Sprial 71 Sby 11/91 8,800
Pe/Pa 19x24 Granite Crystal 72 Sby 11/91 8,800
Smits, Jacob Dut 1855-1928
O/C 26x28 Peasant Family Doy 11/91 32,000
Smitter, J. Eng 19C
W/Pa 9x21 Highland River View 1867 Slo 9/91 300
Smythe, E. L. Am -1910
O/Pn 12x18 Rainy Day Wlf 10/91 200
Smythe, Edward Robert Br 1810-1899
  * See 1990 Edition
Smythe, Eugene Leslie Am 1857-1932
O/Pn 12x18 Rainy Day 1891 Slo 12/91 450
Smythe, Lionel Percy Br 1839-1913
W&G/Pa/B 8x12 Buttercups and Daisies 1883 Sby 7/92 . . 1,100
Smythe, Minnie Eng 19C
  * See 1992 Edition
Smythe, Thomas Br 1825-1906
O/C 18x24 The Mid-Day Rest Sby 6/92 8,250
O/C 14x21 Home from Market on a Winter's Day But 5/92 . 5,500
Snell, Henry Bayley Am 1858-1943
O/C 33x44 Low Tide Chr 3/92 38,500
O/B 22x28 Gloucester Harbor Ald 5/92 3,200
O/B 12x14 Sailboat Ald 5/92 1,300
O/B 10x13 Man on the Path Ald 3/92 350
Snell, James Herbert Eng 1861-1935
  * See 1992 Edition
Snoeyerbosch, Cornelius Johann Dut 1891-1955
O/C 48x30 Irises Slo 7/92 1,600
O/C 48x30 Sunflowers Slo 7/92 1,600
Snow, C. H. Am 20C
O/C 8x16 Landscape with Cows Mys 11/91 220
Snow, W. P.
O/B 16x20 Cape Cod Harbor Scene Eld 4/92 121
Snowman, Isaac Isr 1874-
  * See 1992 Edition
Snyder, Joan Am 1940-
  * See 1991 Edition
Snyders, Frans Flm 1579-1657
O/C 90x66 Table Laden with Long-Billed Snipe Chr 1/92 . 110,000
Soen, Charles
O/C 24x19 Women Along a River Bank Hnz 10/91 500
Soggi, Niccolo It 1474-1552
  * See 1992 Edition
Soglow, Otto Am 1900-1975
Pl/Pa 27x21 Comic Strip. Little King Finds Note 38 Ih 11/91 . 700
Sohler, Alice Ruggles Am 1880-
  * See 1990 Edition
Solana, Jose Guiterrez Spa 1885-1945
  * See 1991 Edition
Solbrig, H. Eur 19C
O/Pn 12x18 The Last Beams Wlf 11/91 1,100
O/Pn 12x18 Shepherd and Flock Slo 2/92 200
Soldi, Andrea It 1703-1771
  * See 1990 Edition

Soldi, Antenore It 1844-1877
  * See 1992 Edition . . . .
Soler, Antonio 19C
  O/C 41x29 Juan Flores, 1st Pres Ecuador 1835 Sby 5/92 . . 6,600
Soliday, Tim Am 20C
  * See 1992 Edition . . . .
Solimena, Francesco It 1657-1747
  O/C 38x39 Vision of Saint Francis Sby 5/92 16,500
Solman, Joseph Am 1883-
  G&H/Pa/B 18x11 Subway Rider; Portrait (2) Sby 12/91 1,320
Solneck, Franz 19C
  * See 1992 Edition . . . .
Solomon, Abraham Br 1824-1862
  * See 1990 Edition . . . .
Solomon, Simeon Br 1840-1905
  * See 1991 Edition . . . .
Solomon, Solomon Joseph Eng 1860-1927
  * See 1991 Edition . . . .
Soltau, nee Suhrlandt, Pauline Ger 1833-1902
  O/C 46x35 The Mother's Favorite Sby 5/92 8,800
Somerby, Frederic Thomas Am 1814-1870
  O/Pn 13x16 Lake Scene 1839 Skn 11/91 770
Somerscales, Thomas Br 1842-1927
  * See 1991 Edition . . . .
Somerset, Richard Gay Br 1848-1928
  * See 1992 Edition . . . .
Sommer, Charles A. Am 1829-1894
  * See 1992 Edition . . . .
Sommer, Otto Am a 1851-1868
  O/C 31x46 Conway, New Hampshire Chr 5/92 17,600
  O/C 34x49 Cattle Beside a Stream 1873 Sel 4/92 1,500
Sommer, William Am 1867-1949
  W&I/Pa 11x13 Figural Composition Wlf 6/92 750
  W/Pa 7x10 Street Scene; Still Life: Two Wlf 10/91 450
  W/Pa 12x16 Horses Grazing 1937 Wlf 3/92 300
Son, Johannes Fr 1859-
  * See 1992 Edition . . . .
Sondag Am
  O/B 8x10 Aboard Ship in San Francisco 1923 Mys 6/92 . . . 330
Sonderland, Fritz Ger 1836-1896
  * See 1992 Edition . . . .
Sonnenstern, Friedrich Schrode 20C
  * See 1991 Edition . . . .
Sonnier, Keith 20C
  Pe,P&K/Pa 13x10 Untitled Sby 11/91 550
Sonntag, William Louis Am 1822-1900
  O/C 36x56 Afterglow, Massanutten Mtns 1865 Chr 12/91 . 33,000
  O/C 40x55 Mountain Stream Chr 5/92 30,800
  O/C 35x50 Duck Hunters on the Ohio River 1850 Chr 5/92 29,700
  O/C 30x50 Mountains in Twilight Chr 6/92 6,820
  O/C 20x30 On the Shenandoah Chr 3/92 6,600
  O/C 20x30 Landscape Wlf 6/92 5,400
  O/C 20x30 On the Potomac Chr 3/92 4,620
  O/C 9x12 Autumn Landscape Sby 12/91 4,400
  O/C 20x24 Landscape Durn 8/92 3,750
  O/C 10x18 Forest Glade Eld 7/92 3,080
  O/C 12x10 Cabin Hidden in Woods Chr 6/92 2,200
  O/C 10x12 The Old Mill Sby 12/91 2,200
  W/Pa 5x8 View Across a Field But 11/91 1,430
Sonntag, William Louis (Jr.) Am 1870-
  O/C 17x52 London and Northwestern Railroad Durn 9/91 . 3,750
  O/B 13x17 Farmhouse and Windmill Hnd 3/92 1,500
Sontag, Herman P. Am 20C
  O/C 15x24 Sheep in a Snowstorm Hnz 5/92 200
Sorbi, Raffaello It 1844-1931
  O/C 16x30 Girotondo 1877 Sby 2/92 57,750
Sorensen, Carl Frederick Dan 1818-1879
  * See 1991 Edition . . . .
Sorgh, Hendrick Maartensz Dut 1611-1670
  O/Pn 19x25 Kitchen Interior with Maid Sby 5/92 8,250

Soriano, Juan Mex 1920-
  O/C 42x32 Paisaje Lirico 51 Chr 11/91 46,200
  O/C 26x61 La Hija de Rapaccini 56 Chr 5/92 28,600
  Dis/Pa 26x20 La Familia 44 Sby 11/91 3,300
  C,I&W/Pa 17x22 Man Sitting on a Park Bench Sby 10/91 . . 2,090
Sormani It 20C
  O/B 9x7 Garden Entrance 1958 Slo 2/92 150
Sorolla Y Bastida, Joaquin Spa 1863-1923
  O/C 20x33 Barcas (Playa de Valencia) Sby 2/92 550,000
  O/Pn 6x10 Barcos en la Playa Sby 10/91 49,500
  O/Pn 5x8 Fiesta Callejera Sby 5/92 44,000
Soto, Jesus Rafael Ven 1923-
  MM 80x85 Construccion en Blanco 1974 Chr 5/92 38,500
Sotomayor Y Zaragoza, Fernando Spa 1875-1960
  * See 1992 Edition . . . .
Sotter, George William Am 1879-1953
  O/C 36x40 Greenville House 1924 Ald 3/92 39,500
  O/B 16x20 Mill at Night Ald 3/92 26,000
  O/B 23x27 Sailing Off the Jersey Coast '48 Wes 11/91 . . . 4,400
  O/Ab 14x12 Evening in the Harbor Brd 8/92 4,290
  O/B 10x12 Seascape Ald 5/92 3,900
  O/B 10x12 Night House Study Ald 5/92 1,600
  O/B 10x12 Hills of Springtown Ald 3/92 1,100
  O/B 10x12 New Hampshire Valley Ald 5/92 650
Sottocornola, Giovanni It 1855-1917
  * See 1991 Edition . . . .
Soucek, Karel Czk 1915-
  * See 1992 Edition . . . .
Soudeikine, Sergei Rus 1883-1946
  O/B 15x20 Two Birds by a Church Ald 5/92 120
Soulacroix, Joseph Frederic C. Fr 1825-1879
  O/C 35x28 Free Beautiful Connoisseurs Chr 10/91 104,500
  O/C/M 36x29 La Demande en Mariage Sby 5/92 31,900
  O/C 24x40 Carnations and Daffodils Sby 10/91 22,000
  O/C 20x12 Lady Seated at a Piano-Forte Chr 5/92 16,500
  O/C 29x14 Elegant Lady Pink Bonnet Chr 10/91 11,000
Soulages, Pierre Fr 1919-
  * See 1992 Edition . . . .
Soulen, Henry James Am 1888-1965
  * See 1992 Edition . . . .
Soulies, Paul Fr a 1850-1859
  * See 1992 Edition . . . .
Souplet, Louis Ulysse Fr 1819-1878
  * See 1991 Edition . . . .
Souter, John Bulloch Br 1890-1972
  O/B 21x16 Diana Sby 5/92 7,150
Southwick, Jeanie Lea Am 1853-
  W/Pa 20x14 Gate with Roses, Bahamas 1831 Yng 2/92 . . . 175
Soutine, Chaim Rus 1894-1943
  O/C 29x21 La Petite Fille en Rose Chr 11/91 638,000
  O/C 26x32 Vue de Montmartre Sby 2/92 275,000
  O/C 35x23 Nature Morte au Faisan Chr 11/91 220,000
  O/C 21x29 Arbres a Ceret Sby 11/91 165,000
Soutner, Theodore Fr 19C
  * See 1992 Edition . . . .
Souverbie, Jean 1891-1981
  O/C 20x24 Repose by the Sea Sby 2/92 9,350
  O/B 18x22 Aphrodite et Helios 1947 Chr 2/92 6,600
Souza-Pinto, Jose Guilio Por 1855-
  * See 1992 Edition . . . .
Soyer, Moses Am 1899-1974
  O/C 23x21 Fortune Teller Sby 12/91 7,150
  O/C 23x17 The Fitting Durn 11/91 5,500
  O/C 20x10 Dancer in Red Skirt 52 Sby 4/92 4,950
  O/C 16x20 Ballet Class 1938 Sby 12/91 3,300
  O/C 14x10 Head of a Girl Chr 6/92 2,860
  O/C 30x25 Composer Virgil Thomson Chr 6/92 1,650
  O/Cb 22x9 A Dancer Resting Chr 11/91 1,430
  O/C 19x15 Girl with a Blue Scarf Hnd 6/92 1,400
  I,K&C/Pa 12x16 Reclining Nude Slo 7/92 1,400
  O/C 19x11 Two Seated Dancers Wlf 6/92 1,000
  C/Pa 19x15 Nude Sleeping Lou 12/91 600

O/C/B 9x7 Portrait of a Young Girl Sby 4/92 412

Soyer, Raphael Am 1899-1987
O/C 32x22 The Conversation Chr 3/92 5,500
O/C 24x18 Blue Cardigan Chr 3/92 3,520
O/C 12x9 Kate Chr 6/92 2,750
O/B 18x18 Woman with a Blue Robe Chr 6/92 1,980
W&Pe/Pa 15x17 Views of Standing Female Nude Sby 4/92 . 1,430
Pe/Pa 19x14 The Women in My Brother's House Sby 4/92 . 1,045
W&Pe/Pa 10x12 The Artist Chr 11/91 715
I&S/Pa 8x10 Reclining Female Nude Slo 9/91 700
P&Pe/Pa 19x15 Before the Bath Chr 6/92 550
Pe/Pa 8x10 Family Mys 6/92 550

Spada, Lionello It 1576-1622
* See 1991 Edition . . . .

Spadaro, Micco It 1609-1675
* See 1992 Edition . . . .

Spadaro, Micco & Codazzi, V. It 1612-1679
O/C 48x71 Figures in Baroque Loggia Sby 5/92 38,500

Spadino (Jr.)
* See 1991 Edition . . . .

Spangenburg, George Am 1907-1964
O/Cb 16x20 Hells Half Acre But 10/91 1,760
O/B 14x18 Devil's Cauldron, Carmel But 6/92 1,650
O/Cb 16x20 Seascape But 10/91 935

Sparks, F.
W/Pa 13x19 H.M.S. Assistance Pioneer Stuck Ice Eld 4/92 . . 385

Sparks, Will Am 1862-1937
O/Pn 20x30 Ancient Village in Mexico 1927 But 10/91 5,500
O/Pn 10x8 Santa Cruz Church, New Mexico 1916 Slo 9/91 . . 650

Spat, Gabriel Am 1890-1967
O/C 15x20 Le Bois de Boulogne Sby 6/92 3,575
O/C 10x14 Park Scene Mys 6/92 715

Spaulding, Henry Plympton Am 1868-
W&G/Pa 13x20 Dutch Waterfront Slo 10/91 275

Spazzali, Luciano 20C
O/M 32x24 Bagnati 60 Chr 5/92 462

Spear, Ruskin Br 1911-
* See 1991 Edition . . . .

Spear, W. H. Br 19C
* See 1992 Edition . . . .

Spears, Ethel Am 1903-
W/Pa/B 14x18 Daylight Bakery Hnd 6/92 100

Speckaert, Hans -1577
O/C 68x67 The Death of Sisera Chr 1/92 77,000

Speer, J. A.
* See 1992 Edition . . . .

Speer, Wil Am 20C
* See 1992 Edition . . . .

Speicher, Eugene E. Am 1883-1962
O/C 16x20 Hudson River Scene Hnz 10/91 1,600
K&Pe/Pa 11x16 Reclining Nude Chr 6/92 275

Spelman, John A. Am 1880-
O/C 30x30 Grey Day Hnd 3/92 3,000
O/C 30x37 Red Barn Chr 6/92 2,090
O/C 28x32 Autumn on the Lake '29 Hnz 10/91 675

Spencer, Howard Bonnell Am 1871-1967
* See 1992 Edition . . . .

Spencer, John C. Am 19C
O/C 20x14 Game Birds 1884 Wes 11/91 990

Spencer, Lilly Martin Am 1822-1902
Pe/Pa 14x10 Woman Holding Oil Lamp Wes 3/92 82

Spencer, Niles Am 1893-1952
Pe/Pa 7x5 Portraits of Waldo Peirce (Pair) Brd 5/92 220

Spencer, Robert S. Am 1879-1931
O/C 11x14 Note of the City, No. 1 Chr 5/92 12,100

Spencer, Stanley Br 1891-1959
* See 1992 Edition . . . .

Sperling, Heinrich Ger 1844-1924
* See 1990 Edition . . . .

Sperling, Johann Christian 1691-1746
O/Cp 19x23 Danae 1724 Chr 1/92 30,800

Sperman, L. Am 20C
O/C 24x20 Dutch Girl Among Tulips Hnd 5/92 2,800

Spero, Nancy
* See 1992 Edition . . . .

Sperry, Reginald T. Am 1845-
O/C 20x14 Landscape Slo 9/91 450

Spey, Martinus 1777-
O/C 27x21 Still Life Grapes, Peaches, Pears Sby 1/92 . . 28,600

Spicuzza, Francesco J. Am 1883-1962
* See 1991 Edition . . . .

Spielter, Carl Johann Ger 1851-1922
* See 1990 Edition . . . .

Spiers, Harry Am 1870-1947
W/Pa 20x16 Park Street Church Yng 4/92 700
W/Pa 15x20 Trappers in a Canoe Ald 3/92 625
W/Pa 28x30 Side Hill, Winter 1924 Dum 12/91 450
W/Pa 16x12 Sunset in the Woods Yng 4/92 225
W/Pa 10x13 Autumn Yng 4/92 100

Spillar, Karel Czk 1871-1939
Y/Pa 11x15 Bathers 1924 Fre 12/91 200

Spinelli, Luca It 1350-1410
* See 1991 Edition . . . .

Spinks, Thomas Br 19C
O/C 20x30 Figures by a River 1898 But 5/92 2,200

Spiridon, Ignace
* See 1991 Edition . . . .

Spiro, Georges Fr 1909-1948
O/M 32x40 Le Soleil et Ses Symboles 1951 Wes 3/92 . . . 2,310
O/M 18x15 Floral Still Life But 5/92 2,200
O/C 18x22 Paysage Surrealiste But 11/91 2,200
O/C 20x24 Sunset 59 Sby 6/92 1,320

Spiro, Professor Eugene Am 20C
O/B 20x16 Chickens 1946 Ald 3/92 125

Spitzer, Walter Pol 1927-
O/C 22x18 Seated Woman in Festive Dress But 11/91 . . . 3,300

Spitzweg, Carl Ger 1808-1885
* See 1992 Edition . . . .

Spode, Samuel Br a 1825-1858
O/C 25x30 Race Horse and Dog in Stable Hnd 12/91 2,700

Spohler
O/Pn 6x9 Dutch Winter Landscape Hnz 10/91 1,000

Spohler, Jan Jacob Dut 1811-1879
* See 1991 Edition . . . .

Spohler, Johannes Franciscus Dut 1853-1894
* See 1992 Edition . . . .

Spohn, Clay 20C
* See 1992 Edition . . . .

Spolander, F. N. Am
O/B 17x20 Fall Colors Hnd 3/92 250

Spolverini, Ilario It 1657-1734
* See 1992 Edition . . . .

Sprague, Howard F. Am a 1871-1899
* See 1992 Edition . . . .

Sprague, Samuel Am 20C
O/B 19x24 Abstract '76 Dum 2/92 45

Spreckels, R. C. Dut 19C
O/Pn 10x14 Cows and Sheep Slo 10/91 950

Sprinchorn, Carl Am 1887-1971
W/Pa 19x24 The North Star Brd 8/92 1,320
G/Pa 12x18 Nat Henson's Camp East Branch 1945 Brd 5/92 . 770
O/M 15x8 Dahlia 1935 Brd 5/92 522

Spring, Alfons Ger 1843-1908
* See 1992 Edition . . . .

Springer, Carl Am 1874-1935
O/C 13x16 Figures by a Fence Lou 9/91 300

Springer, Cornelius Dut 1817-1891
O/Pn 22x29 Wijdstraat te Oudewater 78 Sby 2/92 159,500

Springhorn, Carl
W/Pa 13x17 Winter Creek Ald 3/92 250

Spruance, Benton Am 1904-1967
O/C 36x24 In the Studio Wlf 9/91 1,800

Spruce, Everett Franklin Am 1907-
* See 1991 Edition . . . .

Squires, C. Clyde Am 1883-1970
* See 1992 Edition . . . .

St. Brice, Robert   Hai 20C
O/C 68x35 Twin Loas 55 Sby 5/92 9,350
St. Fleur, J.   Hai 20C
O/Cb 24x20 Figures in Field Slo 12/91 140
St. John, J. Allen   Am 1872-
O/C 20x30 After the Storm Wes 11/91 2,310
St. John, Terry
* See 1992 Edition . . . .
Stable, John   Eng a 1740-1775
O/Tn 4x3 Portrait of a Gentleman 1741 Lou 12/91 100
Stacey, Anna Lee   Am 1865-1943
O/C 24x36 View of Gloucester Bay But 11/91 4,675
Stackhouse, Robert   20C
* See 1991 Edition . . . .
Stackpole, Ralph   Am 1885-1973
* See 1992 Edition . . . .
Stademann, Adolf   Ger 1824-1895
O/Pn 9x13 Winter Landscape Sby 2/92 6,875
O/B 12x18 Faggot Gatherers Winter Landscape Chr 5/92 . . 6,600
O/Pn 5x10 Children in a Winter Landscape Fre 4/92 3,900
Stagliano, Arturo   It 1870-1936
* See 1990 Edition . . . .
Stahl, Benjamin Albert   Am 1910-1987
O/C 18x24 Young Woman in White Blouse Ih 11/91 4,250
Y/Pa 7x6 Portrait of a Black Girl Dum 9/91 40
Stahl, E.   20C
O/C 12x10 Italian Couple 1920 Yng 4/92 100
Stahl, Everett   20C
W/Pa 20x30 The Morning Haul 1936 Yng 4/92 150
Stahl, Fried
O/Pn 13x10 Portrait of Diana Silvarum 1920 Sby 2/92 2,200
Stahr, Paul C.   Am 1883-1953
O/C 25x23 Woman with Torch 34 Ih 5/92 3,500
Stainforth, Martin
O/Ab 21x37 English Horse Race Dum 12/91 1,800
Stalzenburg, C.   Con
O/B 9x6 Old Mill House Lou 6/92 75
Stammel, Eberhard   Ger 1833-1906
O/C/M 17x13 The Nosegay 1863 Sby 1/92 2,750
Stamos, Theodoros   Am 1922-
A/C 96x76 Infinity Field Lefkada Series 1980 Sby 10/91 . . 33,000
O/C 16x42 Cleft 1956 Chr 2/92 11,000
O/M 30x24 Mistra 49 Sby 10/91 10,175
G/Pa 18x24 Untitled Abstraction 1950 Skn 9/91 5,225
O/C 52x56 Infinity Field 1969 Sby 10/91 4,400
A/Pa 22x30 Infinity Field Lefkada Series 1981 Chr 11/91 . . 4,400
O/C 70x23 Star of the Midnight Field 1954 Chr 2/92 4,180
A/Pa 30x22 Infinity Field Lefkada Series 1975 Sby 10/91 . . 3,960
O/B 24x19 Interference Chr 5/92 3,300
A/Pa 24x19 Untitled '74 Chr 2/92 2,200
O/C 16x68 Wm. Blake--Sun Box 1959 Chr 2/92 2,200
O/C 9x12 Untitled 1959 Sby 2/92 1,650
Stan, Walter   Am 1917-
O/C 29x35 At the Piano Fre 10/91 1,450
Stancliff, G.   Eng 19C
Pe&l/Pa 9x10 Guards Engaging the Enemy 1832 Slo 4/92 . . . 200
Stanczak, Julian   Am 1928-
O/Ab 24x36 Abstract '55 Wlf 10/91 125
O/Pn 30x20 Figure Wlf 10/91 70
O/C 34x46 Abstract '56 Wlf 10/91 50
Stanfield, Clarkson   Br 19C
Pl,W&G/Pa 10x14 A Village Square Chr 10/91 3,520
Stanfield, George Clarkson   Br 1828-1878
O/C 27x41 Coastal Scene Slo 9/91 2,750
Stanfield, William Clarkson   Br 1793-1867
O/C 39x51 A Harbor at Dusk 1842 Sby 6/92 4,950
O/C 14x14 Lake Como But 5/92 4,125
W/Pa 8x6 Port Scene Wlf 6/92 650
Stange, Emil
O/C 40x50 Summer Landscape Wlf 3/92 400
Stanier, Henry   Br 1844-1920
W/Pb 24x36 A View of Granada 1883 Chr 2/92 1,320
Stannard, Henry Sylvester   Br 1870-1951
W/Pa 20x13 Evening Mist Over Ellen's Isle Slo 2/92 1,000

Stannard, Lilian   Br 1884-
W/Pa 10x13 English Country Garden Hnd 3/92 2,400
Stannard, Theresa Sylvester   Br 1898-
W/Pa/B 14x10 Perennial Garden w/Sundial 1926 Sby 1/92 . 2,750
Stanwood, Franklin   Am 1856-1888
O/C 18x30 Ships at Anchor 1878 Brd 8/92 8,250
O/C 20x36 Hulk of the Neptune 1883 Brd 8/92 4,400
O/Ab 17x13 Homeless in the Snow 1878 Brd 8/92 3,080
O/C 24x40 Back from the Hunt Brd 8/92 2,200
O/C 14x24 Sunset in the Mountains Brd 8/92 1,540
O/C 12x20 Morning After the Storm 1880 Brd 8/92 880
C/Pa 11x8 Portland Harbor 1885 Brd 8/92 688
W/Pa 5x8 Beached Brd 5/92 99
Stanzione, Massimo   It 1585-1656
O/C 46x61 Adoration of the Shepherds Sby 1/92 . . . 27,500
Stappers, Julien   Bel 19C
* See 1991 Edition . . . .
Stark, Melville F.   Am 1904-
O/C 25x30 North of Hamburg Ald 3/92 1,200
O/C 28x30 Winter Stream 1937 Ald 3/92 1,000
O/C 25x30 Manayunk Bridge Ald 5/92 825
O/B 24x30 The Secret Beach Skn 5/92 550
O/B 12x14 Boat at Dock Ald 5/92 170
W&G/Pa 20x31 Winter Fun Ald 5/92 150
Starkweather, William   Am 1879-1969
W/Pa 19x24 Fantasy Velasquez Theme 1930 Wes 11/91 . . . 660
O/C 18x24 Rain on the Window 1939 Hnd 3/92 400
Starn Twins   Am 1961-
MM 90x240 The Ascension Sby 11/91 41,250
MM/Me 84x192 Blue & Yellow Louvre Floor '85 Chr 2/92 . 15,400
Ph 65x48 Tilted Portrait Sby 5/92 11,000
Ph&L 115x72 Blue Ian Test Strip with Holes '85 Chr 5/92 . . 9,350
MM 39x29 Siamese Twins '90 Chr 11/91 8,800
MM&Ph 72x108 Between Here & There '85 Chr 5/92 5,500
Ph 14x24 Untitled (Horses #61) Chr 5/92 3,520
Ph 11x13 Untitled (Cat) 1982 Chr 11/91 1,320
Ph 10x10 M (Pink) 86 Chr 5/92 1,100
Stea, Cesare
G/Pa/Pa 5x4 Self-Portrait Sby 2/92 1,320
Stead, Fred   Br 1863-1940
O/C 65x30 Admiring the Jewels Chr 5/92 6,050
Steadman, J. T.   Eng a 1880-1891
O/C 18x12 The Harvester 1882 Wlf 6/92 275
Steadman, Ralph   Am 1936-
Pl/Pa 20x27 Nixon and Prime Minister Wilson Ih 5/92 . . . 1,100
Stearns, Junius Brutus   Am 1810-1885
* See 1991 Edition . . . .
Stebbins, Roland Stewart   Am 1833-1974
* See 1991 Edition . . . .
Steele, Daniel   Am 19C
O/C 26x22 Portrait of a Gentleman Wlf 6/92 1,000
Steele, Edwin   Br 1850-
* See 1992 Edition . . . .
Steele, Juliette   Am 1909-1980
T/M 20x24 Circus 1952 But 2/92 3,025
T/M 20x24 Powerline 1952 But 2/92 3,025
Steele, Marian Williams   1916-
O/C 10x20 Lighthouse at Dawn Yng 4/92 550
Steele, Theodore Clement   Am 1847-1926
* See 1991 Edition . . . .
Steele, Thomas Sedgwick   Am 1845-1903
* See 1992 Edition . . . .
Steele, Zulma   Am 1881-1979
O/B 25x21 Abstract Mys 6/92 275
Steell, David George   Br 1856-1930
O/C 12x10 The Messenger 95 Sby 6/92 6,050
Steen, Jan   Dut 1626-1679
* See 1992 Edition . . . .
Steene, William R.   Am 1888-1965
O/C 24x18 Winter in New York Hnz 10/91 600
O/M 24x20 Spring Landscape Hnz 10/91 425
Steer, Philip Wilson   Br 1860-1942
* See 1992 Edition . . . .
Steffani, Luigi   It 1827-1898
* See 1992 Edition . . . .

Steichen, Edward Am 1879-1973
* See 1991 Edition . . . .
Steidman, Eugene M. Am 20C
O/C 40x60 Landscape 1911 Sel 9/91 475
Stein, Georges Fr 20C
O/C 11x16 Boulevard Des Italiens Sby 10/91 7,150
O/Pn 6x9 Place de L'Opera Chr 10/91 7,150
O/Pn 6x9 Place de la Concorde Chr 10/91 5,280
Steinach, Anton Sws 1819-1891
* See 1992 Edition . . . .
Steinberg, Saul Am 1914-
Cp&H/Pa 23x29 Dropouts 1978 Chr 11/91 14,300
WHRs&Gd/Pa 20x30 Watercolor Pyramid 1972 Chr 5/92 . 14,300
Pl&Y/Pa 23x15 #4 Railroad 1958 Chr 5/92 13,200
Rs&Pe/Pa 30x40 71st St. Treaty (Document) 67 Sby 5/92 . 7,700
I&L/Pa 19x13 Hohner Music Machine 1969 Sby 2/92 . . . 5,280
Steiner, G** M** Con 19C
O/C 19x15 Still Lifes Birds: Pair Wes 3/92 440
Steiner, Johann Nepomuk 1725-1793
O/C 18x15 Portrait of Johan Wenzina 1773 Sby 10/91 4,400
Steinlen, Theophile Alexandre Fr 1859-1923
K&S/Pa 15x21 18 Mars au Pere Lachaise 1871 Sby 2/92 . . 7,150
O/C 25x18 Vase de Fleurs et Livres 20 Sby 6/92 6,875
Pl&Y/Pa 13x12 Figures, Head and Cats Hnd 6/92 850
Steinmetz-Noris, Fritz Ger 1860-
O/C 27x18 Morning Joy 87 Slo 4/92 4,000
Steir, Pat 20C
O/C 60x180 Samarai Tree 83 Sby 10/91 20,900
Stella, Frank Am 1936-
MM/Al 120x165 Steller's Albatross, 5X Sby 5/92 363,000
A/C 69x138 Double Scramble '78 Chr 5/92 275,000
MM/Al 96x132 Joatinga I Sby 11/91 220,000
A/C 81x161 Double Concentric Squares Sby 5/92 214,500
A/C 69x69 Scramble: Orange Values '77 Sby 11/91 . . . 198,000
O/M 12x12 Untitled Chr 11/91 143,000
MM/Al 45x40 Shards III, 1X-D Sby 5/92 121,000
MM/Pls 60x84 Bermuda Petrel '81 Sby 11/91 71,500
O/C 12x12 Island No. 10 Sby 10/91 63,250
MM/Pa/L 60x84 Wake Island Rail '77 Chr 11/91 60,500
O/C 12x12 Untitled 61 Sby 11/91 55,000
A/C 12x12 Greek Key Chr 11/91 41,800
Ss&A/Pa/C 60x85 Green Solitaire '81 Chr 5/92 33,000
Fp&Pe/Pa 17x22 Hagmatana 66 Sby 10/91 29,700
O/C 12x12 Palmito Ranch Sby 10/91 29,700
G&Y/Pa 38x38 Polar Co-Ordinates IV '80 Sby 2/92 25,300
MM/Pa 38x38 Polar Coordinate 1980 Sby 10/91 18,700
Cp/Pa 7x7 Untitled 63 Sby 11/91 12,100
Cp&H/Pa 17x22 Working Drawing Chr 11/91 9,350
Stella, Joseph Am 1877-1946
O/C 10x12 Study Battle of Lights, Coney Isl. Chr 3/92 . . 38,500
W/Pa 7x9 Telegraph Poles Chr 9/91 13,200
O/C&/Pn 21x18 Dog on a Balcony, Paris Chr 5/92 12,100
Y&Pe/Pa 22x27 Flower Bud Chr 3/92 12,100
O/C/Al 8x7 Vesuvius Chr 3/92 11,000
O&Pe/C 21x17 Toys 1943 Chr 12/91 9,900
Y/Pa 12x9 Head: Double Chr 9/91 7,700
W/Pa/Pa 10x8 Abstraction: Dance Chr 3/92 6,600
Y&Sv/Pa 22x15 Pink Flower Chr 9/91 5,500
Pe/Pa 8x5 Back of Man Chr 6/92 1,540
Cp&W/Pa 11x9 Hibiscus Blossom Sby 4/92 1,430
O&Y/Pa 10x8 Elephant Slo 7/92 700
Stensen, Matthew C. Am 1870-1942
P/Pa 18x20 Figures in Landscape Mor 11/91 225
Stephan, A. 20C
O/C 33x53 Parlor Scene Dum 7/92 1,200
Stephan, Gary Am 1942-
P/C&Pn 96x60 World 1982 Chr 5/92 4,950
A/C 90x48 Binding Knowledge 1981 Chr 2/92 3,850
Stephane, Micius Hai 20C
O/M 20x24 Photo de Famille Chr 5/92 1,540
O/M 16x24 Peche au Filet Chr 5/92 1,320
Stephens, Alice Barber Am 1858-1932
O&R/B 24x18 Woman on White Horse Ih 11/91 1,600
P,C&W/Pa 20x17 Officer Bowing to Woman Ih 5/92 600

Stephenson, J. G. Am 20C
O/C 28x22 The Model 1925 Hnd 5/92 850
Stephenson, Lionel MacDonald Can 1854-1907
O/B 12x19 Fort Garry, 1869 Sbt 5/92 654
Steppe, Romain Bel 1859-1927
* See 1992 Edition . . . .
Stern, Bernard 20C
* See 1992 Edition . . . .
Stern, Ignaz Stella
* See 1990 Edition . . . .
Stern, Max Ger 1872-1943
O/C 24x30 Peasants by Church at Night Sby 1/92 4,675
Sternberg, Harry Am 20C
* See 1991 Edition . . . .
Sterne, Maurice Am 1878-1957
O/C 29x24 Marigolds in a Vase 1928 Chr 11/91 4,180
O/Pa/B 21x16 Indonesian Woman Sby 12/91 880
Sterner, Albert Am 1863-1946
Pe&P/Pa 17x9 Female Nude Wtf 10/91 200
Steroni It 19C
W/Pa 16x10 Young Girl Seated Mys 11/91 495
Sterrer, Franz Aus 1818-1901
O/C 29x24 Lady with Black Lace Shawl 852 Sby 7/92 . . . 605
Stetson, Charles Walter Am 1858-1911
W/Pa 5x7 Moon Through the Pines Yng 4/92 275
Stettheimer, Florine Am 1871-1944
* See 1992 Edition . . . .
Steuber, Sheila H.
O/C 12x16 Still Life 1992 Ald 5/92 125
Stevaerts Dut 1601-1673
O/C 31x26 Portrait Old Woman, Age 79 1659 Sby 5/92 . . 8,250
Stevaerts Dut 1607-1638
O/Pn 18x24 Military Skirmish on a Bridge Sby 10/91 . . . 14,300
Stevens, Aime Bel 1879-
* See 1990 Edition . . . .
Stevens, Alfred Bel 1823-1906
O/Pn 20x16 Lady in Black Chr 2/92 17,600
O/Pn 8x6 Femme Assise a l'Eventail Chr 10/91 16,500
O/C 16x13 Coucher De Soleil 1902 Wes 11/91 468
Stevens, Dorothy Austin Can 1888-1966
O/C 36x27 Woman and Child Sbt 11/91 1,870
O/Pn 13x16 Nude Bathers on a Rock Sbt 5/92 1,496
Stevens, Edward John Am 20C
O/C 24x18 Mexican Still Life Mys 6/92 165
Stevens, George Br 19C
* See 1992 Edition . . . .
Stevens, George Washington Am 20C
W/Pa 16x29 Sea Battle 1887 Slo 12/91 325
W/Pa 7x10 Landscape 1893 Hnz 5/92 100
Stevens, John Calvin Am 1855-1940
O/C 14x18 View of Casco Bay 07 Brd 8/92 4,400
O/C 17x21 Autumn Sun 15 Brd 8/92 3,960
O/C 13x17 Cape Elizabeth, 1913 Brd 8/92 2,640
O/C 14x18 Winter Day, Delano Park 1903 Brd 8/92 2,420
O/B 14x18 Path Through Delano Park 1913 Brd 8/92 . . . 1,100
Stevens, Marjorie Am 20C
* See 1991 Edition . . . .
Stevens, Pieter Ger 1567-1624
* See 1991 Edition . . . .
Stevens, William Lester Am 1888-1969
O/C 25x30 Coastal Scene Eld 7/92 2,310
O/M 24x36 A Country Lane Wtf 9/91 1,400
O/C 28x35 Winter Landscape with Stream Sby 4/92 1,320
W/Pa 19x24 Farm Scene Mys 6/92 990
O/Cb 20x24 Rocky Coastal View Skn 3/92 935
O/C 18x20 Farm in Autumn Skn 5/92 550
O/Cb 18x24 Farm near a Pond Chr 6/92 220
Stevers Dut 1601-1673
O/Pn 5x6 Elegant Couple in an Interior Sby 1/92 5,500
Steward, Seth Am 1844-1927
O/B 12x23 Greenville...Cove, Squaw Mtn 1875 Brd 8/92 . . 2,860
Stewart, Frank Algernon Br 1887-1945
* See 1990 Edition . . . .

Stewart, Julius   Am 1855-1919
  O/C 21x39 Picnic Under the Trees 96 Chr 9/91 82,500
Stewart, Mary R.   Am 20C
  O/C 18x12 White Roses Slo 7/92 650
Stick, Frank   Am 1884-1966
  * See 1990 Edition . . . .
Stiepevich, Vincent G.   Rus 1841-1910
  O/C 18x24 In the Harem Chr 10/91 6,050
  O/C 30x20 Girl Spinning Thread Slo 9/91 3,250
Stiffler, Ledrue
  O/B 10x18 Funk's Farm Ald 5/92 50
Stifter, Mortiz   Aus 1857-1905
  O/Pn 16x13 The Looking Glass 1890 Sby 10/91 10,450
**Stiglmayer, Johann Babtist   Ger
1791-1844**
  O/C 23x38 Cabin in a Clearing 1842 But 11/91 1,760
Stilke, Hermann Anton   Ger 1803-1860
  * See 1991 Edition . . . .
Still, Clyfford   Am 1904-1980
  * See 1991 Edition . . . .
Stillman, Marie Spartali   Br 1844-
  W,G&H/Pa 31x24 Dante's Vita Nuova '80 Skn 11/91 2,090
Stimpers, Allen C.   Am
  W/Pa 21x37 U.S.S. Waterwitch off Round Island 1849 Eld 7/92 55
Stirling, Dave   Am 1889-1971
  O/Ab 30x36 April Snow, Estes Park Slo 10/91 600
  O/B 24x30 Mountain Sunset Yng 4/92 175
Stivers, Harley E.   Am 1891-
  P/Pa 16x11 Woman in Pink Ih 11/91 425
Stock, H.   Irs 19C
  S/Pa 6x9 Castle in Limerick, Ireland 1837 Hnd 6/92 150
Stocklin, Christian   1741-1795
  O/Pn 26x31 Imaginary Church Interior Chr 5/92 66,000
Stoddard, Alice Kent   Am 1893-1976
  * See 1992 Edition . . . .
Stoiloff, Constantin   Rus 1850-1924
  O/C 27x22 The Cossack's Charge Sby 5/92 3,575
  O/C 27x22 Cossacks in Pursuit Wlf 11/91 2,700
Stoitzner, Constantin   Aus 1863-1934
  O/C 32x21 Elderly Man and a Child Chr 10/91 1,650
  O/Pn 9x6 Sip of Wine Chr 5/92 165
Stoitzner, Rudolph   Aus 1873-1933
  O/C 14x17 Vase of Flowers Lou 6/92 550
Stojanow, C. Pjotr   Rus 19C
  O/C 12x21 Napoleon Riding in a Troika Sby 1/92 2,420
Stojanow, O.   Con 20C
  * See 1992 Edition . . . .
Stokes, Adrian   Eng 1854-1935
  * See 1992 Edition . . . .
Stokes, Frank Wilbert   Am 1854-1927
  O/C 26x34 The Moose Hunt 1920 But 4/92 1,650
Stokes, Frank William   1858-
  W/Pa 6x4 Lady with Stole Yng 4/92 90
Stolker, Jan   1724-1785
  O/Cp 4x3 Portraits of Artists: Five Chr 5/92 5,280
Stoltenberg, Donald   Am 1927-
  O/C 24x36 View of a Cathedral Sel 12/91 275
  O/C 30x40 Urban View Sel 12/91 225
Stoltenberg, Hans John   Am 1879-1963
  O/Ab 9x77 Landscape with Stormy Sky Wlf 3/92 450
Stomer, Mathias   Flm 17C
  * See 1991 Edition . . . .
Stone, Fern Cunningham   Am
  O/C 24x20 End of the Village Durn 9/91 300
Stone, Marcus   Br 1840-1921
  * See 1992 Edition . . . .
Stone, Marland   Am
  P/Pa 25x20 Man Tying Woman's Bowtie 54 Ih 5/92 1,600
Stone, Richard
  G/Pa 23x18 Woman in Yellow w/Umbrella 1954 Ih 11/91 . . 1,100
Stone, Robert   Br 19C
  O/C 6x12 Halloo; Full Cry: Four Sby 6/92 7,150
  O/C 6x12 Meet; Over a Ditch: Four Sby 6/92 6,050
  O/Pn 6x12 On the Scent; The Kill: Pair Sby 6/92 3,850

Stone, W.   Eng 19C
  O/C 17x20 Bettwsy-Coed Wlf 11/91 425
Stone, William R.   Br 19C
  * See 1991 Edition
Stoopendaal, Mosse   Swd 1901-1948
  * See 1992 Edition . . . .
Storch, Frederick   Am 20C
  O/C 16x13 Picking Grapes Mys 6/92 990
Storck, Abraham Jansz.   Dut 1635-1710
  O/Pn 22x19 Men Loading a Ferry 1690 Hnd 10/91 40,000
Storck, Adolf Eduard   Ger 1854-
  O/C 41x30 Landschaft Slo 2/92 700
Storck, Jacobus   Dut 1641-1687
  * See 1992 Edition . . . .
Storer, Charles   Am 1817-1907
  * See 1992 Edition . . . .
Storie, Jose   Bel 1899-
  * See 1991 Edition . . . .
**Storrs, John Henry Bradley   Am
1885-1956**
  O/Cb 10x12 Three People Abstract 45 Chr 5/92 7,700
Stortenbecker, Peter   Dut 1828-1898
  O/Pn 11x13 Barge on a Canal 92 Hnd 5/92 850
Story, George Henry   Am 1835-1923
  O/C 20x18 Portrait of Abraham Lincoln Sby 12/91 22,000
  O/C/M 30x20 The Costume Party Chr 6/92 4,950
Story, Julian Russel   Am 1850-1919
  * See 1992 Edition . . . .
Stout, Myron   1908-1987
  O/C 38x30 Hierophant Chr 11/91 74,800
Strachan, Claude   Br 1865-1929
  * See 1992 Edition . . . .
Stradanus   Dut 1523-1605
  * See 1992 Edition . . . .
Strahlendorf, C.   Ger 20C
  O/B 10x12 Landscapes (2) Mys 11/91 88
Strain, Daniel J.   Am -1925
  O/C 24x36 A Scene in Morocco 1883 Skn 11/91 2,475
Strang, Ray C.   Am 1893-1957
  O/B 27x36 Desert Traveller with a Donkey Chr 6/92 1,650
Strange, Reginald B.   Am 20C
  W/Pa 20x26 Town View with Drawbridge Lou 3/92 70
Stranover, Tobias   Czk 1684-1724
  O/C 55x51 Parrot Perched on a Brass Ring Chr 5/92 17,600
  O/C 37x55 Ducks, Pheasant and Other Birds Sby 5/92 11,000
Strasser, Roland   Am 1880-
  W/Pa 14x17 Horse Corral Mor 6/92 125
Straus, Meyer   Am 1831-1905
  O/C/B 41x70 Grazing Cattle But 6/92 6,600
Strauss, Glen B.   Am 20C
  O/B 14x20 River Landscape 1900 Sel 9/91 150
Strauss, Raphael   Am a 1859-1897
  * See 1990 Edition . . . .
Strawbridge, Anne West   Am 1883-1944
  * See 1990 Edition . . . .
Strawbridge, Edward   20C
  O/B 20x24 Still Life Etched Bottle 1959 Wlf 6/92 150
Strawn, Mel   Am 1885-1952
  O/C 24x18 Portrait Young Man But 6/92 550
Strayer, Paul   Am 1885-
  O/C 34x27 Indian in a Canoe '17 But 4/92 4,675
  O/C 21x15 Elk Collapses at Tree Base (2) 1915 Ih 11/91 . . 1,400
  O/C 31x21 Roaring Rinconada Hnz 5/92 100
  O/C 30x20 An Arab Attack Hnz 5/92 90
Strebelle, Jean Marie   Bel 20C
  P/Pa 21x43 Dessin Rehausse 1960 Slo 12/91 450
Street, J.   Am 19C
  O/C 10x16 River Landscape Sel 4/92 160
Street, Robert   Am 1796-1865
  * See 1992 Edition . . . .
Stretton, Philip Eustace   Br a 1884-1919
  O/C 30x25 His Master's Coat 1922 Sby 6/92 12,100
Strindberg, August   Swd 1849-1912
  * See 1992 Edition . . . .

Stringer, Francis   Br a 1760-1772
  * See 1992 Edition ....
Strisik, Paul   Am 1918-
  O/C 20x30 Rockport Docks Yng 2/92 2,500
Strobel, Oscar   Am 1891-1967
  O/B 14x18 Sunset on the American Desert Dum 1/92 750
Strohling, Peter Eduard   Rus 1768-1826
  * See 1991 Edition ....
Strombotne, James
  * See 1992 Edition ....
Strong, Joseph D.   Am 1852-1899
  * See 1990 Edition ....
Strong, Maud   Am 20C
  O/C 30x40 On the Way to Montauk Wes 3/92 440
Strong, Ray   Am 1905-
  O/B 24x48 California Hillside But 6/92 1,760
  O/C 24x48 California Vista But 6/92 1,540
  O/M 22x28 Hillside Landscape But 6/92 1,540
  O/Cb 24x30 Bolinas Barn But 6/92 880
  O/Cb 12x16 Isabella Valley Farm Mor 6/92 500
Strozzi, Bernardo   It 1581-1644
  * See 1991 Edition ....
Struck, Herman G.   Am 1887-1954
  * See 1991 Edition ....
Struth, Thomas   1954-
  Ph 17x23 Chemin des Courdriers, Geneve 1989 Chr 5/92 .. 3,300
Strutzel, Leopold Otto   Ger 1855-1930
  O/C 43x60 Bluehender Apfelbaum 1914 Sby 10/91 8,800
Stuart, Charles   Br a 1880-1904
  O/C 24x36 Deer in a Mountain Landscape But 5/92 6,050
Stuart, Frederick T.   Am 1837-1913
  W/Pa 10x12 Apple Tree Mys 6/92 94
Stuart, Gilbert   Am 1755-1828
  O/C 30x25 Portrait of Gentleman in White Wig Wes 3/92 .. 3,630
Stuart, James Everett   Am 1852-1941
  O/C 11x17 The Mountain and the Valley: Two Hnz 5/92 900
  O/C 18x12 Glacier Point-Yosemite 1918 Mor 6/92 800
  O/B 10x15 Evening 1905 Wes 5/92 715
  O/C 10x20 Sunset Mt. Hood 1888 Hnd 10/91 375
Stuart, Jane   Am 1814-1888
  * See 1991 Edition ....
Stuart, Raymond J.   Am
  O/C 26x18 Boy in Cowboy Clothes Riding Pig Ih 11/91 ... 4,250
  O/C 24x32 Boy Plays Harmonica 1945 Ih 11/91 1,800
  O/C 20x20 Grandma Falls Asleep Reading Ih 5/92 800
  O/C 18x24 Pike Leaping, Fishermen in Rain Ih 5/92 550
Stubbs, George   Br 1724-1806
  O/C 40x52 Ogilvy's Horse "Trentham" 1771 Sby 6/92 ... 385,000
Stubbs, Kenneth   Am 20C
  O/B 16x11 Seated Woman Abstract 1953 Wes 3/92 358
Stubbs, W. F.   Am
  O/C 24x36 Clipper Ship in a Storm Chr 6/92 1,870
Stubbs, William Pierce   Am 1842-1909
  O/C 24x35 American Schooner "Lottie K Friend" Mor 3/92 .. 2,250
Stuber, Dedrick B.   Am 1878-1954
  O/M 16x20 Near Palm Springs 1941 But 10/91 6,600
  O/C 25x30 Sheltering Trees But 2/92 5,500
  O/C 12x16 Landscape--Sunrise Mor 11/91 1,900
  O/B 10x12 An Interesting Sky Mor 3/92 700
  O/B 12x16 Breaking Surf Mor 6/92 650
Stubney
  O/C 16x11 Elderly Man Dum 4/92 85
Stuempfig, Walter   Am 1914-1970
  O/C 12x18 By the Docks Chr 11/91 2,200
Stuhmuller, Karl   Ger 1858-1930
  O/Pn 14x23 The Cattle Market Chr 2/92 37,400
Stull, Henry   Am 1851-1913
  O/C 20x28 Bay Racehorse with Jockey Up 1892 Slo 7/92 .. 6,500
  O/C 25x29 Bay Racehorse 1902 Sby 6/92 2,200
Stull, John DeForest   Am 1910-1972
  O/C 29x37 Coming Storm '38 Skn 11/91 660
Sturtevant, Elaine   Am 1926-
  * See 1991 Edition ....
Sturtevant, Helena   Am 1872-1946
  O/C 14x17 Landscape Mys 11/91 110

Stuven, Ernst   Ger 1660-1712
  * See 1992 Edition ....
Styka, Adam   Fr 1890-
  O/C 22x27 Two Ouled Nails Dancers Chr 5/92 8,800
  O/C 26x32 Grazing Along the Nile Sby 1/92 2,200
Styka, Jan   Fr 1858-1925
  O/C 30x25 Young Woman in Green 1905 Skn 11/91 1,540
  O/C 46x55 Officer on Horseback 897 Chr 2/92 1,100
Suba, Miklos   Am 1880-1944
  O/C 24x18 Indian Girl 43 Skn 11/91 385
Sugai, Kumi   Jap 1919-
  O/C 58x45 Okina 56 Sby 11/91 35,750
  O/C 45x10 Untitled 1954 Chr 2/92 33,000
Suhrlandt, Carl   Ger 1828-1919
  O/C 20x27 In the Kennel 1885 Sby 6/92 7,700
Suker, Arthur   Eng 1857-
  W/B 22x31 Autumn Perthshire, Scotland Wlf 6/92 1,500
Sullivan, William Holmes   Br -1908
  * See 1990 Edition ....
Sullivant, Thomas S.   Am 1854-1926
  Pl/Pa 13x20 Work Before Pleasure Ih 5/92 1,100
Sully, Jane Cooper   Am 1807-1877
  O/B 10x7 Portrait Francis T. Sully Darley Wes 3/92 715
Sully, Robert Matthew   Am 1803-1855
  Pl/Pa 12x8 Portrait Justice John Marshall 1832 Chr 11/91 .. 4,290
Sully, Thomas   Am 1783-1872
  O/C 22x19 Life Study of Marquis de Lafayette Chr 12/91 .. 121,000
  O/C 36x28 Mother and Child Chr 3/92 35,200
  O/C 30x25 Portrait of William Brown Chr 12/91 26,400
  W/Pa 17x15 Gypsy Maidens 1839 Chr 12/91 17,600
  O/C 30x25 Mrs. Thomas Fitzgerald 1858 Chr 12/91 15,400
  O/C 20x17 Spanish Mother Chr 5/92 5,500
Sultan, Altoon   1948-
  O/C 14x28 Hudson River Mansion 78 Chr 11/91 2,200
Sultan, Donald   Am 1951-
  O&MM/Wd 13x13 Apples, Pears, Lemon 1986 Sby 5/92 .. 27,500
  Pt&MM/M 96x96 Forest Fire July 10, 1984 1984 Sby 11/91 27,500
  C/Pa 60x48 Lemon and Eggs 1986 Sby 10/91 18,700
  C/Pa 60x48 Black Lemons June 3, 1985 1985 Sby 2/92 .. 16,500
  C/Pa 60x48 Lemons and Egg, Jan. 13, 1986 Sby 11/91 .. 16,500
  O&MM/Wd 13x13 Yellow Lemon, Mar 31, 1989 Sby 11/91 16,500
  O&MM/Wd 13x12 Untitled 1978 Sby 5/92 11,000
  C/Pa 61x48 Black Eggs Nov 1 1985 1985 Sby 11/91 ... 9,900
Summers, Alick D.   Eng 1864-1938
  * See 1992 Edition ....
Summers, Robert   Am 1940-
  * See 1990 Edition ....
Sundblom, Haddon Hubbard   Am
1899-1976
  O/C 30x42 Sunny Afternoon Sby 12/91 27,500
  O/C 34x41 Daniel Boone at the Cumberland Gap Ih 11/91 . 4,000
  O/Pa 14x19 Mozart Playing Piano Ih 11/91 750
Sunyer, Joaquin   Spa 1875-1956
  * See 1992 Edition ....
Supplee, Sarah   Am 20C
  P/Pb 19x28 Route 2, Fitchburg, Mass. 1978 Skn 11/91 ... 275
Surdi, Luigi   It 1897-1959
  O/C 24x40 Still Life Cabbage, Corked Bottle But 11/91 ... 2,200
Surrey, Phillip Henry Howard   Can 1910-
  W&Pe/Pa Size? Cafe de la Madeleine 1965 Sbt 5/92 2,338
  O/B 6x8 Deli Lunch Counter, Montreal Sbt 11/91 1,496
  O/B 8x6 Autumn Night, St. Andrew's, N.B. 1964 Sbt 5/92 .. 935
Survage, Leopold   Fr 1879-1968
  O/C 35x46 Paysage de Rousillon '26 But 5/92 24,750
  G/Pa 21x24 Composition with Bird, Leaf, Hand '31 But 5/92 2,750
  Pl/Pa 18x15 Dessin strie 67 Chr 5/92 990
Susenier, Abraham   1620-
  * See 1992 Edition ....
Sustris, Friedrich   1540-1599
  O/C 46x38 The Adoration of the Shepherds Chr 1/92 66,000
Sustris, Lambert   1515-1591
  O/C 30x41 The Birth of the Virgin Sby 5/92 66,000
Sutherland, Graham   Br 1903-1980
  O/C 51x32 Portrait of Douglas Cooper 67 Chr 5/92 46,200
  W,Pe&Bp/Pa 12x10 Portrait of Douglas Cooper 66 Chr 5/92 6,600

218

Sutton, Harry (Jr.) Am 1897-1964
W/Pa 15x22 Red House in Snow '45 Yng 2/92 100
W/Pa 19x24 New England Autumn '48 Yng 2/92 80
W/Pa 19x24 Summer Field '44 Yng 2/92 80
Sutton, Pat Lipsky 20C
A/C 53x69 Acrobat 2 Chr 11/91 550
Suydam, James Augustus Am 1819-1865
* See 1991 Edition
Suzor-Cote, Marc-Aurele De Foy Can 1869-1937
Y/Pa 10x8 Seated Nude 1925 Sbt 11/91 2,805
O/Pn 6x9 Fuentarabia, Espagne 1907 Sbt 11/91 1,402
Svendson, Charles C. Am 1871-1959
* See 1992 Edition
Svendson, Svend Am 1864-1934
O/C 22x36 Winter Scene But 5/92 2,200
O/C 28x18 Winter Forest Scene with River Hnz 5/92 650
O/C 23x37 Winter Twilight Wlf 3/92 550
O/C 32x23 Snowy Winter Scene Sel 12/91 350
O/C 40x12 Floral Still Life 1910 Hnz 5/92 325
O/C 22x28 Mountain Landscape Hnz 5/92 300
Swaine, Francis Br 1740-1782
* See 1991 Edition
Swalley, John F. Am 1887-
O/B 12x9 Portrait of a Boy Dum 9/91 350
Swan, John Macallan Br 1847-1910
* See 1991 Edition
Swane, Sigurd Dan 1879-
O/C 17x23 In the Country 1904 Sby 1/92 6,050
Swanson, Bennett A.
O/C 24x30 Christmas Night 1942 Ald 5/92 180
Swartz, Otto
O/C 12x17 Winter Scene Eld 8/92 468
Swayright, Carol Am 20C
O/C 24x20 Nautical Minded Hnd 5/92 50
Sweerts, Michael Dut 1624-1664
* See 1991 Edition
Swieszewski, Alexander Pol 1839-1895
* See 1992 Edition
Swiggett, Jean Am 1910-
W,G&H/Pa 18x38 Two Mural Studies Skn 3/92 1,320
Swinnerton, James G. Am 1875-1974
O/Pn 14x18 The Coming Storm Chr 11/91 2,200
W/Pa 11x14 House in the Woods Sby 4/92 660
O/Cb 12x16 Desert Palaver Mor 6/92 350
Sword, James Brade Am 1839-1915
O/C 20x30 NH Fishing Excursion 1875 Skn 9/91 3,850
O/C 6x18 Boating on the River Mys 6/92 440
W/Pa 13x20 Ocean Ald 5/92 150
Swords, Cramer Am 20C
* See 1992 Edition
Sychkov, Th. Rus 20C
O/C 32x24 Friends 1930 Sby 2/92 6,600
Syer, John Am 20C
O/B 12x10 Landscape Mys 6/92 138
Sykes, Frederick J. Am 1851-1925
O/C 8x12 Sailboat Evening Wes 3/92 302
Sylluff, G. D.
* See 1992 Edition
Sylvester, Frederick Oakes Am 1869-1915
O/C 22x20 River Landscape at Dusk 1913 Sel 12/91 2,600
O/C 10x8 Landscape '70 Sel 12/91 350
Syme, John Sco 1795-1861
* See 1992 Edition
Symons, George Gardner Am 1863-1930
O/C 25x30 Winter Twilight Chr 9/91 17,600
O/B 8x10 Winter River Mor 3/92 3,250
O/B 4x6 California Landscape But 2/92 3,025
O/B 6x9 Country Landscape Stream But 2/92 3,025
O/B 7x10 Snow Trail Mor 6/92 3,000
O/B 10x12 Country Barn on Hillside But 10/91 2,750
O/Pn 9x12 Beside a Brook But 10/91 2,200
O/B 24x30 Indian Lake Hnz 10/91 1,700
O/B 4x6 New England Landscape Houses But 2/92 1,430

O/B 4x6 New England Landscape Trees But 2/92 1,430
O/B 6x9 Through the Trees But 10/91 1,430
O/Cd 6x4 Landscape Wlf 3/92 600
O/B 4x6 Spring Wlf 3/92 600
Synave, Tancrede Am 1860-
O/C/B 9x7 Portrait of Julius Stewart 1889 Sby 12/91 660
Szafran, Sam Fr 1930-
O/Pa 17x11 Female Nude '59 Wes 11/91 632
Szantho, Maria Hun 1898-1984
O/C 30x24 Two Paintings Chr 11/91 2,420
O/C 24x36 The Artist's Model Slo 2/92 700
Szasz, Paul
* See 1992 Edition
Szvoboda, V. T. Hun a 1920-
O/C 23x30 Peasant in Front of Cottage Wlf 6/92 300
Szyk, Arthur Am 1894-
* See 1992 Edition
Taaffe, Phillip 1955-
A&L/C 65x90 Nativity (Red, White) 1986 Chr 5/92 93,500
A&L/C 24x20 Green Form 1985 Chr 2/92 11,000
A,ESs&I/C 14x17 Braided Arcs 1988 Chr 5/92 7,700
Y/Pa 19x37 Untitled 1987 Chr 5/92 7,700
O&E/Pa 22x34 Untitled Chr 2/92 6,050
H/Pa 19x24 Three Untitled drawings 1986 Chr 5/92 3,520
W,G&Wx/Pa 17x22 Untitled 88 Chr 5/92 3,300
O&E/Pa 22x34 Untitled 1987 Chr 2/92 2,860
W,G&Wx/Pa 17x22 Untitled 88 Chr 2/92 2,750
Tack, Augustus Vincent Am 1870-1949
O/C 40x29 Woman with a Red Rose Chr 5/92 9,900
Tackett, William Am a 1950-1970
* See 1992 Edition
Tafuri, Clemente It 1903-1971
* See 1990 Edition
Tafuri, Raffaele It 1857-1929
O/C 38x28 Il Giovane Cacciatore Sby 10/91 31,900
Tag, Willy Ger 1886-
O/C 19x27 Horses and Cart in Landscape Sby 7/92 3,520
Tait, Arthur Fitzwilliam Am 1819-1905
O/C 36x50 Trappers Following Trail 1851 Chr 5/92 . . . 605,000
O/C 24x36 Ruffed Grouse Shooting 1857 Chr 5/92 . . . 242,000
O/C 29x22 Buck and Doe 1878 Chr 12/91 46,200
O/C 14x22 October in the Forest 1877 Chr 12/91 46,200
O/C 25x30 Chickens Feeding 1870 Dum 9/91 20,000
O/B 9x13 Maternal Affection 1859 Chr 5/92 19,250
O/Pn 10x14 Chicks and Delft Bowl 90 Chr 12/91 16,500
O/C 10x14 Well Retrieved 1886 Doy 12/91 13,000
O/C 40x30 Alert (Adirondacks) 80 But 4/92 12,100
O/B 10x14 Chicks 1865 Wes 3/92 9,900
O/B 8x10 Young Quail 1863 Sby 4/92 8,800
O/B 8x10 Quail Chicks 1866 Slo 10/91 8,500
O/C 22x14 Trespassers 86 Chr 9/91 7,700
O/C 12x16 Spaniel and Canvasback Duck '92 Sby 12/91 . . 6,875
Takashima, Y. Am 20C
O/B 13x18 Tabletop Still Life Peaches Slo 7/92 1,500
Tal-Coat, Pierre Fr 1905-1985
* See 1991 Edition
Talcott, Allen Butler Am 1867-1908
O/C 24x30 The Point/A Landscape 1902 Skn 5/92 4,125
Talizzi, F.
O/C 20x26 Cattle in a Field Hnz 10/91 100
Tallant, Richard H. Am 1853-1934
O/C 24x16 Rocky Mountain Landscape Wes 11/91 385
O/C 12x18 Grand Tetons Mys 11/91 192
Tamarin, Gerona Spa 20C
O/C 21x25 Portuguese Beach Scene Dum 5/92 105
Tamayo, Rufino Mex 1899-1991
O/C 48x34 Retrato De Olga 41 Sby 11/91 962,500
O/C 30x40 Ritmo Obrero 35 Sby 11/91 742,500
O/C 40x30 Atormentado 48 Chr 11/91 650,000
O&Sd/C 38x51 Pareja 68 Sby 11/91 528,000
O/C 38x51 Hombre con Brazos Cruzados 78 Sby 5/92 . . 407,000
A&Sd/C 51x38 Personaje En Rojo 75 Sby 11/91 374,000
O&Sd/C 40x32 La Rubia del Antifaz 78 Sby 5/92 352,000
O/C 31x24 Nido de Pajaros 45 Sby 5/92 308,000
O/C 16x20 Bodegon 28 Sby 5/92 275,000

O/C 20x19 Naturaleza Muerta 30 Sby 5/92 140,000
O/C/B 10x14 Paisaje Con Luna 47 Sby 11/91 77,000
O&Sd/C 14x20 Esfera Flotante 70 Chr 11/91 75,000
G/Pa/B 25x19 Banistas Sby 5/92 60,500
O&Sd/C 12x10 Cabeza 72 Sby 5/92 55,000
W/Pa 9x6 Mujer Sby 11/91 44,000
G/Pa 17x14 Cargador 44 Sby 11/91 38,500
G&Pe/Pa 10x7 Mujer con Baston 42 Chr 5/92 35,200
G/Pa 12x9 Mujer con Rebozo Chr 5/92 33,000
Y&Pe/Pa 10x13 Sandias 68 Chr 5/92 28,600
H&P/Pa 14x18 Guerrero 60 Sby 5/92 23,100
H&Cp/Pa 12x10 Personaje 66 Sby 11/91 22,000
Pe&Y/Pa 10x13 Rostro 67 Chr 11/91 18,700
G/Pa 10x8 Mujeres 31 Sby 5/92 16,500
Pe&Y/Pa 13x10 Hombre 67 Chr 5/92 12,100
W&Pe/Pa 13x10 Cabeza Pre-Columbina 72 Chr 11/91 . . 10,450
Pe&Y/Pa 13x10 Figura 66 Chr 11/91 6,600
H&P/Pa 6x9 Caballo Sby 5/92 5,500
Tamburini, Arnaldo It 1843-
  * See 1991 Edition . . . .
Tamplough, A. Eng 1877-1930
  W/Pa 16x24 Arab Village Near Cairo 1903 Slo 7/92 . . . 1,500
Tanaka, Akira Jap 1918-
  * See 1992 Edition . . . .
Tanguy, Yves Fr 1900-1955
  O/C 11x9 Prodigue Ne Revient Jamais I 43 Sby 11/91 . 247,500
  O/C 11x9 Prodigue Ne Revient Jamais II 43 Sby 11/91 . 247,500
  O/C 11x9 Prodigue Ne Revient Jamais III 43 Sby 11/91 . 247,500
  O/C 11x9 Prodigue Ne Revient Jamais IV 43 Sby 11/91 . 247,500
  G,Pe&W/Pa 8x5 Bacchanale Sby 5/92 2,750
Tanner, H. D. Am 20C
  O/C 20x24 Winter Landscape w/Covered Bridge '47 Fre 4/92 700
Tanner, Henry Ossawa Am 1859-1937
  O/C 11x17 Feeding Sheep Chr 12/91 5,500
Tannert, Louis Ger 19C
  * See 1992 Edition . . . .
Tannert, Volker
  * See 1992 Edition . . . .
Tanning, Dorothea Am 1912-
  O/C 24x12 Soeurs 1953 Chr 11/91 6,050
Tanoux, Adrien Henri Fr 1865-1923
  O/C 40x29 A Picnic in the Fields 1909 Chr 10/91 5,500
  O/C 40x29 The Tailor Shop 1889 Chr 2/92 3,080
Tansey, Mark 1949-
  O/C 39x89 The Myth of Depth 1984 Chr 5/92 242,000
  O/C 40x58 Study for Action Painting II Chr 11/91 77,000
  O/Cb 18x21 Untitled (After Rubens) 79 Chr 5/92 15,400
Tanzi, Leon Louis Antoine Fr 1846-1913
  * See 1990 Edition . . . .
Tanzillo, G. Rippoli 20C
  O/Cb 16x12 Italian Street Scene Yng 4/92 125
Tapies, Antoni Spa 1923-
  E&A/Cd/L 79x55 M Blanc Sby 11/91 176,000
  O&Sd/C 18x15 Figure 8 1963 Chr 5/92 70,400
  MMVC 22x19 Diagonal Relief 1962 Sby 11/91 66,000
Tapiro Y Baro, Jose Spa 1830-1913
  W/Pb 26x19 A Tangerian Beauty Chr 2/92 19,800
  W/Pa 15x11 Holding a Tambourine Chr 5/92 3,080
Tappert, Georg Ger 1880-1957
  * See 1991 Edition . . . .
Taraval, Guillaume-Thomas Fr 1701-1750
  * See 1991 Edition . . . .
Taraval, Hugues Fr 1729-1785
  O/C 17x14 Portrait of a Boy, Half Length Chr 5/92 8,250
Tarbell, Edmund C. Am 1862-1938
  * See 1992 Edition . . . .
Tarenghi, Enrico It 1848-
  W/Pa 31x21 Reading the Litany Sby 1/92 1,210
Tarkay, Itzchak Isr 1935-
  O/C 27x32 Autumn, Ladies in Cafe Doy 11/91 6,250
Taspard, Aida Am 20C
  O/B 12x16 Rockport Scene Mys 11/91 110
Tassel, Jean Fr 1608-1667
  * See 1992 Edition . . . .

Tasset, Tony 1960-
  MM 32x35 Domestic Abstraction 1987 Chr 5/92 825
  MM 14x22 Domestic Abstraction 1987 Chr 5/92 495
Tate, Gayle B. Am 20C
  O/B 10x13 Admit One Wes 11/91 660
Tatlock, Anne Fisher 1916-
  O/B 16x12 Golden Retriever in Snow Yng 4/92 60
Tauber-Arp, Sophie 1889-1943
  G&Pe/Pa 6x3 No. 10 Chr 11/91 39,600
Taubes, Frederick Am 1900-1981
  O/C 35x50 Setting the Table Sby 12/91 5,225
  O/C 20x24 George Washington Bridge Sby 12/91 1,980
  O/C 50x36 Boy in Blue But 2/92 990
  O/C 20x21 The Violinist Fre 12/91 50
Taunay, Nicolas Antoine Fr 1755-1830
  W/Pa 7x10 House With Lake Wes 11/91 440
Taunton, William Eng 19C
  W/Pa Size? River Scene 1870 Mys 11/91 412
Tauzin, Louis Fr a 1867-1914
  * See 1992 Edition . . . .
Tavella, Carlo Antonio It 1668-1738
  K&PVPa 16x11 Farmyard w/Peasants & Animals Chr 1/92 . 3,520
Tavernier, Jules Am 1844-1889
  * See 1992 Edition . . . .
Tavernier, Paul Fr 1852-
  * See 1992 Edition . . . .
Tayler, Albert Chevallier Eng 1862-1925
  O/C 20x16 Portrait Sir Edward James Poynter Sby 1/92 . . 1,760
Taylor Br 19C
  O/C 12x16 Three Masted Ship Yng 2/92 400
Taylor of Bath, John Br 1735-1806
  * See 1991 Edition . . . .
Taylor, Edward Dewitt Am 1871-1962
  O/C 26x30 Haystacks But 6/92 660
Taylor, Edward R. Br 1838-1911
  * See 1991 Edition . . . .
Taylor, Frank Walter Am 1874-1921
  * See 1992 Edition . . . .
Taylor, Grace Martin Am 1903-
  * See 1992 Edition . . . .
Taylor, R. Am 20C
  W/Pa 10x14 Shoe Shine Boys Mys 6/92 93
Taylor, Richard Deane Am
  G/Pa 16x27 Man at Churchill Downs Ih 5/92 275
Taylor, Vernon C. Am 1906-
  O/C 28x21 Calla Lillies with Horse Wlf 6/92 145
Taylor, W. F.
  O/C 16x12 Spring Snowscape Ald 5/92 2,100
Tchelitchew, Pavel Am 1898-1957
  O/C 26x21 Still Life with Pears Chr 5/92 17,600
  O/C 28x23 Still Life, Fruit Skn 9/91 8,800
  G/Pa 26x20 Study for the One Who Fell Sby 2/92 7,700
  G/Pa 22x19 Male Nude Torso 1929 Sby 6/92 7,150
  G/B 8x11 Robert Sby 10/91 6,600
  PI&G/Pa 12x17 Calliope and Apollo Sby 2/92 6,050
  G/Pa 12x18 Costume Design for Concerto Sby 2/92 6,050
  I&S/Pa 11x9 Man and Leaf Children: Two 31 Sby 10/91 . . 6,050
  G/Pa 25x19 Seated Moorish Boy with Fan Sby 10/91 4,675
  G/Pa 10x8 Seated Nude Male Wlf 10/91 4,200
  G/Pa 31x16 Spied, Moroccan Guard '31 Wlf 9/91 4,200
  K&I/Pa 14x10 Head & Figure Studies: Two 1950 Sby 10/91 3,740
  I&S/Pa 11x9 Two Drawings 1946 Sby 10/91 3,740
  PI&G/Pa 14x8 Costume Design: Apollon Musagete Sby 2/92 3,575
  Pe&Y/Pa 22x17 Study of a Male Nude Sby 2/92 3,575
  I&S/Pa 10x8 Circus Performers 32 Sby 11/91 3,300
  PI&S/Pa 11x8 Skull Sby 6/92 3,080
  G/Pa 15x11 Costume Design for Concerto Sby 2/92 3,025
  G/Pa 26x14 Nude Male Studies (2) Wlf 10/91 3,000
  G/Pa 19x15 Portrait of Woman in Red Wlf 9/91 2,800
  P/Pa 14x10 Space Composition 52 Sby 11/91 2,750
  I&S/Pa 10x14 Figure Studies: Two Sby 10/91 2,530
  G&Pe/Pa 14x11 Costume Design for Concerto Sby 10/91 . . 2,200
  G&Pe/Pa 14x8 Costume Design for Concerto Sby 10/91 . . 2,200
  Br&PI/Pa 8x11 Leaf Children Sby 6/92 2,200
  I&S/Pa 11x8 Three Figures 31 Sby 11/91 2,200

G&Pe/Pa 11x15 Costume Design for Concerto Sby 10/91 . . 1,925
G&Pe/Pa 14x8 Costume Design for Concerto Sby 10/91 . . 1,925
G/Pa 11x15 Costume Design for Concerto Sby 2/92 1,870
I&S/Pa 11x8 Women Beneath a Tree: Two 29 Sby 11/91 . . 1,650
Pl,G&S/Pa 11x8 Autumn Leaves 39 Chr 5/92 1,540
W/Pa 14x11 Standing Male Nudes: Pair Sby 6/92 1,540
Pl/Pa 12x8 Study for Hide and Seek 38 Sby 6/92 1,210
G/Pa 13x20 The White Ship 1925 Sby 2/92 1,210
Pe,Br&l/Pa 16x12 Portrait of a Man 35 Chr 5/92 880
Pl/Pa 13x8 Portrait of Igor Stravinski Wtf 10/91 750
W/Pa 12x10 Young Girl Wtf 10/91 750
Pl/Pa 8x8 Circus Figure Wtf 10/91 675

Te Gempt, Bernard   Dut 1826-1879
* See 1992 Edition . . . .

Teague, Donald   Am 1897-
* See 1992 Edition . . . .

Tedeschi, Petrus   1750-1805
O/Cp 26x20 The Visitation 1787 Sby 1/92 2,860

Teed, Douglas Arthur   Am 1864-1929
O/C 56x44 Nude Dancer 1927 Dum 3/92 18,000
O/C 23x35 Pewabic Pottery Vases Dum 3/92 4,000
O/C 24x34 Mosque and Market Scene 1920 Dum 3/92 . . . 3,500
O/C 20x24 Market Scene Dum 2/92 3,250
O/C 22x18 Galleon 1924 Dum 3/92 3,000
O/C 26x36 Market Scene '26 Dum 11/91 3,000
O/C 11x17 Dutch Village 1919 Dum 10/91 1,500
O/C 20x30 Wooded Landscape 1920 Dum 9/91 1,500
O/C 10x12 Arab Street Scene Dum 5/92 700
O/C 26x17 Trees and Forest Scene Dum 5/92 500

Teel, Raymond   Am a 1940-1949
* See 1992 Edition . . . .

Tejada, J. Moreno   Spa 19C
O/C 17x29 A Mexican Market Sby 10/91 17,600

Teles, Jose Jeronimo (Jr.)   Brz 1851-1908
* See 1991 Edition . . . .

Telkessy, Valeria   Hun 1870-
* See 1992 Edition . . . .

Teller, Grif   Am 20C
O/B 11x16 Pair Landscapes Mys 6/92 82

Temple, T.   Br a 1865-1871
* See 1992 Edition . . . .

Ten Compe, Jan   Dut 1713-1761
O/Pn 11x15 Castle Persijn, Near Wassenaar Sby 10/91 . . . 34,100

Ten Kate, Herman Frederik C.   Dut 1822-1891
O/Pn 10x13 The Sitting But 5/92 7,700
O/Pn 7x9 A Good Smoke 1857 Chr 2/92 4,180
O/C 26x34 Mischievous Altar Boys Hnd 3/92 2,600
O/Pn 19x15 The Chemist But 11/91 1,650

Ten Kate, Johan Mari   Dut 1831-1910
* See 1992 Edition . . . .

Ten, Chien Wei   Chi 18C
W/Pa 120x43 Village in Mountainous Landscape Slo 9/91 . . . 600

Teniers, David (the Younger)   Flm 1610-1690
* See 1992 Edition . . . .

Teniswood, George F.   Br a 1856-1876
* See 1992 Edition . . . .

Tenre, Charles-Henry   Fr 1864-1926
* See 1990 Edition . . . .

Tepper, Saul   Am 1899-1987
O/C 21x40 Shipboard Duel with Swords Ih 5/92 4,750
O/C 30x36 Couple at Dentist's Office 1926 Ih 5/92 4,000
O/C 25x36 Woman at Tailor Shop Ih 11/91 2,300

Terbrugghen, Hendrick   Dut 1587-1629
* See 1992 Edition . . . .

Terechkovitch, Constantin   Rus 1902-1978
O/B/C 32x21 La danseuse Chr 5/92 11,000
W,G&Pe/Pa 23x14 Femme debout Chr 5/92 2,200

Terni, A. L.   It 19C
O/C 27x42 The Return Home Chr 10/91 2,750

Terpning, Howard A.   Am 1927-

Terraire, Clovis Frederick   Fr 19C
O/C 49x91 Le Vacher 1905 Sby 10/91 8,800

Teruz, Orlando   Brz 1902-1984
* See 1991 Edition . . . .

Terwesten, Matthaus   Dut 1670-1757
O/C 49x40 Time Revealing Truth Sby 1/92 11,000
O/C 49x40 Time Revealing Truth Sby 5/92 7,700

Tesi, Mauro Antonio   It 1730-1766
K,Pl&S/Pa 11x7 Ornamental Acanthus Spray Chr 1/92 1,540

Tessari, Romolo   It 1868-
O/C 23x29 St. Mark's Square, Venice Yng 4/92 8,500

Testa, Pietro   It 1611-1650
* See 1990 Edition . . . .

Teye
* See 1992 Edition . . . .

Teyral, John   Am 1912-
O/C 26x48 Harbor 1955 Wtf 3/92 300

Thalinger, E. Oscar   Am 1885-1965
O/B 32x33 Coastal Scenes with Ruins of a Pier '47 Sel 2/92 . 175

Thamer, Otto   Ger 1892-
O/C 28x34 Mediterranean Port Scene But 11/91 880

Tharrats, Juan Josep   Spa 1918-
O/C 24x20 Centre galactique 67 Chr 5/92 1,650
O/C 51x38 Aldebaran Slo 12/91 750

Thaulow, Frits   Nor 1847-1906
O/C 24x29 Collecting Water at River's Edge Sby 2/92 . . . 31,900
O/C/B 25x32 Freight Train, Dusk Chr 2/92 31,900
O/C 16x22 The Mill Stream Sby 2/92 22,000
P/Pa 8x12 Horse Drawn Carts in Winter Slo 2/92 6,500
O/C 18x22 Winter in Oslo Chr 2/92 5,720
O/Pn 12x16 Impression of Oslo Chr 2/92 4,400
P/Pa 33x43 Stream in Winter Slo 12/91 1,800

Thayer, Abbott Handerson   Am 1849-1921
* See 1992 Edition . . . .

Thayer, Ethel Randolph   Am 1904-
* See 1992 Edition . . . .

Thayer, Polly   Am 1904-
O/C 20x24 Tending the Garden, Hingham 1940 Skn 9/91 . . . 715

The Perea Master   a 16C
O&Gd/Pn 43x38 Christ Presenting the Redeemed Chr 1/92 55,000

The Spanish Forger
O/Pn 13x9 Approaching Ship; Money Lender: 2 Sby 7/92 . . 1,100

The Torralba Master   15C
O&Gd/Pn 42x32 The Crucifixion Chr 1/92 93,500

The Villalobos Master   a 15C
O&T/Pn 28x28 The Flight Into Egypt Sby 5/92 21,450

Theotokopoulos, Domenikos   1540-1614
* See 1992 Edition . . . .

Therkildsen, Michael   Dan 1850-1925
* See 1990 Edition . . . .

Therrien, Robert   1947-
G/Pa 3x3 Weigh (Blue Keystone) Chr 11/91 2,200

Thevenet, Louis   Bel 1874-1930
O/Cb 12x16 Still Life Porcelain Wes 11/91 440

Thevinin, A. H.   Con 19C
* See 1992 Edition . . . .

Thias, E. J.   Am 20C
W/Pa 14x20 Untitled Sel 2/92 70

Thibesart, Raymond
O/C 11x16 Summer Landscape with Haystacks Sby 10/91 . 1,650

Thiebaud, Wayne   Am 1920-
O/C 24x18 Shelf Pies Chr 11/91 220,000
O/C 12x10 Boxes 1963 Sby 11/91 77,000
O/C 36x36 Hillside 1968 Sby 5/92 66,000
C/Pa 29x23 Seated Woman 1985 Chr 5/92 24,200

Thiebault, Henri Leon   Fr 1855-
* See 1991 Edition . . . .

Thieblin, Reine Josephine   Fr 19C
* See 1992 Edition . . . .

Thiele, Alexander   Ger 1924-
O/C 16x24 Ducks in Marshes Wli 3/92 900
O/Pw 16x24 Ducks on a Lily Pond Wtf 3/92 800

Thielemann, Alfred Rudolph   Dan 1851-1927
O/C/B 27x45 Topographical Landscape Slo 12/91 700

Thielens, Gaspard 1630-1691
* See 1991 Edition . . . .
Thieme, Anthony Am 1888-1954
O/C 30x36 Morning Light Near Charleston Chr 9/91 16,500
O/C 30x36 Italian Whorf, Gloucester 1928 Doy 12/91 9,500
O/C 25x30 Autumn Fields Sby 3/92 7,700
O/C 30x36 Blossoms, Rockport Chr 11/91 7,700
O/C 31x36 Old Rockport Chr 3/92 7,700
O/C 20x24 Sunlight and Shadows Brd 8/92 7,040
O/C 30x36 Seminole Indian Village Chr 11/91 5,500
O/C 24x29 Aniles Street, St. Augustine Dum 11/91 5,250
O/C 25x30 Evening, Florida Chr 3/92 4,950
O/C 30x25 Morning Breeze Yng 4/92 4,500
O/C 25x30 Fishing Boats at the Pier, Rockport Skn 3/92 . . 4,400
O/C 26x30 Lilac Time Chr 11/91 4,400
O/C 27x22 Custom House Tower, Boston Skn 9/91 3,850
O/C 32x32 Harbor Scene Sel 9/91 3,300
O/C 24x30 Harbor Scene Hnd 10/91 2,800
O/M 20x24 Summer in Vermont Sby 4/92 2,750
O/C 24x30 Harbor Scene Hnz 10/91 2,600
O/C 30x36 The Breakers Skn 3/92 2,090
O/C 24x30 Harbor Scene with Fisherman Sel 4/92 1,800
O/Cb 8x10 Corner Market Mor 3/92 1,200
O/B 13x20 Sailboats at a Dock Eld 7/92 990
O/B 8x10 Dutch River Scene Mys 11/91 330
Thierriat, Augustin Alexandre Fr 1789-1870
* See 1992 Edition . . . .
Thirion, Charles Victor Fr 1833-1878
* See 1992 Edition . . . .
Thom, James Crawford Am 1835-1898
O/C 39x72 Christmas Eve Sel 4/92 3,000
O/B 12x10 Pink and White Roses Chr 11/91 2,420
O/Pn 13x9 Lesson in Cookery Hnz 5/92 1,900
O/C Size? Sheep and Children Dum 2/92 1,500
O/C 25x13 Figures by Woodland Pond 1918 Slo 12/91 750
Thomas, Alma Woolsey Am 1896-1978
* See 1992 Edition . . . .
Thomas, Francis Wynne Eng 1920-
O/C 20x23 Woman and Dog Wlf 6/92 300
Thomas, Howard Am 1899-
* See 1992 Edition . . . .
Thomas, Paul Am 1859-
* See 1992 Edition . . . .
Thomas, Stephen Seymour Am 1868-1956
O/Pn 11x14 At Lake Tahoe, 1915 Mor 6/92 325
G/Pa 8x10 Monterey Coastal Mor 11/91 110
Thomassin, Desire Ger 1858-1933
* See 1991 Edition . . . .
Thompson, Alfred Fr a 1862-1876
* See 1992 Edition . . . .
Thompson, Alfred Wordsworth Am 1840-1896
* See 1992 Edition . . . .
Thompson, Bob Am 1937-1966
* See 1992 Edition . . . .
Thompson, Cephas Giovanni Am 1809-1888
O/Pn 28x23 Portrait of a Young Man Chr 11/91 1,650
Thompson, Dorothea Litzinger 1889-1925
O/B 18x24 Sublime Threshold Yng 4/92 150
Thompson, G. Eng 19C
O/C 20x30 Landscape Mys 11/91 302
Thompson, Jerome Am 1814-1886
* See 1992 Edition . . . .
Thompson, John Br 19C
O/C 12x15 Rural Landscape with Shepherds But 5/92 990
Thompson, Leslie P. Am 1880-1963
O/C 30x50 A Summer Picnic Chr 11/91 3,300
Thompson, Michael Can 1954-
* See 1991 Edition . . . .
Thompson, Walter Whitcomb Am 1881-1948
O/C 12x14 Landscape Mys 11/91 250

Thomsen, August Carl Vilhelm Dan 1813-1886
O/C 22x18 Sunday Afternoon Outing 1898 Chr 5/92 7,700
O/C 26x21 Innocence Sel 4/92 2,100
Thomsen, Pauline Dan 1858-1931
* See 1992 Edition . . . .
Thomson, G. F. Br 19C
* See 1992 Edition . . . .
Thomson, Henry Grinnell Am 1850-1939
O/C 18x24 Lyme Farm Scene Mys 6/92 1,925
Thomson, Tom Can 1877-1917
O/B 9x10 Woodland Interior, Winter Sbt 5/92 163,625
O/Pn 8x10 Northern Lake Sbt 11/91 88,825
O/B 11x8 Pine Trees at Sunset Sbt 11/91 88,825
O/Pn 8x10 Forest Interior Sbt 5/92 56,100
Thomson, William John Am 1771-1845
O/Iv 4x3 Portrait of a Gentleman 1816 Lou 12/91 200
Thorburn, Archibald Sco 1860-1935
W/Pa 18x21 November - Woodcock 1907 Sby 6/92 14,300
Thorenfeld, Anton Erik C. Dan 1839-1907
* See 1992 Edition . . . .
Thorn, Diana Eng 1894-
O/Pn 18x24 Polo 1936 Wes 11/91 2,090
Thorrestrup, Jens Christian Dan 1823-1892
O/C 15x14 Meeting by the Church 1864 Chr 2/92 1,320
Thors, Joseph Br 1822-1890
O/C 20x24 Fishing by a Stone Bridge Chr 2/92 3,520
O/C 20x30 Near Dorking Surrey Sel 9/91 2,400
O/C 16x25 Figure; Tending the Flock: Pair Slo 9/91 2,000
O/C 29x43 Figures in a Country Landscape Wlf 3/92 1,700
O/C 8x13 Country Landscape Wlf 9/91 1,500
Thrash, Dox Am 1892-1965
W/Pa 11x15 Fishing Shanty Fre 10/91 60
Thrasher, Leslie Am 1889-1936
O/C 20x16 Man Toasting Nurse and Baby 30 Ih 5/92 3,250
O/C 20x16 Tattooed Man Swallowing Sword 31 Ih 11/91 . . 3,250
Thuma, Marilyn Am 20C
P/Pa 12x9 Abstraction But 11/91 2,200
Thurber, E. E.
W/Pa 15x21 Wadley's Falls Ald 3/92 55
Thurber, James Grover Am 1894-1961
P/Pa 10x8 Man's Head with Four Marginal Dogs Ih 5/92 . . 3,750
Pe/Pa 9x10 Man and Dog Sleep as Woman Longs Ih 11/91 1,800
Pe/Pa 11x9 And Another Thing--! Wes 11/91 220
Thurston, John K. Am 1865-1955
W/Pa 12x15 White Water Hnd 5/92 150
Tiarini, Alessandro It 1577-1668
* See 1991 Edition . . . .
Tielens, Alexandre Bel 1868-1959
O/C 24x18 Yellow Chrysanthemums in a Stein Chr 5/92 . . 1,540
Tiepolo, Giovanni Battista It 1696-1770
Pl&S/Pa 11x8 Study of a Man Chr 1/92 13,200
Tiepolo, Giovanni Domenico It 1727-1804
O/C 16x12 Saint Joseph and the Christ Child Sby 1/92 . . . 88,000
Tiepolo, Lorenzo Baldissera It 1736-1776
K,I&S/Pa 16x11 Beheading of John the Baptist Chr 1/92 . . . 7,150
Tiffany, Louis Comfort Am 1848-1933
W/Pa 12x4 Interior Scene Lou 3/92 400
Tilmans Fr 20C
O/C 16x20 Autumn Landscape Dum 7/92 150
Timen, Frans Helge Swd 1883-1968
O/C 17x12 Landscape with Trees 1904 Fre 12/91 50
Timmermans, Louis Fr 1846-1910
O/C 24x20 The Port of Bruges Chr 2/92 3,850
Timmins, Harry L. Am 1887-1963
G/Pa 21x11 Man and Women Seated Room 40 Ih 11/91 . . . 325
Ting, Wallasse 20C
* See 1992 Edition . . . .
Tinguely, Jean Sws 1925-1991
MM/Pa 9x12 Untitled 83 Chr 11/91 14,300
MM/Pa 17x17 Untitled 88 Chr 11/91 12,100
Tinhof, C.
O/C 9x12 European Castle Dum 9/91 200

Tinkham, Alice   Am 19C
O/C 21x18 Portrait of Edith Lincoln Slo 4/92   65
Tinoco, Carmen Montilla   Ven 1936-
O/C 64x51 Iocasta (from La Selva Interior) 1976 Chr 11/91 . 7,700
Tintoretto   It 1560-1635
O/C 22x20 Portrait of a Man Sby 5/92 14,850
Tippet, W. V.   Br 19C
O/C 20x30 Hay Time Hnd 12/91   650
Tiratelli, Aurelio   It 1842-1900
* See 1992 Edition
Tiribacco   It 20C
O/C 13x11 Cardinal and Parrot Hnz 5/92   900
Tironi, Francesco   It 18C
* See 1991 Edition
Tischbein, Johann (the Elder)   Ger 1722-1789
* See 1992 Edition . . . .
Tisi, Benvenuto   It
* See 1991 Edition . . . .
Tissot, James Jacques Joseph   Fr 1836-1902
O/C 35x47 Portrait de Femme a l'Eventail Sby 10/91 . . . 319,000
W/Pa 14x9 On the River Sby 10/91 77,000
W&Pe/Pa 7x4 Figure of Christ Sby 1/92 4,290
Titcomb, Mary Bradish   Am 1856-1927
* See 1992 Edition . . . .
Titian   It 1488-1576
* See 1992 Edition . . . .
Title, Christian   Am 20C
* See 1991 Edition . . . .
Tittle, Walter   Am 1883-
O/C 26x32 Woman in Yellow '36 Wlf 10/91   325
Tiziani, G.   20C
O/C 12x16 Cabins & Figures Winter Landscape Slo 4/92 . .   130
Tobey, Mark   Am 1890-1976
T/B 18x16 In the Grass No. II 1958 Chr 5/92 60,500
T/Pa 33x24 Other Places, Other Spaces #2 67 Chr 11/91 . 33,000
G/Pa 25x18 World Dust 54 Sby 5/92 22,000
T/Pa/V 15x13 Threaded Plane 59 Chr 11/91 20,900
Pl&K/Pa/B 19x24 Pavanne '52 Chr 5/92 16,500
I&G/Pa 5x8 Chinese Grocery 57 Sby 11/91 13,200
T&W/Pa 18x12 Apparitions '54 Chr 5/92 9,900
T/Pa 5x7 Baroque 60 Chr 11/91 5,500
Tobiasse, Theo   Fr 1927-
O/C 32x39 Les Joueurs de Flute 61 Chr 11/91 24,200
L&O/C 26x21 Les Chanteurs Des Rue 74 Chr 11/91 17,600
O/C 22x18 L'Enfance de Jacob 80 Sby 6/92 14,850
O/C 26x32 Le Fou Qui Danse Sby 2/92 13,200
O/C 24x29 La petite lumiere 71 Chr 5/92 13,200
O/C 26x21 Le Berger et L'Enfant 62 Sby 10/91 12,100
O&L/C 15x18 Lumiere de Venise 75 Chr 11/91 12,100
O/C 31x25 L'Orange et la Bohilloire Fleurie '61 Sby 2/92 . . 11,000
O/C 13x16 View of Notre Dame 74 Sby 2/92 9,900
O/C 15x18 View of Paris Along the Seine '74 Sby 2/92 . . . 9,900
O/C 27x20 Le sacrifice d'Isaac 68 Chr 5/92 9,500
A,Y&L/Pa 28x40 Oiseau Egare dans la Lumiere Chr 2/92 . . 9,350
O,Y&L/Pa 28x20 Fleur de Silence Chr 11/91 7,150
O/C 29x24 Un cheval sur le campanile Hnd 3/92 7,000
MM/Pa 10x14 L'Ombre Orangee du Desir 80 Sby 6/92 3,300
O/C 14x9 L'Oiseau et les Deux (2) Poires Slo 7/92 1,600
Pe&K/Pa 11x9 Les Amoureux 89 Chr 11/91 1,540
Tocque, Louis   Fr 1696-1772
O/C 55x43 Portrait of Monsieur Bouret Seated Sby 5/92 . . 33,000
Todd, Henry George   Br 1847-1898
* See 1991 Edition . . . .
Todhunter, Francis   Am 1884-1963
O/C 24x30 Marin Cove But 2/92 2,750
O/C 28x36 Mill Valley Ranch But 10/91 1,980
W/Pa 19x23 View Across the Bay But 6/92 1,540
O/C 24x30 Avella's Ranch '46 But 2/92 1,430
O/C 24x30 Spring at Greenbrae But 6/92 1,430
O/C 24x30 Approaching Fog But 10/91 1,320
O/C 24x30 Silveira Ranch But 6/92 1,210
O/C 24x30 Cemetery But 2/92 1,100

O/C 24x30 Ranch at Alto But 6/92 1,100
O/C 24x30 Spring at Greenbrae But 10/91   825
O/C 20x26 Church in Landscape Mor 11/91   450
Todt, Max   Ger 1847-1890
* See 1992 Edition
Toeschl, G.   It 19C
O/C 24x16 Flirtation 1876 Chr 2/92 14,300
Tofano, Edouard   It 1838-1920
O/Pn 10x7 Young Woman with a Bouquet Skn 9/91 5,170
W/Pa 26x19 A Pensive Moment Sby 7/92 4,950
O/Pn 8x5 Study Woman in Fancy Dress Wes 3/92 1,870
Toffoli, Louis   Fr 1907-
* See 1992 Edition . . . .
Toft, Peter Petersen   Dan 1825-1901
W&G/Pa 20x26 View of Mexico City 89 Chr 11/91 14,300
Tojetti, Domenico   Am 1806-1892
* See 1990 Edition . . . .
Tojetti, Virgilio   It 1851-1901
O/C 19x27 Bambina con Bambola Sby 2/92 20,900
O/C 24x18 Unrequited Love 1896 Slo 10/91 5,000
Tol, Claes Nicolas Jacobsz   Dut a 1634-1636
* See 1992 Edition . . . .
Toledo, Francisco   Mex 1940-
O&Sd/C 40x50 El Chivo Equivocado Sby 11/91 209,000
O&Sd/C 30x35 El Mago Inexperto Sby 5/92 132,000
O&Sd/C/M 34x46 Nuevo Mapa De Juchitan Sby 11/91 . . . 60,500
MM/L/M 16x20 Autorretrato Chr 5/92 55,000
MM/Pa 37x22 Mujer del Calendario Chr 11/91 49,500
W&G/Pa 22x30 La Bomba de Flit Sby 5/92 46,750
MM&L/Pa 24x32 Tortuga con Pistachos Chr 5/92 44,000
G/Pa 29x22 La Soledad Chr 11/91 33,000
O&Sd/Bu 38x51 El Circo 61 Chr 5/92 30,800
W&H/Pa 16x18 Desinfectando Sby 5/92 26,400
Pl,W&G/Pa 21x30 Matriz Sby 11/91 25,300
MM/Pa 26x15 En Esta Esquina Chr 5/92 22,000
O&Sd/Bu 21x26 Pez 62 Chr 11/91 19,800
G&W/Pa 13x9 El que Perdio las Tijeras Sby 5/92 16,500
W&G/Pa 11x15 Garzas Sby 11/91 9,900
G/Pa 11x15 Mapa De Juchitan Sby 11/91 9,900
G&Pl/Pa 10x13 Cocodrilo, Sapos y Tortugas Chr 5/92 . . . 8,800
O/C/B 12x12 La Ciguena Chr 11/91 8,800
G&Sd/Pa 9x13 Untitled Sby 5/92 8,250
Pl&W/Pa 25x19 Jester (2) Sby 10/91 6,050
G&Gd/Pa 11x14 Mascara Chr 5/92 6,050
G&Pl/Pa 9x10 Payasos 63 Chr 5/92 5,500
G/Pa 15x18 Pareja Y Pescado Sby 11/91 4,950
Pl&G/Pa 8x11 Pajaro Rosado Sby 5/92 2,750
Tolford, Joshua   Am 20C
O/C 30x36 New Snow '38 Wlf 10/91   500
Tolliver, Mose   Am 1919-
O/Pn 36x16 Jig Jag Lady Wlf 10/91   400
E/B 18x16 Big Dick Charlie Wlf 10/91   225
E/B 32x17 George Washington Wlf 10/91   225
Tom of Finland   Am 20C
* See 1992 Edition . . . .
Tomalty, Terry   Can 1935-
O/B 8x10 Point St. Charles Sbt 5/92   468
Tomanek, Joseph   Czk 1889-
O/C 36x44 The Abundance of Nature 1916 Hnd 3/92 2,800
O/C 24x36 Baroque Dining Scene Wlf 11/91   750
Tomaso, Rico   Am 1898-1964
O/C 34x28 Family Sitting on Back Porch 1940 Ih 5/92 4,500
O/C 28x42 Woman Playing Violin Men Enthralled Ih 5/92 . . 1,600
O/C 25x30 Woman in White 1955 Ih 11/91   850
W/Pa 15x15 Cowboy Lou 3/92   150
Tomba, Casimiro   It 1857-1929
O/C 25x18 Flirtatious Cavalier Sby 7/92 5,500
Tominz, Alfredo   It 1854-1936
* See 1992 Edition . . . .
Tomlin, Bradley Walker   Am 1899-1953
O/C 16x19 Number 21 Chr 2/92 13,200
W&H/Pa 10x16 Concarneau 1926 Chr 6/92   110
Tomlinson, Anna C.   Am 20C
O/C 17x14 Winter Night Brd 8/92   192

Tommasi, Adolfo It 1851-1933
O/B 6x8 Vinyards Brd 5/92 3,410
Tommaso It 16C
O/C 37x83 Venus and Adonis Chr 5/92 159,500
Tompkins, Frank Hector Am 1847-1922
O/Cb 8x10 Ice Skating in the City '92 Skn 9/91 715
Toner, Thomas M. Am 20C
O/M 48x52 Surrealistic Composition Sel 9/91 550
Tooker, George Am 1920-
Et/Cd 22x30 Un Ballo in Maschera Sby 12/91 77,000
T/Pn 24x18 White Wall Sby 9/91 60,500
Toorenvliet, Jacob Dut 1635-1719
O/Pn 15x12 Amorous Couple Drinking Sby 5/92 7,700
**Topham, Frank William Warwick Br
1838-1924**
* See 1991 Edition . . . .
Tordi, Sinibaldo It 1876-1955
* See 1991 Edition . . . .
Tordia, Radish Rus 1936-
* See 1992 Edition . . . .
Torgerson, William Am 19C
* See 1991 Edition . . . .
Torr, Helen Am 1886-1967
O/Pn 11x16 Flower Rhythm Sby 12/91 17,600
O/C 10x12 Still Life Chr 9/91 3,080
Pe/Pa 5x7 Landscape Chr 9/91 220
Torreano, John 20C
O&MM/C/Pn 33x33 Space Painting 1973 Sby 10/91 1,650
Torres, Horatio 20C
* See 1991 Edition . . . .
Torres, Jose Samano
* See 1992 Edition . . . .
Torres-Garcia, Joaquin Uru 1874-1949
O/B/Pn 11x16 Canal in Venice Chr 11/91 33,000
O/B/Pn 14x18 La Piazza della Signoria 23 Chr 5/92 30,800
O/C 13x15 The Sail Boat 1922 Chr 5/92 24,200
H,Pl&W/Pa 6x5 Dibujo Constructivo 33 Sby 11/91 19,250
H,Pl&W/Pa 5x6 Caballo 33 Sby 11/91 13,200
Pe/Pa 7x6 Untitled 37 Sby 5/92 8,250
Torrey, Charles Am 1859-1921
* See 1990 Edition . . . .
Torrey, Elliot Bouton Am 1867-1949
* See 1991 Edition . . . .
Torrey, Eugene Am 20C
W/Pa 6x15 House with Red Tile Roof Yng 2/92 50
Torrey, George Burroughs Am 1863-1942
O/C 12x16 Aphrodite Rising from Foam Hnd 3/92 1,400
Torri, Flaminio It 1621-1661
O/C 34x30 A Sibyl Chr 5/92 39,600
Torriglia, Giovanni Battista It 1858-1937
* See 1991 Edition . . . .
Torrini, E. It 19C
* See 1992 Edition . . . .
Torrini, Pietro It 1852-
O/C 24x32 A New Coat of Paint Sby 2/92 6,600
**Toscani, Giovanni Di Francesco It
1370-1430**
* See 1991 Edition . . . .
Toudouze, Edouard Fr 1848-1907
* See 1991 Edition . . . .
Toulmouche, Auguste Fr 1829-1890
O/Pn 36x21 La Toilette 1889 Chr 5/92 35,200
O/C 19x15 The Proposal 1866 Sby 2/92 5,500
O/C 6x5 Portrait of a Woman 1879 Sby 5/92 3,850
Toulouse-Lautrec, Henri de Fr 1864-1901
G/B 33x21 Cavaliers au Bois de Boulogne Chr 5/92 . . . 1.98M
O/C 22x20 Madame Juliette Pascal Sby 5/92 742,500
O/C 22x18 Vieillard a Celeyran Chr 11/91 220,000
C/Pa 19x16 Femme Assisse Chr 11/91 66,000
O/Pa/C 11x9 Portrait de la Femme Sby 11/91 66,000
Pl&H/Pa 8x12 Chevaux Sby 2/92 7,700
H/Pa 6x8 Chevaux and Graffiti: Double Sby 2/92 7,700
Pl/Pa 9x8 Une Loge au Theatre Sby 2/92 4,950
Pl/Pa/B 5x4 Le Bourdelles, Substitut Sby 5/92 2,475
Y/Pa 10x6 Cavalier Hnd 3/92 2,000

Y/Pa 10x6 Etude de Femme Hnd 3/92 1,500
Tourgee, E. C. Am 20C
W/Pa 8x15 Block Island Scenes (2) Mys 6/92 138
Tournon, G. 20C
C,P&W/Pa 19x15 The Flower Sellers 1929 Slo 12/91 140
Tourny, Leon Auguste Fr 1835-
O/C 10x16 Sailboats 1901 Wlf 6/92 900
Toussaint, Fernand Bel 1873-1955
* See 1992 Edition . . . .
Toussaint, Louis Ger 1826-1879
O/C 26x21 Wo Ist Hotel? 1879 Sby 5/92 7,975
Toussaint, Pierre Joseph Bel 1822-1888
* See 1992 Edition . . . .
Tousseau, Theodore Fr 1812-1867
* See 1990 Edition . . . .
Tovar, Ivan Czk 20C
* See 1990 Edition . . . .
Towle, E. M. Am 19C
O/C 22x18 Portrait of a Girl Hnd 6/92 150
Towle, H. Ledyard Am 1890-
* See 1992 Edition . . . .
Town, Harold Barling Can
* See 1991 Edition . . . .
Towne, Charles Br 1763-1840
O/C 39x48 William Yates on Favourite Roadster Sby 6/92 . 79,750
Townley, Charles Br 1746-1800
O/C 36x48 Storm, Groom and Horse 1797 Sby 6/92 27,500
Townsend, A. A. Am 20C
O/B 9x11 View Near Fort Washington, PA Slo 12/91 200
Townsend, Diane 20C
* See 1991 Edition . . . .
Townsend, F. E. 20C
W/Pa 17x14 The Vegetable Seller Slo 7/92 130
Townsend, Frances B. Am 1916-
O/C 20x16 Portrait of St. Bernard Skn 3/92 770
Tozo Am 20C
O/C 27x20 Seated Nude Fre 10/91 500
Tracey, John Michael Am 1844-1893
O/C 10x16 Crusoe Searching Bor 8/92 1,100
Tracy, J. M. Am
* See 1991 Edition . . . .
Traquair, Phoebe Anna Irs 1852-1936
* See 1992 Edition . . . .
Trautsch, Franz Ger 1866-
P/Pa 16x21 Schanbetrieb 1915 Slo 2/92 170
Travers, H. H. Br 19C
O/C 22x18 A Side Entrance 1899 Chr 10/91 1,320
Travis, Paul Am 1891-
W/Pa 20x15 Watering Hole: Double Wlf 3/92 150
Trayer, Jean-Baptiste Jules Fr 1824-1908
W/Pa 15x11 The Fruit Vendor 1888 Wes 11/91 330
Trazzini, Angelo It 19C
O/C 23x18 Peasant Woman on a Snow Hillside Chr 2/92 . . 3,300
Trebilcock, Paul Am 1902-
* See 1992 Edition . . . .
Treganza, Ruth C. Robinson Am 1877-
O/C 25x30 Farm in Pastoral Landscape Slo 4/92 1,700
Treiman, Joyce Am 1922-
* See 1992 Edition . . . .
Treland, Ted
P/Pa 19x9 Football Player '06 Wlf 6/92 100
**Trenholm, William Carpenter Am
1856-1931**
* See 1990 Edition . . . .
Trevisan, A. It 20C
W/Pa 13x20 The Grand Canal, Venice Slo 4/92 800
W/Pa 10x6 Views of Venice: Two Slo 7/92 75
Trevisani, Francesco It 1656-1746
O/C 42x33 Mystic Marriage of Saint Catherine Sby 1/92 . . 22,000
Tribb, C. 19C
O/C 31x23 Portrait of a Lady 1851 Hnd 3/92 950
Tricker, Florence
O/B 10x14 Mountain Ald 5/92 35
Trickett, W. Wasdell Am 20C
* See 1992 Edition . . . .

Triebel, Carl & Von Rentzel, A   Ger 1823-1885
O/C 27x38 Genre Scene Skn 9/91 4,125

Trinquesse, Louis Roland   Fr 1746-1800
* See 1992 Edition . . . .

Tripet, Alfred   Fr 19C
* See 1991 Edition . . . .

Tripp, Wilson B. Evan   Am 1896-
O/C 24x36 Boxing Match at Sharkey's Fre 4/92 1,550

Trivas, Irene
* See 1992 Edition . . . .

Troccoli, Giovanni   1882-1940
O/C 25x20 Still Life Yng 4/92 1,200

Troger, Paul   Aus 1698-1762
* See 1992 Edition . . . .

Tromp, Jan Zoetelief   Dut 1872-1947
O/C 16x22 The Daisy Chain Chr 10/91 10,450

Trompiz, Virgilio   It 20C
* See 1992 Edition . . . .

Trood, William Henry Hamilton   Eng 1848-1899
O/C 22x18 Plow Horses Slo 12/91 950

Troon, Einar   20C
O/C 18x26 Ship in a Breeze 1901 Yng 4/92 600

Troppa, Girolamo   It 1636-1706
* See 1991 Edition . . . .

Trotter, Newbold Hough   Am 1827-1898
O/C 12x17 Cow and Calf 1862 Chr 11/91 1,100
O/C 16x24 Eagle Lake 1885 Ald 3/92 850

Troubetzkoy, Prince Pierre   Am 1864-
* See 1991 Edition . . . .

Trouillebert, Paul Desire   Fr 1829-1900
O/C 15x22 A La Sortie du Village 1893 Sby 5/92 17,600
O/C 18x22 The Mill House Sby 2/92 17,600
O/C 12x16 French River Landscape with Village Chr 2/92 . 13,200
O/C 17x14 Fortuna Sby 2/92 9,900
O/B 9x6 A Wooded Landscape Chr 5/92 1,870

Trova, Ernest   Am 1927-
A&H/C 67x67 Study for Falling Man #82 63 Chr 2/92 . . . 2,420
Cs/C 20x43 Abstract Sel 4/92 300

Troye, Edward   Am 1808-1874
* See 1992 Edition . . . .

Troyon, Constant   Fr 1810-1865
O/Pn 20x28 Cattle Grazing 1857 Chr 5/92 16,500
O/Pn 17x20 Mill Stream with Fishermen Chr 5/92 15,400
O/C 20x24 Watering the Horses Sby 2/92 15,400
O/C 27x36 Vaches a la Mare Chr 5/92 11,000
O/C 22x31 Herder With Cattle Skn 9/91 9,900
O/C 15x18 Cows in a Landscape Chr 2/92 5,500
O/C 24x29 Cow in a Golden Field Fre 10/91 3,500
P/Pa 7x9 Landscape with Cattle Hnd 12/91 1,900
W&Pe/Pa 9x12 Farmers Tending Oxen Wes 3/92 935

Truchet, Abel   Fr 1857-1918
* See 1991 Edition . . . .

True, David   Am 20C
O/C 54x78 Savannah Sea Sby 10/91 3,300
O&B/C 27x36 Symmetry and the Ethiopian 80 Sby 10/91 . 1,760

True, Virginia   Am a 1926-1939
O/C 18x25 Colorado/Autumn 33 Skn 5/92 880

Truesdell, Gaylord Sangston   Am 1850-1899
* See 1992 Edition . . . .

Trumbull, John   Am 1756-1843
* See 1992 Edition . . . .

Trupheme, Auguste Joseph   Fr 1836-1898
* See 1992 Edition . . . .

Truphemus, Jacques   Fr 20C
O/C 15x18 Nue Dans Un Interieur 60 Sby 2/92 6,600

Tryon, A. J.   Am 19C
O/B 14x24 Cow in Farmyard 1885 Slo 7/92 400

Tryon, Benjamin F.   Am 1824-
* See 1992 Edition . . . .

Tryon, Dwight William   Am 1849-1925
O/Pn 11x16 Harbor View 1889 Fre 4/92 2,100
O/Pa/B 12x20 Sheep in a Rock Pasture Hnd 12/91 550

Tsak, P.
O/C 20x16 A Day at the Beach Wtf 3/92 200

Tschaggeny, Charles Philogene   Bel 1815-1894
* See 1991 Edition . . . .

Tschaggeny, Edmond Jean Baptis   Bel 1818-1873
* See 1990 Edition . . . .

Tsingos, Thanos   1914-1965
O/C 24x36 Boats Chr 11/91 2,640

Tsuji, H.   Jap 20C
O/C 29x36 Mount Fuji 1938 Slo 12/91 1,000

Tubby, J. T.   Am 20C
Pe/Pa 8x12 View of Portland Brd 5/92 55

Tucker, *   Eng 19C**
W/Pa 9x14 Sheep in Landscape Slo 10/91 450

Tucker, Allen   Am 1866-1939
O/C 25x30 Cherry Trees Skn 3/92 5,720
O/C 16x20 Washing Day '25 Sby 4/92 1,980
O/B 20x16 Summer Landscape But 11/91 1,650
P/Pa 8x6 Day and Night: Pair Yng 4/92 250

Tucker, M.E.
O/C 21x14 Deer in Landscape 1885 Dum 9/91 150

Tucker, P. A.   Am 20C
P/Pa 22x30 Road by a Pond Yng 2/92 50

Tudgay, F. J.   Am 19C
O/C 20x30 Clipper Ship Macedon off Dover Chr 2/92 5,500
O/C 24x37 On the Open Sea 1860 Chr 2/92 5,500

Tudgay, Frederick   Br a 1850-1877
* See 1991 Edition . . . .

Tunison
W/Pa 22x16 Evening Trees Hnz 10/91 150

Tunnard, John   Br 1900-
* See 1991 Edition . . . .

Turas, Jules   Am 20C
O/C 17x19 Shearing the Sheep Wtf 3/92 650

Turcato, Giulio   It 1912-
O/B 23x16 Abstract Landscape Sby 10/91 6,875

Turchi, Alessandro   It 1578-1649
O/C 74x105 Procris and Cephalus Sby 5/92 17,600

Turnbull, William   20C
* See 1992 Edition . . . .

Turner of Oxford, William   Br 1789-1862
* See 1992 Edition . . . .

Turner, C. E.   Br 20C
O/C 20x30 Changing Guard at Buckingham Palace But 5/92 3,300

Turner, Charles Yardley   Am 1850-1918
O/C 30x45 Harvest Meal 1883 Doy 12/91 6,000
O/C 14x20 Summer Landscape in the Catskills Sby 4/92 . . 1,320
O/C 27x57 The Plainsmen 1912 But 11/91 990

Turner, Francis Calcraft   Eng 1782-1846
* See 1990 Edition . . . .

Turner, George   Br 1843-1910
O/C 24x40 Trent Near Ingleby 1875 Chr 10/91 6,050
O/C 16x24 Feeding the Ducks 1897 Lou 3/92 2,500

Turner, Helen M.   Am 1858-1958
* See 1992 Edition . . . .

Turner, Joseph Mallord William   Br 1775-1851
W/Pa 18x23 Careg Cennen Castle near Llandilo Chr 2/92 . 35,200
W/Pa 6x10 Sands Near... Wtf 6/92 650

Turner, Ross Sterling   1847-1915
W/Pa 13x19 Edge of the Woods Yng 4/92 325

Turtle, Arnold   Am 1892-1954
O/B 16x20 Woodland Image Hnd 6/92 30

Tusquets Y Maignon, Ramon   It -1904
* See 1992 Edition . . . .

Tuttle, Richard   Am 1941-
* See 1992 Edition . . . .

Twachtman, John Henry   Am 1853-1902
O/C 30x25 Tiger Lilies Chr 5/92 165,000
O/C 30x25 Horseneck Falls Chr 5/92 66,000
O/B 9x13 Country Road with Farm Buildings Hnz 5/92 . . . 5,500

Twelvetrees, Charles   Am
G/Pa 24x20 Skating Baby, Waving 1930 Ih 5/92 2,250

Twining, Yvonne Am 1907-
* See 1990 Edition . . . .
Twombly, Cy Am 1929-
O/PtY&Pe/C 79x95 Untitled 1969 Sby 5/92 . . . . . 1.65M
O&H/C 68x85 Untitled 1968 Sby 11/91 935,000
O&Y/C 79x103 Untitled (New York City) Chr 5/92 . . . 660,000
O,Y&Pe/C 76x80 Leda and the Swan 1960 Sby 5/92 . . . 467,500
H/V 11x14 Untitled Sby 10/91 33,000
Bp&Y/Pa 11x10 Untitled 1961 Chr 5/92 4,840
Tworkov, Jack Am 1900-
O/C 70x37 Queen II 57 Sby 11/91 71,500
O/C 40x23 Related to Barrier 63 Sby 11/91 19,800
Tyler, Bayard Henry Am 1855-1931
O/C 14x18 The Hudson 1914 Eld 7/92 550
O/C 14x16 Sandpipers and Surf Skn 9/91 495
Tyler, James Gale Am 1855-1931
O/C 15x22 Going to Windward 1902 Chr 11/91 6,600
O/C 20x31 Sailing Off a Rocky Coast Wes 11/91 6,490
O/B 15x12 Yacht off Rocky Cliffs 1884 Skn 9/91 4,290
O/C 25x30 Clipper Ship at Sea 1918 Sby 12/91 3,025
O/C 17x14 The Squall Skn 3/92 1,210
W/Pa 10x18 Yacht Race Yng 4/92 950
O/C 10x14 Seascape Yng 2/92 900
O/C 18x14 American Whaleship Eld 7/92 880
O/C 10x14 Steamboat in Moonlight Slo 4/92 500
W/Pa 28x21 Schooners in the Moonlight Slo 12/91 450
Tyler, Ron Am 20C
P/Pa 19x12 Bust of a Lady Hnd 12/91 140
Tyler, William Richardson Am 1825-1896
O/C 22x38 The Breakers Sby 12/91 3,850
Tymoshenko, Frederick Joseph Can 1937-
MM/C 24x24 Blue Content '86 Sbt 11/91 374
Tyndale, Thomas Nicholson Br 20C
W/Pb 9x13 Visit from a Neighbor Chr 10/91 550
Tyndale, Walter Br 1855-1943
W/B 15x11 Village in the South Pacific Chr 2/92 660
Tyschler, Alexander
W&Pe/Pa 13x9 Hamlet: Costume Design 1954 Sby 6/92 . . . 660
Tyson, Carroll Am 1878-1956
* See 1992 Edition . . . .
Tytgat, Edgard Bel 1879-1957
* See 1991 Edition . . . .
Tzeytline, Leon Con 20C
O/Pn 18x22 The Charge 1914 Sby 1/92 660
Ubeda, Augustin Spa 1925-
O/C 64x51 Musique Chr 11/91 7,150
O/C 32x40 Las Floras se Oyen Pasar Chr 11/91 6,050
O/C 20x29 Composicion con Dos Figuras Chr 5/92 2,640
O/C 25x32 Ceremonial Figures Hnz 5/92 2,500
O/C 18x25 Naturaleza Muerta Chr 5/92 2,420
O/C 24x29 Still Life Sby 6/92 1,430
Ubertini, Francesco It 1497-1557
* See 1991 Edition . . . .
Uecker, Gunther 20C
MM 32x32 Untitled 1966 Sby 10/91 22,000
Ufer, Walter Am 1876-1936
O/C 20x16 Zuni Women Carrying Water But 11/91 41,250
Ugalde, Manuel
* See 1992 Edition . . . .
Uguccione, Irene It 19C
* See 1992 Edition . . . .
Uhle, A. B. Am 1874-1930
O/C 18x15 Portrait of a Fisherman Fre 10/91 625
Uhle, Bernard Am 1847-1930
O/C 20x16 Portrait of a Lady Fre 10/91 550
Ulianoff, Vsevolod Am 1880-1940
O/B 17x23 View From the Brick Fence But 6/92 1,210
Ulmann, Charles Swd 19C
O/C 20x47 Surveying the Grounds 1862 Skn 11/91 3,300
Ulrich, Charles Frederic Am 1858-1908
Pe&K/Pa 11x14 Friedl; Portrait: (2) 1903 Sby 4/92 1,760
Ulrich, Friedrich Ger 1750-1808
O/C 17x21 Blacksmith's Forge But 11/91 3,025

Ulysse-Roy, Jean Fr 19C
* See 1990 Edition . . . .
Ungerer, Tomi Am 1931-
I&W/Pa 16x17 Man Repairing Vase Elephant Appears 1967 Ilh
11/91 800
Unterberger, Franz Richard Bel 1838-1902
O/C 26x37 Ile de Capri Chr 10/91 44,000
O/Pn 17x15 Road in Pompei, Italy Chr 10/91 28,600
Urban, Humberto Mex 1936-
* See 1990 Edition . . . .
Urban, L. Aus 20C
O/C 19x13 The Violin Player Chr 5/92 1,045
Urlaub, Georg Anton Abraham 1744-1788
* See 1990 Edition . . . .
Urueta, Cordelia Mex 1908-
O/C 48x40 Piramide 89 Chr 5/92 27,500
Ury, Lesser Ger 1861-1931
* See 1992 Edition . . . .
Utrillo, Lucie Valore
O/C 18x22 House with Red Trees 1948 Sby 2/92 3,025
Utrillo, Maurice Fr 1883-1955
O/Pn 32x24 Rue Muller a Montmartre Sby 11/91 880,000
O/C 21x30 La Maison de Mimi Pinson Sby 2/92 187,000
O/C 26x32 L'Eglise de Maillane 1930 Sby 5/92 154,000
O/C 20x24 Place du Tertre a Montmartre Chr 5/92 126,500
O/C 15x18 Le Moulin de la Galette Sby 11/91 115,500
O/C 18x21 Place Saint-Pierre a Montmartre Chr 5/92 . . . 115,500
O/Pa/Pn 14x20 Le Moulin de la Galette Sby 5/92 110,000
O/C 24x20 Montmartre Chr 11/91 99,000
O/C 15x22 Paysage Sous la Neige 1935 Sby 10/91 93,500
O/C 9x13 Le Moulin de Sannois Chr 2/92 88,000
O/C 18x22 L'Eglise de Droue 1936 Sby 5/92 71,500
G/Pa 25x17 Eglise Saint Michel a Limoges 1934 Sby 5/92 . . . 66,000
O/Pn 6x9 Moulin de Sannois Sby 5/92 55,000
O/C 12x14 Rue de l'Abreuvoir a Montmartre Sby 5/92 . . . 55,000
G/Pa 10x13 Eglise Sous la Neige 1922 Sby 5/92 49,500
W&G/Pa 10x13 Scene de Rue Sby 5/92 49,500
O/B 14x11 Plante Dans Un Pot de Tercuite Chr 11/91 . . . 16,500
Utz, Thornton Am 1914-
O/B 16x23 Family Opening Xmas Presents 1952 Ilh 11/91 . . 1,500
Vaarberg, H. Dut 19C
O/Pn 31x24 Selling Fish by Night 66 Hnd 5/92 4,800
Vaccaro, Andrea It 1598-1670
O/C 50x40 Judith Holding Head of Holofernes Chr 5/92 . . 38,500
Vaccaro, Nicola It 1637-1717
* See 1992 Edition . . . .
Vacha, Rudolf Czk 1860-
O/C 28x16 Viconte Guy de Gastines 18-3 Slo 7/92 800
Vacher, Thomas Britain Eng 1805-1880
W/Pa 12x9 Ilfracombe; Rocky Coast 1869 Wlf 11/91 350
Vaillant, Wallerand Dut 1623-1677
* See 1992 Edition . . . .
Valade, Gabrielle Marie Fr 1709-1787
* See 1991 Edition . . . .
Valadon, Suzanne Fr 1865-1938
* See 1992 Edition . . . .
Valbuena, Ricardo Col 1960-
* See 1990 Edition . . . .
Valcin, Gerard Hai 20C
O/C 44x44 Ceremonie pour Agoue 73 Chr 5/92 16,500
O/M 36x48 Carnival 1973 Chr 5/92 5,280
Valckeraere, E. Con 19C
O/C 20x30 Canal in Bruges '90 Hnd 10/91 190
Valencia, Manuel Am 1856-1935
O/C 50x30 Native American Women Yosemite But 6/92 . . . 6,050
O/B 20x26 Cows in Landscape Mor 3/92 1,000
O/C/C 20x30 Cows in Mountain Landscape Mor 3/92 700
O/C/B 24x16 Woman in the Woods But 6/92 550
Valenkamph, Theodore V. C. Am 1868-1924
O/C 22x32 Clipper Ship 1904 Sby 12/91 2,200
O/C 12x18 Sailing by a Hay Field, Cape Ann Brd 8/92 . . . 962
O/C 8x11 Fishing Beach Yng 2/92 900
O/Cb 6x9 Winter Harbor Skn 11/91 412

O/C 10x12 Ships and Schooners Skn 3/92 275

Valentino, Giovanni Domenico   It 17C
O/C 20x26 Kitchen Interior Slo 7/92 1,800

Valeri, Prevot   Con 19C
O/C 16x13 Shepherdess Hnd 3/92 1,500

Valerio, Theodore   Fr 1819-1879
W&G/Pa 12x9 A Man with Cap 1841 Sby 7/92 605

Vallance, R.   Am 20C
O/C 16x20 Haying Scene and Coastal (2) Mys 6/92 330

Vallayer-Coster, Anne   Fr 1744-1818
* See 1992 Edition . . . .

Vallee, Etienne Maxime   Fr 19C
O/Pn 15x18 Peasant Woman Gathering Brush Wes 3/92 . . . 2,860

Vallee, Jack
W/Pa 20x29 Grass Patterns Eld 7/92 77

Vallee, Ludovic   Fr
O/C 25x32 Le Matin Au Parc Sby 10/91 5,500

Vallejo, Boris   Am 1941-
A/Cb 28x18 Montage of Murdered Woman 1978 Ih 11/91 . 1,300

Vallejo, Don Francisco Antonio   Mex a 1752-1784
O/C 32x21 Virgen de Guadalupe 1781 Sby 5/92 33,000

Vallet, Jean Emile   Fr -1899
O/C 33x27 Beaux Arts Ball, 1897: Pair 97 Sby 5/92 4,400

Vallet-Bisson, Frederique   Fr 1865-
* See 1991 Edition . . . .

Vallette, Eveline
W/Pa 9x12 Gibraltar from the Spanish Lines Eld 7/92 66

Vallois, Paul Felix   Fr 19C
O/C/B 19x37 Laundry Day French Village Chr 5/92 3,850

Vallotton, Felix   Sws 1865-1925
* See 1991 Edition . . . .

Valls, Ernesto   Spa 20C
O/C 32x40 Ninos Jugando en la Playa Sby 10/91 27,500
O/C 51x39 Women Collecting Water at Fountain Sby 1/92 . . 9,900

Valmier, Georges   Fr 1855-1937
* See 1992 Edition . . . .

Valtat, Louis   Fr 1869-1952
O/C 29x36 Les Coquelicots Sby 5/92 66,000
O/C 22x18 Vase, Tulipes et Fleurs Blanches Chr 5/92 . . . 41,800
O/Pn 26x20 Femme au Chat et Livres Sby 2/92 40,700
O/C 24x29 Vase de Tulipes Sby 2/92 37,400
O/C 24x29 Les deux bouquets Chr 5/92 33,000
O/C 17x18 Les Bouquets de Fleurs Sby 5/92 31,900
O/C 18x15 Vase de fleurs Chr 5/92 18,700
O/C 24x15 Giroflees, Cruche Marron Chr 2/92 16,500
O/C 29x24 L'Enfant au Costume Marin Bleu Sby 2/92 . . . 16,500
O/C 9x9 Les Coquelicots Chr 11/91 8,800
O/C 22x18 Floral Still Life But 5/92 4,400
C/Pa 9x13 Figures on the Beach Slo 12/91 225
C/Pa 11x8 Still Life: Two Slo 12/91 225

Van Aelst, Pieter Coecke
* See 1990 Edition . . . .

Van Aelst, Willem   Dut 1626-1683
O/C 27x22 Partridge, Pheasant 1675 Chr 10/91 82,500

Van Aenvanck, Theodor   1633-1690
* See 1990 Edition . . . .

Van Anthonissen, Hendrick   Dut 1606-1660
* See 1992 Edition . . . .

Van Asch, Pieter Jansz.   Dut 1603-1678
O/Pn 15x20 Fishermen and Shepherds Chr 5/92 12,100

Van Baburen, Dirck   Dut 1595-1624
O/C 33x26 A Lute Player Chr 1/92 77,000

Van Bassen, Bartholomeus   Dut 1590-1652
* See 1992 Edition . . . .

Van Beers, Jan   Dut 1852-1927
O/C 15x24 A Smoke in the Hammock Sby 5/92 9,625

Van Beyeren, Abraham   Dut 1620-1690
* See 1992 Edition . . . .

Van Bijlert, Jan Harmensz.   Dut 1603-1671
* See 1992 Edition . . . .

Van Blarenberghe, Henri-J & LN   Fr 1741-1826
* See 1992 Edition . . . .

Van Blarenberghe, Jacques G.   Dut 1679-1742
O/Pn 5x6 Market Scene by a Harbor Sby 5/92 27,500

Van Blarenberghe, Louis-N & HJ   Fr 1716-1794
* See 1992 Edition . . . .

Van Blarenberghe, Louis-Nic.   Fr 1716-1794
W&Bc/Pa 16x26 Peasants in Ferry 1776 Chr 1/92 24,200

Van Bloemen, Jan Frans   Flm 1622-1749
* See 1991 Edition . . . .

Van Bloemen, Pieter   Flm 1657-1720
* See 1991 Edition . . . .

Van Bommel, Elias Pieter   Dut 1819-1890
* See 1990 Edition . . . .

Van Boskerck, Robert Ward   Am 1855-1932
* See 1992 Edition . . . .

Van Bouckhorst, Jan   Dut 1588-1631
Pl&K/Pa 3x2 Head of a Man in a Hat Chr 1/92 1,320

Van Bredael, Joseph   Flm 1688-1739
* See 1992 Edition . . . .

Van Bredael, Pieter   Flm 1629-1719
* See 1992 Edition . . . .

Van Brekelenkam, Quiringh G.   Dut 1620-1688
* See 1992 Edition . . . .

Van Bylandt, Alfred Edouard   Dut 1829-1890
O/C 32x27 At the Watering Trough Chr 2/92 7,480

Van Ceulen, Cornelis Janssens   Dut 1593-1664
* See 1992 Edition . . . .

Van Chelminski, Jan   Pol 1851-1925
O/C 20x30 Napoleon's Return 1887 Sby 10/91 10,450

Van Cina, Theodore   Am a 1930-1939
O/C 22x16 Around Santa Barbara Mor 6/92 550

Van Cleve, Cornelis   Fr 1520-1567
* See 1990 Edition . . . .

Van Coppenolle, E.   Con 19C
O/C 50x75 Still Life Potted Plants in Nursery Sby 2/92 . . . 35,750

Van Couver, Jan   Dut 1836-1909
O/C 20x30 On the Meerwede, Holland Sby 1/92 3,960

Van Couwenbergh, Christiaan   Dut 1604-1667
* See 1991 Edition . . . .

Van Cuylenborch, Abraham   Dut 1620-1658
* See 1992 Edition . . . .

Van Dael, Jan Frans   Flm 1764-1840
* See 1992 Edition . . . .

Van De Roye, Jozef   Bel 1861-
* See 1992 Edition . . . .

Van De Tongen, Louis   Dut 1871-1937
O/C 21x18 The Question Bor 8/92 1,700

Van De Velde, Willem (II)   Dut 1633-1707
K,Pl&S/Pa 9x33 A Fleet of Ships Chr 1/92 15,400
Pe/Pa 9x13 An English Two-Decker Chr 1/92 1,760

Van De Venne, Adriaen   Dut 1589-1662
* See 1992 Edition . . . .

Van De Venne, The Pseudo Adria   17C
O/Pn 13x17 Cavaliers Making Merry Sby 5/92 4,400

Van Delen, Dirck   Dut 1605-1671
O/Pn 19x11 View Through Drawn Curtain Chapel Sby 1/92 16,500

Van Den Berg, Anton   Dut
O/C 20x16 Mother Feeding Child Dum 9/91 1,750

Van Den Berg, Willem   Dut 1886-1970
* See 1992 Edition . . . .

Van Den Berghe, Charles   Bel 1883-1939
* See 1991 Edition . . . .

Van Den Berghe, Christoffel   Dut a
1617-1642
  * See 1991 Edition
Van Den Bos, Georges   Bel 1853-1911
  O/C 38x50 A Vase of Yellow Roses Chr 10/91 19,800
  O/C 36x24 Old Dog; a New Trick Slo 12/91 2,250
  O/C 24x15 Matador and Senora Slo 10/91 1,900
Van Den Bossche, Balthasar   1681-1715
  O/C 25x31 Figures at a Table Sby 7/92 2,750
Van Den Broeck, Elias   Dut 1650-1709
  * See 1990 Edition
Van Den Daele, Casimir   Bel 1818-1880
  * See 1992 Edition
Van Den Eycken, Charles   Bel 1859-1923
  O/C 14x18 Kittens by a Sewing Basket 1909 Chr 5/92 9,900
  O/C 27x40 The Intruder 1904 Chr 2/92 9,350
  O/C 14x18 Purrfect Apprentices 1907 Chr 5/92 8,800
Van Der Ast, Balthasar   Dut 1594-1657
  O/Pn 16x24 Wicker Basket with Roses, Tulips Chr 1/92 . . 96,800
Van Der Bilt, Johannes   Am 1882-1943
  W/Pa 14x11 View of Central Park Lou 6/92 200
Van Der Brugghen, Guillaume A.   Dut
1811-1891
  O/Pn 10x12 Young Boy, Mountain Goats, Dog 56 Chr 5/92 . . 770
Van Der Burgh, Hendrik   Dut 1769-1858
  O/Pn 13x10 The Musician But 11/91 3,300
Van Der Cammen, Emile   Dut 20C
  W&C/Pa 19x16 La Femme et L'Oiseau But 5/92 1,980
Van Der Croos, Anthonie Jansz.   Dut
1606-1662
  * See 1992 Edition
Van Der Croos, Pieter   Dut 1610-
  O/Pn 19x24 Dutch Merchant Ships in a Harbor Sby 1/92 . . 3,850
Van Der Haagen, Joris   Dut 1615-1669
  * See 1991 Edition
Van Der Hamen Y Leon, Juan   Spa
1596-1632
  * See 1991 Edition
Van Der Hayden, J.   Dut 20C
  O/Pn 7x14 Boatyard Slo 2/92 135
Van Der Lamen, Christoph J.   Dut
1606-1652
  * See 1992 Edition
Van Der Lisse, Dirck   Dut a 1639-1669
  O/C 45x59 Diana and Actaeon Chr 10/91 17,600
  O/Pn 12x11 Nymphs Dancing Around a Herm Sby 10/91 . . 4,950
Van Der Meide, J. L.   Dut 20C
  O/C 24x36 Seascape Hnd 10/91 300
Van Der Meulen, Edmond   Bel 1841-1905
  * See 1992 Edition
Van Der Mijn, Francis   Dut 1719-1783
  * See 1992 Edition
Van Der Mijn, Hieronymous   Dut 18C
  * See 1992 Edition
Van Der Neer, Aert   Dut 1604-1677
  * See 1992 Edition
Van Der Neer, Eglon Hendrick   Dut
1634-1703
  O/Pn 8x10 Saint John the Baptist Wilderness Sby 5/92 1,980
Van Der Ouderaa, Pierre Jan   Bel
1841-1915
  * See 1992 Edition
Van Der Poel, Egbert   Dut 1621-1664
  O/Pn 14x11 Peasants Extinguishing Cottage Fire Chr 10/91 . 5,280
  O/Pn 17x22 Cottage Ablaze at Night Sby 5/92 2,750
Van Der Pol, Louis   Dut 1896-1982
  O/Pn 10x12 By the Sea Hnd 6/92 600
  G/Pa 9x9 Two Winter Scenes Lou 9/91 450
  O/Pn 7x10 Children on the Beach Hnz 5/92 425
  O/B 10x8 Three Figures Lou 6/92 325
Van Der Poorten, Hendrik Josef   Bel
1789-1874
  * See 1992 Edition

Van Der Stoffe, Jan Jacobsz.   Dut
1611-1682
  O/Pn 13x22 A Cavalry Skirmish Sby 10/91 19,800
Van Der Straet, Jan   Dut 1523-1605
  * See 1992 Edition
Van Der Vaardt, Jan   Dut 1647-1721
  O/C 30x25 Landscape with Figures Sby 10/91 8,250
Van Der Venne, Adolf   Aus 1828-1911
  O/C 11x18 A Gypsy Wagon 1888 Chr 2/92 3,300
Van Der Vin, Paul   Bel 1823-1887
  * See 1992 Edition
Van Der Weele, Herman Johannes   Dut
1852-1930
  O/C 26x36 Herding Sheep Sby 7/92 3,575
Van Der Werff, Adriaen   Dut 1659-1722
  * See 1992 Edition
Van Der Werff, Pieter   Dut 1665-1722
  O/Cp 10x12 Infant Hercules Wrestling w/Snakes Sby 5/92 . 9,900
Van Der Weyde (Jr.)   Am a 1850-
  Pl&S/Pa/B 4x7 Buffalo Hunt 1858 Chr 5/92 4,180
Van Der Willigen, Claes Jansz.   Dut
1630-1676
  O/Pn 25x19 Man Crossing a Wooden Bridge 76 Sby 5/92 . . 8,800
Van Deventer, Johann   Dut 20C
  O/C 24x32 Winter Scene Slo 12/91 575
Van Dieghem, Jacob   Dut 19C
  O/Pn 9x12 Sheep in Landscape Brd 8/92 2,200
Van Diepenbeeck, Abraham   Flm
1596-1675
  K&S/Pa 8x6 Trot a Gauche Chr 1/92 660
Van Doesburg, Theo   Dut 1883-1931
  G,Pl&Pe/Pa 18x15 De l'Espace--Temps III 1924 Chr 11/91 60,500
Van Dongen, Kees   Fr 1877-1968
  O/C 22x13 Nu Fond Vert Doy 11/91 55,000
  W,G&I/Pa/B 9x10 La Mille et Unieme Nuit Sby 5/92 44,000
  W,G&I/Pa 14x10 La Priere Du Pape Chr 11/91 20,900
  P/Pa 20x12 Le Peuplier Sby 10/91 14,850
Van Doust, Jan   Con 20C
  * See 1992 Edition
Van Douw, Simon-Johannes   Flm
1630-1677
  * See 1992 Edition
Van Dyck, Philip   Flm 1680-1753
  * See 1992 Edition
Van Dyck, Sir Anthony   Flm 1599-1641
  * See 1991 Edition
Van Eertvelt, Andries   Flm 1590-1652
  * See 1992 Edition
Van Elten, Hendirk Dirk K.   Am 1829-1904
  O/C 27x42 Returning from Market 1866 Sby 1/92 7,700
  O/C 16x25 Crossing the Bridge by the Mill Dum 8/92 1,200
Van Elven, Pierre Henri T. T.   Dut
1828-1908
  W/Pa 16x12 Vaulted Interior Hnz 10/91 80
Van Es, Jacob   Flm 1596-1666
  * See 1992 Edition
Van Everdingen, Allart   Dut 1621-1675
  O/C 42x64 Landscape with a Watermill Sby 5/92 159,500
Van Everdingen, Caesar Boetuis   Dut a
1617-1678
  * See 1990 Edition
Van Everen, Jay   Am 1875-1947
  Pe/Pa 8x10 Abstraction Chr 11/91 1,100
Van Eydsen, Robert   Dut 1810-1890
  O/Pn 25x29 Lovers Hnd 12/91 1,300
Van Falens, Carel   Flm 1683-1733
  O/Cp 15x19 Extensive Landscape w/Hunting Party Chr 1/92 13,200
Van Gogh, Vincent   Dut 1853-1890
  Pl&Pe/Pa 13x10 Garden with Weeping Tree Sby 11/91 . . . 1.32M
  PeCBr&G/Pa 24x20 La priere Chr 5/92 495,000
Van Goyen, Jan   Dut 1596-1656
  O/Pn 20x27 Fisherfolk/Scheveningen 1644 Chr 1/92 176,000
  O/Pn 25x35 Nymwegen w/Ferryboat 1648 Sby 5/92 104,500
  O/Pn 16x24 River Landscape w/Ferryboats 164* Chr 5/92 . 68,200
  O/Pn 16x22 Three Figures Resting a Cottage Sby 5/92 . . . 38,500

Van Haarlem, Cornelis C.   Dut 1562-1638
  * See 1992 Edition . . . .
Van Haarlem, Johan. (the Elder)   Dut 1628-1691
  * See 1992 Edition . . . .
Van Haensbergen, Jan   Dut 1642-1705
  * See 1992 Edition . . . .
Van Hamme, Alexis   Bel 1818-1875
  * See 1992 Edition . . . .
Van Hasselt, Willem   Dut 1882-1963
  * See 1992 Edition . . . .
Van Heemskerk, Maarten   Dut 17C
  * See 1991 Edition . . . .
Van Hees, Gustav Adolf   Ger 1862-1918
  O/C 21x27 Sailboats Hnd 10/91 800
Van Hofmann, Ludwig   Ger 1862-1945
  Sg/Pa 15x10 Kneeling Female Nude But 5/92 880
Van Hoogstraten, Samuel Dircks   Flm 1627-1678
  O/C 27x21 Annunciation of Death of Virgin Chr 1/92 22,000
Van Horssen, Winand Bastien   Dut 1863-
  O/C 29x21 Still Life Clematis Flowers 1901 Sel 4/92 . . . 4,250
Van Houbraken, Nicola   1660-1723
  * See 1992 Edition . . . .
Van Huysum, Jan   Dut 1682-1749
  O/Pn 32x24 Flowers in Terracotta Vase Sby 1/92 . . . . . 3.52M
  O/C 16x13 A Hollyhock, a French Marigold Chr 1/92 . . . 148,500
  O/Cp 22x35 Arcadian Landscape with Nymphs Sby 5/92 . 57,750
Van Huysum, Justus   Dut 1659-1716
  O/C 38x34 Peonies, Hollyhocks, Roses Chr 1/92 38,500
Van Ingen, Hendrick   Dut 1833-1898
  O/C 24x30 Figures by a Windmill Yng 2/92 100
Van Kalraat, Abraham   Dut 1642-1722
  * See 1990 Edition . . . .
Van Kessel, Jan   Dut 1626-1679
  O/Pn 21x15 Still Life Flowers and Insects Sby 5/92 41,250
Van Laer
  O/Tn 9x7 Haitian Dancer 72 Wlf 3/92 400
  O/Me 9x6 Haitian Welcoming Party '72 Wlf 3/92 225
Van Laer, Alexander T.   Am 1857-1920
  O/C 22x36 Autumnal Fields Skn 3/92 1,100
  O/C 22x18 Marsh Scene Mys 6/92 770
  O/C 12x18 Conn. Winter Scene Mys 11/91 275
Van Leemputten, Cornelis   Bel 1841-1902
  O/C 56x82 Return of the Flock Sby 5/92 19,800
Van Leemputten, Jef Louis   Bel 20C
  O/C 40x59 Het Vaderland Bezet 1918 Chr 10/91 6,600
Van Leen, Willem   Dut 1753-1825
  * See 1992 Edition . . . .
Van Leyden, Aertgen   Fut 1498-1564
  * See 1991 Edition . . . .
Van Lint, Hendrick   Flm 1684-1763
  * See 1991 Edition . . . .
Van Loo, Carle   Fr 1705-1765
  O/C 32x25 Portrait of a Lady, Half Length Chr 5/92 . . . 5,500
Van Loo, Jacob   1614-1670
  O/C 42x37 Portrait of a Lady Chr 10/91 22,000
Van Loo, Jules Cesar Denis   1743-1821
  O/C 25x30 Snowy Winter Landscape Chr 5/92 8,250
Van Loo, Louis Michel   Fr 1707-1771
  * See 1990 Edition . . . .
Van Loon, Hendryk W.   Am 1882-1944
  P/Pa 9x7 Three Illustrations 34 Ih 11/91 250
Van Luppen, Gerard Joseph A.   Bel 1834-1891
  O/Pn 12x9 Path Through the Woods Slo 7/92 800
Van Marcke De Lummen, Emile   Fr 1827-1890
  * See 1992 Edition . . . .
Van Mastenbroek, Johann H.   Dut 1875-1945
  * See 1992 Edition . . . .
Van Mierevelt, Michiel Jans   Dut 1567-1641
  * See 1992 Edition . . . .

Van Mieris, Frans   Dut 1689-1793
  * See 1991 Edition . . . .
Van Mieris, Frans (the Elder)   Dut 1635-1681
  O/Pn 6x5 An Old Woman Singing 1677 Chr 1/92 77,000
Van Mieris, Willem   Dut 1662-1747
  O/Pn 6x4 Gentleman, Small Bust Length 1688 Chr 5/92 . . 26,400
Van Millett, George   Am 1864-
  * See 1992 Edition . . . .
Van Minderhout, Hendrik   Dut 1632-1696
  O/C 65x91 Aerial View of Fort Saint Philippe Sby 1/92 . . . 49,500
Van Montfoort, Anthonie B.   Dut 1532-1583
  * See 1992 Edition . . . .
Van Musscher, Michiel   Dut 1645-1705
  * See 1992 Edition . . . .
Van Muyden, Every Louis   Sws 1853-1922
  O/Pn 12x9 Young Woman Alpine Landscape Skn 9/91 . . . 825
Van Mytens, Martin (II)   1695-1770
  O/C/B 50x38 Portrait of the Artist Chr 10/91 14,300
Van Ness, Frank Lewis   Am 1866-
  O/C 24x20 Four Year Old Girl 1897 Hnd 5/92 650
Van Nieulandt, Willem   Dut 1584-1636
  O/Cp 16x27 Roman Forum w/Shepherds Sby 5/92 38,500
Van Noort, Adrianus Cornelis   Dut 1914-
  O/Pn 12x16 Cote D'Azur Hnd 5/92 3,400
  O/Pn 12x16 On the Beach Hnd 5/92 3,400
  O/Pn 19x28 Picnic by the Shore Wes 3/92 2,640
  O/Pn 20x28 Children on the Beach Hnz 5/92 1,500
  O/Pn 9x12 The Clamdiggers Wes 3/92 1,320
  O/Pn 12x16 Figures on a Beach Wes 5/92 1,100
  O/Pn 9x12 Beach Scene with Child Wes 5/92 1,018
  O/Pn 12x16 Seaside Parasols Hnd 5/92 1,000
  O/Pn 7x10 Children at the Seashore Hnd 5/92 800
Van Notti, Henry   Am 1876-1962
  O/C 22x30 New York Skyline '39 Sel 9/91 1,800
Van Nuyssen, Abraham Janssens   1575-1632
  * See 1992 Edition . . . .
Van Oosten, Isaak   Flm 1613-1661
  * See 1992 Edition . . . .
Van Orley, Barent   Dut 1492-1542
  * See 1991 Edition . . . .
Van Orley, Hieronymus (III)   Dut a 1652-
  * See 1992 Edition . . . .
Van Orley, Richard   Flm 1663-1732
  K&Bc/V 8x6 Susanna and the Elders 1713 Chr 1/92 5,500
Van Os, Georgius Jacobus J.   Dut 1782-1861
  * See 1992 Edition . . . .
Van Os, Jan   Dut 1744-1808
  * See 1991 Edition . . . .
Van Ostade, Adriaen Jansz   Dut 1610-1685
  O/Pn 18x14 Barn Interior with Two Peasants Sby 10/91 . . 13,200
Van Ostade, Isaac   Dut 1621-1649
  Pe,Pl&S/Pa 6x12 Tavern with Peasants Dancing Chr 1/92 . 41,800
Van Plattenberg, Mattias   Flm 1608-1660
  O/C 35x54 Ships Floundering Sby 10/91 8,250
Van Poelenburgh, Cornelis   Dut 1586-1667
  * See 1992 Edition . . . .
Van Pol, Christian   Dut 1752-1813
  * See 1990 Edition . . . .
Van Ravesteyn, Dirck De Quade   Dut 16C
  * See 1990 Edition . . . .
Van Ravesteyn, Jan Anthonisz.   Dut 1570-1657
  O/Pn 48x31 Portrait Joannes De Ruyter 1632 Sby 1/92 . . 170,500
  O/Pn 25x20 Portrait of a Gentleman Chr 5/92 9,900
Van Roestraten, Pieter Gerrits   Dut 1630-1700
  * See 1992 Edition . . . .
Van Roose, Ch.   Bel 20C
  * See 1992 Edition . . . .

Van Ruysdael, Salomon   Dut 1600-1670
* See 1991 Edition ....
Van Ruysdael, Salomon Jacobsz.   Dut 1629-1681
* See 1992 Edition ....
Van Ruzin, P.
O/B 9x16 Landscape with Two Trees Wtf 3/92 225
Van Rysselberghe, Theo   Bel 1862-1926
O/C 36x29 Jacques Copeau Sby 10/91 4,950
Van Savery, William   Dut 19C
W/Pa 22x44 Cows Grazing Mys 11/91 302
Van Schendel, Petrus   Bel 1806-1870
O/Pn 23x17 Candlelit Market 1856 Sby 7/92 14,850
O/C 30x25 Scullery Maid/Young Mistress 1835 Chr 5/92 . 11,000
O/Pn 10x7 Letter by Candlelight 1853 Hnz 5/92 1,500
Van Schooten, Floris Gerritsz   Dut 17C
* See 1991 Edition ....
Van Schrieck, Otto Marseus   Dut 1619-1678
* See 1990 Edition ....
Van Seben, Henri   Bel 1825-1913
O/C 29x25 Playing with Hoola-Hoops 58 Chr 5/92 3,050
O/Pn 14x18 The Tradesmen 1853 Wtf 9/91 2,200
Van Severdonck, Franz   Bel 1809-1889
O/Pn 7x10 Sheep and Poultry Grazing 1883 Chr 10/91 6,600
O/Pn 7x10 Sheep and Ducks 1889 Sby 7/92 3,850
O/Pn 7x10 Gamecocks Fighting 1889 Slo 9/91 2,000
O/Pn 7x10 Fowl in Landscape 1863 Sby 1/92 1,870
O/Pn 6x9 Belle-Cour Avec Pigeons 1861 Skn 9/91 1,760
O/Pn 8x10 Poultry Feeding 1885 Chr 5/92 1,760
Van Severdonck, Franz & Morel   Bel 1809-1889
O/Pn 13x12 Shepherd Tending His Flock 187? Sby 7/92 .. 3,630
Van Sinclair, Gerrit   Am 1890-1955
O/B 12x16 Dan Works Late Mor 3/92 550
Van Sloun, Frank   Am 1879-1938
* See 1991 Edition ....
Van Sluys, Theo   Bel 19C
O/C 22x19 Sheep with Lambs But 11/91 2,475
Van Soelen, Theodore   Am 1890-1964
* See 1992 Edition ....
Van Somer, Hendrick   Dut 1615-1684
* See 1990 Edition ....
Van Son, Joris   Flm 1623-1667
* See 1991 Edition ....
Van Spaendonck, Cornelis   Dut 1756-1840
* See 1990 Edition ....
Van Spaendonck, Gerard   Fr 1746-1822
* See 1992 Edition ....
Van Steenwyck, H. (the Younger)   Dut 1580-1649
O/Cp 8x12 Saint Jerome in Gothic Church 1625 Chr 1/92 . 66,000
Van Streeck, Juriaen   Dut 1632-1687
* See 1992 Edition ....
Van Stry, Abraham   Dut 1753-1826
* See 1992 Edition ....
Van Stry, Jacob   Dut 1756-1815
K,S&W/Pa 10x8 A Seated Old Man Chr 1/92 1,980
Van Strydonck, Guillaume   Bel 1861-1937
* See 1992 Edition ....
Van Swanevelt, Herman   Dut 1600-1655
K&S/V 7x9 River Landscape w/Venus & Adonis Chr 1/92 .. 4,950
Van Tilborch, Gillis   Flm 1578-1623
* See 1991 Edition ....
Van Valkenborch, Martin   Flm 1535-1612
* See 1991 Edition ....
Van Veen, Pieter   Am 1875-1961
O/C 31x25 Summer Landscape Mys 6/92 770
Van Veen, Pieter   Dut 1563-1629
* See 1992 Edition ....
Van Veerendael, Nicolaes   Flm 1640-1691
* See 1990 Edition ....
Van Velde, Bram   Dut 1910-
* See 1990 Edition ....

Van Velde, Geer   Dut 1898-
O/C 18x15 Woman with Vase of Flowers Sby 10/91 22,000
Van Vliet, Hendrik   Dut 1611-1675
* See 1992 Edition ....
Van Vogelaer, Karel   Dut 1653-1695
* See 1992 Edition ....
Van Vreeland, F.   Con 20C
G/Pa 17x26 Picking Blossoms Wes 11/91 220
Van Vreeland, J.   Dut 20C
O/Cd 21x27 Floral Still Life Wtf 3/92 200
Van Vries, Roelof   Dut 1631-1681
O/Pn 13x10 Travellers and Huntsmen: Pair Chr 5/92 11,000
Van Vucht, Gerrit   Dut 1610-1699
* See 1991 Edition ....
Van Walscapelle, Jacob   Dut 1644-1727
O/C 27x22 Still Life Poppies, Peonies, Iris Sby 5/92 ... 60,500
Van Wittel, Gaspar   Dut 1653-1736
* See 1990 Edition ....
Van Woensel, Petronella   1785-1839
O/C 22x18 Still Life Roses, Poppy Sby 10/91 25,300
Van Wyngaerdt, Anthonie J.   Dut 1808-1887
O/Pn 9x15 Cows Grazing in an Open Field Chr 5/92 2,420
Van Wyngaerdt, Petrus Theo.   Dut 1816-1893
O/Pn 21x16 Blowing Bubbles 1846 Chr 2/92 6,050
Van Wyngaerdt, Piet   Dut 1873-1964
O/C 16x24 Cottages by a Riverbank Chr 2/92 950
Van Young, Oscar   Am 1906-
* See 1992 Edition ....
Van Zandt, William   Am 20C
O/C 19x27 Sulky and Rider 87 Sby 4/92 3,575
Van Zevenberghen, Georges A.   Bel 1877-
* See 1990 Edition ....
Vanderbanck, John   1694-1739
O/C 50x40 Portrait of a Lady Sby 1/92 12,100
Vanderbank, M.   Br 18C
O/C 50x40 Portrait of John Warden 1733 But 5/92 2,200
Vanderlyn, John   Am 1775-1852
* See 1992 Edition ....
Vandervelde, Hanny
O/C 30x36 Still Life with Flowers Dum 7/92 900
Vandeverdonek, Francis   Bel 19C
O/Pn 7x10 Ram, Ewe and Lamb 1889 Wtf 3/92 1,500
Vannini, Ottavio   It 1585-1643
* See 1992 Edition ....
Vannutelli, Scipione   It 1834-1894
O/C 24x18 Drawing Room Scene Dum 4/92 4,500
Vanter, Wilhelm Vander   Dut 19C
* See 1992 Edition ....
Vantongerloo, Frans Joseph   Bal 1882-1965
* See 1991 Edition ....
Vantore, Erik Mogens Christian   Dan 1895-
* See 1992 Edition ....
Vanvitelli   Dut 1653-1736
* See 1990 Edition ....
Varady, Frederic   Am 1908-
G/Pn 18x18 Two Men Backstage 1954 Ih 11/91 300
Varese, Edgard   Fr 1888-1965
* See 1992 Edition ....
Vargas, Alberto   Am 1926-1983
W/Pa 13x13 Bust of Woman with Flower Petals Ih 11/91 . 25,000
Varian, Dorothy   Am 1895-
O/C 18x27 Still Life Plums and Melon Sby 12/91 880
Varley, Frederick Horsman   Can 1881-1969
Pe/Pa 12x9 Pear Tree Sbt 11/91 841
Varley, J.   Br 19C
W/Pb 20x13 Old Alpine Cedars on Engsbleu Lake Chr 2/92 . 110
Varo, Remedios   Spa 1908-1963
T/M 37x35 Microcosmos (or Determinismo) Chr 11/91 . 605,000
O&MM/M 34x41 Vuelo Magico 1956 Chr 5/92 440,000

Vasarely, Victor   Fr 1908-
O/C 79x79 Sende 1967 Sby 11/91 35,750
A/C 65x63 Jell 1968 Chr 5/92 22,000
A/C 39x39 Katoltar 1973 Chr 5/92 17,600
A/B 19x19 OND-BV 1968 Sby 2/92 13,200
O/C 41x41 AXO-IX 1975 Chr 11/91 11,000
O/C 41x41 AXO-IX 1975 Chr 5/92 7,150
L/B 16x12 AXO-TER Sby 2/92 6,600
Pe/Pa 7x7 Seated Man Reading 1946 Sel 12/91 120

Vasari, Giorgio   It 1511-1574
* See 1991 Edition

Vasarri, Emilio   It 19C
O/C 35x60 Ladies of Pompeii Sby 10/91 34,100

Vascahallos, S.   Am 20C
O/B 18x30 Venetian Scene Mys 11/91 55

Vassant, G.   Fr 20C
O/B 10x8 Winter Street Scene Wlf 3/92 450

Vasseur, *   Fr 20C**
O/C 14x18 House in Landscape Slo 9/91 225

Vassilev, P.   Rus 20C
P/Pa 10x14 Fields with Cottages '90 Lou 3/92 325

Vassilieff, Marie   Rus 1884-1957
* See 1991 Edition

Vassilion, D.   20C
W/Pa 8x12 Mosque and Arabs: Two Slo 10/91 95

Vatery, L. Sidney   Am
O/C 16x18 Ship in Storm-Tossed Seas Dum 1/92 100

Vauchelet, Theophile Auguste   Fr 1802-1873
* See 1992 Edition

Vaughn
O/C 19x15 Genre Scene 1947 Dum 12/91 150

Vautier, J. C.   20C
O/C 10x14 Baghdad Slo 7/92 1,000

Vavra, Frank   Am 1898-1967
O/C 36x30 Aspen But 11/91 2,200

Vazquez Y Ubeda, Carlos   Spa a 1889-1907
* See 1992 Edition

Veber, Jean   Fr 1868-1928
Pe&K/Pa 6x12 Verre de Vin Hnz 5/92 100

Vecellio, Tiziano   It 1488-1576
* See 1992 Edition

Vecsey   Eur 20C
O/B 12x16 Full Cry Slo 12/91 500

Vedder, Elihu   Am 1836-1923
C&P/Pa/B 6x10 The Labyrinth Chr 9/91 1,760
O/B 11x14 Coastal Scene Hnz 10/91 550
Y/Pa 13x8 Nubia, and Dekkeh: Two Wes 11/91 412
Y/Pa 7x8 Rocks at Aboofoddah 1890 Sel 12/91 80

Veeder, Glenn T.   20C
O/M 18x15 Leopard Slo 7/92 125

Vega Y Munoz, Pedro   Spa 19C
* See 1990 Edition

Veillon, Auguste-Louis   Fr 19C
* See 1991 Edition

Velasco, Jose Maria   Mex 1840-1912
O/C 30x42 Valle De Mexico 1888 Sby 11/91 . . . . 2.42M
O/C 17x24 Valle de Mexico 1887 Chr 5/92 550,000
C&Pe/Pa 13x20 Estudio de Pies 1864 Chr 5/92 9,350

Velasquez, Jose Antonio   LA 1906-1985
O/C 21x27 Iglesia 1958 Sby 2/92 3,300
O/C 18x14 La Escuela 1952 Chr 5/92 2,750

Velier, E.   Fr 19C
O/C 20x15 By the Sea 1885 Chr 5/92 7,700

Vellani, Francesco & Rubbiani   It 1688-1768
O/C 33x56 Still Life Flowers in Vase, Grapes 34 Sby 5/92 . 37,400

Vellay, **
G,Pl&Gd/Pa 22x18 Section D'Or 1935 Sby 10/91 1,265

Velten, Wilhelm   Rus 1847-1929
* See 1992 Edition

Venard, Claude   Fr 1913-
O/C 39x39 Les Oliviers Noirs 63 Chr 11/91 3,850
O/C 40x40 Nature Morte au Poisson Chr 11/91 3,850

O/C 30x30 Nature Morte au Poisson Chr 11/91 3,300
O/C 38x51 Rooftops of Paris Sby 2/92 3,300
O/C 39x39 Nature Morte Sby 2/92 3,080
O/C 38x46 Port Croix Chr 5/92 2,860
O/C 40x39 La Corse '58 But 5/92 2,750
O/C 18x22 La Plage Wes 3/92 2,200
O&Y/C 12x28 Two Paintings Chr 2/92 2,090
O/C 21x26 Nature morte aux pasteques Chr 5/92 1,760
O/C 13x16 Still Life; Composition: Two Sby 6/92 1,650
O/C 15x18 Still Life on a Table Sby 10/91 1,320
O/C 18x22 Le Phare, La Nuit Wes 3/92 1,018

Venat, Victor   Con 19C
W&Pe/Pb 12x22 View of an Alpine Village 1865 Chr 2/92 . . . 440

Venneman, Charles   Bel 1802-1875
O/Pn 16x20 Frolicking Peasants Chr 2/92 6,600

Ventnor, Arthur   Br 20C
O/C 9x11 A Frugal Tea Chr 2/92 2,750

Verbeck, William Francis   Am 1858-1933
Pl&Pe/Pa 7x29 Jonah the Bear Raises Money Ih 5/92 550

Verbeeck, Pieter Cornelisz.   Dut 1610-1654
O/Pn 8x7 Horse and Sleeping Dog Sby 5/92 8,250

Verbeet, Gijsberta   Dut 1838-1916
O/Pn 31x25 Still Life Fruit on Marble Ledge 1854 Sby 2/92 . 8,250

Verboeckhoven, E & Keelhoff, F   Bel 1798-1881
O/C 27x42 A Country Road 1868 Chr 2/92 20,900
O/C 27x43 Sheep and Cattle Grazing Chr 2/92 8,250

Verboeckhoven, Eugene Joseph   Bel 1798-1881
O/C 28x43 Guarding Flock by Coast 1867 Sby 5/92 33,000
O/Pn 22x31 Sheep Gathered in a Barn 1870 Sby 5/92 . . . 12,100
O/C 17x24 Landscape with Cattle Sby 10/91 11,000
O/B 17x22 Peasants Leading Their Herds Doy 11/91 10,500
O/C 22x31 Manger w/Sheep, Lambs, Hens 1870 Skn 3/92 . 6,875
O/Pn 11x14 Spring Lambs Skn 11/91 3,630
C&K/Pa 12x19 Sheep and Poultry Grazing 1870 Chr 10/91 . 1,430
O/Pn 7x10 Sheep in a Meadow Wes 11/91 1,018

Verboeckhoven, Louis   Bel 1802-1889
* See 1992 Edition

Verbruggen, Gaspar (the Elder)   Dut 1635-1687
O/C 27x22 Marigolds, Snowballs, Roses Chr 10/91 7,150

Verbrugghen, Gaspar (the Younger)   Dut 1664-1730
O/C 63x41 Putti Bearing Up Flowers: Pair Sby 10/91 37,400

Verbuecken, J.   Con 19C
O/C 40x31 Still Life Grapes and Shellfish 1870 Sby 7/92 . . 8,800

Verburgh, Dionijs   Dut 1655-1722
O/C 35x47 Travellers Resting on Road Sby 5/92 17,600

Verdaguer, Dionisio Baixeras   Spa 1862-
* See 1992 Edition

Verdi
O/C 20x24 Spanish Countryside Dum 5/92 80

Verdier, Francois   Fr 1651-1730
K/Pa 12x10 St. Utfred Dispensing Alms But 5/92 715

Verdun, Raymond Jean   Fr 19C
* See 1992 Edition

Verelst, John   Flm a 1698-1734
* See 1992 Edition

Verelst, Pieter   Dut 1618-1671
O/C 18x14 Elegant Couples Drinking Sby 1/92 220,000

Verelst, Simon Pietersz   Dut 1644-1721
* See 1991 Edition

Verhaecht, Tobias   Flm 1561-1631
* See 1990 Edition

Verhas, Frans   Bel 1827-1897
O/Pn 24x16 The Green Kimono 1876 Chr 10/91 13,200
O/B 24x18 The Japanese Kimono 1877 Wlf 9/91 12,000

Verheyden, Francois   Bel 1806-1890
O/C 39x31 Young Flower Sellers 1865 Sby 10/91 15,400
O/Pn 8x7 Le Belge Skn 5/92 1,650

Verhoesen, Albertus   Dut 1806-1881
* See 1992 Edition

Verlat, Charles Michel Maria Bel 1824-1890
* See 1990 Edition ....

Verlot, O. Fr 20C
* See 1992 Edition ....

Vermehren, Johan Frederick N. Dan 1823-1910
* See 1990 Edition ....

Vermeulen, Andreas Dut 1821-1884
* See 1991 Edition ....

Vermeulen, Andries 1763-1814
O/C 34x43 Figures Skating 1798 Chr 10/91 63,800
O/Pn 11x17 Traveller Conversing with Shepherd Chr 5/92 .. 9,350

Verne, Alfred Am 1850-1910
* See 1992 Edition ....

Verner, Elizabeth O'Neill Am 1883-
P/L/B 9x9 The Flower Seller Sby 12/91 5,225
O/Cb 13x11 Pipe Smoking Skn 11/91 4,675
P/Pn 18x13 View of Charleston Skn 9/91 3,575

Verner, Frederick Arthur Can 1836-1928
O/C 30x44 In the Kentish Meadows 1890 Hnd 5/92 4,200
W/Pa 10x20 Anne Hathaway's Cottage Sbt 11/91 1,683
W/Pa 17x29 Tending the Flock 1890 Sbt 5/92 1,683
W/Pa 10x14 Farm Yard with Cottage 1896 Sbt 11/91 ... 1,028
W/Pa 8x13 Village at Dusk 1898 Sbt 5/92 935
W/Pa 10x24 View in Caracas 1865 Eld 4/92 275

Vernet, Antoine Charles Horace Fr 1758-1836
Pl&S/Pa 16x23 Startled Horses in a Stable Sby 5/92 .. 3,025

Vernet, Claude Joseph Fr 1714-1789
O/C 120x98 Fishermen; Calm Sea: Pair 1778 Sby 1/92 .. 1.54M

Vernier, Emile Louis Fr 1829-1887
* See 1992 Edition ....

Vernoi, J. T.
Y/Pa 19x25 Race for the Buffalo Eld 4/92 440

Vernon, Emile Fr 19C
* See 1992 Edition ....

Vernon, W. H. Br 1820-1909
O/C 12x20 Cambridgeshire Cottage But 5/92 1,650

Veronese It 1528-1588
* See 1991 Edition ....

Verpoeken, Hendrik Dut 1791-1869
* See 1990 Edition ....

Verschaffelt, Edward
* See 1991 Edition ....

Verschuring, Hendrik Dut 1627-1690
* See 1992 Edition ....

Verschuur, Wouterus Dut 1812-1874
* See 1992 Edition ....

Vertes, Marcel Fr 1895-1961
O/C 11x16 Reclining Woman Hnd 10/91 1,300

Vertin, Pieter Gerard Dut 1819-1893
* See 1991 Edition ....

Vertunni, Achille It 1826-1897
O/C 40x80 Paestum Sby 2/92 12,650
O/Pa 9x6 Roman Ruin, Campagna Slo 7/92 900

Verveer, Elchanon Dut 1826-1900
* See 1992 Edition ....

Verveer, Salomon Leonardus Dut 1813-1876
* See 1990 Edition ....

Verwee, Louis Pierre Bel 1807-1877
* See 1992 Edition ....

Vesin, Jaroslav Fr. Julius Bul 1859-1915
* See 1990 Edition ....

Vespignani, Renzo It 1924-
* See 1992 Edition ....

Vester, Willem Dut 1824-1871
* See 1990 Edition ....

Veyrassat, Jules Jacques Fr 1828-1893
O/C 22x20 The Country Girl 64 Chr 10/91 6,600

Vezin, Charles Am 1858-1942
O/M 12x16 Manhattan Skn 9/91 2,640

Viard, Georges Fr a 1831-1848
* See 1991 Edition ....

Vibert, Jean Georges Fr 1840-1902
O/Pn 29x23 The Diet Chr 5/92 44,000
O/Pn 16x13 Pinch of Snuff 67 Chr 5/92 3,300
W/Pb 14x12 Carmen 1872 Chr 10/91 2,200

Vicente, Esteban Spa 1904-
O/C 16x12 Untitled Chr 2/92 5,280

Vickers, Alfred Br 1786-1868
O/B 7x14 Babbicomb Bay Fre 4/92 6,200
O/C/M 10x18 Figure on a Path But 5/92 2,200
O/C 16x32 Extensive River Landscape But 11/91 1,210
O/C 8x12 Pair: Village; Meadows Sel 9/91 1,050
O/C 12x24 Boats & People on the Beach 1854 Mys 6/92 ... 550

Vickers, Alfred H. Br a 1853-1907
O/C 16x24 Lock-Keeper's Cottage But 5/92 2,750

Vickery, Charles Am 20C
O/C/Ab 14x17 Fall Landscape 1897 Wlf 3/92 325

Vickery, Robert Am 1926-
* See 1992 Edition ....

Victors, Jacobus Dut 1640-1705
* See 1992 Edition ....

Vidal Fr 20C
O/C 18x22 At the Races But 5/92 2,200

Vidal, A. It 20C
O/C 14x20 Gondoliers Along Venetian Canal Slo 7/92 2,000
O/C 16x20 Venetian Canal Fre 4/92 725

Vidal, Louis Fr 1754-1805
O/Pn 28x41 Still Life Flowers, Fruit, Bird Sby 10/91 ... 17,600

Viegers, Bernard Dut 1886-1947
O/C 23x31 The Ferry near Vollenhove, Holland Chr 10/91 .. 7,700

Vieira Da Silva, Maria Helena Fr 1908-
O/C 5x9 Untitled 1967 Sby 10/91 8,800
Bp&G/Pa 6x5 Composition Chr 5/92 6,600

Vien, Joseph-Marie Fr 1716-1809
K/Pa 6x9 Ruins on the Palatine Hill, Rome Chr 1/92 1,100

Vigee-Lebrun, Marie Louise Fr 1775-1842
* See 1991 Edition ....

Vigneron, Pierre RochFr Fr 1789-1872
* See 1991 Edition ....

Vignet, Henri Fr 1857-1920
O/C 18x13 Street Scene in Rouen Sby 7/92 2,310

Vignoles, Andre Fr 1920-
O/C 20x29 Le Sous-Bois 59 Chr 11/91 770

Vignon, Charles
O/C 16x17 Madeleine-Paris Dum 3/92 650

Vignon, Claude Fr 1593-1670
O/C 30x31 Solomon Worshipping False Idol 1626 Sby 1/92 16,500

Vignon, Victor Fr 1847-1909
O/C 22x32 Village de l'Ile de France Chr 2/92 11,000
O/C 18x22 Eglise De Jonay Le Comte 85 Sby 10/91 9,350
O/C 13x16 Spring Landscape Sby 2/92 6,600

Vigny, Andre Fr
* See 1992 Edition ....

Vigon, Louis-Jacques Fr 1897-1985
O/B 21x29 Reims, Esplanade Ceres Chr 11/91 825

Vila Y Prades, Julio Spa 1873-1930
O/C 24x36 Boats in the Harbor at San Tropez Chr 5/92 .. 16,500

Vilaro, Carlos Peaz LA 20C
O/B 28x39 Velorio en Palermo Wes 3/92 1,650

Vilato, Javier Fr 1921-
* See 1992 Edition ....

Villa, Hernando G. Am 1881-1952
W/Pa 23x19 Sailing Along the Coast 48 But 6/92 2,475
O/C 30x24 The Chief 49 But 4/92 1,650
W/Pa 10x14 Crashing Waves But 6/92 990

Villacres, Cesar Ecu 1880-
O/C 20x24 Place Clichy Sby 2/92 1,540
O/C 24x36 View of the Seine at Dusk 1951 Slo 2/92 1,400
O/C 10x13 Retrato de Joven Indio Chr 11/91 605

Villanueva, F. Eur 19C
O/C 10x8 Robin's Nest and Flowers Slo 10/91 225

Villanueva, Leoncio Per 1936-
* See 1991 Edition ....

Villegas Y Cordero, Jose Spa 1848-1922
O/C 24x35 Afternoon by Sea, Biarritz 1906 Chr 10/91 .. 220,000
O/Pn 7x10 Bathers at Biarritz Sby 10/91 24,200

232

W/Pa 34x20 Traje de Luces Doy 11/91 7,000
W/Pa 18x11 Afternoon Nap Sby 1/92 3,410
W/Pa 19x26 Papal Audience But 11/91 2,200

Villegas Y Cordero, Ricardo   Spa 1852-
  * See 1991 Edition . . . .

Villegas, Armando
  * See 1992 Edition . . . .

Villegos, F.   Spa 19C
  O/C 22x27 A Sip of Wine Chr 2/92 1,430

Villon, Jacques   Fr 1875-1963
  O/C 15x18 Jardin a Bernay 47 Sby 10/91 33,000
  O/C 15x18 Celestial Globes 25 Sby 11/91 23,100
  G,S&Pa/Pa 12x14 Le Negre en Bonne Fortune Sby 2/92 . . 15,400
  O/C 10x7 Crane (Memento Mori) 33 Chr 11/91 5,500
  O/C 10x8 Portrait of a Man 1942 Sby 10/91 4,620

Vinall, Joseph Williams Topham   Br 1873-
  * See 1992 Edition . . . .

Vincent, Francois-Andre   Fr 1746-1816
  I&S/Pa 3x5 Study of a Fisherman Slo 7/92 475

Vincent, Harry Aiken   Am 1864-1931
  O/C 28x36 Ships in the Harbor But 11/91 7,700
  O/B 8x10 Beached Boats Brd 8/92 605

Vincent, William   Am 20C
  O/C 12x24 Still Life with Fruit Wlf 10/91 200

Vinckboons, David   Fr 1576-1629
  O/Pn 11x20 Huntsmen Chasing Stags Sby 10/91 28,600

Vinea, Francesco   It 1845-1902
  O/C 32x59 The Visit 1881 Sby 10/91 33,000
  O/C 29x25 Portrait of a Lady Sby 1/92 9,350
  O/Pn 6x4 Peasants on Stone Steps Sby 7/92 3,575

Vines, Roberto   Spa 20C
  O/C/M 48x36 Retrato de Nina 1919 Sby 2/92 10,450

Vinton, Frederick Porter   Am 1846-1911
  O/Ab 16x11 The Chicken Plucker Bor 8/92 1,500

Vinton, John Rogers   Am 1801-1847
  O/C 11x16 Chupko/ Ruins Sugar Hous 1843 Brd 5/92 . . . 16,500
  O/B 5x8 Covered Wagon Brd 5/92 550

Viollet Le Duc, Victor   Fr 1848-1901
  * See 1992 Edition . . . .

Virbicky   Eng 19C
  O/C 27x42 Highland Landscape Sel 9/91 500

Viry, Paul Alphonse   Fr 19C
  O/Pn 30x25 The Proposal 76 Chr 2/92 10,450

Visconti, Alphonse Adolfo   Fr 1850-1924
  * See 1991 Edition . . . .

Viski, Janos   Hun 1891-
  O/C 24x30 Off to the Market Wlf 9/91 1,500
  O/C/B 24x33 Gypsy Encampment Wlf 3/92 350
  O/C/B 22x34 Procession of the Bride and Groom Wlf 3/92 . . 300

Visly, Gene   Fr 20C
  O/C 9x6 Petite Toile Wes 3/92 165

Vitah, E.   It 19C
  W/Pa 9x16 Peasant Girl with Basket Slo 12/91 300

Vital, Pauleus   Hai 20C
  O/M 24x32 Peche au Filet 70 Chr 5/92 1,980

Vitali, E.   It 19C
  W/Pa 13x7 Monks in a Kitchen: Pair Hnd 6/92 600
  W&G/Pa 14x7 Young Woman by a Well Sby 1/92 550
  W/Pa 21x14 Man with Umbrella Dum 5/92 500
  W/Pa 13x17 Fransiscan Holding Skillet; Peeling (2) Fre 12/91 310
  W/Pa 14x7 Monk Riding on a Donkey Hnd 6/92 275
  W/Pa 14x7 Cardinal Reading a Letter Hnd 6/92 225
  W/Pa 14x7 Fransiscan on a Mule Fre 12/91 170
  W/Pa 13x7 Cardinal Reading a Letter Fre 12/91 150

Vitallo, *   It 19C**
  O/C 20x16 Sheep in a Farmyard Wes 3/92 440

Viteri, Alicia
  * See 1992 Edition . . . .

Vivant-Denon, Baron Dominique   Fr 1747-1825
  Pe/Pa 2x3 Woman and Child Watching Slo 7/92 425

Vivarini, Antonio   It 1445-1503
  * See 1991 Edition . . . .

Vivin, Louis   Fr 1861-1936
  * See 1991 Edition . . . .

Vizkeleti, W. E.   Hun 1819-1895
  O/C 20x28 Marketplace Chr 5/92 1,210

Vociare, G.   It 19C
  O/B 8x12 View Towards Sorrento Slo 7/92 225

Voelcker, Gottfried Wilhelm   Ger 1775-1849
  * See 1992 Edition . . . .

Vogel, Valentine   Am -1966
  O/C 30x28 Still Life Sel 9/91 175
  O/C 30x26 Still Life of Flowers Sel 9/91 125

Vogler, Hermann   Ger 1859-
  O/C 32x50 In the Park 91 Sby 2/92 11,000

Vogt, Harry H.   Am 20C
  O/C 24x28 Study of a Pair of Lions Sel 12/91 90

Vogt, Louis G.   Am 1864-
  O/C 16x20 Road to the Village Wlf 9/91 550

Voirin, Leon Joseph
  * See 1991 Edition . . . .

Voiriot, Guillaume   Fr 1713-1799
  * See 1990 Edition . . . .

Voisard-Margerie, Adrien   Fr 19C
  * See 1991 Edition . . . .

Vojnits, Richard   Hun 1942-
  O/Pn 16x12 European Street Scene Dum 11/91 375

Volaire, Pierre Jacques   Fr 1729-1802
  O/C 27x41 Bay of Naples with Mount Vesuvius Chr 1/92 . 99,000
  Pe&S/Pa 4x5 Sitting Man Fre 12/91 210

Volk, Douglas   Am 1856-1935
  O/C 11x16 Figure and House in a Landscape Fre 12/91 425

Volkert, Edward Charles   Am 1871-1935
  O/B 12x9 Farmer in Field; Woodlot: (2) Sby 4/92 3,190
  O/B 12x16 Old Saybrook Mys 6/92 1,760
  O/B 12x16 Morning Light Mys 6/92 550

Volkmar, Charles   Am 1841-1914
  O/C 47x35 Grazing at Water's Edge Chr 9/91 2,750

Volkmour, Carl   Con 19C
  PI/Pa 12x16 Activity on the Canal Fre 10/91 50

Vollerdt, Johann Christian   Ger 1708-1769
  O/C 23x30 Manor House; Farmhouse: Pair 1760 Sby 1/92 37,400
  O/C 23x33 Winter Mountainous Landscape 1762 Sby 1/92 20,900

Vollmar, Ludwig   Ger 1842-1884
  * See 1992 Edition . . . .

Vollmer, Grace L.   Am 1884-1977
  O/B 24x20 Sunflowers But 2/92 2,200

Vollmering, Joseph   Am 1810-1887
  O/C 16x23 Keene Valley, Adirondacks Doy 12/91 1,500

Vollon, A.   Fr 19C
  O/C 15x11 Oxcart and Figures in Landscape Fre 12/91 425

Vollon, Alexis   Fr 1865-
  O/C 95x82 Pierrot, Colombine et Polichinelle Chr 10/91 . . 90,200
  O/C 18x22 French Farming Village Chr 2/92 13,200

Vollon, Antoine   Fr 1833-1900
  O/Pn 9x7 Still Life with Fruit, Chinese Bowl Chr 10/91 . . . 2,860
  O/C 25x34 Still Life Copper Pots Sby 1/92 2,200

Vollweider, Johann Jacob   Ger 1834-1891
  * See 1991 Edition . . . .

Volnay   Fr 20C
  O/C 19x20 Landscape White Building 1961 Hnz 5/92 200

Volti, Antoniucci
  K/Pa 16x13 Crouching Female Nude 1971 Sby 6/92 1,540

Voltz, Friedrich Johann   Ger 1817-1886
  O/Pn 13x26 The Watering Hole 1876 Sby 2/92 23,100
  O/C 12x18 Cattle in a Stream But 5/92 4,675

Von Amerling, Friedrich Ritter   Aus 1803-1887
  O/C 25x20 Die Morgenlanderin 854 Sby 2/92 5,775
  O/Pa 10x10 Young Girl's Head But 5/92 1,100

Von Baranya, Gustov Lorincz   Hun 1886-1938
  * See 1991 Edition . . . .

Von Bartels, Hans   Ger 1856-1913
  G/Pa 18x14 The Day's Catch Sby 1/92 6,875
  G&C/Pa 14x14 Peasant Girl Sby 1/92 1,320

Von Beurden, Alphonse   Flm 1878-1962
O/Cb 23x36 Forest Passage 1911 Slo 2/92   400
Von Blaas, Eugen   Aus 1843-1932
* See 1992 Edition
Von Bremen, Johann Georg Meyer   Ger 1813-1886
O/C 23x17 In the Mountains 1877 Sby 10/91   57,750
O/C 17x14 Das Jungste Bruderchen 1852 Sby 2/92   55,000
O/C 22x15 The Prayer 1844 Chr 5/92   15,400
O/Pn 6x5 Young Woman and Butterfly 1870 But 5/92 . . .   14,300
O/C 15x12 The Letter 1870 Chr 10/91   13,200
W/Pb 8x6 A Young Shepherdess Chr 5/92   3,850
Von Canal, *   Dut 19C**
* See 1992 Edition
Von Chelminski, Jan   Pol 1851-1925
W&G/Pa 15x24 Cossacks Awaiting Fr. Cavalry But 11/91 . .   1,540
Von Defregger, Franz   Ger 1835-1921
O/B 14x10 Jungen Bauern Sby 5/92   8,800
Von Demuth, Anni   Aus 1866-
O/C 37x50 Boating Scene Sby 1/92   3,080
Von Dogsdon, A.   Eur 19C
O/B 10x7 Winter River Hnz 5/92   140
Von Eckenbrecher, Themistocles   Ger 1842-1921
* See 1992 Edition . . . .
Von Faber Du Faur, Otto   Ger 1828-1901
* See 1990 Edition . . . .
Von Ferraris, Arthur   Hun 1856-
* See 1992 Edition . . . .
Von Gegerfelt, Wilhelm   Swd 1844-1920
O/C 13x27 Market Day, Venice Sby 2/92   8,250
Von Gietl, Josua   Ger 1847-1922
* See 1992 Edition . . . .
Von Grutzner, Eduard   Ger 1846-1925
* See 1990 Edition . . . .
Von Gunten, Roger
* See 1992 Edition . . . .
Von Hayek, Hans   Aus 1869-1940
O/M 11x17 A Village Street 17 Chr 5/92   1,320
Von Hoermann, Theodor   Aus 1840-1895
* See 1991 Edition . . . .
Von Huctenburgh, Jan   Dut 1646-1753
* See 1992 Edition . . . .
Von Jawlensky, Alexej   Ger 1864-1931
W&Pl/Pa 10x7 Frauenkopf Sby 11/91   41,250
Von Kaulbach, Friedrich August   Ger 1822-1903
* See 1990 Edition . . . .
Von Keller, Albert   Sws 1844-1920
O/Pn 9x15 Reclining Female Nude Chr 10/91   5,500
Von Klever, Julius Sergius   Rus 1850-1924
* See 1992 Edition . . . .
Von Kobell, Wilhelm A. W.   Ger 1766-1855
W/Pa 15x21 Peasants Meet Infantry 1799 Sby 2/92   49,500
Von Kowalski-Wierusz, Alfred   Pol 1849-1915
O/C 16x20 Soldier on Horseback Wes 3/92   2,200
Von Kreuznach, Konrad Faber   Ger 16C
* See 1990 Edition . . . .
Von Lenbach, Franz Seraph   Ger 1836-1904
O/B 30x27 Young Girl Holding Fruit 1903 Sby 2/92   24,750
Von Madarasz, Gyula   Aus 1858-
* See 1990 Edition . . . .
Von Marr, Carl   Ger 1858-1936
O/C/B 42x35 Die Flagellanten Sby 10/91   13,200
Von Max, Gabriel   Czk 1840-1915
O/C 16x12 Else Wearing a Garland of Flowers Chr 10/91 . .   2,420
Von Menzel, Adolf   Ger 1815-1905
* See 1991 Edition . . . .
Von Muhlenen, Max   Sws 1903-1971
* See 1992 Edition . . . .
Von Perbandt, Carl   Am 1832-1911
* See 1992 Edition . . . .

Von Piloty, Karl Theodor   Ger 1826-1886
O/C 47x69 Henry VIII and Anne Boleyn Sby 10/91   57,750
O/C 16x14 Woman in Profile But 11/91   825
Von Rentzel, August & Triebel   Ger 1810-1891
O/C 27x38 Genre Scene Skn 9/91   4,125
Von Reth, Caspar   Ger 1858-1913
* See 1991 Edition
Von Scheidel, Franz Anton   Aus 1731-1801
* See 1992 Edition
Von Schmidt, Harold   Am 1893-1982
O/Pn 24x50 Bunch Quitters 1931 Sby 12/91   18,700
O/C 30x45 The Searchers 1950 Sby 12/91   16,500
O/C 30x30 Ghost Column 1932 Sby 5/92   8,250
Von Schneidau, Christian   Am 1893-1976
O/C 46x40 Chinese Parasol But 10/91   3,850
O/B 18x23 Sunday on Provincetown(?) Wharf Mor 3/92 . . .   1,900
O/C 64x38 Mood Oriental But 10/91   1,870
O/C 40x34 Mary Philbin But 10/91   1,650
O/C 48x40 Signe (The Artist's Wife) But 6/92   1,540
O/C 36x44 Waves Among the Rocks But 2/92   1,320
O/C 40x36 Whistling Boy But 10/91   1,210
O/C 34x30 Her Fan 1920 But 10/91   1,100
O/C 44x36 Portrait of a Woman But 10/91   1,100
O/C 30x36 Winter Fairyland But 2/92   1,045
O/C 44x34 Self Portrait With Palette 1917 But 10/91   990
O/C 38x28 Self Portrait Carving Wood But 6/92   770
O/B 20x28 Artist's Palette But 6/92   605
O/C 44x36 Studio Dusk But 10/91   550
O/C 24x18 Landscape 1914 Mor 3/92   475
C/Pa 48x40 Five Drawings But 6/92   468
Von Schrotter, Alfred   Aus 1856-
O/Pn 15x12 The Sportsman 1889 Sby 10/91   8,250
O/Pn 6x4 The Conscription Officer 1888 Sby 1/92   3,630
Von Schwind, Moritz   Aus 1804-1871
* See 1992 Edition
Von Sedelmayer, Ferdinand   Ger 19C
* See 1992 Edition
Von Stuck, Franz   Ger 1863-1928
Pe&O/Pn 21x18 Ideal Head 1902 Sby 5/92   27,500
Von Szankowski, Boleslaw   Pol 1873-
* See 1992 Edition
Von Tamm, Franz Werner   1658-1724
O/C 27x22 Still Lifes: Pair Sby 10/91   46,750
Von Volkmann, Hans Richard   Ger 1860-1927
O/C 26x38 Summer Landscape 1920 Sby 1/92   4,950
Von Wedig, Gottfried   1583-1641
O/Pn 17x25 Still Life Fruit, Bread, Wine Sby 5/92   55,000
Von Werner, Anton Alexander   Ger 1843-1915
* See 1992 Edition
Von Wichera, Raimund   Aus 1862-1925
* See 1992 Edition
Von Wiegand, Charmion   Am 1900-1983
L/B 9x8 Counterpoint II 1947 Sby 4/92   4,950
Von Wierusz-Kowalski, Alfred   Pol 1849-1915
* See 1992 Edition
Von Zugel, Heinrich   Ger 1850-1941
O/C 29x38 The Young Shepherd Sby 2/92   88,000
Vonck, Jan   Dut 1630-1660
O/Pn 28x22 Mallard, Kingfisher, Song Birds 1660 Chr 1/92   12,100
Vonnoh, Robert William   Am 1858-1933
O/C 20x24 Springtime Chr 5/92   10,450
O/Pn 13x9 Solitude But 4/92   1,320
Voogd, Hendrick   Dut 1768-1839
* See 1990 Edition
Voorhees, Clark Greenwood   Am 1871-1933
* See 1992 Edition
Voorhout I, Johannes   1647-1773
O/C 31x25 The Crowning with Thorns Chr 5/92   3,850

Vorhay, Louis Dut 1935-
O/C 27x31 Ship at Sea Dum 1/92 300
Vorobieff, Marie (Marevna)
  * See 1992 Edition . . . .
Vos, Hubert Am 1855-1935
P/C 32x60 The Knitting Room 89 Chr 12/91 13,200
Voss, Carl Leopold Ger 1856-1921
  * See 1990 Edition . . . .
Voss, Frank B. Am 1880-1953
O/C 18x24 Horse Auction 1921 Ald 5/92 3,000
Vostell, Wolf 20C
MM/Pa 20x26 Psychogrammen '64 Sby 11/91 8,250
Votoix, L. Fr 20C
O/C 18x22 At the Races Fre 4/92 925
O/C 18x22 Horserace Fre 4/92 525
Vouet, Simon Fr 1590-1649
K/Pa 6x5 Head of an Old Woman Chr 1/92 4,180
Vrancx, Sebastian Flm 1573-1647
  * See 1991 Edition . . . .
**Vrancx, Sebastian & De Momper Flm
1573-1647**
O/C 25x34 Village w/Two Men Fixing Wheel Sby 5/92 . . . 24,200
Vreedenburgh, Cornelis Dut 1880-1946
O/C 24x36 A Shore Scene Skn 9/91 7,150
Vroom, Hendrik Cornelisz Dut 1566-1640
O/Pn 29x23 Old Oak Trees 1607 But 11/91 3,850
Vuillard, Edouard Fr 1868-1940
Pnc/Pa/C 39x22 Mde Hessel Dans Son Salon Sby 5/92 . 632,500
O/B/Pn 12x14 Le Chocolat Chr 11/91 385,000
Det/Pa/C 26x21 Le banc, square Vintimille Chr 5/92 220,000
O/B 14x17 Vase de Fleurs Sby 5/92 77,000
O/C 8x10 Nature Morte aux Prunes Sby 10/91 71,500
C/Pa 9x11 Le Mannequin Sby 5/92 55,000
O/C 12x11 Madame Vuillard a Table Chr 11/91 52,800
I&Pe/Pa 8x10 La Couturiere Sby 5/92 49,500
Dis/Pa/C 20x26 Petite Maison a Saint-Jacut Sby 2/92 . . . 49,500
O/Pa/C 18x15 La Lecture dans le Petit Salon Chr 5/92 . . . 46,200
P/Pa 10x13 Le Pot Vert Sby 11/91 41,800
Pnc&C/Pa/C 29x18 La Robe Noire Chr 2/92 26,400
Pe/Pa 8x5 Portrait Madame Vuillard Sby 5/92 22,000
P/Pa 9x12 Madame Hessel Dans le Jardin Sby 10/91 . . . 18,700
P&Y/Pa 10x13 Femme Dans un Interieur Sby 2/92 16,500
P&C/Pa 15x8 Femme au Bouquet de Fleurs Sby 11/91 . . . 13,200
P&Y/Pa 5x7 Scene de Ville: Double Sby 5/92 9,900
P/Pa 10x9 Portrait de Marie Vuillard Sby 10/91 4,400
Pe/Pa 8x5 Bouquet de Fleurs Fre 10/91 2,200
Pe/Pa 5x7 Seated Woman Sby 10/91 2,200
H/Pa 5x6 Two Figures in a Landscape Sby 2/92 1,760
Vukovik, Marko Am 1892-
O/B 8x10 Peach Yng 2/92 125
Vysekal, Edouard Am 1890-1939
O/C 18x23 Sunshine and Laundry But 2/92 12,100
O/C 13x18 Still Life But 2/92 4,400
O/B 12x9 Luvena in Mandarin Costume But 2/92 1,980
G/Pa 14x19 Silverlake Blvd But 2/92 1,980
W/Pa 16x21 Hollywood But 2/92 1,760
W/Pa 15x22 Neighboring Houses '39 But 2/92 1,430
W/Pa 15x21 Poplars But 2/92 990
W/Pa 11x8 Kutrina But 6/92 825
O/C 11x10 Hilltop, Elysian Park But 6/92 770
O/B 10x12 Our Outlook, Hollywood But 6/92 770
O/C 22x22 Dramatization But 6/92 550
W/Pa 18x24 Nude on Blue 1926 But 6/92 550
W/Pa 13x19 Sunday Afternoon But 6/92 550
O/C 8x11 Neighboring Houses But 6/92 495
O/B 15x10 Spanish Dance But 6/92 440
W/Pa 14x21 Above Silver Lake But 6/92 385
O/C 12x18 Bare Fig Tree But 6/92 385
Vysekal, Luvena Am 1873-1954
O/C 10x14 Ruth and Baby Nell But 2/92 3,025
O/C 10x13 Neighbor Children But 2/92 1,210
O/C 12x10 Boy with Cap (Harold) But 6/92 880
O/C 17x14 Hupa (Indian Child) But 6/92 605
O/B 16x15 Sunflowers But 6/92 440

Vytlacil, Vaclav Am 1892-1984
O/B 11x14 Mountain Landscape in Autumn 1915 Slo 10/91 1,100
O/Cb 13x15 Rocky Coastline 1916 Skn 9/91 825
Wachtel, Elmer Am 1864-1929
O/C 18x24 Pomona Valley But 10/91 24,200
O/C 16x20 Convict Lake But 2/92 15,400
O/Cb 14x18 Alpine Glow-Sierra Nevada Mor 6/92 5,500
W/Pa 12x17 Mission San Juan Capistrano But 2/92 3,575
O/C 14x18 Landscape Mor 11/91 3,250
W/Pa 7x15 Boathouse But 2/92 2,200
W/Pa 10x15 Harbor Scene Mor 3/92 950
**Wachtel, Marion Kavanaugh Am
1875-1954**
W/Pa 16x21 View of Santa Barbara But 10/91 18,700
O/C 24x32 Long Lake But 2/92 17,600
O/C 26x20 Mountain Stream But 10/91 15,400
O/C/B 12x10 Woman in a Flower Garden But 2/92 5,225
W/Pa 16x11 Girl in Blue Apron 1896 Mor 6/92 1,900
W/Pa 17x12 Seated Lady in Peasant Dress 1896 Hnd 12/91 . 475
Wadsworth, Charles Am 20C
O/B 24x12 Submerged Oarlock 1953 Yng 2/92 70
**Wadsworth, Edward Alexander Eng
1889-1949**
W/Pa 11x14 Landscape with Field Workers Wes 3/92 330
Wadsworth, Wedworth Am 1846-1927
  * See 1992 Edition . . . .
Wageman, Thomas Charles Br 1787-1863
Pe/Pa 10x6 Young Man Drawing Hnd 6/92 100
Wagner, Ferdinand Ger 1847-1927
  * See 1992 Edition . . . .
Wagner, Fred Am 1864-1940
  * See 1992 Edition . . . .
Wagner, Fritz Ger 1896-1939
  * See 1992 Edition . . . .
Wagner, Jacob Am 1852-1898
  * See 1991 Edition . . . .
Wagner, M. A.
O/C 26x36 Landscape with Cows 1898 Dum 9/91 200
Wagner, Wilhelm Georg Dut 1814-
  * See 1992 Edition . . . .
Wagoner, Harry B. Am 1889-1950
O/C 16x20 Afternoon Palm Springs 1929 Mor 6/92 850
O/C 12x16 Atmospheric Landscape Mor 6/92 750
W/Pa 10x14 Desert Scene Mys 11/91 192
Wagoner, Robert Am 1928-
W/Pa 8x10 Navajos Sel 5/92 200
Wahlberg, Alfred Swd 1834-1906
  * See 1991 Edition . . . .
Wahlqvist, Ehrnfried Swd 1815-1895
  * See 1991 Edition . . . .
Waidman, Pierre Fr 1860-1937
O/C 19x24 Dans la Vosges Chr 2/92 1,650
Wainewright, Thomas Francis Eng 19C
  * See 1992 Edition . . . .
Wainwright, John Br 19C
  * See 1992 Edition . . . .
Wainwright, William John Br 1855-1931
  * See 1991 Edition . . . .
Wakhevitch, Georges 20C
O/C 70x72 El Amor Brujo: Two Screens Sby 11/91 3,025
W/Pa 15x24 El Amor Brujo: 2 Costume Designs Sby 11/91 . 2,310
G/Pa/B 21x28 Beauty and the Beast: Design Sby 11/91 . . . 1,760
G/Pa 22x30 El Amor Brujo: Two Decor Sby 11/91 1,540
G/Pa 47x13 El Amor Brujo: 3 Costume Design Sby 11/91 . . 1,430
Walbourn, Ernest Br 1872-
O/Pn 11x16 Summer's Day Wes 11/91 990
Walcott, Harry Mills Am 1870-1944
  * See 1991 Edition . . . .
Walde, Alfons 20C
  * See 1991 Edition . . . .
Waldek, H.
  * See 1992 Edition . . . .
Walden, Lionel L. Am 1861-1933
O/Pn 6x9 Capri-The Landing Place Mor 3/92 400

Waldmuller, Ferdinand Georg   Aus 1793-1865
* See 1991 Edition . . . .
Waldo, Frank   Am a 1910-1930
* See 1992 Edition . . . .
Waldo, J. Frank   Am 19C
O/C 14x22 Hayfield 1902   Ald 3/92   2,750
Waldo, Samuel & Jewett, W.
O/C 36x28 Portrait of the Livingston Children   Eld 8/92 . . .   3,740
Waldo, Samuel Lovett   Am 1783-1961
O/C 30x25 Portrait of a Gentleman   Eld 8/92   770
Waldorp, Antoine   Dut 1803-1866
O/C 36x67 Capture of the Den Briel 1862   Chr 2/92   16,500
Waldsperger, M. R.
O/M 17x23 Farm Scene   Dum 10/91   115
Walenta, Edmund   Am 19C
* See 1992 Edition . . . .
Wales, Orlando G.   Am 1865-1933
O/C 24x22 Tabletop Still Life   Slo 7/92   400
O/C 31x22 Still Life   Ald 5/92   280
Walker, Chuck   Am 20C
* See 1992 Edition . . . .
Walker, E.
O/C 8x12 Fisherman's Return   Hnz 10/91   325
Walker, Frederick R.   Am 20C
* See 1992 Edition . . . .
Walker, Henry Oliver   Am 1843-1929
* See 1992 Edition . . . .
Walker, Horatio   Can 1858-1938
O/C 28x36 Hippocrene 1919   Sbt 11/91   6,078
Walker, James   Am 1819-1889
* See 1992 Edition . . . .
Walker, James Alexander   Br 1841-1898
O/Pn 9x7 Portrait of a Cavalryman   Sby 1/92   3,300
Walker, John
* See 1992 Edition . . . .
Walker, John Law   Am 1899-
O/C 40x36 Light Wine 32   But 2/92   1,650
Walker, Matthew
W/Pa 14x20 American Steam & Sail Naval Vessel   Eld 7/92 . .   220
Walker, William Aiken   Am 1838-1921
O/C 15x24 The Wagon's Empty   Chr 12/91   99,000
O/B 9x12 Wash Day   Chr 9/91   11,000
O/C 7x18 Palms at Ponce Park, Florida   Chr 12/91   9,900
O/B 8x4 Full Baskets: Pair   Chr 3/92   8,800
O/Pn 12x7 Cotton Picker with Possum   Sby 3/92   8,250
O/B 9x12 Cotton Pickers in the Field   Sby 3/92   7,150
O/B 6x12 Cabin Scene   Sby 12/91   6,600
O/Pn 6x12 Cabin Scene   Sby 3/92   6,600
O/B 9x12 Cabin Scene   Sby 12/91   6,050
O/Pn 6x12 Picking Cotton by the Cabin   Sby 3/92   6,050
O/B 6x12 Cotton Pickers   Sby 12/91   5,500
O/Pa/B 7x10 Plantation House Along Coast 1870   Sby 12/91   5,500
O/B 6x12 Sharecroppers' Cabin   Skn 11/91   5,500
O/B 6x12 The Cottonfield   Doy 12/91   5,500
O/C 6x18 Beach at Ponce Park, Florida   Chr 12/91   5,280
O/B 10x13 By the Cotton Field   Hnz 5/92   4,500
O/B 6x17 Coastal Beach 1905   Sby 12/91   4,400
O/B 8x4 Cotton Picker   Doy 12/91   2,200
Walkowitz, Abraham   Am 1880-1965
O/Cb 18x24 The Bather   Chr 5/92   6,600
W&Pe/Pa 10x14 Bathers   Chr 3/92   4,620
Pl/Pa 11x7 Abstract Forms 1932   Chr 3/92   3,520
W,Pe&Pl/Pa 14x9 Three Drawings   Chr 9/91   2,090
W/Pa 15x13 Colored Abstraction   Chr 11/91   1,980
Pe&W/Pa 10x8 A Dense Crowd 1909   Chr 11/91   1,430
W&Pe/Pa 14x8 Isadora Duncan Dancing: Two   Sby 4/92 . . .   1,430
Pe&I/Pa 14x19 Isadora Duncan: Pair   Sby 4/92   1,320
Pe/Pa 14x9 Abstractions (2)   Chr 6/92   1,100
W&Pe/Pa 17x23 Figures in a Landscape   Sby 12/91   1,100
Pe&W/Pa 11x7 Swirling Female Figure 1915   Chr 6/92   825
W/Pa 7x2 Isidor Duncan   Mys 6/92   275
Wall, A. Bryan   Am -1937
O/Ab 6x14 Carting Hay   Wtf 10/91   350

Wall, Hermann C.   Am 1875-1915
W&R/Pa 12x15 Couple Walking/Country Road 1912   Ih 5/92 .   475
Wall, W. C.   Am 19C
* See 1992 Edition . . . .
Wall, William Allen   Am 1801-1885
* See 1991 Edition . . . .
Wall, William Guy   Am 1792-1864
* See 1992 Edition . . . .
Wallace, F.   Eng 19C
O/C 17x24 Coastal Scene with Fisherfolk   Sel 2/92   300
Wallace, Harold Frank   Br 1881-1962
W&G/Pb 15x21 The Outcast   Chr 5/92   1,320
Waller, Samuel Edmund   Br 1850-1903
* See 1991 Edition . . . .
Walraven, Jan   Dut 1827-1874
* See 1992 Edition . . . .
Walsh, Tudor E. G.   Eng 19C
O/C 19x14 Still Life of Roses   Slo 10/91   120
Waltensperger, Charles E.   Am 1871-1931
O/C 20x16 Woman with Kettle   Dum 2/92   2,400
O/C 16x13 Dutch Woman with Child   Dum 2/92   1,600
O/Ab 10x14 Morning Sunlight, Gloucester   Dum 11/91   1,100
O/Ab 9x12 Children with Swans   Dum 2/92   1,000
O/Ab 11x14 Harbor Scene   Dum 2/92   1,000
O/C 13x15 Shepherdess, Child and Sheep   Dum 2/92   900
O/Ab 10x12 Children of Fisherman   Dum 11/91   800
O/C Size? Seated Woman Near Window   Dum 8/92   700
O/C 14x18 Two Girls by the Shore   Yng 2/92   350
Walter, Franz Erhard   20C
Pe/Pa 25x20 Untitled   Sby 11/91   550
Walter, Martha   Am 1875-1976
O/C 40x32 Overhead Trestle, Bass Rocks   Sby 12/91   44,000
O/B 14x18 By the Water's Edge   Chr 5/92   17,600
O/B 15x18 Trouville   Sby 5/92   16,500
O/B 9x11 French Family   Chr 9/91   2,640
Walter, Otto   Aus 19C
O/C 24x38 After the Christening   Wtf 9/91   2,900
Walter, William   Am 20C
W/Pa 14x21 Birches in Winter   Slo 10/91   60
Walters, Emile   Am 1893-
O/C 25x30 Summer Storm   But 11/91   1,980
O/B 20x24 Arctic Mountain Landscape   Wes 5/92   550
Walters, G. S.   Br 19C
O/C 14x20 Ship at Sea   Hnd 5/92   650
Walters, George Stanfield   Br 1838-1924
W/Pa 12x19 Meeting the Pilot Boat   Bor 8/92   750
G/Pa 10x14 Ships on Calm Waters   Slo 9/91   700
Walters, H.   20C
O/M 9x13 Still Life Reclining Nude   Slo 7/92   150
Walters, M. J.   Br 19C
W/Pa 10x8 Punt by a Riverbank   Hnd 6/92   225
Walters, Samuel   Br 1811-1882
* See 1992 Edition . . . .
Walther, Charles   Am 1879-1938
* See 1991 Edition . . . .
Waltman, Harry Franklin   Am 1871-1951
O/C 25x20 Two Women   Lou 3/92   500
O/C 25x30 Nearing Sunset   Mys 11/91   495
Walton, Edward Arthur   Eng 1860-1922
* See 1992 Edition . . . .
Walton, Henry   Am 1746-1813
* See 1990 Edition . . . .
Walton, John Whitehead   Br 19C
O/C 46x68 First Trial by Jury 1881   Hnd 10/91   1,600
Wandesforde, Juan   Am 1817-1902
O/C 14x20 Clear Lake   But 6/92   3,025
O/C 20x12 Sentinel Rock   But 10/91   3,025
Wappers, Gustave, Baron   Bel 1803-1874
O/C 41x51 Peter the Great at Zaardam 1836   Sby 5/92 . .   14,300
Ward, Arthur   Br 19C
O/C 20x25 Scottish Terriers and Monkey Pals   Hnd 3/92 . . .   1,500
Ward, Arthur E.   Am 20C
O/C 16x19 The Village Lane   Wtf 3/92   400
Ward, Charles Caleb   Can 1831-1896
O/C 14x10 Indian Basket Weaver 1894   Brd 8/92   880

Ward, Edmund F.   Am 1892-
O/C 28x40 The Fussilade Sby 12/91   1,540
O&R/B 26x31 Woman Embracing Girl 1920 Ih 5/92   1,300
O/C 18x24 The Swimming Hole Sby 12/91   1,100
Ward, Harold Morse   Am 1889-1973
O/B 29x42 The Last Stand #2 But 6/92   660
Ward, James   Br 1769-1859
* See 1991 Edition
Ward, John   Can 1948-
A/C 15x19 Approaching Car 1982 Sbt 5/92   1,496
Ward, William (Jr.)
O/C 27x37 A Boston Harbor Scene Dum 9/91   250
Wardle, Arthur   Br 1864-1949
O/C 22x14 King Charles Spaniel Sby 6/92   17,600
O/C 16x20 Two Fox Terriers Skn 9/91   10,450
O/C 16x20 A Jack Russell Terrier Sby 6/92   7,150
O/B 9x12 An Irish Wolfhound Sby 6/92   5,500
W&G/Pa 21x16 Left in Charge Sby 6/92   4,950
O/C 16x32 Lions on the African Plain Sby 6/92   2,970
P&K/Pb 16x24 Across the Desert Chr 10/91   2,200
Pe&S/Pa 8x15 The Rabbit Hunt Fre 10/91   1,250
O/C 20x14 Woman with Dog 1898 Sel 9/91   1,100
Wardleworth, J. L.   Br 19C
* See 1992 Edition . . . .
Warhol, Andy   Am 1928-1987
Sp,l&HSs/C 83x105 210 Coca-Cola Bottles 62 Chr 5/92 . .   2.09M
l&SpSs/C 49x78 Most Wanted Men No 11 Sby 5/92 . . .   577,500
l&SpSs/C 81x64 16 Jackies Sby 5/92   418,000
SpSs/C 40x40 Red Jackie Sby 11/91   352,000
l&SpSs/C 51x42 Mao Chr 11/91   198,000
SpSs/C 50x42 Mao 73 Sby 11/91   165,000
SpSs/C 36x28 Four Gold/Black Marilyns Sby 5/92   159,500
SpSs/C 36x28 Marilyn (Reversal Series) '86 Chr 5/92 . .   137,500
SpSs/C 23x23 Self Portrait Sby 11/91   104,500
SpSs/C 26x22 Mao 72 Sby 5/92   99,000
SpSs/C 76x52 Shadow 1978 Sby 2/92   99,000
O&Pt/C 9x6 Minestrone Soup Chr 11/91   82,500
Sp&lSs/C 71x49 Knives Chr 11/91   77,000
SpSs/C 20x16 One Red Marilyn Sby 11/91   71,500
l&SpSs/C 24x24 Flowers 64 Chr 11/91   68,200
SpSs/C 24x24 Flowers 64 Sby 11/91   60,500
SpSs/C 20x16 Jackie 64 Sby 10/91   57,750
SpSs/C 22x22 Flowers Sby 5/92   55,000
SpSs/C 76x52 Shadows Sby 5/92   49,500
SpSs/Pa 21x25 Untitled Chr 5/92   46,200
SpSs/C 56x42 Untitled 84 Sby 2/92   24,200
SpSs/C 9x10 Double One Dollar Bill 62 Sby 11/91   20,900
SpSs/C 20x20 Untitled (Guns) 81 Sby 10/91   17,600
SpSs/C 10x8 $ 82 Sby 11/91   16,500
SpSs/C 5x5 Flower 65 Sby 5/92   16,500
SpSs/C 5x5 Flowers 64 Sby 5/92   16,500
SpSs/C 26x22 Soup Can 85 Chr 5/92   16,500
SpSs/C 14x11 Heart Sby 5/92   13,200
A/C 5x5 Untitled 64 Sby 2/92   12,100
Pt&MM/C 14x11 Shadow 1979 Sby 5/92   8,800
SpSs/C 11x14 Shadow 1979 Chr 5/92   6,050
W/Pa 8x11 Cherub with Purple Cat But 5/92   2,475
W/Pa 8x10 Orgy Scene But 5/92   2,200
W/Pa 8x7 Cat Named Sam Dum 9/91   1,900
W/Pa 8x10 Green Shoe But 5/92   1,320
Warner, Albert   Con 20C
O/C/B 11x13 Rocky Seascape Wes 3/92   468
Warner, Everett Longley   Am 1877-1963
O/M 26x32 Winter Morning Chr 3/92   3,080
O/Cb 10x6 Siena--Old Monastery 1904 Skn 9/91   358
Warner, Nell Walker   Am 1891-1970
O/C 20x24 Northeast Shore, Cape Ann But 10/91   2,475
O/C 16x20 Boats Along a Shoreline But 2/92   1,760
O/C 16x20 House Mountain Landscape Mor 6/92   1,200
O/C 24x30 Spring Flowers But 10/91   1,100
O/Cb 8x10 Bickford's Landing - Gloucester Mor 3/92 . . .   950
O/C 18x14 Zinnias in Brown Vase Mor 11/91   500
Warren, Dr.   Can 20C
W/Pa 13x10 Canadian Mountain Lake '44 Dum 4/92   150

Warren, Harold Broadfield   Am 1859-1934
W/Pa 10x14 Lake in the Canadian Rockies 1910 Yng 2/92 . .   125
Warren, Melvin C.   Am 1920-
* See 1990 Edition . . . .
Warshaw, Howard   Am 1920-
O/C 5x8 Sacks 47 Sby 12/91   660
Warshawsky, Abel George   Am 1883-1962
O/C 26x21 Woman of Finisterre But 11/91   2,750
O/Cb 16x20 The Red Barn But 2/92   2,475
O/Pn 15x19 California Coast Scene Chr 6/92   2,420
O/C 13x16 Street Scene Mor 6/92   2,250
O/C 32x26 Seated Nude 1946 Hnd 12/91   2,000
O/B 21x18 Late April in French Countryside Fre 4/92   1,050
O/M 16x13 Still Life Poppies and Daisies Skn 9/91   495
O/C 22x18 Floral Still Life 1929 Fre 10/91   350
Warshburn, Alexander   Am 1887-1945
O/C 26x32 Old Aloes Sby 4/92   2,530
O/Pn 14x18 San Fernando Valley Mor 3/92   650
O/M 18x22 High Sierra Lou 12/91   600
Waschmuth, Ferdinand   Fr 1802-1869
* See 1991 Edition . . . .
Washburn, Cadwallander   Am 1866-1965
O/C 20x22 Early Catch Brd 8/92   880
Washington, Georges   Fr 1827-1910
* See 1992 Edition . . . .
Wasmuller, J. H.   Am 19C
* See 1991 Edition . . . .
Wasson, George Savary   Am 1855-1932
O/B 6x6 Drying Sails off the Block House Brd 8/92   770
Watelet, Louis Etienne   Fr 1780-1866
* See 1992 Edition . . . .
Watelin, Louis   Fr 1838-1905
O/Pn 16x23 French Village Scene Mys 6/92   3,410
Waterbury, Edwin M.   Am 20C
O/C 18x26 Allegheny River: Two Wes 5/92   440
Waterlow, Ernest Albert   Eng 1850-1919
W/Pa 13x20 Fishing Village Stone Haven Bor 8/92   450
Waterman, Marcus A.   Am 1834-1914
O/C 40x22 Merchant and the Genie Chr 3/92   3,850
O/Pa 6x8 Hens and Rooster 1859 Skn 3/92   1,650
Waters, George W.   Am 1832-1912
* See 1992 Edition . . . .
Waters, Susan   Am 1823-1900
* See 1992 Edition . . . .
Watkins, Franklin C.   Am 1894-1972
O/C 24x30 The Blue Bench Chr 6/92   1,980
O/C 22x16 Crucifixtion Fre 4/92   500
Watkins, William Reginald   Am 1890-
O/C 30x25 Moored Sailboats in Harbor 1938 Slo 12/91   500
Watrous, E.   Am 1858-1921
O/C 41x36 Lady in Gray Fre 4/92   525
Watrous, Harry Willson   Am 1857-1940
O/C 20x18 Kwan-Yin Sby 12/91   3,410
O/C 20x16 Orientalist Still Life Skn 5/92   770
Watson, Adele   Am 1875-1947
O/B 11x14 Women Washing Clothes Mor 11/91   850
O/C 18x15 Seated Figure Mor 11/91   600
O/B 15x20 California Coastal Mor 11/91   500
O/Cb 7x10 Monterey Coastal Mor 3/92   375
O/Pn 11x14 House in Landscape Mor 3/92   325
Watson, Charles A.   Am 1857-1923
O/C 16x30 Sunset, Baltimore Harbor, 1897 Wes 5/92   1,650
Watson, Charles H. R.   Irs 20C
* See 1992 Edition . . . .
Watson, Dawson   Eng 1864-
O/B 10x14 Mountainous Landscape Wlf 6/92   250
Watson, Edward Facon   Br 19C
* See 1992 Edition . . . .
Watson, Homer Ransford   Can 1855-1936
O/C 18x24 Toward Evening Sbt 11/91   5,142
O/C 14x18 After Rain '90 Sbt 5/92   2,805
Watson, Jessie N.   Am 1870-1963
O/Pa 14x17 California Landscape 49 Mor 6/92   900
Watson, John Dawson   Eng 1832-1892
* See 1992 Edition . . . .

Watson, P.   19C
O/C 29x48 Landscape with Town View Dum 7/92 750
Watson, P. Fletcher   Eng 1842-1907
W/Pa 12x6 Sheep in a Meadow But 5/92 1,100
Watson, Robert   Am 1923-
O/C 30x40 Italian Landscape Wes 3/92 550
O/C 15x9 Loneliness Wlf 9/91 450
O/B 24x30 Southwind '79 Dum 2/92 175
Watson, Robert   Br 20C
O/C 24x37 Highland Sheep and Cattle: Pair 1894 Sby 1/92 . 4,950
O/C 16x24 Highland Sheep 1898 Brd 5/92 2,750
O/C 16x24 Highland Cattle 1898 Brd 5/92 1,980
Watson, William (Jr.)   Br -1921
O/C 33x26 Sheep Grazing in the Highlands 1903 Sby 5/92 . 6,600
O/C 24x36 By Highland Streams 1907 Sby 5/92 5,500
Watson-Gordon, Sir John   Eng 1790-1864
* See 1991 Edition . . . .
Watteau, Jean-Antoine   Fr 1684-1721
K/Pa 5x8 Studies of Two Girls' Heads Chr 1/92 242,000
K/Pa 7x9 Three Ladies in Profile to Right Chr 1/92 154,000
K/Pa 6x8 Head of Woman and of Man Blowing Chr 1/92 . 38,500
Watts, Frederick Waters   Br 1800-1862
* See 1992 Edition . . . .
Watts, George Frederick   Br 1817-1904
* See 1992 Edition . . . .
Watzelhan, Carl   Ger 1867-1942
* See 1990 Edition . . . .
Waud, Alfred R.   Am 1828-1891
W/Pa 10x7 Self Portrait Brd 5/92 77
Waugh, Frederick Judd   Am 1861-1940
O/C 25x40 Early Morn Sby 3/92 12,100
O/C 36x48 The Channel Chr 5/92 10,450
O/M 36x48 Seascape Sby 3/92 8,800
O/C 25x30 Breaking Waves Chr 9/91 4,950
O/Cb 25x30 Moonlight 26 Chr 11/91 4,400
O/C 22x28 Crashing Waves Chr 6/92 3,740
O/C 24x30 Breaking Surf Fre 4/92 2,500
O/C 28x38 A Rocky Coast Chr 6/92 2,420
O/C 31x30 The Road to Nowhere Sby 12/91 2,310
O/M 22x26 Surf and Rocks Lou 12/91 1,750
O/Cb 23x29 Coming Day Skn 5/92 1,540
O/C 14x20 The Veteran of Monterey But 11/91 1,210
O/C 25x30 Cows in Landscape 1890 Wes 11/91 880
Waugh, Henry J.   Am a 1860-
Pe/Pa 5x3 Tree; Fallen Tree: Two Wes 3/92 110
Wauters, Camille   Bel 1856-1919
O/C 75x43 Female Nude with Red Hair 1890 Sel 4/92 8,500
Way, Andrew John Henry   Am 1826-1888
O/C 10x14 Still Life With Oysters '72 Sby 9/91 18,700
O/B 10x12 A Gourmet's Delight Chr 5/92 17,050
Way, Charles Jones   Can 1834-1919
* See 1991 Edition . . . .
Waycott, Hedley   Am 1865-1937
O/B 24x30 The Lake, Beaver Dam 1934 Hnd 5/92 260
Weatherbee, George Faulkner   Am 1851-1920
* See 1990 Edition . . . .
Weaver, Thomas   Br 1774-1843
* See 1990 Edition . . . .
Webb, Charles Meer   Br 1830-1895
O/C 21x25 The Chess Game 1864 Sby 10/91 2,530
O/C 24x21 The Alchemist 1864 Fre 10/91 1,100
Webb, James   Br 1825-1895
O/C 30x50 Rotterdam, Holland 1876 Sby 10/91 19,800
O/C 30x5 Bamborough Castle Sby 5/92 17,600
O/C 25x37 Fishing Boats at Low Tide 70 Sby 5/92 6,600
Webb, William Edward   Br 1862-1903
O/C 16x24 River at King's Lynn Chr 10/91 4,180
Webber, Wesley   Am 1839-1914
O/C 24x40 Waiting for the Fog to Lift 79 Brd 8/92 7,920
O/C 16x26 Winter Sleigh Ride Brd 8/92 7,700
O/C 30x50 Shepherd with his Flock Chr 6/92 6,050
O/C 22x36 Coastal Scene Hnz 10/91 600
O/C 16x10 Forest Interior Yng 4/92 175

Weber, Carl   Am 1850-1921
O/C 20x36 Evening Effect Antwerp, Belgium Slo 4/92 4,000
O/C 35x25 Rocky Gorge Wes 11/91 1,430
O/C 34x20 Deer by Forest Stream Fre 10/91 1,350
O/C 19x17 Forest Landscape Fre 4/92 600
W/Pa 11x13 Apple Blossoms Mys 6/92 275
Weber, Charles Philipp   Am 1849-
* See 1992 Edition . . . .
Weber, Gottlieb Daniel Paul   Ger 1823-1916
* See 1990 Edition . . . .
Weber, M*   Ger 19C**
O/C 26x10 Woman Examining String of Pearls 83 Sby 7/92 3,300
Weber, Maris   Ger a 1876-
O/Pn 22x11 Woman with a Parasol 1883 Skn 9/91 2,420
Weber, Max   Am 1881-1961
O/C 25x30 Discourse 1950 Sby 9/91 26,400
G/Pa/B 29x19 Soloist at Wanamaker's 1910 Sby 5/92 . . . 26,400
O/C 21x28 Sailors and Girls '39 Lou 6/92 3,250
W&I/Pa 15x12 Study of a Nude Figure But 5/92 1,320
Weber, Otis S.   Am 19C
O/C 26x42 Paddlewheeler Fre 4/92 7,100
Weber, Otto   Ger 1832-1888
* See 1992 Edition . . . .
Weber, Paul   Am 1823-1916
O/C 54x70 Forest Stream 1859 Fre 10/91 9,000
O/C/B 11x14 Katharinensee, Scotland But 5/92 2,475
O/C 14x17 Rural Landscape Sby 12/91 1,870
Weber, Philip   Am 1849-
* See 1992 Edition . . . .
Weber, R.   20C
O/C 23x31 Cottage with Flowers and Gardener Dum 12/91 . 450
Weber, Sarah S. Stilwell   Am 1878-1939
O/C 40x30 Lady with Leopards Skn 11/91 5,225
Weber, Theordore F.   Fr 1838-1907
O/C 34x23 Fishing Boat of Rough Seas Slo 10/91 4,750
O/C 22x34 Entering Rough Seas Chr 5/92 3,800
Webster, Harold T.   Am 1885-1953
Pl/Pa 16x11 Two: Golfing Subjects Ih 5/92 300
Webster, Herman Armour   Am 1878-1970
I/Pa 5x7 Alley in Besalu, Spain Slo 10/91 260
I/Pa 11x11 Farmyard Scene Slo 10/91 120
Webster, Thomas   Br 1800-1886
O/C 21x40 Disruption Outside School 1872 Slo 7/92 3,750
Wedgelan, S.   Eur 19C
O/C 17x36 Break in the Clouds Slo 4/92 120
Weed, M. Stevenson   20C
O/C 25x30 Flowers in a Bowl Yng 4/92 300
Weekes, Henry   Br a 1849-1888
* See 1992 Edition . . . .
Weekes, Herbert William   Br a 1864-1904
O/Pn 12x8 Love's Call; Guilty: Pair But 11/91 3,850
Weeks, Edwin Lord   Am 1849-1903
O/C 19x23 Boy with Monkeys Sby 11/91 10,450
O/C 20x30 Fording a Stream Sby 10/91 8,250
O/Cb 18x11 Young Man on Horseback Skn 11/91 1,320
O/C 17x12 Moor at Prayer Skn 11/91 1,100
O/C 14x10 Indian Gentleman Skn 11/91 935
Weeks, James   Am 1922-
T/B 14x16 Pianist in Blue-Green Room, 1962 But 5/92 . . 11,000
Weeks, R.   Am
O/Ab 9x12 Rooster and Hen Fre 12/91 350
Weenix, Jan Baptist   Dut 1621-1663
O/C 42x55 Harbour Scene w/Merchant, Slaves Sby 10/91 . 17,600
Weerts, Jan Joseph   Fr 1847-1927
O/Pn 15x12 Still-Life Wlf 9/91 1,200
Wegener, Gerda   Dan 1883-1931
W&Pe/Pa 14x11 La Peteite Modele 1922 Sby 6/92 2,860
W&H/Pa 13x11 The Bouquet Sby 6/92 1,760
Wegman, William   Am 1943-
Ph 31x72 Snow 1979 Sby 10/91 9,350
O/C 11x18 Traveling Salesman on Barren Soil Sby 11/91 . 8,800
O/C 16x23 Airplane Chr 11/91 6,050
Ph 29x22 Bargain, Version #2 Chr 5/92 6,050
Pl&Ph 13x11 Untitled (Cup/Socks) Chr 5/92 3,850

Ph 15x36 Throwing Down Chairs 1972 Sby 10/91 3,575
K/Pa 35x24 Neighbor's Yard 1987 Chr 2/92 2,640
Ph 29x22 Lead Baby 1987 Chr 11/91 2,500
L&Ph 13x11 Two Norsemen with Weapons Chr 5/92 2,200
W&H/Pa 8x9 No Solicitors 76 Chr 5/92 1,540
H/Pa 9x11 Two Drawings 74 Chr 2/92 1,540
H/Pa 9x11 Oh, about 2:30 73 Chr 5/92 1,320
Br&l/Pa 9x11 Before After Chr 2/92 990

Wegner, Erich   Ger 1899-
* See 1992 Edition . . . .

Weigall, Arthur Howes   Eng -1877
* See 1991 Edition . . . .

Weiland, Johannes   Dut 1856-1909
* See 1992 Edition . . . .

Weiler, J.   Am 20C
O/C 23x31 Landscape in Spring Bor 8/92 650

Weindorf, Arthur   Am 1885-
O/B 26x44 Jazz 1926 Skn 9/91 1,210

Weindorf, Paul   Am 1887-1965
O/B 20x24 Eucalyptus Landscape Mor 11/91 375
O/C 12x16 Landscape Mor 11/91 175
O/C 12x15 Sierra Landscape Mor 11/91 125

Weiner, Lawrence   20C
Fp/Pa 9x13 One Steel I Beam Sby 11/91 16,500

Weiner, Louis   Am 1892-
O/C 28x32 Farm Landscape Hnz 5/92 225

Weinmann, A.
O/C 8x11 Landscape with Farm Dum 11/91 185

Weinrich, Agnes   Am 20C
P/Pa Var Abstracts (2) Mys 11/91 302
P/Pa Var Houses and Park Scene (2) Mys 11/91 192

Weir, John Ferguson   Am 1841-1926
* See 1992 Edition . . . .

Weir, Julian Alden   Am 1852-1919
O/B 5x9 View of West Point 1871 Doy 12/91 2,100

Weir, Robert Walter   Am 1803-1889
* See 1992 Edition . . . .

Weis, John Ellsworth   Am 1892-
* See 1992 Edition . . . .

Weisbuch, Claude   Fr 1927-
O/C 59x59 La Chute du Cheval Chr 2/92 8,250
O/C 51x38 Femme Nue Chr 2/92 7,700

Weise, Alexander   Rus 1883-
O/C 28x30 Winter Night on a Mountain Top Hnd 12/91 . . . 600
O/C 21x26 Steingarden in Oberbayern Hnd 3/92 550

Weisenborn, Rudolph   Am 20C
C/Pa 25x19 Cubist Woman with Hat 1936 But 5/92 3,575

Weiser, Mary E.   Am 20C
O/C 20x16 Floral Still Life Eld 7/92 330

Weisman, W. H.   Am 19C
O/C 20x12 Waterfall Yng 2/92 225

Weiss, Georges   Fr 1861-
O/Pn 9x7 The Courtship 90 But 11/91 770

Weiss, Johann Baptist   Ger 1812-1879
O/Pn 24x16 Shipping in Rough Waters But 11/91 2,200

Weiss, Jose   Br 1859-1929
O/Pn 10x18 A Riverbank Chr 10/91 1,650

Weisse, Rudolf   Sws 1846-
O/C 70x38 Nubian Guard Chr 10/91 55,000
O/Pn 4x5 An Arab Marketplace Chr 2/92 2,860

Weissenbruch, Jan Hendrik   Dut 1824-1903
* See 1992 Edition . . . .

Weissenbruch, Willem Johannes   Dut 1864-1941
O/Pn 8x14 Woman Knitting Hnz 5/92 5,000
O/C 19x22 Boater near a Windmill But 5/92 2,750

Welch, Thaddeus   Am 1844-1919
O/C 20x36 Grazing by the Sea '94 But 6/92 8,250
O/C 18x30 Tending the Cows 1881 But 6/92 4,400
O/B 11x18 Cows Grazing Mor 6/92 950

Welling, James   1951-
Ph 8x35 Untitled 1981 Chr 5/92 3,300

Welliver, Neil   Am 1929-
O/C 72x72 Reflection Chr 2/92 28,600

Wells, J. S. Sanderson   Br 1872-1955
O/C 16x24 Engligh Horse Racing Scene Dum 2/92 5,100

Wells, K. J.   19C
O/C 14x24 Coastal View Slo 4/92 275

Wendel, Theodore   Am 1857-1932
* See 1992 Edition . . . .

Wendt, William   Am 1865-1946
O/C 24x36 Catalina Island Hnd 5/92 46,000
O/C 28x36 Foothills and Oaks 1909 But 10/91 33,000
O/C 28x36 California Landscape But 2/92 30,250
O/C 30x40 View Through the Trees 1909 But 10/91 30,250
O/C 24x36 Rocky Valley Landscape 1909 Hnd 5/92 22,000
O/C 30x36 The Rock, San Luis Obispo 1940 But 2/92 . . . 22,000
O/C 25x30 Rushing Onward But 2/92 20,900
O/C 25x30 Autumn Vale 1936 But 10/91 19,800
O/C 24x36 California Landscape Hnd 5/92 18,000
O/C 20x30 Winter Landscape - Sierra Mor 3/92 14,000
O/C 24x30 Landscape with Figures Fishing Sby 3/92 . . . 13,200
O/C 18x24 The Brook, San Dimas 1902 But 10/91 10,450
O/C 20x36 Valley Landscape Wlf 3/92 8,000
O/C 16x24 California Sycamores But 6/92 4,950
O/Cb 12x16 California Coastal Mor 11/91 2,500

Wenglein, Josef   Ger 1845-1919
O/B 10x14 Landscape with Cows Skn 3/92 7,150

Wenzell, Albert Beck   Am 1864-1917
* See 1992 Edition . . . .

Werenskiold, Erik Theodor   Nor 1855-1936
* See 1992 Edition . . . .

Weretshchagin, Piotr Petrovitc   Rus 1836-1886
* See 1991 Edition . . . .

Werner, Joseph (the Younger)   Sws 1637-1710
* See 1992 Edition . . . .

Wertheimer, Gustav   Aus 1847-1904
O/C 68x44 Lorelei Hnz 5/92 6,750

Wescott, Gleway
O/B 9x12 Hills Ald 3/92 40

Wescott, Paul   Am 1904-1970
O/C 13x22 Lermond's Cove, Rockland Ald 5/92 1,750

Wesselmann, Tom   Am 1931-
A&L/B 48x60 Still Life #21 Sby 11/91 231,000
E/Al 77x77 Vivienne (3-D) 87 Sby 5/92 93,500
O/C 10x14 Study for Bedroom Painting, #2 Chr 2/92 . . . 33,000
Lq/Pa 40x60 Study Bedroom Painting #51 1982 Sby 10/91 31,900
O/C 10x8 Smoker Study #27 67 Sby 11/91 27,500
O/C/B 7x15 Study Reclining Stockinged Nude 81 Sby 2/92 15,400
O/C 9x9 Study for Mel's Model 83 Sby 2/92 14,300
Lq&H/B 17x19 Blonde Monica in Half-Slip 86 Chr 5/92 . . . 13,200
Pe&Lq/B 4x9 Open-Ended Nude Drawing 80 Sby 5/92 . . . 8,250
Lq&H/B 6x12 Study for Marilyn in Bed 84 Sby 11/91 8,250
Lq&H/B 4x5 Banner Nude 74 Chr 5/92 7,150
H&A/Pa 4x9 Beautiful Kate #15 81 Chr 5/92 7,150
Pe/B 4x9 Nude 89 Sby 6/92 4,950

Wessley, Anton   Aus 1848-
* See 1990 Edition . . . .

Wesson, Robert Shaw   Am 1902-1967
* See 1992 Edition . . . .

West, Benjamin   Am 1738-1820
K&P/Pa 13x8 Figure in Christ Rejected (3) Chr 1/92 . . . 1,100

West, Raphael Lamar   Br 1769-1850
* See 1992 Edition . . . .

West, S.   Am 19C
O/C 12x18 River Landscape 1902 Sel 4/92 210

Westchiloff, Constantin   Rus 1880-1945
* See 1992 Edition . . . .

Westerbeek, Cornelis   Dut 1844-1903
O/C 24x40 Cows in Marshy Landscape Slo 9/91 2,500
O/C 16x24 Landscape with Cows 1885 Lou 9/91 2,500
O/C 20x31 Bringing in the Flock Yng 2/92 2,300

Westermann, H. C.   Am 1922-
* See 1992 Edition . . . .

Westfall, Gertrude B. D.   Am 1889-1962
O/Cb 16x18 Figures/Street Scene Mor 6/92 325

Wetherill, Elisha Kent Kane Am 1874-1929
  * See 1991 Edition . . . .
Weyl, Max Am 1837-1914
  O/C 14x11 Still Life Peaches and Grapes 1874 Slo 9/91 650
  O/C 10x12 Autumn Landscape 1905 Slo 4/92 550
  O/C 11x24 Along the Shore Slo 2/92 475
Whale, John Hicks Can 1829-1905
  O/C 27x34 Landscape with Deer 1876 Sbt 11/91 748
Whalley, J. K. Br 19C
  O/C 30x45 Feeding the Sacred Ibis 1877 Hnd 3/92 4,000
Wheater, J. H. 20C
  W/Pa 5x7 Dock Scenes (2) Yng 4/92 350
  W/Pa 5x7 Railroad Yards (2) Yng 4/92 200
Wheatley, Francis Eng 1747-1801
  O/C 40x45 Portrait Robert and Anne Campbell Sby 1/92 . 110,000
  O/C 29x24 Portrait Miss Fridiswede Moore 1782 Sby 5/92 . 22,000
  O/C 14x11 Mother and her Children: Pair 1794 Chr 1/92 . . 13,200
Wheeler, Alfred Br 1852-1932
  O/C 20x24 Calling Hounds and The End: Pair Sby 6/92 . . 8,800
  O/C 20x24 "Ladas": Dark Brown Racehorse Sby 6/92 . . . 5,500
  O/C 10x16 Last Fence; The Finish: Pair 1896 Sby 6/92 . . . 4,400
Wheeler, J., Sen. of Bath Eng 19C
  O/C 28x36 The Fenian 1873 Slo 4/92 3,500
Wheeler, John Alfred Eng 1821-1903
  O/C 18x24 Full Cry But 11/91 4,400
Wheeler, William R. Am 1832-1894
  * See 1992 Edition . . . .
Wheelwright, Rowland Br 1870-1955
  * See 1990 Edition . . . .
Wheelwright, W. H. Br a 1857-1897
  W/Pa 10x14 Coach and Four 85 Sby 6/92 1,100
Whipple, Seth Arca Am 1855-1901
  * See 1991 Edition . . . .
Whistler, James Abbott McNeill Am 1834-1903
  C&P/Pa 12x8 A Venetian Courtyard Chr 12/91 2,200
Whitaker, George William Am 1841-1916
  O/C 29x36 Cattle by a Pool 1902 Skn 11/91 1,650
  O/C 24x34 Fruit on a Table Mys 6/92 1,320
  O/C 24x34 Still Life with Fruit 93 Sby 4/92 1,320
  O/C 4x6 Still Life Melons and Fruits Skn 3/92 1,210
  O/C 24x34 Still Life Fruit and Wine '93 Wes 11/91 935
  O/C 20x11 The Hay Wain Skn 3/92 550
  W/Pa Size? Cape Mabou, Cape Breton 1882 Eld 4/92 . . . 110
Whitaker, William Am 1943-
  * See 1990 Edition . . . .
Whitcomb, Jon Am 1906-1988
  G/Pa 12x14 Woman Kissing Soldier 1945 Ih 5/92 1,100
  G/Pa 14x10 Woman Admiring Her Smile Ih 11/91 900
Whitcombe, Thomas Br 1760-1824
  O/C 26x39 H.C.S. Canton Leaving Downs 1796 Sby 6/92 . 22,000
White, Clarence Scott Am 1872-
  O/B 6x9 Home Before the Rain Breaks Skn 11/91 412
White, Edith Am 1855-1946
  O/C 10x14 Violets 1909 But 6/92 1,540
  O/C 9x14 Still Life - Yellow Roses Mor 3/92 650
White, Edward Towry Eng 1850-1932
  W/Pa 10x13 Tintgil Castle, North Carawall, 1875 Wlf 6/92 . . . 70
White, Eugene Am 20C
  O/B 19x16 Women in Doorway; Awaiting: Two Wlf 10/91 . . . 100
  O/C 24x20 Old Man; Young Girl: Two Wlf 10/91 80
White, Gabriella Antoinette Am a 1880-1915
  O/C 14x24 Still Life with Lemonade '09 Wes 3/92 1,320
White, George Am 1826-1872
  O/C 35x28 Portrait Annie Palmer Wlf 6/92 2,000
White, Henry Cook Am 1861-1952
  * See 1991 Edition . . . .
White, John Br 1851-1933
  * See 1992 Edition . . . .
White, Kriber
  O/B 20x14 Village at Low Tide Wlf 3/92 250
White, Orrin A. Am 1883-1969
  O/C 18x24 Coastal--Monterey Mor 11/91 17,000

  O/C 25x30 Landscape Mor 6/92 8,000
  O/C 20x24 High Sierra Stream Chr 11/91 3,300
  O/C 24x24 Cathedral in Mexico Mor 11/91 2,000
  O/M 18x14 San Miguel De Allende Mor 11/91 1,900
  O/B 10x12 Coastal Mor 6/92 1,800
  G/Pa 12x16 Coastal Mor 11/91 1,400
White, Robert Am 20C
  O/M 12x16 Still Life with Lemons Fre 10/91 1,200
White, Thomas Gilbert Am 1877-1939
  * See 1990 Edition . . . .
Whitefield, Edwin Am 1816-1892
  * See 1992 Edition . . . .
Whitehead, Frederick William Eng 1853-1938
  * See 1990 Edition . . . .
Whiteside, B. Am 20C
  O/B 33x29 Polo Match, Palm Springs Sby 6/92 2,475
Whiteside, Frank Reed Am 1866-1929
  * See 1992 Edition . . . .
Whitmore, Coby Am 1913-1988
  O/B 9x26 Couple Kissing in the Snow Ih 11/91 1,800
  G/Pa 8x15 Girl Lying in Bed Ih 11/91 1,100
Whittaker, George Am 1841-1916
  O/C 9x10 Landscape with Figures Mys 11/91 302
Whittaker, James Eng 1828-1876
  * See 1990 Edition . . . .
Whittaker, John Barnard Am 1836-1926
  O/C 21x17 The Cobbler's Shop Chr 11/91 1,870
Whitteker, Lilian E. Am 20C
  O/C 15x18 Man in Doorway Lou 3/92 50
Whittemore, William John Am 1860-1955
  * See 1991 Edition . . . .
Whittredge, Thomas Worthington Am 1820-1910
  O/C 19x30 Along the Platte River, Colorado Sby 5/92 . . . 99,000
  O/C 36x48 Happy as a King Chr 12/91 22,000
  O/C 35x48 Evening Service Slo 12/91 9,000
  O/B 4x7 The Campagna from the Via Appia 1857 Slo 2/92 . 3,000
Whorf, John Am 1903-1959
  O/C 21x25 Brooklyn Bridge from Navy Yard Chr 5/92 . . 26,400
  O/C 12x16 Montparnesse-Nuit Blanche Skn 3/92 8,800
  W/Pa 21x30 Winter Waterfront, New York Sby 9/91 . . . 7,150
  W/Pa 15x22 Trout Water Fre 12/91 5,000
  O/B 17x13 Sunday Afternoon Brd 8/92 4,840
  W/Pa 14x19 Street Scene Figures and Horses Hnd 10/91 . 4,000
  W&H/Pa 14x22 Road to the Beach, Winter 21 Skn 3/92 . . 3,300
  W/Pa 14x20 Friendship Sloop at Dock Eld 7/92 2,750
  W/Pa 22x15 Bather in a Landscape Skn 3/92 2,200
  W/Pa 14x21 Dock Scene, Provincetown Wes 5/92 2,200
  W/Pb 10x11 Park, Copley Square, Boston Chr 6/92 1,870
  W/Pa 14x19 Active Coast Fre 10/91 1,500
  W/Pa 23x15 Backyard in Spring Sby 12/91 1,100
  O/B 15x19 The Hay Meadows '18 Brd 5/92 632
  W/Pa 20x25 The Old House Doy 12/91 500
  W/Pa 14x21 Winter Stream Slo 9/91 325
Whyte, D. M. G. Am 20C
  O/C 22x18 Portrait of a Young Girl 05 Sby 4/92 385
Wichera, Raimund Aus 1862-
  * See 1990 Edition . . . .
Wicks, Ron Am 20C
  O/B 24x47 Western Landscape Mys 11/91 55
Wickson, Paul Giovanni Can 1860-1922
  O/C/B 23x15 Study of a Male Nude Sbt 11/91 374
Widdas, Richard Dodd Br 1826-1885
  * See 1991 Edition . . . .
Wider, Wilhelm Ger 1818-1884
  * See 1990 Edition . . . .
Widforss, Gunnar Am 1879-1934
  W/Pa 20x16 View of the Grand Canyon 1926 But 10/91 . . 14,300
  W/Pa 19x27 Monterey Coastal Scene 1924 But 10/91 . . 11,000
  W&G/Pb 41x30 Snowy Mountains 1926 Chr 11/91 9,350
  W/Pa 19x14 Grand Canyon But 6/92 8,800
  W/Pa 13x16 Yosemite Valley in Winter 1925 But 6/92 . . . 7,150
  W/Pa 14x18 Grand Canyon 1934 Skn 3/92 6,600
  W/Pa 9x14 Desert Panorama Skn 3/92 330

Widgery, Frederick John Eng 1861-1942
P/Pa 11x18 Cornish Moor 1896 Slo 9/91 275

Wiegand, Gustave Adolph Am 1870-1957
O/C 31x37 Red Maples; Apple Blossoms: (2) Sby 4/92 . . . 2,200
O/C 30x36 Golden Days, Mount Kearsarge Sby 4/92 1,760
O/B 10x8 Moonlight Lake Sunapee Wes 5/92 990
O/C 20x16 Morning in Spring Slo 4/92 900
O/C 14x20 Marsh Landscape Wlf 9/91 800
O/C 14x20 Cottage by a Lake Brd 8/92 440
O/Cb 6x12 Landscape with Lake Hnd 10/91 350
O/C 18x14 Windy Trees Ald 3/92 225

Wieghorst, Olaf Am 1899-1988
O/C 28x38 Navajo Land Dum 1/92 60,000
O/C 25x30 Moonlight Camp Sby 12/91 14,300
O/C 16x20 Indian Mother and Child Hnd 5/92 10,000
O/C 20x31 Watching Over the Herd 1929 But 11/91 9,900
P/Pa 14x11 Before the Rodeo Chr 11/91 1,320
P/Pa 9x9 Cowboy and Christmas Tree But 4/92 1,320

Wierusz-Kowalski, Alfred Von Pol 1849-1915
* See 1991 Edition

Wiesendanger, Dan Am 1915-
O/B 30x24 What Say Leger? But 6/92 935

Wiesenthal, Franz
O/Ab 16x20 Woman Playing Lute Dum 1/92 225

Wiesner, Hella Ger a 1910-
* See 1991 Edition

Wiggins, Carleton Am 1848-1932
O/C 24x36 Evening Row, Long Island Chr 3/92 6,600
O/C 27x40 On the Chester Meadows '79 Sby 12/91 3,025
O/C 30x36 Spring Plowing, Normandy Eld 7/92 1,430

Wiggins, Guy Carleton Am 1883-1962
O/C 25x30 Double-Decker Bus in Winter Chr 5/92 38,500
O/C 30x25 Old Trinity in Winter Sby 3/92 26,400
O/C 16x12 Washington's Birthday, NY 1927 Chr 5/92 24,200
O/C 25x30 Chicago Blizzard Sby 9/91 20,900
O/C 24x20 Winter's Day Along Nassau Street Sby 5/92 . . . 20,900
O/C 40x50 The Swing Shift Going On 1943 Sby 3/92 20,350
O/C 30x25 The Clock Tower, New Haven Sby 5/92 16,500
O/Cb 12x16 The Plaza, Winter Chr 9/91 13,200
O/C 24x20 Saint Patrick's Cathedral Fre 10/91 13,000
O/Cb 12x16 Winter Weather on Fifth Avenue Chr 9/91 . . . 12,100
O/C 16x12 Entrance to the Plaza Chr 12/91 11,000
O/Cb 12x16 Wall Street Storm But 11/91 8,250
O/C 20x24 Farm in Winter, Connecticut Lou 3/92 8,000
O/C 20x24 Carriages at the Plaza Chr 6/92 6,050
O/Cb 16x12 New York Winter But 11/91 5,500
O/C 30x25 The Rabbit Hunter Wes 11/91 5,500
O/C 20x24 Summer Afternoon, Essex, Conn. Sby 4/92 . . . 5,225
O/C 20x24 Farm in Winter, Kent Doy 12/91 5,000

Wigle, Archie Palmer Am 20C
O/C 20x15 Still Life of Flowers Dum 5/92 250
O/B 23x28 Fall Landscape Dum 1/92 150
O/C 15x20 Cottage Scene Dum 5/92 100
O/C Size? Mountainscape Dum 5/92 100

Wijngaarden, H. v. Dut 19C
O/C 32x28 Still Life of Flowers Sel 4/92 350

Wijsmuller, Jan Hillebrand Dut 1855-1925
* See 1991 Edition

Wilcox, Frank Am 1887-1964
W&Pe/Pa 19x29 Shoreline '52 Wlf 6/92 1,000
W/Pa 16x11 Figures by a Stream Wlf 3/92 425
W/Pa 14x20 Grand Canyon Wlf 6/92 350
W/Pa 9x13 Figures in a Landscape Wlf 3/92 100
W/Pa 7x8 Hunting Scene Wlf 10/91 75

Wilcox, W. S. Am a 1890-1899
O/C 16x34 Blue Flowers with Copper Pot 1894 But 2/92 . . . 935

Wilcox, William H. Am 1831-
* See 1992 Edition

Wilda, Charles Aus 1854-1907
* See 1992 Edition

Wilde, John Am 1919-
* See 1992 Edition

Wildens, Jan Flm 1586-1653
* See 1991 Edition

Wilder Con 19C
W/Pb 20x29 The Grand Canal, Venice Chr 2/92 1,430

Wilder, * 20C**
W/Pa 20x30 Along the Grand Canal Slo 9/91 1,000

Wilder, Tom
O/C 28x34 Beach Scene Hnz 10/91 2,000

Wiles, Irving Ramsay Am 1861-1948
O/C 26x20 In the Garden Chr 12/91 99,000
O/C 27x40 The Enchanted Pool Sby 5/92 30,800
O/C 20x26 Scallopers, Peconic Bay Chr 5/92 26,400
O/C 15x17 Idle Moments Chr 5/92 20,900
G&R/Pa 20x14 Crew Race, Women in Boat Ih 11/91 1,300

Wiles, Lemuel M. Am 1826-1905
O/C 18x12 Melrose Abbey 1883 Chr 6/92 1,100

Wiley, William T. Am 1937-
* See 1992 Edition

Wilhelm, Rudolph Ger 1889-
O/B 16x13 Portrait of a Young Boy 1913 But 5/92 825

Wilke, Hannah 20C
* See 1991 Edition

Wilkes, O. B.
O/C 16x22 Fishing Boats at Anchor Eld 7/92 66

Wilkie, Robert D. Am 1828-1903
O/B 11x17 Boys on Horseback Lou 3/92 200

Wilkinson, Arthur Stanley Br 20C
* See 1992 Edition

Wilks, R. Am 19C
O/C 7x12 Pulling Nets Bor 8/92 500

Will, G. Con 19C
O/C 13x18 Rapallo 1900 Chr 5/92 1,540

Willaerts, Adam Dut 1577-1664
* See 1992 Edition

Willaerts, Isaac Dut 1620-1693
* See 1990 Edition

Willard, Archibald M. Am 1836-1918
O/C 30x24 River Landscape Wlf 10/91 550

Willbright, Monroe Am 20C
O/B 29x36 The Haul Hnd 5/92 500

Willcock, George Barrell Br 1811-1852
O/C 20x24 Fingal Mill Chr 10/91 2,420

Wille, Johann Georg Ger 1715-1808
* See 1992 Edition

Wille, P. A. Ger 1860-1941
O/C 8x10 Landscape with Stream Wlf 6/92 375

Willems, Florent Bel 1823-1905
* See 1992 Edition

Willems, J. Bel 19C
O/C 24x36 Zinneas on a Ledge Chr 2/92 770

Willia Sco 19C
* See 1992 Edition

William, John Haynes Br 19C
* See 1990 Edition

Williams, Alfred Walter Br 1824-1905
* See 1991 Edition

Williams, Edward Charles Eng 1807-1881
O/C 24x42 Along the Upper Thames 67 Sby 7/92 4,400

Williams, Esther Am 1901-
O/B 11x8 Cellist Mys 6/92 440

Williams, Frederick Ballard Am 1871-1956
O/C 30x45 Afternoon Light Slo 9/91 4,000
O/C 40x50 Seven Maidens But 11/91 1,870
O/C 25x30 Women in the Interior of a Forest Lou 6/92 . . . 1,500
O/C 25x30 Music in the Afternoon But 11/91 1,430
O/M 8x10 Ladies in Waiting Hnd 6/92 350

Williams, Frederick Dickinson Am 1829-1915
O/C 18x30 View of Boston 1868 Skn 11/91 15,400
O/C 12x18 Forest of Fontainbleau 1875 Doy 12/91 3,400
O/C 18x26 A Cottage Path 1876 Chr 11/91 1,540

Williams, George A. Am 1875-1932
* See 1991 Edition

Williams, George Augustus Br 1814-1901
PVPa 8x16 City View '98 Lou 6/92 35
Williams, Gluyas Am 1888-1982
PVPa 14x10 Dining Room w/Fathers and Sons llh 11/91 600
Williams, Graham Br 19C
O/C 24x36 Valley of the Teith Dum 1/92 650
O/C 21x31 Landscape with Cows Wading Hnd 12/91 400
Williams, H. Eng 19C
O/C 20x30 Highland Mountain Landscapes Slo 12/91 1,200
Williams, Hamilton Am
PVPa 11x15 Introduction in a Restaurant llh 5/92 400
Williams, James Robert Am 1888-1957
PVPa 13x12 People Leaving Car for Junk llh 5/92 350
Williams, John Haynes Br 19C
   * See 1992 Edition . . . .
Williams, John L. Scott Am 1897-1976
C/Pa 20x19 Couple in Arbor. "Pieces of Eight" llh 5/92 750
Williams, Keith Shaw Am 1905-1951
O/C 30x25 Bee Balm and Bitter Buttons Lou 6/92 600
Williams, Ken Am a 1930-
W/Pa 13x19 Home with the Christmas Tree Hnz 5/92 100
Williams, Mary Belle Am 1873-1928
O/C 20x24 Still Life with Persimmons But 2/92 1,210
O/C 32x24 Eucalyptus Landscape Mor 11/91 750
O/C 28x20 Young Boy with Orange Lou 12/91 600
O/Ab 11x13 Autumn Landscape Slo 9/91 225
O/Ab 10x12 Jack's Graduation All Around 25 Slo 9/91 225
O/Ab 10x12 View Along the Loire 25 Slo 9/91 225
O/Ab 10x12 Cottage on the Hill Slo 10/91 200
O/Ab 9x8 Portrait of a School Boy Slo 10/91 200
O/Ab 10x12 California Landscape 25 Slo 9/91 190
O/C/B 10x12 Desert at Sunset Slo 9/91 190
O/Ab 13x19 Edge of the Forest Slo 9/91 190
O/Ab 10x11 Forest Interior 23 Slo 9/91 190
O/Ab 10x11 Stream through the Fields Slo 9/91 190
O/Ab 9x12 The Farm 23 Slo 9/91 190
O/Ab 8x9 Winter Scene Slo 9/91 190
O/Ab 9x12 Harvest Time Slo 10/91 180
O/Ab 8x9 Cathedral Village Slo 10/91 150
Williams, Neil 20C
   * See 1992 Edition . . . .
Williams, Paul A. Am 1934-
O/C 14x18 Autumn Charm Hnd 12/91 2,200
O/C 12x9 Orange Bicycle Dum 9/91 1,750
O/B 12x10 Blooming Flowers Dum 2/92 1,500
O/B 10x11 Children's Tea Wes 5/92 1,210
O/B 9x12 Tinka II Dum 2/92 1,100
O/C 8x10 Vanilla and Friends Wes 11/91 1,045
O/C 14x10 Breezy Hnd 12/91 1,000
O/C 20x16 Les Fleurs Dum 4/92 1,000
O/C 18x14 Mon Chocolat Dum 9/91 1,000
O/B 10x12 Winter Walk Dum 6/92 1,000
O/B 10x12 Whispers of Spring Wes 3/92 990
O/C 12x16 Crossing the Bay Dum 4/92 900
O/C 8x10 Tinka at the Shore Dum 9/91 700
Williams, Pauline Bliss Am 1888-1962
O/B 10x14 East Gloucester Harbor 1934 Lou 12/91 500
O/B 24x30 Still Life of Lilacs Lou 12/91 500
Williams, Penry Br 1789-1885
   * See 1991 Edition . . . .
Williams, Terrick Br 1860-1936
   * See 1992 Edition . . . .
Williams, V. Am 19C
O/C 20x10 Italian Peasant Woman 1878 Mys 11/91 110
Williams, Virgil Am 1830-1886
O/C 18x30 Landscape with Indians Bud 6/92 8,800
O/C 10x20 Haying Scene 1878 Mys 6/92 880
Williams, Walter Br 1835-1906
   * See 1992 Edition . . . .
Williams, Zoland B. Am 20C
O/C 28x44 Landscape Wlf 3/92 500
Williamson, J. W. Br 19C
O/C 12x16 View of Roslin Castle 1837 Bor 8/92 400
Williamson, John Am 1826-1885
O/C 31x50 Bolton's Landing, Lake George 78 Chr 5/92 . . 35,200

O/B 24x30 River Landscape '66 Wes 11/91 4,950
O/B 8x11 Palisades, Hudson River Chr 6/92 2,750
O/C 8x15 A Marshy Landscape 63 Chr 6/92 1,650
Willis, A. V. Br 19C
O/Pn 11x18 Over the Fence 65 Sby 6/92 4,950
Willis, Henry Brittan Eng 1810-1884
O/C 23x35 Dolgelly, North Wales 55 Chr 2/92 4,400
Willis, J. R. Am 1876-
O/C 7x9 Indian Landscape: Pair 1947 Dum 6/92 400
Willmann, Michael Lucas Leo. 1630-1706
Pe,Pl&S/Pa 8x12 The Death of Priam Chr 1/92 3,080
Willroider, Ludwig Ger 1845-1910
   * See 1990 Edition . . . .
Willson, John Am
W/Pa 10x15 Western Sunset Mor 6/92 125
Wilmarth, Christopher Am 1943-1987
W&H/Pa 31x22 Edge of Long Straight Stray 1978 Chr 5/92 . 2,750
W&H/Pa 15x42 Edges of the Nine Clearings 75 Sby 2/92 . . 2,200
Wilms, Peter Joseph Ger 1814-1892
O/C 13x14 Still Life Fruit, Wine 1871 Skn 11/91 2,970
Wilner, Marie Am 1910-
O/C 30x40 Bears at the Zoo Sby 12/91 1,320
Wilson Con 19C
O/C 20x32 An Extensive Rivertown 1871 Chr 5/92 2,200
Wilson, David Forrester Br 1873-1950
   * See 1992 Edition . . . .
Wilson, Francis Vaux Am 1874-1938
G/Pa 18x17 Woman Wearing Blue Scarf llh 5/92 1,100
Wilson, Howell 20C
W/Pa 18x15 Boaters by a River Yng 4/92 125
Wilson, J. Br 19C
O/C 16x24 Fishing Boats Mys 11/91 908
Wilson, Jane Am 1924-
   * See 1991 Edition . . . .
Wilson, John Eng 19C
O/C 15x21 Two Figures Along a Path Wlf 11/91 275
Wilson, M. B. Am 19C
O/C/B 27x36 Yacht Under Full Sail 1879 Slo 7/92 1,500
Wilson, Mary Loomis 20C
   * See 1991 Edition . . . .
Wilson, Raymond C. Am 1906-1972
W/Pa 15x21 Southern Pacific Railroad But 2/92 1,870
W/Pa 15x23 Houses in the Morning But 2/92 825
Wilson, Richard Br 1714-1782
   * See 1992 Edition . . . .
Wilson, Solomon Am 1896-1974
O/C 46x40 The Torn Sail Chr 6/92 1,760
O/C 12x20 Storm Hnz 5/92 200
Wilson, Thomas Walter Br 1851-
O/C 17x28 Westgate on the Sea 1876 Chr 10/91 2,200
Wilson, W. Eng 19C
O/C 20x30 Sitting on the River Bank Fre 4/92 550
Wilson, W. Reynolds Am 20C
O/C 46x34 The Pose Fre 4/92 925
Wilson, William Am 1884-
W/Pa 20x28 Custer's Last Stand Fre 4/92 200
Wilt, Richard 20C
O/C 30x40 City Mills 1953 Chr 5/92 110
Wimmer, Conrad Ger 1844-1905
   * See 1992 Edition . . . .
Wimperis, Edmund Morison Br 1835-1900
O/C 17x23 Harvesting the Hay Bor 8/92 2,500
Winchell, Paul Am 20C
O/C 27x32 The Bath Wlf 3/92 2,000
O/C 23x30 Reclining Female Nude Wlf 3/92 1,500
O/C 28x36 At the Mill Wlf 9/91 1,200
O/C 30x36 Three Nudes Wlf 9/91 1,100
O/C 25x30 Saying Farewell Wlf 9/91 900
O/C 36x28 Cigarette Girl Wlf 9/91 650
O/C 16x20 Down by the River Mys 11/91 522
O/C 36x28 Nude Female on a White Rocker Wlf 3/92 500
O/C 16x18 Half Portrait of Nude Female Wlf 3/92 375
O/C 18x22 Still Life Plant, Violin and Fruit '32 Wlf 3/92 . . . 350
O/C 35x40 Still Life with Fish Wlf 9/91 300
O/C 24x25 The Entertainers Wlf 3/92 275

O/C 26x39 Two Oils Wlf 3/92 275
O/C 24x20 Seated Female Nude Wlf 3/92 250
O/C 33x30 Waiting for the Steamer Wlf 6/92 250
O/C 30x24 Seated Woman with Black Cat Wlf 3/92 230
O/C 28x24 Nude Girl with Green Jug Wlf 3/92 225
O/C 28x36 Snowy Landscapes: Two Wlf 3/92 220
O/C 48x32 Seated Nude Female Wlf 6/92 200
O/C 28x33 Interested Man Wlf 6/92 175
O/C 36x40 The Captive Wlf 3/92 175
O/C 25x34 Seated Woman in a Green Gown Wlf 3/92 160
O/C 18x24 Pensive Nude Female Wlf 3/92 140
O/C 39x30 Nude Female from Rear Wlf 6/92 125
O/C 15x14 Second Thought Wlf 3/92 125
O/C 36x28 Nude Female Sitting Striped Towel Wlf 3/92 110
O/C 16x19 Two Oils Wlf 3/92 100
O/C 30x24 Woman: Two Wlf 3/92 80
O/C 24x20 Pirate and Parrot Wlf 6/92 70
O/C 24x30 Woman on a Blanket Reading Wlf 3/92 70
O/C 34x25 Female Nude with Blue Cape Wlf 3/92 60
O/C 19x22 Captive on a Sailboat Wlf 3/92 50
O/C 14x18 Farmyard Scene: Two Wlf 3/92 50
O/C 39x32 Seated Female Nude Wlf 3/92 50
O/C 27x21 The Folklore Wlf 10/91 50
O/C 24x18 Woman with Book Wlf 10/91 50
O/C 14x12 Young and Old Men: Three Wlf 6/92 50

Winck, Johann Amandus Ger 1748-1817
O/Cp 12x17 Still Life Peaches, Pears: Pair 1802 Chr 1/92 165,000
O/C 20x15 Still Life Peaches, Grapes, a Melon Sby 10/91 . 77,000

Windhager, Franz Aus 1879-1959
O/C 42x50 A Muse Leaning on a Rock 1906 Sby 1/92 . . . 935

Windmaier, Anton Ger 1840-1896
O/C 20x30 Sunset Over a Rural Landscape 1875 Sby 7/92 . 2,200

Wingfield, James Digman Br -1872
* See 1992 Edition

Winkler, Olaf Am 20C
O/C Size? Alpine Landscape Mys 6/92 138

Winner, William E. Am 1815-1883
* See 1992 Edition

Winter, Andrew Am 1892-1958
O/C 30x40 Coastal Maine Brd 5/92 2,530
O/Cb 12x18 House on the Maine Coast 42 Brd 5/92 1,430
O/Cb 12x16 Light and Gong Brd 8/92 1,430
O/Cb 12x18 View on Monhegan Island, Maine 42 Skn 9/91 . 770

Winter, Charles Allan Am 1869-1942
O/C 24x17 Two Illustrations Skn 3/92 715

Winter, Fritz Ger 1905-1978
* See 1992 Edition

Winter, J. Greenwood Br
O/C 30x24 Woman with a Book Lou 12/91 800

Winter, Lumen Martin Am 1908-
O/C 14x18 Still Life of Mushrooms 1937 Lou 3/92 350

Winter, William Arthur Can 1909-
O/B 10x8 Girl with Bouquet Durn 9/91 50

Winterhalter, Franz Zavier Ger 1806-1873
* See 1991 Edition

Winters, Robin
A&Pe/C 72x60 Another Inadequate Gift 1986 Sby 5/92 4,400

Winters, Terry Am 1949-
O/L 60x84 Stamina I Sby 11/91 55,000
O/L 42x26 Untitled 1983 Chr 11/91 35,200
O/L 48x36 Botanical Subject No. 4 1982 Sby 11/91 30,250
C/Pa 42x30 Untitled Sby 2/92 17,600
G/Pa 11x15 P 1987 Chr 5/92 9,350
G&H/Pa 11x16 N 1987 Chr 5/92 7,700

Winther, Frederik Dan 1853-1916
O/C 34x54 Summer Pond Landscape 1914 Hnd 5/92 . . . 1,500

Wirsum, Karl Am 20C
I&Y/Pa 14x11 A Knock Out 1967 Hnd 12/91 300

Wisby, Jack Am 1870-1940
O/C 24x28 Yosemite Valley But 6/92 4,950
O/C 20x36 Mount Tamalpais But 6/92 3,575

Wisinger-Florian, Olga Aus 1844-1926
* See 1992 Edition

Wissing, Willem 1656-1687
* See 1992 Edition

Wistehuff, Revere F. Am 1900-1971
O/C 21x17 Through the Hoop Sby 4/92 1,870
O/C 23x17 Reclining Girl Writing Love Letter Ih 11/91 . . . 1,400

Witherington, William Frederic Br 1785-1865
* See 1991 Edition

Withington, Elizabeth R. Am 20C
O/B 8x11 Winter Town Mys 11/91 385

Witholm, K. Aus 20C
O/C/B 31x22 Orientalist Beauty Hnd 3/92 425

Witkowski, Karl Am 1860-1910
O/C 24x28 Knucks Down! Slo 10/91 11,000
O/C 21x15 Playing a Tune Chr 3/92 7,700
O/C 24x20 Boy with Parrot Sby 12/91 4,950
O/C 22x18 Peeling an Apple 1900 Chr 11/91 4,400

Wizon, Tod 20C
A/Pn 36x40 Clots Chr 5/92 1,320
A/Pn 11x14 Three Paintings 80 Chr 2/92 275

Woelfle, Arthur Am 1873-1936
O/C 40x30 Lady in White Sby 12/91 3,300

Woffle, J. Ger 20C
O/Pn 7x5 Man with Pipe Hnz 5/92 250

Wohner, Louis Ger 1888-
O/C 46x55 Alpine Mountain View Slo 7/92 3,750

Wojnarowicz, David 1954-
E/M 48x96 Time 1982 Chr 11/91 2,750

Wolcott, Harold C. Am 20C
O/B 20x24 Table Grouping Mys 11/91 110

Wolcott, Wallace Am 20C
W&Pe/Pa 26x36 The Plaza, St. Mark's Square 58 Sby 4/92 . . 440

Wolf, Franz Xavier Aus 1896-1989
O/Pn 19x17 The Letter Chr 2/92 4,400
O/Pn 20x17 The Recital Chr 2/92 2,420

Wolf, Hamilton A. Am 1883-1967
O/M 42x30 The Bridge But 6/92 2,750
O/B 25x19 Atomic Landscape But 6/92 1,100
O/M 11x9 Figures-Church Mor 6/92 425

Wolf, J. L. Am 20C
O/Cb 8x10 Coastal Flowered Banks Mor 6/92 175

Wolf, Joseph Br 1820-1899
O/C 28x20 A Greenland Gyr-Falcon But 5/92 71,500

Wolfe, Edward Br 1897-1982
* See 1991 Edition

Wolff, Henrik Dan 19C
O/C 14x18 Still Life with Potted Bluebells 1837 Sby 5/92 . . 6,600

Wolff, Robert Jay Am 1905-
* See 1992 Edition

Wolffort, Artus 1581-1641
* See 1992 Edition

Wolfson, William Am 1894-
O&G/Pb 29x27 Miners Chr 6/92 1,100

Wolke, Jurgen 20C
O/C 16x13 Untitled 74 Chr 2/92 110

Wollaston, John Eng a 1738-1775
O/C 30x25 Portrait of an Officer Chr 10/91 4,400
O/C 30x25 Portrait of a Gentleman Chr 10/91 2,200
O/C 30x25 Portrait of a Gentleman Hnz 10/91 500

Wolstenholme, Charles Dean Br 1798-1883
O/Pn 16x22 Party of Anglers Fishing Sby 6/92 19,800

Wolstenholme, Dean (Sr.) Eng 1757-1837
* See 1990 Edition

Wolter, Jan Hendrik Dut 1873-1952
* See 1991 Edition

Wolter, Max Am 1916-1988
Pl&W/Pa 16x15 Twenty Advertisements 1972 Ih 11/91 . . . 75

Woltze, Berthold Ger 1829-1896
O/C 29x23 Off to America Sby 10/91 13,200

Wonner, Paul Am 1924-
O/C 30x20 Flowers on Chair But 5/92 8,800
A/Pa 39x28 Untitled Sby 5/92 5,500
Cs&Pe/Pa 23x18 Zinnia But 5/92 1,750
Cs&Pe/Pa 18x15 Landscape with Flowers But 5/92 1,430
Cs,P&Pe/Pa 13x17 Under the Light of the Moon But 5/92 . . . 880

Wontner, William Clarke Br 19C
* See 1991 Edition . . . .
Wood, A. A. Am 20C
O/C 20x36 Goose Girl Besides a Roadway 1889 Hnz 5/92 . . 200
Wood, Charles Haigh Br 1856-1927
* See 1991 Edition . . . .
Wood, George Albert Am 1845-1910
O/C 22x36 Clams Served at All Hours Skn 11/91 2,310
Wood, George Bacon (Jr.) Am 1832-1910
W/Pa 12x19 Cat Sleeping by Spinning Wheel Fre 4/92 550
Wood, Grant Am 1891-1942
* See 1992 Edition . . . .
Wood, H. Am 20C
O/C 18x24 Ship at Sea Fre 10/91 350
Wood, H. Br 19C
O/C/B 20x24 Peasants Hnd 3/92 500
Wood, Harrie Morgan Am 1902-1974
O/C 30x24 Still Life Calla Lily Lou 3/92 200
Wood, Henry
O/C 9x12 Afternoon Sunlight Dum 11/91 400
Wood, Hunter Am 1908-
O/C 25x30 Top Side Mys 11/91 275
Wood, John T. Am 1845-1919
O/C 14x17 Country Road Brd 8/92 550
O/C 12x18 The Woods in Snow Brd 8/92 550
Wood, Michael Eng 20C
O/C 20x30 Before the Hunt Slo 4/92 700
O/C 20x30 Setting Off Slo 4/92 700
Wood, Nan Am 1874-
O/B 9x12 Arroy Seco Hnd 10/91 300
Wood, Peter Br 1914-
O/C 16x20 On the Arun River But 5/92 660
Wood, Robert Am 1889-1979
O/C 16x20 Blue Bonnets Spring in Texas Dum 4/92 6,000
O/C 25x30 Rocky Coastal Hillside Sby 12/91 3,410
O/C 25x30 Mountain Lake But 2/92 2,750
O/C 14x18 Incoming Tide But 2/92 2,475
O/C 14x18 Scrub Brush in Bloom But 6/92 2,475
O/C 22x32 Coastal - "Wood's Cove" Mor 3/92 2,000
O/C 25x30 The Pond Hnz 10/91 1,200
O/C 24x30 Landscape with Cactus Flowers Lou 3/92 1,000
O/C 25x30 Landscape Mor 3/92 850
Wood, Robert E. Am 1926-1979
O/C 28x35 Landscape Wlf 9/91 1,500
Wood, Thomas Waterman Am 1823-1903
O/C 18x14 Woman in a Shawl 1858 Skn 9/91 5,500
Wood, W. T.
W/Pa 7x11 Mazigne Lake, British Columbia Dum 4/92 75
Wood-Thomas, A. Am 20C
O/B 13x23 Strange Fruits 1947 Hnd 5/92 425
Woodbury, Charles Herbert Am 1864-1940
O/Ab 8x10 Ogunquit Summer Brd 8/92 9,900
O/C 20x27 Ogunquit Beach Brd 8/92 7,700
O/C 29x36 The Rushing Wave Chr 11/91 4,400
W/Pa 10x20 Dawn Fishing Cove '89 Yng 4/92 4,000
O/C 14x20 Beached Ship 86 Brd 8/92 2,860
O/B 12x19 Summer-Castine Yng 2/92 2,300
O/C 17x21 Heavy Swell Yng 4/92 2,250
O/C 36x48 Winter Coastline 1927 But 4/92 2,200
O/C 17x21 Midwinter, Ogunquit Yng 4/92 2,000
O/B 10x14 Surf and Rocks Brd 8/92 1,320
Woodcock, Hartwell L. Am 1853-1929
O/C 28x41 View of the Harbor at Belfast, ME 1889 Brd 8/92 . 935
W/Pa 14x9 Bahama Harbour 1925 Brd 8/92 798
Woodhouse, H. J. Br 19C
O/C 24x18 Bird Dog and Pheasant Hnd 10/91 6,000
Woodhouse, William Br 1857-1935
O/C 30x25 The Blacksmith's Shop Chr 5/92 5,500
O/C 12x16 Still Life; After the Hunt Slo 10/91 950
Woodside, John Archibald Am 1781-1852
O/C 16x20 Still Life with Fruit 1824 Fre 4/92 5,250
Woodward, Ellsworth
W/Pa 14x20 New Orleans Street Scene Ald 3/92 375

Woodward, Mabel May Am 1877-1945
W&Pe/B 15x22 Afternoon at the Beach Chr 12/91 27,500
O/C/M 16x19 An Afternoon at the Beach Chr 9/91 24,200
O/C 10x13 Polperro and Venice: Pair Sby 12/91 5,225
O/Cb 16x20 Monterey Coast, California Sby 12/91 1,980
O/M 10x13 Rockport Pier Skn 11/91 1,980
O/C/B 13x10 First Baptist Meeting House Sby 12/91 1,100
O/Cb 8x10 Florida Beach Slo 12/91 650
G/Pa 14x11 Canal in Holland Yng 4/92 60
Woodward, Stanley Wingate Am 1890-1970
O/Cb 12x16 Moonlit Calm Skn 5/92 770
O/C 22x26 Dry-Docked Boat '50 Wes 11/91 468
O/B 12x16 White Barn Eld 7/92 330
Woodworth, P. D.
Pe/Pa 15x22 Elb Sunk at Sea 1895 Eld 7/92 248
Woog, Raymond Fr 1875-
* See 1990 Edition . . . .
Wool, Christopher 1955-
Pt/Al&St 81x60 Untitled 1988 Sby 11/91 55,000
Pt/Al 72x48 Untitled (P.16) '87 Chr 5/92 44,000
MM/Al 48x32 Untitled (S.23) '88 Chr 2/92 19,800
Pt/Al 48x24 Untitled Study #13 '87 Sby 2/92 17,600
Pt/Pa 50x38 Untitled 1988 Chr 11/91 11,000
Pt/Pa 66x36 Untitled Chr 5/92 9,900
Pt/Pa 74x38 Untitled 1990 Chr 5/92 7,700
Pt/Pa 66x36 Untitled Chr 2/92 6,600
A/Pa 39x25 Untitled Chr 5/92 4,950
Woolf, Samuel Johnson Am 1880-1948
O/C 40x60 The Lower East Side Chr 12/91 60,500
O/C 62x43 In the Morning Chr 5/92 16,500
C&Cw/Pa 12x19 Scene; Coal Miner: Two 1929 Wes 11/91 . . 330
C&K/Pa 19x24 City Hall, New York Wes 3/92 248
C&Cw/Pa 18x23 Streetscene; Ben Franklin: Two Wes 11/91 . 165
C/Pa 11x26 Political Rally Sel 12/91 80
Woolmer, Alfred Joseph Br 1805-1892
* See 1991 Edition . . . .
Woolrych, Francis Humphrey Am 1868-
W/Pa 24x20 Dutch Girl Reading a Letter Lou 6/92 500
W/Pa 19x13 Boy with Sword Lou 9/91 350
O/C 24x30 Nude Lou 6/92 300
W/Pa 18x14 Nymphs in Landscape Lou 12/91 300
Woolsey, Carl Am 1902-
O/C 32x45 Western Village, Taos But 4/92 5,500
Wooster, Austin C. Am 19C
* See 1992 Edition . . . .
Wootton, John Br 1683-1764
* See 1991 Edition . . . .
Wopfner, Joseph Aus 1843-1927
* See 1991 Edition . . . .
Worcester, Albert Am 1871-1935
O/C 20x25 Iviza Balearic, Spain 1935 Dum 5/92 250
Wores, Theodore Am 1859-1939
O/Cb 12x9 View from an Archway But 6/92 1,100
Worms, Jules Fr 1832-1924
W/Pa 14x10 Femme a la Fontaine Sby 1/92 1,100
Worth, Thomas Am 1834-1917
O/C 18x32 Out for a Sleigh Ride Mys 6/92 990
Wostry, Carlo It 1865-1943
O/C 30x47 Exchanging Secrets 1894 But 5/92 18,700
Wouters, Frans Flm 1614-1658
O/Cp 22x16 Aeneas Fleeing Troy Sby 10/91 7,150
Wouwerman, Philips Dut 1619-1668
O/Pn 19x25 Elegant Hawking Party Heading Out Sby 5/92 467,500
Wouwermans, Pieter Dut 1623-1682
* See 1992 Edition . . . .
Wright, Don Am 20C
W/Pa 10x7 Young Boy in Woods '74 Lou 6/92 130
Wright, George Br 1860-1942
O/C 16x24 Cub Hunting Morning Sby 6/92 17,600
O/C 16x24 Hunting Scenes: Pair Chr 10/91 16,500
O/C 12x16 Off Lightly and Over Fence: Pair Sby 6/92 . . . 15,950
O/C 7x10 Before the Polo Match Sby 6/92 15,400
O/C 14x20 Breaking Cover Sby 6/92 6,050
O/C 12x16 Full Cry Sby 6/92 4,950

O/C 20x30 Full Cry Sby 6/92 4,620
O/C 13x17 Border Collie Puppies Sby 6/92 4,400
O/C 13x17 Jack Russell Terriers Sby 6/92 4,400
O/C 14x20 The Fox Hunt Wes 11/91 2,970

Wright, George Hand   Am 1873-1951
C&W/Pa 17x11 People Around Gondola in Venice Ih 11/91 . 900
C&W/Pa 12x10 People Looking at Movie Posters Ih 5/92 ... 800
Pe/Pa 19x14 City Folks in the Country Ih 11/91 275

Wright, Gilbert Scott   Br 1880-1958
* See 1992 Edition ....

Wright, James Couper   Am 1906-1969
W/Pa 12x18 Landscape 1938 Mor 3/92 250

Wright, John   Am a 1860-1869
* See 1992 Edition ....

Wright, Joseph   Am 1756-1793
O/C 32x25 Portrait of Benjamin Franklin Chr 5/92 55,000

Wright, Joseph (of Derby)   Br 1734-1797
* See 1990 Edition ....

Wright, Larry
Pe/Pa 5x10 Caricature "Poltergeist III" 86 Dum 1/92 65
Pe/Pa 5x10 Caricature Coming Soon People Mover Dum 1/92 . 35

Wright, Mary Catherine   Am 20C
O/Cb 20x24 Rainy Night, New York City Lou 3/92 100

Wright, P. J.   Eng 19C
O/C 40x30 Coaching Scene Sel 9/91 1,400

Wright, Robert C.   Am 20C
O/C 18x24 Autumnal Landscape Sel 12/91 325

Wright, Rufus   Am 1832-
O/C 22x16 Still Life Peaches 1870 Sby 12/91 3,575

Wrinch, Mary Evelyn   Can 1877-1969
* See 1992 Edition ....

Wtewael, Joachim   Dut 1566-1638
* See 1990 Edition ....

Wucherer, Fritz   Sws 1873-1948
W/Pa 10x14 Scene with Three Figures '25 Lou 6/92 200

Wuchters, Abraham   1610-1682
O/Pn 28x20 Old Woman Wearing Fur Hat 1652 Sby 10/91 18,700

Wuermer, Carl   Am 1900-1982
O/C 19x29 December Afternoon Doy 12/91 3,600

Wuerpel, Edmund Henri   Am 1866-1958
* See 1992 Edition ....

Wunder, George   Am 20C
Pl&S/Pa 18x27 U.S. Air Force to China Hnd 12/91 100

Wunder, Wilhelm Ernst   1713-1787
O/C 15x17 Still Life Fruit in a Wan Li Bowl Sby 10/91 ... 12,100

Wunderlich, Paul   Ger 1927-
* See 1992 Edition ....

Wunnenberg, Carl   Ger 1850-1929
* See 1992 Edition ....

Wust, Alexander   1837-1876
C/Pa 9x14 Driving the Cow Yng 4/92 150
C/Pa 7x16 Gathering Seaweed Yng 4/92 100

Wuttke, Carl   Ger 1849-1927
O/Pn 5x8 An Orientalist View Chr 2/92 110

Wyant, Alexander Helwig   Am 1836-1892
O/C 18x30 Autumn Landscape Chr 12/91 22,000
O/C 20x30 A Path to the River Chr 5/92 8,800
O/C 20x16 Woodland Stream Lou 12/91 4,250
O/C 12x16 Moonlit Landscape Wtf 9/91 3,000
O/C/M 28x41 New England Landscape Doy 12/91 3,000
O/C 17x24 Autumn Landscape Slo 12/91 2,500
W/Pa 12x16 Around the Country Door Chr 6/92 2,200
O/C 10x14 Bear Creek, Jefferson County Slo 10/91 1,900
O/C 16x12 Landscape Rocky Outcrop Hnd 6/92 1,400
O/B 12x7 Landscape with Castle Ruins Slo 9/91 1,400
O/C 15x13 Landscape with Two Cows Dum 9/91 1,400
O/Pn 19x25 A Wooded Clearing Chr 6/92 1,320
O/Pn 5x8 West Rock, Connecticut Skn 11/91 660

Wyant, Arabella L.   Am -1919
O/B/Pn 28x35 Autumn Skn 11/91 468

Wydeveld, Arnoud   Am a 1855-1862
O/C 30x22 Floral Still Life Fre 12/91 10,000

Wyeth, Andrew   Am 1917-
I&S/Pb 15x21 Study of Pine, Maine Sby 3/92 21,450

Wyeth, Caroline   Am 1909-
O/C 30x36 A Stand of Fir Trees Sby 12/91 6,600

Wyeth, Henriette   Am 1907-
* See 1992 Edition ....

Wyeth, Jamie   Am 1946-
O/C 60x72 The Raven Sby 3/92 34,100

Wyeth, Newell Convers   Am 1882-1945
O/C/B 23x49 A Garden Meeting 1931 Sby 3/92 14,300
O/C 30x39 Man with Butterfly Net 1920 Ih 11/91 7,000

Wyld, William   Br 1806-1889
W/Pa 11x17 Santa Maria Della Salute Slo 7/92 2,600
O/Pn 15x12 Venice Wtf 3/92 1,050

Wyllie, Charles William   Br 1853-1923
* See 1992 Edition ....

Wyman, M. A.   Am 20C
O/B 11x15 Summer Play 1915 Brd 5/92 1,980

Wynants, Jan   Dut 1630-1684
* See 1991 Edition ....

Wyngardt, A. V.   Dut 19C
W/Pa 15x21 Sheep in a Farmyard Wes 11/91 605

Wysmuller, Jan Hillebrand   Dut 1855-1925
O/C 16x24 Dutch Canal View; Spring Slo 4/92 950

Wysocki, M.   Aus 20C
O/Pn 11x9 Pair: Bavarian Men Sel 2/92 450
O/Pn 12x10 Pair: Bavarian Men Sel 2/92 350

Wysor, Jeanne   Am 20C
O/C 40x24 Joe Louis Mys 11/91 275

Xavery, Jacob   1736-1769
* See 1992 Edition ....

Xceron, John   Am 1890-1967
W,G&I/Pa/B 8x11 Abstract Composition 58 Sby 10/91 ... 1,320

Xul Solar, Alejandro   Arg 1887-1963
W&Pl/Pa 11x15 Fecha Patria 1925 Chr 5/92 55,000
O/Pn 8x8 La Sombra del Caminante Chr 11/91 35,200
W/Pa 7x12 Careo 1922 Sby 11/91 14,300
W&I/Pa 20x17 Nitra 1954 Chr 5/92 11,000

Yankel, Jacques   1920-
O/C 40x40 L'atelier de l'artiste Chr 5/92 2,860

Yanosky, Thomas R.   Am 1918-
O/C 24x32 Blue Mosaic 1953 Slo 7/92 200

Yarber, Robert   Am 1943-
K/Pa 30x44 Untitled 86 Chr 2/92 3,080

Yard, Sydney Janis   Am 1855-1909
W/Pa 15x22 Sheep Grazing But 2/92 2,200
O/Pa 15x21 Landscape Mor 3/92 1,300

Yarz, Edmond   Fr 20C
* See 1992 Edition ....

Yates, Cullen   Am 1866-1945
O/C 40x36 Orange and Yellow Marigolds Fre 10/91 6,750
O/B 20x24 Woodland Brook But 4/92 4,400
O/B 9x7 Village Scene Mys 6/92 825

Yates, Thomas   Br -1796
* See 1991 Edition ....

Yatrides, Georges   Fr 1931-
O/C 40x18 The Lady '58 Wtf 9/91 6,500

Yeckley, Norman   Am 1914-
O/B 8x10 Desert Landscape Yng 2/92 325

Yektai, Manoucher   Am 1922-
O/C 22x26 Still Life 1951 Slo 12/91 350

Yelland, Raymond Dabb   Am 1848-1900
O/C 40x72 Yosemite 1883 Sby 3/92 55,000
O/C 12x10 Landscape: Yosemite Mor 6/92 1,900

Yens, Karl   Am 1868-1945
O/Cot 54x44 The Boys of Yosemite 1919 But 2/92 10,450
O/C 56x60 Sacred Solitude, Retreat But 2/92 4,125
O/B 33x42 Half Dome, Yosemite 1919 But 2/92 3,575

Yepes, Tomas   Spa a 1642-1674
* See 1991 Edition ....

Yewell, George Henry   Am 1830-1923
* See 1992 Edition ....

Yip, Richard   Am 1919-1981
W/Pa 15x22 Walk Along the Coast But 2/92 1,430

Yoakum, Joseph E.   Am 1886-1973
* See 1991 Edition ....

Yohn, Frederick C. Am 1875-1933
G/Pa 19x12 Couple on Steps 1915 lh 5/92 1,400
Yokuchi
W/Pa 9x25 Cherry Blossom in Emperor's Garden Sel 4/92 .. 250
Yon, Edmond Charles Joseph Fr
1836-1897
* See 1990 Edition ....
York, William Am 19C
O/C 19x26 The Ship Mobile 1862 Sby 12/91 5,500
Yorke, William G. Am 1817-1883
* See 1992 Edition ....
Yorke, William Howard Br 1858-1913
O/C 12x18 Ship-Holme Force Fre 4/92 4,900
Yoshida, Hiroshi Jap
* See 1992 Edition ....
Yoshida, R. Jap 20C
O/Pn 14x23 An Oriental Genre Scene Skn 9/91 1,320
Young, Arthur Am 1866-1943
S&I/Pa 11x9 Parachutist Looking for a Lift lh 5/92 200
Young, August Am 1837-1913
* See 1992 Edition ....
Young, Charles Morris Am 1869-1964
O/C 22x36 September Landscape 1893 Fre 10/91 1,400
Young, E. Ger 19C
O/B 10x6 Bavarian Gentleman w/Walking Stick Slo 4/92 100
Young, Gordan Am 20C
* See 1992 Edition ....
Young, Harvey Otis Am 1840-1901
O/B 18x26 Colorado Landscape Hnz 10/91 850
MM 10x13 Walk by the Old Gnarled Tree Eld 8/92 165
Young, Mahonri Am 1877-1957
* See 1992 Edition ....
Young, Michael 20C
Sd&A/C 82x78 Rhizome 1986 Sby 2/92 7,700
Young, Murat "Chic" Am 1901-1973
Pl&W/Pa 4x18 Comic Strip. Dagwood's Grandma 30 lh 11/91 750
Pl&W/Pa 4x18 Cartoon Strip. Dagwood 31 lh 11/91 650
Pl/Pa 14x17 Comic Strip. "Blondie" 39 lh 5/92 500
Young, Walter 1906-
W/Pa 14x11 The "Ellie" at Dock Yng 4/92 90
Young, William S. Am a 1850-1870
O/C 24x41 Hudson River Landscape Yng 2/92 2,250
Youngerman, Jack Am 1926-
* See 1992 Edition ....
Yrisarry, Mario Am 1933-
A/C 96x96 Untitled Hnd 5/92 50
Yuan, S. C. Am 20C
O/B 12x16 Tidal Pools But 6/92 2,475
Yuzbasiyan, Arto Can 1948-
O/C 24x34 Queen Street East, 1980 Sbt 11/91 5,610
O/B 12x16 Dundas St. near Parliament St. Sbt 5/92 1,496
W/Pa 12x14 Changing Harbourfront 1990 Sbt 5/92 654
Yvon, Adolphe Fr 1817-1893
O/C 22x18 Portrait D'Une Femme 1867 Sby 5/92 1,650
W/Pa 6x4 Officer Smoking Yng 4/92 80
Zabaleta, Vladimir Ven 1944-
* See 1992 Edition ....
Zacharie, Ernest Philippe Fr 1849-1915
* See 1991 Edition ....
Zack, Leon Rus 1892-
* See 1992 Edition ....
Zadkine, Ossip Fr 1890-1967
G/Pa 26x22 Meditation (Portrait of Carol) 37 Chr 2/92 ... 10,450
W&G/Pa 28x22 L'Homme et le Cheval 32 Sby 5/92 9,350
G/Pa 25x19 Quatre Figures 51 Sby 10/91 7,150
Bp/B 10x8 Embracing Figures Sby 6/92 880
Zaganelli, Francesco It 1460-1532
O/C 25x21 Madonna and Child before a Parapet Chr 5/92 .. 55,000
Zais, Giuseppe It 1709-1784
* See 1992 Edition ....
Zak, Eugene Pol 1884-1926
* See 1992 Edition ....
Zakanitch, Robert Am 1935-
* See 1991 Edition ....

Zaice, Alfredo Mex 1908-
O/M 24x33 Boat Landing Wes 3/92 7,260
O/M 28x48 Jardin Central 62 Chr 5/92 6,050
Zalopany, Michele 20C
C&P/Pa 88x97 Untitled Sby 10/91 6,050
Zamacois Y Zabala, Eduardo Spa
1842-1871
W/Pa 16x11 The Court Jester 67 Chr 2/92 5,280
Zambella, M.
O/C 28x27 Pastoral Landscape Yng 4/92 300
Zampighi, Emiliano It 19C
O/C 20x25 Two and Two are Four Chr 5/92 3,850
Zampighi, Eugenio Eduardo It 1859-1944
O/C/Pn 30x50 The Grandfather's Visit Sby 2/92 44,000
O/C 29x42 The Happy Family Hnd 3/92 26,000
O/C 29x42 Happy Days Sby 10/91 23,100
O/C 30x22 Musicians and Dancer Sby 10/91 11,000
O/C 18x15 The Mandolin Player Chr 5/92 8,580
O/C 22x30 Frugal Meal Wtf 6/92 7,500
W/Pa 15x22 Preparing the Baby's Bath Sby 7/92 6,600
W/Pa 21x15 Grandfather's Favorite Hnd 5/92 3,600
W/Pa 21x14 For the Hot Sun Hnd 5/92 2,800
Zanchi, Antonio It 1631-1722
* See 1992 Edition ....
Zandini It 19C
O/C 29x40 Piazza San Marco la Notte Sby 2/92 8,800
Zandomeneghi, Federico It 1841-1917
O/C 29x36 En Promenade Sby 2/92 907,500
P&C/Pa 22x17 Study for Signora All'Aperto Chr 10/91 ... 22,000
Zang, John J. Am 19C
* See 1990 Edition ....
Zao-Wou-Ki Chi 1921-
W/Pa 19x19 Composition '54 But 11/91 3,850
Zapeda, Ernesto Am 20C
O/C 14x18 Burro '83 Dum 1/92 50
O/C 16x20 Indian Boy Dum 1/92 40
Zapkus, Kes Am 1938-
* See 1992 Edition ....
Zaragoza, Fernando Alvared
* See 1991 Edition ....
Zarate 19C
O/C 79x47 Monja Coronada-Retrato 1840 Sby 11/91 33,000
Zardo, Alberto It 1876-1959
O/C 22x18 Fishing Village at Sunset Chr 10/91 2,420
O/B 12x17 Water's Edge Slo 10/91 1,300
O/Pn 11x15 Watering Cow Slo 10/91 700
Zaritzky, Joseph Isr 20C
* See 1991 Edition ....
Zarraga, Angel Mex 1886-1946
O/C 39x32 Jugada de Futbol Chr 11/91 24,200
O/C 14x11 Paisaje con Figuras Sby 5/92 20,900
Zatzka, Hans Aus 1859-1945
O/C 27x19 Lady in Waiting Sby 2/92 8,250
O/C 23x31 Sleeping Beauty Sby 7/92 7,975
O/C 22x31 Sea Nymphs Sby 2/92 7,150
O/C 30x25 Still Life of Flowers Sby 1/92 7,150
O/C 30x25 Ornate Still Life on a Ledge Chr 2/92 4,180
Zeedijk, A.
O/C 18x21 Seascape Dum 2/92 50
Zeeman Dut 1623-1664
* See 1992 Edition ....
Zehme, Werner 20C
* See 1991 Edition ....
Zenil, Nahum 20C
* See 1992 Edition ....
Zenkevich, Boris Rus 1888-1972
I&S/Pa 10x8 Costume Designs: Two Hnd 3/92 300
I&W/Pa 7x15 Theatre Set Design Hnd 3/92 200
C&P/Pa 18x22 Landscapes: Ten Hnd 3/92 120
I/Pa 18x22 Figural Studies: Six Hnd 3/92 100
C/Pa 18x22 Train Stations: Two Hnd 3/92 100
C&S/Pa 22x18 War Office Scenes: Seven Hnd 3/92 100
C&W/Pa 12x14 Two Cats, Dog, Parrot: Three Hnd 3/92 80
Zeno, Jorge Am 1956-
O/C 48x36 Silencio Chr 11/91 15,400

O/C 40x33 Lluvia 89 Chr 5/92 11,000

Zerbe, Karl Am 1903-1972
O/C 36x24 Dog under the Table 1946 Chr 6/92 1,100
N/C 32x30 Marion Square, Charleston 1941 Lou 6/92 1,100
N/Pn 29x32 Marion Square, Charleston 1940 But 11/91 550

Zermett, J. It 19C
O/C 18x23 Flirtation Slo 10/91 550

Zewy, Karl Aus 1855-1929
O/C 42x27 The White Lillies Chr 2/92 4,730

Zick, Januarius Ger 1730-1797
O/C 27x33 Shepherds Wooing Shepherdess Chr 1/92 ... 79,200

Ziegler, Eustace Paul Am 1881-1969
O/Cb 9x11 Mother and Child 1936 But 4/92 2,200

Ziegler, Matt Am 20C
O/B 28x36 Mines at St. Genevieve Sel 2/92 170

Ziegler, Nellie E. Am 1874-1948
O/C 25x30 The Arroyo But 2/92 3,575
O/B 18x22 Suburban Road 1922 Wlf 6/92 475
O/C 10x13 Landscape Lou 9/91 350

Zieler, F. Aus 19C
O/C 12x16 The Scholar Fre 10/91 325

Ziem, Felix Francois Georges Fr 1821-1911
O/C 22x36 Venetian Scene Chr 2/92 35,200
O/C 27x45 Venice showing the Doge's Palace Chr 5/92 .. 33,000
O/C 30x42 View of Venice Chr 9/91 33,000
O/C 27x42 Les Eaux Douces, Constantinople Chr 5/92 .. 26,400
O/C 21x34 Venetian Regatta Chr 2/92 26,400
O/C 22x32 Departure for Mecca Chr 2/92 22,000
O/C 21x33 Venetian Scene Sunset Chr 2/92 19,800
O/Pn 15x29 A Venetian Regatta Chr 5/92 18,700
O/C 23x28 Jour de Fete Grand Canal Chr 10/91 16,500
O/C 22x34 Le Grand Canal, Venise Sby 5/92 16,500
O/Pn 18x22 Along the Grand Canal Skn 5/92 8,250
O/Pn 25x16 Drapeaux sur un Canal a Venise Sby 5/92 ... 7,150
O/Pn 15x22 View of the Piazza San Marco Chr 10/91 6,600
O/B 13x18 Canal Scene Hnz 10/91 4,600
O/Pn 10x14 Venetian Canal Scene Sel 4/92 2,400
O/Pn 8x10 Figures Around a Table Sel 4/92 550

Zier, Francois Edouard Fr 1856-1924
O/C 18x13 The Young Scholar 1877 Chr 5/92 3,300

Zietlen
O/C 36x24 Genre Interior Scene Dum 11/91 1,000

Zille, Heinrich Ger 1858-1929
* See 1992 Edition ....

Zim, Marco Am 1880-
* See 1992 Edition ....

Zimmer, Wilhelm Carl August Ger 1853-1937
* See 1991 Edition ....

Zimmerman, Carl Am 1900-
* See 1992 Edition ....

Zimmerman, Eugene Am 1878-1935
O/B 15x12 Ragpicker Wlf 3/92 425

Zimmerman, Frederick Am 1886-1974
* See 1992 Edition ....

Zimmerman, Karl Ger 1796-1857
* See 1990 Edition ....

Zimmerman, Reinhard Sebastian Ger 1815-1893
O/C 13x9 Jilted But 11/91 1,540

Zimmermann, Jan Wendel G. Dut 1816-1887
O/C 30x39 Deerhound in a Landscape Sby 10/91 7,700

Zini, Fratelli It 20C
W/Pa 16x10 Grand Canal, Venice: Two Slo 2/92 70

Zinnogger, Leopold Aus 1811-1872
* See 1992 Edition ....

Zipin, Martin Am 20C
O/C 20x34 Woman Playing Guitar Fre 4/92 50

Zobel, Fernando Spa 1924-
A/C 31x31 Interior 1967 Mys 11/91 7,975

Zoboli, Jacopo It 1681-1767
* See 1992 Edition ....

Zocchi, Guglielmo It 1874-
O/Pn 15x12 Nude with Mirror Skn 9/91 3,410

Zogbaum, Rufus Fairchild Am 1849-1925
O/C 24x20 West Point Trooper 89 But 4/92 2,750
O/C 24x18 Moose Hunting Ald 5/92 220

Zoir, Emil Swd 1867-1936
* See 1992 Edition ....

Zolan, Donald James Am 20C
O/Pn 11x8 Flower Vendor Hnz 5/92 160

Zona, Antonio It 1813-1892
O/C 56x41 A Neapolitan Beauty 1875 Chr 2/92 8,800

Zorach, Marguerite Am 1888-1968
O/C 30x22 The Sisters 1922 Chr 3/92 38,500
O/C 20x30 Lonely Campfire 1934 Brd 5/92 9,900

Zorach, William Am 1887-1966
O/C 46x39 Springtime in the High Sierras Sby 12/91 ... 44,000
W&H/Pa 10x14 New England Village 1917 Sby 12/91 ... 3,850
W/Pa 10x14 Family at Rest 15 Chr 11/91 2,420
W/Pa 14x18 Cottages Near a Woodland Path 1937 Chr 11/91 1,650

Zorn, Anders Swd 1860-1920
O/C 32x26 Daughters/Subercasseaux 92 Sby 5/92 ... 550,000

Zornes, James Milford Am 1908-
W/Pa 21x29 Morro Beach '61 But 6/92 1,870
W/Pa 22x30 Village Street Scene 1952 But 10/91 1,760
W/Pa 20x28 Treasure Island 70 But 2/92 1,540
W/Pa 20x28 Rocky Coast 70 But 2/92 1,430
W/Pa 20x28 The Arch, Laguna '73 But 6/92 1,210
W/Pa 22x28 Crater Lake 64 But 6/92 1,045
W/Pa 22x29 Mining Town 50 But 6/92 825
W/Pa 20x28 South From Dana Point '68 But 6/92 770
W/Pa 11x15 From Randsburg 1941 Mor 6/92 600
W/Pa 14x20 Ancient Bridge in Castile 1963 But 11/91 550
W/Pa 10x22 Death Valley and The Panamints 54 But 11/91 . 550

Zox, Larry Am 1936-
* See 1992 Edition ....

Zsissly Am 20C
W/Pa 20x14 Dock Scene 1941 Hnz 5/92 100

Zuber, Henri Fr 1844-1909
* See 1991 Edition ....

Zuber-Buhler, Fritz Sws 1822-1896
O/C 14x11 La Toilette Sby 10/91 8,800
O/C 58x45 Mother and Child Chr 5/92 7,700

Zuccarelli, Francesco It 1702-1788
* See 1992 Edition ....

Zucker, Jacques Am 1900-
O/C 24x29 Figures on a Bench Sby 4/92 880
O/C 26x22 The Guitar Player Sby 4/92 880
O/C 23x27 Street in Bievres, France Fre 10/91 600

Zucker, Joe Am 1941-
* See 1992 Edition ....

Zuckerberg, Stanley Am 1919-
G/Pa 16x23 Man Drying Woman's Tears Ih 11/91 1,200

Zugel, Heinrich Johann Ger 1850-1941
O/Pn 14x21 At the Stable Door Chr 10/91 104,500

Zugno, Francesco It 1709-1787
O/C 26x13 Vision of Saint Teresa of Avila Chr 5/92 5,280

Zuloaga Y Zabaleta, Ignacio Spa 1870-1945
* See 1992 Edition ....

Zuniga, Francisco Mex 1913-
C&W/Pa 20x26 Dos Mujeres Sentadas 1972 Sby 11/91 .. 11,000
W,Y&K/Pa 26x20 Madre y Nino 1966 Chr 5/92 9,900
C&P/Pa 27x40 Chamulas 1981 Chr 5/92 9,350
Pl&W/Pa 26x20 Dos Mujeres 1963 Sby 11/91 9,350
P&C/Pa 19x27 Sin Titulo 1979 Chr 11/91 8,800
C&P/Pa 20x26 Tehuana En Una Silla 1972 Sby 11/91 .. 8,800
P/Pa 20x28 Mujer Sentada 1979 Sby 11/91 8,250
Sg&C/Pa 20x26 Mujer con Naranjas 1967 Chr 5/92 ... 7,700
C/Pa 22x30 Dos Mujeres Sentadas 1977 Chr 11/91 ... 6,600
C/Pa 20x26 Mujer Sentada 1966 Sby 5/92 6,600
C&P/Pa/B 20x26 Seis Comadres 1965 Sby 11/91 6,600
C&Sg/Pa 20x26 Mujer Sentada 1964 Chr 5/92 6,050
C&P/Pa 20x26 Study of Women 1966 Sby 10/91 5,775
C/Pa 20x28 Desnudo Reclinado 1978 Chr 5/92 5,500
P&Y/Pa 38x20 Mujer con Pescados 1981 Chr 5/92 5,500

C&P/Pa 20x28 Seated Woman 1978 But 5/92 5,500
C&P/Pa 22x30 Mujer Sentada 1977 Slo 10/91 5,000
C/Pa 22x28 Mestiza Dormida 1976 Chr 11/91 4,620
P&C/Pa 23x35 Mujer Acostada 1973 Sby 5/92 4,400
P/B 20x26 Seated Old Woman 1965 Sby 10/91 4,400
C/Pa 22x29 Seated Women Candlelight 1968 Yng 2/92 . . . 3,900
C&P/Pa 26x20 Desnudo de Frente 1972 Sby 5/92 3,300

Zupan, Bruno   Yug 20C
O/C 15x18 Detail From My Work Table '72 Wes 3/92 358
O/C 32x24 Natasha on a Rocking Horse '68 Wes 3/92 165

Zusi, A.
O/Pn 9x11 Russian Troika Pulling Officer Dum 11/91 2,900

Zwann, Cornelisz C.   Dut 1882-1964
O/C 30x25 Floral Still Life Dum 6/92 3,000

Zwengauer, Anton   Ger 1810-1884
* See 1992 Edition . . . .

ILLUSTRATION ART AT AUCTION

Mead Schaeffer

Our auctions receive maximum exposure to the specialized audience of collectors, dealers and museum curators involved in the entire spectrum of original illustration art: advertising, book illustration, pulp & paperback, calendar art and magazine cover paintings. The sales include many subjects of special interest: Brandywine, children, fantasy, western, romance, detective, automotive, fashion, science fiction, movies, aviation, etc.

Because this is our area of expertise, we consistently out-perform other auction houses for illustration and cartoon art, and have established record prices in every category.

Illustration House, Inc.
96 Spring Street, 7th Floor
New York, NY 10012-3923
℗ 212/966-9444 • fax 212/966-9425

Walt Reed   •   Roger Reed   •   Frederic Taraba